THE COMPLETE HANDY REFERENCE

DICTIONARY

THESAURUS

GUIDE TO ENGLISH USAGE

This edition first published in 1992
by Reed Consumer Books
part of Reed International Books Limited
Michelin House, 81 Fulham Road, London SW3 6RB
and Auckland, Melbourne, Singapore and Toronto

Chancellor Press is an imprint of Reed Consumer Books

Third impression

ISBN 1 851 52311 1

A catalogue record for this book is available
from the British Library

Printed in India

THE COMPLETE HANDY REFERENCE

DICTIONARY

THESAURUS

GUIDE TO ENGLISH USAGE

ENGLISH DICTIONARY

Foreword

The Newnes Pocket English Dictionary gives concise and accurate definitions of about 12 000 of the most important words in current use in English. Special attention has been taken to cover modern, technical, and informal meanings. An additional feature is the inclusion of over 2000 idioms and idiomatic phrasal verbs (such as *take off*). Distinct senses of words are numbered separately, with the most common or important meaning placed first. Easy-to-read pronunciations based on the International Phonetic Alphabet have been given only for words that might cause some difficulty (see *Key to symbols used in pronunciation* below).

The wide coverage of this dictionary with its emphasis on modernity, together with its compact size and clear typeface, will make it an invaluable aid at school, at the office and in the home.

Abbreviations used in the Dictionary

adj	adjective	*infin*	infinitive	*pt*	past tense
adv	adverb	*interj*	interjection	*r*	reflexive
aux	auxiliary	*n*	noun	*s*	singular
cap	capital	*neg*	negative	*sl*	slang
conj	conjunction	*pl*	plural	*tab*	taboo
def art	definite article	*poss*	possessive	*Tdmk*	trademark
esp	especially	*pp*	past participle	*US*	United States
f	feminine	*prep*	preposition	*v*	verb
indef art	indefinite article	*pres*	present tense	*vi*	verb intransitive
inf	informal	*pron*	pronoun	*vt*	verb transitive

Key to symbols used in pronunciation

Vowels

iː	*meet*	u	*put*	aɪ	*fly*
ɪ	*bit*	uː	*shoot*	au	*how*
e	*get*	ʌ	*cut*	ɔɪ	*boy*
æ	*hat*	ə	*ago*	ɪə	*here*
ɑː	*heart*	əː	*sir*	ɛə	*air*
ɔ	*hot*	eɪ	*late*	uə	*poor*
ɔː	*ought*	ou	*go*		

Consonants

θ	*thin*	ʃ	*ship*
ð	*then*	ʒ	*measure*
ŋ	*sing*	tʃ	*chin*
j	*yes*	dʒ	*gin*

ˈ indicates that the following syllable is stressed, as in ago (əˈgou)

ˌ placed under an *n* or *l* indicates that the *n* or *l* is pronounced as a syllable, as in *button* (ˈbʌtn̩) and *flannel* (ˈflænl̩)

Irregular verbs

Infinitive	Past Tense	Past Participle	Infinitive	Past Tense	Past Participle
abide	abode *or* abided	abode *or* abided	**beware**[2]		
			bid	bid	bidden *or* bid
arise	arose	arisen	**bind**	bound	bound
awake	awoke *or* awaked	awoke *or* awaked	**bite**	bit	bitten *or* bit
			bleed	bled	bled
be	was	been	**blow**	blew	blown
bear[1]	bore	borne *or* born	**break**	broke	broken
beat	beat	beaten	**breed**	bred	bred
become	became	become	**bring**	brought	brought
begin	began	begun	**build**	built	built
bend	bent	bent	**burn**	burnt *or* burned	burnt *or* burned
bet	bet	bet			

Infinitive	Past Tense	Past Participle
burst	burst	burst
buy	bought	bought
can	could	
cast	cast	cast
catch	caught	caught
choose	chose	chosen
cling	clung	clung
come	came	come
cost	cost	cost
creep	crept	crept
crow	crowed *or* crew	crowed
cut	cut	cut
deal	dealt	dealt
dig	dug *or* digged	dug *or* digged
do	did	done
draw	drew	drawn
dream	dreamed *or* dreamt	dreamed *or* dreamt
drink	drank	drunk
drive	drove	driven
dwell	dwelt	dwelt
eat	ate	eaten
fall	fell	fallen
feed	fed	fed
feel	felt	felt
fight	fought	fought
find	found	found
flee	fled	fled
fling	flung	flung
fly	flew	flown
forbid	forbade *or* forbad	forbidden *or* forbid
forget	forgot	forgotten *or* forgot
forgive	forgave	forgiven
forsake	forsook	forsaken
freeze	froze	frozen
get	got	got
give	gave	given
go	went	gone
grind	ground	ground
grow	grew	grown
hang[3]	hung *or* hanged	hung *or* hanged
have	had	had
hear	heard	heard
hide	hid	hidden *or* hid
hit	hit	hit
hold	held	held
hurt	hurt	hurt
keep	kept	kept
kneel	knelt	knelt
knit	knitted *or* knit	knitted *or* knit
know	knew	known
lay	laid	laid
lead	led	led
lean	leant *or* leaned	leant *or* leaned
leap	leapt *or* leaped	leapt *or* leaped
learn	learnt *or* learned	learnt *or* learned
leave	left	left
lend	lent	lent
let	let	let
lie	lay	lain
light	lit *or* lighted	lit *or* lighted
lose	lost	lost
make	made	made
may	might	
mean	meant	meant
meet	met	met
mow	mowed	mown
must		
ought		
panic	panicked	panicked
pay	paid	paid
picnic	picnicked	picnicked
put	put	put
quit	quitted *or* quit	quitted *or* quit
read	read	read
rid	rid *or* ridded	rid *or* ridded
ride	rode	ridden
ring	rang	rung
rise	rose	risen
run	ran	run
saw	sawed	sawn *or* sawed
say	said	said
see	saw	seen
seek	sought	sought
sell	sold	sold

Irregular verbs

Infinitive	Past Tense	Past Participle
send	sent	sent
set	set	set
sew	sewed	sewn *or* sewed
shake	shook	shaken
shall	should	
shear	sheared	sheared *or* shorn
shed	shed	shed
shine	shone	shone
shoe	shod	shod
shoot	shot	shot
show	showed	shown
shrink	shrank *or* shrunk	shrunk *or* shrunken
shut	shut	shut
sing	sang	sung
sink	sank	sunk
sit	sat	sat
sleep	slept	slept
slide	slid	slid
sling	slung	slung
slink	slunk	slunk
slit	slit	slit
smell	smelt *or* smelled	smelt *or* smelled
sow	sowed	sown *or* sowed
speak	spoke	spoken
speed	sped *or* speeded	sped *or* speeded
spell	spelt *or* spelled	spelt *or* spelled
spend	spent	spent
spill	spilt *or* spilled	spilt *or* spilled
spin	spun	spun
spit	spat *or* spit	spat *or* spit
split	split	split
spread	spread	spread
spring	sprang	sprung
stand	stood	stood
steal	stole	stolen
stick	stuck	stuck
sting	stung	stung
stink	stank *or* stunk	stunk
stride	strode	stridden
strike	struck	struck

Infinitive	Past Tense	Past Participle
string	strung	strung
strive	strove	striven
swear	swore	sworn
sweep	swept	swept
swell	swelled	swollen *or* swelled
swim	swam	swum
swing	swung	swung
take	took	taken
teach	taught	taught
tear	tore	torn
tell	told	told
think	thought	thought
throw	threw	thrown
thrust	thrust	thrust
traffic	trafficked	trafficked
tread	trod	trodden *or* trod
wake	woke	woken
wear	wore	worn
weave	wove	woven *or* wove
weep	wept	wept
will	would	
win	won	won
wind	wound	wound
wring	wrung	wrung
write	wrote	written

[1] when *bear* means *give birth to* the past participle is always *born*.

[2] used only in the infinitive or as an imperative.

[3] the preferred form of the past tense and past participle when referring to death by hanging is *hanged*.

A

a, an *indef art* one; each; every; any; some.

aback *adv* **taken aback** taken by surprise; disconcerted; flabbergasted.

abandon *vt* **1** leave behind with no intention of returning; desert; forsake. **2** give up; fail to complete. **abandon oneself (to)** yield, submit, or give in (to).

abashed *adj* ashamed; embarrassed.

abate *vi* lessen; die down. *vt* reduce; subdue; suppress. **abatement** *n*.

abattoir (ˈæbətwɑː) *n* slaughterhouse.

abbess *n* female head of nuns in an abbey or nunnery.

abbey *n* **1** community of monks or nuns. **2** buildings occupied by such a community. **3** church attached to such a community.

abbot *n* male head of monks in an abbey or monastery.

abbreviate *vt* shorten (a word or phrase). **abbreviation** *n*.

abdicate *vi,vt* renounce or relinquish (the throne, one's powers, etc.). **abdication** *n*.

abdomen *n* lower part of the body between the diaphragm and pelvis; belly. **abdominal** *adj*.

abduct *vt* take (a person) away unlawfully; kidnap. **abduction** *n*. **abductor** *n*.

aberration *n* deviation from the usual, right, or natural course, condition, etc. **aberrant** *adj*.

abet *vt* (-tt-) assist or encourage in crime or wrongdoing.

abeyance *n* **in abeyance** in a state of inactivity; suspended.

abhor *vt* (-rr-) have an intense horror of; loathe; detest. **abhorrence** *n*. **abhorrent** *adj*.

abide *vt* (abode *or* abided) tolerate; bear. *vi* **1** stay; remain. **2** reside; dwell. **abide by** keep to; remain close or faithful to.

ability *n* **1** power; capacity; means. **2** competence; skill.

abject *adj* **1** downcast; humiliated. **2** despicable; shocking. **3** humble. **abjectly** *adv*.

ablaze *adj* **1** on fire; in flames; burning fiercely. **2** displaying strong passion or ardour.

able *adj* **1** having the power, capacity, opportunity, or means (to). **2** competent; skilled. **ably** *adv*. **able-bodied** *adj* physically fit; strong.

abnormal *adj* irregular; unnatural; deviant. **abnormality** *n*. **abnormally** *adv*.

aboard *adv,prep* on or in(to) a ship, aircraft, etc.

abode[1] *n* place of residence; dwelling; home.

abode[2] *v* a *pt* and *pp* of **abide.**

abolish *vt* do away with; put an end to; ban. **abolition** *n*.

abominable *adj* loathsome; detestable; dreadful. **abominably** *adv*.

Aborigine (æbəˈridʒini) *n also* **Aboriginal** person belonging to a race of original native inhabitants, esp. of Australia. **Aboriginal** *adj*.

abort *vt* **1** terminate (a pregnancy); perform an abortion on. **2** cancel or destroy (a project, mission, etc.) before completion. *vi* **1** miscarry. **2** fail to function successfully; terminate before completion. **abortive** *adj*. **abortion** *n* **1** operation carried out to remove a foetus from the womb. **2** miscarriage. **3** disastrous failure.

abound *vi* exist or have in great quantity; be plentiful.

about *prep* **1** of; concerning; relating to; connected with. **2** near or close to; around. **about to** ready or preparing to; on the point of. ~*adv* **1** approximately. **2** nearby; close at hand. **3** around; here and there; to and fro.

above *adv* higher up; overhead. *prep* **1** over; higher than. **2** more or greater than. **3** in authority over; superior to. **4** beyond (suspicion, reproach, etc.). *adj also* **above-mentioned** mentioned or written above or before. **above all** more than anything. **aboveboard** *adv* openly; without deception. *adj* open; straightforward; honest; legal.

abrasion *n* **1** wearing down by rubbing. **2** graze on the skin. **abrasive** *adj* **1** producing abrasion. **2** harsh; grating. *n* something used for wearing down or smoothing a surface.

abreast *adv* side by side; level with. **keep abreast of** keep up or up-to-date with.

abridge *vt* cut (a novel, play, etc.); condense. **abridgement** *n*.

abroad *adv* **1** in or to a foreign country. **2** in circulation; at large.

abrupt *adj* **1** unexpected and sudden. **2** curt; short; brusque. **abruptly** *adv*. **abruptness** *n*.

abscess *n* pus-filled sore.
abscond *vi* leave without permission; run away, esp. after committing a crime. **absconder** *n*.
absent *adj* (ˈæbsənt) **1** away; not in attendance. **2** lacking; missing; not present. *v* **absent oneself** (əbˈsent) stay away. **absence** *n*. **absentee** *n* person, such as an employee or landlord, who is absent. **absenteeism** *n*. **absent-minded** *adj* forgetful or vague, esp. when preoccupied. **absent-mindedly** *adv*. **absent-mindedness** *n*.
absolute *adj* total; utter; complete. **absolutely** *adv*.
absolve *vt* release from blame, sin, obligation, etc.; pardon; exonerate. **absolution** *n*.
absorb *vt* **1** take in or soak up. **2** assimilate. **3** engross; engage fully. **absorbent** *adj*. **absorbing** *adj*. **absorption** *n*.
abstain *vi* **1** refrain from registering one's vote. **2** refrain from indulging in certain pleasures, such as drinking alcohol. **abstention** *n* withholding of one's vote. **abstinence** *n* state or period of self-denial.
abstract *adj* (ˈæbstrækt) having no material existence; not concrete; conceptual. *n* (ˈæbstrækt) brief account; summary; résumé. *vt* (əbˈstrækt) take away; remove. **abstraction** *n*. **abstract art** *n* art depicting ideas or objects through form, colour, and line rather than natural or actual representation.
absurd *adj* ridiculous; silly; ludicrous. **absurdity** *n*. **absurdly** *adv*.
abundant *adj* plentiful. **abundance** *n*. **abundantly** *adv*.
abuse *vt* (əˈbjuːz) **1** use or treat badly or unfairly; misuse. **2** insult; be rude to. *n* (əˈbjuːs) **1** ill-treatment; misuse; violation. **2** insulting behaviour or language. **abusive** *adj*.
abyss (əˈbis) *n* deep bottomless pit or gulf. **abysmal** (əˈbizməl) *adj* **1** bottomless; deep. **2** dreadful; shocking. **abysmally** *adv*.
academy *n* **1** school or college offering specialized training. **2** association of distinguished scholars. **academic** *adj* **1** relating to a university, college, etc. **2** theoretical or intellectual rather than practical or technical. *n* university teacher or researcher. **academically** *adv*.
accelerate *vt,vi* make or become faster; speed up. **acceleration** *n*. **accelerator** *n* control pedal in a motor vehicle that is used for regulating speed; throttle.
accent *n* (ˈæksent) **1** type of pronunciation associated with a particular region, social class, etc. **2** stress placed on a syllable or word. **3** written or printed symbol occurring in some languages to indicate stress, vowel quality, etc. **4** emphasis. *vt* (əkˈsent) stress; mark with an accent. **accentuate** *vt* emphasize; draw attention to. **accentuation** *n*.
accept *vt* **1** take something that is offered; receive. **2** agree (to); admit. **3** tolerate; put up with. **acceptable** *adj*. **acceptance** *n*.
access *n* **1** way in or to; approach. **2** opportunity, means, or permission to enter, reach, use, etc. **accessible** *adj* reachable; approachable.
accessory *n* **1** one of an additional set of items. **2** person who assists in or conceals knowledge of a crime.
accident *n* unforeseen event or occurrence, often having unpleasant consequences. **by accident** by chance; unexpectedly. **accidental** *adj*. **accidentally** *adv*.
acclaim *vt* show approval by cheering; applaud; hail; praise. *n also* **acclamation** enthusiastic approval; applause; praise.
acclimatize *vt,vi* make or become conditioned or used (to). **acclimatization** *n*.
accommodate *vt* **1** provide room or space for; house; shelter. **2** adjust (to); reconcile. **accommodation** *n*.
accompany *vt* go with; escort; join in or take part in with. **accompaniment** *n* **1** something that belongs or occurs with something else. **2** music that is played to support a solo performance.
accomplice *n* partner in crime or wrongdoing.
accomplish *vt* achieve; attain; complete successfully. **accomplished** *adj* talented; skilful; proficient, esp. in social graces; refined. **accomplishment** *n* **1** successful completion; achievement. **2** skill; refinement; proficiency.
accord *vt,vi* agree; correspond; match up (to). *n* harmony; agreement. **of one's own accord** on one's own initiative; voluntarily. **accordance** *n*. **in accordance with** in agreement with; conforming to. **according** *adv* **according to 1** as laid down or stipulated by. **2** as stated or shown by; on the evidence of. **3** in relation to; dependent on. **accordingly** *adv* **1** therefore; so. **2** as the situation demands.

accordion *n* portable box-shaped musical instrument with bellows and keys

accost *vt* **1** approach (someone) in order to converse, question, etc. **2** solicit.

account *n* **1** report of an event, etc. **2** explanation. **3** banking service or a credit service at a store, etc. **4** sum of money deposited at a bank. **5** statement of money transactions. **6** importance; esteem. **on account** on credit. **on account of** because of. **on any/no account** for no reason whatever. **take into account** *or* **take account of** allow for. *vi* **account for 1** give reasons for; explain. **2** make a reckoning of; count. **3** capture; kill. **accountable** *adj* responsible (for). **accountant** *n* professional person who investigates the business and financial transactions of an individual or organization. **accountancy** *n*.

accumulate *vt,vi* amass or collect over a period of time; pile up. **accumulation** *n*. **accumulative** *adj*.

accurate *adj* precise; correct; exactly right. **accuracy** *n*. **accurately** *adv*.

accuse *vt* charge (a person) with a crime, mistake, fault, etc.; blame. **accusation** *n*.

accustom *vt* familiarize; acquaint; acclimatize.

ace *n* **1** playing card having a single pip. **2** pilot who has destroyed a large number of enemy aircraft. **3** champion. *adj sl* first-rate; excellent.

ache *vi* **1** feel a steady dull pain. **2** yearn; long (for). *n* steady dull pain.

achieve *vt* accomplish; attain; gain. **achievement** *n*.

acid *n* sour-tasting chemical compound that turns litmus red and dissolves in water to produce hydrogen ions. *adj* **1** sharp; sour-tasting. **2** sarcastic; caustic. **acidic** *adj*. **acidity** *n*.

acknowledge *vt* **1** recognize that something is true or right; admit. **2** respond to. **acknowledgment** *or* **acknowledgement** *n*.

acne ('ækni) *n* skin disorder affecting mainly the face and upper part of the body, which become covered with pimples and blackheads.

acorn *n* nut that is the fruit of the oak.

acoustic *adj* relating to sound or the sense of hearing. **acoustics** *n* **1** *s* branch of physics concerned with the study of sound-waves. **2** *pl* properties of a concert hall, room, etc., that affect the way sounds are heard.

acquaint *vt* inform; familiarize; introduce. **acquaintance** *n* **1** someone one knows, but not as a close or intimate friend. **2** personal knowledge. **acquaintanceship** *n*.

acquiesce *vi* agree tacitly; assent; comply. **acquiescence** *n*. **acquiescent** *adj*.

acquire *vt* obtain, esp. gradually or with some effort; take possession of; get. **acquisition** *n*. **acquisitive** *adj* eager to possess.

acquit *vt* (-tt-) pronounce not guilty; discharge. **acquit oneself** perform; behave; conduct oneself.

acre *n* unit of land area equal to approx. 4000 sq m (4840 sq yds). **acreage** *n* total number of acres in any given area.

acrobat *n* performer on a trapeze, tightrope, etc., gymnast. **acrobatic** *adj*. **acrobatics** *n s or pl* gymnastic feats or exercises.

across *prep,adv* **1** from one side to another. **2** over on the other side (of). **come across** meet or discover unexpectedly.

acrylic *adj* relating to a type of synthetic fibre.

act *vi* **1** operate; function; behave; perform; do (something). **2** perform in a play. **3** pretend; feign. *vt* take the role of; play. *n* **1** single deed; action. **2** law passed by Parliament. **3** major division of a play, opera, etc., consisting of a number of scenes. **4** performer(s) in a show, circus, etc., or the performance itself.

action *n* **1** process of doing something; act; deed. **2** gesture; movement. **3** mechanism; movement of mechanical parts. **4** lawsuit.

activate *vt* make active; stir; agitate; cause to react.

active *adj* **1** in operation; functioning. **2** taking a positive part. **3** lively; busy. **actively** *adv*. **activist** *n* person working for a particular political cause.

activity *n* **1** movement; motion. **2** something that keeps one occupied or busy.

actor *n* performer in the theatre, on television, or in films. **actress** *f n*.

actual *adj* having real existence; not imaginary. **actually** *adv* really; as a matter of fact; in fact.

actuary *n* expert adviser on insurance, pensions, etc. **actuarial** *adj*.

acupuncture *n* Eastern method of medical treatment using sharp needles to puncture certain areas of the skin.

acute *adj* **1** having a keen sense of hearing, smell, etc. **2** perceptive; quick-witted; shrewd. **3** severe; critical. **4** *med* reaching crisis point; not chronic. **acute accent** *n* symbol placed over certain vowels in some languages, as in *café*. **acute angle** *n* angle of less than 90°. **acutely** *adv*. **acuteness** *n*.

adamant *adj* insistent; firm. **adamantly** *adv*.

Adam's apple *n* popular name for the thyroid cartilage of the larynx.

adapt *vt* modify to suit a different purpose or situation. *vi* adjust to a new environment or set of conditions. **adaptable** *adj*. **adaptation** *n*. **adaptor** *n*.

add *vt,vi* **1** put together; join; give as something extra. **2** calculate the sum (of); total. **3** state further; go on to say. **add to** supplement; increase. **addition** *n*. **additional** *adj* extra. **additive** *adj,n*.

adder *n* viper.

addict *n* ('ædikt) **1** person who has become physically dependent on something, esp. a drug. **2** enthusiast; fanatic. **be(come) addicted to** (ə'diktid) be(come) totally dependent on. **addiction** *n*. **addictive** *adj*.

address *n* **1** postal location of a house, office, etc. **2** speech given before an audience. *vt* **1** write the address on. **2** speak directly to. **addressee** *n*.

adenoids *pl n* mass of enlarged tissue in the pharynx.

adept *adj* skilful; adroit; deft. **adeptly** *adv*. **adeptness** *n*.

adequate *adj* **1** sufficient; just enough; acceptable; satisfactory. **2** able to cope; capable. **adequacy** *n*. **adequately** *adv*.

adhere *vi* stick; hold. *vt* stick; glue; gum. **adhere to** keep to; uphold; observe strictly; abide by. **adherent** *adj*. **adhesion** *n*. **adhesive** *n* substance such as glue, gum, or paste, used for sticking things together. *adj* relating to such a substance.

ad hoc *adj* used for a specified purpose.

adjacent *adj* adjoining; situated beside; next to.

adjective *n* part of speech qualifying a noun. **adjectival** *adj*.

adjoin *vt* be situated next to; border on. **adjoining** *adj*.

adjourn *vt,vi* discontinue or suspend (a meeting, court session, etc.) with the intention of resuming at a later time. **adjournment** *n*.

adjudicate *vi,vt* judge; settle; select (a winner). **adjudication** *n*. **adjudicator** *n*.

adjust *vt* make a minor alteration to; modify; change. *vi* change to fit in with new requirements; adapt. **adjustable** *adj*. **adjustment** *n*.

ad-lib *vi* (-bb-) compose (a speech, lines in a play, etc.) without previous preparation; improvise.

administer *vt* **1** *also* **administrate** govern; control as an official. **2** dispense; hand out; issue. **administrative** *adj*. **administrator** *n*. **administration** *n* **1** management; control; process of governing. **2** body of managers, governors, etc.

admiral *n* highest ranking naval officer. **admiralty** *n* state department responsible for naval affairs.

admire *vt* have a high regard for; respect; look up to; approve of. **admirable** *adj*. **admiration** *n*. **admirer** *n*.

admit *vt* (-tt-) **1** grant entry to. **2** confess; accept blame for. **3** accept as true; agree to. **admissible** *adj* acceptable; allowable. **admission** *n* **1** permission or opportunity to enter. **2** fee charged for entrance. **3** confession. **4** acknowledgment; acceptance. **admittance** *n* right of entry; access.

ado *n* fuss; confused excitement; commotion.

adolescence *n* period between puberty and adulthood. **adolescent** *n,adj*.

adopt *vt* **1** take (another person's child) into one's own family as a legal guardian. **2** take up (someone else's suggestion, plan, etc.). **3** give formal approval to; choose. **adoption** *n*.

adore *vt* love ardently; worship; have great affection for. **adorable** *adj*. **adoration** *n*.

adorn *vt* decorate; embellish; enhance. **adornment** *n*.

adrenaline *n* hormone secreted in the body or produced synthetically that is used to accelerate heart action, raise blood sugar levels, etc.

adrift *adj* **1** cut loose from a mooring; unattached; drifting. **2** off the point; not concise.

adroit *adj* skilfully quick; resourceful; adept. **adroitly** *adv*. **adroitness** *n*.

adulation *n* **1** unqualified or uncritical praise. **2** flattery. **3** unquestioning devotion.

adult *n* **1** person who is grown up or mature. **2** fully grown animal or plant. *adj* **1** mature; of age; fully grown. **2** intended for adults. **adulthood** *n*.

adultery *n* extra-marital sexual intercourse.

advance *vi* **1** move forwards or upwards; proceed. **2** show improvement; progress. *vt* **1** take further; move ahead. **2** pay out (money) before it is due. *n* **1** movement forwards. **2** progress. **3** amount paid before payment is due. *adj* issued in advance. **advancement** *n*. **in advance** beforehand; ahead.

advantage *n* favourable position, circumstances, etc.; privilege; benefit. **advantageous** *adj*.

adventure *n* exciting journey or experience, usually involving risks or hazards. **adventurous** *adj* daring; bold; willing to take risks. **adventurously** *adv*.

adverb *n* part of speech qualifying a verb. **adverbial** *adj*.

adverse *adj* hostile; in opposition; antagonistic. **adversity** *n* distressing circumstances; misfortune.

advertise *vt,vi* give public information (of goods for sale, vacancies, etc.); announce. **advertiser** *n*. **advertisement** *n* public announcement in the press, on televison, etc.; note of goods for sale, etc.

advice *n* opinion or recommendation given in order to help someone make a decision.

advise *vt,vi* give advice (to); recommend. **adviser** *n*. **advisable** *adj* wise; worth recommending.

advocate *vt* ('ædvəkeit) recommend; urge. *n* ('ædvəkət) **1** supporter; believer. **2** (in Scotland) barrister.

aerial *n* system of conducting rods for receiving or transmitting radio or television signals; antenna. *adj* of, in, or from the air. **aerially** *adv*.

aerodynamics *n* study of the behaviour of aircraft, missiles, etc., in relation to airflow. **aerodynamic** *adj*. **aerodynamically** *adv*.

aeronautics *n* study of flight. **aeronautic** *or* **aeronautical** *adj*.

aeroplane *n* aircraft propelled by jet engines or propellers and kept aloft by aerodynamic forces.

aerosol *n* container dispensing a fine spray of pressurized liquid, gas, etc.

aesthetic (i:s'θetik) *adj* **1** pleasing to one's sense of beauty. **2** relating to aesthetics. **aesthetics** *n* branch of philosophy concerned with the concept and study of beauty, esp. in art.

afar *adv* far away; from or at a distance.

affair *n* **1** matter; concern; business. **2** sexual relationship, esp. an extra-marital one; liaison. *pl n* personal, business, or political matters.

affect[1] *vt* **1** influence; alter; cause to change. **2** move; arouse emotionally.

affect[2] *vt* feign; simulate; pretend. **affectation** *n* falseness of manner or style; insincerity.

affection *n* fondness; love; strong liking. **affectionate** *adj*. **affectionately** *adv*.

affiliate *vt,vi* join or unite (with) as a member; associate. **affiliation** *n*.

affinity *n* **1** relationship, esp. by marriage. **2** close connection; resemblance. **3** empathetic attraction; strong liking.

affirm *vt,vi* testify as to truth or validity; substantiate; assent. **affirmation** *n*. **affirmative** *adj* positive; assertive. *n* the answer 'yes'.

affix *vt* (ə'fiks) fasten; attach. *n* ('æfiks) prefix or suffix.

afflict *vt* cause distress, pain, or suffering; torment. **affliction** *n* **1** torment; grief. **2** disease; sickness; disability.

affluent *adj* wealthy; prosperous; rich. **affluence** *n*.

afford *vt* **1** have money, time, etc., to spare (for). **2** be able to risk. **3** offer; provide; allow.

affront *vt* insult or offend, esp. publicly. *n* public insult; display of disrespect.

afield *adv* far away; a long way off.

afloat *adj,adv* **1** floating. **2** solvent.

afoot *adj,adv* under way; in the offing.

aforesaid *adj also* **aforementioned** previously referred to.

afraid *adj* **1** frightened; apprehensive; fearful. **2** sorry; regretful.

afresh *adv* from the beginning; again; anew.

aft *adv* towards or at the stern.

after *prep* **1** following; later than. **2** in pursuit of. **3** in spite of; in view of. **4** concerning. **5** in imitation of. **after all** when everything is considered. ~*adv* **1** behind. **2** subsequently. **take after** resemble. ~*conj* subsequent to the time that. **after-care** *n* help, treatment, supervision, etc., given to a person discharged from hospital or prison. **after-effect** *n* delayed effect, esp. of a drug. **afterlife** *n* life after death. **aftermath** *n* **1** period of devastation following a war, disaster, etc. **2** disastrous consequence. **afternoon** *n* period between midday and evening. **afterthought** *n* thought or idea that occurs later or incidentally. **afterwards** *adv* at a later time; subsequently.

again *adv* **1** once more; any more. **2** additionally; further; besides. **again and again** repeatedly; many times.

against *prep* **1** in contact with; next to; close to; up as far as. **2** in opposition to; competing with. **3** not in favour of. **4** contrasting with. **5** in order to prevent.

age *n* **1** period of time during which a person or thing has existed. **2** era; epoch; period. **3** *also pl inf* a long time. *vi,vt* grow or cause to grow or look old(er). **aged** *adj* **1** ('eidʒid) very old. **2** (eidʒd) of the age of.

agenda *n* list of items to be discussed or dealt with; programme.

agent *n* **1** person representing or working on behalf of a client. **2** something that produces a change or effect. **agency** *n* **1** company providing services or goods and operating on behalf of a client. **2** influence; mediating power.

aggravate *vt* **1** make worse; exacerbate. **2** irritate; annoy. **aggravation** *n.*

aggression *n* feeling or display of hostility, anger, etc. **aggressive** *adj.* **aggressively** *adv.* **aggressor** *n.*

aggrieved *adj* suffering from injustice; feeling unfairly treated.

aghast *adj* horrified; dumbfounded; shocked.

agile *adj* quick; alert; nimble. **agility** *n.*

agitate *vt* **1** shake or stir violently. **2** worry; make anxious; trouble. *vi also* **agitate for** publicly campaign and fight for. **agitator** *n.*

aglow *adj* glowing; shining; alight.

agnostic *n* person who believes that an immaterial being such as God cannot be the subject of real knowledge. **agnosticism** *n.*

ago *adv* in the past.

agog *adj* eager and excited.

agony *n* intense and prolonged pain or suffering; torment; anguish. **agonize** *vi,vt* suffer or cause agony or extreme distress.

agrarian *adj* relating to agricultural land or landed property.

agree *vi* **1** consent. **2** correspond; match; tally. **3** think or feel the same (as). **4** make a joint decision. **5** suit; go well with. *vt* **1** settle; arrange terms of. **2** acknowledge; concede; consent to. **agreeable** *adj* **1** willing to consent. **2** pleasant. **agreement** *n* **1** consent; permission. **2** deal or contract between parties. **3** accordance; harmony.

agriculture *n* practice or study of farming. **agricultural** *adj.* **agriculturalist** *n.*

ahead *adv* further on; in front; in advance. **go ahead** continue; proceed; advance.

aid *vt,vi* help; assist; facilitate. *n* help; assistance; support. **in aid of** for; in order to help.

ailment *n* particular illness or disease.

aim *vt,vi* **1** point or direct (a gun, etc.) towards a target. **2** direct (one's efforts, remarks, etc.) towards a particular object. **aim at** *or* **for 1** try to achieve; strive for. **2** mean or intend for. ~*n* **1** act of aiming. **2** goal; target; purpose. **aimless** *adj* having no particular goal or purpose. **aimlessly** *adv.* **aimlessness** *n.*

air *n* **1** mixture of gases, consisting chiefly of nitrogen (78 per cent) and oxygen (21 per cent), that is essential for respiration. **2** layer of air surrounding the earth; atmosphere. **3** light breeze. **4** impression or aura. **5** bearing; manner. **6** tune; melody. **by air** transported by aircraft. **clear the air** remove tension or discord. **in the air** not yet settled. **into thin air** without a trace; completely. **on/off the air** being/not being broadcast. **walk** *or* **tread on air** feel elated. **airs** *pl n* affectations. ~*vt* **1** expose to fresh air; ventilate. **2** declare openly; make public. *vt,vi* dry in warm air. **airborne** *adj* in or supported or carried by air. **airtight** *adj* preventing the passage of air into or out of; impermeable. **airy** *adj* **1** open to the fresh air; well ventilated. **2** carefree; unconcerned. **3** light as air; graceful. **4** insubstantial; speculative. **airily** *adv.* **airiness** *n.*

air-conditioning *n* system for controlling flow and humidity of air within a building.

aircraft *n* machine, such as an aeroplane, helicopter, or glider, that is capable of flight through the air.

aircraft carrier *n* warship with special decks for operational aircraft.

airfield *n* extensive level area for take-off and landing of aircraft.

airforce *n* branch of a nation's armed services concerned with military aircraft.

airgun *n* gun discharged by compressed air.

air hostess *n* stewardess on an aircraft.

airlift *n* transportation by air of people, food, etc., esp. in an emergency when surface routes are cut. *vt* transport using an airlift.

airline *n* organization offering transportation by scheduled flights for people and cargo. **airliner** *n.*

airmail *n* **1** letters and parcels conveyed by

aircraft. **2** system for sending such mail. *vt* send (mail) by air.

airport *n* system of buildings, runways, hangars, etc., providing facilities for aircraft, passengers, and cargo.

air-raid *n* military attack by enemy aircraft.

airship *n* self-propelled aircraft kept aloft by buoyancy.

aisle *n* **1** gangway or open passageway separating blocks of seats in a theatre, church, etc. **2** area on either side of a church, usually separated from the nave by a series of pillars and arches.

ajar *adj,adv* partially open.

alabaster *n* form of gypsum that is white and opaque or translucent, used for statues, ornaments, etc.

alarm *n* **1** warning signal, such as a bell or shout. **2** sudden fear or anxiety; panic; fright. *vt* **1** frighten; shock; horrify. **2** alert to possible danger.

alas *interj* expression of regret, sadness, etc.

albatross *n* large sea-bird with webbed feet.

albeit *conj* even though; although.

albino *n* person or animal with unnatural colouring in skin and eyes.

album *n* **1** book used for the display of photographs, stamps, etc. **2** long-playing record.

alcohol *n* **1** intoxicating substance produced by fermenting sugar in a liquid. **2** any drink containing such a substance. **alcoholic** *adj* containing alcohol. *n* person addicted to alcohol. **alcoholism** *n* addiction to alcohol.

alcove *n* recess or niche.

alderman *n* senior councillor of a city or borough.

ale *n* type of light-coloured beer.

alert *adj* watchful; quick to respond. **alertness** *n*.

algebra *n* branch of mathematics in which numbers, quantities, and variables are represented by symbols whose manipulation is governed by generalized rules and relationships. **algebraic** *adj*.

alias *adv* also known as. *n* assumed name; pseudonym.

alibi *n* claim that someone accused of a crime was elsewhere at the time that it was committed.

alien *adj* **1** foreign; strange. **2** not part of; contrary. *n* foreigner. **alienate** *vt* estrange; cast out; cause to become indifferent or detached, esp. from society. **alienation** *n*.

alight[1] *adj* **1** on fire; lit up. **2** bright; shining.

alight[2] *vi* (alighted *or* alit) **1** dismount; get down (from). **2** settle or perch (on). **alight on** find unexpectedly; seize; light on.

align *vt,vi* **1** bring into line (with); line up; straighten. **2** form an alliance (with); cooperate. **alignment** *n*.

alike *adj* similar; appearing the same; resembling. *adv* similarly; in the same way.

alimentary canal (æli'mentəri) *n* system of organs in the body, including the stomach and intestines, through which food passes.

alimony *n* allowance paid to one marriage partner by the other following a legal separation.

alive *adj* **1** living; existing. **2** active; vigorous.

alkali ('ælkəlai) *n* chemical base that is soluble in water. **alkaline** *adj*.

all *adj* **1** every one of; the whole of. **2** complete; total. *adv* entirely; completely; totally. **all but** very nearly; almost. **all in all** taking everything into consideration. **in all** altogether; in total.

allay *vt* alleviate; assuage; appease; relieve.

allege (ə'ledʒ) *vt* claim as true; assert; avow. **allegation** (æli'geiʃən) *n*.

allegiance (ə'li:dʒəns) *n* loyalty, esp. to a sovereign; fidelity.

allegory ('æligəri) *n* story, painting, etc. in which moral values and other qualities are personified. **allegorical** (æli'gɔrikḷ) *adj*.

alleluia *interj,n* hallelujah.

allergy ('ælədʒi) *n* physical reaction of the body caused by extreme sensitivity to certain substances. **allergic** (ə'lə:dʒik) *adj*.

alleviate *vt* relieve (pain or suffering); allay. **alleviation** *n*.

alley *n* **1** *also* **alleyway** narrow passageway or street. **2** lane used in skittles, ten-pin bowling, etc.

alliance *n* **1** treaty of mutual friendship and help between nations. **2** relationship so formed. **3** nations so involved. **4** close relationship; union. **allied** *adj* **1** joined by alliance; united. **2** related; connected.

alligator *n* large reptile, chiefly of the southern US, related to the crocodile but having a shorter broader snout.

alliteration *n* repetition of the initial sound, usually a consonant, in a group of words.

allocate *vt* assign; distribute; share out. **allocation** *n*.

allot *vt* (-tt-) allocate. **allotment** *n* **1** plot of rented land for cultivation. **2** assignment.

allow *vt* **1** permit; let. **2** set aside. **3** grant; permit to have; concede. **allow for** make provision for. **allowable** *adj* permissible. **allowance** *n* **1** regular amount of money paid to a dependant. **2** sum of money allocated for certain tasks, responsibilities, etc. **3** concession; toleration. **make allowances for 1** excuse. **2** take into account.

alloy *n* metallic material consisting of a mixture of metals, as in bronze and brass, or of metals and nonmetals, as in steel.

allude *v* **allude to** refer indirectly to.

allure *vt* entice; attract; fascinate. *n* attraction; fascination. **allurement** *n*.

ally *n* ('ælai) **1** member of an alliance. **2** sympathetic person; supporter. *vt,vi* (ə'lai) unite; join (with).

almanac ('ɔːlmənæk) *n* book containing a calendar, with astronomical and astrological information, etc., for the year.

almighty *adj* **1** omnipotent; supremely or divinely powerful. **2** *sl* tremendous; great. **the Almighty** *n* God.

almond *n* **1** tree related to the plum and peach. **2** smooth oval nut in a hard shell produced by this tree. *adj* of an oval shape like an almond.

almost *adv* nearly; close to; not quite.

alms (ɑːmz) *pl n* money or gifts donated as charity to the poor. **almshouse** *n* building founded to provide accommodation and food for the poor and aged.

aloft *adj,adv* high up; overhead.

alone *adj,adv* by oneself; by itself; apart; isolated; separate; unaccompanied.

along *prep* **1** from one end to the other. **2** on any part of the length of. *adv* **1** onwards; forwards. **2** together (with); accompanying. **all along** all the time. **alongside** *adv,prep* along the side of; beside; parallel to.

aloof *adj* distant; haughty or reserved; uninvolved. *adv* at a distance; with reserve.

aloud *adv* using a normal speaking voice; not silently; out loud.

alphabet *n* system of letters or other symbols used for writing in a particular language. **alphabetical** *adj* following the order of the letters of the alphabet. **alphabetically** *adv*.

alpine *adj* relating to mountains or a mountainous region.

already *adv* by now, by then; previously.

Alsatian *n* breed of dog resembling a wolf in appearance and often used by the police or as a guard dog.

also *adv* in addition; as well; too; besides.

altar *n* **1** table in a Christian church at which the Eucharist is celebrated. **2** table or platform used for offerings or sacrifices to a deity.

alter *vt,vi* change; give or take on a new form or appearance; modify. **alteration** *n*.

alternate *adj* (ɔl'təːnət) every other or second one; first one then the other. *vi,vt* ('ɔltəneit) switch repeatedly from one to the other; take or arrange in turn. **alternately** *adv*. **alternation** *n*. **alternative** *n* the second of two possibilities or choices. *adj* offering a choice between two things.

although *conj* though; even though; in spite of the fact that.

altitude *n* height of an aircraft, mountain, etc., esp. that above sea level.

alto *n* **1** male singing voice or musical instrument with a range between tenor and treble. **2** contralto.

altogether *adv* **1** completely; totally; absolutely; all; utterly; entirely. **2** on the whole. **3** added together; in total.

aluminium *n* silvery metallic element extracted mainly from bauxite and widely used in lightweight alloys.

always *adv* all the time; without exception; regularly.

am *v* 1st person singular form of **be** in the present tense.

amalgamate *vi,vt* join together; merge; unite; combine. **amalgamation** *n*.

amass *vt,vi* bring or come together; accumulate; collect.

amateur *n* person who is an unpaid participator in an activity such as sport or the arts. *adj* **1** not professional. **2** *also* **amateurish** lacking in skill or polish; of a rather low standard.

amaze *vt* fill with surprise or wonder; astonish; astound. **amazement** *n*. **amazingly** *adv*.

ambassador *n* minister or diplomat sent abroad by the Government as an official representative.

amber *n* yellowish-brown fossil resin often used for jewellery. *adj* **1** of a yellowish-brown or dull orange colour. **2** made of amber.

ambidextrous *adj* able to use either hand with equal skill. **ambidexterity** *n.*

ambiguous *adj* having more than one possible meaning; open to interpretation. **ambiguity** *n.* **ambiguously** *adv.*

ambition *n* **1** desire or will to achieve fame, power, position, etc. **2** desired object or goal; aim. **ambitious** *adj.* **ambitiously** *adv.*

ambivalent (æmˈbivələnt) *adj* having conflicting or uncertain feelings; undecided. **ambivalence** *n.* **ambivalently** *adv.*

amble *vi* **1** walk at an easy and leisurely pace; stroll; saunter. **2** (of a horse) move slowly lifting both legs on the same side of the body together. *n* leisurely pace.

ambulance *n* vehicle designed and equipped to convey sick or injured people to hospital.

ambush *n* **1** act of lying in wait in order to make a surprise attack. **2** such an attack, the concealed place from which such an attack is launched, or the attackers themselves. *vt* attack (an enemy) by ambush.

amen *interj* word meaning 'so be it' spoken or sung at the end of a prayer, hymn, etc.

amenable *adj* **1** willing; agreeable; responsive. **2** legally responsible; answerable. **3** capable of being tested or judged.

amend *vt* rectify; correct; modify. **make amends** make up (for); compensate. **amendment** *n.*

amenity *n often pl.* useful service or facility intended to make life easier or more comfortable.

amethyst *n* precious stone of crystallized quartz that is usually purple or mauve.

amiable *adj* pleasant; likeable; friendly. **amiability** *n.* **amiably** *adv.*

amicable *adj* friendly; not hostile. **amicably** *adv.*

amid *or* **amidst** *prep* among or amongst; in the midst of.

amiss *adj* faulty; defective; wrong. *adv* wrongly; incorrectly. **take amiss** feel wronged or hurt (by), often unjustifiably.

ammonia *n* colourless pungent gas, containing nitrogen and hydrogen, used in the manufacture of fertilizers and of other chemicals.

ammunition *n* **1** bullets, missiles, etc., that can be fired from a gun or other offensive weapon. **2** information or points of argument used against someone in debate, criticism, etc.

amnesty *n* general pardon given esp. to political prisoners.

amoeba *n* microscopic single-celled animal having a constantly changing shape.

among *or* **amongst** *prep* **1** in the middle of; surrounded by; in company with; together with. **2** between; shared by.

amoral (eiˈmɔrəl) *adj* outside the sphere of morality. **amorality** *n.*

amorous *adj* concerned with or displaying love; affectionate. **amorously** *adv.* **amorousness** *n.*

amorphous *adj* having no distinct form, shape, or structure.

amount *n* **1** quantity; extent; whole. **2** sum; total. *v* **amount to 1** add up to; come to. **2** be equal or equivalent to; have the same function as.

ampere *n* unit used to measure electric current.

amphetamine *n* drug that stimulates the central nervous system, used for the relief of nasal congestion, hay fever, etc.

amphibian *n* **1** cold-blooded animal, such as the frog or newt, that usually lives on land as an adult but breeds in water. **2** vehicle able to function both on land and water. **amphibious** *adj.*

amphitheatre *n* large arena enclosed by rising tiers of seats.

ample *adj* **1** plenty; more than enough; sufficient. **2** of generous proportions; large. **amply** *adv.*

amplify *vt* increase the intensity of (an electrical signal). *vt,vi* explain in greater detail; expand (on). **amplification** *n.* **amplifier** *n* electrical device, used in radios, televisions, etc., for reproducing a signal at increased intensity.

amputate *vt,vi* sever (a limb or part of a limb) usually by surgery. **amputation** *n.*

amuse *vt* **1** entertain, esp. by speaking or acting in a humorous way. **2** keep pleasantly busy or occupied. **amusement** *n.*

an *indef art* used before an initial vowel sound and sometimes *h*. See **a.**

anachronism *n* **1** representation of an object, event, etc., in too early a historical period; chronological error. **2** something no longer useful or suitable in the present age. **anachronistic** *adj.*

anaemia *n* deficiency of red blood cells causing pale appearance of the skin, fatigue, etc. **anaemic** *adj.*

anaesthetic (æṇisˈθetik) *n* substance administered before an operation to produce loss of sensation or unconsciousness. **anaesthetist** *n* (əˈniːsθətist) person trained to administer anaesthetics. **anaesthetize** *vt* (əˈniːsθətaiz) administer anaesthetics to.

anagram *n* word or phrase whose letters can be transposed to form a new word or phrase.

anal (ˈeinəl) *adj* relating to the anus.

analogy (əˈnælədʒi) *n* comparison that serves to draw attention to a similarity between things. **analogous** (əˈnæləgəs) *adj*.

analyse (ˈænəlaiz) *vt* break down (a substance, situation, etc.) into constituent parts or stages for examination. **analysis** *n, pl* **analyses** (əˈnælisiːz). **analytic** (ænəˈlitik) *or* **analytical** *adj*. **analyst** (ˈænəlist) *n* **1** person who analyses. **2** psychoanalyst.

anarchy (ˈænəki) *n* **1** form of society in which established forms of government and law are not recognized. **2** disorder; lawlessness. **anarchist** *n* supporter of anarchy.

anatomy (əˈnætəmi) *n* study or science of the physical structure of animals and plants. **anatomical** (ænəˈtɔmikəl) *adj*. **anatomist** (əˈnætəmist) *n*.

ancestor (ˈænsestə) *n* person from whom one is descended; forefather. **ancestral** (ænˈsestrəl) *adj*. **ancestry** (ˈænsəstri) *n*.

anchor *n* **1** heavy steel or iron object used for holding fast a vessel in the water. **2** something that offers security and stability. *vt,vi* hold fast with the anchor. **anchorage** *n* **1** place where a vessel may be anchored or the fee charged. **2** stability, firm or sound basis.

anchovy (ˈæntʃəvi) *n* small fish of the herring family with a strong salty flavour.

ancient *adj* **1** relating to a very early or remote historical period. **2** very old.

ancillary *adj* auxiliary; secondary; subsidiary.

and *conj* **1** as well as; in addition to. **2** then; after. **3** also; too.

anecdote (ˈænikdout) *n* short witty account or story.

anemone (əˈneməni) *n* **1** woodland plant producing white, red, or deep blue flowers. **2** sea anemone.

anew *adv* afresh; again.

angel *n* **1** spiritual being in the Christian religion who is one of God's attendants and messengers, usually depicted as having human form with wings. **2** sweet kind-hearted person. **angelic** (ænˈdʒelik) *adj*.

anger *n* feeling of intense annoyance or irritation; rage. *vt* make angry; enrage; infuriate.

angle[1] *n* **1** difference in direction between two intersecting lines or planes, measured in degrees. **2** shape formed by such lines or planes. **3** projecting corner. **4** point of view; aspect. *vt* **1** move or place at an angle; bend into an angle. **2** direct at a particular audience; bias.

angle[2] *vi* **1** fish with a rod, line, and bait. **2** *also* **angle for** seek (compliments, favours, etc.), esp. by devious means. **angler** *n*.

Anglican *adj* relating to the Church of England. *n* member of the Church of England. **Anglicanism** *n*.

angry *adj* **1** extremely cross or annoyed; enraged. **2** sore and inflamed. **angrily** *adv*.

anguish *n* intense anxiety and distress; agony; torment.

angular *adj* **1** having sharp corners or many angles. **2** bony; gaunt.

animal *n* living organism capable of spontaneous movement; creature. *adj* **1** relating to an animal or animals. **2** physical as opposed to spiritual; carnal.

animate *adj* (ˈænimət) living; capable of spontaneous movement. *vt* (ˈænimeit) give life or movement to; make active. **animation** *n*.

aniseed *n* seed yielding an aromatic oil with a strong liquorice flavour, used in medicines, drinks, etc.

ankle *n* joint that connects the foot and the leg.

annex *vt* (əˈneks) **1** take possession of by conquest. **2** join; attach; incorporate. *n* (ˈæneks) *also* **annexe** additional building usually set apart from the main block of a hotel, hospital, etc.

annihilate *vt* wipe out completely; destroy; obliterate. **annihilation** *n*.

anniversary *n* **1** date of a significant event which occurred in some previous year. **2** celebration of this.

announce *vt* declare; proclaim; make known. **announcement** *n*. **announcer** *n* person who introduces programmes, reads news bulletins, etc., on radio or television.

annoy *vt,vi* irritate; bother; vex. **annoyance** *n*.

annual *adj* **1** occurring once a year. **2** valid for one year. **3** lasting for one growing season. *n*

1 plant that lasts for one growing season only. 2 book or periodical published in a new edition each year. **annually** *adv*.

annuity (ə'nju:iti) *n* sum of money paid out in instalments at regular intervals.

annul (ə'nʌl) *vt* (-ll-) declare (a law, marriage contract, etc.) invalid or no longer binding; revoke.

anoint *vt* rub or smear with oil, esp. ritually as an act of consecration. **anointment** *n*.

anomaly (ə'nɔməli) *n* something that is out of place or deviates from the common rule. **anomalous** *adj*.

anonymous (ə'nɔniməs) *adj* **1** *sometimes shortened to* **anon** having no acknowledged author. **2** faceless; unknown. **anonymity** (ænə'nimiti) *n*.

anorak *n* waterproof jacket with a hood.

another *adj* **1** additional; further. **2** different; separate. *pron* **1** one more. **2** a different or new one. **3** a comparable or similar one.

answer *n* **1** reply or response (to a question). **2** solution (to a problem). *vt,vi* reply or respond (to); acknowledge. *vt* solve. **answer for** accept responsibility or blame for. **answer to** match or correspond to (a description). **answerable** *adj* responsible; liable; accountable.

ant *n* small insect that typically lives in a complex highly organized colony.

antagonize *vt* provoke; incite; arouse hostility by attacking. **antagonism** *n*. **antagonist** *n*. **antagonistic** *adj*.

antelope *n* deer-like animal with hollow horns such as the gazelle or springbok.

antenatal *adj* relating to the period of pregnancy; before birth.

antenna (æn'tenə) **1** *pl* **antennae** (æn'teni:) one of a pair of sensitive organs on the head of an insect, crustacean, etc.; feeler. **2** *pl* **antennas** radio aerial.

anthem *n* patriotic song; hymn of praise.

anthology *n* collection of poems, stories, articles, etc.

anthropology *n* study of mankind and man's social and cultural relationships. **anthropological** *adj*. **anthropologist** *n*.

anti-aircraft *adj* designed for defence against enemy aircraft.

antibiotic (æntibai'ɔtik) *n* chemical substance, such as penicillin, used to destroy certain bacteria. *adj* relating to an antibiotic.

antibody *n* protein in the blood that counteracts harmful bacteria.

anticipate *vt* **1** realize or recognize beforehand; predict; foresee. **2** expect; look forward to; await. **anticipation** *n*.

anticlimax *n* drop in mood from excitement to flatness, seriousness to absurdity, etc.

anticlockwise *adj,adv* moving in a direction opposite to that followed by the hands of a clock.

antics *pl n* playful jokes, tricks, or gestures.

anticyclone *n* area of high atmospheric pressure producing calm settled weather.

antidote ('æntidout) *n* substance or agent used to counteract harmful effects; remedy.

antifreeze *n* substance that lowers the freezing point of a liquid, used esp. in car radiators.

antique *n* valuable piece of furniture, work of art, etc., belonging to an earlier period. *adj* **1** old and valuable. **2** antiquated. **antiquated** *adj* obsolete; out-of-date; old-fashioned. **antiquity** (æn'tikwiti) *n* **1** quality of being very old. **2** period before the Middle Ages; distant past.

anti-Semitic (æntisə'mitik) *adj* discriminating against Jews. **anti-Semite** (ænti'semait) *n*. **anti-Semitism** (ænti'semitizəm) *n*.

antiseptic *adj* relating to the destruction of undesirable microorganisms; preventing decay. *n* an antiseptic substance.

antisocial *adj* **1** contrary to the norms of society. **2** unsociable; shunning the company of others.

antithesis (æn'tiθisis) *n, pl* **antitheses** (æn'tiθisi:z) direct contrast; opposite. **antithetical** (ænti'θetikəl) *adj*.

antler *n* branched bony outgrowth on the head of a male deer or similar animal.

anus *n* opening at the lower end of the rectum.

anvil *n* iron or steel block on which metal is hammered and shaped.

anxious *adj* **1** nervous; worried; uneasy; apprehensive; tense. **2** keen; eager. **anxiety** *n*. **anxiously** *adv*.

any *adj* **1** some; several. **2** whichever; no matter which. **3** one of many; every. **at any rate/in any case** anyway; moreover; besides; anyhow; however. ~*pron* **1** anybody; anything. **2** some. *adv* at all; to an extent. **anybody** *pron, n* a person; no matter who; anyone. **anyhow** *adv* **1** besides; anyway. **2** haphazardly; with no particular care or organization; not systematically. **anyone** *pron,n* anybody. **anything** *pron,n* a thing; no matter what or which; something. ~*adv* at all; remotely. **anyway** *adv* **1** in any case; well; besides; anyhow; after all. **2** carelessly; anyhow. **anywhere** *adv* **1** to or at any place. **2** at all; anything.

apart *adv* **1** separately; independently. **2** into parts or pieces. **3** at a distance; away. **apart from** after considering; aside from; other than.

apartheid (ə'pɑ:taid) *n* system of racial segregation, esp. in South Africa

apartment *n* **1** *chiefly US* flat, usually in a block. **2** suite of rooms.

apathy *n* lack of sympathy, feeling, interest, etc.; listlessness; complete indifference. **apathetic** *adj*.

ape *n* short-tailed or tailless primate, such as the chimpanzee or gorilla.

aperture *n* **1** opening or slit. **2** diaphragm in a lens system that limits the diameter of a light beam entering a camera, etc. **3** diameter of such a diaphragm.

apex ('eipeks) *n, pl* **apexes** *or* **apices** ('æpisi:z) highest point; vertex; tip; pinnacle.

aphid ('eifid) *n* small insect that feeds on plant juices.

apiece *adv* each; for each one.

apology *n* **1** statement expressing regret for an offence, error, failure, etc. **2** poor substitute. **apologetic** *adj* sorry; making an apology. **apologetically** *adv*. **apologize** *vi* make an apology or excuse.

apostle (ə'pɔsəl) *n* one of Christ's twelve disciples.

apostrophe (ə'pɔstrəfi) *n* written or printed symbol (') used to show omission of a letter or letters, or to denote the possessive case.

appal *vt* (-ll-) fill with abhorrence; shock; horrify; disgust.

apparatus *n* equipment, machinery, tools, etc., required for a particular purpose.

apparent *adj* **1** seeming; ostensible. **2** evident; clear; obvious. **apparently** *adv*.

appeal *vi* **1** apply to a higher authority for the reversal of a decision. **2** plead; beseech; call (for). **3** appear attractive (to); please. *n* **1** application to a higher authority. **2** plea; request; entreaty. **3** attractiveness; ability to arouse interest. **appealing** *adj* attractive; arousing interest, sympathy, pity, etc.

appear *vi* **1** come into view; become visible. **2** arrive. **3** seem; give the impression (of). **4** become clear or obvious; emerge. **5** give a public performance. **6** become available. **7** present oneself in court, before a tribunal, etc. **appearance** *n* **1** coming into view. **2** arrival. **3** outward manifestation; impression; aspect; look. **4** public performance. **5** attendance in court. **keep up appearances** maintain an outward show of respectability, affluence, etc.

appease *vt* **1** pacify; soothe. **2** assuage; ease; allay; relieve. **appeasement** *n*.

appendix *n, pl* **appendixes** *or* **appendices** (ə'pendisi:z) **1** small blind functionless tube attached to the lower abdomen. **2** section containing supplementary information at the end of a book. **appendicitis** *n* inflammation of the appendix.

appetite *n* **1** desire to satisfy bodily needs, esp. for food. **2** craving; capacity. **appetizing** *adj* able to stimulate the appetite; tasty.

applaud *vi,vt* **1** show appreciation (of) by clapping. **2** commend; praise. **applause** *n*.

apple *n* edible round fruit with a red, green, or yellow skin.

apply *vt* **1** use in a practical or appropriate way; employ; put into practice. **2** cover with; put on. **3** concentrate; give attention to. *vi* **1** make a formal request (for a job, money, etc.). **2** be appropriate; have a bearing (on). **appliance** *n* piece of equipment; tool; machine; instrument. **applicable** *adj* relevant; appropriate; able to be applied. **applicant** *n* person applying for a job, place, etc.; candidate. **application** *n* **1** formal request; claim. **2** putting into practice (of relevant knowledge, skills, etc.). **3** act of applying (paint, ointment, etc.). **4** close attention; concentration.

appoint *vt* **1** select for a job, position, etc. **2** assign; allocate. **3** arrange for a particular time; fix. **appointment** *n* **1** fixed meeting; engagement. **2** selection or nomination for a job, position, etc. **3** job or position for which a person is selected.

apportion *vt* share out; allot; distribute. **apportionment** *n*.

appraise *vt* estimate the quality or value of; assess. **appraisal** *n*.

appreciate *vt* **1** be grateful for; recognize the worth of. **2** realize; understand; be aware of. *vi* increase in value. **appreciation** *n*. **appreciable** *adj* considerable; large enough to be assessed.

apprehend *vt* **1** arrest and take into custody. **2** be anxious about; fear; dread. *vt,vi* comprehend; grasp. **apprehension** *n* **1** anxiety; fear; caution; dread. **2** understanding; conception. **3** arrest. **apprehensive** *adj* worried; anxious; cautious; uneasy; doubtful.

apprentice *n* person under contract to an employer whilst learning a trade. *vt* engage or place as an apprentice.

approach *vt,vi* draw close or closer (to); near; advance. *vt* **1** make contact with in order to obtain advice, a favour, etc. **2** begin to tackle; start working on; deal with. **3** approximate; come close to being. *n* **1** act of drawing near; advance. **2** initial contact; overture. **3** method of working, acting, thinking, etc. **4** approximation. **5** way in or to; access. **approachable** *adj* **1** accessible; able to be contacted. **2** friendly; easy to get on with.

appropriate *adj* (ə'proupriət) suitable for a particular purpose or set of circumstances; relevant; apt. *vt* (ə'proupriεit) **1** take possession of; take for one's own use. **2** set aside; allocate. **appropriately** *adv.* **appropriation** *n.*

approve *vt* give consent for; sanction. **approve of** have a favourable opinion of; believe to be good or right. **approval** *n* **1** consent; permission. **2** favourable opinion. **on approval** on free trial before deciding whether or not to buy.

approximate *adj* (ə'prɔksimət) roughly calculated; estimated; about right. *vt,vi* (ə'prɔksimeit) come close to what is required or expected; be roughly right. **approximately** *adv.*

apricot *n* small fleshy fruit that is similar to the peach, with a soft reddish-orange skin.

April *n* fourth month of the year.

apron *n* **1** loose covering worn over the front of the body to protect one's clothes and tied round the waist. **2** part of a stage that projects in front of the curtain.

apse *n* semicircular domed recess situated at the east end of a church.

apt *adj* **1** fitting; appropriate; to the point. **2** likely; inclined; liable. **3** quick to learn; clever. **aptly** *adv.* **aptitude** *n* talent, skill, or ability; flair.

aquarium *n, pl* **aquariums** *or* **aquaria** (ə'kwεəriə) tank or pool for fish and aquatic plants.

Aquarius (ə'kwεəriəs) *n* eleventh sign of the zodiac represented by the water carrier.

aquatic *adj* relating to or living in water.

aqueduct *n* channel constructed to direct a flow of water, esp. one built as a bridge.

arable *adj* (of land) able to be ploughed in order to produce crops.

arbitrary *adj* **1** not fixed by law; discretionary. **2** impulsive; capricious. **arbitrarily** *adv.*

arbitrate *vt,vi* settle (a dispute); mediate (between). **arbiter** *or* **arbitrator** *n.* **arbitration** *n.*

arc *n* **1** curved segment of a circle. **2** something shaped like an arc, such as a rainbow. **3** luminous electrical discharge between two electrodes. *vi* form an arc.

arcade *n* **1** series of arches and columns. **2** covered passageway or gallery, esp. one lined with shops.

arch[1] *n* **1** curved structure built to bear a load over an opening. **2** *also* **archway** opening, passageway, gateway, etc., with an arch. **3** curve; bow. **4** part of the sole of the foot between the ball and heel. *vt,vi* **1** span with an arch; curve over. **2** produce or form into a curve or bow.

arch[2] *adj* **1** chief; principal. **2** mischievous; cunning.

archaeology (ɑ:ki'ɔlədʒi) *n* scientific study of ancient remains and artefacts. **archaeological** (ɑ:kiə'lɔdʒikəl) *adj.* **archaeologist** (ɑ:ki'ɔlədʒist) *n.*

archaic (ɑ:'keiik) *adj* no longer in current use; out-of-date; old; belonging to the past.

archbishop *n* bishop having jurisdiction over an ecclesiastical province.

archduke *n* prince of the imperial dynasty of Austria. **archduchess** *n* **1** wife or widow of an archduke. **2** princess of the imperial dynasty of Austria. **archduchy** (ɑ:tʃ'dʌtʃi) *n* territory ruled by an archduke or archduchess.

archery *n* art of shooting with a bow and arrows. **archer** *n.*

archetype ('ɑ:kitaip) *n* **1** prototype. **2** ideal or completely typical example or model; standard type. **archetypal** *or* **archetypical** (ɑ:ki'tipikəl) *adj.*

archipelago (ɑ:ki'peləgou) *n* chain or scattered group of islands.

architecture *n* **1** art of designing buildings and other constructions. **2** style of building or design. **3** buildings taken collectively.

architect *n* **1** person trained in architecture. **2** planner; organizer; mastermind.

archives (ˈɑːkaivz) *pl n* **1** collection of historical records and documents. **2** place where such a collection is kept. **archivist** (ˈɑːkivist) *n* person in charge of archives.

arctic *adj* **1** relating to regions surrounding the earth's North Pole. **2** extremely cold.

ardent *adj* fervent; zealous; vigorously enthusiastic; earnest; passionate **ardently** *adv*. **ardour** *n*.

arduous *adj* hard and laborious; extremely difficult; exhausting; requiring great effort. **arduously** *adv*.

are *v* plural form of **be** in the present tense.

area *n* **1** extent of a specific surface, piece of ground, geometric figure, etc. **2** open space; region; locality. **3** section or part. **4** range or scope of something.

arena *n* **1** central area for performers in an amphitheatre, stadium, etc. **2** scene of activity.

argue *vi* quarrel; attack verbally. *vi,vt* debate; have a heated discussion (about); present (a case) for or against; reason. **argument** *n*. **argumentative** *adj* quarrelsome; inclined to argue.

arid *adj* **1** extremely dry and infertile; parched. **2** dull; not stimulating. **aridity** *n*.

Aries (ˈɛəriːz) *n* first sign of the zodiac represented by the ram.

arise *vi* (arose; arisen) **1** rise; get up; stand up. **2** come about; occur; happen; start.

aristocracy *n* **1** class of privileged people of the highest rank; nobility. **2** government by such a class. **aristocrat** *n*. **aristocratic** *adj*.

arithmetic *n* (əˈriθmətik) **1** manipulation of numbers by addition, subtraction, multiplication, and division. **2** mathematical calculations. *adj* (æriθˈmetik) *also* **arithmetical** relating to arithmetic.

arm[1] *n* **1** upper limb extending from the shoulder to the wrist. **2** sleeve. **3** support for the arm on a chair or seat. **4** anything resembling an arm in appearance or function. **armchair** *n* easy chair with supports for the arms. **armhole** *n* opening in a garment for the arm to pass through. **armpit** *n* hollow under the arm where it joins the shoulder.

arm[2] *vt,vi* **1** equip (with weapons and ammunition). **2** prepare (for a confrontation, discussion, etc.). **arms** *pl n* weapons; firearms.

armament *n* **1** equipment for fighting; weaponry. **2** armed force. **3** preparation for a war or battle.

armour *n* **1** protective covering of metal formerly worn in battle. **2** hard protective shell or covering of certain animals. **armour-plated** *adj also* **armoured** fitted with a protective covering of steel against bullets, shells, torpedoes, etc.

army *n* **1** organized military force. **2** horde; large organized group.

aroma *n* distinctive smell given off by food, wine, perfume, etc. **aromatic** *adj*.

arose *v pt* of **arise.**

around *prep* **1** round the outside of; surrounding; enclosing. **2** from place to place within; about; at various points on. **3** round rather than straight across. **4** at approximately; about. *adv* **1** on all sides; in a circle. **2** somewhere near; in the vicinity; about. **3** round; with a circular movement. **get around** travel widely; circulate.

arouse *vt* stimulate; provoke interest, anger, etc., in; awake. *vt,vi* rouse; wake. **arousal** *n*.

arrange *vt* **1** put into some kind of order or pattern; form. **2** fix; make plans for. **3** come to agreement about; settle on. **4** adapt (music) for a different instrument. **arrangement** *n*. **arranger** *n*.

array *n* **1** arranged selection or display; assortment. **2** dress; clothing. *vt* **1** dress lavishly; adorn. **2** arrange in order; set out.

arrears *pl n* outstanding payments; accumulated debts. **in arrears** behind in one's payments.

arrest *vt* **1** seize and detain by lawful authority; apprehend. **2** hinder; check; stop. *n* **1** act of arresting or state of being arrested. **2** hindrance; check; stoppage. **under arrest** held in detention. **arresting** *adj* attracting attention.

arrive *vi* **1** reach a destination. **2** happen; occur. **3** *inf* achieve success. **arrive at** reach. **arrival** *n*.

arrogant *adj* proud: haughty; conceited. **arrogance** *n*. **arrogantly** *adv*.

arrow *n* **1** slender pointed missile shot from a bow. **2** symbol used to indicate direction, etc.

arsenic *n* poisonous brittle grey metallic element.

arson *n* crime of maliciously setting fire to property.

art *n* **1** process of creative activity, esp. painting and drawing. **2** works resulting from such a process. **3** creative or practical skill. **arts** *n pl or s* university course(s) such as modern languages, literature, history, and philosophy.

artefact *n also* **artifact** man-made object.

artery *n* **1** thick-walled tubular vessel that conveys oxygenated blood from the heart. **2** major road, railway, or other channel of communication. **arterial** *adj.*

artful *adj* cunning; crafty; ingenious. **artfully** *adv.*

arthritis *n* painful inflammation of a joint or joints. **arthritic** *adj.*

artichoke *n* **1** *also* **globe artichoke** thistle-like plant with large edible fleshy flower heads. **2** *also* **Jerusalem artichoke** sunflower with an edible tuber.

article *n* **1** small object; item. **2** newspaper or magazine report. **3** clause or section in a document. **4** the words *a* or *an (indefinite articles)* or *the (definite article)* preceding a noun or noun phrase. **articled** *adj* bound by written contract; apprenticed.

articulate *v* (ɑːˈtikjuleit) *vt,vi* speak clearly. *vt* express precisely or coherently. *adj* (ɑːˈtikjulit) **1** fluent; coherent. **2** able to speak. **articulated** *adj* having two or more jointed or pivoted sections. **articulation** *n.*

artifact *n* artefact.

artificial *adj* **1** man-made; synthetic. **2** feigned; not spontaneous. **artificial respiration** *n* method for restoring natural breathing. **artificially** *adv.*

artillery *n* **1** large-calibre guns; cannon. **2** troops or military units trained in their use.

artist *n* **1** creative person, esp. a painter or sculptor. **2** skilful practitioner of a craft, etc. **3** professional performer. **artistic** *adj* **1** creative; skilled. **2** beautiful; aesthetically pleasing. **3** relating to art. **artistically** *adv.*

as *conj* **1** when; just at the time that. **2** in the manner that; like. **3** that which; what; whatever. **4** because; since. *prep,conj* to the extent (that); of the same amount (that). *prep* in the role or capacity of.

asbestos *n* any of several incombustible fibrous minerals used for thermal insulation and in flameproof and building materials.

ascend *vt,vi* climb; mount; rise. **ascent** *or* **ascension** *n.* **the Ascension** ascent of Christ into heaven.

ascertain *vt* determine by inquiry; discover; find out.

ascribe *vt* attribute (a work of art, blame, etc.); assign.

ash[1] *n* widespread deciduous tree with compound leaves, winged seeds, and a durable wood used as timber.

ash[2] *n* **1** grey powdery residue of something that has been burnt. **2** fine material thrown from an erupting volcano. **ashes 1** human remains after cremation. **2** ruins. **ashen** *adj* pallid. **ashtray** *n* receptacle for cigarette ends, ash, etc.

ashamed *adj* **1** full of shame (for); remorseful. **2** reluctant or refusing (to).

ashore *adv,adj* towards or on land.

aside *adv* **1** on or to one side. **2** into a secluded place. **3** out of one's thoughts, consideration, etc. **4** in reserve. **aside from** apart from. ~*n* confidential or seemingly confidential statement.

ask *vt,vi* **1** put a question to (concerning). **2** make a request for. *vt* **1** enquire about. **2** invite. **ask after** request news of. **ask for trouble/it** behave provocatively.

askew *adv* at an angle; awry. *adj* crooked.

asleep *adj* sleeping. **fall asleep** pass into a state of sleep.

asparagus *n* young edible shoots of a plant of the lily family.

aspect *n* **1** direction towards which something faces; outlook. **2** appearance. **3** point of view; angle.

asphalt *n* dark naturally occurring material used in road surfacing and roofing materials. *vt* cover with asphalt.

aspire *vi* have ambitious plans, desires, etc.; yearn for. **aspiration** *n.*

aspirin *n* mild pain-relieving drug, usually taken in tablet form.

ass *n* **1** donkey. **2** fool; stupid person.

assail *vt* attack; assault. **assailant** *n,adj.*

assassinate *vt* murder (a public figure), esp. for political reasons. **assassin** *n* murderer; hired killer. **assassination** *n.*

assault *n* **1** violent or sudden attack. **2** *law* threat of attack. *vt* **1** make an assault on. **2** rape.

assemble *vt,vi* **1** come or bring together; collect. **2** fit together; construct. **assembly** *n.*

assent *n* **1** agreement; acceptance. **2** consent. *vi* agree to; accept.

assert *vt* **1** declare as true. **2** insist upon; maintain. **assert oneself** act authoritatively or boldly. **assertion** *n*. **assertive** *adj*.

assess *vt* **1** determine the value or amount of; evaluate. **2** judge the worth or importance of. **assessment** *n*.

asset *n* possession, quality, etc., that is useful or of value. **assets** *pl n* capital; property.

assign *vt* **1** allot; give to; set apart for; fix. **2** nominate; select for; appoint to. **assignation** *n* arrangement to meet secretly or illicitly; tryst. **assignment** *n*.

assimilate *vt,vi* **1** absorb or become absorbed; incorporate. **2** adjust or become adjusted. *vt* digest (food). **assimilation** *n*.

assist *vt,vi* help; give support (to); work in a subordinate capacity (for). **assistance** *n*. **assistant** *n*.

associate *v* (ə'sousieit) **associate with** *vt* link or connect (with). *vi* keep company (with). *n* (ə'sousiit, -eit) **1** partner; colleague. **2** acquaintance; companion. *adj* (ə'sousiit) **1** having equal or nearly equal status with others. **2** having only partial rights. **association** *n* **1** connection. **2** organized group; society.

assorted *adj* **1** of various kinds; miscellaneous. **2** classified; sorted. **ill-assorted** badly matched. **assortment** *n*.

assuage *vt* make less severe; ease; lessen.

assume *vt* **1** take for granted; accept; suppose. **2** undertake; take on. **3** adopt; feign; affect. **assumed** *adj* **1** false; fictitious. **2** taken for granted. **assumption** *n*.

assure *vt* **1** make certain; ensure. **2** inform confidently; promise; guarantee. **assurance** *n* **1** promise; guarantee. **2** certainty. **3** self-confidence. **4** life or endowment insurance. **assuredly** *adv* definitely.

asterisk *n* symbol (*) used in print to indicate an omission, cross reference, etc. *vt* mark with an asterisk.

asthma ('æsmə) *n* disorder, often allergic, causing difficulty in breathing, wheezing, etc. **asthmatic** *adj,n*.

astonish *vt* fill with surprise or wonder; amaze; astound. **astonishment** *n*.

astound *vt* surprise greatly; astonish.

astray *adv,adj* away from what is right or expected.

astride *adv,adj,prep* with a leg on each side (of).

astrology *n* prediction of human characteristics, activities, etc., based on the motion and relative positions of celestial bodies. **astrological** *adj*. **astrologer** *n*.

astronaut *n* person trained and adapted to space travel. **astronautical** *adj*. **astronautics** *n*.

astronomy *n* study of the universe and the celestial bodies contained in it. **astronomer** *n*. **astronomical** *or* **astronomic** *adj* **1** relating to astronomy or the celestial bodies. **2** huge; immense.

astute *adj* cunning; sly; clever; perceptive; quick. **astutely** *adv*. **astuteness** *n*.

asunder *adv,adj* apart; in(to) pieces.

asylum *n* **1** temporary refuge; place of shelter; sanctuary. **2** mental hospital.

at *prep* **1** in; close to; next to. **2** towards; in the direction of. **3** towards or around a specified time. **4** in a state of; engaged in. **5** during. **6** in exchange for; for the price of. **7** about; concerning.

ate *v pt of* **eat.**

atheism *n* disbelief in the existence of God. **atheist** *n*.

athlete *n* person skilled in running, hurdling, shot putting, or other track and field sports. **athletics** *n* track and field sports. **athletic** *adj*.

atlas *n* book containing maps.

atmosphere *n* **1** gaseous layer surrounding the earth or other celestial body. **2** air in an enclosed space. **3** gaseous medium. **4** prevailing mood; feeling. **5** unit of pressure. **atmospheric** *adj*.

atom *n* **1** minute entity of which chemical elements are composed, consisting of a central nucleus around which electrons orbit. **2** very small amount. **atom bomb** *n also* **atomic bomb** bomb in which energy is derived from nuclear fission. **atomic** *adj*. **atomic energy** *n* energy derived from nuclear fission or fusion. **atomize** *vt* reduce (a liquid, such as perfume) to a fine spray by forcing it through a nozzle. **atomizer** *n*.

atone *vi* make amends (for a sin, error, etc.); expiate. **atonement** *n*.

atrocious *adj* **1** extremely cruel; wicked; appalling; horrifying. **2** *inf* of very poor quality. **atrociously** *adv*. **atrocity** *n* cruel and appalling act or behaviour.

attach *vt,vi* join; connect; fasten. *vi* **1** attribute;

ascribe. 2 adhere; be inherent in. **attached to** 1 fond of; devoted to. 2 assigned or brought in as a specialist. **attachment** *n*.

attaché *n* member of staff of an embassy or legation. **attaché case** *n* small rectangular case for carrying documents, etc.

attack *vt* 1 make a physical or verbal assault on, assail; set upon. 2 seize upon; take up with vigour. 3 act or play offensively. 4 affect adversely. *n* 1 physical or verbal assault. 2 offensive action. 3 bout of illness.

attain *vt,vi* succeed in reaching; achieve; obtain; get. **attainable** *adj*. **attainment** *n*.

attempt *vt* try (to do or accomplish something); endeavour. *n* 1 effort, often unsuccessful. 2 attack.

attend *vt,vi* be present (at); go regularly (to). *vi* pay attention (to); listen (to). **attend to** 1 deal with; handle; manage. 2 look after; tend; minister. **attendance** *n* 1 act of attending; presence 2 number of persons present. **attendant** *n* person employed to assist, guide, look after, etc. *adj* associated or accompanying. **attention** *n* 1 concentrated thought. 2 observation; notice. **call** *or* **bring attention to** point out. **pay attention to** 1 take notice of; attend. 2 take care of. **stand to attention.** adopt a formal alert stance, esp. on military occasions. **attentive** *adj* 1 listening carefully; observant. 2 thoughtful; polite.

attic *n* room just below the roof; garret.

attitude *n* 1 opinion; judgement; policy; disposition. 2 position of the body; pose. **strike an attitude** assume a theatrical pose.

attorney *n* 1 person with legal authority to act for another. 2 *US* lawyer.

attract *vt* 1 excite pleasure, anticipation, etc., in; fascinate. 2 cause to approach; draw towards. **attraction** *n*. **attractive** *adj* 1 pleasing to look at; alluring; appealing. 2 interesting; pleasing.

attribute *vt* (əˈtribju:t) **attribute to** consider as produced by, resulting from, or belonging to; ascribe to. *n* (ˈætribju:t) property; quality; feature. **attribution** *n*.

atypical (eiˈtipikəl) *adj* not typical; unrepresentative.

aubergine *n* tropical plant with a deep purple egg-shaped fruit, eaten as a vegetable.

auburn *n,adj* reddish-brown.

auction *n* public sale in which items are sold to the highest bidder. *vt* sell by auction. **auctioneer** *n* person conducting an auction.

audacious *adj* 1 fearlessly bold. 2 impudent; forward.

audible *adj* able to be heard. **audibly** *adv*.

audience 1 group of spectators, listeners, etc. 2 formal hearing or interview granted by someone in authority.

audiovisual *adj* involving both hearing and sight.

audit *n* professional examination of business accounts. *vt,vi* examine by or perform audit(s). **auditor** *n*.

audition *n* trial in which an actor, singer, musician, etc., demonstrates his ability or his aptitude for a role. *vt,vi* give a trial hearing (to).

auditorium *n, pl* **auditoriums** *or* **auditoria** part of a theatre, hall, etc., where the audience is seated.

augment *vt,vi* increase; enlarge; extend. **augmentation** *n*.

August *n* eighth month of the year.

aunt *n* 1 sister of one's mother or father. 2 wife of one's uncle.

au pair *n* foreign girl who undertakes housework, etc., in return for board and lodging. *adv* as an au pair.

aura *n* 1 distinctive air or quality of a person or thing; charisma. 2 apparent emanation surrounding an object, etc.

aural *adj* relating to hearing.

austere *adj* severe; strict; harsh; not luxurious. **austerely** *adv*. **austerity** *n*.

authentic *adj* genuine; real; not faked; from a reliable source. **authentically** *adv*. **authenticity** *n*.

author *n* 1 writer of a book, script, article, etc. 2 originator; creator. **authorship** *n*.

authoritative *adj* possessing, exercising, or claiming authority. **authoritatively** *adv*. **authorize** *vt* empower; sanction; give permission for. **authorization** *n*.

authority *n* 1 power or right to command and enforce obedience. 2 official body or group having such power. 3 position commanding such power. 4 delegated power. 5 acknowledged expert or trustworthy written work. 6 power or influence. **authoritarian** *adj* favouring the enforcement of obedience; opposed to individual freedom; nondemocratic. *n* an authoritarian person.

autistic *adj* living in a fantasy world; abnormally introspective. **autism** *n*.

autobiography *n* person's biography written by that person; personal biography. **autobiographical** *adj*.

autograph *n* handwritten signature. *vt* write an autograph in; sign.

automatic *adj* **1** operated or regulated by mechanical means; self-acting. **2** performed or produced without conscious thought or effort. **3** inevitable. *n* self-loading weapon firing continuously on depression of the trigger. **automatically** *adv*. **automation** *n* automatic operation of industrial processes or equipment.

autonomous *adj* self-governing; self-sufficient; independent. **autonomously** *adv*. **autonomy** *n*.

autumn *n* season between summer and winter.

auxiliary *adj* additional; supporting; extra; ancillary. *n* helper; assistant. **auxiliary verb** verb used to express tense, mood, etc., of another verb.

avail *n* **to** *or* **with no avail** in vain; without success. *v* **avail oneself of** make use of; help oneself to.

available *adj* obtainable; ready for use; accessible. **availability** *n*.

avalanche *n* **1** heavy fall of snow and ice down a mountainside. **2** large pile or heap that has accumulated suddenly and rapidly.

avenge *vt,vi* seek vengeance (for); punish in retaliation.

avenue *n* **1** wide road or drive, esp. one lined with trees. **2** means of achieving; way; opening.

average *n* **1** sum of a set of numbers or quantities divided by their total number; mean value. **2** representative or typical amount, value, etc. **on average** typically; usually. ~*adj* **1** typical; representative; usual. **2** constituting or worked out as an average. *vt* **1** perform or receive an amount calculated as an average. **2** calculate an average. *vi* amount to an average.

averse *adj* disinclined; unwilling; against. **aversion** *n* strong dislike; repulsion.

aviary *n* enclosure or large cage for birds.

aviation *n* art or science of flying aircraft. **aviator** *n* airman; pilot.

avid *adj* eager; enthusiastically dedicated or keen. **avidity** *n*. **avidly** *adv*.

avocado (ævə'kɑːdou) *n* *also* **avocado pear** fleshy pear-shaped tropical fruit with a dark green or purple skin.

avoid *vt* keep away from or out of; evade; refrain from. **avoidable** *adj*. **avoidance** *n*.

avow *vt* declare; claim; admit openly. **avowal** *n*.

await *vt* **1** wait for; expect. **2** be ready or in store for.

awake *v* (awoke *or* awaked; awaked) *vt,vi* wake; wake up; rouse. *vt* arouse; stir; stimulate.

awaken *vt,vi* awake.

award *vt* give as a prize; grant. *n* prize; grant.

aware *adj* conscious (of); having knowledge; well-informed. **awareness** *n*.

away *adv* **1** to or at a place further off. **2** apart; at a distance; separately. **3** out of one's possession. **4** without hesitation; immediately. **5** until there is nothing left. **do away with 1** abolish; get rid of. **2** murder; kill. **get away with** do without being noticed or caught. ~*adj* absent; not at home.

awe *n* feeling of absolute wonder, fear, reverence, etc. *vt* fill with awe; dumbfound. **awe-inspiring** *adj* overwhelming; magnificent; tremendous. **awesome** *adj* capable of producing awe. **awe-struck** *adj* *also* **awe-stricken** filled with awe.

awful *adj* terrible; dreadful; very bad. **awfully** *adv inf* very; extremely.

awhile *adv* briefly; for a while.

awkward *adj* **1** clumsy, ungainly. **2** difficult to deal with; tricky; inconvenient. **awkwardly** *adv*. **awkwardness** *n*.

awl *n* small tool used for boring holes in leather, wood, etc.

awning *n* sheet of canvas attached to a frame to provide cover and protection from the weather.

awoke *v pt of* **awake.**

awry (ə'rai) *adj* **1** crooked; askew. **2** wrong; amiss

axe *n* chopping tool with a long handle and a broad blade. **have an axe to grind** act from selfish motives or a vested interest. ~*vt* **1** chop or fell with an axe. **2** cut back or reduce drastically.

axis *n, pl* **axes** ('æksiːz) **1** line about which something rotates or is symmetrical. **2** reference line on a graph by which a point is located. **3** main central stem of a plant.

axle *n* rod or shaft that allows an attached wheel to revolve.

azalea *n* flowering shrub related to the rhododendron.

B

babble *vi,vt* **1** speak incoherently and continuously: chatter. **2** burble; murmur. *n* **1** fast incoherent speech. **2** burbling sound; murmur.

babe *n* baby.

baboon *n* large monkey.

baby *n* **1** newborn child; infant. **2** newborn animal. *vt* treat as a baby; lavish care on. **babyish** *adj.* **baby-sit** *vi* (-tt-) look after a baby for a short time while the parents are out. **baby-sitter** *n.*

bachelor *n* **1** unmarried man. **2** person who holds a first degree from a university or college.

bacillus *n* any of various rod-shaped bacteria.

back *n* **1** that part of the body extending from the base of the neck to the buttocks. **2** corresponding part of an animal. **3** spine; backbone. **4** side or part that is opposite the front; reverse. **5** place furthest away from the front; rear. **6** part of a garment that covers the back. **7** defence player in football, hockey, etc. **behind one's back** without one's knowledge; deceitfully. **get/put one's back up** antagonize; provoke; anger. ~*vt* **1** bet on to win. **2** support; sponsor. **3** provide a musical accompaniment for. *vt,vi* move backwards; reverse. **back down** withdraw a claim, challenge, etc.; admit fault. **back onto** have the back or rear bordering on. **back out** withdraw one's support. **back up** support; encourage; confirm. ~*adv* **1** backwards; towards the rear. **2** in or into the past. **3** to a previous or earlier place, state, condition, owner, etc. **4** in reply; in return. **back to front** with the back and front reversed. **go back on** break (a promise). **take back** revoke; cancel. ~*adj* **1** situated behind. **2** from the past; overdue; not current.

backbencher *n* British member of Parliament without a ministerial position.

backbone *n* **1** spine. **2** stamina; courage; spirit.

backdate *vt* make effective from an earlier date.

backfire *vi* **1** produce an explosion of fuel mixture in an internal-combustion engine. **2** have unintended and unfortunate consequences.

backgammon *n* board game for two players, each using fifteen pieces, which are moved according to the throws of two dice.

background *n* **1** place, setting, scene etc., at the back or in the distance. **2** person's class, education, experience, etc. **3** context through which historical, political, or social events may be understood.

backhand *n* stroke in tennis made with the back of the hand facing the direction of the shot. **backhanded** *adj* **1** relating to a backhand. **2** with underlying sarcasm.

backing *n* **1** sponsorship; support. **2** musical accompaniment.

backlash *n* **1** recoil occurring when machinery parts are badly worn or faulty. **2** hostile reaction; repercussions.

backlog *n* accumulated work, arrears, etc., requiring attention.

backside *n inf* buttocks; bottom.

backstage *adv* **1** behind the stage, esp. in the wings, dressing-rooms, etc. **2** at the back of the stage. *adj* taking place behind or at the back of the stage.

backstroke *n* type of stroke made when swimming on one's back.

backward *adj* **1** slow to learn or progress; underdeveloped. **2** directed towards the back or rear. **3** towards or fixed in the past. **4** bashful; shy. *adv* backwards. **backwardness** *n.*

backwards *adv* **1** towards the back or rear. **2** in reverse. **3** into the past. **4** back to a poorer state or condition. **know backwards** know thoroughly.

backwater *n* **1** stretch of water cut off from the main stream. **2** isolated place unaffected by changes occurring elsewhere.

bacon *n* cured meat from the back or sides of a pig.

bacteria *pl n* group of microscopic vegetable organisms causing putrefaction, fermentation, disease, etc. **bacterial** *adj.*

bad[1] *adj* **1** not good; below standard; poorer than average. **2** disobedient; naughty. **3** harmful; injurious. **4** sinful; wicked. **5** sick; unwell. **6** not fresh; rotten. **7** distressing; upsetting. **8** unpleasant; distasteful. **badly** *adv* **1** unsatisfactorily; poorly. **2** very much; urgently; seriously. **bad-tempered** *adj* cross; irritable.

bad[2] *v* a *pt* of **bid.**
bade (beid. bæd) *v* a *pt* of **bid.**
badge *n* **1** emblem worn or displayed to indicate rank, membership, etc. **2** distinguishing mark or characteristic.
badger *n* nocturnal burrowing animal with a black and white striped head. *vt* pester.
badminton *n* game similar to tennis played with lightweight rackets and a shuttlecock.
baffle *vt* perplex; bewilder; stump; mystify.
bag *n* **1** container of leather, paper, etc., used for carrying things in. **2** loose or sagging fold of skin. *v* (-gg-) *vt* **1** put into a bag. **2** *inf* claim; seize first. *vi* hang loosely; sag; bulge. **baggage** *n* luggage. **baggy** *adj* hanging loosely; not tight. **bagginess** *n*. **bagpipes** *pl n* musical instrument consisting of a set of reed pipes and a wind-bag. **bagpiper** *n*.
bail[1] *n* **1** sum of money that is pledged to secure the release of a person from custody on condition that he appears in court on a specified date. **2** procedure allowing such a sum of money to be pledged. *vt* **bail out** rescue (a person, company, etc.) esp by giving financial assistance.
bail[2] *n* small wooden bar placed across the stumps of a wicket.
bail[3] *vt,vi also* **bail out** remove (water) from the bottom of a boat with a bucket or can.
bailiff *n* **1** official employed by a sheriff to serve writs, collect fines, summon juries, etc. **2** landowner's agent.
bait *n* **1** things such as worms, maggots, etc., used by an angler to lure and catch fish. **2** food or other enticement used to lure animals into a trap. **3** enticement; temptation. *vt* **1** prepare (a line or trap) with bait. **2** lure; entice. **3** taunt; persecute.
bake *vi,vt* cook (bread, cakes, etc.) in an oven. **baker** *n* person who bakes or sells bread, cakes, etc. **bakery** *n* **1** room where bread, cakes, etc., are baked. **2** baker's shop.
balance *n* **1** apparatus for weighing consisting of two pans suspended from either end of a horizontal bar, which has a central pivot. **2** equilibrium. **3** emotional or mental stability; rationality. **4** compatibility; equality of distribution; harmony. **5** equality between credit and debit totals. **6** remainder; amount left over. **in the balance** not yet decided. ~*vt* **1** weigh on a balance. **2** keep or put in a state of balance. **3** calculate the totals of. *vi* have equal totals. *vt,vi* place in or achieve equilibrium. **balance sheet** *n* statement of accounts showing a company's financial position for a given period.
balcony *n* **1** enclosed platform built on to the outside of a wall of a building usually with access from within. **2** gallery of seats above the circle in a theatre.
bald *adj* **1** having no hair, esp. on the head. **2** threadbare; badly worn. **3** bare; having no vegetation. **4** plainly expressed; blunt. **baldly** *adv*. **baldness** *n*.
bale[1] *n* large bundle or package. *vt* pack into a bale.
bale[2] *vi* **bale out** make an emergency parachute jump.
ball[1] *n* **1** spherical object used in games such as football, golf, or tennis. **2** any spherical object. **3** rounded fleshy part of the thumb, sole of the foot, etc. **balls** *pl n sl* testicles. **on the ball** aware; quick to react
ball[2] *n* grand social event with music and dancing, refreshments, etc. **have a ball** enjoy oneself enormously. **ballroom** *n* hall or large room used for dancing.
ballad *n* narrative poem that is usually set to music.
ballast *n* **1** any heavy material used to stabilize a ship, balloon, etc. **2** mixture of gravel and sand used in building.
ballerina *n* female ballet dancer.
ballet *n* **1** theatrical dance form requiring a conventional and highly developed technique **2** performance in which a story is told through dance and mime. **3** music written for such a performance. **4** company of dancers.
ballistics *n* study of the motion of projectiles. **ballistic** *adj* relating to projectiles or ballistics.
balloon *n* **1** inflatable coloured rubber bag used as a toy or for decoration. **2** large impermeable bag filled with gas lighter than air that enables it to rise in the air, often having a basket for passengers, scientific instruments, etc. *vi* fly in a balloon. *vt,vi* inflate or swell.
ballot *n* **1** system of voting using tickets, cards, slips, etc. **2** tickets or cards used in voting. **3** number of votes cast. *vt,vi* vote or put to the vote by ballot.
bamboo *n* tropical treelike grass with hard hollow stems, which are often used for making furniture.
ban *vt* (-nn-) prohibit; declare to be illegal.

forbid. *n* order or rule prohibiting certain goods, behaviour, etc.

banal (bəˈnɑːl) *adj* commonplace; trite; mundane.

banana *n* tropical fruit that is long or crescent shaped with a thick yellow skin.

band[1] *n* **1** small group of people. **2** group of musicians, esp. one playing woodwind, brass, and percussion instruments for dancing or marching. *v* **band together** form into a united group.

band[2] *n* **1** flat strip of cloth, rubber, metal, etc., used as a fastening or for decoration. **2** coloured stripe. **3** waveband.

bandage *n* strip of cloth used to keep a dressing in place over a wound, support a sprain, etc. *vt* cover with a bandage.

bandit *n* outlawed robber.

bandy *adj* bow-legged. *vt* **1** exchange (words, blows, etc.). **2** throw or pass to and fro.

bang *n* **1** loud noise as of an explosion; report. **2** knocking noise. **3** slam. **4** sharp hit or blow. *vt,vi* **1** make a loud explosive sound. **2** knock loudly, rap. **3** slam. **4** hit; strike. **banger** *sl* **1** sausage. **2** old car. **3** firework that explodes with a bang.

bangle *n* ornamental band worn as a bracelet.

banish *vt* **1** exile; expel. **2** dispel. **banishment** *n*.

banister *n* support rail on a staircase.

banjo *n* long-necked instrument of the guitar family with a circular body.

bank[1] *n* **1** slope; embankment. **2** large mound or pile. *vt also* **bank up** form into a mound; heap up.

bank[2] *n* **1** institution dealing in deposits and withdrawals of money, loans, exchange of currencies, etc. **2** building occupied by such an institution. **3** place reserved for the safekeeping of some valuable commodity. *vt* deposit in a bank. *vi* have an account with a bank. **bank on** rely on. **bankbook** *n* book containing a record of a person's financial transactions with a bank. **banker** *n* professional expert in banking; financier. **banking** *n* business of running a bank or similar institution. **bank holiday** *n* public holiday on which banks are traditionally closed. **banknote** *n* paper note issued by a bank as money. **Bank Rate** *n* rate of interest charged by the Bank of England to the banking system.

bankrupt *adj* insolvent. *n* person who is declared bankrupt by a court. **bankruptcy** *n*.

banner *n* **1** flag or ensign, esp. one carried in a procession. **2** something that represents a principle, particular cause, etc.

banquet *n* lavish entertainment and feast given for a large number of guests.

baptize *vt,vi* initiate into the Christian faith with the rite of immersing in or sprinkling with water. **baptism** *n*. **Baptist** *n* member of a Christian denomination believing in baptism as an expression of personal faith. *adj* relating to such a denomination.

bar *n* **1** straight piece of wood, metal, etc., used as part of an enclosure, lever, etc. **2** stripe; band. **3** slab of chocolate, soap, etc. **4** barrier; obstruction. **5** counter from which drinks or refreshments are served. **6** room in a hotel or public house where alcoholic drinks are served. **7** *also* **barline** vertical stroke on a stave in a musical score. **8** notes or music occurring between such strokes. **the Bar** professional body of barristers. **barmaid** *n* woman employed to serve drinks in a hotel or public house. **barman** *n*.

barbarian *n* savage or uncivilized person. *adj* uncivilized; not cultured. **barbaric** *adj also* **barbarous** cruel; savage; brutal; inhuman. **barbarism** *n also* **barbarity** cruelty; brutality; uncivilized behaviour.

barbecue (ˈbɑːbikjuː) *n* **1** grid or grill used on an open fire for cooking meat, vegetables, etc. **2** party held in the open air at which barbecued food is served. *vt* cook on a barbecue.

barber *n* person who cuts men's hair, trims beards, etc.

barbiturate *n* drug used as a sedative.

bare *adj* **1** unclothed; naked. **2** uncovered; unadorned. **3** plain; undecorated. **4** having no vegetation. **5** mere; hardly sufficient. *vt* uncover; make bare. **bareness** *n*. **barefoot** *adj,adv* having no covering on the foot. **barely** *adv* **1** hardly; only just; scarcely. **2** austerely; not elaborately.

bargain *n* **1** agreement between parties; deal. **2** something bought cheaply; good buy. **into the bargain** moreover; besides. ~*vi* barter; haggle; make a deal. **bargain for** be prepared for; expect.

barge *n* large flat-bottomed boat used esp. for carrying cargo on canals. *vi* **1** bump (into); collide; push rudely. **2** interrupt; enter noisily.

baritone *n* male singing voice or musical instrument with a range between bass and tenor.

bark[1] *n* **1** loud cry of a dog or wolf. **2** gruff angry voice. *vi,vt* **1** (of a dog or wolf) utter a loud harsh cry. **2** speak in a gruff voice.

bark[2] *n* outer covering of the trunk and branches of a tree. *vt* scrape the skin or outer layer of.

barley *n* cereal plant with spiked ears used for food and to make malt for brewing and distilling. **barley-sugar** *n* boiled sweet made from sugar.

barn *n* farm building used for storing hay, housing livestock, etc.

barnacle *n* crustacean that attaches itself to rocks, the timber of boats, etc.

barometer *n* **1** instrument for measuring atmospheric pressure. **2** anything that indicates or warns of change.

baron *n* **1** nobleman of the lowest rank. **2** *inf* magnate. **baronial** *adj*. **baroness** *n* **1** wife or widow of a baron. **2** woman of a rank that is equivalent to that of a baron. **baronet** *n* man of a rank between that of a baron and a knight. **baronetcy** *n*.

barracks *n pl or s* building used for the accommodation of soldiers.

barrel *n* **1** cylindrical wooden or metal container. **2** tube of a gun through which the bullet or shell is discharged. *vt* put into a barrel.

barren *adj* **1** infertile; sterile. **2** unproductive; bare. **3** dull; uninteresting. **barrenness** *n*.

barricade *n* obstruction hastily set up as a barrier against an advancing enemy. *vt* block with a barricade.

barrier *n* **1** gate, fence, etc., intended to prevent access. **2** something that screens or protects. **3** hindrance; impediment.

barrister *n* lawyer having the right to practise in a court of law.

barrow[1] *n* cart pushed by hand; wheelbarrow.

barrow[2] *n* burial mound.

barter *vi,vt* trade by exchanging goods or commodities. *vi* haggle. *n* exchange of goods by bartering.

base[1] *n* **1** bottom; support on which something is constructed or rests. **2** foundation; basis. **3** main ingredient or element. **4** starting point. **5** headquarters. **6** establishment set up by the armed forces. **7** marked position on a baseball pitch. **8** sour-tasting chemical substance that turns litmus blue. *vt* **1** take as a foundation or starting point. **2** locate; situate. **baseball** *n* game for two sides of nine players each, on a diamond-shaped pitch using a hard ball and wooden bat. **basement** *n* room or set of rooms built below ground level.

base[2] *adj* **1** mean; despicable. **2** inferior; worthless. **baseness** *n*.

bash *inf vt* hit hard; slog. *n* rough blow. **have a bash** try; attempt.

bashful *adj* shy; embarrassed. **bashfully** *adv*. **bashfulness** *n*.

basic *adj* **1** fundamental; main. **2** elementary; primary. **3** relating to a chemical base. **basics** *pl n* fundamental or underlying principles. **basically** *adv*.

basin *n* **1** bowl used for mixing foods, holding liquids, etc. **2** sink; washbasin. **3** area of land drained by a river.

basis *n, pl* **bases** ('beisi:z) **1** underlying principle; foundation. **2** main part.

bask *vi* **1** expose oneself to the warmth of the sun, a fire, etc. **2** display enjoyment of publicity, glory, etc.

basket *n* **1** receptacle made of cane, straw, etc. **2** metal hoop with a net attached used as the goal in basketball. **basketball** *n* game for two sides of five or six players each, using a large ball which must be shot through a metal hoop fixed to a board in order to score. **basketry** *n* art of making baskets.

bass[1] (beis) *n* **1** lowest range of male singing voice. **2** musical instrument having the lowest range of its type. **3** double bass.

bass[2] (bæs) *n, pl* **bass** sea fish with a spiny dorsal fin; perch.

bassoon *n* woodwind instrument that is lower in tone than an oboe and having a mouthpiece fitted with a double reed. **bassoonist** *n*.

bastard *n* **1** illegitimate child. **2** *inf* unpleasant or cruel person.

bat[1] *n* wooden implement used for hitting a ball in various games. **off one's own bat** unassisted and on one's own initiative. ~*vi,vt* (-tt-) strike or play with a bat. **batsman** *n, pl* **-men** person who bats in cricket.

bat[2] *n* small nocturnal mammal that is able to fly.

batch *n* **1** quantity of loaves, cakes, etc., baked at the same time. **2** set; group.

bath *n* **1** large tub that is filled with water and used for washing the whole body. **2** act of sitting or lying in a bath in order to wash oneself. **3** water in a bath. **baths** *pl n* building housing public baths, swimming pool, etc. ~*vi,vt* wash in a bath. **bathroom** *n* room containing a bath and often a toilet and washbasin.

bathe *vi* **1** swim. **2** have a bath. *vt* **1** wash in order to cleanse or soothe. **2** cover with light, colour, etc. **bathing costume** *n* garment worn when bathing, swimming, etc.

baton *n* **1** small stick used to conduct an orchestra. **2** stick carried by the runner in a relay race. **3** staff of office.

battalion *n* military unit of three or four companies.

batter[1] *vt,vi* beat severely and repeatedly; pound.

batter[2] *n* mixture of flour, eggs, and milk used in cooking.

battery *n* **1** electrical device used as the source of current in radios, torches, vehicles, etc. **2** collection of cages for intensive rearing of chickens, turkeys, etc. **3** unlawful attack on a person. **4** prepared position for artillery, the artillery itself, or a military unit operating it. **5** array; number.

battle *n* **1** fighting between organized forces or armies. **2** hard struggle; fight. *vi* **1** fight in a battle. **2** struggle; strive. **battlefield** *n* site of a battle. **battleship** *n* large armoured warship.

battlement *n* parapet with indentations, used for defence.

bauxite *n* claylike substance that is the chief ore of aluminium.

bawl *vt,vi* shout or cry loudly; howl; bellow *n* howl.

bay[1] *n* coastal inlet.

bay[2] *n* **1** window area projecting beyond the face of a building. **2** recess; alcove. **3** area set aside for parking or loading and unloading a vehicle. **4** storage area in an aircraft.

bay[3] *n* type of laurel tree whose aromatic leaves are used as a seasoning.

bay[4] *n* bark or deep cry of a hound. **at bay 1** facing and warding off a pursuer. **2** in check; at a distance. ~*vt,vi* bark; howl.

bay[5] *n* horse with a reddish-brown body and black mane and tail. *adj,n* reddish-brown.

bayonet *n* short blade attached to the muzzle of a rifle. *vt* stab with a bayonet.

be *vi* (*pres t s* am, are, is; *pl* are. *pt s* was, were, was; *pl* were. *pp* been) **1** exist. **2** occur; take place. **3** equal; have the character of. **4** remain; stay. **5** continue to do or act. *v aux* (used to form the passive).

beach *n* expanse of sand, pebbles, etc., on the seashore. **beachcomber** *n* person who makes a living by collecting things washed ashore by the sea.

bead *n* **1** small ball strung together with others to make a necklace, rosary, etc. **2** small drop; globule. *vt* decorate with beads.

beak *n* horny jaw of a bird; bill.

beaker *n* **1** glass for drinking from; tumbler. **2** small glass cylinder used in chemical experiments.

beam *n* **1** thick piece of timber or steel used to support a floor or roof; joist; girder. **2** shaft of light; ray. **3** radio or radar signal. **4** radiant smile. *vt,vi* **1** send out (a ray of light, radio signal, etc.). **2** smile radiantly.

bean *n* **1** type of plant producing pods containing seeds. **2** pod or seeds of such a plant often eaten as a vegetable. **full of beans** cheerful and energetic; ebullient.

bear[1] *v* (bore; borne) *vt* **1** take the weight of; support. **2** hold; carry. **3** accept responsibility for. **4** *pp* **born** give birth to. **5** yield (fruit); produce. **6** tolerate; endure. **7** display; wear. **8** possess; have. **9** conduct (oneself). *vi* follow or move in the direction of. **bring to bear** exert influence; effect. **bear on 1** push or press against. **2** be relevant to; relate to. **bear out** confirm; furnish proof of. **bear up** cope cheerfully; manage. **bearer** *n*.

bear[2] *n* **1** large carnivorous mammal with black, brown, or white shaggy fur. **2** person who sells stocks and buys them back after the price has dropped.

beard *n* **1** hair growth on the chin and sides of the face. **2** tuft or growth resembling a beard.

bearing *n* **1** person's carriage, posture, deportment, etc. **2** relevance; significance. **3** angle measured from north or some other fixed direction. **4** machine part that supports or guides another moving part. **bearings** *pl n* **1** position or direction determined by reference to fixed points. **2** awareness of one's situation; orientation.

beast *n* **1** animal, esp. when distinguished from man. **2** brutal person. **beastly** *inf adj* disgusting, nasty. **beastliness** *n*.

beat *v* (beat; beaten) *vt* **1** strike hard; hit. **2**

thrash; flog. **3** hammer; bang. **4** whisk; stir vigorously. **5** flap; move up and down. **6** defeat in a contest. **7** do better than; surpass. **8** overcome. *vi* **1** throb; pulsate. **2** pound; bang. **3** produce a rhythmical sound. **4** move up and down. **beat up** assault and injure severely. ~*n* **1** throb; pulsation. **2** blow; bang; stroke. **3** rhythmical sound. **4** basic unit by which the duration of musical notes is measured. **5** stressed syllable or note in poetry or music. **6** type of popular music with a strongly marked rhythm and beat.

beauty *n* **1** quality or qualities appealing to the senses or intellect and conforming to a certain standard of excellence, attractiveness, etc. **2** exceptionally lovely woman. **3** exceptionally good example of something. **beautiful** *adj.* **beautifully** *adv.*

beaver *n* **1** aquatic rodent with webbed feet and a strong broad tail. **2** fur of the beaver. *vi* work hard and enthusiastically.

because *conj* for the reason that; since. **because of** on account of; due to.

beckon *vi,vt* summon with a gesture of the hand or head. *n* summoning gesture.

become *v* (became; become) *vi* **1** grow, change, or develop into; start to be. **2** happen (to); befall. *vt* suit; make attractive. **becoming** fetching; attractive.

bed *n* **1** piece of furniture designed for sleeping on. **2** small plot of ground for growing flowers or vegetables. **3** bottom of the sea, a river, etc. **4** layer of rock. *vt* (-dd-) **1** plant in a bed. **2** *sl* have sexual intercourse with. **bed down** find a place to sleep. **bedclothes** *pl n* covers used on a bed. **bedding** *n* mattress, covers, pillows, etc., used on a bed. **bedridden** *adj* confined to bed, esp. through illness. **bedroom** *n* room used for sleeping in. **bedsitter** *n also* **bed-sit** one-roomed accommodation, usually with cooking and washing facilities. **bedspread** *n* top cover for a bed.

bedraggled *adj* spattered with mud or dirt.

bee *n* insect that produces wax and converts nectar into honey. **have a bee in one's bonnet** be obsessed or fanatical. **beehive** *n* box-like or domed construction for keeping bees in.

beech *n* deciduous tree with a smooth bark and shiny oval leaves.

beef *n* **1** meat from a cow, bull, etc. **2** cow, bull, etc., used for its meat. **beefy** *adj* **1** containing or having the flavour of beef. **2** muscular and strong.

been *v pp* of **be.**

beer *n* alcoholic drink made from malt and flavoured with hops.

beet *n* **1** *also* **beetroot** plant with a round red root, which is eaten as a vegetable. **2** *also* **sugar beet** plant with a whitish root, which is used as a source of sugar.

beetle *n* insect with wings, which are modified to form a hard protective shell.

befall *vi,vt* (befell; befallen) happen (to); occur, esp. by chance.

befit *vt,vi* (-tt-) be right or suitable (for).

before *adv* on a previous occasion; earlier. *prep* **1** previous to. **2** in front of. **3** in the presence of. *conj* **1** until or up to the time that. **2** rather than; sooner than. **beforehand** *adj,adv* early; in advance.

befriend *vt* take care of as a friend.

beg *vt,vi* (-gg-) **1** ask for (money, food, etc.). **2** beseech; implore; plead (with). **beggar** *n.*

begin *vt,vi* (-nn-) (began; begun) start; commence; bring into being. **beginner** *n* person at an early stage of learning; novice. **beginning** *n* start; starting place; early stage; outset. **beginnings** *pl n* **1** origin; early background. **2** early indication of potential or development.

begonia *n* plant with showy red, green, or greyish leaves and red, yellow, or white flowers.

begrudge *vt* resent; wish to deny; grudge.

beguile *vt,vi* charm; bewitch; hoodwink.

behalf *n* **on behalf of** in the name of; representing.

behave *vi* **1** act; react; function. **2** conduct (oneself). **behaviour** *n.*

behead *vt* execute by severing the head; decapitate.

behind *adv,adj* **1** following; after. **2** in a place that is further back. **3** behindhand. *prep* **1** at the back of; beyond. **2** not so advanced as. **3** remaining; left over. *n inf* buttocks. **behindhand** *adj,adv* in arrears; late.

behold *vt,vi* (beheld) see; look (at). *interj* look!

beige *adj,n* light greyish-brown; fawn.

being *n* **1** living creature. **2** existence; living state.

belated *adj* arriving or happening too late. **belatedly** *adv.*

belch *vi,vt* **1** expel wind noisily fron the stomach

through the mouth. **2** send out in large quantities; gush. *n* **1** act of belching. **2** blast; burst.

belfry *n* tower in which bells are hung.

belie *vt* **1** give the wrong impression of. **2** show to be false.

believe *vt,vi* **1** consider to be true or right; accept. **2** think; assume. *vi* subscribe to a particular faith. **believe in** have faith in; trust; be convinced of the existence of. **believable** *adj*. **believer** *n*. **belief** *n* **1** something believed; opinion. **2** creed; faith. **3** trust; acceptance.

belittle *vt* undervalue; disparage.

bell *n* **1** hollow metal instrument that produces a ringing sound when struck. **2** electrical device that produces a ringing or buzzing sound. **ring a bell** seem vaguely familiar.

belligerent *adj* warlike; aggressive. **belligerence** *n*. **belligerently** *adv*.

bellow *vi,vt* roar loudly; bawl. *n* deep-throated roar or shout.

bellows *n pl or s* device that expands and contracts to produce a strong draught of air.

belly *n* **1** abdomen. **2** stomach. **3** part of something that bulges.

belong *v* **belong to 1** be owned by. **2** be a member of. **3** be part of a set with; go with; fit. *vi* have an allotted place. **belongings** *pl n* personal possessions.

below *adv* at a place lower down; underneath. *prep* lower or further down than; under.

belt *n* **1** strip of leather, cloth, etc., worn round the waist. **2** band; strip. **3** region or zone with specific characteristics. **4** slap; blow; sharp hit. **below the belt** unfairly; against the rules. ~*vt* **1** fasten with a belt. **2** *sl* strike; beat. **3** *also* **belt out** sing, play, or shout loudly. *vi* race; travel fast. **belt up** *sl* stop talking.

bemoan *vt,vi* moan (about); lament; deplore.

bemused *adj* **1** lost in thought. **2** dazed; confused.

bench *n* **1** long wooden or stone seat. **2** work table; counter. **3** seat occupied by a judge or magistrate.

bend *v* (bent) *vt* **1** make into a bow or curved shape. **2** turn or curve in a particular direction. **3** subdue; coerce. *vi* **1** curve. **2** stoop; bow. *n* curve. **round the bend** mad; crazy.

beneath *adv* underneath; below. *prep* **1** concealed under; lower than. **2** in an inferior or subordinate position than. **3** unacceptable to.

benefactor *n* person who donates a large sum of money; patron.

benefit *n* **1** advantage; privilege; good. **2** welfare or insurance payment. *vt,vi* do good to or be good for. **beneficial** *adj* advantageous; helpful. **beneficiary** *n* recipient of a legacy, annuity, etc.

benevolent *adj* **1** kindly; good-natured. **2** charitable; generous. **benevolence** *n*. **benevolently** *adv*.

benign (bi'nain) *adj* **1** gentle; friendly. **2** not malignant.

bent *v pt* and *pp* of **bend.** *adj* **1** crooked; curved. **2** *sl* dishonest; corrupt. **bent on** determined to. ~*n* inclination; penchant.

benzene *n* colourless sweet-smelling liquid containing carbon and hydrogen and used as a solvent.

bequeath *vt* leave (money, property, etc.) esp. by will. **bequest** *n* something bequeathed.

bereaved *adj* deprived (of) by death. **bereavement** *n*.

bereft *adj* deprived; completely lacking (in).

beret ('berei) *n* flat circular cap of wool, felt, etc.

berry *n* soft stoneless fruit of various trees or bushes.

berserk (bə'zə:k) *adj* in a frenzy; wild and violent.

berth *n* **1** sleeping place in a ship, train, caravan, etc. **2** mooring place. *vi,vt* moor; dock.

beseech *vt* implore; entreat.

beset *vt* (besetting; beset) **1** trouble; plague. **2** attack; assail.

beside *prep* at the side of; adjacent to; by. **beside oneself** overcome; out of control. **besides** *adv* **1** moreover; furthermore; anyway. **2** additionally; as well. *prep* in addition to; apart from.

besiege *vt* **1** surround and attack (a city, fortress, etc.). **2** assail with demands, requests, etc.

best *adj* **1** of the highest quality. **2** most suitable or desirable. *adv* in the best way. *n* the highest possible standard; utmost. **best man** *n* man who looks after a bridegroom. **bestseller** *n* book or other product that sells exceptionally well.

bestial *adj* **1** brutal; coarse and savage; carnal. **2** relating to a beast.

bestow *vt* give; confer; endow. **bestowal** *n*.

bet *n* **1** pledge between parties to pay a sum of money to the one who successfully predicts the outcome of a future event. **2** sum of money pledged. **3** predicted outcome. **4** course of action. *vt,vi* (-tt-; bet) **1** place a bet (on); gamble. **2** *inf* predict. **betting shop** *n* premises of a bookmaker.

betray *vt* **1** disclose information about or expose to an enemy. **2** be unfaithful or disloyal to. **3** show signs of; reveal inadvertently. **betrayal** *n*.

better *adj* **1** of a higher quality; superior. **2** more suitable or desirable. **3** no longer sick; recovering. **better off** richer; having a greater advantage. *adv* more; to a greater extent. **had better** ought to; should. ~*n* **1** the more excellent or desirable. **2** superior; person of higher worth. **get the better of** outwit; defeat. ~*vt* improve upon. **betterment** *n* improvement.

between *prep* **1** in a space or interval separating two places, moments in time, etc. **2** shared by. **3** through joint effort or contribution. *adv* in or towards the middle.

beverage *n* any drink except water.

beware *vt,vi* be wary (of); take heed (of).

bewilder *vt* puzzle; confuse; perplex. **bewilderment** *n*.

bewitch *vt* charm as if by a spell; enchant.

beyond *prep* **1** farther away than; on the far side of. **2** outside the control or limits of. *adv* farther away.

biannual *adj* occurring twice a year. **biannually** *adv*.

bias *n* **1** prejudice; distorted outlook. **2** tendency; inclination. **3** diagonal line or cut. **biased** *adj* partial; prejudiced.

bib *n* **1** piece of cloth worn under the chin by a baby whilst eating. **2** part of an apron, pinafore, etc., that covers the front of the body above the waist.

Bible *n* collection of sacred writings of the Christian Church. **biblical** *adj*.

bibliography *n* list of works relating to a particular subject, author, etc. **bibliographical** *adj*. **bibliographer** *n*.

biceps *pl n* muscles of the upper arm.

bicker *vi* squabble; quarrel, esp. over trivial matters.

bicycle *also* **cycle** *or* **bike** *n* vehicle with two wheels propelled by pedalling. *vi* ride a bicycle.

bid *v* (-dd-; bad, bade, *or* bid; bidden *or* bid) *vt,vi* **1** offer to buy for a certain sum, esp at an auction. **2** ask; command. *vt* express in greeting. **bidder** *n*.

bidet ('bi:dei) *n* small bath used for washing the genital area.

biennial *adj* occurring once every two years or lasting for two years. *n* plant with a two-year life cycle. **biennially** *adv*.

big *adj* **1** large; great; not small. **2** important; substantial. **3** generous. *adv* with authority; in a big way.

bigamy *n* crime of marrying another partner when a former marriage is still valid. **bigamist** *n*., **bigamous** *adj*.

bigot *n* offensively intolerant or prejudiced person. **bigoted** *adj*. **bigotry** *n*.

bike *n,vi* short for **bicycle.**

bikini *n* woman's two-piece bathing costume.

bile *n* fluid secreted by the liver. **bilious** *adj* suffering from excessive secretion of bile in the liver.

bilingual *adj* able to speak two languages.

bill[1] *n* **1** statement of money owed; invoice. **2** law or act of Parliament in draft form. **3** poster or notice. **4** programme of events. **5** *US* banknote. *vt* **1** present an account to; invoice. **2** put on a programme; schedule.

bill[2] *n* bird's beak.

billiards *n* game played with a long cue and a number of balls on a table usually fitted with pockets.

billion *n* **1** (in Britain) one million million. **2** (esp. in the US) one thousand million.

billow *n* **1** large sea-wave. **2** surging mass. *vi, vt* swell up; surge.

bin *n* storage container.

binary *adj* **1** composed of two parts. **2** relating to the number two.

bind *v* (bound) *vt,vi* **1** tie or entwine; wrap round tightly. **2** cohere; stick. *vt* **1** restrict; place under an obligation or contract. **2** confine; trap; constrain. **3** fasten together (pages) inside a cover. **4** sew the edge of to prevent fraying, for decoration, etc. *n inf* restricting circumstance; constraint. **binder** *n* folder with clasps for holding together loose sheets of paper. **binding** *n* **1** cover of a book. **2** edging material or tape *adj* restricting;

obligatory. **bindweed** *n* plant that twines round a support or the stems of other plants.

bingo *n* gambling game in which players match up numbers on a chart with those picked out at random.

binoculars *pl n* optical instrument consisting of a pair of small telescopes joined together.

biochemistry *n* study of the chemical compounds occurring in plants and animals. **biochemical** *adj*. **biochemist** *n*.

biography *n* account of a person's life written by someone else. **biographical** *adj*. **biographer** *n*.

biology *n* study of living organisms. **biological** *adj*. **biologically** *adv*. **biologist** *n*.

birch *n* **1** tree with a slender grey or white trunk. **2** bundle of birch twigs used as a whip. *vt* flog; thrash.

bird *n* warm-blooded feathered egg-laying vertebrate with forelimbs modified as wings.

birth *n* **1** act of being born or producing offspring. **2** origin; beginning. **3** descent; lineage. **birth certificate** *n* official document issued when a child's birth is registered. **birth control** *n* method or practice of contraception. **birthday** *n* anniversary of a person's birth. **birthmark** *n* blemish on the skin formed before birth. **birth rate** *n* ratio of live births in relation to a given population.

biscuit *n* crisp flat cake made from baked dough.

bisect *vt* **1** divide into two equal parts. **2** split; cut across. **bisection** *n*.

bisexual *adj* able to respond sexually to a person of either sex. *n* person who is bisexual.

bishop *n* **1** high-ranking clergyman with authority over a diocese. **2** chess piece able to move diagonally across squares of the same colour.

bison *n* N American animal of the ox family with a shaggy coat and humped back; buffalo.

bistro ('bi:strou) small restaurant or bar.

bit[1] *n* **1** small piece or amount. **2** short while. **a bit** a little; somewhat; rather. **bit by bit** gradually. **do one's bit** do one's duty; contribute. **every bit as** equally as. **not a bit** not at all.

bit[2] *n* **1** mouthpiece attached to a bridle for controlling a horse. **2** metal drill used with a brace.

bitch *n* **1** female dog. **2** *sl* malicious woman. *vi* speak maliciously; grumble. **bitchy** *adj*. **bitchiness** *n*.

bite *vt,vi* (bit; bitten) **1** press, cut, or sink into with the teeth. **2** have a tendency to attack with the teeth, fangs, etc. **3** sting; smart. **4** corrode; eat into. **5** take bait. **6** grip; hold fast. *n* **1** act of biting. **2** piece bitten off; morsel. **3** mark or swelling caused by biting. **4** something to eat; snack. **5** strong grip. **biting** *adj* **1** harsh; keen. **2** sarcastic; hurtful.

bitter *adj* **1** having a harsh taste. **2** resentful; rancorous; deeply hostile. **3** distressing; hard to bear. **4** extremely cold; icy. *n* type of beer with a strong flavour of hops. **bitterly** *adv*. **bitterness** *n*.

bivalve *n* mollusc having two shells hinged together.

bizarre *adj* weird; odd; strange.

black *adj* **1** of the colour of coal, jet, etc. **2** extremely dark; unlit. **3** extremely dirty. **4** grim; bleak. **5** enraged; angry. **6** dark-skinned. **black market** *n* system of illicit trading. **black pudding** sausage made from pork fat and blood. ~*n* **1** dark colour having no hue. **2** darkness. **3** *cap* Negro; dark-skinned person. **black and blue** heavily bruised. ~*vt* **1** blacken. **2** *inf* boycott; ban. **black out 1** obliterate. **2** extinguish; plunge into darkness. **3** pass out; lose consciousness. **blackout** *n* **1** power failure. **2** extinguishing of lights in cities, etc., in order to prevent identification by enemy aircraft. **3** temporary loss of consciousness or memory. **blackness** *n*. **blacken** *vt,vi* make or become black; darken. *vt* defame.

blackberry *n* edible purplish-black fruit of the bramble.

blackbird *n* songbird in which the male has black plumage with a yellow beak and the female is brown.

blackboard *n* large board that can be written on with chalk.

blackcurrant *n* small round edible black berry that grows on a cultivated bush.

blackguard ('blægɑ:d) *n* scoundrel; rogue.

blackhead *n* spot with a black surface that clogs a pore on the skin.

blackleg *n* person who acts against the interests of a trade union, esp. by refusing to strike. *vi* (-gg-) act as a blackleg.

blackmail *n* crime of demanding payment in exchange for not disclosing discreditable information. *vt* threaten by means of blackmail. **blackmailer** *n*.

blacksmith *n* craftsman who works with iron.

bladder *n* sac in the body that functions as a receptacle for urine.

blade *n* **1** sharp-edged or cutting part of a knife, sword, etc. **2** long flat leaf of grass. **3** shoulder blade. **4** flat broad end of a propeller, oar, etc.

blame *n* responsibility for a crime, error, fault, etc. *vt,vi* attribute blame (to); find fault (with). **blameless** *adj* innocent; faultless.

blanch *vt* **1** make lighter in colour; bleach. **2** plunge (vegetables, meat, etc.) into boiling water. *vi* become pale with fear, nausea, etc.

blancmange (blə'mɔndʒ) *n* dessert made from milk, cornflour, and flavouring.

bland *adj* **1** not highly flavoured or seasoned. **2** mild; temperate. **3** unemotional; without passion. **blandly** *adv*. **blandness** *n*.

blank *adj* **1** not written on or filled in. **2** bare; undecorated. **3** uncomprehending; expressionless. **4** uninspired. **blank verse** unrhymed verse. ~*n* **1** empty space. **2** mental confusion. **3** written or printed dash. **4** gun cartridge having powder but no bullet. **draw a blank** fail to obtain the required information during an investigation. *v* **blank out** blot out; obliterate.

blanket *n* **1** woollen bed cover. **2** thick layer; cover. *vt* cover up.

blare *vt,vi* **1** shout or sound loudly; proclaim. **2** shine harshly. *n* **1** loud noise; blast. **2** blinding light; glare; blaze.

blasé ('blɑːzeɪ) *adj* no longer capable of being shocked, excited, etc.; cool and sophisticated.

blaspheme *vi* curse; swear; utter profanities. *vt* act irreverently towards. **blasphemous** *adj*. **blasphemy** *n*.

blast *n* **1** explosion. **2** loud explosive noise; blare. **3** strong sudden rush of air, flames, water, etc. *interj sl* exclamation of anger, frustration, etc. *vt,vi* **1** blow up; destroy by explosion. **2** produce a sudden loud noise. **3** force an opening (in); breach. **blastoff** *n* launching of a rocket.

blatant *adj* flagrant; conspicuous; undisguised. **blatancy** *n*. **blatantly** *adv*.

blaze *n* **1** roaring fire; bright flame. **2** bright light; glare. **3** passionate display; outburst. *vi* **1** burn vigorously; flare. **2** glare; shine harshly.

blazer *n* jacket, esp. one worn as part of a school or club uniform.

bleach *vt,vi* whiten through heat or the action of chemicals. *n* substance used for bleaching clothes, the hair, etc.

bleak *adj* **1** desolate and exposed. **2** grim; dismal; unfavourable. **bleakly** *adv*. **bleakness** *n*.

bleat *vt,vi* **1** (of a sheep or goat) utter a high-pitched cry. **2** moan plaintively; whine; complain. *n* cry of a sheep or goat.

bleed *v* (bled) *vi* **1** lose blood. **2** suffer extreme anguish. *vt* **1** drain blood from. **2** draw off (liquid, gas, etc.). **bleeding** *adj* utter. *adv sl* extremely; very.

bleep *n* noise produced by an electronic device. *vi* make a short high-pitched sound.

blemish *n* **1** discoloured mark on the skin. **2** stain or flaw. *vt* spoil; mar; tarnish.

blend *vt,vi* **1** mix (different varieties of tea, tobacco, etc.). **2** combine (colours). **3** merge; form a mixture. *vi* harmonize; mix well. *n* blended mixture. **blender** *n* machine for blending vegetables, liquids, etc.

bless *vt* **1** make holy; consecrate. **2** call for God's aid or protection for. **blessed with** (blest) endowed or favoured with; granted. **blessed** ('blesid) *adj* holy; sacred. **blessing** *n* **1** statement or ceremony invoking God's aid or protection. **2** divine gift; sanction. **3** good fortune.

blew *v pt of* **blow**.

blight *n* **1** plant disease caused by fungi, insects, etc. **2** something that mars or impedes growth. *vt* **1** cause blight in. **2** spoil; destroy.

blind *adj* **1** deprived of the power of sight. **2** unable or unwilling to understand or tolerate. **3** made reckless by passion. **4** concealed; unseen. **5** closed at one end. *adv also* **blindly** **1** without being able to see. **2** without proper information or preparation. *vt* **1** make blind. **2** dazzle. **3** deprive of reason or judgment. *n* length of material on a roller used as a shade for a window. **blindness** *n*. **blindfold** *n* strip of cloth placed over the eyes and tied at the back of the head. *vt* place a blindfold over (the eyes).

blink *vt,vi* **1** rapidly open and shut (the eyes). **2** flash on and off. *n* **1** rapid opening and shutting of the eyes. **2** flash; twinkle. **blinkers** *pl n* **1** direction indicators on a motor vehicle. **2** part of a horse's bridle that prevents sideways vision.

bliss *n* state of ecstatic happiness. **blissful** *adj*. **blissfully** *adv*.

blister *n* **1** small swelling or bubble on the skin produced by friction, burning, etc. **2** bubble of paint. *vt,vi* produce blisters.

blithe *adj* **1** carefree; light-hearted. **2** thoughtless; casual. **blithely** *adv*. **blitheness** *n*.

blitz *n* heavy attack, such as an air-raid. *vt* make an intensive attack on.

blizzard *n* violent snowstorm.

bloat *vt,vi* swell; inflate.

blob *n* **1** drop of liquid, dirt, etc. **2** blurred shape or form. *vt* (-bb-) splash or mark with blobs.

bloc *n* united group of countries, political parties, etc.

block *n* **1** solid piece of stone, wood, etc.; slab; brick; chunk. **2** building comprising a number of offices, flats, etc. **3** group of things fastened together or arranged in rows. **4** obstruction; obstacle; blockage. **5** psychological or mental barrier. *vt also* **block up 1** obstruct; cause a blockage in; stop up. **2** veto; impede; prevent. **blockade** *n* obstruction, esp. of a port or harbour by military forces. *vt* obstruct with a blockade. **blockage** *n* something that blocks, obstructs, or impedes.

bloke *n inf* man.

blond *adj* fair-haired. *n* man with fair hair. **blonde** *f n*. **blondness** *n*.

blood *n* **1** red fluid circulating through the veins and arteries of the body. **2** lineage; descent. **in cold blood** ruthlessly; in a calculated way. **bloodcurdling** *adj* terrifying; ghastly. **blood pressure** *n* pressure of the blood against the inner walls of the arteries. **bloodshed** *n* violent killing; slaughter. **bloodstream** *n* flow of blood through the body. **bloodthirsty** *adj* sadistic; delighting in violence. **bloodthirstiness** *n*. **bloody** *adj* covered or stained with blood; gory. *adj,adv sl* damned; extremely. *vt* stain with blood. **bloodiness** *n*. **bloody-minded** *adj* obstinate; pig-headed; perverse. **bloody-mindedness** *n*.

bloom *n* **1** flower(s); blossom. **2** healthy glow. **3** shiny surface of various fruits. *vi* **1** flower; blossom. **2** flourish; develop vigorously.

blossom *n* flower(s), esp. of a fruit tree. *vi* **1** flower; produce blossom. **2** begin to grow or develop.

blot *n* **1** ink stain. **2** eyesore. **3** damage to one's character or reputation. *vt* (-tt-) **1** stain; mark. **2** use an absorbent material to soak up. **blot out** obscure completely; obliterate. **blot one's copybook** spoil one's reputation or record; blunder. **blotting paper** *n* absorbent paper used esp. to soak up excess ink.

blotch *n* stain; discolouration; patch. *vt,vi* produce stains or patches. **blotchy** *adj*.

blouse *n* woman's garment that is similar to a shirt.

blow[1] *v* (blew; blown) *vt,vi* **1** send out (air) through the mouth or nose; exhale. **2** move through or by air or wind. **3** produce the sound of a whistle, trumpet, the wind, etc. **4** fuse; burn out. **blow out** extinguish or be extinguished. **blow over** subside; pass. **blow up 1** explode or cause an explosion. **2** lose one's temper. **3** inflate. **4** enlarge (a photograph). ~*n* **1** expulsion of air; puff. **2** act of blowing or sound produced by a whistle, trumpet, etc. **blowy** *adj* windy; blustery.

blow[2] *n* **1** heavy stroke or hit with the hand or a weapon. **2** sudden shock or disappointment; setback. **come to blows** start to fight.

blubber *n* thick layer of subcutaneous fat of a whale, seal, etc. *vt,vi* sob; cry noisily.

blue *n* colour in the spectrum that is the colour of a clear sky. **out of the blue** suddenly; without warning; from nowhere. **the blues 1** state of depression; dejectedness. **2** type of music created by Black Americans. ~*adj* **1** of the colour blue. **2** depressed; unhappy. **3** *inf* obscene. **bluebell** *n* woodland plant with blue bell-shaped flowers. **blue-blooded** *adj* of royal or aristocratic descent. **blueprint** *n* **1** photocopy of plans or drawings. **2** original model; prototype.

bluff *vt,vi* feign confidence in order to deceive about one's true motives, resources, etc. *n* act of deception. **call someone's bluff** act in a way that forces someone to reveal his true motives, resources, etc.; challenge.

blunder *n* stupid, tactless, or clumsy mistake. *vi* **1** make a stupid or tactless mistake. **2** move clumsily; stumble.

blunt *adj* **1** not sharp; unable to cut well. **2** outspoken; forthright; direct. *vt,vi* make or become blunt(er). *vt* make less sensitive; dull. **bluntly** *adv*. **bluntness** *n*.

blur *vt,vi* (-rr-) **1** make or become hazy, indistinct, or vague. **2** smear; smudge. *n* **1** something that is indistinct in outline or vague. **2** smudge.

blurt *vt,vi also* **blurt out** reveal (a secret), esp. when confused or under pressure.

blush *vi* become red in the face with embarrassment, shame, etc.; flush. *n* **1** reddening of the cheeks. **2** hint of redness on a flower, fruit, etc.

bluster *vt,vi* speak or act in a forceful and often boastful manner; swagger. *vi* blow strongly; be windy. **blustery** *adj.*

boar *n* **1** wild pig. **2** uncastrated male domestic pig.

board *n* **1** plank of wood. **2** shaped piece of wood or other material designed for a specific purpose, such as an ironing board or chess board. **3** cardboard. **4** notice board or blackboard. **5** body of directors, governors, or other officials; committee. **6** meals provided for residents in a hotel, hostel, etc. **go by the board** be ignored or rejected. **on board** on a ship, aircraft, etc.; aboard. ~*vt,vi* go on to a ship, aircraft, etc.; embark. *vt also* **board up** enclose or cover with boards of wood. *vt* provide lodgings for. *vi* live in lodgings. **boarder** *n* **1** child at boarding school. **2** lodger. **boarding house** *n* small private establishment offering cheap accommodation. **boarding school** *n* school with living accommodation for pupils. **board room** *n* committee room where a board meets.

boast *vi* exaggerate or speak proudly of one's own achievements or qualities; brag. *vt* be the proud possessor of. *n* exaggerated or proud statement. **boastful** *adj.* **boastfully** *adv.* **boastfulness** *n.*

boat *n* small vessel for travelling on water. **in the same boat** in the same situation or predicament. **miss the boat** miss an opportunity. ~*vi* travel in a boat, esp. for pleasure.

bob *vt,vi* (-bb-) **1** move up and down esp. in a liquid. **2** nod or jerk (the head). **3** bow or curtsy. *n* **1** jerky movement. **2** bow or curtsy.

bodice *n* top part of a woman's dress.

body *n* **1** the whole physical structure of a human being or other vertebrate. **2** torso; trunk. **3** corpse. **4** main or central part. **5** mass; expanse. **6** corporate group of people. **7** object or solid. **8** consistency or fullness, esp. of wine. **bodily** *adj* physical; corporeal. *adv* by lifting or using the body. **bodyguard** *n* person giving physical protection to another. **bodywork** *n* covering for the shell or framework of a vehicle.

bog *n* **1** area of waterlogged land, usually of peat. **2** *sl* lavatory. **bogged down** unable to make progress; hindered. **boggy** *adj.*

bogus *adj* fake; sham.

boil[1] *vt,vi* **1** produce gas or vapour from a liquid by the action of heat. **2** cook by heating in liquid. *vi* seethe; become agitated. **boil down** reduce in quantity by boiling. **boil down to** amount to; result in. **boil over** overflow or spill whilst boiling. *n* **on the boil** **1** approaching boiling point. **2** in operation; functioning well. **boiler** *n* vessel producing steam to drive an engine. **boiling point** *n* **1** temperature at which a liquid boils. **2** moment at which one loses one's temper or a situation becomes explosive.

boil[2] *n* inflamed pus-filled sore on the skin.

boisterous *adj* unruly; noisy and unrestrained. **boisterously** *adv.* **boisterousness** *n.*

bold *adj* **1** courageous; unafraid; daring. **2** clear; distinct. **boldly** *adv.* **boldness** *n.*

bolster *n* long pillow or cushion. *vt also* **bolster up** reinforce; encourage; boost.

bolt *n* **1** metal bar used to fasten a door, window, etc. **2** screw or pin used with a nut. **3** clap of thunder or flash of lightning. **make a bolt for it** run away quickly. ~*vt* **1** secure or fasten with a bolt. **2** eat hurriedly; gulp down. *vi* **1** jump up suddenly. **2** run off unexpectedly. *adv* **bolt upright** with one's back straight and rigid.

bomb *n* explosive device. **go like a bomb** **1** travel at high speed. **2** be highly successful. ~*vt,vi* attack with bombs. **bombard** *vt* **1** attack repeatedly with bombs, missiles, etc. **2** direct series of questions, complaints, etc., at. **bombardment** *n.* **bombardier** (bɔmbəˈdiə) *n* noncommissioned officer below a sergeant in the Royal Artillery. **bomber** *n* **1** aircraft designed to carry bombs. **2** person who attacks with bombs. **bombshell** *n* unexpected event causing great shock or distress.

bond *n* **1** something that binds, such as a rope or chain. **2** close intimate relationship; tie. **3** obligation; duty. **4** company or government certificate issued as a guarantee of repayment of money lent. **bonded warehouse** warehouse storing imported goods until duty is paid. **bondage** *n* slavery.

bone *n* hard tissue that makes up the skeleton of the body. **have a bone to pick** have something to criticize or quarrel about. **make**

no bones about have no hesitation or doubt about. ~*vt* remove the bones from (meat). **bonemeal** *n* animal food or fertilizer made from crushed bones. **bony** *adj* **1** having many bones. **2** having prominent bones. **3** resembling a bone.

bonfire *n* fire lit out of doors.

bonnet *n* **1** hat kept in place with ribbons tied under the chin. **2** hinged section at the front of a vehicle that covers the engine or luggage compartment.

bonus *n* additional payment, dividend, etc.

booby trap *n* **1** concealed or disguised explosive device intended to blow up when touched. **2** object or trap used by a practical joker to surprise or scare an unsuspecting victim. **booby-trap** *vt* (-pp-) set up a booby trap in or for.

book *n* **1** set of printed pages bound together; volume **2** written work, such as a novel or textbook. **3** pack of stamps, tickets, etc. **by the book** strictly according to the rules. ~*vt,vi* reserve (a seat, ticket, etc.) in advance. *vt* record (a person's name) prior to prosecution on a minor charge. **bookkeeping** *n* accounting system or practice of keeping records of business transactions. **bookkeeper** *n*. **booklet** *n* small book; brochure. **bookmaker** *n* person running a business to accept bets, esp. in horseracing.

boom *vi* **1** produce a deep resonant sound. **2** thrive; prosper. *n* **1** deep resonant sound. **2** period or state of prosperity.

boomerang *n* curved piece of wood used as a missile and designed to follow a course back to the user when thrown.

boor *n* uncouth coarse person. **boorish** *adj*

boost *n* **1** push or shove upwards. **2** increase; rise. **3** encouragement; help. *vt* **1** lift up with a push. **2** increase; expand. **3** improve; promote. **booster** *n*.

boot *n* **1** type of footwear usually covering the leg up to the knee. **2** stout shoe worn for walking, climbing, playing football, etc. **3** luggage compartment in a vehicle, usually situated at the rear. **4** *inf* kick. **the boot** *sl* dismissal; sack. ~*vt* **1** kick. **2** *also* **boot out** expel or dismiss unceremoniously.

booth *n* **1** enclosed cubicle. **2** covered stall at a market or fair.

booze *inf n* alcoholic drink. *vi* drink heavily.

border *n* **1** stretch of land constituting a frontier or boundary. **2** edge; margin. **3** flower bed along the edge of a lawn, path, etc. *vt,vi* function as a border or boundary (to). **border on 1** lie adjacent to. **2** verge on; come close to. **borderline** *n* **1** boundary line. **2** intermediate area or category. *adj* marginal; in between.

bore[1] *vt,vi* **1** drill (a hole) in. **2** dig or make (a tunnel, shaft, etc.), esp. in order to extract oil, minerals, etc. *n* **1** tunnel or shaft. **2** hollow part of a gun barrel. **3** calibre of a gun.

bore[2] *vt* exhaust or frustrate by being dull, repetitious, etc. *n* tedious or dreary person, task, etc. **boredom** *n*.

bore[3] *v pt* of **bear**[1].

born *v pt* of **bear**[1] (def 4) when used in the passive. *adj* possessing a specified innate quality.

borne *v pp* of **bear**[1].

borough *n* **1** town or district represented in Parliament. **2** area having its own local council.

borrow *vt,vi* **1** take or accept on loan. **2** incorporate into one's own language; adopt. **borrower** *n*.

borstal *n* establishment for young offenders.

bosom *n* **1** breast or chest, esp. of a woman; bust. **2** centre of love or comfort.

boss *inf n* employer, manager, or foreman. *vt,vi* control or manage, esp. domineeringly. **bossy** *adj* overbearing; inclined to dominate. **bossiness** *n*.

botany *n* science or study of plants. **botanical** *adj*. **botanist** *n*.

botch *vt,vi* bungle; make a bad job of *n* mess; clumsy repair.

both *pron,adj* each of two taken together. *conj*, **both...and...** firstly...and secondly...

bother *vt* disturb; worry; annoy; trouble. *vi* concern oneself; take trouble or care. *n* **1** fuss; commotion. **2** trouble; anxiety. *interj* exclamation of mild impatience or annoyance. **bothersome** *adj*.

bottle *n* long glass or plastic vessel with a narrow neck, for holding liquids. *vt,vi* pour into a bottle. **bottle up** repress or hide (emotions). **bottleneck** *n* something that restricts the flow of traffic, goods on a production line, etc.

bottom *n* **1** lowest part; base; foot. **2** seabed, riverbed, etc. **3** worst or most inferior position. **4** *inf* buttocks. **at bottom** fundamentally;

basically. **get to the bottom of** investigate the truth or cause of. ~*adj* lowest. **bottomless** *adj* 1 extremely deep. 2 seemingly endless or inexhaustible. **bottommost** *adj* 1 very lowest. 2 most basic.

bough *n* branch of a tree.

bought *v pt* and *pp* of **buy.**

boulder *n* large stone or rock.

bounce *vi,vt* **1** rebound or cause to spring back after striking or being thrown. **2** jump or throw up and down; jerk. *vi* (of a cheque) be returned by a bank as unacceptable. *n* **1** rebound; springing back. **2** jump; jerk. **3** exuberance; ebullience. **bouncing** *adj* very healthy or robust. **bouncy** *adj* exuberant; high-spirited. **bounciness** *n.*

bound[1] *v pt* and *pp* of **bind.** *adj* **bound to** certain to; sure to. **bound up with** *or* **in** closely involved with.

bound[2] *vi* leap; spring. *n* jump; bounce; leap.

bound[3] *vt* restrict; limit. *n* boundary; limit. **boundless** *adj* inexhaustible; limitless.

bound[4] *adj* heading towards; destined for.

boundary *n* something that marks the edge or limit of an area of land.

bouquet *n* **1** (bou'kei, bu:-) bunch of flowers, esp. one elaborately arranged or displayed. **2** (bu:'kei) aroma of a wine.

bourgeois ('buəʒwɑ:) *adj* of the middle class, esp. when regarded as conservative and materialistic. *n* member of the middle class. **bourgeoisie** (buəʒwɑ:'zi:) *n* middle class.

bout *n* **1** boxing contest; fight. **2** short period; spell.

boutique *n* small shop, esp. one selling clothes.

bow[1] (bau) *vt,vi* bend (the body or head) forwards as an act of respect, submission, etc. *vi* yield; submit; comply. **bow down 1** yield. **2** submit. ~*n* bending of the body or lowering of the head.

bow[2] (bou) *n* **1** weapon from which arrows are shot, consisting of a supple piece of wood pulled into a curved shape by a taut string. **2** rod strung with horsehair used for playing a violin, cello, etc. **3** decorative knot having two loops and two loose ends. **4** curve; arc. *vi,vt* **1** draw a bow across (a violin, cello, etc.). **2** curve; bend. **bow-legged** (bou'legid, -'legd) *adj* having the legs curving outwards; bandy.

bow[3] (bau) *n* front or forward end of a ship or boat.

bowels *pl n* **1** intestines. **2** deepest or innermost part.

bowl[1] *n* shallow basin or dish. **bowler** *n also* **bowler hat** hat with a hard rounded crown and narrow brim.

bowl[2] *n* heavy ball used in bowls, tenpin bowling, etc. *vt,vi* **1** roll (a ball) or travel smoothly along the ground. **2** deliver (a ball) to the batsman in cricket. **bowl along** travel fast and comfortably. **bowl over 1** knock to the ground. **2** overwhelm; astound. **bowler** *n* person who bowls in cricket. **bowling** *n* tenpin bowling or skittles. **bowls** *n* game played with weighted balls on a level grass pitch.

box[1] *n* **1** flat-bottomed container sometimes with a lid. **2** compartment for a small number of spectators, situated at the side of an auditorium. **3** cubicle; booth. **4** horsebox. **5** witness box. **6** section of printed matter enclosed within a border. **the box** *sl* television. ~*vt* pack into a box. **box in 1** enclose; board up. **2** corner or jam so as to prevent movement. **Boxing day** *n* first weekday after Christmas day. **box office** *n* booking office in a theatre, cinema, etc.

box[2] *vi,vt* **1** fight in a boxing match (against). **2** punch; hit with the fist. *n* blow of the fist; punch, cuff. **boxer** *n* **1** person who fights in a boxing match. **2** breed of smooth-haired dog, similar to a bulldog. **boxing** *n* sport in which two opponents fight with the fists using padded gloves.

boy *n* male child. **boyhood** *n.* **boyish** *adj.* **boyfriend** *n* male friend, esp. one with whom one has a romantic relationship.

boycott *vt* refuse to deal with (another nation, group, etc.) or buy (goods). *n* practice or instance of boycotting.

bra *n also* **brassiere** woman's undergarment worn to support the bosom.

brace *n* **1** tool into which a drill or bit is fitted for boring holes. **2** beam or girder used for strengthening or supporting a wall. **3** metal band fixed to the teeth to correct their alignment. **4** pair, esp of game birds. **braces** *pl n* pair of straps worn over the shoulders and fastened to the waistband of a pair of trousers. ~*vt* strengthen or support with a brace. *vt,vi* invigorate; freshen. **brace oneself** prepare oneself for impending pain, shock, etc.

bracelet *n* ornamental chain or band worn round the wrist.

bracken *n* type of large fern.

bracket *n* 1 right-angled support for a shelf. 2 one of a pair of written or printed symbols used to enclose additional information, etc. 3 classified group of people, esp. an income group. *vt* 1 fix with a bracket. 2 enclose within brackets. 3 place in the same category.

brag *vi* (-gg-) boast. *n* card game similar to poker. **braggart** *n* boastful person.

braid *n* 1 plait. 2 band of material made from plaited or twisted threads. *vt* plait; interweave (strands).

Braille *n* system of writing using embossed dots enabling the blind to read by touch.

brain *n* 1 mass of nerve fibre situated inside the skull, forming the main part of the central nervous system. 2 *also* **brains** intelligence. *vt inf* kill by striking violently on the head. **brainwash** *vt* indoctrinate or condition totally. **brainwave** *n* 1 voltage and current waves produced by the brain. 2 brilliant idea or inspiration. **brainy** *adj inf* intelligent.

braise *vt,vi* cook in a small amount of liquid in an airtight container.

brake *n* device on a vehicle that stops or slows down the motion of the wheels. *vi,vt* stop or slow down by applying the brake.

bramble *n* bush with thorny stems, esp. a blackberry bush.

branch *n* 1 limb of a tree or shrub that grows from the trunk or main stem; bough. 2 subdivision; offshoot. 3 local shop, bank, etc., that is part of a larger organization. *vi* 1 produce branches. 2 *also* **branch off** subdivide, diverge; fork. **branch out** extend one's interests.

brand *n* 1 class of product, esp. one marketed under a trademark. 2 type, variety; sort. 3 identifying mark on cattle, sheep, etc. 4 *also* **branding iron** iron rod that is heated and used for marking animals for identification. 5 stigma. *vt* 1 mark with a brand. 2 denounce as; label. 3 impress permanently on the mind; scar. **brand-new** *adj* absolutely new and unused.

brandish *vt* hold or wave (a weapon) threateningly or defiantly. *n* triumphant wave; flourish.

brandy *n* spirit distilled from the fermented juice of grapes.

brash *adj* 1 coarse; loud. 2 reckless, impetuous. **brashly** *adv*. **brashness** *n*.

brass *n* 1 yellowish-gold alloy of copper and zinc. 2 family of musical instruments that includes the trumpet and trombone. 3 engraved memorial tablet made of brass. **get down to brass tacks** start to consider or discuss the most important aspects of an issue or situation. **brassy** *adj* 1 of or like brass. 2 vulgar and showy; shameless.

brassiere *n* bra.

brave *adj* courageous; not cowardly; bold. *vt* face or tackle courageously; defy. *n* warrior of an American Indian tribe. **bravely** *adv*. **bravery** *n*.

brawl *n* noisy uncontrolled fight. *vi* fight or quarrel noisily.

brawn *n* 1 well-developed muscles. 2 muscular strength. 3 dish made of chopped meat from the head of a pig or calf and compressed into a mould.

bray *n* 1 harsh cry of a donkey. 2 shout or harsh laugh. *vi,vt* 1 (of a donkey) utter a harsh cry. 2 shout or laugh harshly.

brazen *adj* 1 shamelessly defiant; bold. 2 made of or like brass; brassy. *v* **brazen out** face or carry out boldly or defiantly.

brazil *n also* **brazil nut** nut with an edible kernel and hard rough shell that grows in a cluster inside a large capsule.

breach *n* 1 infringement or violation of the terms of a contract or agreement. 2 split between factions or parties. 3 gap; hole; crack. *vt* 1 infringe; violate. 2 break open; make a hole in.

bread *n* 1 food made from flour, milk, yeast, etc., baked in the form of loaves or rolls. 2 *sl* money. **breadwinner** *n* person responsible for earning money to support a family.

breadth *n* 1 measurement or extent from one side to another; width; broadness. 2 extent. 3 open-mindedness; tolerance.

break *v* (broke; broken) *vt,vi* 1 shatter or separate into pieces; fragment; smash; burst. 2 damage or cease to function. 3 pause; adjourn; stop for a while. *vt* 1 fail to keep (a promise, agreement, etc.). 2 bankrupt; ruin financially. 3 destroy; crush. 4 fracture (a bone). 5 reveal or disclose (news, a secret, etc.). 6 succeed in giving up (a habit). 7 surpass or improve on (a previous record, achievement, etc.). 8 reduce the impact of. *vi*

1 become known; be made public. 2 change; come to an end. 3 be overcome or overwhelmed with grief, strain, etc. 4 (esp. of the male voice at puberty) undergo a change. *n* 1 fracture; split; crack. 2 pause; recess; interval. 3 disconnection; discontinuation. 4 change of routine or habit. 5 sudden escape. 6 *inf* opportunity; stroke of luck. **break away** 1 escape. 2 form or join a new group. **breakaway** *n* 1 escape. 2 split. **break down** 1 stop functioning because of mechanical failure. 2 fail. 3 collapse with emotion. 4 analyse. **breakdown** *n* 1 failure. 2 mental collapse; nervous breakdown. 3 analysis; detailed account. **break even** cover one's expenses with neither profit nor loss. **break in(to)** 1 force entry, esp. in order to steal. 2 interrupt. 3 tame and train (a horse). **break-in** *n* forced entry. **break off** 1 detach a piece (from). 2 discontinue (a relationship). 3 stop abruptly, esp. when speaking. **break out** 1 escape (from prison). 2 begin suddenly or violently. 3 develop (a rash, pimples, etc.). **break through** 1 penetrate. 2 achieve after a long struggle. **breakthrough** *n* important discovery or achievement. **break up** 1 disintegrate. 2 split up; separate; part. **break-up** *n* 1 disintegration. 2 split; separation. **breakable** *adj*. **breakage** *n* 1 act of breaking. 2 the thing broken or its value.

breakfast *n* first meal of the day. *vi* eat breakfast.

breast *n* 1 front part of the body from the neck to the abdomen; chest. 2 mammary gland. 3 centre of affection, patriotic feelings, etc. **make a clean breast of** confess. **breaststroke** *n* stroke in swimming performed face downwards with the arms and legs making circular movements.

breath *n* 1 inhalation and exhalation of air. 2 air inhaled or exhaled. 3 slight gust of air or wind. 4 hint; suggestion; vague rumour. **out of breath** unable to breathe properly. **take one's breath away** dumbfound; astound. **under one's breath** in a low voice or whisper. **breathless** *adj* out of breath. **breathy** *adj*. **breathtaking** *adj* amazing; thrilling.

breathe *vt,vi* 1 inhale and exhale (air). 2 whisper; murmur; blow gently. **breather** *n inf* pause for rest. **breathing space** *n* sufficient room to move or function.

breed *vt,vi* (bred) 1 bear and produce (offspring). 2 propagate; reproduce. 3 generate; give rise to. *n* 1 group within a species, having common characteristics. 2 type; variety; brand. **breeder** *n*. **breeding** *n* 1 reproduction; propagation. 2 socially acceptable upbringing or background.

breeze *n* light wind. *vi inf* move about in a carefree manner. **breezy** *adj*.

brethren *n pl* of **brother,** esp. in a religious context.

brevity *n* briefness; conciseness.

brew *vt,vi* 1 make (beer) by fermentation. 2 make (tea, coffee, etc.) by infusion. *vt* concoct. *vi* 1 undergo fermentation or infusion. 2 be in the process of formation. *n* 1 brand of beer. 2 concoction. **brewery** *n* establishment where beer is brewed.

bribe *n* payment offered in order to influence a person to act in one's favour, esp. illegally. *vt,vi* persuade with a bribe. **bribery** *n*.

brick *n* 1 block of stone or baked clay used in building. 2 small block of wood used as a toy. 3 slab. *vt also* **brick up** seal or enclose with bricks. **bricklayer** *n* person skilled in building with bricks. **bricklaying** *n*. **brickwork** *n* construction with bricks.

bride *n* woman preparing for marriage or recently married. **bridegroom** *n* husband of a bride. **bridesmaid** *n* female attendant who looks after the bride.

bridge[1] *n* 1 construction spanning a river, valley, etc. 2 top part of the nose. 3 platform from which a ship is piloted or navigated. 4 small block supporting the strings of a violin, guitar, etc. 5 something that serves to connect. *vt* 1 place a bridge over; span. 2 form a connection between.

bridge[2] *n* card game developed from whist.

bridle *n* part of a harness, including the headpiece, bit, and reins, for controlling a horse. *vt* 1 fit or control with a bridle. 2 curb; check. *vi* express contempt, anger, etc., by drawing in the chin or jerking the head. **bridlepath** *n* narrow track that is suitable for horses.

brief *adj* 1 lasting a short time. 2 concise. 3 curt; abrupt. *n* 1 document in which a solicitor sets out details of his client's case for a barrister. 2 set of instructions. **briefs** *pl n* short underpants or knickers. ~*vt* prepare or instruct with a brief. **briefly** *adv*. **briefness** *n*. **briefcase** *n* bag or case used to hold papers, documents, etc. **briefing** *n* meeting at which information and instructions are given, esp. for a military operation.

brigade *n* **1** military unit forming part of a division. **2** group of people trained to perform a special task. **brigadier** (brigə'diə) *n* army officer holding a rank below that of major general and above a colonel and usually in command of a brigade.

bright *adj* **1** giving off a strong light. **2** of a strong colour; vivid. **3** shiny; gleaming. **4** cheerful. **5** *inf* clever; intelligent. *adv also* **brightly** in a bright manner. **brightness** *n*. **brighten** *vt,vi* make or become bright(er).

brilliant *adj* **1** shining brightly; glittering. **2** extremely clever or talented. **3** displaying great imagination. **4** outstanding. **brilliance** *n*. **brilliantly** *adv*.

brim *n* **1** rim of a cup, dish, etc. **2** edge of a hat projecting from the crown. *vt,vi* (-mm-) fill or be full so as to overflow.

bring *vt* (brought) **1** carry or convey (to or towards). **2** accompany. **3** produce; yield. **4** cause. **5** force or persuade. **bring about** cause to happen. **bring back** reintroduce; restore. **bring down 1** force down. **2** reduce. **3** humiliate or depress. **bring forward 1** produce; present. **2** fix for an earlier time. **bring in 1** introduce; initiate. **2** yield; earn. **3** include. **bring off** achieve by striving or by taking risks. **bring on 1** cause to start; induce. **2** help to develop; encourage. **bring out 1** cause to show or appear. **2** publish. **bring round 1** make conscious again, esp. after fainting. **2** persuade; convert; convince. **bring up 1** rear; educate from an early age. **2** vomit. **3** introduce or mention.

brink *n* **1** edge of a high or steep place, body of water, etc. **2** threshold; verge.

brisk *adj* **1** quick; lively. **2** invigorating; fresh. **briskly** *adv*. **briskness** *n*.

bristle *n* **1** short tough hair of an animal such as the pig. **2** hair, wire, fibre, etc., of a brush. **3** hair of a man's beard; stubble. *vi* **1** (of fur, hair, etc.) stand on end; be stiff or rigid. **2** display signs of annoyance, indignation, etc. **bristle with** be crowded or overrun with. **bristly** *adj*.

brittle *adj* **1** easily broken, shattered, or cracked. **2** irritable; short-tempered. **brittleness** *n*.

broach *vt* **1** introduce or suggest tentatively. **2** pierce or open in order to draw off liquid; tap.

broad *adj* **1** wide; not narrow. **2** extensive. **3** from one side to another; across; in width. **4** general; not specific. **5** direct; not subtle. **6** crude; coarse; vulgar. **7** displaying features of dialect or non-standard speech. **8** tolerant. **in broad daylight** openly; without attempting to conceal. **broad bean** *n* bean having large flat seeds, which are eaten as a vegetable. **broaden** *vt,vi* make or become broad(er); widen. **broad-minded** *adj* having tolerant or liberal views; not bigoted. **broad-mindedness** *n*.

broadcast *v* (-cast *or* -casted) *vt,vi* transmit via radio or television. *vi* appear on a radio or television programme. *vt* **1** publicize. **2** sow (seed) by hand. *n* radio or television transmission or programme. **broadcaster** *n*. **broadcasting** *n*.

brocade *n* heavy fabric woven with embossed designs.

broccoli *n* type of cabbage having edible green or purple flower heads.

brochure *n* pamphlet or booklet containing information, advertisements, etc.

broke *v pt* of **break.** *adj* penniless; bankrupt.

broken *v pp* of **break. broken-hearted** *adj* overwhelmed with grief, sorrow, disappointment, etc.

broker *n* agent for insurance, shares, securities, loans, etc.

bronchi ('brɔŋkai) *pl n, s* **bronchus** ('brɔŋkəs) *also* **bronchial tubes** two main branches of the windpipe. **bronchial** *adj*. **bronchitis** *n* inflammation of the bronchi.

bronze *n* **1** reddish-gold alloy of copper and tin, sometimes with zinc and lead added. **2** statue or ornament of bronze. *adj* **1** reddish-gold. **2** *also* **bronzed** suntanned. *vt,vi* make or become suntanned.

brooch *n* ornamental pin or clasp fastened to the front of the clothing.

brood *n* **1** group of young birds hatched at the same time. **2** *inf* children in a family; offspring. *vt,vi* **1** sit on and hatch (eggs). **2** think or worry (about) for a long time. **broody** *adj*.

brook *n* small stream.

broom *n* **1** implement for sweeping with a head of bristles or fibres and a long handle. **2** evergreen shrub with bright yellow flowers, that is able to grow on poor soil.

brother *n* **1** son of the same parents as another **2** fellow member, comrade. **3** unordained or lay male member of a religious order. **brotherhood** *n* **1** relationship as a brother. **2** fraternity; fellowship. **3** religious community of men. **brother-in-law** *n, pl* **brothers-in-law** **1** husband of one's sister. **2** brother of one's wife or husband. **3** husband of the sister of one's wife or husband. **brotherly** *adj* affectionate or loyal as a brother.

brought *v pt* and *pp* of **bring.**

brow *n* **1** eyebrow. **2** forehead. **3** crest of a hill. **browbeat** *vt* (-beat; -beaten) intimidate; oppress; bully.

brown *n* the colour of earth; very dark orange or yellow. *adj* **1** of the colour brown. **2** suntanned. *vt,vi* make or become brown. **browned off** *adj* disillusioned; bored; fed up. **brownish** *adj.*

browse *vi* **1** look through or examine a book, items for sale, etc., unhurriedly or casually. **2** feed on vegetation; graze.

bruise *n* rupture of the blood vessels causing discoloration of the skin. *vt,vi* **1** produce a bruise. **2** offend; hurt the feelings (of).

brunette *n* woman or girl with dark hair. *adj* dark; brown.

brunt *n* full impact of force, shock, etc.

brush *n* **1** implement with a head of bristles or fibres and a handle. **2** stroke made with a brush. **3** light touch. **4** short unpleasant meeting or contact. **5** fox's tail. *vt* **1** wipe, clean, apply, etc., with a brush. **2** touch lightly. **brush aside** dismiss as irrelevant; disregard. **brush up** **1** revise; refresh the memory. **2** make neat and tidy.

brusque *adj* curt; brisk; abrupt. **brusquely** *adv.* **brusqueness** *n.*

Brussels sprout *n* type of cabbage having small edible heads of tightly overlapping leaves growing on one stem.

brute *n* **1** animal, esp. when contrasted with man; beast. **2** cruel, tyrannical, or ignorant person. *adj* **brute force/strength** sheer physical force/strength; brawn. **brutal** *adj* cruel; savage; barbaric. **brutality** *n.* **brutally** *adv.*

bubble *n* **1** globule of air or gas contained within a film of liquid. **2** gurgling sound. *vt,vi* form bubbles, effervesce. *vi* gurgle.

buck *n* male of animals such as the rabbit, hare, or deer. *vi* rear in an attempt to unseat a rider. *vt* unseat; throw off. **buck up** **1** hurry. **2** cheer up.

bucket *n* container with a circular bottom and a handle. **kick the bucket** die.

buckle *n* **1** clasp with a prong used for securing a belt or strap. **2** distorted curve; bulge; twist. *vt,vi* **1** fasten with a buckle. **2** force or be forced out of shape through stress, heat, etc.; warp.

bud *n* undeveloped flower or leaf shoot. **nip in the bud** prevent the development of. ~*vi* (-dd-) produce buds. **budding** *adj* beginning to show talent; promising.

Buddhism ('budizəm) *n* Eastern religion, founded by Buddha, that teaches self-awareness through the denial of passion or desire. **Buddhist** *n,adj.*

budge *vt,vi* move; shift.

budget *n* **1** estimate of expected income and expenditure. **2** money allocated for a project. *vt,vi* **1** allow for or include in a budget. **2** spend according to a budget; economize (on).

buffalo *n* **1** African animal of the ox family having curved horns. **2** bison.

buffer *n* **1** shock absorber fitted to a train or placed at the end of a railway track. **2** person or thing that serves to reduce the threat of attack or lessen the impact of a collision.

buffet[1] ('bʌfei) *n* **1** counter or table from which refreshments are served. **2** refreshments set out for guests to help themselves.

buffet[2] ('bʌfit) *vt* **1** blow or toss about; batter. **2** fight or push through.

bug *n* **1** type of insect that feeds on plant juices or the blood of animals. **2** *inf* infection caused by certain microorganisms. **3** concealed device, such as a microphone, used to obtain secret information. **4** *sl* obsession; craze. *vt* (-gg-) **1** annoy; bother; nag. **2** conceal a microphone in.

bugle *n* brass instrument similar to the trumpet but without valves. *vi* play a bugle.

build *vt,vi* (built) **1** construct using materials such as brick, stone, or wood. **2** commission or finance a construction. *vt* **1** establish and develop (a business, etc.). **2** create or design for a particular purpose. **build up** **1** work on in order to strengthen, increase, or enhance. **2** accumulate. **build-up** *n* **1** gradual increase. **2** promotion of a commodity. **builder** *n.* **building** *n* **1** construction having walls and a roof **2** business or process of constructing houses, shops, etc. **building society** *n* company advancing loans for mortgages using funds deposited by investors. **built-in** *adj* constructed as an integral part.

bulb *n* **1** rounded organ of a plant, such as the tulip or onion, that grows underground. **2** plant growing from such an organ. **3** light bulb. **bulbous** *adj*.

bulge *n* swelling; protuberance. *vi* swell; stick out.

bulk *n* **1** large quantity or volume. **2** greater part. **3** cargo, esp. before packaging. **4** human body, esp. when large or fat. **bulky** *adj* large and cumbersome. **bulkiness** *n*.

bull *n* **1** adult male member of the ox family. **2** male of animals such as the elephant or seal. **3** person who buys stocks and sells them after the price has risen. **4** *sl also* **bullshit** nonsense; exaggerated statement. **bulldog** *n* breed of short-haired dog with a sturdy body, muscular legs, and a large head. **bulldoze** *vt* **1** demolish or clear with a bulldozer. **2** barge through; shove. **bulldozer** *n* heavy tractor used for clearing rubble, earth, etc. **bullfight** *n* public entertainment common in Spain, Portugal, and S America in which a matador fights a bull. **bullfighter** *n*. **bullring** *n* arena used for a bullfight.

bullet *n* projectile discharged from a gun. **bullet-proof** *adj* able to protect from bullets.

bulletin *n* public notice or announcement giving official news or information.

bullion *n* gold or silver, esp. before it has been minted.

bully *vt,vi* threaten or act violently towards someone weaker; intimidate. *n* person who bullies.

bum *n sl* buttocks.

bump *vt,vi* **1** collide (with); bang (into); knock. **2** injure or hurt by banging. *vi also* **bump along** jolt; travel jerkily. **bump into** meet unexpectedly. **bump off** *sl* murder. ~*n* **1** collision; jolt; knock. **2** swelling; lump. **3** small mound; bulge. **bumpy** *adj*. **bumper** *n* protective bar fitted to either end of a vehicle.

bun *n* **1** small sweet baked roll. **2** hair coiled into a knot at the back of the head.

bunch *n* **1** number of things growing or arranged in a cluster. **2** group of people; set. *vt,vi also* **bunch up** gather together; cluster; huddle.

bundle *n* pile of things loosely wrapped or tied together. *vt* **1** *also* **bundle up** make into a bundle. **2** push hurriedly out of sight.

bung *n* stopper for a bottle, barrel, etc. *vt* **1** *also* **bung up** stop up or seal with a bung; block. **2** *sl* throw; chuck.

bungalow *n* single-storeyed house.

bungle *vt,vi* spoil by acting clumsily or incompetently; botch.

bunk *n* **1** narrow bed, esp. on a ship. **2** *also* **bunk bed** one of a pair of beds fitted one above the other in a single framework.

bunker *n* **1** storage container for coal, oil, etc. **2** sand-filled hollow functioning as a hazard on a golf course. **3** fortified underground shelter.

buoy *n* anchored float used as a navigation guide or for mooring a vessel. *v* **buoy up 1** keep afloat. **2** sustain optimism or cheerfulness in. **buoyant** *adj* **1** able to float. **2** optimistic; light-hearted **buoyancy** *n*. **buoyantly** *adv*.

burble *vt,vi* gurgle; babble. *n* gurgling sound.

burden *n* **1** heavy load. **2** responsibility, suffering, etc., that is hard to cope with. *vt* **1** overload; weigh down with. **2** oppress, cause to suffer. **burdensome** *adj*.

bureau ('bjuərou) *n*, *pl* **bureaux** ('bjuərou) *or* **bureaus 1** agency or government department dealing in employment, tourist information, etc. **2** writing desk fitted with drawers, pigeonholes, etc.

bureaucracy (bjuə'rɔkrəsi) *n* **1** system of government or administration by paid officials rather than elected representatives. **2** officials working within such a system. **3** excessive use of official administrative procedures; red tape. **bureaucrat** *n*. **bureaucratic** *adj*.

burglary *n* crime of breaking into a building at night with intent to commit certain offences. **burglar** *n*. **burgle** *vt,vi* commit burglary (in or on).

burial *n* burying, esp. of a body at a funeral.

burn *v* (burnt *or* burned) *vt,vi* damage or become damaged by fire, heat, or acid. *vi* **1** be combustible or inflammable. **2** produce heat or light; blaze; glow. **3** feel painfully hot or sore; smart. **4** be consumed with desire, anger, jealousy, etc. *vt* **1** use in order to produce heat or light. **2** make (a hole, mark, etc.) by fire, heat, or acid; scorch. **burn out 1** wear out by heat or friction. **2** use up one's energy; become exhausted. ~*n* **1** injury caused by fire, heat, or acid. **2** mark or hole caused by burning. **burning** *adj* **1** urgent; vital. **2** intense; passionate.

burrow *n* underground hole or tunnel dug by an animal for shelter. *vt,vi* tunnel or dig deeply (into). *vi* delve; search.

burst *vt,vi* (burst) break or split open, esp. under pressure; explode. **burst in(to) 1** enter noisily. **2** interrupt rudely. **burst into song/tears, etc.** start to sing, cry, etc., loudly and suddenly. ~*n* **1** split; rupture. **2** sudden loud noise; explosion. **3** spurt of activity, energy, etc.; surge.

bury *vt* **1** place (a corpse) in a grave or tomb; inter. **2** place underground. **3** conceal by covering. **4** embed; stick into. **5** engross. **6** repress; forget.

bus *n, pl* **buses** *or* **busses** large motor vehicle scheduled to carry passengers along a fixed route. *vi,vt* (-ss-) travel or carry by bus.

bush *n* **1** large plant with woody stems; shrub. **2** thick mass. **the bush** area of rough uncultivated land, esp. in Australia or S Africa; scrubland. **beat about the bush** act evasively; prevaricate. **bushy** *adj* **1** thick and shaggy. **2** covered with bushes.

bushel *n* unit of capacity equal to 2219 cubic inches. **hide one's light under a bushel** be modest about one's abilities or skills.

business *n* **1** commerce; trade. **2** occupation; profession. **3** commercial company; trading organization; firm. **4** affair; matter; concern. **business-like** *adj* conforming to certain standards of business procedure; efficient. **businessman** *n, pl* **-men** man engaged in commerce or trade, esp. as an executive. **businesswoman** *f n*.

bust[1] *n* **1** bosom or breast. **2** sculpture depicting a person's head and shoulders.

bust[2] *vt,vi* (busted *or* bust) **1** break; smash. **2** ruin; make or become bankrupt. **3** *sl* raid or search, esp. in order to arrest. **bust up 1** disrupt. **2** split or part after a quarrel. **bust-up** *n* **1** brawl. **2** separation after a quarrel.

bustle *vt,vi* hurry; be or make busy. *n* busy activity; commotion.

busy *adj* **1** fully occupied; active; engaged. **2** crowded; bustling. *v* **busy oneself** take up time with; occupy oneself. **busily** *adv*. **busybody** *n* person who gossips or meddles.

but *conj* **1** however; yet; nevertheless. **2** except; apart from; other than. *prep* with the exception of. **but for** without; were it not for. ~*adv* merely, just. **all but** almost; nearly.

butane *n* flammable hydrocarbon gas used as a fuel.

butcher *n* **1** person who prepares and sells meat. **2** savage murderer. *vt* **1** slaughter and prepare (meat). **2** murder, esp. with a knife, axe, etc.; slaughter; slay. **butchery** *n*.

butler *n* male servant, usually having special responsibility for wines.

butt[1] *n* **1** blunt thick end of a rifle, tool, etc. **2** cigarette end; stub.

butt[2] *n* **1** person who bears the brunt of ridicule, scorn, etc. **2** mound situated behind the target on a shooting range. **3** target.

butt[3] *vt,vi* push hard with the head or horns; ram. **butt in** interrupt; interfere. ~*n* violent push with the head or horns.

butter *n* yellowish-white solid fat produced by churning cream. *vt* spread with butter. **butter up** flatter. **buttercup** *n* wild flower with bright yellow petals. **butterscotch** *n* brittle toffee made with butter and sugar.

butterfly *n* **1** insect with large wings, which are often brightly coloured or patterned. **2** person who is unable to settle or sustain interest in anything for very long.

buttocks *pl n* fleshy lower part of the body on which a person sits; bottom.

button *n* **1** small disc sewn on to a garment and able to pass through a buttonhole or loop as a fastening, or used for decoration. **2** small knob that is pushed to operate a machine, doorbell, etc. **3** anything small and round that resembles a button. *vt also* **button up** fasten with a button. **buttonhole** *n* **1** hole edged with stitching, through which a button is passed. **2** flower or spray worn in a buttonhole. *vt* **1** stitch round a buttonhole. **2** corner in order to engage in conversation.

buttress *n* **1** structure of stone or brick built to support a wall. **2** source of strength or support. *vt* **1** strengthen with a buttress. **2** give moral support to.

buxom *adj* having a full bosom; plump.

buy *vt,vi* (bought) obtain in exchange for money; purchase. **buy up** buy all that is available of a particular commodity. ~*n* thing bought; purchase. **buyer** *n* person who buys, esp. one purchasing merchandise for resale.

buzz *n* **1** low continuous noise; hum. **2** *inf* telephone call; ring. **3** *sl* pleasant sensation caused by certain drugs, alcohol, etc. *vt,vi* **1** produce a low vibrating hum. **2** signal or call using a buzzer. **3** *inf* phone; ring. *vi* **1** move hurriedly from place to place. **2** produce an atmosphere of excitement. **buzz off** go away; leave. **buzzer** *n* electrical device producing a harsh continuous signal.

by *prep* **1** through the agency, means, or authorship of. **2** via; past. **3** beside; close to; near. **4** no later than. **5** to a greater or lesser extent than. **6** multiplied with. **7** with a second dimension of. **8** during; in the course of. **by and by** eventually; after a while. **by-election** *n* election held when a particular seat becomes vacant, as after the resignation or death of a Member of Parliament. **bylaw** *n* law made by a local authority and operational only within its own area. **bypass** *n* road constructed to direct the flow of traffic away from a town centre. *vt* **1** go round in order to avoid. **2** ignore (regulations, procedures, etc.) in order to proceed without delay.

C

cab *n* **1** driver's compartment of a lorry, bus, etc. **2** taxi.

cabaret ('kæbərei) *n* entertainment provided by a nightclub, restaurant, etc.

cabbage *n* vegetable with a short stalk and a head of green or purplish tightly packed leaves.

cabin *n* **1** small functional house, hut, or shelter. **2** living quarters on a ship; berth. **3** section of an aircraft for passengers or crew. **cabin cruiser** *n* motor boat with cabin accommodation.

cabinet *n* **1** piece of furniture for storing crockery, glassware, medicine, etc.; cupboard. **2** filing cabinet. **3** outer case of a radio or television set. **the Cabinet** body of Government ministers responsible for policy-making.

cable *n* **1** strong rope of twisted wire, hemp, etc. **2** set of insulated wires used for conducting electricity. **3** overseas telegram. **4** *also* **cable stitch** knitting stitch producing a twisted pattern. *vt,vi* send an overseas telegram (to).

cache (kæʃ) *n* hidden supply or store, esp. of weapons.

cackle *vi* **1** squawk like a hen. **2** laugh or shriek raucously. *n* **1** squawk. **2** raucous laugh or shriek.

cactus *n, pl* **cacti** ('kæktai) *or* **cactuses** plant adapted to grow in desert regions with tough spiny stems and bright showy flowers.

cadence *n* **1** sequence of chords marking the end of a musical phrase or section. **2** modulation of the voice; intonation.

cadet *n* young trainee, esp. in the armed forces or police force.

cadge *vt vi* acquire or ask for without intending to pay; beg. **cadger** *n* person who cadges.

café *n* small restaurant serving snacks.

cafeteria *n* self-service restaurant or canteen.

caffeine *n* mild stimulant found in some plants, esp. coffee.

cage *n* **1** enclosure or box with bars used for confining animals or birds. **2** lift in a mine shaft. *vt* put or keep in a cage.

cajole *vt,vi* wheedle; coax; persuade by flattery.

cake *n* **1** sweet food made from flour, sugar, eggs, etc., and baked. **2** flattish compact mass, as of soap. **a piece of cake** *inf* something easily achieved or obtained. ~*vt* cover with a hard dry mass.

calamity *n* disaster; misfortune. **calamitous** *adj.*

calcium *n* silvery metallic element found in limestone, marble, and other rocks and in bones and teeth.

calculate *vt,vi* work out mathematically. *vt* **1** estimate; believe; suppose. **2** design; plan; intend. **calculating** *adj* ruthless; scheming. **calculation** *n*. **calculator** *n* electronic device used for mathematical calculation.

calendar *n* **1** system for determining the length of a year, order of months, etc. **2** chart showing the divisions of a year. **3** list or diary of events and engagements.

calf[1] *n, pl* **calves** **1** young of cattle. **2** young seal, whale, elephant, etc.

calf[2] *n* fleshy part of the back of the lower leg.

calibre *n* **1** diameter of a gun bore, bullet, etc. **2** worth; merit.

call *vt,vi* **1** shout out in order to summon, attract attention, etc. **2** telephone; ring. *vi also* **call on** visit. *vt* **1** name; christen. **2** describe as; label. **3** convene (a meeting). **call for 1** fetch; collect. **2** require; demand. **call in 1** drop by on a visit. **2** request the services of (a doctor, specialist, etc.). **call off 1** cancel or postpone. **2** order to stop attacking. **call on** appeal to; request. **call out 1** summon. **2** bring out on strike. **call to mind** recall. **call**

up 1 conscript. **2** reach by telephone. ~*n* **1** characteristic cry of a bird or animal. **2** shout. **3** visit. **4** telephone conversation. **5** duty; obligation. **6** demand; need. **on call** available for duty. **caller** *n*. **callbox** *n* public telephone box. **calling** *n* vocation. **call-up** *n* conscription.

callous *adj* cruelly indifferent to suffering. **callously** *adv*. **callousness** *n*.

calm *adj* **1** not excited or anxious; serene; untroubled. **2** peaceful. **3** still; hardly moving. *n also* **calmness** stillness; tranquillity; peace. *vt,vi also* **calm down** make or become calm(er); quieten; soothe. **calmly** *adv*.

calorie *n* unit of heat energy, used esp. for measuring the energy value of foods.

came *v pt of* **come.**

camel *n* long-legged largely domesticated mammal with one or two humps on its back, commonly found in desert areas of N Africa.

camera *n* **1** optical device for producing a photographic image. **2** *also* **television camera** device for converting optical images into electrical signals. **in camera** in private; not open.

camouflage *n* **1** use of certain materials as a disguise to prevent a person, military equipment, etc., from being seen by an enemy. **2** colour or markings of an animal that make it less conspicuous in a certain environment. *vt* make less noticeable by use of camouflage.

camp[1] *n* **1** site having tents, huts, etc., for use as temporary accommodation. **2** military base housing soldiers temporarily; encampment. **3** group of people with common political views. *vi also* **camp out** live in a tent or other temporary living accommodation. **camper** *n*. **camping** *n*.

camp[2] *adj* of a style that exaggerates or parodies what is thought to be appropriate homosexual behaviour. *n* exaggerated or effeminate style of behaviour.

campaign *n* **1** series of planned military operations. **2** technical activities designed to promote a political cause or candidate, commercial product, etc. *vi* mount a campaign; fight. **campaigner** *n*.

campus *n* area and buildings occupied by a university or college.

can[1] *v aux* (*pt* could) **1** be able or willing to; know how to. **2** have permission or opportunity to.

can[2] *n* metal container or tin. **carry the can** accept responsibility or blame. ~*vt* (-nn-) put or store in a can.

canal *n* **1** man-made waterway or channel for navigation, irrigation, etc. **2** passage or duct in the body.

canary *n* small yellow songbird of the finch family.

cancel *vt* (-ll-) **1** prevent (a planned event) from taking place; call off. **2** stop; discontinue. **3** make invalid by crossing through or stamping with a special mark. **cancel out** offset; compensate (for). **cancellation** *n*.

cancer *n* malignant growth or tumour in the body. **Cancer** fourth sign of the zodiac represented by the crab.

candid *adj* honest; frank; open; fair. **candidly** *adv*. **candour** *n*.

candidate *n* **1** person nominated or applying for a particular office, job, or position. **2** person sitting an examination.

candle *n* cylinder of wax with a central wick, which burns slowly when lit. **burn the candle at both ends** exhaust oneself by living strenuously.

cane *n* **1** pliant hollow stem of the bamboo or various palms, often used for making furniture. **2** sugar cane. **3** thorny stem of a raspberry or blackberry bush. **4** thin rod used as a walking stick or as an implement for inflicting punishment. *vt,vi* punish by beating with a cane.

canine *adj* **1** of the dog family. **2** like a dog.

canister *n* cylindrical metal storage container; can.

cannabis *n* **1** hemp plant. **2** marijuana.

cannibal *n* **1** person who eats human flesh. **2** animal that feeds on its own kind. **cannibalism** *n*. **cannibalize** *vt* take parts from (motor vehicles, etc.) to repair others.

cannon *n, pl* **cannons** *or* **cannon** heavy mounted gun that discharges large shells. *v* **cannon into** collide with; barge into.

cannot *v aux* **1** be unable or unwilling to. **2** be forbidden or have no opportunity to.

canoe *n* small narrow portable boat propelled with a paddle. *vi* travel or transport by canoe.

canon *n* **1** ecclesiastical law. **2** list of Christian saints. **3** priest attached to a cathedral or various religious orders. **4** moral principle; standard; criterion. **5** musical form in which the same melody is introduced at overlapping intervals by two or more voices. **canonical** *adj*. **canonize** *vt* recognize officially as a saint.

canopy *n* ornamental awning suspended above a throne, bed, etc.

canteen *n* **1** restaurant for the use of employees of a company, children at school, etc. **2** box of cutlery. **3** flask carried by soldiers, campers, etc.

canter *n* gait of a horse between a trot and a gallop. *vi,vt* move or take at a canter.

canvas *n* **1** hard-wearing waterproof material of flax or hemp. **2** piece of such material used for painting on in oils.

canvass *vi,vt* seek support or opinions from (potential voters, customers, etc.). **canvasser** *n*.

canyon *n* deep narrow valley or gorge; ravine.

cap *n* **1** flat closely fitting hat, sometimes with a peak. **2** small lid or cover. **3** natural or artificial covering of a tooth. **4** *also* **dutch cap** diaphragm used as a contraceptive device. *vt* (-pp-) **1** cover the top or surface of. **2** outdo; top. **to cap it all** in addition; on top; as a finishing touch.

capable *adj* **1** having the potential or capacity for. **2** able; competent. **capability** *n*. **capably** *adv*.

capacity *n* **1** power to contain a quantity. **2** amount that a container can hold; volume. **3** maximum number that can be accommodated. **4** ability to perform or behave in a particular way. **5** power or function of an office or rank.

cape [1] *n* short cloak.

cape [2] *n* headland.

capital *n* **1** city that is the seat of government of a country. **2** wealth or assets, esp. when used for investment or profit. **3** *also* **capital letter** large or upper case form of a written or printed letter of the alphabet. *adj* **1** *inf* excellent; first-class. **2** carrying the penalty of death. **capitalism** *n* economic system whereby private owners control the means of production and distribution. **capitalist** *adj,n*. **capitalize** *vt* **1** use, provide, or convert into capital. **2** write or print in capital letters. **capitalize on** exploit; take advantage of.

caprice (kə'pri:s) *n* whim. **capricious** (kə'priʃəs) *adj* subject to or indicative of whim; changeable.

Capricorn *n* tenth sign of the zodiac, represented by the goat.

capsicum *n* tropical plant bearing edible fruit (peppers).

capsize *vi,vt* overturn; upset.

capsule *n* **1** soluble shell enclosing a dose of oral medicine. **2** pressurized compartment of a space vehicle. **3** closed structure containing seeds, spores, or fruits. **capsular** *adj*.

captain *n* **1** person in charge of a vessel or aircraft. **2** naval officer ranking above a commander and below a rear admiral. **3** army officer ranking above a lieutenant and below a major. **4** leader of a sports team. *vt* act as captain of. **captaincy** *n*.

caption *n* **1** brief description accompanying an illustration. **2** heading or title; headline, subtitle. *vt* provide with a caption.

capture *vt* **1** take prisoner. **2** gain control or possession of. *n* act of capturing. **captivate** *vt* fascinate; charm; enchant. **captivation** *n*. **captive** *n* prisoner. *adj* **1** imprisoned. **2** restrained; confined. **captivity** *n*.

car *n* **1** small wheeled vehicle for personal transport. **2** vehicle containing passengers, such as a railway carriage.

carafe (kə'ræf, 'kærəf) *n* decorative bottle used for serving wine or water at the table.

caramel *n* **1** burnt sugar used for flavouring and colouring. **2** chewy kind of toffee.

carat *n* **1** measure of the purity of gold in an alloy. **2** measure of weight of precious stones, esp. diamonds.

caravan *n* **1** covered vehicle equipped for living in and capable of being drawn by a car, horse, etc. **2** company of travellers in desert regions. *vi* (-nn-) travel by caravan.

caraway *n* Eurasian plant whose aromatic fruits (caraway seeds) are used in cooking.

carbohydrate *n* organic compound, such as starch or sugar, containing carbon, hydrogen, and oxygen.

carbon *n* **1** widely distributed nonmetallic element occurring as diamond, graphite, or charcoal and forming many organic and inorganic compounds. **2** *also* **carbon paper** *n* paper coated on one side with a dark pigment, used to duplicate writing or typing. **carbon dioxide** *n* colourless incombustible gas present in the atmosphere, formed during respiration and the combustion of organic compounds.

carburettor *n* part of a petrol engine where the fuel is mixed with air.

carcass *n* dead body, esp. of an animal sold for food.

card *n* **1** piece of stiff paper used for filing, as proof of identity or membership, advertising, etc. **2** similar piece of paper, often illustrated, used for sending greetings, congratulations, etc. **3** any of a set of cardboard pieces, marked with symbols, used for playing games or telling fortunes. **a card up one's sleeve** thing or action kept in reserve to be used to gain an advantage. **on the cards** probable; likely. **put one's cards on the table** *or* **show one's cards** reveal one's intentions, plans, etc. **cardboard** *n* thin stiff board made of paper pulp.

cardigan *n* close-fitting woollen jacket.

cardinal *n* senior dignitary of the Roman Catholic Church, ranking next below the Pope. *adj* of prime importance; fundamental. **cardinal number** *n* number denoting quantity rather than order. **cardinal point** *n* one of the points of the compass, N, S, E, or W.

care *n* **1** solicitous attention. **2** caution. **3** supervision; charge; responsibility. **4** anxiety; trouble; worry. **care of** at the address of. ~*vi* feel interest or concern. **care for 1** feel affection for. **2** look after; tend. **3** wish for; want. **carefree** *adj* free from worry, anxiety, and responsibility. **careful** *adj* **1** cautious; wary. **2** meticulous; painstaking. **carefully** *adv*. **careless** *adj* **1** lacking sufficient thought or attention; negligent. **2** unconcerned; indifferent. **carelessly** *adv*. **carelessness** *n*. **caretaker** *n* person employed to look after and maintain a school, office, etc.

career *n* **1** pursuit of a profession or occupation. **2** course; progression. *vi* move rapidly, esp. in an uncontrolled way; hurtle.

caress *n* light gentle stroke of affection. *vt* stroke gently and affectionately; fondle.

cargo *n* goods carried in a ship or aircraft; freight; load.

caricature *n* satirical representation of a person that grossly exaggerates particular characteristics. *vt* represent as a caricature.

carnal *adj* sensual; not spiritual; of the flesh. **carnal knowledge** *n* sexual intercourse. **carnally** *adv*.

carnation *n* cultivated flower having fragrant pink, white, or red blooms.

carnival *n* public celebration, festivities, and revelry, esp. just before Lent.

carnivorous *adj* meat-eating. **carnivore** *n* meat-eating animal, esp. a mammal.

carol *n* joyous song, esp. to celebrate Christmas. *vi* (-ll-) sing joyfully.

carpenter *n* person skilled in using wood in building, making furniture, etc. *vi,vt* work as a carpenter. **carpentry** *n*.

carpet *n* **1** thick textile floor covering. **2** thick layer or covering. *vt* cover with or as if with a carpet.

carriage *n* **1** horse-drawn four-wheeled vehicle. **2** section of a train, often comprising several compartments. **3** movable gun-support. **4** part of a typewriter holding and moving paper. **5** deportment; bearing. **carriageway** *n* road, or part of a road, used by vehicles.

carrot *n* plant whose long orange root is eaten as a vegetable. **carroty** *adj* orange.

carry *vt,vi* take (something) from one place to another; transport; transmit; convey. *vt* **1** hold; bear; keep. **2** contain; include. **3** sustain; keep in operation. **4** influence. **carry oneself** conduct oneself; behave. **carry on** continue; persevere. **carrier** *n* **1** person or thing that carries. **2** *also* **carrier-bag** large paper or polythene bag with handles. **3** person or animal carrying disease.

cart *n* strong two-wheeled open vehicle used by farmers, tradesmen, etc. *vt,vi* **1** transport in a cart. **2** *inf* carry with difficulty.

cartilage *n* strong flexible tissue often developing into bone; gristle. **cartilaginous** *adj*.

carton *n* small light container, esp. of cardboard.

cartoon *n* **1** simple humorous or satirical drawing. **2** animated film. **3** sketch made in preparation for a painting, tapestry, etc. **cartoonist** *n*.

cartridge *n* **1** small cylindrical case containing explosives, a bullet, or shot. **2** large type of cassette for a tape recorder. **3** film cassette. **4** device fitted to the pickup arm on a gramophone that contains the stylus. **5** removable container filled with ink for a fountain pen. **cartridge paper** *n* strong white paper for drawing.

carve *vi,vt* **1** shape with a knife, chisel, etc. **2** cut (meat) into pieces or slices. **carve up 1** *inf* injure by an attack with a knife. **2** *sl* endanger by aggressive driving. **carver** *n*. **carving** *n* **1** act of carving. **2** artefact carved from wood, stone, etc.

cascade *n* **1** waterfall. **2** something that falls in folds or drapes. *vi* fall like a cascade.

case[1] *n* box, container, or protective outer covering.

case[2] **1** instance; circumstance; example. **2** instance of a medical condition. **3** legal suit, or grounds for suit. **4** patient or client dealt with by a doctor, social worker, lawyer, etc. **5** grammatical relationship of a noun, pronoun, or adjective to other parts of a sentence, sometimes shown by inflectional endings. **in case** in the event that. **in any case** whatever happens.

cash *n* money, esp. in the form of notes and coins. *vt* convert into cash. **cash in on** *inf* profit from; exploit.

cashier[1] *n* person employed to receive and pay out cash in a bank, shop, etc.

cashier[2] *vt* discharge dishonourably from the army.

cashmere *n* very fine soft woven hair of the Kashmir goat.

casino *n* building equipped for gambling.

casket *n* small box or case, esp. for jewels.

casserole *n* **1** heavy pan or dish for long slow cooking. **2** meal cooked in a casserole. *vt* cook in a casserole.

cassette *n* sealed container holding spools of film, magnetic tape, etc., for use in a camera, tape-recorder, etc.

cassock *n* long black tunic worn by various members of the clergy.

cast *vt* (cast) **1** throw; hurl; fling. **2** discard; shed; drop. **3** project; direct. **4** make (a vote). **5** allocate (parts) for a play. **6** make (shape of metal, glass, etc.) by pouring into a mould. **cast off** discard; throw away; reject. **castoff** *n* discarded thing or person. **cast on/off** form the first/last row of stitches of a piece of knitting. ~*n* **1** all the actors in a play. **2** throw, as of dice. **3** mould. **4** casing for a broken bone. **5** slight squint.

castanets *pl n* pair of hollow shells of hard wood or ivory held in the hand and clicked together to accompany music and dancing.

caste *n* **1** one of four hereditary social divisions in Hindu society. **2** social class.

castle *n* **1** large fortified building functioning as a fortress or stronghold. **2** (in chess) rook. **castellated** *adj* having battlements, turrets, etc., as a castle.

castrate *vt* remove the testicles of. **castration** *n*.

casual *adj* **1** accidental; not planned; chance. **2** informal. **3** not regular; temporary. **casually** *adv*.

casualty *n* victim of a serious accident, battle, etc.

cat *n* **1** small domestic animal, kept esp. as a pet. **2** feline mammal, such as the lion, tiger, or leopard. **cat's eye** *n* glass stud set into the road surface to mark traffic lanes as a guide to motorists at night.

catalogue *n* comprehensive orderly list of books in a library, goods for sale, etc. *vt* list or insert in a catalogue.

catapult *n* **1** device for hurling small rocks and stones. **2** equipment for launching aircraft from ships, etc. *vt* throw or hurl as from a catapult.

cataract *n* **1** powerful waterfall. **2** heavy rainstorm or flood. **3** eye disorder in which the lens becomes opaque.

catarrh *n* inflammation of a mucous membrane in the nose or throat, as during a cold.

catastrophe *n* major disaster; calamity. **catastrophic** *adj*. **catastrophically** *adv*.

catch *v* (caught) *vt* **1** grasp (something that has been thrown or is falling). **2** capture; seize. **3** discover by surprise; detect. **4** board or take (a train, bus, etc.). **5** hear or grasp the meaning of. **6** contract (an infection or disease). **7** strike; hit. **8** portray accurately or convincingly. **9** make contact with; find. **10** deceive; swindle. *vi,vt* **1** ignite or become ignited by. **2** become tangled (with) or hooked up (on). **catch on 1** learn or grasp. **2** become fashionable. **catch up 1** reach or get level after following. **2** make up (arrears, a backlog, etc.). ~*n* **1** act of catching. **2** something caught. **3** device for fastening. **4** *inf* difficulty; snag. **5** *inf* highly eligible person. **6** ball game. **catchy** *adj inf* (esp. of a tune) easy to remember or imitate.

catechism *n* religious instruction, esp. in a dialogue form.

category *n* class; group; division. **categorical** *adj* absolutely; definite; explicit. **categorically** *adv*. **categorize** *vt* place in a category; classify.

cater *vi* provide food, entertainment, etc. **cater for** supply whatever is necessary. **caterer** *n*.

caterpillar *n* **1** larva of a moth, butterfly, etc. **2**

continuous band of steel plates fitted instead of wheels to a vehicle such as a tractor or tank.

cathedral *n* principal church in a diocese.

catholic *adj* widespread; liberal; of general interest. **Catholic** *adj, n* Roman Catholic. **Catholicism** *n.*

catkin *n* cluster of small flowers of the willow, hazel, etc., resembling a cat's tail.

cattle *pl n* cows, bulls, etc., collectively.

catty *adj inf* spiteful.

caught *v pt* and *pp* of **catch.**

cauliflower *n* variety of cabbage cultivated for its large edible white flower head.

cause *n* **1** something that produces an effect. **2** motive; grounds; reason. **3** general aim or set of ideals for which a person or group campaigns. *vt* be the cause of; bring about; make happen. **causal** *adj.* **causation** *or* **causality** *n.*

causeway *n* raised road or path over treacherous ground, water, etc.

caustic *adj* **1** burning or corrosive. **2** cutting; sarcastic. *n* substance that corrodes or burns. **caustic soda** *n* sodium hydroxide.

caution *n* **1** prudence; care; watchfulness. **2** warning. *vt* warn; advise caution. **cautionary** *adj* advising caution; intended as a warning. **cautious** *adj* careful; prudent; wary. **cautiously** *adv.*

cavalry *n* unit of troops, originally mounted on horseback but now equipped with armoured cars, tanks, etc.

cave hollow area in a rock or under a cliff. *vt* hollow out. **cave in** collapse; give way; subside. **cavern** *n* large underground cave. **cavernous** *adj.*

caviar *n* salted roe of the sturgeon, eaten as a delicacy.

cavity *n* **1** hollow space. **2** hollow part of a tooth caused by decay.

cayenne *n* hot red pepper produced from capsicum seeds.

cease *vt,vi* stop; end; discontinue; finish. *n* **without cease** endlessly; continuously. **ceasefire** *n* truce, esp. a temporary one. **ceaseless** *adj* incessant; endless.

cedar *n* large coniferous evergreen tree with hard sweet-smelling wood.

cede *vt,vi* concede or yield territory, rights, etc.

ceiling *n* **1** upper surface of a room. **2** upper limit of prices, wages, etc.

celebrate *vt* **1** mark or honour with festivity and rejoicing. **2** officiate at a religious or public ceremony. *vi* rejoice, make merry. **celebrated** *adj* famous. **celebrity** *n* **1** well-known or famous person. **2** fame; renown; notoriety.

celery *n* vegetable grown for its long greenish-white edible stalks.

celestial *adj* heavenly; of the sky.

celibate *adj* **1** unmarried **2** abstaining from sexual intercourse. *n* person who is celibate, esp. one who has taken religious vows. **celibacy** *n.*

cell *n* **1** independent unit of an organism. **2** small room occupied by a monk, prisoner, etc. **3** device producing or storing electric current by chemical action. **4** small group working within a larger political or religious movement. **cellular** *adj.*

cellar *n* **1** underground room, used esp. for storage. **2** store of wine.

cello *n* musical instrument of the violin family, held between the knees when played. **cellist** *n.*

Cellophane *n Tdmk* thin transparent packaging material.

Celluloid *n Tdmk* inflammable material made from cellulose nitrate and camphor, used esp. as a coating for film.

cellulose *n* carbohydrate forming walls of plant cells.

cement *n* **1** substance made from limestone and clay mixed with water that hardens to form concrete. **2** substance used to fill cavities of the teeth. *vt* **1** join or spread with cement. **2** unite; bind together; strengthen.

cemetery *n* burial ground, esp. one not attached to a church.

censor *n* person authorized to examine and ban material in films, books, letters, etc., considered to be harmful, dangerous, or immoral. *vt* act as a censor of. **censorship** *n.* **censorious** *adj* critical; harsh.

censure *n* disapproval; blame; harsh criticism. *vt* reprimand; criticize; blame.

census *n* official population count.

cent *n* **1** US coin equivalent to one hundredth of a dollar. **2** coin of various other countries. **per cent** by the hundred; in a hundred. **hundred per cent** complete; absolute; total.

centenary *n* hundredth anniversary. *adj* relating to a period of a hundred years.

centigrade *adj* relating to a temperature scale

on which the freezing point of water is 0° and its boiling point 100°.

centime *n* **1** French coin equivalent to one hundredth of a franc. **2** coin of various other countries.

centimetre *n* one hundredth of a metre.

centipede *n* small crawling animal having a body made up of several segments, each segment bearing a pair of legs.

central *adj* **1** of the centre. **2** principal; most important. **central heating** *n* system of heating a building with radiators, air vents, etc., connected to a central source. **centralize** *vt* **1** bring to a central point. **2** unite (several duties, powers, etc.) under one central authority. *vi* come to a central point. **centralization** *n*.

centre *n* **1** middle point of a circle, line, sphere, etc. **2** main point or focus of interest, attention, administration, importance, etc. *vt,vi* be concentrated (on); have a centre at or in. **centre-forward** *n* player in football, hockey, etc., positioned at the centre of the front line. **centre-half** *n, pl* **-halves** player in football, hockey, etc., positioned at the centre of the defence line.

century *n* **1** one hundred years. **2** one of the periods of a hundred years numbered before and since the birth of Christ. **3** score of a hundred runs in cricket.

ceramics *n* art of making pottery from clay, porcelain, etc. **ceramic** *adj,n*.

cereal *n* **1** crop yielding edible grain. **2** breakfast dish made from cereals.

ceremony *n* **1** formal or public act, religious rite, etc. **2** formal politeness. **stand (up)on ceremony** insist on exaggerated politeness or formality. **ceremonial** *adj* ritual; formal; pertaining to ceremony. *n* prescribed form of ceremonies; ritual. **ceremonially** *adv*. **ceremonious** *adj* elaborately correct, dignified, or precise. **ceremoniously** *adv*.

certain *adj* **1** sure; convinced; positive. **2** definite; inevitable. **3** indicating someone or something specific but unnamed. **certainly** *adv*. **certainty** *n*.

certificate *n* written declaration of a fact, such as success in an examination, ownership of shares, public status, etc. **certify** *vt* **1** declare; authorize; guarantee; endorse. **2** declare officially to be insane.

cervix *n, pl* **cervixes** *or* **cervices** ('sə:visi:z) **1** lower part of the uterus. **2** neck. **cervical** *adj*.

chafe *vt,vi* rub until sore or roughened. *n* soreness.

chaffinch *n* small European songbird of the finch family.

chain *n* **1** flexible line of connected metal links. **2** range of mountains. **3** series of connected events. *vt* fasten or restrict with or as with a chain. **chain reaction 1** chemical or nuclear process in which the product of each step initiates the next step. **2** series of rapid interconnected events. **chain-smoke** *vi* smoke continuously, esp. by lighting one cigarette from the stub of the last. **chain-smoker** *n*. **chain-store** *n* one of a number of shops owned and managed by the same organization.

chair *n* **1** movable seat usually with four legs and a back, for one person. **2** seat of dignity or authority. **3** chairmanship. **4** professorship. *vt* preside over; act as chairman of. **chairman** *n, pl* **-men 1** principal director of a company. **2** person presiding over a meeting, committee, etc. **chairmanship** *n*.

chalet *n* **1**. wooden Swiss house with a steep overhanging roof. **2** house or bungalow built in this style, esp. for holidays.

chalk *n* **1** soft white rock consisting of calcium carbonate. **2** piece of chalk or similar material used for writing or drawing. *vt,vi* write or treat with chalk.

challenge *vt* **1** invite to a duel or other contest. **2** defy; dispute; call for an answer to. *n* **1** summons to a contest. **2** questioning of right; calling to account.

chamber *n* **1** room, esp a bedroom. **2** meeting hall. **3** enclosed cavity. **chambers** *pl* barrister's or judge's conference rooms. **chambermaid** *n* hotel maid in charge of bedrooms. **chamber music** *n* music written for a small ensemble of solo instruments.

chamberlain *n* **1** officer managing a royal household. **2** high-ranking Court official.

chameleon (kə'mi:liən) *n* type of lizard capable of changing its skin colour to match its surroundings.

champagne *n* type of sparkling French wine.

champion *n* **1** winner; victor; person excelling all others. **2** upholder of a cause. *adj* excellent. *vt* defend; stand up for. **championship** *n* **1**

competition or series of contests to find a champion. 2 status or conduct of a champion.

chance *n* 1 unexpected or inexplicable event. 2 risk. 3 possibility; opportunity. **by chance** accidentally; fortuitously. ~*adj* fortuitous; accidental. *vi,vt* 1 happen (to). 2 risk; dare.

chancel *n* eastern part of a church near the altar, reserved for the clergy and choir.

chancellor *n* 1 chief minister or other high official. 2 titular head of a university. **Chancellor of the Exchequer** *n* principal government finance minister.

chandelier *n* decorative branched fitting that hangs from a ceiling and supports a number of lights.

change *n* 1 substitution of one thing for another; alteration; variance. 2 money returned as balance for payment; coins of small value. *vt* 1 alter; substitute; make different. 2 give coins of smaller denomination in exchange for a larger coin or note. *vi* become different. *vt,vi* 1 put on (different clothes). 2 board (another train, bus, etc.). **changeable** *adj.*

channel *n* 1 navigable part of a harbour, river bed, etc. 2 comparatively narrow stretch of sea. 3 radio or television waveband. 4 tube; passage; groove. 5 means of communication, commerce, etc. *vt* (-ll-) 1 provide, use, or supply through a channel. 2 direct; find an outlet for.

chant *n* song, esp. intoned sacred music. *vt,vi* 1 sing, esp. in monotone. 2 recite.

chaos *n* disorder; confusion. **chaotic** *adj.*

chap[1] *vt,vi* (-pp-) (of skin) roughen and crack through excessive cold, etc.

chap[2] *n inf* man; fellow.

chapel *n* 1 small subordinate church often attached to a college, institution, etc. 2 small part of a larger church containing a separate altar. 3 association of printers or journalists.

chaplain *n* clergyman attached to a particular household, institution, unit of soldiers, etc.

chapter *n* 1 one of the principal divisions of a book. 2 governing body of a cathedral.

char[1] *vt,vi* (-rr-) scorch; singe; blacken; burn.

char[2] *n also* **charwoman** *or* **charlady** *inf* person employed to do housework. *vi* (-rr-) do rough housework.

character *n* 1 sum of particular qualities distinguishing an individual. 2 personality created by a writer. 3 distinguishing feature, mark, handwriting, etc. 4 eccentric or amusing person. **characteristic** *adj* distinctive; typical. *n* distinctive quality or trait. **characteristically** *adv.* **characterize** *vt* 1 distinguish (by); typify. 2 portray; describe. **characterization** *n.*

charcoal *n* carbon made from burnt wood, coal, etc.

charge *n* 1 price; liability to pay. 2 accusation. 3 responsibility; duty. 4 quantity, esp. of explosive, with which anything is loaded. 5 property of matter responsible for electrical phenomena and having two forms, positive and negative, which cause mutual attraction. 6 sudden attacking rush. **in charge of** with responsibility for. ~*vt,vi* 1 demand as a price. 2 rush aggressively towards. *vt* 1 accuse. 2 burden. 3 load; fill up. 4 supply (with electricity). **charge-hand** *n* workman or assistant in charge of others; foreman.

chariot *n* two-wheeled horse-drawn vehicle formerly used for races and battle. **charioteer** *n.*

charisma *n* spiritual quality inspiring great devotion and trust. **charismatic** *adj.*

charity *n* 1 quality of love, kindness, or generosity; compassion. 2 institution or organization founded for the benefit of others. **charitable** *adj* 1 kind; lenient; generous. 2 of a recognized charity.

charm *n* 1 ability to fascinate and delight by personal qualities. 2 magic spell, act, trinket, etc., thought to bring good fortune. *vt,vi* 1 attract; delight; enthrall. 2 enchant by magic. **charming** *adj* delightful.

chart *n* graph, plan, or map. *vt* record progress by means of a chart.

charter *n* document granting a right, establishing a university, etc. *vt* 1 establish by charter. 2 let or hire, esp. a ship or aircraft. **chartered** *adj* qualified according to established rules.

chase *vt* hunt; pursue; run after; drive away. *n* pursuit; hunt.

chasm ('kæzəm) *n* deep gulf or inlet; abyss.

chassis ('ʃæsi) *n, pl* **chassis** basic frame, esp. of a motor car, on which other parts are mounted.

chaste *adj* pure or virtuous, esp. sexually. **chastity** *n.*

chastise *vt* punish, esp. by beating. **chastisement** *n.*

chat *vi* (-tt-) talk in a friendly informal way. *n*

easy informal conversation. **chatty** *adj inf* talkative.

chatter *vi* **1** talk rapidly and thoughtlessly. **2** (of monkeys, birds, etc.) make an excited rapid rattling noise. *n* **1** idle talk; gossip. **2** rattling noise. **chatterbox** *n inf* talkative person.

chauffeur ('ʃoufə) *n* person employed to drive another's car; driver. *vt* act as chauffeur for.

chauvinism ('ʃouvinizəm) *n* excessive aggressive patriotism. **male chauvinism** belief of men in their superiority over women. **chauvinist** *n,adj.*

cheap *adj* **1** inexpensive; low in price. **2** inferior; vulgar; shoddy. **cheaply** *adv.* **cheapness** *n.* **cheapen** *vt,vi* decrease in price or quality.

cheat *vt* defraud; swindle; trick. *vi* attempt to succeed by dishonest means. *n* person who cheats; fraud.

check *vt* **1** restrain; hinder; halt. **2** verify; test the truth of; inspect. *n* **1** obstruction; hindrance. **2** supervision; careful watch; verification. **3** move in chess threatening the opponent's King. **4** pattern of squares. **5** *US* bill; account; cheque. **checkmate** *n* stage in chess where a threat to the King cannot be countered. *vt* defeat at checkmate. **checkpoint** *n* place where traffic is halted and inspected by police, etc. **check-up** *n* careful detailed examination, esp. for medical purposes.

cheek *n* **1** side of the face below the eye. **2** *inf* impudence; rudeness; impertinence. *vt inf* speak impertinently to. **cheeky** *adj inf* impudent; saucy. **cheekily** *adv.* **cheekiness** *n.* **cheekbone** *n* bone of the face just below the eye.

cheer *n* **1** shout of approval or joy. **2** entertainment; comfort. **3** disposition; attitude. *vt* comfort; encourage. *vi,vt* shout with joy or approval. **cheer up** become more cheerful. **cheerful** *adj* happy; jovial; lively. **cheerfully** *adv.* **cheerfulness** *n.*

cheese *n* protein-rich food of many varieties made from the curd of milk.

cheetah *n* swift-running member of the cat family, resembling a leopard.

chef *n* master cook.

chemical *adj* pertaining to chemistry. *n* substance made by or used in chemical processes. **chemist** *n* **1** one qualified to sell drugs and medicine. **2** researcher or student of chemistry. **chemistry** *n* science concerned with the properties and interactions of elements and compounds.

cheque *n* signed order, written generally on a printed form, to a bank to pay out money from a customer's account.

chequer *n* pattern of squares. **chequered** *adj* **1** variegated; diversified in colour. **2** marked by fluctuations in fortune, nature, etc.

cherish *vt* protect; preserve; hold dear; nurture.

cherry *n* small red or yellow stone fruit.

cherub *n* one of the orders of angels, generally depicted as a plump winged child.

chess *n* game of skill for two players using thirty-two pieces (chessmen) on a board with sixty-four black and white squares.

chest *n* **1** upper front part of the body. **2** large strong box. **chest of drawers** *n* piece of furniture fitted with a set of drawers, used esp. for storing clothes or linen.

chestnut *n* **1** deciduous tree (sweet-chestnut, bearing edible nut, or horse-chestnut, bearing inedible nut). **2** fruit of these trees. **3** dark reddish-brown horse. *n,adj* dark reddish-brown.

chew *vt,vi* grind between the teeth. **chew over** wonder; ruminate. ~*n* act of chewing. **chewing gum** *n* sweetened flavoured preparation of resin or gum for chewing.

chick *n* **1** young bird, esp. a chicken. **2** *sl* girl.

chicken *n* **1** fowl reared for its eggs and meat. **2** *inf* young person. *adj sl* cowardly. **chickenpox** *n* mild infectious disease usually contracted by children, characterized by a blistery rash.

chicory *n* plant whose leaves are used in salads and whose root is ground to flavour coffee.

chief *adj* main; major; most important; principal. *n* **1** leader; superior head of a department, organization, etc. **2** *also* **chieftain** leader of a tribe or clan. **chiefly** *adv* mainly; principally.

chilblain *n* painful itchy red swelling on the hands and feet caused by extreme cold, bad circulation, etc.

child *n* **1** young person; infant; boy or girl. **2** son or daughter. **childbirth** *n* act of giving birth to a child. **childhood** *n* state or period of being a child. **childish** *adj* immature; foolish; naive. **childishly** *adv.* **childlike** *adj* trusting or innocent like a child.

chill *n* **1** coldness. **2** slight cold preceding fever. **3** discouraging influence. *vt,vi* make or become cold or cool. **chilly** *adj* **1** slightly cold; cool. **2** unfriendly.

chilli *n* pod of a capsicum, often dried and ground into the hot pungent spice, Cayenne pepper.

chime *n* melodious sound as of bells, esp. when ringing in sequence. *vt,vi* **1** ring musically. **2** agree; concur.

chimney *n* construction allowing smoke to escape from a fireplace, furnace, etc.

chimpanzee *n* small African ape.

chin *n* part of the face below the mouth.

china *n* crockery, esp. made of fine porcelain.

chink[1] *n* crevice, narrow opening; slit.

chink[2] *n* sharp clinking sound, as of coins or glasses struck together. *vi* clink; jingle.

chip *n* **1** small fragment or splinter of glass, wood, etc. **2** small oblong piece of deep-fried potato. **3** small crack or missing piece in china, glass, etc. **4** counter or token used in gambling games. **have a chip on one's shoulder** bear a grudge. ~*vt* (-pp-) **1** crack or break a small piece from. **2** cut (potatoes) into oblongs. **3** carve with a small tool. **chip in** contribute.

chiropody *n* treatment of minor foot disorders. **chiropodist** *n*.

chirp *vi* make the short shrill cry of a bird. *n* chirping sound. **chirpy** *adj inf* lively and cheerful.

chisel *n* steel cutting tool with wedge-shaped edge used in carpentry, masonry, etc. *vi,vt* (-ll-) cut or shape with a chisel.

chivalry *n* **1** courtesy or protectiveness, esp. as shown by men to women. **2** code of behaviour of medieval knights. **chivalrous** *adj*.

chive *n* small plant of the onion family whose leaves are used as a seasoning in cooking.

chlorine *n* greenish-yellow poisonous corrosive gaseous element, used as a disinfectant and bleach.

chlorophyll *n* green colouring matter present in plants, necessary for photosynthesis.

chocolate *n* preparation of cocoa mixed with sugar, milk, etc., eaten as a sweet, used for flavouring, etc. *adj,n* dark brown.

choice *n* **1** act of choosing. **2** variety to choose from. **3** thing chosen. *adj* of excellent quality; selected.

choir *n* **1** body of singers performing in public, esp. in a church. **2** part of a church or cathedral reserved for singers, above the nave and below the altar. **chorister** *n* member of a church choir.

chòke *vt* **1** throttle or obstruct the breathing of; suffocate. **2** block; obstruct. *vi* **1** become choked. **2** become speechless through emotion. *n* **1** action or sound of choking. **2** valve controlling air supply, as in a carburettor.

cholera *n* highly infectious, often fatal disease characterized by feverish vomiting and diarrhoea.

choose *vt* select or take something in preference to something else. *vi* decide; determine.

chop[1] *vt* (-pp-) **1** cut with sharp blows. **2** cut into small pieces. *n* **1** act of chopping. **2** slice of pork or lamb containing part of a rib. **chopper** *n* axe or hatchet.

chop[2] *vi* (-pp-) make a sudden change of direction or attitude. **chop and change** change or alter repeatedly.

chopstick *n* one of a pair of small sticks used, esp. in the Far East, as an implement for eating.

choral *adj* written for or sung by a choir or chorus.

chord *n* **1** simultaneous sounding of several notes in music. **2** string of a musical instrument. **3** straight line linking two points on a curve.

chore *n* routine or repetitive task, esp. housework.

choreography *n* art of dance composition and notation. **choreographer** *n*.

chorus *n* **1** group of performers speaking, singing, or dancing together, esp. as separate from the action of a drama. **2** combined speech or song, esp. the refrain of a ballad, etc. *vt,vi* speak or sing as a group.

chose *v pt* of **choose.**

chosen *v pp* of **choose.**

Christ *n* title given to Jesus acknowledging him to be the Saviour foretold in the Old Testament.

christen *vt* give a name to, esp. at a Christian baptismal service. **christening** *n* ceremony of baptizing and naming a child in a church.

Christian *n* one professing to follow the teaching of Christ. *adj* **1** believing in Christ. **2** charitable; forgiving; unselfish. **3** of or pertaining to Christ. **Christian name** *n* personal name, esp. as given at a christening. **Christianity** *n* Christian faith, teaching, spirit, or way of life.

Christmas *n* celebration of the birth of Christ. **Christmas Day** December 25th.

chromatic *adj* **1** concerned with or having colours. **2** relating to a musical scale consisting of semitones.

chrome *n* chromium.

chromium *n* silvery-white metallic element used for highly polished coatings on other metals.

chromosome *n* small rod-like body found in living cells, responsible for the transmission of genetic information.

chronic *adj* **1** (esp. of a disease) of a long-standing or constantly recurring nature. **2** *inf* dreadful; tedious; objectionable. **chronically** *adv.*

chronological *adj* in order of time; according to time of occurrence. **chronologically** *adv.* **chronology** *n.*

chrysalis *n* pupa or insect larva, esp. enclosed in a sheath during its resting stage.

chrysanthemum *n* autumn-flowering garden plant with large blooms.

chubby *adj* plump and round-faced. **chubbiness** *n.*

chuck *vt,vi inf* **1** throw; toss. **2** give up. **chuck out 1** throw away or out. **2** eject forcibly.

chuckle *n* quiet burbling laugh. *vi* laugh quietly.

chunk *n* thick piece or portion. **chunky** *adj* thick and bulky.

church *n* **1** whole body of Christians or of one of the Christian denominations. **2** building used for Christian or other religious services. **3** the clergy. **churchyard** *n* burial ground surrounding a church.

churn *n* **1** vessel used for converting milk or cream into butter. **2** large cylindrical container used for transporting milk. *vt,vi* rotate or agitate vigorously, as in a churn. **churn out** produce rapidly and in great quantity.

chute *n* **1** sloping track or passage down which water, rubbish, laundry, etc., may be shot. **2** narrow waterfall.

chutney *n* sweet spicy relish made from pickled fruit and vegetables.

cider *n* drink made from pressed fermented apples.

cigar *n* roll of tobacco leaves for smoking.

cigarette *n* shredded tobacco leaves rolled in thin paper for smoking.

cinder *n* piece of burnt or charred wood, coal, etc.

cinecamera *n* camera used for taking motion pictures.

cinema *n* **1** the film industry. **2** building in which films are shown.

cinnamon *n* sweet pungent spice made from the bark of a type of laurel found largely in S and SE Asia.

circle *n* **1** plane figure bounded by an unbroken line, which is at every point the same distance from the centre. **2** ring. **3** group of people with a common interest. **4** gallery in a theatre. *vt,vi* move round in a circle.

circuit *n* **1** circular path; distance or way round. **2** journey taken regularly through a specific area, esp. by a judge or barrister in performance of professional duties. **3** path of an electric current. **circuitous** *adj* roundabout; long-winded; devious.

circular *adj* **1** relating to a circle. **2** round. **circulate** *vi,vt* move or pass around. **circulation** *n* **1** act of moving or passing around. **2** movement of blood through veins and arteries. **3** distribution or sale of newspapers, magazines, etc.

circumcise *vt* cut off the foreskin. **circumcision** *n.*

circumference *n* outer rim of a circle.

circumscribe *vt* **1** restrict or contain within certain limits. **2** draw a line around.

circumstance *n* incident; fact; detail. **circumstances** *n pl* **1** facts attendant on or relating to others; condition; state. **2** financial position. **circumstantial** *adj* **1** of or derived from circumstances. **2** fully detailed.

circus *n* **1** group of travelling entertainers, clowns, acrobats, performing animals, etc. **2** arena or amphitheatre. **3** place where several roads converge.

cistern *n* water tank, esp. supplying water to a lavatory.

cite *vt* **1** quote as an example or authority. **2** summon to appear in court. **citation** *n* **1** quotation. **2** summons. **3** mention, esp. for bravery, in military dispatches.

citizen *n* **1** resident of a city. **2** member of a state. **citizenship** *n.*

citrus *n* genus of fruit trees including orange, lemon, and lime.

city *n* large or important town, esp. containing a cathedral. **the City** financial centre of London.

civic *adj* of a city or local community. **civics** *pl* *n* science of government, esp. local government.

civil *adj* **1** courteous; polite. **2** of a citizen or the community. **3** not military. **4** (of legal proceedings, etc.) not criminal; disputed between ordinary citizens. **civil engineering** *n* branch of engineering concerned with designing and building roads, bridges, etc. **civil engineer** *n*. **civil service** *n* body of officials employed by the state in an administrative capacity. **civil servant** *n*. **civil war** *n* war between citizens of the same state.

civilian *n* one not in the employ of the armed forces.

civilization *n* **1** moral, social, intellectual, and artistic standards of a specific society. **2** advanced nonbarbaric condition or society. **civilize** *vt* bring out of a primitive condition; refine.

clad *adj* clothed; dressed.

claim *vt* **1** demand as a right. **2** ask or call for. *vt,vi* assert; maintain. *n* **1** demand or request by right. **2** that which is claimed or asserted. **3** right or title. **claimant** *n* person who makes a claim, esp. in law.

clam *n* edible bivalve shellfish. *v* **clam up** refuse to speak.

clamber *vi* climb, esp. with effort or difficulty. *n* awkward climb.

clammy *adj* damp and sticky.

clamour *n* raucous outcry; uproar. *vi* demand vociferously. **clamorous** *adj*. **clamorously** *adv*.

clamp *n* device used in carpentry, metalwork, surgery, etc., to hold things firmly in place. *vt* fasten or hold with a clamp. **clamp down on** *inf* suppress.

clan *n* large family or tribal group, esp. in Scotland. **clansman** *n*.

clandestine *adj* concealed; secret.

clang *n* resounding metallic sound, as of a large bell. *vt,vi* make or cause a clang. **clanger** *n* *inf* blunder.

clank *n* loud metallic sound, as of a heavy chain. *vt,vi* make or cause a clank.

clap *n* **1** sudden noise as of the palms of the hands brought sharply together. **2** sound of thunder. *vt,vi* (-pp-) **1** applaud with the hands. **2** place (down) suddenly. **3** throw (into prison, etc.). **clapper** *n* tongue suspended inside a bell. **like the clappers** very energetically or quickly.

claret *n* red wine from Bordeaux.

clarify *vt,vi* make or become clear. **clarification** *n*.

clarinet *n* musical wind instrument with a single reed. **clarinetist** *n*.

clarity *n* clearness.

clash *n* **1** loud banging noise, as of colliding metal objects. **2** opposition; dispute; conflict. *vt* bang noisily together. *vi* **1** strike against. **2** come into opposition; conflict. **3** (of colours) be displeasing or disharmonious when placed together.

clasp *n* **1** hinged or interlocking fastening. **2** embrace; grasp of the hand. *vt* **1** fasten with a clasp. **2** embrace; grasp with the hand.

class *n* **1** kind; sort; category. **2** social group defined according to occupation, position, wealth, birth, social status, etc. **3** group of students or pupils undergoing the same course of instruction. **4** division denoting standard of comfort in an aeroplane, train, etc. *vt* form into or place in a class.

classic *adj* widely recognized as standard, typical, or of great merit. *n* work of art, esp. literature, noted for its lasting excellence. **classical** *adj* **1** of ancient Greece or Rome, esp. in formalized literary or architectural style. **2** (of music) belonging to great serious European tradition, esp. if composed before 1800. **classics** *pl n* language, literature, and philosophy of ancient Greece and Rome. **classicist** *n* student of classics.

classify *vt* arrange in classes or categories; place in a class. **classification** *n*.

clatter *n* loud repetitive rattling noise. *vt,vi* make or cause a clatter.

clause *n* **1** part of a sentence with a subject, predicate, and finite verb. **2** subsection in a legal contract, will, agreement, etc.

claustrophobia *n* morbid dread of enclosed or confined places. **claustrophobic** *adj*.

claw *n* hard hooked nail of an animal or bird. *vt* seize or tear with claws or nails.

clay *n* heavy sticky fine-grained soil material, plastic when moist, and used in pottery, brick-making, etc.

clean *adj* free from dirt, marks, impurity, guilt, disease, etc. *adv* completely. *vt* make clean. **clean out** clean thoroughly; empty. **clean up** **1** tidy. **2** suppress crime, vice, etc. **3** gain a large profit, advantage, etc. **cleanliness** *n*.

cleanse *vt* clean (something) thoroughly; make pure. **cleanser** *n*.

clear *adj* **1** unclouded; bright; transparent. **2** obvious; distinct; straightforward. **3** net; after deductions. **4** without obstruction. *adv* completely. *vt* **1** clarify. **2** empty. **3** acquit; declare innocent. **4** pass without touching. **5** verify; justify. **6** receive (net). *vi* become clear. **clear off** *or* **out** leave hurriedly. **clear up 1** solve. **2** tidy. **3** become fine or sunny. **clearance** *n* **1** act of clearing. **2** space between moving and stationary objects. **3** certificate permitting passage through Customs, esp. of a ship. **clear-headed** *adj* lucid; intelligent; sensible. **clearing** *n* **1** act of making or becoming clear. **2** area free from trees, esp. in a forest.

clef *n* musical symbol denoting pitch of the notes written on the stave.

clench *vt* **1** grasp; grip; press (teeth, the fist, etc.) firmly together. **2** secure tightly; rivet.

clergy *n* priests and ordained ministers of a Christian church. **clergyman** *n, pl* **-men** priest, esp. in the Church of England.

clerical *adj* **1** of a clerk. **2** of a clergyman; religious.

clerk *n* **1** employee dealing with records, correspondence, etc., in an office. **2** person holding a particular administrative position in local government, the law, etc.

clever *adj* **1** intelligent; bright. **2** ingenious; cunning. **cleverly** *adv*. **cleverness** *n*.

cliché *n* hackneyed expression or phrase.

click *n* short sharp sound, as of a latch closing. *vi,vt* make a click.

client *n* customer; person employing another for business or professional purposes. **clientele** (kli:ən'tel) *n* clients.

cliff *n* steep high rock, esp. facing the sea.

climate *n* **1** general weather conditions of a region. **2** prevailing public attitude, economic situation, etc.

climax *n* **1** ultimate culmination of a series of events. **2** moment of supreme elation, terror, etc. **3** orgasm. **climactic** *adj*.

climb *vi,vt* **1** ascend or go up using hands and feet; scale. **2** rise; mount. *n* **1** distance or route to be climbed. **2** act of climbing. **climb down** admit to having been wrong; withdraw.

cling *vi* (clung) **1** adhere or stick to closely. **2** refuse to abandon a belief, idea, etc.

clinic *n* **1** hospital department or health centre for the diagnosis and treatment of specific disorders. **2** private nursing home. **clinical** *adj* **1** relating to a clinic. **2** of, used, or carried out in a hospital. **3** concerned with treatment of disease in the patient. **4** not biased or emotionally involved.

clink *n* **1** short ringing sound, as of metal, glass, etc., struck together. **2** *sl* prison. *vt,vi* make a clink.

clip[1] *n* **1** device for holding paper, etc., together. **2** hairgrip. *vt* (-pp-) fasten with a clip.

clip[2] *vt* (-pp-) **1** trim; cut closely; shorten. **2** smack; hit sharply. *n* **1** act of clipping. **2** piece clipped off. **3** sharp blow. **4** short extract from a film.

clitoris *n* female sexual organ similar to a rudimentary penis. **clitoral** *adj*.

cloak *n* long loose sleeveless garment fastening at the neck. *vt* disguise; mask. **cloakroom** *n* room in a public building, etc., where coats are left.

clock *n* instrument for telling or measuring time. *vt* **1** time (a runner). **2** *sl* hit; strike. **clock in** *or* **on/out** *or* **off** record the time of starting/finishing work. **clockwise** *adv* in the same direction as the hands of a clock. **clockwork** *n* mechanism of a clock or one working like that of a clock. **like clockwork** with perfect regularity and precision.

clog *n* heavy shoe with a sole and sometimes upper of wood. *vi* (-gg-) (of drains, pipes, etc.) become obstructed or blocked. *vt* block; obstruct.

cloister *n* **1** covered arcade surrounding a monastery quadrangle. **2** monastery, abbey, or nunnery. **cloistered** *adj* shut away; secluded.

close *adj* (klous) **1** nearby; near. **2** mean; stingy. **3** stuffy; sultry. **4** confined; restricted. **5** thorough. **6** intimate. *n* (klous for 1,2; klouz for 3) **1** alley; dead-end street or road; enclosure. **2** cathedral precinct. **3** end. *adv* (klous) tightly; leaving no space. **close-up** *n* ('klousʌp) film-shot or photograph giving a detailed view. ~*v* (klouz) *vt* **1** shut. **2** pull together; unite. **3** finish; end; complete. *vi* come to an end; terminate. **close in** surround and move in on. **close down** terminate; cease functioning. **close up** shut completely. **closed-shop** *n* factory employing only union members. **closure** *n*.

closet *n* **1** small private room. **2** cupboard. **3** lavatory. **closeted** *adj* shut away; kept secret.

clot *n* **1** small solidified mass of blood, mud, etc. **2** *sl* fool. *vt,vi* (-tt-) form into clots; congeal; coagulate.

cloth *n* **1** small piece of fabric used for polishing, mopping, covering, etc. **2** woven fabric from which clothing, curtains, etc., are cut and sewn.

clothe *vt* **1** provide with clothes; dress. **2** cover; disguise. **clothing** *n* clothes; garments in general. **clothes** *pl n* **1** garments; materials fashioned to be worn on the person; dress. **2** bed-coverings. **in plain clothes** (of a policeman, etc.) not wearing uniform.

cloud *n* **1** visible mass of small droplets of water floating in the sky, from which rain or snow falls. **2** mass of dust, smoke, etc., resembling a cloud. **3** anything depressing or threatening. *vt,vi* **1** fill or cover with clouds. **2** make or become murky or opaque. **3** fill or cover with gloom, doubt, etc. **cloudy** *adj* **1** covered or scattered with clouds. **2** opaque; not clear.

clove[1] *n* dried flower-bud of an aromatic tropical tree, used as a spice.

clove[2] *n* small bulb, esp. of garlic, that forms part of a larger one.

clover *n* small flowering plant with three-lobed leaves, often grown as cattle fodder.

clown *n* comic fool, esp. in a circus. *vi* play the fool.

club *n* **1** association of people with a common interest in a social, cultural, or sporting activity, etc. **2** the building, etc., used by such a group. **3** thick heavy stick. **4** stick used in golf. **clubs** *pl n* one of the four suits in cards. ~*vt* (-bb-) beat with a club. **club together** unite for a common end; contribute to a collection.

cluck *n* sound made by a hen. *vi* make such a sound.

clue *n* **1** hint or suggestion leading to the solution of a mystery. **2** information; idea. **clueless** *adj inf* stupid.

clump *n* **1** cluster of trees, bushes, etc. **2** heavy tread. *vi* **1** tread heavily. **2** group together.

clumsy *adj* **1** inclined to stumble, drop things, etc.; awkward. **2** tactless; gauche. **clumsily** *adv*. **clumsiness** *n*.

cluster *n* closely packed group, as of flowers, diamonds, stars, etc. *vi* grow or be gathered together.

clutch *vt* grasp or seize tightly. *n* **1** grasp; grip. **2** mechanical coupling device allowing gradual engagement of gears, etc. **3** number of eggs laid at one time.

clutter *n* confused jumble. *vt* crowd with a confused or untidy mass.

coach *n* **1** bus, esp. one used for long trips. **2** large horse-drawn carriage. **3** railway carriage. **4** tutor training people for exams, athletic events, etc. *vt* prepare for examination, contest, etc.; train.

coagulate *vi* solidify; clot; congeal. **coagulation** *n*.

coal *n* solid black mineral consisting of carbonized vegetation and mined for use as fuel. **coalmine** *n* workings from which coal is obtained; pit.

coalition *n* short-term alliance, esp. between political parties.

coarse *adj* **1** rough in texture; not fine. **2** vulgar; base; impolite. **coarsely** *adv*. **coarseness** *n*.

coast *n* land bordering the sea. *vi* sail or drift along. **coastal** *adj*. **coastguard** *n* person employed to watch the coast and sea for ships in danger, smuggling, etc. **coastline** *n* line of the shore, esp. as seen from the sea or air or as shown on a map.

coat *n* **1** outer garment with sleeves. **2** hair, fur, etc., covering an animal; pelt. **3** layer of paint, etc., on a surface. *vt* cover with a layer.

coax *vt* persuade, esp. by soothing or flattery; cajole.

cobble *n* rounded stone used for paving, road-making, etc. *vi,vt* mend or repair clumsily or shoddily.

cobbler *n* one who makes or mends shoes and boots.

cobra *n* poisonous hooded snake found in Asia and Africa.

cobweb *n* spider's web.

cock *n* **1** male bird, esp. of domestic fowl. **2** water-tap. **3** hammer of a gun. **4** *inf* chap; fellow. **5** *sl* penis. *vt* **1** tilt; turn to one side; set at a jaunty angle. **2** pull back the hammer of (a gun). **cocky** *adj* cheeky; self-assured; impudent. **cockiness** *n*.

cockle *n* edible bivalve mollusc with a heart-shaped shell.

Cockney *n* **1** Londoner, esp. one born within the sound of Bow Bells. **2** dialect of a Cockney.

cockpit *n* pilot's compartment in an aircraft.

cockroach *n* brown or black insect with long antennae.

cocktail *n* **1** drink made from a mixture of spirits and flavourings. **2** dish made from mixed fruit or prawns, etc.
cocoa *n* powder from the ground seeds of the cacao tree, used to make chocolate or to flavour drinks.
coconut *n* large fruit of a tropical palm-tree, with edible flesh, juice resembling milk, and a hard hairy husk.
cocoon *n* protective silky coating spun by various insect larvae before becoming pupae.
cod *n, pl* **cod** large edible sea fish.
coddle *vt* **1** boil lightly. **2** pamper; indulge; be protective towards.
code *n* **1** system of symbols for secret or esoteric communication. **2** system of regulations, laws, social customs, or moral principles. *vt* put into a code.
codeine *n* pain-killing drug obtained from opium.
coeducation *n* education of children of both sexes at the same school.
coerce (kou'ɔːs) *vt* persuade forcefully; compel. **coercion** *n*. **coercive** *adj*.
coexist *vi* exist at the same time, esp. in harmony. **coexistence** *n*.
coffee *n* drink made from the roasted ground seeds (beans) of the coffee tree. *adj,n* light brown.
coffin *n* wooden box in which a corpse is placed for burial.
cog *n* one of the teeth on the rim of a wheel. **cogwheel** *n* wheel fitted with cogs, used in engineering, etc., for transmitting movement; gearwheel.
cognac *n* French brandy.
cohabit *vi* live together as man and wife. **cohabitation** *n*.
cohere *vi* stick together; remain consistent. **coherence** *n*. **cohesion** *n*. **coherent** *adj* clear; comprehensible; articulate; consistent.
coil *vt,vi* wind in rings; twist. *n* **1** piece of rope, string, etc., coiled into rings. **2** coil of wire in an electrical circuit.
coin *n* stamped metal disc used as official currency. *vt* **1** form or stamp coins in a mint. **2** invent (an expression or phrase). **coinage** *n*.
coincide *vi* **1** occur at the same time or place. **2** agree; concur. **coincidence** *n* **1** act or state of coinciding. **2** striking accidental concurrence of events.
colander *n* large strainer for draining vegetables.
cold *adj* **1** not hot; chilly; low in temperature. **2** unfriendly; indifferent; unemotional. *n* **1** lack of heat. **2** acute nasal inflammation. **coldly** *adv*. **coldness** *n*. **cold-blooded** *adj* **1** having a blood temperature varying with that of the surrounding water or air. **2** unemotional; callous; ruthless. **cold-bloodedly** *adv*. **cold-bloodedness** *n*. **cold war** *n* period or state of political and military hostility between nations, involving no armed conflict.
collaborate *vi* **1** co-operate; work together. **2** co-operate with an enemy. **collaboration** *n*. **collaborator** *n*.
collapse *vi* **1** break or fall down; fail totally; give up. **2** fold away. *n* **1** breakdown; physical or mental exhaustion. **2** falling down of a structure. **collapsible** *adj*.
collar *n* **1** part of a garment encircling the neck. **2** leather strap worn round the neck by a dog, horse, etc. *vt inf* seize; tackle. **collarbone** *n* prominent frontal bone linking the ribs to the shoulder blades.
colleague *n* associate, esp. someone following the same profession as oneself.
collect *vt* **1** gather together; seek out and acquire. **2** solicit (money) for a cause. **3** fetch; pick up. **collection** *n* **1** group of objects collected together. **2** act of collecting, esp. for a charity, church, etc. **collective** *adj* taken as a whole. **collectively** *adv*.
college *n* **1** place of higher or specialized education. **2** autonomous group of people. **collegiate** *adj*
collide *vi* **1** strike violently; crash into. **2** come into conflict. **collision** *n*.
colloquial *adj* of informal everyday speech. **colloquialism** *n* informal phrase; slang; idiom.
colon *n* punctuation mark (:) used to indicate a definite pause or division in a sentence.
colonel *n* military officer of a rank between lieutenant-colonel and brigadier.
colony *n* group of settlers from another country. **colonize** *vt* take over as a colony. **colonial** *adj* from or of a colony. *n* inhabitant of a colony.
colossal *adj* extremely large; enormous; gigantic; huge.
colour *n* **1** sense impression produced by light of different wavelengths, or the property of objects or light producing this. **2** pigment; hue. **3** skin pigmentation. **4** quality of vividness or distinction. **5** false quality. **colours** *pl*

n **1** military flag or standard. **2** award for membership of a team. **off colour** unwell. ~*vt* **1** impart colour to. **2** give a false or biased impression of. *vi* take on a colour. **coloration** *n*. **colour-bar** *n* discrimination against people of coloured or dark-skinned races. **colour-blind** *adj* unable to distinguish or identify specific colours. **colour-blindness** *n*. **coloured** *adj* **1** having a colour. **2** (of a person) of a non-White race. **3** deceptive; biased. **colourful** *adj* **1** full of colour. **2** picturesque; vivid.

colt *n* young male horse.

column *n* **1** tall pillar, esp. one supporting a building. **2** row or line of people, figures, etc. **3** newspaper or magazine article or report. **columnist** *n* journalist providing regular articles for a newspaper or magazine.

coma *n* condition of very deep unconsciousness. **comatose** *adj* **1** drowsy. **2** in a coma.

comb *n* **1** small toothed instrument for separating and tidying hair, wool, etc. **2** group of wax cells made by bees. **3** crest of certain birds, esp. cocks. *vt* **1** untangle and tidy hair, wool, etc. **2** search thoroughly.

combat *vt,vi* fight against; oppose. *n* fight; struggle; battle. **combatant** *n*. **combative** *adj*.

combine *vt,vi* (kəm'bain) join together; unite; amalgamate. *n* ('kɔmbain) association of several similar companies, institutions, etc. **combine harvester** *n* mechanical corn harvester. **combination** *n* mixture; amalgamation.

combustion *n* process of burning. **combustible** *adj* capable of burning; flammable.

come *vi* (came; come) **1** arrive; be delivered; reach. **2** happen; occur. **3** originate; be caused by. **4** be available; be supplied. **come across** discover or meet by chance. **come back** return. **come off 1** become separated or broken. **2** be successfully completed. **come out 1** emerge. **2** be issued. **3** erupt. **come round 1** recover consciousness. **2** be persuaded. **come to 1** recover consciousness. **2** amount to. **come up** arise; appear. **come up with** suggest; think of; produce. **comeback** *n* **1** return or success after an absence or failure. **2** retort. **comedown** *n* **1** anticlimax. **2** reduction in status, quality, etc.

comedian *n* entertainer who performs comic songs or plays, tells jokes, etc.

comedy *n* humorous, amusing, or light-hearted play.

comet *n* heavenly body having a luminous head and a long tail, which always points away from the sun.

comfort *n* **1** encouragement; relief. **2** ease; peacefulness; lack of anxiety or pain. *vt* relieve; console; cheer. **comfortable** *adj* **1** providing or enjoying comfort. **2** fairly affluent. **comfortably** *adv*.

comic *adj* **1** funny; amusing. **2** relating to comedy. *n* **1** comic person; comedian. **2** children's paper consisting mainly of strip cartoons. **comical** *adj* ridiculous; absurd; laughable. **comically** *adv*.

comma *n* punctuation mark (,) used to indicate a slight pause, to separate clauses, etc.

command *vt* order; control; have authority or influence over; dominate. *n* order; rule; authority; control. **in command** in charge. **commander** *n* **1** someone who commands; leader. **2** naval officer ranking below a captain.

commandeer *vt* take over or seize arbitrarily or by force, esp. for military purposes.

commandment *n* order; command. **Ten Commandments** *pl n* laws given by God to Moses according to the Old Testament.

commando *n, pl* **commandos** *or* **commandoes** soldier specially trained to carry out dangerous raids.

commemorate *vt* celebrate the memory of; provide a memorial to. **commemoration** *n*.

commence *vt,vi* begin; start. **commencement** *n*.

commend *vt* **1** praise; recommend. **2** entrust. **commendable** *adj*. **commendation** *n*.

comment' *n* brief, critical, or explanatory remark expressing an opinion, reaction, etc. *vi* make a comment. **commentary** *n* **1** series of comments, esp. analysing a book. **2** description of and comments on a sporting event, state occasion, etc., esp. when broadcast. **commentator** *n* one who provides a commentary, esp. on radio or television.

commerce *n* business; trade. **commercial** *adj* relating to commerce or business. **commercial traveller** *n* representative employed by a firm as a salesman.

commission *n* **1** document conferring authority, position, agency, etc. **2** body of people holding an enquiry and producing a report. **3**

piece of work, esp. a work of art, specifically ordered. **4** percentage payment taken by an agent, salesman, etc. *vt* **1** give authority to. **2** put in an order for. **commissioner** *n* one holding or appointed by a commission.

commit *vt* (-tt-) **1** entrust; charge with. **2** perform; do; perpetrate (a crime, etc.). **3** promise; pledge. **4** send to prison or for further trial. **commit oneself** take on an obligation or duty. **commitment** *n*.

committee *n* small group instructed by a larger organization to deal with specific matters.

commodity *n* particular type of goods, produce, or merchandise.

common *adj* **1** shared by or belonging to all or to many. **2** usual; frequent. **3** general; widespread. **4** relating to the public. **5** habitual. **6** ordinary; familiar; well-known. **7** coarse; vulgar; low. *n* piece of land belonging to the community and available for public use. **in common** in joint use; of mutual interest; shared. **commonly** *adv*. **commonness** *n*. **common law** unwritten law based on custom or tradition. **common sense** *n* practical sense; good judgment; normal mental capacity. **commonplace** *adj* ordinary; not remarkable. *n* trite remark; cliché. **commonwealth** *n* **1** people of a state or nation, esp. when viewed as a political entity. **2** federation of self-governing units or former colonies.

commotion *n* disturbance; public disorder; uproar

communal *adj* relating to or belonging to a commune or community; public; common.

commune[1] *vi* (kə'mju:n) converse or act intimately or spiritually. *n* ('kɔmju:n) intimate conversation; communion.

commune[2] ('kɔmju:n) *n* **1** smallest administrative division of some countries, such as France or Belgium. **2** group or small community organized to promote mutual interests and goals.

communicate *vt* **1** give or transmit; impart. **2** make known. *vi* **1** exchange thoughts or information in a way that may be easily understood. **2** be connected, as by a passage. *vt,vi* administer or receive the Eucharist. **communicant** *n,adj*. **communication** *n*.

communion *n* **1** participation; act of sharing. **2** fellowship. **3** intimate exchange of thoughts and feelings. **Communion** *also* **Holy Communion** the Eucharist or its celebration.

communism *n* belief or social system based on the doctrine that all goods, property, and means of production belong to the community or state. **communist** *adj,n*.

community *n* **1** group of people living in the same area or sharing a common culture. **2** joint possession or ownership.

commute *vi* travel regularly, usually over relatively long distances, from home to work. *vt* reduce (a prison sentence, penalty, etc.). *vt,vi* transform; substitute. **commuter** *n*.

compact[1] *adj* (kəm'pækt) **1** packed neatly and closely together. **2** concentrated; dense. **3** terse; pithy. *vt* (kəm'pækt) pack closely together; condense; compress. *n* ('kɔmpækt) small hinged container, usually with a mirror, for holding face powder. **compactly** *adv*. **compactness** *n*.

compact[2] ('kɔmpækt) *n* agreement or contract between parties.

companion *n* **1** mate; comrade. **2** person who accompanies another or shares the same experience. **3** something that matches another. **companionable** *adj*. **companionship** *n* fellowship; friendship.

company *n* **1** gathering of persons, as for social purposes; group. **2** guest or guests. **3** association for business. **4** officers and crew of a ship. **5** infantry unit of two or more platoons. **6** troupe of actors, dancers, or singers. **part company** end association or friendship (with).

compare *vt* notice or identify similarities; liken. *vi* be in relation to. **comparable** *adj* capable or worthy of being compared. **comparably** *adv*. **comparative** *adj* **1** relating to or involving comparison. **2** not absolute or positive; relative. **comparatively** *adv*. **comparison** *n*.

compartment *n* **1** part or parts into which an enclosed space is partitioned or divided off; section; division. **2** section of a railway carriage.

compass *n* **1** instrument for determining bearings, usually by means of a magnetized needle that always points north. **2** limit or scope. **compasses** *pl n* small instrument with two hinged arms, used for drawing circles, arcs, etc. *vt* encircle; surround.

compassion *n* deeply felt pity or sympathy **compassionate** *adj*.

compatible *adj* **1** able to live or exist well or

harmoniously together. **2** consistent; not contradictory. **compatibility** *n.* **compatibly** *adv.*

compel *vt* (-ll-) **1** force or bring about by force. **2** subdue; overpower.

compensate *vt,vi* pay money (to) in acknowledgement of loss, damage, or injury; recompense. *vt* offset. *vi* modify or exaggerate one's behaviour to make up for a fault or shortcoming. **compensation** *n.*

compete *vi* strive against others. **competitor** *n.* **competition** *n* **1** competing; rivalry; opposition. **2** contest to show worth or ability, often with a prize for the winner. **competitive** *adj.* **competitively** *adv.*

competent *adj* **1** skilful; able; properly qualified. **2** sufficient; adequate. **competence** *or* **competency** *n.* **competently** *adv.*

compile *vt* assemble; make or put together (a book, its parts, etc.) from various materials or sources. **compilation** *n.* **compiler** *n.*

complacent *adj* self-satisfied. **complacency** *n.* **complacently** *adv.*

complain *vi* express unhappiness or lack of satisfaction; grumble; moan. **complaint** *n* **1** statement of a grievance, wrong, etc. **2** illness.

complement *n* **1** something that serves to complete or make whole or perfect. **2** full allowance, quantity, etc. **complementary** *adj.*

complete *adj* **1** whole, finished, full; perfect. **2** utter; absolute. *vt* finish; make whole, perfect, or full. **completely** *adv.* **completion** *n.*

complex *adj* **1** involved; intricate; complicated. **2** having many facets or parts. *n* **1** whole composed of many parts, often different or distinct. **2** set of mental attitudes, often subconscious, that affect personality. **complexity** *n.*

complexion *n* **1** texture, colour, and quality of the skin, esp. of the face. **2** aspect; appearance.

complicate *vt* make difficult, intricate, or involved. **complication** *n.*

compliment *n* ('kɔmplimənt) remark expressing praise, admiration, respect, etc. *vt* ('kɔmpliment) pay a compliment to; congratulate; praise. **complimentary** *adj* **1** expressing a compliment; flattering. **2** free of charge.

comply *vi* do as one is asked; consent; conform. **compliance** *n.* **compliant** *adj.*

component *n* essential or constituent part of something.

compose *vt* **1** create or write (a literary or musical work). **2** constitute; make up. **3** make of various parts or elements; fashion. **4** set type in lines. *vi* write music. **compose oneself** calm or settle oneself. **composer** *n* writer of music. **composite** *adj* made up of different parts. **composition** *n* **1** putting together of parts or elements to form a whole. **2** parts that form the whole; make-up. **3** piece of music. **4** artistic creation. **5** short essay, esp. one written at school. **composure** *n* calmness of mind; serenity.

compost *n* decomposed matter, manure, etc., used as fertilizer.

compound[1] *adj* ('kɔmpaund) composed of separate parts or substances. *vt* **1** (kəm'paund) assemble into a whole; combine. **2** complicate, increase. *n* ('kɔmpaund) **1** something formed by putting together separate substances, ingredients, or components. **2** chemical substance composed of atoms of two or more elements held together by chemical bonds.

compound[2] ('kɔmpaund) *n* enclosure containing houses or other buildings.

comprehend *vt,vi* **1** understand; grasp. **2** include. **comprehensible** *adj.* **comprehension** *n.* **comprehensive** *adj* **1** inclusive, covering everything; broad. **2** able to understand fully. *n also* **comprehensive school** state secondary school taking in pupils from a given area irrespective of ability.

compress *vt* (kəm'pres) **1** force or squeeze together. **2** make smaller in bulk, size, etc. *n* ('kɔmpres) pad or cloth for applying pressure, moisture, etc., to a bodily part. **compression** *n.*

comprise *vt* contain; include; consist of.

compromise *n* **1** settlement of a dispute or disagreement by giving up part of a claim. **2** something between two extremes, courses of action, etc. **3** exposure to jeopardy, suspicion, loss of reputation, etc. *vi* settle a dispute through a compromise. *vt* expose to jeopardy, etc.

compulsion *n* **1** impulse or urge that cannot be resisted. **2** act of compelling. **compulsive** *adj* acting on a sudden urge or impulse. **compulsively** *adv.* **compulsiveness** *n.* **compulsory** *adj* **1** obligatory; required. **2** compelling; employing compulsion. **compulsorily** *adv.*

computer *n* electronic apparatus that performs

calculations, processes data, etc., usually equipped with a memory and able to print out required information.

comrade *n* **1** close associate or companion; mate. **2** fellow member of a communist group or party. **comradeship** *n*.

concave *adj* curved inwards; being hollow and curved. *n* concave surface or part.

conceal *vt* **1** hide. **2** keep secret. **concealment** *n*.

concede *vt* admit having lost. *vt,vi* **1** acknowledge to be true. **2** yield.

conceit *n* excessive estimation of one's achievements, abilities, or worth; vanity. **conceited** *adj*.

conceive *vt,vi* **1** become pregnant with (a child). **2** form (an idea); imagine. **conceivable** *adj*.

concentrate *vt,vi* **1** direct (one's attention or energies) towards a particular objective. **2** make or become less diluted; condense. **3** place or be confined in a dense mass. *n* concentrated solution. **concentration** *n*. **concentration camp** *n* (esp. during World War II) place, such as a guarded compound, for the detention of political prisoners, racial minorities, etc.

concentric *adj* having a common centre.

concept *n* abstract notion; idea; thought. **conceptual** *adj*. **conception** *n* **1** fertilization; start of pregnancy. **2** idea; concept. **3** plan; design.

concern *vt* be of interest to; relate to; affect; worry. *n* **1** care; regard; anxiety; interest. **2** affair; matter. **3** business; firm; company. **concerning** *prep* about; regarding; relating to.

concert *n* ('kɔnsət) **1** public musical entertainment. **2** agreement; union; harmony. *vt* (kən'sɜ:t) plan together; arrange by agreement. **concerted** *adj*.

concertina *n* musical instrument with bellows and button-like keys.

concerto (kən'tʃɛətou) *n* musical piece for solo instrument and orchestra.

concession *n* **1** act of conceding or yielding. **2** that which is conceded or yielded. **3** franchise or privilege; grant. **concessionary** *adj*.

concise *adj* brief; terse; succinct. **concisely** *adv*.

conclude *vt,vi* bring or come to an end; finish. *vt* **1** settle; arrange or agree finally. **2** say or declare in ending or finishing. **conclusion** *n*. **conclusive** *adj*.

concoct *vt* **1** prepare with various ingredients; make a mixture of. **2** make up; devise; invent. **concoction** *n*.

concrete *adj* **1** real; not abstract. **2** relating to a specific object or case. *n* building material formed from sand, cement, water, etc., that hardens as it dries. *vt* cover over with concrete.

concur *vi* (-rr-) **1** agree; have the same opinion. **2** occur together; coincide. **concurrent** *adj*.

concussion *n* injury to the brain, caused by a blow, fall, etc., often causing loss of consciousness. **concuss** *vt* cause concussion in.

condemn *vt* **1** blame; find guilty. **2** pronounce judicial sentence against. **3** judge to be unfit for service or use. **condemnation** *n*.

condense *vt* **1** concentrate; make more solid, compact, or dense. **2** abridge; put into a few or fewer words. **3** change (a gas or vapour) to a liquid, esp. by cooling. *vi* become liquid or solid. **condensation** *n* anything condensed from a vapour, esp. fine droplets of water on a window, etc., condensed from the atmosphere.

condescend *vi* **1** lower oneself to the level of one's inferiors. **2** be gracious or patronizing. **condescension** *n*.

condition *n* **1** state or mode of existence. **2** state of health. **3** stipulation; restriction. **conditions** *pl n* **1** circumstances. **2** terms of an agreement, contract, etc. ~*vt* **1** accustom (someone) to. **2** affect; change. **conditional** *adj* tentative; not absolute; dependent on certain conditions. **conditionally** *adv*.

condolence *n* expression of sympathetic grief.

condone *vt* overlook; forgive; pardon.

conduct *v* (kən'dʌkt) *vt,vi* **1** transmit (heat, electricity, etc.). **2** control (an orchestra) during a performance or rehearsal. *vt* **1** guide; lead. **2** direct; manage; control. *n* ('kɔndʌkt) **1** behaviour. **2** execution or handling of business. **conduction** *n* transfer of heat or electricity through a medium. **conductor** *n* **1** director of an orchestra, choir, etc. **2** leader; guide. **3** person who collects fares from passengers on public transport vehicles. **4** that which conducts electricity, heat, etc.

cone *n* **1** solid figure with a circular base and tapering to a point. **2** fruit of certain trees, such as the pine or fir. **3** anything shaped like or resembling a cone.

confectioner *n* person who makes or sells sweets, cakes, etc. **confectionery** *n* **1** sweets, chocolate, etc. **2** confectioner's trade or business.

confederate *adj* (kən'fedərit) united; allied. *n* (kən'fedərit) ally; accomplice. *vt,vi* (kən'fedəreit) unite in an alliance, conspiracy, etc. **confederation** *or* **confederacy** *n*.

confer *v* (-rr-) *vt* grant as a favour, gift, honour, etc. *vi* talk with; compare opinions.

conference *n* meeting for discussion.

confess *vt,vi* **1** admit or acknowledge (a crime, sin, etc.). **2** concede; agree. **confession** *n*. **confessor** *n* priest who gives absolution to those who confess their sins.

confetti *n* small bits of coloured paper for throwing at weddings, etc.

confide *vi also* **confide in** divulge information (to); disclose in secret. **confidence** *n* **1** feeling of trust, assurance, etc.; firm belief. **2** self-assurance. **confident** *adj*. **confidently** *adv*. **confidential** *adj* secret; private. **confidentially** *adv*.

confine *vt* (kən'fain) **1** imprison; shut in. **2** keep in bed or in the house. **3** limit; keep within limits. **confines** ('kɔnfainz) *pl n* limits; restrictions. **confinement** *n*.

confirm *vt* **1** verify; substantiate; make valid. **2** give a firm undertaking of. **3** administer confirmation to. **confirmation** *n* **1** verification. **2** rite by which baptized persons are admitted into full membership of the Church.

confiscate *vt* seize by authority; appropriate. **confiscation** *n*.

conflict *n* ('kɔnflikt) **1** struggle; trial of strength. **2** opposition or clash of interests, ideas, etc. *vi* (kən'flikt) be inconsistent or at odds with; clash.

conform *vi also* **conform to** comply (with); agree to certain standards, rules, etc.; fit in (with). **conformist** *n,adj*. **conformity** *n*.

confound *vt* **1** baffle; perplex. **2** mix up; confuse. **confounded** *adj* **1** astonished; utterly confused. **2** dreadful; irritating.

confront *vt* **1** face; present. **2** bring face to face with. **confrontation** *n*.

confuse *vt* **1** throw into disorder. **2** mix mentally; obscure. **3** bewilder; muddle. **confusion** *n*.

congeal *vt,vi* **1** solidify by freezing or cooling. **2** coagulate; stiffen. **congealment** *n*.

congenial *adj* **1** pleasing; agreeable. **2** similar in disposition; compatible. **congenially** *adv*.

congenital *adj* existing at birth.

congested *adj* **1** crowded; overcrowded; blocked. **2** (of an organ or part) excessively suffused with blood. **congestion** *n*.

congratulate *vt* acknowledge the good fortunes or achievements of; praise; compliment. **congratulation** *n*.

congregate *vi* assemble; flock together; gather. **congregation** *n* **1** act of congregating. **2** assembly of people, esp. those who gather in a church to worship.

congress *n* **1** assembly; conference. **2** legislative body. **congressional** *adj*.

conical *adj also* **conic** relating to or having the shape of a cone.

conifer *n* tree, such as the pine or fir, having evergreen needle-shaped leaves and bearing cones. **coniferous** *adj*.

conjugal *adj* marital; relating to husband and wife.

conjugate *vt* ('kɔndʒugeit) inflect (a verb) in its various forms. *adj* ('kɔndʒugit) joined together in pairs; coupled. **conjugation** *n*.

conjunction *n* **1** union; association. **2** simultaneous occurrences; combination of events. **3** part of speech joining words, phrases, etc. **conjunctive** *adj*.

conjure *vt also* **conjure up** **1** call or produce as if by magic. **2** imagine; evoke; recall. *vi* practice or perform tricks of illusion or magic. **conjurer** *n*.

connect *vt,vi* link; join; fasten together. *vt* associate in the mind. **connection** *n* **1** link; joining together. **2** association; relationship. **3** public transport, esp. a train, timed to meet another train for the transfer of passengers. **connections** *pl n* influential business or social contacts.

connoisseur *n* person who is an expert, esp. in matters of taste and art.

connotation *n* suggestion or implication of a word in addition to its chief meaning. **connotative** *adj*.

conquer *vt,vi* **1** overcome (an enemy) by force; defeat. **2** surmount. *vt* gain possession of by force; take over. **conqueror** *n*. **conquest** *n*.

conscience *n* **1** mental sense of right and wrong. **2** feeling of guilt. **conscientious** *adj* **1**

paying attention to conscience; scrupulous. **2** painstaking; hard-working. **conscientiously** *adv*.

conscious *adj* **1** aware of one's surroundings; awake. **2** sensitive to or recognizing some truth, fact, etc. **3** performed or registered with full awareness. **4** intended; deliberate. **consciously** *adv*. **consciousness** *n*.

conscript *vt* (kən'skript) enrol compulsorily into service, esp. in the armed forces; call up. *n* ('kɔnskript) person who has been conscripted. **conscription** *n*.

consecrate *vt* **1** make sacred or holy; sanctify. **2** devote; dedicate. **consecration** *n*.

consecutive *adj* in unbroken or logical order or succession. **consecutively** *adv*.

consent *vi* agree (to); give assent. *n* **1** permission. **2** agreement.

consequence *n* **1** effect or result; conclusion. **2** significance; importance. **in consequence** as a result. **consequent** *adj*.

conservative *adj* **1** opposed to change, as in social or political conditions; traditional. **2** moderate. *n* person who is conventional or opposed to change. **Conservative Party** *n* British political party which generally favours private enterprise. **conservatively** *adv*.

conservatory *n* glassed-in room for growing blooming or exotic plants, esp. one attached to an outside wall of a house.

conserve *vt* preserve; keep from decay, change, etc. *n* jam made with whole fruit. **conservation** *n* preservation, esp. of the natural environment.

consider *vt,vi* **1** think about; reflect on; contemplate; examine. **2** suppose; think to be; believe. **3** look upon with respect, sympathy, etc. **considerable** *adj* **1** somewhat large in amount, extent, or degree. **2** important; great. **considerably** *adv*. **considerate** *adj* thoughtful; kind. **consideration** *n* **1** thought; contemplation; reflection. **2** payment; financial reward. **3** thoughtfulness for others. **4** importance. **take into consideration** take into account; bear in mind. **considering** *prep* in view of.

consign *vt* **1** hand over formally; commit (to). **2** give over to another's custody; entrust. **consignment** *n*.

consist *vi* be composed or made up (of). **consistency** *n* **1** degree of solidity, density, or firmness. **2** agreement; correspondence; accordance; regularity. **consistent** *adj* harmonious; not contradictory; regular. **consistently** *adv*.

console *vt,vi* comfort in distress or grief; cheer. **consolation** *n*.

consolidate *vt,vi* **1** make or become firm or solid; strengthen. **2** combine; unite. **consolidation** *n*.

consonant *n* **1** speech sound made by constriction or stoppage of the breath stream. **2** letter or symbol representing this, such as *p, t,* or *s*.

conspicuous *adj* easily seen; noticeable; standing out. **conspicuously** *adv*.

conspire *vt,vi* plot (an evil or criminal act) in secret. *vi* act together; contribute in combination. **conspiracy** *n*. **conspirator** *or* **conspirer** *n*.

constable *n* police officer of the lowest rank. **constabulary** *n* local police force.

constant *adj* **1** always present, happening, or continuing. **2** unchanging; permanent. *n* quantity or value that does not vary. **constancy** *n*. **constantly** *adv*.

constellation *n* star group, esp. one with a given name.

consternation *n* dismay; anxiety.

constipation *n* difficulty or infrequency in evacuating the bowels.

constituency *n* body of electors or area served by a member of Parliament.

constituent *adj* **1** serving to make up a whole; component. **2** having power to elect. *n* **1** component or essential part. **2** elector; voter.

constitute *vt* **1** set up; establish. **2** be an element of; make up. **3** appoint; make into. **constitution** *n* **1** manner in which something is made up. **2** state of physical or mental health. **3** character; temperament; disposition. **4** principles or laws by which a state is governed. **constitutional** *adj*.

constrain *vt* **1** compel. **2** confine; restrain; restrict. **constraint** *n*.

constrict *vt* make narrower or tighter; compress. **constriction** *n*.

construct *vt* (kən'strʌkt) **1** put together; build; make. **2** devise; formulate; fabricate. *n* ('kɔnstrʌkt) something constructed; formulation. **construction** *n*. **constructive** *adj* useful; helpful.

consul *n* official state representative, residing and performing administrative duties in a foreign city. **consular** *adj*. **consulate** *n* **1** premises occupied by a consul. **2** period of office of a consul.

consult *vt* seek advice or information from; refer to. **consultant** *n* **1** person qualified to give expert professional advice. **2** medical or surgical specialist. **consultation** *n*.

consume *vt* **1** use up. **2** eat or drink up. **3** destroy as by burning or decomposition. **4** spend (time, money, etc.), esp. foolishly or wastefully. **5** engross; absorb. **consumer** *n* person who buys or uses a commodity or service. **consumption** *n*.

contact *n* **1** touching or being in touch. **2** connection; association. **3** person exposed to a contagious disease. **4** person who may be useful to one socially or for business purposes. *vt,vi* get in touch, be in contact, or communicate (with). **contact lenses** *pl n* optical lenses that fit directly on to the surface of the eye to correct visual defects.

contagious *adj* **1** (of an infectious disease) transmitted directly or indirectly from one person to another. **2** (of an infected person) able to spread disease to others. **3** tending to spread or influence; catching. **contagion** *n*.

contain *vt* **1** hold; enclose. **2** comprise; include; have room for. **contain oneself** control or restrain oneself. **container** *n* something able to hold a product, substance, etc.; receptacle.

contaminate *vt* **1** make impure by mixture or contact; pollute. **2** corrupt; spoil. **3** make dangerous or worthless by being exposed to radioactivity. **contamination** *n*.

contemplate *vt* **1** gaze upon, esp. thoughtfully. **2** meditate on. **3** intend; plan. *vi* consider carefully; meditate. **contemplation** *n*.

contemporary *adj* **1** of roughly the same date or age. **2** of the present; reflecting current styles, fashions, etc.; modern. *n* person of the same age or time as another. **contemporaneous** *adj*.

contempt *n* **1** scorn. **2** disrespect. **3** lack of regard for authority, esp. for the rules of a court or legal body. **contemptible** *adj*. **contemptuous** *adj*.

contend *vi* struggle; fight for; compete. *vt* assert; claim; maintain. **contention** *n*.

content[1] ('kɔntent) *n* **1** capacity. **2** proportion of a substance contained; subject matter. **contents** *pl n* **1** items placed in a container. **2** list of chapters or divisions in a book.

content[2] (kən'tent) *adj* **1** satisfied; happy. **2** willing; resigned. *vt* make content; please. *n* *also* **contentment** happiness; satisfaction.

contest *n* ('kɔntest) **1** competition; match. **2** conflict; struggle. *vt* (kən'test) fight for; dispute; struggle against. **contestant** *n* person who takes part in a contest; competitor.

context *n* **1** text or section preceding or following a particular passage, word, etc. **2** facts or circumstances relating to an event, situation, etc.; background. **contextual** *adj*.

continent *n* major land mass of the earth. **continental** *adj*. **Continental** *adj* relating to the mainland of Europe or to Europeans. *n* inhabitant of the mainland of Europe. **continental quilt** *n* duvet.

contingency *n* chance occurrence; unforeseen event or circumstance; possibility; eventuality. **contingent** *adj* dependent upon an uncertain event or condition; possible. *n* representative group in a body of people.

continue *vt,vi* **1** go on; carry on; proceed (with). **2** remain existing; persist. **3** resume; take up again. **continual** *adj* occurring at regular intervals; constant; persistent. **continually** *adv*. **continuation** *n* **1** extended or connected part or section. **2** prolonged action. **3** resumption; renewal. **continuity** *n* **1** continuous flow; logical sequence. **2** complete film scenario, script, etc. **continuous** *adj* without interruption; unbroken. **continuously** *adv*.

contour *n* outline or shape of a body or figure. *vt* form the outline or shape of. **contour line** *n* line on a map that passes through all points that have equal elevation.

contraband *n* **1** illegal importing or exporting. **2** smuggled goods.

contraception *n* prevention of conception; birth control. **contraceptive** *adj* serving to prevent conception. *n* agent or device that prevents conception.

contract *n* ('kɔntrækt) agreement, esp. legally binding, between two or more persons, groups, etc. *v* (kən'trækt) *vt,vi* **1** make or become smaller or more compressed. **2** ('kɔntrækt) enter into or settle by agreement. **3** draw or be drawn together. *vt* **1** shorten by omitting parts, elements, etc. **2** acquire (a disease, liability, etc.). **contraction** *n*.

contradict *vt* **1** state the opposite of (a statement, etc.). **2** deny; refute. *vt,vi* be inconsistent (with). **contradiction** *n*. **contradictory** *adj*.

contralto *n* female alto voice.

contraption *n* strange or cumbersome invention, machine, etc.

contrary *adj* **1** opposite. **2** opposed in direction, tendency, or nature. **3** perverse. *n* exact opposite. *adv* in opposition.

contrast *vt,vi* (kən'tra:st) show or display dissimilarity. *n* ('kɔntra:st) striking difference or distinction.

contravene *vt* **1** infringe; conflict with; violate. **2** contradict; dispute. **contravention** *n*.

contribute *vt,vi* **1** pay with others to a common fund. **2** supply or give as one's share in a discussion, task, etc. **contribution** *n*. **contributor** *n*. **contributory** *adj*.

contrive *vt* **1** devise; design. **2** succeed in bringing about; manage. *vi,vt* plot; conspire. **contrivance** *n*. **contrived** *adj* unnatural; not spontaneous.

control *vt* (-ll-) **1** command; dominate. **2** check; curb; restrain. **3** verify or test by a standard comparison. *n* **1** domination; command. **2** restraint; check. **3** standard of comparison. **controls** *pl n* devices for regulating or guiding a machine, as an aircraft, car, etc.

controversy *n* debate; dispute; argument. **controversial** *adj*.

convalesce *vi* recover from illness. **convalescence** *n* period of recovery. **convalescent** *adj,n*.

convenience *n* **1** suitability; usefulness. **2** personal comfort; ease. **3** public lavatory. **convenient** *adj* **1** well adapted to one's purpose; suitable. **2** helpful; useful; handy. **conveniently** *adv*.

convent *n* **1** religious community, esp. of nuns. **2** buildings occupied by sucn a community.

convention *n* **1** large assembly, conference, or formal meeting. **2** traditionally observed custom or rule; norm. **conventional** *adj* conforming to accepted standards.

converge *vi* tend to meet or move towards the same point; approach. **convergence** *n*. **convergent** *adj*.

converse (kən'və:s) *vi* talk or hold a conversation (with). **conversation** *n* talk; exchange of thoughts, opinions, etc.

converse[2] ('kɔnvə:s) *adj* opposite; reverse. *n* statement with the terms of another interchanged; opposite. **conversely** *adv*.

convert *vt* (kən'və:t) **1** modify or change into something different; adapt. **2** change in outlook, religion, opinion, etc. *n* ('kɔnvə:t) person who has been converted, esp. to a particular religion. **conversion** *n*. **convertible** *adj* capable of being converted. *n* car with a folding or removable roof.

convex *adj* curved outwards; bulging.

convey *vt* **1** carry; transport. **2** communicate. **conveyance** *n* **1** transfer of property from one person to another. **2** transportation. **conveyor belt** *n* endless flexible belt used to convey goods, esp. in a factory.

convict *vt* (kən'vikt) prove or declare guilty. *n* ('kɔnvikt) imprisoned criminal.

conviction *n* **1** firm belief; certainty. **2** verdict of guilt.

convince *vt* satisfy by argument or evidence; persuade.

convoy *n* **1** escort of naval vessels, armed forces, etc., provided for protection. **2** group of vehicles moving together.

cook *vt,vi* **1** prepare (food) by roasting, boiling, etc. **2** subject or be subjected to heat; burn. *n* person who prepares food, esp. professionally. **cooker** *n* oven; stove. **cookery** *n* art or practice of cooking.

cool *adj* **1** somewhat cold. **2** unexcited; calm. **3** lacking interest or friendliness. *vt,vi* make or become cool(er). *n* cool part, place, time, etc. **cool one's heels** be kept waiting. **coolly** *adv*. **coolness** *n*.

coop *n* pen or cage for poultry. *vt also* **coop up** confine in a small space.

cooperate *vi* work together; act jointly. **cooperation** *n*. **cooperative** *adj* helpful; willing to cooperate. *n* joint enterprise based on collective principles.

coordinate *vt* (kou'ɔ:dineit) bring into order as parts of a whole; combine harmoniously. *adj* (kou'ɔ:dinit) combined; harmonious. *n* (kou'ɔ:dinit) combination.

cope *vi* deal with; manage satisfactorily.

copper[1] *n* **1** soft reddish lustrous metal, used in electrical wiring, plumbing, etc. **2** coin made or formerly made of copper. *adj,n* red or reddish-gold.

copper[2] *n sl* policeman.

copulate *vi* have sexual intercourse. **copulation** *n*.

copy *n* **1** reproduction or imitation; duplicate. **2** single specimen of a book. **3** matter for printing. *vt,vi* **1** make a copy (of); duplicate. **2** imitate. **copyright** *n* exclusive legal right to produce or dispose of copies of a literary or artistic work over a given period of time. *vt* secure a copyright on.

coral *n* **1** hard red or white substance secreted by sea polyps, often forming reefs or islands. **2** polyps producing this. **3** ornament, etc., fashioned from coral.

cord *n* **1** thin rope or thick string. **2** ribbed fabric, such as corduroy. *vt* furnish or fasten with cord.

cordial *adj* sincere; warm; hearty. *n* concentrated fruit juice. **cordially** *adv*.

cordon *n* **1** ornamental cord or badge. **2** line of police, troops, etc., guarding an area.

corduroy *n* thick cotton fabric with a corded or ribbed surface.

core *n* **1** central or innermost part of anything. **2** middle part of an apple or other fleshy fruit, containing the seeds. *vt* remove the core of.

cork *n* **1** porous outer bark of a certain tree (cork oak), used for making bottle stoppers, floats, etc. **2** piece of cork used as a bottle stopper. *vt* stop up with a cork. **corkscrew** *n* device for extracting corks from bottles, usually consisting of a sharp pointed metal spiral.

corn[1] *n* **1** edible grain, esp. the small hard seeds of cereal plants. **2** *US* maize. **cornflakes** *n* breakfast cereal made from flakes of roasted maize. **cornflour** *n* finely ground flour from maize, used mainly to thicken gravies, sauces, etc. **cornflower** *n* blue flower commonly found growing in cornfields.

corn[2] *n* horny growth on the toe or foot, caused by friction of shoes.

corner *n* **1** angle or area formed when two sides, surfaces, or lines meet. **2** nook; secluded place. *vt* **1** force or drive into a difficult position. **2** establish a monopoly.

cornet *n* **1** brass musical instrument with three valves, similar to but smaller and more mellow than a trumpet. **2** cone-shaped wafer for ice cream.

coronation *n* ceremony of crowning a monarch.

coroner *n* public official in charge of an inquest in cases of suspicious death.

coronet *n* small crown.

corporal[1] *adj* relating to the body; physical.

corporal[2] *n* noncommissioned officer below a sergeant in the army or airforce.

corporation *n* **1** body of persons, usually in business, legally authorized to function as an individual. **2** municipal authority or council. **corporate** *adj*.

corporeal *adj* physical; material; not spiritual.

corps (kɔː) *n* **1** military unit comprising several divisions. **2** group of dancers, actors, etc. **3** body of officials, esp. diplomats.

corpse *n* dead human body.

corpuscle (ˈkɔːpʌsəl) *n* small free-floating cell present in the blood.

correct *vt* **1** set right. **2** point out faults or errors. **3** neutralize; counteract. *adj* **1** factual; true; accurate. **2** proper; conforming to a custom or standard. **correction** *n*. **correctly** *adv*.

correlate *vt,vi* have or bring into mutual relation. *n* either of two related things that imply each other. **correlation** *n*.

correspond *vi* **1** conform; match. **2** be similar or equivalent. **3** communicate by exchanging letters. **correspondence** *n* **1** agreement; conformity. **2** communication by letters. **correspondent** *n* **1** person who communicates by letters. **2** person employed by a newspaper, etc., to cover a special area or to report from a foreign country. *adj* similar.

corridor *n* long passageway connecting rooms, railway compartments, etc.

corrode *vt* eat away; eat into the surface of. **corrosion** *n*. **corrosive** *adj,n*.

corrupt *adj* **1** dishonest; open to bribery. **2** depraved; evil. **3** rotten; putrid; tainted. *vt* **1** cause to be dishonest. **2** pervert; debase. **3** taint. **corruptible** *adj*. **corruption** *n*.

corset *n* close-fitting stiffened undergarment that supports and shapes the stomach, worn esp. by women.

cosmetic *n* preparation to beautify the complexion or the hair. *adj* relating to cosmetics.

cosmic *adj* relating to or forming part of the universe.

cosmonaut *n* Soviet astronaut.

cosmopolitan *adj* **1** relating to all parts of the world; worldwide. **2** widely travelled; urbane. *n* person who is widely travelled or sophisticated.

cosmos *n* **1** universe. **2** harmonious system; order.

cost *n* **1** price of something. **2** loss; sacrifice; penalty. **3** expenditure of time, labour, money, etc. **at all costs** *or* **at any cost** regardless of the cost. ~*vt* (cost) **1** have as the price. **2** result in a loss, sacrifice, or penalty. **3** determine or estimate the cost of. **costly** *adj*.

costume *n* style of dress, esp. one indicating a particular period, nationality, etc.

cosy *adj* snug; comfortable. *n* padded cover for keeping a teapot, boiled egg, etc., warm. **cosily** *adv*.

cot *n* **1** child's bed with high sides. **2** portable bed or hammock.

cottage *n* small house, esp. in the country.

cotton *n* **1** plant producing white downy fibres that cover its seeds. **2** thread or cloth produced from these fibres. *v* **cotton on** realize; grasp. **cotton-wool** *n* raw bleached cotton, esp. as used for surgical dressings.

couch *n* upholstered furniture that seats two or more persons. *vt* express in a particular style.

cough *vi* expel air from the lungs with effort and noise. **cough up** *sl* produce; hand over. ~*n* act or sound of coughing.

could *v pt* of **can.**

council *n* administrative or legislative body, esp. one elected to govern a town or district. **councillor** *n*.

counsel *n* **1** advice; guidance. **2** barrister. **3** consultation; debate. *vt* (-ll-) give advice to; recommend. **counsellor** *n* adviser.

count[1] *vt,vi* **1** enumerate; add; reckon up; calculate. **2** list or name numerals in sequence. *vt* take into account; consider. *vi* be of importance; matter. **count on** rely or depend on. **count out** exclude. ~*n* **1** reckoning; calculation. **2** total number. **countdown** *n* period immediately before firing a missile, launching a spacecraft, etc., timed by counting backwards to zero. **countless** *adj* innumerable.

count[2] *n* nobleman of certain European countries, corresponding to a British earl.

counter[1] *n* **1** table or other surface on which money is counted, business transacted, etc. **2** long narrow table at which food is served. **3** small disc used as a token. **under the counter** **1** conducted in a secret or dishonest manner. **2** reserved for special persons, favoured clients, etc.

counter[2] *adv* in the opposite or reverse direction. *adj,n* opposite. *vt,vi* oppose; contradict.

counterattack *n* military attack launched just after an enemy attack. *vt,vi* make such an attack (on).

counterfeit *adj* not genuine; fake; forged. *vt* imitate with intent to deceive; forge. *n* something counterfeited.

counterfoil *n* stub of a cheque, receipt, etc., kept as a record.

counterpart *n* person or thing having an identical or equivalent function.

countess *n* **1** wife or widow of a count or earl. **2** woman of a rank equivalent to a count or earl.

country *n* **1** nation; territory; state. **2** population of a nation. **3** land of birth or residence. **4** rural area as opposed to a town.

county *n* major administrative, political, or judicial division of certain countries or states.

coup (ku:) *n* successful and often unexpected attack, stroke, etc.

couple *n* **1** pair. **2** two people in a relationship. **a couple of** a small number of; a few. ~*vt* **1** link or fasten together. **2** associate mentally. *vi* **1** associate in pairs. **2** unite sexually; copulate.

coupon *n* detachable slip or ticket used when ordering goods, claiming discount, etc.

courage *n* capacity to deal with danger; bravery; boldness. **courageous** *adj*. **courageously** *adv*.

courgette *n* small vegetable marrow.

courier *n* **1** special or express messenger. **2** person employed to take care of tourists and their travel arrangements.

course *n* **1** movement in space or time. **2** direction of movement; route. **3** type of action or conduct. **4** duration. **5** area or stretch of land over which a race is run, golf is played, etc. **6** series of lessons, sessions, etc. **7** any of the sequential parts of a meal. **in the course of** during. **of course** certainly; in fact. ~*vi* move or flow quickly.

court *n* **1** *also* **courtyard** space enclosed by buildings. **2** area marked off or enclosed for playing games, such as tennis or squash. **3** household or establishment of a sovereign. **4** body with judicial powers; tribunal. **5** building or room in which a trial or tribunal is held. **6** attention; homage. *vt,vi* **1** seek the affection of (a member of the opposite sex). **2** seek the approval or support of. **court card** *n* playing card that is a king, queen, or jack; face card. **court-martial** *n pl* **courts-martial** court of officers for trying naval, airforce, or army offences. **courtship** *n* courting of a woman.

courtesy *n* polite behaviour or disposition. **courteous** *adj*.

cousin *n* son or daughter of one's uncle or aunt.

cove *n* **1** small inlet; sheltered bay. **2** nook or recess.

covenant *n* **1** agreement; bargain. **2** sealed contract or one of its clauses. *vt,vi* agree to or enter into a covenant.

cover *vt* **1** place or spread over. **2** overlie. **3** shield or conceal. **4** include. **5** protect by insurance. **6** report (an event) for a newspaper, etc. *n* **1** anything that covers. **2** funds to meet possible liability or loss. **coverage** *n* extent, amount, or risk covered.

cow *n* **1** female of the ox family, esp. one kept by farmers for milk. **2** female of certain other animals, such as the elephant, whale, and seal. **cowboy** *n* herdsman in charge of cattle on the western plains of North America, esp. one on horseback.

coward *n* person given to fear. **cowardice** *n*. **cowardly** *adj*. **cower** *vi* crouch in fear or shame; tremble.

coy *adj* shy; modest; slow to respond, esp. deliberately. **coyly** *adv*. **coyness** *n*.

crab *n* **1** ten-legged shellfish. **2** flesh of the crab, used as food. **3** ill-tempered person. **4** species of small apple. *vi* (-bb-) criticize; find fault.

crack *vi,vt* **1** break into pieces; form fissures. **2** make or cause to make a sharp sound. **3** change suddenly in tone; become hoarse. *vt* **1** strike sharply. **2** *inf* open; break into. **3** *inf* find the solution to. **4** tell (a joke). *vi also* **crack up** have a physical or mental breakdown. *n* **1** sharp explosive noise. **2** split or fissure. **cracker** **1** thin crisp biscuit. **2** exploding firework. **3** paper and cardboard Christmas toy that emits a bang when pulled apart. **crackle** *n* **1** sound of rapid repeated cracking. **2** network of fine cracks. *vi* emit a sharp crackling sound.

cradle *n* **1** infant's bed. **2** supporting frame. **3** origin or home. *vt* hold in or as if in a cradle.

craft *n* **1** skilled trade. **2** manual skill. **3** cunning. **4** boat; vessel. **craftsman** *n*. **craftsmanship** *n*. **crafty** *adj* cunning; artful. **craftily** *adv*.

crag *n* rugged projecting rock or rock mass.

cram *v* (-mm-) *vt* fill or pack tightly. *vt,vi* **1** study intensively, as just before an examination. **2** eat greedily.

cramp[1] *n* sudden painful involuntary contraction of a muscle.

cramp[2] *n* clamp for holding things together. *vt* **1** hold with a cramp. **2** hem in; keep within too narrow limits; hinder. **cramp someone's style** hinder someone from doing his best, etc.

crane *n* **1** large wading bird with long legs, neck, and bill. **2** machine for moving heavy objects. *vi* stretch the neck (for a better view).

crash *n* **1** violent noisy impact, fall, etc. **2** burst of mixed loud sound, such as thunder. **3** sudden downfall or collapse. *vi,vt* **1** make or cause to make a crash. **2** fall or strike with a crash. **3** involve or be involved in a collision.

crate *n* large packing case. *vt* pack in a crate.

crater *n* **1** bowl-shaped cavity or depression, such as one made by a meteorite on the earth or moon or by an exploding bomb. **2** mouth of a volcano. **cratered** *adj*.

crave *vt,vi* have a strong desire (for); yearn (for). **craving** *n*.

crawl *vi* **1** move along on the ground, etc., on the stomach or on the hands and knees. **2** move or progress very slowly. **3** creep or go stealthily or abjectly. **4** behave abjectly. *n* **1** act of crawling. **2** *also* **front crawl** fast swimming stroke.

crayfish *n* freshwater shellfish resembling a lobster.

crayon *n* stick of coloured chalk or wax used for drawing.

craze *n* **1** mania, tremendous liking. **2** temporary fashion. *vt* **1** impair mentally; drive insane. **2** make small cracks in. *vi* become insane. **crazy** *adj* **1** insane; mad. **2** eccentric; peculiar. **3** unsound; shaky. **4** *inf* wildly enthusiastic or excited (about). **crazily** *adv*. **craziness** *n*.

creak *vi* make a sharp squeaking or grating sound. *n* such a sound. **creaky** *adj*.

cream *n* **1** fatty part of milk. **2** dish or delicacy resembling or made of cream. **3** creamlike substance, esp. a cosmetic. **4** best part of anything. *n,adj* yellowish-white. *vt* **1** beat (a mixture, etc.) until light and smooth. **2** remove the cream from. **3** apply a cream to. **creamy** *adj*.

crease *n* **1** line made by folding. **2** wrinkle. *vt,vi* make or develop creases.

create *vt* **1** bring into being. **2** give rise to. **3** make; produce. **creation** *n* **1** act of creating or state of being created. **2** something created, esp. an original design, work of art, etc. **3** universe and all living creatures. **creative** *adj* having the ability to create; original; inventive. **creativity** *n.*

creature *n* **1** living being, esp. an animal. **2** contemptible or pitiful person.

crèche *n* **1** nursery for infants. **2** model of the Nativity scene.

credible *adj* believable; worthy of belief.

credit *n* **1** system of doing business without immediate receipt or payment of cash. **2** power to purchase items, services, etc., by deferred payment. **3** money at one's disposal in a bank, etc. **4** belief; trust. **5** source of honour, reputation, etc. **6** good name; reputation. **7** influence; respect; commendation. **8** acknowledgement of authorship, direction, performance, etc. *vt* **1** believe; trust; have faith in. **2** attribute; acknowledge. **3** give credit for. **credit card** *n* card that identifies and authorizes the holder to obtain goods or services on deferred payment. **creditor** *n* person, etc., to whom money is owed.

creep *vi* (crept) **1** move like a snake; crawl. **2** move stealthily, quietly, or very slowly. **3** feel a shrinking shivering sensation due to fear, repugnance, etc. *n* **1** creeping movement. **2** *sl* servile or unpleasant person. **creeps** *pl n* feeling of fear, repugnance, etc. **creeper** *n* plant, such as ivy, that trails over ground, etc., by means of roots, tendrils, etc., along its stem.

cremate *vt* dispose of (a corpse) by burning. **cremation** *n.* **crematorium** *n* place where corpses are cremated.

crept *v pt* or *pp* of creep.

crescent *n* **1** waxing or waning moon. **2** narrow curved and pointed figure or symbol. **3** curved row of houses.

cress *n* plant of the mustard family, whose leaves are used in salads or as a garnish.

crest *n* **1** comb or tuft on an animal's head. **2** plume on top of a helmet. **3** top of a wave, mountain ridge, etc. *vt* reach or lie on the top of. *vi* form or rise into a crest. **crestfallen** *adj* dejected.

crevice *n* fissure; narrow split or crack.

crew *n* persons that man a boat, ship, aircraft, etc.

crib *n* **1** child's cot. **2** barred rack for fodder. *vt,vi* (-bb-) *inf* copy unfairly; plagiarize.

cricket[1] *n* chirping leaping insect.

cricket[2] *n* **1** team game played on a grass pitch with bats, ball, and wickets. **2** *inf* fair play.

cried *v pt* or *pp* of **cry.**

crime *n* **1** serious violation of the law. **2** wicked act; sin; grave offence. **3** *inf* senseless or foolish act. **4** unlawful acts in general. **criminal** *n* person guilty or convicted of crime. *adj* **1** relating to or involving crime or its punishment; guilty of crime. **2** wicked; senseless.

crimson *n,adj* deep rich red.

cringe *vi* cower; crouch; shrink back. *n* act of cringing.

crinkle *vt,vi,n* **1** wrinkle; twist. **2** rustle.

cripple *n* lame or disabled person. *vt* **1** disable; maim; make a cripple of. **2** damage, esp. financially. **crippling** *adj* damaging.

crisis *n, pl* **crises** ('kraisi:z) **1** time of acute danger, stress, suspense, etc. **2** turning point; decisive moment.

crisp *adj* **1** brittle; dry; crackling. **2** brisk. **3** clear-cut; sharp; lively. **4** fresh. *n* fine slice of fried potato. **crisply** *adv.* **crispness** *n.*

criterion *n, pl* **criteria** (kraiˈtiəriə) standard of judgement or comparison; test.

critic *n* **1** person who passes judgment or criticizes. **2** expert in assessing the merits of works of art, literature, drama, etc. **critical** *adj* **1** given to judging, fault-finding, etc. **2** of great importance; decisive. **3** involving suspense or risk. **4** relating to critics or criticism. **critically** *adv.* **criticism** *n* **1** severe judgment; disapproval. **2** assessment; review; analysis; evaluation. **criticize** *vt,vi* **1** judge severely; censure. **2** examine critically; evaluate.

croak *n* deep hoarse cry or sound. *vi,vt* utter or speak with a croak. **croakily** *adv.* **croaky** *adj.*

crochet *n* type of knitting done with a single hooked needle. *vt,vi* do such work.

crockery *n* china or earthenware vessels.

crocodile *n* **1** large predatory amphibious reptile of the tropics, with armour-like skin, long tapering snout, and massive jaws. **2** long line of schoolchildren.

crocus *n* small bulbous plant with yellow, purple, or white flowers.

crook *n* **1** criminal; swindler. **2** hooked staff. **3** sharp turn or bend. *vt* bend; curve; make a crook in. **crooked** *adj* **1** bent; curved. **2** set at an angle; askew. **3** *inf* dishonest.

crop *n* **1** cultivated produce. **2** harvest of this. **3** group of things occurring together. **4** pouch in a bird's gullet. **5** stock of a whip. **6** hunting or riding whip. **7** closely cut head of hair. *vt* (-pp-) **1** clip; cut short; cut off. **2** raise or harvest produce. **crop up** *inf* occur, arise, etc., unexpectedly.

croquet *n* lawn game played with wooden balls and mallets and wire hoops.

cross *n* **1** upright stake with a transverse bar. **2** model, mark, or figure of a cross, esp. as a Christian emblem or symbol of Christianity. **3** sign of the Cross made with the hand. **4** intermixture of breeds, qualities, etc. **5** misfortune; trouble. **the Cross 1** cross on which Jesus died. **2** model or picture of this. ~*vt* **1** place so as to intersect. **2** make the sign of the Cross on or over. **3** pass across. **4** meet and pass. **5** mark with lines across. **6** oppose; thwart. **7** modify a breed of animals or plants by intermixture. *vi* **1** intersect. **2** pass over. *adj* **1** out of temper. **2** transverse. **3** intersecting. **4** contrary; adverse. **cross-examine** *vt* examine a witness already examined by the other side. **cross examination** *n*. **cross-eyed** *adj* having a squint. **cross-fire** *n* **1** sharp verbal exchange. **2** crossing of two or more lines of fire. **crossing** *n* **1** act of crossing. **2** intersection of roads, rails, etc. **3** special place for crossing easily, safely, etc. **cross-question** *vt* cross-examine. **cross-reference** *n* reference from one word, part, etc., in a book to another. *vt,vi also* **cross-refer** make a cross-reference. **crossword** *n* puzzle in which words are written horizontally and vertically in numbered spaces according to numbered clues.

crotchet *n* musical note or symbol equal to quarter of a semibreve. **crotchety** *adj inf* cross; quick-tempered.

crouch *vi* **1** huddle down close to the ground, floor, etc. **2** cringe; fawn. *n* crouching position.

crow[1] *n* large black bird with glossy feathers.

crow[2] *vi* **1** *inf* boast. **2** utter a shrill cry.

crowd *vi* flock together. *vt* **1** cram or pack. **2** fill with people. *n* large number; throng. **crowded** *adj*.

crown *n* **1** monarch's headdress. **2** wreath for the head. **3** royal power. **4** former coin. **5** top, as of the head. **6** completion; perfection. *vt* **1** put a crown on. **2** make a king or queen. **3** honour; reward; invest with dignity, etc. **4** bring to completion or perfection. **crown prince** *n* male next in line to the throne.

crucial *adj* decisive; critical.

crucifix *n* cross, esp. one with a figure of Jesus crucified on it. **crucifixion** *n* crucifying, esp. of Jesus. **crucify** *vt* **1** put to death by nailing or tying to a cross. **2** treat severely; torment.

crude *adj* **1** in the natural or raw state. **2** unfinished; rough. **3** without grace; unpolished. **4** blunt; vulgar. **crudely** *adv*. **crudeness** *or* **crudity** *n*. **crude oil** *n* petroleum before it is made into petrol or other products.

cruel *adj* **1** delighting in the pain or suffering of others; heartless. **2** enjoying the infliction of pain on others. **3** distressing; painful. **cruelty** *n*.

cruise *vi* **1** sail about, esp. for pleasure. **2** fly, drive, etc., at moderate speed. *n* act of cruising. **cruiser** *n* armed high-speed naval ship of light or medium displacement.

crumb *n* small particle; fragment, esp. of bread. *vt* break into or cover with crumbs.

crumble *vt,vi* **1** break into small fragments. **2** decay; fall to pieces. *n* baked fruit pudding with a crumbled cake-like topping.

crumple *vt,vi,n* crease; wrinkle.

crunch *vt,vi* crush, grind, or chew noisily. *n* **1** act or sound of crunching. **2** *sl* critical moment.

crusade *n* **1** *also* **Crusade** medieval Christian war to recover the Holy Land from the Turks. **2** campaign in favour of a cause. *vi* participate in a crusade.

crush *vt* **1** compress so as to break, bruise, or crumple. **2** break into small pieces. **3** defeat utterly. *n* **1** act of crushing. **2** crowded mass, esp. of people.

crust *n* **1** hard outer surface of bread. **2** any hard or firm outer part, deposit, or casing. **3** surface of the earth. *vt,vi* cover with or form a crust. **crusty** *adj* **1** having or like a crust. **2** ill-tempered. **crustily** *adv*.

crustacean *n* hard-shelled animal with antennae, usually living in water, such as a crab or lobster.

crutch *n* **1** support for a lame person that fits under the armpit. **2** something needed for moral or psychological support.

crux *n* **1** real issue. **2** hard problem.

cry *vi* **1** weep; shed tears. **2** cry out; shout. **3**

(esp. of animals) utter a characteristic sound. *vt* utter or implore loudly. **cry for** beg for. **cry off** break a promise; withdraw from an agreement. ~*n* **1** loud utterance. **2** call of an animal or bird. **3** fit of weeping. **a far cry 1** long way. **2** very different.

crypt *n* underground chamber or vault, esp. one beneath a church, used for burials, etc. **cryptic** *adj* secret; hidden; mysterious.

crystal *n* **1** transparent piece of mineral **2** form of certain substances having a definite internal structure and external surfaces that intersect at characteristic angles. **3** very clear glass. **4** cut-glass vessels. **5** something made of or resembling crystal. **crystalline** *adj*. **crystallize** *vt,vi* **1** form into crystals. **2** become or cause to be definite or certain.

cub *n* **1** young of certain animals, such as lions or bears. **2** inexperienced person.

cube *n* **1** regular solid figure bounded by six equal squares. **2** cube-shaped or nearly cube-shaped block. **3** product obtained by multiplying a number by itself twice. **cubic** *adj* **1** having the shape of a cube. **2** relating to volume or volume measure. **3** having three dimensions.

cubicle *n* small room or walled-off space, as for sleeping, dressing, studying, etc.

cuckoo *n* widely distributed bird named from the sound of its call.

cucumber *n* long fleshy green edible fruit, commonly used in salads.

cuddle *vt* hug; fondle. *vi* lie close. *n* hug; affectionate embrace.

cue[1] *n* **1** words or actions used as a guide or signal. **2** hint.

cue[2] *n* long tapered rod with a soft tip used to strike the ball in billiards, etc.

cuff[1] *n* end of a sleeve; wrist-band. **off the cuff** without preparation; improvised.

cuff[2] *vt* hit with the open hand. *n* such a blow.

culinary *adj* relating to or used in cooking or the kitchen.

culprit *n* guilty person; offender.

cult *n* **1** system of religious worship. **2** devotion to or pursuit of some object.

cultivate *vt* **1** raise (crops) on land; grow. **2** develop; improve; refine. **cultivation** *n*.

culture *n* **1** intellectual, behavioural, and artistic ideas, beliefs, etc., of a particular group, time, or place. **2** particular form or stage of civilization. **3** development and training of the mind. **4** refinement of taste, manners, etc. **5** cultivation. **cultural** *adj*. **cultured** *adj* **1** refined. **2** grown in an artificial medium.

cumbersome *adj* **1** troublesome; vexatious. **2** clumsy; unwieldy.

cunning *n* **1** dexterity; skill. **2** skill in deceit or evasion. *adj* having such qualities or characteristics. **cunningly** *adv*.

cup *n* **1** drinking vessel, esp. one with a handle. **2** any cup-shaped formation, depression, cavity, etc. **3** prize in the shape of a cup. **4** fruit-flavoured wine, cider, etc. **one's cup of tea** what especially or particularly suits one; what one likes. ~*vt* (-pp-) form (one's hand) into a hollow shape.

cupboard *n* closed cabinet, usually with shelves.

curate *n* assistant to a parish priest or vicar.

curator *n* person in charge of a museum, a specific collection, etc.

curb *n* **1** check or means of restraint; control. **2** framework or border that encloses. *vt* restrain; control, check.

curd *n* substance obtained by coagulating milk, used as food or in cheese-making. **curdle** *vt vi* form into curd.

cure *vt* **1** heal; remedy. **2** preserve (fish, skins, etc.). *n* **1** remedy. **2** course of medical treatment. **3** restoration to health.

curfew *n* **1** restriction on movement after nightfall or a signal indicating that this is to be enforced. **2** time at which such a signal is given.

curiosity *n* **1** eagerness to know; inquisitiveness. **2** strange, rare, or odd object.

curious *adj* **1** eager to know; inquisitive. **2** prying; tending to meddle. **3** exciting interest. **4** odd; eccentric. **curiously** *adv*.

curl *vt,vi* bend into a curved shape or spiral. *n* **1** spiral lock of hair. **2** spiral or curved form, state, or motion. **curly** *adj*. **curling** *n* game played on ice with large rounded stones.

currant *n* small seedless raisin.

currency *n* **1** time during which anything is current. **2** state of being in use. **3** money.

current *adj* **1** in general use or circulation. **2** going on; not yet superseded. *n* **1** moving body of water or air. **2** flow of something, such as a river. **3** movement of electric charge through a conductor or the rate of its flow.

curry *n* **1** oriental dish flavoured with hot spices.

2 spicy seasoning. *vt* add curry to (food) while cooking.

curse *n* **1** obscene or profane utterance. **2** utterance designed to destroy or harm someone. **3** affliction; bane; scourge. *vi* swear. *vt* **1** abuse by uttering curses at. **2** call on supernatural powers to bring harm to (someone).

curt *adj* **1** short. **2** rudely brief. **curtly** *adv*. **curtness** *n*.

curtail *vt* cut short; end. **curtailment** *n*.

curtain *n* **1** cloth, etc., hung as a screen in front of a window or door. **2** screen between the audience and a stage. **3** end to an act or scene. *vt* provide or cover with a curtain.

curtsy *n* formal woman's bow made as a sign of respect, greeting, etc. *vi* make such a bow.

curve *n* **1** line with no straight parts. **2** bend in a road, etc. **3** curved form or object. *vt,vi* bend in a curve. **curvature** *n*.

cushion *n* **1** bag or pad filled with soft stuffing or air, used to sit on, lean against, etc. **2** something that absorbs shocks, jolts, etc. *vt* provide or protect with a cushion.

custard *n* cooked dessert of flavoured eggs and milk.

custody *n* **1** safe-keeping; guardianship. **2** imprisonment. **custodian** *n* person having custody of someone or something.

custom *n* **1** established or habitual practice, usage, etc. **2** business patronage. **3** customers of a shop, business, etc. **customs** *pl n* **1** duties levied on certain imports. **2** area in an airport, etc., where such duties are collected. **customary** *adj* usual. **customer** *n* **1** buyer; patron. **2** *inf* fellow; chap.

cut *vt* (-tt-; cut) **1** sever; penetrate. **2** divide; separate. **3** detach, trim, or shape by cutting. **4** abridge; shorten. **5** ignore (someone). **6** strike (with a whip, sword, etc.). **cut down 1** reduce. **2** fell (trees). **3** *inf* kill. **cut it fine** leave very small margin of time, etc. **cut off 1** discontinue supply of (gas, etc.). **2** interrupt. **3** separate; isolate. **cut out 1** cut (pieces, etc.) from something. **2** remove. **3** suit or equip for. **4** cease to operate. **cut up 1** chop into small pieces. **2** *inf* upset; distress. ~*n* **1** act or result of cutting. **2** incision. **3** engraving. **4** piece cut off. **5** division. **a cut above** superior to. *adj* **cut and dried** settled. **cut-price** *adj* below the normally charged price. **cutting** *n* **1** act of cutting or thing cut off or out. **2** newspaper clipping. **3** piece cut from a plant for replanting.

cute *adj* **1** quaint; sweet. **2** clever; sharp. **cutely** *adv*. **cuteness** *n*.

cuticle *n* skin at the edges of the nails.

cutlery *n* **1** knives and other cutting implements. **2** eating implements.

cutlet *n* small piece of meat, esp. for frying or grilling.

cycle *n* **1** recurrent or complete series or period. **2** development following a course of stages. **3** series of poems, etc. **4** short for **bicycle.** *vi* **1** move in cycles. **2** ride a bicycle. **cyclic** *or* **cyclical** *adj*. **cyclist** *n* person who rides a bicycle.

cyclone *n* system of winds moving round a centre of low pressure.

cygnet *n* young swan.

cylinder *n* **1** tube-shaped figure, usually with a circular base. **2** piston chamber of an engine. **cylindrical** *adj*.

cymbal *n* saucer-shaped piece of brass used as a musical instrument of percussion.

cynic *n* sceptical or distrusting person. **cynical** *adj*. **cynicism** *n*.

cypress *n* coniferous tree having dark foliage and durable wood.

cyst *n* abnormal sac containing bodily secretions.

czar *n* tsar.

D

dab *vt,vi* (-bb-) touch gently; apply with a light touch. *n* **1** gentle blow. **2** small lump of soft substance.

dabble *vt,vi* move about in water or other liquid. *vi* engage in some activity in a superficial manner. **dabbler** *n*.

dad *n inf* father.

daffodil *n* variety of yellow narcissus.

daft *adj* silly; feeble-minded.

dagger *n* short stabbing weapon with a double-edged blade.

daily *adj* performed, occurring, etc., every day. *adv* every day. *n* **1** daily newspaper. **2** non-resident domestic help.

dainty *adj* **1** pretty; elegant. **2** fastidious; delicate. **daintily** *adv*. **daintiness** *n*.

dairy *n* place for keeping, processing, or supplying milk and milk products. **dairy farm** *n* farm producing milk and milk products.

daisy *n* small white-petalled flower with a yellow centre.

dam[1] *n* barrier to hold back water. *vt* (-mm-) obstruct or hold back with a dam.

dam[2] *n* female parent, esp. of an animal.

damage *vt,vi* injure; harm; impair; spoil. *n* harm; injury. **damages** *pl n* financial compensation awarded by law for loss or harm.

dame *n* lady, esp. a mistress of a household or school. **Dame** title of a female member of an order of knighthood.

damn *vt* **1** curse; doom; condemn to hell. **2** censure. *interj* expression of anger or annoyance. **damnable** *adj* **1** deserving condemnation. **2** wretched. **damnation** *n* state of being damned.

damp *adj* moist; slightly wet. *n* moisture. *vt also* **dampen 1** moisten. **2** depress; discourage.

damson *n* small purple fruit of the plum family.

dance *n* **1** sequence of rhythmical steps usually performed to music. **2** social gathering for dancing. *vt,vi* **1** perform (a dance). **2** move quickly, energetically, or gracefully. **dance attendance (on)** attend constantly. **dancer** *n*.

dandelion *n* plant with bright yellow flowers and leaves with jagged edges.

dandruff *n* flakes of scurf formed on the scalp.

danger *n* exposure to risk of harm; peril; risk. **dangerous** *adj*. **dangerously** *adv*.

dangle *vt,vi* swing loosely; hang freely.

dare *vt,vi* be brave enough (to do something). *vt* challenge; defy. *n* challenge to do something. **daring** *adj* bold; adventurous. *n* boldness; audacity.

dark *adj* **1** without light. **2** deeply tinted; brown or almost black. **3** mysterious; secret; evil. *n* **1** absence of light; night. **2** ignorance; secrecy. **darkness** *n*. **darken** *vt,vi* make or become dark(er).

darling *n* person greatly loved; favourite. *adj* greatly loved or desired.

darn *vt,vi* mend (a hole in fabric) by stitching over. *n* repair so made.

dart *n* **1** small pointed missile, such as a short arrow. **2** swift sudden movement. **3** short seam or tuck in a garment. *vi,vt* move swiftly and suddenly; shoot out. **darts** *n* game in which darts are thrown at a circular board (dartboard).

dash *vi* rush hastily. *vt* **1** hurl; thrust; knock violently. **2** discourage; ruin. *n* **1** sudden rush. **2** small quantity, esp. as a flavouring in food or drink. **3** punctuation mark (-) used to indicate a pause, change of subject, etc. **4** energy; vigour. **dashing** *adj* **1** showy; stylish. **2** impetuous; spirited. **dashboard** *n* instrument panel of a motor vehicle.

data *n s or pl* facts, figures, statistics, etc., used as a basis for discussion or calculation.

date[1] *n* **1** day on which an event occurs or a statement of this in days, months, and years. **2** *inf* appointment; rendezvous. **3** person with whom one has an appointment. *vt* **1** determine the date of. **2** *inf* make an appointment, esp. with a member of the opposite sex. **date from** originate from a certain date.

date[2] *n* sweet oblong single-stoned fruit of the date palm.

daughter *n* **1** female offspring, esp. in relation to her parents. **2** any female descendant. **daughter-in-law** *n, pl* **daughters-in-law** son's wife.

dawdle *vi* move slowly; loiter; fall or lag behind. **dawdler** *n*.

dawn *n* **1** period during which the sun rises; daybreak. **2** beginning. *vi* **1** begin to grow light. **2** begin to appear or develop. **dawn upon** become evident to.

day *n* **1** period between sunrise and sunset. **2** period of 24 hours beginning at midnight. **daybreak** *n* dawn. **daydream** *n* pleasant sequence of thoughts or musing while awake. *vi* have daydreams. **daylight** *n* light from the sun.

daze *vt* stupefy; bewilder; stun. *n* state of being dazed or stunned; drowsiness.

dazzle *vt* **1** blind temporarily with brilliant light. **2** confuse or surprise with brilliance, beauty, etc.

dead *adj* **1** without life; having died. **2** dull; numb; resembling death. **3** extinct; no longer active. **deaden** *vt* make insensible; numb; dull the vitality of. **deadline** *n* time by which some task must be completed. **deadlock** *n* complete standstill in which further progress is impossible. **deadly** *adj* **1** fatal; poisonous. **2** like death.

deaf *adj* **1** lacking or deficient in the sense of hearing. **2** unwilling to listen. **deafen** *vt* **1** make deaf. **2** make impervious to sound. **deafness** *n*.

deal *v* (dealt) *vt,vi* distribute, esp. playing cards to the players. *vt* inflict; deliver. *vi* do business; trade. **deal with** manage; settle. ~*n* **1** business transaction. **2** distribution of playing cards. **3** *inf* amount. **dealer** *n*.

dean *n* **1** head clergyman of a cathedral. **2** college or university official.

dear *adj* **1** much loved; precious. **2** expensive; costly. *n* someone much loved. *adv* at high cost. **dearly** *adv* **dearness** *n*.

death *n* **1** end of life; state of being dead. **2** dying. **3** cause of death. **deathly** *adj* resembling death; lifeless; pale.

debase *vt* undervalue; lower in value; degrade.

debate *n* **1** formal public discussion. **2** argument; controversy. *vt,vi* discuss; argue (about). **debatable** *adj* open to discussion; questionable.

debit *n* **1** record in an account of money owed. **2** debt; something owed. *vt* record as money owing; charge.

debris *n* wreckage; fragments.

debt *n* **1** something owed. **2** obligation. **in debt** **1** owing money. **2** having an obligation. **debtor** *n* person who is in debt to another.

decade *n* period of ten years.

decadent *adj* **1** declining or deteriorating, esp. morally. **2** corrupted. **decadence** *n*.

decant *vt* pour liquid gently from one vessel to another. **decanter** *n* glass vessel for serving wine.

decapitate *vt* sever or chop off the head of. **decapitation** *n*.

decay *vi* **1** decompose, rot. **2** deteriorate, decline. *n* **1** decomposition. **2** deterioration, decline.

decease *n* death. *vi* die.

deceive *vt,vi* mislead deliberately; delude; cheat. **deceit** *n*. **deceitful** *adj*. **deceitfully** *adv*.

December *n* twelfth month of the year.

decent *adj* **1** respectable; proper; modest. **2** *inf* fairly good; adequate. **decency** *n*. **decently** *adv*.

deceptive *adj* tending to deceive or give a false impression. **deception** *n*.

decibel *n* unit for measuring intensities of sounds.

decide *vt* give judgment on; settle. *vi* make up one's mind; conclude. **decided** *adj* **1** certain; definite. **2** resolute. **decidedly** *adv*.

deciduous *adj* **1** (of leaves, teeth, etc.) shed periodically. **2** (of trees) shedding leaves annually.

decimal *adj* based on the number ten, numbered or proceeding by tens. *n also* **decimal fraction** fraction having a denominator that is a power of ten, written with a dot in front of the numerator.

decipher *vt* **1** decode. **2** make out the meaning of.

decision *n* **1** judgment, settlement; conclusion. **2** firmness; determination. **decisive** *adj* **1** conclusive; deciding. **2** resolute; firm. **decisively** *adv*.

deck *n* **1** horizontal platform forming the floor of a ship, bus, etc. **2** pack of cards. *vt* adorn, decorate. **deckchair** *n* portable folding chair with a canvas back.

declare *vt,vi* **1** announce formally; proclaim; assert. **2** state that one has an income, goods, etc., on which duty or tax must be paid. **3** close an innings in cricket before all the wickets have fallen. **declaration** *n*.

declension *n* **1** change in form of a noun, pronoun, or adjective depending on its case. **2** decline; deterioration.

decline *vt,vi* **1** slope downwards. **2** deteriorate; decay. **3** refuse. *n* gradual deterioration; loss of strength, vigour, etc.

decode *vt* interpret from a code; decipher.

decompose *vt,vi* putrefy; rot; decay. **decomposition** *n*.

decorate *vt* **1** embellish; adorn. **2** restore with new paint, wallpaper, etc. **3** invest with a medal, badge, etc. **decoration** *n*. **decorative** *adj*. **decorator** *n*.

decoy *n* something used to attract others into a trap; lure.

decrease *vt,vi* diminish; make or grow less; reduce. *n* process of or amount of lessening; reduction.

decree *n* official decision, judgment, or law. *vt,vi* command; judge, order.

decrepit *adj* worn out; old and useless.

dedicate *vt* **1** devote solemnly or wholly. **2** set apart for a special purpose. **3** inscribe or address as a compliment. **dedication** *n*.

deduce *vt* draw as a conclusion from given facts; infer. **deduct** *vt* take away; subtract. **deduction** *n* **1** act of deducting. **2** amount deducted. **3** logical reasoning from given facts. **4** the conclusion reached.

deed *n* **1** something done; action; exploit. **2**

legal document stating terms of a contract, rights, etc.

deep *adj* **1** extending far down, in, or across. **2** at or of a specified distance down or in. **3** profound; intense; serious. **4** absorbed; engrossed. **5** low-pitched. **6** dark-coloured. *adv also* **deeply** so as to be deep. *n* deep place, esp. in the sea. **deepness** *n*. **deepen** *vt,vi* make or become deep(er). **deep-freeze** *n* refrigerator to keep food fresh for long periods. **deeply** *adv* strongly; profoundly; extremely. **deep-seated** *adj* firmly established; not superficial.

deer *n, pl* **deer** ruminant, the male of which has deciduous antlers.

deface *vt* spoil the appearance or surface of; disfigure. **defacement** *n*.

defame *vt* injure the good name or reputation of, as by libel, slander, etc. **defamation** *n*. **defamatory** *adj*.

default *n* **1** absence; want. **2** failure to act or appear. *vi* fail to act or appear as required. **defaulter** *n*.

defeat *vt* conquer; vanquish; overcome; beat. *n* act of being beaten or conquered.

defect *n* ('di:fekt) failing; blemish; imperfection; fault; flaw. *vi* (di'fekt) desert one's country, duty, etc.; switch allegiance. **defection** *n*. **defector** *n*. **defective** *adj* imperfect; faulty; deficient.

defend *vt,vi* **1** protect against attack. **2** justify, as in answer to a legal charge. **defence** *n*. **defences** *pl n* **1** fortifications. **2** self-protective attitudes. **defensive** *adj* protective; resisting attack. **defensively** *adv*.

defer[1] *vt,vi* (-rr-) postpone; put off.

defer[2] *vi* (-rr-) make concessions; submit (to). **deference** *n* respectful submission to another's will. **deferential** *adj*.

defiant *adj* stubbornly or aggressively hostile; insolent. **defiance** *n*. **defiantly** *adv*.

deficient *adj* incomplete; defective; lacking. **deficiency** *n*.

deficit *n* lack or shortage, esp. of money.

define *vt* **1** mark out; show the limits of. **2** describe exactly; give the meaning of.

definite *adj* **1** certain; fixed; exact. **2** clear distinct. **definite article** *n* the word 'the **definitely** *adv*.

definition *n* **1** act of defining. **2** brief description or explanation, esp. of a word or phrase. **3** quality of distinctness or clarity.

deflate *vt,vi* **1** release air from or lose air. **2** reduce economic inflation. **3** lessen the dignity or conceit of. **deflation** *n*. **deflationary** *adj*.

deflect *vt,vi* turn or move at an angle. **deflection** *n*.

deform *vt* spoil the shape of; make ugly; disfigure. **deformation** *n*. **deformity** *n*.

defraud *vt* cheat; swindle; deprive by fraud.

defrost *vt* remove ice from.

deft *adj* skilful; nimble. **deftly** *adv*. **deftness** *n*.

defunct *adj* obsolete; no longer used.

defy *vt* **1** challenge; resist stubbornly. **2** disobey.

degenerate *vi* (di'dʒenəreit) decline in standard or qualities; deteriorate. *adj* (di'dʒenərət) degraded; depraved. *n* (di'dʒenərət) degenerate person. **degeneration** *or* **degeneracy** *n*.

degrade *vt,vi* **1** reduce in grade or rank. **2** lower in character; debase; humiliate. **degradation** *n*.

degree *n* **1** grade; stage; relative position; extent. **2** academic rank awarded for proficiency or as an honour. **3** unit of measurement in temperature scales. **4** unit of angular measure; 1/360th part of a complete turn.

dehydrate *vt* remove water from. **dehydration** *n*.

deity *n* god or goddess.

dejected *adj* depressed; despondent; sad; miserable.

delay *vt* cause to be late; postpone. *vi* be late; linger. *n* act of delaying; fact or period of being delayed; postponement.

delegate *vt* ('deligeit) **1** send or elect as a representative. **2** entrust to as a deputy. *n* ('deligət) representative; deputy; agent. **delegation** *n* **1** number of delegates in a group. **2** act of delegating.

delete *vt* strike out; erase; remove. **deletion** *n*.

deliberate *vi* (di'libəreit) reflect; consider carefully. *adj* (di'libərət) **1** intentional; purposeful. **2** slow in deciding; cautious. **deliberately** *adv*. **deliberation** *n*.

delicate *adj* **1** finely made or prepared; pleasing. **2** sensitive; easily hurt or damaged. **3** refined; fastidious. **delicacy** *n* **1** sensitivity; tact. **2** refinement; gracefulness. **3** attractive and tasty food. **delicately** *adv*.

delicatessen *n* shop specializing in foreign food, cooked meats, delicacies, etc. *pl n* the foods sold.

delicious *adj* **1** pleasing, esp. to the senses of taste or smell. **2** delightful.

delight *vt* give great pleasure to. **delight in** take pleasure in. ~*n* intense pleasure or joy or a cause of this. **delightful** *adj*. **delightfully** *adv*.

delinquency *n* neglect of duty; wrongdoing; petty crime. **delinquent** *n,adj*.

deliver *vt* **1** set free; liberate. **2** hand over or distribute (mail, goods, etc.). **3** give forth; discharge. **4** pronounce; utter. **5** assist at the birth of. **deliverance** *n* liberation; rescue. **delivery** *n* **1** delivering of mail, goods, a speech, etc. **2** childbirth.

delta *n* fan-shaped area of land at the mouth of a river.

delude *vt* deceive; mislead. **delusion** *n*. **delusive** *adj*.

deluge *n* violent flood. *vt* rush upon or at, as a flood; inundate.

delve *vt,vi* **1** dig. **2** *also* **delve into** research deeply (into).

demand *vt* **1** ask for; claim; request urgently. **2** require; need. *n* pressing request or requirement.

democracy *n* **1** government by the people, esp. by majority vote; equality of rights. **2** state or community so governed. **democrat** *n*. **democratic** *adj*.

demolish *vt* destroy; pull down. **demolition** *n*.

demon *n* **1** devil; evil spirit. **2** cruel or wicked person. **demonic** *adj*.

demonstrate *vt* show by reasoning or practical example; prove; explain. *vi* manifest opposition or sympathy in public; make a protest. **demonstrable** *adj*. **demonstration** *n*. **demonstrator** *n*.

demoralize *vt* **1** lower the morale of; cause to lose courage. **2** harm morally; corrupt.

demure *adj* modest; reserved; sedate. **demurely** *adv*.

den *n* **1** wild animal's retreat or resting place. **2** hiding-place of thieves. **3** private room for work.

denial *n* **1** contradiction. **2** refutation; rejection. **3** refusal of a request.

denim *n* strong cotton fabric.

denomination *n* **1** name or designation. **2** class of units in money, weights, etc. **3** name of a group of people, esp. a religious sect.

denominator *n* lower number in a fraction; divisor. **common denominator** *n* something possessed in common by all members of a group.

denote *vt* **1** mark out; distinguish. **2** stand for; indicate. **denotation** *n*.

denounce *vt* **1** condemn strongly or publicly. **2** inform against. **3** repudiate.

dense *adj* **1** thick; closely packed. **2** opaque. **3** *inf* stupid. **density** *n* **1** thickness. **2** mass per unit volume.

dent *n* small hollow left by a blow or by pressure. *vt,vi* make a dent in or become marked by a dent.

dental *adj* of or relating to the teeth. **dentist** *n* person who treats decayed teeth, fits false teeth, etc. **dentistry** *n*. **denture** *n* set of false teeth.

deny *vt* **1** declare to be untrue; contradict. **2** reject; repudiate. **3** refuse. **deny oneself** abstain from.

deodorant *n* substance that counteracts offensive smells.

depart *vi* **1** go away; leave. **2** die. **departure** *n*.

department *n* **1** subdivision; branch; separate section of an organization. **2** field of activity special concern.

depend *v* **depend (up)on 1** be conditional or contingent on. **2** rely on; trust. **dependable** *adj* reliable. **dependant** *n* person relying upon another for maintenance or support. **dependent** *adj*. **dependence** *n*.

depict *vt* represent in words or pictures; portray; describe. **depiction** *n*.

deplete *vt* exhaust; empty; reduce. **depletion** *n*.

deplore *vt* **1** regret deeply; lament. **2** disapprove of. **deplorable** *adj*.

deport *vt* expel from a country; banish. **deportation** *n*.

deportment *n* manner of standing, walking, etc.; bearing.

depose *vt* remove from office, esp. from a high position. *vi* bear witness; testify. **deposition** *n*.

deposit *vt* **1** set down. **2** put aside for safekeeping or as a pledge of faith. *n* **1** money entrusted to a bank, etc., or as part-payment of a transaction. **2** layer of ore or sediment in the earth. **depository** *n* place for safekeeping, esp. a store for goods.

depot *n* **1** store or military headquarters. **2** central garage for buses.

deprave *vt* corrupt morally; pervert. **depravity** *n*.

deprecate *vt* express disapproval of.

depreciate *vt,vi* **1** lower or fall in price or value. **2** disparage. **depreciation** *n*.

depress *vt* **1** press down; lower. **2** lessen the activity of. **3** make humble or gloomy. **depression** *n* **1** lowered surface; hollow. **2** low spirits; dejection. **3** state or period of reduced economic activity; slump. **4** region of low barometric pressure in the atmosphere.

deprive *vt* prevent from possessing or using; take away from. **deprivation** *n*.

depth *n* **1** distance downwards; deepness. **2** intensity or extent, as of emotion. **3** profundity of thought or explanation. **4** lowness of pitch. **5** most extreme or intense point. **out of one's depth** unable to understand or cope with a subject, situation, etc. **the depths** *pl n* **1** deepest part. **2** condition of low spirits or dejection.

deputize *vi,vt* act or appoint as an agent or representative. **deputation** *n* body of persons sent to represent others. **deputy** *n* assistant; representative; delegate.

derail *vt* cause (a train) to leave the rails. **derailment** *n*.

derelict *adj* abandoned; in a poor condition; dilapidated. *n* something abandoned. **dereliction** *n* neglect, esp. of duty.

deride *vt* mock at; scorn. **derision** *n*. **derisive** *adj*.

derive *vt* obtain or receive from. *vi* originate (from); be descended (from). **derivation** *n*. **derivative** *n,adj*.

derogatory *adj* insulting; not complimentary; damaging.

descend *vt,vi* move, come, or bring down. *vi* **1** move or slope downwards. **2** originate (from). **descendant** *n* person descended from another, offspring. **descent** *n* **1** descending; going down. **2** downward slope or path. **3** ancestry; transmission by inheritance.

describe *vt* **1** give a detailed account of, esp. in words. **2** trace or mark out. **description** *n*. **descriptive** *adj*.

desert[1] (ˈdezət) *n* waterless and uninhabited region. *adj* barren; lonely.

desert[2] (diˈzəːt) *vt* abandon; leave. *vi* leave service, esp. the army, without permission. **deserter** *n*. **desertion** *n*.

desert[3] (diˈzəːt) *n* something deserved, as a reward or punishment.

deserve *vt* be entitled to by conduct or qualities; merit. *vi* be worthy.

design *vt* **1** plan; make sketches for. **2** intend. *n* **1** plan; scheme; project. **2** art of making designs or patterns. **designer** *n*.

designate *vt* (ˈdezigneit) **1** indicate; point out; name. **2** appoint to office. *adj* (ˈdezignət) appointed to but not yet holding office. **designation** *n*.

desire *vt* **1** wish for greatly; yearn for; want. **2** request. *n* **1** longing; craving; urge; appetite. **2** request. **3** thing or person desired. **desirable** *adj*.

desist *vi* refrain; cease; stop.

desk *n* table with a flat or sloping writing surface.

desolate *adj* (ˈdesələt) **1** abandoned; lonely. **2** dreary; gloomy. *vt* (ˈdesəleit) **1** lay waste; destroy. **2** make unhappy. **desolation** *n*.

despair *n* loss of hope; hopelessness; despondency. *vi* lose hope.

desperate *adj* **1** very serious or dangerous; beyond hope. **2** reckless; violent; careless of risk. **desperation** *n*.

despise *vt* feel contempt for; scorn. **despicable** *adj*.

despite *prep* in spite of

despondent *adj* dejected; lacking hope or courage. **despondency** *n*.

despot *n* tyrant; cruel ruler or master. **despotic** *adj*.

dessert *n* fruit, confectionery, etc., served as the final course of a meal. **dessertspoon** *n* spoon of a size between a tablespoon and a teaspoon.

destine *vt* **1** determine the future of; doom. **2** set apart for a special purpose; intend. **destination** *n* place towards which a person travels or a thing is sent; end of a journey. **destiny** *n* **1** fate; supernatural or divine power. **2** that which is destined to happen.

destitute *adj* in extreme poverty; penniless. **destitution** *n*.

destroy *vt* demolish; annihilate; ruin. **destruction** *n*. **destructive** *adj*.

detach *vt* separate; disconnect. **detached** *adj* **1** disconnected. **2** aloof; impartial. **detachment** *n*.

detail *n* small part of a whole; item; fact; piece of information. **in detail** thoroughly; fully.

~*vt* **1** give particulars of. **2** appoint for special duty.

detain *vt* **1** keep waiting; prevent from leaving; delay. **2** keep possession of; withhold. **3** hold in custody. **detainee** *n*. **detention** *n*.

detect *vt* **1** notice; see. **2** find out; discover. **detection** *n*. **detective** *n* person, esp. a policeman, who investigates crimes.

deter *vt* (-rr-) discourage or dissuade from action, esp. by fear of consequences. **deterrent** *n,adj*.

detergent *n* cleansing substance. *adj* cleansing.

deteriorate *vt,vi* make or become worse; degenerate. **deterioration** *n*.

determine *vt* **1** be the cause of or deciding factor in. **2** set limits to; fix. *vi* resolve; decide. **determination** *n*.

detest *vt* dislike intensely; loathe; hate. **detestable** *adj*.

detonate *vt,vi* explode. **detonation** *n*. **detonator** *n* detonating device.

detour *n* diversion; deviation from a usual route.

detract *vt* disparage. **detract from** diminish, spoil.

devalue *vt* reduce the value of. **devaluation** *n*.

devastate *vt* destroy wholly; demolish. **devastation** *n*.

develop *vi* evolve; grow; open out. *vt* **1** bring to a more advanced stage. **2** bring forth; reveal. **3** treat (photographic film) to make the image visible. **development** *n*.

deviate *vi* diverge; turn away from what is normal or expected. **deviant** *adj,n*.

device *n* **1** mechanical contrivance; apparatus, appliance, or machine. **2** plot; scheme.

devil *n* **1** demon; wicked fiend. **2** *sl* lively or energetic person; rascal. **the Devil** personification of evil; Satan. **devilish** *adj*.

devious *adj* **1** roundabout; winding; erratic. **2** deceitful.

devise *vt* **1** invent; contrive. **2** bequeath.

devoid *adj* **devoid of** empty (of); lacking in.

devolve *vt* to delegate or transfer (power, responsibility, etc.). *vi* to be transferred. **devolution** *n* the act of devolving, esp. the transfer of government from a central to a regional organisation.

devote *vt* give up wholly, esp. to some cause or person; dedicate. **devotion** *n* **1** great loyalty, dedication. **2** religious worship. **devotee** *n*.

devour *vt* **1** eat greedily; consume. **2** absorb mentally with great eagerness.

devout *adj* **1** pious. **2** earnest; solemn.

dew *n* droplets of moisture deposited on ground surfaces at night.

dexterous *adj* skilful; deft; clever. **dexterity** *n*.

diabetes (daɪəˈbiːtɪs) *n* disease of the pancreas, characterized by allergy to sugar and abnormal discharge of urine. **diabetic** *n,adj*.

diagonal *adj* joining two opposite corners; slanting; oblique. *n* diagonal line. **diagonally** *adv*.

diagram *n* sketch, drawing, or plan, used esp. to illustrate or demonstrate something. **diagrammatic** *adj*.

dial *n* **1** graduated face or disc on a watch, compass, or other instrument. **2** numbered disc on a telephone. *vt* (-ll-) call using a telephone dial.

dialect *n* regional variation of a language.

dialogue *n* **1** conversation. **2** passage of written work in conversational form.

diameter *n* **1** straight line across a circle passing through the centre. **2** length of this line; thickness.

diamond *n* **1** very hard precious stone of pure carbon. **2** equilateral parallelogram. **3** playing card of the suit marked with a red diamond-shaped pip, or the symbol itself.

diaphragm *n* **1** muscular membrane between the chest and the abdomen. **2** thin vibrating disc in certain instruments. **3** contraceptive device inserted over the mouth of the cervix to act as a barrier to sperm.

diarrhoea (daɪəˈrɪə) *n* abnormal looseness of the bowels.

diary *n* daily record of events, or book in which such a record is kept.

dice *n pl or s* small cube with faces marked with between one and six spots, used in games of chance. *vt* cut into small cubes. **dice with** gamble with; deal with recklessly.

dictate *vt* (dɪkˈteɪt) **1** say or read for another to write down. **2** prescribe; command. *n* (ˈdɪkteɪt) authoritative command. **dictation** *n* act of dictating for another to write down or the matter so dictated. **dictator** *n* absolute ruler. **dictatorial** *adj* of or resembling a dictator, autocratic. **dictatorship** *n* **1** office of or government by a dictator. **2** country so ruled.

dictionary *n* **1** book containing an alphabetical list of words and their meanings, pronunciation, etc. **2** reference book relating to a particular subject, with items listed in alphabetical order.

did *v pt* of **do.**

die *vi* (dying) cease to live; perish. **die down** gradually diminish or become less forceful.

diesel *n* internal-combustion engine fuelled by oil or a vehicle driven by this.

diet *n* **1** regulated allowance of food, esp. one prescribed for slimming or medical reasons. **2** the food a person normally eats. *vi* to eat a special diet.

differ *vi* be unlike; disagree. **difference** *n* degree of differing or point in which things differ; disagreement. **different** *adj.* **differently** *adv.* **differentiate** *vi* **1** constitute a difference between. **2** become unlike; diverge. *vt* distinguish between. **differentiation** *n.*

difficult *adj* not easy; hard to do or understand. **difficulty** *n.*

dig *v* (-gg-; dug) *vt,vi* cut into or remove earth, esp. with a spade; excavate. *vt* poke or prod. *n* **1** prod. **2** sarcastic remark. **3** archaeological excavation.

digest *vt* (di'dʒest) **1** dissolve (food) in the stomach for bodily absorption. **2** classify or summarize to aid mental assimilation. **3** reflect on; absorb. *n* ('daidʒest) **1** summary. **2** publication containing condensed versions of other articles, books, etc. **digestion** *n* natural assimilation of food into the bodily system.

digit *n* **1** any number from nought to nine. **2** finger or toe.

dignified *adj* stately; exalted; noble.

dignity *n* **1** stateliness; gravity; distinction of mind or character. **2** high office or title.

digress *vi* stray from the main point or theme of a story, argument, etc. **digression** *n.*

dike *n,vt* dyke.

dilapidated *adj* decayed; neglected; in ruins. **dilapidation** *n.*

dilemma *n* situation in which alternative choices are equally unattractive; difficult predicament.

diligent *adj* industrious; conscientious. **diligence** *n.*

dilute *vt* reduce the strength of by adding water, water down. **dilution** *n.*

dim *adj* **1** not bright; indistinct; obscure. **2** *also* **dim-witted** *inf* stupid, not intelligent. *vt,vi* (-mm-) make or become dim(mer).

dimension *n* measurement of length, breadth, height, etc.; extent; size.

diminish *vt,vi* make or become smaller or less; lessen; reduce. **diminutive** *adj* extremely small.

dimple *n* small hollow, esp. in the surface of the skin on the face.

din *n* loud continuous noise. *vt* (-nn-) **1** subject to din. **2** repeat (facts, opinions, etc.) insistently.

dine *vi* eat dinner. *vt* entertain at dinner.

dinghy *n* small open boat.

dingy *adj* **1** shabby; dirty. **2** badly lit; gloomy. **dinginess** *n.*

dinner *n* **1** chief meal of the day. **2** formal banquet.

dinosaur *n* large extinct reptile.

diocese ('daiəsis) *n* district under a bishop's jurisdiction. **diocesan** (dai'ɔsizən) *adj.*

dip *vt* (-pp-) **1** submerge briefly in liquid; immerse. **2** lower. *vi* **1** sink briefly under the surface of a liquid. **2** slope downwards. *n* **1** act of dipping. **2** downward slope. **3** bathe.

diphthong *n* union of two vowel sounds in one syllable.

diploma *n* document conferring some privilege, title, or qualification.

diplomacy *n* **1** management of international relations. **2** tact or skill in dealing with others. **diplomat** *n* person engaged in international diplomacy. **diplomatic** *adj.*

direct *vt* **1** give orders; manage; control. **2** give directions to; point; indicate a route to. *adj* straight; straightforward; immediate. **direct object** *n* word in a sentence receiving the direct action of the main verb. **direction** *n* **1** instruction; command. **2** course to which anything moves, faces, etc. **director** *n* **1** person who directs, esp. the production of a film or play. **2** member of a board controlling a company or organization. **directory** *n* book listing names with addresses, telephone numbers, etc.

dirt *n* **1** any unclean substance; filth. **2** soil; earth. **dirty** *adj.*

disable *vt* incapacitate; cripple. **disability** *n.* **disabled** *adj.*

disadvantage *n* unfavourable circumstance or situation; handicap.

disagree *vi* **1** differ in opinion; dissent. **2** be incompatible. **disagreeable** *adj.* **disagreement** *n.*

disappear *vi* vanish; go out of sight. **disappearance** *n.*

disappoint *vt* fail to fulfil the desires or expectations of; frustrate. **disappointment** *n*.
disapprove *vt,vi* fail to approve; have an unfavourable opinion (of). **disapproval** *n*.
disarm *vt* **1** deprive of weapons; make defenceless. **2** win over; conciliate. *vi* lay down weapons; reduce national military forces. **disarmament** *n*.
disaster *n* extreme misfortune; calamity. **disastrous** *adj*.
disc *n* **1** thin flat circular plate. **2** *inf* gramophone record. **disc jockey** *n* person who plays recorded music on the radio, at parties, etc.
discard *vt,vi* throw out; cast off; reject.
discern *vt* see clearly; detect; distinguish. **discerning** *adj* having good taste; discriminating. **discernment** *n*.
discharge *vt* (dis'tʃɑ:dʒ) **1** release; send forth. **2** dismiss. **3** unload. *n* ('distʃɑ:dʒ) **1** matter discharged. **2** state of being discharged; release.
disciple *n* follower; loyal pupil.
discipline *n* **1** obedience and orderliness; self-control. **2** training or system of rules that produces such conduct. *vt* **1** subject to strict rules of conduct; train. **2** punish.
disclose *vt* reveal; make known. **disclosure** *n*.
disconcert *vt* upset; take aback; dismay.
disconnect *vt* break connection between; separate.
disconsolate *adj* unhappy; lacking hope or comfort.
discontinue *vt,vi* cease to continue; leave off.
discord *n* lack of harmony; disagreement; strife.
discotheque *n* public place for dancing to recorded pop music.
discount *n* ('diskaunt) reduction in the price of anything. *vt* (dis'kaunt) **1** reduce the value or price of. **2** leave out of consideration; ignore.
discourage *vt* **1** lessen the courage or confidence of; dishearten. **2** oppose by expressing disapproval; deter. **discouragement** *n*.
discover *vt* **1** find out; learn about. **2** uncover; reveal. **discoverer** *n*. **discovery** *n*.
discreet *adj* careful; prudent; tactful.
discrepancy *n* difference; inconsistency; variance.
discrete *adj* separate; distinct.
discretion *n* **1** prudence; tact. **2** freedom to act or choose as one likes.
discriminate *vt,vi* **1** make or see distinctions; distinguish. **2** treat persons, groups, etc., as different from others. **discrimination** *n*.
discus *n* heavy disc thrown in athletic contests.
discuss *vt* argue or write about in detail; debate. **discussion** *n*.
disease *n* illness; condition of impaired health.
disembark *vt,vi* set or go ashore from a ship; land.
disfigure *vt* spoil the appearance of; deform. **disfigurement** *n*.
disgrace *n* shame; dishonour. *vt* bring shame or discredit on; humiliate.
disgruntled *adj* discontented; sulky.
disguise *vt* conceal the true nature or appearance of; misrepresent. *n* clothing, make-up, etc., worn to give a false appearance.
disgust *n* extreme dislike; loathing; repugnance. *vt* cause disgust in; offend greatly.
dish *n* **1** shallow vessel or basin for food. **2** particular variety or preparation of food.
dishearten *vt* discourage; make despondent.
dishevelled *adj* untidy; scruffy; bedraggled.
dishonest *adj* not honest; insincere; deceitful. **dishonesty** *n*.
dishonour *n* **1** state of shame or disgrace. **2** cause of this. *vt* **1** bring shame or discredit on; disgrace. **2** treat with disrespect. **3** fail to pay (a debt, etc.). **dishonourable** *adj*.
disillusion *vt* cause to lose illusions; disenchant. **disillusionment** *n*.
disinfect *vt* free from infection; remove infectious germs from; sterilize. **disinfection** *n*. **disinfectant** *n* substance that prevents or removes infection.
disinherit *vt* deprive of inheritance. **disinheritance** *n*.
disintegrate *vt,vi* break into fragments; crumble. **disintegration** *n*.
disinterested *adj* impartial; objective; free from selfish or private motives.
disjointed *adj* **1** disconnected. **2** incoherent.
dislike *vt* feel aversion to; disapprove of. *n* aversion; disapproval.
dislocate *vt* put out of joint; displace. **dislocation** *n*.
disloyal *adj* not loyal; unfaithful. **disloyalty** *n*.
dismal *adj* gloomy; depressing; dreary. **dismally** *adv*.
dismantle *vt* take apart, esp. carefully or piece by piece.
dismay *vt* fill with alarm or fear. *n* apprehension; anxiety.

dismiss *vt* **1** send away; discharge from a job. **2** give only brief consideration to. **dismissal** *n*.
disobey *vt* refuse or fail to obey. **disobedience** *n*. **disobedient** *adj*.
disorder *n* **1** lack of order or organization; confusion. **2** breach of the peace; riot. **3** illness; ailment. **disordered** *adj* upset; disturbed; badly arranged. **disorderly** *adj* unruly; badly organized.
disown *vt* refuse to acknowledge; repudiate.
disparage *vt* speak scornfully of; belittle. **disparagement** *n*.
dispassionate *adj* without emotion or prejudice; objective.
dispatch *vt* **1** send off. **2** finish off. *n* **1** sending off. **2** speed; promptness. **3** official message or report.
dispel *vt* (-ll-) clear away; make disappear; scatter.
dispense *vt* **1** deal out; administer. **2** make up (medicines). **dispense with** do without; get rid of. **dispensary** *n* place where medicines are made up.
disperse *vt,vi* scatter; spread widely. **dispersal** *n*.
displace *vt* **1** move out of place. **2** remove from office. **3** take the place of. **displacement** *n*.
display *vt* exhibit; show; expose to view. *n* **1** exhibition. **2** ostentatious show.
dispose *vt* **1** arrange; set in order. **2** make willing or inclined. **dispose of** get rid of; deal with. **disposal** *n*. **disposition** *n* **1** arrangement. **2** inclination; tendency. **3** temperament.
dispossess *vt* deprive of rights, possessions, etc.
disprove *vt* prove false; refute.
dispute *v* (dɪˈspjuːt) *vi,vt* argue, debate, or disagree. *vt* **1** doubt or question the truth of. **2** compete to win (something). *n* (ˈdɪspjuːt) argument; quarrel.
disqualify *vt* **1** make ineligible or unsuitable. **2** ban from competing in sports, etc., for a breach of the rules. **3** deprive of legal or other rights, etc. **disqualification** *n*.
disregard *vt* **1** take no notice of; ignore. **2** treat with no respect. *n* lack of respect.
disrepute *n* ill repute. **disreputable** **1** discreditable. **2** shabby.
disrespect *vt* have or show no respect for. *n* lack of respect or courtesy. **disrespectful** *adj*.
disrupt *vt* **1** cause chaos or disorder. **2** interrupt the continuity of. **disruption** *n*. **disruptive** *adj*.
dissect *vt* **1** cut up and examine (an animal or plant). **2** analyse in detail. **dissection** *n*.
dissent *vi* **1** disagree. **2** express views opposing established or orthodox doctrines, esp. of a church. **dissension** *n*. **dissenter** *n*.
dissimilar *adj* not similar; different. **dissimilarity** *n*.
dissolve *vi,vt* **1** disperse or cause to disperse into a solution. **2** dismiss (a company, organization, etc.). *vi* vanish. **dissolution** *n*.
dissuade *vt* discourage from an intention by persuasion.
distance *n* length of a space between two points. **keep (someone) at a distance** refuse to allow someone to become friendly. **keep one's distance** behave in a reserved or formal way. **distant** *adj* **1** far away. **2** remote. **3** reserved.
distaste *n* dislike. **distasteful** *adj* unpleasant; objectionable.
distil *v* (-ll-) *vt* **1** boil (a liquid) and condense the vapour. **2** purify by this process. **3** obtain the essential part of something. *vi* undergo distillation. **distillation** *n*. **distillate** *n* product of distillation. **distillery** *n* place where alcoholic spirits are produced.
distinct *adj* **1** easily understood; clear. **2** noticeable. **distinct from** different; not the same as. **distinction** *n* **1** act of distinguishing things as different or distinct. **2** mark of difference. **3** mark of superiority or excellence. **distinctive** *adj* of distinguishing characteristic.
distinguish *vt* **1** be able to see a difference; discriminate. **2** characterize. **3** recognize; perceive. **distinguish oneself** do something with distinction.
distort *vt* **1** twist; deform. **2** give an untrue impression of. **distortion** *n*.
distract *vt* **1** divert the attention of. **2** confuse; disturb. **3** entertain or amuse. **distraction** *n*. **distractive** *adj*.
distraught *adj* **1** agitated or bewildered. **2** frantic.
distress *vt* cause acute mental or physical discomfort. *n* **1** state of acute anxiety or anguish. **2** state of danger, extreme discomfort, etc.
distribute *vt* **1** give out in shares; allot. **2** spread; scatter. **3** divide into groups or categories. **distribution** *n*.

district *n* geographical, political, or administrative region.

distrust *vt* have no trust in; suspect. *n* lack of trust.

disturb *vt* **1** interrupt; disrupt. **2** cause disorder; disarrange. **3** cause worry or anxiety. **disturbance** *n* **1** act of disturbing or being disturbed. **2** disturbing of the public peace.

ditch *n* narrow trench dug for drainage purposes. *vi* repair or dig ditches. *vt inf* throw away; abandon.

ditto *n* the same as above; used in accounts, lists, etc., to save repetition.

divan *n* **1** low backless cushioned couch set against a wall. **2** *also* **divan bed** type of bed with an enclosed base and no visible frame.

dive *vi* **1** jump into water headfirst or in a controlled fashion. **2** throw oneself forward headlong. **3** (of a submarine) submerge. *vi,vt* **1** move in a steep downward path through the air. *n* **1** act of diving. **2** *inf* shabby disreputable café, pub, etc. **diver** *n*.

diverge *vi* **1** turn off and go in different directions; move apart. **2** differ. **divergence** *n*.

diverse *adj* varied; different. **diversify** *vt,vi* make or become diverse. **diversification** *n*.

divert *vt,vi* turn (a person or thing) from a previously intended course. *vt* distract. **diversion** *n* **1** act of diverting. **2** temporary detour caused by repairs, etc., on a road. **3** distraction; amusement.

divide *vt,vi* **1** separate or split into two or more parts. **2** distribute. **3** find out how many times a number is contained in another. *vt* cause a disagreement (between).

dividend *n* **1** money paid to shareholders as interest, profit, etc. **2** number to be divided by another.

divine *adj* **1** relating to God, a god, or theology. **2** sacred; religious; heavenly. *vt,vi* guess or discover intuitively. **divinely** *adv*. **divinity** *n* **1** state or quality of being divine. **2** god; deity. **3** theology.

divisible *adj* able to be divided.

division *n* **1** act of dividing. **2** part of a unit or whole. **3** administrative or legislative body. **4** military unit larger than a regiment.

divorce *n* **1** legal termination of a marriage. **2** total or radical separation. *vt,vi* obtain a divorce (from). *vt* separate. **divorcé(e)** *n* man (woman) who is divorced.

divulge *vt* reveal; disclose; let out (a secret, etc.).

dizzy *adj* **1** experiencing a sensation of confusion, being unsteady, or whirling; giddy. **2** causing such a sensation. **dizzily** *adv*. **dizziness** *n*.

do *v* (does; did; done) *vt* **1** perform; act. **2** deal with; complete. **3** serve; provide. **4** fix; arrange. **5** have as a job or occupation. **6** *inf* swindle; defraud. *vi* **1** suffice; be accepted. **2** manage; cope. **3** make progress. *v aux* used in certain interrogative, negative, or emphatic statements. **do in** *sl* kill; murder. **do up 1** tie; fasten. **2** make smart. **make do (with)** manage with what is available. ~*n inf* function; social event.

docile *adj* willing to be trained; tame; gentle; obedient.

dock[1] *n* area or wharf for mooring, loading, repairing ships, etc. *vt,vi* bring or come in to dock; moor. **docker** *n* person employed to load and unload cargo. **dockyard** *n* enclosure with docks for repairing, equipping, or building ships.

dock[2] *n* **1** solid part of an animal's tail. **2** stump remaining after clipping a tail. *vt* **1** cut (an animal's tail). **2** deduct from.

dock[3] *n* section in a lawcourt where the accused is seated.

doctor *n* **1** person qualified to practise medicine. **2** person holding the highest diploma or degree of a university. *vt* **1** treat medically. **2** falsify; adulterate.

doctrine *n* **1** teaching of a school, church, political group, etc. **2** dogma; belief.

document *n* ('dɔkjumənt) printed or written evidence or information. *vt* ('dɔkjument) furnish with evidence, references, etc. **documentation** *n*. **documentary** *adj* relating to a document. *n* detailed factual film.

dodge *vi,vt* move quickly, so as to avoid; evade. *n* clever plan or move.

does *v* 3rd person singular of **do** in the present tense.

dog *n* domesticated or wild four-footed animal of various breeds. *vt* (-gg-) pursue steadily; tail; hound. **dog-collar** *n inf* clergyman's collar. **dogged** ('dɔgid) *adj* persistent; stubborn; tenacious.

dogma *n* system of beliefs, such as those of a church; doctrine. **dogmatic** *adj* **1** relating to dogma. **2** asserting beliefs or opinions with persistent arrogance. **dogmatically** *adv.*

dole *n* money or food given charitably or for maintenance. **on the dole** receiving unemployment benefit. *v* **dole out** give or share out; distribute.

doll *n* **1** child's toy in the image of a person. **2** *sl* attractive girl or young woman. *v* **doll up** dress up in fine clothes.

dollar *n* unit of currency of the US and various other countries, comprising 100 cents.

dolphin *n* sea mammal resembling but larger than a porpoise.

domain *n* **1** territory ruled over, as by a sovereign. **2** field of interest, influence, etc.; province.

dome *n* large high rounded roof.

domestic *adj* **1** relating to the home or household matters. **2** not foreign. **3** (of animals) tame. **domestic science** *n* study or art of cooking, needlework, household management, etc. **domesticate** *vt* tame; train for domestic purposes. **domesticity** *n* home life, matters concerning the home or a household.

dominate *vt,vi* **1** rule; control; govern. **2** be the most important or conspicuous feature (of). **domination** *n.* **dominant** *adj* **1** prevailing, having power, authority, or priority. **2** prominent, most important. **dominance** *n.* **domineer** *vi* behave in an overbearing or arrogant manner. **dominion** *n* **1** sovereignty, governing authority, rule. **2** land controlled by a government; domain. **3** name formerly given to the self-governing countries of the Commonwealth of Nations.

domino *n, pl* **dominoes** small rectangular brick marked with various combinations of spots for use in various games.

donate *vt* give. **donation** *n* gift, esp. for charity. **donor** *n* person making a donation.

done *v pp* of **do.**

donkey *n* **1** long-eared member of the horse family, used esp. as a beast of burden; ass. **2** *sl* fool.

doodle *vi,vt* draw or scribble casually, esp. while attending to some other matter. *n* scribbled drawing or shape. **doodler** *n.*

doom *n* **1** fate; destiny. **2** unfavourable judicial sentence; condemnation. *vt* **1** sentence; condemn. **2** destine to an unhappy end or fate.

door *n* **1** hinged or sliding structure fitted across a passage or entrance. **2** *also* **doorway** entrance to a building, room, etc.

dope *n* **1** kind of varnish used for waterproofing. **2** drug, esp. a narcotic. **3** *sl* information. **4** *sl* stupid person; dunce. *vt,vi* drug or take drugs. **dopey** *adj also* **dopy 1** drugged; drowsy. **2** stupid.

dormant *adj* inactive.

dormitory *n* large room containing a number of beds.

dormouse *n, pl* **dormice** hibernating rodent similar to but smaller than a squirrel.

dorsal *adj* relating to or on the back.

dose *n* **1** amount of a medicine, etc., to be given or taken at one time. **2** bout; spell. *vt* give medicine or doses (to). **dosage** *n* **1** giving of medicine in doses. **2** amount of medicine to be given.

dot *n* small point or spot, speck. *vt* (-tt-) **1** mark with dots, spot. **2** place a dot over a letter, after a musical note, etc.

dote *vi* be silly or mentally weak. **dote on** be excessively fond of. **dotage** *n* silliness or childishness in old age; feeble-mindedness.

double *adj* **1** two of a kind together, of two kinds. **2** twice as much. **3** having two functions, uses, etc. **4** suitable for two. **5** having extra weight, thickness, width, etc. **6** ambiguous. *adv* **1** twice. **2** in pairs. *n* **1** something or someone exactly like another. **2** quantity that is twice that of another. **3** sharp backward turn or bend. **4** evasion; trick; shift. *vt,vi* **1** make or become twice as great. **2** multiply by two. **3** fold in half. **4** turn sharply. **double up** be contorted with pain, laughter, etc. **double bass** *n* largest instrument of the violin family. **double-cross** *vt* betray. *n* betrayal. **double-dutch** *n inf* nonsense; gibberish. **doubly** *adv* to twice the extent.

doubt *vt* **1** hesitate to accept, fail to believe immediately. **2** suspect. *n* uncertainty, lack of conviction or belief. **no doubt** probably, presumably. **doubtful** *adj.* **doubtless** *adv,adj.*

dough *n* flour or meal mixed with water and kneaded before baking. **doughnut** *n* small round cake made of dough and sugar and fried in deep fat.

douse *vt,vi also* **dowse** plunge into water, immerse, drench. *vt* extinguish (a light).

dove *n* bird belonging to the pigeon family.

dowdy *adj* drab, shabby.

down[1] *adv* **1** from a higher to a lower place or

position. **2** to or at the bottom; towards or on the ground. **3** below the horizon. **4** from an earlier to a later time. **5** into a worse physical or mental condition. *prep* **1** towards, at, in, or near a lower place, rank, condition, etc. **2** in the same direction as; with. *adj* dejected; miserable; depressed.

down[2] *n* **1** fine soft feathers of young ducks or other birds. **2** fine hair.

downcast *adj* **1** looking or directed downwards. **2** dejected.

downfall *n* **1** ruin; destruction. **2** cause of overthrow or destruction. **3** falling, as of rain or snow.

downhearted *adj* dejected in spirits; depressed.

downhill *adv* down a hill; downwards. *adj* descending; sloping.

downpour *n* heavy fall of rain.

downright *adj* in plain terms; straightforward. *adv* absolutely; thoroughly.

downstairs *adv* **1** down the stairs. **2** towards or on a lower floor. *adj* relating to or situated on a lower floor. *n* lower floor.

downstream *adv* down or in the direction of flow of a stream. *adj* farther down or moving with the current.

downtrodden *adj* trodden or trampled down; oppressed.

downward *adj* moving or extending from a higher to a lower place. **downwards** *adv* from a higher place to a lower; in a descending course.

dowry *n* money, goods, or property that a woman brings to her husband at marriage.

dowse *vt,vi* douse.

doze *vi* sleep lightly or for a short time. *n* light or brief sleep.

dozen *n* group of twelve. **dozens** *pl n* many.

drab *adj* **1** of a dull colour. **2** monotonous; not exciting.

draft *n* **1** first or rough copy, outline, sketch, etc. **2** detachment of soldiers. **3** conscription. **4** written order for money. *vt* **1** prepare a first or rough copy of. **2** send or select (a detachment of soldiers). **3** conscript; recruit.

drag *v* (-gg-) *vt,vi* **1** pull; draw or be drawn along. **2** trail. **3** search or sweep with a net, hook, etc. *vi* move slowly; lag. **drag out** prolong, esp. unnecessarily. ~*n* **1** device used for dragging. **2** something that slows movement or progress. **3** *sl* something or someone that is tedious or a waste of time. **4** *inf* puff or inhaling of a cigarette. **in drag** (of a man) wearing women's clothing.

dragon *n* **1** fire-breathing monster usually depicted as a winged reptile. **2** *inf* fierce or fiery person, esp. a woman; tyrant. **dragonfly** *n* long-bodied insect with large delicate wings.

drain *vt* **1** draw off (liquid) so as to empty or leave dry. **2** exhaust; consume utterly; empty. *vi* **1** flow out or away. **2** become dry or empty. *n* **1** pipe, channel, or ditch for drawing off water, sewage, etc. **2** steady depletion or expenditure. **drainage** *n* **1** act or process of draining. **2** system of pipes or channels for draining. **3** substance drained. **draining board** *n* sloping surface beside a sink on which wet dishes, etc., are placed to dry. **drainpipe** *n* pipe channelling water, sewage, etc.

drake *n* male bird of the duck family.

dram *n* **1** unit of weight, equal to one sixteenth of an ounce. **2** small amount of alcoholic drink; tot.

drama *n* **1** story performed by actors; play. **2** plays collectively. **3** compelling event or series of events. **dramatic** *adj* **1** relating to or resembling drama. **2** vivid; forceful. **dramatically** *adv*. **dramatics** *pl n* acting by an amateur company. **dramatist** *n* person who writes drama; playwright. **dramatize** *vt* **1** act out or put into the form of a drama. **2** express vividly or forcefully or in an exaggerated manner.

drank *v pt* of **drink.**

drape *vt* cover, esp. with cloth or fabric. *vt,vi* hang in folds (about). *n* arrangement of folds. **draper** *n* person who deals in cloth, linen, etc. **drapery** *n* **1** cloth or other fabrics. **2** business of a draper.

draught *n* **1** current of air, esp. in an enclosed space. **2** act of pulling or that which is pulled. **3** quantity drunk in one go. **4** drawing of beer, wine, etc., from a barrel or cask. **5** dose of medicine. **draughts** *n* game played with round flat pieces on a board marked off in squares. **draughtsman** *n, pl* **-men** **1** person skilled in mechanical drawing. **2** *also* **draught** piece used in draughts.

draw *v* (drew; drawn) *vt,vi* **1** pull; haul; drag. **2** bring or come nearer; approach. **3** portray in lines; sketch. *vt* **1** pull out; extract; withdraw; take. **2** inhale. **3** infer; deduce. **4** describe. **5** obtain by lot. **6** attract. *vi* **1** finish a game with an equal score for both sides, tie **2** permit the circulation of air. **draw on 1** use as a resource. **2** approach. **draw up** draft (a will, contract, etc.). ~*n* **1** attraction. **2** raffle; lottery. **3** game ending in a tie. **drawback** *n* disadvantage. **drawbridge** *n* bridge that can be raised

drawer *n* sliding compartment in a desk, chest, etc. **drawers** *pl n inf* underpants or knickers.

drawing *n* **1** art or practice of portraying in lines; sketching. **2** image or sketch so done. **drawing pin** *n* short pin with a flat head, fixed by pushing with the thumb. **drawing room** *n* room for the reception or entertaining of guests; living room.

drawl *vt,vi* speak slowly, esp. with elongated vowel sounds. *n* such speech.

dread *vt* anticipate with great fear or apprehension. *n* great apprehension or fear, terror. **dreadful** *adj* **1** causing dread. **2** *inf* unpleasant, bad. **dreadfully** *adv inf* terribly; awfully; very.

dream *n* **1** sequence of thoughts or images during sleep. **2** something hoped for. **3** vision. *vi,vt* (dreamt *or* dreamed) have dreams (of).

dreary *adj* gloomy; not exciting, dull. **dreariness** *n*.

dredge *n* device for bringing up mud and other material from the bottom of a river, etc. *vt* bring up, clean, etc., with a dredge.

dregs *pl n* sediment.

drench *vt* wet completely, soak.

dress *vt,vi* put clothes on. *vt* arrange for show, decorate; adorn. **3** prepare (meat, fish, etc.) by trimming, gutting, etc. **4** treat (a wound, etc.) by applying a dressing. *n* **1** clothing. **2** female outer garment consisting of a bodice and skirt. **3** formal evening wear. **dress circle** *n* first gallery above the floor in a theatre or cinema. **dressmaker** *n* person skilled in making dresses. **dress rehearsal** *n* final rehearsal of a stage production, in which the actors appear in full costume

dresser[1] *n* kitchen sideboard.

dresser[2] *n* person assisting an actor with costume changes.

dressing *n* **1** sauce applied to various foods. **2** stuffing. **3** something applied to a wound to aid healing. **dressing-gown** *n* loosely fitting robe or gown, usually worn over night attire. **dressing-room** *n* special room, esp. in a theatre, where one dresses. **dressing-table** *n* small table, usually with a mirror, for cosmetics etc.

drew *v pt of* **draw.**

dribble *vi,vt* **1** flow or allow to flow in small drops, trickle. **2** propel (a ball) with a series of small kicks. *n* drop, trickle

drier *n* appliance for drying clothes, hair, etc.

drift *n* **1** snow, sand, etc., piled up by the wind **2** general meaning. **3** deviation from a plan, course, etc. **4** general movement, progress, etc. *vi* **1** be carried, as by air or water currents. **2** move without purpose or direction. **driftwood** *n* wood carried ashore by water

drill[1] *n* **1** tool or device for boring holes. **2** routine exercises or training. *vt,vi* **1** bore (a hole) in. **2** exercise, esp. by repetition.

drill[2] *n* **1** small trench for seed. **2** machine or device for sowing seed in drills.

drink *v* (drank, drunk); *vt,vi* swallow (liquid). *vt* **1** absorb, take in. **2** consume (alcoholic drinks). *n* **1** amount of liquid suitable for consumption; beverage. **2** alcohol.

drip *vi,vt* (-pp-) fall or let fall in drops. *n* process of dripping or that which falls by dripping. **drip-dry** *adj* (of clothing, etc.) drying without creases if hung up when wet. **dripping** *n* fat that drips from a roasting joint.

drive *vt,vi* (drove, driven) **1** move by force, power, etc. **2** urge onward; compel. **3** control or steer (an animal, vehicle, etc.). **4** transport or be transported in a vehicle. **5** move or fix by striking, hitting, etc. *n* **1** act of driving. **2** trip in a vehicle. **3** road, esp. a private one leading to a house. **4** energy, force, motivation. **driver** *n*.

drivel *vi* (-ll-) **1** let secretions flow from the mouth or nose, dribble. **2** talk or act foolishly. *n* nonsense, silly talk.

drizzle *vi* rain lightly. *n* fine rain.

droll *adj* witty, satirical, wry.

dromedary *n* camel with one hump.

drone *n* **1** male bee. **2** idle person. **3** deep buzz or hum. **4** monotonous voice, tone, etc. *vi* **1** buzz or hum continuously. **2** speak in a low monotonous voice.

drool *vi* **1** gloat, gush. **2** drivel, dribble.

droop *vi,vt* bend or hang down limply, sag. *vi* become disheartened, languish. *n* drooping state or condition.

drop *n* **1** small spherical amount of liquid, globule. **2** very small amount of anything. **3** steep descent, fall. **4** distance through which something falls. **5** round sweet. *v* (-pp-) *vt,vi* **1** fall or permit to fall. **2** lower; decrease; sink. *vt* **1** cease to consider or discuss. **2** mention casually. **3** allow (passengers, goods, etc.) to disembark or be unloaded. **4** omit; cease to make use of. **drop in** make a casual visit. **drop off 1** fall asleep. **2** decline; decrease. **drop out** cease to compete, complete one's education, etc. **dropout** *n* person who rejects society's norms, fails to complete an educational course, etc.

drought *n* prolonged period during which no rain falls.

drove[1] *v pt of* **drive.**

drove[2] *n* herd or flock, esp. when on the move.

drown *vt,vi* kill or die by suffocating in water. *vt* **1** overpower; extinguish; destroy. **2** cover completely; flood. **3** shut out (sound); muffle.

drowse *vi,vt* be or make sleepy. *n* condition of being sleepy or half asleep. **drowsy** *adj* **1** sleepy or sluggish. **2** inducing sleep; soporific. **drowsily** *adv.* **drowsiness** *n.*

drudge *vi* work hard; slave. *n* person doing menial work. **drudgery** *n* hard menial work; toil.

drug *n* substance, esp. a narcotic. *vt* (-gg-) **1** mix a drug or drugs with (food, drink, etc.) **2** administer a drug (to).

drum *n* **1** percussion instrument having skin, etc., stretched tightly over a hollow chamber. **2** large cylindrical container for oil, water, etc. *vt,vi* (-mm-) **1** beat or play (a drum). **2** beat, tap, or strike continuously. *vt* instil by insistent repetition. **drummer** *n.*

drunk *adj* **1** *also* **drunken** intoxicated; inebriated. **2** emotionally overcome. *n also* **drunkard** person who is drunk, esp. habitually.

dry *adj* **1** not wet or moist. **2** having little or no rainfall, arid. **3** thirsty or causing thirst. **4** not yielding milk, water, etc. **5** not stimulating; dull. **6** caustically clever or witty. **7** not permitting the legal sale or consumption of alcohol. *vt,vi* make or become dry(er). **dry-clean** *vt* clean with chemical solvents rather than water.

dual *adj* **1** relating to two or a pair. **2** having two parts; double. **dual carriageway** *n* major road with opposite lanes separated by a barrier, area of grass, etc. **duality** *n.* **dually** *adv.*

dubious *adj* causing doubt; suspicious; questionable.

ducal *adj* relating to a duke or duchy.

duchess *n* **1** wife or widow of a duke. **2** woman holding a rank equivalent to that of a duke. **duchy** *n* territory ruled by a duke or duchess.

duck[1] *n* wild or tame edible bird with webbed feet. **duckling** *n* young duck.

duck[2] *vi* **1** bend down or lower suddenly; bob. **2** plunge temporarily under water. **3** avoid; dodge.

duct *n* channel or tube for conveying liquid, secretions, etc. **ductile** *adj* **1** (of gold, copper, etc.) capable of being drawn out into wire or hammered very thin. **2** flexible; pliant.

due *adj* **1** payable at once. **2** fitting; usual; proper; adequate. **3** expected to arrive or be ready. **due to** attributed or ascribed to. ~*n* fair share. **dues** *pl n* fee; charges.

duel *n* **1** fight with pistols, swords, etc., between two persons. **2** contest between two parties. *vi* (-ll-) fight a duel.

duet *n* composition for two musicians or performers.

dug *v pt and pp of* **dig.**

duke *n* **1** nobleman ranking next below a prince. **2** ruler of a small state (duchy).

dulcimer *n* percussion instrument having a set of strings, which are struck with hammers.

dull *adj* **1** lacking intelligence; stupid. **2** having no feelings; insensible. **3** not clear or sharp. **4** tedious. **5** moving slowly; sluggish. **6** overcast. **7** blunt. *vt,vi* make or become dull. **dullness** *n.* **dully** *adv.*

duly *adv* as expected; properly; in a fitting manner.

dumb *adj* **1** incapable of uttering speech sounds. **2** temporarily unable to speak. **3** silent. **4** *sl* stupid. **dumbfound** *vt* amaze into silence; astound. **dumbly** *adv.* **dumbness** *n.*

dummy *n* **1** model of a human being used esp. for displaying clothes. **2** imitation; copy. **3** *inf* inactive or silent person. **4** rubber teat sucked by a baby.

dump *vt* **1** throw down in a pile or heap. **2** unload; dispose of. *n* **1** place where rubbish is dumped; tip. **2** *inf* messy, dirty, or ugly place, room, etc. **down in the dumps** depressed; dejected; miserable. **dumpling** *n* ball of dough cooked in a stew, etc. **dumpy** *adj* short and fat; plump.

dunce *n* person who is slow to learn or mentally dull.

dune *n* ridge or hill of sand.

dung *n* excrement; manure.

dungeon *n* underground cell or prison, esp. in a castle.

duplicate *adj* (ˈdjuːplikət) **1** resembling or exactly like another. **2** occurring in pairs; double. *n* (ˈdjuːplikət) exact copy. *vt* (ˈdjuːplikeit) reproduce exactly; copy. **duplication** *n*. **duplicator** *n* machine for producing stencilled copies.

durable *adj* resisting decay or wear; lasting. **durability** *n*.

duration *n* period of time that something lasts.

during *prep* **1** throughout the period, existence, or activity of. **2** in the course of.

dusk *n* period of the evening before darkness falls; twilight. **dusky** *adj* **1** dark-skinned. **2** dim; shadowy.

dust *n* dry fine particles of earth, mineral deposits, etc. *vt,vi* wipe the dust (from). *vt* sprinkle; powder. **dusty** *adj*. **dustbin** *n* container for refuse, ashes, etc. **duster** *n* cloth used to wipe dust from furniture, etc. **dustman** *n, pl* **-men** person employed to remove refuse, empty dustbins, etc.

duty *n* **1** obligation, esp. of a moral or legal nature. **2** allocated work or task. **3** tax on imported or exported goods; tariff. **on/off duty** at work/not at work, esp. as a nurse, doctor, soldier, etc. **duty-free** *adj* requiring no duty to be paid. **dutiful** *adj* respectful; obedient. **dutifully** *adv*.

duvet (ˈduːvei) *n* quilt for a bed, padded with feathers, down, etc.; continental quilt.

dwarf *n, pl* **dwarfs** *or* **dwarves 1** person of exceptionally small stature or size. **2** plant or animal of a smaller type than average. **3** supernatural being in the form of a small ugly man. *vt* **1** restrict the growth of. **2** cause to appear relatively small, insignificant, etc., by comparison.

dwell *vi* (dwelt *or* dwelled) reside as a permanent occupant; live (in). **dwell (up)on** emphasize; concentrate on. **dwelling** *n* place where someone lives; abode; house.

dwindle *vi* grow gradually less in size, number, etc.; decrease.

dye *n* substance used for colouring fabric, the hair, etc. *v* (dyeing; dyed) *vt* colour (fabric, hair, etc.) with a dye. *vi* become coloured with a dye.

dying *v pres p* of **die. dying to/for** having a strong desire to/for.

dyke *n also* **dike 1** embankment for holding back sea or river water. **2** ditch; trench. *vt* hold back or drain with a dyke.

dynamic *adj* **1** relating to force or energy; not static. **2** forceful; ambitious. **dynamically** *adv*. **dynamics** *n* branch of science concerned with forces and their effects on motion.

dynamite *n* high explosive of nitroglycerine and other substances.

dynamo device that converts mechanical energy into electrical energy.

dynasty *n* **1** unbroken line of hereditary rulers of the same family. **2** period of their rule.

dysentery *n* disease of the intestines.

dyslexia *n* condition leading to impaired reading ability. **dyslexic** *adj,n*.

E

each *adj,pron,adv* every separate one considered individually.

eager *adj* **1** strongly desirous. **2** keen; willing. **eagerly** *adv*. **eagerness** *n*.

eagle *n* large bird of prey having very keen eyesight.

ear[1] *n* **1** one of two organs of hearing, situated on either side of the head. **2** sense of hearing or appreciation of sound, esp. music. **3** attention. **be all ears** be listening attentively. **eardrum** *n* membrane in the inner part of the ear that vibrates when struck by sound waves. **earmark** *vt* designate for a special purpose. **earphone** *n* small loudspeaker placed in or over the ear for listening to a radio or telephone communication. **earring** *n* jewellery worn on or hanging from the ear lobe.

ear[2] *n* spike of a cereal plant containing the seed.

earl *n* British nobleman ranking next above a viscount.

early *adj,adv* **1** before the expected or appointed time. **2** at or near the beginning of a period or season. **earliness** *n*.

earn *vt,vi* gain (money, etc.) by working. *vt* deserve. **earnings** *pl n* wages or salary.

earnest *adj* **1** sincere; serious. **2** zealous; determined. **earnestly** *adv*.

earth *n* **1** third planet from the sun, lying between Venus and Mars and orbited by the moon, on which life has developed; world. **2** surface of this planet. **3** soil; ground. **4** home of a fox, etc. **5** connection of an electrical apparatus to the ground, assumed to be at zero voltage. **down-to-earth** sensible; realistic. **earthenware** *n* domestic pottery of coarse baked clay. **earthly** *adj* **1** of the earth or world. **2** likely; conceivable. **earthquake** *n* violent natural movement of the earth's crust; tremor. **earthworm** *n* worm that lives in and eats soil. **earthy** *adj* coarse; basic; crude.

earwig *n* small insect having pincers on the tail.

ease *n* **1** freedom from work, pain, or exertion; comfort; relaxation. **2** lack of difficulty (in doing something). *vt,vi* make or become less painful, difficult, etc.

easel *n* frame for supporting a blackboard or artist's canvas.

east *n* **1** one of the four cardinal points of the compass situated to the front of a person facing the sunrise. **2** part of a country, area, etc., lying towards the east. *adj also* **eastern** of, in, or facing the east. *adv,adj also* **easterly** **1** towards the east. **2** (of winds) from the east. **easterner** *n*. **eastward** *adj* facing or moving towards the east. **eastwards** *adv* in the direction of the east.

Easter *n* annual Christian festival in the spring, celebrating Christ's resurrection.

easy *adj* **1** requiring little effort; not difficult. **2** relaxed; comfortable. **3** tolerant; casual. **easily** *adv*. **easiness** *n*. **easygoing** *adj* tolerant; relaxed.

eat *v* (ate; eaten) *vt,vi* consume (food) through the mouth; have (a meal). *vt* **1** corrode; wear away. **2** use up in great quantities.

eavesdrop *vi* (-pp-) listen secretly to a private conversation. **eavesdropper** *n*.

ebb *n* **1** tidal falling back of the sea away from land. **2** decline; decay. *vi* **1** flow back from the land. **2** decline; diminish; wane.

ebony *n* hard almost black wood, obtained from a tropical or subtropical tree.

ebullient *adj* fervent; enthusiastic; full of life. **ebullience** *n*.

eccentric *adj* **1** not having the same centre; having a noncentral axis. **2** unconventional; odd. *n* eccentric person. **eccentricity** *n*.

ecclesiastic *adj also* **ecclesiastical** of or relating to the Church or clergymen. *n* clergyman.

echo *n, pl* **echoes** **1** sound like or repeating a first sound, caused by reflection of sound waves by a solid object. **2** anything that repeats or mimics. *vt,vi* reverberate; repeat; imitate.

éclair *n* cake made of light pastry and filled with cream.

eclipse *n* phenomenon in which light from one heavenly body is blocked by another, esp. a **solar eclipse,** where the moon moves between the earth and the sun. *vt* **1** cause an eclipse of. **2** throw into obscurity; surpass.

ecology *n* **1** relationship between natural things and their surroundings, and the effect of technology on this. **2** study of this. **ecological** *adj*. **ecologist** *n*.

economic *adj* **1** of or relating to economics. **2** worth doing; profitable. **3** economical. **economical** *adj* **1** frugal; thrifty. **2** not wasteful; giving value for money. **economically** *adv*. **economics** *n* study of the causes of and relationships between production, exchange, distribution, and consumption. **economize** *vt,vi* reduce expenditure or consumption to save money. **economy** *n* **1** arrangement or condition of trade, production, and commerce of an area. **2** thrift; frugality.

ecstasy *n* **1** intense joy; bliss. **2** state of extreme religious fervour. **ecstatic** *adj*.

edge *n* **1** outer side or margin. **2** cutting side of a blade. **3** keenness; sharpness. **4** slight advantage. **on edge** tense. ~*vt* **1** sharpen. **2** be or provide the border of. *vi,vt* move gradually; inch. **edgy** *adj* tense.

edible *adj* that may be eaten; not poisonous; not disgusting to the palate.

edit *vt* **1** prepare (a manuscript) for publication. **2** prepare the final form of (a film).

edition *n* set of books, newspapers, etc., printed at the same time. **editor** *n* **1** person who edits. **2** person who directs content and coverage of a newspaper, etc. **editorial** *adj* of or relating to the task of an editor. *n* newspaper article containing the opinions of its editor.

educate *vt* **1** give teaching to; instruct. **2** bring up; raise. **3** refine; improve. **education** *n* **1** process of gaining knowledge; training; schooling. **2** state of being educated. **3** upbringing. **educational** *adj*.

eel *n* snakelike fish.

eerie *adj* frighteningly strange; weird; ghostly. **eerily** *adv*. **eeriness** *n*.

effect *n* **1** change produced by an action; result. **2** impression on the mind, eyes, etc. **in effect**

actually; virtually. **take effect** start; become operative. ~*vt* bring about; cause. **effective** *adj* **1** producing a result, esp. a considerable one. **2** causing a pleasant or striking effect or impression. **3** taking effect. **effectively** *adv*.

effeminate *adj* (of a man) like a woman; not masculine or virile.

effervesce *vi* (of a liquid) give off bubbles of gas; fizz. **effervescent** *adj* **1** bubbling; fizzy. **2** merry; lively. **effervescence** *n*.

efficient *adj* producing the desired effect without waste; competent; effective. **efficiency** *n*. **efficiently** *adv*.

effigy *n* model or solid representation of a person.

effort *n* **1** exertion of energy. **2** attempt; try. **effortless** *adj* needing or using little effort; easy. **effortlessly** *adv*.

egg[1] *n* **1** oval object consisting of the embryo of birds, reptiles, etc., within a protective shell. **2** egg of certain birds, esp. hens, eaten as food.

egg[2] *v* **egg on** encourage or incite; urge; persuade.

ego *n* **1** the self; part of the mind that is conscious of itself. **2** self-centredness; conceit. **egocentric** *adj* self-centred; conceited. **egoism** *n* characteristic of thinking only of oneself; self-centredness. **egoist** *n*. **egoistic** *adj*. **egotism** *n* characteristic of talking only or too much about oneself; arrogance; conceit. **egotist** *n*. **egotistic** *or* **egotistical** *adj*.

eiderdown *n* **1** fine down from the eider duck. **2** bed cover or quilt filled with down, feathers, etc.

eight *n* **1** number equal to one plus seven. **2** group of eight things or people. **3** *also* **eight o'clock** eight hours after noon or midnight. *adj* amounting to eight. **eighth** *adj* **1** coming between seventh and ninth in sequence. *n* **1** eighth person, object, etc. **2** one of eight equal parts; one divided by eight. *adv* after the seventh.

eighteen *n* **1** number that is eight more than ten. **2** eighteen things or people. *adj* amounting to eighteen. **eighteenth** *adj,adv,n*.

eighty *n* **1** number equal to eight times ten. **2** eighty things or people. *adj* amounting to eighty. **eightieth** *adj,adv,n*.

either *adj,pron* one or each of two. *conj* used to introduce a choice between alternatives. *adv* (after negatives) as well; furthermore; anyway.

ejaculate *vt,vi* **1** say (something) suddenly; exclaim. **2** discharge; eject. **ejaculation** *n*.

eject *vt* throw out; expel; send forth; discharge. **ejection** *n*.

eke *v* **eke out** cause to last; supplement; draw out.

elaborate *adj* (i'læbərət) complicated; intricate; detailed. *vt,vi* (i'læbəreit) make more detailed; give further explanation of. **elaborately** *adv*. **elaboration** *n*.

elapse *vi* (of time) pass; go by.

elastic *adj* easily stretched; flexible; able to return to its original shape after being distorted, etc. *n* material made elastic by interwoven strips of rubber, used in clothes. **elasticity** *n*.

elated *adj* very happy and excited; overjoyed; high-spirited. **elatedly** *adv*. **elation** *n*.

elbow *n* **1** joint between the forearm and upper arm. **2** part of a coat, etc., covering this. **elbow grease** *n inf* hard work. ~*vt* push (one's way) through, towards, etc.

elder[1] *adj* older of two, esp. two brothers or sisters; senior. *n* **1** older person. **2** official in some churches. **elderly** *adj* old; aged.

elder[2] *n* bush or small tree with whitish flowers and purple or black berries.

eldest *adj* oldest of three or more people.

elect *vt* appoint or choose by voting. *vi* choose; decide. **elector** *n*. **election** *n* process of choosing and voting for candidates for office, esp. for Parliament.

electric *adj* **1** *also* **electrical** of, relating to, or worked by electricity. **2** charged with emotion; tense. **electrically** *adv*.

electrician *n* person whose job is to install or mend electrical equipment.

electricity *n* **1** phenomenon caused by motion of electrons or by excess of electric charge. **2** electric current; electric charge.

electrify *vt* **1** supply with or adapt to work by electric power. **2** startle; shock; thrill. **electrification** *n*.

electrocute *vt* kill by passing an electric charge through the body. **electrocution** *n*.

electrode *n* metal plate or wire by which an electric current enters or leaves a device.

electron *n* elementary particle with negative electric charge that moves round the nucleus of an atom.

electronic *adj* relating to or operated by the conduction of electrons through a vacuum, gas, or semiconductor **electronics** *n* **1** *s* study and technology of electronic equipment **2** *pl* circuits in electronic equipment

elegant *adj* tasteful; refined; graceful **elegance** *n* **elegantly** *adv*

element *n* **1** constituent part **2** chemical substance that cannot be broken down into simpler substances by chemical reactions **3** small amount; suggestion **elements** *pl n* **1** weather, rain, wind, etc **2** basic ideas **elemental** *adj*

elementary *adj* **1** easy; simple; basic **2** relating to the earliest stages of teaching or development

elephant *n* largest land mammal, found in India and Africa, having a trunk and two tusks of ivory **elephantine** *adj* enormous

elevate *vt* **1** make higher in physical position, raise, lift up **2** promote in rank **3** make more refined or cultured **elevation** *n* **1** act of elevating or state of being elevated **2** altitude; height **elevator** *n US* **lift** (def 2)

eleven *n* **1** number that is one greater than ten **2** eleven things or people *adj* amounting to eleven **eleventh** *adj,adv,n*

elf *n, pl* **elves** small magical being in human form, fairy **elfin** *adj*

eligible *adj* having the necessary qualities or qualifications to be chosen, suitable

eliminate *vt* get rid of, remove **elimination** *n*

elite *n* select group of people

ellipse *n* geometric figure having an oval shape **elliptical** *adj also* **elliptic** oval-shaped

elm *n* tall deciduous tree

elope *vi* run away with one's lover to get married secretly **elopement** *n*

eloquent *adj* speaking persuasively or expressively **eloquence** *n* **eloquently** *adv*

else *adv* **1** other, different **2** more **or else** otherwise, if not **elsewhere** *adv* to, in, or at another place

elucidate *vi* explain the meaning of, clarify **elucidation** *n*

elude *vt* **1** escape from, avoid capture **2** escape (a person's mind or memory) **elusive** *adj* **1** hard to find, catch, or see **2** evasive

emaciated *adj* very thin, esp through starvation or illness **emaciation** *n*

emanate *vi* come from, originate from **emanation** *n*

emancipate *vt* free from slavery or legal or social restraint, esp by giving the right to vote **emancipation** *n*

embalm *vt* preserve (a corpse) by removing internal organs and applying chemicals, etc

embankment *n* artificial mound or ridge piled up to carry a railway, etc, or hold back water, as along a river

embargo *n, pl* **embargoes** order prohibiting ships from entering or leaving port, veto, prohibition (esp on trade)

embark *vi,vt* go or put on board a ship, aircraft, etc **embark on** begin, start **embarkation** *n*

embarrass *vt* **1** cause awkwardness or shyness in, disconcert **2** hinder; hamper **embarrassment** *n*

embassy *n* **1** ambassador's official residence **2** staff of an ambassador **3** mission or message of an ambassador

embellish *vt* **1** make more beautiful, decorate, adorn **2** add greater detail or description to **embellishment** *n*

ember *n* piece of wood or coal in a dying fire, glowing cinder

embezzle *vt* misuse or misappropriate (money in one's care), defraud **embezzlement** *n* **embezzler** *n*

embitter *vt* cause to feel bitterness or rancour

emblem *n* sign or symbol representing an idea, principle, etc **emblematic** *adj*

embody *vt* **1** represent in physical form **2** include, comprise **embodiment** *n* person or thing representing a quality, etc personification

emboss *vt* impress (a raised design, lettering, etc) on (a surface)

embrace *n* clasp, hug *vt,vi* hug, as to show affection or welcome *vt* **1** take up (a religion etc), adopt **2** include, cover

embroider *vt,vi* sew (a pattern) on to (fabric) using coloured silks and fancy stitches *vt* add untrue details to **embroidery** *n*

embryo *n* **1** unborn young of animals during early stages of development **2** early stage of development **embryonic** *adj*

emerald *n* bright green precious stone *n adj* bright green

emerge *vi* **1** come into view, as from concealment, appear **2** become revealed or known **emergence** *n* **emergent** *adj* beginning to develop

emergency *n* unforeseen and dangerous situation requiring immediate action, crisis

emigrate *vi* leave a country to live permanently in another. **emigrant** *n,adj.* **emigration** *n.*
eminent *adj* **1** famous and respected; distinguished; high; exalted. **2** outstanding or obvious. **eminence** *or* **eminency** *n.* **eminently** *adv.*
emit *vt* (-tt-) give forth; make (sounds, etc.). **emission** *n.*
emotion *n* feeling, esp. strong feeling; anger, hate, love, etc. **emotional** *adj* given to strong or changeable emotion. **emotionally** *adv.* **emotive** *adj* arousing emotion; provocative.
empathy *n* ability to imagine and share the feelings of another person.
emperor *n* ruler of an empire.
emphasis *n* **1** calling of special attention to an important fact, etc.; stress. **2** accent on a particular or important word, phrase in music, etc. **emphasize** *vt* represent as important; give emphasis to; lay stress on. **emphatic** *adj* **1** stressed; accented. **2** sure; decided. **emphatically** *adv.*
empire *n* group of territories or countries ruled by one person or government.
empirical *adj* based on experience or experiment; not theoretical. **empirically** *adv.*
employ *vt* **1** hire (a person) to work for money; provide work for. **2** make use of. **3** occupy; use. **employment** *n.* **employee** *n* person hired to work for money. **employer** *n* person, firm, etc., employing people.
empower *vt* invest with the power (to); authorize.
empress *n* **1** female ruler of an empire. **2** wife or widow of an emperor.
empty *adj* **1** containing nothing; unoccupied. **2** lacking significance or feeling; meaningless; dull. **3** lacking force or substantiation. *vt,vi* discharge; vacate; leave empty; evacuate. **emptiness** *n.* **empty-handed** *adj* **1** carrying nothing. **2** having won or gained nothing. **empty-headed** *adj* not thinking deeply about important matters; silly.
emu *n* large flightless Australian bird.
emulate *vt* imitate (a person or thing admired or envied); try to equal. **emulation** *n.*
emulsion *n* **1** mixture in which one liquid is suspended in the form of tiny droplets in another. **2** household paint consisting of an emulsion of oil paint in water. **3** light-sensitive coating on photographic film or plates. **emulsify** *vt,vi* make into or become an emulsion.
enable *vt* make able (to); make possible for (a person) to do something.
enact *vt* **1** make into a law or statute. **2** represent on or as if on a stage; perform. **enactment** *n.*
enamel *n* **1** opaque glossy substance applied by fusion to metal for protection or decoration. **2** glossy paint. **3** protective outer layer of the teeth. *vt* (-ll-) coat or decorate with enamel.
enchant *vt* **1** cast a magic spell on; charm. **2** be delightful or fascinating to; bewitch. **enchantment** *n.*
encircle *vt* **1** make a circle round; surround. **2** pass round (the waist, etc.).
enclose *vt* **1** place within a surround, wall, etc.; shut in. **2** put in an envelope for posting, esp. as an additional item. **enclosure** *n* **1** act of enclosing or something enclosed. **2** fencing off of land, esp. common land. **3** area of a sports ground, etc., reserved for spectators, officials, or others.
encore *interj* call from an audience to a performer to repeat a piece of music, etc., or perform an additional item. *n* song or item so performed.
encounter *vt* **1** meet unexpectedly; come across. **2** be faced or confronted with. *n* meeting or confrontation.
encourage *vt* cause to feel more hopeful or confident. **encouragement** *n.*
encroach *vi* overstep the proper limits; intrude on (another's property, area of responsibility, etc.).
encumber *vt* **1** weigh down; be a burden to. **2** hamper; impede. **encumbrance** *n.*
encyclopedia *n* reference book or books giving information on a wide range of topics or on one particular subject. **encyclopedic** *adj*
end *n* **1** final or last part; furthest point. **2** conclusion or completion. **3** aim; object. **4** death. **at a loose end** having nothing to do. **in the end** finally; at last. *~vi,vt* come or bring to an end; finish; conclude. **endless** *adj* without end; never ceasing. **endlessly** *adv*
endanger *vt* bring into danger; put at risk.
endeavour *vt,vi* try hard (to do something); attempt. *n* act of trying; attempt.
endemic *adj* always present in a particular country or area.
endorse *vt* **1** sign the back of (a cheque, etc.). **2** enter a motoring offence in (a driving licence). **3** support; uphold. **endorsement** *n.*

endow *vt* **1** give money or property to (a college, etc.). **2** bestow (beauty, kindness, etc.) upon; bless with. **endowment** *n*.
endure *vi* last; continue in existence. *vt* tolerate; bear. **endurance** *n*. **endurable** *adj* bearable. **enduring** *adj* longlasting.
enemy *n* **1** person hostile to or hated by one; foe; opponent; antagonist. **2** nation with which one is at war.
energy *n* **1** capacity to do work. **2** physical strength; vitality; force. **energetic** *adj*. **energetically** *adv*.
enfold *vt* fold in; hold tightly; embrace.
enforce *vt* **1** force (a law) to be carried out or obeyed. **2** force; compel. **enforcement** *n*.
engage *vt* **1** hire; employ. **2** promise; pledge, esp. to marry someone. **3** occupy. **4** begin fighting against; attack. *vt,vi* (of gears, etc.) lock in position; mesh. **engagement** *n* **1** state of being engaged; act of engaging. **2** appointment to meet; date. **3** military encounter; battle.
engine *n* **1** machine able to convert energy into mechanical work. **2** railway locomotive. **3** any mechanical apparatus or device. **engineer** *n* **1** person skilled in a branch of engineering. **2** someone in charge of engines, esp. on a ship. **3** planner or organizer. *vt* **1** plan, supervise, or construct as an engineer. **2** plan or arrange skilfully; contrive. **engineering** *n* **1** practical application of scientific knowledge in the design, construction, or management of machinery, roads, bridges, buildings, etc. **2** planning or contrivance.
engrave *vt* **1** cut (letters, designs, etc.) into a hard surface. **2** print from an engraved and inked surface. **3** make a deep impression on. **engraver** *n*. **engraving** *n* **1** print made from an engraved surface. **2** engraved surface. **3** art of engraving.
engross *vt* occupy the attention of; absorb.
engulf *vt* swallow up. **engulfment** *n*.
enhance *vt* raise in importance or prominence; heighten; intensify. **enhancement** *n*.
enigma *n* **1** puzzle; riddle. **2** baffling or perplexing person, situation, etc. **enigmatic** *or* **enigmatical** *adj*. **enigmatically** *adv*.
enjoy *vt* **1** take pleasure in. **2** have the use or benefit of; possess **enjoy oneself** feel pleasure, amusement, satisfaction, etc. **enjoyable** *adj*. **enjoyment** *n*.
enlarge *vt,vi* make or become larger; increase in size, scope, extent, etc. **enlarge on** *or* **upon** treat more fully. **enlargement** *n*.
enlighten *vt* impart knowledge or information to, esp. to free from ignorance, superstition, etc. **enlightenment** *n*.
enlist *vt,vi* **1** enrol in some branch of the armed forces. **2** secure or join in support of a person, cause, etc. **enlistment** *n*.
enmity *n* hatred between enemies; hostility; animosity.
enormous *adj* very great; huge; gigantic. **enormity** *n*. **enormously** *adv*.
enough *adj* adequate for the purpose; sufficient. *n* adequate amount; sufficiency. *adv* **1** sufficiently; adequately; tolerably. **2** fully.
enquire *vt,vi* **1** ask questions or seek information (about). **2** inquire. **enquiry** *n* **1** act of enquiring. **2** question. **3** inquiry.
enrage *vt* fill with rage; anger.
enrich *vt* **1** make wealthy or wealthier. **2** make more splendid in appearance; adorn. **3** increase the value or quality of.
enrol *v* (-ll-) *vt* place (a name) or write the name of (a person) on a list, register, etc. *vt,vi* make or become a member enlist. **enrolment** *n*.
ensemble (ɑːnˈsɑːmbəl) *n* **1** collection of parts. **2** group of performers **3** outfit; set of matching clothes and accessories.
ensign *n* **1** flag of a nation, regiment, etc. **2** badge or emblem of office.
enslave *vt* make a slave of. **enslavement** *n*
ensue *vi* come about or follow, esp as a consequence.
ensure *vt* **1** make sure or certain. **2** make safe; secure.
entail *vi* have as a consequence; inevitably involve. **entailment** *n*.
entangle *vt* **1** catch or snare in a mesh, net, etc. **2** make tangled. **3** involve in difficulties, complications, etc. **entanglement** *n*.
enter *vt,vi* **1** come or go in(to). **2** penetrate; pierce. **3** be or cause to be admitted (to). *vt* **1** put into; insert. **2** become a member of. **3** write down in a record, list, etc. **4** begin upon. **enter into** take part in; become a party to. **enter upon** **1** begin; set out on. **2** come into enjoyment or possession of.
enterprise *n* **1** undertaking or project, esp. an important one. **2** boldness, daring, or adventurousness; initiative. **3** commercial undertaking; business.
entertain *vt,vi* **1** divert, amuse, or interest. **2**

give hospitality (to); receive (guests). *vt* consider; cherish. **entertainment** *n*.

enthral *vt* (-ll-) captivate; enchant. **enthralment** *n*.

enthusiasm *n* intense interest, admiration, approval, etc.; zeal; fervour. **enthusiast** *n*. **enthusiastic** *adj*. **enthusiastically** *adv*. **enthuse** *vi* display enthusiasm.

entice *vt* lure or attract by exciting hope of reward, gratification, etc.; tempt. **enticement** *n*. **enticingly** *adv*.

entire *adj* **1** whole; complete; undivided; unbroken; intact. **entirely** *adv* **entirety** *n*.

entitle *vt* **1** give a particular title or name to. **2** give a right, claim, or legal title to. **entitlement** *n*.

entity *n* **1** something that has real existence; thing; object. **2** being; existence.

entrails *pl n* **1** internal organs of an animal, esp. the intestines. **2** internal parts of anything.

entrance[1] ('entrəns) *n* **1** act of entering. **2** place of entry, such as a doorway, passage, etc. **3** admission. **4** act or instance of an actor coming on stage.

entrance[2] (en'trɑːns) *vt* delight; charm; captivate; enthral.

entreat *vt,vi* beseech; implore; beg. **entreaty** *n*.

entrench *vt* **1** fortify or defend by digging trenches. **2** establish firmly and securely. **entrenchment** *n*.

entrepreneur (ɑntrəprə'nəː) *n* someone who sets up and organizes business enterprises.

entrust *vt* give into the care of; trust with; invest or charge with a duty, etc.

entry *n* **1** act or instance of entering. **2** place for entering, esp. a passageway or hall; entrance. **3** access or admission. **4** entering of an item in a record, ledger, etc., or the item entered. **5** contestant in a race, competition, etc.

entwine *vt,vi* twist or tangle together; interweave (with).

enumerate *vt* **1** mention or specify one by one, as in a list; itemize. **2** count. **enumeration** *n*.

enunciate *vt,vi* say or pronounce (a word or words). *vt* state, declare, or proclaim, esp clearly and carefully. **enunciation** *n*.

envelop (en'veləp) *vt* **1** wrap or cover up. **2** surround, enclose, or engulf. **3** obscure; conceal. **envelopment** *n*.

envelope ('envəloup) *n* **1** covering or container for a letter. **2** any enclosing structure, etc.

environment *n* all the external influences, surroundings, conditions, etc., immediately affecting a person or other organism. **environmental** *adj*.

envisage *vt* contemplate as actual or real; visualize.

envoy *n* **1** diplomatic representative ranking just below an ambassador. **2** any messenger or agent.

envy *n* **1** feeling of discontent caused by the possessions, status etc., of someone else. **2** desire to have or enjoy an advantage, possession, etc., of another. **3** object of such feelings. *vt* view with envy. **enviable** *adj*. **envious** *adj*. **enviously** *n*.

enzyme *n* any of numerous organic substances that are produced in living cells and act as catalysts for biochemical changes.

epaulet *n also* **epaulette** decorative shoulder piece, esp. as worn on military uniforms.

ephemeral *adj* lasting only for a short time; transitory; fleeting.

epic *n* **1** long narrative poem in formalized style relating the exploits of a hero or heroes. **2** film, novel, etc., resembling this in style or content.

epidemic *adj* spreading rapidly among people in a certain area. *n* widespread occurrence of a disease, etc.

epilepsy *n* disorder of the nervous system characterized by convulsions and, usually, loss of consciousness. **epileptic** *adj,n*.

epilogue *n* **1** speech made to an audience at the end of a play by one of the actors. **2** concluding part of a novel, television or radio broadcast, etc.

episcopal *adj* **1** of or relating to a bishop. **2** governed by bishops.

episode *n* **1** incident or occurrence in the course of a series of events. **2** digression in a narrative, piece of music, etc. **3** instalment of a book, play, etc., serialized on television or radio. **episodic** *adj*.

epitaph *n* **1** inscription on a tomb or other monument. **2** anything serving as a memorial.

epitome (i'pitəmi) *n* **1** summary; abstract. **2** representative or typical characteristic. **epitomize** *vt* **1** summarize; abstract. **2** typify.

epoch *n* **1** period of time, esp. one considered as distinctive; era. **2** beginning of an important era in the history of anything.

equable *adj* **1** uniform or steady in effect,

operation, motion, etc.; unvarying. **2** tranquil; even; serene.

equal *adj* **1** as great as another in extent, size, degree, etc.; equivalent. **2** having the same rank, value, quality, etc., as another. **3** evenly proportioned. **4** uniform; equable. **5** adequate in quantity, powers, ability, etc. **6** smooth; even; level. *n* someone or something equal to another. *vt* (-ll-) be equal to or the same as. **equality** *n*. **equalize** *vt* make equal. *vi* reach a score equal to an opponent's.

equate *vt* **1** treat or regard as equal or equivalent. **2** put in the form of an equation. **equation** *n* **1** mathematical expression of the equality of two quantities. **2** representation in symbols of a chemical reaction.

equator *n* circle round the earth dividing the Northern hemisphere from the Southern hemisphere. **equatorial** *adj*.

equestrian *adj* **1** of or relating to horses, horsemen, or the skill of riding. **2** on horseback. *n* rider on horseback, esp. an entertainer or competitor.

equilateral *adj* having all sides equal.

equilibrium *n* **1** state of poise or balance prevailing when equal and opposing forces, influences, etc., counter each other in effect. **2** mental composure or stability.

equinox *n* either of the two dates in the year, at the beginning of spring and auntumn, when day and night are of equal length.

equip *vt* (-pp-) provide with necessary equipment, skills, etc. **equipment** *n* **1** equipping or being equipped. **2** collection of tools, implements, resources, etc., necessary for a task or undertaking.

equity *n* **1** fairness; impartiality. **2** system of law co-existing with and supplementing Common Law. **3** total ordinary shares of a limited company. **equitable** *adj*.

equivalent *adj* **1** equal in value, significance, force, etc. **2** corresponding in meaning, function, etc. *n* something equivalent. **equivalence** *n*.

equivocal *adj* **1** uncertain; ambivalent. **2** ambiguous; debatable.

era *n* **1** period of time with its own distinctive flavour, trends, characteristics, etc.; age; epoch. **2** system of dating from a particular event, etc., in the past.

eradicate *vt* wipe out; destroy; obliterate. **eradication** *n*.

erase *vt* **1** rub or scratch out (something written). **2** remove all trace of; wipe out. **eraser** *n*.

erect *adj* **1** upright; vertical. **2** raised or directed upwards. **3** stiff or firm. *vt* **1** build, construct, or elevate. **2** set up; establish. **erection** *n*.

ermine *n* **1** stoat with a brown summer coat and white winter fur. **2** white fur of the animal used to trim judges' robes, etc. **3** rank or functions of a judge.

erode *vt* wear or eat away by gradual action. **erosion** *n*.

erotic *adj* of, relating to, or exciting sexual desire. **eroticism** *n*.

err *vi* **1** be mistaken; make an error. **2** deviate from a moral code; sin.

errand *n* short task entrusted to someone, esp. a short journey to deliver or fetch something.

erratic *adj* **1** irregular; random. **2** irresponsible unpredictable.

error *n* **1** something incorrect; mistake. **2** sin.

erudite *adj* learned; having great knowledge or wisdom. **erudition** *n*.

erupt *vi* **1** (of a volcano) emit lava, etc. **2** burst out; emit suddenly. **eruption** *n*.

escalate *vt,vi* increase by stages or in intensity **escalator** *n* moving staircase consisting of steps in an endless belt.

escape *vt,vi* **1** free oneself from; get away (from). **2** avoid (harm, punishment, etc.) *vi* become free; leak out. *vt* be forgotten by elude. *n* **1** act of escaping or means by which this occurs. **2** sport, pastime, or other release from pressure or reality. **escapism** *n* avoidance of unpleasant reality by fantasy etc. **escapist** *adj,n*.

escort *n* ('eskɔ:t) **1** person or group acting as guard or protection for others on a journey **2** man accompanying a woman to a social function. *vt* (e'skɔ:t) accompany as an escort

esoteric *adj* **1** restricted to a specialized group **2** difficult to understand; obscure in meaning

especial *adj* **1** outstanding; notable; special **2** particular. **especially** *adv*.

espionage *n* spying; obtaining secret information.

esplanade *n* wide level road or walk, esp. one constructed along the shore.

essay *n* **1** ('esei) short prose composition **2** (e'sei) attempt; try; test. *vt,vi* (e'sei) attempt try; test.

essence *n* **1** characteristic fundamental feature

or nature of something. **2** oil or other constituent of a plant, extracted as a perfume, flavouring, etc. **essential** *adj* **1** highly important; indispensable; necessary. **2** constituting the essence; fundamental. **3** absolute; perfect. *n* something that is essential.

establish *vt* **1** make secure or permanent. **2** found; bring about. **3** set up in a position, business, etc. **4** cause to be accepted. **establishment** *n* **1** act or an instance of establishing something. **2** permanent large business or government organization. **3** institution. **4** small business premises, club, hotel, etc. **5** large private household. **the Establishment** *n* group of people and institutions thought of as holding the power in a country.

estate *n* **1** country property with extensive land. **2** new building development for housing or light industry. **3** person's collective assets and liabilities. **4** position in society; social standing. **estate agent** *n* person whose business is the management, lease, and sale of houses and land. **estate car** *n* car with a long body and rear doors, designed to carry goods as well as passengers.

esteem *vt* **1** think highly of; respect. **2** consider; regard. *n* judgment or opinion, esp. a favourable one.

estimable *adj* **1** deserving respect; worthy. **2** able to be estimated; calculable.

estimate *vt* ('estimeit) **1** calculate roughly; gauge. **2** judge. *n* ('estimət) **1** approximation. **2** judgment. **estimation** *n* **1** act or result of estimating. **2** regard; esteem.

estuary *n* tidal mouth of a river.

etch *vt* **1** produce (a design, picture, etc.) on a metal plate by cutting into a wax coating and removing exposed metal with acid. **2** eat away by chemical action. **etching** *n* etched plate or a print made from this.

eternity *n* **1** endless time. **2** time after death. **eternal** *adj* **1** lasting for ever; timeless; without end. **2** continual; incessant. **eternally** *adv*.

ether ('i:θə) **1** volatile highly flammable liquid formerly used as an anaesthetic. **2** hypothetical weightless substance once thought to permeate all space. **ethereal** (i'θiəriəl) *adj* **1** light and airy. **2** spiritual; heavenly.

ethics *n* **1** *s* branch of philosophy concerned with moral conduct, right and wrong, etc. **2** *pl* moral principles; rules or standards of conduct. **ethical** *adj*. **ethically** *adv*.

ethnic *adj* **1** relating to a group of people of a particular culture, religion, language, etc. **2** relating to the racial classification of man.

etiquette *n* customs and rules determining good behaviour; manners.

etymology *n* study of the derivation of words and changes in their meaning and form. **etymological** *adj*. **etymologist** *n*.

eucalyptus *n* tree native to Australasia yielding an aromatic oil, which is used medicinally.

Eucharist *n* **1** Christian sacrament of communion, commemorating the Last Supper. **2** consecrated bread or wine offered at communion.

eunuch *n* male who has been castrated.

euphemism *n* **1** socially acceptable word or phrase used in place of one considered offensive or impolite. **2** practice of using euphemisms. **euphemistic** *adj*.

euphoria *n* feeling of bliss or elation. **euphoric** *adj*.

euthanasia *n* act of killing a person, esp. one experiencing intense pain or suffering; mercy killing.

evacuate *vi,vt* leave or remove from (an unsafe place). *vt* empty; discharge; vacate. **evacuation** *n*.

evade *vt* avoid; escape; elude.

evaluate *vt* **1** determine the quantity or worth of. **2** judge critically; appraise. **evaluation** *n*.

evangelist *n* preacher, esp. one not attached to a particular church. **Evangelist** any one of the four writers of the Gospels. **evangelical** *adj* **1** relating to the Gospels. **2** relating to certain Protestant groups that stress the importance of personal religious experiences and missionary work.

evaporate *vt,vi* **1** change from a solid or liquid state to a vapour. **2** lose or cause to lose some liquid, leaving a concentrated residue. **3** disappear; vanish. **evaporation** *n*.

eve *n* **1** evening or day before a holiday, festival, etc. **2** period immediately preceding an event.

even *adj* **1** level; flat; plane. **2** uniform; regular. **3** calm; placid. **4** equally balanced; fair. **5** (of numbers) divisible by two. **6** exact. *adv* **1** still; yet. **2** used to emphasize comparative forms. **3** used when the content of a phrase or sentence is unexpected. **4** used to modify a statement or add precision to it. *vt,vi* make or become even;

balance. **evenly** *adv*. **even-tempered** *adj* calm; not easily upset or angered.

evening *n* **1** latter part of the day or early night. **2** concluding or final period.

event *n* **1** anything that takes place; occurrence. **2** outcome; result. **3** sports contest.

eventual *adj* final; ultimate; last. **eventually** *adv*.

ever *adv* **1** at any time. **2** by any possibility. **3** always. **evergreen** *adj* (of trees, shrubs, etc.) having foliage that remains green throughout the year. *n* evergreen tree or shrub. **everlasting** *adj* **1** endless; unending. **2** perpetual; of long duration. **evermore** *adv* always; forever; constantly.

every *adj* **1** each. **2** all possible. **every other** every second or alternate. **everybody** *pron* each person; everyone. **everyday** *adj* **1** daily. **2** commonplace; ordinary. **3** suitable for normal days; not special. **everyone** *pron* each person; everybody. **everything** *pron* **1** each thing, aspect, factor, etc. **2** a great deal; something very important. **everywhere** *adv* towards or in all places, parts, etc.

evict *vt* eject or expel (a person) from a house, building, etc. **eviction** *n*.

evidence *n* proof; ground for belief. **evident** *adj* apparent; obvious; plain. **evidently** *adv*.

evil *adj* **1** wicked; sinful. **2** harmful; malicious. **3** offensive; vile. *n* wickedness; sin; depravity.

evoke *vt* **1** summon; call forth. **2** excite; provoke. **evocation** *n*.

evolution *n* **1** natural process of very gradual continuous change in all plants and animals. **2** development; unfolding. **evolutionary** *adj*.

evolve *vt,vi* develop; unroll. *vi* undergo evolution.

ewe *n* female sheep.

exacerbate *vt* **1** aggravate; heighten. **2** exasperate; irritate; provoke. **exacerbation** *n*.

exact *adj* **1** completely correct. **2** precise. **3** very same; particular. **4** rigorous; strict. *vt* **1** extort. **2** demand; require authoritatively. **exactly** *adv*.

exaggerate *vt,vi* represent (something) as being greater or more than it really is. *vt* make more noticeable. **exaggeration** *n*.

exalt *vt* **1** raise; elevate. **2** praise. **exaltation** *n*.

examine *vt* **1** inspect; observe. **2** investigate; study. **3** test (a person's skill, knowledge, etc.). **examiner** *n*. **examination** *n* **1** act of being examined. **2** questions or tasks intended to test skill or knowledge. **3** medical inspection of the body.

example *n* **1** specimen; sample. **2** someone or something worthy of emulation. **3** precedent.

exasperate *vt* irritate; provoke; incense. **exasperation** *n*.

excavate *vt,vi* **1** dig out. **2** hollow out. **3** expose (buried objects) by digging. **excavation** *n*. **excavator** *n* machine for digging and moving soil, gravel, etc.

exceed *vt,vi* be greater than (another). *vt* overstep the limit of. **exceedingly** *adv* very; greatly.

excel *v* (-ll-) *vt,vi* surpass; be superior to. *vi* do extremely well (in).

excellency *n* term of address used for ambassadors, governors, high-ranking government officials, etc.

excellent *adj* of the best quality; thoroughly good and praiseworthy. **excellence** *n*.

except *prep* with the exception of; save. *vt* exclude; omit. **exception** *n* **1** act of being excepted. **2** instance to be excepted; unusual situation, person, thing, etc. **exceptional** *adj* **1** relating to an exception; irregular. **2** having higher than average intelligence, skill, talent, etc. **exceptionally** *adv*.

excerpt *n* selected passage from a book; extract.

excess *n* (ek'ses) **1** surplus. **2** amount, degree, etc., by which something is exceeded by another. *adj* ('ekses) over and above what is normal, necessary, or required. **excessive** *adj*. **excessively** *adv*.

exchange *vt* **1** barter; trade for something. **2** interchange; trade (information). **3** replace; substitute. *n* **1** act of exchanging. **2** anything that substitutes for or replaces something offered. **3** argument. **4** central office or station. **5** place where brokers, dealers, etc., buy and sell securities and certain commodities.

exchequer *n* **1** department of the treasury dealing with accounting. **2** treasury or government department of a country, state, etc., controlling financial matters.

excise *n* ('eksaiz) **1** tax levied on certain commodities or for certain licences. **2** branch of the civil service responsible for collecting such taxes. *vt* (ek'saiz) impose excise on; tax; levy.

excite *vt* **1** arouse; awaken; provoke. **2** stir up;

instigate. **3** disturb; agitate. **excitable** *adj.* **excitement** *n.*

exclaim *vt* cry out; shout. **exclamation** *n* **1** act of exclaiming; outcry. **2** interjection; emphatic word, phrase, or sentence. **exclamation mark** *n* punctuation mark (!) used after an exclamation.

exclude *vt* **1** keep out; bar. **2** deny inclusion or consideration of. **exclusion** *n.* **exclusive** *adj* **1** barring or excluding everything else. **2** sole; not shared; individual. **3** fashionable; select. **exclusively** *adv.*

excommunicate *vt* bar (someone) from church membership or receiving certain sacraments. **excommunication** *n.*

excrete *vt* (of an animal) discharge (waste, such as urine, sweat, etc.) from the body. **excrement** *n* waste matter, esp. solid, discharged from the body. **excreta** *pl n* waste matter discharged from the body.

excruciating *adj* agonizing; tortuous; intensely painful.

excursion *n* **1** short journey, pleasure trip, or outing. **2** group or party taking an excursion.

excuse *vt* (ik'skju:z) **1** pardon; forgive. **2** justify or make allowances for. **3** exempt or release (from). *n* (ik'skju:s) **1** justification; reason. **2** explanation offered to explain bad behaviour, rudeness, etc. **3** pretext; pretence. **excusable** *adj.*

execute *vt* **1** kill, esp. following a legal decision; put to death. **2** perform; achieve; carry out. **3** administer; enforce. **execution** *n.* **executive** *adj* relating to administration, the execution of a duty, etc. *n* person or group running or administrating a company, project, etc. **executor** (ig'zekjutə) *n* person who carries out a duty, esp. someone responsible for dealing with the provisions of a will.

exempt *vt* release or excuse from a duty, obligation, etc. *adj* released from a duty, obligation, etc. **exemption** *n.*

exercise *n* **1** physical exertion, esp. for the purpose of training or to maintain health. **2** task undertaken to improve one's skill or competence. **3** operation or use of one's power, right, etc. *vt,vi* give exercise to or take exercise. *vt* **1** use; employ. **2** put into action; carry out. **3** exert; wield.

exert *vt* use the power of (strength, influence, etc.); exercise. **exert oneself** make an effort; strive. **exertion** *n.*

exhale *vi,vt* breathe out; force (air) out of the lungs. **exhalation** *n.*

exhaust *vt* **1** drain; empty; consume completely. **2** use, discuss, etc., to the full. *n* **1** gases that are expelled from an engine as waste. **2** expulsion of such gases. **exhaustion** *n.* **exhaustive** *adj.* **exhaustively** *adv.*

exhibit *vt* **1** present for viewing or inspection. **2** indicate; disclose; demonstrate. *n* something presented for public viewing. **exhibitor** *n.* **exhibition** *n* **1** act of exhibiting. **2** public show or display. **exhibitionism** *n* practice of or tendency towards showing off or drawing undue attention to oneself in public. **exhibitionist** *adj,n.*

exhilarate *vt* enliven; animate; stimulate. **exhilaration** *n.*

exhume *vt* dig up (a corpse) after burial.

exile *n* **1** banishment; ostracism. **2** banished person; outcast. *vt* banish; expel (from a country).

exist *vi* **1** be; have reality. **2** endure; continue. **3** be present in a particular place or situation. **existence** *n* life; state of being. **existent** *adj.*

exit *n* **1** way out. **2** departure; withdrawal. *vi* go out or away; depart.

exonerate *vt* **1** absolve; acquit. **2** release; exempt. **exoneration** *n.*

exorbitant *adj* excessive; extravagant; enormous. **exorbitantly** *adv.*

exorcize *vt* deliver from evil spirits, demons, etc. **exorcism** *n.* **exorcist** *n.*

exotic *adj* unusual; foreign; not native.

expand *vt,vi* **1** make or become greater in size, range, scope, etc. **2** swell; fill out; extend. **3** develop (a theme, story, etc.). **expansion** *n.* **expansive** *adj.* **expanse** *n* continuous surface that extends or spreads; stretch.

expatriate *vt* (eks'peitrieit) **1** banish; exile. **2** move (oneself) away from one's own country. *adj* (eks'peitriit) expatriated. *n* (eks'peitriit) expatriated person. **expatriation** *n.*

expect *vt* **1** consider as probable. **2** await; look forward to. **3** rely on; require; want. *vt,vi* be pregnant (with). *vi* suppose; anticipate. **expectant** *adj.* **expectation** *n* **1** act of expecting. **2** goal; aim; hope. **3** something expected or anticipated.

expedient *adj* **1** proper; suitable. **2** advantageous; profitable. **expediency** *n.*

expedition *n* **1** organized journey for exploration, hunting, etc. **2** group or party on such a journey.

expel *vt* (-ll-) eject; drive out; ban.

expend *vt* use up; spend; consume. **expenditure** *n* money spent; outgoings.

expense *n* **1** cost; charge; outlay. **2** something costing a great deal. **expensive** *adj* costly; high-priced; dear.

experience *n* **1** direct personal observation, knowledge, practice, etc. **2** specific situation that one has undergone. **3** process of gaining knowledge, esp. when not through study. **4** acquired knowledge. *vt* **1** undergo; encounter. **2** feel; be moved by. **experienced** *adj* fully trained or qualified; expert.

experiment *n* **1** trial, test, or examination to discover something by observation. **2** original or new attempt. *vi* perform an experiment. **experimental** *adj*. **experimentation** *n*. **experimenter** *n*.

expert *n* person having great knowledge, experience, skill, etc., in a particular subject. *adj* **1** relating to an expert. **2** knowledgeable; specialist; skilled. **expertise** *n* specialist skill or knowledge.

expiate *vt* atone for; redeem. **expiation** *n*.

expire *vi* **1** end; terminate; conclude. **2** exhale. **3** die. **expiry** *n* termination; lapsing; end.

explain *vt,vi* **1** make clear or understandable. **2** interpret; expound. **3** account for; justify. **explanation** *n*. **explanatory** *adj*. **explicable** *adj*.

expletive *n* exclamation; swearword or curse.

explicit *adj* **1** clear; precise; definite. **2** open; unreserved. **explicitly** *adv*

explode *vt,vi* **1** burst; blow up. **2** destroy or be destroyed by bursting. *vi* suddenly or violently display anger, rage, etc. **explosion** *n* **1** act of exploding. **2** any rapid or very large increase, as in population. **explosive** *adj* **1** characterized by or capable of explosion. **2** potentially violent, turbulent, or dangerous. *n* substance or device capable of exploding. **explosively** *adv*.

exploit *n* ('eksplɔit) heroic act, deed, or feat. *vt* (ik'splɔit) **1** take unjust advantage of. **2** utilize fully. **exploitation** *n*. **exploitative** *adj*.

explore *vt* investigate thoroughly and methodically. *vt,vi* go to or into (distant lands, areas, etc.) to investigate. **exploration** *n*. **explorer** *n*.

exponent *n* person or thing that functions as an example, representation, or symbol.

export *vt,vi* (ik'spɔ:t) sell or send (goods) out of a country for foreign sale. *n* ('ekspɔ:t) commodity sold or sent to a foreign country. **exporter** *n*.

expose *vt* **1** uncover; disclose; lay open. **2** subject; make liable. **3** make familiar with. **4** subject (camera films, etc.) to light. **exposure** *n* **1** act of exposing. **2** direction in which the main wall of a house or building faces. **3** frame of photographic film that has been exposed to light.

expound *vt* explain in detail.

express *vt* **1** utter; verbalize; speak. **2** represent or symbolize as in a painting, piece of music, etc. *adj* **1** clear; plain; definite. **2** special; particular. *n* train, bus, etc., stopping only at major stations. **expression** *n* **1** verbal communication. **2** manifestation; representation. **3** saying; phrase; term. **4** look on the face that expresses a particular emotion. **expressionless** *adj*. **expressive** *adj*. conveying emotion. **expressly** *adv* particularly; especially; explicitly.

exquisite *adj* delicate; refined; excellent; rare. **exquisitely** *adv*.

extend *vt,vi* **1** stretch; reach out; spread. **2** prolong or last (for). *vt* **1** offer; give. **2** expand; broaden. **extension** *n* **1** act of extending. **2** additional room(s) built on to a house, etc. **3** additional telephone apparatus connected to a central switchboard or having the same number as another. **4** delay or additional period. **extensive** *adj* **1** wide, large. **2** comprehensive; far-reaching. **extensively** *adv* **extent** *n* degree to which something extends; range; scope.

exterior *n* outside; outward appearance. *adj* outer; outside; external.

exterminate *vt* annihilate, destroy or kill. **extermination** *n*.

external *adj* **1** situated at or coming from the outside; outer. **2** foreign; alien. **3** (of medicines, etc.) not to be taken internally. **externally** *adv*.

extinct *adj* **1** (of plants, animals, etc.) no longer existing. **2** obsolete; out-of-date. **3** (of volcanoes) inactive; incapable of further eruption. **extinction** *n*.

extinguish *vt* **1** put out or suppress (fire, lights, etc.). **2** destroy completely. **extinguisher** *n*.

extort *vt* obtain by force or threats. **extortion** *n*.

extra *adj* additional; supplementary. *n* **1** something additional. **2** special edition of a newspaper. **3** actor taking part in crowd scenes, etc.

extract *vt* (ik'strækt) **1** draw or pull out; remove. **2** derive or develop (an idea, theory, etc.). **3** select (from a written work). *n* ('ekstrækt) **1** quotation; excerpt. **2** essence; vital principle or substance. **extraction** *n*.

extramural *adj* related to but not under direct control of an academic institution.

extraneous (ik'streiniəs) *adj* not strictly necessary or central; external; extra.

extraordinary *adj* remarkable; unusual; amazing. **extraordinarily** *adv*.

extravagant *adj* **1** wasteful. **2** free or generous. **3** excessive; inordinate; exorbitant. **3** ornate; fussy. **extravagance** *n*. **extravagantly** *adv*.

extreme *adj* **1** greatest; highest; most intense. **2** immoderate; unreasonable. **3** drastic; radical. **4** most distant or remote; utmost. *n* **1** highest or greatest degree. **2** upper or lower limit of a scale, range, etc. **extremely** *adv*. **extremity** *n* **1** utmost or farthest point or degree. **2** end part of a limb; hand or finger or foot or toe.

extricate *vt* disengage; clear; set free (from). **extrication** *n*.

extrovert *n* gregarious outgoing person. *adj also* **extroverted** gregarious; outgoing; not shy.

exuberant *adj* **1** joyful; vigorous; lively. **2** lavish; prolific; abundant. **exuberance** *n*.. **exuberantly** *adv*.

exude *vt,vi* emit; ooze; gush.

eye *n* **1** organ of sight. **2** *also* **eyesight** sight; vision. **3** gaze; look; glance. **4** ability to inspect, judge, or observe. **5** aperture in a camera, etc., through which light can pass. **6** small hole in a needle, etc. **7** calm centre of a hurricane, tornado, etc. **8** bud on a potato, etc. *vt* inspect carefully; scrutinize. **eyeball** *n* round ball-shaped part of the eye. **eyebrow** *n* **1** fringe of hair growing on the ridge above the eye. **2** ridge above the eye; brow. **eye-catching** *adj* stunning; attracting attention. **eyelash** *n* short hair growing out of the edge of the eyelid. **eyelid** *n* fold of skin that can be closed over the eyeball. **eye-opener** *n* revelation; startling occurrence. **eye shadow** *n* cosmetic applied to colour the eyelids and draw attention to the eyes. **eyesore** *n* extremely ugly or offending building, object, etc. **eyestrain** *n* fatigue and tiredness of the eye. **eye-witness** *n* someone who has been present at and has observed a particular event.

F

fable *n* **1** tale with a moral, whose characters are often animals. **2** fictional story or account.

fabric *n* **1** woven or knitted cloth. **2** structure or basis, as of society, personality, etc. **fabricate** *vt* **1** manufacture or construct, esp. by putting together components. **2** invent; give a false account of. **fabrication** *n*.

fabulous *adj* **1** wonderful; marvellous. **2** almost impossible; unbelievable. **3** mythical. **fabulously** *adv*.

facade (fə'sɑːd) *n* **1** front of a building, esp. when considered for its artistic merit. **2** image that a person presents, esp. when misleading.

face *n* **1** front part of the head, including the mouth, nose, eyes, etc. **2** particular expression of the face. **3** outward attitude or pose, as of self-confidence. **4** any outward appearance. **5** most prominent or front part, as of a cliff, building, etc. **6** dial of a clock or watch. **7** flat surface of something, such as a coin, crystal, etc. **save/lose face** maintain/lose one's dignity or prestige. ~*vt,vi* position or be positioned to point in a particular direction. *vt* **1** come into contact with; meet. **2** confront; challenge. **3** apply to or cover (a surface). **face up to** accept and deal with realistically. **faceless** *adj* anonymous. **facelift** *n* **1** surgical operation to tighten the skin on the face and improve the appearance. **2** any improvement in appearance, as by decoration; renovation. **facepack** *n* cream or paste applied to the face to improve the skin. **face value** *n* **1** stated monetary value. **2** apparent value or meaning of something. **facial** *adj* relating to the face. *n* cosmetic treatment for the face.

facet *n* **1** flat surface of a polished gem. **2** aspect of a situation, subject, or personality.

facetious (fə'siːʃəs) *adj* meant or attempting to be amusing, sometimes inappropriately. **facetiously** *adv*.

facile *adj* **1** easy; simple. **2** glib; superficial; too easy.

facility *n* **1** ease or skill. **2** equipment or means enabling execution of an action. **facilitate** *vt* make easier or simpler.

facsimile (fæk'simili) *n* exact copy; reproduction.

fact *n* something that actually happened, existed, or exists; provable statement. **in fact** *or* **as a matter of fact** really; truly. **factual** *adj* true or truthful; actual.

faction *n* dissenting group within a larger group.

factor *n* **1** something that contributes towards a result. **2** number that can be divided into another number evenly.

factory *n* building equipped with manufacturing machinery.

faculty *n* **1** ability or power, as the senses, etc. **2** department of a university or its staff.

fade *vt,vi* make or become pale, less clear, etc. **fade out** disappear gradually.

fag *n* **1** difficult chore. **2** *sl* cigarette. *vt,vi* (-gg-) *also* **fag out** make or become tired through arduous work; exhaust.

Fahrenheit *adj* relating to a temperature scale on which the freezing point of water is 32° and its boiling point 212°.

fail *vi,vt* have no success (at). *vi* **1** become inoperative; break down. **2** be inadequate or insufficient. **3** omit; forget. *vt* **1** judge to have failed. **2** disappoint; let down. *n* instance of failing. **without fail** certainly; definitely. **failing** *n* inadequacy; fault. **failure** *n* person or thing that fails.

faint *adj* **1** lacking in clarity, contrast, etc. **2** without conviction; weak; feeble. **3** feeling as though one is going to lose consciousness. **4** cowardly; timid. *vi* lose consciousness for a short time. *n* short period of loss of consciousness. **faint-hearted** *adj* cowardly; timid.

fair[1] *adj* **1** impartial; just; without bias. **2** conforming to regulations. **3** (of a person) having light colouring. **4** beautiful or unblemished. **5** acceptable; good. **6** sunny; cloudless. **fair and square** legitimate; correct. **fairness** *n*. **fairly** *adv* **1** moderately; rather. **2** justly; deservingly. **fair-minded** *adj* just; impartial.

fair[2] *n* **1** event, usually out of doors, with various entertainments and sideshows. **2** cattle market. **3** gathering of people dealing in similar products for trade purposes. **fairground** *n* place where a fair is held.

fairy *n* imaginary being having small human form and supernatural or magical powers. **fairytale** *n* a story containing imaginary or supernatural characters, usually intended for children.

faith *n* **1** belief; trust. **2** any religion. **faithful** *adj* **1** loyal; true. **2** remaining close to the original. **faithfully** *adv*. **faith-healing** *n* healing by means of supernatural or religious powers.

fake *vt,vi* forge; pretend. *n* counterfeit; forgery. *adj* not real; counterfeit.

falcon *n* bird of prey, which is sometimes trained for sport.

fall *vi* (fell; fallen) **1** descend quickly; drop. **2** collapse from an upright position. **3** decrease; decline. **4** diminish in tone. **5** extend towards a lower level; hang down. **6** be defeated or overthrown; submit. **7** pass into sleep or a similar condition. **8** occur at a specified time. **9** be transferred. **10** be classified into. **fall back on** have recourse to for support. **fall for** *inf* **1** be deceived by. **2** develop a deep affection for. **fall in with 1** become acquainted with. **2** agree to. **fall on one's feet** emerge successfully from a precarious situation. **fall out** quarrel; disagree. ~*n* **1** act or instance of falling or dropping. **2** lowering; decline. **3** distance over or through which something falls. **4** capture or decline of a city, civilization, etc. **falls** *pl n* waterfall; cataract. **fallout** *n* descent of particles of radioactive substances, which contaminate the air after a nuclear explosion.

fallacy *n* incorrect opinion or belief; deceptive notion. **fallacious** *adj*.

fallible *adj* **1** liable to make mistakes or be deceived. **2** likely to contain errors.

fallow *adj* (of land) left uncultivated for one or more seasons.

false *adj* **1** untrue; incorrect. **2** unfaithful; given to deceit. **3** synthetic; not genuine, artificial. **falsehood** *n* lie or fallacy. **false pretences** *pl n* forgeries and misrepresentations for illegally obtaining money, property, etc. **falsify** *vt* **1** make false or incorrect, esp. to mislead. **2** prove incorrect; disprove.

falsetto *n* male voice pitched within a range that is higher than normal. *adj,adv* using such a voice.

falter *vi* hesitate; waver; stumble. *vt* say with hesitation; stammer.

fame *n* state of being well known; reputation. **famed** *adj* acknowledged; recognized.

familiar *adj* **1** well-known or easily recognizable. **2** often used or frequented; customary. **familiar with** well acquainted with. **familiarize** *vt* make knowledgeable about a subject, place, etc.

family *n* **1** group consisting of parents and their children. **2** group of related people. **3** any interrelated group of things.

famine *n* widespread shortage of food, esp. because of drought or crop failure.

famished *adj* extremely hungry; starved.

famous *adj* **1** well-known; celebrated. **2** *inf* fantastic; splendid.

fan[1] *n* **1** device for causing a flow of air for cooling, such as a folding wedge-shaped device held in the hand. **2** anything shaped like a fan. *vt,vi* (-nn-) **1** cool by means of a fan. **2** *also* **fan out** spread or move in the shape of a fan; separate.

fan[2] *n* enthusiastic admirer of a pop star, actor, etc.

fanatic *n* **1** person with extreme and irrational dedication to a cause. **2** *inf* person dedicated to a particular pestime. **fanatical** *adj*.

fancy *adj* **1** elaborate, decorated, or ornamental. **2** high in quality. **3** coming from the imagination. *n* **1** whim; pleasure. **2** poetic imagery. *vt* **1** imagine; picture in the mind. **2** like; be attracted by. **fancy dress** *n* costume worn for a masquerade. **fanciful** *adj* **1** not factual; imaginary. **2** produced creatively or imaginatively.

fanfare *n* short musical piece played on trumpets.

fang *n* long pointed tooth, as of a snake or dog.

fantasy *n* **1** unrestrained imagination. **2** something imagined, esp. when bizarre. **3** imagined sequence that fulfils some unsatisfied need; daydream. **4** hallucination. **5** notion that is not based on fact. **fantastic** *adj* **1** strange or eccentric in design, appearance, etc. **2** exaggerated or incredible. **3** *inf* very large or great. **4** *inf* fabulous; splendid.

far *adv* **1** at, to, or from a long way or great distance. **2** at or to a distant time. **3** very much. **as far as** to the point that. **by far** by a great deal. **far and near** *or* **far and wide** everywhere; over a great distance or area. **far gone 1** in an advanced condition. **2** mad; crazy. **3** *inf* drunk. **far out** *sl* strange; unconventional. **in so far as** to the extent that. ~*adj* **1** long way away. **2** extending or protruding a great distance. **3** remote; isolated. **far-away** *adj* **1** distant; removed. **2** preoccupied; daydreaming. **far-fetched** *adj* improbable; exaggerated. **far-off** *adj* distant; remote. **far-reaching** *adj* having extensive effects or importance.

farce *n* **1** form of drama in which characters, plot, etc., are presented as highly comical or ridiculous. **2** absurdly silly event or situation. **farcical** *adj*.

fare *n* **1** amount of money paid for a journey, etc. **2** menu; type of food.

farewell *interj,n* goodbye.

farinaceous *adj* made of or containing flour or grain.

farm *n* tract of land, with buildings, used for the rearing of livestock or cultivation of crops. *vi,vt* rear livestock or cultivate (land) for a living. **farm out** distribute. **farmer** *n*. **farmyard** *n* enclosed area adjacent to farm buildings.

farther *adv* **1** to or at a distant place or time; further. **2** in addition (to). **farthest** *adv* to or at the most distant place or time; furthest. *adj* most remote in place or time.

fascinate *vt* make curious or interested; captivate. **fascination** *n*.

fascism *n* ideology or government that is authoritarian and undemocratic. **fascist** *adj,n*.

fashion *n* **1** style of dress, makeup, etc. **2** custom; behaviour. **3** kind; type. *vt* make or form. **fashionable** *adj* relating to a current trend, style, or fashion.

fast[1] *adj* **1** moving or able to move rapidly; quick. **2** lasting only a short period. **3** (of a timepiece) indicating a more advanced time than is accurate. **4** promiscuous. **5** retaining colour; not prone to fading. *adv* **1** quickly; rapidly; swiftly. **2** securely; tightly. **3** soundly.

fast[2] *vi* abstain from food, esp. for religious reasons or as a protest. *n* *also* **fasting** abstinence from food.

fasten *vt,vi* attach; secure; tie.

fastidious *adj* difficult to please; fussy.

fat *n* **1** greasy semi-solid chemical substance. **2** animal tissue containing such substances. *adj* **1** overweight; obese. **2** containing fat. **3** thick. **4** rewarding or promising. **fatten** *vt,vi* make or become fat(ter). **fatty** *adj*.

fatal *adj* **1** leading to death. **2** disastrous; tragic. **fatality** *n* **1** accident that has resulted in death. **2** person so killed. **3** condition causing death.

fate *n* **1** force or power that determines events. **2** fortune; destiny. **fated** *adj* determined by fate. **fateful** *adj* awful; dreadful.

father *n* **1** male parent. **2** person who has founded a field of study, movement, etc. *vt* be the father (of). **father-in-law** *n, pl* **fathers-in-law** father of one's husband or wife. **fatherland** *n* person's native country or that of his ancestors.

fathom *n* unit used to measure depth of water, equal to 6 feet. *vt* **1** measure the depth of (water). **2** probe into (a problem, situation, etc.) and discover its meaning.

fatigue *n* **1** tiredness; weariness. **2** strain, esp. in fibres, metals, etc. *vt* make tired or weak.

fatuous *adj* silly; foolish.

fault *n* **1** flaw; defect. **2** mistake. **3** misdemeanour; wrong. **4** accountability for a mistake or error. **at fault** to blame. **find fault** criticize; find a mistake in. **to a fault** excessively. ~*vt* find a mistake in. **faulty** *adj*.

fauna *n, pl* **faunas** *or* **faunae** ('fɔːniː) all animal life of a particular time or region.

favour *n* **1** kind gesture of good will. **2** good will. **3** partiality. **4** token or gift. **in favour of** **1** commending. **2** to the advantage of. *vt* **1** prefer. **2** advocate or endorse. **favourable** *adj* advantageous; encouraging. **favourably** *adv*. **favourite** *adj* given preference to over others; best liked. *n* someone or something regarded preferentially.

fawn[1] *n* young deer. *adj,n* greyish or yellowish brown.

fawn[2] *vi* seek attention or favour servilely.

fear *n* **1** feeling of alarm or terror. **2** something causing this. **3** reverence. **4** anxiety; apprehension. **for fear of** so as to avoid. ~*vt,vi* feel fear (of). **fearless** *adj*. **fearful** *adj* **1** afraid. **2** *inf* very great.

feasible *adj* **1** able to be done. **2** suitable or likely. **feasibility** *n*.

feast *n* **1** lavish meal; banquet. **2** periodic religious celebration. **3** something lavishly pleasing. *vi* **1** eat at a feast. **2** take extreme pleasure in. *vt* **1** provide with a feast. **2** please; delight.

feat *n* deed or action, esp. when noteworthy.

feather *n* one of the external structures that form a bird's outer covering. *vt* cover or fill with feathers. **feathery** *adj*.

featherweight *n* **1** boxer of a weight under 126 lbs. **2** something extremely lightweight or of little consequence.

feature *n* **1** part of the face, such as mouth, eyes, etc. **2** characteristic or quality. **3** full-length cinema film. **4** particular article in a periodical. *vi* be a distinctive characteristic of. *vt* offer as or make a feature; give main importance to.

February *n* second month of the year.

feckless *adj* weak; ineffectual.

federal *adj* **1** relating to a league of nations or states. **2** relating to a system of government in which states retain a degree of autonomy under a central government. **federally** *adv*. **federate** *vi,vt* join in a federation or league. **federation** *n*.

fee *n* amount of money due for a service, right of entrance, etc.

feeble *adj* **1** weak or exhausted, either physically or mentally. **2** deficient in strength or force. **feeble-minded** *adj* lacking in intelligence.

feed *v* (fed) *vt* **1** offer food or other essential materials to. **2** offer as food. *vi* eat. *n* **1** food, esp. as for infants, livestock, etc. **2** amount of food or material allowed. **fed up** disgruntled with a particular situation.

feel *v* (felt) *vt* **1** sense or examine by touching. **2** experience (an emotional or physical sensation). **3** have an emotional or physical reaction to. *vi* produce a sensation as specified. **feel for** sympathize with. **feel like** want. **feel up to** be well enough to. ~*n* **1** instance of feeling. **2** nature of something as perceived by touch or by intuition. **feeler** *n* organ in some animals especially adapted for touch. **feeling** **1** ability to experience a sensation or a sensation itself. **2** mood; attitude; emotion. **3** impression; premonition. *adj* **1** sensitive; sympathetic. **2** showing emotion.

feet *n pl of* **foot.**

feign *vt* pretend; invent; imitate.

feint *n* deceptive movement, action, etc. *vi* make such a movement.

feline *adj* **1** of the cat family. **2** like a cat. *n* animal in the cat family.

fell[1] *v pt of* **fall.**

fell[2] *vt* bring down or cause to fall.

fellow *n* **1** man; boy **2** companion; colleague. **3**

member of the same class, kind, etc. **4** member of a learned society. **fellowship** *n* **1** sharing of interests, activities, etc. **2** group sharing such things; brotherhood. **3** position of being a fellow, esp. in a learned society, university, etc. **4** religious communion.

felon *n* criminal. **felony** *n*.

felt[1] *v pt* and *pp* of **feel.**

felt[2] *n* fabric whose fibres have not been woven but joined together by pressure.

female *n* person or animal of the sex that conceives and gives birth. *adj* designating a female. **feminine** *adj* **1** considered suitable to or representative of women or girls. **2** of a grammatical gender normally denoting females. **feminism** *n* **1** ideology or movement that advocates the equality of women. **feminist** *n,adj*.

fence *n* **1** structure enclosing an area or forming a barrier. **2** *inf* distributor of illegally obtained goods. **on the fence** indecisive; neutral. ~*vt* build a fence around or on. *vi* **1** participate in the sport of fencing. **2** evade questions or arguments. **fencing** *n* sport or activity of fighting with swords.

fend *v* **fend off** ward off (something). **fend for** provide for; support.

ferment *vt,vi* (fə'ment) undergo or cause fermentation. *n* ('fə:ment) **1** agent, such as yeast, that causes fermentation. **2** tumult; commotion. **fermentation** *n* chemical reaction in which sugar is changed into alcohol by action of microorganisms.

fern *n* plant with green feathery leaves that forms spores.

ferocious *adj* fierce; savage.

ferret *n* weasel-like animal used for hunting rabbits and rats. *vt* **1** drive out from cover. **2** *also* **ferret out** find; search out; seek.

ferry *n* boat or service used for transportation across a body of water. *vt,vi* transport or travel over water.

fertile *adj* **1** able to produce young. **2** capable of sustaining vegetation. **fertility** *n*. **fertilize** *vt* **1** cause the union of (a female reproductive cell) with sperm or a male reproductive cell. **2** make fertile. **fertilizer** *n* substance added to soil to increase crop yield.

fervour *n* ardour; zeal; passion. **fervent** *adj*.

fester *vi* **1** form pus. **2** become gradually resentful, bitter, etc.

festival *n* **1** celebration or feast. **2** series of cultural performances. **festivity** *n* **1** gaiety; merry-making. **2** feast or celebration.

festoon *n* **1** decorative chain of flowers, foliage, etc.; garland. **2** something that resembles a festoon. *vt,vi* decorate with or form festoons.

fetch *vt* **1** go and get; bring. **2** cost or sell for. **fetching** *adj* becoming or charming.

fete (feit) *n* **1** festival or celebration, esp. in aid of charity. **2** holiday. *vt* **1** entertain. **2** celebrate with a fete.

fetid *adj* smelling stale or rotten.

fetish *n* **1** object believed to have magic powers in certain cultures. **2** object or activity to which one is blindly devoted.

fetlock *n* part of a horse's leg above the hoof.

fetter *n* chain fastened to the ankle; shackle. *vt* restrain with fetters; shackle.

feud *n* long bitter hostility between two families, factions, etc. *vi* participate in a feud.

feudal *adj* of a social system based on land ownership and on ties between lords and vassals. **feudalism** *n*.

fever *n* **1** abnormally high body temperature. **2** disease characterized by fever. **3** extreme excitement. **feverish** *adj*.

few *adj* not many; small number of. *n* small number. **quite a few** large number.

fiancé *n* engaged man. **fiancée** *f n*.

fiasco *n* disaster; absolute failure.

fib *inf n* harmless lie. *vi* (-bb-) tell fibs. **fibber** *n*.

fibre *n* **1** yarn or cloth or the filaments from which they are made. **2** thread; filament. **3** structure or substance. **4** character; nature. **fibreglass** *n* **1** fabric made from pressed or woven glass fibres. **2** material made by binding glass fibres with synthetic resin.

fickle *adj* not faithful; changeable.

fiction *n* **1** literary works not based on fact. **2** falsehood; lie. **3** act of lying. **fictional** *adj*. **fictitious** *adj* not genuine; false.

fiddle *n* **1** *inf* violin. **2** *inf* illegal or fraudulent dealing or arrangement. *vi* **1** play on a fiddle. **2** fidget or tamper with. *vt* do something deceptively or illegally.

fidelity *n* **1** faithfulness or devotion to duty, a cause, person, etc.; loyalty. **2** truthfulness. **3** faithfulness of reproduction in sound recording.

fidget *vi* **1** be restless or uneasy. **2** play with or handle something in a restless manner. **fidgety** *adj*.

field *n* **1** open plot of land, esp. one for pasture

or crops. **2** tract of land on which sports are played; pitch. **3** battleground. **4** area rich in minerals, etc. **5** area of knowledge, study, etc. **6** area away from normal working quarters where new data or material can be collected. **7** the side that is not batting in a game of cricket. *vt* stop or recover (the ball) in cricket. **fieldwork** *n* work done away from normal working quarters for purposes of research, investigation, etc.

fiend *n* **1** evil spirit. **2** wicked or cruel person. **3** *inf* fanatic; addict. **fiendish** *adj* cruel; wicked.

fierce *adj* savage; wild; ferocious.

fiery *adj* **1** of or like fire. **2** emotional; passionate. **3** causing a feeling of burning.

fifteen *n* **1** number that is five more than ten. **2** fifteen things or people. *adj* amounting to fifteen. **fifteenth** *adj,adv,n.*

fifth *adj* coming between fourth and sixth in a sequence. *n* **1** one of five equal parts; one divided by five. **2** fifth person, object, etc. *adv* after the fourth.

fifty *n* **1** number equal to five times ten. **2** fifty things or people. *adj* amounting to fifty. **fiftieth** *adj,adv,n.*

fig *n* plant bearing sweet fleshy fruit, which is sometimes dried

fight *n* **1** battle; combat. **2** quarrel; conflict. **3** boxing contest. *vt,vi* (fought) **1** struggle against (a person) in physical combat. **2** contend with (a person, situation, etc.). **3** support or campaign (for). **4** box. **fighter** *n.*

figment *n* invention; fiction.

figurative *adj* not literal; metaphorical.

figure *n* **1** symbol for a number. **2** amount; number. **3** shape; form. **4** person. **5** pattern; design. *vt,vi* **1** calculate. **2** mark with a pattern, diagram, etc. *vi* be important; feature. **figure out** *inf* solve; think out. **figurehead** *n* person who is an apparent leader, but with no real power.

filament *n* **1** thin wire inside a light bulb. **2** single strand of fibre.

file[1] *n* **1** holder for the orderly storage of documents. **2** correspondence or information on a particular subject, person, etc. **3** row or line. **on file** in a file; recorded. ~*vt* **1** keep or put in a file. **2** institute (a legal suit). *vi* proceed in a row. **filing cabinet** *n* cabinet designed for orderly storage of documents.

file[2] *n* **1** hand tool with a blade that has small cutting teeth. **2** nailfile.

filial *adj* of or suitable to a son or daughter.

fill *vt* **1** make full to capacity. **2** extend; permeate. **3** insert material into (an opening). **4** fulfil (a requirement). **5** cover, as with writing, etc. **6** do or perform the duties of (a job). **7** hire or elect for. **fill in 1** supply information on a form. **2** be a substitute for. **3** insert. **4** fill up (a hole, gap, etc.). **fill out** become or make fuller. *n* **one's fill** enough; one's limit.

fillet *n* piece of boneless meat or boned fish. *vt* remove the bones from (meat or fish).

filly *n* female horse or pony of under four years.

film *n* **1** cellulose that has been specially treated for making photographs, negatives, etc. **2** sequence of pictures projected onto a screen in a cinema or transmitted on television, etc. **3** thin layer or coating. *vt* take moving pictures with a cinecamera. *vt,vi* cover or be covered with a film.

filter *n* **1** substance or device through which fluid is passed to remove particles, impurities, etc. **2** device which allows only certain signals, kinds of light, etc., to pass through. *vt,vi* pass through a filter. *vi* become known or occur slowly.

filth *n* **1** dirt, squalor, or pollution. **2** obscenity. **filthy** *adj.*

fin *n* wing-like organ of a fish, used for locomotion.

final *adj* **1** last; ultimate. **2** decisive; conclusive. **finally** *adv.* **finalize** *vt* conclude or arrange.

finance (fi'næns, 'fainæns) *n* study or system of public revenue and expenditure. *vt* provide funds for. **finances** *pl n* monetary affairs, resources, etc. **financial** *adj.* **financially** *adv.* **financier** *n* person engaged in finance, esp. on a large scale.

finch *n* small bird that feeds mainly on seeds.

find *vt* (found) **1** discover or come upon. **2** become aware of. **3** regard or consider as being. **4** determine; arrive at (a conclusion). **5** provide. *n* lucky discovery, bargain, etc.

fine[1] *adj* **1** superior in quality, skill, or ability. **2** pleasurable. **3** minute, powdered, or thin. **4** (of weather) clear and dry. **5** in good health or condition. **6** subtle or acute. **7** refined; well-mannered. *adv inf* very well; in good health. **finely** *adv.* **fine arts** *pl n* painting, sculpture, architecture, etc.

fine[2] *n* amount of money paid as a penalty for a crime, offence, etc. *vt* impose a fine on.

finery *n* showy or elaborate dress, jewellery, etc.

finesse (fi'nes) *n* delicate or subtle skill.

finger *n* any of the five appendages attached to the hand. *vt* handle; touch with the fingers. **fingermark** *n* smudge made by a finger. **fingerprint** *n* impression of the pattern on the underside of the end joint of a finger.

finish *vt,vi* end; complete; conclude; terminate. *vt* **1** use up; consume. **2** perfect. **3** put a finish on. *n* **1** final stage; completion; conclusion; end. **2** surface or texture of a material or a preparation used to produce this. **3** refinement; elegance.

finite *adj* bounded or limited.

fiord *n also* **fjord** narrow inlet of the sea between high cliffs.

fir *n* coniferous tree with needle-like leaves.

fire *n* **1** state of burning or combustion. **2** mass of burning material. **3** any device for heating a room. **4** something that resembles a fire. **5** discharge of a firearm. **6** passion or enthusiasm. **7** liveliness or brilliance. *vt,vi* (of a firearm or explosive) discharge or be discharged. *vt* **1** *inf* terminate (someone's) employment. **2** expose to heat, as clay in a kiln. **3** provide the fuel for. **firearm** *n* weapon from which a bullet, etc., is propelled by means of an explosion. **fire brigade** *n* group of persons trained in fire-fighting. **fire drill** *n* practice of emergency measures to be taken in case of fire. **fire engine** *n* motor vehicle equipped with fire-fighting apparatus. **fire-escape** *n* staircase or other means of escape in the event of a fire. **fireman** *n, pl* **-men** man specially trained in fire-fighting. **fireplace** *n* recess in a wall for a fire. **fire station** *n* building where fire engines are housed and where firemen are stationed. **firework** *n* device made from combustible material that is lit for entertainment. **firing squad** *n* group of men who carry out a death sentence by shooting.

firm[1] *adj* **1** hard; solid. **2** stationary; secured. **3** settled; established. **4** steadfast; resolute. **firmly** *adv*. **firmness** *n*.

firm[2] *n* business concern; company.

first *adj* coming before all others. *adv* **1** before any other. **2** for the first time. *n* **1** beginning. **2** highest honours degree. **first aid** *n* emergency medical aid administered before professional help is available. **first-class** *adj* best or most expensive; belonging to the highest grade. *adv* by first-class means. **first-hand** *adj,adv* from the original source. **first person** *n* form of a pronoun or verb when the speaker is the subject. **first-rate** *adj* of the best kind or class.

fiscal *adj* relating to state finances.

fish *n, pl* **fish** *or* **fishes 1** any of a large group of aquatic animals, usually having gills and fins. **2** flesh of this animal used for food. *vi* **1** catch or attempt to catch fish. **2** *also* **fish out** obtain from an inaccessible place. **3** draw out, as by hinting or questioning. *vt* fish in (a particular body of water). **fisherman** *n, pl* **-men** man who catches fish for a living. **fishmonger** *n* person who sells fish.

fission *n* **1** breaking into parts or bits. **2** *also* **nuclear fission** splitting of the nucleus of atoms, used in atom bombs and as a source of energy.

fist *n* closed or clenched hand.

fit[1] *vt,vi* (-tt-) **1** make or be suitable or well adapted for. **2** be proper or correct for. **3** adjust to make (something) appropriate. **4** qualify or make competent. **5** alter (clothing) for a particular person. *adj* **1** suitable or well adapted. **2** competent. **3** healthy; well. **4** worthy. **5** ready or inclined to. *n* **1** way in which something fits. **2** something that fits. **3** process of fitting. **fitting** *adj* appropriate; suitable.

fit[2] *n* **1** attack; seizure; convulsion. **2** period or spell of emotion, activity, etc. **fitful** *adj* coming on in or characterized by sudden irregular spells.

five *n* **1** number equal to one plus four. **2** group of five persons, things, etc. **3** *also* **five o'clock** five hours after noon or midnight. *adj* amounting to five.

fix *vt,vi* fasten; secure; attach. *vt* **1** settle; determine. **2** assign; allot. **3** repair; mend; correct. *n* **1** *inf* predicament; dilemma. **2** *sl* injection of a narcotic. **fixation** *n* compulsive preoccupation with or concentration on (a particular object, idea, etc.). **fixture** *n* **1** household appliance that is firmly or permanently attached. **2** person regarded as being permanently installed in a particular place, position, etc. **3** scheduled football match, sports meeting, etc.

fizz *vi* bubble; effervesce. *n* **1** hiss. **2** effervescence. **3** drink containing soda water or sparkling wine.

fizzle *vi* **1** hiss; make bubbling sounds. **2** *inf also* **fizzle out** die out after an energetic start.

fjord *n* fiord.

flabbergasted *adj* amazed; astonished.

flabby *adj* **1** without firmness; soft. **2** having limp flesh. **3** lacking vitality; listless. **flabbiness** *n*.

flag[1] *n* piece of cloth decorated with an emblem or symbol. *vt* (-gg-) **1** decorate with flags. **2** signal with flags.

flag[2] *vi* (-gg-) become limp or weak; tire.

flagon *n* vessel for holding liquids.

flagrant *adj* blatant; glaring.

flair *n* **1** ability or aptitude. **2** style; elegance.

flake *n* thin layer or piece. *vt,vi* **1** peel off in flakes or chips. **2** cover with flakes. **flaky** *adj*.

flamboyant *adj* showy; ostentatious; extravagant. **flamboyance** *n*.

flame *n* **1** blaze or fire. **2** ardour; passion. *vt,vi* burn. *vi* flash; be inflamed.

flamingo *n, pl* **flamingos** *or* **flamingoes** large wading bird with bright pinkish red plumage and long legs.

flammable *adj* capable of burning; inflammable.

flan *n* open tart, either savoury or sweet.

flank *n* **1** part of the body of man or animals between the ribs and hip. **2** cut of beef from this area. **3** either side of a body of armed troops, ships, etc. *vt,vi* **1** place or be next to. **2** go round the flank of (an enemy).

flannel *n* **1** light fabric with a short nap. **2** piece of cloth used for washing the body. **3** *inf* evasive speech, explanation, etc. *vt* (-ll-) clean or polish with a flannel.

flap *v* (-pp-) *vt,vi* swing or flutter. *vi* panic; become agitated or upset. *n* **1** action or sound made by flapping. **2** flat sheet attached at one end, used to cover an opening, etc. **3** *inf* state of panic or distress.

flare *vt,vi* **1** burn with an unsteady or sudden flame. **2** spread outwards in a wedge shape. *vi* develop quickly; break out. **flare up** suffer a sudden outburst of anger, violence, etc. ~*n* **1** sudden burst of flame, sometimes used as a signal. **2** spreading or tapering section. **3** sudden burst of emotion, etc.

flash *n* **1** flame; flare. **2** outburst. **3** instant; moment. **4** display. *adj also* **flashy** **1** ostentatious or gaudy. **2** counterfeit; false. *vi* **1** move quickly; race. **2** occur suddenly. **3** send out a sudden intermittent bright light. *vt* **1** send a signal or message by means of a flash. **2** *inf* display ostentatiously. **flashback** *n* abrupt change of scene to one earlier in time in a play, film, etc. **flashbulb** *n* bulb producing a bright flash used to take photographs. **flashlight** *n* **1** source of intermittent or flashing light. **2** electric torch.

flask *n* bottle or similar container for liquids.

flat[1] *adj* **1** horizontal; level; even or smooth. **2** low; prostrate. **3** collapsed or deflated. **4** unqualified; outright. **5** dull; lifeless. **6** insipid; stale. **7** pointless. **8** having a pitch below the true pitch; half a semitone below a specified note. *adv* **1** horizontally. **2** absolutely; definitely. *n* **1** flat surface, piece of land, etc. **2** deflated tyre. **3** flat musical note. **flatfish** *n, pl* **-fish** fish that swims horizontally and has both eyes on the uppermost side of the body, such as plaice, sole, etc. **flat-footed** *adj* having feet with flattened arches. **flatten** *vt,vi* make or become flat.

flat[2] *n* room or set of rooms in a building, used as a self-contained dwelling.

flatter *vt,vi* **1** praise insincerely or immoderately. **2** show to advantage. **3** please by paying compliments or attention to. **flattery** *n*.

flaunt *vt,vi* **1** show off. **2** wave or flutter.

flautist *n* person who plays the flute.

flavour *n* **1** taste. **2** seasoning or extract. **3** essence; characteristic quality. **4** smell; aroma. *vt* give a flavour to. **flavouring** *n* seasoning.

flaw *n* defect; imperfection; blemish. **flawless** *adj*.

flax *n* plant producing fibres used in the manufacture of linen, paper, etc.

flea *n* small blood-sucking insect, a parasite on mammals and birds, noted for its ability to leap.

fleck *n* speck; spot.

flee *vt,vi* (fled) run away (from).

fleece *n* **1** woollen coat of a sheep, etc. **2** something resembling this. *vt* **1** shear (a sheep). **2** swindle.

fleet[1] *n* **1** large number of warships functioning as a unit. **2** nation's navy. **3** group of aeroplanes, motor vehicles, ships, etc., operated by the same company.

fleet[2] *adj* moving quickly; fast. **fleeting** *adj* passing quickly; transitory.

flesh *n* **1** soft body tissue of animals or man. **2** skin; body surface. **3** thick pulpy part of a fruit or vegetable. **4** man's physical nature, as opposed to his spiritual side. **5** one's family. **fleshy** *adj.*

flew *v pt* of **fly**[1].

flex *vt,vi* bend. *n* insulated cable for connecting an appliance with a source of electricity. **flexible** *adj* **1** pliable; supple. **2** adaptable or yielding. **flexibility** *n.*

flick *n* sudden light stroke. *vt* strike, move, or remove with a sudden jerky movement. **the flicks** *pl n inf* cinema.

flicker *vi,n* **1** flash; glimmer. **2** flutter; flap.

flight[1] *n* **1** act, ability, or manner of flying. **2** route taken by an airborne animal or object. **3** trip or journey of or on an aircraft or spacecraft. **4** soaring mental digression. **5** fin fitted to a dart, arrow, etc., to stabilize its flight. **6** set of steps or stairs. **flighty** *adj* irresponsible; frivolous or erratic.

flight[2] *n* act of fleeing, as from danger.

flimsy *adj* **1** weak or insubstantial. **2** (of paper, fabrics, etc.) thin.

flinch *vi* **1** withdraw suddenly, as if from pain or shock; wince. **2** avoid; shirk.

fling *v* (flung) *vt* **1** toss or hurl; throw forcefully. **2** cast aside; abandon. *vi* move quickly and violently. *n* **1** instance of flinging. **2** period of unrestrained or irresponsible behaviour. **3** any of several lively Scottish dances.

flint *n* **1** hard dark grey stone. **2** small piece of this stone used for striking fires.

flip *v* (-pp-) *vt* toss lightly or carelessly. *vt,vi* move with a jerky motion; flick. *n* **1** tap; flick. **2** alcoholic drink containing egg. **flipper** *n* **1** broad flat limb of certain aquatic animals, used for swimming. **2** paddle-like device worn on the feet for use in swimming.

flippant *adj* impertinent or impudent. **flippancy** *n.*

flirt *vi* **1** behave as if one is amorously attracted to another person. **2** trifle or toy (with an idea, situation, etc.). **flirtation** *n.* **flirtatious** *adj.*

flit *vi* (-tt-) **1** dart; skim along; flutter. **2** pass or pass away quickly. *n* rapid movement; flutter.

float *vt,vi* **1** suspend or be suspended on the surface of a liquid. **2** move lightly through the air or through a liquid. **3** come or bring to mind vaguely. *vt* **1** circulate (a rumour, idea, etc.). **2** offer (stocks, bonds, etc.) for sale on the market. *n* **1** something that floats. **2** small floating object attached to a fishing line. **3** light electrically powered vehicle, as for delivering milk, etc.

flock[1] *n* **1** group of sheep, goats, birds, etc., that keep or are kept together. **2** crowd of people. *vi* **1** gather or cluster together. **2** go or attend in large numbers.

flock[2] *n* **1** tuft of wool, cotton, etc. **2** wool remnants used for mattress stuffing, etc.

flog *vt* (-gg-) **1** beat or whip. **2** *sl* sell.

flood *n* **1** overflowing of water on usually dry ground. **2** great outpouring or gush. **3** rising tide. *vt,vi* **1** cover or be covered in quantities of water. **2** overflow or cause to overflow. **3** overwhelm or be overwhelmed with a great quantity of something. **4** cover or fill completely; saturate. *vi* flow copiously; gush. **floodlight** *n* artificial light that illuminates an area evenly. *vt* illuminate with or as if with a floodlight.

floor *n* **1** lowest horizontal surface of a room, compartment, etc. **2** storey. **3** bottom of a river, ocean, cave, etc. **4** area used for a particular purpose. *vt,vi* cover with or make a floor. *vt* **1** knock over or down. **2** defeat or confound. **floorboard** *n* board in a wooden floor.

flop *v* (-pp-) *vi,vt* **1** fall or drop quickly or clumsily. **2** flap; flutter clumsily. *vi inf* fail. *n* failure.

flora *n, pl* **floras** *or* **florae** ('flɔːriː) **1** plant life of a particular area or time period. **2** catalogue of such plant life. **floral** *adj* of flowers. **florist** *n* person who sells flowers or plants.

flounce[1] *vi* move or go with angry or jerky movements. *n* instance of flouncing.

flounce[2] *n* ruffle used to ornament a garment, etc.

flounder[1] *vi* stumble or plod; move or act with difficulty.

flounder[2] *n* common marine flatfish.

flour *n* powdered wheat or other grain, used in baking and cooking. *vt* **1** make into flour or a fine powder. **2** sprinkle or cover with flour.

flourish *vi* **1** thrive; prosper. **2** make a display; show off. *vt* wave in the air. *n* **1** ostentation; show. **2** embellishment. **3** showy musical passage.

flout *vt,vi* mock; show contempt (for).

flow *vi* **1** (of liquids) move in a stream; circulate. **2** move or proceed as if in a stream. **3** hang loosely. **4** abound. *n* **1** act or rate of flowing. **2** current; stream. **3** continuity. **4** amount that flows. **5** outpouring; flood; overflowing.

flower *n* 1 blossom or a plant that bears a blossom. 2 finest period, part, example, etc. 3 ornament or embellishment. *vi* 1 bear flowers; blossom. 2 mature; develop fully. *vt* cover or adorn with flowers. **flowery** *adj* 1 covered with flowers. 2 ornate; highly embellished.

flown *v pp* of **fly**[1].

fluctuate *vi* waver; change; vary. **fluctuation** *n*.

flue *n* pipe or passage conducting hot gases, air, etc., from a fireplace or boiler.

fluent *adj* 1 speaking or writing a foreign language well. 2 spoken or written well and with ease. 3 flowing, smooth, or graceful. **fluency** *n*. **fluently** *adv*.

fluff *n* light downy particles or material. *vt,vi* make or become fluffy or like fluff. **fluffy** *adj*.

fluid *n* 1 liquid substance. 2 (in physics) liquid or a gas. *adj* 1 capable of flowing. 2 changing; not stable.

flung *v pt* and *pp* of **fling.**

fluorescent *adj* giving off light by the influence of radiation, electrons, etc.; luminous. **fluorescence** *n*.

fluoride *n* 1 chemical compound of fluorine. 2 sodium fluoride added to the water supply to reduce tooth decay.

fluorine *n* yellow poisonous corrosive gaseous element.

flush[1] *vt,vi* 1 blush or make blush; glow. 2 flow or cause to flow with water, etc. *vt* excite; exhilarate. *n* 1 blush; rosy colour; ruddiness. 2 emotion; exhilaration. 3 hot feeling; fever.

flush[2] *adj,adv* level; even. *adj* 1 *inf* affluent. 2 *inf* plentiful; easily obtainable. 3 vigorous. 4 full; almost overflowing.

fluster *vt,vi* make or become nervous or confused. *n* state of nervousness or confusion.

flute *n* 1 musical wind instrument made of wood or metal. 2 narrow rounded channel or groove, as in pillars, etc. *vt* cut flutes in.

flutter *vt,vi* 1 wave or flap. 2 make or be nervous; fluster. *vi* 1 fall or move with irregular motion. 2 move uneasily or aimlessly. *n* 1 flap; wave. 2 state of nervousness. 3 excitement; sensation. 4 distortion of higher frequencies in record-players, radios, etc. 5 *inf* gamble; wager.

flux *n* 1 flow. 2 continuous change.

fly[1] *v* (flew, flown) *vi* 1 move through the air; take wing; soar. 2 move quickly or rapidly. 3 vanish; disappear. *vt,vi* 1 travel in or operate (an aircraft). 2 float; glide; flutter. 3 transport or be transported by aircraft. *n* strip of fabric concealing the zip on trousers. **flyover** *n* road intersection having a bridge that passes over another road.

fly[2] *n* any of certain two-winged insects, such as the housefly.

foal *n* horse, ass, etc., less than one year old. *vt,vi* (of horses, etc.) give birth (to).

foam *n* 1 mass of tiny bubbles, as soap suds. 2 sweat of a horse. 3 frothy saliva. 4 lightweight porous substance made from rubber, plastic, etc. *vi,vt* produce foam; froth; lather.

focus *n, pl* **focuses** *or* **foci** ('fousai) 1 point to which light converges or from which it appears to diverge by the action of a lens or curved mirror. 2 central point, as of attraction or interest. *vt,vi* 1 bring or come to a focus. 2 concentrate (on). **focal** *adj*.

fodder *n* feed for livestock.

foe *n* enemy; opponent.

foetus *n* young of an animal or person while still developing in the womb.

fog *n* 1 cloudlike mass of water vapour near the ground. 2 bewilderment; confusion. *vt,vi* (-gg-) 1 surround or be surrounded with fog. 2 blur; confuse; obscure. **foggy** *adj*. **foghorn** *n* loud horn used to signal warning to ships, etc., in foggy weather.

foible *n* slight weakness or fault; failing.

foil[1] *vt* frustrate; thwart.

foil[2] *n* thin flexible metal sheet.

foil[3] *n* light flexible sword used in fencing.

foist *vt* impose or force (unwanted or inferior goods, etc.).

fold[1] *vt,vi* bend or double (paper, etc.) over itself. *vt* 1 position (the arms) with one round the other. 2 wrap up. 3 wind; bend; enclose. *vi inf* fail; flop. *n* 1 section or mark made by folding. 2 act of folding.

fold[2] *n* enclosure for livestock, esp. sheep.

foliage *n* leaves of a plant.

folk *n* 1 people in general. 2 family; relatives. **folkdance** *n* traditional dance having common or popular origins. **folklore** *n* traditional legends, proverbs, etc., of a people. **folksong** *n* 1 song whose words and music have been passed down through the common people. 2 composition imitating such a song. **folktale** *n* traditional legend or tale.

follicle *n* small cavity or gland, such as that from which a hair grows.

follow *vt,vi* **1** go or come after. **2** result from; ensue. **3** comprehend or understand. **4** watch closely; monitor. *vt* **1** accompany. **2** keep to (a path, road, etc.); trace. **3** comply with; observe; conform to. **4** be interested in. **follower** *n*.

folly *n* **1** foolishness. **2** elaborate nonfunctional building erected to satisfy a whim, fancy, etc.

fond *adj* **1** affectionate; loving. **2** doting; indulgent. **be fond of** have a liking for; be pleased by. **fondness** *n*.

fondant *n* creamy sugary paste, used for sweets, icing, etc.

fondle *vt* touch or handle tenderly or with affection.

font *n* receptacle for baptismal water in a church.

food *n* **1** substance, esp. when solid, eaten for nourishment. **2** something that provides nourishment or stimulation.

fool *n* **1** senseless, silly, or stupid person. **2** jester; buffoon. *vt* deceive; trick; take in. *vi* act like a fool; joke or tease. **fool (around) with** behave stupidly or irresponsibly with. **foolish** *adj* **1** silly; senseless. **2** unwise; thoughtless. **foolishly** *adv*.

foot *n, pl* **feet** **1** part of the end of the leg below the ankle. **2** similar part in animals. **3** unit of length equal to 12 inches (30.48 centimetres). **4** anything resembling a foot in form or purpose. **5** bottom or base. **6** way of walking. **on foot** walking or running. **football** *n* any of various team games in which a ball is kicked towards a goal. **footballer** *n*. **footbridge** *n* bridge for pedestrians. **foothold** *n* **1** place capable of providing support for a foot. **2** secure situation or position. **footing** *n* **1** foothold. **2** foundation or base. **3** status or level. **footlights** *pl n* row of lights along the front of the stage floor in a theatre. **footnote** *n* note printed on the bottom of a page giving additional information to the main text. **footprint** *n* mark made by a foot. **footwear** *n* articles worn on the feet, as shoes, boots, etc.

for *prep* **1** with the intention of. **2** intended to belong to. **3** towards. **4** over or across. **5** in support of. **6** to obtain. **7** suited to. **8** over a particular period or length of time. **9** instead of. **10** because of. **11** with regard to a norm. **12** as. **13** at a particular time. **14** to join in. **15** in spite of. *conj* because.

forage *n* **1** fodder. **2** search for food. *vt,vi* search for food, etc.

forbear *vt,vi* (-bore; -borne) abstain or refrain (from).

forbid *vt* (-dd-; -bad *or* -bade; -bidden) **1** prohibit. **2** hinder.

force *n* **1** strength; intensity; energy. **2** power or might. **3** power to affect; influence. **4** organized military group. **5** group of people organized for a particular purpose. **6** violence; coercion. **7** effectiveness; potency. **8** influence producing motion or strain in an object or material. *vt* **1** compel or oblige. **2** obtain through effort or by overpowering. **3** propel or drive. **4** break down or open; overpower. **5** impose; urge upon. **6** strain; labour. **forceful** *adj*. **forcefully** *adv*. **forcible** *adj* having or done through force. **forcibly** *adv*.

forceps *pl n* surgical pincers.

ford *n* area of a river, etc., shallow enough to be crossed on foot, horseback, etc. *vt* cross (a river, etc.) in this manner.

fore *adj* at or towards the front. *n* front section or area. *adv* at or towards the bow of a ship or boat.

forearm[1] ('fɔːrɑːm) *n* part of the arm between the elbow and wrist.

forearm[2] (fɔːr'ɑːm) *vt* arm beforehand.

forebear *n* ancestor.

forecast *vt,vi* predict; foretell. *vt* herald; anticipate. *n* prediction; estimate.

forecourt *n* court in front of a building, petrol station, etc.

forefather *n* ancestor; forebear.

forefinger *n* finger next to the thumb; index finger.

forefront *n* most outstanding or advanced position.

foreground *n* nearest part of a scene or view.

forehand *adj* **1** made or relating to the right side of a right-handed person or the left side of a left-handed person. **2** foremost; most important. *n* forehand stroke in tennis, squash, etc.

forehead *n* part of the face between the hairline and eyebrows.

foreign *adj* **1** in, from, dealing with, or relating to another country, people, or culture. **2** not familiar; alien. **3** not coming from or belonging to the place where found. **4** not pertinent or applicable; inappropriate. **foreigner** *n*.

foreleg *n* one of the front legs of a four-legged animal.

forelock *n* lock of hair growing above the forehead.

foreman *n, pl* **-men** person who supervises workers.

foremost *adj,adv* first in order, prominence, etc.

forensic *adj* relating to courts of law.

forerunner *n* **1** predecessor; forebear. **2** herald.

foresee *vt* (-saw; -seen) see or realize beforehand; anticipate.

foresight *n* **1** prudence, forethought, or precaution. **2** forecast.

forest *n* **1** large tree-covered tract of land. **2** anything resembling this in appearance, density, etc.

forestall *vt* **1** thwart or foil beforehand. **2** anticipate; consider in advance.

foretaste *n,vt* sample or taste in advance.

foretell *vt* (-told) predict, prophesy.

forethought *n* foresight, anticipation.

forfeit *n* **1** fine or penalty. **2** something lost in order to pay a fine or penalty. *vt* surrender or lose (something) as a forfeit. **forfeiture** *n*.

forge[1] *n* **1** place or furnace where metal is heated and worked. **2** device for hammering heated metal into shape. *vt* **1** hammer (heated metal) into a form. **2** make or produce. **3** invent or make up (a story, etc.). **4** duplicate or copy (a signature, money, etc.) **forgery** *n* act or result of illegally duplicating (a signature, money, etc.).

forge[2] *vi* move ahead or make progress, esp. slowly and with difficulty.

forget *v* (-got; -gotten) *vt,vi* fail to remember or recall. *vt* **1** neglect or ignore. **2** leave behind unintentionally. **forget oneself 1** behave improperly. **2** forget one's position or station.

forgive *vt,vi* (-gave, -given) **1** pardon; excuse; acquit. **2** cease to blame or harbour ill will (for). **forgiveness** *n*.

forgo *vt* (-went; -gone) do without; deny oneself.

fork *n* **1** pronged instrument for holding and lifting, esp. one used at table or for gardening. **2** branching or dividing of a road, river, etc. **3** tuning fork. *vi,vt* divide as or with a fork.

forlorn *adj* **1** abandoned; deserted; forsaken. **2** desolate; miserable.

form *n* **1** shape; structure. **2** variety; type. **3** nature. **4** printed document with blank spaces to be filled in. **5** long backless bench. **6** class in a school. **7** conventional social behaviour. **8** formula; conventional procedure. **9** fitness or level of performance, as in a sport. *vt,vi* **1** make into or assume a particular shape, arrangement, or condition. **2** develop. **3** constitute; make up. **formation** *n*.

formal *adj* **1** relating or adhering to set conventions, rituals, behaviour, etc. **2** precise or symmetrical in form. **formally** *adv*. **formality** *n* **1** something done solely for the sake of custom or appearance. **2** state of being formal. **3** rigorous observation of ceremony, protocol, etc.

formation *n* **1** forming. **2** arrangement, as of a group of soldiers, aircraft, etc.

formative *adj* **1** relating to growth or development. **2** giving form.

former *adj* previous. *n* first of two things mentioned. **formerly** *adv*.

formidable *adj* **1** fearful; threatening; menacing. **2** difficult to resolve, conquer, etc. **3** awe-inspiring.

formula *n, pl* **formulas** *or* **formulae** ('fɔːmjuliː) **1** standard procedure or method for doing or expressing something. **2** mathematical relationship expressed, esp. in the form of an equation. **3** representation of the chemical structure of something. **formulaic** *adj*. **formulate** *vt* express in exact form or formula. **formulation** *n*.

forsake *vt* (-sook, -saken) **1** leave; desert; abandon. **2** renounce; forgo.

fort *n also* **fortress** fortified building or enclosure. **hold the fort** maintain or control during the absence of those usually in charge.

forte (fɔːt, 'fɔːtei) *n* person's strong point or particular ability.

forth *adv* **1** forwards, onwards. **2** out or away from. **forthcoming** *adj* **1** happening soon; imminent. **2** willing to talk; open; forward.

fortify *vt* strengthen or enrich. **fortification** *n*.

fortnight *n* two weeks, fourteen days. **fortnightly** *adv* every two weeks.

fortress *n* fort.

fortune *n* **1** amount of great wealth; bounty. **2** fate; destiny. **3** good luck. **fortunate** *adj* lucky; happy; favourable. **fortunately** *adv*. **fortune-teller** *n* person who predicts future events.

forty *n* **1** number equal to four times ten. **2** forty things or people. *adj* amounting to forty. **fortieth** *adj,adv,n*.

forum *n, pl* **forums** *or* **fora** ('fɔːrə) **1** meeting for discussion. **2** court or tribunal.

forward *adv* **1** onward; ahead; in advance. **2** out or forth. *adj* **1** well-advanced; ahead. **2** ready; prompt; eager. **3** bold; impertinent. **4** radical; progressive. **5** early; premature. *n* an attacking player in certain team games. *vt* send (a letter) on to a new address. **forwards** *adv* **1** towards the front; ahead. **2** into the future.

forwent *v pt* of **forgo.**

fossil *n* **1** remains or impression of a plant or animal of an earlier geological age. **2** *inf* old-fashioned person or thing. **fossilize** *vt,vi* make into or become a fossil.

foster *vt* **1** promote; encourage; further. **2** bring up; rear; nourish. **3** cherish; care for. **foster-parent** *n* person who takes care of another's child.

fought *v pt* and *pp* of **fight.**

foul *adj* **1** offensive; disgusting; repulsive. **2** filthy; squalid; polluted. **3** stormy; tempestuous. **4** wicked; shameful; infamous. **5** obscene; smutty; profane. **6** unfair; dishonourable; underhanded. *n* breaking of the rules (of a sport, game, etc.). *vt* **1** soil; defile; stain. **2** commit a foul on. *vt,vi* entangle or clog. *adv* unfairly. **foul play** *n* unfair or underhanded goings-on or behaviour.

found[1] *v pt* and *pp* of **find.**

found[2] *vt* set up; establish; organize. *vt,vi* base (on). **founder** *n.* **foundation** *n* **1** base or basis. **2** supporting base of a building, structure, etc. **3** organization or institution supported by an endowment. **4** cosmetic used to cover the skin.

founder *vt,vi* sink; fill with water. *vi* **1** break down or collapse. **2** stumble or fail.

foundry *n* place where metal is cast.

fountain *n* **1** jet or gush of water. **2** decorative structure producing jets of water. **fountain pen** *n* pen with a built-in ink reservoir or cartridge.

four *n* **1** number equal to one plus three. **2** group of four persons, things, etc. **3** *also* **four o'clock** four hours after noon or midnight. *adj* amounting to four. **fourth** *adj* coming between third and fifth in sequence. *adv* after the third. **four-poster** *n* bed having a post at each corner and sometimes a canopy. **foursome** *n* group of four.

fourteen *n* **1** number that is four more than ten. **2** fourteen people or things. *adj* amounting to fourteen. **fourteenth** *adj,adv,n.*

fowl *n* **1** hen or cock; chicken. **2** any bird that is hunted as game or used or bred for food. **3** flesh of these birds.

fox *n* **1** undomesticated doglike mammal having pointed ears and muzzle and a bushy tail. **2** fur of this animal. **3** sly or crafty person. *vt inf* trick or perplex. **foxhound** *n* hound trained and kept for foxhunting. **foxhunting** *n* sport in which people on horseback pursue a fox that is being chased by a pack of hounds.

foxglove *n* wild flower having trumpet-like purple or white flowers.

foyer ('fɔijei) *n* lobby or entrance hall.

fraction *n* **1** small part of something. **2** quantity that is not a whole number, often expressed as one number divided by another. **fractional** *adj* being a part, esp. a small part.

fracture *n* act of breaking or something broken, esp. a bone. *vt,vi* break.

fragile *adj* easily broken, marred, or damaged; frail. **fragility** *n.*

fragment *n* ('frægmənt) **1** broken-off part; chip. **2** incomplete portion or part. *vt,vi* (fræg'ment) break into fragments or bits. **fragmentation** *n.*

fragrant *adj* perfumed; sweet-smelling; aromatic. **fragrance** *n.*

frail *adj* **1** weak; delicate; feeble. **2** fragile; breakable; brittle. **frailty** *n.*

frame *n* **1** supporting structure of anything. **2** form; basis. **3** surrounding structure, such as a border around a picture or mirror. **4** small glass structure for growing plants. **5** single picture in a film or television transmission. *vt* **1** surround with a frame. **2** support with a frame. **3** form the basic outlines of (a plan, theory, etc.). **4** *sl* incriminate (someone) by falsifying evidence. **framework** *n* **1** basis or outline. **2** structure that supports or sustains.

franc *n* monetary unit of France, Belgium, Switzerland, and several other countries.

franchise *n* **1** rights of citizenship, esp. the right to vote. **2** privilege granted by the government. **3** permission to market a product in a specified area.

frank *adj* **1** straightforward; honest; candid. **2** blunt; unrestrained; outright. **3** undisguised; avowed. *vt* mark (mail) so as to authorize for free delivery.

frankfurter *n* thin smoked sausage made of

beef or pork that is served hot, usually in a roll.

frantic *adj* agitated; frenzied; raving. **frantically** *adv*.

fraternal *adj* **1** of or relating to a brother. **2** brotherly; showing affection or support. **fraternally** *adv*. **fraternity** *n* **1** group of people with common interests or goals. **2** brotherhood; brotherly consideration and affection. **fraternize** *vi* associate or be friendly (with). **fraternization** *n*.

fraud *n* **1** deceit; trickery; deception. **2** something false or forged; counterfeit. **3** person who practises fraud. **fraudulent** *adj*.

fraught *adj* abounding in; full of.

fray[1] *n* noisy argument or brawl.

fray[2] *vt,vi* **1** unravel or wear away. **2** strain; vex; annoy. **3** rub or rub against.

freak *n* **1** deformed person, animal, or plant. **2** abnormal or odd thing, event, etc. **3** *sl* person deeply interested in something.

freckle *n* small brownish spot on the skin. *vt,vi* cover or be covered with freckles.

free *adj* **1** at liberty; independent; unfettered. **2** not restricted or regulated. **3** clear, immune, or exempt. **4** easy; firm or unimpeded. **5** loose; unattached. **6** available; unoccupied. **7** costing nothing; without charge. **8** frank or open. **9** liberal; generous. *vt* (freed) **1** liberate; set free; release. **2** exempt. **3** rid; clear. *adv* **1** *also* **freely** in a free manner. **2** without cost. **freedom** *n* **1** state or quality of being free; liberty. **2** immunity or privilege. **3** ease; facility. **4** frankness. **5** familiarity; lack of formality. **freehand** *adj* done by hand without the use of other aids. **freehold** *n* absolute ownership of land, property, etc. **freeholder** *n*. **freelance** *n also* **freelancer** self-employed writer, artist, etc. *adj* relating to a freelance. *adv* in the manner of a freelance. **free will** *n* doctrine that people have free choice and that their actions are not predetermined.

freeze *v* (froze; frozen) *vt,vi* **1** change into a solid by a drop in temperature. **2** cover, be, or become covered or blocked with ice. **3** attach (to). **4** be or cause to be motionless through terror, fear, surprise, etc. **5** be or make very cold. *vt* **1** preserve (food) by subjecting to extreme cold. **2** stabilize and prevent increases in (prices, incomes, etc.). *n* fixing of levels of prices, incomes, etc. **freezer** *n* refrigerator in which food can be deep-frozen; deep freeze.

freezing point *n* temperature at which a liquid freezes.

freight *n* **1** cargo; shipment; load. **2** transportation of goods.

French bean *n* thin green seed pod used as a vegetable.

French dressing *n* salad dressing made from oil and vinegar and usually seasoned.

French horn *n* coiled brass instrument with a mellow tone.

French window *n* door made of glass and wood that opens outwards.

frenzy *n* wild excitement or enthusiasm; rage. *vt* make very excited; enrage. **frenzied** *adj*.

frequent *adj* ('fri:kwənt) **1** occurring often and at short intervals. **2** habitual; usual. *vt* (fri'kwent) visit regularly or repeatedly. **frequently** *adv*. **frequency** **1** state of being frequent. **2** rate of occurrence. **3** rate of repetition of a periodic process per unit time.

fresco *n, pl* **frescoes** *or* **frescos** technique or example of wall-painting in which pigments are applied to the plaster before it has dried.

fresh *adj* **1** new; recent. **2** additional; more. **3** (of food) not preserved in any way. **4** (of water) not salt. *adv* in a fresh manner. **freshly** *adv*. **freshness** *n*. **freshen** *vt,vi* make or become fresh. **freshwater** *adj* relating or indigenous to fresh water.

fret[1] *vt,vi* (-tt-) **1** worry; irritate; vex. **2** wear away; erode. *n* **1** annoyance; irritation; vexation. **2** erosion; eating away. **fretful** *adj*.

fret[2] *n* ornamental geometric pattern. *vt* (-tt-) adorn with such a pattern. **fretsaw** *n* fine narrow saw with a curved frame used for cutting designs. **fretwork** *n* interlacing geometric designs cut in thin wood.

friar *n* male member of a religious order supported by alms.

friction *n* **1** resistance met when two surfaces are rubbed together. **2** discord; conflict.

Friday *n* sixth day of the week.

fridge *n inf* refrigerator.

friend *n* **1** companion; intimate. **2** acquaintance; colleague. **3** ally. **friendly** *adj* **1** relating or fitting to a friend. **2** amicable or helpful. **friendliness** *n*. **friendship** *n* **1** being friends or a friend. **2** goodwill; benevolence.

frieze *n* ornamental band or border on a column, wall, etc.

fright *n* scare; alarm; dismay. **look a fright** look terrible or grotesque. **frighten** *vt* **1** scare.

terrify. **2** cause to worry or feel apprehensive about something. **frightful** *adj* dreadful; terrible. **frightfully** *adv* **1** dreadfully; terribly. **2** *inf* very.

frigid *adj* cold in manner, feeling, temperature, etc. **frigidity** *n.*

frill *n* **1** decorative ruffle. **2** trimming; ornamentation. *vt* decorate with frills.

fringe *n* **1** border or edging having hanging thread, tassels, flaps, etc. **2** section of hair cut short to hang over the forehead. **3** outer region; margin. *vt* provide with a fringe. *adj* additional; supplementary.

frisk *vi,vt* move about playfully. *vt inf* search or rob (a person) by examination of clothing. **frisky** *adj.*

fritter[1] *vt* waste (money, time, etc.).

fritter[2] *n* type of pancake dipped in batter and deep-fried.

frivolity *n* gaiety; revelry; merriment. **frivolous** *adj* **1** unimportant; trifling; petty. **2** idle; silly; foolish.

frizz *vt,vi* make or become tightly curled or kinky. **frizzy** *adj.*

frizzle[1] *vt,vi* frizz. *n* tight wiry curl.

frizzle[2] *vi* emit a hiss or sizzling noise. *vt* cook (meat, etc.) until crisp and dry.

fro *adv* from or back. **to and fro** back and forth.

frock *n* **1** dress. **2** monk's cloak. *vt* install (a cleric) in office.

frog *n* smooth-skinned web-footed amphibian. **have a frog in one's throat** speak hoarsely. **frogman** *n, pl* **-men** underwater diver.

frolic *n* gaiety or merry occasion. *vi* (-ck-) act in a lively playful manner. **frolicsome** *adj.*

from *prep* **1** indicating the original place or circumstance. **2** starting at. **3** indicating a distance between (two places). **3** indicating removal or restraint.

front *n* **1** forward position or side that is usually closest to a viewer or user. **2** beginning or opening part or section. **3** leading position. **4** separating area between two different masses of air. **5** *inf* cover; outward appearance. **6** alliance; coalition. *vt,vi* face (on). **frontal** *adj.* **frontally** *adv.*

frontier *n* **1** unexplored or unsettled area. **2** boundary.

frost *n* **1** (formation of) ice particles that are white in appearance. **2** below-freezing temperature. **3** *inf* coldness of attitude, manner, etc. *vt,vi* coat or be coated with frost or something similar. **frostbite** *n* injury to the body caused by exposure to extreme cold. **frostbitten** *adj.* **frosty** *adj.*

froth *n,vi,vt* foam.

frown *vi,n* scowl. **frown on** disapprove of.

froze *v pt of* **freeze.** **frozen** *v pp of* **freeze.**

frugal *adj* economical; thrifty. **frugality** *n.* **frugally** *adv.*

fruit *n* **1** produce of a plant, usually eaten raw or cooked as a sweet. **2** result; product. *vi* bear fruit. **fruit machine** *n* gambling machine with pictures of fruits as variables. **fruitful** *adj* prolific; fertile; productive. **fruitfully** *adv.* **fruitfulness** *n.* **fruitless** *adj* **1** yielding nothing; useless. **2** barren; sterile. **fruitlessly** *adv.* **fruition** (fru:ˈiʃən) *n* **1** fulfilment or maturity. **2** bearing of fruit.

frustrate *vt* baffle; disconcert; foil. **frustration** *n.*

fry *vt,vi* cook in oil or fat.

fuchsia (ˈfju:ʃə) *n* ornamental plant or shrub yielding hanging red, purple, or white flowers.

fudge *n* thick sweet made of butter, sugar, cream, and flavouring.

fuel *n* substance that can be used to supply energy. *vt,vi* (-ll-) provide with or receive fuel.

fugitive *n* person who flees or hides.

fulcrum *n, pl* **fulcrums** *or* **fulcra** (ˈfulkrə) **1** pivot. **2** support; prop.

fulfil *vt* (-ll-) **1** carry out; complete. **2** perform; do; obey. **3** satisfy; gratify. **4** complete; terminate. **fulfilment** *n.*

full *adj* **1** filled to capacity. **2** having eaten as much as one can. **3** entire; complete. **4** enjoying all rights and privileges. **5** ample or plump. **full of** preoccupied with. ~*adv also* **fully** entirely; exactly. *n* **in full** in entirety. **to the full** to capacity. **full-length** *adj* **1** relating to the complete length; unabridged. **2** (of dresses and skirts) reaching the floor. **full stop** *n* punctuation mark (.) used to mark the end of a sentence. **full-time** *adj,adv* relating to or lasting normal working hours.

fumble *vi* **1** handle something clumsily. **2** grope; find one's way clumsily. *vi,vt* utter (something) in an awkward manner. **fumbler** *n.*

fume *vi* storm; rage. *vt,vi* smoke; give off (smoke). *n* smoke; vapour.

fun *n* enjoyment; pleasure; amusement. **make fun of** ridicule; tease. **funfair** *n* fair; amusement park.

function *n* **1** purpose; special or natural activity.

2 formal gathering. **3** variable factor. *vi* perform (as). **functional** *adj* **1** relating to a function. **2** useful rather than decorative or ornamental. **functionally** *adv*.

fund *n* store or reserve, esp. of money, resources, etc. *vt* supply with a fund or funds.

fundamental *adj* **1** basic; underlying; principal. **2** original; first. *n* principle; rule. **fundamentally** *adv*.

funeral *n* burial ceremony.

fungus *n, pl* **fungi** (ˈfʌndʒai) plant lacking chlorophyll, such as a mould, mushroom, etc.

funnel *n* **1** hollow tapering apparatus for transferring a substance to a more narrow-necked container. **2** something shaped like a funnel. *vt,vi* (-ll-) **1** pour through a funnel. **2** direct or channel. **3** fix attention or focus (on).

funny *adj* amusing; comical; humorous. **funnily** *adv*.

fur *n* **1** dense coat of an animal. **2** *inf* sediment caused by hard water. *v* (-rr-) *vt* decorate with fur. *vi,vt inf* cover or be covered with sediment.

furious *adj* raging; angry; violent. **furiously** *adv*.

furnace *n* apparatus equipped to produce steam, etc., by burning fuel.

furnish *vt* **1** provide furniture, carpets, etc., for. **2** equip or supply (with).

furniture *n* movable items such as tables, chairs, or beds, found in a house, office, etc.

furrow *n* **1** trench. **2** groove or line, esp. in the forehead. *vt,vi* make or become wrinkled or lined.

further *adv* **1** *also* **furthermore** moreover. **2** to a greater degree or distance. *adj* more. *vt* assist; help along. **furthest** *adv* to the most extreme degree or place. *adj* most.

furtive *adj* secret; sly. **furtively** *adv*.

fury *n* **1** passion; anger; frenzy. **2** violence; turbulence.

fuse[1] *vi,vt* **1** melt. **2** combine; blend. *n* safety device in plugs, electric wiring, etc. **fusion** *n* act of fusing; coming together.

fuse[2] *n* combustible wire or device leading to and capable of setting off an explosive. *vt* provide with a fuse.

fuselage *n* body of an aeroplane.

fuss *n* activity; ado; bustle. *vi* worry; be unduly preoccupied with. **fussy** *adj* **1** fussing; worrying. **2** preoccupied with petty details. **3** particular.

futile *adj* **1** ineffective; useless; unsuccessful. **2** trivial; frivolous. **futility** *n*.

future *n* **1** time that is yet to come. **2** prospects. *adj* yet to come.

fuzz *n* **1** fluffy or curly hairy mass. **2** blur. *vt,vi* make or become like fuzz. **fuzzy** *adj*.

G

gabble *vi,vt* speak rapidly and inarticulately. *n* rapid inarticulate speech.

gable *n* triangular part of a wall immediately below that part of a pitched roof that juts out.

gadget *n* ingenious, novel, or useful tool, device, or appliance. **gadgetry** *n* gadgets collectively.

gag[1] *n* something placed in or over the mouth in order to silence or control. *vt* (-gg-) place a gag on.

gag[2] *n inf* comedian's joke.

gaiety *n* jollity; light-heartedness; merriment.

gaily *adv* in a gay manner; light-heartedly.

gain *vt* **1** obtain; acquire; win; earn. **2** reach; attain. *vi* **1** increase; gather speed. **2** profit. *n* **1** advantage; win; profit. **2** increase; advancement. **gainful** *adj* profitable.

gait *n* manner of walking.

gala *n* special performance or display; festival.

galaxy *n* **1** large grouping of stars, such as the Milky Way. **2** impressive group of famous people. **galactic** *adj*.

gale *n* strong wind.

gallant *adj* (ˈgælənt) **1** dashing and brave; courageous. **2** (ˈgælənt, gəˈlænt) chivalrous. *n* (ˈgælənt) **1** brave knight or nobleman. **2** attentive suitor. **gallantly** *adv*. **gallantry** *n*.

galleon *n* large sailing ship originally used by Spain.

gallery *n* **1** building or room(s) exhibiting works of art. **2** block of seats above the circle in a theatre. **3** upper floor or section opening out on to the interior of a hall, church, etc.

galley *n* **1** ship's kitchen. **2** warship propelled by oars. **3** long tray for holding metal type.

gallon *n* measure of liquid equal to approx. 4.5 litres (8 pints).

gallop *n* **1** the fastest gait of a horse or similar animal. **2** rapid movement or course. *vi,vt* ride at a gallop. *vi* race; move rapidly.

gallows *s n* wooden structure used for execution by hanging.

galore *adv* in abundance.

galvanism *n* process of producing electricity by chemical action. **galvanize** *vt* **1** coat with a metal by galvanism. **2** stimulate into action. **galvanic** *adj.*

gamble *vi,vt* **1** place a bet (on); stake. **2** risk; hazard; speculate. *vi* play at games of chance, esp. in order to win money. *n* risk; something of uncertain outcome; chance. **gambler** *n.*

game *n* **1** something played for amusement or sport. **2** match; contest. **3** certain wild animals that are hunted for sport or food. *vi* take part in games of chance such as roulette. *adj* willing; plucky. **gamekeeper** *n* person employed to take care of animals, fish, etc., on an estate, to prevent poaching, etc.

gammon *n* lower end of a side of bacon.

gander *n* male goose.

gang *n* **1** group of people, esp. one engaged in unlawful activity. **2** band of workers. *v* **gang up (on)** band together in order to attack. **gangster** *n* armed criminal, usually operating in a gang.

gangrene *n* death and putrefaction of part of a living organism caused by lack of blood supply.

gangway *n* **1** aisle or passageway separating blocks of seats. **2** movable bridge placed between a ship and the quay.

gaol *n,vt* jail. **gaoler** *n.*

gap *n* **1** opening, hole or space between two things. **2** interval; pause.

gape *vi* **1** stare in a stupid way, with astonishment, etc. **2** be wide open. *n* **1** open-mouthed stare. **2** split, hole, breach.

garage *n* **1** small building or shelter for a vehicle, esp. a car. **2** commercial premises selling petrol, repairing motor vehicles, etc.; service station.

garble *vt* give a muddled or misleading account of.

garden *n* **1** plot of land adjoining a house, where flowers, vegetables, etc., are cultivated. **2** small park. *vi* engage on work in a garden. **gardener** *n.* **gardening** *n.*

gargle *vi* rinse out the mouth and throat with liquid, which is kept moving by the action of air drawn up from the lungs. *n* mouthwash; rinse.

gargoyle *n* carved stone face, usually of a grotesque form and often functioning as a waterspout.

garish (ˈgɛəriʃ) *adj* gaudy; vulgar in taste, colour, etc.

garland *n* flowers, leaves, etc., woven into a ring and worn for decoration round the neck or on the head. *vt* decorate with a garland.

garlic *n* plant with a pungent bulbous root, which is used as a seasoning.

garment *n* item of clothing.

garnish *vt* add extra decoration, seasoning, etc., to (food). *n* trimmings or seasoning used to decorate or enhance the flavour of food.

garrison *n* military establishment where troops are stationed. *vt* station (troops, etc.) in a garrison.

garter *n* elasticated band worn round the leg to hold up a stocking or sock.

gas *n* **1** substance, such as nitrogen, oxygen, or carbon dioxide, that has no fixed volume or shape. **2** fuel in the form of gas. *vt* (-ss-) poison or asphyxiate with gas. **gaseous** (ˈgæsiəs, ˈgeiʃəs) *adj.*

gash *n* deep cut, wound, or tear. *vt* cut deeply; slash.

gasket *n* asbestos sheet used as a seal in an engine cylinder.

gasp *vi* **1** struggle to breathe; pant. **2** catch one's breath in surprise, shock, etc. **3** *inf* crave; long (for). *n* **1** sudden sharp intake of air. **2** strangled cry of surprise, etc.

gastric *adj* relating to the stomach.

gastronomic *adj* relating to the art of good eating. **gastronomy** *n.*

gate *n* wooden or metal structure forming a barrier across an opening in a fence, wall, etc. **gatecrash** *vt,vi* force one's way into (a party, meeting, etc.) as an uninvited guest. **gatecrasher** *n.*

gâteau *n, pl* **gâteaus** *or* **gâteaux** (ˈgætou) rich cake decorated with cream, fruit, nuts, etc.

gather *vi,vt* **1** collect together in a crowd or group; assemble; congregate. **2** increase in speed, intensity, etc. **3** draw thread through material to form pleats or folds. *vt* **1** amass; accumulate; collect. **2** pick or pluck (flowers, berries, etc.). **3** assume, understand, believe. **gathering** *n* assembly of people; congregation.

gauche (gouʃ) *adj* awkward, clumsy; ill at ease. **gaucheness** *n.*

gaudy *adj* brightly coloured; showy; garish. **gaudiness** *n.*

gauge (geidʒ) *n* **1** instrument for measuring

speed, temperature, pressure, etc. **2** standard or criterion. **3** thickness of metal. **4** width of a railway track. *vt* **1** measure or estimate the measurement of. **2** assess; judge.

gaunt *adj* thin and bony; haggard; angular.

gauze *n* thin loosely woven fabric used for surgical dressings, curtains, etc.

gave *v pt* of **give.**

gay *adj* **1** cheerful; bright; light-hearted; merry. **2** vivid; of a bright colour. *adj,n sl* homosexual.

gaze *vi* stare fixedly or for a considerable time. *n* fixed or long look or stare.

gazelle *n* small antelope of Africa and Asia.

gear *n* **1** mechanism consisting of a set of toothed wheels, such as that on a motor vehicle used for transmitting motion from the engine to the road wheels. **2** the engaging of a particular gear. **3** *inf* equipment or apparatus required for a particular activity. *vt* set up or arrange one thing to fit in with another.

geese *n pl* of **goose.**

gelatine *n also* **gelatin** yellowish protein obtained by boiling animal bones and skin, used in the manufacture of glue, jellies, etc. **gelatinous** *adj.*

gelignite *n* type of dynamite.

gem *n also* **gemstone** jewel created from a polished stone.

Gemini *n* third sign of the zodiac, represented by the Twins.

gender *n* **1** category, such as masculine, feminine, or neuter, into which nouns may be placed in some languages. **2** sexual identity.

gene *n* part of a chromosome carrying hereditary information.

genealogy *n* **1** descent through a line of ancestors; lineage. **2** family tree. **genealogical** *adj.*

general *adj* **1** not specific or particular; broad. **2** common; widespread; usual. **3** vague; indefinite. *n* military officer of a rank below that of field marshal. **general election** *n* nationwide election held to elect parliamentary representatives. **generalize** *vi,vt* come to a general conclusion from particular statements or facts. **generalization** *n.* **generally** *adv* **1** usually. **2** widely; commonly. **general practitioner** *n* doctor dealing with a wide range of cases rather than specializing in any particular area of medicine.

generate *vt* **1** create. **2** produce (electricity). **generation** *n* **1** production; creation. **2** whole range of people within the same general age group. **3** particular genealogical stage. **4** span of about 30 years. **generator** *n* machine producing electrical energy.

generic *adj* **1** relating to a genus. **2** representing a whole group or class.

generous *adj* **1** unselfish; not mean; kind. **2** tolerant; liberal. **3** ample; lavish. **generosity** *n.* **generously** *adv.*

genetic *adj* relating to genes or genetics. **genetics** *n* study of heredity.

genial *adj* amiable; friendly; warm. **geniality** *n.*

genitals *pl n* male or female sexual organs. **genital** *adj.*

genius *n* **1** person of exceptionally high intelligence or talent. **2** remarkable talent or ability.

genteel *adj* displaying extremely refined manners or taste.

gentile *n* non-Jewish person, esp. a Christian. *adj* non-Jewish.

gentle *adj* **1** not rough or violent. **2** mild. **3** docile; tame. **4** gradual. **gentleness** *n.* **gently** *adv.* **gentleman** *n, pl* **-men 1** man who is cultured and well-mannered. **2** aristocrat or nobleman.

genuine *adj* **1** real; authentic; not false or artificial. **2** sincere. **genuinely** *adv.*

genus ('dʒenəs, 'dʒi:nəs) *n, pl* **genera** ('dʒenərə) biological subdivision containing one or more species.

geography *n* **1** study of the features of the earth's surface. **2** physical features of a region. **geographer** *n.* **geographical** *adj.*

geology *n* study of the composition and evolution of the earth. **geological** *adj.* **geologist** *n.*

geometry *n* branch of mathematics concerned with the properties of figures in space. **geometric** *or* **geometrical** *adj.*

geranium *n* garden or house plant having pink, scarlet, or white flowers and roundish leaves.

germ *n* any microbe that causes disease.

German measles *n* contagious disease characterized by a rash and swelling of the glands.

germinate *vi,vt* **1** develop through warmth and moisture from a seed into a plant. **2** create; spring up. **germination** *n.*

gesticulate *vi* make wild or broad gestures. **gesticulation** *n.*

gesture *n* **1** movement of the arms or head. **2**

act of friendship, sympathy, etc. *vi,vt* express by means of gestures.

get *v* (-tt-; got) *vt* **1** obtain; acquire; gain possession of. **2** fetch. **3** cause to happen or be done. **4** *inf* grasp; understand. **5** make; force; persuade. *vi* **1** become; grow. **2** start. **3** go; proceed. **get about** *or* **around 1** be active. **2** move about; circulate. **get across** communicate so as to be understood. **get ahead** progress; continue. **get along 1** manage; cope. **2** succeed. **get at 1** reach. **2** intend; imply. **get away** escape. **get away with** remain undetected or unpunished. **get by** just about manage to cope adequately. **get down 1** descend. **2** depress; make unhappy. **get down to** begin to concentrate on. **get off 1** dismount or disembark. **2** be permitted to leave. **3** escape punishment. **get on 1** board (a bus, train, etc.). **2** mount (a horse, etc.). **3** make successful progress. **4** have a friendly relationship (with). **get over** recover from; come to terms with. **get round 1** cajole; persuade; bribe. **2** solve or resolve (a difficulty, problem, etc.) by using a different technique or approach. **get round to** find time for. **get through (to) 1** contact by telephone. **2** make (someone) understand or listen. **get up 1** stand up. **2** get out of bed. **3** organize; arrange. **get up to** engage in, esp. when not being watched or controlled. **getaway** *n* escape.

geyser *n* **1** natural hot spring. **2** gas-fuelled water heater.

ghastly *adj* dreadful; shocking; gruesome; horrific.

gherkin *n* small cucumber used for pickling.

ghetto *n, pl* **ghettos** *or* **ghettoes 1** poor district or quarter in a city; slum area. **2** (formerly) poor Jewish quarter in a city.

ghost *n* supernatural being believed to be a dead person's soul, which returns to haunt the living; spirit. *vt,vi* write (a book) for another person, who is then acknowledged as the author.

giant *n* **1** abnormally tall person. **2** prominent or powerful person. **3** one of a race of huge mythological people with superhuman powers. *adj* huge; enormous.

gibberish *n* nonsense; gabbling speech.

gibbon *n* small long-armed ape.

giddy *adj* **1** dizzy. **2** frivolous. **giddiness** *n*.

gift *n* **1** present; donation. **2** talent. **gifted** *adj* talented.

gigantic *adj* very large; huge.

giggle *vi* laugh in a silly or uncontrolled manner. *n* silly laugh; chuckle.

gild *vt* (gilded *or* gilt) coat with gold, gold paint, etc.

gill[1] (gil) *n* respiratory organ of aquatic animals.

gill[2] (dʒil) *n* liquid measure equal to one quarter of a pint.

gimmick *n* device or method used to gain publicity, promote sales, etc.

gin *n* alcoholic drink made by distilling barley or rye and flavoured with juniper berries.

ginger *n* plant whose pungent root is used as a flavouring for drinks, confectionery, etc. *n,adj* reddish-orange; auburn. *v* **ginger up** *inf* enliven; give energy to.

gingerly *adv* cautiously; warily; uncertainly.

gingham *n* cotton fabric patterned with coloured checks or stripes.

Gipsy *n* Gypsy.

giraffe *n* African mammal with a mottled hide and very long neck.

girder *n* iron or steel beam; joist.

girdle *n* **1** cord or thin belt worn round the waist. **2** light corset. **3** band or circle. *vt* **1** fasten with a girdle. **2** encircle.

girl *n* **1** female child; young woman. **girlish** *adj*. **girlhood** *n*. **Girl Guide** *n* female member of an organization with aims similar to those of the Scouts.

giro *n* banking system whereby transfers between accounts may be made by special cheques.

girth *n* **1** leather strap secured under a horse's belly to hold a saddle in position. **2** measurement of circumference. *vt* secure with a girth.

give *v* (gave; given) *vt* **1** present as a gift; donate. **2** place into the hands of; offer; hand. **3** provide; supply. **4** be the cause of. **5** transmit or transfer. **6** yield; produce. **7** *also* **give out** emit or radiate. **8** grant; award; confer. **9** pay; offer to buy for. **10** set aside; allow; spare. **11** act as the host for (a party, meal, etc.). **12** administer (drugs, a punishment, etc.). **13** communicate; make known; tell. **14** inflict; cause to suffer. **15** utter. *vi* **1** donate. **2** be flexible or elastic. **3** *also* **give way** collapse or break under strain or pressure. **give away 1** dispose of; offer for no payment. **2** reveal; disclose. **give in** submit;

surrender. **give up** abandon; cease to do, study, care for, etc. ~*n* elasticity; flexibility.

glacier *n* mass of ice extending over a large area. **glacial** *adj*.

glad *adj* happy; pleased. **gladly** *adv*. **gladness** *n*. **gladden** *vt,vi* make or become glad; cheer.

gladiolus *n, pl* **gladioli** (glædiˈəulai) *or* **gladioluses** plant with long narrow leaves and one stem bearing a brightly coloured flower.

glamour *n* attraction or attractiveness; allure; glittering charm. **glamorous** *adj*. **glamorize** *vt* make attractive or glamorous; exaggerate the charms of; idealize.

glance *vi* **1** take a brief look. **2** flash; shine. **glance off** bounce off sharply. ~*n* **1** brief look; glimpse. **2** quick movement of the eyes. **3** flash; spark.

gland *n* one of various organs in the body that secrete different substances. **glandular** *adj*.

glare *vi* **1** shine fiercely or dazzlingly. **2** stare angrily; glower; scowl. *n* **1** harsh blinding light; dazzle. **2** angry look.

glass *n* **1** hard brittle transparent material used in windows, vessels, etc. **2** drinking vessel made of glass. **3** mirror. **4** telescope. *vt* glaze. **glasses** *pl n* **1** spectacles. **2** binoculars. **glasshouse** *n* greenhouse or conservatory. **glassy** *adj* of or like glass.

glaze *vt,vi* **1** fit with glass. **2** apply or have a thin glassy coating. *n* shiny coating, esp. on ceramics.

gleam *n* beam of light; glow. *vi* shine; beam; glow.

glean *vt,vi* **1** gather (remnants of corn) after reaping. **2** collect painstakingly.

glee *n* mirth; cheerfulness; joy. **gleeful** *adj*. **gleefully** *adv*.

glen *n* (in Scotland) narrow valley.

glib *adj* smooth but insincere in manner. **glibly** *adv*. **glibness** *n*.

glide *vi,vt* move smoothly and noiselessly. *n* smooth flowing movement. **glider** *n* aircraft without an engine that moves according to air currents.

glimmer *vi* shine dimly or faintly. *n* **1** faint light. **2** slight hint or suggestion of hope, intelligence, etc.

glimpse *n* fleeting look; glance; brief view. *vt* see very briefly; get a partial view of.

glint *n* flash; sparkle; gleam. *vi* sparkle; glitter.

glisten *vi* sparkle; shine brightly.

glitter *vi* shine brilliantly; flash; twinkle. *n* sparkle; twinkle.

gloat *vi* take malicious pleasure in one's own greed, another's misfortune, etc.

globe *n* **1** the earth. **2** model of the earth. **3** spherical object; ball. **global** *adj*. **globule** *n* small drop, particle, or bubble.

gloom *n* **1** dim light; semi-darkness; shadow. **2** pessimism; cynicism; despondency; depression. **gloomy** *adj*. **gloomily** *adv*.

glory *n* **1** state of being highly honoured, revered, etc.; exaltation. **2** magnificence; splendour. **3** fame; renown. **glorify** *vt* exalt, treat with great reverence; worship or admire. **glorification** *n*. **glorious** *adj* **1** overwhelmingly beautiful; magnificent. **2** stunning. **3** highly distinguished; great. **gloriously** *adv*.

gloss *n* **1** bright or reflective surface or appearance; sheen; lustre. **2** *also* **gloss paint** type of paint giving a smooth shiny finish. *vt* polish; shine. **gloss over** try to hide; cover up mistakes, etc. **glossy** *adj* shiny.

glossary *n* explanatory list of specialist or technical terms or words.

glove *n* covering for the hand with individual sections for each finger and the thumb. *vt* cover with a glove.

glow *vi* **1** burn with a steady light; shine warmly or brightly. **2** radiate excitement, pride, enthusiasm, etc. *n* steady bright light; blaze. **glow-worm** *n* small beetle, the female of which possesses organs that give off a luminous greenish light.

glower (ˈglauə) *vi* scowl; frown; stare angrily. *n* angry stare; scowl.

glucose *n* type of sugar obtained from grapes and other fruits.

glue *n* substance used as an adhesive, made from gelatine, resin, etc. *vt* **1** stick with glue. **2** attach firmly.

glum *adj* disconsolate; unhappy; gloomy; sullen. **glumly** *adv*. **glumness** *n*.

glut *n* surfeit; excess. *vt* (-tt-) supply with an excess amount; provide with too much. *vi* gorge; overeat. **glutton** *n* **1** excessively greedy person; one who habitually overeats. **2** fanatic. **gluttony** *n*.

gnarled *adj* twisted and knotty; misshapen, lumpy.

gnash *vt* grind or clench (the teeth); grate. *n* grinding action or sound.

gnat *n* small mosquito.

gnaw *vt,vi* **1** bite continuously (on); chew. **2** corrode; wear away. **3** torment persistently. *n* act of gnawing.

gnome *n* mythological being living underground and having a dwarflike appearance.

go *v* (went; gone) *vi* **1** move; proceed. **2** function; work; operate. **3** depart; leave. **4** make a trip or take a walk with a particular purpose. **5** vanish; disappear. **6** extend as far as; reach. **7** become. **8** be put; belong. **9** be ordered; have as a sequence. **10** be used for. **11** fail; break down; collapse. **12** attend; be a member of. **13** be decided (by). **14** be able to fit. **15** be applicable or relevant. **16** be awarded. **17** be allowed to escape. *vt* **1** take or follow (a route, path, etc.). **2** travel (a specified distance). **go against** defy; infringe. **go down** **1** descend. **2** be reduced. **3** deflate. **4** be received or appreciated by an audience. **go for** **1** aim at. **2** attack suddenly. **go in for** take up as a hobby, career, etc. **go off** **1** explode. **2** cease to be interested in. **3** happen. **4** (of food) turn bad. **go on** **1** proceed; continue. **2** criticize or nag incessantly. **3** appear (on stage, TV, etc.). **4** take place; occur. **go out** **1** be extinguished. **2** cease to be fashionable. **3** attend a social function. **go over** **1** repeat; re-examine. **2** cross. **3** be communicated. **go slow** work slowly to enforce one's demands for more pay, etc. **go through** **1** suffer; have to bear; experience. **2** make a search of. **3** inspect. **go under** succumb; sink. ~*n* **1** turn. **2** *inf* energy; drive. **go-between** *n* person acting as a messenger between parties; intermediary.

goad *n* **1** sharp pointed stick used for driving cattle. **2** provocation; stimulus. *vt* **1** drive or prod with a goad. **2** urge; incite; provoke.

goal *n* **1** area between two posts through which a ball must pass in games such as football or hockey in order to score. **2** winning post on a race track. **3** point scored by getting a ball through the goal. **4** aim; object; target. **goalkeeper** *n* player who guards the goal area.

goat *n* brownish-grey mammal often domesticated for its milk or wool. **get one's goat** irritate; annoy.

gobble[1] *vt,vi* eat quickly or greedily; gulp; bolt.

gobble[2] *vi* (of a turkey cock) make a harsh gurgling sound. *n* harsh gurgling sound.

goblet *n* drinking vessel with a long stem.

goblin *n* mythological being that is malevolent or mischievous; demon.

god *n* **1** supernatural being having power over mankind who is worshipped and revered; deity. **2** any object of worship or idolatry. **God** *n* spiritual being who is the creator and ruler of mankind. *interj* exclamation of disgust, horror, surprise, etc. **the gods** highest gallery in a theatre. **godchild** *n, pl* **-children** child for whom a godparent acts. **goddaughter** *n* female godchild. **godfather** *n* male godparent. **godfearing** *adj* intensely religious; pious. **godless** *adj* **1** having no religious beliefs. **2** wicked; evil. **godmother** *n* female godparent. **godparent** *n* person who acts as a sponsor for a child at baptism. **godsend** *n* timely and fortunate event or gift. **godson** *n* male godchild.

goddess *n* **1** female god. **2** extremely beautiful woman.

goggle *vi* **1** stare stupidly; gape. **2** roll the eyes. **goggles** *pl n* protective covering worn over the eyes.

going *n* **1** departure; leaving. **2** manner of travelling. *adj* thriving. **going to** intending to.

gold *n* **1** valuable yellow metal used for coins, jewellery, etc. **2** coins of this metal. **3** wealth; money; riches. *adj,n* bright yellowish-orange. **golden** *adj* **1** made of gold. **2** of the colour of gold. **3** valuable; precious. **golden syrup** *n* kind of treacle of a pale golden colour. **goldfinch** *n* European finch with gold and black plumage. **goldfish** *n* reddish-gold freshwater fish. **goldmine** *n* **1** place where gold ore is mined. **2** source of great wealth. **goldsmith** *n* craftsman who works with gold.

golf *n* sport played on a grass course with the aim of driving a small ball into a succession of holes with a long club. **golfer** *n*.

gondola *n* long narrow open boat traditionally used on the canals in Venice. **gondolier** *n* person who makes a living by transporting passengers in a gondola.

gone *v pp of* **go.**

gong *n* percussion instrument consisting of a large metal disc, which is struck with a hammer.

gonorrhoea (gɔnə'riə) *n* type of venereal disease.

good *adj* **1** of a high quality; not bad. **2** obedient; not naughty. **3** pleasing; attractive. **4** virtuous. **5** efficient; suitable. **6** kind;

benevolent. 7 beneficial. 8 correct; accurate. 9 able; competent. 10 fitting; apt. 11 considerable. 12 safe; not harmful. 13 full; complete. *n* 1 use; point. 2 benefit; advantage. 3 virtue. **for good** for ever; definitely and finally. **Good Friday** *n* Friday before Easter when Christ's Crucifixion is commemorated. **good-humoured** *adj* affable; in a good mood. **good-looking** *adj* handsome; attractive. **good-natured** *adj* kind; genial; easygoing. **goods** *pl n* 1 merchandise; products. 2 items; articles. 3 possessions; property. **good will** *n* 1 generosity; kindness. 2 assets, such as clientele, reputation, etc., taken into consideration when a business is bought or sold.

goose *n, pl* **geese** 1 web-footed bird that is similar to but larger than a duck. 2 foolish or timid person.

gooseberry *n* small edible green berry that grows on a bush with thorny stems.

gore[1] *n* blood that flows from a wound.

gore[2] *vt* stab and wound by ramming with horns or tusks.

gorge *n* 1 steep-sided river valley; ravine. 2 lavish feast. *vi,vt* stuff (oneself) with food; overeat; glut.

gorgeous *adj* very beautiful; magnificent; wonderful.

gorilla *n* large African ape.

gorse *n* prickly evergreen shrub with bright yellow flowers.

gory *adj* 1 covered with blood. 2 bloodthirsty; involving bloodshed. 3 horrifying.

gosh *interj* exclamation of surprise.

gosling *n* young goose.

gospel *n* something taken as the truth; doctrine. **Gospel** *n* one of the first four books of the New Testament, namely Matthew, Mark, Luke, and John.

gossip *vi* talk, esp. in a way that spreads scandal, rumours, etc. *n* 1 act of gossiping. 2 casual or malicious talk; news; scandal. 3 person who gossips.

got *v pt* and *pp* of **get. have got** possess; hold; own. **have got to** must.

gouge *vt* 1 carve a deep hole in with a sharp instrument. 2 tear or scoop out.

goulash *n* stew seasoned with paprika that is a traditional Hungarian dish.

gourd *n* large fruit of various plants, having a tough outer skin and a large number of seeds.

gourmand *n* glutton.

gourmet *n* connoisseur of good food and wine.

govern *vt,vi* 1 rule; reign (over); control. 2 participate in a government. *vt* 1 check; restrain. 2 determine; influence completely. **governess** *n* woman employed as a tutor in a private household. **government** *n* 1 control; rule. 2 body of representatives who govern a country, state, etc. **governor** *n* 1 ruler, esp. of a colony, province, etc. 2 person in charge of a prison. 3 chief controller of a state in the US. 4 *inf* boss. **governorship** *n*.

gown *n* 1 woman's dress, esp. for evening wear. 2 loose light garment, often signifying academic or official status; robe.

grab *vt,vi* (-bb-) 1 take hold of hastily, clumsily, or greedily; seize; snatch. 2 take possession of by force; confiscate. *n* 1 act of grabbing. 2 mechanical device for gripping large objects.

grace *n* 1 elegance, beauty, or charm of movement, style, etc. 2 good will; magnanimity; mercy. 3 short prayer of thanks offered before or after a meal. *vt* serve to add elegance or beauty to; adorn. **graceful** *adj*. **gracefully** *adv*. **gracious** *adj* 1 elegant; dignified. 2 benevolent; courteous; kind. *interj also* **good gracious!** expression of surprise or alarm.

grade *n* 1 position on a scale or in a category. 2 mark or score awarded in an examination, test, etc. *vt* 1 place in a category according to size, quality, etc. 2 award a mark or score to. **gradation** *n* 1 step or stage within a system or on a scale. 2 gradual progression or transition.

gradient *n* slope of a road, railway, etc., measured by the increase in height per distance travelled.

gradual *adj* 1 slowly changing. 2 not steep. **gradually** *adv*.

graduate *vi* ('grædju:eit) 1 receive a degree or diploma from a university, college, etc. 2 change gradually; move along a scale. 3 progress. *n* ('grædju:it) person holding a degree, diploma, etc. **graduation** *n*.

graffiti *pl n* scribbled messages or drawings on walls, public buildings, etc.

graft *n* 1 small plant shoot that is united with another plant in order to produce a new plant. 2 transplanted bone or skin tissue. *vt,vi* 1 propagate by means of a graft. 2 transplant or be transplanted.

grain *n* 1 fruit or seed of a cereal plant. 2 cereal

crops. **3** small particle or granule of sand, sugar, etc. **4** pattern, texture, or arrangement of layers of a piece of timber, rock, etc. **5** minute quantity or proportion.

gram *n also* **gramme** metric unit of weight equivalent to approx. 0.035 ozs.

grammar *n* **1** system of rules governing the correct use of a language. **2** branch of linguistics concerned mainly with syntax and word formation. **grammar school** *n* (in Britain) state secondary school that selects pupils at the age of eleven by means of examination. **grammatical** *adj* relating or conforming to the rules of grammar. **grammatically** *adv.*

gramophone *n* machine for playing records, having a turntable, amplifier, and pick-up arm fitted with a stylus; record player.

granary *n* storage place for grain.

grand *adj* **1** impressively large; magnificent; tremendous. **2** haughty; elegant. **3** marvellous; great. **4** admirable; worthy. **5** final and complete. *n also* **grand piano** large piano whose strings are arranged horizontally rather than vertically. **grandeur** *n.* **grandly** *adv.* **grandchild** *n* grandson or granddaughter. **granddaughter** *n* daughter of one's son or daughter. **grandfather** *n* father of one's father or mother. **grandmother** *n* mother of one's father or mother. **grandparent** *n* grandfather or grandmother. **grandson** *n* son of one's son or daughter. **grandstand** *n* covered block of seats for spectators at a race meeting, football match, etc.

granite *n* hard greyish-white crystalline rock.

granny *n inf* grandmother.

grant *vt* **1** give as a favour. **2** admit; concede. **3** give (a sum of money). *n* sum of money given for research, education, etc.

granule *n* small grain. **granular** *adj.*

grape *n* small sweet green or purple fruit that is eaten raw, dried, or pressed to make wine. **grapevine** *n* **1** vine producing grapes. **2** informal or underground information network.

grapefruit *n* large round citrus fruit with a yellow peel.

graph *n* chart or diagram for depicting the relationship between variables, particular sets, quantities, etc. **graphic** *adj* **1** clearly or imaginatively expressed. **2** relating to writing or drawing. **3** in graph form.

graphite *n* soft black carbon, used in pencils, electrodes, etc.

grapple *vi* struggle physically; wrestle; tussle. **grapple with** attempt to deal with (a problem, difficult situation, etc.). ~*n* **1** iron hook. **2** grip in wrestling; hold.

grasp *vt,vi* **1** take hold (of) firmly in the hands; grip; clasp. *vt* understand; comprehend. *n* **1** firm grip. **2** knowledge; understanding. **3** power to dominate.

grass *n* **1** plant with green spiky blades. **2** lawn, field, or pasture of such plants. **3** *sl* marijuana. *vt,vi* sow with grass. *vi sl* act as an informer, esp. to the police. **grassy** *adj.* **grasshopper** *n* greenish-brown insect renowned for its characteristic chirping sound produced by friction of the hind legs against the wings. **grass roots** *pl n* **1** section of the population regarded as representing true political or public opinions at a local level. **2** underlying or essential principles.

grate[1] *vt* cut or shred (cheese, vegetables, etc.) by rubbing against a rough surface. *vt,vi* **1** produce a harsh squeak by scraping. **2** annoy; jar. *n* harsh squeak.

grate[2] *n* iron structure or rack placed in a fireplace to hold fuel and allowing air to circulate underneath.

grateful *adj* thankful; appreciative of kindness, a gift, opportunity, etc. **gratefully** *adv.*

gratify *vt* **1** seek or obtain satisfaction of (one's desires); indulge. **2** please; make happy. **gratification** *n.*

grating *n* cover or guard made of a network of metal bars; grille.

gratitude *n* feeling or expression of appreciation; thankfulness.

gratuity *n* gift of money; tip. **gratuitous** *adj* **1** free of charge. **2** not asked for or solicited; unjustified.

grave[1] *n* trench or hole dug in the ground for a coffin. **have one foot in the grave** be feeble or near to death.

grave[2] *adj* **1** serious; solemn. **2** dangerous; bad. **gravely** *adv.*

gravel *n* coarse mixture of fragments of rock.

gravity *n* **1** force of attraction between objects with mass, exerted by the earth, moon, etc., to pull objects towards their centre. **2** seriousness; solemn importance. **gravitate** *vi* **1** be drawn by the force of gravity. **2** be attracted to a certain place. **gravitation** *n*

gravy *n* stock or juice produced by cooking meat, often thickened for a sauce.

graze[1] *vi,vt* feed or allow to feed on grass or other vegetation in a pasture.

graze[2] *vt,vi* touch lightly; scrape. *vt* produce a scratch or cut on the skin by scraping. *n* abrasion; scratch.

grease *n* **1** melted animal fat. **2** lubricant; oil. *vt* **1** cover or smear with grease. **2** lubricate. **greasy** *adj*. **greasepaint** *n* waxy substance used by actors as make-up for the stage.

great *adj* **1** large; big; huge; vast; tremendous. **2** excellent. **3** famous. **4** important; significant. **5** impressive; grand. **greatly** *adv*. **greatness** *n*.

greed *n* **1** desire to overeat; gluttony. **2** desire to take more than one's fair share of wealth, power, etc. **greedy** *adj*. **greedily** *adv*.

green *n* **1** colour of grass; spectral colour. **2** grass pitch or field. *adj* **1** of the colour green. **2** inexperienced; naive. **3** jealous; envious. **4** unripe. **greenery** *n* green vegetation; foliage. **greenfly** *n* green aphid. **greengage** *n* fruit of the plum family with a yellowish-green skin. **greengrocer** *n* person who sells fruit and vegetables. **greengrocery** *n*. **greenhouse** *n* shed with walls and roof mainly of glass, used for housing and cultivating plants. **greens** *pl n* leaves of green vegetables, such as cabbage or spinach.

greet *vt* **1** welcome. **2** send good wishes to. **3** be present at the arrival of; meet. **greeting** *n* statement or act of welcome, good wishes, etc.

gregarious *adj* enjoying other people's company; sociable.

grenade *n* small explosive shell thrown by hand or fired from a gun.

grey *n* colour between black and white, having no hue. *adj* **1** of a grey colour. **2** having grey hair. **3** dull; gloomy. **greyish** *adj*. **greyhound** *n* breed of smooth-haired dog with a slender body and pointed muzzle, often used for racing.

grid *n* **1** network of squares printed or placed over a map or drawing. **2** network of electricity cables, water pipes, etc.

grief *n* sorrow; distress; remorse. **grief-stricken** *adj* suffering intense grief; heart-broken. **grievance** *n* complaint; feeling of being hurt or offended. **grieve** *vi,vt* feel or cause great sorrow or distress.

grill *n* rack or section of an oven on or under which food is cooked. *vt,vi* cook on or under a grill. *vt inf* interrogate; cross-question.

grille *n* framework of metal bars forming an ornamental screen or grating.

grim *adj* **1** bleak; unpleasant; formidable. **2** stern; unbending; severe. **grimly** *adv*.

grimace *n* facial expression of disgust, hatred, etc. *vi* screw up the face in a grimace.

grime *n* **1** soot. **2** dirt. **grimy** *adj*.

grin *n* broad happy smile. *vi,vt* (-nn-) smile with the lips widely parted.

grind *vt,vi* (ground) **1** crush or pound into powder or small particles. **2** sharpen (a blade) or smooth by friction. **3** oppress; enslave. **4** grate or gnash (the teeth). *n* hard toil; repetitious routine. **grinder** *n* appliance for grinding coffee beans, etc.

grip *n* **1** firm hold or clasp; grasp. **2** strength of the fingers. **3** handle of a racquet or bat. **4** understanding; comprehension. **5** holdall; bag. **get** *or* **come to grips with** learn to control; master; tackle. ~*vt,vi* (-pp-) **1** hold firmly; clasp. **2** mesmerize; enthrall.

gripe *vi* moan; nag; complain. *vi,vt* feel or cause sudden pain.

gristle *n* cartilage, esp. when present in meat.

grit *n* **1** small pieces of gravel, sand, etc. **2** *inf* courage; stamina. *v* **grit one's teeth** (-tt-) **1** clench the teeth. **2** bear suffering bravely and without complaint.

groan *n* **1** low cry of pain, distress, disappointment, etc. **2** harsh noise made by the wind. **3** complaint, grumble. *vi,vt* **1** utter or sound like a groan. **2** complain; moan.

grocer *n* shopkeeper selling food, household articles, etc. **grocery** *n* trade or business of a grocer. **groceries** *pl n* items purchased from a grocer.

groin *n* part of the body where the legs join the abdomen.

groom *n* **1** person employed to look after horses. **2** bridegroom. *vt* **1** rub down (a horse). **2** keep (hair, clothes, etc.) clean and neat. **3** train or instruct for a particular role.

groove *n* **1** narrow channel cut into the surface of something; rut; furrow. **2** monotonous routine. *vt* cut a groove (into).

grope *vi* **1** search by touch; handle uncertainly; fumble. **2** seek (a solution) with difficulty. *n* fumbling touch.

gross *adj* **1** offensively fat. **2** vulgar; crude. **3** excessive; extreme. **4** before deductions. *n* **1**

pl **gross** quantity of 144 (12 dozen). **2** majority; bulk. *vt* earn before deductions. **grossly** *adv*.

grotesque *adj* extremely ugly; bizarre.

grotto *n* small cave; cavern.

ground[1] *n* **1** surface of the earth; land; soil. **2** enclosure or pitch. **3** area of knowledge; field. **down to the ground** perfectly; entirely. ~*vt* **1** prevent the take-off of (an aircraft). **2** give basic but thorough instructions to. **grounds** *pl n* **1** justification; valid reasons. **2** land attached to a large house, castle, etc. **3** coffee dregs. **groundsheet** *n* waterproof sheet used when camping in a tent. **groundsman** *n, pl* **-men** caretaker or gardener employed on an estate, park, sports ground, etc. **groundwork** *n* basic preparation for a job or project.

ground[2] *v pt* and *pp* of **grind.**

group *n* number of people or things placed or classed together; set. *vt,vi* form into a group or set; assemble.

grouse[1] *n* game bird with reddish-brown or black plumage.

grouse[2] *vi* grumble; nag; complain. *n* complaint; grievance.

grove *n* area of trees; plantation.

grovel *vi* (-ll-) **1** humiliate oneself; behave in a servile manner. **2** crawl in an undignified manner.

grow *v* (grew; grown) *vi* **1** become larger, taller etc.; mature. **2** increase in size or number. **3** develop; arise; become. *vt* produce; bring forth; yield. **grow up** become adult. **grown-up** *n* adult person. *adj* mature; adult. **growth** *n* **1** process of growing. **2** amount by which something grows. **3** increase; development. **4** cancer or tumour.

growl *vt,vi* **1** (esp of an animal such as a dog) utter a low warning or hostile sound. **2** say in a low angry voice. *vi* rumble; grumble. *n* low hostile sound.

grub *n* **1** larva of certain insects, esp. a beetle. **2** *sl* food *vt,vi* (-bb-) dig or root (in).

grubby *adj* dirty; grimy; soiled. **grubbiness** *n*.

grudge *n* grievance; feeling of resentment. *vt* resent; feel grieved about; begrudge. **grudgingly** *adv*.

gruelling *adj* extremely strenuous; exhausting; taxing; rigorous.

gruesome *adj* ghastly; horrible; spine-chilling.

gruff *adj* rough in manner or voice; rough. **gruffly** *adv*.

grumble *vt,vi* express dissatisfaction; groan; complain. *vi* rumble. *n* **1** expression of discontent; groan. **2** rumble.

grumpy *adj* inclined to grumble; cross; bad-tempered. **grumpiness** *n*.

grunt *vi,vt* **1** (esp. of a pig) snort. **2** say in a low incoherent manner. *n* **1** snort. **2** low incoherent noise.

guarantee *n* **1** statement that goods supplied conform to a certain standard or that they will be repaired or replaced. **2** formal undertaking to honour another's debts. **3** assurance that something is right or will happen. *vt* give a guarantee of; assure; undertake. **guarantor** *n* person giving a guarantee.

guard *vt,vi* **1** keep watch (over) in order to defend, protect, or prevent entry or escape. **2** shield; protect. *vt* restrain; control. **guard against** take precautions to avoid. ~*n* **1** person who guards, esp. a warder. **2** military or police escort. **3** sentry; keeper. **4** person officially in charge of a train. **5** safety device fitted to a machine, fire, etc. **6** safeguard; precaution. **on/off one's guard** alert or watchful/unwary. **guarded** *adj* cautious. **guardian** *n* **1** person having custody of another, esp. a minor. **2** defender; protector; keeper.

guerrilla *n also* **guerilla** member of a group of fighters waging war against regular military forces, using tactics of ambush, sabotage, etc.

guess *vt,vi* **1** attempt to judge or find an answer or solution (to) without having sufficient information; estimate. **2** give the right answer (to); discover correctly. *n* attempt at solving; estimate. **guesswork** *n* **1** process of guessing. **2** conclusion reached by guessing.

guest *n* **1** person invited as a visitor. **2** person whom one entertains or treats to a meal. **3** person staying at a hotel. **guesthouse** *n* small private hotel or boarding house.

guide *vt* **1** lead; show the way to; conduct. **2** influence; direct. **3** steer; control the movement of. *n* **1** person who guides, esp. one who conducts tourists or sightseers round places of interest. **2** *also* **guidebook** book giving information on places of interest. **3** book containing practical information on a subject; manual. **4** *also* **guideline** suggested principle or standard. **5** Girl Guide. **guidance** *n*.

guild *n* **1** society of craftsmen or merchants of the Middle Ages. **2** association; society.

guile *n* cunning; slyness; deceit. **guileless** *adj.*

guillotine *n* **1** execution device used to behead people. **2** machine fitted with a sharp blade for cutting and trimming paper, metal, etc. *vt* use a guillotine on.

guilt *n* **1** fact of having committed a criminal or other offence. **2** deep feeling of shame or remorse at having been responsible for a crime, error, omission, etc. **guiltless** *adj.* **guilty** *adj.* **guiltily** *adv.*

guinea *n* former British gold coin worth 21 shillings (£1.05).

guinea pig *n* **1** small tailless rodent often kept as a pet or used for experiments. **2** person used as the subject of experiment.

guitar *n* long-necked musical instrument, usually with six strings, which are plucked. **guitarist** *n.*

gulf *n* **1** large bay or inlet of the sea. **2** chasm or abyss. **3** great discrepancy; irreconcilable difference. *vt* engulf.

gull *n* seabird with white or grey plumage and webbed feet.

gullet *n* **1** oesophagus. **2** throat.

gullible *adj* easily cheated or taken in. **gullibility** *n.*

gulp *vt,vi* **1** swallow (food) quickly and noisily; bolt. **2** inhale noisily; choke; gasp. *n* act of gulping.

gum[1] *n* **1** sticky substance produced by various plants and used as an adhesive. **2** chewing gum. *v* (-mm-) *vt* stick with gum. *vt,vi also* **gum up** smear or become smeared with gum; clog.

gum[2] *n* pink fleshy tissue in which the teeth are rooted.

gun *n* any type of weapon capable of discharging bullets or shells from a barrel. **jump the gun** begin too soon or without adequate preparation. **stick to one's guns** keep to one's opinions or principles; persevere. ~*vt* (-nn-) *also* **gun down** shoot at with a gun. **gun for** pursue with determination. **gunman** *n, pl* **-men** person who uses a gun to commit a crime. **gunpowder** *n* explosive mixture of sulphur, charcoal, and saltpetre. **gunrunning** *n* smuggling of firearms. **gunrunner** *n.*

gurgle *vi* **1** (esp. of flowing water) make a bubbling or rushing sound. **2** produce a throaty chuckle; bubble. *n* gurgling sound.

guru *n* Hindu or Sikh religious teacher.

gush *vt,vi* **1** pour out with great force; flow; stream. **2** utter with exaggerated enthusiasm or sentiment. *n* sudden stream or flow.

gust *n* blast of wind, smoke, etc.

gut *n* **1** alimentary canal or any part of it. **2** strong type of thread made from an animal's intestines. *vt* (-tt-) **1** remove the entrails of (fish). **2** reduce to a shell; destroy. **guts** *pl n* **1** intestines or bowels. **2** courage; tenacity; determination. **3** essential part; core.

gutter *n* drainage channel at the side of a road or attached to the eaves of a roof.

guy[1] *n* **1** *inf* man. **2** effigy of Guy Fawkes that is burnt on Nov. 5th.

guy[2] *n* rope or chain used to keep a tent, mast, etc., in position.

guzzle *vt,vi* eat or drink greedily or noisily.

gymkhana (dʒimˈkɑːnə) *n* horseriding event in which competitors are judged for their skill or speed in various contests.

gymnasium *n, pl* **gymnasiums** *or* **gymnasia** (dʒimˈneiziə) building or hall equipped with gymnastic apparatus and also used for various indoor sports. **gymnastics** *n* method of physical training that includes exercises in balance, vaulting, etc. **gymnast** *n.* **gymnastic** *adj.*

gynaecology *n* branch of medicine concerned with diseases peculiar to women. **gynaecological** *adj.* **gynaecologist** *n.*

gypsum *n* white mineral consisting of calcium sulphate, used to make plaster of Paris.

Gypsy *n also* **Gipsy** member of a nomadic race living in many parts of Europe and N America.

gyrate (dʒaiˈreit) *vi* rotate. **gyration** *n.*

H

haberdasher *n* shop or shopkeeper selling pins, thread, lace, etc. **haberdashery** *n.*

habit *n* **1** custom; usual practice or way of behaving. **2** type of garment worn by monks, nuns, etc. **habit-forming** *adj* causing addiction. **habitual** *adj* **1** usual; customary. **2** having a specified habit or addiction. **habitually** *adv.*

habitable *adj* fit to be lived in.

hack[1] *vi,vt* cut, chop, or strike roughly or clumsily. *vi inf* cough dryly and spasmodically. *n* rough cut or blow. **hacksaw** *n* saw for cutting metal, consisting of a narrow blade in a U-shaped frame.

hack[2] *n* **1** horse that can be hired. **2** old overworked horse. **3** writer or journalist who produces poor work fast and for little money. **hackneyed** *adj* unoriginal; said too often; trite.

had *v pt* and *pp* of **have.**

haddock *n, pl* **haddock** common N Atlantic food fish, related to the cod.

haemorrhage *n* profuse bleeding. *vi* to bleed profusely.

hag *n* ugly old woman; witch.

haggard *adj* looking ill, tired, or pale; gaunt.

haggis *n* Scottish dish of sheep's offal and oatmeal boiled in a sheep's stomach.

haggle *vi* dispute noisily (over) a price, etc.; wrangle.

hail[1] *n* **1** *also* **hailstones** pellets of frozen rain. **2** shower of hail. **3** profusion or shower of insults, abuse, or bullets. *vi* fall as hail.

hail[2] *vt* **1** greet or salute. **2** call out to; attract the attention of. **hail from** be a native of. *n* shout; greeting.

hair *n* **1** threadlike growth on or from the skin of mammals. **2** mass of hairs, esp. that on the human head. **hair's breadth** very short distance or margin. **keep your hair on!** keep calm! **let one's hair down** act informally and without reserve. **not turn a hair** show no fear or surprise. **split hairs** make petty unimportant distinctions. **hairy** *adj.* **hairdo** *n* arrangement of a woman's hair, esp. by a hairdresser. **hairdresser** *n* **1** person who cuts and arranges hair. **2** shop employing such persons. **hairdressing** *n.* **hairgrip** *n also* **hairpin** clip for securing women's hair. **hairpiece** *n* false hair worn to hide baldness, etc. **hair-raising** *adj* frightening; terrifying.

half *n, pl* **halves** **1** amount obtained by dividing a whole into two equal or nearly equal parts. **2** either of the parts. **3** half a pint, esp. of beer. **better half** one's wife or husband. **go halves** share equally. ~*adv* **1** to the extent of a half. **2** partially; nearly. *adj* amounting to a half in number. *pron* amount of half in number. **half-and-half** *adj* neither one thing nor the other. **half-back** *n* player or position in rugby, soccer, etc., behind the forwards. **half-baked** *adj* foolish; not properly thought out. **half-breed** *n* **1** person having parents of different races; half-caste. **2** domestic animal having parents of different breeds. *adj* relating to a half-breed. **half-brother** *n* brother related through only one parent. **half-caste** *n,adj* half-breed. **half-hearted** *adj* not enthusiastic. **half-heartedly** *adv.* **half-sister** *n* sister related through only one parent. **half-term** *n* point or holiday in the middle of a scholastic term. **half-time** *n* point or interval in the middle of a football match, etc. **halfway** *adv,adj* equally far from two points. **halfwit** *n* **1** idiot; cretin. **2** stupid or foolish person. **halfwitted** *adj.*

halibut *n, pl* **halibut** large N Atlantic flat fish, important as a food fish.

hall *n* **1** large room for dining, lectures, etc. **2** public building for dances, meetings, etc. **3** *also* **hallway** passage or room leading from an entrance to other rooms. **4** large country house. **5** students' residence, hostel, or college.

hallelujah *interj,n, also* **alleluia** cry of praise to God.

hallmark *n* **1** stamp of an official body on a silver or gold article, indicating its purity. **2** typical characteristic proving authenticity; distinguishing feature.

hallowed *adj* **1** holy; consecrated. **2** revered; respected.

Hallowe'en *n* Oct 31st, eve of All Saints Day, when witches are supposed to ride at night and graves give up their dead.

hallucination *n* **1** alleged but imaginary perception of an object, sound, etc., because of illness or through taking certain drugs. **2** act of such perception. **hallucinate** *vi* experience hallucinations.

halo *n* **1** circle of light around the head of Christ, an angel, saint, etc., as shown in paintings. **2** circle of light around the sun or moon, caused by refraction by ice particles.

halt *vi,vt* stop. *n* **1** act of stopping; stop. **2** place, as on a train or bus route, at which it stops briefly.

halter *n* **1** rope by which horses, etc., can be led or tethered. **2** *also* **halterneck** neckline of a woman's dress that leaves the back bare.

halve *vt* **1** divide in half; share equally. **2** cut by half.

ham *n* **1** salted, sometimes smoked meat from the thigh of a pig. **2** back of the thigh; thigh and buttocks. **3** actor who overacts. **4** amateur radio operator. **ham-fisted** *adj* clumsy.

hamburger *n* fried cake of seasoned minced beef often served in a bread roll.

hammer *n* **1** tool with a head fitted at right angles to a handle for driving in nails, beating metal, etc. **2** any device for striking, knocking, etc. **3** heavy metal sphere with a flexible wire handle, thrown by athletes. **go at it hammer and tongs** argue or fight fiercely. ~*vt,vi* strike or pound with a hammer. *vt* **1** strike violently. **2** defeat conclusively. **3** criticize severely. **hammer away at** work hard to do or produce. **hammer in(to)** teach by repetition. **hammer out** settle or work out after much discussion or dispute.

hammock *n* bed of canvas, rope, etc., suspended between two supports.

hamper[1] *vt* prevent from moving or working easily; hinder; impede.

hamper[2] *n* basket or case in which food and other things can be packed.

hamster *n* tailless ratlike animal with pouched cheeks, kept as a pet.

hand *n* **1** part of the arm below the wrist. **2** help; assistance; role. **3** manual worker, labourer **4** indicator, esp. on a clock. **5** single game at cards or the cards so dealt. **6** position or direction. **change hands** pass to another owner. **a free hand** complete freedom. **from hand to mouth** precariously, in poverty. **hand and foot** completely. **hand in glove** in close cooperation. **in good hands** well cared for. **in/out of hand** under/beyond control. **on/at/to hand** near; close by. **on the other hand** in contrast. **take in hand** discipline; control. **wash one's hands of** disclaim responsibility. **win hands down** win easily. ~*vt* **1** pass to; give. **2** *also* **hand on, hand down** pass on; transmit. **handbag** *n* small bag for carrying personal items, etc. **handbook** *n* book of useful hints or information manual; guide. **handbrake** *n* manual brake on cars, etc. **handful** *n* **1** small amount or number. **2** person that is difficult to control **handmade** *adj* made by a person rather than a machine **hand-pick** *vt* select very carefully **handstand** *n* vertical upside-down position maintained by balancing on one's hands. **handwriting** *n* **1** writing done by hand, **2** individual's style of handwriting. **handwritten** *adj*.

handicap *n* **1** something that hinders, disadvantaga; defect; drawback. **2** mental or physical defect or disability. **3** disadvantage given to certain sports competitors to equalize everybody's chances. *vt* (-pp-) be a disadvantage to. **handicapped** *adj*.

handicraft *n* skilled manual work, often artistic, such as pottery.

handiwork *n* **1** skilled or artistic manual work. **2** result of someone's actions or plans.

handkerchief *n* piece of absorbent material on which to blow or wipe one's nose.

handle *n* part of a tool, machine, case, etc., by which to hold, carry, or control it. **fly off the handle** lose one's temper. ~*vt* **1** hold or feel with one's hands. **2** control or use (a machine, etc.). **3** deal with; cope with, manage. **handlebars** *pl n* metal crosspiece by which a bicycle, etc., is steered.

handsome *adj* **1** good-looking. **2** generous or ample. **handsomely** *adv*.

handy *adj* **1** useful; easy or convenient to use. **2** capable of doing manual jobs well. **3** easily accessible. **handyman** *n, pl* **-men** person adept at odd jobs.

hang *vi,vt* (hung *or for def. 2* hanged *or* hung). **1** suspend or be suspended from above **2** execute or be executed by strangling with a noose. *vt* **1** suspend by a hook, attach, fix or stick in position. **2** keep (meat, esp. game) suspended until ready for eating. **hang around** *or* **about** linger; loiter; wait without purpose **hang back** hesitate. **hang on** wait; persevere; cling to. **hang out 1** live, frequent. **2** display; hang outside. **hang up** replace (telephone receiver). *n* **get the hang of** understand or begin to be able to do. **hanger** *n* coathanger. **hangover** *n* after-effects of excessive drinking, esp. a headache.

hanker *vi* desire persistently; yearn (for). **hankering** *n* lingering desire or wish.

haphazard *adj* happening or arranged without planning, by chance, or at random. *adv also* **haphazardly** by chance; at random.

happen *vi* occur, take place, esp. by chance. **happen to** (**one**) befall; affect. **happen to** chance to (be, do, know, etc.). **happening** *n* occurrence; event, esp. a social one characterized by spontaneity.

happy *adj* **1** feeling, indicating, or causing contentment, pleasure, or joy. **2** fortunate **3** willing (to). **4** suitable; apt. **5** mildly drunk **happily** *adv*. **happiness** *n*.

harass *vt* annoy, pester, or pursue (someone)

continually. **harassed** *adj* nervous; irritated; bothered. **harassment** *n*.

harbour *n* **1** sheltered coastal area providing safe anchorage for ships, etc. **2** place for shelter or safety. *vt* **1** give refuge to (a hunted criminal, etc.); shelter. **2** cherish or maintain secretly. *vi* take shelter (in).

hard *adj* **1** not easily cut, dented, etc.; rigid. **2** difficult to do or understand. **3** violent or strenuous; arduous. **4** unfair; harsh or strict; severe; distressing. **5** unfeeling or insensitive. **6** (of water) impairing the lathering of soap. **hard and fast** strict; rigid. **hard cash** paper money and coins rather than cheques, etc. **hard to come by** difficult to obtain. **hard drugs** addictive drugs. **hard of hearing** deaf or slightly deaf. **hard up** having little money. ~*adv* **1** with force; violently. **2** with effort or vigour. **3** closely; with careful scrutiny. **hard at it** working strenuously. **hard put to** finding difficulty in. **harden** *vt,vi* **1** make or become hard(er). **2** make or become insensitive or accustomed to pain or suffering.

hardback *n* book with stiff cardboard covers.

hardboard *n* sheeting formed from compressed sawdust and woodchips, used as a building material, etc.

hard-boiled *adj* **1** (of eggs) boiled until the whole inside is solid. **2** cynical; callous.

hard-headed *adj* practical or shrewd, esp. in business. **hard-headedness** *n*.

hard-hearted *adj* not feeling or showing sympathy for the sufferings of others; cruel. **hard-heartedly** *adv*. **hard-heartedness** *n*.

hardly *adv* scarcely; not quite; barely.

hardship *n* lack of material comforts; deprivation; suffering.

hardware *n* **1** household utensils, tools, etc.; ironmongery. **2** computer equipment.

hardy *adj* **1** able to tolerate difficult physical conditions; tough; robust. **2** (of plants) able to survive outdoors all year round.

hare *n* animal resembling a rabbit but having longer legs and ears. *vi* rush (about, after, etc.), esp. in a confused manner. **hare-brained** *adj* stupid; rash; foolish.

hark *vi* listen (to). **hark back** revert (to a previous question or topic).

harm *n* damage or injury. *vt* cause damage or injury to. **harmful** *adj*.

harmonic *adj* relating to or characterized by harmony. *n* component of a musical note whose frequency is a multiple of, the note's pitch. **harmonically** *adv* with or in harmony. **harmonics** *n* study of musical sounds.

harmonica *n* small musical instrument played by blowing into a small case in which metal reeds are set; mouth-organ.

harmony *n* **1** pleasant relationship of musical sounds. **2** friendly agreement in personal relationships. **3** pleasant arrangement, as of colours. **harmonious** *adj*. **harmoniously** *adv*. **harmonize** *vt,vi* come or bring into harmony; reconcile. *vi* sing or play in harmony (with). **harmonization** *n*.

harness *n* **1** complete set of straps and other parts fitted to a working horse. **2** fitment for a baby, etc., used for controlling, guiding, etc. *vt* **1** put a harness on (a horse). **2** gain control over (a form of energy, etc.).

harp *n* triangular musical instrument played by plucking or drawing the fingers over strings. *v* **harp on** talk repeatedly about.

harpoon *n* spear with a line attached that is fired or thrown when hunting whales, etc. *vt,vi* catch (whales, etc.) using a harpoon.

harpsichord *n* pianolike musical instrument.

harsh *adj* **1** not soft; coarse; rough. **2** severe; cruel; unkind. **3** jarring on the senses; strident; too bright or loud. **harshly** *adv*. **harshness** *n*.

harvest *n* **1** act of cutting and gathering ripe crops. **2** the crop itself. **3** result; product. *vt,vi* **1** gather in ripe crops. **2** get the benefit from.

has *v* 3rd person singular of **have** in the present tense.

hashish *n also* **hash** intoxicating drug prepared from dried leaves, flower tops, etc., of Indian hemp.

hasten *vi,vt* hurry or cause to hurry; rush. **haste** *n* **1** speed; hurry; urgency. **2** rashness. **hastily** *adv*. **hasty** *adj*.

hat *n* shaped covering for the head. **keep (something) under one's hat** keep secret. **old hat** old-fashioned; no longer novel.

hatch[1] *vi,vt* to emerge or cause to emerge from an egg. *vt also* **hatch up** think up (a plot, surprise, or idea).

hatch[2] *n* **1** small door covering an opening in a wall, esp. between two rooms. **2** cover for an opening on the deck of a boat or ship providing access below decks.

hatchet *n* small axe. **bury the hatchet** make peace after a quarrel.

hate *vt,vi* dislike fiercely; abhor. *n* **1** *also* **hatred** feeling of strong dislike or abhorrence. **2** person or thing so disliked. **hateful** *adj* loathsome.

haughty *adj* proud and arrogant; condescending; supercilious. **haughtily** *adv*. **haughtiness** *n*.

haul *vt,vi* pull or drag along with great effort; transport. *n* **1** something hauled. **2** act of hauling or the effort involved. **3** distance hauled or travelled. **4** result or amount obtained from an enterprise.

haunch *n* part of the body from the hip to the thigh.

haunt *vt,vi* visit as or be visited by a ghost. *vt* **1** go to habitually; frequent. **2** be continually in the thoughts of; obsess. **3** pester. **4** pervade. *n* place one frequents.

have *v* (*3rd person s present* has; *pp and pt* had) *vt*. **1** be characterized by. **2** own, possess. **3** hold; keep. **4** experience or undergo. **5** bear (children or young). **6** eat or drink (something). **7** take or receive. **8** must; be forced (to). **9** cause to happen or be done. **10** tolerate; put up with; allow. **11** cheat or deceive. *v aux* (used to form the perfect and pluperfect tenses). **have had it** be near death, no longer usable, tolerable, etc. **have on 1** wear. **2** fool; hoax.

haven *n* **1** place of shelter; refuge. **2** harbour.

haversack *n* canvas bag carried on the back or over the shoulder while hiking, etc.

havoc *n* disorder or confusion.

hawk *n* type of small long-tailed bird of prey.

hawthorn *n* thorny tree or bush with white, pink, or red flowers.

hay *n* dried grass used as fodder. **hayfever** *n* allergic reaction to inhaled pollen or dust, causing sneezing, runny eyes, etc. **haystack** *n* pile of hay in a field. **haywire** *adj* **go haywire** go badly wrong, become disorganized.

hazard *n* **1** danger; peril; risk. **2** something causing danger or risk; obstacle. *vt* **1** risk, gamble. **2** venture (an opinion, etc.). **hazardous** *adj*.

haze *n* **1** light mist that impairs visibility. **2** vague or confused state of mind. **hazy** *adj* **1** slightly misty. **2** dimly or imperfectly remembered or remembering. **hazily** *adv*. **haziness** *n*.

hazel *n* small tree producing edible nuts. *adj,n* light to medium brown.

he *pron* male person or animal.

head *n* **1** part of the body above the neck. **2** intelligence; mental power. **3** chief person; commander; ruler. **4** highest or foremost point or part; top. **5** *pl* **head** person or animal considered as a unit in a group. **6** short for **headmaster** or **headmistress**. **bite someone's head off** rebuke sharply. **come to a head** reach a critical point. **give someone his head** allow greater freedom. **go to one's head** make proud, rash, etc. **head over heels (in love)** madly in love. **keep/lose one's head** keep calm/become flustered. **not make head nor tail of** completely fail to understand. **off one's head** crazy. **over someone's head** to someone of greater authority. ~*vt,vi* be, form, or put at the head of. *vt* hit (a football) with one's head. **head for** be directed towards (a place, trouble, etc.). **heady** *adj* intoxicating; affecting the mind or senses.

headache *n* **1** pain in the head. **2** troublesome person or thing.

headgear *n* any covering for the head.

heading *n* title at the beginning of an article, chapter of a book, etc.

headland *n* area of land jutting out to sea; cape.

headlight *n also* **headlamp** powerful light on the front of a car, etc.

headline *n* words in large or heavy type at the top of a newspaper article.

headlong *adv also* **headfirst 1** with the head foremost. **2** rashly; impetuously.

headmaster *n* chief male teacher in a school. **headmistress** *f n*.

headphones *pl n* pair of receivers fitted over the ears for communications purposes.

headquarters *pl n* chief office of a military force or other organization.

headstrong *adj* **1** obstinate, wilful. **2** rash, impetuous.

headway *n* **1** movement forward by a vessel. **2** progress, as in a struggle or problem.

heal *vt* cure; restore to health. *vi* (of a wound) close up.

health *n* **1** person's general bodily condition. **2** condition of being well, freedom from illness. **3** general condition of a business, country, etc. **healthy** *adj* **1** in good health. **2** conducive to good health. **3** promising or encouraging. **healthily** *adv.*

heap *n* **1** jumbled mass; pile; mound. **2** *also* **heaps** great deal. **3** something no longer useful. *vt* place (things) in a heap.

hear (heard) *vt,vi* **1** perceive (sound) with the ears. **2** become informed (about news). *vt* listen to. **hear from** receive news, etc., from. **hear of 1** obtain news or information about. **2** allow the possibility of. **hear out** allow (a person) to finish what he is saying. **hear, hear!** exclamation of agreement, approval, etc. **hearing** *n* **1** sense by which one hears; ability to hear. **2** range in which a person may be heard. **3** chance or opportunity to be heard.

hearse *n* car or carriage for carrying a corpse to burial or cremation.

heart *n* **1** muscular internal organ that pumps blood round the body. **2** symbolic seat of love, sympathy, or courage; these feelings themselves. **3** soul; inner thoughts. **4** centre; core. **5** heart-shaped symbol. **6** playing card marked with one or more red hearts. **hearts** *pl or s n* suit of cards each marked thus. **after someone's own heart** exactly of the type someone likes or approves of. **break someone's heart** upset or disappoint someone, esp. in love. **by heart** from memory. **heart of hearts** inmost feelings. **heart to heart** (discussion that is) intimate. **set one's heart on** want very much. **take to heart** be greatly influenced by. **wear one's heart on one's sleeve** make one's feelings, esp. of love, very obvious. **with all one's heart 1** with deep love. **2** willingly.

heart attack *n* sudden very painful, often fatal, malfunction of the heart.

heartbeat *n* single pulsation of the heart.

heartbroken *adj* very unhappy, disappointed, etc.

hearth *n* **1** place where a domestic fire is lit. **2** the whole fireplace. **3** the home.

heartless *adj* cruel; unfeeling; unsympathetic. **heartlessly** *adv.*

hearty *adj* **1** jovial; cheerful. **2** cordial; sincere. **3** in good health; vigorous. *n* fellow; comrade. **heartily** *adv.*

heat *n* **1** form of energy resulting from the motion of atoms and molecules in an object, etc. **2** degree of hotness, esp. when great. **3** hot weather. **4** strong or deep feeling; anger; enthusiasm. **5** pressure, intensity. **6** period of sexual excitement in female animals. **7** preliminary race or contest. *vt,vi* make or become hot. *vi* become agitated or nervous. **heated** *adj.* **heater** *n* domestic appliance for heating rooms, water, etc. **heatwave** *n* period of very hot weather.

heath *n* **1** area of open uncultivated ground. **2** heather.

heathen *adj* **1** not believing in the same god or religion as oneself; pagan. **2** uncivilized; barbaric. *n* person who is heathen.

heather *n also* **heath** small evergreen plant having small purplish or white bell-shaped flowers. **heathery** *adj.*

heave *vt,vi* pull or drag (something heavy); haul. *vt* **1** throw with great effort. **2** give out (a sigh, etc.). *vi* **1** move up and down rhythmically. **2** retch. *n* act of heaving.

heaven *n* **1** abode of God, the angels, and the good after death. **2** great happiness; intense pleasure. **3** place or state that induces this. **4** *also* **heavens** sky. **move heaven and earth** do everything possible to effect. **heavenly** *adj.*

heavy *adj* **1** of great or considerable weight. **2** difficult to move or lift because of weight. **3** serious; weighty; considerable. **4** difficult to bear, fulfil, digest, read, etc. **5** violent; of great force. *n* **1** role of a villain in a play or film. **2** actor playing this. **heavily** *adv.* **heaviness** *n.* **heavyweight** *n* boxer who weighs 175 pounds or more.

Hebrew *n* **1** language of the ancient Jews and modern Israel. **2** Jew; Israelite.

heckle *vt,vi* try to disconcert a public speaker by continual taunts. **heckler** *n.*

hectic *adj* **1** very busy or active. **2** hurried and confused; agitated. **hectically** *adv.*

hedge *n* **1** closely planted row of bushes and small trees forming a fence, etc. **2** barrier. *vt* **1** provide or surround with a hedge. **2** give an answer that does not reveal one's true thoughts. **hedge one's bets** make a safe bet, investment, etc., to protect oneself. **hedgehog** *n* small animal with long prickles on its back.

heed *vt,vi* take careful notice of. *n* **1** attention; notice. **2** caution; care. **take heed!** be careful!

heel[1] *n* **1** back part of a the foot. **2** part of a sock, stocking, etc., that covers the heel. **3** part of a shoe or boot beneath the heel. **4** despicable man. **Achilles' heel** person's only weak point. **down at heel** shabbily dressed. **cool one's heels** be kept waiting. **take to one's heels** run away. **to heel** under control. ~*vt* repair the heel of (a shoe).

heel[2] *vi also* **heel over** 1 tilt to one side; list. 2 fall to the ground.

hefty *adj* 1 strong and muscular. 2 forceful.

height *n* 1 distance from bottom to top. 2 altitude. 3 most successful point; culmination. 4 most extreme or exaggerated form. **heights** high place or point. **heighten** *vt,vi* 1 make or become higher. 2 accentuate; be increased.

heir *n* 1 male person who inherits the wealth, rank, etc., of another when the latter dies. 2 successor, as to a tradition. **heiress** *f n*. **heirloom** *n* object passed down to succeeding generations in a family.

held *v pt* and *pp* of **hold**.

helicopter *n* aircraft powered by large overhead horizontally rotating blades.

helium *n* light inert rare gaseous element.

hell *n* 1 abode of Satan; place of eternal damnation for the wicked after death. 2 extreme suffering; torture; difficulty. 3 place or situation causing this. **a hell of a** very much of a. **for the hell of it** for fun. **give someone hell** 1 cause much trouble to. 2 scold severely. **like hell** 1 very much, fast, etc. 2 certainly not.

hello *interj* exclamation of greeting, surprise, etc.

helm *n* 1 steering device on a boat; tiller or steering-wheel. 2 position of control or authority. **helmsman** *n*.

helmet *n* 1 soldier's protective metal headgear worn during battle. 2 protective headgear worn by miners, firemen, motorcyclists, etc.

help *vt,vi* 1 give assistance (to); aid. 2 cause improvement in. *vt* 1 be of use in (doing). 2 avoid (doing); prevent oneself from. 3 serve with food or drink. **it can't be helped** it cannot be avoided or rectified. **help oneself (to)** 1 take without permission, payment, etc. 2 serve oneself. **help out** give assistance to, esp. in time of need. ~*n* 1 assistance, aid, cooperation. 2 domestic servant. **helper** *n*. **helpful** *adj*. **helpfully** *adv*. **helpless** *adj* 1 weak; dependent. 2 powerless.

hem *n* edge of a piece of cloth or clothing turned over and sewn. *vt* (-mm-) sew a hem on. **hem in** surround; encircle.

hemisphere *n* 1 half a sphere. 2 half of the earth. **hemispherical** *adj*.

hemp *n* 1 tough-fibred Asian plant from which the drug cannabis is obtained. 2 cannabis. 3 rope or coarse cloth made from the fibres.

hen *n* 1 female bird, esp. a chicken. 2 old woman. **hen party** *n* gathering for women only.

hence *adv* 1 and so; therefore; for this reason. 2 from this time forward. 3 from this place.

henna *n* reddish dye for hair, etc., obtained from an Asiatic shrub.

her *adj* belonging to a female person. *pron* that particular woman or girl. **herself** *r pron* 1 her own self. 2 her normal self.

herald *n* 1 official who makes public or ceremonial announcements. 2 person or thing that indicates the approach of something. *vt* usher in; proclaim.

heraldry *n* practice and rules governing official coats of arms, etc. **heraldic** *adv*.

herb *n* plant, such as parsley, that can be used as a flavouring in cooking, as a medicine, etc. **herbal** *adj*. **herbaceous** *adj* relating to plants with fleshy stems that die down after flowering. **herbivore** *n* animal feeding on plants. **herbivorous** *adj*.

herd *n* 1 large group of wild or domestic animals that live and feed together. 2 mass of people; rabble. *vt,vi* 1 gather or be gathered into a herd. 2 drive or be driven (forward or back). **herdsman** *n* man who tends a herd.

here *adv* 1 in or to this place. 2 at this point in time or space. **here and there** 1 in or to several places. 2 scattered around. **be neither here nor there** be irrelevant or unimportant. ~*n* this place.

heredity *n* 1 biological process by which characteristics, etc., are transmitted from parents to children in the genes. 2 characteristics so transmitted. **hereditary** *adj*.

heresy *n* belief or doctrine, esp. religious, that is contrary to established order. **heretic** *n* person originating or believing a heresy. **heretical** *adj*. **heretically** *adv*.

heritage *n* 1 culture or tradition passed on to successive generations. 2 something inherited at birth, esp. property or family characteristics.

hermit *n* 1 person living completely alone to pray or undergo mystic experiences. 2 person who lives a solitary life; recluse. **hermitage** *n* dwelling of a hermit.

hero *n, pl* **heroes** **1** man admired for his courage, nobleness, or fortitude. **2** central male character in a book, play, or film. **3** person who suffers much without complaint. **heroic** *adj.* **heroically** *adv.* **heroine** *f n.* **heroism** *n.*

heroin *n* addictive narcotic drug obtained from morphine.

heron *n* long-legged wading bird.

herring *n, pl* **herring** *or* **herrings** marine food fish. **red herring** misleading fact or argument.

hers *pron* belonging to her. **herself** *r pron* her own self; her normal self.

hesitate *vi* pause through doubt; waver; falter; be unwilling (to). **hesitancy** *n.* **hesitant** *adj.* **hesitation** *n.*

heterosexual *n* person sexually attracted to members of the opposite sex. **heterosexuality** *n.*

hexagon *n* six-sided geometric figure. **hexagonal** *adj.*

hibernate *vi* (of animals) spend the winter in a sleeplike state. **hibernation** *n.*

hiccup *n also* **hiccough** one of a series of sudden involuntary coughlike noises. *vi* (-pp-) *also* **hiccough** experience such a spasm; make such a noise.

hide[1] *vt* (hid; hidden) **1** keep from sight; conceal. **2** keep secret. *vi* conceal oneself. *n* place where someone is concealed, esp. for observing birds.

hide[2] *n* skin of some large animals, usually hairless, esp. when tanned. **tan someone's hide** beat or flog someone.

hideous *adj* **1** extremely ugly. **2** morally repulsive. **3** of an extreme nature. **hideously** *adv.*

hiding[1] *n* act or place of concealment.

hiding[2] *n* **1** beating or thrashing. **2** conclusive defeat in a contest.

hierarchy *n* strictly graded structure, as of society or some other system. **hierarchical** *adj.*

high *adj* **1** having or being at a considerable or specified height. **2** being at a peak; considerable; relatively great in value or amount. **3** important; exalted. **4** main; chief. **5** noble; lofty; admirable. **6** slightly intoxicated by liquor or drugs. **high and dry** stranded; abandoned. **high and low** in every place possible. **high time** the correct or appropriate time. ~*adv* **1** at or to a high point or place. **2** for considerable gambling stakes. *n* **1** high point; peak. **2** high place. **highly** *adv* greatly; considerably.

highbrow *adj* relating to very intellectual tastes in music, literature, art, etc. *n* person having such tastes.

high-fidelity *adj* reproducing sounds electronically without distortion.

high jump *n* athletic event in which competitors leap over a high, continuously elevated bar. **be for the high jump** be in trouble. **high-jumper** *n.*

highland *n also* **highlands** hilly or mountainous region, esp. in Scotland.

highlight *n* **1** small concentration of light on something shiny. **2** best or most impressive or enjoyable part. *vt* **1** put highlights in. **2** put emphasis on; accentuate.

highness *n* **1** condition of being high. **2** honorary address to a royal person.

highway *n* public road, esp. a main road.

hijack *vt* **1** board and capture (an aeroplane, etc.) and threaten to destroy it or kill its passengers unless one's demands are met. **2** steal (a lorry, etc.) with its load. *n* instance of hijacking. **hijacker** *n.*

hike *n* long walk or walking holiday in the country; ramble. *vi* go for a hike. **hiker** *n.*

hilarious *adj* very funny; causing much amusement. **hilariously** *adv.* **hilarity** *n.*

hill *n* **1** elevated area of ground; small mountain. **2** slope, as in a road. **hilly** *adj.*

him *pron* that particular man or boy. **himself** *r pron* **1** his own self. **2** his normal self.

hind *adj* in or at the back or rear; posterior. **hindsight** *n* ability to guess or act correctly when looking back on an event.

hinder *vt* cause obstruction or delay to; impede. **hindrance** *n* **1** obstruction; delay. **2** person or thing causing this.

hinge *n* **1** joint by which a door, lid, etc., is attached to a frame, container, etc., so that it can open and close. **2** central fact or argument on which all else depends. *vi* **hinge on** depend on.

hint *n* suggestion; piece of helpful advice. *vt,vi* make suggestions (about).

hip *n* side of the body from the upper thigh to the waist.

hippopotamus *n, pl* **hippopotamuses** *or* **hippopotami** (hipə'pɔtəmai) very large thick-skinned African mammal living in and around rivers.

hire *vt* obtain the temporary use or services of, for payment. *n* **1** act of hiring. **2** charge of hiring.

his *pron* belonging to him.

hiss *vi* **1** produce a whistling sound like a prolonged *s*. *vt,vi* display scorn or disapproval (for) by making such a noise. *n* such a noise.

history *n* **1** development and past events of a country, etc. **2** study concerned with this. **3** book, play, or other chronological account about past events. **make history** do something important or influential. **historian** *n* scholar or student of history. **historic** *adj* **1** important or memorable in history. **2** *also* **historical** relating to history.

hit *vt,vi* (-tt-; hit) **1** give a blow to; knock; strike. **2** reach (a target, etc.). *vt* **1** come upon by chance; find. **2** wound; injure. **hit it off with** get on well (with somebody). **hit on** *or* **upon** guess or find (an answer, etc.) by chance. **hit out** (**at** *or* **against**) speak angrily or critically (about). ~*n* **1** blow or knock. **2** act of reaching a target. **3** great success.

hitch *vt* pull up roughly. *vt,vi* **1** fasten or become fastened (on to); become entangled or caught. **2** procure (a lift) from a driver. *n* **1** abrupt pull. **2** unexpected difficulty or obstacle causing a delay. **3** type of knot. **hitched** *adj* married. **hitch-hike** *vi* **1** procure free travel in a motor vehicle. **2** travel around by such means. **hitch-hiker** *n*.

hive *n* **1** structure in which bees are kept. **2** bees kept in a hive. **3** very busy or industrious place. *vt* gather (bees) into a hive.

hoard *n* **1** accumulated store, often hidden or secret. **2** hidden or buried treasure. **3** *also* **hoards** great quantity (of). *vt,vi* amass (a hoard). **hoarder** *n*.

hoarding *n* **1** temporary wooden fence on which advertising posters are often stuck. **2** structure intended for posters, etc.

hoarse *adj* **1** coarse and husky; raucous. **2** having a harsh voice, esp. from shouting or due to a cold. **hoarsely** *adv*.

hoax *n* mischievous deception; practical joke. *vt,vi* play a hoax on.

hobble *vi* walk lamely or clumsily; limp. *vt* tie together two legs of a horse, etc., to prevent it from straying. *n* clumsy or lame walk.

hobby *n* favourite leisure occupation; pastime.

hockey *n* **1** team game in which a ball is hit with curved wooden sticks into opposing goals. **2** ice hockey.

hoe *n* long-handled horticultural tool with transversely set blade, used to weed, break up ground, etc. *vt,vi* weed, break up, etc., with a hoe.

hoist *vt* raise or lift, esp. using a mechanical device. *n* **1** act of hoisting. **2** device for doing this.

hold[1] (held) *vt* **1** grasp, grip, or support. **2** reserve or keep; maintain; control. **3** have; occupy; use. **4** contain. **5** cause to take place; conduct. **6** think that; consider. *vi* **1** withstand. **2** remain in a certain attitude or condition; remain valid. **3** maintain beliefs, etc. **4** refrain; forbear. **hold back** restrain; hesitate. **hold down** keep a job, esp. when difficult. **hold forth** talk at length or pompously. **hold good** remain valid. **hold off 1** keep or stay at a distance. **2** stay aloof. **hold on 1** cling to. **2** wait. **hold one's own** maintain one's position, as in an argument. **hold one's tongue** say nothing. **hold out 1** resist successfully; remain firm. **2** last; be sufficient. **hold up 1** cause delay in. **2** rob while threatening with a gun. **holdup** *n* **1** delay. **2** armed robbery. **hold water** remain true or logical under analysis. **hold with** agree with out of principle. ~*n* **1** act or method of holding. **2** something to grasp. **3** control or influence. **get hold of 1** grasp. **2** get in contact with. **holdall** *n* large bag or case.

hold[2] *n* cargo storage area below the deck of a vessel.

hole *n* **1** empty or hollow space in something; cavity; gap; opening; rupture or tear. **2** animal's burrow. **3** squalid or dingy room or house. **4** dull place. **5** predicament; difficulty. **make a hole in** use up a large part. **pick holes in** find faults with. ~*vt,vi* produce a hole in.

holiday *n* **1** time or period of rest from work, esp. when spent away from home. **2** day of rest or recreation, esp. a public one. **3** day for celebrating a religious event; festival. *vi* spend a holiday.

hollow *adj* **1** having an empty interior or a cavity inside. **2** having a depression in it; sunken. **3** insincere; flattering. **4** without substance; unreal. **5** dull or muffled. **6** hungry. *n* **1** hollow part of something. **2** sunken place; depression; cavity. **3** shallow valley. *vt also*

hollow out scoop out a hollow in. *adv* in a hollow way. **beat hollow** defeat completely. **hollowness** *n*.

holly *n* evergreen tree or shrub having shiny prickly leaves and red berries.

hollyhock *n* tall garden plant having large showy open flowers.

holster *n* leather case for a pistol.

holy *adj* **1** of God or a religion; sacred. **2** worshipped as sacred; sanctified. **3** saintly; pious. **holiness** *n* condition of being holy. **Holiness** title or term of address of the Pope.

homage *n* **1** loyalty; allegiance; reverence. **2** act of respect or reverence rendered to someone.

home *n* **1** place where a person lives; family residence. **2** place where something originated or is situated. **3** native country or town. **4** institution for the old or infirm. **at home** feeling comfortable. **at home with** familiar with. ~*adv* **1** at or towards home. **2** to a required point, target, etc. **come/bring home to** realize/cause to realize fully. **homely** *adj* plain; simple; unpretentious. **homeliness** *n*. **homesick** *adj* feeling great longing or nostalgia for one's home or native country. **homework** *n* pupil's work that is to be done outside school hours.

homosexual *n* person sexually attracted to members of his or her own sex. *adj* relating to such people. **homosexuality** *n*.

honest *adj* **1** not lying, deceiving, or cheating. **2** not given to stealing or other criminal activities. **3** sincere; open; frank. **4** trustworthy or conscientious. **honestly** *adv*. **honesty** *n*.

honey *n* **1** sweet liquid made from nectar by bees. **2** something sweet, soothing, flattering, etc. **honeycomb** *n* **1** waxy structure of hexagonal cells in which bees store their honey and eggs. **2** intricate system of passages and tunnels. **honeymoon** *n* holiday of a newly married couple. *vi* spend one's honeymoon (in). **honeysuckle** *n* sweet-smelling climbing shrub.

honorary *adj* **1** given or conferred as an honour. **2** acting or done without pay.

honour *n* **1** good reputation; public esteem; integrity; respect. **2** person or thing bringing honour. **3** mark of respect, etc. **4** act of courtesy. **5** title or address, esp. of a judge. **do the honours** act as host. ~*vt* **1** treat with honour; show respect or courtesy for. **2** confer an honour on. **3** keep a promise or bargain. **4** accept as valid. **honourable** *adj*. **honourably** *adv*.

hood *n* **1** loose covering for the head and neck. **2** collapsible or removable cover for a car or pram. **3** hood-shaped structure. **hooded** *adj* (of the eyes) half closed.

hoof *n* horny part of the foot of horses, cows, etc.

hook *n* **1** small implement curved or bent at one end, by which something is hung, pulled, fastened, etc. **2** something shaped like a hook. **3** swerving blow or stroke. **off the hook** out of trouble or difficulty. ~*vt* **1** connect, hang, fasten, catch, etc., with a hook. **2** put in the shape of a hook; crook. **hooked on** addicted to.

hooligan *n* wild, violent, or destructive person; vandal. **hooliganism** *n*.

hoop *n* circular band or ring, used as a binding, toy, etc. *vt* bind with a hoop.

hoot *vi* **1** make or give out a hollow noise like the cry of an owl. **2** laugh noisily. **3** express derision with a hoot. *n* **1** such a noise. **2** cause of great amusement. **hooter** *n* **1** mechanical device giving out a hoot as a time signal. **2** *inf* nose.

hop[1] *vi* (-pp-) **1** jump on one leg. **2** move by hopping or jumping. **hop it!** go away! ~*n* **1** act of hopping. **2** short distance or journey. **3** small dance. **on the hop** unprepared.

hop[2] *n* climbing plant whose flowers are used in flavouring beer.

hope *n* **1** desire; expectation. **2** person or thing expected to bring desired success, etc. *vt,vi* wish (for); expect or trust (that). **hopeful** *adj*. **hopefully** *adv*.

horde *n* large number or group; throng; gang. *vi* gather together in a horde.

horizon *n* **1** line where the sea or land appears to meet the sky. **2** limit of a person's hopes, intellect, or ambition. **horizontal** *adj* parallel to the horizon; lying flat; level. **horizontally** *adv*.

hormone *n* biochemical substance produced in certain glands and secreted into the blood to trigger or stimulate certain processes. **hormonal** *adj*.

horn *n* **1** hard pointed growth projecting from the head of certain animals. **2** drinking vessel made from a hollowed horn. **3** curved projection. **4** metal musical wind instrument. **5** siren or hooter on a car, etc. **draw in one's**

horns reduce one's expenditure. ~*vt* injure with a horn.

hornet *n* large wasp.

horoscope *n* astrological prediction.

horrible *adj* **1** causing horror or great fear. **2** horrid. **horribly** *adv*.

horrid *adj* **1** unpleasant; nasty; cruel. **2** shocking; repulsive. **horridly** *adv*.

horrify *vt* cause to feel horror; shock. **horrific** *adj*.

horror *n* **1** great fear; disgust. **2** thing causing such feeling. **3** ugly thing. **4** annoying or disagreeable person. **horror-struck** *adj* overwhelmed with horror.

hors d'oeuvres *n* (ɔː'dəːv) course before the main course of a meal, esp. a light savoury or appetizing fruit dish.

horse *n* **1** large hoofed domestic animal that may be ridden or used as a draught animal. **2** wooden frame for drying or airing clothes. **3** large wooden box over which gymnasts vault. **dark horse** person with hidden or unknown merit. **flog a dead horse** work at or revive a lost or hopeless cause. *vi* **horse about** act noisily or foolishly. **horsy** *adj* **1** relating to a horse. **2** interested in horses and riding. **horsebox** *n* large trailer or van for transporting horses. **horse chestnut** *n* large tree with clusters of white or red flowers and shiny brown nuts enclosed in a prickly case. **horsepower** *n* unit of power, as of a car engine. **horseradish** *n* plant whose pungent root is made into a thick sauce.

horticulture *n* growing of flowers, fruit, and vegetables; gardening. **horticultural** *adj*. **horticulturist** *n*.

hose *n* long narrow flexible pipe for transporting liquids, directing water, etc. *vt* direct water at.

hospitable *adj* offering a friendly welcome to guests; sociable. **hospitably** *adv*. **hospitality** *n*.

hospital *n* institution where the sick or injured are cared for or treated by doctors, nurses, etc.

host[1] *n* **1** person who receives and entertains guests. **2** person who runs an inn, hotel, etc. **3** animal or plant on which parasites live.

host[2] *n also* **hosts** large number of people, such as an army.

hostage *n* person seized and kept under threat until his captors' demands are fulfilled.

hostel *n* residential house or hall for students, hikers, or workers.

hostess *n* **1** female host. **2** female attendant on an aeroplane, etc.

hostile *adj* showing enmity or opposition; aggressive; unfriendly. **hostility** *n*.

hot *adj* **1** having a high temperature; very warm. **2** highly spiced; pungent. **3** violent; passionate. **4** recently occurring, produced, etc.; following closely. **hot air** meaningless or boastful talk. **hot stuff** person or thing exciting or excellent. **hot water** trouble. ~*adv* in a hot manner; hotly. **blow hot and cold** repeatedly enthuse then hesitate. *vt,vi* (-tt-) **hot up** make or become more exciting, powerful, etc. **hotly** *adv* with ardour or deep feeling. **hot-blooded** *adj* passionate. **hot dog** *n* hot sausage in a bread roll or sandwich. **hothouse** *n* artificially heated greenhouse. **hot-tempered** *adj* losing one's temper easily.

hotel *n* building offering accommodation and service to travellers, etc.

hound *n* **1** dog that hunts by following the scent of its quarry. **2** despised person. *vt* pursue or persecute ruthlessly.

hour *n* **1** unit or period of time; sixty minutes. **2** correct or appointed time. **3** destined time, as of a person's death. **hours** *pl n* **1** normal time of operation, as of a shop. **2** long time. **the eleventh hour** the last possible moment. **hourly** *adj* **1** occurring or done every hour. **2** measured by the hour.

house *n* (haus) **1** building designed for living in; residence; home. **2** building used for a special purpose. **3** household. **4** important or noble family. **5** part of a school. **6** business firm. **7** legislative assembly. **8** theatre audience. **bring the house down** cause great merriment or applause. **get on like a house on fire** get on very well. **on the house** free. **safe as houses** very safe. ~*vt* (hauz) **1** contain; enclose. **2** put in a house; provide shelter for.

housebound *adj* unable to leave the house.

household *n* those living together in a house. **household word** *or* **name** very well-known name, as of a product.

housekeeper *n* **1** woman hired to cook and look after someone else's house. **2** woman servant in charge of other servants in a large household. **housekeeping** *n* **1** domestic management. **2** money allowed or required for this.

houseman *n, pl* **-men** junior resident doctor in a hospital.

House of Commons *n* lower house of the British legislative assembly consisting of representatives elected by the people; parliament.

House of Lords *n* upper house of the British legislative assembly consisting of non-elected hereditary peers and life peers and acting also as the supreme court of judicial appeal.

housewife *n, pl* **-wives** married woman who stays at home to run the house instead of working.

housing *n* **1** houses collectively. **2** provision of houses by the government, etc.

hover *vi* **1** remain suspended in air, almost motionless. **2** remain close, as to help or protect. **hovercraft** *n* passenger craft that moves above a water or land surface on a cushion of air.

how *adv* **1** in what way or manner; by what method or means. **2** in what condition. **3** to what extent or degree. **4** why; for what reason. **5** to what a great degree or amount. **however** *conj* nevertheless; in spite of this. *adv* in any way; by whatever means.

howl *vi* **1** make a prolonged mournful cry. **2** cry loudly. **3** laugh uncontrollably. *n* **1** loud or mournful cry. **2** loud laugh. **howler** *n* ridiculous or amusing mistake.

hub *n* **1** centre of a wheel from which the spokes radiate. **2** central point, as of activity.

huddle *vi,vt* crowd or be crowded together, as for warmth or protection. *n* confused heap. **in/into a huddle** in/into a private discussion.

hue *n* **1** attribute of colour that enables different colours, red, yellow, blue, etc., to be distinguished. **2** colour; shade. **hue and cry** public outcry.

huff *n* angry, offended, or sulky fit of temper. **huffish** *or* **huffy** *adj.*

hug *v* (-gg-) *vt,vi* clasp affectionately; cuddle. *vt* keep close to. *n* affectionate clasp; cuddle.

huge *adj* extremely large; vast; immense. **hugely** *adv* very much.

hulk *n* **1** old, useless, abandoned, or partially dismantled ship. **2** large clumsy person. **hulking** *adj* large and clumsy.

hull *n* basic frame of a ship, without masts, etc.

hum *v* (-mm-) *vi* **1** make a continuous musical sound like singing but with the mouth shut. **2** make a prolonged low buzzing noise. **3** be alive with activity, rumour, etc. *vt* sing (a tune, etc.) by humming. *n* **1** sound like a prolonged 'm'. **2** low buzz or drone. **3** sound of great activity.

human *adj* **1** relating to man or mankind. **2** having or appealing to human kindness, weakness, etc. *n also* **human being** person; man or woman. **humane** *adj* sympathetic; merciful; kind; compassionate. **humanely** *adv.* **humanity** *n* **1** mankind. **2** compassion for others.

humble *adj* **1** not proud or conceited; modest. **2** unimportant or lowly; subjected; submissive. *vt* **1** cause to feel humble; shame. **2** make humble or lowly. **eat humble pie** apologize in a humble way. **humbly** *adv.*

humdrum *adj* commonplace; dull; monotonous.

humid *adj* damp; moist. **humidity** *n.*

humiliate *vt* cause to feel humble, foolish, or ashamed. **humiliation** *n.*

humility *n* condition of being humble; meekness; modesty.

humour *n* **1** ability to see or appreciate what is funny. **2** humorous or amusing quality. **3** temper; mood. *vt* indulge someone's whims or ideas. **humorous** *adj* causing laughter; funny; amusing; droll; witty. **humorously** *adv.*

hump *n* **1** natural lump on the backs of camels. **2** rounded deformity on the back of humans. **3** any curved protuberance, such as a small hill. *vt* lift clumsily. *vt,vi* arch.

hunch *n* suspicion; intuitive guess. *vt* **1** draw (one's shoulders) up, as when sitting. **2** thrust out or arch (one's back). **hunchback** *n* **1** lumplike deformity on the back. **2** person with such a deformity.

hundred *n* **1** number equal to ten times ten. **2** hundred things or people. **hundreds** very many. *adj* consisting of or amounting to a hundred or about a hundred. **hundredth** *adj,adv,n.* **hundredweight** *n* measure of weight equal to 112 pounds; one twentieth of a ton.

hung *v pt* and *pp* of **hang.**

hunger *n* **1** sensation that one needs or desires to eat. **2** lack of food; famine. **3** deep desire or need; craving. *vi* **1** feel hungry. **2** lack food. **hunger for** *or* **after** desire or crave. **hunger-strike** *n* refusal to eat, as when in prison, as a protest. **hungry** *adj.*

hunt *vt,vi* **1** chase or pursue wild animals to kill them for food or sport. **2** search (for); seek. *vt* chase or pursue a criminal, etc. **hunt down**

capture after pursuing ruthlessly. ~*n* **1** practice or instance of hunting animals. **2** group of people and working animals so involved. **3** search; pursuit. **hunter** *n*.

hurdle *n* **1** light frame used as a temporary fence. **2** framelike barrier over which an athlete (**hurdler**), show jumper, etc., must leap. **3** problem to be overcome; obstacle. *vi,vt* jump over (hurdles) in a race.

hurl *vt* **1** throw with great effort or force. **2** shout; yell.

hurrah *interj,n* *also* **hurray** exclamation of pleasure or applause.

hurricane *n* **1** very strong wind. **2** violent storm; tropical cyclone.

hurry *vi,vt* **1** move or cause to move more quickly or with haste. **2** do quickly. *n* **1** haste; bustle. **2** need for haste; urgency.

hurt *vt,vi* (hurt) **1** cause physical pain or injury (to). **2** offend; distress. **3** affect adversely; damage. *n* **1** pain; injury; wound. **2** harm; damage. *adj* **1** injured. **2** offended.

hurtle *vi* rush violently; move very fast.

husband *n* man to whom a woman is married.

hush *vt,vi* **1** make or become quiet or silent. **2** make or become soothed. **hush up** keep secret; suppress. ~*n* quiet; silence. *interj* be quiet!

husk *n* dry outer covering of some seeds. *vt* remove the husk from.

husky *adj* hoarse or whispery. **huskily** *adv*.

hustle *vt,vi* hurry along or be hurried along roughly. *vi* act quickly and efficiently. *n* rush of activity; bustle; jostling.

hut *n* small wooden building, esp. a temporary or ramshackle one.

hutch *n* small wooden cage for pet rabbits, etc.

hyacinth *n* plant that grows from a bulb and produces a spike of white, pink, or blue fragrant flowers in spring.

hybrid *n* **1** plant or animal that is a cross between two different species or varieties. **2** blend of two dissimilar things.

hydraulic *adj* **1** worked by the flow or pressure of fluids, esp. water. **2** relating to fluids and their use in engineering. **hydraulics** *n* study of fluid flow.

hydrocarbon *n* organic compound containing only carbon and hydrogen.

hydro-electric *adj* relating to the generation of electricity by the force of falling water. **hydro-electricity** *n*.

hydrogen *n* inflammable gas that is the lightest element and occurs in water and most organic compounds.

hyena *n* doglike carnivorous animal.

hygiene *n* **1** cleanliness; healthy practices. **2** science of preserving health. **hygienic** *adj*.

hymn *n* religious song; song of praise to God.

hyphen *n* mark (-) in writing or printing used to compound two words or syllables or when a word is split at the end of a line. **hyphenate** *vt* insert a hyphen in. **hyphenation** *n*.

hypnosis *n* **1** induced relaxed state of semiconsciousness during which a person will obey suggestions or commands made to him. **2** hypnotism. **hypnotic** *adj* **1** having the power to hold the attention; fascinating. **2** of or like hypnosis; lulling or trancelike. **hypnotism** *n* induction of hypnosis. **hypnotist** *n*. **hypnotize** *vt* **1** induce hypnosis in. **2** fascinate; dominate the will or mind of.

hypochondria *n* obsessive concern with one's own health. **hypochondriac** *adj,n*.

hypocrisy *n* **1** feigning of beliefs or feelings one does not have; insincerity. **2** false virtue. **hypocrite** *n*. **hypocritical** *adj*. **hypocritically** *adv*.

hypodermic *n* **1** syringe or needle used to administer injections below the skin. **2** such an injection. *adj* relating to the tissue area below the skin.

hypothesis *n* idea or suggestion put forward for discussion or verification; proposition. **hypothetic** *or* **hypothetical** *adj* not based on facts. **hypothetically** *adv*.

hysterectomy *n* surgical removal of the womb or part of the womb or uterus.

hysteria *n* **1** neurotic uncontrollable outbursts of panic or other emotions. **2** any uncontrollable emotion. **hysterical** *adj* **1** relating to hysteria. **2** extremely funny. **hysterically** *adv*.

I

I *pron* used as the subject to refer to oneself.

ice *n* **1** water frozen until solid. **2** ice-cream. *vt* **1** produce ice in; freeze. **2** put icing on (a cake). **3** chill (a drink) with ice. **iceberg** *n* large floating mass of ice in the sea. **ice-cream** *n* dessert made of flavoured frozen cream, custard, etc. **ice lolly** *n* confectionery consisting of flavoured ice on a short stick. **ice**

hockey *n* team game similar to hockey, played on ice. **ice rink** *n* an area of ice for skating, esp. one kept frozen artificially. **ice-skate** *vi* skate on ice. *n* **1** shoe fitted with a narrow metal runner for skating on ice. **2** such a runner.

icicle *n* thin tapering piece of hanging ice.

icing *n* mixture of fine sugar (icing sugar) and water, egg whites, etc., spread over cakes as a decoration.

icon *n* sacred image of Christ, saints, angels, etc.

icy *adj* **1** so cold as to cause ice. **2** relating to ice. **3** (of roads) slippery. **4** unfriendly; aloof; distant. **icily** *adv*. **iciness** *n*.

idea *n* **1** mental concept; anything thought of in the mind. **2** opinion; belief. **3** plan or suggestion. **4** impression of what something is like.

ideal *adj* **1** of the best that could be imagined; perfect. **2** conforming to a notion of excellence or purity. *n* **1** standard of excellence or complete perfection. **2** principle or aim that is pure or noble. **3** concept of perfection in a person, object, etc. **ideally** *adv*. **idealistic** *adj* **1** having or cherishing ideals or high-minded principles. **2** relating to such principles. **idealist** *n,adj*. **idealism** *n*. **idealize** *vt* **1** consider that (a person or thing) conforms to an ideal or standard of excellence. **2** present or write about (a person or thing) as if ideal. **idealization** *n*.

identical *adj* exactly the same. **identically** *adv*. **identify** *vt* recognize or prove the identity of. **identify with** associate oneself or give support to (a group, person, etc.). **identity** *n* **1** fact of being who one is or what something is. **2** exact sameness.

ideology *n* body of related ideas or doctrines of a religious, political, or economic system. **ideological** *adj*. **ideologically** *adv*.

idiom *n* **1** phrase or expression meaning something other or more than its literal meaning. **2** language restricted to a particular type of speaker, period, group, etc. **idiomatic** *adj*. **idiomatically** *adv*.

idiosyncrasy *n* individual and unusual tendency or characteristic. **idiosyncratic** *adj*.

idiot *n* **1** foolish or stupid person. **2** mentally subnormal person. **idiotic** *adj* foolish; silly. **idiotically** *adv*.

idle *adj* **1** not doing anything; inactive. **2** (of a machine) not in use. **3** lazy. **4** vain or ineffectual; useless. **5** frivolous. *vi,vt* waste (time) doing nothing. *vi* (of an engine) turn over gently while not providing drive. **idleness** *n*. **idly** *adv*.

idol *n* **1** image, esp. a sculpture, of a god or something that is worshipped as a god. **2** god of another religion from one's own. **3** very popular or admired person or thing, esp. a pop star or film star. **idolatry** *n* **1** worship of idols. **2** excessive admiration. **idolater** *n*. **idolatrous** *adj*. **idolize** *vt* treat or worship as an idol.

idyllic *adj* charmingly simple, peaceful, or poetic. **idyllically** *adv*.

if *conj* **1** in case that; supposing that. **2** whether. **3** even though; allowing that.

igloo *n* Eskimo's dome-shaped hut made of blocks of hard snow.

ignite *vt,vi* **1** set or be set on fire; kindle. **2** cause or reach a temperature at which combustion takes place. **3** arouse the passion of or be so aroused. **ignition** *n* **1** act or fact of igniting. **2** starting system in an internal-combustion engine.

ignorant *adj* **1** lacking knowledge. **2** lacking education or upbringing. **ignorance** *n*.

ignore *vt* **1** fail to notice or take into account; disregard. **2** refuse to acknowledge or greet.

ill *adj* **1** in bad health; sick. **2** bad; wicked. **3** hostile; malicious. **4** rude. **5** unfavourable; indicating misfortune. **ill at ease** embarrassed; uneasy. ~*adv* badly. *n* misfortune; harm. **ill-bred** *adj* lacking good manners or refinement; badly brought up. **illness** *n* **1** state of being ill; sickness; ill health. **2** specific complaint or disease. **ill-treat** *vt* treat cruelly or carelessly; abuse. **ill-treatment** *n*. **ill will** *n* feeling of dislike, jealousy, or hatred; malice.

illegal *adj* not in accordance with the law; unlawful. **illegally** *adv*.

illegible *adj* not able to be read; badly written; partially obliterated.

illegitimate *adj* **1** born of parents who are not married to each other. **2** contrary to the law; unlawful. **illegitimacy** *n*.

illicit *adj* not permitted or authorized; unlawful. **illicitly** *adv*.

illiterate *adj* **1** unable to read or write. **2** ignorant, uneducated, or uncultured. **illiteracy** *n*.

illogical *adj* **1** contrary to logic; irrational. **2** not thinking logically. **illogically** *adv*.

illuminate *vt* **1** light up; provide light for. **2** clarify. **3** decorate with bright gay lights or floodlighting. **4** decorate (a manuscript) by adding painted ornamentation. **illumination** *n*.

illusion *n* **1** something that is falsely or mistakenly thought to exist or be so. **2** deception; delusion; hallucination. **3** conjuring trick. **illusionist** *n* conjurer. **illusory** *adj* based on illusion; not real; deceptive.

illustrate *vt* **1** provide pictures for (a book, talk, etc.). **2** provide examples for; clarify. **illustration** *n*.

illustrious *adj* eminent.

image *n* **1** representation or likeness of a person or thing. **2** exact likeness. **3** view of an object as seen in a mirror, lens, etc. **4** mental concept; idea. **5** figure of speech, esp. a metaphor or simile in poetry, etc. **6** way the personality or character of a person, company, etc., is presented to others, esp. the general public. **7** symbol; emblem. **imagery** *n* **1** metaphorical language. **2** repetition or use of certain symbols, as in a cultural tradition.

imagine *vt,vi* **1** form a mental image or idea (of). **2** suppose; believe. **imaginary** *adj* created by the imagination; not real. **imagination** *n* **1** power or ability to create mental concepts or images. **2** act of imagining. **3** baseless or fanciful belief or idea. **imaginative** *adj* **1** having considerable powers of creative imagination. **2** relating to or characterized by imagination. **imaginatively** *adv*.

imbecile *n* idiot.

imitate *vt* **1** copy the behaviour, appearance, etc., of; take as a model. **2** impersonate or mimic. **3** be or look like. **imitation** *n* **1** act of imitating. **2** impersonation or copy. *adj* made of a synthetic material.

immaculate *adj* **1** completely free from dirtiness or untidiness. **2** free from sin; pure. **immaculately** *adv*.

immature *adj* **1** not yet fully grown or developed. **2** lacking adult judgment or stability. **immaturity** *n*.

immediate *adj* **1** without delay; instant. **2** very close or near. **3** without another intervening; next. **immediacy** *n*. **immediately** *adv*.

immense *adj* **1** very large; vast; huge. **2** very great in number, quantity, etc. **immensely** *adv* **1** to an immense degree. **2** very greatly; very much. **immensity** *n*.

immerse *vt* **1** put into water or other liquid; plunge or steep. **2** absorb or engross. **3** involve (someone) in an affair; entangle. **4** baptize (a person) by plunging him in a river, special bath, etc. **immersion** *n*.

immigrate *vi* come to a country other than one's own in order to take up permanent residence. **immigration** *n*. **immigrant** *n* person who immigrates.

imminent *adj* likely to happen very soon. **imminence** *n*. **imminently** *adv*.

immobile *adj* **1** not moving; still or fixed. **2** not capable of moving or being moved. **immobility** *n*. **immobilize** *vt* make incapable of moving. **immobilization** *n*.

immoral *adj* not in accordance with morals; against moral laws. **immorality** *n*.

immortal *adj* **1** never dying or ceasing. **2** never forgotten. **immortality** *n*.

immovable *adj* unable to be moved or altered; rigid. **immovably** *adv*.

immune *adj* **1** protected from a disease, etc., esp. because of previous exposure or inoculation. **2** not affected or moved emotionally (by). **3** free or safe (from). **immunity** *n*. **immunize** *vt* render immune to a disease. **immunization** *n*. **immunology** *n* science dealing with immunity to disease.

imp *n* **1** mischievous small fairy; sprite; goblin. **2** naughty, impudent, or mischievous child. **impish** *adj*.

impact *n* (ˈimpækt) **1** act of one object colliding with another. **2** force with which an object collides with something. **3** effect or impression. *vt* (imˈpækt) press forcefully into something or together.

impair *vt* reduce the effectiveness, value, or strength of. **impairment** *n*.

impart *vt* give (information, news, enthusiasm, etc.) to

impartial *adj* not favouring either side; fair; disinterested; not biased. **impartiality** *n*. **impartially** *adv*.

impatient *adj* **1** not willing to wait or delay. **2** irritated; vexed. **3** intolerant (of). **impatience** *n*. **impatiently** *adv*.

impeach *vt* **1** charge with (a crime, esp. of treason). **2** cast doubt on; call in question. **3** accuse or try to discredit. **impeachment** *n*.

impeccable *adj* without fault; perfect. **impeccably** *adv*.

impediment *n* **1** something that prevents something happening or working properly; obstacle. **2** speech defect, such as a stammer or lisp.

imperative *adj* **1** urgent or necessary; essential. **2** commanding; authoritative. **3** designating that form of a verb used in commands. *n* **1** command. **2** form of a verb used in commands.

imperfect *adj* not perfect; defective, faulty, or incomplete. **imperfection** *n* defect or flaw.

imperial *adj* **1** relating to an emperor or empire. **2** commanding in manner; majestic. **imperialism** *n* form of government in which one state establishes and extends its rule over foreign lands and people. **imperialist** *n,adj*.

impermeable *adj* impervious.

impersonal *adj* **1** not personal; formal; unfriendly. **2** (of verbs) limited in use to the third person singular form with *it* as the subject. **3** (of pronouns) not specifying; indefinite. **impersonally** *adv*.

impersonate *vt* pretend to be (another person). **impersonation** *n*.

impertinent *adj* rude; cheeky; impudent. **impertinence** *n*. **impertinently** *adv*.

impervious *adj* **1** not absorbing liquid; watertight. **2** not affected by criticism, etc.; insensitive.

impetuous *adj* done or acting without due consideration; rash. **impetuosity** *n*. **impetuously** *adv*.

impetus *n* **1** driving force or momentum. **2** incentive.

impinge *vi* come into contact or collision (with). **impinge (up)on 1** have an effect or bearing on. **2** encroach or infringe on. **impingement** *n*.

implement ('impləmənt) *n* tool; instrument. *vt* ('implәment) put (a law, etc.) into force. **implementation** *n*.

implicit *adj* **1** implied though not expressly stated. **2** unquestioning; unqualified; absolute. **implicitly** *adv*.

implore *vt* beg or plead.

imply *vt* **1** state or show in an indirect way. **2** insinuate; suggest; hint at. **3** indicate as a logical consequence. **implication** *n*.

import *vt* (im'pɔːt) **1** bring (goods) into a country from another for resale, etc. **2** mean; signify. *n* ('impɔːt) **1** imported commodity. **2** act or practice of importing. **3** importance. **4** meaning; consequence. **importer** *n*.

important *adj* **1** of significance or consequence; notable. **2** wielding power or influence. **3** pompous; self-satisfied. **importance** *n*. **importantly** *adv*.

impose *vt* **1** force to comply with. **2** force to pay (a tax). **3** take advantage of. **4** foist (one's company) on. **imposition** *n*. **imposing** *adj* of grand or impressive appearance or nature.

impossible *adj* **1** not possible; unable to be done. **2** difficult to deal with; annoying. **impossibility** *n*. **impossibly** *adv*.

impostor *n* person who pretends to be someone else in order to cheat or defraud.

impotent *adj* **1** not able to act; powerless or helpless. **2** (of men) not able to have an erection of the penis. **impotence** *or* **impotency** *n*. **impotently** *adv*.

impound *vt* **1** take legal possession of; confiscate. **2** confine; enclose.

impress *vt* **1** have a great effect or influence on the mind or feelings of. **2** cause to remember. **3** press a mark into; stamp. **impressive** *adj* producing a great or lasting effect; remarkable. **impressively** *adv*.

impression *n* **1** effect on the mind or feelings. **2** idea or memory, esp. when vague or general. **3** mark or stamp left when something is pressed on something. **4** imitation or impersonation. **5** printing of a book, esp. a subsequent one with no amendments. **impressionable** *adj* easily impressed. **impressionism** *n* late 19th-century movement in the arts, using effects of light, sound, form, etc., to give a general impression of the subject.

imprint *vt* (im'print) **1** stamp or print on to. **2** make a lasting impression on. *n* ('imprint) **1** mark or print on something. **2** publisher's or printer's mark, as on the title page of a book.

improbable *adj* unlikely; not very probable. **improbability** *n*.

impromptu *adj,adv* made or done without preparation, rehearsal, or consideration. *n* short piece of music.

improper *adj* **1** not proper; not conforming to rules of etiquette, morality, etc. **2** unsuitable; inappropriate. **improperly** *adv*.

improve *vi,vt* become or make better or more valuable. **improvement** *n*.

improvise *vt,vi* **1** make or do (something)

without preparation or proper materials. **2** play (music) without rehearsal or with the addition of one's own embellishments. **improvisation** *n*.

impudent *adj* rude; cheeky; insolent; impertinent. **impudence** *n*. **impudently** *adv*.

impulse *n* **1** sudden desire for something; whim. **2** thing that drives or forces something to happen. **3** electrical signal in certain machines. **impulsive** *adj* done or acting on impulse. **impulsively** *adv*.

impure *adj* **1** not pure; mixed with other substances. **2** not chaste; indecent. **impurely** *adv*. **impurity** *n*.

in *prep* **1** on the inside of; within. **2** at or to (a place). **3** during. **4** according to. **5** involved with. **6** through the medium of; using. **7** made of. **8** wearing. *adv* **1** inside; on the interior. **2** at home. **3** so as to have power. **4** so as to be fashionable. **5** accepted as a friend. **in for** going to receive or experience. **in on** knowing about. *n* **ins and outs** complicated details.

inability *n* lack of ability, power, or means.

inaccurate *adj* not accurate; wrong; incorrect. **inaccuracy** *n*. **inaccurately** *adv*.

inadequate *adj* **1** not adequate; insufficient. **2** not able to cope or deal with a task, etc. **inadequacy** *n*. **inadequately** *adv*.

inadvertent *adj* **1** done, said, etc., by accident. **2** not paying attention; careless; heedless. **inadvertently** *adv*.

inane *adj* **1** having no sense; silly. **2** having no content; empty; void. **inanely** *adv*. **inaneness** *or* **inanity** *n*.

inarticulate *adj* **1** not able to voice one's thoughts or feelings fluently. **2** not clearly said or expressed. **inarticulately** *adv*.

inasmuch *adv* **inasmuch as** since; because.

inaugurate *vt* **1** declare open or in use with ceremony. **2** install in office ceremonially. **inaugural** *adj*. **inauguration** *n*.

incapable *adj* **1** not able (to). **2** not capable; lacking the necessary powers. **incapacity** *n*. **incapacitate** *vt* render incapable or unfit; disable.

incendiary *adj* **1** relating to fires, esp. intentional fires. **2** stirring up strong feelings, esp. of revolt against authority. *n* **1** person who illegally sets fire to buildings, etc. **2** person who stirs up revolt, violence, etc. **3** type of bomb causing fires.

incense[1] *n* ('insens) substance that gives off sweet or aromatic smells when burnt.

incense[2] *vt* (in'sens) enrage.

incessant *adj* never-ending; constant; ceaseless. **incessantly** *adv*.

incest *n* illicit sexual intercourse between closely related members of the same family. **incestuous** *adj*.

inch *n* unit of length equal to one twelfth of a foot or 2.54 centimetres. *vi* move forward very slowly.

incident *n* event or occurrence. **incidence** *n* degree or scope of occurrence of something. **incidental** *adj* **1** happening at the same time as or as a natural part of. **2** not specially planned; chance; casual. **3** less important or significant. **incidentally** *adv* **1** in an incidental manner. **2** by the way.

incisor *n* tooth adapted for cutting.

incite *vt* stir up in; inflame; urge on. **incitement** *n*.

incline *v* (in'klain) *vt,vi* **1** slope or slant. **2** tend or cause to tend towards. *vt* **1** bend or bow (the head, etc.). **2** influence (someone) towards; dispose. *n* ('inklain, in'klain) slope; gradient. **inclination** *n*.

include *vt* **1** contain as a part or member; comprise. **2** regard as a part of a category, class, etc. **inclusion** *n*. **inclusive** *adj*.

incognito *adj,adv* in disguise; under an assumed identity.

incoherent *adj* not easy to understand because of being rambling, inconsistent, or illogical. **incoherently** *adv*.

income *n* money gained, esp. regularly, from work done, investments, etc.

incompatible *adj* **1** not able to agree or remain on friendly terms together. **2** not capable of or suitable for existing, working, etc. (with or together). **incompatibility** *n*.

incompetent *adj* **1** lacking the necessary skill or knowledge. **2** not capable or able; inefficient. *n* person who is incapable or inefficient. **incompetence** *or* **incompetency** *n* **incompetently** *adv*.

incongruous *adj* out of place; irrelevant; not suitable. **incongruously** *adv*.

inconsistent *adj* **1** not consistent. **2** changing one's opinions often. **3** not agreeing or compatible. **inconsistency** *n*. **inconsistently** *adv*.

inconvenient *adj* not convenient; causing

trouble or difficulty. **inconvenience** *n.* **inconveniently** *adv.*

incorporate *vt,vi* unite, blend, or mix into another body or thing. **incorporation** *n.*

increase *vt,vi* (in'kri:s) make or become more, larger, or greater; multiply; enlarge. *n* ('inkri:s) **1** act or fact of increasing. **2** amount increased by. **increasingly** *adv* more and more.

incredible *adj* **1** not able to be believed; unlikely or amazing. **2** very surprising; extraordinary. **incredibly** *adv.*

incubate *vt* (of birds, reptiles, etc.) sit on eggs to hatch them. *vi* **1** (of eggs) hatch. **2** undergo incubation. **incubation** *n* **1** hatching of eggs. **2** stage of a disease between infection and the appearance of symptoms. **incubator** *n* **1** heated apparatus in which delicate or premature new-born babies are protected. **2** similar device for hatching eggs, growing bacteria, etc.

incur *vt* (-rr-) bring upon oneself; become liable or responsible for.

indecent *adj* **1** shameful; immodest. **2** improper or unseemly. **indecency** *n.* **indecently** *adv.*

indeed *adv* **1** certainly. **2** in fact. *interj* really!

indefinite *adj* **1** not clearly or exactly stated, limited, or defined. **2** not precise or fixed; vague; unsure. **3** (of pronouns) impersonal. **indefinite article** *n* 'a' or 'an'. **indefinitely** *adv* **1** in an indefinite manner. **2** for an unknown, esp. a long, period of time.

indent *vt* **1** put or cut notches or regular recesses in. **2** set lines (such as the first line of a paragraph) in printed or written matter further from the margin than the rest. **indentation** *n* **1** act of indenting. **2** notched portion as formed. **3** series of such notches or recesses.

independent *adj* **1** not under the control or authority of someone or something else; free; self-governing. **2** not relying or dependent on other people or things; self-sufficient. **3** without any connection (with) or reference (to). **independence** *n.* **independently** *adv.*

index *n, pl* **index** *or* **indices** ('indisi:z) **1** alphabetical list of names, subjects, etc., at the end of a book, indicating where or on what page they are mentioned. **2** pointer on a dial, etc. **3** indication; sign. *vt* provide an index for (a book). **index finger** *n* finger next to the thumb.

indicate *vt* **1** show, as by sign or gesture; point out. **2** imply; mean. **indication** *n.* **indicative** *adj* suggestive (of); meaning or implying (that). *adj,n* (of or designating) grammatical mood of verbs expressing simple statements, not wishes, etc. **indicator** *n* **1** person or thing that indicates, esp. a directional signal on a car. **2** chemical substance that changes colour when certain reactions take place.

indifferent *adj* **1** not caring (about); not interested (in). **2** mediocre. **indifference** *n.* **indifferently** *adv.*

indigenous *adj* originally belonging (to); native.

indigestion *n* **1** inability to digest food or difficulty in digesting. **2** pain in the stomach caused by this. **indigestible** *adj* not easy to digest.

indignant *adj* righteously angry, as at something one considers justifies anger. **indignantly** *adv.* **indignation** *n.*

indirect *adj* not direct, straightforward, or explicit. **indirectly** *adv.*

individual *adj* of, for, or characteristic of one particular person or thing. *n* **1** single person, as distinguished from a group. **2** any person. **individuality** *n.* **individually** *adv.*

indoctrinate *vt* teach (someone) rigidly so that he does not question or think for himself. **indoctrination** *n.*

indolent *adj* lazy; idle. **indolence** *n.* **indolently** *adv.*

indoor *adj* done or suitable for inside a house or other building. **indoors** *adv* in, into, or inside a house or other building.

induce *vt* **1** have the effect of; cause; produce. **2** persuade or influence. **inducement** *n.*

indulge *vi,vt* yield to or satisfy (a desire, whim, etc.). *vt* pamper; spoil. **indulgence** *n.* **indulgent** *adj.*

industry *n* **1** system of manufacturing goods using mechanization. **2** particular branch of this; trade. **3** hard work or diligent application. **industrial** *adj* relating to industry. **industrially** *adv.* **industrialism** *n.* **industrialist** *n.* **industrialize** *vt* bring industry, factories, etc., to. **industrialization** *n.*

inebriate *vt* intoxicate.

inept *adj* **1** not suitable or appropriate. **2** stupid; slow, as to learn. **ineptly** *adv.* **ineptness** *n.* **ineptitude** *n* **1** ineptness. **2** inept remark, etc.

inequality *n* state or instance of a person or

thing being unequal, esp. in having fewer rights or advantages.

inert *adj* **1** not showing movement, activity, or change; sluggish. **2** not chemically active. **inertly** *adv*. **inertia** *n* lack of activity or movement.

inevitable *adj* unavoidable; certain to happen. **inevitability** *n*. **inevitably** *adv*.

inextricable *adj* unable to be separated, parted, or solved. **inextricably** *adv*.

infallible *adj* **1** never failing; always successful, correct, or effective. **2** certain; inevitable. **infallibility** *n*. **infallibly** *adv*.

infamous ('infəməs) *adj* **1** notorious; disreputable. **2** shocking; scandalous. **infamy** *n*.

infant *n* **1** small child. **2** person under eighteen and therefore not legally independent or responsible; minor. **infancy** *n* **1** period of being an infant. **2** early stages of development. **infantile** *adj* childishly immature.

infantry *n* foot soldiers.

infatuated *adj* wildly or foolishly in love or obsessed, esp. temporarily. **infatuation** *n*.

infect *vt* **1** transmit a disease or germs to. **2** communicate a feeling to. **3** pollute; contaminate. **infectious** *adj*. **infection** *n* **1** act of infecting or state of being infected. **2** disease or organism causing disease.

infer *vt* (-rr-) deduce; conclude. **inference** *n*.

inferior *adj* lower in position, rank, value, or quality. *n* person lower in rank or authority; subordinate. **inferiority** *n*.

infernal *adj* **1** of, like, or found in hell or the underworld. **2** wicked; diabolical. **3** annoying; confounded. **infernally** *adv*.

infest *vt* (of vermin, pests, etc.) swarm over or into; overrun. **infestation** *n*.

infidelity *n* **1** unfaithful or disloyal act or behaviour. **2** adultery.

infiltrate *vt* enter (a country, political group, etc.) gradually and stealthily as to subvert it. **infiltration** *n*. **infiltrator** *n*.

infinite *adj* without end or limit; boundless or countless. **infinity** *n*. **infinitely** *adv* **1** without limit or end. **2** extremely; very.

infinitive *n* grammatical form of verbs, usually preceded by *to,* and not indicating tense, person, or subject.

infirm *adj* **1** in poor health; ill or weak. **2** not resolute; uncertain. **infirmity** *n*.

inflame *vt* **1** cause a part of the body, etc., to become red and swollen, as when hit or infected. **2** anger or excite. **3** make more intense or worse. **inflammable** *adj* **1** likely to ignite; easy to burn. **2** excitable. **inflammation** *n* **1** act of inflaming or state of being inflamed. **2** swelling or redness.

inflate *vt,vi* **1** fill with gas; blow or swell up. **2** raise (prices) or increase in price. **inflation** *n* persistent fall in the value of money leading to continuously rising prices. **inflationary** *adj*.

inflection *n* **1** modulation of tone and stress in speech. **2** alteration in the form of a word to denote a grammatical change, as in the tense, number, case, etc.

inflict *vt* make (a person) suffer, undergo, or endure (something unpleasant); impose. **infliction** *n*.

influence *vt* have an impression on; affect; persuade, often indirectly. *n* **1** power to influence others. **2** person or thing that influences. **influential** *adj*.

influenza *n also inf* **flu** contagious viral disease characterized by fever, breathing difficulties, and muscular aches and pains.

influx *n* sudden abundant flow or large increase.

inform *vt* **1** tell; instruct; impart knowledge (to). **2** give character to; inspire. **inform on** reveal a person's activities, esp. secret or discreditable ones, to a higher authority. **informer** *n* person who informs on others. **information** *n* knowledge acquired from another source; news; relevant facts. **informative** *adj*.

informal *adj* casual; easy-going; not formal. **informality** *n*. **informally** *adv*.

infringe *vi* go beyond the limits or boundaries of. *vt* break or disobey (a law or rule). **infringement** *n*.

infuriate *vt* annoy or irritate intensely.

infuse *vt* impart; inspire. *vt,vi* soak or steep in a liquid, esp. to extract flavour. **infusion** *n*.

ingenious *adj* inventive; cleverly contrived; resourceful; cunning. **ingenuity** *n*.

ingenuous *adj* innocent or naive; not sophisticated.

ingredient *n* constituent; something that forms part of a mixture.

inhabit *vt* live or reside in. **inhabitable** *adj*. **inhabitant** *n* person living in a place; occupier.

inhale *vt,vi* draw into the lungs; breathe in.

inherent *adj* existing as an essential part (of). **inherently** *adv*.

inherit *vt,vi* have as a legacy; become heir (to).

vt possess (a family trait); derive from one's family. **inheritance** *n*.

inhibit *vt* prevent; restrain; hold back. **inhibition** *n*.

inhuman *adj* cruel; barbarous; unfeeling. **inhumanity** *n*.

initial *adj* existing at the beginning or outset; early, first. *n* first letter of a name. *vt* (-ll-) sign one's initials on.

initiate *vt* (ɪˈnɪʃɪeit) **1** begin; originate. **2** introduce; admit. *n* (iˈniʃiit) initiated person. **initiation** *n*.

initiative *n* **1** capacity to be enterprising and efficient. **2** first step; introductory move.

inject *vt* **1** drive (liquid) into living tissue using a syringe. **2** introduce vigorously. **injection** *n*.

injure *vt* hurt; harm; damage. **injury** *n* **1** damage. **2** wound. **3** something causing damage or offence.

injustice *n* **1** lack of fairness; practice of being biased or unjust. **2** wrong; unjust act.

ink *n* coloured liquid used in writing, printing, etc.

inkling *n* hint; vague idea; notion.

inland *adj* **1** situated in the interior of a country or region; away from the coast. **2** operating inside a country; domestic. *adv* towards an inland area. *n* interior of a country or region. **Inland Revenue** *n* **1** money obtained by taxes and duties levied within a country and on residents living abroad. **2** government body that collects and administers this money.

inmate *n* **1** person confined to an institution. **2** occupant.

inn *n* public house, esp. one that serves meals and offers lodgings.

innate *adj* inherent in one's nature. **innately** *adv*.

inner *adj* **1** situated or occurring further in, inside, or within. **2** not superficial; hidden.

innings *n pl or s* turn of a batsman or team of batsmen in cricket.

innocent *adj* **1** ignorant of evil; uncorrupted; naive; unsophisticated. **2** not guilty. **3** not harmful. *n* innocent person. **innocence** *n*. **innocently** *adv*.

innocuous *adj* totally harmless.

innovation *n* a newly introduced device, procedure, method, or change. **innovate** *vt,vi* make an innovation.

innuendo *n, pl* **innuendoes** malicious or obscene implication or reference.

innumerable *adj* too many to be calculated; countless.

inoculate *vt,vi* introduce a vaccine into the body to immunize against a specific disease. **inoculation** *n*.

input *n* amount, material, or data put into or supplied to a machine, factory, project, etc.

inquest *n* **1** judicial inquiry, esp. one into an unnatural death. **2** any official investigation.

inquire *vi* investigate; request information. *vt,vi* enquire. **inquiry** *n* **1** investigation; official examination of the facts. **2** enquiry.

inquisition *n* lengthy, thorough, and painful investigation or interrogation. **The Inquisition** tribunal set up by the Roman Catholic Church to abolish heresy. **inquisitor** *n*.

inquisitive *adj* **1** fond of inquiring into other people's affairs; curious. **2** eager to learn. **inquisitively** *adv*. **inquisitiveness** *n*.

insane *adj* **1** mentally ill or out of control; mad; crazy. **2** dangerously foolish. **insanely** *adv*. **insanity** *n*.

insatiable *adj* unable to be satisfied; voracious; greedy.

inscribe *vt* write, engrave, or mark (names, words, etc.). **inscription** *n*.

insect *n* **1** invertebrate animal or class of animals with six legs, a segmented body, and wings, such as beetles, butterflies, flies, and ants. **2** *inf* any similar animal, such as a spider. **insecticide** *n* substance used to kill insects.

insecure *adj* **1** not balanced; wobbly; unsafe. **2** lacking confidence or stability. **insecurely** *adv*. **insecurity** *n*.

inseminate *vt* implant semen into (a female). **insemination** *n*.

insensible *adj* **1** insensitive; indifferent. **2** unconscious; unable to experience sensations.

insensitive *adj* **1** thick-skinned; not sensitive. **2** heartless; cruel; ruthless.

insert *vt* put or place in, among, or between; introduce into. **insertion** *n*.

inside *n* **1** inner area, surface, or side; interior. **2** *inf* stomach. *adj* relating to the inside. *adv* **1** on or in the inside; indoors. **2** *inf* in prison. *prep also* **inside of** within; on the inside of.

insidious *adj* **1** secretly spreading; tending to corrupt or destroy. **2** intended to trap; treacherous. **insidiously** *adv*. **insidiousness** *n*.

insight *n* **1** perception; discernment; sympathetic understanding. 2 sudden revealing glimpse.

insinuate *vt* 1 imply or hint (something unpleasant). 2 introduce covertly or gradually. **insinuation** *n*.

insist *vt,vi* 1 declare or assert emphatically or repeatedly. 2 demand strongly; persist in urging. **insistence** *n*. **insistent** *adj* persistent; demanding attention.

insolent *adj* insulting; impertinent; rude. **insolence** *n*. **insolently** *adv*.

insoluble *adj* 1 not soluble. 2 unable to be solved.

insolvent *adj* unable to meet debts; bankrupt. *n* insolvent person. **insolvency** *n*.

insomnia *n* inability to get to sleep. **insomniac** *n* person suffering from insomnia.

inspect *vt* examine; scrutinize; look into; investigate. **inspection** *n*. **inspector** *n* 1 person, esp. an official, who inspects. 2 police officer inferior in rank to a superintendent and superior to a sergeant.

inspire *vt* 1 stimulate; fill with creative or intellectual urges or impulses. 2 arouse; excite. 3 communicate or produce by superhuman influence. **inspiration** *n* 1 artistic genius or impulse. 2 sudden bright idea.

instability *n* lack of stability, esp. in mood or character.

install *vt* 1 fix (apparatus) in position ready for use. 2 place in office. 3 settle; set (oneself) down. **installation** *n*.

instalment *n* one portion of something that appears, is sent, or paid in parts at regular intervals or over a period of time.

instance *n* example; illustration of a general statement or truth. **for instance** for example. **in the first instance** to begin with; firstly.

instant *adj* 1 occurring immediately or at once; immediate; urgent. 2 requiring little or no preparation. *n* 1 precise moment. 2 brief time. **instantaneous** *adj* occurring or done immediately or with little delay. **instantaneously** *adv*. **instantly** *adv* immediately; at once.

instead *adv* as an alternative. **instead of** in place of; rather than.

instep *n* 1 top part of the foot between the toes and ankle. 2 part of a shoe, etc., that covers the instep.

instigate *vt* stir up; urge; incite; bring about. **instigation** *n*. **instigator** *n*.

instil *vt* (-ll-) gradually introduce (ideas, values, etc.) into the mind. **instillation** *n*.

instinct *n* 1 innate impulse or feeling. 2 mode of behaviour that is innate and not learned or acquired through experience. **instinctive** *adj*. **instinctively** *adv*.

institute *vt* establish; start up. *n* society or establishment, esp. for promoting the arts or sciences or for education. **institution** *n* 1 act of instituting. 2 established law, procedure, custom, or practice. 3 establishment set up for educational, medical, social, or corrective purposes. **institutional** *adj*.

instruct *vt* teach; direct; order. **instruction** *n* 1 act of instructing. 2 information. **instructions** *pl n* directions as to use, etc.; orders. **instructive** *adj* informative.

instrument *n* 1 implement; tool; mechanical device. 2 object played to produce music. 3 person exploited by another as a means to an end. **instrumental** *adj*. **instrumentalist** *n* person who plays a musical instrument. **instrumentation** *n* arrangement of music for instruments; orchestration.

insubordinate *adj* disobedient; rebelling against authority. *n* insubordinate person. **insubordination** *n*.

insular *adj* 1 inward-looking; narrow-minded; remote; aloof. 2 relating to an island. **insularity** *n*.

insulate *vt* 1 protect against heat or sound loss or the passage of electric current by means of nonconducting material. 2 isolate or separate by means of a barrier. **insulation** *n*.

insulin *n* hormone secreted by the pancreas to control blood sugar levels.

insult *vt* (in'sʌlt) speak or act in order to hurt a person's pride or dignity; abuse. *n* ('insʌlt) insulting remark or action.

insure *vt* 1 safeguard against loss, damage, illness, etc., by paying insurance. 2 ensure. **insurance** *n* 1 act, system, or business of insuring. 2 state of being insured. 3 money paid to provide financial compensation in the event of illness, injury, loss of or damage to property, etc. 4 financial protection so obtained.

intact *adj* 1 whole; complete. 2 unharmed; untouched.

intake *n* amount or number taken in, admitted, or consumed.

integer ('intidʒə) *n* whole number.

integral *adj* **1** being an essential part (of). **2** complete; entire.

integrate *vt* combine or mix parts to make a whole; coordinate; unify. **integration** *n*.

integrity *n* **1** uprightness; honesty; soundness of character. **2** unity; wholeness.

intellect *n* **1** ability to absorb knowledge and think rationally; intelligence. **2** person of great intelligence; brilliant mind. **intellectual** *adj* **1** relating to the intellect. **2** having or revealing great powers of mind. *n* person of high intellect and cultural tastes, esp. one interested in ideas.

intelligence *n* **1** ability to learn, to reason, and to use the mental faculties. **2** information, esp. secret information about an enemy. **intelligent** *adj* possessing or showing intelligence; clever. **intelligently** *adv*. **intelligible** *adj* comprehensible; capable of being easily understood.

intend *vt* have as a purpose; mean.

intense *adj* **1** extreme. **2** strenuous; strong. **3** violent; deeply felt; passionate. **4** unable to relax; tense. **intensely** *adv*. **intensify** *vt,vi* make or become stronger, greater, brighter, or more extreme. **intensification** *n*. **intensity** *n* **1** quality or state of being intense. **2** strength; power; concentration. **intensive** *adj* **1** thorough and organized; exhaustive; concentrated. **2** requiring and using large amounts of labour or capital. **intensively** *adv*.

intent *adj* **1** determined; resolved; having in mind. **2** concentrating (on). *n* purpose; motive. **to all intents and purposes** as good as; more or less; pretty well. **intention** *n* aim; purpose; plan of action; design; motive. **intentional** *adj* meant; on purpose. **intentionally** *adv*.

inter (in'tə:) *vt* (-rr-) bury.

interact *vi* have an effect upon other things; influence. **interaction** *n*.

intercept *vt* stop or seize during transit; interrupt the progress of. **interception** *n*.

interchange *vt,vi* **1** exchange; switch. **2** substitute; alternate. *n* **1** exchange, alternation. **2** motorway junction of interconnecting roads and bridges. **interchangeable** *adj*.

intercourse *n* **1** dealings; interchange of ideas, benefits, etc. **2** *also* **sexual intercourse** copulation.

interest *n* **1** curiosity; concern; involvement. **2** cause of such a feeling. **3** pursuit; pastime; hobby. **4** personal advantage. **5** right, share, or claim, as in a business. **6** charge or payment for a financial loan. *vt* arouse the curiosity of; take an interest in. **interested** *adj* **1** having or showing interest. **2** personally involved.

interfere *vi* meddle; concern oneself with others' affairs. **interfere with** have a bad effect on; impede; hinder; molest. **interference** *n* **1** act of interfering. **2** interruption of broadcast signals by atmospheric conditions, etc.

interim *n* time between; time that has elapsed; meantime. *adj* temporary.

interior *n* **1** inside, esp. of a house or room. **2** inland regions of a country. *adj* of, on, or in the interior.

interjection *n* exclamation; sudden interrupting remark. **interject** *vt* interpose, interrupt with.

interlock *vi,vt* lock together; join firmly or inextricably.

interlude *n* **1** intermission; interval. **2** intervening period or episode of contrasting activity.

intermediary *n* go-between; mediator. *adj* **1** acting as an intermediary. **2** intermediate.

intermediate *adj* coming or existing between; in between.

intermission *n* **1** short interval; pause between the parts of a performance, film show, etc. **2** respite; rest.

intermittent *adj* occurring at intervals; sporadic; periodic. **intermittently** *adv*.

intern *vt* confine to a particular area, camp, or prison, esp. during wartime. **internee** *n*.

internal *adj* **1** concerning the interior workings or inside of something. **2** domestic; within a country. **3** essential; intrinsic. **internally** *adv*.

international *adj* of, between, or shared by a number of countries. *n* **1** member of a national team. **2** international match or contest.

interpose *vt,vi* **1** put in or between; interrupt (with). **2** intervene; mediate.

interpret *vt,vi* **1** translate. **2** reveal the meaning or significance of. **3** take to mean; understand. **interpretation** *n*. **interpreter** *n* person who makes an immediate verbal translation of speech.

interrogate *vt* ask (a prisoner or suspect) a series of questions; cross-examine; cross-question. **interrogation** *n*. **interrogator** *n*. **interrogative** *adj* **1** questioning; in the form of a query. **2** describing a word, such as *who* or *which*, used in or forming a question. *n* interrogative word.

interrupt *vt,vi* **1** stop the flow, passage, or progress (of). **2** break in (on); disturb. *vt* obstruct. **interruption** *n*.

intersect *vt,vi* divide by crossing; cut across; cross. **intersection** *n* **1** act of intersecting. **2** place or point where two things cross.

interval *n* **1** period of time between two events, acts, or parts; intermission. **2** intervening space.

intervene *vi* **1** occur or come between. **2** interfere or step in in order to prevent, hinder, or protest. **intervention** *n*.

interview *n* **1** formal meeting or discussion. **2** conversation between a journalist and a newsworthy person. **3** article resulting from this. *vt* have an interview with. **interviewer** *n*.

intestines *pl n* portion of the digestive tract between the stomach and anus. **intestinal** *adj*.

intimate[1] ('intimit) *adj* **1** close; dear; being a good friend. **2** deep; profound; private. **3** sexual; having sexual relations. *n* close friend. **intimacy** *n*.

intimate[2] ('intimeit) *vi* hint; imply.

intimidate *vt* **1** frighten; make nervous or timid; bully. **2** discourage by threats. **intimidation** *n*.

into *prep* **1** in; to the inside of. **2** to; from one point or condition to another.

intolerable *adj* **1** unbearable; unendurable. **2** extremely annoying. **intolerably** *adv*.

intolerant *adj* not tolerant; narrow-minded; bigoted. **intolerance** *n*.

intonation *n* **1** variation of pitch in the speaking voice. **2** correct pitching of musical notes.

intoxicate *vt* **1** make drunk; inebriate. **2** excite; inflame; exhilarate. **intoxication** *n*.

intransitive *adj* describing a verb that does not take or need a direct object.

intricate *adj* complex; complicated; difficult to work out or solve. **intricacy** *n*. **intricately** *adv*.

intrigue *n* ('intri:g) **1** plot; conspiracy; secret plan. **2** illicit love affair. *v* (in'tri:g) *vt* fascinate; stimulate the curiosity or wonder of. *vi* plot; conspire.

intrinsic *adj* real; fundamental; essential. **intrinsically** *adv*.

introduce *vt* **1** bring in; put forward. **2** bring into use; first establish. **3** present and identify (a stranger) to another or others; make acquainted. **4** insert. **introduction** *n* **1** act of introducing. **2** something introduced. **3** preface; foreword; opening. **4** preliminary guide; basic handbook. **introductory** *adj*.

introspective *adj* mentally inward-looking; aware of and critical of one's mental processes.

introvert *n* withdrawn or introspective person.

intrude *vt,vi* force (one's presence, etc.) uninvited. **intruder** *n*. **intrusion** *n*. **intrusive** *adj*.

intuition *n* **1** ability to perceive and understand things instinctively. **2** knowledge acquired through this ability; hunch. **intuitive** *adj* using or revealing powers of intuition rather than logic or rationality. **intuitively** *adv*.

inundate *vt* flood; overwhelm; swamp. **inundation** *n*.

invade *vt,vi* attack or forcibly enter (another's country or territory) *vt* violate; intrude or encroach on. **invader** *n*. **invasion** *n*.

invalid[1] ('invali:d) *n* sick, disabled, or permanently bedridden person. *vt also* **invalid out** send home or retire (military personnel) because of ill health or injury.

invalid[2] (in'vælid) *adj* not valid; not legally justifiable or effective. **invalidate** *vt* render invalid. **invalidation** *n*.

invaluable *adj* of great worth or usefulness; priceless.

invariable *adj* constant; unvarying; not changing; usual. **invariably** *adv* always; constantly.

invent *vt* **1** think up (something untrue or imaginary). **2** design or devise (something new or original). **inventor** *n*. **invention** *n* **1** act of inventing. **2** thing invented. **3** ability to invent; ingenuity. **inventive** *adj* good at thinking up or creating new ideas or things; ingenious.

invert *vt* turn upside down; put back to front; reverse. **inverse** *adj* inverted; back to front; contrary. **inversion** *n*.

invertebrate *adj* having no backbone. *n* invertebrate animal.

invest *vt,vi* put in (money, capital, time, effort, etc.) in order to make a profit. *vt* **1** endow; provide. **2** confer a rank or office upon with ceremony. **investor** *n*. **investiture** *n* ceremonial conferring of office. **investment** *n* **1** act of investing. **2** thing invested.

investigate *vt* make enquiries about; look into; examine; inquire into. **investigation** *n*. **investigator** *n*.

invincible *adj* unconquerable.

invisible *adj* **1** incapable of being seen. **2** hard to see; not conspicuous. **invisibility** *n*.

invite *vt* **1** request (a person) to be present or take part. **2** ask for (comments, questions, etc.). **3** court; provoke. **invitation** *n* **1** act of inviting. **2** spoken or written request for a person's presence.

invoice *n* bill listing goods sold or services rendered with prices charged. *vt* present with or make an invoice of.

invoke *vt* summon the powers of; appeal or call for. **invocation** *n*.

involve *vt* **1** include. **2** embroil; entangle. **3** engross. **4** entail; mean. **involvement** *n*.

inward *adj* **1** inner. **2** existing in the mind or emotions; situated within. **inwardly** *adv* inside; deep down. **inwards** *adv* towards the inside or middle.

iodine *n* chemical element found in seawater and seaweed and used in photography and the manufacture of antiseptics and dyes.

ion *n* positively or negatively charged atom or group of atoms. **ionize** *vt,vi* convert into ions.

iridescent *adj* shimmering with rainbow colours. **iridescence** *n*.

iris *n* **1** circular coloured area around the pupil of the eye. **2** garden plant with narrow leaves and purple or yellow flowers.

iron *n* **1** malleable magnetic metallic element that is easily corroded and widely used in alloyed form, esp. steel. **2** heated appliance for removing creases from clothes, etc. **3** iron or steel tool, usually heated. **4** great hardness, strength, or resolution. **5** golf club with a metal head. *vt,vi* remove creases from (clothes, etc.) with a hot iron. **iron out** settle; put right. **Iron Curtain** *n* the ideological, cultural, and social barrier that exists between the Soviet dominated countries of Eastern Europe and most of Western Europe. **ironmonger** *n* person selling hardware, tools, etc. **ironmongery** *n* **1** hardware, tools, etc. **2** shop or business of an ironmonger.

irony *n* **1** subtle use of words to imply a meaning opposite to the literal one. **2** incongruous usually unfortunate situation or sequence of events. **ironic** *or* **ironical** *adj*. **ironically** *adv*.

irrational *adj* not rational or consistent; illogical. **irrationality** *n*. **irrationally** *adv*.

irreconcilable *adj* not capable of being reconciled or made compatible. **irreconcilably** *adv*.

irregular *adj* **1** not occurring regularly. **2** not symmetrical; uneven; not uniform. **3** contravening customs, rules, or laws. **4** not following the usual grammatical pattern. **irregularity** *n*. **irregularly** *adv*.

irrelevant *adj* not relevant or applicable. **irrelevance** *n*.

irresistible *adj* **1** impossible to resist. **2** extremely delightful or charming; fascinating. **irresistibly** *adv*.

irrespective *adv* **irrespective of** not taking into consideration; regardless of.

irresponsible *adj* not behaving in a responsible manner; unreliable. **irresponsibly** *adv*.

irrevocable (iˈrevəkəbəl) *adj* unable to be reversed; unalterable. **irrevocably** *adv*.

irrigate *vt* keep (land) constantly supplied with water using ditches, pipes, etc. **irrigation** *n*.

irritate *vt* **1** annoy; exasperate. **2** sore; itch; chafe. **irritation** *n*. **irritable** *adj* easily annoyed.

is *v* 3rd person singular form of **be** in the present tense.

Islam *n* **1** Muslim faith based on a belief in one God, Allah, and on the teachings of his prophet, Mohammed, set down in the Koran. **2** Muslim culture; Muslim world. **Islamic** *adj*.

island *n* **1** area of land surrounded by water. **2** anything resembling an island in being isolated from its surroundings. **islander** *n*. **isle** *n* small island.

isolate *vt* **1** set apart or keep separate. **2** put in quarantine. **isolation** *n*.

issue *vi* **1** emerge; come, go, or pour out. **2** result; be derived. *vt* **1** give out; offer; distribute. **2** publish. *n* **1** something issued at one time, such as stamps or copies of a magazine or journal. **2** outflow; discharge. **3** disputed point; question; topic. **4** result. **5** offspring. **at issue** in dispute; under discussion. **take issue** disagree; dispute.

it *pron* **1** that or this thing, animal, group, etc., when not specified or identified precisely or when previously mentioned. **2** used as the subject with impersonal verbs such as 'rain', 'snow', etc. **3** used as the subject or object when referring to a following clause or phrase.

italic *adj* in or denoting a style of type with letters sloping to the right. *n also* **italics** italic type, sometimes used to isolate or emphasize a word or phrase.

itch *n* **1** irritating sensation of the skin causing a desire to scratch. **2** constant craving; restless desire. *vi* have or feel an itch. **itchy** *adj*.

item *n* **1** one unit or object from a list or collection. **2** piece of news or information. **itemize** *vt* list.

itinerary *n* **1** detailed plan of a journey; route. **2** account of a journey. **itinerant** *adj* travelling from place to place. *n* itinerant worker.

its *adj* belonging to it. **itself** *r pron* of its own self.

ivory *n* hard smooth cream-coloured highly prized material forming the tusks of the elephant, walrus, etc.

ivy *n* trailing evergreen plant with shiny leaves.

J

jab *vt,vi* (-bb-) poke; thrust; stab. *n* **1** sharp thrust or poke. **2** *inf* injection.

jack *n* **1** tool used for raising heavy objects, esp. a vehicle. **2** lowest court card in a pack; knave. *vt,vi also* **jack up** raise by using a jack. **jackpot** *n* accumulated sum of money given as a prize.

jackal *n* wild animal of the dog family.

jackdaw *n* large black bird of the crow family.

jacket *n* **1** short coat. **2** *also* **dust jacket** detachable paper cover of a book. **3** skin of a baked potato.

jade *n* semiprecious hard stone of a green or whitish colour, valued as a gemstone.

jaded *adj* worn out or stale; weary.

jagged ('dʒægid) *adj* having rough sharp points or edges.

jaguar *n* wild animal of the cat family resembling the leopard.

jail *or* **gaol** *n* prison. *vt* imprison. **jailer** *n*.

jam[1] *v* (-mm-) *vt* **1** crush or squeeze into a confined space; cram; clog. **2** *also* **jam on** apply (brakes) suddenly and forcefully. *vt,vi* stick or become stuck; wedge. *n* congestion or blockage, esp. of a number of vehicles on the road.

jam[2] *n* preserve made by boiling fruit and sugar together.

jangle *vi,vt* produce a harsh or discordant metallic ringing sound. *n* harsh metallic ringing sound.

janitor *n* caretaker; porter; warden.

January *n* first month of the year.

jar[1] *n* glass or earthenware vessel used for preserves, pickles, etc.

jar[2] *vi,vt* (-rr-) **1** vibrate with an unpleasant grating sound. **2** grate (on the nerves). *n* jolt; grating vibration.

jargon *n* **1** idiomatic or specialized language developed by a particular group, trade, or profession. **2** any talk or writing difficult to understand.

jasmine *n* shrub of the olive family having sweet-scented yellow, red, or white flowers.

jaundice *n* disease caused by excessive bile pigment in the blood, characterized by a yellowing of the skin. **jaundiced** *adj* affected or distorted by prejudice, jealousy, etc.

jaunt *n* **1** short trip or excursion. **2** spree; carefree adventure.

jaunty *adj* sprightly; brisk; lively. **jauntily** *adv*.

javelin *n* long slender spear thrown as a field event in athletics.

jaw *n* bony structure forming the bottom of the face or head in which the teeth are set. **jaws** *pl n* gripping part of a machine, tool, etc. ~*vi inf* gossip; chatter. **jawbone** *n* either of the two bones of the jaw.

jazz *n* popular music of Negro origin, often improvised and making use of syncopation.

jealous *adj* experiencing strong feelings of resentment or envy, esp. towards a rival in love. **jealously** *adv*. **jealousy** *n*.

jeans *pl n* trousers of a strong cotton or denim material.

jeep *n* open-sided motor truck used esp. by military personnel.

jeer *vi* shout insults; scorn; scoff; mock. *n* mocking remark or shout; taunt.

jelly *n* **1** type of confectionery made from gelatin, sugar, and fruit flavouring. **2** gelatinous substance produced when meat is boiled. **jellyfish** *n* small marine creature with tentacles and a soft gelatinous body.

jeopardize *vt* place at risk; endanger. **jeopardy** *n*.

jerk *vt* pull or push sharply; tug. *vi* move quickly

and suddenly; jolt. *n* **1** sharp tug. **2** spasm. **jerky** *adj*. **jerkily** *adv*. **jerkiness** *n*.

jersey *n* **1** woollen jumper. **2** type of knitted fabric. **Jersey** breed of dairy cattle.

jest *n* witty or amusing joke or trick. *vi* joke light-heartedly. **jester** *n* **1** clown or fool formerly employed at the court of a king or nobleman. **2** joker in a pack of cards.

Jesuit (ˈdʒezjuit) *n* member of a religious order (Society of Jesus) founded by Ignatius Loyola.

Jesus *n also* **Jesus Christ** founder of Christianity.

jet[1] *n* **1** fast stream of water, gas, etc., forced by pressure through a nozzle. **2** aircraft propelled by a jet of gas.

jet[2] *n* type of hard black coal used for jewellery. **jet black** *adj,n* deep glossy black.

jetty *n* small pier.

Jew *n* person belonging to or following the religion of the race which is descended from the ancient Israelites. **Jewish** *adj*.

jewel *n* precious stone worn or used for adornment; gem. **jewellery** items such as necklaces, rings, or brooches; jewels. **jeweller** *n*.

jig[1] *n* **1** lively folk-dance. **2** music for such a dance, usually in triple time. *vi,vt* (-gg-) **1** dance or play (a jig). **2** bounce or jog up and down.

jig[2] *n* cutting tool or a guide for such a tool. **jigsaw** *n also* **jigsaw puzzle** puzzle consisting of a number of specially shaped pieces of cardboard or wood, which interlock to make up a complete picture.

jiggle *vt,vi* jerk or shake up and down; rattle.

jilt *vt* forsake (a lover, intended husband or wife, etc.).

jingle *vt,vi* produce a light ringing sound; tinkle. *n* **1** light metallic sound. **2** catchy tune or song.

job *n* **1** employment; occupation; work. **2** specific task; assignment. **a good job** a fortunate thing or occurrence.

jockey *n* professional rider of racehorses. *vt,vi also* **jockey for** jostle; manoeuvre.

jocular *adj* given to joking; jolly. **jocularity** *n*.

jodhpurs (ˈdʒɔdpəz) *pl n* type of close-fitting trousers worn when riding a horse.

jog *v* (-gg-) *vi* **1** knock or push lightly; nudge; jerk. **2** move slowly but steadily; trot or plod. *vt* stimulate (the memory). *n* nudge; light blow.

joggle *vt,vi* jolt; jerk; jiggle; shake; jog. *n* slight shake or jolt.

join *vt,vi* **1** bring or come together; fasten; connect. **2** become a member (of). **3** *also* **join up** enlist (in). *vt also* **join in** accompany; take part in with. *n* seam. **joinery** *n* craft of making wooden doors, window frames, etc. **joiner** *n*.

joint *n* **1** connection of two parts or components. **2** junction at which two bones connect. **3** large piece of meat including a bone. **4** *inf* marijuana cigarette. **5** *inf* bar or club. **6** *inf* place. *adj* shared; combined. *vt* cut up (meat) into joints. **jointly** *adv*.

joist *n* steel or timber beam or girder.

joke *n* something done or said to cause amusement or laughter; jest. *vi* speak or act amusingly or wittily. **joker** *n* **1** person who jokes. **2** one of two extra cards in a pack with a picture of a clown or jester.

jolly *adj* cheerful; funny; jovial. *adv* very. **jollity** *n*.

jolt *vt,vi* shake or bump sharply; lurch; jerk. *n* **1** sudden sharp jerk. **2** shock.

jostle *vi,vt* push or move so as to gain more room or a better position. *n* rough push.

journal *n* **1** periodical; newspaper or magazine. **2** diary or logbook recording daily events. **journalism** *n* art or practice of writing for the press. **journalist** *n*.

journey *n* process of travelling or distance travelled; trip; voyage; excursion. *vi* travel; take a trip.

jovial *adj* hearty; jolly; good-humoured.

joy *n* delight; pleasure; gladness. **joyful** *or* **joyous** *adj*. **joyfully** *adv*.

jubilant *adj* joyful; rejoicing; triumphant. **jubilance** *or* **jubilation** *n*.

jubilee *n* celebration of a particularly significant anniversary.

Judaism *n* Jewish religion or tradition.

judge *n* **1** person presiding over a trial in a court of law. **2** person who chooses the winner(s) of a competition; adjudicator. **3** critic; assessor. *vt,vi* act as a judge (for). **judgment** *or* **judgement** *n*. **judicial** *adj* relating to a judge, court of law, or justice. **judiciary** *adj* relating to judgment. *n* **1** method or administration of justice. **2** judges collectively. **judicious** *adj* wise; well-judged; sensible. **judiciously** *adv*.

judo *n* Japanese sport embracing certain principles of self-defence by unarmed combat.

jug *n* vessel with a handle and spout or lip, used for holding or serving liquids.

juggernaut *n* large articulated lorry.

juggle *vi,vt* **1** perform tricks (with) by tossing and catching (various objects). **2** manipulate or rearrange, esp. in order to deceive. **juggler** *n.*

juice *n* liquid from fruit, vegetables, etc. **juicy** *adj* **1** containing plenty of juice. **2** suggesting scandal. **juiciness** *n.*

jukebox *n* coin-operated record-player found mainly on commercial premises.

July *n* seventh month of the year.

jumble *vt,vi* mix up; place or be out of sequence. *n* muddled heap or mixture. **jumble sale** *n* sale of second-hand articles, which have been donated, esp. in aid of charity.

jump *vi* **1** leap into the air, spring. **2** move involuntarily, esp. in reaction to a noise, shock, etc. **3** jerk. **4** increase, rise, or switch suddenly. *vt* leap over or across; clear. **jump at** take advantage of or seize (an opportunity) eagerly. ~*n* **1** leap; spring. **2** obstacle to be cleared by jumping. **3** spasm; jerk. **4** sudden increase, rise, or switch. **jumpy** *adj* nervous; tense.

jumper *n* garment fitting the upper part of the body, often made of wool; sweater.

junction *n* **1** joining place or point of intersection. **2** place where railway lines converge or intersect. **3** point of contact between different electrical circuits.

juncture *n* **1** critical point in time. **2** junction; connection.

June *n* sixth month of the year.

jungle *n* **1** area of land in tropical regions, having thick dense vegetation and undergrowth. **2** situation or environment characterized by ruthless competition, lack of law and order, etc.

junior *adj* of a lower rank or status; not senior. *n* person who is younger or of a lower rank or status; subordinate. **junior school** *n* school for children after primary but before secondary levels.

juniper *n* conifer producing pungent purple cones, which are used in medicines, distilling, etc.

junk[1] *n* discarded articles regarded as worthless; rubbish; trash. **junkie** *n also* **junky** *sl* drug addict.

junk[2] *n* flat-bottomed square-sailed ship of Chinese origin.

junta *n* **1** self-appointed group that seizes political power. **2** administrative council in some parts of Latin America.

Jupiter *n* largest of the planets, orbiting between Mars and Saturn.

jurisdiction *n* legal power, authority, or administration.

jury *n* **1** body of persons required to hear evidence and deliver a verdict at a trial. **2** panel of judges. **juror** *n* member of a jury.

just *adj* **1** fair in the administration of justice; impartial; unbiased. **2** deserved; proper. *adv* **1** a moment earlier; recently. **2** exactly; precisely. **3** barely; hardly. **4** at the same time (as). **5** merely; only. **justly** *adv.*

justice *n* moral or legal correctness; fairness; lawfulness. **do justice to** treat according to merit.

justify *vt* give sufficient or valid reasons for; uphold; defend. **justifiable** *adj.* **justification** *n.*

jut *vi* (-tt-) *also* **jut out** stick out; extend beyond a particular point; protrude.

jute *n* strong natural fibre used for ropes or sacking.

juvenile *adj* **1** immature; young; childish. **2** intended for young people. *n* young person; child or adolescent. **juvenile delinquency** *n* criminal behaviour by young offenders. **juvenile delinquent** *n.*

juxtapose *vt* place immediately next to. **juxtaposition** *n.*

K

kaftan *n also* **caftan** traditional loose full-length tunic of the Near East.

Kaiser *n* (formerly) German emperor.

kaleidoscope (kəˈlaɪdəskoup) *n* sealed tube containing at one end pieces of coloured glass whose reflections produce patterns when the tube is turned or shaken.

kangaroo *n* Australian marsupial with powerful hind limbs and a broad tail.

karate (kəˈrɑːti) *n* Oriental system of self-defence by unarmed combat employing smashes, chops, or kicks with the hands, elbows, head, or feet.

kebab *n* Middle Eastern dish of small cubes of

meat and vegetables cooked on a skewer over a charcoal grill.

keel *n* timber or plate running along the length of the bottom of a ship's hull. **on an even keel** maintaining a steady course; stable. *v* **keel over** capsize; overturn.

keen *adj* **1** enthusiastically willing or interested. **2** anxious; eager. **3** perceptive; observant; shrewd. **4** having a sharp cutting edge. **5** bitingly cold. **6** intense; strong. **keen on** very interested in. **keenly** *adv*. **keenness** *n*.

keep *v* (kept) *vt* **1** hold in one's possession; retain. **2** detain. **3** maintain in a particular state or condition. **4** own and look after or care for. **5** abide by; observe; comply with. **6** store; have in stock. **7** restrain; deter; prevent. **8** provide for; earn money for. **9** make a record in. *vi* **1** remain; stay. **2** carry on; continue to. **3** stay fresh. **keep on 1** continue to employ. **2** nag; persist. **3** proceed. **keep to** proceed as planned; stick or adhere to. **keep up (with)** maintain the same rate of progress (as). ~*n* **1** cost of maintaining. **2** fortified central tower of a castle. **keeper** *n* **1** person in charge of animals in a zoo. **2** museum or gallery attendant. **3** warder; jailer. **keeping** *n* **in keeping with** in accordance with; conforming or appropriate to. **keepsake** *n* memento, token gift or souvenir.

keg *n* small barrel.

kennel *n* **1** small shed for housing a dog. **2** *also* **kennels** establishment breeding and caring for dogs.

kerb *n* edge of a pavement.

kernel *n* edible central part of a nut or fruit stone.

kestrel *n* small falcon.

kettle *n* metal vessel with a lid, spout, and handle, used for boiling water. **kettledrum** *n* large percussion instrument having a hollow body with a skin stretched tightly over the top.

key *n* **1** metal instrument cut and shaped to fit a particular lock. **2** lever on a typewriter. **3** lever on a piano and certain woodwind instruments. **4** set of notes in a musical scale. **5** crucial piece of information, component, etc. **6** guide to coded information or symbols used. *adj* most important or vital. **keyed up** tense with anticipation. **keyboard** *n* set of levers or keys on a piano, typewriter, etc.

khaki ('kɑ:ki) *adj,n* yellowish-brown, often used as the colour for military uniforms.

kibbutz (ki'buts) *n, pl* **kibbutzim** (kibut'si:m) collective farm in Israel.

kick *vt,vi* strike or aim (at) with the foot. *vi* raise or shake the feet or legs. **kick up** create (a fuss, trouble, etc.). ~*n* **1** blow or jerky movement of the foot. **2** *inf* thrill. **kick-off** *n* start of play in football.

kid[1] *n* **1** young goat. **2** *inf* child; young person. **3** soft goatskin.

kid[2] *vt,vi* (-dd-) *inf* deceive by teasing; hoax.

kidnap *vt* (-pp-) seize and carry off (a person), esp. in order to obtain ransom. **kidnapper** *n*.

kidney *n* one of a pair of bodily organs that filters the blood and removes waste products, which are discharged to the bladder as urine. **kidney bean** *n* reddish-brown kidney-shaped bean.

kill *vt,vi* **1** cause the death (of). **2** destroy completely. **3** *inf* cause pain, suffering, etc., to; exhaust. **kill time** find something to do whilst waiting. ~*n* act of killing, esp. a hunted animal or prey. **killer** *n*.

kiln *n* large oven used for baking clay, bricks, etc.

kilogram *n* *also* **kilogramme** *or* **kilo** one thousand grams (approx. 2.2 lbs.).

kilometre ('kiləmi:tə, ki'lɔmitə) *n* one thousand metres (approx. 0.6 miles).

kilowatt *n* one thousand watts.

kilt *n* pleated tartan skirt, traditionally worn by Highland Scotsmen.

kimono *n* full-length wide-sleeved dress with a wide sash, traditionally worn by Japanese women.

kin *n* *also* **kindred** one's relatives.

kind[1] *adj* **1** *also* **kind-hearted** friendly; generous; helpful; considerate. **2** mild; not harmful. **kindness** *n*. **kindly** *adj* sympathetic; warm-hearted. *adv* **1** in a kind manner; sympathetically. **2** please.

kind[2] *n* sort; type; class.

kindergarten *n* nursery group or school for children under primary school age.

kindle *vt* **1** set light to. **2** arouse or excite (interest, passion, etc.). *vi* catch fire.

kindred *adj* **1** of one's kin. **2** compatible, in sympathy. *n* kin.

kinetic *adj* relating to motion.

king *n* **1** male monarch or sovereign. **2** most influential or prominent person or thing. **3** highest court card ranking above a queen and often below an ace. **4** key chess piece, able to move one square at a time in any direction. **kingdom** *n* **1** nation ruled by a king or queen; realm. **2** one of three major divisions into which animals, plants, or minerals may be classified. **kingfisher** *n* fish-eating river bird having bright blue and orange plumage. **king-size** *adj also* **king-sized** of a larger than average size.

kink *n* **1** twist, loop, or curl in a piece of rope, string, hair, etc. **2** *inf* perversion. *vi,vt* form into kinks; bend; curl. **kinky** *adj sl* sexually deviant; perverted.

kiosk *n* **1** public telephone booth. **2** small open-fronted shop selling newspapers, cigarettes, etc.

kipper *n* herring or similar fish that has been salted and smoked.

kiss *vt,vi* caress or touch with lips as a token of love, affection, reverence, etc. *n* act of kissing.

kit *n* **1** items of clothing and equipment issued to a member of the armed forces. **2** equipment or tools used by a workman, sportsman, etc. **3** collection of parts sold for assembly by the purchaser. *vt* (-tt-) *also* **kit out** supply or issue with a kit.

kitchen *n* room equipped for cooking. **kitchen garden** *n* garden where vegetables, herbs, etc., are grown.

kite *n* **1** light framework of wood, paper, etc., that can be flown in the air at the end of a long string. **2** type of hawk.

kitten *n* young cat.

kitty *n* pooled sum of money; fund.

kiwi *n* large bird native to New Zealand that is unable to fly.

kleptomania *n* compulsion to steal. **kleptomaniac** *n,adj.*

knack *n* skilful or intuitive ability; aptitude; flair.

knave *n* **1** jack in a pack of cards. **2** rogue; scoundrel.

knead *vt* shape and mould (dough, clay, etc.) with the hands.

knee *n* joint connecting the upper and lower leg. **kneecap** *n* flat bone at the front of the knee. **kneedeep/kneehigh** *adj* so deep/high as to reach the knees.

kneel *vi* (knelt *or* kneeled) rest or bend with the knees on the ground.

knickers *pl n* woman's undergarment covering the lower half of the body.

knife *n, pl* **knives** cutting implement consisting of a sharpened blade set into a handle. *vt* stab or wound with a knife. **on a knife-edge** in a state of extreme tension or anxious anticipation.

knight *n* **1** medieval nobleman of high military rank. **2** person honoured by the sovereign with a non-hereditary rank below that of the nobility. **3** chess piece usually in the shape of a horse's head. **knighthood** *n* rank of a knight.

knit *vi,vt* (-tt-; knitted *or* knit) **1** make (a garment, fabric, etc.) by winding and looping wool or yarn round two or more long needles in a particular way. **2** join together; mesh; interlock. **knitwear** *n* knitted garments.

knob *n* **1** rounded handle on a door, drawer, etc. **2** round switch on a radio, TV set, etc. **3** lump; swelling. **knobbly** *adj also* **knobby** lumpy; bumpy; having knobs.

knock *n* **1** blow; bang; tap. **2** tapping noise. *vt,vi* **1** tap; bang; hit; strike. **2** produce a tapping sound; rattle. **3** *inf* criticize; find fault (with). **knock about** *or* **around** **1** travel around. **2** be in a group (with). **3** beat; batter. **knock down** **1** hit and push over. **2** sell in an auction. **3** reduce in price. **knock off** *sl* **1** finish work. **2** pilfer; steal. **3** complete hurriedly. **4** deduct. **knock out** **1** cause to lose consciousness. **2** exhaust; tire. **knockout** *n* **1** blow that renders (someone) unconscious. **2** contest in which competitors are eliminated by heats. **3** person of stunningly attractive appearance. **4** overwhelming experience. **knock up** **1** assemble quickly. **2** rouse; waken. **knocker** *n* hinged metal bar attached to a door and used for knocking.

knot *n* **1** tight loop tied in a piece of rope, string, ribbon, etc. **2** small bunch of people. **3** irregular lump in a piece of wood. **4** unit used to measure the speed of a ship or aircraft equal to one nautical mile per hour. *vt,vi* (-tt-) form into a knot; tangle; tie.

know *v* (knew; known) *vt,vi* **1** be aware or certain of (a fact). **2** understand; have experience (of). *vt* **1** be acquainted or familiar with. **2** have a grasp of or skill in. **3** be able to distinguish. **know how** be able (to); have the skill (to). **knowhow** *n inf* skill; ability. **knowing** *adj* **1** shrewd; aware. **2** intentional; deliberate. **knowingly** *adv.* **knowledge** *n* **1** information or facts. **2** experience; awareness; consciousness. **3** familiarity; understanding. **4**

learning; wisdom. **knowledgeable** *adj* well-informed. **knowledgeably** *adv*.

knuckle *n* joint of the finger. *v* **knuckle down** get on with a task. **knuckle under** submit to authority or pressure.

kosher *adj* conforming to the requirements for the preparation of food under Jewish law.

kung fu *n* Chinese system of self-defence combining the principles of both karate and judo.

L

label *n* **1** slip of paper, card, etc., affixed to luggage, a parcel, etc., for identification; tag. **2** name or description. *vt* (-ll-) **1** affix a label to. **2** describe as; name.

laboratory *n* room or building equipped for scientific experiments, manufacture of drugs, etc.

laborious *adj* **1** requiring great effort or hard work. **2** painstaking; hardworking. **laboriously** *adv*.

labour *n* **1** work; toil; task. **2** period of childbirth. **3** body of people available for employment; workers. *vi* **1** work hard; toil. **2** move with difficulty; struggle. *vt* go into excessive detail about. **labourer** *n* unskilled manual worker. **Labour Party** *n* British political party representing the interests of the working class and trade unions.

labrador *n* breed of dog with a golden or black coat.

laburnum *n* small tree bearing clusters of drooping yellow flowers.

labyrinth *n* **1** complex network of paths, tunnels, caves, etc. **2** complicated system, situation, etc.

lace *n* **1** delicate fabric woven from cotton, silk, etc. **2** cord for fastening a shoe or boot. *vt* **1** *also* **lace up** tie (footwear) with a lace. **2** add a dash of alcohol to. **lacy** *adj*.

lack *n* deficiency; absence; shortage. *vt,vi* be without or short (of).

lacquer *n* **1** resinous substance for varnishing wood. **2** hairspray. *vt,vi* coat or spray with lacquer.

lad *n inf* boy or young man.

ladder *n* **1** framework for climbing consisting of two uprights fitted with horizontal bars or rungs. **2** flaw in knitting where vertical threads have unravelled. **3** means of moving within a social structure. *vt* produce a ladder in (stockings, tights, etc.).

laden *adj* **1** loaded; weighed down. **2** overburdened.

ladle *n* spoon with a long handle and deep bowl for serving soups, stews, etc. *vt also* **ladle out** serve by using a ladle.

lady *n* woman, esp. one who is wealthy or noted for her good manners. **Lady** title, rank, or form of address of certain female members of the nobility. **ladylike** *adj* refined and well-mannered as befits a lady. **Your/Her Ladyship** *n* form of address used to/of certain women with the rank of Lady.

ladybird *n* small beetle having a red back with black spots.

lag[1] *vi* (-gg-) fall behind. *n* interval; lapse.

lag[2] *vt* (-gg-) protect (pipes, etc.) with insulating material.

lager *n* type of beer stored in a cool place and served chilled.

laid *v pt* and *pp* of **lay**.

lain *v pp* of **lie**.

laity *n* persons who are not members of the clergy; laymen.

lake *n* inland expanse of water.

lamb *n* young sheep or its meat.

lame *adj* **1** unable to walk properly; crippled or limping. **2** feeble; unconvincing. *vt* make lame; cripple. **lame duck** *n* liability, worthless cause, etc.

lament (lə'ment) *vi,vt* express great sorrow or grief (for); mourn. *n* song or poem expressing grief or mourning. **lamentable** ('læməntəbəl) *adj* deplorable.

lamp *n* device producing light by electricity, oil, etc., usually having a shade for protection.

lance *n* **1** long spear. **2** *also* **lancet** sharp surgical knife. *vt* pierce with a lance. **lance corporal** *n* noncommissioned officer of the lowest rank in the British Army.

land *n* **1** solid mass forming the earth's surface. **2** country, nation. **3** soil; ground. **4** domain, sphere. *vi* **1** arrive on the shore or ground after a journey by ship or aircraft; disembark. **2** come to the ground after falling or jumping. *vt* **1** bring (a ship) to shore or (an aircraft) to the ground. **2** catch (a fish). **3** obtain (a job, contract, etc.). *vt,vi* place or be in a difficult situation. **landing** *n* **1** flat area at the top of a flight of stairs. **2** act of bringing a ship or aircraft to land. **landlady** *n* **1** woman who rents out rooms to tenants or guests. **2** female owner or manager of a public house. **landlord** *n* **1** person who owns and rents out property, land, rooms, etc. **2** male owner or manager of a public house. **landmark** *n* **1** prominent feature of the landscape. **2** significant historical event or achievement. **landscape** *n* **1** scenery of an area. **2** painting, drawing, etc., depicting this. *vt,vi* design and lay out (a park, garden, etc.).

lane *n* **1** narrow road, esp. in the country. **2** marked division of a motorway, racing track, etc. **3** prescribed route for shipping or aircraft.

language *n* **1** structured system of speech sounds used by a community. **2** written form of such a system. **3** any system of communication. **4** style of expression of speech or writing.

languid *adj* lacking energy; weakened; listless; inert. **languish** *vi* become languid; lose strength through neglect, deprivation, etc. **languor** *n*.

lanky *adj* tall and thin.

lantern *n* lamp with a light enclosed in a glass case.

lap[1] *n* **1** part formed by the area from the waist to the thighs when a person is sitting down. **2** comfortable or safe place.

lap[2] *vt,vi* (-pp-) **1** drink by licking up with the tongue. **2** wash gently against with a soft slapping sound. **lap up** take in (information) greedily. ~*n* gentle slapping movement or sound.

lap[3] *n* one circuit of a racing track. *vt* (-pp-) **1** wrap round; overlap; envelop. **2** overtake so as to be one or more laps ahead.

lapel *n* front part of a garment that folds back to join the collar.

lapse *n* **1** error; deviation; aberration; fault. **2** decline to a lower standard. **3** interval or passing of time. *vi* **1** decline; fall into disuse. **2** cease to subscribe to or be a member of a club, organization, religion, etc. **3** elapse; pass slowly. *vt* cancel the subscription of.

larceny *n* theft.

larch *n* type of deciduous conifer.

lard *n* pig fat melted down for use in cooking. *vt* **1** smear with lard. **2** embellish (a speech, story, etc.).

larder *n* room used for storing food; pantry.

large *adj* **1** of considerable size, weight, extent, etc.; great; big. **at large 1** free; unchecked. **2** on the whole; generally. **largely** *adv* mostly; to a great extent.

lark[1] *n* small songbird; skylark.

lark[2] *n* piece of fun or mischief; prank; spree. *v* **lark about** act mischievously.

larva *n, pl* **larvae** ('lɑːviː) immature form of an insect such as the butterfly or an animal such as the frog. **larval** *adj*.

larynx *n* organ containing the vocal cords, situated at the base of the tongue. **laryngitis** *n* inflammation of the larynx resulting in temporary loss of voice.

lascivious (lə'siviəs) *adj* lewd; lustful; lecherous.

laser *n* electronic device for producing a narrow parallel very intense beam of light of a single wavelength.

lash[1] *n* **1** whip, esp. the flexible part or thong. **2** stroke of a whip. **3** cutting remark. **4** beating or impact of waves, rain, etc. **5** eyelash. *vt* **1** whip; thrash. **2** scold; criticize sharply. **3** strike forcefully and repeatedly. **4** move like a whip. **lash out 1** attack wildly. **2** spend extravagantly.

lash[2] *vt* bind with ropes.

lass *n inf* girl or young woman.

lasso *n, pl* **lassoes** *or* **lassos** long rope with a noose for catching horses, etc. *vt* catch with a lasso.

last[1] *adj* **1** coming at the end; final. **2** most recent; latest. **3** one remaining. **4** ultimate; most conclusive. *adv* **1** at the end; after the rest. **2** most recently. *n* person or thing at the end. **at last** finally; eventually. **lastly** *adv* as a conclusion.

last[2] *vi* **1** exist or continue for a specified time. **2** endure; remain useful or in good condition; keep. **lasting** *adj* permanent; continuing.

latch *n* bar or lever for securing a door or gate. *vt* fasten with a latch. **latch on (to)** *inf* **1** attach oneself to. **2** grasp; come to understand.

late *adj* **1** not punctual. **2** happening or continuing after the normal or expected time. **3** occurring towards the end of a period, stage, etc. **4** former; recent. **5** deceased. *adv* **1** after the expected time. **2** at an advanced stage. **lately** *adv also* **of late** recently.

latent *adj* present but not yet developed or apparent; potential. **latency** *n*.

lateral *adj* directed to or coming from the side.

lathe *n* machine for holding and shaping or cutting wood, metal, etc.

lather *n* **1** foam produced by soap or detergent; suds. **2** frothy sweat, esp. of a horse. *vi,vt* produce lather; foam; froth.

latitude *n* angular distance north or south of the equator.

latrine *n* lavatory, esp. a temporary one for use at a camp site, barracks, etc.

latter *adj* **1** relating to the second of two things. **2** occurring in the second half. **latterly** *adv* lately.

lattice *n* network of strips of wood, metal, etc., arranged to form a pattern of squares, diamonds, etc.

laudable *adj* praiseworthy; commendable.

laugh *vi,vt* utter a sound of amusement, scorn, etc. **laugh at** make fun of; mock. *n* **1** single sound uttered in amusement, scorn, etc. **2** *inf* something that is fun to do or watch. **laughable** *adj* ridiculous. **laughter** *n* act or sound of laughing.

launch[1] *vt* **1** send (a ship) into the water for the first time. **2** send (a rocket) into space. **3** propel; hurl. **4** start off on a new course or enterprise. **launch into** start without hesitation or introduction.

launch[2] *n* small open motorboat.

launder *vt,vi* wash and press or iron (clothes, sheets, etc.). **Launderette** *n Tdmk* public laundry equipped with coin-operated machines. **laundry** *n* **1** place where clothes, sheets, etc., are laundered. **2** items to be laundered.

laurel *n* evergreen tree with smooth broad aromatic leaves; bay. **laurels** *pl n* honours; credit for achievement. **rest on one's laurels** cease to strive after having attained victory or success.

lava *n* molten rock from an erupting volcano.

lavatory *n* water-closet or the room where it is situated; toilet.

lavender *n* bush bearing fragrant mauve flowers. *n,adj* mauve.

lavish *adj* done on a generous scale; abundant; lush. *vt* bestow; spend generously. **lavishly** *adv*.

law *n* **1** binding regulation laid down by a government, council, or sovereign. **2** scientific rule or principle **3** code of behaviour. **the law 1** legal profession. **2** body of legal regulations. **3** *inf* police. **lay down the law** behave domineeringly, dogmatically, or tyrannically. **law-abiding** *adj* obedient according to the law. **lawful** *adj* permitted by law; legal; legitimate. **lawsuit** *n* instance of bringing a case before a court of law; action. **lawyer** *n* practising member of the legal profession.

lawn *n* area of grass laid out in a garden or park. **lawn-mower** *n* machine for cutting grass.

lax *adj* **1** not strict. **2** loose; slack. **3** having open or loose bowels. **laxative** *n* medicine taken to relieve constipation.

lay[1] *v* (laid) *vt* **1** place gently on the ground or a surface; rest; deposit. **2** set (a table) for a meal. **3** fit (a carpet). **4** place a bet on; stake. **5** *tab* copulate with. *vt,vi* produce (eggs). **lay down** surrender; sacrifice; relinquish. **lay off 1** dismiss (workers) temporarily. **2** *sl* stop; desist. **lay on** provide; organize. **lay out 1** spread out, arrange for display. **2** prepare (a body) for burial. **3** spend. **lay up** incapacitate. **layabout** *n* lazy person. **layby** *n* parking space at the side of a road. **layout** *n* arrangement of material for a book, newspaper, etc.

lay[2] *v pt of* **lie** .

lay[3] *adj* relating to people, duties, etc., concerned with the laity. **layman** *n, pl* **-men 1** person who is not a member of the clergy. **2** person who has an amateur rather than a professional knowledge of something.

layer *n* **1** coating spread over a surface. **2** stratum; band. **3** strip placed over or resting on another. **4** shoot of a plant pegged underground so that it will produce its own roots. *vi,vt* form or place in layers. *vt* propagate by means of a layer.

lazy *adj* not inclined to work; idle; inactive. **lazily** *adv*. **laziness** *n* **laze** *vi,vt* be lazy; spend (time) idly.

lead[1] (led) *n* **1** tough malleable bluish-grey metal, used for pipes, as a roofing material, etc. **2** graphite used for pencils. **leaden** *adj* **1** made of lead. **2** heavy or sluggish.

lead[2] (li:d) *v* (led) *vi,vt* **1** show the way (to); guide; conduct. **2** act as the leader or head (of); control. **3** be in or take first place; be ahead (of). *vi* **1** be a means of reaching. **2** follow a particular direction. *vt* live; follow (a particular way of life). **lead astray** persuade to do wrong; corrupt. **lead on** entice; provoke. **lead up to** move towards; prepare for; approach. ~*n* **1** clue; hint; guideline. **2** position in front or ahead of others. **3** main role in a play, film, etc. **4** flex, cord, or cable for an electrical appliance. **5** leash. **leader** *n* **1** person in charge; head of a political party, movement, etc. **2** person in a winning position. **3** principal violinist in an orchestra. **4** editorial in a newspaper. **leadership** *n.* **leading** *adj* main; principal; chief.

leaf *n, pl* **leaves 1** flat photosynthetic organ of a plant. **2** page of a book. **turn over a new leaf** make a fresh start by reforming one's behaviour. ~*vi* produce leaves. **leaf through** glance through (a book, papers, etc.) by turning the pages quickly. **leaflet** *n* **1** advertisement or notice printed on a single sheet of paper. **2** small undeveloped leaf.

league *n* **1** political alliance; coalition. **2** association of sports teams. **in league (with)** conspiring (with); allied (to). ~*vt,vi* bring or come together in a league.

leak *n* **1** crack or hole through which liquid, gas, etc., escapes. **2** disclosure of confidential information. *vi,vt* **1** escape or allow to escape through a leak. **2** divulge; disclose. **leaky** *adj.* **leakage** *n* process of leaking or the amount leaked.

lean[1] *vt,vi* (leaned *or* leant) place or be in a sloping position; tilt; incline. **lean on 1** rest against; use for support. **2** rely or depend on. **3** *sl* threaten; intimidate. **lean towards** favour; have a bias towards. **leaning** *n* tendency; bias; inclination.

lean[2] *adj* **1** (of meat) having very little fat. **2** thin; skinny. **3** not productive, barren; of a poor quality or standard. **leanness** *n*

leap *vi,vt* (leapt *or* leaped) **1** jump or spring high into the air, bound. **2** increase sharply. *n* **1** high or sudden jump. **2** abrupt change of position. **leap at** take advantage of eagerly. **leapfrog** *n* game in which one person bends over for another to leap or vault over him. *vi* (-gg-) **1** play leapfrog. **2** move erratically. **leap year** *n* year having one day (i.e. Feb. 29th) more than the usual 365.

learn *vi,vt* (learned *or* learnt) **1** acquire knowledge (of) or skill by studying or being taught. **2** experience. **3** obtain information (of); hear (about). **learned** ('lɜːnid) *adj* scholarly; wise, having great learning. **learning** *n* academic knowledge or study; scholarship.

lease *n* contract drawn up between a landlord and tenant. *vt* grant or take possession of by lease. **leasehold** *adj* held by lease. *n* tenure by lease. **leaseholder** *n.*

leash *n* strap for attaching to a dog's collar as a means of control; lead. *vt* attach a leash to.

least *adj* smallest in amount or importance. *n* smallest amount. **at least 1** as a minimum. **2** even if nothing else. **not in the least** not at all, not in the slightest; not to any extent. ~*adv* of the lowest amount.

leather *n* strong material made from the cured hide of certain animals. **leathery** *adj* of or resembling leather.

leave[1] *v* (left) *vt,vi* **1** go away or depart (from). **2** cease to attend. **3** cease to be a member (of) or participant (in). *vt* **1** forget to take; lose. **2** deposit; place. **3** result in. **4** cause a visible sign (of). **5** bequeath. **6** cause to remain. **7** fail to complete; postpone. **8** keep open, free, or vacant. **9** abandon; forsake. **leave out** omit, fail to consider.

leave[2] *n* **1** permission. **2** time off from duty or work. **take one's leave (of)** depart (from); say goodbye (to).

leaves *n pl* of **leaf.**

lecherous *adj* lewd; lascivious; lustful. **lecher** *n.* **lechery** *n.*

lectern *n* stand for the Bible in a church.

lecture *n* **1** formal talk given to instruct an audience, esp. as part of a university course. **2** rebuke; reproof; scolding; reprimand. *vt,vi* deliver a lecture (to). **lecturer** *n.* **lectureship** *n.*

ledge *n* narrow horizontal shelf projecting from a wall, window, cliff, etc.

ledger *n* book in which credits and debits of an account are recorded.

leech *n* **1** blood-sucking wormlike animal living usually in water. **2** person who lives off another's efforts.

leek *n* vegetable related to the onion, having a long edible greenish-white bulb.

leer *vi* stare lustfully, mockingly, or slyly. *n* lascivious, mocking, or sly look. **leery** *adj.*

left[1] *v pt* and *pp* of **leave**.

left[2] *adj* of or on the side of a person or thing that is turned towards the west when facing north. *adv* towards the left side. *n* direction, location, or part that is on the left side. **the Left** party or political group following radical or socialist policies. **left-hand** *adj* on the side towards the left. **left-handed** *adj* using the left hand for writing, etc. **left wing** *n* the Left. *adj* **left-wing** relating to the left wing.

leg *n* **1** limb used for walking, standing, running, etc. **2** upright support of a chair, table, etc. **3** part of a garment covering the leg. **4** particular stage of a journey, race, or competition. **not have a leg to stand on** be unable to defend oneself; have no justifiable case. **on its/one's last legs** about to disintegrate or collapse; worn out. **pull someone's leg** hoax; tease; deceive jokingly. *v* **leg it** (-gg-) walk; go on foot.

legacy *n* gift of property left by will; bequest.

legal *adj* **1** relating to law. **2** authorized or required by law; legitimate; lawful. **legality** *n*. **legally** *adv*. **legalize** *vt* make legal; sanction by law. **legalization** *n*.

legend *n* traditional story popularly believed to concern actual people or events. **legendary** *adj* known from legend; renowned.

legible *adj* written so as to be clear to read; easily deciphered.

legion *n* **1** military unit of Ancient Rome comprising several thousand soldiers. **2** vast number; multitude.

legislate *vi,vt* formulate officially and pass laws (about). **legislation** *n*. **legislative** *adj*. **legislator** *n*. **legislature** *n* body of statesmen who pass laws; parliament.

legitimate *adj* **1** permitted by law; legal. **2** conforming to rules; allowable; permissible. **3** logical; justifiable. **4** born of parents who are legally married. **legitimacy** *n*. **legitimately** *adv*.

leisure *n* period outside working hours; free time. **at leisure** when free; at a convenient time. **leisurely** *adj* without haste; unhurried. *adv* at an easy or unhurried rate or pace.

lemon *n* sharp-tasting citrus fruit with a bright yellow skin. *n,adj* bright light yellow.

lend *vt* (lent) **1** give with the expectation of repayment or return; loan. **2** add to the quality or character of; impart. **lend a hand** help; cooperate; assist. **lender** *n*.

length *n* **1** measurement of something from one end to another. **2** time taken from beginning to end; duration. **3** piece of cloth, rope, wire, etc. **at arm's length** at a distance; apart. **at length 1** in great detail; for a long time. **2** eventually. **lengthen** *vt,vi* make or become longer. **lengthways** *adj,adv also* **lengthwise** measured from one end to another. **lengthy** *adj* long and detailed.

lenient *adj* not strict; inclined not to punish severely. **leniency** *n*. **leniently** *adv*.

lens *n* piece of transparent material with curved surfaces for converging or diverging a beam of light.

Lent *n* period of forty days before Easter, traditionally observed by Christians as a time for fasting and penitence.

lentil *n* plant producing brownish-orange seeds, which are eaten as a vegetable, used to thicken soups, etc.

Leo *n* fifth sign of the zodiac, represented by the Lion.

leopard *n* large animal of the cat family having a yellowish coat with black markings.

leprosy *n* infectious disease characterized by skin inflammation and disfigurement. **leper** *n* person suffering from leprosy.

lesbian *n* woman who has a sexual relationship with someone of her own sex; female homosexual. **lesbianism** *n*.

less *adj,adv* not as much; to a smaller extent; not as often. *prep* minus. *pron* a smaller amount. **lessen** *vt,vi* make or become less; reduce; decrease. **lesser** *adj* smaller; less important.

lesson *n* **1** period of time spent learning or teaching. **2** something that is learned or taught. **3** short reading from the Bible given during a service.

lest *conj* in case; for fear that; so as to avoid.

let *vt* (-tt-; let) **1** allow; permit. **2** rent or hire (accommodation, etc.). **let alone 1** leave alone. **2** not to mention; apart from. **let down 1** lower; take down. **2** deflate. **3** disappoint; fail to keep a promise. **let (someone) know** inform; tell. **let off 1** excuse; pardon; refrain from punishing. **2** cause to explode. **3** release; allow to escape. **let on** divulge; tell; reveal. **let out 1** allow to leave. **2** divulge; leak. **3** alter (a garment) so as to be larger. **4** utter; emit. **let up** cease; become less persistent. **let-down** *n* disappointment; anticlimax.

lethal *adj* likely to cause death; highly dangerous.

lethargy ('leθədʒi) *n* extreme lack of energy or vitality; inertia; sleepiness; idleness; sluggishness. **lethargic** (le'θɑːdʒik) *adj*.

letter *n* **1** written message or account that is

sent to someone. 2 written or printed alphabetical symbol or character. **letter of the law** the law when interpreted literally. **lettering** *n* art or practice of inscribing letters.

lettuce *n* vegetable with broad green leaves used in salads.

leukaemia *n* disease in which an excessive number of white corpuscles in the blood is produced.

level *adj* **1** having an even surface or plane; horizontal. **2** not tilted or sloping. **3** equal; even. **4** *also* **level-headed** calm and sensible; not inclined to panic. *n* **1** measured height or altitude. **2** flat even surface or area. **3** standard or status; grade. **4** instrument or device for measuring or checking that something is horizontal or level. **5** layer; stratum. **on the level** *inf* honest; straightforward. ~*vt* (-ll-) **1** make level or horizontal; line up. **2** equalize; bring to the same standard or status; even up. **3** raze; demolish. **4** take aim with; point. **5** direct (a remark, gaze, etc.). **levelly** *adv*. **levelness** *n*. **level crossing** *n* intersection of a road and railway track.

lever *n* **1** bar or rod used to move a heavy object, set machinery in motion, etc. **2** means of persuasion or coercion. *vt,vi* use a lever (on); prise. **leverage** *n* **1** force or action of a lever. **2** means of exerting power or influence.

levy *n* tax; duty; toll. *vt,vi* impose a levy (on).

lewd *adj* **1** lecherous; lustful. **2** vulgar; crude; obscene; indecent.

liable *adj* **1** obliged by law; subject (to). **2** likely; apt; inclined. **liability** *n* **1** legal obligation. **2** likelihood; probability. **3** tendency; inclination. **4** responsibility; burden; disadvantage; drawback.

liaison *n* **1** close working relationship; association; cooperation. **2** illicit sexual relationship. **liaise** *vi* work together; cooperate.

liar *n* person who tells lies.

libel *n* **1** written defamatory statement. **2** crime of publishing such a statement. *vt* (-ll-) publish libel about. **libellous** *adj*.

liberal *adj* **1** tolerant, esp. on political or religious matters. **2** progressive; enlightened. **3** generous; free. **Liberal** *n* member or supporter of the Liberal Party. **Liberal Party** *n* British political party advocating individual freedom and occupying a position to the right of the Labour Party but to the left of the Conservative Party.

liberate *vt* set free; release; emancipate. **liberation** *n*.

liberty *n* freedom from restraint, restriction, or control. **take liberties (with)** take unfair advantage (of).

Libra *n* seventh sign of the zodiac, represented by the Scales.

library *n* **1** room or building housing a collection of books. **2** collection of films, documents, etc. **librarian** *n* person working in a library. **librarianship** *n*.

libretto *n* text of an opera, operetta, etc.

lice *n pl* of **louse.**

licence *n* **1** official document or certificate of authorization. **2** permission granted by an authority. **3** misuse of freedom; lack of self-control. **4** allowable deviation from a particular convention, esp. in art or literature. **license** *vt* grant or authorize a licence (for). **licensee** *n* person holding a licence, esp. to sell alcoholic drinks.

lichen ('laikən, 'litʃən) *n* moss-like plant that grows on tree-trunks, rocks, etc.

lick *vt,vi* **1** touch or stroke with the tongue. **2** *inf* beat or defeat soundly. **3** *inf* thrash; flog. **lick into shape** improve or groom by special training or instruction. ~*n* **1** stroke of the tongue. **2** *inf* pace; rate; speed.

lid *n* **1** cover for a container. **2** eyelid.

lie[1] *n* untrue statement, esp. one deliberately intended to deceive. *vi* (lying) tell a lie or lies.

lie[2] *vi* (lying; lay; lain) **1** be stretched out or placed in a horizontal position; rest. **2** be situated. **3** be buried. **4** be the responsibility (of). **lie in** remain in bed for longer than usual. **lie low** remain in hiding.

lieu (luː) *n* **in lieu of** instead of; in place of.

lieutenant (lef'tenənt) *n* **1** military officer of a rank below that of captain. **2** naval officer of a rank below that of lieutenant commander. **lieutenant colonel** *n* military officer of a rank below that of colonel. **lieutenant commander** *n* naval officer of a rank below that of commander.

life *n, pl* **lives** **1** condition of existing or being alive; being. **2** *also* **lifetime** period of existence; length of time lived. **3** all living things. **4** biographical account. **5** liveliness; vivacity; vitality. **6** way of living; mode of existence. **7** maximum prison sentence that can be awarded. **come to life 1** recover consciousness; be revived. **2** become lively or animated. **lifeboat** *n* boat used for searching for those in distress at sea or one carried by a ship in case of emergency. **lifeguard** *n* person who patrols the shore, attends a swimming pool, etc., for the safety of swimmers. **lifelike** *adj* resembling something real. **lifeless** *adj* **1** dead. **2** motionless; seemingly dead. **3** dull; uninspired. **lifeline** *n* **1** rope used in life-saving. **2** something that ensures survival. **lifelong** *adj* lasting throughout one's life; permanent. **life-saving** *n* practice or method of rescuing someone in distress, esp. at sea. *adj* able to save life.

lift *vt* **1** take or carry upwards; pull up; haul; raise. **2** turn or direct upwards. **3** put into a happy or cheerful mood; gladden. **4** exalt; elevate. **5** revoke or cancel (a ban, restriction, etc.). **6** *inf* steal; shoplift. **7** *inf* copy or borrow (an idea, piece of text, etc.). **8** dig up (plants). *vi* **1** move upwards; rise. **2** (of fog, mist, etc.) clear; disperse. *n* **1** act of lifting or raising. **2** boxlike compartment driven hydraulically, mechanically, or by electricity that moves vertically between floors of a building. **3** free ride in someone else's vehicle. **4** something that gives one energy or makes one cheerful or happy. **lift-off** *n* launching of a rocket; blast-off.

light[1] *n* **1** brightness emitted by the sun, a lamp, etc. **2** daylight. **3** source of illumination. **4** match, etc., that produces a flame. **5** aspect; context; view. **6** enlightenment; knowledge. **7** small window pane. **bring/come to light** make/become known or apparent. **in the light of** taking into account; with the knowledge of. **set light to** ignite or kindle. **shed** *or* **throw light on** clarify; explain. ~*adj* **1** not dark; illuminated. **2** of a pale or pastel shade or colour. **3** fair-haired. *vt,vi* (lit *or* lighted) **1** set light to; ignite. **2** provide with light or illumination. **light up 1** illuminate; make bright. **2** apply a match to. **3** cause to sparkle or shine; brighten. **light bulb** *n* glass bulb containing a metal filament, which lights up when an electrical current is passed through it. **lighten** *vt,vi* brighten; make or become light(er). **lighter** *n* device producing a flame for lighting cigarettes, etc. **lighthouse** *n* tower situated on or near the coast that sends out a powerful light as a guide or warning to shipping.

light[2] *adj* **1** not heavy; weighing little. **2** not forceful; gentle; not hard. **3** of a small amount; slight. **4** not overpowering; subtle. **5** buoyant. **6** *also* **light-headed** giddy; faint; dizzy. **7** *also* **light-hearted** cheerful; not serious; happy. **8** not severe or strict; lenient. **9** airy; spongy; porous. **10** not classical or highbrow. **11** nimble; graceful or quick. **12** not arduous; simple or easy. **make light of** treat as unimportant; make no fuss about. ~*adv* without being weighed down; comfortably. *vi* (lighted *or* lit) settle or perch; alight. **light (up)on** come across by chance; discover. **lightly** *adv*. **lightness** *n*. **lighten** *vt,vi* **1** make or become less heavy. **2** make or become more cheerful, optimistic, etc.; lift. **lightweight** *adj* **1** light in weight. **2** not intellectually demanding; superficial. *n* boxer whose weight is between 126 lbs and 135 lbs.

lightning *n* electricity discharged in the atmosphere producing a flash of light and usually accompanied by thunder. **like lightning** with tremendous speed.

like[1] *prep* **1** very similar to; in the manner of; the same as. **2** for example; such as. **3** as though; as if. **feel like 1** desire; want; be tempted or inclined to. **2** have the sensation of; resemble; feel similar to. **like-minded** *adj* having the same or similar views or opinions. **liken** *vt* compare; draw an analogy or find a resemblance (between). **likeness** *n* **1** resemblance; similarity. **2** representation in a painting, photograph, etc. **likewise** *adv* **1** similarly; in the same way. **2** moreover; furthermore; also.

like[2] *vt* be fond of; find pleasing, attractive, agreeable, etc. *vi,vt* wish; prefer; choose.

likely *adj* probable; to be expected; liable. *adv* probably; possibly. **likelihood** *n*.

lilac *n* hardy shrub having fragrant purple, mauve, or white flowers.

lilt *n* **1** rhythmic or melodious quality in speech or music. **2** tune or song with such a quality. *vi,vt* sing, speak, or sound with a lilt.

lily *n* bulb producing large white, purple, yellow, or orange flowers. **lily-of-the-valley** *n* small plant having fragrant white bell-shaped flowers and broad leaves.

limb *n* **1** part of the body attached to the trunk,

such as an arm or leg. **2** branch; bough. (**out**) **on a limb** isolated and vulnerable.

limbo *n* **1** supposed state of those who have died without being baptized. **2** state of being unwanted, cast aside, or without a proper place.

lime[1] *n* **1** *also* **quicklime** calcium oxide; white substance made from limestone. **2** *also* **slaked lime** calcium hydroxide; white substance produced by adding water to quicklime. *vt* treat with lime. **limelight** *n* **in the limelight** attracting a great deal of public notice or acclaim. **limestone** *n* whitish rock composed of calcium carbonate.

lime[2] *n* green-skinned citrus fruit similar to a lemon.

limerick *n* humorous five-lined poem.

limit *n* **1** extent to which something is possible or permissible. **2** most acceptable amount; minimum or maximum. **3** boundary. *vt* place a restriction on. **limitation** *n* restriction; limiting circumstance.

limp[1] *vi* walk in an abnormal way because of injury or disablement; be lame. *n* act of limping.

limp[2] *adj* **1** sagging; not rigid; floppy. **2** feeble; weak.

limpet *n* marine mollusc having a conical shell that clings to rocks, etc.

line[1] *n* **1** mark drawn in pencil, paint, etc., across a surface. **2** groove; crease; furrow. **3** row; column. **4** outline; edge. **5** boundary; limit. **6** cable, rope, cord, or string used for a particular purpose. **7** means of transport; route. **8** railway track. **9** policy; method or system. **10** direction taken by a missile. **11** field of research; area of interest. **12** single horizontal row of written or printed words. *vt* **1** draw lines on. **2** produce grooves or furrows in. **3** form a row along; border. **line up 1** set in a straight or orderly row or line. **2** provide; organize.

line[2] *vt* provide with an inside covering or layer of material.

lineage *n* line of descent from a common ancestor.

linear (ˈliniə) *adj* **1** relating to a line. **2** made up of lines. **3** of one dimension only.

linen *n* **1** strong fabric of woven flax. **2** sheets, tablecloths, etc., made esp. of linen.

liner *n* ship designed to carry a large number of passengers.

linger *vi* **1** be reluctant to hurry away; stay behind; loiter. **2** remain or persist, esp. as a memory.

lingerie (ˈlɑːnʒəri) *n* women's underwear and nightwear.

linguist *n* **1** person who is able to speak one or more foreign languages skilfully. **2** student of linguistics. **linguistic** *adj* relating to language, linguistics, or speech. **linguistics** *n* study of the structure or history of language.

lining *n* material used to line a coat, curtain, etc.

link *n* **1** single loop forming part of a chain. **2** connecting part or piece in a mechanism. **3** connection or relationship between people, different places, times, etc. *vt,vi* form a link (between); connect; relate.

linoleum *n also* **lino** material having a canvas backing coated with linseed oil, cork, etc., used as a floor covering.

linseed *n* seed of flax from which oil is extracted.

lion *n* **1** large mammal of the cat family, the male of which has a shaggy mane. **2** powerful or strong person. **lioness** *f n*.

lip *n* **1** one of two fleshy parts surrounding the opening of the mouth. **2** that part of the rim of a jug, etc., that channels liquid being poured out. **3** *sl* impudent remark. **lip-read** *vi,vt* (-read) interpret (speech) by following a person's lip movements. **lipstick** *n* cosmetic used to add colour to the lips.

liqueur *n* sweet alcoholic drink generally taken after a meal.

liquid *n* substance that can flow but cannot easily be compressed. *adj* **1** relating to a liquid; capable of flowing. **2** harmonious; flowing. **3** (of assets) readily convertible into cash. **liquidate** *vt* **1** settle (debts). **2** dissolve (a company) by realizing assets in order to pay off creditors, shareholders, etc. **3** dispose of (an enemy, spy, etc.) by violent means. **liquidize** *vt,vi also* **liquefy** make or become liquid.

liquor *n* any alcoholic drink, esp. a spirit.

liquorice *n* black substance extracted from the root of a shrub for use in medicines, confectionery, etc.

lira (ˈliərə) *n, pl* **lire** (ˈliəri) *or* **liras** standard monetary unit of Italy.

lisp *n* manner of pronunciation in which *s* and *z* sound like *th* (θ and ð). *vt,vi* pronounce or speak with a lisp.

list[1] *n* record or statement placing a number of items one after the other. *vt* place on a list; make a list of.

list[2] *vi* (of a ship) lean to one side. *n* leaning to one side.

listen *vi* **1** pay attention or concentrate in order to hear. **2** take notice; heed. **listener** *n*.

listless *adj* not energetic; lethargic; weary.

lit *v* a *pt* and *pp* of **light**[1] and **light**[2].

literal *adj* **1** not metaphorical. **2** interpreted or translated word for word. **literally** *adv*.

literary *adj* concerning literature, authorship, or scholarship.

literate *adj* able to read and write. **literacy** *n*.

literature *n* body of written material, such as novels, poetry, or drama.

lithe *adj* supple; moving easily or gracefully.

litmus *n* type of vegetable dye that turns red in acids and blue in alkalis.

litre *n* unit of volume equal to one thousand cubic centimetres.

litter *n* **1** rubbish or refuse that is dropped or left lying about, esp. in a public place. **2** set of offspring produced by a sow, bitch, etc., at one birth. *vt* **1** cover or make untidy with litter. **2** scatter or be scattered untidily on.

little *adj* **1** small; tiny; not big or tall. **2** not important; trivial. **3** brief; not lasting long. *pron* not much. *adv* not often; hardly at all. **a little** *pron* a small number or quantity. *adv* to a small extent. **little by little** gradually.

live[1] (liv) *vi* **1** exist; be alive; have life. **2** have one's home (in); reside; stay. **3** continue, flourish. **4** make a living. *vt* **1** spend (one's life). **2** have as a fundamental part of one's life. **live up to** match (required standards or expectations).

live[2] (laiv) *adj* **1** alive; not dead; living. **2** stimulating; interesting. **3** (of a shell, cartridge, etc.) not yet exploded. **4** broadcast directly without being previously recorded. **5** carrying electric current. **livestock** *n s or pl* animals kept or reared on a farm, such as cattle, pigs, or poultry.

livelihood *n* means of earning a living.

lively *adj* **1** active; having energy; vigorous. **2** busy; fully occupied. **3** alert; quick. **4** bright; cheerful. **liveliness** *n*.

liver *n* reddish-brown organ situated below the diaphragm in the body that secretes bile, neutralizes toxic substances, etc.

livid *adj* **1** extremely angry; furious. **2** discoloured, as when bruised.

living *adj* still alive; not yet dead or extinct. *n* **1** livelihood. **2** way of life. **living room** *n* room in a house used for recreation, receiving guests, etc.

lizard *n* reptile having four limbs, a long tail, and a scaly body.

llama *n* mammal related to but smaller than a camel, valued for its fleece.

load *n* **1** something carried or transported. **2** cargo. **3** burden; weight of responsibility, etc. **4** *inf* large amount; lot; heap. *vt,vi* **1** place a load on or in (a lorry, ship, etc.). **2** burden. **3** put ammunition in (a gun).

loaf[1] *n, pl* **loaves** baked bread in a particular shape.

loaf[2] *vi* pass time idly; lounge; loiter.

loan *n* something lent, such as a sum of money or a book from a library. **on loan** borrowed. ~*vt,vi* lend.

loathe *vt* hate; detest; abhor. **loathsome** *adj* detestable; abhorrent.

lob *vt,vi* (-bb-) hit or bowl (a ball) so as to form a high arc. *n* ball hit or bowled in such a way.

lobby *n* **1** entrance hall, waiting room, or corridor. **2** group seeking to persuade officials, members of parliament, etc., to support or oppose a particular policy or piece of legislation. *vt,vi* seek to influence as a lobby.

lobe *n* **1** lower fleshy part of the ear. **2** subdivision of certain organs such as the lung or brain.

lobster *n* large edible crustacean with long claws or pincers.

local *adj* **1** belonging to or concerning a particular district or locality. **2** affecting a particular part of the body. *n* **1** person belonging to the locality. **2** *inf* public house nearest to one's home or place of work. **locality** *n* neighbourhood; vicinity; district. **localize** *vt* **1** limit to a particular part of the body. **2** make local.

locate *vt* **1** look for and find the position of. **2** situate; place; position. **location** *n* **1** place; site; position. **2** act of locating or finding. **3** place other than a studio, where a film is shot.

loch *n* (in Scotland) lake or narrow sea inlet.

lock[1] *n* **1** device for securely fastening a door, drawer, box, etc., operated usually by means of a key. **2** section of a canal or river enclosed within a barrier or gate, which can be opened or shut to control the water level. **3** wrestling hold in which a limb or the head is unable to move. *vt,vi* **1** fasten or become secure with a lock. **2** jam; fix so as to be unable to move. **3** interlock.

lock[2] *n* length or curl of hair from or on the head.

locker *n* cupboard provided esp. in a public building, used for storing personal property, clothes, etc.

locket *n* small case containing a portrait, memento, etc., attached to a chain and worn as a necklace.

locomotion *n* power of motion. **locomotive** *n* engine driven by steam, electricity, or diesel power, used to draw a train along a railway track.

locust *n* insect of the grasshopper family that travels in swarms stripping vegetation over a wide area.

lodge *vt,vi* **1** provide or be provided with accommodation, esp. in a private household. **2** embed or become embedded (in); wedge. *vt* **1** make (a formal complaint). **2** deposit for safekeeping *n* **1** small house located near or at the gate of a park, estate, etc. **2** cabin or house used by hunters, skiers, etc. **lodger** *n* person lodging in a private household. **lodgings** *pl n* accommodation, such as rented rooms in a private household.

loft *n* **1** room or space immediately below the roof of a house. **2** upper floor of a barn, stable, etc., where hay is stored. **3** building constructed as a shelter for racing pigeons. **lofty** *adj* **1** high and imposing. **2** idealistic; noble. **3** haughty; arrogant.

log *n* **1** section of a felled branch or tree trunk. **2** regular or daily record kept during a voyage, flight, etc. *vt* (-gg-) **1** fell or saw (logs). **2** record as a log. **logbook** *n* book in which records or logs are kept.

logarithm *n* power to which a base number, usually 10, is raised to give a specified number, tabulated as an aid to calculation. **logarithmic** *adj*.

logic *n* **1** branch of philosophy concerned with determining the validity of particular statements according to certain principles of reasoning. **2** consistency of method or practice; validity of reasoning. **logical** *adj*. **logically** *adv*.

loins *pl n* lower part of the back and sides of the body.

loiter *vi* lurk; linger; move about aimlessly. **loiterer** *n*.

loll *vi* laze; lounge. *vt,vi* droop; sag; hang loosely.

lollipop *n* **1** boiled sweet on a small stick. **2** ice lolly.

lonely *adj* **1** without friends; isolated; alone. **2** remote; desolate. **loneliness** *n*. **lone** *adj* solitary; single.

long[1] *adj* **1** of considerable extent from one end to another; not short. **2** lasting for a considerable time. **3** of a particular length or duration. **4** having a large number of entries. parts, etc. **in the long run** over a long period. *adv* for a particular time. **as long as** on condition that; provided that. *n* **before long** after a short time; soon. **for long** for a long time. **no/any longer** no/any more. **long-sighted** *adj* **1** able to see clearly at a distance **2** having imagination or foresight. **long-standing** *adj* having been in effect over a long period. **longwinded** *adj* using an excessive number of words; tediously long.

long[2] *v* **long for** crave; yearn for; desire **longing** *n*.

longevity *n* relatively long life span or state of living to a great age.

longitude *n* angular distance east or west of a standard meridian (through Greenwich)

loo *n inf* lavatory or toilet.

look *vi* **1** *also* **look at** direct the eyes (towards) in order to see. **2** *also* **look at** begin to examine; attend (to). **3** seem; appear; be likely to be. **4** face; overlook. **5** *also* **look for** search (for); seek. **6** *also* **look through** read; glance at; scan. *vt* **1** direct one's gaze at; stare or glance at. **2** have the appearance of being. correspond to. **look after** take care of; tend. be in charge of. **look down on** regard as inferior or worthy of contempt. **look forward (to)** anticipate with pleasure. **look out** be cautious; heed. **look up** begin to improve **look up to** admire; respect. ~*n* **1** act of looking. **2** appearance; impression. **lookout** *n* **1** person placed on guard, to watch out for danger, etc. **2** *inf* matter for personal concern. affair. **looks** *pl n* physical appearance.

loom[1] *n* machine for weaving by hand or mechanically.

loom[2] *vi* **1** approach or appear menacingly. **2** give an impression of greatness; dominate.

loop *n* shape of a circle, oval, spiral, etc.

formed by string, wire, etc.; coil. *vt,vi* form a loop.

loophole *n* flaw or ambiguity in a law, contract, etc., that enables one to evade obligations, penalties, etc.

loose *adj* **1** not tight; slack. **2** not fastened or fitted securely. **3** not put in a bundle or tied together. **4** free; not confined. **5** not compact. **6** approximate; rough. **7** promiscuous. **8** not careful; sloppy. **9** not controlled. **at a loose end** having nothing in particular to do; not occupied. ~*adv also* **loosely** in a loose manner. *vt* **1** liberate; set free; allow to escape. **2** loosen; slacken. **loosen** *vt,vi* make or become loose(r); slacken; unfasten.

loot *n* money, property, etc., stolen or seized, esp. during a battle or riot. *vt,vi* steal; plunder. **looter** *n*.

lop *vt* (-pp-) chop or sever (branches, a limb, etc.) swiftly and in one movement.

lopsided *adj* tilted to one side, uneven or crooked; not symmetrical.

lord *n* nobleman. **Lord 1** title, rank, or form of address of certain male members of the nobility. **2** title of certain high officials in the Church or of the law. **the Lord 1** God. **2** Jesus Christ. **the Lords** House of Lords. *v* **lord (it) over** be master of; dominate. **lordship** *n* rank of a lord. **Your/His Lordship** form of address used to/of certain men with the rank of Lord and also bishops and judges of the high court.

lorry *n* motor vehicle for carrying heavy loads, transporting goods, etc.; truck.

lose *v* (lost) *vt* **1** drop or leave (something) and be unable to find it again. **2** decrease in power, speed, etc. **3** be deprived of as through death, accident, etc. **4** be unable to maintain (a particular state, belief, etc.). **5** fail to take advantage of or use. *vt,vi* **1** fail to win; suffer defeat (in). **2** (of a watch, clock, etc.) be slow (by). **loser** *n*. **loss** *n* act of losing or that which is lost. **at a loss** helpless; incapable.

lot *pron* **a lot** a large number or quantity; much or many; a great deal. *n* **1** group; collection; bunch. **2** assigned task. **3** article or set of items in an auction. **draw lots** select at random by using tickets, slips, etc. *adv* **a lot 1** to a great extent. **2** often; regularly.

lotion *n* liquid preparation used as a skin cleanser, antiseptic, etc.

lottery *n* **1** system of raising money by selling tickets, one or more of which are drawn at random to entitle the holder to a prize. **2** situation governed by luck or chance.

lotus *n* **1** mythical fruit that induces laziness or forgetfulness. **2** variety of tropical water lily.

loud *adj* **1** of a relatively high volume of sound; not quiet. **2** of a vulgar style; garish. *adv also* **loudly** in a loud manner. **out loud** aloud. **loudness** *n*. **loud-mouthed** *adj* rude; abusive, brash. **loudspeaker** *n* device for converting electrical signals into sound that can be heard over a wide area.

lounge *n* **1** sitting room. **2** room or area at an airport, hotel, etc., where one may sit or wait. **3** *also* **lounge bar** saloon bar. *vi* laze; move or sit idly.

louse *n, pl* **lice** wingless bloodsucking insect that is a parasite of mammals. **lousy** *adj* **1** infested with lice. **2** *inf* very bad; awful.

lout *n* uncouth person.

love *n* **1** feeling of deep passion, desire, affection, or fondness. **2** score of nil in tennis, squash, etc. **make love (to)** have sexual intercourse (with). ~*vt,vi* feel love (for). **lover** *n*. **lovesick** *adj* pining; suffering through love.

lovely *adj* **1** giving pleasure; nice; highly enjoyable. **2** beautiful, attractive. **loveliness** *n*.

low[1] *adj* **1** not tall or high; relatively close to the ground. **2** close to the bottom of a particular scale, grade, etc.; poor. **3** inferior, below average. **4** mean, despicable. **5** depressed or ill. **6** almost empty; having only a small amount left. **7** deep and quiet. *adv* towards or into a low position, state, or condition. **lie low** remain hidden, esp. to avoid capture. **lowness** *n*. **lowbrow** *adj* relating to a style or taste, esp. in the arts, that is not very sophisticated or intellectual, not highbrow. **lower** *vt,vi* **1** decrease, reduce. **2** move downwards. **lower case** *n* printed letters of the alphabet that are not capitals. **lowland** *n* region or area that is relatively flat. **lowlander** *n*.

low[2] *vt,vi,n* (of cattle) moo.

loyal *adj* faithful, maintaining allegiance; patriotic. **loyally** *adv* **loyalty** *n*

lozenge *n* **1** small tablet eaten as a sweet for medicinal purposes. **2** diamond-shaped equilateral figure.

LSD *n* **lysergic acid diethylamide:** synthetic hallucinatory drug.

lubricate *vt* apply oil or grease to. **lubrication** *n*. **lubricant** *n* lubricating substance; oil. *adj* serving to lubricate.
lucid *adj* **1** expressed in a way that is easily understood; clear. **2** shining; bright. **lucidity** *n*.
luck *n* **1** state of affairs, event, etc., apparently occurring at random; chance; fortune. **2** good fortune. **lucky** *adj* having or bringing good luck; fortunate. **luckily** *adv* fortunately.
lucrative *adj* profitable.
ludicrous *adj* absurd; ridiculous.
lug *vt* (-gg-) pull or carry with effort; drag.
luggage *n* suitcases, bags, etc., carried on a journey; baggage.
lukewarm *adj* **1** tepid; moderately warm. **2** not enthusiastic.
lull *vt* soothe; make calm or drowsy. *n* brief respite or period of tranquillity. **lullaby** *n* soothing song intended to lull a child to sleep.
lumbago *n* backache.
lumber[1] *n* **1** (esp. in North America) timber or logs. **2** large unwanted furniture or other household articles. *vt* **1** store or fill with household lumber. **2** *inf* burden with an unpleasant duty, boring person, etc. **lumberjack** *n* (esp. in North America) person who fells trees and cuts timber.
lumber[2] *vi* move clumsily and heavily.
luminous *adj* reflecting light.
lump *n* **1** solid mass, usually irregular in shape. **2** swelling; bump. *vt also* **lump together** place in or consider to be one group or mass. **lumpy** *adj* having many lumps; bumpy.
lunar *adj* relating to the moon.
lunatic *n* insane person. **lunacy** *n* madness; insanity.
lunch *n also* **luncheon** midday meal. *vi* eat lunch.
lung *n* one of a pair of respiratory organs situated in the thorax that oxygenates the blood.
lunge *n* **1** thrust of a sword in fencing. **2** sudden forward movement. *vi* make or move with a lunge.
lupin *n* plant with a tall stem bearing bright flowers of various colours.
lurch[1] *vi* stagger; sway; jerk or jog violently. *n* sudden violent jerk or stagger.
lurch[2] *n* **leave in the lurch** abandon at a critical time; forsake.
lure *vt* entice in order to trap; tempt.
lurid *adj* **1** sensational; shocking; scandalous. **2** having strange bright colours.
lurk *vi* loiter; lie in wait; remain hidden.
luscious *adj* **1** gorgeous; delightful. **2** having a rich flavour; succulent.
lush *adj* **1** characterized by rich dense growth; luxuriant; abundant. **2** luxurious.
lust *n* **1** strong sexual desire. **2** craving; passion; greed. **lustful** *adj* consumed with lust. **lusty** *adj* robust; hearty; vigorous.
lustre *n* brightness or gloss of a surface; sheen; shine; radiance. **lustrous** *adj*.
lute *n* pear-shaped stringed instrument of the 14th–17th centuries, related to the guitar. **lutenist** *n*.
luxury *n* **1** condition of having all that one needs to gratify one's desires. **2** item not regarded as a necessity. **luxuriant** *adj* abundant; lush. **luxurious** *adj* providing luxury. **luxuriously** *adv*.
lynch *vt* (of a mob) hunt down and kill without legal trial.
lynx *n* long-eared wild cat inhabiting forest regions in parts of Europe, North America, and Africa.
lyre *n* stringed instrument of ancient Greece, resembling a small harp.
lyric *adj* relating to a style of poetry expressing personal feelings, originally recited to a lyre accompaniment. **lyrical** *adj* **1** expressive of the emotions of love, sorrow, etc. **2** enthusiastically eloquent. **lyrics** *pl n* words of a song.

M

mac *n* short for **mackintosh.**
macabre (məˈkɑːbrə) *adj* suggesting or associated with death; frightening.
macaroni *n* type of pasta shaped into thin tubes.
mace[1] *n* **1** hammer-like medieval weapon with a spiked metal head. **2** ceremonial staff that is a symbol of office.
mace[2] *n* spice produced from nutmeg.
machine *n* **1** apparatus that performs useful work using applied forces. **2** mechanism, such as a car or aeroplane. **3** highly organized controlling body. *vt,vi* use a machine to shape, cut, or work on something. **machine gun** *n* automatically loaded and repeatedly firing gun. **machine-gun** *vt* (-nn-) shoot at with a

machine gun. **machinery** *n* **1** machines or machine parts. **2** system or way of organization. **machinist** *n* person who makes or works on machines.

mackerel *n, pl* **mackerel** *or* **mackerels** marine food fish with a silvery belly and green stripes on its back.

mackintosh *n* light coat worn esp. as protection from rain; raincoat.

mad *adj* **1** mentally disturbed; insane. **2** eccentric, crazy. **3** *inf* extremely pleased, angry, enthusiastic, noisy, etc. **drive** *or* **make someone mad** annoy. **go mad** become very excited, angry, pleased, etc. **madly** *adv* **madness** *n* **madden** *vt,vi* anger; excite; irritate.

madam *n* polite form of address to a woman.

made *v pt* and *pp* of **make.**

Madonna *n* Virgin Mary, esp. when painted or a statue.

madrigal *n* **1** love poem or song. **2** part song performed usually by six or seven voices without musical accompaniment.

magazine *n* **1** paper-covered periodical containing contributions from various writers and usually illustrated. **2** place where arms, explosives, etc., are stored. **3** replaceable metal containers for cartridges inserted into some automatic guns or rifles.

maggot larva of a housefly, etc., often breeding in decaying matter.

magic *n* **1** art of producing certain effects with the help of supernatural forces; witchcraft. **2** art of producing seemingly inexplicable results by means of tricks. **3** mysterious power or agency. *adj* **1** relating to magic. **2** *also* **magical** as if by magic; miraculous; enchanting. **magician** *n* person who is skilled in tricks or in spells.

magistrate *n* person who officiates in a lower court of law; justice of the peace. **magisterial** *adj* **1** relating to a magistrate. **2** dictatorial; authoritative.

magnanimous *adj* generous; noble; not petty. **magnanimity** *n* **magnanimously** *adv*

magnate *n* wealthy highly influential person, esp. in industry.

magnet *n* piece of iron or steel that can attract iron or steel objects and point north when suspended. **magnetic** *adj* **1** relating to a magnet or magnetism. **2** attractive; alluring. **magnetism** *n* **1** science or attractive properties of magnets. **2** charm; attractiveness. **magnetize** *vt* **1** make magnetic. **2** attract.

magnificent *adj* remarkable; splendid. **magnificence** *n*. **magnificently** *adv*.

magnify *vt* **1** make apparently larger, esp. by means of a lens or microscope. **2** exaggerate. **magnification** *n*.

magnitude *n* **1** size; extent. **2** importance; significance.

magnolia *n* shrub or tree with large, usually sweet-smelling creamy-pink flowers.

magpie *n* bird with a long tail, black-and-white plumage, and a chattering call.

mahogany *n* tropical American tree, the hard reddish-brown wood of which is used for furniture.

maid *n* **1** girl. **2** female servant. **old maid** old unmarried woman; spinster. **maiden** *n* young single woman. **maiden aunt** *n* unmarried aunt. **maiden name** *n* family name before a woman marries. **maiden speech** *n* first speech.

mail *n* **1** letters, parcels, etc., sent or received by post. **2** postal service. **mailing list** *n* list of names and addresses of persons to whom specific information is regularly sent. **mail order** *n* order and delivery of goods by post.

maim *vt* disable, cripple.

main *adj* chief, principal, most important. *n also* **mains** principal pipe or cable for gas, water or electricity supply. **mainly** *adv* **mainland** *n* land mass, such as a country or continent, excluding its islands. **mainspring** *n* **1** chief spring of a clockwork mechanism. **2** driving force; chief motivation. **mainstream** *n* leading trend.

maintain *vt* **1** keep going; keep in fair condition; support. **2** assert. **maintenance** *n* **1** act or way of keeping or supporting a person or thing. **2** financial support, as after a divorce.

maize *n* tall annual grass grown for its yellow grain, used as food and fodder, and for its oil.

majesty *n* grandness; splendour; stateliness. **Majesty** term of address for a queen or king or the spouse or widow of a sovereign. **majestic** *adj* stately; dignified.

major *adj* **1** of greater importance, extent, size, etc. **2** of or relating to a musical scale in which the third and fourth and the seventh and eighth notes are a semitone apart. *n* military officer ranking below a lieutenant colonel and above a captain. **major general** *n* military officer ranking above a brigadier.

majority *n* **1** greater number, part, etc.; more than half. **2** number by which a winning vote in an election, etc., exceeds the runner-up. **3** state or time of reaching full legal age.

make *v* (made) *vt* **1** create; produce; construct; form; prepare; establish. **2** cause to be, become, or seem. **3** cause; force. **4** amount to; constitute. **5** earn; acquire. **6** develop into. **7** do; perform. **8** appoint. *vt,vi* cause to become or become (happy, sad, merry, etc.). *n* brand; style; way things are made. **on the make** *inf* seeking an easy profit or conquest. **make do (with)** be content with; improvise with. **make for** go towards. **make good 1** repair. **2** be successful in. **make it** achieve or reach a goal. **make off (with)** go or run off (with). **make out 1** understand. **2** see; discern. **3** write out or fill in (a cheque, etc.). **4** attempt to establish; represent as. **make up 1** complete; form. **2** invent; compose; fabricate. **3** reconcile or become reconciled. **4** apply cosmetics to the face, esp. for theatrical effect. **make-up** *n* **1** cosmetics. **2** person's constitution or personality. **make up for** compensate or atone for. **make up one's mind** decide; resolve.

make-believe *n* pretence; fantasy.

makeshift *adj* provisional; acting as a substitute. *n* makeshift object, method, etc.

maladjusted *adj* not adjusted or adapted properly to personal environment. **maladjustment** *n*.

malaria *n* infectious tropical disease transferred by mosquitoes and characterized by chills and high fever.

male *adj* **1** of or related to the sex that produces young by fertilizing the female, masculine **2** composed of or for men or boys. *n* male person or animal.

malevolent *adj* harmful; evil; spiteful, malicious. **malevolence** *n*. **malevolently** *adv*.

malfunction *vi* fail to function properly. *n* failure to function properly.

malice *n* intention to inflict harm on another; spite. **malicious** *adj*. **maliciously** *adv*.

malignant *adj* **1** inclined to cause suffering, showing ill will. **2** (of disease) likely to cause death if not treated successfully. **malign** *vt* insult; slander. *adj* evil. **malignancy** *n*.

malleable *adj* (esp. of metal) easily shaped or treated.

mallet *n* hammer-shaped tool, usually with a wooden head.

malnutrition *n* defective or inadequate nutrition.

malt *n* grain, often barley, soaked then dried for use in brewing beers or distilling spirits.

maltreat *vt* treat in an abusive or cruel manner. **maltreatment** *n*.

mammal *n* any of the class of warm-blooded animals whose offspring are fed by mother's milk. **mammalian** *adj*.

mammoth *n* huge extinct elephant. *adj* huge; immense.

man *n, pl* **men 1** human male adult. **2** individual; person. **3** mankind. **4** husband or lover. **5** workman; male employee. **6** piece in draughts, chess, etc. **man in the street** *n* person considered as representative of an average member of society. **to a man 1** unanimously. **2** completely; utterly. ~*vt* (-nn-) supply with people for a specific purpose. **manly** *adj* denoting conduct and qualities expected of a man. **manliness** *n*.

manage *vt,vi* control; be in charge (of); handle. *vt* succeed in; be successful in. *vi* cope. **manageable** *adj*. **management** *n* **1** managing techniques. **2** body of persons in charge of a business. **3** administration. **manager** *n* person managing or controlling a business, etc. **manageress** *f n*. **managerial** *adj*.

mandarin *n* **1** high-ranking official in imperial China. **2** high-ranking or pompous official. **3** small orange-like fruit. **Mandarin** *n* official Chinese dialect.

mandate *n* **1** authorization; official command. **2** sanction or support given to a government by the electorate. **mandatary** ('mændətərı) *n* person, body, or state holding a mandate. **mandatory** ('mændətərı) *adj* **1** having the nature or command of a mandate. **2** compulsory.

mandolin *n* musical instrument of the lute family with eight strings tuned and plucked in pairs.

mane *n* long growth of hair on the back of the neck of a horse, lion, etc.

mange *n* contagious skin disease of domestic animals, esp. dogs. **mangy** *adj* **1** having mange. **2** scruffy.

mangle[1] *vt* **1** disfigure as by severe cuts, etc; mutilate. **2** spoil by errors.

mangle[2] *n* machine with two rollers used for removing water from and smoothing clothes, etc. *vt* put through a mangle.

mango *n, pl* **mangos** *or* **mangoes** pear-shaped tropical fruit with sweet yellowish flesh, borne on an evergreen tree.

manhandle *vt* **1** treat roughly; use physical violence on. **2** use physical rather than mechanical force.

manhole *n* hole, covered by a lid, that serves as an access to a sewer, pipe, etc.

mania *n* **1** excessive excitement. **2** obsession or excessive liking for something. **3** condition characterized by abnormal excitement and often manifestations of violence. **maniac** *n* **1** person showing excessive enthusiasm for something; fanatic. **2** mad person; lunatic. **manic** *adj* relating to mania.

manicure *n* care or treatment of hands and fingernails. *vt* treat (fingernails) by cutting, varnishing, etc.

manifest *adj* quite apparent and obvious; visible. *vt* reveal clearly. **manifest itself** show itself; appear. **manifestation** *n*. **manifestly** *adv*.

manifesto *n* written declaration by a sovereign or body of people proclaiming certain principles or rights.

manifold *adj* of many parts, aspects, or uses; varied. **manifoldly** *adv*.

manipulate *vt* **1** operate skilfully; use; handle. **2** exercise shrewd control over; influence cleverly. **3** exercise treatment on. **manipulation** *n*. **manipulator** *n*.

mankind *n* human race.

man-made *adj* artificially produced.

manner *n* **1** way something happens or is done. **2** style. **3** particular way a person behaves towards others. **4** kind; sort. **manners** *pl n* social conduct. **mannerism** *n* gesture, speech habit, etc., particular to an individual.

manoeuvre (mə'nu:və) *n* planned, calculated, or strategic movement, as in a war; clever plan. *vt,vi* **1** make or perform manoeuvres. **2** move or cause to move into a desired direction or position.

manor *n* **1** feudal territorial unit occupied and worked by serfs paying rent in crops and service to their lord. **2** *also* **manor house** residence of the lord with its grounds. **3** mansion on an estate.

manpower *n* number of people needed or supplied for something.

mansion *n* large stately residence; manor house.

manslaughter *n* unlawful but unintentional killing of a person.

mantelpiece *n* structure above and around a fireplace, often incorporating a shelf.

mantle *n* **1** loose sleeveless cloak. **2** something covering or concealing. **3** net-like luminous cover over a gas lamp. *vt* cover with or in a mantle.

manual *adj* of the hands; done or operated by hand; not mechanical. *n* book containing fundamentals of a subject; textbook; handbook. **manually** *adv*.

manufacture *n* **1** commercial production or processing of goods, usually on a large scale. **2** manufactured product. *vt,vi* make (goods); produce; process. *vt* fabricate; concoct. **manufacturer** *n*.

manure *n* animal excrement used for fertilizing soil. *vt* apply manure to (soil).

manuscript *n* author's original piece of writing or document before its printing.

many *adj* much more than few; numerous. *n,pron* large number of people or things.

map *n* two-dimensional representation of a geographical area. *vt* (-pp-) produce a map of.

maple *n* deciduous tree or shrub with hard close-grained wood, used for furniture, etc.

mar *vt* (-rr-) spoil; ruin.

marathon *n* **1** long-distance race run over a distance of 42 km. **2** any long and trying task or contest.

marble *n* **1** hard, usually veined, limestone rock, used in a polished form, esp. in architecture. **2** small glass ball. **marbles** *n* game played with such balls.

march *vi* **1** walk with regular steps in an orderly military fashion. **2** proceed steadily. *vt* force to go or march. *n* **1** act or instance of marching. **2** distance or route marched. **3** piece of music composed for marching.

March *n* third month of the year.

marchioness *n* (mɑ:ʃə'nes) wife or widow of a marquess.

mare *n* female horse.

margarine *n* food product, similar to butter, usually made from vegetable fats.

margin *n* **1** border. **2** empty space on the sides

of a text. **3** vertical line bordering this. **4** limit of something. **5** tolerable excess. **marginal** *adj* **1** relating to a margin. **2** close to a limit. **3** insignificant. **marginally** *adv.*

marguerite *n* garden plant resembling a large daisy.

marigold *n* plant having orange or yellow flowers.

marijuana (mæri'wɑːnə) *n* dried hemp leaves or flowers smoked for euphoric effect.

marinade *n* **1** seasoned mixture of vinegar or wine with oil in which meat, vegetables, etc., are steeped before cooking. **2** food thus steeped. **marinate** *vt,vi also* **marinade** soak (meat, fish, etc.) in marinade.

marine *adj* **1** of or relating to the sea and sea life. **2** of navigation and shipping or the navy. *n* **1** soldier trained to serve both on land and the sea. **2** sea vessels collectively.

marital *adj* relating to marriage.

maritime *adj* **1** relating to the sea, shipping, or navigation. **2** of a place or area by the sea.

marjoram *n* plant with sweet-scented leaves, which are used in cooking.

mark[1] *n* **1** visible trace on a surface, such as a stain, dot, scratch, etc. **2** sign or symbol indicating or distinguishing something. **3** figure or letter evaluating a piece of work, examination, etc. **4** distinguishing quality. **5** target. *vt* **1** put a mark on. **2** distinguish, characterize, indicate, or show, as by a mark. **3** select; designate. *vt,vi* **1** stain; scratch. **2** evaluate and correct (an examination paper, essay, etc.). **marked** *adj* **1** noticeable; evident. **2** watched with suspicion; singled out. **markedly** *adv.* **marksman** *n, pl* **-men** a person who shoots a gun skilfully and accurately.

mark[2] *n* German monetary unit.

market *n* **1** place, usually with outdoor stands, where food, clothes, etc., are sold. **2** area of trade in certain goods. **3** demand for goods. *vt,vi* offer for sale. **market garden** *n* establishment where fruit and vegetables are grown for sale. **market research** *n* research into consumers' needs and preferences.

marmalade *n* jelly-like preserve usually made from oranges.

maroon[1] *n,adj* brownish-red.

maroon[2] *vt* abandon or isolate on an island, etc., without resources.

marquee *n* large tent used for exhibitions, etc.

marquess *n also* **marquis** ('mɑːkwis) nobleman ranking below a duke and above an earl or count. **marquise** (mɑː'kiːz) *n* wife of a marquess.

marriage *n* **1** relationship or legal bond between a man and woman, making them husband and wife. **2** harmonious union of two things.

marrow *n* **1** soft nutritious tissue inside bones that is vital for production of certain blood cells. **2** *also* **vegetable marrow** plant with a long, rounded, and usually green striped fruit, eaten as a cooked vegetable. **marrowbone** *n* bone containing marrow used in cooking, esp. for making stock.

marry *vi* become husband and wife. *vt* **1** make (a person) one's spouse; join or take in marriage. **2** unite.

Mars *n* fourth planet from the sun, lying between earth and Jupiter. **Martian** *adj.*

Marseillaise (mɑːsə'leiz) *n* French national anthem.

marsh *n* low, poorly drained, and usually very wet ground. **marshy** *adj.*

marshal *n* **1** highest military rank in certain countries. **2** official in charge of ceremonies, parades, etc. *vt* (-ll-) **1** arrange in proper order. **2** assemble. **3** conduct.

marshmallow *n* sweet with a soft spongy texture.

marsupial *n* any of the group of mammals, including the kangaroo, whose young are carried in and complete their development in a pouch.

martial *adj* relating to war.

martin *n* kind of swallow.

martini *n* drink made of gin and vermouth.

martyr *n* person who endures suffering out of religious or some other conviction. *vt* kill, torture, or persecute as a martyr. **martyrdom** *n.*

marvel *n* something wonderful. *vi,vt* (-ll-) feel wonder or surprise (at). **marvellous** *adj* wonderful; excellent. **marvellously** *adv.*

Marxism *n* political theory describing the historical change of capitalism into a classless society as the outcome of the struggle of the working classes against their exploitation. **Marxist** *n,adj.*

marzipan *n* sweet paste of ground almonds and sugar, moulded into small fruits or used in cakes, etc.

mascara *n* cosmetic for painting eyelashes.

mascot *n* object believed to bring luck.

masculine *adj* **1** relating to or characteristic of a man. **2** of a grammatical gender normally denoting males. **masculinity** *n*.

mash *n* **1** mixture of warm water and crushed grain, etc., used as fodder, in brewing, etc. **2** mashed potatoes. *vt* crush into a soft pasty mass.

mask *n* **1** facial covering, worn, esp. as a disguise. **2** pretence; disguise. *vt* **1** put a mask on. **2** disguise; hide.

masochism *n* condition in which a person suffers voluntarily in order to experience pleasure, esp. sexual. **masochist** *n*. **masochistic** *adj*.

mason *n* person who works with building stone. **masonry** *n* profession or work of a mason.

masquerade *n* **1** ball, etc., where people wear masks, costumes, and other disguises. **2** pretence; false show. *vi* wear a disguise.

mass[1] *n* **1** bulk of matter that is not particularly shaped. **2** large number or quantity of something. **3** measure of the amount of matter in a body. *vt,vi* form or gather into a large crowd. **mass media** *pl n* newspapers, television, radio, etc., informing and influencing the public. **mass-produce** *vt* manufacture on a very large scale. **mass production** *n*.

mass[2] *n* **1** *also* **Mass** celebration of the Eucharist, esp. in the Roman Catholic Church. **2** music composed for this occasion.

massacre *n* ruthless killing, esp. of innocent people; slaughter. *vt* kill indiscriminately.

massage *n* treatment of muscles in order to relax them by rubbing and kneading. *vt* give a massage to. **masseur** *n* person who practises massage. **masseuse** *f n*.

massive *adj* **1** large and solid. **2** considerable.

mast *n* **1** vertical pole for supporting a vessel's sails and rigging. **2** any high upright pole.

mastectomy *n* surgical removal of a breast.

master *n* **1** person who controls others. **2** expert in a special field. **3** employer of servants. **4** male teacher. **5** form or mould for making duplicates; original. *vt* **1** become highly skilled in. **2** gain control over; overcome. **masterful** *adj* **1** highly capable; skilful. **2** showing authority; dominant. **mastermind** *n* person who creates or plans a major project or activity. *vt* plan with great skill. **masterpiece** *n* great work of art; example of excellence or skill.

masturbate *vi,vt* excite oneself or another to orgasm by manipulation or rubbing of the genitals. **masturbation** *n*.

mat[1] *n* **1** piece of fabric, used to cover floors, stand or sit on, wipe shoes on, etc. **2** piece of material placed under vases, plates, etc. **3** tangled mass. *vi* (-tt-) become tangled.

mat[2] *adj* matt.

matador *n* man who kills the bull in bullfights.

match[1] *n* slender strip of wood with a coated head that bursts into flame when rubbed.

match[2] *n* **1** person or thing that resembles or corresponds to another. **2** contest; team game. **3** marriage or person eligible for marriage. *vt* **1** equal or be equal to. **2** be the match of. **3** make to fit or correspond; adapt. *vi* correspond in shape, size, colour, etc.; harmonize. **matchless** *adj* incomparable; having no equal.

mate *n* **1** one of a couple or pair, esp. a pair of breeding animals. **2** husband or wife. **3** friend; one's equal; fellow worker. **4** officer of a merchant ship ranking below a captain. *vt,vi* **1** join or pair. **2** (of animals) unite in order to produce young.

material *n* **1** stuff or substance of which anything is made. **2** raw data; facts. **3** cloth; fabric. **materials** *pl n* elements or tools required to make or perform something. ~*adj* **1** composed of matter; not spiritual; relating to physical well-being or wealth. **2** essential; important. **materialist** *n* person who values possessions and physical well-being more than ideas or spiritual beliefs. **materialism** *n*. **materialistic** *adj*. **materialize** *vi,vt* appear or cause to appear out of nothing. *vi* assume solid, material, or bodily form; become fact.

maternal *adj* **1** relating to a mother or mothers; motherly. **2** related through a mother. **maternalistic** *adj*.

maternity *n* state of being a mother. *adj* relating to mothers or the period of their pregnancy.

mathematics *n* science concerned with the logical study of space, numbers, relationships, etc., using various forms of analysis and special symbols. **mathematical** *adj*. **mathematician** *n*.

matinée *n* afternoon or first evening performance at a theatre, cinema, etc.

matrimony *n* state of being married. **matrimonial** *adj*.

matrix *n, pl* **matrices** (ˈmeitrisiːz) **1** mould for casting or shaping objects. **2** anything that encloses or gives form to something.

matron *n* **1** married woman, esp. one of at least middle age. **2** woman in charge of nurses or domestic arrangements in a school, hospital, or other institution. **matronly** *adj* of or like a matron; dignified.

matt *adj also* **matte, mat** dull; without lustre; not shiny.

matter *n* **1** stuff or substance of which the physical universe is composed. **2** any physical or bodily substance. **3** topic or issue; thing; concern. **4** difficulty or trouble. **5** content of a book, etc. *vi* be of significance or importance.

mattress *n* flat case filled with soft or firm supporting material, used as a bed or placed on a bed frame.

mature *adj* **1** fully developed; ripe. **2** complete in growth; grown-up. **3** characteristic of an adult; mentally developed; sensible. **4** perfected; complete. *vi,vt* become or make mature. **maturity** *n*.

maudlin *adj* over-sentimental; tearfully drunk.

maul *vt* treat roughly; attack savagely; injure badly.

mausoleum *n* **1** stately building used as a tomb or housing tombs. **2** large depressing building.

mauve *n,adj* pale bluish purple.

maxim *n* condensed general truth or principle of conduct.

maximum *adj* greatest; highest. *n, pl* **maximums** *or* **maxima** ('mæksimə) greatest or highest amount, extent, degree, etc. **maximize** *vt* **1** increase to a maximum. **2** make the most of.

may *v aux* (*pt* might) **1** be able or permitted to. **2** be likely or probable that. **maybe** *adv* perhaps; possibly.

May *n* fifth month of the year. **May Day** *n* first day of May, celebrated with various festivities, parades, etc. **maypole** *n* decorated pole around which persons dance on May Day.

mayonnaise *n* thick dressing for salads, etc., consisting usually of egg yolk, oil, and vinegar.

mayor *n* official head of a town corporation. **mayoress** *f n*.

maze *n* **1** intricate network of interconnecting paths, passages, etc. **2** confused state.

me *pron* form of **I** when used as the object.

meadow *n* grassland, often used for grazing or growing hay.

meagre *adj* lacking quality or quantity; insufficient; scanty; thin.

meal[1] *n* **1** food, esp. when eaten at regular times during the day. **2** occasion or time of eating.

meal[2] *n* coarsely ground grain, used esp. as fodder.

mean[1] *vt,vi* (meant) **1** signify; intend; intend to express; denote. **2** be resolved to; be serious about.

mean[2] *adj* **1** stingy; petty; not generous. **2** low in quality, character, rank, or performance. **3** not important; having little consequence. **4** offensive; nasty. **meanly** *adv*. **meanness** *n*.

mean[3] *adj* **1** halfway between two extremes, values, numbers, etc.; intermediate. **2** average. *n* anything intermediate or between two extremes, values, etc.; average.

meander (mi'ændə) *vi* wander; move about aimlessly; follow a winding course. *n* winding course of a river or stream.

meaning *n* **1** significance; import. **2** sense of a word, phrase, etc.; definition. **meaningful** *adj*. **meaningless** *adj*.

means *pl n* **1** method for achieving a purpose or function. **2** financial or material resources. **by all means** certainly; without fail or hesitation. **by no means** most definitely not; on no account, not at all.

meantime *n* intervening time. *adv also* **meanwhile** during or in an intervening time; at the same time.

measles *n* **1** infectious viral disease producing a red rash, common in childhood. **2** German measles.

measure *n* **1** size, quantity, extent, etc., of something, determined by comparing it with a standard. **2** unit of size, quantity, etc. **3** criterion. **4** vessel or instrument for determining size, quantity, etc. **5** certain amount, extent, or degree. **6** regular beat or movement in music, poetry, etc.; rhythm. **for good measure** as something extra; as an addition. **take measures** do things to achieve some goal or purpose. ~*vt* determine the size or quantity of; judge; estimate. *vi* have a specified measure. **made to measure** (of clothes) fitted to the individual. **measure up** live up to expectations; be adequate for. **measurement** *n*.

meat *n* **1** flesh of animals used as food, often excepting fish and poultry. **2** edible part of anything. **3** main principle of something; essence.

mechanical *adj* **1** relating to machinery. **2** operated or produced by machines; automatic. **3** not requiring thought; spontaneous. **mechanic** *n* person skilled in repairing, building, or using machinery. **mechanics 1** *s n* study of the action of forces on physical bodies and the motions they produce. **2** *pl n* technical aspects or workings of something.

mechanism *n* **1** machine or its structure or parts. **2** means by which a machine works. **3** way in which anything works or operates.

mechanize *vt* **1** make mechanical. **2** substitute mechanical power as a source of production or energy. **3** operate by machines or machinery. **mechanization** *n*.

medal *n* flat piece of metal, usually round, with a design or inscription to commemorate an event or given as an award. **medallion** *n* **1** large medal. **2** circular decorative design or panel.

meddle *vi* **1** *also* **meddle in** concern oneself with things that are not one's business. **2** *also* **meddle with** interfere; tamper.

media *pl n* newspapers, radio, and television; collective means of communication.

medial *adj also* **median** relating to or situated in the middle. **median** *n* middle point, part, value, etc.; dividing line or plane.

mediate *vt* **1** settle; reconcile. **2** serve as the medium for communicating, conveying, etc. *vt,vi* intervene to bring about a reconciliation or compromise. **mediation** *n*.

medicine *n* **1** practice and profession of preserving or restoring health. **2** drugs or other agents used to treat bodily diseases or disorders. **medicinal** *adj*. **medical** *adj* **1** relating to medicine. **2** relating to treatment that does not require surgery. *n* physical examination by a doctor. **medication** *n* **1** use of medicine or medical agents. **2** drug or other medical agent.

medieval *adj* **1** relating to the Middle Ages. **2** *inf* primitive; crude.

mediocre *adj* between good and bad; of only average quality or excellence; ordinary. **mediocrity** *n*.

meditate *vi* engage in deep mental reflection; contemplate. *vt* think about doing; plan. **meditation** *n*. **meditative** *adj*.

medium *n* **1** means; agency. **2** middle degree or quality; mean. **3** substance through or in which something is transmitted, conveyed, or effected. **4** material used by an artist. **5** environment. **6** person claiming to be able to communicate with spirits. **7** *pl* **media** means of mass communication, such as the press, radio, or television. *adj* average; intermediate.

meek *adj* humble; submissive; lacking in spirit; mild. **meekly** *adv*.

meet *v* (met) *vt* **1** encounter; come across. **2** be present at the arrival point of. **3** satisfy; handle; cope with. *vi* come together; come into contact; join. *vt,vi* **1** be introduced (to). **2** gather for a meeting, etc. (with). **3** fight; confront. *n* assembly of people and animals prior to a hunt. **meeting** *n* **1** coming together; encounter. **2** gathering; assembly of persons, esp. for a common cause. **3** joining of things.

megaphone *n* instrument shaped like a funnel, used to amplify the voice or direct sound.

melancholy *n* depression; sadness; tendency to be morose. *adj* depressing; sad; gloomy. **melancholic** *adj*.

mellow *adj* **1** not harsh; rich and full. **2** genial; warm. **3** rendered receptive and friendly, as through advancing years, alcoholic drink, etc. *vt,vi* make or become mellow.

melodrama *n* **1** play or drama displaying violent or exaggerated emotions. **2** over-emotional language or behaviour. **melodramatic** *adj*.

melody *n* **1** agreeable or pleasing music or tune. **2** recognizable sequence of musical notes. **melodic** *adj* relating to melody. **melodious** *adj* pleasing to listen to; tuneful.

melon *n* plant of the gourd family, the edible fruit of which has a hard rind and juicy flesh.

melt *vi,vt* **1** liquefy by heat; thaw; pass or convert from solid to liquid. **2** soften; dissolve. **3** disappear; disperse. **4** blend; merge. *n* act of melting or state of being melted. **melting point** *n* temperature at which a solid becomes liquefied.

member *n* **1** person who belongs to a group, society, or organization. **2** distinct part of a whole. **3** limb or other bodily organ. **membership** *n* **1** state of being part of a group or society. **2** total number of persons who are part of a group, etc.

membrane *n* thin pliable sheet of tissue that lines, connects, or covers an organ or part.

memento *n, pl* **mementoes** *or* **mementos** reminder; souvenir; keepsake.

memoir *n* record of facts or events written from experience or gathered through research. **memoirs** *pl n* biography or autobiography; published reminiscences.

memorable *adj* easily or worthy to be remembered.

memorandum *n, pl* **memorandums** *or* **memoranda** (memə'rændə); *also* **memo 1** note to aid the memory. **2** short informal communication to colleagues, business firms, clients, etc.

memorial *n* object or custom in memory of a person, event, etc.; monument. *adj* preserving the memory of a person or event; commemorative.

memory *n* **1** faculty of recalling to mind or recollecting. **2** something remembered. **3** capacity to remember. **4** commemoration. **5** part of a computer where information is stored. **memorize** *vt* commit to memory.

men *n pl* of **man.**

menace *n* something that threatens or constitutes a threat. *vt* threaten; intimidate.

menagerie *n* exhibition of caged animals.

mend *vt* **1** repair; make whole; put right. **2** make better; improve; correct. *vi* improve in health. *n* improvement; repair. **on the mend** recovering; improving in health.

menial *adj* lowly; servile. *n* servile person; domestic servant.

menopause *n* time of life during which women cease to menstruate, usually between the ages of 45 and 50.

menstrual *adj* relating to the monthly discharge from the womb of blood and cellular material in women. **menstruate** *vi* produce menstrual discharge. **menstruation** *n.*

mental *adj* **1** relating to the mind or intellect; done or existing in the mind. **2** *sl* insane; mad; crazy. **mental hospital** *n* institution for treating persons with disorders of the mind. **mentality** *n* mental or intellectual capacity; mind.

menthol *n* substance obtained from peppermint oil, used esp. as a flavouring.

mention *vt* speak of; refer to. *n* remark about or reference to a person or thing.

menu *n* **1** list of dishes available to be served, with their prices. **2** dishes served.

mercantile *adj* **1** relating to merchants or commerce; commercial. **2** engaged in commerce or trade.

mercenary *adj* working simply for reward or gain. *n* professional soldier serving a foreign country.

merchandise *n* **1** goods or commodities bought and sold in commerce or trade. **2** stock of a store. *vt,vi* buy and sell; promote the sale (of).

merchant *n* wholesale trader, esp. with foreign countries. **merchant bank** *n* bank chiefly involved in foreign commerce. **merchant navy** *n* **1** ships of a nation engaged in commerce. **2** officers and crews of merchant ships.

mercury *n* heavy silvery toxic metallic element, normally liquid, used in thermometers, barometers, etc. **Mercury** nearest planet to the sun. **mercurial** *adj* lively; changeable.

mercy *n* **1** compassion; kindness; pity. **2** forgiveness of an injustice, transgression, or injury by someone with the power to inflict punishment. **3** act of compassion, kindness, etc. **at the mercy of** completely in the power of; defenceless. **merciful** *adj* compassionate. **mercifully** *adv.* **merciless** without mercy; cruel. **mercilessly** *adv.*

mere *adj* nothing more than; only. **merely** *adv.*

merge *vt,vi* **1** blend; mingle. **2** combine; unite. **merger** *n* commercial combination of two or more companies.

meridian *n* **1** position of the sun at noon. **2** highest point or period of development of something. **3** imaginary circle encompassing the earth and passing through both poles. *adj* **1** relating to a meridian. **2** relating to or at noon.

meringue (mə'ræŋ) *n* **1** mixture of sugar and beaten egg whites, slightly browned, used as an icing, etc. **2** small cream-filled cake of meringue.

merit *n* **1** worth; excellence. **2** commendable quality. *vt* be worthy of. **meritorious** *adj.*

mermaid *n* mythical sea creature with the head, arms, and torso of a woman and the tail of a fish.

merry *adj* **1** joyous; cheerful; festive; happy; gay. **2** slightly drunk. **merry-go-round** *n* fairground amusement consisting of a rotating platform fitted with models of animals, cars, etc., on which one may ride; roundabout **merrily** *adv.* **merriment** *or* **merriness** *n.*

mesh *n* net; network. *vt* catch in a mesh. *vi* **1**

(of gearwheels) engage. **2** merge; blend; harmonize.

mesmerize *vt* **1** hypnotize. **2** fascinate greatly.

mess *n* **1** untidy state or condition. **2** state of confusion or disorder. **3** difficult or embarrassing situation. **4** place where military personnel, etc., take their meals. **5** meals taken by military personnel, etc. **6** *inf* person who is untidy, sloppy, or dirty. *vt also* **mess up** make dirty or untidy. **mess around** *or* **about** busy oneself in an ineffective or aimless manner.

message *n* **1** spoken or written communication. **2** moral conveyed in a literary or artistic work. **messenger** *n* person who conveys a message, does errands, etc.

metabolism *n* sum of the chemical changes in an animal or plant that result in growth, production and use of energy, etc. **metabolic** *adj.*

metal *n* **1** chemical element, such as iron, tin, or silver, that is usually lustrous, easily worked, and often a good conductor of heat and electricity. **2** alloy. **metallic** *adj.* **metallurgy** *n* study and technology of metals. **metallurgical** *adj.* **metallurgist** *n.*

metamorphosis *n* **1** complete change in form. **2** marked change in character, etc. **3** relatively rapid transformation of certain larvae into adult form, as tadpole to frog. **metamorphic** *adj.*

metaphor *n* figure of speech in which a word is applied to something for which it does not literally stand. **metaphorical** *adj.*

meteor *n* small body from space that burns up in the earth's atmosphere producing a bright streak. **meteoric** *adj* **1** relating to meteors. **2** rapid; transient. **meteorite** *n* larger body able to reach earth.

meteorology *n* study of the earth's atmosphere, climate, and weather. **meteorological** *adj.* **meteorologist** *n.*

meter *n* measuring or recording instrument or device. *vt* measure with a meter.

methane *n* inflammable gas occurring in natural gas and used as a fuel and in chemical manufacture.

method *n* **1** way of doing something. **2** systematic or orderly procedure. **methodical** *adj* systematic; orderly.

Methodist *n* adherent of the Christian beliefs and tenets (Methodism) of a Protestant nonconformist denomination founded by John Wesley. *adj* relating to Methodists or Methodism.

meticulous *adj* extremely careful about small details.

metre *n* **1** unit of length equal to 1.09 yards. **2** rhythmic arrangement of syllables in verse. **metric** *adj.* **metric system** *n* system of scientific units based on the metre, the kilogram or gram, and the second. **metrication** *n* conversion to the metric system.

metropolitan *adj* **1** relating to or characteristic of the capital or any large city. **2** relating to the characteristics or attitudes of a city dweller; sophisticated. **metropolis** *n* chief or major city; capital.

miaow *n* sound a cat makes. *vi* make such a sound.

mice *n pl* of **mouse.**

microbe *n* microorganism, esp. one causing disease; germ.

microorganism *n* microscopic animal or plant, such as a bacterium or virus.

microphone *n* instrument for converting sound waves into electrical currents or voltages that can then be amplified.

microscope *n* instrument for magnifying very small objects, usually consisting of at least two lenses mounted in a tube. **microscopic** *adj* visible only under a microscope; tiny.

midday *n* noon.

middle *adj* **1** equidistant from two extremes; intermediate; mean. **2** central. *n* **1** something intermediate or equidistant from two extremes. **2** central area of the body; waist. **middle-aged** *adj* relating to the age between youth and old age; aged about 40 to 65. **Middle Ages** *n* historical period now usually regarded as being from about the fifth to the late fifteenth century. **middle class** *n* generally well-educated class of people in commerce, the professions, etc., who often hold conformist views. **middle-class** *adj* relating to the middle class.

midget *n* **1** very small person. **2** anything unusually small of its kind.

midnight *n* middle of the night; 12 o'clock at night.

midst *n* middle; central part, stage, or point. **in the midst of** surrounded by; among.

midwife *n, pl* **-wives** woman who assists others in childbirth. **midwifery** *n.*

might[1] *v pt* of **may.** *v aux* used to express likelihood or possibility.

might[2] *n* strength; power. **mighty** *adj.*

migraine *n* severe headache.

migrate *vi* **1** leave one country, region, etc., to settle or work in another. **2** (of certain birds, animals, etc.) move seasonally from one region to another. **migrant** *n.* **migration** *n.* **migratory** *adj.*

mike *n sl* microphone.

mild *adj* **1** moderate; gentle; not harsh or drastic. **2** not having a sharp taste. **mildly** *adv.*

mildew *n* destructive fungus or fungal disease that attacks plants or objects exposed to damp.

mile *n* **1** unit of length equal to 1760 yards or 1.61 kilometres. **2** *also* **miles** great distance. **mileage** *n* **1** total number of miles travelled. **2** distance in miles between two points. **3** travel expenses based on a given sum per mile. **mileometer** *n* device for measuring and recording the number of miles travelled. **milestone** *n* **1** roadside stone showing number of miles to the next large city or town. **2** important event or turning point in history, a person's life, etc.

militant *adj* **1** aggressive; forceful. **2** engaged in warfare. *n* aggressive person. **militancy** *n.*

military *adj* relating to the armed forces, soldiers, or warfare. *n* soldiers collectively; armed forces.

milk *n* **1** whitish liquid produced in the mammary glands of female mammals, used to feed their young. **2** cow's or goat's milk, used as food. **3** whitish juice of various plants or fruits. **cry over spilt milk** regret or complain about something that cannot be undone or remedied. ~*vt* **1** extract milk from the udder of. **2** draw off from. **milkman** *n, pl* **-men** person who sells or delivers milk. **Milky Way** *n* faint band of light in the night sky that consists of millions of stars and is part of our galaxy.

mill *n* **1** machinery for grinding grain into flour. **2** machinery for manufacturing paper, textiles, steel, etc. **3** building containing such machinery. **4** small machine for grinding pepper corns, coffee beans, etc. *vt* grind, work, or shape in or as if in a mill. **millstone** *n* **1** either of two large round slabs of stone between which grain, etc., is ground. **2** heavy emotional burden.

millennium *n, pl* **millenniums** *or* **millennia** (mi'leniə) thousand years.

millet *n* cereal grass cultivated for its small seeds or grain.

milligram *n* one thousandth of a gram.

millimetre *n* one thousandth of a metre.

million *n* **1** number or numeral, 1 000 000, equal to 1000 multiplied by 1000. **2** *also* **millions** extremely large number or amount. **3** million units of money, etc. *adj* amounting to a million. **millionth** *adj,n.* **millionaire** *n* **1** person worth a million pounds, dollars, etc. **2** very rich person.

mime *n* **1** art or practice of wordless acting. **2** person who performs wordless acting. *vt,vi* act or express in mime.

mimic *n* person or animal that imitates or copies others. *vt* (-ck-) imitate in action, speech, etc.; copy; caricature. **mimicry** *n.*

minaret *n* slender tower of a mosque, from which the faithful are called to prayer.

mince *vt* **1** cut or chop into small pieces. **2** utter with affected carefulness. *vi* speak or act in an affected way. *n* minced meat.

mind *n* **1** thinking faculties or consciousness. **2** intellect. **3** memory. **4** person of great intelligence. **5** sanity; reason. **6** way of thinking; opinion; temper. **7** attention. **bear in mind** continue to remember. **be of one mind** be in total agreement with. **be of two minds** be undecided. **make up one's mind** decide. **out of one's mind** mad; highly agitated; confused. **take (someone's) mind off** help (someone) stop worrying about something; distract. ~*vt,vi* **1** object (to); be upset or concerned (about). **2** pay attention (to). **3** be careful (about). *vt* attend to; look after. **mind out** be careful; watch.

mine[1] *pron* that belonging to me.

mine[2] *n* **1** deep hole or shaft in the ground for extracting coal, metals, etc. **2** associated buildings, etc. **3** underground or surface deposit of minerals. **4** rich source of something. **5** explosive device, detonated on impact. *vt,vi* **1** dig or extract (minerals) from a mine. **2** make a mine in or under.

mineral *n* **1** inorganic substance that occurs in the earth and has a definite chemical composition. **2** nonliving matter. **mineralogy** *n* study of minerals. **mineral water** *n* **1** water containing dissolved minerals or gases. **2** fizzy nonalcoholic drink.

minestrone (mini'strouni) *n* Italian soup containing vegetables, etc.

mingle *vt,vi* **1** blend; mix; combine. **2** mix in company.

miniature *n* **1** very small painting, esp. a portrait. **2** model, copy, etc., greatly reduced in size. *adj* small-scale; reduced; tiny.

minim *n* musical note half the length of a semibreve.

minimum *n* least possible or lowest quantity, number, degree, etc. **minimal** *adj*. **minimize** *vt* **1** reduce to or estimate at a minimum. **2** belittle; underestimate.

mining *n* act, process, or industry of extracting minerals, coal, etc., from mines.

minister *n* **1** person authorized to conduct religious services; clergyman. **2** person in charge of a government department. **3** diplomatic representative. *vi* give aid or service (to). **ministerial** *adj*.

ministry *n* **1** functions or profession of a clergyman or clergymen. **2** profession or department of a government minister. **3** building in which government offices are located. **4** act of giving service.

mink *n* **1** animal of the weasel family with highly valued brownish fur. **2** garment made of mink fur.

minor *adj* **1** lesser in size, extent, significance, etc. **2** of or relating to a musical scale in which the second and third and the fifth and sixth notes are a semitone apart. *n* **1** person under full legal age. **2** person or thing of inferior importance, rank, etc. **minority** *n* **1** smaller number, part, etc.; less than half. **2** group whose race, religion, etc., is different from most others in the same country or community. **3** state or period of being under full legal age.

minstrel *n* medieval musician or singer.

mint[1] *n* **1** aromatic herb. **2** sweet with a peppermint or similar flavouring.

mint[2] *n* **1** place where money is officially minted. **2** large amount, esp. of money. *vt,vi* make (coins and paper money) under government authority. **mint condition** perfect condition.

minuet *n* **1** slow stately dance in triple time. **2** music in the rhythm of this dance.

minus *prep* **1** less by the deduction of; decreased by. **2** without; lacking. *adj* **1** indicating deduction or subtraction. **2** negative. **3** lacking. *n also* **minus sign** symbol denoting subtraction.

minute[1] ('minit) *n* **1** one sixtieth of an hour; 60 seconds. **2** short time. **3** one sixtieth of a degree of angular measure. **4** memorandum. **up to the minute** current; very latest; modern. **minutes** *pl n* summary of a meeting.

minute[2] (mai'nju:t) *adj* **1** very small. **2** insignificant; trivial. **3** precise; detailed. **minutely** *adv*.

miracle *n* **1** supernatural event. **2** something wonderful; marvel. **miraculous** *adj*.

mirage *n* **1** optical illusion caused by intense heat, etc. **2** something unreal or illusory.

mirror *n* **1** polished surface that reflects images of objects, esp. glass backed with metal. **2** any reflecting surface, as of water. **3** something that gives a true representation or portrayal. *vt* reflect or represent faithfully.

mirth *n* merriment; festive or joyous gaiety.

misbehave *vi* behave badly. **misbehaviour** *n*.

miscarriage *n* **1** expulsion of a foetus from the womb before it is capable of living independently. **2** failure to carry out or attain a desired result. **miscarry** *vi* **1** undergo a miscarriage. **2** fail; go wrong.

miscellaneous *adj* **1** varied; mixed; assorted. **2** having various qualities or aspects; many-sided. **miscellany** *n* miscellaneous collection.

mischance *n* bad luck; misfortune; unlucky accident.

mischief *n* **1** teasing or annoying conduct. **2** source of annoyance or harm. **mischievous** *adj*. **mischievously** *adv*.

misconceive *vt,vi* misunderstand; interpret incorrectly. **misconception** *n*.

misconduct *n* improper conduct.

misdeed *n* evil or criminal deed.

miser *n* person who hoards money. **miserly** *adj*.

miserable *adj* **1** extremely unhappy or uncomfortable. **2** causing misery. **3** characterized by wretched poverty and neglect. **4** pitiable. **miserably** *adv*. **misery** *n* condition or cause of great suffering or distress.

misfire *vi* **1** fail to fire correctly or on time. **2** fail to be successful or have a desired effect. *n* failure to fire.

misfit *n* **1** person who does not fit in socially

with others. **2** something that does not fit properly.

misfortune *n* bad luck; calamity.

misgiving *n* feeling of fear, doubt, or mistrust.

misguided *adj* mistaken; misled.

mishap *n* unlucky or unfortunate accident.

mislay *vt* (-laid) put something in a place later forgotten.

mislead *vt* (-led) lead astray; deceive, esp. by giving incorrect or inadequate information or advice.

misplace *vt* **1** lose; put in the wrong place. **2** place or bestow unwisely or improperly.

misprint *n* mistake in printing.

miss[1] *vt* **1** fail to hit, find, reach, notice, catch, etc. **2** *also* **miss out** omit; pass over. **3** notice or regret the absence of. **4** fail. **5** escape; avoid. *vi* **1** (of an engine) fail to fire. **2** fail to hit or attain something. **miss the boat** fail to take advantage of an opportunity. ~*n* failure.

miss[2] *n* girl; young woman. **Miss** form of address for an unmarried young woman or girl.

missile *n* object or weapon that can be thrown or fired, esp. a rocket-propelled weapon.

mission *n* **1** group of persons sent to a foreign country as envoys or missionaries. **2** official business or task of an envoy or missionary. **3** aim or calling in life. **4** military operation against an enemy. **5** any duty, esp. one that has been assigned. **missionary** *n* person sent to convert natives or primitive peoples to his religion, educate them, etc.

mist *n* **1** water vapour in fine drops; thin fog. **2** something that blurs or dims. *vt,vi* be, become, or make dim or blurred. **misty** *adj.*

mistake *n* error in thought or action. *vt* (-took; -taken) **1** form a wrong opinion about; misunderstand. **2** take (a person or thing) for another; confuse.

Mister *n* form of address for an adult male: normally written *Mr.*

mistletoe *n* evergreen plant with white berries that grows as a partial parasite on other trees.

mistress *n* **1** woman teacher. **2** woman who employs others. **3** woman with whom a man has a continuing sexual relationship outside marriage.

mistrust *n* lack of trust. *vt* regard with lack of trust; distrust.

misunderstand *vt,vi* (misunderstood) fail to understand correctly or properly. **misunderstanding** *n* **1** failure to understand. **2** slight quarrel.

misuse *n* (mis'ju:s) wrong or improper use. *vt* (mis'ju:z) **1** use wrongly. **2** treat badly.

mitre *n* **1** bishop's tall pointed hat. **2** corner joint formed by two pieces of wood, etc., that meet at equal angles. *vt* join so as to form a mitre joint.

mitten *n* glove with one compartment for the four fingers and a separate one for the thumb.

mix *vt,vi* combine; blend. *vi* associate with others freely or easily. *vt* form by blending. **mix up 1** confuse. **2** blend. **mixture** *n* **1** product of mixing. **2** combination of two or more ingredients, elements, types, qualities, etc. **mix-up** *n* confusion; muddle.

moan *n* low sound, usually indicating pain or suffering. *vi,vt* **1** utter or say with a moan. **2** grumble; complain.

moat *n* deep wide ditch, originally filled with water, round a castle or town.

mob *n* disorderly crowd of people. *vt* (-bb-) crowd round; attack in a crowd.

mobile *adj* **1** capable of movement. **2** easily moved. **3** expressive. *n* ornament consisting of a delicate hanging construction of balanced parts, which move with the air current. **mobility** *n.* **mobilize** *vt* **1** prepare (armed forces) for active service. **2** organize for a task. **3** put into motion or use. *vi* be ready or assembled for battle.

mock *vt,vi* make fun of by imitating; scoff or jeer (at). **mockery** *n* **1** ridicule. **2** derisive action or imitation.

mode *n* manner; style; method; fashion.

model *n* **1** representation of an object made to scale. **2** pattern to be followed; design; style. **3** person or object worthy of imitation. **4** person who poses for an artist, etc. **5** person who wears and displays clothing for potential customers. *v* (-ll-) *vt,vi* **1** make a model (of). **2** form or work (clay, etc.). **3** wear and display (clothing) for potential customers. *vi* pose for an artist, etc.

moderate *adj* ('mɔdərit) **1** not going to extremes. **2** of medium quantity, quality, or extent; not excessive. *n* ('mɔdərit) person of moderate views. *vt,vi* ('mɔdəreit) make or become less violent or excessive. **moderately** *adv.*

modern *adj* relating to or characteristic of

present and recent time. **modernize** *vt* make modern; bring up to date. **modernization** *n*.

modest *adj* **1** unassuming; shy; not vain. **2** free from pretension; not showy. **3** moderate. **modestly** *adv*. **modesty** *n*.

modify *vt* **1** make small changes in. **2** tone down. **3** qualify. **4** make less severe. **modification** *n*.

modulate *vt* **1** vary the tone, pitch, or volume of. **2** regulate; adjust; soften. *vi* change from one musical key to another. **modulation** *n*.

module *n* **1** separable compartment of a space vehicle. **2** standard or unit of measurement. **3** removable framework or assembly.

mohair *n* yarn or fabric made from the soft silky hair of the Angora goat or made to resemble it.

moist *adj* damp; slightly wet. **moistly** *adv*. **moisten** *vt,vi* make or become moist. **moisture** *n* **1** water or other liquid diffused as a vapour or condensed on a surface. **2** dampness. **moisturize** *vt* give or restore moisture to.

mole[1] *n* small dark birthmark on the skin.

mole[2] *n* small nocturnal burrowing animal with a smooth silky pelt.

molecule *n* simplest unit of a chemical compound, consisting of two or more atoms. **molecular** *adj*.

molest *vt* **1** disturb or annoy by interfering with. **2** interfere with improperly, esp. sexually.

mollusc *n* soft-bodied invertebrate, such as the snail, oyster, or octopus, usually with a hard shell.

molten *adj* liquefied by intense heat.

moment *n* **1** very short space of time. **2** appropriate time. **at the moment** now. **in a moment 1** soon; shortly. **2** quickly; instantly. **momentary** *adj* lasting a moment. **momentarily** *adv*. **momentous** *adj* important.

momentum *n* **1** mass multiplied by velocity of a moving body. **2** impetus; driving strength.

monarch *n* sovereign head of a country; king or queen. **monarchic** *or* **monarchical** *adj*. **monarchy** *n* **1** form of government in which authority is vested, constitutionally or traditionally, in the monarch. **2** country of a monarch.

monastery *n* house occupied by a community of monks. **monastic** *adj* relating to monks or their way of life.

Monday *n* second day of the week.

money *n* **1** official medium of exchange of a country, consisting of coins and paper currency of various denominations. **2** amount or sum of money; income. **3** funds; assets. **monetary** *adj* relating to money.

mongrel *n* dog of mixed breeds.

monitor *n* **1** pupil appointed to special duties in a school. **2** person who warns or advises. **3** control or checking device on a machine or system. **4** person who officially listens to and records foreign broadcasts. *vt* listen to in order to record or check.

monk *n* member of a male community, having taken final religious vows.

monkey *n* **1** long-tailed primate usually living in forests. **2** mischievous child. *vi also* **monkey around** *or* **about** play or fool (with).

monochrome *n* something of one colour or in black and white.

monogamy *n* custom or state of being married to only one person at a time. **monogamous** *adj*.

monologue *n* **1** prolonged talk by a single speaker. **2** dramatic work or part to be performed by one speaker.

monopoly *n* exclusive control or possession of a trade, privilege, etc. **monopolize** *vt* obtain or exercise sole control or possession of.

monosyllable *n* word of one syllable. **monosyllabic** *adj*.

monotone *n* sound, note, or voice of an unvaried pitch. **monotonous** *adj* lacking variation; dull; tedious. **monotonously** *adv*. **monotony** *n*.

monsoon *n* **1** seasonal wind of S Asia and the Indian Ocean, blowing from the southwest in summer. **2** rainy season that accompanies the wind from this direction.

monster *n* **1** legendary animal of a combination of forms. **2** grossly deformed animal or plant. **3** evil person. **4** something huge. **monstrous** *adj* **1** very great; huge. **2** ugly; hideous. **3** outrageous; revolting.

month *n* any of the 12 periods into which a year is divided. **monthly** *adj* **1** occurring, done, etc., once a month. **2** lasting a month. *adv* once a month.

monument *n* **1** something, esp. a statue, that commemorates. **2** statue, structure, etc., of historical importance. **3** written record. **monumental** *adj* **1** colossal; massive; stupendous. **2** relating to or serving as a monument.

moo *n* sound a cow makes. *vi* make a sound like a cow.

mood[1] *n* **1** state of mind and feelings. **2** depressed or sulky state of mind. **moody** *adj* changeable in mood.

mood[2] *n* form of a verb that indicates a particular function, such as the imperative, subjunctive, conditional, etc.

moon *n* **1** cratered and mountainous body that revolves around the earth in about 27.3 days, changing in apparent shape. **2** apparent shape of the moon; phase. *vi also* **moon around** *or* **about** go about idly, dreamily, listlessly, etc. **moonlight** *n* light from the sun reflected from the moon to the earth.

moor[1] *n also* **moorland** tract of open waste land, often hilly and covered with heather. **moorhen** *n* black red-billed water bird living on rivers, etc.

moor[2] *vt,vi* secure or fasten (a ship, etc.) with cables or ropes or be secured so. **mooring** *n* place for securing a vessel. **moorings** *pl n* ropes, etc., used in securing a vessel.

mop *n* sponge or bundle of yarn, cloth, etc., fastened to the end of a handle for cleaning floors, etc. *vt* (-pp-) *also* **mop up** clean or wipe with a mop.

mope *vi* be depressed. **mope about** *or* **around** act aimlessly. **mopes** *pl n* dejected state.

moped *n* motorized bicycle.

moral *adj* **1** relating to or concerned with right and wrong conduct; ethical. **2** of good conduct; virtuous; honest. *n* practical lesson, esp. one taught by a fable or other story. **morally** *adv*. **morale** (məˈrɑːl) *n* discipline and spirit of a group of persons. **morality** *n* **1** virtuous conduct. **2** moral principles. **moralize** *vt* interpret or explain in a moral sense; derive a moral from. *vi* make moral reflections; talk about morality. **morals** *pl n* personal conduct, or principles.

morbid *adj* **1** gloomy; unpleasant. **2** unhealthy. **morbidly** *adv*.

more *adj* **1** greater in quantity, number, or degree. **2** additional; extra. *n* additional quantity, number, or degree. *adv* to a greater extent; in addition. **more or less** approximately; roughly. **moreover** *adv* besides; further.

morgue *n* room or building where dead bodies are taken to await identification before burial.

morning *n* early part of the day, usually up to noon or lunchtime.

moron *n* **1** mentally deficient person. **2** foolish person. **moronic** *adj*.

morose *adj* sullen; gloomy; unsociable.

morphine *n* drug to relieve severe pain.

Morse Code *n* signalling system in which numbers and letters are represented by combinations of dots and dashes.

mortal *adj* subject to or causing death. *n* human being. **mortality** *n* **1** condition of being subject to death. **2** large loss of life. **3** frequency of death; death rate.

mortar *n* **1** mixture of lime, sand, and water for holding bricks and stones together. **2** vessel in which substances are pounded or ground. **3** short cannon for throwing shells at high angles. *vt* fix or plaster with mortar.

mortgage *n* conveyance of property pledged as security for a debt until the loan is repaid. *vt* pledge (property) by mortgage.

mortify *vt* **1** humiliate. **2** subdue by self-denial. **mortification** *n*.

mortuary *n* place where dead bodies are temporarily kept before burial.

mosaic *n* picture or pattern made of small pieces of coloured stone, glass, etc.

Moslem *n,adj* Muslim.

mosque *n* Muslim place of worship.

mosquito *n, pl* **mosquitoes** *or* **mosquitos** blood-sucking insect that can transmit a disease such as malaria.

moss *n* small plant that grows in dense clumps on moist surfaces. **mossy** *adj*.

most *adj* greatest in size, number, or degree; nearly all. *n* greatest amount or degree. **at (the) most** not over; at maximum. **make the most of** use to the greatest advantage. *~adv* in the greatest degree. **mostly** *adv* mainly; almost entirely; usually.

motel *n* roadside hotel, often consisting of private cabins with parking space in front.

moth *n* usually nocturnal insect similar to the butterfly. **motheaten** *adj* decrepit; damaged; filled with holes.

mother *n* **1** female parent. **2** head of a religious community of women. *vt* care for or protect as a mother. **motherhood** *n* state or qualities of being a mother. **mother-in-law** *n, pl* **mothers-in-law** mother of one's husband or wife. **mother superior** *n* head of a religious community of women.

motion *n* **1** movement. **2** manner or power of movement. **3** formal proposal at a meeting. **in motion** in operation, functioning. ~*vi* make a gesture, as with the hand. *vt* direct or guide by a gesture. **motionless** *adj* not moving; still.

motive *n* **1** reason; cause; intention; incentive. **2** chief idea in a work of art. *adj* causing motion or action. **motivate** *vt* provide with a motive. **motivation** *n*.

motor *n* **1** engine. **2** machine that transforms electrical into mechanical energy to produce motion. *vi* travel by car. **motorboat** boat powered by a motor. **motor car** *n* car. **motorcycle** *n also* **motorbike** two-wheeled road vehicle, heavier and more powerful than a moped. **motorist** *n* person who drives a (motor) car. **motorway** *n* main road with separate carriageways of several lanes and limited access.

motto *n, pl* **mottoes** *or* **mottos** **1** saying adopted as a rule of conduct. **2** short phrase or sentence inscribed on a coat of arms, etc.

mould[1] *n* **1** hollow form or container in which molten metal, plastic, etc., is cast or shaped. **2** anything cast or shaped in a mould. **3** character; type. *vt* form; shape; model.

mould[2] *n* fungal growth caused by dampness; mildew. **mouldy** *adj*.

moult *vi,vt* shed (feathers, skin, fur, etc.). *n* act or process of moulting.

mound *n* **1** pile, as of earth or stones; heap. **2** small hill. *vt* form into a mound.

mount[1] *vt,vi* **1** go up; ascend; climb. **2** get up on (a horse, platform, etc.). *vt* **1** set at a height or elevation. **2** provide with or place on a horse. **3** fix in a setting, backing, or support. *vi* rise; increase. *n* **1** act of mounting. **2** something mounted. **3** setting, backing, or support on which something is mounted.

mount[2] *n* mountain; hill.

mountain *n* **1** natural and usually very high and steep elevation of the earth's surface. **2** large pile or heap. **mountainous** *adj*. **mountaineer** *n* person who climbs mountains. *vi* climb mountains.

mourn *vi* feel sorrow. *vt* grieve for.

mouse *n, pl* **mice** small long-tailed rodent. **mousy** *adj* **1** like or suggestive of a mouse. **2** (of hair) fair but not blond(e).

mousse *n* dish made with whipped cream, beaten eggs, etc.

moustache *n* hair growing on the upper lip.

mouth *n* (mauθ) **1** cavity between the lips and the throat, containing the teeth, tongue, etc., in which food is chewed and speech sounds are formed. **2** opening into anything hollow. **3** entrance to something. **4** part of a river where its waters empty into a sea, lake, etc. *v* (mauð) *vt* form (words) with the lips without speaking. *vi* declaim. **mouthpiece** *n* **1** end of something intended to be put between or near the lips. **2** person who speaks for others. **mouth-watering** *adj* appetizing.

move *vt,vi* **1** change the place or position (of). **2** stir. *vt* **1** propose. **2** affect with emotion. *vi* **1** change one's place of residence. **2** make progress; advance. *n* act of moving; movement. **get a move on** *inf* hurry up. **movable** *adj* capable of being moved; not fixed. **movement** *n* **1** process or act of moving. **2** moving parts of a mechanism, as of a watch. **3** main division of a musical work, esp. of a symphony. **4** group engaged in or activities directed towards some goal or end. **5** trend.

mow *vt,vi* (mowed; mown *or* mowed) cut or cut down (grass, grain, etc.). **mower** *n*.

Mr abbreviation for **Mister.**

Mrs abbreviation for **mistress**; used as a form of address for a married woman.

much *adj* in great quantity or degree. *n* **1** large amount. **2** notable or important matter or thing. *adv* in or to a great degree. **as much** exactly that. **make much of** **1** make sense of. **2** give importance to. **not much of** not really. **not think much of** have a poo opinion of.

muck *n* **1** manure. **2** filth; dirt. *vt* make dirty. **muck about** *sl* mess or fool about. **muck in** *sl* join in to achieve something. **muck out** clean out; remove muck from. **muck up** *sl* ruin; spoil. **mucky** *adj*.

mud *n* wet soft earth. **mudguard** *n* guard over a wheel to protect against mud. **mudslinging** *n* reckless accusations or abuse. **muddy** *adj* **1** covered with or abounding in mud. **2** mudlike in colour or texture. **3** vague; obscure; not clear. *vt,vi* make or become muddy.

muddle *vt* **1** confuse; bewilder. **2** mismanage; mix up in a confused way. **muddle through** succeed in spite of inadequate planning, etc. ~*n* muddled state or condition; mess.

muffle *vt* **1** wrap or cover up with something

warm. **2** wrap up to deaden sound. **3** deaden (sound). **4** conceal. *n* something that muffles.

mug *n* **1** large drinking cup with a handle. **2** *sl* face or mouth. **3** fool; gullible person. *vt,vi* (-gg-) *sl* attack and rob. **mug up** obtain (information) or study during a short intensive period. **mugger** *n sl* person who assaults and robs someone.

mulberry *n* tree that bears dark red edible berries.

mule[1] *n* sterile offspring of a mare and a donkey. **mulish** *adj* stubborn.

mule[2] *n* slipper with an exposed heel.

multiple *adj* have many parts, elements, etc. *n* quantity that contains another quantity an exact number of times.

multiply *vt,vi* **1** find the mathematical product of two or more numbers or quantities. **2** increase or cause to increase in number or amount. **multiplication** *n*.

multitude *n* **1** great number of persons; crowd; throng. **2** the common people.

mum *n inf* mother.

mumble *vt,vi* speak or utter indistinctly. *n* indistinct talk or sound.

mummy[1] *n* dead body preserved by embalming or other techniques. **mummify** *vt* preserve as a mummy.

mummy[2] *n inf* mother.

mumps *n* contagious viral disease, esp. of children, marked by a swelling of the glands in the neck.

munch *vt,vi* chew vigorously and often noisily.

mundane *adj* ordinary; everyday; common.

municipal *adj* relating to the local government of a city or town. **municipality** *n* city or town with local self-government.

mural *n* painting executed on a wall.

murder *n* **1** unlawful and deliberate killing of a human being. **2** *inf* difficult or unpleasant task. *vt* **1** kill. **2** *inf* ruin; destroy. *vi* commit murder. **murderer** *n*. **murderess** *f n*.

murmur *n* **1** low and continuous sound. **2** grumble; complaint. *vt* utter in a low voice. *vi* **1** make a murmur. **2** complain.

muscle *n* **1** specialized body tissue that produces movement by contracting. **2** strength; brawn. **muscular** *adj*.

muse *vi* ponder; meditate; be lost in thought.

museum *n* building housing objects or illustrations of art, science, history, etc., for observation and study.

mushroom *n* fungus, esp. an edible variety, having a cap on the end of a stem. *vi* **1** increase, grow, or expand rapidly. **2** gather mushrooms.

music *n* **1** organization of vocal or instrumental sounds into a pleasing or stirring rhythm or harmony. **2** sequence of pleasing sounds. **3** art of producing music. **4** record of notes for reproducing music. **musical** *adj* **1** relating to music. **2** liking or skilled in music. *n* light stage or film entertainment with songs and dancing. **musician** *n* composer or performer of music.

Muslim *n also* **Moslem** adherent of Islam. *adj also* **Moslem** relating to the religion or culture of Islam.

muslin *n* fine cotton fabric.

mussel *n* mollusc with a dark elongated hinged shell.

must *v aux* be obliged to; be certain to; be resolved to. *n* something imperative.

mustard *n* strong-flavoured yellowish or brownish paste or powder prepared from the seeds of the mustard plant, used as a condiment and seasoning.

mute *adj* **1** silent; soundless. **2** dumb; not capable of speech. *n* person unable to speak. *vt* deaden the sound of; soften.

mutilate *vt* injure, disfigure, or make imperfect, as by damaging parts, removing a limb, etc. **mutilation** *n*.

mutiny *n* revolt or rebellion against authority, esp. by soldiers or sailors. *vi* engage in mutiny. **mutinous** *adj*.

mutter *vt,vi* utter indistinctly or in a low tone; mumble. *n* muttered sound; complaint.

mutton *n* flesh of mature sheep, used as food.

mutual *adj* done, felt, possessed, etc., by each of two with respect to the other; common to both or all. **mutually** *adv*.

muzzle *n* **1** open end of the barrel of a firearm. **2** projecting nose and mouth of an animal. **3** device placed over the mouth of an animal to prevent it from biting. *vt* **1** put a muzzle on. **2** prevent from speaking.

my *pron* belonging to or associated with me. **myself** *pron* reflexive or emphatic form of **me** or **I**.

myrrh (mɜː) *n* aromatic gum exuded from certain shrubs, used as perfume, incense, etc.

mystery *n* secret, puzzling, or obscure thing. **mysterious** *adj*. **mysteriously** *adv*.

mystic *n* person who claims spiritual knowledge or insight, as by following mysticism. **mystical** *adj also* **mystic** **1** of hidden, spiritual, or occult nature or significance. **2** mysterious. **3** relating to mysticism. **mysticism** *n* belief in direct communion with God and awareness of divine truth by means of contemplation and love alone.

mystify *vt* **1** bewilder; confuse; perplex. **2** make obscure or mysterious. **mystification** *n*.

mystique *n* atmosphere of mystery associated with or investing certain activities, doctrines, arts, etc.

myth *n* **1** ancient story or legend, usually with supernatural characters or events. **2** imaginary or fictitious event, person, or thing. **mythical** *adj*. **mythology** *n* **1** collection of myths. **2** study of myths. **mythological** *adj*.

N

nag *vt,vi* (-gg-) annoy, pester, or be troubled with constant complaints, reminders, worries, or pain.

nail *n* **1** narrow flat-headed piece of metal hammered in as a means of joining or for use as a peg. **2** hard horny covering on the tip of a finger or toe. **as hard as nails** cold; ruthless; tough. **hit the nail on the head** describe exactly; pinpoint (a problem, situation, etc.). ~*vt* **1** join or fasten with a nail. **2** *inf* get hold of (a person); catch. **nail down** make (a person) declare his aims or opinions. **nailfile** *n* small metal file for shaping fingernails.

naive *adj* **1** unsophisticated; ingenuous. **2** credulous; gullible. **naively** *adv*. **naiveté** *or* **naivety** *n*.

naked *adj* without clothes or protection; bare. **nakedly** *adv*. **nakedness** *n*.

name *n* **1** word or words by which a person or thing is known or identified. **2** reputation. **3** *inf* celebrity. *vt* **1** give a name to; identify. **2** declare (a price, terms, etc.). **namely** *adv* that is to say. **namesake** *n* person or thing having the same name as another.

nanny *n* **1** woman employed to look after children, esp. in a private household. **2** *inf* grandmother.

nap[1] *n* short period of sleep, esp. during the day. *vi* (-pp-) sleep for a short period.

nap[2] *n* surface fibres on cloth.

napalm *n* jellied mixture of petrol and acids used in bombs, etc.

nape *n* back of the neck.

napkin *n* square of cloth or paper used for protecting clothes and wiping the mouth and fingers during meals.

nappy *n* square of cloth or disposable pad worn by a baby to absorb excreta.

narcissus *n, pl* **narcissi** (nɑːˈsisai) bulb producing yellow or white flowers.

narcotic *n* addictive drug, such as morphine, that induces sleep and dulls the senses. *adj* inducing sleep or insensibility.

narrate *vt* relate or tell (a story). **narration** *n*. **narrator** *n*. **narrative** *n* story; account. *adj* consisting of or relating to a narrative.

narrow *adj* **1** measuring little across. **2** strict; accurate. **3** bigoted; not liberal. **4** limited; restricted. *vt,vi* make or become narrow or narrower. **narrowly** *adv*. **narrowness** *n*. **narrow-minded** *adj* having rigid and narrow views.

nasal *adj* **1** relating to the nose. **2** (of sounds) formed by breathing through the nose.

nasturtium *n* garden plant having orange, yellow, or red flowers and roundish leaves.

nasty *adj* **1** unpleasant. **2** spiteful. **3** offensive; disgusting. **nastily** *adv*. **nastiness** *n*.

nation *n* **1** country; land. **2** large group of people having a common cultural background, history, and language. **nationwide** *adj,adv* throughout the country.

national *adj* **1** relating to a country as a whole. **2** typical of a particular country. **3** controlled by the government. **nationally** *adv*. **national anthem** *n* country's official song. **national insurance** *n* state scheme to provide financial aid during unemployment, sickness, widowhood, etc. **national service** *n* compulsory military training. **nationalism** *n* patriotism; belief in national unity. **nationalist** *n,adj*. **nationality** *n* citizenship of a particular country. **nationalize** *vt* transfer (an industry or property) to public ownership and control. **nationalization** *n*.

native *adj* **1** relating to the place of birth or origin. **2** innate. **3** indigenous. **4** relating to the indigenous population. *n* **1** person born or living in or animal found in a certain country or area. **2** person belonging to a race of original inhabitants of a country. **nativity** *n* **1**

birth. **2** *also* **nativity play** play or artistic representation of the birth of Christ.

natural *adj* **1** produced by, present in, or relating to the physical world; not artificial. **2** innate. **3** normal; to be expected; automatic. **4** unaffected. **5** not domesticated or civilized. *n* **1** *inf* person naturally equipped for a particular skill or job. **2** musical note or key that is neither sharp nor flat. **naturally** *adv*. **natural gas** *n* gas formed like oil in natural deposits and burned for cooking, heating, etc. **natural history** *n* study of animals and plants. **natural science** *n* science, such as chemistry or zoology, that is concerned with laws and processes of the external physical world. **naturalize** *vt,vi* **1** confer or adopt citizenship of a country. **2** introduce or adapt to another country or area. **naturalization** *n*.

nature *n* **1** external physical world and its laws, plants, and animals. **2** character or temperament; characteristics. **3** kind or sort.

naughty *adj* **1** mischievous. **2** indecent; suggestive. **naughtily** *adv*. **naughtiness** *n*.

nausea *n* **1** feeling of sickness; desire to vomit. **2** absolute disgust. **nauseous** *adj*. **nauseate** *vt* **1** induce a feeling of sickness. **2** disgust; repel.

nautical *adj* relating to ships, seamen, or navigation.

naval *adj* relating to the equipment, personnel, or activities of a navy.

nave *n* central seating area of a church up to the chancel.

navel *n* small pit in the abdomen left by the severed umbilical cord.

navigate *vt,vi* direct or plan the course or route of (a ship, car, etc.). *vt* **1** follow the course of (a river). **2** sail across. **navigator** *n*. **navigable** *adj* **1** (of water) deep enough to admit ships. **2** able to be navigated. **navigation** *n* **1** theory and practice of navigating. **2** shipping.

navy *n* **1** fleet of warships with sea aircraft. **2** personnel of the fleet. **navy blue** *n,adj* dark blue.

near *prep* at or within a short time or distance. *adj* **1** close in position or time. **2** intimate; dear. **3** only just avoided; narrow. *adv* close (to). **nearness** *n*. **nearby** *adv,adj* close by; not far away. **nearly** *adv* almost. **nearside** *n* the side of a car, traffic lane, etc., nearest to the kerb. **near-sighted** *adj* short-sighted.

neat *adj* **1** tidy; carefully arranged. **2** skilful; deft. **3** well-planned; clever. **4** precise. **5** undiluted. **neatly** *adv*. **neatness** *n*. **neaten** *vt* make neat; tidy up.

necessary *adj* **1** essential; needed. **2** logical. **necessarily** *adv*. **necessity** *n* **1** essential requirement. **2** pressing need. **3** logical consequence.

neck *n* **1** part of the body connecting the head and shoulders. **2** *also* **neckline** part of a garment round the neck and shoulders. **3** long narrowed portion of land, slender part of a bottle, etc. **neck and neck** abreast in a race or contest. **stick one's neck out** act defiantly and risk censure. ~*vi inf* kiss and cuddle lengthily (with). **necklace** *n* neck ornament.

nectar *n* **1** sweet liquid that bees obtain from certain flowers for making honey. **2** very sweet, soothing drink.

née (nei) *adj* having a maiden name of; born.

need *vt* require; lack. *vi* be obliged to; be necessary to. *v aux* **need I, you, he?, etc.** must I, you, he?, etc. **I, you, he, etc., need not** I, you, he, etc., do/does not have to. ~*n* **1** circumstances in which something is needed. **2** misfortune; poverty. **3** requirement. **needy** *adj* poor.

needle *n* **1** sharp pointed sliver of steel with a hole at one end to take thread for sewing. **2** plastic or metal rod for knitting. **3** gramophone stylus. **4** indicator arrow on a compass, dial, etc. **5** pointed part of a hypodermic syringe. **6** sharply pointed leaf of a conifer. **needlework** *n* hand-sewing.

negate *vt* **1** deny. **2** cancel out; make void. **negation** *n*.

negative *adj* **1** indicating *no*, not affirmative. **2** not productive or positive. **3** indicating opposition or disapproval. **4** denoting numbers less than zero. **5** with light and dark areas reversed. **6** designating the electrical charge carried by an electron. *n* **1** word(s) indicating a denial or refusal. **2** negative number. **3** negative photographic plate.

neglect *vt* **1** fail to care for. **2** omit; overlook. *n* act or result of neglecting. **negligent** *adj* careless; not paying proper attention. **negligence** *n*. **negligently** *adv*. **negligible** *adj* so minor as to be not worth considering. **negligibly** *adv*.

négligé ('neglɪʒei) *n* woman's dressing gown, usually of a light or flimsy material.

negotiate *vi* reach an agreement through discussion. *vt* **1** settle through discussion. **2** successfully come through or deal with (an obstacle). **3** obtain cash settlement for. **negotiation** *n*. **negotiator** *n*.

Negro *n, pl* **Negroes** black-skinned person of African descent.

neigh *vi* (of a horse) produce a braying sound. *n* cry of a horse; bray.

neighbour *n* **1** person living nextdoor or nearby. **2** thing situated near or adjacent to another. *v* **neighbour on** border on; adjoin. **neighbourhood** *n* (people living in) the vicinity; surrounding area.

neither *adj,pron* not either (one). *conj* nor yet.

neon *n* gaseous element used in strip lighting and advertising display.

nephew *n* son of one's brother or sister, or of one's husband's or wife's brother or sister.

nepotism *n* favouritism shown to relatives in unfairly procuring positions or promotion for them. **nepotist** *n*.

Neptune *n* outer giant planet lying beyond Uranus.

nerve *n* **1** bundle of fibres that connects the central nervous system with all parts of the body transmitting sensory and motor impulses. **2** courage; confidence. **3** *sl* impudence; cheek. **nerves** *pl n* anxiety; hysteria; irritability. **get on one's nerves** irritate. **nervy** *adj* anxious; tense. **nerve-racking** *adj* causing emotional strain; worrying.

nervous *adj* **1** tense; excitable. **2** timid; anxious. **3** vigorous; spirited. **4** relating to the nerves. **nervous breakdown** *n* severe mental and emotional collapse. **nervous system** *n* body mechanism coordinating internal functions and external impulses.

nest *n* **1** shelter made of twigs, grass, etc., where birds, reptiles, mice, etc., lay eggs or give birth. **2** protective or comfortable place in which young animals are reared. *vi* **1** make a nest. **2** look for nests. **nest egg** *n* savings.

nestle *vi* cuddle; settle comfortably.

net[1] *n* **1** *also* **netting** open mesh of knotted string, wire, etc., used for catching fish, birds, etc., or to protect against birds, insects, etc. **2** mesh barrier dividing playing areas in tennis and other games or to enclose a goal area. *vt,vi* (-tt-) **1** catch or cover with nets. **2** snare. **3** construct a net. **netball** *n* sport in which goals are scored by throwing a ball into a net. **network** *n* **1** complex connected pattern or system of wires, roads, etc. **2** series of linked radio or television stations.

net[2] *adj* remaining after deductions. *vt* (-tt-) earn as net profit or income.

nettle *n* plant with toothed leaves and stinging hairs. *vt* irritate.

neurosis *n* nervous disorder involving irrational anxiety, obsessions, or other abnormal behaviour. **neurotic** *adj* **1** relating to a neurosis or to the nerves. **2** prone to anxiety or hysteria. *n* neurotic person.

neuter *adj* **1** of neither masculine nor feminine gender. **2** sexually underdeveloped. **3** deprived of sexual organs. *n* neuter word, animal, plant, etc. *vt* make neuter.

neutral *adj* **1** impartial; not taking sides. **2** belonging to neither side. **3** having no definite characteristics. **4** neuter. **5** neither alkali nor acid. **6** neither positive nor negative. **7** (of gears) not engaged. *n* **1** person, country, etc., who favours no side or who does not take part in an argument, war, etc. **2** (of gears) state of being not engaged. **neutrality** *n*. **neutralize** *vt* **1** make neutral. **2** render powerless; deaden.

neutron *n* minute uncharged particle occurring in the nuclei of all atoms except hydrogen.

never *adv* **1** at no time. **2** not at all. **never mind!** don't worry! **well I never!** how surprising!

nevertheless *adv* even so; in spite of that.

new *adj* **1** of recent origin or existence; not old; freshly produced. **2** recently acquired or discovered. **3** modern; novel; different. **4** another. **new at** *or* **to** unaccustomed to; unfamiliar with. ~*adv also* **newly** freshly; recently. **newcomer** *n* recently arrived person; beginner. **New Year** *n* **1** coming year. **2** first or first few days of January.

news *s n* **1** current information about recent events. **2** broadcast information about local, national, and international events. **newsagent** *n* shopkeeper who sells newspapers, journals, etc. **newspaper** *n* daily or weekly publication containing news, features, specialist information, and advertisements. **newsreel** *n* filmed report of current events.

newt *n* small lizard-like amphibian.

next *adj* **1** following; subsequent. **2** adjacent; neighbouring. **3** closest. *adv* after this or that.

nib *n* pointed writing end of a pen.

nibble *n* **1** small bite. **2** morsel. *vt,vi* take a nibble (at); eat in nibbles.

nice *adj* **1** pleasant; attractive. **2** good; virtuous. **3** refined. **4** precise; subtle; delicate. **nicely** *adv*.

niche *n* **1** alcove or recess, often used for shrines or statues. **2** suitable or comfortable place or position.

nick *n* tiny notch. **the nick** *sl* jail. **in the nick of time** just in time. ~*vt* **1** make a nick in. **2** *sl* steal; pinch.

nickel *n* **1** hard silvery metal used for plating and coin-making. **2** *US* five-cent coin.

nickname *n* name by which a person is known affectionately or mockingly. *vt* give a nickname to.

nicotine *n* narcotic found in tobacco.

niece *n* daughter of one's brother or sister, or of one's husband's or wife's brother or sister.

nigger *n abusive* Negro.

night *n* period of time between evening and morning; darkness. **nightclub** *n* place of entertainment open at night providing food and drink. **nightdress** *n also* **nightgown** woman's sleeping garment. **nightly** *adv* **1** during the night. **2** every night. **nightmare** *n* **1** terrifying dream. **2** frightening experience; trauma. **night-time** *n* period of darkness between sunset and sunrise. **night watchman** *n* person employed to guard premises at night.

nightingale *n* red-brown European songbird noted for its nocturnal trilling song.

nil *n* nothing.

nimble *adj* agile; deft; quick. **nimbly** *adv*.

nine *n* **1** number equal to one plus eight. **2** group of nine persons, things, etc. **3** *also* **nine o'clock** nine hours after noon or midnight. *adj* amounting to nine. **nine days wonder** something that causes short-lived excitement or admiration. **ninth** *adj* coming between eighth and tenth in sequence. *n* **1** ninth person, object, etc. **2** one of nine equal portions; one divided by nine. *adv* after the eighth.

nineteen *n* **1** number that is nine more than ten. **2** nineteen things or people. **talk nineteen to the dozen** talk fast and unceasingly. ~*adj* amounting to nineteen. **nineteenth** *n,adj,adv*.

ninety *n* **1** number equal to nine times ten. **2** ninety things or people. *adj* amounting to ninety. **ninetieth** *adj,adv,n*.

nip *vt,vi* (-pp-) **1** catch, pinch, or bite sharply. **2** check the growth (of). *vi inf* go quickly; pop. *n* **1** small bite or pinch. **2** touch of frost. **nippy** *adj* cold; sharp; frosty.

nipple *n* **1** suckling teat of a breast or bottle. **2** device similar in shape or function to a nipple.

nit *n* **1** egg of a head louse or other parasite. **2** *sl* fool.

nitrogen *n* colourless gas forming 78 per cent of the air and used esp. in the manufacture of fertilizers.

nitroglycerine *n* unstable chemical used in dynamite and other explosives.

no *adv* **1** not any; not one. **2** not in any way; not at all. **3** not. **4** expressing denial, refusal, etc. *n* statement of denial, refusal, etc.; negative.

noble *adj* **1** courageous; worthy; high-minded. **2** aristocratic. **3** stately; splendid. *n also* **nobleman** member of the nobility; aristocrat; peer. **nobility** *n* **1** hereditary class of the highest status; aristocracy. **2** moral courage, worthiness, or endurance.

nobody *pron* **1** no-one. **2** person of no importance or of low birth.

nocturnal *adj* of, occurring in, or active during the night. **nocturnally** *adv*.

nod *vt,vi* (-dd-) bend (the head) forward to indicate (agreement or approval). *vi* doze. *n* nodding motion.

noise *n* sound. **noisy** *adj* loud. **noisily** *adv*. **noisiness** *n*.

nomad *n* **1** member of a tribe constantly on the move in search of new pasture. **2** habitual wanderer; roamer. **nomadic** *adj*.

nominal *adj* **1** not actual; existing in name only. **2** very small; token. **nominally** *adv*.

nominate *vt* **1** propose as a candidate. **2** appoint. **nomination** *n*. **nominee** *n* person who is nominated.

non- *prefix* indicating negation, absence, etc.

nonchalant *adj* coolly casual; offhand. **nonchalance** *n*. **nonchalantly** *adv*.

nondescript *adj* having no distinguishing characteristics; dull.

none *pron* **1** not any (of them or it). **2** no part or section. **3** no such person. *adv* not at all; in no way.

nonentity *n* **1** insignificant person or thing. **2** non-existent thing.

nonsense *n* **1** meaningless or foolish words or ideas. **2** trifle. **nonsensical** *adj.*

noodle *n* thin strip of pasta.

nook *n* secret or sheltered corner or hiding place.

noon *n* midday; 12 o'clock in the daytime.

no-one *pron* no person at all; nobody.

noose *n* loop of rope with a slipknot to tighten it, used esp. for execution by hanging.

nor *conj* also not; not either.

norm *n* **1** usual or recognized standard or pattern. **2** expected or potential output.

normal *adj* **1** usual; ordinary, average. **2** not physically or mentally handicapped. **normality** *n.* **normally** *adv.*

north *n* **1** one of the four cardinal points of the compass situated to the left of a person facing the sunrise. **2** part of a country, area, etc., lying towards the north. *adj also* **northern** of, in, or facing the north. *adv,adj also* **northerly** **1** towards the north. **2** (of winds) from the north. **northerner** *n.* **northeast** *n* point situated midway between the north and east. *adj also* **northeastern** of, in, or facing the northeast. *adv,adj also* **northeasterly** **1** towards the northeast. **2** (of winds) from the northeast. **northward** *adj* facing or moving towards the north. **northwards** *adv* in the direction of the north. **northwest** *n* point situated midway between north and west. *adj also* **northwestern** of, in, or facing the northwest. *adv,adj also* **northwesterly** **1** towards the northwest. **2** (of winds) from the northwest.

nose *n* **1** central projection in the face used for breathing and smelling. **2** ability to smell out or discover. **be led by the nose** follow blindly. **keep one's nose to the grindstone** work persistently. **pay through the nose** pay too much. **poke one's nose into** interfere in. **turn one's nose up (at)** reject contemptuously. **under one's (very) nose** in one's presence; in full view. ~*vt,vi* smell or sniff (at).

nostalgia *n* **1** sentimental longing for things past. **2** homesickness. **nostalgic** *adj.*

nostril *n* one of the two openings of the nose.

nosy *adj* unpleasantly inquisitive. **nosiness** *n.*

not *adv* expressing negation, denial, refusal, etc.

notable *adj* important; remarkable; conspicuous. *n* important person. **notably** *adv.*

notation *n* **1** act or process of organizing a scheme of signs that represent scientific, musical, or other concepts. **2** such a scheme or method.

notch *n* V-shaped cut in a piece of wood, etc. *vt* cut a notch in, esp. as a way of keeping count. **notch up** score.

note *n* **1** short written record, summary, or comment. **2** short letter. **3** piece of paper money. **4** written promise to pay. **5** (symbol indicating) a musical sound of a certain pitch. **6** distinction; fame; importance. **7** notice; attention. **8** certain quality. *vt* **1** make a note of. **2** take note of; observe. **noteworthy** *adj* **1** deserving attention; worth noting. **2** remarkable.

nothing *n* **1** not anything; no thing. **2** no part. **3** something of no importance or value. **4** something requiring no effort. **5** zero; nought. **for nothing** **1** free of charge. **2** with no purpose. **think nothing of** do without hesitation. ~*adv* not in any way.

notice *vt,vi* **1** observe; take note of. **2** comment on, esp. favourably. *n* **1** attention; observation. **2** piece of displayed written information. **3** public announcement. **4** warning. **5** official announcement or notification of the termination of employment. **6** critical review. **at short notice** with little warning or preparation time. **noticeable** *adj.*

notify *vt* let (a person) know; inform officially. **notification** *n.*

notion *n* impression; view; idea; concept. **notional** *adj* **1** expressing a concept; not based on fact. **2** nominal.

notorious *adj* infamous; having a bad reputation. **notoriety** *n.* **notoriously** *adv.*

notwithstanding *adv* nevertheless. *prep,conj* in spite of.

nougat *n* chewy white sweet containing nuts.

nought *n* zero; nothing. **noughts and crosses** *n* game played on a criss-cross grid in which the object is to get three noughts or crosses in a row.

noun *n* word used to denote a thing, person, concept, act, etc.

nourish *vt* **1** give food to. **2** encourage or harbour (feeling). **nourishment** *n* food.

novel[1] *adj* new and different. **novelty** *n* **1** quality of being novel. **2** cheap often gaudy small article for sale.

novel[2] *n* sustained work of prose fiction longer than a short story. **novelist** *n.*

November *n* eleventh month of the year.

novice *n* **1** beginner; learner. **2** nun or monk who has not yet taken final vows.

now *adv* **1** at present. **2** immediately; this minute. **3** recently. **4** presently. **5** at this point; currently. **6** consequently. **now and then** every so often; occasionally. *~conj also* **now that** since; as a consequence of. **nowadays** *adv* these days; in modern times.

nowhere *adv* not in any place; not anywhere. **get nowhere** be unsuccessful; fail to achieve something.

noxious *adj* poisonous.

nozzle *n* tube or spout through which liquid or gas is let out.

nuance *n* subtle variation in meaning, shade, etc.

nuclear *adj* **1** of, forming, or relating to a nucleus or central core. **2** relating to the structure or splitting of atoms. **nuclear fission/fusion** *n* splitting of a heavy atom/fusion of light atoms attended by enormous release of energy. **nuclear physics** *n* science relating to the behaviour of atoms. **nuclear reactor** *n* device for generating power from nuclear fission. **nuclear weapon** *n* bomb or missile using energy from nuclear fission or fusion.

nucleus *n, pl* **nuclei** ('nju:kliai) *or* **nucleuses 1** central or most active part of a movement, organization, etc. **2** positively charged central mass of an atom consisting of protons and neutrons.

nude *adj* naked. *n* naked figure, esp. one depicted in a painting, sculpture, etc. **in the nude** naked. **nudity** *n*.

nudge *n* deliberate slight push with the elbow; prod. *vt* give a nudge (to).

nugget *n* **1** small hard irregularly shaped lump, esp. of gold. **2** small valuable piece.

nuisance *n* thing or person causing annoyance, trouble, or offence.

null *adj* **1** without value or feeling. **2** having no legal force. **null and void** legally invalid. **nullity** *n*. **nullify** *vt* make null. **nullification** *n*.

numb *adj* without feeling, sensation, or emotion. *vt* make numb or insensitive. **numbness** *n*.

number *n* **1** mathematical concept of quantity, each unit of which has a unique value, enabling them to be used in counting. **2** numeral. **3** sum; quantity; aggregate. **4** one of a series; issue. **5** short musical piece. **6** exclusive article. **a number of** several. **number one** oneself. **without** *or* **beyond number** too many to be counted. *~vt* **1** assign a number to. **2** add up to. **3** enumerate; list. **numberless** *adj* countless; innumerable.

numeral *n* symbol or group of symbols, such as 6 or VI, denoting a number.

numerate *adj* ('nju:mərət) able to understand and use mathematical concepts. *vt* ('nju:məreit) number; count. **numeracy** *n*.

numerical *adj* relating to or consisting of numbers. **numerically** *adv*.

numerous *adj* great in number; abundant.

nun *n* woman who has taken final vows in a religious order. **nunnery** *n* community of nuns; convent.

nurse *n* **1** person trained and employed to care for the sick under the direction of doctors. **2** woman employed to look after very small children. *vt,vi* **1** act as a nurse (to). **2** suckle. *vt* cherish; foster; nurture; encourage. **nursing home** *n* small privately run hospital for convalescent, aged, or chronically ill patients.

nursery *n* **1** playroom. **2** place for growing or stocking plants. **nursery rhyme** *n* traditional children's song or verse. **nursery school** *n* school for children under five; kindergarten.

nurture *vt* foster; rear; feed. *n* upbringing; education.

nut *n* **1** hard shelled fruit with a single sometimes edible kernel. **2** small regularly shaped metal block with a central threaded hole used for securing bolts. **3** *sl* fanatic; enthusiast. **4** *sl* insane or peculiar person. **nuts** *sl adj* crazy. **nutcracker** *n also* **nutcrackers** device having pincers for cracking nutshells. **nutmeg** *n* seed of an East Indian tree, ground as a spice. **nutshell** *n* woody covering of a nut kernel. **in a nutshell** precisely; concisely expressed.

nutrient *n* nourishing substance taken in, esp. by a plant

nutrition *n* **1** digestion and assimilation of food. **2** feeding; nourishment. **nutritious** *adj* nourishing; health-giving.

nuzzle *vt,vi* rub or push (against) with the nose.

nylon *n* synthetic plastic fibre or material made from it. **nylons** *pl n* woman's stockings.

nymph *n* **1** minor Greek or Roman goddess inhabiting and guarding trees, rivers, etc. **2** beautiful young girl.

O

oak *n* deciduous acorn-bearing tree with hard wood and jagged leaves.

oar *n* wooden pole with one end flattened into a blade, used to propel a boat through water. **put one's oar in** interfere. **oarsman** *n pl* **-men** one who rows with an oar.

oasis *n, pl* **oases** (ou'eisi:z) fertile area in a desert.

oath *n* **1** solemn binding declaration of the truth of one's statement. **2** casual use of a solemn word or name in anger or irritation; swear-word. **on** *or* **under oath** sworn to tell the truth.

oats *pl n* grains of a hardy cereal plant, widely used as human and animal food. **sow one's wild oats** indulge in pleasures, esp. irresponsible sexual relationships, while young. **oatmeal** *n* coarse flour made from oats used for porridge, biscuits, etc.

obese *adj* extremely fat; gross. **obesity** *n*.

obey *vt,vi* do what is commanded by a person, law, instinct, etc. **obedient** *adj* ready and willing to obey; dutiful. **obedience** *n*. **obediently** *adv*.

obituary *n* notice of death, esp. in a newspaper, often including a short biography.

object *n* ('ɔbdʒekt) **1** thing discernible by the senses. **2** aim, goal, or intention. *vt,vi* (əb'dʒekt) oppose, disapprove, or protest against. **objection** *n* **1** act of or reason for objecting. **2** feeling or statement of dislike or disapproval. **objective** *adj* **1** separate; detached. **2** impartial; viewed fairly and dispassionately. *n* point or situation to be aimed at; goal. **objectively** *adv*. **objectivity** *n*.

oblige *vt* **1** allow no choice; insist or force. **2** do a favour for. **3** make indebted to. **obligation** *n* duty enforceable by law, morality, a contract, promise, etc. **obligatory** (ə'bligətəri) *adj* necessary and binding.

oblique 1 slanting away from the horizontal or vertical. **2** indirect; devious; not straightforward. **obliquely** *adv*.

obliterate *vt* leave no trace of; destroy; blot out. **obliteration** *n*.

oblivion *n* state of forgetfulness or lack of awareness. **oblivious** *adj* **1** absent-minded; unaware. **2** unaffected by; impervious to. **obliviously** *adv*.

oblong *n* figure, esp. a rectangle, longer than it is broad. *adj* shaped like an oblong.

obnoxious *adj* **1** repulsive; causing disgust. **2** extremely rude or insulting.

oboe *n* woodwind instrument having a mouthpiece fitted with a double reed. **oboist** *n*.

obscene *adj* offending against decency or morality; vulgar; lewd. **obscenely** *adv*. **obscenity** *n*.

obscure *adj* **1** vague; enigmatic; not easily understood. **2** dim; gloomy; indistinct. **3** not famous or well-known. **obscurely** *adv*. **obscurity** *n*.

observe *vt,vi* **1** see, notice, or watch. **2** keep to the rules of a custom, law, religion, etc. **3** remark or comment. **observer** *n*. **observance** *n* adherence to the rules of law, religion, custom, etc. **observant** *adj* attentive; taking notice. **observation** *n* **1** careful watching; recognizing and noting. **2** comment or remark. **observatory** *n* building used for astronomical observation.

obsess *vt* be an obsession of; preoccupy. **obsessive** *adj*. **obsession** *n* fixed idea or addiction that fascinates and preoccupies the mind to an exaggerated or dangerous extent.

obsolete *adj* out-of-date; antiquated; disused. **obsolescent** *adj* becoming obsolete. **obsolescence** *n*.

obstacle *n* any snag or obstruction hindering progress or action.

obstinate *adj* stubborn; hard to persuade; unyielding. **obstinacy** *n*. **obstinately** *adv*.

obstruct *vt,vi* **1** block off; prevent access or progress. **2** impede or delay any action. **obstruction** *n*.

obtain *vt,vi* gain possession (of); get; secure or acquire. **obtainable** *adj*.

obtrusive *adj* interfering; impertinent. **obtrusion** *n*.

obtuse *adj* dull; blunt; not sharp or acute. **obtuse angle** *n* angle greater than 90° but less than 180°.

obvious *adj* evident; clear; apparent. **obviously** *adv*.

occasion *n* **1** particular time of an event, ceremony, etc. **2** suitable opportunity or chance. **3** reason; need. **rise to the occasion** display the necessary or suitable qualities. ~*vt* give rise to; bring about or cause. **occasional** *adj* infrequent; sporadic. **occasionally** *adv*.

Occident *n* the West, esp. W. Europe and America. **Occidental** *adj,n*.

occult *adj* supernatural; magical; mysterious. **the occult** *n* supernatural or magical knowledge or experience.

occupy *vt* **1** take or hold possession of (a country, building, etc.). **2** employ. **occupant** *n* one who possesses or lives in a particular place. **occupancy** *n*. **occupation** *n* **1** employment; pastime; job. **2** state or act of occupying or being occupied.

occur *vi* (-rr-) **1** happen; take place. **2** exist; be found at. **3** come into the mind. **occurrence** *n*.

ocean *n* one of the five vast areas of sea surrounding the continents of the globe. **oceanic** *adj*.

octagon *n* geometric figure, design, building, etc., having eight sides. **octagonal** *adj*.

octane *n* inflammable hydrocarbon present in petrol. **high-octane** *adj* denoting a superior grade of petrol.

octave *n* **1** range of eight notes in a musical scale. **2** set of eight.

October *n* tenth month of the year.

octopus *n, pl* **octopuses** *or* **octopi** ('ɔktəpai) eight-armed mollusc.

odd *adj* **1** strange; bizarre; peculiar. **2** uneven; irregular. **3** (of a number) not divisible by two. **odd man out** one remaining when others have formed a pair, class, group, etc. **oddly** *adv*. **oddity** *n* **1** strangeness; peculiarity. **2** remarkable or unlikely event, person, object, etc. **oddment** *n* scrap; remnant; leftover. **odds** *pl n* **1** chances; possibilities. **2** ratio between two stakes in a wager. **at odds** in disagreement. **odds and ends** small miscellaneous scraps.

ode *n* poem addressed to a particular person or object.

odious *adj* hateful; loathsome. **odium** *n*.

odour *n* smell; fragrance.

oesophagus (i:'sɔfəgəs) *n, pl* **oesophagi** (i:'sɔfəgai) tube running from the pharynx to the stomach; gullet.

oestrogen *n* female sex hormone.

oestrus *n* period of sexual receptiveness in most female mammals.

of *prep* **1** belonging to. **2** originating from. **3** created or produced by. **4** from the period relating to. **5** made with. **6** containing; holding. **7** towards or away from a specified place. **8** that is the same as. **9** for. **10** separated from.

off *prep* **1** so as to be away or distant from. **2** not present at or attending to. **3** removed or deducted from. **4** no longer interested in. **5** by the means of. *adv* **1** distant; away. **2** so as to be removed or rid of. **3** so as to stop or disengage. *adj* **1** cancelled or postponed. **2** not attached. **3** not working or turned on. **on the off chance** with the possibility or hope.

offal *n* edible internal organs or parts of an animal.

offend *vt* cause displeasure or pain to. *vi* sin; do wrong. **offence** *n* **1** crime or infringement of the law. **2** any cause of anger, grievance, or pain. **to take/give offence** to be/cause hurt. **offensive** *adj* aggressive; repellent; obnoxious. *n* attack.

offer *vt* give; present or hold out for acceptance. *vi* volunteer; be available or on hand. *n* **1** act of offering. **2** something offered.

offhand *adj* **1** impromptu; unprepared. **2** casual; impolite.

office *n* **1** position of authority, esp. public or governmental. **2** place of business. **3** government department. **4** rite or religious service. **officer** **1** person holding a responsible position in a government, club, organization, etc. **2** holder of a commission in the armed forces. **3** policeman. **official** *n* one who holds an office. *adj* **1** authorized or vouched for. **2** relating to an office. **officially** *adv*. **officious** *adj* bossy; interfering.

offing *n* **in the offing** in view; near; likely to happen.

off-licence *n* shop licensed to sell alcoholic drink for consumption off the premises.

off-peak *adj,adv* at a less popular or less busy time.

off-putting *adj* discouraging; repelling.

offset *vt* (-tt-; -set) compensate for; balance out.

offshore *adj,adv* from or far from the shore or land.

offside *adj* in a part of a football field, etc., between the ball and the opponents' goal, where it is not allowable to kick the ball. *n* the right-hand side of a vehicle, horse, etc.

offspring **1** child or children. **2** any issue or result.

offstage *adj,adv* not visible to the audience in a theatre.

often *adv* frequently; repeatedly.

ogre *n* **1** monstrous man-eating giant of fairy tales and folklore. **2** cruel person; tyrant.

oil *n* viscous liquid obtained from many mineral and vegetable sources, lighter than and insoluble in water. **burn the midnight oil** work or study until late at night. ~*vt* apply oil to. **oily** *adj*. **oil painting** *n* **1** picture painted in oil-based paints (oils). **2** art or practice of painting such pictures. **oilskin** *n* cloth or clothing treated with oil to make it waterproof.

ointment *n* soothing or medicated cream applied to the skin.

old *adj* **1** aged; having existed for many years. **2** out-of-date; obsolete; belonging to an earlier age; stale. **old age** *n* last years of life. **old-fashioned** *adj* out-of-date; obsolete; quaint. **old hand** *n* experienced person.

olive *n* small oily Mediterranean fruit eaten either unripe (green olive) or ripe (black olive). *n,adj also* **olive green** brownish green.

omelette *n* eggs beaten together, fried, and flavoured with herbs, vegetables, cheese, etc.

omen *n* sign supposedly prophesying a future event.

ominous *adj* threatening; suggesting future trouble.

omit *vt* (-tt-) leave out; fail to do. **omission** *n*.

omnibus *n* bus. *adj* containing several assorted ingredients, items, etc.

omnipotent *adj* all-powerful. **omnipotence** *n*.

on *prep* **1** placed or being in contact with the top or surface of. **2** supported by or attached to. **3** during a particular day. **4** close to or by the side of; along. **5** being broadcast by or performed at. **6** at the time or occasion of. **7** with the support of. **8** concerning; about. **9** by means of. *adv* **1** so as to work or function. **2** so as to be covered with. **3** ahead. **on and off** sporadically. **on and on** repeatedly; continuously. ~*adj* **1** taking place; planned. **2** attached. **3** working; functioning; performing.

once *adv* **1** on a single occasion. **2** in the past. **at once 1** immediately. **2** simultaneously. **once and for all** finally.

one *adj* **1** single; individual. **2** only. **3** being a united entity. *n* **1** the smallest whole number represented by the symbol 1 or I. **2** particular or specified single person, thing, example, etc. **3** *also* **one o'clock** the first hour after noon or midnight. *pron* **1** a person; any person; each person. **2** *formal* I or me. **one another** each other; one to or with the other. **oneself** *r pron* **1** a or any person's own self. **2** yourself. **be/feel oneself** be/feel normal, natural, etc. **one-sided** *adj* unfairly biased. **one-way** *adj* **1** allowing traffic in one direction only. **2** not reciprocal.

onion *n* vegetable whose rounded pungent bulb is used in cooking.

onlooker *n* spectator; observer.

only *adj* being a single one or one of few; sole. *adv* **1** exclusively; solely. **2** merely; just. *conj* but; however.

onset *n* beginning; start; attack.

onslaught *n* violent assault.

onus *n* responsibility; duty; burden.

onward *adj* moving forwards. **onwards** *adv* forwards; towards the front.

onyx ('ɔniks) *n* quartz having bands or layers of different colours.

ooze *vi,vt* seep; leak; flow gradually.

opal *n* quartz-like mineral characterized by iridescent colours, often used as a gemstone.

opaque *adj* obscure; transmitting no light. **opacity** *n*.

open *adj* **1** not closed or sealed. **2** allowing access. **3** ready or available for business or trade. **4** free from obstruction. **5** vacant; unoccupied; free. **6** not yet settled or decided. **7** candid; honest; not prejudiced. **8** vulnerable; liable. *vt,vi* **1** make or become open. **2** undo; unfold. **3** start; give an introduction (to). *vt* **1** disclose; reveal. **2** declare officially to be open to the public. *n also* **the open air** outdoors; outside. **in the open** so as to be known or made public. **openly** *adv*. **openness** *n*. **open-ended** *adj* limitless. **opener** *n* gadget for opening tins, bottles, etc. **open-handed** *adj* generous. **open-hearted** *adj* frank; sincere. **opening** *n* **1** gap; space. **2** start; beginning. **3** opportunity; chance. **open-minded** *adj* not biased or prejudiced; liberal. **open-mouthed** *adj* astonished; aghast. **open-plan** *adj* having few or no internal walls to separate rooms.

opera *n* musical drama, largely or wholly sung. **operatic** *adj*.

operate *vi,vt* **1** work or function. **2** perform surgery (on). **operative** *adj*. **operator** *n*. **operation** *n* **1** working; action; function; effect. **2** instance of surgery. **operational** *adj*.

operetta *n* short, light, or comic opera.
ophthalmology *n* branch of medicine dealing with eye disorders. **ophthalmologist** *n*.
opinion *n* judgment; view; belief. **opinionated** *adj* dogmatic; stubborn. **opinion poll** *n* organized questioning to determine public opinion on a particular issue.
opium *n* narcotic, sedative, or stimulant drug prepared from juice of certain poppies. **opiate** *n* drug containing opium. *adj* made from opium; inducing sleep.
opponent *n* antagonist; one who opposes. *adj* opposing; adverse.
opportunity *n* favourable chance or occasion. **opportune** *adj* lucky; well-timed.
oppose *vt* set against; resist; obstruct or contest. **opposite** *adj* **1** facing; in front of. **2** opposed or contrary (to). *n* opposite person or thing; antithesis. *adv,prep* in an opposite position, direction, etc. **opposite number** *n* person holding a similar or equivalent position in another country, company, etc. **opposition** *n* **1** resistance; hostility. **2** state or position of being opposite. **3** most distant positioning of two stars or planets. **the Opposition** major political party not in office.
oppress *vt* **1** weigh down or overwhelm. **2** persecute severely. **oppression** *n*. **oppressive** *adj* **1** harsh; cruel. **2** (of weather) sultry.
opt *vt* choose; settle for; decide between. **option** *n* **1** choice; alternative. **2** right, freedom, or opportunity to purchase. **optional** *adj* not obligatory.
optical *adj* relating to the eyes; visual. **optician** *n* person who makes or sells glasses, lenses, etc.
optimism *n* feeling or belief that the best will happen; hopefulness. **optimist** *n*. **optimistic** *adj*.
opulent *adj* rich; lavish; sumptuous. **opulence** *n*.
or *conj* **1** with the alternative of. **2** and also; as well as.
oral *adj* **1** spoken. **2** relating to the mouth.
orange *n* round juicy citrus fruit with reddish-yellow peel. *n,adj* reddish-yellow. **orangeade** *n* orange-flavoured fizzy drink.
oration *n* eloquent public speech or address. **orator** *n*. **oratory** *n*.
orbit *n* **1** path followed around a planet or star by a satellite. **2** sphere of influence. **3** eye socket. **orbital** *adj*.
orchard *n* enclosed area of fruit trees.
orchestra *n* **1** company of instrumental musicians. **2** *also* **orchestra pit** semicircle between the stage and seats in a theatre. **orchestra stalls** *pl n* front seats in a theatre. **orchestral** *adj*. **orchestrate** *vt* arrange (music) for an orchestra. **orchestration** *n*.
orchid *n* one of a family of perennial plants with complicated specialized, often exotic, flowers.
ordain *vt* **1** decree; order. **2** appoint as a priest or minister. **ordination** *n*.
ordeal *n* severe trial of stamina or endurance.
order *n* **1** arrangement; sequence. **2** command; rule. **3** tidiness. **4** class or group. **5** religious body. **in order 1** in a proper state or condition. **2** correct or appropriate. **in order to** so as to; with the intention or purpose of. ~*vt* **1** command; instruct. **2** arrange; organize. **3** send for. **orderly** *adj* methodical; tidy; well-controlled. *n* **1** soldier serving an officer. **2** attendant in a hospital.
ordinal number *n* number, such as first, second, etc., that denotes order, quantity, or rank in a group.
ordinary *adj* usual; common; familiar; plain. *n* **out of the ordinary** unusual; exceptional. **ordinarily** *adv*.
ore *n* mineral from which metal may be obtained.
organ *n* **1** differentiated part of an animal or plant performing a particular function. **2** large musical wind instrument with a keyboard and pipes, often used in churches. **3** means or method of communication. **organist** *n*.
organic *adj* **1** relating to or derived from plants or animals. **2** inherent; structural. **3** (of food) grown without application of any non-organic fertilizer, pesticide, etc. **4** relating to chemical compounds of carbon. **organically** *adv*.
organism *n* any animal, plant, bacterium, or virus.
organize *vt* arrange, group, classify, or prepare. *vi* form a political group, union, etc. **organization** *n* **1** organized group, system, company, etc. **2** act of organizing.
orgasm *n* culmination of a sexual act, characterized by ejaculation in the male and vaginal contractions in the female.
orgy *n* drunken riotous revelry. **orgiastic** *adj*.
Orient *n* the East or the countries of Asia. **Oriental** *adj,n*.

orientate *vt* find the bearings of in relation to surroundings, conditions, etc. **orientation** *n*.

origin *n* source; beginning; starting point. **original** *adj* **1** existing since the beginning. **2** new; not copied; novel; creative. *n* the source from which copies, translations, etc., are made. **originate** *vt,vi* start or initiate; have as a source. **origination** *n*.

Orlon *n Tdmk* lightweight synthetic fibre used for clothing, etc.

ornament *n* ('ɔ:nəmənt) **1** decoration; adornment. **2** item or article used for show. *vt* ('ɔ:nəment) embellish; decorate. **ornamentation** *n*. **ornamental** *adj* decorative.

ornate *adj* elaborately or flamboyantly decorative.

ornithology *n* study of birds. **ornithologist** *n*.

orphan *n* child whose parents have died. *adj* bereaved of parents. *vt* leave bereaved of parents. **orphanage** *n* institution for bringing up orphans.

orthodox *adj* having sound, correct, or established views, esp. in religion. **orthodoxy** *n*.

orthopaedic *adj* intended to cure deformity.

oscillate *vi* **1** move from side to side as a pendulum. **2** waver; fluctuate. **oscillation** *n*.

ostensible *adj* apparent; seeming. **ostensibly** *adv*.

ostentatious *adj* showy; flamboyant; vulgar. **ostentation** *n*.

osteopath *n* one who manipulates the bones and muscles in order to cure diseases. **osteopathy** *n*.

ostracize *vt* isolate, shun, or bar from society. **ostracism** *n*.

ostrich *n* large fast-running long-necked bird that is native to Africa.

other *adj* alternative; remaining; different; additional. **on the other hand** alternatively. **the other day** recently. *~pron* second or additional person or thing. *adv* **other than 1** in addition to; apart from. **2** in a different way from. **others** *pl pron* remaining, different, or additional ones. **otherwise** *conj* or else. *adv* in a different way; in other respects. *adj* different.

otter *n* fish-catching aquatic mammal having a smooth coat and webbed feet.

ought *v aux* **1** have an obligation or duty. **2** need; will be wise or advised. **3** will be likely or liable. **4** will be pleased.

ounce *n* unit of weight equal to one sixteenth of a pound (approx. 28 grams).

our *adj* belonging to us. **ours** *pron* something or someone belonging to us. **ourselves** *r pron* **1** our own selves. **2** our normal selves.

oust *vt* eject or dispossess; usurp or replace.

out *adv* **1** away; towards the outside. **2** not present. **3** no longer in power. **4** on strike. **5** not accurate. **6** available to the public. **7** not alight or switched on. **8** no longer in fashion. **9** so as to eliminate or omit. **10** so as to project or protrude. **11** so as to appear. **12** acting with the intention of. **13** into a state of unconsciousness. *prep* away through. **out-of-date** *adj,adv* old-fashioned; obsolete.

outboard motor *n* engine that can be attached to the exterior of a small boat.

outbreak *n* eruption, epidemic, or sudden appearance.

outburst *n* sudden or violent expression of feelings.

outcast *n* one rejected by society; exile.

outcome *n* result; consequence.

outcry *n* eruption of public protest.

outdo *vt* (-does; -did; -done) excel or surpass.

outdoor *adj* used or existing outdoors. **outdoors** *adv* in the open air; outside any building.

outer *adj* external; further out. **outermost** *adj* furthest out or away. **outer space** *n* vast untravelled area beyond the known planets.

outfit *n* **1** complete equipment, such as a suit of clothes, for a specific purpose. **2** *inf* gang; group of people. **outfitter** *n* shop or dealer selling men's clothes.

outgoing *adj* **1** resigning; retiring; departing. **2** extrovert; gregarious. *n* expenditure.

outgrow *vt* (-grew; -grown) **1** grow larger or taller than. **2** grow too large for. **outgrowth** *n* something growing from a main stem, part, etc.

outhouse *n* shed; small building separate from larger one.

outing *n* excursion; pleasure trip.

outlandish *adj* extraordinary; eccentric; bizarre.

outlaw *n* fugitive from justice; bandit. *vt* ban; prohibit.

outlay *n* expenditure. *vt* (-laid) spend; expend.

outlet *n* **1** means of escape, expression, etc. **2** market or shop handling a particular commodity.

outline *n* **1** rough sketch or draft. **2** silhouette.

vt **1** produce an outline of. **2** give a preliminary account of.

outlive *vt* live longer than; survive.

outlook *n* **1** mental attitude; point of view. **2** prospect; forecast.

outlying *adj* remote; on the outside; far away.

outnumber *vt* surpass in number; be more than.

outpatient *n* non-resident patient who visits hospital for treatment.

outpost *n* position or station far away from headquarters.

output *n* quantity or amount produced by a factory, industry, person, etc.

outrage *n* **1** atrocity; intolerable act. **2** indignation or anger over such an act. *vt* shock; scandalize. **outrageous** *adj* **1** monstrous; appalling; horrifying. **2** absurdly ridiculous. **outrageously** *adv*.

outright *adj* **1** direct; thorough. **2** blatant; total. *adv* at once; completely.

outshine *vt* (-shone) be more successful than; surpass; overshadow.

outside *n* outer surface or side. *adj* exterior; on the outside. *adv* out of doors; not inside. *prep* beyond. **outsider** *n* **1** one not belonging to a particular group, society, party, etc. **2** competitor in a race, etc., considered to have very little chance of winning.

outsize *adj* larger than average.

outskirts *pl n* outer surrounding area or district; suburbs.

outspoken *adj* exceedingly frank and candid; forthright.

outstanding *adj* **1** prominent; conspicuous; exceptional. **2** not yet paid.

outstrip *vt* (-pp-) **1** do better than; surpass. **2** run faster than.

outward *adj* **1** towards the outside. **2** superficial; apparent; external. *adj,adv* away from home. **outwardly** *adv* ostensibly; apparently; on the surface. **outwards** *adv* out; away from the centre.

outweigh *vt* be more important, valuable, or heavy than.

outwit *vt* (-tt-) defeat by superior cunning or ingenuity.

oval *adj* egg-shaped. *n* something that is oval.

ovary *n* **1** one of the two female reproductive organs producing eggs. **2** part of a flower containing ovules.

ovation *n* enthusiastic applause.

oven *n* compartment enclosed by metal, brick, etc., and heated for baking, roasting, etc.; kiln; furnace.

over *prep* **1** above; higher than. **2** on the top or surface of; so as to cover. **3** across; on the other side of. **4** during. **5** in excess of; more than. **6** throughout. **7** about; concerning. **8** recovered from; finished with. **9** better than. **10** superior in rank to. **11** by means of. **12** whilst occupied with. *adv* **1** across. **2** throughout; during. **3** from start to finish. **4** so as to fall or bend. **5** so as to remain. **6** so as to be finished. **over and over (again)** repeatedly. ~*n* series of six balls bowled in cricket.

overall *adj,adv* including or considering everything. *n* light coat or apron worn to protect clothes from dirt. **overalls** *pl n* hard-wearing trousers with a high front and straps over the shoulders.

overbearing *adj* domineering; bossy.

overboard *adv* over the side of a boat or ship. **go overboard** enthuse.

overcast *adj* cloudy; gloomy.

overcharge *vt,vi* charge too much money.

overcoat *n* heavy coat.

overcome *vt* (-came; -come) **1** conquer; vanquish; get the better of. **2** overwhelm; affect totally.

overdo *vt* (-does; -did; -done) **1** do something to excess; exaggerate. **2** cook for too long.

overdose *n* too large a dose.

overdraw *vt,vi* (-drew; -drawn) draw from a bank more money than exists to one's credit. **overdraft** *n* amount by which debit exceeds credit in a bank account.

overdue *adj* late; past the time when due.

overeat *vi* (-ate; -eaten) eat excessively; gorge.

overestimate *vt* value too highly.

overfill *vt* flood; fill too full.

overflow *vt* (-flowed; -flown) flow over the edge of; reach beyond the limits of; be excessively full of. *n* **1** flood or profusion. **2** outlet for excess water.

overgrown *adj* covered with vegetation, weeds, etc.

overhang *vt,vi* (-hung) jut over. *n* jutting ledge.

overhaul *vt* **1** check thoroughly for faults. **2** repair; renovate; restore. *n* check-up, service.

overhead *adv,adj* above the head; in the sky. **overheads** *pl n* regular unavoidable expenses of administration.

overhear *vt* (-heard) eavesdrop; hear words intended for others by accident or design.

overjoyed *adj* ecstatic; thrilled; delighted.

overland *adj,adv* mainly or entirely by land.

overlap *vt,vi* (-pp-) **1** extend partly beyond the edge of. **2** coincide partly. *n* overlapping part or area.

overlay *vt* (-laid) **1** cover the surface of. **2** cover; disguise with. *n* something laid over as a cover; decoration, etc.

overleaf *adv* on the other side of the page.

overload *vt* load, fill, or weigh down excessively.

overlook *vt* **1** view from a higher place. **2** disregard or take no notice of; choose to ignore.

overnight *adv,adj* **1** during the night. **2** all night. **3** lasting for one night.

overpower *vt* **1** conquer by superior strength, weight, etc. **2** subdue; overwhelm; overcome.

overrate *vt* overestimate.

overreach *vt* **1** reach or extend too far for comfort. **2** outwit.

overrule *vt* rule against or annul by virtue of greater authority.

overrun *vt* (-nn-; -ran; -run) **1** swarm over and take possession of; infest. **2** extend beyond.

overseas *adv,adj* abroad; across the sea.

overshadow *vt* **1** cast a shadow over. **2** outshine.

overshoot *vt* (-shot) shoot or go over or beyond.

oversight *n* **1** omission; mistake; failure to take into account. **2** supervision.

oversleep *vi* (-slept) sleep longer than intended.

overspill *n* surplus, esp. of the population of a town.

overstep *vt* (-pp-) exceed; go beyond (a limit, constraint, etc.).

overt *adj* openly done; public; not concealed. **overtly** *adv*.

overtake *vt* (-took; -taken) **1** catch up with and pass. **2** come up on suddenly.

overthrow *vt* (-threw; -thrown) **1** defeat utterly. **2** overturn; demolish. *n* defeat; ruin.

overtime *n* time worked beyond usual working hours or payment for this.

overtone *n* implication; suggestion.

overture *n* **1** instrumental prelude to an opera, ballet, etc. **2** opening negotiations or approach.

overturn *vt* upset, overthrow, or abolish.

overweight *adj* heavier than permissible or normal. *n* excess weight.

overwhelm *vt* **1** conquer by superior might. **2** overpower emotionally. **overwhelmingly** *adv*.

overwork *vt,vi* work or cause to work too hard. *n* excess work.

overwrought *adj* over-excited; in a state of nervous agitation.

ovulate *vi* produce and discharge an egg from an ovary. **ovulation** *n*.

ovule *n* part of a plant that contains the egg cell, which develops into a seed after fertilization.

owe *vt* be indebted for; be under an obligation. **owing to** because of.

owl *n* nocturnal bird of prey with a large head and eyes, small hooked beak, and a hooting cry.

own *adj* relating to oneself, itself, etc. **get one's own back** take revenge. **hold one's own** succeed in keeping one's position; acquit oneself well. **on one's own** by oneself; independently. ~*vt* possess; have. **own up** confess. **owner** *n*. **ownership** *n*.

ox *n pl* **oxen** castrated male of domestic cattle. **oxtail** *n* tail of an ox used esp. in soups and stews.

oxygen *n* colourless tasteless gaseous element present in air, water, and most minerals. **oxygenate** *vt,vi also* **oxygenize** fill with oxygen.

oyster *n* edible marine bivalve mollusc.

P

pace *n* **1** single step or its approximate length. **2** speed, esp. of walking or running. **put through one's paces** test (someone) for speed, talent, etc. ~*vi* walk with a regular step. *vt* measure out (distance) by pacing.

pacifism *n* opposition to or nonparticipation in warfare or violence. **pacifist** *n,adj*. **pacify** *vt* calm; soothe; placate; appease.

pack *n* **1** bundle; load; heap. **2** container; small package, as of cigarettes. **3** set of playing cards. **4** group of wolves, hounds, etc. **5** gang of people. **6** forwards in a Rugby team. **pack of lies** false story. ~*vt,vi* arrange (clothes, etc.) in a case, etc. *vt* **1** form into a bundle; roll up; put away. **2** crowd into; press together; cram. **3** make compact. **pack off** send away. **send packing** send away abruptly; dismiss. **packhorse** *n* horse used to carry supplies, goods, etc.

package *n* **1** parcel; object or objects in a container, wrapping, etc. **2** group of separate items, services, ideas, etc., offered for sale or acceptance as a single unit. *vt* make a package of or for; wrap. **packaging** *n* materials or containers and wrappings used to package goods.

packet *n* **1** small package. **2** *sl* large sum of money.

pact *n* agreement; treaty; contract.

pad[1] *n* **1** piece of material used to fill out, cushion, or protect. **2** fleshy cushion on the underside of an animal's paw or foot. **3** covering or guard to protect part of the body. **4** sheets of writing paper fastened together. **5** *sl* flat or residence, esp. a small one. *vt* (-dd-) **1** stuff, fill, or protect with soft cushion-like material. **2** expand or extend with irrelevant or unnecessary information. **padding** *n*.

pad[2] *vt,vi* (-dd-) traverse on foot; trudge. *n* soft dull sound.

paddle[1] *n* **1** short oar flattened at one or both ends used without rowlocks in small boats, canoes, etc. **2** structure or implement shaped like a paddle. **3** spell of paddling. *vt,vi* move on water using a paddle.

paddle[2] *vi* dabble one's feet or hands in shallow water. *n* act or instance of paddling.

paddock *n* **1** small field used for grazing horses. **2** enclosure where racehorses assemble before a race.

paddyfield *n also* **paddy** field used for growing rice.

padlock *n* detachable lock having a hinged loop released by a key. *vt* secure with a padlock.

paediatrics *n* branch of medicine dealing with children and childhood diseases. **paediatric** *adj*. **paediatrician** *n*.

pagan *adj* heathen; relating to a religion other than Christianity, Judaism, or Islam. *n* pagan person.

page[1] *n* one side of a leaf of a book, newspaper, etc.

page[2] *n* **1** attendant in a hotel, etc. **2** junior servant of a king or nobleman. **3** boy attendant at a wedding. *vt* summon by calling out a name over a public address system.

pageant *n* lavish public spectacle, procession, or play, esp. of historical significance. **pageantry** *n*.

pagoda *n* Oriental temple with a tower of concave sloping roofs.

paid *v pt* and *pp* of **pay.**

pain *n* **1** physical or mental distress or discomfort. **2** *sl also* **pain in the neck** irritating or annoying person or thing. *vt* hurt; cause to feel physical or mental distress. **painful** *adj*. **painfully** *adv*.

painstaking *adj* careful; meticulous. **painstakingly** *adv*.

paint *n* colouring or covering matter on or for a surface. *vt* **1** apply paint or liquid to. **2** represent or depict in words. *vt,vi* portray or design using paint. **painter** *n*. **painting** *n* **1** picture; artist's representation in paint. **2** art or procedure of applying paint to a canvas.

pair *n* **1** two matched objects designed to be used or worn together. **2** two persons, animals, things, etc., normally found together. **3** single object consisting of two similar interdependent parts. *vt,vi* arrange in twos; make a pair.

pal *n inf* friend; mate; chum. *v* (-ll-) **pal up** *inf* become friends.

palace *n* present or former residence of a royal family, bishop, or archbishop. **palatial** *adj*.

palate *n* **1** roof of the mouth. **2** sensitive or refined sense of taste, esp. for wine. **palatable** *adj* **1** agreeable to the taste. **2** acceptable to the mind.

pale *adj* **1** light in shade; lacking in colour. **2** faint; dim. *vi* lose importance or significance (before). **paleness** *n*.

palette *n* **1** flat board used by artists for mixing colours. **2** range of colours used by a particular artist or school of painters.

pallid *adj* pale; sickly looking. **pallor** *n*.

palm[1] *n* cushioned underside of the hand between the fingers and wrist. *v* **palm off** (**on**) pass to or impose by trickery; get rid of.

palm[2] *n* tropical and subtropical tree with a straight branchless trunk and a crest of large fan-shaped leaves at the top. **Palm Sunday** *n* Church festival on the Sunday before Easter commemorating Christ's triumphal entry into Jerusalem.

palmistry *n* practice or skill of foretelling the future by inspecting lines on the palm of the hand. **palmist** *n*.

pamper *vt* spoil; over-indulge.

pamphlet *n* leaflet or short publication containing information of current interest.

pan *n* **1** metal or earthenware vessel in which food is cooked or served. **2** container resembling such a vessel. *vt,vi* (-nn-) wash (sand, gravel, etc.) in a pan to separate out any gold, silver, etc. **pancake** *n* thin round cake of batter that is fried on both sides.

pancreas *n* gland situated near the stomach that secretes insulin.

panda *n* large black and white bearlike mammal that is native to China.

pander *v* **pander to** minister to or gratify vices, weakness, etc.

pane *n* sheet of glass cut to fit a window or door.

panel *n* **1** section of a wall, door, etc., when framed, raised, or sunk. **2** vertical strip of material in a dress, skirt, etc. **3** small group of persons meeting for a specific purpose. *vt* (-ll-) cover with or provide panels for.

pang *n* sharp stabbing pain.

panic *n* fear or terror, often resulting in rash ill-considered behaviour. *vi,vt* (-ck-) feel or cause to feel panic. **panic-stricken** *adj*.

panorama *n* uninterrupted view of a landscape spread over a wide area. **panoramic** *adj*.

pansy *n* **1** garden plant with white, yellow, purple, or red flowers. **2** *sl* homosexual.

pant *vi,vt* gasp for breath. *vi* long or yearn (for). *n* gasping noise.

panther *n* leopard, esp. a black leopard.

pantomime *n* traditional English Christmas entertainment for children.

pantry *n* room adjoining a kitchen with shelves for storing provisions, etc.

pants *pl n* undergarment covering area of the body from the waist to the thighs.

papal *adj* relating to the Pope or his official function.

paper *n* **1** material produced by processing wood, rags, etc., used for books, packaging, etc. **2** examination; essay; report. **3** newspaper. *vt* cover with paper or wallpaper. **paperback** *n* book in a cheap edition with a paper cover. **paperclip** *n* piece of twisted wire used to fasten single sheets of paper together. **paperwork** *n* routine clerical work.

papier-mâché *n* pulped paper used in making models, masks, etc.

papist *n abusive* follower of the Pope and the Roman Catholic faith.

paprika *n* powdered sweet red pepper.

par *n* **1** equality; equal or even footing; average or usual value or level. **2** (in golf) standard score. **at par** (of shares, etc.) at face value. **on a par with** equal or equivalent to.

parable *n* story designed to illustrate a moral or philosophical point; allegory.

parachute *n* device that assumes an umbrella shape to slow down the descent of a person jumping from an aircraft, etc. *vi,vt* descend or land by parachute.

parade *n* **1** procession; march. **2** show; ostentatious display. **3** promenade. *vi* walk or march (through) in or as in a procession. *vt* flaunt; exhibit openly.

paradise *n* heaven; state of bliss.

paradox *n* **1** statement that appears selfcontradictory or absurd. **2** person or thing having self-contradictory qualities. **paradoxical** *adj*. **paradoxically** *adv*.

paraffin *n* light oil distilled from petroleum, used for domestic heating and as aircraft fuel.

paragraph *n* subdivision of the printed page containing several sense-connected sentences and indicated by indentation of the first word.

parallel *adj* **1** remaining equidistant to infinity. **2** similar; analogous. *n* **1** comparable situation. **2** circle marking a degree of latitude. *vt* (-ll-) compare with; correspond to.

paralyse *vt* **1** immobilize or cripple through damage to or destruction of a nerve function. **2** transfix; make immobile. **paralysis** *n, pl* **paralyses** (pə'rælisi:z) pathological condition of crippling due to loss of muscle control. **paralytic** *adj,n*.

paramount *adj* chief; supreme; most important.

paranoia *n* mental disorder characterized by delusions of grandeur, persecution, etc. **paranoid** *adj,n*.

parapet *n* low protective wall built along the edge of a balcony, bridge, etc.

paraphernalia *n* **1** equipment; assorted personal possessions. **2** complicated procedure; rigmarole.

paraphrase *vt* express the sense of a passage by using other words. *n* passage thus reworded.

parasite *n* **1** animal or plant depending on another for sustenance. **2** person who lives off others. **parasitic** *adj*.

paratrooper *n* member of an army unit trained in parachute jumping.

parcel *n* wrapped object, esp. in paper. *vt* (-ll-) **1** make a parcel of. **2** divide (up); apportion.

parch *vt,vi* dry up. *vt* make thirsty.

parchment *n* **1** skin of a sheep or goat processed for use as paper. **2** old document.

pardon *vt* **1** forgive; excuse. **2** waive legal consequences of an offence for (a prisoner). *n* **1** forgiveness. **2** waiver of a penalty.

pare *vt* peel; skin; trim. **pare down** make smaller or more compact.

parent *n* **1** mother or father. **2** animal or plant that has produced one of its kind. **parental** *adj*. **parenthood** *n* state of being a parent.

parenthesis *n, pl* **parentheses** (pə'renθisi:z) either of a pair of characters used to separate or enclose matter in a written or printed text.

parish *n* ecclesiastical subdivision of a county with its own church and clergyman.

park *n* large enclosed area of land laid out for ornamental or recreational purposes. *vt,vi* position or leave (a car, etc.) in a place temporarily. *vt inf* put or leave.

parliament *n* democratic assembly of elected representatives constitutionally empowered to govern by legislation following free discussion. **parliamentary** *adj*.

parlour *n* sitting room or lounge.

parochial *adj* **1** relating to a parish. **2** provincial; limited; narrow.

parody *n* **1** imitation of a work or of an author or musician's style with comic or satirical intent. **2** poor imitation; travesty. *vt* imitate; mock.

parole *n* **1** early or temporary release from prison on condition of good behaviour. **2** period of such release. *vt* grant parole to.

parrot *n* brightly coloured tropical bird capable of imitating human speech.

parsley *n* mildly aromatic herb with curly green leaves.

parsnip *n* white tapering root vegetable.

parson *n* clergyman; minister. **parsonage** *n* residence of a clergyman.

part *n* **1** portion; piece; segment; component. **2** role; responsibility; duty. **3** actor's role. **4** melodic line in choral or orchestral music. **5** *also* **parts** region; area. **take part in** become involved in; join in. ~*vt,vi* **1** divide; separate; come, break, or take apart. **2** leave or stop seeing one another; keep apart. **part with** give up; relinquish. ~*adv* partially; in part. **partly** *adv*. **parting** *n* **1** leave-taking; separation. **2** division; splitting up. **3** line between two sections of hair that have been combed in opposite directions. **part-time** *adj,adv* for or during less than normal working time.

partake *vi* (-took; -taken) **1** participate. **2** have or receive a share or portion.

partial *adj* **1** incomplete; relating to a part. **2** biased; unfair. **3** having a liking for; fond of. **partially** *adv*.

participate *vi* take part (in); share (in). **participant** *n*. **participation** *n*.

participle *n* adjective derived from various verb forms, e.g. *laughing, loving, given,* or *written*.

particle *n* **1** tiniest visible portion; speck. **2** microscopic body of matter.

particular *adj* **1** relating to a single person, object, etc. **2** extraordinary; notable. **3** careful, fastidious; exact. **particulars** *pl n* details, features. **particularly** *adv*.

partisan *n* **1** supporter of a party, cause, etc. **2** guerrilla fighter in enemy-occupied territory.

partition *n* **1** division; separation into parts. **2** structure erected to separate rooms, areas, etc. *vt* divide into parts; separate.

partner *n* **1** associate; colleague; member of a partnership. **2** one of a pair in dancing, cards, etc. *vt* join with someone, esp. in a game or dance. **partnership** *n* legal relationship between two or more persons operating a joint business venture.

partridge *n* small European game bird.

party *n* **1** group united by a common belief or purpose, esp. political. **2** social gathering. **3** person or persons involved in a legal action.

pass *vt,vi* **1** go by or through; move ahead or on; proceed. **2** move or cause to move. **3** exchange or be exchanged. **4** undergo (an exam, trial, etc.) with favourable results. **5** elapse or allow to elapse. *vt* **1** hand over; transfer; throw. **2** surpass; exceed. **3** pronounce; utter. **4** adopt, approve (legislation, etc.). *vi* happen; occur; come to an end. **pass out** faint. ~*n* **1** favourable examination result, without honours. **2** ticket, authorization, etc., to enter or leave at will, without charge, etc. **3** critical position. **4** narrow passage between mountains. **5** amorous advance. **passable** *adj* **1** able to be crossed, passed, etc. **2** mediocre; fairly good. **password** *n* prearranged word used as a code for entry, etc.

passage *n* **1** corridor; channel; route. **2** state of transit; voyage; journey. **3** section of a book, etc **passenger** *n* **1** person travelling in but not controlling a motor vehicle, boat, etc. **2** *sl* person in a team, etc. who does not do his share of the work.

passion *n* **1** intense or ardent emotion. **2** strong liking or enthusiasm. **3** object of such liking. **passionate** *adj*. **passionately** *adv*.

passive *adj* **1** inactive; inert; not participating. **2** submissive; yielding. **3** denoting a sentence or construction in which the logical subject of a verb is the recipient of the action. **passively** *adv*.

Passover *n* Jewish festival commemorating the deliverance of the Hebrews from Egypt.

passport *n* official document issued by a country that identifies the bearer, permits his travel abroad, and requests safe passage while there.

past *adj* **1** relating to an earlier time; gone by; just over; finished. **2** previous; former. **3** relating to a verb tense used to express an action or condition occurring in the past. *n* **1** period prior to the present; past time. **2** person's past life, career, activities, etc. *prep* beyond. *adv* by; ago. **past participle** *n* verb form functioning as an adjective or used with an auxiliary verb to denote past or completed action, e.g. *grown, written,* or *spoken*.

pasta *n* food, such as spaghetti, macaroni, etc. made from a flour and water dough and boiled.

paste *n* **1** pliable, malleable, or sticky mess. **2** preparation of meat, fish, etc. mashed to a spreadable consistency. **3** glue; adhesive. *vt* stick, fix or cover with paste.

pastel *n* **1** crayon made from colour pigments and gum. **2** drawing made with these crayons. *adj* pale; light.

pasteurize *vt* partially sterilize (milk, beer, etc.) by heating in order to kill bacteria, limit fermentation, etc. **pasteurization** *n*.

pastime *n* recreation; amusement; hobby.

pastoral *adj* **1** of the country; rural. **2** (of land) used for grazing. **3** peaceful; idyllic. **4** relating to a clergyman or his duties.

pastry *n* **1** flour paste used for pies, tarts, etc. **2** baked foods.

pasture *n* **1** grass, etc., suitable for grazing cattle. **2** meadow; field. *vt* put to pasture.

pasty[1] ('peɪstɪ) *adj* **1** relating to paste. **2** (of a person's appearance) pale, unhealthy, white-skinned.

pasty[2] ('pæstɪ) *n* small pie filled with meat, vegetables, etc.

pat[1] *vt* (-tt-) **1** tap; touch lightly. **2** stroke softly; caress. **3** flatten by beating gently. *n* light blow; slap; tap.

pat[2] *adj* **1** apt; perfect. **2** presumptuous; glib. *adv* **1** exactly; perfectly. **2** aptly.

patch *n* **1** piece of material used to repair something. **2** irregular or small area, piece, plot of land, etc. **3** protective covering for an eye, etc. *vt* repair; mend. **patchwork** *n* **1** patches of material stitched together to form a pattern. **2** something made of different parts, pieces, etc.

pâté *n* paste or spread made from liver, meat, fish, etc.

patent ('pætn̩t) *n* **1** government permit granting sole rights for an invention, process, etc., for a set period of time. **2** something under such a permit. *adj* ('peɪtn̩t) obvious; evident. **patent leather** *n* leather treated to produce a hard lacquered appearance. ~*vt* obtain a patent for.

paternal *adj* **1** fatherly; characteristic of a father. **2** pertaining to a father or a father's side of a family. **paternally** *adv*. **paternity** *n* **1** fatherhood. **2** descent from a father.

path *n* **1** *also* **pathway** track worn by pedestrians, animals, etc. **2** walk in a park, garden, etc. **3** means; procedure; course of action.

pathetic *adj* **1** pitiful; evoking sadness. **2** *inf* poor; of low quality. **pathetically** *adv*.

pathology *n* study of diseases. **pathological** *adj*. **pathologist** *n*.

patience *n* ability to persevere or endure without complaint.

patient *n* person under the care of a doctor, dentist, etc. *adj* marked by or exhibiting patience. **patiently** *adv*.

patio *n* paved area adjoining a house.

patriarch *n* **1** male head of a family, tribe, etc. **2** elder; senior member of a community. **3** any of several Old Testament personages regarded as a father of the human race. **4** bishop of the Eastern Orthodox Church. **patriarchal** *adj*.

patriot *n* person who loves his country intensely. **patriotic** *adj*. **patriotism** *n*.

patrol *n* **1** regular inspection of an area or building to ensure security, orderliness, etc. **2** person or persons carrying out this inspection.

3 military detachment with the duty of reconnaissance. *vt,vi* (-ll-) take part in a patrol (of).

patron *n* **1** regular customer of a shop, etc. **2** one who offers financial support to a cultural or educational enterprise. **patronage** *n* **1** support given by a patron. **2** trade given a business by its customers. **3** power to bestow political favours, make appointments, etc. **patronize** *vt* **1** visit regularly; support. **2** behave condescendingly (towards someone). **3** be a benefactor of; sponsor.

patter[1] *n* **1** glib inconsequential speech. **2** rapidly delivered lines of a salesman, comedian, etc. **3** *inf* jargon; expressions used by a clique. *vi,vt* talk glibly, rapidly, etc.

patter[2] *vi* **1** make a sound like tapping. **2** walk with a patter. *n* light tapping sound.

pattern *n* **1** design; arrangement. **2** example; model; plan. **3** usual way of doing something. *vt* model after a pattern; imitate.

pause *n* temporary stop or break. *vi* **1** stop temporarily. **2** hesitate; linger.

pave *vt* **1** cover (a road, etc.) with a hard surface. **2** prepare; facilitate. **pavement** *n* paved path for pedestrians alongside a road.

pavilion *n* **1** building on a sportsground housing changing rooms, etc. **2** large tent erected temporarily at fairs, weddings, etc. **3** summerhouse; light ornamental building or structure.

paw *n* foot of certain mammals, esp. cats and dogs. *vi,vt* touch or strike with a paw or leg. *vt inf* caress clumsily; grope.

pawn[1] *vt* leave (an article) as security in exchange for a loan until repayment is made. **pawnbroker** *n* person who lends money on security of personal possessions.

pawn[2] *n* **1** chessman of least value whose second and subsequent moves are limited to one square in a forward direction. **2** manipulated person.

pay *v* (paid) *vt,vi* **1** give (money, etc.) to for, or in return for; recompense. **2** discharge (a debt, etc.). **3** *also* **pay off** be profitable or worthwhile; benefit. *vt* **1** bestow; give. **2** make (a visit, etc.). **pay back 1** repay (a loan, etc.). **2** retaliate against. **pay for** suffer or be punished because of. **pay off 1** pay wages of and discharge. **2** pay in total. ~*n* **1** money paid for work; salary; wages. **2** paid employment. **payment** *n* **1** act of paying. **2** sum of money paid. **3** due reward. **payoff** *n* **1** *inf* outcome; climax of events. **2** full payment. **payroll** *n* **1** list of employees to be paid and their salaries or wages. **2** total of or amount equal to a company's salary or wage expenditure.

pea *n* annual climbing plant whose round green seeds are eaten as a vegetable.

peace *n* **1** state of amity; absence of war. **2** tranquillity; period of rest or quiet. **peaceful** *adj*. **peacefully** *adv*.

peach *n* tree yielding a round juicy yellowish fruit with down-covered skin. *n,adj* bright pinkish-yellow.

peacock *n* brightly coloured male of a large pheasant with a crested head and a tail which can fan out to display bright blue and green markings. **peahen** *f n*.

peak *n* **1** any pointed edge or projection. **2** top of a mountain; summit. **3** projecting brim of a cap. **4** sharp increase or the highest point or value reached. *vi* reach the highest point or value. **peaked** *adj*.

peal *n* loud resounding sound, such as bells ringing, laughter, or thunder. *vt,vi* sound with a peal; ring out.

peanut *n* edible seed rich in food value and yielding oil.

pear *n* tree yielding a sweet juicy fruit whose shape is rounded and tapers towards the stalk.

pearl *n* **1** smooth lustrous creamy precious gem formed on the inside of a clam or oyster shell or synthesized. **2** highly valued person or thing. **pearly** *adj*.

peasant *n* **1** agricultural labourer; countryman; rustic. **2** *inf* uncultured and unsophisticated person. **peasantry** *n*.

peat *n* solid partially carbonized and decomposed vegetable matter used as a garden fertilizer and a fuel. **peaty** *adj*.

pebble *n* small rounded stone. *vt,vi* pave or cover with pebbles. **pebbly** *adj*.

peck *vt* **1** strike with the beak or something sharp. **2** *inf* kiss quickly on the cheek. *n* **1** quick strike or blow. **2** *inf* quick kiss on the cheek.

peckish *adj inf* hungry.

peculiar *adj* strange; odd; unusual. **peculiar to** special or specific to. **peculiarity** *n*. **peculiarly** *adv*.

pedal *n* foot lever of a machine, bicycle, piano, etc. *vt,vi* (-ll-) **1** operate by using pedals. **2** ride a bicycle.

peddle *vt,vi* sell from door to door; hawk. **pedlar** *n*.

pedestal *n* **1** plinth or base supporting an upright object. **2** position of superiority or eminence.

pedestrian *n* person who goes about on foot. *adj* plodding; dull; unimaginative.

pedigree *n* **1** record of an animal's ancestors, kept esp. for animals of good breeding. **2** animal of pedigree stock. **3** ancestral line. **pedigreed** *adj*.

peel *n* rind; outer layer of fruit, vegetables, etc. *vt,vi* strip or whittle (off) an outer skin or surface.

peep *vi* **1** look quickly or furtively. **2** appear briefly or partially. *n* quick look or glance.

peer[1] *n* **1** member of the nobility. **2** person equal in rank or social standing. **peerage** *n* **1** nobility as a group. **2** position, rank, or title of a peer.

peer[2] *vi* **1** look closely or intently (at). **2** appear partially; peep.

peevish *adj* irritable; bad-tempered. **peevishly** *adv*. **peevishness** *n*.

peg *n* **1** small piece of wood or metal used for hanging or fastening things. **2** pin or stake pushed into the ground, a scoreboard, or other surface. **3** pin on a guitar, violin, etc., used for tuning the strings. **4** hinged or grooved pin for hanging clothes on a line. **take down a peg** teach a lesson; humble. **off the peg** (of clothes) ready-made. ~*vt* (-gg-) **1** pierce with or insert a peg. **2** secure with a peg.

pejorative *adj* deprecatory; uncomplimentary.

pelican *n* water bird with white plumage and a large beak with a pouch used for catching fish.

pellet *n* **1** small ball of something solid. **2** piece of shot.

pelmet *n* wood or fabric used to conceal a curtain rail.

pelt[1] *n* skin or hide of a fur-bearing animal.

pelt[2] *vt* assail with a shower of missiles, blows, abuse, etc. *n* blow; knock; stroke.

pelvis *n* cavity or structure found in the lower part of the trunk in most vertebrates. **pelvic** *adj*.

pen[1] *n* instrument with a pointed nib used for writing with ink. **penfriend** *n* person, often living in a different country, with whom one corresponds. **penknife** *n* small folding knife usually carried in the pocket.

pen[2] *n* small enclosure for farm animals. *vt* (-nn-) enclose in a pen; confine.

penal *adj* relating to punishment, esp. for breaking a law. **penal code** *n* body of criminal law. **penalize** *vt* **1** punish; subject to penalty. **2** handicap; disadvantage. **3** award a point or points to an opposing team. **penalization** *n*. **penalty** *n* **1** punishment; price exacted as a punishment. **2** loss; suffering. **3** free kick at goal afforded to one football team because of a breach of rules by the other. **penance** *n* **1** self-imposed punishment. **2** regret; sorrow.

pence *n pl of* **penny** (def. 3).

penchant ('pɑːnʃɑːn) *n* liking; strong inclination.

pencil *n* writing instrument consisting of a thin rod of graphite encased in wood. *vt* (-ll-) write or draw with a pencil.

pendant *n* **1** hanging ornament, esp. on a necklace. **2** hanging lamp or chandelier.

pending *adj* about to be decided, confirmed, completed, etc. *prep* while waiting for.

pendulum *n* suspended weight that swings back and forth under the influence of gravity.

penetrate *vt,vi* **1** pass into or through. **2** enter or permeate. *vt* **1** see through. **2** unravel; understand. *vi* be understood. **penetrable** *adj*. **penetration** *n*.

penguin *n* large flightless black and white aquatic bird of Antarctica.

penicillin *n* antibiotic drug produced from a mould and capable of preventing the growth of certain bacteria.

peninsula *n* strip of land jutting into the sea. **peninsular** *adj*.

penis *n* male organ of copulation.

penitent *adj* repentent; remorseful. *n* penitent person. **penitence** *n*. **penitently** *adv*.

penniless *adj* having no money; very poor; destitute.

penny *n* **1** *also* **new penny** bronze coin worth one-hundredth of a pound sterling. **2** former bronze coin worth one-twelfth of a shilling. **3** *pl* **pence** unit of currency of such a value. **not worth a penny** worthless. **spend a penny** *inf* urinate.

pension *n* periodical payment by state or employer to the retired, disabled, widowed, etc. *vt* grant a pension to. **pensioner** *n* person receiving a pension.

pensive *adj* engaged in serious or sad thought. **pensively** *adv*.
pentagon *n* five-sided figure. **pentagonal** *adj*.
penthouse *n* subsidiary structure attached to the main part of a building, often a small house or flat on the roof.
penury *n* poverty; destitution.
people *pl n* **1** human beings in general. **2** racial group. **3** one's family. *vt* populate; fill as with people.
pepper *n* **1** pungent condiment made from the dried berries of a pepper plant. **2** red or green slightly pungent fruit of other types of pepper plant. *vt* flavour with pepper. **peppercorn** *n* dried berry of the pepper plant. **peppermill** *n* instrument for grinding peppercorns. **peppermint** *n* **1** aromatic and pungent herb of the mint family. **2** lozenge flavoured with oil from this mint.
per *prep* **1** for each. **2** by means of.
perambulator *n formal* pram.
perceive *vt* **1** see; discern. **2** be or become aware of. **3** understand. **perceivable** *adj*.
per cent *adv* in each hundred.
percentage *n* **1** number forming a proportion in each hundred. **2** interest paid per hundred.
perception *n* **1** process or power of becoming aware of something. **2** insight; discernment. **perceptible** *adj* noticeable; discernible. **perceptive** *adj* **1** able or quick to notice. **2** intelligent. **perceptively** *adv*.
perch[1] *n, pl* **perch** edible spiny-finned freshwater fish.
perch[2] *n* **1** pole, bar, or branch for birds to roost or sit on. **2** secure seat in a high position. *vi,vt* sit or place on a perch.
percolate *vt,vi* filter or trickle (through). *vi* gradually become known. **percolator** *n* apparatus for percolating water through coffee grounds.
percussion *n* **1** impact; collision. **2** production of noise by striking or tapping. **3** musical instruments, such as the drum, that are struck to produce a note.
perennial *adj* **1** continuing through the year or from year to year. **2** (of plants) living more than two years. **3** perpetual. **perennially** *adv*.
perfect *adj* ('pə:fikt) faultless; complete; functioning correctly; exact. *vt* (pə'fekt) make perfect or complete; finish. **perfection** *n*. **perfectly** *adv*.
perforate *vt,vi* make a hole or holes through, often in a line for easy separation. **perforation** *n*.
perform *vt,vi* **1** do; carry out; complete. **2** act. **performer** *n*. **performance** *n* **1** act of performing; carrying out of something. **2** piece of work; exhibition or entertainment. **3** manner or achievement in working.
perfume *n* **1** sweet-smelling substance applied to the body. **2** pleasant odour; fragrance. *vt* impart fragrance to.
perhaps *adv* maybe; possibly.
peril *n* danger; risk. **perilous** *adj*. **perilously** *adv*.
perimeter *n* circumference; boundary; length of outline of a plane figure.
period *n* **1** stretch of time; phase; era. **2** interval between recurrent phases. **3** full stop. **4** *inf* menstruation. **periodic** *adj*. **periodical** *adj* periodic; issued or occurring at roughly regular intervals. *n* magazine published at stated intervals of more than one day. **periodically** *adv*.
peripheral *adj* **1** of or on the circumference, boundary, or outskirts. **2** of less than central importance. **periphery** *n*.
periscope *n* tube with mirrors for viewing objects above eye level.
perish *vt* destroy; ruin; cause to decay. *vi* **1** die; decay; be ruined or destroyed. **2** distress with hunger and cold. **perishable** *adj*.
perjure *vt* **perjure oneself** lie deliberately under oath. **perjurer** *n*. **perjury** *n*.
perk *v* **perk up 1** look up jauntily. **2** make (oneself) smarter. **3** recover spirits or energy. *n inf* legitimate extra gain attached to a job, not included in wages.
permanent *adj* lasting or intended to last indefinitely. *n also inf* **perm** artificially induced and long-lasting waving of the hair. **permanently** *adv*.
permeate *vt,vi* spread through, pervade, or be pervaded. **permeation** *n*.
permission *n* act of permitting; allowing; consent. **permissible** *adj*. **permissive** *adj* granting permission or liberty; lenient; tolerant. **permissively** *adv*. **permissiveness** *n*.
permit *vt,vi* (pə'mit) (-tt-) grant leave; allow; concede; make possible. *n* ('pə:mit) written permission; warrant; licence.
permutation *n* **1** changing of the order of a set of objects. **2** each arrangement of these objects.

peroxide *n* **1** oxide containing more oxygen than normal oxide. **2** *inf* hydrogen peroxide, an antiseptic and bleach.

perpendicular *adj* upright; vertical; at right angles (to). *n* vertical position; perpendicular line. **perpendicularly** *adv*.

perpetual *adj* **1** never ceasing; not temporary. **2** continuously blooming through the growing season. **3** applicable or valid for ever or for an indefinite time. **perpetually** *adv*. **perpetuate** *vt* **1** make perpetual. **2** prolong indefinitely. **3** preserve from extinction or oblivion. **perpetuity** *n* quality or condition of lasting indefinitely.

perplex *vt* confuse; present difficulties or intricacies to bewilder; tease with suspense or doubt. **perplexity** *n*.

persecute *vt* **1** harass; treat cruelly; persistently attack. **persecution** *n*.

persevere *vi* continue in spite of obstacles; keep on striving. **perseverance** *n*.

persist *vi* **1** continue firmly or obstinately, esp. against opposition. **2** continue to exist; remain. **persistence** *n*. **persistent** *adj*. **persistently** *adv*.

person *n* **1** human being. **2** body of a person. **in person** physically present or active. **personal** *adj* **1** one's own; individual; of private concern. **2** relating to bodily appearance. **3** offensive to an individual; insulting. **personally** *adv*. **personality** *n* **1** state of having an identity. **2** celebrity. **3** total intellectual, emotional, or physical qualities of an individual, esp. as presented to others. **personify** *vt* **1** regard as a person. **2** embody; symbolize in human form. **personification** *n*.

personnel *n* persons engaged together in some work; work force.

perspective *n* **1** method of portraying relative size and distance of objects on a plane surface. **2** relative importance and true relationship of facts, ideas, etc.

perspex *n* tough transparent unsplinterable plastic material.

perspire *vi,vt* exude moisture through skin pores; sweat. **perspiration** *n*.

persuade *vt* induce by argument; cause to believe; convince. **persuasion** *n*. **persuasive** *adj*. **persuasively** *adv*.

pert *adj* **1** forward; saucy; cheeky. **2** open; brisk; flourishing. **pertly** *adv*.

pertain *vi* **1** belong as part of; be connected with. **2** have reference or relevance to. **3** be suitable for or appropriate to. **pertinent** *adj*. **pertinently** *adv*.

perturb *vt* disturb greatly; cause alarm or anxiety to. **perturbation** *n*.

pervade *vt* penetrate; diffuse through the whole of; permeate. **pervasion** *n*. **pervasive** *adj*.

perverse *adj* obstinately turning aside from right or truth; unreasonably contradictory. **perversely** *adv*. **perversion** *n*. **pervert** *vt,vi* (pəˈvəːt) turn from proper use or sense; corrupt or be corrupted. *n* (ˈpəːvəːt) one who is thought to deviate in sexual desires or practice. **perversion** *n*.

peseta *n* monetary unit of Spain.

peso *n* monetary unit of Argentina, Mexico, the Philippines, and various other countries.

pessimism *n* tendency to look on the worst side of things; despondency. **pessimist** *n*. **pessimistic** *adj*.

pest *n* **1** troublesome or destructive person, etc. **2** insect, fungus, etc., destructive of cultivated plants. **pesticide** *n* chemical for destroying pests.

pester *vt* cause slight but repeated annoyance to.

pet[1] *n* **1** tame animal kept as a companion, etc. **2** favourite; dearly loved and pampered person, esp. a child; darling. *v* (-tt-) *vt* treat as a pet; pamper; fondle. *vi* indulge in amorous caressing.

pet[2] *n* childish fit of aggrieved sulkiness; huff. *vi* (-tt-) be peevish; sulk.

petal *n* leaflike part, sometimes brightly coloured, of a flower.

peter *v* **peter out** gradually diminish to nothing; fade away.

petition *n* **1** humble or solemn entreaty. **2** formal request to an authority often signed by a number of persons. *vt,vi* make or receive a humble or formal request.

petrify *vt,vi* **1** turn into or become like stone; fossilize. **2** fix in amazement or horror.

petrol *n* inflammable liquid from refined petroleum, used esp. as fuel in motor-vehicle engines.

petroleum *n* dark thick oily mixture of hydrocarbons, other organic compounds, etc., found in rock deposits.

petticoat *n* woman's underskirt.

petty *adj* **1** unimportant; trivial; insignificant. **2** contemptible, spiteful, or mean over small matters. **petty cash** *n* cash fund in an office for small items of receipt or expenditure. **petty officer** *n* noncommissioned naval officer. **pettiness** *n*.

petulant *adj* peevishly impatient, irritated, or capricious. **petulance** *n*. **petulantly** *adv*.

pew *n* enclosed compartment or fixed bench with a back and sides, as in a church.

pewter *n* **1** alloy of tin and lead and sometimes other metals. **2** vessel, plate, or utensil made of pewter.

pfennig *n, pl* **pfennigs** *or* **pfennige** (ˈpfenigə) West German copper coin equal to one hundredth of a mark.

phallus *n* **1** male sexual organ; penis. **2** representation of the penis. **phallic** *adj*.

phantom *n* **1** supernatural apparition; ghost; immaterial form. **2** visual illusion.

pharmacy *n* **1** art or practice of preparing and dispensing medicines. **2** chemist's dispensary. **pharmacist** *n*. **pharmaceutical** *adj* relating to medical drugs.

pharynx *n* cavity behind nose and mouth forming the upper part of the gullet and the opening into the larynx.

phase *n* **1** transitory stage in a cycle. **2** appearance of a moon or planet at a particular stage of its orbit. **3** aspect or appearance of anything at any stage. *vt* separate into stages of activity or development. **phase out** bring to terminal stage; extinguish gradually; discontinue.

pheasant *n* **1** long-tailed game bird, brightly coloured in the male. **2** flesh of this bird as food.

phenomenon *n, pl* **phenomena** (fəˈnominə) **1** anything perceived by the senses; observed event. **2** anything striking or exceptional. **phenomenal** *adj* of or like a phenomenon; extraordinary; exceptional; remarkable. **phenomenally** *adv*.

philanthropy *n* benevolence; active generosity in social action; love of mankind. **philanthropic** *adj*. **philanthropist** *n*.

philately *n* study and collection of postage and revenue stamps. **philatelist** *n*.

philosophy *n* **1** study of the ultimate nature of existence. **2** any specified system of thought in this. **3** general mental and moral outlook on life; reasoning. **philosopher** *n*. **philosophical** *adj* **1** relating to philosophy or philosophers. **2** calmly reasonable; wise. **3** stoical; bearing misfortune well.

phlegm (flem) *n* **1** thick slimy fluid secreted in the throat and chest and discharged by coughing. **2** apathy; sluggish indifference. **phlegmatic** (flegˈmætik) *adj* **1** not easily excited or perturbed; placid. **2** sluggish; apathetic; stolid. **phlegmatically** *adv*.

phobia *n* fear, often irrational; dread; dislike.

phoenix *n* bird fabled to burn itself to death every 500 years and be reincarnated from its own ashes.

phone *n,vt,vi* short for **telephone.**

phonetic *adj* relating to the sounds of spoken language. **phonetically** *adv*. **phonetics** *n* study of speech sounds.

phoney *adj* counterfeit; unreal; insincere.

phosphate *n* chemical salt containing phosphorus, used in fertilizers.

phosphorescent *adj* emitting a faint light, similar to fluorescence, esp. after bombardment by radiation. **phosphorescence** *n*.

phosphorus *n* nonmetallic chemical element having an unreactive red form and a toxic inflammable phosphorescent white form, used in matches.

photo *n* short for **photograph.**

photocopy *vt* reproduce an exact copy of by a photographic process. *n* copy produced in this way.

photogenic *adj* suitable for and making a pleasing photograph.

photograph *n* image of something produced by the action of light on chemically sensitized surfaces. *vt* make a photographic image of. **photographer** *n*. **photography** *n* art or process of producing photographs. **photographical** *adj*.

phrase *n* **1** group of words forming a subdivision of a sentence. **2** idiomatic expression. *vt* choose fitting words to express. **phrasebook** *n* collection of idioms and commonly used phrases of a language.

physical *adj* **1** pertaining to the natural world of matter and energy or its study. **2** relating to the body. **physically** *adv*. **physical education** *n* promotion of bodily fitness by exercising the body.

physician *n* doctor; person legally qualified to treat disease by medicines but not surgery.

physics *n* study of the properties of matter and energy. **physicist** *n*.

physiology *n* study of physical processes in living beings. **physiological** *adj*. **physiologist** *n*.

physiotherapy *n* treatment of disease, weakness, or disability by exercise, massage, heat, etc. **physiotherapist** *n*.

physique *n* bodily appearance and constitution.

pi *n* ratio of the circumference of a circle to its diameter, equal to about 3.142.

piano *n* keyboard instrument with strings struck by hammers. **pianist** *n*.

piccolo *n* small high-pitched woodwind instrument of the flute family.

pick[1] *vt,vi* **1** choose; select carefully. **2** gather (fruit, etc.). *vt* **1** poke at with the fingers. **2** provoke. **3** steal from (a pocket, etc.). **pick and choose** select with excessive care. **pick at** nibble at food, esp. due to loss of appetite. **pick on** select, esp. to blame or be unpleasant to. **pick out 1** select. **2** recognize; distinguish; make obvious. **pick up 1** lift or gather in the hands. **2** improve. **3** take on (passengers, etc.). **4** learn gradually and casually. **5** *inf* meet casually and get acquainted. **6** *inf* arrest. ~*n* **1** choice; selection. **2** best choice. **pickpocket** *n* one who steals from others' pockets. **pick-up** *n* **1** device for converting vibrations, as of a record-player stylus, into electric current. **2** recovery. **3** act of picking up or one picked up.

pick[2] *n* **1** *also* **pickaxe** tool having a long cross-bar with sharp or pointed ends, used for breaking up stone, etc. **2** any sharp or pointed instrument for picking.

picket *n* **1** striker or group of strikers outside their workplace to dissuade other workers from working. **2** vigil in a public place by a person or group expressing political or social protest. *vt,vi* surround with or act as a picket.

pickle *n* **1** brine or vinegar solution in which food is preserved. **2** vegetable so preserved. **3** *inf* plight. *vt* preserve in pickle. **pickled** *adj sl* drunk.

picnic *vi* (picnicking; picnicked) take a casual meal outdoors for pleasure. *n* **1** meal so eaten. **2** outing for such a purpose.

pictorial *adj* **1** having or expressed by pictures. **2** relating to painting or drawing. *n* magazine comprising mainly pictures. **pictorially** *adv*.

picture *n* **1** two-dimensional arrangement of lines and colours intended to have aesthetic value. **2** embodiment; representation; mental image. **3** impressive sight. **4** film shown at a cinema. **5** vivid verbal description. **in the picture** well-informed; in possession of the facts. **the pictures** *pl n* cinema. ~*vt* depict or represent in a picture, the mind, or in words.

picturesque *adj* suitable for a picture; graphic; quaint.

pidgin *n* trade language or jargon having elements from two or more languages.

pie *n* dish of meat, fish, vegetables, or fruit baked with a pastry covering. **easy as pie** very easy.

piece *n* **1** part or item of a whole; bit; portion. **2** example; specimen. **3** musical, artistic, or literary composition. **4** small object, as used in board games. **go to pieces 1** lose one's self-control. **2** disintegrate. **piecemeal** *adv* bit by bit; in pieces. **piecework** *n* work paid according to the amount done rather than the time taken. *v* **piece together** assemble; fit together; mend.

pier *n* **1** jetty; landing stage; breakwater. **2** column supporting an arch or bridge. **3** load-bearing brickwork between windows or doors.

pierce *vt* **1** penetrate; make a hole in; enter or force a way into. **2** be seen, heard, or felt through. **3** afflict; touch or move deeply.

piety *n* willing and devout observance of religious duties; devotion to God.

pig *n* **1** domesticated mammal with thick bristly skin and a long snout, bred for its meat. **2** coarse, dirty, or greedy person. **pig in a poke** something bought without examination. **pigheaded** *adj* stupidly stubborn; obstinate. **pigheadedly** *adv*. **pig-iron** *n* iron in rough bars as first extracted from its ore. **piglet** *n* young pig. **pigsty** *n* **1** pen in which pigs are kept. **2** very untidy or dirty house or room. **pigtail** *n* hair twisted into a bunch to form a plait or hang loose.

pigeon *n* widely distributed bird of the dove family. **pigeonhole** *n* **1** small compartment for storing or classifying papers. **2** compartment of the mind. **3** entrance to a dovecote or pigeon's nest. *vt* **1** put in a pigeonhole. **2** put aside; defer considering. **3** classify methodically.

piggyback *n* ride astride someone's back or shoulders. *adv* on someone's back or shoulders.

pigment *n* paint; any colouring matter; substance giving colour to living tissue. **pigmentation** *n* coloration by pigments.

pike *n, pl* **pike** large voracious freshwater fish with a pointed snout.

pilchard *n* small food fish, similar to the herring.

pile[1] *n* **1** heap of objects. **2** *inf* large sum or amount of money, work, etc. *vt,vi also* **pile up.** heap up; collect into a mound. *vi* move quickly and haphazardly as in a group. **pile-up** *n inf* accumulation of things, esp. of cars as a result of a multiple crash, traffic jam, etc.

pile[2] *n* post driven into the ground to support a structure. **piledriver** *n* **1** machine for driving piles into the ground. **2** (in games) powerful stroke; kick.

pile[3] *n* **1** fine soft hair; down. **2** raised yarn on cloth such as velvet or towelling.

pilfer *vt,vi* steal petty articles in small quantities.

pilgrim *n* **1** person journeying to a shrine for religious reasons. **2** wanderer. **pilgrimage** *n* journey to a sacred or revered place. **Pilgrim Fathers** *pl n* original settlers of New England.

pill *n* oral medicine formed into or contained in a small ball, capsule, etc. **bitter pill** something disagreeable that has to be accepted. **the pill** contraceptive pill.

pillar *n* **1** column supporting a structure or standing alone as a monument. **2** person who is a prominent supporter. **pillar-box** *n* short hollow red pillar in which letters are posted; letter box.

pillion *n* seat for a second person on a horse or motorcycle behind the rider or driver. *adv* on a pillion.

pillow *n* soft cushion to support a sleeper's head; padded support. *vt* rest one's head; serve as a pillow for. **pillowcase** *n* washable cover for a pillow.

pilot *n* **1** person qualified to conduct ships in harbours, channels, etc. **2** person qualified to operate flying controls of an aircraft. **3** person steering a ship. *vt* steer; navigate; guide. **pilot scheme** preliminary, experimental, or trial approach or procedure.

pimento *n* red pepper used for stuffing olives, in salads, and as a vegetable.

pimple *n* small swelling on the skin. **pimply** *adj.*

pin *n* **1** short stiff pointed piece of wire with a rounded or flat head. **2** anything resembling a pin in form or function. **3** brooch; badge. *vt* (-nn-) **1** fasten, attach, or secure by a pin. **2** hold or fix in position; immobilize. **pin down 1** force to keep a promise, agreement, etc. **2** define exactly. **pin on** attribute to; blame. **pinpoint** *n* **1** point of a pin. **2** anything very tiny or minute. *vt* locate; define very exactly. **pinstripes** *n* repeated narrow stripes in a material pattern, etc. **pin-up** *n* **1** picture of a nude or seminude girl pinned up on wall. **2** one whose picture is thus displayed.

pinafore *n* apron. **pinafore dress** *n* sleeveless dress worn over a jumper, etc.

pincers *pl n* **1** gripping tool with jaws and handles on a pivot. **2** pair of grasping clawlike parts, as in a crab. **pincer movement** *n* attack by two converging forces.

pinch *vt,vi* **1** squeeze sharply between finger and thumb or be squeezed between two hard objects. **2** inconvenience or be inconvenienced by a lack (of something). *vt* **1** *sl* steal. **2** *sl* arrest. *n* **1** squeeze. **2** emergency. **3** small amount. **at a pinch** if absolutely necessary.

pine[1] *n* coniferous tree with evergreen needle-shaped leaves.

pine[2] *vi* **1** become feeble from mental or physical suffering. **2** languish with longing; yearn (for).

pineapple *n* tropical plant yielding a large edible fruit having yellow flesh and a tuft of leaves on top.

Ping-Pong *n Tdmk* table-tennis.

pinion *n* small wheel with teeth engaging with a larger wheel or rack, one imparting motion to the other.

pink *adj,n* pale red; light rose. *n* garden plant resembling the carnation.

pinnacle *n* **1** small ornamental turret or spire. **2** slender mountain peak. **3** highest point or degree. *vt* **1** set on a pinnacle. **2** adorn with pinnacles.

pint *n* **1** measure of liquid capacity equal to an eighth of a gallon (0.57 litre). **2** *inf* this amount of beer.

pioneer *n* one of the first to attempt, explore, research, or colonize; one who takes the lead. *vt,vi* be or act as a pioneer.

pious *adj* devout; faithful in religious duties. **piously** *adv.*

pip[1] *n* small seed of fleshy fruits.

pip[2] *n* shrill note repeated as a signal in broadcasting or telephoning.

pip[3] *n* spot on a playing card, domino, or die.

pipe *n* **1** tube for conveying water, etc. **2** vessel for smoking loose tobacco. **3** simple wind instrument. **4** note of a bird; shrill voice. **pipes** *pl n* bagpipes. ~*vt* **1** convey by pipe. **2** provide pipes or piping for. **3** play on a pipe. **pipe down** make less noise. **pipe up** begin to speak unexpectedly. **pipedream** *n* wishful daydream; futile hope or plan. **pipeline** *n* **1** long line of pipes conveying water or oil. **2** direct communication line. **in the pipeline** on the way.

piquant *adj* **1** pleasantly pungent; tasty. **2** rousing keen interest. **piquancy** *n*.

pique *n* ill-feeling; resentment; anger. *vt* **1** annoy; offend. **2** arouse (interest, etc.).

pirate *n* **1** one who attempts robbery or unlawful capture of ships at sea. **2** privately owned radio transmitter or operator without a licence. **3** one who infringes copyright or trading rights. *vt* infringe copyright or trading laws. **piracy** *n*.

pirouette *n* act of spinning on tiptoe, esp. in dancing. *vi* spin thus.

Pisces *n* twelfth sign of the zodiac, represented by the Fishes.

pistol *n* small hand gun.

piston *n* short cylinder moving to and fro in a cylindrical tube as part of an engine or pump.

pit *n* **1** hole, sunken area; depression. **2** mine shaft. **3** sunken area for an orchestra in front of a stage. **4** area near a race track in which cars are serviced or refuelled. **pit of the stomach** hollow below the breastbone. ~*vt,vi* (-tt-) make a hole in or become marked with hollows. **pit against** set to fight against; match against. **pitfall** *n* hidden danger or unexpected difficulty.

pitch[1] *vt,vi* **1** throw; fling. **2** set up (camp); erect (a tent). *vt* **1** set the slope or level of. **2** give a particular slant or character to. **3** sing or play (a note, etc.) accurately. *vi* toss up and down, as by waves. *n* **1** slope; gradient. **2** playing field. **3** frequency of a musical note. **4** *inf* persuasive sales talk. **pitchfork** *n* long-handled two-pronged fork for pitching hay. *vt* **1** lift and throw with a pitchfork. **2** assign work or responsibility to hastily or roughly.

pitch[2] *n* black viscous tarry liquid that sets hard on cooling and is used for roads, paths, etc. *vt* apply pitch to.

piteous *adj* arousing pity; pathetic.

pith *n* **1** core of spongy tissue in plant stems, feathers, etc. **2** white fibre inside the rind of oranges, lemons, etc. **3** essence; concentrated meaning; importance. **4** physical strength; mastery. **pithy** *adj*.

pittance *n* meagre allowance or portion.

pituitary gland *n* small gland in the brain that controls or influences hormone action.

pity *n* **1** compassion for suffering and the misfortunes of others; mercy. **2** cause of disappointment or regret. *vt* feel pity for. **pitiful** *adj* **1** arousing pity; pathetic; miserable. **2** contemptible. **pitifully** *adv*. **pitiless** *adj* merciless; cruel.

pivot *n* **1** pin or fixed point on which something turns. **2** person or thing on which all depends. *vt,vi* mount or turn on a pivot. *vi* depend on.

pizza *n* Italian dish consisting of a breadlike base with a topping of tomato sauce, cheese, and garnishes.

placard *n* public notice; written or printed display. *vt* **1** publicize by a placard. **2** fix a placard to.

placate *vt* appease the hostility or resentment of.

place *n* **1** geographical point; location; area. **2** position; state; rank. **3** space; room; seat. **4** house; residence. **5** duty; right. **6** job; appointment. **7** relative position in a race. **go places** *inf* become successful. **out of place** unsuitable; inappropriate. **in place of** instead of. **take place** occur; happen. ~*vt* **1** put or set in a particular or suitable position or order. **2** identify by some past link. **3** make; put. **4** appoint. **place with** put under the care of.

placenta *n* mass of tissue within the womb by which a connection is made between the foetus and the mother and which is discharged after birth. **placental** *adj*.

placid *adj* calm; unruffled. **placidly** *adv*.

plagiarize *vt,vi* steal from writings or ideas of another and use as one's own. **plagiarism** *n*. **plagiarist** *n*.

plague *n* **1** deadly highly infectious epidemic disease. **2** calamity; curse. **3** troublesome or annoying person or thing. *vt* be a persistent trouble to; pester.

plaice *n* edible flatfish having a brown body marked with orange spots.

plaid *n* cloth with a tartan or a chequered pattern.

plain *n* **1** tract of level land; open country. **2** simple knitting stitch. *adj* **1** level; flat; even. **2** clear; obvious. **3** simple; not ornate, decorated, or embellished. 4 neither beautiful nor ugly. 5 outspoken; straightforward. *adv also* **plainly** distinctly; bluntly; frankly. **plain-clothes** *adj* (of police, etc.) wearing ordinary clothes as opposed to a uniform. **plain sailing** *n* smooth and unhindered progress.

plaintive *adj* mournful; lamenting; complaining. **plaintively** *adv*.

plait *n* braid in which three or more strands or bunches of hair, etc., are passed over one another in turn. *vt* braid; intertwine.

plan *n* 1 scheme; project; method. 2 map of an area. 3 diagram of a structure. *vt,vi* (-nn-) 1 make a plan of or for; devise methods of doing. 2 regulate by a central authority.

plane[1] *n* 1 level or even surface. 2 level of existence or standard of performance, etc. 3 short for **aeroplane.** *adj* level; flat. *vi* skim over a water surface.

plane[2] *n* tool for levelling or smoothing surfaces, cutting grooves, etc. *vt* 1 use a plane on. 2 shave off by means of a plane.

planet *n* nonluminous celestial body that orbits around a star, esp. the nine bodies, including earth, that orbit around the sun. **planetary** *adj*.

plank *n* long broad length of cut timber. *vt* cover or supply with planks.

plankton *n* small animals and plants that inhabit the surface of a body of water and on which many larger animals feed.

plant *n* 1 living organism that synthesizes its own food from inorganic substances and lacks sense organs and powers of locomotion. 2 any herbaceous plant, as distinct from a tree or shrub. 3 factory; manufacturing works. 4 *inf* person or thing introduced into a group, place, etc., to throw guilt on innocent people. *vt* 1 put in the ground to grow. 2 establish; fix. **plantation** *n* large estate, esp. in tropical countries, where crops are grown. **planter** *n* 1 owner or supervisor of a plantation. 2 decorative holder for a house plant.

plaque 1 ornamental plate or disc intended to be mounted or hung for display. 2 hard white deposit that forms around the teeth.

plasma *n* clear yellowish fluid part of blood or lymph in which cells are suspended.

plaster *n* 1 mixture of sand, lime, and water that is applied to walls and ceilings to make them smooth. 2 self-adhesive bandage for minor wounds. *vt* cover or coat with or as if with plaster. **plaster of Paris** *n* hard refined plaster suitable for use in sculptures, casts, etc.

plastic *n* widely used synthetic material that can be moulded into a desired shape when soft. *adj* 1 made of plastic. 2 pliable; elastic. 3 easily influenced. **plastic surgery** *n* surgery concerned with the repair, sometimes cosmetic, of external tissue.

Plasticine *n Tdmk* soft modelling material.

plate *n* 1 shallow dish or receptacle. 2 thin coating of metal, esp. gold or silver. 3 item or items coated with gold or silver. 4 illustration or print in a book. 5 thin sheet, esp. of glass. *vt* coat with a thin layer of metal. **platelayer** *n* person who lays and maintains railway tracks.

plateau *n* 1 large level area of high land. 2 long stable period during development.

platform *n* 1 raised area, as for a speaker at a meeting. 2 waiting area at a railway station, etc. 3 statement of policy or plan of a political party, etc.

platinum *n* pliable silvery precious metal that is very durable and much used, esp. in jewellery.

platonic *adj* without physical desires.

platter *n* large dish or plate, used esp. for serving food.

plausible *adj* reasonable, likely, or believable. **plausibility** *n*. **plausibly** *adv*.

play *vt,vi* 1 occupy or amuse oneself (in a game, sport, etc.). 2 fill a particular role in a team game. 3 act as; imitate. 4 operate a musical instrument, radio, record player, etc., or be operated. *vt* 1 compete with. 2 act the part of. 3 give a dramatic performance of. *n* 1 drama; dramatic production. 2 games, diversions, etc. 3 manner or way of playing. 4 fun; lightheartedness. 5 liberty of action; scope. **playable** *adj*. **player** *n*. **playboy** *n* man who devotes himself to the pursuit of irresponsible pleasures. **playground** *n* outdoor area for children to play in. **playgroup** *n* nursery group for very young children. **playhouse** *n* 1 theatre for live drama. 2 toy house for children. **playing card** *n* one of a pack of fifty-two cards having a set value in one of the four suits into which the cards are divided. **playing field** *n* field used for playing team games. **playmate** *n* companion in play, esp. for children. **playschool** *n* playgroup. **playwright** *n* writer of plays; dramatist.

plea *n* **1** sincere claim or appeal. **2** something pleaded on behalf of a defendant in a legal trial.

plead *vt,vi* **1** appeal (to); beseech; implore. **2** offer an argument (for). *vt* **1** give as an excuse or justification. **2** declare oneself as being (guilty or not guilty) in a court of law.

pleasant *adj* pleasing; agreeable; enjoyable. **pleasantly** *adv*. **please** *vt,vi* gratify or delight (someone). *adv* used in making polite requests, asking favours, etc. **pleasure** *n* **1** delight; happiness; enjoyment. **2** something giving these things.

pleat *n* permanent fold or repeated crease in a fabric, esp. in skirts or dresses. *vt* make pleats in.

plectrum *n,pl* **plectrums** *or* **plectra** ('plektrə) implement or pick for plucking a musical string.

pledge *n* **1** solemn oath or promise. **2** guarantee; security. **3** token; symbol. *vt,vi* **1** promise solemnly. **2** give as a pledge. *vt* bind or secure by a pledge.

plenty *n* **1** enough; adequate supply. **2** abundance; profusion; large number. *adj* enough; very many. **plentiful** *adj*.

pliable *adj* **1** flexible; easily bent. **2** compliant; yielding; manageable.

plight *n* dilemma; difficult situation.

plimsoll *n* rubber-soled canvas shoe worn for sport.

plod *v* (-dd-) *vt,vi* walk along in a slow dogged manner. *vi* work slowly and steadily. *n* act or sound of plodding.

plonk *n inf* cheap wine.

plop *n* sound made by dropping an object into water. *v* (-pp-) *vt,vi* drop or make fall with a plop. *vi* make a plop.

plot[1] *n* **1** secret plan; outline; scheme. **2** story of a play, novel, etc. *v* (-tt-) *vt,vi* plan or conspire secretly. *vt* chart (a course) or make a map of.

plot[2] *n* small patch of ground.

plough *n* device for turning over soil when planting crops. *vt,vi* till or make a furrow with a plough.

pluck *vt* **1** pick off (feathers, flowers, etc.) from. **2** draw sound from (the strings) of (a musical instrument) by pulling them. **3** pull; tug. *n* courage. **plucky** *adj* brave; courageous.

plug *n* **1** piece of material used to fill a hole or stop up a gap. **2** device that connects an electrical appliance to an electricity supply. **3** *inf* unscheduled advertisement for or mention of a product. *vt* (-gg-) **1** attach to an electricity supply by means of a plug. **2** stop up or fill. **3** *inf* mention favourably or advertise.

plum *n* small tree bearing purple or green fruit with an oval stone. *adj inf* comfortable; pleasant.

plumage *n* feathers on a bird.

plumb *n* lump of heavy material, esp. when attached to a length of string (**plumbline**) and used to ensure that a wall, etc., is vertical. *vt* measure the depth of (the sea, etc.) with or as if with a plumb.

plumber *n* person who installs and repairs water pipes, baths, sinks, etc. **plumbing** *n* **1** profession of a plumber. **2** pipes and other appliances connected with the supply of water to a building.

plume *n* feather, esp. a long ornamental one.

plump[1] *adj* fleshy; chubby; fat. *vt,vi* make or become plump.

plump[2] *vi* fall or drop heavily or noisily. **plump for** choose; select.

plunder *vt,vi* steal (from) by force; rob. *n* **1** anything stolen or taken by force; loot. **2** act of plundering.

plunge *vt,vi* **1** thrust or be thrust, esp. into a liquid. **2** bring or be brought suddenly (into a certain condition). **3** rush madly in a certain direction. **4** throw oneself enthusiastically (into). *n* **1** act of plunging. **2** leap; mad dash.

plural *adj* consisting of or relating to more than one. *n* **1** linguistic number category in which plural nouns are placed. **2** plural form of a noun.

plus *prep* added to; with. *adv* or more. *n also* **plus sign** sign indicating addition.

plush *adj also* **plushy** very comfortable and expensive; luxurious.

Pluto *n* ninth and furthest known planet from the sun.

ply[1] *vt* **1** travel regularly around (an area) selling (goods, etc.). **2** supply continuously. **3** work at; engage in.

ply[2] *n* layer of material, esp. wood, or a strand of yarn. **plywood** *n* material consisting of layers or strips of wood glued together.

pneumatic *adj* relating to or operated by air, esp. compressed air.

pneumonia *n* disease marked by inflammation of the lungs, usually caused by bacteria or a virus.

poach[1] *vi,vt* **1** catch or take (game, fish, etc.) illegally. **2** trespass; encroach. **3** steal; pinch. **poacher** *n*.

poach[2] *vt* cook in gently boiling liquid.

pocket *n* **1** small pouch or bag, esp. one sewn into a garment. **2** cavity; hollow. **3** isolated area of group of people. **out of pocket** having made a financial loss. ~*vt* steal; appropriate. **pocket money** *n* small weekly sum of money given by parents to a child.

pod *n* fruit of the pea, bean, and related plants.

poem *n* composition usually written in regular rhythmic lines and often employing rhyme, metaphor, etc., to stimulate the imagination. **poetic** *adj*. **poet** *n* writer of poems. **poetess** *n f*. **poetry** *n* **1** verse. **2** art or work of a poet. **3** poetic qualities.

point *n* **1** sharp tapering end. **2** any projection, esp. a tapering one, such as a piece of land jutting out into the sea. **3** mark or dot made by something with a sharp point. **4** punctuation mark or accent used in writing, esp. a full stop. **5** something that has a position but no spatial extent. **6** definite place on a scale; specific moment. **7** stage in a course of action, procedure, etc., esp. an important or decisive stage. **8** element or part of something, esp. the most essential part, as of a topic, joke, etc. **9** reason; aim; meaning; significance. **10** unit of counting used in scoring games; mark. **on the point of** about to commit the act of. **make a point of** insist on as being important. **point of view** outlook; personal position or attitude. **stretch a point** be prepared to make an exception to one's usual practice. **to/off the point** relevant/irrelevant. **point-blank** at a range so close that one cannot miss; directly. ~*vt,vi* direct or aim (one's finger, etc.) at. *vt also* **point out** **1** indicate the position of. **2** turn someone's attention to. *vi* indicate or face in the direction of. **pointed** *adj* **1** having a point. **2** referring obviously to someone or something; emphatic; incisive. **pointer** *n* **1** something used for pointing. **2** indicator on a dial. **3** hint; suggestion. **4** breed of hunting dog. **pointless** *adj* lacking relevance, meaning, significance, etc.

poise *n* **1** calmness of manner; composure. **2** balance; stability. *vt,vi* **1** balance or be balanced. **2** hold a position, esp. in mid-air; hover.

poison *n* substance that causes illness or death because of its chemical properties. *vt* **1** kill or injure by administering poison. **2** put poison into (food, water, etc.). **poisonous** *adj*.

poke *vt,vi* **1** probe; prod; pierce. **2** push or thrust. *n* prod; push; thrust.

poker[1] *n* metal rod used for stirring the embers of a fire.

poker[2] *n* gambling card game.

pole[1] *n* long usually slender cylindrical rod used for support, measurement, propulsion, etc. **pole-vault** *n* athletic event in which a competitor propels himself over a high bar by means of a pole. *vt,vi* perform the pole-vault over a barrier.

pole[2] *n* **1** either of the two extreme ends of the axis of a planet or other globe. **2** two ends of a magnet, terminals of an electric battery, etc. **Pole Star** star almost directly over the earth's North Pole. **polar** *adj*. **polarize** *vt,vi* form into two or more distinct opposing groups.

polemic *n* controversial dispute or argument or an article, essay, etc., containing this. *adj also* **polemical** of or concerning a polemic.

police *n* **1** authority in a country responsible for keeping order, preventing crime, and enforcing laws. **2** *pl* members of this authority. *vt* control or keep law and order in. **policeman** *n, pl* **-men** police officer. **police station** *n* headquarters of a local branch of the police.

policy[1] *n* **1** course or line of action, esp. one adapted by a government in running state affairs. **2** wise or sensible way of doing things.

policy[2] *n* document stating the details of a contract between an individual and an insurance company.

polio *n also* **poliomyelitis** acute infectious disease, usually of children, that can paralyse various muscle groups.

polish *vt,vi* put a shine on something. *vt* improve (one's language, manners, etc.). *n* **1** substance applied to something to make it smooth or shiny. **2** shine or smoothness resulting from polishing. **3** act of polishing. **4** elegance or superior quality, as of a person's behaviour.

polite *adj* **1** demonstrating good manners and good behaviour; courteous. **2** refined and elegant. **politely** *adv*. **politeness** *n*.

politic *adj* **1** wise. **2** clever; cunning.

political *adj* **1** of or connected with politics or a party, in politics. **2** of or relating to a state government or its administration. **politically**

adv. **politician** *n* person concerned with politics, esp. one who holds a public office in a government. **politics** *n* **1** *s* science or profession concerned with government. **2** *pl* political affairs, principles, or ideas.

polka *n* **1** lively Bohemian dance. **2** music composed for this dance. *vi* dance a polka.

poll *n* **1** mass vote, as at an election. **2** number of votes cast. **3** list of people drawn up for voting or taxation purposes. **4** *also* **opinion poll** process in which a selection of people are interviewed as a means of assessing public opinion. *vt* **1** receive votes in an election. **2** interview to test public opinion.

pollen *n* dustlike material produced by flowering plants that serves as a fertilizing agent. **pollinate** *vt* transfer pollen to (a plant) for purposes of fertilization. **pollination** *n*.

pollute *vt* **1** make foul or poisonous; contaminate. **2** corrupt the morals of. **pollutant** *n* something that pollutes. **pollution** *n*.

polygamy *n* practice of marrying or the situation of being married to more than one woman at a time. **polygamist** *n*. **polygamous** *adj*.

polygon *n* geometric figure having three or more sides.

polymer *n* substance containing long chains of atoms joined together, as in cellulose, plastics, synthetic fibres, etc.

polyp *n* **1** type of individual of such organisms as corals or sea anemones, having tentacles and a mouth. **2** *also* **polyps** small pathological growth, as in the nose.

polytechnic *n* type of college of higher education originally set up to teach scientific subjects but now also teaching social sciences.

polythene *n* widely used type of plastic. *adj* made of polythene.

pomegranate *n* large round usually red fruit with a tough rind and inner parts divided into chambers containing edible seeds.

pommel *n* **1** raised front end of a saddle. **2** knob on the top of a sword.

pomp *n* **1** stately splendour. **2** ostentatious or empty show; vain display. **pompous** *adj* **1** overdignified; self-important. **2** ostentatious or inflated. **pompously** *adv*.

pond *n* small lake; pool.

ponder *vt,vi* reflect or think deeply; meditate.

pony *n* small horse.

poodle *n* breed of dog having thick curly hair.

pool[1] *n* **1** small body of water; pond; puddle. **2** any small amount of liquid. **3** still deep part in a river.

pool[2] *n* **1** group or association of mutually cooperative members. **2** combination of things, esp. a set of services or financial facilities shared by a number of people or groups. **3** all the stakes in a game. *vt,vi* combine to form a pool. **the pools** *n* system of betting on the results of football matches.

poor *adj* **1** having or characterized by little wealth or resources. **2** deficient in something necessary or desirable; inferior; unsatisfactory; scanty. *n* **the poor** poor people in general. **poorly** *adv* badly. *adj inf* ill.

pop[1] *v* (-pp-) *vt,vi* **1** make or cause to make a short sharp sound. **2** burst open or cause to burst open with a pop. *vi* come or go quickly. *n* **1** popping sound. **2** nonalcoholic fizzy drink. **pop off 1** depart. **2** die suddenly. **pop the question** propose marriage. ~*adv,interj* with or expressing a popping sound. **popcorn** *n* type of maize that bursts and puffs up when roasted.

pop[2] *n* type of music usually having a distinctive and persistent rhythmic beat and making extensive use of electronically aided instruments.

Pope *n* head of the Roman Catholic Church.

poplar *n* tall tree of the willow family having a spirelike appearance.

poppy *n* plant bearing red, orange, or white flowers.

popular *adj* **1** liked or enjoyed by a large number of people. **2** of or connected with the people. **3** normal among or suitable for the people. **popularity** *n*. **popularly** *adv*. **populate** *vt* **1** live in; inhabit. **2** introduce a population into; people. **population** *n* people considered collectively, esp. all the people living in a town, city, country, etc.

porcelain *n* type of delicate pottery; china.

porch *n* **1** exterior roofed entrance to a house. **2** veranda.

porcupine *n* animal of the rodent family whose body is covered with stiff sharp spines or quills.

pore[1] *v* **pore over** think or ponder deeply about; study.

pore[2] *n* tiny opening, esp. in the skin or a leaf, to allow the passage of perspiration or other moisture.

pork *n* flesh or meat obtained from pigs. **porker** *n* pig being fattened for slaughter.

pornography *n* literature or art dealing with obscene subjects and intended to arouse sexual desires. **pornographic** *adj.*

porous *adj* full of little holes like a sponge, which allow the passage of water or air.

porpoise *n* aquatic mammal with a blunt snout, related to the whale.

porridge *n* breakfast dish consisting of oatmeal, water, and often milk.

port[1] *n* a place, city, etc., where ships may load or unload cargoes.

port[2] *n* left side of a ship or aeroplane for someone facing towards the front.

port[3] *n* sweet fortified usually dark red wine.

portable *adj* able to be carried easily by hand. *n* portable object.

porter[1] *n* person employed to carry people's luggage, as at a railway station or hotel.

porter[2] *n* dark bitter ale.

portfolio *n* **1** large flat case for carrying documents, drawings, etc. **2** collection of documents concerned with a government department. **3** office of a government minister. **4** list of securities held by a person, bank, etc.

porthole *n* opening in a ship's side fitted with glass to let in air and light.

portion *n* **1** piece; share. **2** amount of food served to one person. *vt* **1** give as a share. **2** divide or share.

portrait *n* **1** picture of a person, usually a painting. **2** lively written description of a person. **portraiture** *n* **1** art of producing portraits. **2** portraits collectively.

portray *vt* **1** play the part of (someone), as in a play. **2** describe a person or his character. **portrayal** *n.*

pose *n* **1** way of standing or behaving deliberately adopted to give an effect. **2** pretence. *vi* **1** act (as something one is not). **2** stand or sit in a certain way to be photographed or painted. *vt* ask (a question); present (a problem).

posh *adj inf* **1** smart; showing style. **2** upper-class; snobbish.

position *n* **1** place. **2** situation or condition. **3** opinion; attitude. **4** way of standing, sitting, etc. **5** job; employment; office; rank. *vt* **1** put into place. **2** find the place of. **positional** *adj.*

positive *adj* **1** definite. **2** certain; sure. **3** real, true, or actual. **4** useful or helpful. **5** hopeful; optimistic. **6** denoting numbers greater than zero. **7** designating or having the electric charge of a proton. **8** (of a photograph) corresponding in colour or tone to the scene photographed. *n* positive photograph, electric terminal, etc. **positively** *adv.*

possess *vt* have or control; own. **possessed** *adj* mad or frenzied, esp. when under the control of an evil spirit. **possession** *n* **1** something one owns. **2** act of possessing or state of being possessed. **3** condition of occupying property. **4** overseas colony. **possessive** *adj* **1** concerning possession. **2** selfishly dominating or controlling a person. **3** denoting the case or form of a word used to indicate possession. *n* possessive case or a pronoun in it.

possible *adj* **1** able to exist, occur, be done, etc. **2** that may perhaps happen. **3** potential. *n* person or thing that is possible. **possibly** *adv.* **possibility** *n* something that is possible. **possibilities** *pl n* likely prospects.

post[1] *n* **1** stout wooden pole driven into the ground, esp. to support a roof, gate, or door. **2** place where a race starts or ends. *vt* **1** put up (a notice) on a wall, etc. **2** announce to the public by putting up a notice or sign.

post[2] *n* **1** job or duty. **2** place where a soldier carries out his duties. **3** fort or military camp. **4** remote settlement. *vt* **1** assign a task or duty to. **2** send to (a military camp). **3** appoint to (a certain job).

post[3] *n* **1** national system or organization for carrying letters, parcels, etc. **2** letters and parcels handled for delivery; mail. **3** act or time of collecting or delivering mail. *vt* send through the post. **keep posted** keep informed. **postage** *n* money paid for the use of the post. **postal** *adj.* **postal order** *n* money order that can be bought or cashed only at a post office. **postbox** *n* box in which letters are placed for collection. **postcard** *n* card, sometimes having a picture on one side, used to send short messages. **postman** *n, pl* **-men** official who delivers letters.

poster *n* placard, esp. used as an advertising announcement.

posterior *adj* placed or following behind something else. *n* buttocks.

posterity *n* future generations.

postgraduate *adj* relating to studies carried out

by a student who has already gained his first degree. *n* postgraduate student.

posthumous *adj* **1** happening or produced after a person's death. **2** published after an author's death. **posthumously** *adv.*

postmortem *n* **1** medical examination of a corpse to find out the cause of death. **2** analysis of reasons for failure of a plan, etc., of something after it is over. *adj,adv* after death.

postpone *vt* delay; put off; defer. **postponement** *n.*

postscript *n* additional note added at the end of a letter or document, after the signature.

postulate *n* ('pɔstjulit) **1** idea or principle temporarily adopted as the basis of an argument, etc.; assumption. **2** unproved or self-evident scientific statement. *vt* ('pɔstjuleit) **1** claim; demand. **2** adopt as a postulate.

posture *n* **1** way of standing or walking. **2** situation or condition. *vi* act in an unnatural way to achieve an effect.

posy *n* small bunch of flowers.

pot[1] *n* **1** round vessel or container. **2** vessel used for cooking food or from which tea or coffee is served. **3** jar. **go to pot** fall into a state of ruin. **pot shot** easy shot with a gun, etc. ~*v* (-tt-) *vt,vi* **1** place plants, etc., in a pot. **2** put food in jars to preserve it. *vt* strike (a billiard ball) into a pocket.

pot[2] *n* marijuana.

potassium *n* soft silvery-white metallic element whose compounds are much used in drugs and fertilizers.

potato *n, pl* **potatoes** tuber of certain plants used as a vegetable.

potent *adj* **1** powerful; strong; influential. **2** (of men) able to perform sexually. **potency** *n.*

potential *adj* **1** capable of existing, becoming effective, etc. **2** not yet using one's power. *n* capacity or ability not yet realized or used. **potentiality** *n.* **potentially** *adv.*

pothole *n* **1** small pit in a road. **2** deep hole in rock, often large enough to be explored. **potholer** *n.*

potion *n* drink of a medicinal, magical, or poisonous nature.

potter[1] *n* person who makes pottery.

potter[2] *vi* move or act aimlessly.

pottery *n* **1** earthenware vessels. **2** material from which such vessels are made. **3** factory where pots are made.

pouch *n* **1** small bag, esp. one for carrying money, food, tobacco, etc. **2** baglike or pocket-like part of the body on certain animals, esp. the one in which kangaroos, wallabies, etc., carry their young.

poultice *n* soft moistened mass applied to the body for medicinal purposes. *vt* place a poultice on.

poultry *n* domesticated fowls. **poulterer** *n* person who sells poultry and game.

pounce *vi* leap suddenly (upon); swoop. *n* sudden leap or swoop.

pound[1] *vt,vi* beat with a succession of heavy blows. *vt* reduce to dust; crush. *vi* thump; throb. *n* thump.

pound[2] *n* **1** unit of weight, divided into sixteen ounces, equivalent to 0.45 kilograms. **2** basic unit of British currency or the system of currency used in Great Britain (**pound sterling**) and several other countries.

pound[3] *n* enclosure, esp. one for sheltering, confining, or catching animals.

pour *vt,vi* **1** flow or cause to flow out. **2** emit or cause to emit continually and quickly. **3** rain heavily.

pout *vi* push out the lips as when angry, sullen, etc. *vt* say in a sulky manner. *n* **1** act or gesture of pouting. **2** sulk.

poverty *n* state or condition of being poor; lack of wealth. **poverty-stricken** *adj* without means; destitute.

powder *n* **1** solid substance in the form of tiny loose particles, usually produced by grinding or crushing. **2** type of powder used as a cosmetic, medicine, etc. *vt,vi* make into or become a powder; crush or be crushed. *vt* apply powder to. **powdery** *adj.*

power *n* **1** ability or means to do something. **2** capacity of mind or body. **3** strength, energy, or force. **4** control; influence; authority. **5** country or state having international influence. **6** divine or supernatural being. **7** rate at which work is done or energy is transferred. *vt* **1** provide energy, force, etc., for. **2** provide with an engine or motor. **powerful** *adj.* **powerfully** *adv.* **powerless** *adj.*

practicable *adj* able to be done or used.

practical *adj* **1** concerned with practice or action. **2** capable of or suitable for use. **3** concerned with the ordinary activities in the world. **4** inclined towards actual or useful work; not philosophical or interested in theory.

5 aware of possibilities; experienced. **practically** *adv* 1 almost; nearly. 2 in a practical manner.

practice *n* 1 custom; habit. 2 exercises done to gain skill in something. 3 action that corresponds to a theory. 4 work or clients of a lawyer, doctor, etc. **practise** *vt,vi* 1 do as a habit or do repeatedly to gain skill. 2 train (at). 3 take an action that corresponds to a theory. 4 work as a lawyer, doctor, etc. **practitioner** *n* person who works at a profession, esp. a doctor.

pragmatic *adj* 1 making judgments based on causes and results. 2 acting in a practical manner. **pragmatically** *adv*.

prairie *n* large usually fertile area of grassland without trees.

praise *vt* 1 show approval or admiration for. 2 give glory to (God, etc.). *n* 1 admiration or approval. 2 glory or homage expressed to God. **praiseworthy** *adj*.

pram *n* wheeled carriage for a baby.

prance *vi* 1 jump or move by jumping from the hind legs, as a horse does. 2 walk about pompously; swagger. *n* jump; spring; swagger.

prank *n* childish trick.

prattle *n* meaningless chatter. *vi* chatter meaninglessly.

prawn *n* edible marine animal resembling but larger than a shrimp.

pray *vt,vi* make an earnest request for, esp to God or a god; make a prayer. **prayer** *n* 1 earnest request made to God or a god. 2 special set of words used in praying. 3 strong wish or desire.

preach *vt,vi* 1 speak publicly on a religious theme or in support of a religion. 2 give strong moral encouragement (to); advocate. 3 give unwelcome moral advice (to). **preacher** *n*.

precarious *adj* insecure; unsafe; uncertain. **precariously** *adv*. **precariousness** *n*.

precaution *n* action taken to stop something unpleasant or dangerous from happening. **precautionary** *adj*.

precede *vt* 1 go in front of. 2 be earlier than. 3 be more important or of higher rank than. **precedence** *n* 1 act of preceding. 2 relative importance or rank 3 right resulting from rank, birth, or important office. **precedent** *n* earlier case or decision that is taken as guidance in dealing with subsequent situations.

precept *n* rule or guide for behaviour; maxim.

precinct *n* enclosed area, esp. the grounds of a cathedral, school, etc.

precious *adj* 1 valuable; of great price. 2 well loved. 3 affected; excessively refined. *adv* very. **preciously** *adv*.

precipice *n* high, vertical, and steep cliff.

precipitate (priˈsipiteit) *vt* 1 cause to happen before required or expected; hasten. 2 throw down; hurl. 3 cause dissolved matter to separate from solution in solid form. *n* (priˈsipitit) solid precipitated matter. **precipitation** *n*.

précis *n* shortened form of a longer statement, document, etc. *vt* make a summary of.

precise *adj* 1 accurate; exact. 2 clear; definite. **precisely** *adv*. **precision** *n*.

precocious *adj* advanced in development.

preconceive *vt* form an opinion beforehand. **preconception** *n*.

predator *n* 1 animal that lives by hunting and killing other animals for food. 2 plunderer; thief. **predatory** *adj*.

predecessor *n* person who precedes someone else in a particular office, job, or duty.

predestine *vt* decide the fate of beforehand. **predestination** *n*.

predicament *n* awkward or dangerous situation.

predicate *n* (ˈpredikit) 1 part of a sentence that contains what is said about the subject. 2 statement relating to something. *vt* (ˈpredikeit) declare as a characteristic. **predication** *n*. **predicative** *adj*.

predict *vt* describe future events before they happen; foretell; prophesy. **predictable** *adj*. **prediction** *n*.

predominate *vi* 1 be the most numerous. 2 have the most power or strength. **predominance** *n*. **predominant** *adj*.

pre-eminent *adj* better than anyone or anything else; excellent; very distinguished. **pre-eminence** *n*. **pre-eminently** *adv*.

preen *vt,vi* 1 (of a bird) clean and straighten the feathers with the beak. 2 prepare or dress oneself tidily. 3 show self-satisfaction.

prefabricate *vt* manufacture parts or sections of (a building, etc.) ready for assembling and erection.

preface *n* 1 written introduction in a book; foreword. 2 similar introduction to a speech or play. *vt* introduce with a preface. **prefatory** *adj.*

prefect *n* senior pupil with some authority over other pupils at a school.

prefer *vt* (-rr-) **1** like better. **2** give special attention to. **3** present or make (a statement, charge, etc.). **4** promote. **preferable** *adj.* **preference** *n* **1** preferring or being preferred. **2** something preferred. **3** advantage or right granted to particular people, countries, etc. **preferential** *adj.*

prefix *n* affix added to the beginning of a word to alter or otherwise affect its meaning. *vt* attach at the beginning of something.

pregnant *adj* **1** (of a woman or female animal) being with child or young. **2** full of; abounding in. **3** very significant. **pregnancy** *n.*

prehistoric *adj* of or occurring in the period before history was written down.

prejudice *n* **1** judgment or opinion reached prematurely or on insufficient evidence. **2** unfavourable opinion or bias. *vt* **1** cause to be prejudiced; bias. **2** injure; harm. **prejudicial** *adj.*

preliminary *adj* occurring beforehand; introductory. *n* first action or occurrence; introductory or preparatory step, event, etc.

prelude *n* **1** short piece of music, esp. introducing an opera, suite, or fugue. **2** any introduction. *vt* form a prelude or introduction to.

premarital *adj* before marriage.

premature *adj* before the right time; too early.

premeditate *vt* think of or decide upon beforehand; plan. **premeditation** *n.*

premier *adj* of the highest importance; first; leading. *n* prime minister.

premiere *n* first showing or performance of a film, play, etc.

premise *n* **1** *also* **premiss** assumption. **2** introduction to a document, such as a lease. **premises** *pl n* house or other building, including the grounds. ~*vt* state as a premise.

premium *n* **1** prize; bonus. **2** additional payment to a standard rate, wage, etc. **3** amount paid periodically to renew an insurance policy. **at a premium** very valuable. **premium bond** government bond that pays no interest but offers the chance of monthly cash prizes.

preoccupied *adj* **1** concentrating on one thought above others; engrossed; absorbed. **preoccupation** *n.*

prepare *vt,vi* **1** make or become ready or suitable for something. **2** make; manufacture; construct. **3** equip. **preparatory** *adj.* **preparation** *n* **1** preparing or being prepared. **2** something prepared, esp. a medicine or cosmetic. **3** *also inf* **prep** school work done by a pupil at home; homework.

preposition *n* word placed before a noun or pronoun indicating relationship in time, space, etc. **prepositional** *adj.*

preposterous *adj* ridiculous; stupid; absurd. **preposterously** *adv.*

prerogative *n* privilege; right.

Presbyterian *adj* relating to a Protestant Church governed by elders (presbyters), traditionally following the teachings of Calvin. *n* member of such a Church.

prescribe *vt,vi* **1** order or require (medicine, treatment, etc.). **2** make certain rules about. **prescription** *n* **1** written instructions issued by a doctor indicating required medicine, treatment, etc. **2** act of prescribing.

presence *n* **1** state or condition of being present. **2** closeness; nearness. **3** demeanour; bearing. **4** dignity; importance. **presence of mind** ability to act quickly and intelligently when faced by difficulty or danger.

present[1] ('prezənt) *adj* **1** being here within sight or hearing. **2** being at a particular place at a certain time. **3** existing now; indicating this time now. *n* **1** time being lived through now. **2** tense in a language indicating this. **presently** *adv* soon; before long. **present participle** *n* verb form functioning as an adjective or used with an auxiliary verb to denote continuous action, e.g. *changing, living,* or *speaking.*

present[2] *n* ('prezənt) gift. *vt* (prə'zent) **1** give, esp. formally; bestow. **2** introduce, esp. in a formal way. **3** organize (a performance, etc.). **4** show to the public. **5** offer or put forward for consideration, etc. **6** raise (a weapon) in salute. **presentation** *n.* **presentable** *adj* fit to be introduced, displayed, etc.

preserve *vt* **1** keep safe or undamaged. **2** save from decay, change, etc. *n* **1** preserved food, such as jam. **2** area of country protected or kept private, as for hunting. **3** right; privilege. **preservation** *n.* **preservative** *n,adj.*

president *n* **1** person having highest authority in a republic. **2** someone presiding over an assembly, society, company, etc. **presidency**

n. **preside** *vi* **1** sit in authority over a meeting, debate, etc. **2** exercise control or authority.

press[1] *vt,vi* **1** apply weight, force, or pressure to, so as to squeeze, crush, flatten, etc. **2** obtain liquid, juice, oil, etc., by pressure. **3** hold close; grasp. **4** attack hard, as in battle. **5** insist on; compel; urge; entreat. **6** oppress; harass. **7** iron. **press on** continue with an activity. ~*n* **1** machine for printing. **2** newspapers and magazines collectively. **3** machine for exerting pressure, as in extracting liquids. **4** large crowd of people. **press stud** *n* fastener for clothes having two parts pressed together.

press[2] *vt* force into service, esp. military service. **pressgang** *n* men formerly employed to force people into the army or navy. ~*vt* force (someone) into doing something.

pressure *n* **1** act of pressing. **2** force exerted by pressing; force per unit area acting on a surface. **3** compulsion; constraint. **4** cause of distress; burden. **pressure group** *n* group of people seeking to influence public opinion, government, etc. **pressure cooker** *n* special pot in which food is cooked at a high temperature under pressure. **pressurize** *vt* **1** maintain normal air pressure in (an aircraft cabin, etc.). **2** urge or compel, esp. to a course of action.

prestige *n* **1** high reputation gained through success, rank, etc.; status. **2** power to influence and impress. **prestigious** *adj.*

presume *vt,vi* **1** assume; suppose. **2** dare or venture, esp. with excessive boldness. **presumption** *n.* **presumable** *adj.* **presumably** *adv.*

pretend *vt,vi* **1** feign or affect (to do or be something). **2** lay claim to, esp. dubiously. **3** state or profess falsely. **4** venture; attempt. **5** fancy or imagine oneself as being. **pretender** *n* **1** claimant to a throne, inheritance, etc. **2** someone who pretends. **pretence** *n.*

pretentious *adj* **1** claiming or attempting things beyond one's ability. **2** affecting dignity, importance, etc. **3** ostentatious; showy. **pretentiousness** *n.* **pretentiously** *adv.* **pretension** *n* **1** laying claim to something. **2** dubious or unsupportable claim, esp. made indirectly, to some merit, importance, etc. **3** pretentiousness.

pretext *n* pretended reason or motive that conceals the real one; excuse.

pretty *adj* **1** attractive, charming, or appealing in a delicate way. **2** neat; dainty. **3** *inf* fine; good. **4** *inf* considerable. **a pretty penny** great deal of money. ~*adv* fairly; quite. **prettily** *adv.* **prettiness** *n.*

prevail *vi* **1** be or prove dominant, effective, superior, etc.; be victorious. **2** be used or exist widely; predominate. **prevail on** persuade.

prevalent *adj* used or occurring widely; common. **prevalence** *n.*

prevaricate *vi* make misleading statements; answer evasively. **prevarication** *n.*

prevent *vt* make impossible; hinder; stop. **prevention** *n.* **preventive** *adj.*

preview *n* advance showing of a play, film, exhibition, etc., before presentation to the public. *vt* see in advance.

previous *adj* **1** before something else in time or position; prior. **2** *inf* too early; premature. **previously** *adv.*

prey *n* **1** animal hunted for food. **2** habit of hunting for prey. **3** victim, as of an enemy, illness, etc. *v* **prey on 1** hunt for food. **2** make profits out of; exploit. **3** have a destructive or depressing influence (on); weigh heavily (on).

price *n* **1** amount of money, goods, etc., for which something is bought or sold. **2** cost at which something is acquired. **3** value; worth. *vt* **1** set a price on. **2** estimate or find out the price of. **priceless** *adj* **1** valuable beyond price; invaluable. **2** *inf* very funny or absurd. **pricey** *adj inf* expensive.

prick *vt* pierce; puncture; make holes in with a sharp point. *vi,vt* feel or cause to feel sharp mental or physical pain; sting. **prick up one's ears** listen attentively. ~*n* **1** pricking or being pricked. **2** small injury or puncture caused by a sharp point. **3** sharp painful sensation. **4** *sl* penis. **prickle** *n* **1** small sharp thorn or spine. **2** tingling or prickling sensation. *vt,vi* tingle. **prickly** *adj.*

pride *n* **1** self-respect based on a true sense of personal worth. **2** arrogance about or exaggerated belief in one's own merits, achievements, etc. **3** satisfaction. **4** source of pride, esp. something splendid. **5** group of lions. **take pride in** be proud about.

priest *n* minister who officiates at religious

ceremonies and rituals. **priestess** *f n.* **priesthood** *n.*

prim *adj* excessively formal or proper in attitude or behaviour.

primary *adj* **1** first or most important. **2** simple; elementary; basic; fundamental. **primarily** *adv.* **primary colours** *pl n* three colours, for example red, green, and blue, that can be combined to give any other colour. **primary school** *n* school for children below the age of eleven (or sometimes nine).

primate *n* **1** high-ranking clergyman, such as an archbishop. **2** member of the order of mammals that includes man, apes, and monkeys.

prime *adj* **1** first or most important; primary. **2** excellent; very good. **3** necessary; essential. *n* period when something is at its best or strongest, usually the earliest period. *vt,vi* **1** put explosive into. **2** fill with food. **3** supply with information. **prime minister** *n* chief minister; leader of the government. **prime number** *n* number, such as seven, able to be divided only by itself and one. **primer** *n* **1** book for beginners. **2** cap or tube containing explosive used to set off a charge. **3** first coat of paint.

primitive *adj* **1** at the beginning of development. **2** barbarous; savage. **3** not sophisticated; rough; simple. *n* primitive person or thing.

primrose *n* wild plant bearing pale yellow flowers. *n,adj* pale yellow.

prince *n* **1** son or close male relative of a king or queen. **2** nobleman. **3** ruler of a minor state. **princely** *adj.* **princess** *n* **1** daughter or close female relative of a king or queen. **2** wife of a prince.

principal *adj* **1** chief; main. **2** of the highest rank. *n* **1** person who plays a leading part in an activity. **2** head of a university, college, or school. **3** capital sum that is borrowed or lent at interest. **principally** *adv.*

principality *n* rule of a prince or the country or state over which he rules.

principle *n* **1** basic rule, esp. one that governs one's life. **2** fundamental truth or doctrine. **3** important element of something. **4** moral behaviour.

print *vt,vi* **1** produce (letters, text, pictures, etc.) by pressing inked types, plates, etc., directly onto paper. **2** publish (a book, magazine, etc.) in this way. **3** write in separated letters or block capitals. **4** produce a picture from a negative. **5** leave (a mark, etc.) by or as if by pressing or stamping. *n* **1** printed text. **2** picture produced from an engraved or etched plate or a photographic negative. **3** cloth with a pattern printed on it. **4** mark made by or as if by pressure. **out of print** (of a book, etc.) sold out; not available. **printable** *adj* fit to appear in print. **printer** *n.*

prior[1] *n* head of a monastery.

prior[2] *adj* **1** coming before; earlier. **2** of greater importance. **prior to** before; previous to. **priority** *n* **1** greater importance; superiority. **2** state of being earlier. **3** condition of being or right to be dealt with earlier.

priory *n* religious house presided over by a prior, often attached to an abbey.

prise *vt* lift or open by means of a lever, etc.

prism *n* **1** solid figure usually having rectangular sides and triangular ends of equal size. **2** triangular prism of transparent material, used esp. for splitting light into its component colours. **prismatic** *adj.*

prison *n* **1** building used for the confinement of convicted criminals. **2** any place of confinement. **prisoner** *n* criminal or other captive kept in prison.

private *adj* **1** not public or official; secret; confidential. **2** connected with an individual; personal. **3** out of the way; isolated. *n* soldier of the lowest army or marine rank. **privacy** *n.* **privately** *adv.*

privet *n* evergreen shrub commonly used for hedges.

privilege *n* **1** right granted to a person or group. **2** advantage connected with such a right. *vt* grant a privilege to; give a special advantage to.

prize[1] *n* **1** reward won in a competition. **2** something valuable captured in war, etc.

prize[2] *vt* hold in high estimation; place a high value on.

probable *adj* likely to occur or be true. **probability** *n* likelihood, esp. when mathematically calculated. **probably** *adv.*

probation *n* **1** period during which a person is tested for his ability or suitability. **2** system by which a convicted offender is set free on condition that he reports regularly to an official and behaves well. **probationary** *adj.*

probe *vt,vi* seek for information; investigate; examine. *n* **1** investigation. **2** surgical instrument used to probe wounds, etc. **3** spacecraft capable of exploration.

problem *n* **1** difficult issue or situation. **2** matter deserving profound consideration. **3** question requiring a solution by calculation. **problematic** *adj.*

procedure *n* **1** method of doing something; technique. **2** established manner of behaviour in a given situation. **3** rules governing the conduct of business, as in parliament. **procedural** *adj.*

proceed *vi* **1** go forward; advance. **2** start or continue a course of action. **proceed from** be the result of. **proceed against** bring a legal action against. **proceeds** *pl n* profit from a sale, etc.

process *n* **1** series of connected actions; course of action. **2** method by which legal action is conducted. **3** method of making or manufacturing something. **4** bone, organ, or part that sticks out or projects. *vt* **1** preserve (food), as by drying, freezing, etc. **2** use special methods to manufacture or do something.

procession *n* **1** large number of people moving along in an ordered manner. **2** long series of things or events.

proclaim *vt* announce or make known officially or openly. **proclamation** *n.*

procreate *vt,vi* give birth to or produce (offspring). **procreation** *n.* **procreator** *n.*

procure *vt* **1** get; obtain. **2** bring about; cause. **procurement** *n.*

prod *vt* (-dd-) **1** poke; nudge. **2** urge; encourage; rouse; stir. *n* **1** poke; nudge. **2** reminder.

prodigy *n* **1** wonder; marvel; miraculous event or thing. **2** person, esp. a child, having exceptional ability or talent. **prodigious** *adj* **1** enormous. **2** extraordinary; wonderful.

produce *v* (prəˈdjuːs) *vt,vi* bring forth; bear; yield. *vt* **1** cause; bring into existence. **2** manufacture or make. **3** organize or finance (a play, film, etc.). **4** bring out; show. *n* (ˈprɔdjuːs) anything that is produced, brought forth, or made, esp. fruit or crops. **producer** *n.* **production** *n.* **product** *n* **1** something produced. **2** result of multiplying two or more numbers. **productive** *adj* able to produce, esp. effectively or efficiently. **productivity** *n.*

profane *adj* **1** showing contempt or disrespect for sacred or holy things. **2** vulgar or coarse, esp. in language. *vt* **1** defile or otherwise spoil (something holy, sacred, or pure). **2** treat with callous disrespect. **profanely** *adv.* **profanity** *n.*

profess *vt* **1** declare or claim in public. **2** pretend; declare falsely.

profession *n* **1** job or career for which special training and mental skills are required. **2** body of people in a particular profession. **3** public declaration or claim. **professional** *adj* **1** connected with a profession or those who practise it. **2** earning one's living by playing a sport. *n* professional person.

professor *n* **1** head of a teaching department in a university or similar institution. **2** someone who professes a religious belief.

proficient *adj* skilled; capable; expert; experienced. **proficiency** *n.*

profile *n* **1** view or drawing of a face seen from the side. **2** outline or sectional drawing. **3** journalistic character outline of someone; brief biography. *vt* give, present, or draw an outline of.

profit *n* **1** advantage, benefit. **2** money left over after the necessary expenses of a transaction have been paid. *vt,vi* **1** gain advantage (from). **2** be of advantage. **3** obtain profits. **profitable** *adj.*

profound *adj* **1** extremely deep. **2** felt deeply; strong; intense. **3** requiring considerable concentration; obscure; difficult. **profoundly** *adv.* **profundity** *n.*

profuse *adj* **1** unrestrained; lavish; generous. **2** very plentiful; abundant to the point of excess. **profusely** *adv.* **profusion** *n.*

programme *n* **1** list of items or events in a theatrical performance, concert, etc., or at a meeting. **2** performance consisting of several items or parts. **3** radio or television broadcast. **program** *n* list of operations and data used in or prepared for a computer. *vt,vi* (-mm-) prepare data for a computer. **programmer** *n.*

progress *n* (ˈprougres) **1** forward motion. **2** advance; development; increase or growth. *vi* (prəˈgres) **1** move forward; advance. **2** improve; get better. **progression** *n* **progressive** *adj* **1** characterized by progress. **2** supporting political or social reforms; enlightened. **3** increasing regularly; accumulative. *n* person supporting social and political reform. **progressively** *adv.*

prohibit *vt* forbid or prevent, esp. by law; stop; ban; restrict. **prohibition** *n.* **prohibitive** *adj.*

project *n* (ˈprɔdʒekt) scheme being planned or

already being worked on. *v* (prəˈdʒekt) *vt,vi* stick out; protrude; jut out. *vt* **1** throw; thrust; drive forward. **2** cast (the mind) forward to think about the distant future; plan ahead. **3** shine light or an image on something, as with a film projector. **projection** *n*. **projectile** *n* object propelled through the air; missile. **projectionist** *n* person who works a projector at a cinema. **projector** *n* machine for projecting films or picture slides on a screen.

proletariat *n* social class that owns no property and earns its living by the sale of its labour; working class.

proliferate *vt,vi* bring or come forth in increasing abundance, produce or reproduce more and more. **proliferation** *n*. **prolific** *adj* **1** plentiful, abundant. **2** producing much. **3** having numerous offspring.

prologue *n* **1** section of a book, play, poem, etc., that comes before the main part; introduction. **2** any preliminary to something more important.

prolong *vt* make longer in time or space.

promenade *n* **1** place along which one may walk, esp. near the sea. **2** short walk; stroll. *vi* walk along freely, stroll.

prominent *adj* **1** famous, well-known. **2** obvious; clear. **3** projecting, sticking out. **prominence** *n*. **prominently** *adv*.

promiscuous *adj* **1** indiscriminate, esp. in sexual relations. **2** confused; lacking order; casual. **promiscuity** *n*. **promiscuously** *adv*.

promise *n* **1** declaration; vow. **2** assurance given to do or not to do something. **3** grounds or hope for future excellence, achievement, etc. *vt,vi* make a promise (of).

promote *vt* **1** advance to a higher or more important rank, position, etc. **2** encourage the development, progress, or growth of. **3** work to make successful, acceptable, or popular. **promotion** *n*.

prompt *adj* **1** quick to act, respond, or do. **2** punctual. **3** acted on or accomplished without delay. *vt* **1** instigate; incite. **2** inspire. *vi,vt* provide or help by providing cues or suggestions. *n* act of prompting or something that prompts. **promptly** *adv*.

prone *adj* lying with the face or front of the body downwards, stretched out. **prone to** liable, inclined, or disposed (to).

prong *n* pointed end, as of a fork; spike; narrow projection.

pronoun *n* word such as *you, my, who,* or *someone,* used as a substitute for a noun.

pronounce *vt,vi* make a speech sound, esp. in a specific manner; utter; articulate. *vt* state formally; declare officially. *vi* voice an opinion (on). **pronounced** *adj* obvious, marked. **pronouncement** *n* declaration. **pronunciation** *n* act or manner of making speech sounds, esp. with regard to correctness.

proof *n* **1** irrefutable evidence, reasoning, or facts. **2** anything that serves to establish validity or truth. **3** trial; demonstration; test. **4** alcoholic strength proved or maintained by certain standards. *adj* of standard or proved strength or quality. **proof against** unable to be penetrated, invulnerable. **proofread** *vt,vi* (-read) read and correct (trial printed matter).

prop[1] *n* **1** rigid support, such as a beam or pole. **2** person or thing giving support. *vt* (-pp-) **1** *also* **prop up** prevent from caving in or falling; support. **2** place or rest against something.

prop[2] *n* object placed on stage or used by actors.

propaganda *n* false, biased, or self-serving information, usually designed to harm or discredit another person, group, etc.

propagate *vt* **1** cause to increase or multiply. **2** reproduce or transmit in reproduction. **3** spread. *vi* **1** breed; multiply. **2** move (through); be transmitted. **propagation** *n*.

propel *vt* (-ll-) cause to move forwards; drive. **propeller** *n* powered device, usually consisting of blades mounted on a revolving shaft, for propelling aircraft, ships, etc.

proper *adj* **1** suitable; appropriate; right; apt. **2** having good manners, correct. **3** within the technical or strict meaning of a term, etc. **properly** *adv*. **proper noun** *n also* **proper name** noun that refers to a specific person, place, or thing.

property *n* **1** possession(s). **2** piece of land; estate. **3** ownership. **4** quality or characteristic associated with something.

prophecy (ˈprɔfisi) *n* **1** prediction. **2** divine revelation. **3** prophetic declaration. **prophesy** (ˈprɔfisai) *vt* **1** predict; proclaim; foretell. **2** reveal by divine inspiration. *vi* declare what is to come. **prophet** *n* **1** person who speaks by divine inspiration. **2** person who predicts future events, etc. **3** inspired leader, etc. **prophetic** *adj*.

proportion *n* **1** relative size or magnitude, ratio,

comparative relation. **2** symmetry; harmony. **3** part of a whole; share; portion. **proportions** *pl n* size. ~*vt* adjust or arrange proportions of. **proportional** *adj*.

propose *vt* **1** submit for consideration; suggest. **2** recommend for membership, office, etc. **3** intend; plan to do. *vi* make a proposal of marriage. **proposal** *n* **1** act of proposing. **2** plan; scheme. **3** offer of marriage.

proposition *n* **1** suggested plan; scheme. **2** statement; assertion. **3** point or subject offered for discussion. *vt* suggest a plan, scheme, etc., to.

proprietor *n* person who owns a business.

propriety *n* **1** suitability; correctness; aptness. **2** good conduct.

propulsion *n* **1** act of propelling or state of being propelled. **2** impulse; force.

prose *n* speech, writing, or printed matter, esp as distinguished from poetry.

prosecute *vt* bring legal action against. *vi* seek legal redress. **prosecutor** *n*. **prosecution** *n* **1** act of prosecuting or state of being prosecuted. **2** lawyers acting for the Crown in a criminal lawsuit.

prospect *n* **1** expectation; probability; future outlook. **2** scenic view; outlook. **prospects** *pl n* chances of success, good fortune, etc. ~*vt,vi* search, esp. for oil or valuable minerals; explore. **prospective** *adj* anticipated; expected; likely.

prospectus *n* statement or pamphlet giving details of a coming event or of school or academic courses or describing an organization, etc.

prosperous *adj* **1** successful; flourishing. **2** having plenty of money, well-off. **3** favourable; promising. **prosperity** *n* wealth; success. **prosper** *vi* be successful; thrive.

prostitute *n* woman who charges money for sexual intercourse. *vt* **1** offer (oneself) for sexual intercourse for money. **2** sell for immediate gain; put to a base or unworthy use. **prostitution** *n*.

prostrate *adj* ('prɔstreit) **1** lying with the face downwards. **2** helpless; defenceless; exhausted. *vt* (prɔ'streit) **1** throw (oneself) down in an act of submission, humility, etc. **2** force or throw to the ground. **3** render helpless; overcome.

protagonist *n* leading character, actor, participant, spokesman, etc.

protect *vt* guard; defend; shield from harm, etc. **protection** *n*. **protective** *adj*.

protégé *n* person under the protection or guidance of another.

protein *n* type of complex organic compound, found esp. in meat, eggs, and milk, essential for metabolism.

protest *n* ('proutest) **1** serious or formal objection, disapproval, or dissent. **2** act of objecting or declaring formally. *vt,vi* (prou'test) **1** object; complain. **2** affirm seriously or solemnly.

Protestant *n* member or adherent of any of various Christian Churches outside the Roman Catholic Church.

protocol *n* etiquette, esp. in formal or diplomatic situations.

proton *n* stable positively charged particle that occurs in the nucleus of an atom.

prototype *n* first model, design, or pattern; original.

protrude *vt,vi* project or thrust out. **protuberance** *n*.

proud *adj* **1** feeling intensely pleased with an achievement, etc. **2** showing or having self-esteem, often excessive. **3** very creditable. **proudly** *adv*. **proudness** *n*.

prove *vt* **1** demonstrate to be true or genuine. **2** test; verify; demonstrate by using, etc. **3** show to be as expected or specified. *vi* turn out (to be).

proverb *n* short common saying, expressing a general truth. **proverbial** *adj*.

provide *vt* **1** equip; supply; furnish. **2** yield. *vi* supply money or means of support (for). **providing** *conj also* **provided** on condition (that).

province *n* **1** administrative division of a country. **2** area of learning, interest, or activity. **provinces** *pl n* parts of a country distinct from the leading financial, cultural, or government centres. **provincial** *adj* **1** relating to a province; not national. **2** lacking sophistication; rustic. *n* unsophisticated person.

provision *n* **1** supplying of something needed. **2** arrangement in advance. **3** stipulation. **4** something provided. **provisions** *pl n* food and other necessities. **provisional** *adj* temporary; serving only a limited function, need, etc.

proviso *n* condition; stipulation.

provoke *vt* **1** make angry; irritate; enrage. **2**

arouse; move to action. **3** cause to happen; induce. **provocation** *n*. **provocative** *adj*.

prow *n* front part of a ship or boat; bow.

prowess *n* **1** bravery; courage. **2** accomplishment, esp. showing unusual ability.

prowl *vt,vi* move about stealthily, esp. in search of something. *n* act of prowling.

proximity *n* nearness; near neighbourhood.

prude *n* person who is excessively prim or modest. **prudish** *adj*.

prudent *adj* **1** wisely cautious or careful. **2** showing caution, good judgment, etc. **prudence** *n*.

prune[1] *n* dried plum, dark brown in colour.

prune[2] *vt* **1** trim; cut off, esp. from trees and shrubs. **2** remove (excesses, etc.).

pry *vi* look inquisitively; enquire closely or furtively; examine with intrusive curiosity.

psalm *n* religious song or hymn.

pseudonym *n* false name used by a writer, etc., to conceal his identity.

psychedelic *adj* relating to or producing a joyful state of expanded consciousness.

psychiatry *n* branch of medicine concerned with treating mental illness. **psychiatric** *adj*. **psychiatrist** *n*.

psychic *adj* **1** relating to the mind or mental activities. **2** relating to unusual mental powers, such as telepathy. **3** involving a nonphysical force or influence.

psychoanalysis *n* technique or system of bringing subconscious conflicts into awareness. **psychoanalyst** *n*. **psychoanalyse** *vt* treat by psychoanalysis.

psychology *n* scientific study of mental attitudes and human or animal behaviour. **psychologist** *n*. **psychological** *adj* **1** relating to psychology. **2** arising in the mind; irrational.

psychopath *n* person suffering from severe mental and emotional instability. **psychopathic** *adj*.

psychosis *n* serious mental illness. **psychotic** *adj*.

psychosomatic *adj* relating to a physical disorder that is caused or aggravated by the emotional state.

pub *n inf also* **public house** building licensed for the sale and consumption of alcoholic drinks. **publican** *n* person responsible for running a pub.

puberty *n* age at which a person becomes sexually mature.

public *adj* **1** relating or belonging to the people of a community, country, etc. **2** general; available to all; not private. *n* **1** people in general. **2** followers; admirers. **public relations** *n* business or activity of promoting goodwill for an organization, individual, etc. **public school** *n* private independent fee-paying school.

publication *n* act or product of publishing.

publicity *n* **1** state or condition of being generally known. **2** business, activity, or methods of informing the public about a person, product, campaign, etc.

publicize *vt* make public; bring to general notice.

publish *vt,vi* produce and issue (books, etc.) for sale. *vt* make known to the public. **publisher** *n*.

pucker *vt,vi* gather into wrinkles or folds. *n* uneven fold; wrinkle.

pudding *n* **1** cooked dish of various ingredients, such as suet or sponge with fruit or meat. **2** course following the main meal; sweet; dessert.

puddle *n* small pool of water or other liquid.

puff *n* **1** brief burst of air, smoke, vapour, etc.; gust of wind. **2** draw at a cigarette, cigar, or pipe. *vi,vt* **1** send out puffs of air, smoke, etc. **2** *also* **puff up** *or* **out** swell; inflate. **3** smoke. *vi* breathe in short gasps; pant.

pull *vt,vi* tug (at) forcefully; haul; jerk. *vt* **1** move forward by means of or using force; draw. **2** tear or rip (apart, out, etc.). **3** remove from the natural or normal position by pulling. **pull apart** criticize severely. **pull faces** grimace. **pull a fast one** trick; deceive. **pull in 1** draw into a station, kerb, etc., and stop. **2** attract. **pull off** succeed in accomplishing something. **pull oneself together** regain self-control. **pull one's weight** make a significant contribution towards a common task. **pull out** withdraw; abandon; leave. **pull someone's leg** tease. **pull strings** use personal influence. **pull through** recover. **pull up 1** stop. **2** draw level in a race. ~*n* act or force of pulling. **pullover** *n* sweater; jumper.

pulley *n* wheel for raising weights by pulling downwards on a cord, etc., passing over its grooved rim.

pulp *n* **1** mass of soft moist matter. **2** moist

mixture of wood particles, rags, etc., from which paper is made. *vt,vi* reduce or be reduced to pulp.

pulpit *n* raised stand or platform from which a clergyman preaches.

pulsate *vi* beat or throb, esp. rhythmically; quiver; vibrate. **pulsation** *n*. **pulse** *n* **1** periodic throbbing of the arteries, caused by successive contraction and relaxation of the heart. **2** transient change in voltage, current, etc.

pulverize *vt,vi* grind or pound to a fine powder or be so reduced. *vt* demolish.

pump *n* machine for forcing liquids or gases to a different level, container, etc., for reducing fluid pressure, etc. *vt,vi* raise, clear, inflate, etc., with a pump. *vt* **1** move up and down repeatedly. **2** elicit by repeated questioning. **3** question for information.

pumpkin *n* large orange-coloured edible gourd.

pun *n* play on words, esp. those with similar sounds. *vi* (-nn-) make puns.

punch[1] *n* **1** sharp forceful blow, esp. with the fist. **2** forcefulness; drive. **3** tool for stamping, piercing, etc. *vt* **1** hit sharply, esp. with the fist. **2** prod; poke. **3** stamp, pierce, etc., with a punch.

punch[2] *n* drink usually made in quantity by mixing wine or spirits with fruit, spices, etc.

punctual *adj* on time; prompt. **punctuality** *n*.

punctuate *vt* **1** mark (sentences, etc.) with full stops, commas, brackets, etc. **2** give emphasis to; stress. **3** interrupt at intervals. *vi* use punctuation. **punctuation** *n* **1** various marks inserted in sentences, etc., to clarify meaning. **2** act of punctuating.

puncture *n* **1** tiny hole made by pricking or piercing. **2** loss of pressure in a tyre resulting from this. *vt* **1** prick; pierce. **2** deflate by a puncture.

pungent *adj* **1** smelling or tasting sharp or acrid. **2** caustic; biting. **pungency** *n*. **pungently** *adv*.

punish *vt* **1** inflict a penalty on; make to suffer for some offence, fault, etc.; discipline. **2** hurt; injure. **punishment** *n*.

punt[1] *n* boat with a flat bottom, moved by aid of a pole. *vt,vi* propel (a boat) by using a pole.

punt[2] *vi,n* gamble; bet.

pup *n* young dog, seal, or similar animal.

pupa *n, pl* **pupae** ('pju:pi:) inactive stage of development of an insect, between larva and adult forms. **pupal** *adj*.

pupil[1] *n* student; schoolchild.

pupil[2] *n* variable aperture in the iris of the eye through which light enters.

puppet *n* **1** figure with movable limbs controlled by strings or wires; marionette. **2** person, group, etc., under the control of another.

puppy *n* **1** young dog. **2** conceited young man.

purchase *vt* buy; obtain by payment. *n* **1** something bought. **2** act of buying. **3** leverage. **4** hold; grip. **purchase tax** *n* tax levied on purchased goods, being added to the selling price.

pure *adj* **1** not contaminated; free from mixture with anything else. **2** simple; not complicated. **3** innocent; chaste. **4** mere. **purely** *adv* entirely; solely. **purity** *n*.

purgatory *n* **1** place where souls of the dead go for punishment of earthly sins before entering heaven. **2** state or condition of temporary pain, suffering, etc.

purge *vt* **1** cleanse; remove by cleaning. **2** rid of waste, unwanted elements, etc.; clear; eliminate; remove. *vi* become cleansed, purified, etc. *n* **1** act of purging. **2** something that purges. **3** *also* **purgative** drug or agent aiding defecation.

purify *vt,vi* make or become pure. *vt* free from undesirable elements, etc. **purification** *n*.

Puritan *n* member of an extreme reform group of 16th- and 17th-century Protestants. **puritan** person who is excessively strict, esp. in matters of religion or morals. **puritanical** *adj*.

purl *n* knitting stitch that is an inverted plain stitch. *vt,vi* knit in purl.

purple *n,adj* reddish-blue or bluish-red. **purplish** *adj*.

purpose *n* **1** end or aim towards which any view, action, etc., is directed; intention. **2** reason. **on purpose** intentionally.

purr *n* low murmuring sound, as made by a contented cat. *vi* utter such a sound.

purse *n* small pouch or bag for holding coins, etc.

pursue *vt* **1** trail; follow closely; chase. **2** attend. **3** seek to gain or accomplish. **4** continue (with or on). **pursuit** *n* **1** act of pursuing. **2** hobby; pastime.

pus *n* yellowish-white matter discharged from an infected wound.

push *vt,vi* **1** press (against) forcefully; impel by

pressure. **2** urge; promote. *vt* thrust (away, through, forward, etc.) with or by force. **pushed** (**for**) *inf* short of. ~*n* **1** act of pushing. **2** *inf* drive; self-assertion. **3** *inf* special effort. **4** *inf* dismissal. **pushchair** *n* small chair on wheels for carrying infants.

pussy *n inf* cat.

put *vt* (-tt-; put) **1** place, deposit, lay, set, or cause to be in any position, situation, or place. **2** render; transform. **3** express; propose. **put across** *or* **over** communicate. **put (it) at** estimate (it) as. **put away 1** store. **2** save. **3** imprison; lock up. **put down 1** record; write. **2** quell. **3** kill (an animal). **put forward** suggest; propose. **put off 1** delay; defer. **2** discourage. **3** switch off. **put on 1** dress in. **2** assume; adopt. **3** wager; bet. **4** switch on. **put out 1** annoy; disturb. **2** extinguish; switch off. **put up 1** build. **2** accommodate. **3** provide; give. **put up with** tolerate. **stay put** remain; not move.

putrid *adj* **1** rotten; decaying. **2** having a foul smell. **3** *inf* awful; of poor quality. **putrefy** *vi,vt* rot; decompose. **putrefaction** *n*.

putt *vt,vi* hit a golfball so that it rolls towards the hole. *n* putted stroke. **putting** *n* game like golf involving putted strokes only.

putty *n* pliable material that sets rigid, used for holding panes of glass in frames, etc. *vt* repair, fill, etc., with putty.

puzzle *vt,vi* confuse or perplex or be confused or perplexed. **puzzle over** strain to discover a solution; expend effort to find a meaning. ~*n* **1** something that poses a problem to be worked out. **2** something that perplexes. **3** jigsaw.

PVC *n* polyvinyl chloride: man-made plastic material, either flexible or rigid, with a wide variety of uses.

Pygmy *n* member of a central African hunting people of small stature. **pygmy** very small person.

pyjamas *pl n* loose trousers and jacket for sleeping in.

pylon *n* tall structure, used esp. to convey high-voltage electric cables over open country.

pyramid *n* **1** solid figure consisting usually of a square base and triangular sloping faces that meet at the top. **2** enormous pyramid-shaped stone monument, esp. of ancient Egypt.

Pyrex *n Tdmk* heat-resistant glass or glassware.

python *n* large snake that kills its prey by squeezing.

Q

quack[1] *n* harsh cry of a duck. *vi* make such a sound.

quack[2] *n* medical practitioner who is unqualified or unreliable.

quadrangle *n* **1** quadrilateral. **2** *also inf* **quad** quadrilateral courtyard, esp. within a school. **quadrangular** *adj*.

quadrant *n* quarter section of a circle.

quadrilateral *n* figure with four sides and four angles. *adj* having four sides and four angles.

quadruped *n* animal with four legs. *adj* having four legs.

quadruple *vt,vi* increase fourfold. *adj* **1** four times as much. **2** having four members, parts, etc.

quadruplet *n* **1** *also inf* **quad** one of four children born at the same time to the same mother. **2** group having four members or parts.

quail[1] *n* small game bird.

quail[2] *vi* shrink with dread or fear; tremble.

quaint *adj* pleasingly odd or old-fashioned. **quaintly** *adv*.

quake *vi* tremble or shake. *n inf* short for **earthquake.**

Quaker *n* member of a pacifist Christian sect advocating simplicity of worship, dress, etc.

qualify *vt,vi* make or become suitable, appropriate, or acceptable (for). *vi* reach a required standard or level. *vt* **1** restrict or modify (a statement, proposal, etc.). **2** temper or moderate. **qualification** *n*.

quality *n* **1** distinguishing attribute or characteristic. **2** degree of fineness or excellence. **3** excellence. **4** accomplishment. **qualitative** *adj*.

qualm *n* pang of conscience; misgiving.

quandary *n* dilemma; perplexed turmoil.

quantify *vt* assess or ascertain the amount of. **quantification** *n*.

quantity *n* **1** amount. **2** large amount.

quarantine *n* careful isolation imposed on people, animals, etc., to prevent the spread of an infectious disease. *vt* put into quarantine; isolate.

quarrel *n* **1** disagreement or dispute. **2** cause for complaint. *vi* (-ll-) argue or disagree; squabble; dispute.

quarry[1] *n* shallow mine or pit from which stone, slate, etc., is excavated. *vt* mine (stone, etc.) from a quarry.

quarry[2] *n* animal, person, or other object of pursuit; game; prey.

quart *n* liquid or dry measure equal to two pints (approx. 1.1 litres) and one quarter of a bushel respectively.

quarter *n* **1** one of four equal parts or portions; one divided by four. **2** *US* twenty-five cents or a coin having this value. *vt* **1** cut or divide into quarters. **2** place or provide someone, esp. soldiers, with lodgings. **quarterly** *adj,adv.* **quarterdeck** *n* rear section of the upper deck of a ship, often reserved for officers. **quartermaster** *n* **1** petty officer on a ship responsible for steering, signals, etc. **2** officer, esp. in the army, responsible for the provision of food, clothing, lodging, etc. **quarters** *pl n* living accommodation.

quartet *n* group of four persons or things, esp. four singers or musicians.

quartz *n* common colourless crystalline mineral.

quash *vt* **1** subdue; suppress. **2** annul or invalidate (a decision, law, etc.).

quaver *n* musical note lasting one eighth the time of a semibreve. *vi* quiver; quake; tremble.

quay *n* man-made landing place to which ships may come to load or unload; wharf.

queasy *adj* **1** feeling or causing nausea; sickly. **2** ill at ease. **queasily** *adv.* **queasiness** *n.*

queen *n* **1** female monarch or wife of a king. **2** woman, thing, etc., regarded as very fine or outstanding. **3** fertile female in a colony of wasps, bees, ants, etc. **4** court card whose value is higher than the jack and lower than the king. **5** most powerful chess piece able to move any distance in a straight or diagonal line. **6** *sl* homosexual male. **queenly** *adj.*

queer *adj* **1** odd; peculiar; strange. **2** *sl* homosexual. *n sl* homosexual. *vt sl* ruin or spoil. **queerly** *adv.*

quell *vt* suppress; subdue; calm.

quench *vt* **1** satisfy (a thirst, etc.). **2** extinguish or smother something such as a fire.

query *n* **1** question. **2** point of doubt. **3** question mark. *vt,vi* raise (a question); ask for (an answer or clarification).

quest *n* search or hunt, esp. one carried on fervently. *vi* engage in a quest; search.

question *n* **1** request for information, a decision, clarification, etc. **2** point of doubt; uncertainty. **3** problem or matter for discussion; issue. *vt,vi* ask questions (of). *vt* cast doubt upon; challenge. **beyond question** indisputable. **call into question** cast doubt upon. **out of the question** impossible. **question mark** *n* mark (?) used at the end of a sentence, phrase, or word to indicate a question. **questionnaire** *n* written list of questions used to gather information, obtain opinions, etc.

queue *n* line of people or things waiting their turn to do or obtain something. *vi* form or wait in a queue.

quibble *n* trivial or petty objection, criticism, evasion, etc. *vi* argue about trivial points; evade by petty criticism or objection.

quick *adj* fast or sudden; swift. *adv* rapidly; swiftly. *n* sensitive flesh at the edge of a fingernail or toenail. **the quick and the dead** the living and the dead. **cut to the quick** hurt or offend deeply. **quicken** *vt,vi* **1** hasten; accelerate. **2** stimulate; revive. **quicksand** *n* soft wet sand into which objects are liable to sink. **quicksilver** *n* mercury. **like quicksilver** moving very swiftly. **quickstep** *n* **1** quick marching step. **2** fast ballroom-dancing step. **quick-tempered** *adj* having a hasty or hot temper; easily angered. **quick-witted** *adj* thinking swiftly; alert.

quid *n, pl* **quid** *sl* pound (money).

quiet *adj* **1** free from harsh noise or disturbance. **2** tranquil; calm. **3** subdued; restrained. *n* calmness; stillness; tranquillity. **quietly** *adv.* **quieten** *vt,vi also* **quiet** make or become quiet; subdue; ease.

quill *n* **1** large feather from the wing or tail of a bird. **2** such a feather made into a pen for writing. **3** one of the spines of a hedgehog, porcupine, etc.

quilt *n* bed covering made of two layers of material filled with some soft fabric and sewn together. *vt,vi* make a quilt (of).

quinine *n* alkaline substance originally obtained from the bark of a tree and used medicinally, esp. in treating malaria.

quintet *n* group of five persons or things, esp. five singers or musicians.

quirk *n* **1** unusual or odd trait or characteristic. **2** sudden twist or turn.

quit *vt,vi* (-tt-; quitted *or* quit) **1** stop; cease. **2**

give up; relinquish; resign. **3** discharge (a debt, etc.). **4** depart (from); leave.

quite *adv* **1** wholly or entirely. **2** *inf* fairly; moderately. **3** positively. *interj* expression of agreement or concurrence.

quiver[1] *vi* shake; tremble; quake. *n* act of quivering; tremble.

quiver[2] *n* case or sheath for holding arrows.

quiz *n* series of questions, often taking the form of a competition between two or more people. *vt* (-zz-) question closely.

quizzical *adj* **1** comical or odd. **2** questioning; perplexed. **3** teasing. **quizzically** *adv*.

quoit *n* ring of rubber, metal, etc., used in a game by being thrown at an upright peg in an attempt to encircle it.

quota *n* prescribed share or amount of something that is allotted to or expected from a person, group, etc.; allotment.

quote *vt* **1** repeat (a passage, sentence, etc.) from a written or spoken source. **2** cite as an example. **3** state the price or cost of. *vi* use a quotation or quotations. *n* quotation. **quotation** *n* **1** *also* **quote** something quoted. **2** act of quoting. **quotation marks** *pl n* punctuation marks ' and ' or " and " used to enclose and indicate a quotation.

R

rabbi *n* **1** Jewish priest. **2** scholar and teacher of the Jewish law.

rabbit *n* small burrowing animal of the hare family with long ears, a short tufty tail, and soft fur. *vi* hunt rabbits.

rabble *n* noisy crowd or throng; mob.

rabid *adj* **1** fervent; wildly enthusiastic. **2** raging; violent. **3** relating to or having rabies.

rabies *n* fatal viral disease that is transmitted by the bite of an infected animal, esp. a dog.

race[1] *n* **1** contest of speed between people or animals in running, swimming, driving, etc. **2** any contest in which people compete to be the first to do or achieve something. *vi* **1** take part in a race. **2** hurry; go quickly. *vt* **1** run a race or compete with. **2** cause (a horse, car, etc.) to take part in a race. **racecourse** *n* track on which races, esp. horseraces, are held. **racehorse** *n* horse trained and used for racing.

race[2] *n* **1** group of people connected by common ancestry or blood. **2** subdivision of mankind to which people belong by virtue of their hereditary physical characteristics. **3** any group of people, plants, or animals regarded as a distinct class. **race relations** *pl n* relationships between people of different races, esp. within a single society. **racial** *adj* of or relating to race or races. **racially** *adv*.

rack *n* **1** framework, holder, or container; storage or display unit. **2** former instrument of torture on which people were tied and stretched. *vt* **1** torture on the rack. **2** torment. **3** arrange on or in a rack. **rack one's brains** strive to remember or understand something.

racket[1] *n* **1** noisy disturbance; uproar. **2** *sl* any illegal or dishonest scheme, activity, business, etc.

racket[2] *n* bat used in tennis, squash, etc., consisting of a rounded frame across which strings are stretched. **rackets** *n* kind of tennis played in a walled court.

radar *n* system for determining the presence and position of an object, such as a ship, by transmitting a beam of radio waves and measuring the direction and time taken for the echo to return from the object.

radial *adj* **1** branching out from a central point; radiating. **2** of or relating to a radius.

radiant *adj* **1** glowing with heat or brightness; shining. **2** glowing with happiness, joy, hope, etc. **3** emitted in rays.

radiate *v* ('reidieit) *vt,vi* **1** emit radiation. *vt* transmit or give out a particular emotion or feeling. *vi* spread or branch out from a central point. *adj* ('reidiit) having rays or radiating from a centre. **radiation** *n* **1** emission of energy in the form of light, heat, sound, electrons, etc. **2** energy so emitted and propagated. **3** radiate arrangement. **radiator** *n* **1** heating device through which hot air, water, steam, etc., passes. **2** device by which a car engine is kept cool.

radical *adj* **1** basic; fundamental. **2** essential; complete. **3** favouring fundamental political, social, or other reforms. **4** of or arising from a root. *n* person favouring radical reforms.

radio *n* **1** transmission of information by waves transmitted through the atmosphere. **2** device for receiving radio broadcasts; wireless. **3** broadcasts so received. *vt,vi* transmit a message, etc., by radio.

radioactivity *n* spontaneous disintegration of

unstable atomic nuclei with the emission of radiation. **radioactive** *adj* undergoing or relating to radioactivity.

radish *n* small crisp white or red root of a plant of the mustard family, usually eaten raw.

radium *n* radioactive metallic element.

radius *n, pl* **radii** (ˈreidiai) *or* **radiuses 1** line from the centre of a circle or sphere to its perimeter or surface. **2** length of such a line. **3** any radiating or raylike part. **4** circular area defined by the length of its radius. **5** range or extent of experience, influence, activity, etc.

raffia *n* fibre obtained from the leafstalks of a Madagascan palm, used for weaving baskets, matting, etc.

raffle *n* scheme for raising money in which tickets give the purchaser the chance of winning a prize, the winning tickets being randomly selected. *vt* offer as a prize in a raffle.

raft *n* buoyant material, such as logs, fastened together into a platform to transport goods or people by water.

rafter *n* sloping timber or beam on which a roof is supported.

rag[1] *n* **1** scrap of cloth; torn, dirty, or worthless fragment. **2** *sl* newspaper or magazine, esp. one of poor quality. **rags** *pl n* old or tattered clothing. **ragged** *adj* **1** rough, tattered, or torn. **2** uneven; jagged. **3** irregular or imperfect.

rag[2] *vt* (-gg-) **1** tease or play jokes on. **2** scold. *n* **1** joke or escapade. **2** organized series of games, events, etc., by students to publicize the collection of money for charity.

rage *n* **1** extreme anger; fury. **2** violence or intensity of fire, wind, disease, etc. **3** intensity of emotion, appetite, or enthusiasm. **4** anything arousing widespread enthusiasm. *vi* **1** display violent anger. **2** move, continue, prevail, etc., with great intensity or violence.

raid *n* surprise attack, esp. one undertaken to capture goods, personnel, etc. *vt,vi* make a surprise attack (on).

rail *n* **1** horizontal bar of wood or metal acting as a barrier, support, etc. **2** fence. **3** one of a pair of parallel metal bars laid as a track for trains, etc. **4** railway transportation. *vt* enclose with a rail; fence. **railing** *n* fence or framework of rails. **railway** *n* **1** permanent track of rails on which trains may transport passengers, goods, etc. **2** complete network of such tracks together with stations, land, etc.

rain *n* **1** drops of water falling from clouds, condensed from atmospheric water vapour. **2** an instance of this; shower. **3** rapid heavy fall or occurrence of anything. *vt,vi* fall or cause to fall as or like rain. *vt* give (praise, gifts, etc.) in large quantities. **rain cats and dogs** rain very heavily. **rainbow** *n* banded arc of spectral colours visible in the sky during or just after a shower of rain. **rainfall** *n* **1** fall of rain; shower. **2** amount of water falling as rain, snow, etc., in a given area within a given period of time.

raise *vt* **1** elevate; lift up. **2** build; erect. **3** bring up for consideration. **4** initiate or inspire; provoke. **5** bring up (children, etc.); rear. **6** collect or gather. **7** increase in degree, size, intensity, etc. **8** evoke; suggest. **9** promote in rank, dignity, etc. **10** summon up. **11** bring back to life. **12** remove or lift (a ban, siege, etc.).

raisin *n* sweet dried grape.

rajah *n* king, prince, or chief, esp. in India.

rake *n* tool with a long handle and teeth or prongs at one end used for gathering leaves, etc. *vt* **1** gather, collect, or smooth with a rake. **2** gather in or collect up. **3** search through carefully. *vi* use a rake. **rake up** bring up or reveal (something, esp. from the past).

rally *vt,vi* **1** reassemble. **2** bring or come together for some common purpose. *vi* **1** gather to support or assist a person, cause, etc. **2** regain strength or vigour; recover. *n* **1** recovery. **2** gathering of people supporting a cause, taking part in a sporting event, etc.

ram *n* **1** male sheep. **2** device used to batter, crush, or drive against something. *vt* (-mm-) **1** strike or crash against with great force. **2** force, cram, or press.

ramble *vi* **1** wander about; stroll. **2** grow in or follow a meandering course. **3** talk or write aimlessly or incoherently. *n* walk taken for pleasure. **rambler** *n*.

ramp *n* sloping surface joining two levels.

rampage *vi* rush about wildly or destructively. *n* wild, violent, or destructive behaviour. **on the rampage** very angry; engaged in destructive behaviour.

rampant *adj* **1** rife; unchecked. **2** violent in opinion, action, etc.

rampart *n* 1 mound of earth, usually surmounted by a parapet, fortifying a castle, fort, etc. 2 any defence or protection.

ramshackle *adj* loosely constructed or held together; shaky; derelict.

ran *v pt of* **run.**

ranch *n* large farm, esp. in America, for rearing cattle, horses, or sheep. **rancher** *n.*

rancid *adj* having an unpleasant stale smell or taste; rank.

rancour *n* angry resentment; bitterness.

random *adj* happening, done, etc., without aim or purpose; chance; haphazard. *n* **at random** without choice, purpose, method, etc. **randomly** *adv.*

rang *v pt of* **ring.**

range *n* 1 limits within which variation is possible. 2 extent or scope. 3 possible distance of movement, flight, etc. 4 place with targets for shooting practice. 5 chain of mountains. 6 row or line. 7 class, set, or series. 8 large cooking stove. *vt* 1 arrange in order, esp. in rows or lines. 2 dispose or place in a particular group, class, etc. 3 travel through or over; roam. *vi* 1 vary within specified limits. 2 extend or run, esp. in a given direction. 3 roam or wander (over). 4 occur within a certain area or time. 5 have a particular range.

rank[1] *n* 1 position or standing in a scale or graded body. 2 row or line, esp. of soldiers. *vt* 1 arrange in a row or rank. 2 assign to a certain position, station, class, etc. *vi* hold a certain position. **rank and file** *n* body of soldiers in an army or people in any other organization, as opposed to the officers or leaders. **ranks** *pl n* soldiers as opposed to officers.

rank[2] *adj* 1 growing vigorously or producing luxuriant vigorous growth. 2 having a strong unpleasant smell or taste. 3 utter; complete. **rankly** *adv.* **rankness** *n.*

rankle *vi* annoy; hurt one's pride.

ransack *vt* 1 search thoroughly or energetically. 2 plunder.

ransom *n* 1 redeeming of a kidnapped person, captured goods, etc., for a price. 2 price paid or demanded. *vt* release from captivity, detention, etc., by paying the price demanded.

rant *vi* shout angrily; rage.

rap *vt,vi* (-pp-) 1 knock, strike, or tap, esp. quickly. 2 *also* **rap out** say sharply. *n* 1 quick light blow; tap. 2 sound of this. 3 *sl* blame or punishment, esp. a prison sentence.

rape *n* 1 crime of having sexual intercourse with a woman without her consent. 2 act of taking by force. *vt,vi* commit rape (on). **rapist** *n.*

rapid *adj* quick; fast; swift. **rapids** *pl n* part of a river where the water flows very swiftly. **rapidity** *n.* **rapidly** *adv.*

rapier *n* sword with a slender pointed blade used for thrusting.

rapt *adj* 1 enthralled; enchanted. 2 totally absorbed or engrossed.

rapture *n* ecstatic delight; joy; pleasure. **rapturous** *adj.*

rare[1] 1 seldom occurring, found, experienced, etc. 2 remarkable or unusual, esp. in excellence. 3 of low density. **rarely** *adv.* **rarity** *n.*

rare[2] *adj* not completely cooked; underdone.

rascal *n* 1 scoundrel; rogue. 2 mischievous child or animal. **rascally** *adj,adv.*

rash[1] *adj* hasty in speech or action; reckless.

rash[2] *n* skin eruption, as of spots.

rasher *n* thin slice of bacon.

rasp *vt,vi* grate; sound harsh. *n* harsh grating sound.

raspberry *n* shrub of the rose family producing small juicy red edible fruit.

rat *n* 1 long-tailed rodent resembling but larger than the mouse. 2 *sl* despicable person. **smell a rat** be suspicious about. ~*v* (-tt-) **rat on** *sl* desert or betray (friends, a cause, etc.).

rate *n* 1 quantity, amount, degree, etc., relative to a unit of something else. 2 price. 3 speed of movement, action, etc. 4 tax paid by householders, companies, etc., to cover the supply of local services and amenities. *vt* 1 appraise the value or worth of. 2 esteem; consider. 3 deserve. 4 determine (prices, etc.) at a certain rate. *vi* 1 be classed or ranked. 2 have status, value, position, etc.

rather *adv* 1 more readily; preferably. 2 somewhat; quite. 3 with more reason, justice, etc. 4 more accurately or properly. 5 on the contrary.

ratio *n* fixed numerical relation between two similar magnitudes; proportion.

ration *n* fixed allowance; share. *vt* 1 apportion; share out. 2 restrict to or provide with rations.

rational *adj* 1 of, relating to, or based on reason. 2 able to reason. 3 reasonable; sensible. **rationality** *n.* **rationally** *adv.* **ration-**

alize *vt* **1** make rational; justify unconscious behaviour. **2** make (an industry, process, etc.) more efficient; streamline. *vi* think in a rational manner; reason.

rattle *vi,vt* make or cause to make a series of short sharp sounds; vibrate noisily. *vi also* **rattle on** chatter. *vt* **1** say or do rapidly. **2** *sl* confuse or disturb (someone). *n* **1** rapid succession of short sharp sounds. **2** device producing a rattling sound, such as a baby's toy.

raucous *adj* rough or harsh sounding. **raucously** *adv*.

ravage *n* **1** violent destructive action. **2** devastation; damage. *vt* damage or devastate. *vi* cause great damage.

rave *vi,vt* talk or utter wildly or incoherently. *vi also* **rave about** talk or write very enthusiastically (about). *n* **1** act of raving. **2** extravagant praise.

raven *n* large bird of the crow family with shiny black plumage and a harsh cry. *adj,n* shiny black.

ravenous *adj* **1** extremely hungry. **2** greedy for praise, recognition, etc. **ravenously** *adv*.

ravine steep valley; gorge; canyon.

ravioli *n* small pieces of pasta enclosing chopped meat, etc., usually served in a tomato sauce.

ravish *vt* **1** seize and carry away forcibly. **2** rape. **3** enrapture.

raw *adj* **1** not cooked. **2** in a natural state; unprocessed. **3** inexperienced. **4** painfully open or exposed, as a wound. **5** crude; vulgar. **6** harsh; unfair; unpleasant. **rawness** *n*.

ray *n* **1** narrow beam of light, etc. **2** tiny amount of hope, comfort, etc.; spark. **3** line or structure radiating from a centre. *vi,vt* radiate.

rayon *n* man-made textile or fibre made from cellulose.

raze *vt* demolish or destroy (buildings, etc.) completely.

razor *n* instrument fitted with cutting edges, used esp. for shaving hair.

reach *vt* **1** get to; arrive at; attain; come to. **2** establish contact with. **3** amount to; total. *vt,vi* extend as far as. **reach for** stretch up or out for in order to grasp and bring closer. ~*n* **1** act of reaching. **2** range; extent covered.

react *vi* **1** reciprocate. **2** respond to a stimulus. **3** act in opposition or in reverse. **4** interact. **reaction** *n* **1** reciprocal action, movement, or tendency. **2** response to a stimulus. **3** response to an event, idea, etc. **4** tendency or movement in politics towards extreme conservatism. **5** interaction between chemicals. **reactionary** *adj* relating to reaction, esp. in politics. *n* reactionary person.

read *v* (read) *vt,vi* **1** apprehend the meaning of (letters, words, etc.). **2** *also* **read out** utter (printed or written matter) aloud. **3** be occupied in reading. **4** study (a subject). **5** learn of by reading. *vt* **1** interpret. **2** register; indicate. **3** predict; foretell. *vi* have a certain wording. **read between the lines** deduce an implied meaning not openly stated. ~*n* act of reading. **reader** *n*.

readjust *vt* adjust again or afresh; rearrange; readapt.

ready *adj* **1** fully prepared. **2** willing. **3** prompt; quick. **4** inclined; apt. **5** likely or liable (to). **6** immediately available. **get ready 1** prepare. **2** dress oneself. *n* **at the ready** in position. **readily** *adv* willingly; without delay.

real *adj* **1** true; genuine; authentic. **2** actual; not imaginary or fictitious. **really** *adv* **1** in fact; actually. **2** truly; genuinely. **reality** *n*. **realism** *n* interest in or concern for the real or actual. **realist** *n*. **realistic** *adj*. **realistically** *adv*.

realize *vt,vi* comprehend; appreciate; be aware. *vt* **1** bring to fruition. **2** convert into cash. *vi* be sold for; bring as proceeds; gain. **realization** *n*.

realm *n* **1** kingdom; domain. **2** region or sphere in which something rules or predominates.

reap *vt,vi* cut or harvest (grain). *vt* obtain as a result or recompense.

rear[1] *n* **1** back part of anything. **2** position behind or in the rear. **3** buttocks. *adj* of, at, or in the rear. **rear admiral** *n* naval officer ranking immediately below a vice-admiral. **rearguard** *n* military detachment that brings up and protects the rear, esp. in retreat.

rear[2] *vt* **1** care for and bring to maturity. **2** lift up; erect. *vi* rise up on the hind legs. **rear up** rise up in anger, resentment, etc.

reason *n* **1** ground, cause, or motive. **2** justification; explanation. **3** mental ability of logical argument. **4** good sense. **5** sanity. *vi,vt* **1** think or argue logically (about). **2** conclude or infer (that). **3** urge or persuade by reasoning. **reasonable** *adj* **1** amenable to reason. **2** based on reason; sensible or sound. 3 able to reason. 4 not excessive; moderate. **reasonably** *adv*.

reassure *vt* allay (fears, doubts, etc.); restore confidence or tranquillity to. **reassurance** *n*.

rebate *n* return of part of an amount paid for goods, a service, etc.

rebel *n* (ˈrebəl) person who defies authority or control. *vi* (riˈbel) (-ll-) resist; oppose. **rebel against** show or feel strong aversion (for). **rebellion** *n*. **rebellious** *adj*.

rebound *vt,vi* (riˈbaund) spring back or cause to spring back. *n* (ˈri:baund) act of rebounding; recoil.

rebuff *vt* treat scornfully; turn away; snub. *n* rejection; abrupt dismissal.

rebuke *vt,n* reprimand.

recalcitrant *adj* unwilling to submit; wayward; wilful; stubborn. **recalcitrance** *n*.

recall *vt* 1 remember. 2 call back. 3 revoke or withdraw. *n* 1 act or instance of recalling. 2 memory.

recede *vi* 1 move back; retreat. 2 become more distant. 3 slope backwards. 4 withdraw from a bargain, promise, etc. 5 decline in value, etc.

receipt *n* 1 written acknowledgement of payment or delivery. 2 act of receiving; fact of being received. *vt* mark (a bill) as paid. *vt,vi* write or give a receipt for. **receipts** *pl n* amount received.

receive *vt* 1 take into one's possession; gain; get. 2 encounter, experience, or undergo. 3 bear; sustain. 4 gain knowledge of; learn. 5 welcome; admit. *vi* 1 receive something. 2 buy and sell stolen goods. **receiver** *n* 1 someone or something that receives. 2 device for converting electrical signals into their desired form.

recent *adj* occurring, appearing, done, etc., just before the present time; fresh; not remote. **recently** *adv*.

receptacle *n* 1 container. 2 portion of a plant stem bearing a flower or flower head.

reception *n* 1 act of receiving or being received. 2 manner of being received. 3 formal social gathering. 4 area in an office, hotel, etc., where visitors are received. 5 quality attained in receiving radio signals, etc. **receptionist** *n* person employed to receive visitors, answer the telephone, etc. **receptive** *adj* able, quick, or willing to receive suggestions, requests, etc.

recess (riˈses, ˈri:ses) 1 part or area that is set back; alcove. 2 *also* **recesses** secluded inner place or area. 3 *US* temporary break; holiday. *vt* 1 place in a recess. 2 make a recess in or of.

recession *n* 1 withdrawal. 2 receding part. 3 decline or falling off in business activity.

recipe *n* formula or method, esp. for preparing a dish in cookery.

recipient *n* person who receives.

reciprocal *adj* 1 given, felt, etc., on both sides; mutual. 2 given, done, etc., in return. *n* reciprocal relationship; equivalent; counterpart. **reciprocate** *vt,vi* 1 do, feel, etc., (something similar) in return. 2 give and receive; interchange.

recite *vt,vi* repeat aloud, as from memory. *vt* read or narrate before an audience. **recital** *n* 1 musical performance, poetry reading, etc. 2 detailed account; statement; description.

reckless *adj* careless of consequences; heedless; rash. **recklessly** *adv*.

reckon *vt,vi* add (up); calculate. *vt* consider; regard as; think. **reckon with** 1 settle accounts with. 2 take into consideration.

reclaim *vt* 1 render useable for cultivation, habitation, etc. 2 recover from waste products. 3 bring back from error, sin, etc. **reclamation** *n*.

recline *vi,vt* lean back or cause to lean back. **reclinable** *adj*.

recluse *n* hermit.

recognize *vt* 1 identify; know again. 2 perceive; realize. 3 acknowledge or accept the existence, truth, etc., of. 4 show appreciation of by a reward, etc. **recognition** *n*. **recognizable** *adj*.

recoil *vi* 1 draw or shrink back, as in fear, horror, etc. 2 spring back when released, as a firearm. 3 rebound or react upon. *n* act or instance of recoiling.

recollect *vt,vi* recall; remember. **recollection** *n*.

recommend *vt* 1 speak or write of favourably; commend. 2 urge as advisable; advise. 3 entrust to. 4 make acceptable or likeable. **recommendable** *adj*. **recommendation** *n*.

recompense *vt* 1 compensate, repay, or reward. 2 compensate for (a loss, etc.). *n* compensation; repayment; remuneration.

reconcile *vt* 1 make no longer opposed or hostile. 2 settle. 3 make consistent or compatible. **reconciliation** *n*.

reconstruct *vt* **1** rebuild. **2** recreate from surviving information. **reconstruction** *n*.

record *v* (riˈkɔːd) *vt* **1** set down for future reference, esp. in writing. **2** produce in a lasting form, as on magnetic tape. **3** register; indicate. *vi* record music, etc. *n* (ˈrekɔːd) **1** written account. **2** something preserving evidence of the past. **3** aggregate of past achievements, actions, etc.; career. **4** attainment, occurrence, etc., that surpasses all others. **5** flat disc with a spiral groove played on a gramophone to reproduce music, etc. **6** list of a person's crimes. **on record** stated or known publicly. **recorder** *n* wind instrument similar to the flute.

recount *vt* **1** relate or tell in detail. **2** enumerate.

recover *vt* **1** regain; retrieve; reclaim. **2** secure compensation for; make up for. *vi* **1** regain health, composure, balance, etc. **2** get back to a former or normal position, state, etc. **recovery** *n*.

recreation *n* **1** refreshment and relaxation afforded by exercise, a pastime, etc. **2** hobby, exercise, or other diversion providing this. **recreational** *adj*.

recriminate *vi* accuse one's accuser. **recrimination** *n*.

recruit *n* recently enlisted member, esp. of the armed forces. *vt,vi* enlist (new personnel, etc.). **recruitment** *n*.

rectangle *n* four-sided figure with four right angles. **rectangular** *adj*.

rectify *vt* set or put right; remedy; correct. **rectification** *n*.

rector *n* clergyman of a parish formerly returning tithes. **rectory** *n* residence of a rector.

rectum *n* lower end of the intestine.

recuperate *vi* recover from illness or fatigue. *vt* recover (financial losses). **recuperation** *n*.

recur *vi* (-rr-) **1** occur again; be repeated. **2** return to the mind, in conversation, etc. **recurrence** *n*.

red *n* **1** colour of the spectrum that is the colour of fresh blood, ripe tomatoes, etc. **2** *also* **Red** someone who is radical in politics, esp. a communist. **in the red** in debt. **see red** become very angry. ~*adj* of the colour red. **reddish** *adj*. **redness** *n*. **redcurrant** *n* shrub bearing small red edible berries. **redden** *vt,vi* make or become red. *vi* blush. **red-handed** *adj,adv* in the act of performing a deed, committing a crime, etc. **red tape** *n* complicated official or administrative procedure.

redeem *vt* **1** buy or get back; recover; pay off. **2** convert (bonds, etc.) into cash. **3** fulfil (a pledge, etc.). **4** make amends for. **5** deliver from sin. **redemption** *n*.

redress *vt* set right; remedy; repair; adjust. *n* compensation; reparation.

reduce *vt,vi* make or become smaller or less; diminish; decrease. *vt* **1** bring or force into a certain state, form, etc. **2** lower; weaken; subdue. **reduction** *n*.

redundant *adj* **1** excessive; superfluous; unnecessary. **2** deprived of a job through being superfluous, etc. **redundancy** *n*.

reed *n* **1** hollow straight stem of any of various tall grasses. **2** vibrating piece of cane or metal in some wind instruments. **3** wind instrument that sounds by means of a reed.

reef *n* narrow ridge of sand, rocks, etc., at or just under the surface of water.

reek *vi* smell strongly or unpleasantly; stink. *vt* emit (smoke, etc.). *n* strong unpleasant smell.

reel[1] *n* cylinder, frame, or spool on which thread, wire, film, etc., may be wound. *vt* wind on a reel. **reel off** say, write, or produce easily and quickly.

reel[2] *vi* sway; rock; stagger; whirl. *n* act of reeling; stagger.

refectory *n* large communal dining hall.

refer *v* (-rr-) *vt,vi* direct attention, etc., (to). *vt* submit; assign. **refer to 1** be concerned with; relate to. **2** resort to for help, information, etc. **3** mention or allude (to). **referee** *n* **1** person to whom something is referred for decision. **2** umpire in certain games. **3** person who supplies a written reference. *vi* act as a referee. **reference** *n* **1** act of referring. **2** mention or allusion. **3** direction of attention to a person or thing. **4** written statement as to character, abilities, etc. **5** relation; regard. **referendum** *n, pl* **referendums** *or* **referenda** (refəˈrendə) referring of legislative measures to the direct vote of the electorate for approval or rejection.

refine *vt,vi* **1** make or become fine; purify; separate out. **2** make or become more polished, elegant, etc. **refined** *adj*. **refinement** *n*. **refinery** *n* establishment for refining oil, sugar, etc.

reflation *n* government action taken to stimulate the economy. **reflationary** *adj*.

reflect *vt,vi* **1** cast or throw back light, heat, etc.

2 produce an image (of). *vt* 1 mirror; express; reproduce. 2 rebound; bring as a consequence. *vi also* **reflect on** 1 think about; contemplate. 2 cast credit, dishonour, etc., on. **reflection** *n*. **reflector** *n* surface or device that reflects light, heat, sound, etc.

reflex *n* involuntary reaction; automatic response. **reflexive verb** *n* verb having an identical subject and direct object.

reform *vt* improve by removing abuses, inequalities, etc.; change for the better. *vi,vt* abandon or cause to abandon (evil habits, crime, etc.). *n* act or instance of reforming; improvement. **reformation** *n*.

refract *vt,vi* appear to bend or be bent by the action of light or other waves. **refraction** *n*.

refrain[1] *vi* keep oneself from; forbear.

refrain[2] *n* recurring phrase or verse.

refresh *vt,vi* revive; restore; renew. *vt* stimulate or revive (the memory). **refreshment** *n* food or drink. **refreshments** *pl n* light meal.

refrigerator *n* cabinet in which food, drink, etc., may be kept at a low temperature. **refrigerate** *vt,vi* freeze, chill, or keep cool in a refrigerator. **refrigeration** *n*.

refuge *n* 1 shelter or protection from danger, trouble, etc. 2 place or person affording this. **refugee** *n* person who flees from warfare, persecution, etc., esp. to a foreign country.

refund *vt* (riˈfʌnd) pay back; reimburse. *n* (ˈriːfʌnd) repayment; sum repaid.

refuse[1] (riˈfjuːz) *vt* decline to do, accept, give, grant, etc. *vi* withhold or decline acceptance, consent, compliance, etc.

refuse[2] (ˈrefjuːs) *n* rubbish; waste.

refute *vt* prove to be false or in error.

regain *vt* 1 win or get back; recover. 2 reach or attain again.

regal *adj* 1 of, like, or befitting a king; royal. 2 stately; dignified; elegant.

regard *vt* 1 consider; look upon; take into account; heed. 2 have or display respect for; esteem. 3 relate to; concern. *vt,vi* look steadily (at). *n* 1 attention; heed. 2 respect; esteem. 3 reference; connection. **regards** *pl n* greetings. **regardless** *adj* heedless or careless (of). *adv* without regard for expense, difficulties, etc.

regatta *n* event in which yachts and other boats are raced.

regent *n* person ruling in a kingdom during the minority, illness, incapacity, etc., of the sovereign. **regency** *n,adj*.

regime *n* 1 system or method of government. 2 prevailing system or authority.

regiment *n* (ˈredʒimənt) 1 military unit of ground forces commanded by a colonel. 2 large quantity. *vt* (ˈredʒiment) organize strictly, esp. into disciplined groups. **regimentation** *n*.

region *n* 1 part; area; district. 2 range; scope. 3 sphere of activity. **regional** *adj*.

register *n* 1 official record or list of names, items, etc. 2 book in which this is kept. 3 range of a voice or an instrument. *vt,vi* 1 enter in a register. 2 record. 3 show by facial expression, reaction, etc. **registration** *n*. **registrar** *n* official keeper of a register or record.

regress *vi* 1 move or go backwards. 2 revert to a former, esp. worse, state. **regression** *n*. **regressive** *adj*.

regret *vt* (-tt-) 1 feel sorrow or remorse for. 2 remember with sadness or remorse. 3 mourn. *n* 1 remorse. 2 sorrow or grief, esp. for a loss. **regretful** *adj*. **regrettable** *adj*.

regular *adj* 1 usual; normal. 2 conforming to a rule, principle, etc. 3 symmetrical. 4 recurring at fixed times or distances; unvarying; periodic. 5 habitual. *n* 1 soldier in a permanent army. 2 habitual customer or visitor of a place. **regularity** *n*. **regularly** *adv*.

regulate *vt* 1 control by rule, principle, etc. 2 adjust to function accurately, conform to some standard, etc.; put in order. **regulatory** *adj*. **regulation** *n* 1 rule; law; requirement. 2 control; adjustment.

rehabilitate *vt* 1 restore to normal by treatment or training. 2 restore to a former position or standing. **rehabilitation** *n*.

rehearse *vt,vi* practise in private before giving a public performance. **rehearsal** *n*.

reign *n* 1 period of rule, esp. of a sovereign. 2 dominance or rule. *vi* 1 rule as a sovereign. 2 prevail; predominate.

reimburse *vt* repay or refund, esp. for expense incurred, time lost, etc. **reimbursement** *n*.

rein *n* 1 long narrow strap fastened to a bit for controlling a horse. 2 restraint; curb. **give free rein to** allow complete freedom or licence. ~*vt* 1 put a rein on. 2 check; guide.

reincarnation *n* 1 belief that the soul returns after death in a new bodily form. 2 rebirth of the soul in a new body. **3** new bodily form taken.

reindeer *n, pl* **reindeer** large deer having branched antlers, found in arctic regions.

reinforce *vt* strengthen; give support to; stress. **reinforcement** *n*.

reinstate *vt* restore to a former state or position.

reject *vt* (ri'dʒekt) refuse to take, keep, accept, grant, etc. *n* ('ri:dʒekt) something rejected as imperfect, useless, etc. **rejection** *n*.

rejoice *vt,vi* make or become joyful; gladden.

rejuvenate *vt,vi* make or become young again; restore or be restored in vigour, freshness, etc. **rejuvenation** *n*.

relapse *vi* **1** fall or slip back to a former state or condition. **2** become ill again after apparent recovery. *n* act of relapsing.

relate *vt* **1** tell of; recount. **2** establish or perceive connection or relationship. *vi* refer to; have relation to. **relation** *n* **1** connection; association. **2** kinship. **3** relative. **4** reference; respect. **5** narration. **relations** *pl n* connections, feelings, etc., between people, countries, etc. **relationship** *n* connection; relation; mutual response.

relative *adj* **1** considered or existing in relation to something else; comparative. **2** related to; connected with. **3** relevant. **4** proportionate. *n* someone connected to another by birth or marriage. **relatively** *adv*. **relative pronoun** *n* word, such as *who* or *which*, that introduces a subordinate clause and refers back to a previous word or words.

relax *vt,vi* **1** make or become less rigid, tense, or firm. **2** make or become less strict, severe, or intense. **3** rest from or cease (work, effort, worry, etc.). **relaxation** *n*.

relay *n* **1** fresh supply or group of horses, men, etc., relieving others. **2** *also* **relay race** race between teams, each member covering part of the distance before being relieved by another. **3** broadcast; transmission. *vt* broadcast; transmit.

release *vt* **1** free; let go; give up; surrender. **2** permit to be issued, published, etc. **3** discharge. *n* **1** act of releasing; discharge. **2** something released for public sale, exhibition, publication, etc.

relent *vi* become less severe, firm, or harsh; soften; abate. **relentless** *adj* ruthless.

relevant *adj* to the point; pertinent. **relevance** *or* **relevancy** *n*.

reliable *adj* dependable; trustworthy. **reliability** *n*. **reliant** *adj* dependent; trusting. **reliance** *n*.

relic *n* **1** something associated with or surviving from the past. **2** object treasured in remembrance. **3** something associated with a saint, martyr, etc., revered as holy.

relief *n* **1** easing or alleviation of pain, distress, etc. **2** feeling resulting from this. **3** anything that eases. **4** aid; assistance. **5** pleasing change. **6** release from a post or duty. **7** person taking over. **8** raising of a siege. **9** elevation of figures, forms, etc., from a flat surface or the appearance of this. **10** distinct contrast. **relieve** *vt* **1** ease; lessen; alleviate. **2** help; aid. **3** free from anxiety, etc. **4** break the monotony of. **5** bring into relief; provide contrast. **6** release from duty; take over the duties of. **7** deprive.

religion *n* **1** belief in and worship of a god or gods. **2** a particular system of belief and worship. **3** associated ritual, conduct, doctrines, etc. **4** anything revered or zealously pursued. **religious** *adj* **1** relating to religion. **2** pious. **3** conscientious; scrupulous. **religiously** *adv*.

relinquish *vt* **1** give up; abandon. **2** let go, release. **3** surrender.

relish *vt* take delight in; enjoy; look forward to. *n* **1** enjoyment; keen anticipation. **2** appetizing taste or flavour. **3** sauce; spicy food.

relive *vt* experience again through the imagination or memory.

reluctant *adj* unwilling; marked by unwillingness. **reluctance** *n*. **reluctantly** *adv*.

rely *v* **rely on** trust in; depend on; have confidence in.

remain *vi* **1** stay behind in a place. **2** be left over or behind. **3** continue to be. **remains** *pl n* **1** remnants; relics; surviving fragments. **2** dead body; corpse. **remainder** *n* **1** something remaining or left over. **2** quantity remaining after subtraction or division.

remand *vt* send (a prisoner or accused person) back to prison pending further inquiries or proceedings. *n* act of remanding or state of being remanded. **remand home** *n* home for juvenile offenders.

remark *n* comment; observation. *vt,vi* say; comment (about). *vt* notice; perceive. **remarkable** *adj* worthy of notice; striking; unusual. **remarkably** *adv*.

remedy *n* **1** medicinal cure or treatment. **2** cure or correction for a wrong, evil, etc. **3** legal redress. *vt* **1** cure or heal. **2** put right; correct; redress. **remedial** *adj.*

remember *vt* retain in or recall to the memory. *vi* hold in one's memory. **remembrance** *n* memory; keepsake.

remind *vt* cause to remember or think of again. **reminder** *n* thing that reminds.

reminiscence *n* thing remembered or act of evoking old memories. **reminiscent** *adj.*

remiss *adj* negligent; at fault.

remission *n* **1** forgiveness; pardon. **2** reduction of a prison sentence.

remit *v* (-tt-) *vt* **1** send, esp. money. **2** pardon; refrain from inflicting (a sentence, etc.). *vt,vi* slacken. **remittance** *n* money sent; payment.

remnant *n* fragment; remainder; relic.

remorse *n* feeling of deep regret, guilt, etc. **remorseful** *adj.* **remorseless** *adj* **1** relentless. **2** not penitent.

remote *adj* **1** far away; removed; isolated. **2** slight; unlikely. **remotely** *adv.*

remove *vt* **1** take away or off; withdraw. **2** dismiss from a post or appointment. **removal** *n.*

remunerate *vt* grant as earnings, reward, etc.; pay or repay. **remuneration** *n.* **remunerative** *adj.*

renaissance *n* revival, esp. of learning. **the Renaissance** *n* period of radical artistic, scientific, and social development in Europe from the 14th to 16th centuries.

renal *adj* relating to the kidney.

render *vt* **1** give back; return. **2** serve; present for approval, action, etc.; supply with. **3** give a version or interpretation of; represent. **4** melt down. **rendition** *n.*

rendezvous *n* meeting place or time of meeting. *vi* meet by appointment.

renew *vt,vi* make or become new again; revive. *vt* **1** restore; replace; repair; renovate. **2** grant for a further period. **3** begin again. **renewal** *n.*

renounce *vt* **1** give up; abandon, esp. formally. **2** disown; break ties with. **renunciation** *n.*

renovate *vt* make fit or habitable again; restore. **renovation** *n.*

renown *n* fame; great distinction; notoriety.

rent *n* regular payment for the use of land, a house, buildings, etc. *vt* grant or use in exchange for rent; hire. **rental** *n* amount charged or paid in rent.

rep *n* short for (sales) **representative** or **repertory** (company).

repair *vt* **1** mend; restore; renew. **2** make up for; make good; remedy. *n* **1** mend. **2** act or process of repairing. **reparation** *n* compensation; amends; remedy.

repartee *n* witty reply or retort.

repatriate *vt* send (someone) back to his own country. **repatriation** *n.*

repay *vt,vi* (-paid) **1** pay back; refund. **2** return (a kindness, compliment, etc.).

repeal *vt* annul; revoke; cancel. *n* annulment; cancellation.

repeat *vt* say or do again; reproduce; echo. *n* second performance; something repeated. **repeatedly** *adv.*

repel *vt* (-ll-) **1** drive or force back or away; resist. **2** disgust. **repellent** *adj* **1** revolting; disgusting. **2** unpleasant. *n* substance used to keep flies, pests, etc., away.

repent *vi,vt* feel penitent (about); regret (one's sins). **repentance** *n.* **repentant** *adj.*

repercussion *n* **1** indirect or unintended consequence or result. **2** recoil.

repertoire *n* stock of plays, songs, etc., that a theatrical company, singer, etc., can offer.

repertory *n* **1** theatrical company performing a selection of plays, operas, etc., over a relatively short period. **2** repertoire; stock.

repetition *n* **1** act of repeating or being repeated. **2** something said or done again. **repetitious** *adj* repeated in a boring manner. **repetitive** *adj* **1** having a constant rhythm or beat. **2** characterized by repetition.

replace *vt* **1** put back. **2** find or be a substitute for. **replacement** *n.*

replenish *vt* fill up or supply again.

replica *n* copy or reproduction, esp. of a work of art.

reply *vi,vt* answer; respond. *n* answer; response.

report *vt,vi* **1** relate. **2** make, give, or bring back an account (of). **3** take down or write for publication. *vt* name as an offender; inform against. *vi* present (oneself); register (with). *n* **1** rumour. **2** account of something. **3** bang; sharp noise. **reporter** *n* person who reports, esp. for a newspaper.

repose *vi,vt* take rest or give rest to; recline; relax. *n* **1** rest; sleep; relaxed state. **2** tranquillity; composure.

represent *vt* **1** depict; stand for; symbolize. **2** act as a deputy or agent for. **3** portray; describe. **representation** *n*. **representative** *adj* serving to represent; typical. *n* **1** person or thing that represents or typifies. **2** *also* **sales representative** person selling a company's products. **3** agent; delegate.

repress *vt* keep down or under. **repressive** *adj*. **repression** *n* **1** restraint. **2** exclusion of thoughts and tendencies from consciousness.

reprieve *vt* **1** suspend execution of. **2** relieve temporarily from harm, punishment, etc. *n* **1** respite from punishment. **2** temporary relief.

reprimand *n* sharp rebuke; severe scolding. *vt* give a reprimand to.

reprint *vt* print again; print a new copy of. *n* reproduction or copy of something previously printed.

reprisal *n* retaliation; vengeful action.

reproach *vt* scold; rebuke. *n* scolding; rebuke. **reproachful** *adj*.

reproduce *vt* **1** produce again. **2** make a copy of; duplicate; imitate. *vt,vi* produce (offspring). **reproduction** *n*. **reproductive** *adj*.

reptile *n* cold-blooded egg-laying vertebrate, such as a snake, lizard, or turtle. **reptilian** *adj*.

republic *n* form of state in which supreme power rests in the people and their elected representatives. **republican** *adj,n*.

repudiate *vt* **1** reject. **2** disown; cast off. **repudiation** *n*.

repugnant *adj* distasteful; offensive. **repugnance** *n*.

repulsion *n* distaste; aversion. **repulsive** *adj*.

reputation *n* **1** what is generally thought about a person or thing. **2** good repute. **reputable** *adj* of good repute; respectable. **repute** *n* reputation, esp. a favourable one. **reputed** *adj* considered; reckoned.

request *n* act of asking for something or a thing asked for; demand. *vt* ask for (something) or ask (someone) to do something, esp. a favour.

requiem *n* **1** mass for the dead. **2** music composed for this.

require *vt* **1** need. **2** demand; order. **requirement** *n*.

rescue *vt* save or deliver from danger, etc. *n* delivery or release from harm or danger.

research *n* investigation, esp. into a scientific field in order to discover facts. *vt,vi* investigate. **researcher** *n*.

resemble *vt* look like or be similar to. **resemblance** *n*.

resent *vt* feel indignant at; dislike; be bitter about. **resentful** *adj*. **resentment** *n*.

reserve *vt* **1** hold back; set apart; keep for future use. **2** book (tickets, seats, etc.) in advance. *n* **1** something reserved. **2** part of an army, etc., kept back for use in emergency. **3** self-restraint; lack of familiarity. **in reserve** kept back for future use. **reservation** *n* **1** act of reserving; something reserved. **2** advance booking. **3** qualification; limitation. **reserved** *adj* **1** set aside for future use; held back. **2** booked in advance. **3** quiet; self-restrained; reticent.

reservoir *n* **1** place functioning as a store. **2** place for holding a large quantity of water.

reside *vi* dwell; have as one's home; live. **reside in** live in; be present or inherent. **residence** *n* state of residing or the place where a person resides. **resident** *adj* residing. *n* person staying in a place permanently or for a long time. **residential** *adj* relating to housing, residences, etc.; not commercial.

residue *n* what is left over; remainder. **residual** *adj*.

resign *vt* give up; surrender; relinquish. *vi* give up an office, commission, employment, etc. **resign oneself** (**to**) accept as unavoidable. **resignation** *n*.

resilient *adj* **1** elastic; rebounding. **2** capable of recovering quickly from a shock, injury, etc. **resilience** *n*.

resin *n* **1** sticky substance manufactured or obtained from various plants or trees. **2** synthetic substance used in making plastics, varnish, etc.

resist *vt,vi* **1** withstand; oppose. **2** overcome (a temptation). **resistance** *n*. **resistant** *adj*.

resit *vt* (-tt-; -sat) take (an examination) again after failing it.

resolute *adj* firm; determined. **resolutely** *adv*.

resolution *n* **1** firmness; determination; resolve. **2** act or state of resolving or being resolved. **3** decision of a court. **4** vote of an assembly, etc. **5** explanation; solution.

resolve *vt* **1** make clear. **2** determine; decide. **3** form by a vote or resolution. **4** find a solution to (a problem, etc.). **5** agree to (an action, course, etc.) formally. *vt,vi* separate into component parts; analyse. *n* **1** something resolved. **2** determination; strong intention.

resonance *n* increase or prolonging of vibrations, as of sound. **resonant** *adj.* **resonate** *vi,vt* undergo or cause resonance.

resort *vi also* **resort to** go for help to; turn to. *n* holiday or recreation place.

resound *vi* echo; ring; continue sounding.

resource *n* skill in devising means. **resources** *pl n* **1** means of supplying a want. **2** supplies, etc., that can be drawn on. **resourceful** *adj.*

respect *n* **1** reference; relation. **2** deference; esteem. **3** point or aspect. *vt* treat with esteem; admire. **respectable** *adj.* **respectability** *n.* **respectful** *adj.* **respective** *adj* relating to two or more persons or things regarded individually. **respectively** *adv* individually in the order mentioned.

respite (ˈrespit) *n* **1** delay. **2** period of rest or relief. **3** suspension of execution; reprieve.

respond *vi* **1** answer; reply. **2** react. **response** *n.*

responsible *adj* **1** liable to answer for something. **2** of good credit or position. **responsibility** *n.*

responsive *adj* **1** answering; making reply. **2** acting in response.

rest[1] *n* **1** quiet repose; sleep. **2** refreshing break from activity. **3** freedom or relief. **4** calm; tranquillity. **5** stopping or absence of motion. **6** prop or support; something that steadies. **7** pause in music, rhythm, etc. *vi,vt* **1** take rest or give rest to. **2** support or steady or be supported or steadied. **restful** *adj.* **restless** *adj* **1** unable to remain at rest. **2** uneasy; unquiet. **3** never still or motionless. **4** without rest. **5** characterized by constant activity.

rest[2] *n* **1** remainder; that which is left. **2** others; everyone else. *vi* remain; continue to be.

restaurant *n* place where meals are bought and eaten.

restore *vt* **1** build up again; repair; renew. **2** establish again. **3** give back. **restoration** *n.* **restorative** *adj,n.*

restrain *vt* check; hold back; repress. **restraint** *n.*

restrict *vt,vi* place limits (on); confine; restrain. **restriction** *n.* **restrictive** *adj.*

result *n* **1** thing caused or produced; effect; outcome; consequence. **2** solution; answer. **3** final score. *vi* be the result. **result in** end in.

resume (riˈzju:m) *vt,vi* start to take up again after an interval or pause. *vt* occupy (a seat) again. **resumption** *n.*

résumé (ˈrezju:mei) *n* summary, esp. of one's career or background.

resurrect *vt* **1** bring to life again. **2** use again; express new interest in. **resurrection** *n.*

retail *n* sale of goods in small quantities to the public, usually through a shop; not wholesale. *adv* sold in such a way. *vt,vi* sell or be sold by retail. **retailer** *n.*

retain *vt* **1** keep back; continue to hold. **2** hold in the mind or memory. **3** continue to employ; keep for future use. **retention** *n.* **retentive** *adj.*

retaliate *vi* fight back; answer an attack. **retaliation** *n.*

retard *vt* hold back or slow down the development of; delay. **retardation** *n.*

retch *vi* attempt or begin to vomit.

reticent *adj* reserved; modest; shy; not forthcoming. **reticence** *n.*

retina *n, pl* **retinas** *or* **retinae** (ˈretini:) membrane of the eyeball that is sensitive to light and transmits images to the brain.

retire *vi* **1** leave one's employment at the end of one's working life. **2** go to bed. **3** leave or withdraw. *vt* cease to employ after a certain age. **retirement** *n.*

retort[1] *vi,vt* reply rudely or abruptly; answer back. *n* rude or angry reply.

retort[2] *n* round glass vessel with a long neck attached at an angle, used esp. in a laboratory for distilling or heating certain substances.

retrace *vt* **1** follow (a route) again in exactly the same way. **2** go over again; recount or recall.

retract *vt,vi* **1** draw or pull inwards. **2** withdraw (an earlier statement, promise, etc.); go back on. **retractable** *or* **retractible** *adj.* **retraction** *n.*

retreat *vi* **1** move back, esp. from an advancing army. **2** seek shelter or refuge. *n* **1** act of retreating. **2** safe place; refuge; haven; sanctuary.

retribution *n* punishment; revenge.

retrieve *vt* **1** fetch, find again, recover; regain. **2** rescue from difficulty or harm. **retrieval** *n.*

retrograde *adj also* **retrogressive** **1** moving or pointing backwards; reverse. **2** tending to retrogress or decline into a worse condition. **retrogress** *vi* **1** move backwards; recede. **2** revert; decline; deteriorate. **retrogression** *n.*

retrospect *n* **in retrospect** looking back in time; with hindsight. **retrospective** *adj.*

return *vi* **1** come or go back to a former place,

situation, etc. **2** reappear. **3** reply; answer back. *vt* **1** give, send, or take back. **2** respond to; react to; acknowledge. **3** yield as a rate of interest. **4** elect by voting. *n* **1** act of coming or going back. **2** yield on investment; revenue. **3** reappearance. **4** form to be filled in for tax purposes. **returnable** *adj*.

reveal *vt* **1** display; show. **2** divulge; disclose; betray. **revelation** *n* dramatic or sudden disclosure of the truth, esp. as revealed by God to mankind.

revel *v* (-ll-) **revel in** derive enormous satisfaction or pleasure from; bask in. **revels** *pl n also* **revelry** merrymaking; festivities.

revenge *n* act of retaliation to offset a previous crime or wrong; vengeance. *vt* avenge; retaliate for.

revenue *n* income, esp. from taxation or goods sold.

reverberate *vi* vibrate noisily; resound; echo. **reverberation** *n*.

reverence *n* feeling or act of deep respect, esp. towards something sacred. **Reverence** title used when addressing a priest or high-ranking clergyman. **reverent** *adj*. **revere** *vt* treat with reverence; idolize or worship.

reverse *vt* **1** change the direction or order of; turn back. **2** revoke; alter (a former decision, attitude, etc.). *vi* drive or move backwards. *n* **1** opposite side of a coin, sheet of paper, etc. **2** gear engaged on a vehicle for moving backwards. **3** opposite of what has been stated. *adj* opposite. **reversal** *n* **1** turning round; reversing. **2** revoking of a law, etc.; cancellation.

revert *vt* return to a former state or condition. **reversion** *n*.

review *vt* **1** look back over; examine, check, or consider again. **2** give a critical report of (a book, play, etc.). *n* **1** critical report. **2** general analysis or report; survey. **reviewer** *n*.

revise *vt* **1** alter (one's attitudes, opinions, etc.). **2** rewrite. *vi,vt* study in preparation for an examination. **revision** *n*.

revive *vt,vi* **1** bring or return to consciousness. **2** introduce again; restore. **revival** *n*.

revoke *vt* cancel, esp. a law or rule; repeal.

revolt *vi* rebel; protest or act against authority. *vt* disgust; repel. *n* rebellion; uprising; mutiny. **revolting** *adj* disgusting; repulsive.

revolution *n* **1** large-scale rebellion resulting in the overthrowing of those in power and radical social and political change. **2** dramatic change. **3** movement around a point or axis; orbit or rotation. **revolutionary** *n* person in favour of or working for political revolution. *adj* **1** relating to political revolution. **2** radical, changing dramatically. **3** revolving or rotating. **revolutionize** *vt* cause a radical change in; alter dramatically.

revolve *vt,vi* move around a point or axis; orbit or rotate. **revolve around** be centred on or totally engaged with. **revolver** *n* small firearm capable of discharging several shots before reloading.

revue *n* light entertainment with music, satirical or comic sketches, etc.

revulsion *n* **1** repugnance; feeling of extreme distaste or hatred. **2** violent withdrawal or recoil.

reward *n* **1** something, such as a sum of money or prize, awarded in acknowledgment of a particular deed, act of service, etc. **2** profit; gain; benefit. *vt* repay; give a reward to. **rewarding** *adj* satisfying.

rhetoric *n* **1** art of public speaking; oratory. **2** eloquence. **rhetorical** *adj* **1** relating to rhetoric. **2** concerned more with style or effect of language than with meaning or content. **rhetorical question** *n* question to which no answer is required, used esp. as a literary device for its dramatic effect.

rheumatism *n* inflammation of the muscles, joints, etc. **rheumatic** *adj*.

rhinoceros *n* large mammal inhabiting tropical or subtropical regions, having one or two horns and a tough hide.

rhododendron *n* evergreen shrub having showy red, pink, or white flowers.

rhubarb *n* plant with large flat leaves and edible pink stalks.

rhyme *n* **1** identical or similar form of sounds occurring esp. at the end of two or more words, e.g. *try* and *buy* or *relieve* and *believe*. **2** verse using rhymes. *vi,vt* occur or make use of as a rhyme.

rhythm *n* **1** alternation of strong and weak stress or beats in music, speech, etc. **2** recurring pattern or form of movement, flow, etc. **rhythmic** *or* **rhythmical** *adj*.

rib *n* **1** one of the curved bones forming the wall of the chest. **2** anything resembling such a bone. **3** ridged stitch in knitting. *vt* (-bb-) **1**

knit using alternate plain and purl stitches. **2** *inf* tease; make fun of in a gentle way.

ribbon *n* **1** strip of satin, cotton, etc., used for decoration, trimming, etc. **2** long narrow strip of land, water, etc. **3** narrow band impregnated with ink for use on a typewriter or similar machine.

rice *n* type of grass whose grains are used as a staple food.

rich *adj* **1** having a large amount of money; wealthy. **2** having an abundant supply. **3** sumptuous; luxurious. **4** having a high proportion of cream or fat. **5** having a full flavour or consistency. **6** of a deep or vivid colour. **richly** *adv*. **richness** *n*. **riches** *pl n* wealth; valuable possessions.

rickety *adj* liable to collapse or break.

rickshaw *n* two-wheeled passenger vehicle drawn by hand, traditionally used in parts of Asia.

rid *vt* (-dd-; rid *or* ridded) free; clear away completely. **get rid of** dispose of entirely; do away with; banish or abolish. **good riddance (to)** *n* welcome relief (from).

riddle[1] *n* complicated puzzle or problem in the form of a verse or question, employing puns, hidden meaning, etc.

riddle[2] *vt* make a series of holes in.

ride *v* (rode; ridden) *vi* **1** be carried on the back of a horse, donkey, etc. **2** travel in a vehicle. **3** *inf* continue without interference. *vt* **1** travel by sitting on an animal's back. **2** drive or propel (a vehicle). *n* journey on horseback, in a vehicle, etc. **take for a ride** swindle; defraud. **rider** *n* **1** person who rides. **2** additional remark, observation, etc.

ridge *n* **1** long elevated stretch of land; range. **2** furrow; raised or projecting section. **3** area of high atmospheric pressure between two depressions.

ridicule *n* mockery; scorn. *vt* treat as absurd; mock; deride. **ridiculous** *adj* stupid; extremely silly; absurd; ludicrous. **ridiculously** *adv*.

rife *adj* prevalent; rampant; widely distributed.

rifle[1] *n* firearm that is effective over a relatively long range, having spiral grooves cut inside a long barrel.

rifle[2] *vt* ransack; loot; plunder.

rift *n* **1** crack or opening caused by a geological fault. **2** split or disagreement.

rig *vt* (-gg-) **1** equip (a vessel) with sails, masts, etc. **2** fix (prices, an election, etc.) by fraudulent means. **rig up** construct or set up, esp. in a makeshift fashion. ~*n* **1** arrangement of sails, masts, etc. **2** equipment or installation used in drilling for oil or gas. **rigging** *n* ropes, chains, etc., supporting sails or masts on a ship.

right *adj* **1** correct; accurate. **2** true; of an expected standard. **3** suitable; appropriate. **4** normal. **5** on the side of the body opposite the heart. **6** conservative or reactionary. *adv* **1** accurately; correctly; properly. **2** directly; all the way. **3** completely; totally. **4** towards the right side. **5** immediately. *n* **1** legal or moral entitlement; due. **2** direction, location, or part that is on the right side. **3** conservative or reactionary group. *vt* correct; restore. *vt,vi* make or become upright again. **rightly** *adv*. **rightful** *adj* proper; entitled; justified. **right angle** *n* angle of 90°. **right-hand** *adj* on the side towards the right. **right-handed** *adj* using the right hand for writing, etc. **right wing** *n* political group representing conservative attitudes. *adj* **right-wing** relating to the right wing.

righteous ('raitʃəs) *adj* virtuous; pious; upright. **righteousness** *n*.

rigid *adj* **1** straight and stiff; not flexible. **2** strict; not allowing variation. **rigidity** *n*. **rigidly** *adv*.

rigour *n* harshness; severity; hardship. **rigorous** *adj*. **rigorously** *adv*.

rim *n* outer or top edge of a container, wheel, etc.

rind *n* **1** tough outer skin of certain fruits; peel. **2** hard layer or coating of a piece of bacon or cheese.

ring[1] *n* **1** circle. **2** band worn on the finger. **3** circular course, track, route, etc. **4** group of people in a circle. **5** circular arena, esp. for a circus performance. **6** raised platform for a boxing match. *vt,vi* **1** encircle; surround. **2** fit rings on (birds, etc.) for identification. **ringleader** *n* main organizer, esp. of crime, etc. **ringlet** *n* long curl of hair. **ringside** *n* seats nearest the ring at a boxing or wrestling match.

ring[2] *v* (rang; rung) *vt,vi* **1** produce a clear metallic sound. **2** sound (a bell). **3** *also* **ring up** telephone; call. *vi* **1** resound. **2** experience a vibrating hum in the ears. **ring true/false** sound right/wrong. ~*n* **1** sound produced by a bell, telephone, etc. **2** echo. **3** telephone call. **4** quality; characteristic; hint.

rink *n* building or arena used for ice-skating.

rinse *vt* wash through in water, esp. in order to remove soap. *n* **1** application of clean water. **2** temporary dye for the hair; tint.

riot *n* **1** public disturbance causing a breakdown of law and order; uprising. **2** showy display; blaze. **3** *inf* hilarious occasion or person. *vi* participate in a riot. **rioter** *n*. **riotous** *adj* uproarious; disorderly.

rip *vt,vi* (-pp-) tear clumsily or violently. *n* torn part; split. **rip off** *sl* **1** cheat; overcharge. **2** steal. **rip-off** *n sl* **1** swindle. **2** exploitation for profit.

ripe *adj* **1** ready to be eaten or harvested. **2** fully matured. **3** having reached the appropriate stage of development. **ripen** *vi,vt* become or make ripe.

ripple *n* **1** slight movement of liquid; small wave. **2** continuous gentle sound. *vi* **1** form small waves; undulate. **2** gently rise and fall.

rise *vi* (rose; risen) **1** move upwards; ascend. **2** stand up; arise. **3** get out of bed. **4** progress to a higher rank or status. **5** become more cheerful, animated, etc. **6** increase in price or value. **7** rebel; revolt. **8** be able to tackle or cope. *n* **1** pay increase. **2** upward movement or progression; ascent. **3** slope; incline. **give rise to** cause; produce.

risk *n* possibility of harm, loss, etc.; gamble; chance. *vt* take a chance on; gamble; hazard. **risky** *adj*.

rissole *n* ball of minced meat fried with a coating of egg and breadcrumbs.

rite *n* formal ceremony having deep religious or cultural significance. **ritual** *adj* relating to rites. *n* **1** formalized procedure for performing certain rites or ceremonies. **2** rigid routine.

rival *n* person, organization, etc., in competition with others. *vt* (-ll-) **1** compete with. **2** be equal to. **rivalry** *n*.

river *n* **1** body of fresh water flowing usually into the sea or a lake. **2** flow; stream.

rivet *n* short bolt or nail. *vt* fasten with rivets. **riveted** *adj* unable to move or avert one's gaze; fixed.

road *n* **1** *also* **roadway** stretch of prepared land for vehicles. **2** street. **3** way.

roam *vi,vt* wander freely (over); travel widely. *n* leisurely walk; ramble. **roamer** *n*.

roar *vi* (esp. of lions) utter a loud noise. *vi,vt* **1** bellow; produce a loud angry or wild sound. **2** burn fiercely. *n* **1** loud cry of a lion, bull, etc. **2** angry or wild noise of a crowd, the wind, etc. **roaring trade** brisk profitable trade.

roast *vt,vi* **1** cook in an oven. **2** brown, scorch. *n* joint of meat for roasting.

rob *vt* (-bb-) **1** steal from. **2** deprive of. **robbery** *n* stealing by force or by threat of violence. **robber** *n*.

robe *n* long loose gown, often signifying office held. *vt,vi* dress, esp officially.

robin *n* small brown songbird, the male of which has a red breast.

robot *n* man-like machine capable of performing certain human tasks and functions.

robust *adj* strong, healthy; vigorous. **robustly** *adv*.

rock[1] *n* **1** large solid mass of minerals. **2** cliff; boulder; large stone. **3** hard stick of sugar. **on the rocks 1** in serious financial trouble. **2** served with ice-cubes. **rock-bottom** *n* lowest possible level. **rockery** *n also* **rock garden** area in which small plants grow between specially placed rocks. **rocky** *adj* having or strewn with rocks.

rock[2] *vt,vi* sway, move gently from side to side, shake. **rocker** *n* curved wooden or metal support for a rocking-chair, cradle, etc. **off one's rocker** mentally unbalanced. **rocky** *adj* shaky; unsteady.

rocket *n* cylindrical object propelled at speed into the sky to launch spaceships, direct bombs, or act as a warning or decorative firework. *vi* move like a rocket.

rod *n* **1** long straight stick of wood, bar of metal, etc. **2** *also* **fishing rod** rod used to suspend a line over water.

rode *v pt* of **ride.**

rodent *n* mammal, such as a rat, vole, or squirrel, with four strong incisors for gnawing and no canine teeth.

roe *n* **1** *also* **hard roe 1** mass of eggs in a female fish. **2** *also* **soft roe** sperm of a male fish.

rogue *n* villain; rascal; scoundrel; criminal. **roguery** *n*. **roguish** *adj*.

role *n* **1** actor's part. **2** function; task.

roll *vt,vi* **1** move along by rotating; turn over. **2** move on wheels. **3** billow; undulate. **4** rotate; move up and down. **5** sway or move from side to side. **6** form into a ball or cylinder, coil. **7** produce a loud noise; roar. *vi* pass; move onwards. *vt* use a roller on. **roll in** *or* **up**

arrive; turn up. ~*n* **1** act of rolling. **2** something rolled into a cylinder or ball. **3** small round or oblong of baked dough. **4** undulation. **5** roar. **6** rapid drumbeat. **rollcall** *n* calling of names to check attendance. **rolling pin** *n* cylindrical kitchen utensil for rolling pastry, dough, etc.

roller *n* **1** cylindrical part of a machine for pressing, rolling, winding, etc **2** small cylindrical hair-curler. **3** long swelling wave. **roller-skate** *n* skate with wheels. *vi* move on roller-skates.

Roman Catholic *n* member of that part of the Christian Church owing allegiance to the Pope. *adj* relating to the Roman Catholic Church. **Roman Catholicism** *n*.

romance *n* **1** love affair; idealized love. **2** inclination for adventure, excitement, etc. **3** atmosphere of mystery, nostalgia, etc. **4** love story, esp remote and idealized. **5** heroic medieval legend, verse, etc. **6** flight of imagination or fancy. *vi* tell extravagant or untrue stories. **romantic** *adj* **1** concerned with or given to romance. **2** fantastic, extravagant; imaginative. *n* person with romantic views. **romanticize** *vt,vi* attach romantic qualities to an otherwise unromantic object, story, etc.

romp *vi* frolic and play together, esp. boisterously. **romp home** win easily. ~*n* boisterous game. **rompers** *pl n* one-piece garment for a young child.

roof *n* **1** upper covering of a building, vehicle, etc. **2** top limit; highest point. **hit the roof** become furious. **raise the roof** **1** complain noisily. **2** cause confusion. ~*vt* cover with a roof.

rook[1] **1** black raucous gregarious type of crow. **2** *sl* swindler; cheat. *vt sl* swindle; cheat; overcharge. **rookery** *n* tree-top colony of rooks.

rook[2] *n also* **castle** chess piece that can move forwards, backwards, or sideways over any number of empty squares.

room *n* **1** unoccupied space. **2** partitioned part of a building with a specific purpose. **3** opportunity; scope. **make room** clear a space, bring about an opportunity. **roomy** *adj* spacious.

roost *n* bird's perch or sleeping place. **rule the roost** be in charge; dominate. ~*vi* settle for sleep.

root[1] *n* **1** part of a plant anchoring it to the ground and through which it absorbs water and nutrients. **2** essential element, basic part or cause; origin. **3** one of a specified number of equal factors of a number or quantity. *vi* **1** form roots; become established. **2** have a basis or origin (in). **root out** **1** dig out. **2** remove; destroy.

root[2] *v* **root about** *or* **around** search (for).

rope *n* thick twisted cord. **give enough rope** allow enough freedom. **know the ropes** be familiar with the method, rules, etc. ~*vt* catch or tie with rope. **rope in** persuade to take part, enlist. **rope off** partition or enclose with a rope. **ropy** *adj sl* meagre; of poor quality.

rosary *n* **1** series of Roman Catholic prayers, counted on a string of beads. **2** beads so used.

rose[1] *n* **1** prickly shrub or climbing plant having red, yellow, pink, or white flowers, often fragrant. **2** rose-shaped ornament, window, etc. *n,adj* deep pink. **bed of roses** luxurious state. **through rose-coloured spectacles** *or* **glasses** with unjustified optimism. **rosette** *n* **1** cluster of ribbons in the shape of a rose, often worn or presented as a trophy. **2** carving in the shape of a rose. **rosy** *adj* **1** rose-coloured. **2** promising, hopeful.

rose[2] *v pt of* **rise.**

rot *vi,vt* (-tt-) decay or cause to decay; deteriorate, putrefy. *n* **1** decay, corruption. **2** disease causing localized decay in plants, animals, timber, etc. *n,interj inf* nonsense! rubbish!

rota *n* list of duties, names, etc., which may be performed or used in rotation.

rotate *vt,vi* **1** move or cause to move on an axis; spin. **2** recur or cause to recur in regular succession. **rotation** *n*. **rotary** *adj* **1** turning like a wheel, moving round an axis. **2** acting by rotation. **rotor** *n* rotating part of a machine.

rotten *adj* **1** unsound, decayed, putrefied. **2** corrupt; contemptible. **3** *inf* unfortunate; annoying; badly done.

rouge *n* pink cosmetic powder for the cheeks.

rough *adj* **1** not smooth, coarse; uneven. **2** turbulent; violent. **3** unkind; rude. **4** harsh; grating. **5** unfinished; casual. **rough and ready** primitive but effective. **rough and tumble** *or* **rough house** disorderly brawling behaviour. **rough diamond** person who is worthy but lacking refinement. **rough on** **1** unfortunate for. **2** severe towards. ~*n* **1** rough ground. **2** preliminary sketch, stage, etc. *v* **rough it** live primitively. **rough up 1** *sl* attack; beat up. **2** produce a preliminary sketch, etc. **roughen** *vt,vi* make or become rough. **roughly** *adv* **1** in a rough way **2** approximately. **roughness** *n*.

roulette *n* gambling game in which bets are laid on which numbered socket a ball will find when dropped onto a rotating wheel.

round *adj* **1** circular; ring-shaped; spherical; curved. **2** complete; whole. *n* **1** habitual journey; single circuit, turn, session, etc. **2** meeting; session. **3** outburst; volley. **4** distribution of drinks to members of a group. **5** song in which voices sing in turn. *adv,prep* **1** continuously. **2** around; about; from place to place. **3** in a reverse or sideways direction. **4** with a circular movement. **5** so as to arrive. **6** so as to be conscious again. **round the bend** crazy. **get round** persuade; overcome. ~*vt,vi* make or become round, curved, etc. *vt* go or move around. **round off** bring to completion. **round on** attack, esp. verbally. **round up** gather or collect together. **roundup** *n* gathering; collection.

roundabout *n* **1** merry-go-round at a fairground. **2** road junction where traffic circulates in only one direction. *adj* indirect; circuitous.

rouse *vt,vi* **1** waken from sleep; stir. **2** incite to fury, passion, etc.; provoke. **rousing** *adj* exciting; thrilling; vigorous.

route *n* course or way to be followed to a destination. *vt* direct along or plan (a particular route).

routine *n* regular unvarying repeated course of action.

rove *vt,vi* stray; wander, ramble.

row[1] (rou) *n* line of several persons, objects, etc.

row[2] (rou) *vt,vi* propel by oars *vt* carry or transport in a boat propelled by oars. *vi* take part in races in such a boat. *n* act or instance of rowing.

row[3] (rau) *n* **1** noisy brawl; squabble **2** disturbance; noise; din. *vi* quarrel noisily.

rowdy *adj* noisily boisterous and exuberant. **rowdiness** *n*.

royal *adj* **1** of or relating to a king or queen; regal; majestic. **2** splendid; lavish; magnificent. **royally** *adv*. **royalty** *n* **1** the rank of a king or queen. **2** member(s) of a reigning family. **3** share of profits made on the sale of books, records, etc., paid to the author, composer, etc.

rub *vt,vi* (-bb-) **1** move a hand, cloth, etc., briskly or forcefully over the surface (of); polish; smooth. **2** irritate; grate. **rub (it) in** emphasize. **rub off on** affect through association. **rub out** obliterate; erase. **rub up** polish; improve. **rub up the wrong way** annoy. ~*n* act of rubbing; massage.

rubber *n* **1** elastic material made from the milky juice of certain tropical trees or synthesized. **2** piece of rubber used to erase pencil marks, etc.

rubbish *n* **1** waste materials; litter. **2** nonsense.

rubble *n* loose fragments of stone, rock, etc. esp. from demolished buildings.

ruby *n* deep red precious stone. *n,adj* deep red.

rucksack *n* large bag carried on the back by walkers, etc.

rudder *n* vertical pivoted piece of wood, metal, etc., at the stern of a boat or aircraft, used to steer it.

rude *adj* **1** impolite; impertinent. **2** primitive; unsophisticated. **3** vulgar; coarse. **rudely** *adv*. **rudeness** *n*.

rudiments *pl n* **1** basic elements; first principles of a subject. **2** undeveloped form. **rudimentary** *adj* undeveloped; primitive; elementary.

rueful *adj* regretful; repentant **ruefully** *adv*.

ruff *n* **1** starched lacy collar or frill. **2** prominent growth of feathers or hair around the neck of a bird or animal.

ruffian *n* rogue; villain; bully.

ruffle *vt,vi* **1** disturb; wrinkle; rumple. **2** annoy or become annoyed **3** erect (feathers) in anger or display. *n* frill at the neck or wrist.

rug *n* **1** small thick carpet. **2** thick woollen blanket.

rugby *n also* **rugby football** *or* **rugger** form of football in which players may use their hands to carry the ball or to tackle opponents.

rugged *adj* **1** uneven, rough; craggy. **2** strong; unbending; harsh. **ruggedly** *adv*. **ruggedness** *n*.

ruin *n* **1** collapse; devastation; total destruction. **2** complete loss of social, financial, or moral reputation. *vt* bring to ruin; spoil; destroy. **ruins** *pl n* remains of a partly destroyed or derelict building, etc. **in ruins** destroyed; decayed. **ruinous** *adj*.

rule *n* **1** regulation; law; maxim; code of discipline; procedure. **2** period of control.

authority, etc. **as a rule** generally. **work to rule** decrease efficiency or output by observing rules precisely. ~*vt,vi* **1** govern; dominate. **2** decree (that); decide officially (that). *vt* draw a straight line. **rule out** exclude. **ruler 1** person who rules. **2** instrument for measuring, drawing straight lines, etc.

rum *n* alcoholic drink distilled from sugar cane.

rumble *vi* make a low rolling noise, as of distant thunder. *vt sl* see through; guess correctly. **rumble along** *or* **past** move or pass making a rumble. ~*n* low rolling noise.

ruminant *n* any of various cud-chewing, hoofed animals, such as the cow, sheep, or deer. **ruminate** *vi* **1** chew the cud. **2** meditate; ponder; consider carefully.

rummage *vt,vi* ransack; search (through).

rumour *n* hearsay; gossip; unverified talk.

rump *n* rear part of a person or animal; buttocks.

rumple *vt,vi* crease; crumple; ruffle.

run *v* (-nn-; ran; run) *vi* **1** proceed on foot at a fast pace. **2** gallop or canter. **3** make a quick journey. **4** function; operate. **5** be valid; endure or last. **6** go; proceed. **7** be inherited from. **8** fall in a stream; flow. **9** spread; become diffused. *vt* **1** do whilst running. **2** roll; push; drive. **3** cover quickly. **4** operate; manage; control. **5** be affected by. **6** cause to flow. **run across** *or* **into** meet unexpectedly. **run away** escape; abscond. **run down 1** slow down. **2** find or capture. **3** criticize; speak badly of. **run for** seek election for. **run out** become exhausted; have no more. **run to** be adequate for. ~*n* **1** act or pace of running; race. **2** continuous series. **3** sort; type. **4** unlimited freedom or access. **5** strong demand. **6** score of one in cricket. **in the long run** eventually; after a long while. **on the run** escaping from the police, etc.

rung[1] *n* bar forming a spoke of a wheel, step of a ladder, crosspiece on a chair, etc.

rung[2] *v pp* of **ring.**

runner *n* **1** person that runs; athlete. **2** lateral shoot of a plant. **3** narrow strip of wood, metal, or cloth on which something is supported or runs. **runner bean** *n* climbing bean plant with scarlet flowers and long edible green pods. **runner-up** *n* competitor finishing just after the winner.

running *adj* **1** continuous; without interruption. **2** taken at a run. **3** moving easily; flowing. *n* **1** condition of the ground on a race course. **2** management; operation. **in/out of the running** with a/no chance of winning.

runny *adj* discharging liquid; streaming.

runway *n* **1** long wide track used by aircraft for landing or taking off. **2** ramp. **3** channel; groove.

rupture *n* act of bursting; state of being burst or broken; breach; split. *vt,vi* break; burst.

rural *adj* **1** of the countryside. **2** rustic.

rush[1] *vi,vt* hurry or cause to hurry; hasten; proceed recklessly. *vi* come, flow, etc., quickly. *vt* make a sudden attack on. *n* sudden speedy advance. **rush hour** *n* time of day when traffic is heaviest.

rush[2] *n* plant growing in wet places, the stems of which can be used for chair seats, baskets, etc.

rust *n* powdery brownish coating formed on iron and steel by the action of air and moisture. *vi,vt* become or make rusty; corrode. **rusty** *adj* **1** covered in rust; corroded. **2** inefficient through disuse; spoilt by neglect. **rustiness** *n.*

rustic *adj* unsophisticated; rural; simple. *n* **1** country dweller. **2** unsophisticated person.

rustle *vi,vt* make or cause to make a soft sound, as of dry leaves, silk, etc. *vt* steal (cattle, etc.). **rustle up** improvise; procure hastily. ~*n* rustling sound.

rut *n* **1** sunken furrow in a path or track; groove. **2** dreary or boring way of life.

ruthless *adj* without mercy or pity; cruel; heartless. **ruthlessly** *adv.* **ruthlessness** *n.*

rye *n* cereal grain used as animal fodder and for making flour and whisky.

S

Sabbath *n* day set aside for rest and worship, Saturday for Jews and Sunday for Christians.

sabotage *n* deliberate destruction for political, military, or private ends. *vt* destroy or disrupt by sabotage. **saboteur** *n.*

saccharin *n* intensely sweet powder used as a non-fattening sugar substitute. *adj* cloyingly sweet.

sachet *n* small sealed bag containing perfume, shampoo, etc.

sack *n* **1** large coarse bag made of flax, hemp, etc., used for coal, flour, corn, etc. **2** *inf* dismissal from employment. *vt inf* dismiss from employment.

sacrament *n* religious ceremony (Baptism, Matrimony, Holy Orders, etc.) regarded as conferring an outward sign of inward divine grace. **sacramental** *adj.*

sacred *adj* holy; dedicated to God; inviolate. **sacredly** *adv.* **sacredness** *n.*

sacrifice *vt* **1** give up (something) so that greater good or a different end may result. **2** offer to or kill in honour of a deity. *n* **1** offering of something to a god. **2** giving or offering up (anything), esp. with a worthy motive. **sacrificial** *adj.*

sacrilege *n* desecration of a sacred place, person, or thing. **sacrilegious** *adj.*

sad *adj* **1** sorrowful; dejected; downcast. **2** unfortunate. **sadly** *adv.* **sadness** *n.* **sadden** *vt,vi* make or grow sad.

saddle *n* rider's seat fitted to a horse, bicycle, etc. *vt* **1** put a saddle on. **2** load or burden (with).

sadism *n* perversion in which pleasure, esp. sexual pleasure, is derived from inflicting pain. **sadist** *n.* **sadistic** *adj.*

safari *n* expedition, esp. for hunting big game.

safe *adj* **1** secure; free from danger. **2** dependable; reliable. **safe and sound** unharmed. ~*n* strong box for keeping valuables secure against theft. **safely** *adv.* **safeguard** *n* proviso; precaution. *vt* protect; guard. **safekeeping** *n* custody.

safety *n* security; freedom from danger or risk. **safety belt** *n* strong strap to secure a passenger in the seat of an aircraft, car, etc. **safety pin** *n* bent pin with the point protected by a guard. **safety valve** *n* **1** machine valve that opens when pressure becomes too great for safety. **2** harmless outlet for anger, passion, etc.

sag *vi* (-gg-) **1** droop; bend; sink. **2** give way under weight or pressure.

saga *n* **1** heroic prose tale in old Norse literature. **2** long chronicle, esp. of generations of one family.

sage[1] *n* very wise man. *adj* of great wisdom, discretion, prudence, etc. **sagacity** *n.* **sagely** *adv.*

sage[2] *n* grey-green aromatic herb widely used in cookery.

Sagittarius *n* ninth sign of the zodiac, represented by the Archer.

said *v pp* and *pt* of **say.**

sail *n* **1** large sheet of canvas, etc., spread to catch the wind and propel a boat. **2** arm of a windmill. **3** trip in a sailing vessel. *vt,vi* **1** move by sail power; travel by sea. **2** glide or pass smoothly and easily. **set sail** start on a voyage. **sail close to the wind** narrowly avoid danger, ruin, etc. **sailor** *n* member of ship's crew. **good/bad sailor** one not/very liable to seasickness.

saint *n* holy person canonized or famous for extreme virtue. **saintly** *adj.*

sake *n* purpose; benefit; behalf. **for the sake of** for the advantage or purpose of; in order to help, protect, etc.

salad *n* cold meal of vegetables seasoned and served raw. **fruit salad** mixture of raw fruits. **salad dressing** *n* mixture of oil, vinegar, seasoning, herbs, etc., used to flavour salad.

salamander *n* lizard-like creature of the newt family.

salary *n* fixed payment given periodically for non-manual work. **salaried** *adj* earning a salary.

sale *n* **1** exchange of goods for money. **2** fast disposal of unwanted stock at reduced prices or by auction. **saleable** *adj* easy to sell. **salesman** *n, pl* **-men** person employed to sell. **saleswoman** *f n.* **salesmanship** *n* skill in persuading customers to buy.

saline *adj* of or containing salt. **salinity** *n.*

saliva *n* spittle; colourless odourless juice secreted into the mouth, esp. for moistening food. **salivate** *vi* produce saliva, esp. in excess. **salivation** *n.*

sallow *adj* **1** with skin of a pale yellow colour. **2** unhealthy looking.

salmon *n, pl* **salmon** *or* **salmons** large fish, popular as a food, that goes up rivers to spawn. **salmon pink** *n,adj* orange-pink colour of salmon flesh.

salon *n* **1** large elegant reception room. **2** regular gathering of distinguished guests. **3** exhibition of paintings. **4** premises or shop where dressmakers, hairdressers, etc., receive clients.

saloon *n* **1** large public room in a hotel, ship, train, etc. **2** *also* **saloon bar** more comfortably furnished bar room in a public house. **3** car with an enclosed body.

salt *n* **1** white crystalline compound, sodium chloride, used as food seasoning, preservative, etc. **2** any crystalline compound formed from an acid and base. *vt* season or treat with salt. **salt-cellar** *n* small container for holding salt. **saltpetre** *n* nitrogen compound used in explosives, fertilizers, etc.

salute *n* gesture of greeting, recognition, or respect. *vt,vi* make a salute (to).

salvage *n* act of or reward for saving a ship, property, etc., from destruction or waste. *vt* save from loss or destruction.

salvation *n* act of saving from loss, destruction, or sin.

salve *vt* anoint, heal, or soothe. *n* ointment; balm; whatever soothes or heals.

same *adj* **1** identical. **2** indicating no change. *adv* **the same** in an identical manner; with no change. **all the same** even so; in spite of that; nevertheless. ~*pron* that same or identical thing or person.

sample *n* specimen; example; small quantity showing properties of something. *vt* test or try a sample.

sanatorium *n, pl* **sanatoria** (sænə'tɔːriə) *or* **sanatoriums 1** hospital, esp. for convalescent, tubercular, mentally unbalanced, or chronically ill patients. **2** place where sickness is treated in a school, college, etc.

sanctify *vt* make holy or sacred; revere.

sanction *vt* allow; authorize; confirm. *n* **1** penalty or reward intended to enforce a law. **2** confirmation; authorization; permission.

sanctity *n* holiness; sacredness.

sanctuary *n* **1** recognized place or right of refuge. **2** part of a church beyond the altar rails. **3** protected reserve for birds, animals, etc.

sand *n* mass of tiny fragments of crushed rocks covering deserts, seashores, etc. *vt* rub with sandpaper. **sandpaper** *n* heavy paper coated with sand or other abrasive and used for smoothing, polishing, etc. **sandy** *adj* **1** covered in sand. **2** of the colour of sand.

sandal *n* open shoe secured by straps.

sandwich *n* two slices of bread enclosing jam, meat, etc. *vt* squeeze (one thing) between two others.

sane *adj* of sound mind; sensible; rational. **sanely** *adv.* **sanity** *n.*

sang *v pt of* **sing.**

sanitary *adj* concerning or conducive to health, esp. in regard to cleanliness and hygiene. **sanitary towel** *n* absorbent pad for use during menstruation. **sanitation** *n* sanitary methods and equipment, esp. concerning sewage disposal, drainage, clean water, etc.

sank *v pt of* **sink.**

sap *n* vital juice, esp. of plants. *vt* (-pp-) drain the sap or energy from. **sapling** *n* young tree.

sapphire *n* gemstone, usually brilliant blue, akin to the ruby. *adj* brilliant blue.

sarcasm *n* mocking, sneering, or ironic language. **sarcastic** *adj.* **sarcastically** *adv.*

sardine *n* young pilchard often packed tightly with others and tinned in oil.

sari *n* Indian or Pakistani woman's garment worn over a blouse, consisting of a long bolt of cloth that is wrapped around the waist and over the shoulder.

sash[1] *n* band of material worn around the waist or over the shoulder.

sash[2] *n* sliding frame holding panes of glass in a window.

sat *v pt and pp of* **sit.**

Satan *n* the Devil. **satanic** *adj.*

satchel *n* small bag with shoulder straps, esp. for holding school books.

satellite *n* **1** heavenly body or spacecraft revolving round a planet or star. **2** disciple; hanger-on; underling.

satin *n* glossy closely woven silk fabric. *adj* of or like satin.

satire *n* **1** use of irony, ridicule, or sarcasm to mock or denounce. **2** literary work exhibiting this. **satirical** *adj.*

satisfy *vt,vi* fulfil the needs or wishes of. *vt* be sufficient for; give enough to; appease. **satisfaction** *n.* **satisfactory** *adj.*

saturate *vt* imbue or soak completely; cause to be thoroughly absorbed in. **saturation** *n.*

Saturday *n* seventh day of the week.

Saturn *n* outer giant planet lying between Jupiter and Uranus and having a system of rings around its equator.

sauce *n* **1** liquid poured over food to add piquancy or relish. **2** *inf* cheeky impudence. **saucy** *adj* **1** cheeky; impertinent; bold. **2** smart; pert. **saucily** *adv.* **sauciness** *n.*

saucepan *n* long-handled cooking pan.

saucer *n* **1** shallow indented dish placed under a cup. **2** anything of similar shape.

sauna *n also* **sauna bath 1** steam bath. **2** room used for this.

saunter *vi* wander idly; stroll; amble. *n* gentle stroll; ramble.

sausage *n* short tube, esp. of animal gut, stuffed with minced seasoned meat.

savage *adj* ferocious; violent; uncivilized. *n* **1** primitive person. **2** one with savage characteristics; brute. *vt* attack and wound.

save[1] *vt* rescue or protect from evil, danger, loss, damage, etc. *vt,vi* **1** store up; set aside for future use. **2** be economical or thrifty. **savings** *pl n* sum of money set aside for future use.

save[2] *prep* except; not including.

saviour *n* one who saves another person, etc., from serious trouble; redeemer. **Saviour** *n* Christ.

savoury *adj* not sweet but with a pleasant appetizing taste. *n* savoury course of a meal.

saw[1] *n* tool with a long toothed metal blade used for cutting wood, etc. *vt,vi* use a saw (on). **sawdust** *n* tiny fragments of wood produced by sawing and used in packaging, etc.

saw[2] *v pt of* **see.**

saxophone *n* brass wind instrument with a single reed and about twenty keys. **saxophonist** *n*.

say *vt,vi* (said) **1** state, utter, or speak in words. **2** declare; tell; repeat. **3** assume; take as an example. *n* **1** chance or turn to speak. **2** authority. **saying** *n* maxim; proverb; something commonly said.

scab *n* **1** crust formed over a healing wound. **2** *sl* blackleg.

scaffold *n* **1** temporary raised platform, esp. for supporting workmen. **2** platform on which criminals are executed. **scaffolding** *n* scaffold or system of scaffolds.

scald *vt* **1** burn with hot liquid. **2** clean or cook with boiling water. **3** bring (milk, etc.) almost to boiling point. *n* burn caused by hot liquid.

scale[1] *n* **1** graded table used as a scheme for classification or measurement. **2** series of musical notes ascending at fixed intervals. **3** range; compass; scope. *vt* clamber up; climb. **scale down** make smaller proportionately.

scale[2] *n* **1** one of the small thin plates protecting fish, reptiles, etc. **2** thin film or layer. *vt,vi* peel off (scales). **scaly** *adj* dry; flaky; hard.

scale[3] *n* **1** dish forming one side of a balance. **2** *also* **scales** weighing machine.

scalp *n* skin covering the head. *vt* tear off scalp and hair from.

scalpel *n* small surgical knife.

scampi *pl or s n* large prawns.

scan *v* (-nn-) *vt* **1** scrutinize carefully. **2** glance briefly over. **3** cast a beam over. **4** classify (verse) by metre. *vi* follow metrical pattern. *n* act of scanning.

scandal *n* **1** act or behaviour outraging public opinion. **2** malicious gossip; slander. **scandalize** *vt* shock by scandal. **scandalous** *adj*. **scandalously** *adv*.

scant *adj* scarcely enough; not plentiful. **scanty** *adj* meagre; inadequate.

scapegoat *n* one forced to bear the blame for others' faults.

scar *n* mark left by a wound. *vt* (-rr-) mark with a scar.

scarce *adj* in short supply; rare. **make oneself scarce** *inf* go away. **scarcely** *adv* **1** hardly; barely; only just. **2** not quite. **scarcity** *n*.

scare *vt* startle; frighten away; alarm. *n* sudden or unreasonable panic. **scary** *adj inf* frightening. **scarecrow** *n* device, often resembling a man, to frighten birds away from crops.

scarf *n, pl* **scarves** piece of material worn over the head or around the neck.

scarlet *adj* brilliant red.

scathing *adj* scornful; showing contempt.

scatter *vt* strew; sprinkle; throw loosely about. *vi* disperse; separate. **scatter-brained** *adj* easily distracted; unable to concentrate.

scavenge *vt,vi* search through litter and rubbish and take (anything of value). **scavenger** *n*.

scenario *n* outline of the plot of a film or play.

scene *n* **1** setting for an action, play, film, etc. **2** short division of an act in a play or film. **3** description of an incident. **4** noisy public outburst. **behind the scenes** not for public view or knowledge. **scenery** *n* **1** theatrical backdrops, properties, etc. **2** natural features of landscape. **scenic** *adj* **1** concerning natural scenery. **2** dramatic; theatrical.

scent *n* **1** individual smell, aroma, or fragrance. **2** mixture of fragrant essences; perfume. **3** sense of smell. *vt* **1** perceive odour of. **2** sense; suspect. **3** impart scent to.

sceptic *n* one unwilling to believe and inclined to question or doubt. **sceptical** *adj*. **scepticism** *n*.

sceptre *n* staff carried as a symbol of regal or imperial power.

schedule *n* **1** timetable; order of events. **2**

inventory or list. *vt* make a schedule of; plan; arrange. **on schedule** as arranged; on time.

scheme *n* **1** planned systematic arrangement. **2** cunning plot. *vt,vi* plan; contrive; plot.

schizophrenia *n* psychosis marked by delusions and inability to distinguish fantasy from reality and often leading to a double personality. **schizophrenic** *adj,n*.

scholar *n* **1** learned person. **2** student or holder of a scholarship. **scholarly** *adj* studious; learned; intellectually thorough. **scholarship** *n* **1** grant awarded to a promising student. **2** erudition; learning.

school[1] *n* **1** place of education, esp. for children. **2** group of students of a particular branch of learning. **3** followers or imitators of a particular theory, artist, etc. *vt* **1** instruct. **2** control. **scholastic** *adj* of schools, learning, etc.

school[2] *n* large body of fish, whales, etc.

schooner *n* **1** swift two-masted sailing ship. **2** large beer or sherry glass.

science *n* knowledge or branch of knowledge obtained by experiment, observation, and critical testing. **science fiction** *n* fiction based on imagined sensational changes or developments of environment, space travel, etc. **scientific** *adj* **1** to do with science. **2** systematic, careful, and exact. **scientist** *n*.

scissors *pl n* cutting tool with two pivoted blades.

scoff[1] *vi* mock or jeer; show scorn and derision. *n* expression of contempt.

scoff[2] *vt sl* eat greedily, ravenously, or quickly. *n sl* food.

scold *vt* find fault with; reprimand.

scone *n* small round plain cake eaten with butter and jam.

scoop *n* **1** small short-handled shovel. **2** journalist's exclusive story. *vt* hollow out or lift as with a scoop.

scooter *n* **1** child's two-wheeled vehicle with handles and a platform, propelled by pushing against the ground with one foot. **2** small low-powered motorcycle.

scope *n* range; extent; field of action.

scorch *vt,vi* **1** burn slightly, so as to discolour but not destroy. **2** dry up with heat; parch.

score *n* **1** tally or record of relative charges, achievements, or points gained. **2** incised line. **3** written musical composition. **4** set of twenty. *vt* **1** gain and record points. **2** furrow or mark with lines. **3** orchestrate. *vi inf* achieve a success. **know the score** know the hard facts. **scoreboard** *n* board on which a score is recorded.

scorn *vt* **1** despise; hold in contempt. **2** refuse contemptuously; disdain to. *n* derision; contempt; mockery. **scornful** *adj*. **scornfully** *adv*.

Scorpio *n* eighth sign of the zodiac, represented by a scorpion.

scorpion *n* member of the spider family with pincers and a joined head and thorax.

scoundrel *n* rascal; villain; rogue.

scour[1] *vt* clean or polish thoroughly by rubbing. *n* act of scouring. **scourer** *n*.

scour[2] *vt* search thoroughly through.

scout *n* one sent out or ahead to bring back information. *vi* act as scout. **Scout** *also* **Boy Scout** boy belonging to an organization founded to encourage high principles, self-reliance, etc.

scowl *vi* frown angrily or sullenly. *n* bad-tempered sullen frown.

scramble *vi* make one's way fast and awkwardly, esp. as to race others to a goal. *vt* **1** mix or muddle. **2** alter the frequencies of (a radio message, etc.) so as to render it unintelligible. *n* **1** undignified rush. **2** motorcycle race over rough ground. **scrambled eggs** eggs beaten and cooked.

scrap *n* **1** morsel; fragment. **2** rubbish; leftovers. **3** *inf* fight; quarrel. *vt* (-pp-) discard; throw away. **scrapbook** *n* blank book into which newspaper cuttings, photographs, etc., are pasted. **scrap iron** *n* fragments of metal useful only for remelting.

scrape *vt* smooth or damage by rubbing with a sharp edge. **scrape through** succeed by a narrow margin. **scrape up** *or* **together** gather with difficulty, diligence, or thrift. ~*n* **1** scratch. **2** *inf* awkward predicament.

scratch *vt,vi* **1** mark or cut with something sharp or be susceptible to such marking. **2** rub the nails over (the skin) to relieve itching. *vt* cancel; erase. *n* mark or sound made by scratching. **from scratch** from the very beginning. **up to scratch** *inf* acceptable; up to standard. **scratchy** *adj* **1** marked with scratches. **2** ragged; irregular. **3** irritable.

scrawl *vt,vi* scribble; write fast and unintelligibly. *n* illegible writing.

scream *vt,vi* shriek or cry out in a high loud

voice. *n* **1** piercing cry. **2** *inf* hilarious joke. **screamingly** *adv* hilariously.

screech *vi* cry out in a harsh shrill voice. *n* sound made by screeching.

screen *n* movable board or partition acting as a room divider, surface to project films, protection from heat or observation, etc. *vt* **1** hide or shelter. **2** display on a cinema or television screen. **3** subject to tests to determine weakness, disease, qualities, etc. **screenplay** *n* script for a film.

screw *n* spiral grooved metal shaft used as a fastening device. **have a screw loose** be mentally deficient. **put the screws on** extort by blackmail. ~*vt* fasten; tighten; compress with a screw. *vt,vi tab* have sexual intercourse (with). **screw up 1** tighten firmly with a screw. **2** twist; distort; crumple. **3** summon up. **screwdriver** *n* tool with metal wedge-shaped blade, which slots into the groove on the head of a screw to turn it. **screwy** *adj sl* crazy.

scribble *vt,vi* write carelessly, fast, or meaninglessly. *n* careless or meaningless writing. **scribbler** *n*.

script *n* **1** text of a film, play, speech, etc. **2** handwriting or print resembling it. **scriptwriter** *n* one who writes scripts, dialogues, television series, etc.

scripture *n* the Bible. **scriptural** *adj*.

scroll *n* **1** roll of parchment or paper. **2** ornamental design resembling a scroll.

scrounge *vt,vi inf* cadge; sponge; wheedle or scrape together. **scrounger** *n*.

scrub[1] *vt,vi* (-bb-) clean by rubbing hard with a brush and water. *n* act of scrubbing.

scrub[2] *n* landscape of low stunted trees, bushes, and shrubs.

scruffy *adj* untidy; unkempt; messy. **scruffily** *adv*. **scruffiness** *n*.

scruple *n* moral doubt or hesitation. *vi* hesitate because of scruple.

scrupulous *adj* conscientious; attentive to details. **scrupulously** *adv*.

scrutinize *vt* examine closely, critically, or in great detail. **scrutiny** *n*.

scuffle *n* close confused struggle or fight. *vi* fight in a disorderly manner.

scullery *n* small room for rough kitchen work, dish washing, etc.

sculpture *n* **1** art of making figures, statues, etc., by carving or moulding. **2** work or works made in this way. **sculpt** *vt,vi* make a sculpture (of). **sculptor** *n*.

scum *n* **1** foam on the surface of a liquid. **2** worthless or disgusting residue.

scurf *n* crust of small flakes of dead skin, esp. on the scalp; dandruff.

scythe *n* implement with a large curved blade for cutting grass. *vt* cut with a scythe.

sea *n* **1** continuous expanse of salt water that covers most of the earth's surface. **2** large body of salt water partially bounded by land. **3** large lake. **4** condition, turbulence, waves, etc., of an ocean or sea. **5** something suggestive of the sea in being vast or overwhelming. **at sea 1** on the ocean. **2** confused. **go to sea 1** become a sailor. **2** start an ocean voyage. **put to sea** leave port.

sea anemone *n* common marine animal whose arrangement of tentacles resembles a flower.

seacoast strip of land bordering on an ocean or sea.

seafront *n* area of a seaside resort directly facing the sea and having a promenade, hotels, etc.

seagull *n* gull frequenting the sea or coast.

seahorse *n* **1** marine fish that swims in an upright position and has a head shaped like that of a horse. **2** walrus.

sea-kale vegetable having broad green leaves.

seal[1] *n* **1** impression on wax or metal serving as an authorization, guarantee, etc. **2** anything used to close tightly to prevent leaking or opening. *vt* mark, attest, or close firmly with a seal. **set the seal on** formally conclude.

seal[2] *n* carnivorous marine mammal with flippers, a short tail, and a long body covered in dense fur. **sealskin** *n* close short furry hide of the seal, sometimes used for clothing.

sea-level *n* level of the sea midway between high and low tide.

sea-lion *n* large seal having visible external ears.

seam *n* join formed by sewing together or attaching two pieces of material. **seamy** *adj* squalid.

seaman *n, pl* **-men** sailor, esp. below the rank of officer. **seamanship** *n* skill or techniques of ship management, operation, and navigation.

seaplane *n* aeroplane equipped to land on or take off from the water.

search *vt,vi* examine, probe, or investigate closely hoping to find something. *n* investigation; exploration; enquiry. **search me!** *si* I have no idea! **searchlight** *n* lamp emitting a strong beam of artificial light used to scan an area, the sky, etc.

seashore *n* seacoast.

seasick *adj* nauseated by the movement of a vessel at sea. **seasickness** *n*.

seaside *n* seacoast. *adj* relating to or located at the seacoast.

season *n* **1** one of the four climatic divisions of the year. **2** appropriate time; short spell. **in season 1** (of game, fish, foxes, etc.) allowed to be legally hunted or caught. **2** ripe; ready for use. ~*vt* **1** flavour with salt, pepper, etc **2** accustom; mature. **seasonable** *adj* appropriate to the moment or occasion; timely. **seasonal** *adj* occurring at or changing with the season. **seasoned** *adj* **1** experienced. **2** flavoured; tempered. **seasoning** *n* **1** food flavouring, such as salt, pepper, or herbs. **2** processing of timber. **season ticket** *n* ticket valid for repeated use over a set period.

seat *n* **1** chair or part of a chair, place to sit **2** position in Parliament, a council, etc., to which one is elected or appointed. **3** basis, central location or site **4** manner of sitting (on a horse, etc.). **5** buttocks; bottom. *vt* place on a seat; accommodate in a chair or chairs. **seat-belt** *n* safety belt.

seaweed *n* plant or alga growing in the ocean.

seaworthy *adj* (of a vessel) fit for sailing. **seaworthiness** *n*.

secluded *adj* hidden or shut off from observation or company. **seclusion** *n* privacy, solitude.

second[1] *adj* **1** coming between the first and the third. **2** another; additional; extra. **3** alternate, alternative. *adv* in second place. *n* person or thing in second place. *vt* support (another's proposal or nomination). **secondly** *adv*. **second best** *adj* inferior to the best. **second-class** *adj* of second or inferior class, quality, etc. **second-hand** *adj* not new; having belonged to another. **second nature** *n* habit or tendency that has become automatic or instinctive. **second-rate** *adj* of inferior quality or value; shoddy.

second[2] *n* **1** period of time equal to one sixtieth of a minute. **2** moment; instant. **3** unit by which time is measured.

secondary *adj* subordinate; of less importance; coming second. **secondary school** *n* school teaching children over the age of eleven.

secret *adj* concealed; hidden; private; not made known. *n* whatever is made or kept secret. **secrecy** *n*. **secretly** *adv*. **secret agent** *n* spy.

secretary *n* **1** one employed to help with correspondence, keep records, etc. **2** principal assistant to a minister, ambassador, etc. **secretarial** *adj*.

secrete *vt* (of a gland, cell, etc.) produce and release (substances such as saliva, etc.). **secretion** *n*.

secretive *adj* reticent; given to undue secrecy; uncommunicative.

sect *n* group of people following a particular leader or holding specific views. **sectarian** *n,adj*.

section *n* division or portion; part. *vt* cut or separate into parts.

sector *n* **1** part of a circle bounded by two radii and an arc. **2** area; part; scope of activity.

secular *adj* temporal, lay, not spiritual or monastic. *n* priest bound by no monastic rule.

secure *adj* **1** safe; free from danger. **2** reliable, certain. **3** not movable. *vt* **1** make safe, certain, or sure. **2** obtain. **securely** *adv*. **security** *n* **1** safety; freedom from anxiety, danger, or want. **2** pledge, document, or certificate of ownership; bond or share. **3** precautions against espionage, theft, etc.

sedate *adj* **1** calm, placid, tranquil. **2** staid, dignified. **sedately** *adv*. **sedateness** *n*. **sedation** *n* act of calming or state of calmness induced by sedatives. **sedative** *adj* calming, soporific. *n* sedative drug.

sediment *n* dregs or residue at the bottom of a liquid. **sedimentary** *adj*.

seduce *vt* **1** entice, lure, or tempt, esp. into evil. **2** persuade to have sexual intercourse. **seducer** *n*. **seduction** *n*. **seductive** *adj*.

see[1] *v* (saw; seen) *vi* **1** have the power of sight. **2** find out, investigate. **3** attend (to). *vt* **1** look at; perceive; be aware of; observe. **2** experience. **3** visit. **4** realize; consider. **5** discover **6** consult. **7** make sure; check; take care. *vt,vi* understand; comprehend. **see through 1** fail to be deceived by. **2** finish, remain with until completion.

see[2] *n* office or diocese of a bishop.

seed *n* **1** tiny cell containing an embryonic plant. **2** germ; first principle. *vt* **1** sow. **2**

remove the seed from. **run to seed** deteriorate; decay. **seedling** *n* young plant grown from seed.

seedy *adj* shabby.

seek *vt,vi* (sought) look for; try to find; search (for).

seem *vi* appear to be; give the impression of being. **seeming** *adj* apparent. **seemingly** *adv*. **seemly** *adj* appropriate; decent.

seep *vi* ooze; percolate; leak through. **seepage** *n*.

seesaw *n* plank so balanced that children seated on either end can ride up or down alternately. *vi* move or vacillate like a seesaw.

seethe *vi* surge or be agitated (with extreme fury, excitement, etc.).

segment *n* **1** part of a circle bounded by a chord and arc. **2** section; portion. *vt,vi* divide into segments. **segmentary** *adj*. **segmentation** *n*.

segregate *vt* separate from others; isolate; group apart, esp. racially. **segregation** *n*.

seize *vt* take possession of, esp. suddenly or by force. **seize up** become jammed or stuck. **seizure** *n* **1** act of seizing. **2** sudden attack of illness; fit.

seldom *adv* rarely; only occasionally.

select *vt* choose; pick out for preference. *adj* choice; exclusive. **selection** *n* **1** act or result of choice; discrimination. **2** item or items selected. **3** scope or range of selected items. **selective** *adj* **1** able to select or discriminate. **2** tending to select very carefully. **selectively** *adv*.

self *n, pl* **selves 1** person or thing regarded as individual. **2** personality or ego.

self-assured *adj* confident; not shy. **self-assurance** *n*.

self-aware *adj* able to view oneself objectively. **self-awareness** *n*.

self-centred *adj* preoccupied with oneself; selfish. **self-centredness** *n*.

self-confident *adj* having confidence in oneself. **self-confidence** *n*.

self-conscious *adj* shy; embarrassed. **self-consciously** *adv*. **self-consciousness** *n*.

self-contained *adj* **1** reserved; absorbed in oneself. **2** (of accommodation) complete; not approached through another's property.

self-defence *n* protection of oneself or one's rights, property, etc.

self-discipline *n* control of one's own behaviour, emotions, etc. **self-disciplined** *adj*.

self-employed *adj* working for oneself; freelance.

self-expression *n* voicing or demonstrating one's own personality or beliefs.

self-interest *n* desire for benefit or advantage to oneself.

selfish *adj* motivated by self-interest; showing little regard for others. **selfishly** *adv*. **selfishness** *n*.

self-pity *n* pity for oneself; feeling of being sorry for oneself. **self-pitying** *adj*.

self-portrait *n* picture painted by an artist of himself.

self-respect *n* pride; dignity; integrity.

self-righteous *adj* excessively confident in one's own merits, judgment, etc.; hypocritical. **self-righteously** *adv*. **self-righteousness** *n*.

self-sacrifice *n* subordination of one's own desires or rights to another's.

selfsame *adj* (the) very same; exactly the same.

self-satisfied *adj* smug; conceited.

self-service *adj* (of a restaurant, shop, etc.) where the customer serves himself.

self-sufficient *adj* **1** needing nothing from outside oneself. **2** economically independent. **self-sufficiency** *n*.

self-will *n* obstinacy. **self-willed** *adj*.

sell *vt* (sold) **1** exchange for money. **2** betray for an ignoble motive. **3** extol; praise the virtues of. **sell off** sell cheaply to clear stock. **sell out 1** sell whole stock in trade. **2** betray for profit. **sell up 1** sell a debtor's goods in settlement. **2** sell a business.

Sellotape *n Tdmk* transparent adhesive cellulose tape. *vt* attach, stick down, etc., with adhesive tape.

selves *n pl* of **self.**

semaphore *n* means of signalling by flags. *vt,vi* signal using flags.

semen *n* fluid and cells produced by the male reproductive organs.

semibreve *n* musical note equal to two minims or four crotchets.

semicircle *n* half a circle. **semicircular** *adj*.

semicolon *n* punctuation mark (;) showing a sentence division that is stronger than a comma but less marked than a colon.

semiconductor *n* substance whose electrical conductivity increases with added impurities.

used in transistors and other electronic components.

semidetached *adj* (of a house) joined to another on one side.

semifinal *n* last round of a tournament before the final. **semifinalist** *n*.

seminar *n* class of advanced students working on a specific subject.

semiprecious *adj* (of stones) valuable, but not rare or valuable enough to be classed as precious.

semiquaver *n* musical note half the length of a quaver.

semitone *n* musical interval between a note and its sharp or flat.

semolina *n* particles of fine hard wheat used for making milk puddings, pasta, etc.

senate *n also* **Senate 1** legislative or governing body of ancient Rome, modern British universities, etc. **2** upper house of government of the US, Australia, Canada, etc. **senator** *n*.

send *vt* (sent) **1** cause (mail, goods, a message, etc.) to be transmitted or taken. **2** direct; convey. **3** drive or force into a particular condition or state. **send for** ask to come; demand the services of.

senile *adj* weak or deteriorating through old age. **senility** *n*.

senior *adj* older, higher, or more experienced or advanced. *n* one who is senior. **seniority** *n*.

sensation *n* **1** feeling; perception through the senses. **2** public or melodramatic excitement. **sensational** *adj* exciting; thrilling; startling. **sensationally** *adv*.

sense *n* **1** faculty of sight, hearing, smell, touch, or taste. **2** sensation; feeling. **3** awareness; perception. **4** intelligence; common sense. **5** meaning or definition, esp. of a word or phrase. **make sense** be logical, reasonable, or coherent. ~*vt* **1** feel; be aware of. **2** comprehend, esp. intuitively. **senseless** *adj* **1** meaningless; motiveless; foolish. **2** unconscious.

sensible *adj* **1** wise; reasonable; practical. **2** aware. **3** appreciable by the senses. **sensibly** *adv*. **sensibility** *n* delicacy or capacity of emotional, mental, or moral responses.

sensitive *adj* **1** easily affected by another's emotions, actions, plight, etc. **2** easily irritated by certain stimuli. **sensitively** *adv*. **sensitivity** *or* **sensitiveness** *n*.

sensual *adj* **1** relating to the senses. **2** seeking pleasure or gratification of the senses. **3** voluptuous; licentious. **sensuality** *n*. **sensually** *adv*.

sensuous *adj* relating or pleasing to the senses. **sensuously** *adv*. **sensuousness** *n*.

sent *v pt* and *pp* of **send.**

sentence *n* **1** number of words forming a grammatical unit, usually containing a subject, predicate, and finite verb. **2** punishment allotted to an offender in court. *vt* pronounce judgment on (a person) in a court of law.

sentiment *n* thought or opinion at least partly dictated by emotion. **sentimental** *adj* **1** over-emotional; mawkish. **2** having romantic or tender feelings. **sentimentality** *n*.

sentry *n* soldier, etc., posted to stand guard.

separate *v* ('sepəreit) *vt* set or keep apart; divide. *vi* go, move, or live apart. *adj* ('seprit) distinct; divided; individual. **separable** *adj*. **separately** *adv*. **separation** *n*.

September *n* ninth month of the year.

septic *adj* putrefying because of the presence of bacteria.

sequel *n* result; consequence; whatever succeeds, follows, or happens next.

sequence *n* **1** order of succession; series. **2** scene from a film. **sequential** *adj*. **sequentially** *adv*.

sequin *n* tiny sparkling piece of foil used to decorate clothing.

serenade *n* piece of music traditionally played at night by a lover under his lady's window. *vt* entertain with a serenade.

serene *adj* tranquil; calm; placid. **serenely** *adv*. **serenity** *n*.

serf *n* medieval farm labourer or peasant bound to the land. **serfdom** *n*.

sergeant *n* **1** noncommissioned officer ranking above a corporal. **2** police officer ranking between constable and inspector. **sergeant-major** *n* highest grade of noncommissioned officer.

serial *adj* forming a series; in instalments. *n* story told in instalments. **serialize** *vt* divide (a story, film, etc.) into instalments or episodes.

series *n, pl* **series** sequence; succession of things, episodes, etc., with similar characters, subjects, or purposes.

serious *adj* solemn; grave; earnest; not comic or frivolous. **seriously** *adv*. **seriousness** *n*.

sermon *n* speech, esp. one delivered from a pulpit, with a strong scriptural or moral lesson.

serpent *n* snake. **serpentine** *adj* **1** relating to serpents. **2** twisting; convoluted.

servant *n* person employed to serve another.

serve *vt,vi* **1** work for; wait upon. **2** be of use to; help. **3** act or offer as a host. **4** deliver (the ball) in certain games. **5** spend (a specified period of time, enlistment, etc.). *vt* **1** obey or honour. **2** deliver (a summons, etc.) to. **serve someone right** be an appropriate punishment. ~*n* act or turn of delivering the ball in certain games.

service *n* **1** work, position, or duty of a servant. **2** religious rite or ceremony. **3** supply, maintenance, or repair. **4** set of dishes, etc. **5** act of serving or turn to serve the ball in tennis, etc. **6** supply or system of a public utility. **7** branch of government or public employment. **8** help; assistance. **(the) services** *pl n* Army, Navy, and Air Force. ~*vt* do maintenance work on. **serviceable** *adj* useful; durable but not decorative. **service station** *n* roadside garage providing petrol and repair services.

serviette *n* table napkin.

servile *adj* **1** of servants or slaves. **2** menial; cringing. **servility** *n*.

session *n* period during which a court, Parliament, etc., sits, universities function, or meetings or interviews take place.

set *v* (-tt-; set) *vt* **1** place; position; put. **2** cause or prompt. **3** fix; regulate; mend. **4** make firm or hard. **5** put (hair) in rollers, etc., to produce waves or curls. **6** bring into contact with fire; ignite; light. **7** establish as a standard, record, etc. **8** require the completion of (an examination, task, etc.). *vi* **1** become firm or hard; solidify. **2** (of the sun) fall below the horizon. **3** (of bones, etc.) mend. **set about** begin to deal with. **set in** become established. **set off** *or* **out** begin a journey; leave. **set up** start (a business, scheme, etc.); establish; found. ~*adj* **1** fixed; settled; determined; not alterable. **2** ready; prepared. *n* **1** group of people; class. **2** number of things that match or are designed to be used together. **3** scenery used for a play. **4** studio or area used when making a film, TV broadcast, etc. **setback** *n* relapse; check; halt. **setting** *n* frame, background, scenery, environment, etc., in which anything is set.

settee *n* long upholstered seat with a back and arms; couch; sofa.

settle *vt* **1** place at rest or in comfort, peace, order, etc. **2** decide finally. **3** give money to; resolve (debts). *vi* **1** subside; come to rest; sink. **2** take up residence. **3** reach a decision. **settle down** take up a settled normal established way of life. **settle for** agree to accept. **settle in** adapt to a new environment, circumstances, etc. **settle up** balance accounts; pay. **settlement** *n* **1** act or state of settling, paying, etc. **2** group of social workers in an underprivileged community. **3** newly established colony. **4** sinking or subsidence.

seven *n* **1** number equal to one plus six. **2** group of seven persons, things, etc. **3** *also* **seven o'clock** seven hours after noon or midnight. *adj* amounting to seven. **seventh** *adj* coming between sixth and eighth in sequence. *n* **1** seventh person, object, etc. **2** one of seven equal parts; one divided by seven.

seventeen *n* **1** number that is seven more than ten. **2** seventeen things or people. *adj* amounting to seventeen. **seventeenth** *adj,adv,n*.

seventy *n* **1** number equal to seven times ten. **2** seventy things or people. *adj* amounting to seventy. **seventieth** *adj,adv,n*.

sever *vt,vi* separate; cut; end. **severance** *n*.

several *adj* **1** more than one; a few. **2** separate; distinct; various.

severe *adj* **1** harsh; strict; violent. **2** grave; serious. **3** unadorned; plain, austere. **severely** *adv*. **severity** *n*.

sew *vt,vi* (sewed; sewn *or* sewed) work on, fasten, join, embroider, etc., with a needle and thread; stitch.

sewage *n* used water supply containing domestic refuse and waste matter. **sewer** *n* underground pipe or drain for carrying sewage. **sewerage** *n* provision or system of sewers.

sex *n* **1** characteristics distinguishing male from female. **2** males or females. **3** sexual desires, instincts, or intercourse.

sextet *n* **1** group of or work composed for six musicians. **2** group of six.

sexual *adj* relating to sex or sex organs. **sexuality** *n* awareness of one's own sexual characteristics.

sexy *adj* sexually attractive or stimulating. **sexily** *adv*. **sexiness** *n*.

shabby *adj* **1** worn; dilapidated; ragged. **2** despicable; dishonourable. **shabbily** *adv*. **shabbiness** *n*.

shack *n* rough hut.
shade *n* **1** comparative darkness caused by shelter from light or sun. **2** screen against light. **3** gradation of colour. **4** small amount; tiny degree. *vt* shield from light; darken. **shady** *adj* **1** out of bright sunlight. **2** *inf* dishonest; of dubious reputation.
shadow *n* **1** dark outline of an object placed in front of light or sun. **2** mere insubstantial copy. **3** constant companion. *vt* **1** shade from light. **2** follow closely and secretly. **shadowy** *adj*. **shadow cabinet** *n* group of leading Opposition politicians determining policy should their party return to power.
shaft *n* **1** long straight narrow rod, handle, beam of light, column, etc. **2** vertical passage into a mine.
shaggy *adj* unkempt; tangled. **shaggily** *adv*.
shake *v* (shook; shaken) *vt* agitate; move with small fast gestures. *vi* tremble; be agitated. **shake off** get rid of. **shaky** *adj* unreliable; precarious; wobbling.
shall *v aux* used to express future probability or intention.
shallot *n* small onion similar to but milder than garlic.
shallow *adj* **1** not deep. **2** not profound; superficial. **shallowness** *n*.
shame *n* **1** feeling of humiliation caused by guilt, failure, disgrace, etc. **2** sense of modesty, pride, or dignity. **3** disappointing or unlucky event. *vt* bring shame upon. **put to shame** cause to feel inferior. **shameful** *adj* **shamefully** *adv*. **shamefaced** *adj* embarrassed; humiliated; ashamed.
shampoo *n* preparation for washing hair, carpets, upholstery, etc. *vt* rub clean with shampoo.
shamrock *n* type of small three-leaved plant, used as the Irish emblem.
shandy *n* drink made by mixing beer with lemonade or ginger beer.
shanty[1] small roughly built cabin or shack.
shanty[2] *n* rousing sailors' song.
shape *n* **1** external appearance of an object or figure; outline; form. **2** condition; situation; state. **take shape** begin to develop or take on a definite form. ~*vt* **1** make a particular shape of. **2** develop; fit. **shapeless** *adj* not having the proper or appropriate shape. **shapely** *adj* well shaped.
share *n* **1** part; portion or division given to or contributed by an individual. **2** fixed equal part of a company's capital. *vt* divide into shares. **share out** distribute; allot. **shareholder** *n* one holding a share, esp. in a company.
shark *n* large long-bodied voracious and often dangerous marine fish.
sharp *adj* **1** having a fine edge or point; cutting; piercing. **2** acid; shrill, painful; intense. **3** clear-cut. **4** quick; lively. **5** artful; dishonest. **6** (in music) above true pitch; a semitone higher than the note. *adv* **1** punctually. **2** too high in pitch. **look sharp** hurry. **sharp-sighted** *adj* **1** having excellent eyesight. **2** shrewd; sharp-witted. **sharpen** *vt,vi* become or make sharp.
shatter *vt,vi* **1** smash or break into fragments. **2** wreck; exhaust; destroy.
shave *vt,vi* scrape off a superficial layer, esp. of facial hair. *n* act of shaving. **close shave** narrow escape; near miss.
shawl *n* folded square of material worn loosely around the shoulders or wrapped around a baby.
she *pron* female person; the 3rd person singular as the subject.
sheaf *n, pl* **sheaves 1** large bundle of cereal crops tied together after reaping. **2** bundle of papers.
shear *vt* (sheared; shorn *or* sheared) clip or cut off hair or wool, esp. from sheep. **shears** *pl n* cutting implement resembling large scissors.
sheath *n* tightly fitting case or covering for a blade, insects' wings, etc. **sheathe** *vt* enclose in a sheath.
shed[1] *vt* (-dd-; shed) cast off; let fall; pour out. **shed light on** reveal; illuminate.
shed[2] *n* small simple building; hut.
sheen *n* glow; radiance; lustre.
sheep *n, pl* **sheep** wild or domesticated ruminant mammal reared for meat and wool. **black sheep** rogue. **sheepish** *adj* embarrassed through being wrong, etc. **sheepishly** *adv*. **sheepdog** *n* dog trained to herd sheep. **sheepskin** *n* skin of a sheep used for rugs, coats, etc.
sheer[1] *adj* **1** perpendicular; very steep. **2** unqualified; complete; utter. *adv* **1** vertically. **2** outright.
sheer[2] *vi* swerve; deviate. **sheer off 1** move away. **2** snap off with a clean break.
sheet[1] **1** large thin rectangle of cotton, linen,

nylon, etc., for a bed. **2** thin rectangular piece of paper, metal, etc.

sheet[2] *n* rope attached to a sail of a boat.

sheikh *n* head of an Arab family or tribe. **sheikhdom** *n* area ruled by a sheikh.

shelf *n, pl* **shelves** horizontal board set into a wall, bookcase, cupboard, etc. **on the shelf** (usually of a woman) not married and unlikely to be so.

shell *n* **1** hard outer case enclosing an egg, nut, shellfish, tortoise, etc. **2** framework; outline. **3** explosive device fired from heavy guns. *vt* **1** remove shell from. **2** bombard. **shell out** *inf* pay. **shellfish** *n* aquatic mollusc or crustacean with a shell.

shelter *n* place or thing providing safety from weather, attack, danger, etc. *vt* shield; protect. *vi* take cover.

shelve *vt* **1** provide with or put on a shelf. **2** postpone indefinitely.

shepherd *n* one who guards and herds sheep. *vt* guide and herd like a shepherd. **shepherdess** *f n.*

sherbet *n* fizzy drink or powder for making it.

sheriff *n* chief Crown officer of a county, responsible for keeping the peace, administering courts, etc.

sherry *n* fortified wine, esp. from Spain.

shield *n* **1** broad piece of armour carried to protect the body. **2** anything serving as shelter, protection, or defence. *vt* protect; screen.

shift *vt,vi* move; change position (of). *vi* manage; make do. *n* **1** movement; change of position. **2** period of work on a rota or relay system. **3** undergarment.

shilling *n* former British coin or unit of currency worth five new pence.

shimmer *vi* glisten; gleam with faint diffuse light. *n* faint light.

shin *n* **1** front of the human leg below the knee. **2** beef from the lower part of the leg. *vi* climb up (a tree, rope, etc.) quickly, using only the arms and legs.

shine *vi* (shone) **1** give off or reflect light; beam; glow. **2** excel; be conspicuous or animated. *vt* (shined) polish (shoes, etc.). *n* sheen; lustre. **shiny** *adj.*

ship *n* large floating sea-going vessel. *vt* (-pp-) carry or send by ship. **shipment** *n* **1** cargo; goods shipped together. **2** shipping goods. **shipping** *n* **1** business of transporting goods by sea. **2** number of ships, esp. of a country or port. **shipshape** *adj* well-ordered; clean; neat. **shipwreck** *n* destruction or loss of a ship at sea. *vt,vi* cause or suffer shipwreck; ruin. **shipyard** *n* dock or yard where ships are built and repaired.

shirk *vt,vi* evade (duties or obligations). **shirker** *n.*

shirt *n* loose garment covering the top half of the body, esp. with sleeves, collar, and cuffs. **shirty** *adj sl* bad-tempered; irritable.

shiver *vi* tremble or quiver with cold, excitement, or fear. *n* tremble; shivering motion.

shock[1] *n* **1** alarming startling experience. **2** violent collision or impact. **3** bodily condition of near or complete collapse because of rapid falling of blood pressure. **4** *also* **electric shock** condition resulting from bodily contact with a strong electric current. *vt* shake or alarm by violent impact, frightening experience, improper outrageous behaviour, etc. **shock absorber** *n* device for diminishing vibration in vehicles.

shock[2] *n* thick shaggy mass, esp. of hair.

shoddy *adj* of inferior quality; cheap and nasty. *n* cloth made from scraps of other materials. **shoddily** *adv.* **shoddiness** *n.*

shoe *n* **1** outer covering for the foot. **2** anything resembling a shoe. *vt* (shod) provide shoes for.

shone *v pt* and *pp* of **shine.**

shook *v pt* and *pp* of **shake.**

shoot *v* (shot) *vt,vi* **1** fire (a gun). **2** propel (a bullet, arrow, etc.). **3** send out suddenly; project. **4** sprout; put out buds. **5** photograph or film. *vt* injure or kill with a gun. *vi* hunt game for sport with a gun. *n* **1** young branch or sprout. **2** hunting or shooting party. **3** inclined plank or trough down which water, rubbish, coal, etc., may be thrown; chute. **good/bad shot** good/bad marksman.

shop *n* **1** place where goods are sold. **2** place where industrial work is carried out. **on the shop floor** amongst the workers in a factory, workshop, etc. **talk shop** discuss one's own occupation or job. ~*vi* (-pp-) visit shops to buy goods. **shop around** compare values at different shops. **shopkeeper** *n* owner or manager of a shop. **shoplifter** *n* one who steals goods from a shop. **shoplifting** *n.* **shop steward** *n* trade union's elected departmental delegate.

shore[1] *n* land bordering a river, lake, or sea.

shore[2] *vt* support or prop up (a building, ship, etc.). *n* prop.

shorn *v pp* of **shear.**

short *adj* **1** of relatively little length; not long or tall. **2** lasting for a little while; brief. **3** brusque; abrupt; curt. **4** not plentiful; sparse; inadequate; insufficient. **5** abbreviated; cut. *adv* abruptly. *n* **in short** as a summary; briefly. **shorts** *pl n* short trousers, worn esp. when participating in certain sports. **shortness** *n*. **shortage** *n* lack; deficiency. **shortbread** *n* crisp biscuit made from butter, flour, and sugar. **shortcoming** *n* failure; deficiency. **shorten** *vt,vi* decrease; reduce. **shorthand** *n* system of symbols used for writing at speed. **shorthanded** *adj* short of staff; undermanned. **shortlived** *adj* transitory; brief. **shortly** *adv* **1** soon; in a short time. **2** briefly; abruptly. **short-sighted** *adj* **1** unable to see clearly at a distance. **2** without imagination or foresight. **short-sightedly** *adv*. **short-sightedness** *n*. **short-tempered** *adj* liable to lose one's temper easily; irritable. **short-term** *n* immediate future.

shot *n* **1** act of shooting or the missile shot. **2** photograph. **3** attempt; try. **4** hypodermic injection. **be/get shot of** be/get rid of. **like a shot** with great speed. **shot in the arm** encouragement. **shot in the dark** mere guess. ~*adj* of changing colour. *v pt* and *pp* of **shoot. shotgun** *n* smooth bore gun firing small shot.

should *v aux* **1** used to express obligation, duty, or likelihood. **2** used to form the conditional tense. **3** used in indirect speech.

shoulder *n* **1** part of the body where the arm is attached. **2** corresponding part in animals and birds. **3** prominent part of a hillside, bottle, vase, etc. **4** roadside verge. **give the cold shoulder to** snub. **rub shoulders with** mix with; get to know. ~*vt* **1** push, lift, or jostle with the shoulder. **2** accept (responsibility). **shoulder-blade** *n* broad flat bone of the upper back.

shout *n* loud cry or call. *vt,vi* utter (with) a shout.

shove *vt,vi* push; thrust; jostle. *n* hard push. **shove off 1** push a boat away from the shore. **2** *sl* leave.

shovel *n* broad often short-handled spade for lifting coal, earth, etc. *vt* (-ll-) move with or as if with a shovel.

show *v* (showed; shown) *vt* **1** display; allow to be seen. **2** conduct; guide. **3** reveal; indicate. **4** demonstrate; instruct. **5** prove; give evidence of. *vi* **1** be able to be seen; be revealed or displayed. **2** be evident; prove. **show off** behave in a pretentious way. ~*n* **1** exhibition or display. **2** entertainment with dancers, singers, etc. **show business** *n* profession of theatrical entertainers, variety artists, etc. **showcase** *n* glass-fronted display cabinet. **showdown** *n* open conflict or challenge. **show-jumping** *n* horse-jumping displayed in competition. **showmanship** *n* skill in displaying goods, theatrical productions, etc., to the best advantage. **showroom** *n* room in which goods may be viewed.

shower *n* **1** short fall of rain, bullets, blows, etc. **2** large supply; abundant flow. **3** bathroom fitting from which water is sprayed from above. *vt* fall or pour out, as in a shower. **showery** *adj*. **showerproof** *adj* impervious to showers.

shrank *v pt* of **shrink.**

shred *n* strip; fragment. *vt* (-dd-; shredded *or* shred) cut or tear into shreds.

shrew *n* **1** small mammal resembling a mouse and also having an elongated snout. **2** bad-tempered woman.

shrewd *adj* **1** discerning; astute; wise. **2** cunning; sly. **shrewdly** *adv*. **shrewdness** *n*.

shriek *n* high piercing cry or scream. *vt,vi* utter (with a shriek).

shrill *adj* high-pitched, piercing, and insistent. *vt,vi* utter in a shrill manner. **shrillness** *n*. **shrilly** *adv*.

shrimp *n* **1** tiny edible crustacean smaller than and similar to a prawn. **2** *inf* small person.

shrine *n* **1** place hallowed by associations with a saint. **2** casket containing holy relics.

shrink *vi* (shrank; shrunk *or* shrunken) become smaller; contract, esp. when wet. **shrink (back) from** recoil or flinch from; shun.

shrivel *vi* (-ll-) *also* **shrivel up** become shrunken, withered, and wrinkled.

shroud *n* **1** sheet wrapped around a dead body. **2** anything that veils or wraps round. **3** set of ropes forming part of a ship's rigging. *vt* cloak or cover (in secrecy, antiquity, etc.).

Shrove Tuesday *n* day of confession and subsequent merrymaking before Lent.

shrub *n* low bush with no central trunk. **shrubbery** *n* area or group of shrubs.

shrug *vt,vi* (-gg-) raise the shoulders to express indifference, doubt, or dislike. *n* act of shrugging. **shrug off** shake off with indifference.

shrunk *v* a *pp* of **shrink.**

shrunken *v* a *pp* of **shrink.**

shudder *n* shiver, esp. with horror, fear, etc. *vi* **1** tremble as with horror. **2** vibrate.

shuffle *vt,vi* **1** move slowly without lifting the feet from the ground. **2** mix randomly, esp. playing cards. *n* act of shuffling.

shun *vt* (-nn-) avoid; stay away from.

shunt *vt,vi* **1** divert (a train) to another track. **2** bypass; sidetrack. *vi inf* move; go away. *n* **1** act of shunting. **2** electrical conductor diverting current.

shut *v* (-tt-; shut) *vt* **1** move (a door, the eyes, mouth, etc.) so as to be no longer open; close. **2** fasten; secure; lock or bolt. **3** cease to operate, trade, etc. *vi* become closed. **shut up 1** become silent. **2** lock up or in. **shutter** *n* **1** wooden or metal window covering. **2** device controlling light admitted to a camera lens.

shuttlecock *n* small piece of cork, plastic, etc., stuck with feathers and struck by a racket in badminton, etc.

shy *adj* bashful; timid; lacking self-confidence. *vi* move (away from); recoil (from). **shyly** *adv.* **shyness** *n.*

sick *adj* **1** unwell; ill. **2** inclined to vomit. **3** gruesome; macabre. **sick of** tired of; bored with. **sicken** *vi,vt* become or make sick, weary, or disgusted. **sickening** *adj* nauseating; annoying. **sickly** *adj* **1** prone to ill-health; feeble. **2** so sweet as to be nauseating. **sickness** *n* **1** illness; disease. **2** vomiting; nausea.

side *n* **1** one of the surfaces of an object. **2** that part of something other than the top and bottom or back and front. **3** surface of a piece of paper, cloth, etc. **4** left or right part of the body, face, etc. **5** area to the left or right of the centre of something. **6** one of the teams or groups in a match, competition, debate, etc. **7** facet; aspect; part. **side by side** together; in juxtaposition. **take sides** favour one side more than the other in a dispute. *v* **side with** take sides with one rather than the other. **sideboard** *n* piece of dining-room furniture holding or displaying plates, cutlery, etc. **sideboards** *pl n* side whiskers on the face. **side effect** *n* secondary unplanned and often undesirable effect of an action, drug, etc. **sideline** *n* subsidiary or additional occupation. **sideshow** *n* minor show or fairground entertainment. **sidestep** *vt* (-pp-) neatly evade; avoid or step aside from. **sidetrack** *vt* lead away from a subject; divert. **sideways** *adv, adj* on or towards one side. **siding** *n* short stretch of railway track used for shunting.

sidle *vi* **1** move sideways; edge along. **2** fawn; cringe.

siege *n* attempt to conquer a fortified place by surrounding and preventing access to it.

sieve *n* utensil with a perforated container for straining liquids, separating coarse from fine grains, or pulping solids. *vt* put through a sieve; sift.

sift *vt* **1** pass through or separate with a sieve. **2** examine minutely.

sigh *n* long deep breath expressing weariness, sadness, relief, etc. *vt,vi* utter (with) a sigh.

sight *n* **1** ability or power to see; vision. **2** something seen or viewed. **3** something that is messy, ugly, or untidy; mess. **4** appearance. **5** *inf* a lot; much more. **at first sight** on the first occasion of seeing. ~*vt* see; observe; spot. **sightless** *adj* blind. **sightread** *vt,vi* (-read) read, play, or sing music at first sight. **sightseeing** *n* visiting tourist attractions, beauty spots, etc. **sightseer** *n.*

sign *n* **1** symbol. **2** gesture; gesticulation. **3** hint; implication; clue; trace. **4** recognizable symptom. **5** advertisement or notice. *vt,vi* **1** write one's name or signature (on). **2** signal; communicate with signs. **sign on** *or* **up** enrol; enlist.

signal *n* visible or audible sign, esp. prearranged or well-known. *vt,vi* (-ll-) make signals (to).

signature *n* **1** signed name, esp. for use as authentication. **2** act of signing. **3** mark showing key and time at the beginning of a musical score. **signature tune** *n* tune used to announce and identify a particular performer or programme on stage, radio, television, etc.

significant *adj* meaningful; noteworthy; important. **significance** *n.* **significantly** *adv.* **signify** *vt* mean; indicate; be a sign of. *vi* matter; be important.

silence *n* absence of sound, speech, or communication. *vt* make silent; suppress. **silencer** *n* device rendering car exhaust, a gun, etc., more quiet. **silent** *adj* without a sound; noiseless; quiet. **silently** *adv*.

silhouette *n* outline figure, esp. in black on a white background. *vt* show in silhouette.

silk *n* fine soft fibre spun by silkworms and woven into fabric. **silkworm** *n* caterpillar of the mulberry-eating moth, which spins silk. **silky** *adj* soft, fine, and gleaming like silk. **silkiness** *n*.

sill *n* ledge or slab below a window or door.

silly *adj* foolish; fatuous; imprudent; unwise. **silliness** *n*.

silo *n* granary.

silt *n* sediment left by water in a river, harbour, etc. *vt,vi* fill (up) with silt.

silver *n* **1** white shining malleable valuable metallic element, widely used in coinage, jewellery, tableware, electrical contacts, alloys, etc. **2** *also* **silverware** cutlery, dishes, etc., made from silver or an alloy of silver. *adj* **1** made of silver. **2** of the colour of silver. **silver wedding** *n* twenty-fifth wedding anniversary. **silvery** *adj* **1** looking like silver. **2** having a clear soft sound.

similar *adj* like; resembling; exactly the same. **similarity** *n*. **similarly** *adv*.

simile *n* figure of speech in which two apparently unlike things are compared.

simmer *vt,vi* **1** cook slowly at boiling point. **2** have emotions (esp. anger) barely in check. **simmer down** calm down. ~*n* state of simmering.

simple *adj* **1** easy; plain; ordinary. **2** not complex. **3** mere. **simple-minded** *adj* ingenuous; foolish. **simple-mindedly** *adv*. **simple-mindedness** *n*. **simplicity** *n* condition of being simple. **simplify** *vt* make less complicated; clarify. **simplification 3** absolutely.

simulate *vt* feign or reproduce (a situation, condition, etc.). **simulation** *n*.

simultaneous *adj* occurring at the same time. **simultaneously** *adv*.

sin *n* moral or religious offence. *vi* (-nn-) commit a sin. **sinful** *adj*.

since *adv* from that time until now; subsequently; ago. *prep* after; from the time of. *conj* **1** from the time that. **2** because; seeing that.

sincere *adj* honest; straightforward; genuine. **sincerely** *adv*. **sincerity** *n*.

sinew *n* tendon joining a muscle to a bone. **sinewy** *adj* wiry; muscular.

sing *vi,vt* (sang; sung) **1** utter (words or a tune) melodiously; produce musical notes. **2** celebrate in poetry. **singer** *n*.

singe *vt,vi* scorch or burn (the surface, edge, or end of). *n* slight burn.

single *adj* **1** individual; only one. **2** separate; solitary. **3** unmarried. **4** unique. *n* **1** short gramophone record played at 45 revolutions per minute. **2** one-way train or bus ticket. **3** single thing, event, etc. **singles** *pl n* tennis match, etc., between two players. *v* **single out** select from many for a specific purpose. **singly** *adv*. **single-handed** *adj* alone; unaided. **single-minded** *adj* intent; with one driving force or set aim. **single-mindedly** *adv*. **single-mindedness** *n*.

singular *adj* **1** indicating a single person, place, or thing. **2** odd; extraordinary; unusual. **singularity** *n*. **singularly** *adv*.

sinister *adj* malignant; suggestive of evil.

sink *v* (sank; sunk) *vt,vi* **1** submerge. **2** drop; lower. **3** lower or become lower in cost, value, etc. *vi* **1** pass (into) a state, condition, etc. **2** become weaker, unwell, etc. *vt* drive (a stake, post, etc.) into the ground. *n* fitted basin for washing, etc. **sink or swim** fail or succeed.

sinner *n* one who commits sin.

sinus *n* bodily cavity or passage, esp. communicating with the nose. **sinusitis** *n* inflammation of the sinus.

sip *vt,vi* (-pp-) drink in small mouthfuls. *n* small mouthful of liquid.

siphon *n* **1** bent pipe or tube for drawing off liquids. **2** bottle for dispensing soda water, etc., by means of a siphon. *vt,vi* draw (off) using a siphon.

sir *n* title used in a formal letter or to address a knight, baronet, or a man superior in age, rank, dignity, etc.

siren *n* apparatus producing a loud wailing noise or signal.

sirloin *n* upper part of a loin of beef.

sister *n* **1** daughter of the same parents as another. **2** nun. **3** nurse in charge of a hospital ward. **sisterhood** *n* community of nuns or other women. **sister-in-law** *n, pl* **sisters-in-law** brother's wife or husband's or wife's sister. **sisterly** *adj*.

sit *v* (-tt-; sat) *vi* **1** be in the position of having one's buttocks resting on the ground, a chair, etc. **2** be placed; rest. **3** be a member (of a committee, etc.). *vt* **1** seat; place in a sitting position. **2** allocate a place at table to. *vt,vi* take (an examination). **sit-in** *n* mass occupation of premises as a form of protest.

site *n* place, setting, or ground on which a building, town, etc., stands. *vt* locate.

sitting *n* **1** session; business meeting. **2** time spent posing for a portrait, etc. **sitting room** *n* room used for sitting comfortably; living room.

situated *adj* **1** located; sited. **2** placed with respect to money, housing, or other considerations. **situation** *n* **1** position; condition. **2** job.

six *n* **1** number equal to one plus five. **2** group of six persons, things, etc. **3** *also* **six o'clock** six hours after noon or midnight. **at sixes and sevens** confused; in a muddle. ~*adj* amounting to six. **sixth** *adj* coming between fifth and seventh in sequence. *n* **1** sixth person, object, etc. **2** one of six equal parts; one divided by six. *adv* after the fifth.

sixteen *n* **1** number that is six more than ten. **2** sixteen things or people. *adj* amounting to sixteen. **sixteenth** *adj,adv,n.*

sixty *n* **1** number equal to six times ten. **2** sixty things or people. *adj* amounting to sixty. **sixtieth** *adj,adv,n.*

size *n* **1** extent; dimensions; importance. **2** measurement categorizing individual proportions. *vt* categorize by size. **size up** judge roughly; weigh up. **sizable** *adj* of considerable size or importance.

sizzle *vi* **1** hiss and splutter as during frying. **2** *inf* be very hot. *n* sizzling noise.

skate[1] *n* boot fitted with a blade or wheels allowing the wearer to glide smoothly over ice or other hard surfaces. *vi* move on or as if on skates. **skate on thin ice** deal with or be in a precarious situation. **skater** *n.*

skate[2] *n* large flatfish with an elongated snout.

skeleton *n* **1** framework of bones within a human or animal body. **2** outline, sketch, nucleus, or framework of anything. **skeleton in the cupboard** secret domestic disgrace.

sketch *n* **1** rough or unfinished drawing, draft, or outline. **2** very short usually amusing play. *vt,vi* draw or outline roughly. **sketchy** *adj* incomplete; rough; inadequate. **sketchily** *adv.*

ski *n* **1** one of two long narrow pointed pieces of wood, metal, etc., attached to boots allowing wearer to slide quickly over snow. **2** short for **water-ski.** *vi* (skiing; skied *or* ski'd) travel on skis. **skier** *n.* **ski-lift** *n* seats slung on a cable transporting skiers up slopes.

skid *n* **1** wooden or metal support on which a ship, aeroplane, car, etc., may be rested, moved, or slid. **2** act of skidding. *vi* (-dd-) (of a vehicle, etc.) slide sideways, esp. out of control. **skid row** haunt or condition of vagrants, drunkards, etc.

skill *n* accomplishment; craft; expert knowledge. **skilled** *adj.* **skilful** *adj.* **skilfully** *adv.*

skim *vt* (-mm-) **1** remove scum, cream, etc., from the surface of a liquid. **2** pass over lightly, scarcely touching. **skim over** *or* **through** read cursorily; glance at. **skimmed milk** milk without cream.

skin *n* **1** tissue forming the outer covering of the body. **2** outer covering of a fruit. **3** leather pelt obtained from an animal. **4** layer; thin coating. *vt* (-nn-) remove the skin of or from. **skinny** *adj* unpleasantly thin. **skin-tight** *adj* extremely close-fitting.

skip *vt,vi* (-pp-) **1** jump or hop lightly, esp. from one foot to the other or over a twirling rope. **2** omit; leave out. *n* skipping movement.

skipper *n* captain of a ship, aircraft, etc.

skirmish *n* small unplanned fight or clash, as between hostile armies, etc. *vi* engage in a skirmish.

skirt *n* **1** woman's garment extending downwards from the waist or this part of a dress. **2** edge; extremity; border. *vt* pass around or along the edge of.

skittle *n* bottle-shaped target used in ninepin or tenpin bowling.

skull *n* bony framework of the head enclosing the brain.

skunk *n* small carnivorous black North American mammal with bushy tail, white-striped back, and a gland that sprays a powerful offensive scent.

sky *n* upper atmosphere; heavens; apparent canopy of air seen from the earth. **sky-high** *adj,adv* extremely high. **skylark** *n* lark that sings while hovering in the air. *vi inf* indulge in practical jokes, frolics, etc. **skyscraper** *n* very tall building of many storeys.

slab *n* thick flat piece of stone, metal, cake, chocolate, etc.

slack *adj* **1** loose; not taut or stretched; limp. **2** lazy; remiss. *n* slack part of a rope. **slacks** *pl n* trousers for casual or informal wear.

slacken *vi,vt* **1** make or become slack(er). **2** relax; abate; delay.

slam *vt,vi* (-mm-) shut or put down violently and noisily. *n* noise of something slammed.

slander *n* false, defamatory, or injurious report. *vt* injure by spreading false malicious gossip. **slanderer** *n*. **slanderous** *adj*.

slang *n* colloquial language not regarded as good, educated, or acceptable. *vt* berate abusively. **slanging match** bitter exchange of verbal insults.

slant *vt,vi* **1** slope; turn obliquely. **2** write or present (material) in a biased or prejudiced manner. *n* **1** slope. **2** angle of approach; attitude.

slap *n* blow with hand or anything flat. **slap in the face** insult; rebuff. ~*vt* (-pp-) smack; strike with a slap. **slapdash** *adj* careless; haphazard. **slapstick** *n* rough boisterous comedy.

slash *vt,vi* **1** cut with long violent random strokes. **2** economize or reduce drastically. *n* long cut or slit.

slat *n* narrow strip of wood, metal, etc.

slate *n* **1** dull grey fine-grained rock that can be split into smooth even pieces. **2** thin piece of this used as a writing tablet, roofing tile, etc.

slaughter *n* killing, esp. of many people or animals at once; massacre. *vt* **1** kill or slay ruthlessly, esp. in large numbers. **2** kill (an animal) for market. **slaughterhouse** *n* place where animals are killed for market; abattoir.

slave *n* **1** person legally owned by another. **2** person forced to work against his will. **3** person under the control or influence of someone or something. *vi* work like a slave. **slavery** *n* **1** state or condition of being a slave. **2** extremely hard unrewarding work.

sledge *n* vehicle on runners for transporting goods or people over snow; sleigh.

sledgehammer *n* large heavy hammer.

sleek *adj* **1** smooth and glossy. **2** suave; elegant. *vt* make smooth and glossy. **sleekly** *adv*. **sleekness** *n*.

sleep *n* resting state during which the body is relaxed and consciousness is suspended. *vi* (slept) take rest in sleep. **sleep on it** postpone a decision overnight. **sleepless** *adj*. **sleepily** *adv*. **sleepiness** *n*. **sleepy** *adj*. **sleeper** *n* **1** one who sleeps. **2** horizontal beam supporting the rails of a railway track. **3** sleeping car or compartment on a train.

sleepwalk *vi* walk while asleep. **sleepwalker** *n*.

sleet *n* rain falling as half-melted hail or snow. *vi* fall as sleet.

sleeve *n* **1** part of a garment covering the arm. **2** tube covering a rod, pipe, etc. **3** cover for gramophone record. **up one's sleeve** held secretly in reserve.

sleigh *n* sledge, esp. one pulled by horses.

slender *adj* **1** slim; thin. **2** meagre; insufficient.

slice *n* **1** thin flat piece cut from something. **2** utensil for lifting and serving fish, etc. *vt* **1** cut into slices. **2** cut a slice from. **3** hit (a golfball, tennis ball, etc.) so that it curves in flight.

slick *adj* **1** sleek; smooth. **2** deft; cunning. **slickness** *n*.

slide *v* (slid) *vt,vi* **1** move or glide smoothly over a surface. **2** move or be moved unobtrusively. *vi* **1** pass gradually. **2** slip or fall. **let slide** allow to take a natural course. ~*n* **1** transparent photograph. **2** smooth inclined surface for children, goods, etc., to slide down. **3** clasp for the hair. **slide-rule** *n* mechanical device used for calculating.

slight *adj* **1** frail; slim; flimsy. **2** insignificant; unimportant. *n* snub; hurtful act. *vt* disregard; treat as if of no importance. **slightly** *adv* a little; somewhat.

slim *adj* **1** slender; thin. **2** small; slight; meagre. *vi* (-mm-) try to lose weight by means of diet, exercise, etc. **slimmer** *n*. **slimness** *n*.

slime *n* thin oozing mud or anything resembling it. **slimy** *adj* **1** resembling or covered with slime. **2** vile; repulsive.

sling *n* **1** piece of material for supporting an injured arm, hand, etc. **2** band or pocket attached to strings for throwing stones, hoisting or supporting weighty objects, etc. *vt* (slung) **1** throw casually. **2** support with or hang from a sling.

slink *vi* (slunk) move stealthily and quietly; sneak. **slinky** *adj* **1** close-fitting. **2** sinuous and graceful.

slip[1] *v* (-pp-) *vi* **1** slide; glide. **2** become unfastened or less secure. **3** lose one's balance, grip, etc. **4** become less efficient, careful, etc. **5** move quietly or without being noticed. **6** forget; make a mistake. *vt* **1** pull or push easily or hastily. **2** drop; let fall. **slip up** make a mistake. ~*n* **1** sliding; act of slipping. **2** mistake; small error. **3** petticoat. **slipway** *n* sloping area from which a vessel is launched.

slip[2] *n* narrow strip of wood, paper, etc.
slipper *n* loose comfortable indoor shoe.
slippery *adj* **1** so smooth, greasy, etc., as to make slipping likely. **2** elusive; unstable. **slipperiness** *n.*
slit *n* **1** long cut. **2** narrow opening. *vt* (-tt-) **1** make a long cut in. **2** cut into long strips.
slither *vi* slide unsteadily.
slog *vi,vt* (-gg-) **1** hit violently. **2** work hard and determinedly. *n* **1** long spell of hard work. **2** heavy blow.
slogan *n* catchy word or phrase used in advertising, etc.
slop *n* **1** liquid waste. **2** semiliquid unappetizing food. *vt,vi* (-pp-) spill carelessly and messily. **sloppy** *adj* **1** messy; careless; untidy. **2** muddy, slushy, or watery. **3** sentimental; maudlin. **sloppily** *adv.* **sloppiness** *n.*
slope *n* **1** inclined surface. **2** deviation from the horizontal; slant. *vi* have or take a sloping position or direction.
sloshed *adj inf* drunk.
slot *n* groove, channel, or slit into which a bolt, coin, etc., may fit or be inserted. *vt* (-tt-) **1** make fit into. **2** provide with or pass through a slot. **slot together** fit neatly together.
slovenly *adj* **1** careless; slipshod. **2** lazy and dirty. **slovenliness** *n.*
slow *adj* **1** taking a long time. **2** not quick; gradual. **3** behind correct time. **4** dull-witted or unresponsive. *vt* delay; retard. **slow down** *or* **up** lessen; slacken in speed. **slowly** *adv.* **slowness** *n.*
slug small shell-less mollusc, destructive to garden plants.
sluggish *adj* lazy; slow-moving. **sluggishly** *adv.* **sluggishness** *n.*
sluice *n* sliding gate or valve controlling a flow of water in a channel, drain, etc. *vt,vi* flush or wash down with running water.
slum *n* squalid overcrowded housing.
slump *n* **1** sudden fall or decline. **2** economic depression. *vi* **1** collapse in a heap. **2** suddenly lose value.
slung *v pt* and *pp* of **sling.**
slunk *v pt* and *pp* of **slink.**
slur *vt,vi* (-rr-) **1** sound (words) indistinctly. **2** pass over lightly. **3** disparage. *n* **1** smudge; blur. **2** indistinct noise. **3** slight, insult, or blame.
slush *n* **1** watery mud or snow. **2** excessive sentimentality. **slushy** *adj.*

sly *adj* **1** cunning. **2** devious; deceitful. **slyly** *adv.* **slyness** *n.*
smack[1] *vt* strike sharply with the palm of the hand. **smack the lips** make a smacking sound with the lips. ~*n* act or sound of smacking. *adv inf* immediately; directly.
smack[2] *n* slight trace or flavour. *vi* suggest; have the flavour (of).
small *adj* not large; of little size, strength, importance, quantity, etc. **feel small** feel humiliated. **small talk** polite trivial conversation. ~*n* narrow part (of the back, etc.). **smallness** *n.* **smallholding** *n* small farm or rented plot of agricultural land. **small-minded** *adj* petty; narrow-minded. **smallpox** *n* serious contagious disease causing eruptions and subsequent scars on the skin.
smart *adj* **1** fashionable; elegant. **2** clever; ingenious; witty. *vi* feel sharp pain or resentment. **smartly** *adv.* **smartness** *n.* **smarten** *vt* make cleaner, tidier, more fashionable, etc.
smash *vt,vi* **1** shatter; break into fragments. **2** hit or throw violently. *n* **1** sound or act of smashing. **2** violent collision, esp. of motor vehicles. **smashing** *adj inf* wonderful; excellent.
smear *n* **1** dirty greasy mark. **2** slur on one's reputation. **3** specimen taken for pathological testing. *vt* **1** spread or cover with something thick or greasy. **2** discredit publicly. **3** blur by smearing.
smell *n* **1** odour; stink; fragrance. **2** ability to distinguish smells. **3** suggestion; hint. *vt* detect or distinguish by the sense of smell. *vi* give off a smell. **smell out** discover by investigation. **smell a rat** become suspicious. **smelly** *adj* having a strong or unpleasant smell.
smile *vi* turn up the corners of the lips to express pleasure, approval, amusement, etc. *n* act of smiling; happy expression. **smilingly** *adv.*
smirk *vi* give an unpleasant, knowing, silly, or self-satisfied smile. *n* act of smirking; smirking expression.
smock *n* full long loose shirt.
smog *n* combination of smoke and fog. **smoggy** *adj.*
smoke *n* **1** visible cloud of fine particles given off during burning. **2** cigarette, cigar, etc. *vi* give off smoke. *vi,vt* inhale fumes of burning

tobacco in a cigarette, pipe, etc. *vt* cure (meat, fish, etc.) by treatment with smoke. **smoker** *n* **1** person who smokes tobacco. **2** train compartment where smoking is allowed. **smoky** *adj.*

smooth *adj* **1** having an even surface. **2** level; even. **3** unruffled; calm. **4** easy; comfortable. *vt,vi also* **smoothen** make or become smooth. *vt* **1** soothe; comfort. **2** facilitate; make easy or easier. **smoothly** *adv.* **smoothness** *n.*

smother *vt* **1** suffocate; prevent access of air with a thick covering, heavy smoke, etc. **2** suppress or conceal.

smoulder *vi* **1** burn slowly without a flame. **2** exist in a suppressed or undetected condition.

smudge *n* smear; dirty mark. *vt* mark or be marked with a smudge; smear.

smug *adj* self-satisfied; complacent. **smugly** *adv.* **smugness** *n.*

smuggle *vt,vi* import or export (goods) illegally. *vt* bring or take in secretly or illegally. **smuggler** *n.*

smut *n* **1** particle of soot or dust. **2** small dark mark. **3** bawdiness; obscenity. **smutty** *adj.*

snack *n* light quick meal.

snag *n* small problem, hitch, drawback, etc. *vt* (-gg-) **1** hinder; prevent. **2** catch or tear on a small sharp protuberance.

snail *n* small slow-moving hard-shelled mollusc.

snake *n* **1** long scaly legless reptile with a forked tongue and neither eyelids nor ears. **2** treacherous deceitful person.

snap *vt,vi* (-pp-) **1** bite suddenly. **2** speak sharply or irritably. **3** shut or break suddenly. **snap up** seize hastily. ~*n* **1** act or sound of snapping. **2** simple card game. **3** *inf* snapshot. **snapshot** *n* informal photograph.

snarl *vi* growl, speak, or show the teeth threateningly or angrily. *n* act, sound, or expression of snarling.

snatch *vt,vi* seize or grab suddenly, violently, or when an opportunity arises. *n* **1** act of snatching. **2** fragment or bit.

sneak *vi* move or creep in a furtive cowardly or underhand way. *vt* take secretly; steal. *n* one who sneaks.

sneer *n* cynical contemptuous expression or remark. *v* **sneer at** scorn; mock.

sneeze *vi* eject sudden convulsive involuntary breath through the nose. **not to be sneezed at** not to be treated as insignificant. ~*n* act or sound of sneezing.

sniff *vi* inhale sharply and noisily through the nose. *vt* smell. **sniff at** show scorn. ~*n* act or sound of sniffing.

snip *vt,vi* (-pp-) clip or cut off with or as with scissors. *n* **1** act of snipping. **2** small piece snipped off.

snipe *vi* shoot at an enemy or enemies from a concealed position. *n* long-billed wading bird. **sniper** *n.*

snivel *vi* (-ll-) **1** have a runny nose. **2** whine or whimper tearfully. *n* act or sound of snivelling. **sniveller** *n.*

snob *n* one who admires and imitates those he considers his superior in class, wealth, or rank and who despises his inferiors. **snobbish** *adj.* **snobbery** *n.*

snooker *n* game resembling billiards using fifteen red balls and six of other colours.

snoop *vi* pry; investigate secretly. **snooper** *n.*

snooty *adj* supercilious; haughty; disdainful. **snootily** *adv.* **snootiness** *n.*

snooze *n* short sleep; cat nap. *vi* doze; take a snooze.

snore *vi* breathe noisily while asleep. *n* act or sound of snoring.

snort *vi* exhale noisily and sharply through the nose, often in anger. *n* act or sound of snorting.

snout *n* **1** animal's projecting nose. **2** part of machinery, etc., resembling a snout.

snow *n* atmospheric vapour frozen and falling as flakes of white crystals. *vi* shower or fall as snow. **snowed under** overwhelmed with work, problems, etc. **snowed up** confined in a house, car, etc., by fallen snow. **snowy** *adj.*

snowdrop *n* tiny white-flowered bulbous plant of early spring.

snub *vt* (-bb-) humiliate or slight pointedly or sarcastically. *n* snubbing act or rebuff. **snub-nosed** *adj* having a short turned-up nose.

snuff[1] powder (esp. tobacco) inhaled through the nose.

snuff[2] *vt* extinguish (a candle).

snug *adj* cosy, comfortable, and warm. **snugly** *adv.*

snuggle *vt,vi* cuddle closely together or into blankets, etc., for warmth and comfort.

so *adv* **1** to such an extent; very. **2** in such a manner. **3** consequently; then. **4** also; as well. **and so on** and continuing; et cetera. ~*pron* **1** something similar. **2** as anticipated. *adj* correct; right; true. **so-and-so** *n* **1** particular but unnamed person. **2** awkward or difficult person; nuisance.

soak *vt,vi* steep or be steeped in liquid. *vt* drench; permeate. **soak up** draw into itself; absorb. ~*n* **1** act of soaking. **2** heavy downpour.

soap *n* substance used for cleansing, forming a lather with water. **soap opera** *n* serialized drama, esp. broadcast on daytime television. ~*vt* **1** rub with soap. **2** *inf* flatter. **soapy** *adj*.

soar *vi* rise upwards; fly or glide at great height. *n* act of soaring.

sob *v* (-bb-) *vi* catch one's breath noisily in involuntary spasms as a result of emotion; weep; cry. *vt* utter while sobbing. *n* act of sobbing.

sober *adj* **1** not drunk. **2** temperate in the use of intoxicants. **3** moderate; well-balanced. **4** serious; sedate. *vt,vi* make or become sober. **soberly** *adv*. **sobriety** *or* **soberness** *n*.

sociable *adj* **1** friendly. **2** fond of or conducive to social interaction. **sociability** *n*. **sociably** *adv*.

social *adj* **1** of or concerning interaction or relations between persons. **2** forming a society, group, or community. **3** gregarious; convivial. **4** pertaining to fashionable circles. *n* gathering for companionship. **socially** *adv*. **social class** *n* members of a community sharing a similar position in economic and social structure. **social security** *n* scheme(s) providing for the welfare of the public. **social work** *n* social service to improve the welfare of the public. **social worker** *n*.

socialism *n* political and economic theory of society which tends towards centralized planning and ownership of the means of production, distribution, and exchange and operation of the free market. **socialist** *adj,n*.

society *n* **1** group sharing territory, language, customs, laws, and political and economic organization. **2** fellowship; companionship. **3** any group of people organized for a purpose. **4** rich, aristocratic, and exclusive social group.

sociology *n* study of human societies, their structure, organization, and customs. **sociological** *adj*. **sociologist** *n*.

sock[1] *n* short stocking. **pull one's socks up** make greater efforts.

sock[2] *vt,n sl* punch; hit.

socket *n* **1** device which receives an electric plug. **2** natural or artificial indentation functioning as a receptacle.

soda *n* term applied to compounds of sodium. **soda-water** *n* aerated solution of sodium bicarbonate.

sodium *n* soft silvery reactive metallic element.

sofa *n* upholstered couch with a back and arms.

soft *adj* **1** yielding; malleable; smooth. **2** gentle. **3** lenient. **4** tender; sympathetic. **5** (of sound) low in volume. **6** (of colour) not very bright. **7** *inf* feeble-minded; foolish. **softly** *adv*. **softness** *n*. **soften** *vt,vi* make or become soft(er). **soft-hearted** *adj* easily moved to tenderness, pity, etc. **soft-heartedly** *adv*. **soft-heartedness** *n*. **software** *n* written or printed data used in the operation of computers; program.

soggy *adj* soaked; marshy; sodden. **soggily** *adv*. **sogginess** *n*.

soil[1] *n* top layer of the earth, composed of organic and inorganic substances; ground.

soil[2] *vt,vi* make or become dirty, stained, or polluted.

solar *adj* **1** of or from the sun. **2** measured by the movement of the earth relative to the sun. **3** radiating like the sun's rays. **solar system** *n* our sun with the planets, asteroids, comets, etc., that revolve round it. **solar plexus** *n* network of nerves radiating from behind the stomach.

sold *v pt* and *pp* of **sell.**

solder *n* alloy with a low melting temperature used for joining metals. *vt* join, mend, or patch with solder.

soldier *n* noncommissioned member of an armed force. *v* **soldier on** keep fighting or struggling towards something. **soldierly** *adj*.

sole[1] *n* flat underside of a foot, shoe, etc. *vt* put a sole on.

sole[2] *n* edible flatfish.

sole[3] *adj* only; single; solitary. **solely** *adv*.

solemn *adj* **1** grave; serious. **2** marked by formal or religious ceremony; arousing awe and reverence. **3** impressive; dignified; pompous. **solemnity** *n*. **solemnly** *adv*.

solicit *vt,vi* **1** ask (for) persistently. **2** make unlawful sexual offers or requests (to).

solicitor *n* lawyer who prepares deeds, manages cases, and who acts in lower courts only but prepares cases for barristers.

solicitous *adj* considerate; concerned; eager; anxious. **solicitude** *n*.

solid *adj* **1** firm; compact. **2** having three dimensions; not hollow. **3** heavy; strongly built. **4** reliable; steady. **5** unanimous. *n* solid substance; substance that is neither liquid nor gaseous. **solidity** *n*. **solidly** *adv*. **solidarity** *n* unanimous whole-hearted coherence in action or attitude. **solidify** *vt,vi* make or become solid.

solitary *adj* **1** existing, living, or going without others. **2** happening, done, or made alone. **3** secluded. **4** lonely; single; sole. **solitary confinement** *n* isolation of a prisoner from all others. **solitude** *n* absence of company; seclusion.

solo *n* **1** musical composition for a single voice or instrument. **2** card game in which players act individually and not in partnership. **3** flight during which the pilot is unaccompanied. *adv* alone; by oneself. **soloist** *n*.

solstice *n* time of year when the sun reaches its farthest points north and south of the equator, producing the shortest or longest day.

soluble *adj* **1** capable of being dissolved in liquid. **2** capable of being solved. **solubility** *n*.

solution *n* **1** method or process of solving a problem. **2** explanation or answer. **3** liquid containing a dissolved solid.

solve *vt* find the correct solution to; settle; clear up; explain.

solvent *adj* **1** able to pay debts. **2** able to dissolve another substance. *n* liquid capable of dissolving another substance. **solvency** *n* ability to pay off debts.

sombre *adj* dark; dismal; gloomy. **sombrely** *adv*. **sombreness** *n*.

sombrero *n* wide-brimmed hat with a tall crown, traditionally worn in Spain and Latin America.

some *adj* **1** certain (people or things). **2** a few; a number; an amount or quantity. **3** particular proportion. *pron* a number of people or things. *adv* about; approximately. **somebody** *pron* **1** particular but unnamed person. **2** important or famous person. **somehow** *adv* **1** in some way or other. **2** for some reason. **someone** *pron* somebody. **something** *pron* particular but unnamed thing, action, characteristic, etc. **something like** approximately; about; almost. *adv* to a certain extent. **sometime** *adv* on some occasion; at some time. **sometimes** *adv* occasionally; from time to time. **somewhat** *adv* to a certain extent; rather. **somewhere** *adv* **1** in or to some particular but unspecified place. **2** placed approximately.

somersault *n* **1** leap or roll in which one turns heels over head. **2** complete reversal of opinion or attitude. *vi* make a somersault.

son *n* **1** male offspring, esp. in relation to his parents. **2** any male descendant. **son-in-law** *n, pl* **sons-in-law** daughter's husband.

sonata *n* musical composition of three or four movements and featuring a solo instrument.

song *n* **1** musical piece that is sung. **2** songs in general. **3** characteristic call of certain birds. **song and dance** *inf* fuss.

sonic *adj* **1** relating to sound. **2** having a speed approximately equal to the speed of sound.

sonnet *n* poem of fourteen lines with a set rhyming pattern.

soon *adv* in a short time; without delay; quickly. **as soon as** at the moment that.

soot *n* black powdery substance given off by burning coal, wood, etc. **sooty** *adj*.

soothe *vt* calm; comfort; allay.

sophisticated *adj* **1** refined or cultured in taste and manner; urbane. **2** attractive to refined tastes. **3** over-refined; unnatural. **4** (of machines, etc.) complex. **sophistication** *n*.

soprano *n* **1** highest range of an adult female voice. **2** singer capable of this range of notes. **3** part written for this voice.

sordid *adj* **1** filthy; squalid. **2** degrading; base. **3** greedy or selfish. **sordidly** *adv*. **sordidness** *n*.

sore *adj* **1** painful; tender; inflamed. **2** grieved, vexed, or bitter. *n* injured or diseased spot; wound. **soreness** *n*. **sorely** *adv* severely; distressingly; greatly.

sorrow *n* mental pain caused by loss or misfortune. **sorrowful** *adj*. **sorrowfully** *adv*.

sorry *adj* **1** feeling pity, regret, sadness, sympathy, etc. **2** pitiful; miserable. **3** poor; shabby. *interj* expression of apology.

sort *n* **1** class; kind; type. **2** character; nature. **sort of** *inf* in some way; rather. **out of sorts** not in good health or spirits. ~*vt,vi* **1** classify. **2** group (with). **sort out 1** separate out. **2** solve (a problem); resolve (a situation). **3** *inf* punish; reprimand.

soufflé *n* light fluffy dish made with eggs.

sought *v pt* and *pp* of **seek.**

soul *n* **1** immortal spiritual part of man. **2** innermost depth, being, or nature; core. **3**

nobler feelings and capacities of the human being; conscience. **4** person. **5** music derived from Black American gospel singing. **soul-destroying** *adj* eroding identity; sapping effort or vigour; making inhuman. **soulful** *adj* having, expressing, or affecting deep or lofty feelings. **soulfully** *adv*. **soulless** *adj* inhuman; mechanical; lacking emotion or identity.

sound[1] *n* **1** noise perceptible to the ear. **2** mere noise without meaning. *vt,vi* **1** cause or emit a sound. **2** signal by a sound. *vi* seem; give an impression of being. **soundless** *adj*. **soundlessly** *adv*.

sound[2] *adj* **1** in good condition; healthy; whole and complete. **2** reasoned; prudent; reliable. **3** (of sleep) deep; unbroken. **soundly** *adv*. **soundness** *n*.

soup *n* liquid food made by boiling meat or vegetables in water. **in the soup** *sl* in trouble or difficulties.

sour *adj* **1** sharp or acid to the taste; not sweet. **2** turned or rancid. **3** embittered; morose. **sour grapes** pretending to dislike what one cannot have. **sourly** *adv*. **sourness** *n*.

source *n* **1** spring; origin; starting point or cause. **2** document or work providing authority, validity, or inspiration.

south *n* **1** one of the four cardinal points of the compass situated to the right of a person facing the sunrise. **2** part of a country, area, etc., lying towards the south. *adj also* **southern** of, in, or facing the south. *adv,adj also* **southerly** **1** towards the south. **2** (of winds) from the south. **southerner** *n*. **southeast** *n* point situated midway between the south and east. *adj also* **southeastern** of, in, or facing the southeast. *adv,adj also* **southeasterly** **1** towards the southeast. **2** (of winds) from the southeast. **southward** *adj* facing or moving towards the south. **southwards** *adv* in the direction of the south. **southwest** *n* point situated midway between south and west. *adj also* **southwestern** of, in, or facing the southwest. *adv,adj also* **southwesterly** **1** towards the southwest. **2** (of winds) from the southwest.

souvenir *n* memento or keepsake by which memory of some person, place, or event is cherished.

sovereign *n* **1** monarch; supreme ruler. **2** former English gold coin worth a pound. *adj* **1** supreme; utmost. **2** excellent. **sovereignty** *n*.

sow[1] (sou) *v* (sowed; sown *or* sowed) *vt,vi* scatter or put (seeds, plants, etc.) in the ground. *vt* disseminate; suggest. **sower** *n*.

sow[2] (sau) *n* adult female pig.

soya bean *n* seed of an east Asian plant, rich in oil and protein.

spa *n* resort having mineral water springs in its locality.

space *n* **1** three-dimensional expanse. **2** period of time or the distance between events, places, etc. **3** blank or unused area. **4** universe; area beyond the earth's atmosphere. *vt* arrange at or divide into intervals. **spacecraft** *n* vehicle launched into space for research purposes, exploration, etc. **spacious** *adj* having ample room; extensive; wide. **spaciously** *adv*.

spade[1] *n* digging tool with a broad flat blade.

spade[2] *n* playing card of the suit marked with a black heart-shaped pip and a stem or the symbol itself.

spaghetti *n* pasta in the form of long thin cords.

span *n* **1** extent of something stretched out; stretch of space or time. **2** distance between two points, as between pillars, supports of arches, bridges, etc. *vt* **1** extend; stretch across. **2** measure with an extended hand.

spaniel *n* breed of medium-sized dog with long drooping ears and a silky coat.

spank *vt* strike with the open hand, a slipper, etc., esp. on the buttocks; slap. *n* blow or series of blows with the flat of the hand, etc.; smack.

spanner *n* tool for manipulating nuts and bolts. **spanner in the works** deliberate hindrance; sabotage.

spare *vt* **1** be merciful to; refrain or release from punishment, suffering, etc. **2** give away freely; be able to do without. *adj* **1** left over; not used or needed; extra. **2** freely available; kept in reserve. **3** lean; thin. **4** scanty; meagre. *n* spare part. **sparing** *adj* thrifty; economical.

spark *n* **1** glowing particle thrown out by a burning substance. **2** brief flash of light, as that accompanying an electric discharge. **3** vitality; life. *vi* emit sparks. *vt* **1** produce (sparks). **2** kindle; excite.

sparkle *vi* **1** glitter; twinkle; emit sparks or flashes. **2** be gay, clever, or witty. *n* **1** act of glittering; brilliance. **2** gaiety; wit; lively intelligence. **3** appearance of effervescence, as in champagne.

sparrow *n* any of various small brown birds.

sparse *adj* thinly distributed; scanty. **sparsely** *adv*. **sparseness** *or* **sparsity** *n*.

spasm *n* **1** involuntary muscular contraction. **2** strong but short-lived movement, action, or emotion. **spasmodic** *adj* **1** intermittent; not continuous. **2** relating to spasms. **spasmodically** *adv*.

spastic *adj* suffering from spasms and lack of muscular control due to damage to the brain. *n* person who suffers so.

spat *v pt* and *pp* of **spit.**

spatial *adj* of, in, or concerning space or the placement of objects in space. **spatially** *adv*.

spatula *n* broad blunt-bladed knife or flattened spoon.

spawn *n* eggs of fish, frogs, molluscs, etc., laid in water. *vt,vi* deposit (eggs).

speak *v* (spoke; spoken) *vi* **1** utter words; talk. **2** give a speech, lecture, sermon, etc. *vt* declare; pronounce. **nothing to speak of** nothing worth mentioning. **so to speak** as one might put it. **speak for** speak on behalf of. **speak for oneself** express personal views. **speak up** speak so as to be sure to be heard. **speak up for** speak in favour of; defend. **speaker** *n*.

spear *n* **1** long weapon consisting of a shaft with a sharp pointed head. **2** anything so shaped. *vt,vi* kill or pierce with a spear.

spearmint *n* aromatic garden mint or the flavour of this.

special *adj* **1** distinctive; peculiar; for a particular purpose. **2** detailed; exceptional. *n* special thing or person. **specially** *adv*. **specialist** *n* person having comprehensive knowledge of a subject, etc.; authority. **speciality** *n* particular characteristic, product, etc., for which a person, shop, etc., is renowned. **specialize** *vi* limit oneself to one particular area for intensive study. **specialization** *n*.

species *n, pl* **species** group of animals or plants of the same genus, capable of interbreeding.

specific *adj* **1** of or particular to one definite kind or type. **2** explicit; precise; exact. **specifically** *adv*. **specify** *vt* **1** make explicit; mention particularly. **2** set down as a requisite. **specification** *n*.

specimen *n* individual, object, or portion regarded as typical or a sample for purposes of study or collection.

speck *n* small spot; minute particle. *vt* mark with specks.

spectacle *n* **1** exhibition; show; pageant. **2** unusual or ridiculous sight. **spectacles** *pl n* glasses worn to correct vision, etc. **spectacular** *adj* impressive; outstanding; amazing. *n* flamboyant show. **spectacularly** *adv*.

spectator *n* person watching a show, contest, etc.; onlooker.

spectrum *n* **1** range of colours in order of wavelength produced when sunlight is split into colours on passing through a prism. **2** wide range; graduated series. **spectral** *adj*.

speculate *vi* **1** theorize; reflect; make conjectures. **2** take risks, esp. in buying and selling, in the hope of quick gain. **speculation** *n*. **speculative** *adj*. **speculator** *n*.

speech *n* **1** that which is spoken; language. **2** act or faculty of speaking; manner of speaking. **3** oration; talk addressed to an audience. **speechless** *adj* **1** temporarily deprived of speech. **2** unable to speak.

speed *n* rate of movement; quickness; velocity. *v* (sped *or* speeded) *vi,vt* move rapidly or quickly. *vi* drive a vehicle at high speed or in excess of the speed limit. *vt* **1** further; hasten. **2** send forth with good wishes. **speedy** *adj*. **speedily** *adv*.

spell[1] *v* (spelt *or* spelled) *vt,vi* say or write in order the letters that constitute (a word). *vt* **1** (of letters) form; make up. **2** amount to. **spell out** explain in very simple and exact terms.

spell[2] *n* **1** magical formula or incantation. **2** enchantment; irresistible attraction. **spellbound** *adj* under a spell or influence; fascinated.

spell[3] *n* short period of time; bout.

spend *vt* (spent) **1** give; pay out. **2** expend; use; exhaust. **3** pass (time). **spendthrift** *n* person who wastes money.

sperm *n* **1** semen. **2** male reproductive cell.

sphere *n* **1** ball; globe. **2** scope; range. **3** field of activity or influence; world. **spherical** *adj*.

spice *n* **1** strong aromatic and pungent seasoning of vegetable origin. **2** that which adds excitement or interest. *vt* season with spice. **spicy** *adj*. **spicily** *adv*. **spiciness** *n*.

spider *n* eight-legged insect-like animal that spins webs to catch prey. **spidery** *adj* **1** spider-like. **2** having thin angular lines.

spike *n* sharp pointed rod, esp. of metal. *vt* fix or pierce with a spike. **spiky** *adj*.

spill *vt,vi* (spilt *or* spilled) **1** allow (liquid) to fall, esp. by accident. **2** overflow or cause to overflow. **spill the beans** reveal a secret. ~*n* **1** fall from a vehicle, horse, etc. **2** spilling.

spin *vt,vi* (spun) **1** rotate rapidly. **2** draw out and twist (wool, etc.) into thread. **3** (of spiders, etc.) form webs or cocoons. *n* **1** act or speed of rotating. **2** *inf* pleasure drive in a vehicle, etc.

spine *n* **1** backbone surrounding and protecting nerve tissue. **2** long thin ridge. **3** spiked extremity on a plant, fish, etc. **4** bound edge of a book. **spinal** *adj*. **spiny** *adj*. **spine-chilling** *adj* terrifying. **spineless** *adj* **1** having no spine. **2** weak; irresolute.

spinster *n* unmarried woman.

spiral *n* **1** curve that winds around and away from a fixed point or axis. **2** upward or downward trend in prices, wages, etc. *adj* resembling a spiral; twisting. *v* (-ll-) *vt,vi* take or make into a spiral course or shape. *vi* increase or decrease with ever-growing speed.

spire *n* **1** tall slender tower tapering to a point. **2** long slender flower or stalk; shoot.

spirit *n* **1** moving force; inner life; soul. **2** underlying meaning; true significance. **3** vitality; courage. **4** mood. **5** any distilled alcoholic beverage. **6** active essence of a drug, compound, etc. **spirited** *adj* lively; animated. **spirited away** *adj* mysteriously or secretly carried off.

spiritual *adj* **1** of or like a spirit or soul. **2** religious; sacred. **3** ideal; unworldly; not materialistic. *n* American Negro religious song originating in the time of slavery. **spiritually** *adv*.

spit[1] *n* saliva. *v* (-tt-; spat *or* spit) *vt,vi* eject (something) from the mouth. *vi* drizzle lightly and irregularly.

spit[2] *n* spike for roasting meat.

spite *n* malevolence; vindictiveness; desire to injure. **in spite of** notwithstanding; in defiance of. ~*vt* injure or grieve maliciously. **spiteful** *adj*. **spitefully** *adv*.

splash *vt,vi* **1** scatter or cause (a liquid) to scatter; spatter. **2** fall or cause to fall on in drops or waves. *n* **1** act or sound of splashing. **2** liquid splashed. **3** mark so made. **make a splash** cause a sensation.

splendid *adj* **1** magnificent; brilliant. **2** *inf* excellent; very good. **splendidly** *adv*. **splendour** *n* glory; brilliance; magnificence.

splint *n* rigid piece of wood tied to a limb to keep a broken bone in place. *vt* support with splints.

splinter *n* sliver of wood, glass, metal, etc. *vt,vi* break up into splinters. **splinter group** *n* members who break away from a main group.

split *vt,vi* (-tt-; split) **1** break or divide into separate pieces, groups, etc. **2** break off from a whole. **3** tear; rend. **4** separate because of disharmony, disagreement, etc. **5** share or divide among persons. **6** *sl* go away; leave. *n* **1** act or process of splitting. **2** result of splitting; division; gap.

splutter *vi* **1** gasp and spit jerkily. **2** speak incoherently as in rage. **3** eject drops of liquid. *n* act or noise of spluttering.

spoil *v* (spoilt *or* spoiled) *vt* **1** damage, destroy, or impair the beauty, usefulness, or value of. **2** cause (a child, etc.) to become selfish by excessive indulgence. *vi* deteriorate. **spoils** *pl n* plunder; booty. **spoil-sport** *n* person who spoils the enjoyment of others.

spoke[1] *v pt of* **speak.**

spoke[2] *n* **1** bar radiating from the hub towards the rim of a wheel. **2** rung of a ladder.

spoken *v pp* of **speak.**

spokesman *n, pl* **-men** person authorized to speak on behalf of others.

sponge *n* **1** pad of any porous elastic substance. **2** marine animal with fibrous skeleton. **3** act of applying or removing liquid with a sponge. **4** light baked or steamed pudding. *vt,vi* **1** apply a sponge to absorb; wipe off. **2** *inf* live or obtain by presuming on the generosity of others. **spongy** *adj*.

sponsor *vt* **1** vouch for good character of; act as surety. **2** act as godparent. **3** finance; fund. *n* person who sponsors. **sponsorship** *n*.

spontaneous *adj* **1** impulsive; uninhibited; unconstrained. **2** produced of itself without external cause. **spontaneity** *n*. **spontaneously** *adv*.

spool *n* small cylinder, bobbin, or reel for winding yarn, photographic film, etc., on.

spoon *n* utensil consisting of a small bowl on a handle. *vt,vi* transfer with or as if with a spoon.

sporadic *adj* occasional; occurring irregularly. **sporadically** *adv*.

sport *n* **1** activity or game indulged in for pleasure. **2** amusement; fun; joke. **3** *inf* good-humoured person. *vt* wear conspicuously.

sporty *adv.* **sportive** *adj* merry; playful. **sports car** *n* low-bodied usually two-seater car with high acceleration. **sportsman** *n* **1** person fond of sport. **2** one who bears defeat, inconvenience, etc., cheerfully. **sportsmanship** *n.*

spot *n* **1** small mark or patch. **2** small area or quantity. **3** skin blemish. **in a spot** in difficulties. **soft spot** liking; fondness. ~*vt* (-tt-) **1** mark with spots. **2** notice; observe; discover. **spotless** *adj* **1** without blemish. **2** very clean. **spotlight** *n* strong beam of light focused on one spot. **spotty** *adj* having spots, esp. on the face.

spouse *n* wife or husband of someone.

spout *n* **1** narrow projecting tube through which contents of a vessel are poured. **2** jet of liquid. *vt,vi* pour out conspicuously.

sprain *vt* twist or wrench muscles or ligaments (of a foot, hand, etc.) without dislocation of a joint. *n* **1** act of spraining muscles. **2** swelling and pain caused by this.

sprang *v pt* of **spring.**

sprawl *vi* **1** lie or sit with stretched-out limbs. **2** be spread untidily over a wide area. *n* **1** act or position of sprawling. **2** untidy spread, esp. of buildings.

spray[1] *n* **1** fine drops of liquid blown through the air. **2** apparatus for doing this. *vt,vi* squirt, disperse, or become spray.

spray[2] small shoot or branch of a plant; sprig.

spread *vt,vi* (spread) **1** extend or cause to extend or cover widely; stretch or be stretched. **2** circulate. *n* **1** extent. **2** act or degree of spreading or the area covered. **3** feast. **4** substance for spreading on bread, etc.

spree *n* lively outing; session of reckless activity or amusement.

sprig *n* small shoot; twig.

sprightly *adj* vivacious; brisk; lively. **sprightliness** *n.*

spring *v* (sprang; sprung) *vi* **1** leap; jump. **2** bounce; rebound; recoil. **3** move suddenly or violently. **4** have as a cause; originate; start. **5** produce shoots, leaves, etc.; sprout. *vt* **1** leap over; jump. **2** produce suddenly. *n* **1** leap; jump; bounce. **2** season following winter and preceding summer. **3** coil of wire, metal, etc., that cushions impact, causes movement of parts in a mechanism, etc. **4** natural flow of water forced by pressure from underground. **spring-clean** *n* thorough house-cleaning associated with springtime. *vt* clean in this way. **springy** *adj* **1** elastic; resilient; well-sprung. **2** able to leap or recoil.

springbok *n* African antelope.

sprinkle *vt,vi* scatter in small drops. *n* small quantity dispersed in drops; light shower.

sprint *vi* race or run very fast for a short distance. *n* short race at full speed.

sprout *vt* develop (shoots or buds). *vi* begin to grow; send forth. *n* **1** young bud or shoot. **2** short for Brussels sprout.

sprung *v pp* of **spring.**

spun *v pt* and *pp* of **spin.**

spur *n* **1** spiked or pointed device on the heel of a rider's boot for urging a horse on. **2** incitement; stimulus. **3** projecting small branch or hill range. **on the spur of the moment** on impulse. ~*vt,vi* (-rr-) goad; hasten.

spurt *vt,vi* **1** make a sudden intense effort. **2** send out a sudden jet or stream; spout. *n* **1** brief spell of intense activity. **2** sudden jet of liquid.

spy *n* secret agent watching others and collecting information. *vi* **1** watch. **2** ascertain; detect.

squabble *vi* dispute in a noisy way. *n* petty quarrel; wrangle. **squabbler** *n.*

squad *n* **1** small group of soldiers. **2** group or working party acting together.

squadron *n* **1** group of military aircraft. **2** group of warships forming part of a fleet.

squalid *adj* sordid; dirty; uncared for. **squalidly** *adv.* **squalor** *n* state of being squalid; repulsive dirtiness.

squander *vt* spend carelessly and wastefully.

square *n* **1** right-angled figure having four equal sides. **2** total obtained by multiplying a number by itself. **3** area of land, courtyard, etc., usually bounded on four sides by buildings. *adj* **1** of the shape of a square. **2** broad and straight. **3** relating to a measurement of area. **4** equal or fair. *adv* so as to be square. *vt* **1** form into a square. **2** multiply (a number) by itself. **3** make equal or fair. **square with** be equal or in agreement with; match up to. **squarely** *adv.* **squareness** *n.*

squash *vt,vi* crush or become crushed into or as if into a pulp. *n* **1** drink made from diluted fruit juice. **2** ball game played with racquets. **3** crushed mass or tight-packed crowd.

squat *vi* (-tt-) **1** sit down with knees bent up and heels against buttocks; crouch. **2** occupy a building or land without the consent of the legal owner. *adj* short and thick. **squatter** *n*.

squawk *vi* utter a loud raucous cry. *n* loud harsh cry.

squeak *vi* emit shrill note or cry. *n* shrill weak cry or grating noise. **squeaky** *adj*. **squeakiness** *n*.

squeal *vi* utter a long shrill cry of pain, terror, or excitement. *n* long shrill cry.

squeamish *adj* easily distressed, shocked, or disgusted; too sensitive.

squeeze *vt,vi* **1** subject or be subjected to pressure; press or be pressed out. **2** pack tightly; cram. **3** extort by threats. *n* **1** act of squeezing; state of being tightly pressed or packed. **2** government restrictions placed on commercial or financial activities.

squid *n* edible marine mollusc having a slender body and triangular tail fins.

squiggle *n,vi* twist; wriggle.

squint *vi* **1** be unable to focus both eyes in the same direction. **2** look obliquely; glance. *n* **1** defect in the alignment of the eyes. **2** sidelong or stealthy glance.

squire *n* country landowner, esp. of an old established family. *vt* attend or escort (a lady).

squirm *vi* **1** twist and turn; wriggle. **2** feel embarrassed or humiliated. *n* wriggling movement.

squirrel *n* **1** small nimble bushy-tailed rodent. **2** *inf* person who hoards.

squirt *vt,vi* eject or be ejected in a stream. *n* jet; stream.

stab *v* (-bb-) *vt* **1** wound or pierce with a pointed weapon. **2** give a sharp throbbing pain. *vt,vi* jab or strike (at). *n* act of stabbing; blow or wound.

stable[1] *adj* **1** firmly established or steady; unchanging. **2** not easily upset or overturned; constant. **stably** *adv*. **stability** *n* quality or state of being stable; steadiness. **stabilize** *vt,vi* make or become stable or permanent. **stabilizer** *n*.

stable[2] *n* **1** building where horses, etc., are kept. **2** group of horses, etc., kept by a particular owner or trainer. *vt,vi* provide with or keep in a stable.

stack *n* orderly pile or heap. *vt* **1** place in a stack; heap. **2** load; fill. **stack the cards** dishonestly or unfairly arrange (something) against the interests of others.

stadium *n, pl* **stadiums** *or* **stadia** ('steidiə) sports arena.

staff *n, pl* **staffs** *or* (for 3–6) **staves** **1** people employed by a company, individual, authority, etc. **2** officers appointed to assist a commanding officer. **3** rod; stick. **4** flag pole. **5** something capable of sustaining or supporting. **6** series of horizontal lines used in musical notation. *vt* provide with a staff.

stag *n* adult male deer. **stag party** *n* social gathering of men only.

stage *n* **1** elevated or allocated arena on which a performance takes place. **2** theatrical profession. **3** stopping place on a journey. **4** level or period of development. *vt* **1** put (a play, etc.) on the stage before an audience. **2** do for effect; contrive dramatically. **3** arrange and carry out. **stage manager** *n* person who organizes rehearsals, scenery, staging, etc., of a play.

stagger *vi,vt* move or walk unsteadily; totter. *vt* **1** startle; shock. **2** arrange at intervals. *n* unsteady movement; tottering gait. **staggeringly** *adv*.

stagnant *adj* **1** still; not flowing. **2** foul; putrid from standing still. **3** inert; languid. **stagnantly** *adv*. **stagnate** *vi* **1** cease to flow; putrefy. **2** fail to develop; become sluggish. **stagnation** *n*.

stain *n* **1** discoloration; spot; blemish. **2** dye or tint. *vi,vt* soil or discolour. *vt* **1** taint. **2** colour or dye. **stainless** *adj*. **stained glass** *n* glass coloured by metallic pigments fused into its surface.

stair *n* one in a series of steps. **stairs** *pl n* series of steps from one level to another. **staircase** *n* flight of stairs usually having a banister and containing structure.

stake[1] *n* **1** pointed stick or post for fixing into the ground. **2** post to which persons were tied and burnt to death. *vi* **1** tie or join with or to a stake. **2** mark a boundary with stakes. *vt* **1** register (a claim) to a plot of land, rights, etc. **2** support by tying to a stake.

stake[2] *n* **1** money risked in gambling. **2** amount that may be won. **at stake** in danger of being lost; at risk, at issue. ~*vt* bet; wager; risk.

stale *adj* **1** (of food, etc.) not fresh; altered by age. **2** out of condition or practice. **staleness** *n*.

stalemate *n* **1** one type of draw in a game of

chess. **2** deadlock. *vt* cause to suffer a stalemate.

stalk[1] *n* **1** stem of a plant. **2** slender support; shaft.

stalk[2] *vt,vi* **1** walk stealthily (after); go after (prey). **2** walk stiffly or haughtily.

stall *n* **1** place for a single animal in a stable. **2** bench, table, booth, or barrow for displaying goods for sale. **3** theatre seat on the ground floor. **4** church seat, esp. for the choir. **5** covering for a finger or toe. *vt,vi* **1** stop (a car, motor, etc.) or make stop because of incorrect adjustment or handling. **2** put off; evade; delay.

stallion *n* male horse, esp. one kept for breeding.

stamina *n* power of endurance; strength.

stammer *n* speech defect in which particular sounds are uttered falteringly and sometimes repeated involuntarily. *vi,vt* speak or say with a stammer; utter brokenly.

stamp *vt,vi* crush or tread (on) heavily with the feet. *vt* **1** make a mark, symbol, or design on. **2** affix a postage stamp to. **3** make a deep impression; scar. **stamp out** suppress or abolish completely. ~*n* **1** heavy tread or pressure with the feet. **2** *also* **postage stamp** small piece of paper printed with a design, for affixing to mail as proof of postage paid. **3** seal, symbol, or mark. **4** device for producing a particular symbol or mark. **5** characteristic quality.

stampede *n* **1** sudden rush of frightened animals. **2** any impulsive action by a mass of people. *vi,vt* flee or cause to flee in panic. *vt* press a person into rash action.

stand *v* (stood) *vi* **1** be erect with the feet supporting the weight of the body. **2** move into such a position; rise; get up. **3** be positioned or located. **4** have a particular point of view. **5** remain; stay; adhere (to). **6** be a candidate; be nominated. *vt* **1** place; position; rest. **2** take the strain of; bear. **3** tolerate; put up with. **4** treat; pay for. **5** be subjected to (a trial). **stand by 1** be ready to act if needed. **2** remain loyal to. **stand down** give up a post, claim, etc. **stand for** represent; tolerate. **stand out** be conspicuous or prominent. **stand up for** defend; protect; fight for. ~*n* **1** platform. **2** article or piece of furniture for supporting something. **3** stall at a market, exhibition, etc. **4** position or point of view to be defended. **stand-by** *n* person or thing that may be relied upon in an emergency. **standing** *n* **1** rank; status; reputation. **2** duration; length of experience, etc. *adj* **1** erect. **2** permanent or continuing. **3** stagnant. **standstill** *n* complete cessation of movement or progress.

standard *n* **1** guideline; example. **2** principle; integrity. **3** flag; banner; emblem. **4** commodity on which a monetary system is based. **5** fruit or rose tree having a straight stem and no lower branches. *adj* serving as or conforming to a standard; average; accepted. **standardize** *vt* cause to conform to a standard; remove variations from. **standardization** *n*.

stank *v pt* of **stink.**

stanza *n* group of lines of verse forming a division of a poem.

staple[1] *n* bent length of wire for fastening. *vt* fasten with a staple or staples. **stapler** *n*.

staple[2] *n* **1** basic essential food. **2** grade of fibre in wool, flax, etc. *adj* basic; indispensable; standard.

star *n* **1** incandescent body in outer space seen in the night sky as a twinkling light. **2** figure with five or six pointed rays. **3** highly popular public entertainer. **4** asterisk. **5** planet influencing one's luck according to astrology; fate. *vt* (-rr-) **1** mark or cover with stars. **2** play the leading part or present as the leading performer. **3** mark with an asterisk. **starfish** *n* star-shaped invertebrate fish. **starry** *adj*.

starboard *n,adj* right-hand side of a vessel when one is facing forward.

starch *n* **1** carbohydrate present in many plants and vegetables. **2** this substance used as a stiffener after laundering fabrics. *vt* stiffen with starch. **starchy** *adj*. **starchily** *adv*. **starchiness** *n*.

stare *vi* look with fixed eyes. *n* act of staring.

stark *adj* **1** bleak; harsh; grim. **2** unelaborated; blunt. *adv* completely. **starkly** *adv*. **starkness** *n*.

starling *n* small gregarious bird with blackish feathers.

start *vt* **1** begin; set up. **2** set in motion. *vi* jump involuntarily as because of fright. *n* **1** beginning. **2** jerk; jump. **starter** *n*.

startle *vt* give a shock to; alarm; take aback. *vi* feel slight shock or alarm; be taken aback. **startlingly** *adv*.

starve *vi,vt* **1** die or make die from lack of food. **2** suffer or make suffer from hunger. *vi* be very hungry. **starvation** *n*.

state *n* **1** condition; situation; circumstances. **2** form; structure. **3** political community under a government. **4** status; rank. **5** splendour; dignified style. **6** *inf* distressed or anxious condition. *vt* declare; specify; utter. **stately** *adj* imposing; magnificent; dignified. **stateliness** *n*. **statement** *n* **1** act of stating. **2** something stated. **3** formal account. **4** financial account in detail.

statesman *n* wise revered politician. **statesmanlike** *adj*. **statesmanship** *n* skill and abilities involved in being a statesman.

static *adj* **1** at rest; unmoving. **2** not causing movement. **3** relating to interference in reception of radio signals. *n* disturbance in radio or television reception caused by electrical disturbances.

station *n* **1** fixed stopping place for a bus, train, etc. **2** position; status. **3** office or headquarters of the police, etc. *vt* assign a place or post to. **station-master** *n* official in charge of a railway station.

stationary *adj* fixed; still; permanently located.

stationer *n* person who sells writing materials, etc. **stationery** *n* writing materials, esp. notepaper and envelopes.

statistics *pl n* numerical data used to make analyses. *s n* study of the analysis of numerical data. **statistical** *adj* relating to numerical data. **statistically** *adv*. **statistician** *n* expert in statistics.

statue *n* sculpture or representation of a person, group, or an animal.

stature *n* **1** height of a person or animal standing upright. **2** moral or intellectual greatness.

status *n* **1** official or social position. **2** prestige; high rank. **status quo** the existing situation. **status symbol** object desired or owned for prestige purposes.

statute *n* **1** act, law, or decree made by Parliament or some other legislative body. **2** rule laid down by an institution or authority. **statutory** *adj* prescribed; authorized by statute.

stave *n* **1** strip of wood, esp. on the side of a barrel. **2** series of five lines on which music is written. **staves** *pl* of **staff** (defs 3–6).

stay[1] *vi* remain or be (for a time). *vt* check; delay. **stay the course** be able to finish in spite of difficulties. ~*n* **1** period of time spent; visit. **2** postponement.

stay[2] *n* support; prop; rope or cable supporting a ship's mast, etc. **stays** *pl n* corsets.

steadfast *adj* **1** unwavering. **2** resolute; loyal. **steadfastly** *adv*. **steadfastness** *n*.

steady *adj* **1** firmly balanced or supported. **2** regular; controlled; fixed. **3** constant. **4** reliable; sober. *vt,vi* make or become steady. **steadily** *adv*. **steadiness** *n*.

steak *n* thick slice of meat or fish.

steal *v* (stole; stolen) *vt* **1** unlawfully take away (another person's property). **2** obtain secretly; snatch. *vi* **1** thieve. **2** move quietly and unobtrusively; creep. **stealth** *n* furtive behaviour; secrecy; evasion. **stealthy** *adj*. **stealthily** *adv*.

steam *n* **1** vapour produced by boiling water. **2** mist left by water vapour. **get up steam** become excited or emotional. **let off steam** release pent-up emotion or energy harmlessly. ~*vi* **1** emit steam. **2** move by steam power. *vt* cook, iron, etc., using steam. **steamy** *adj*.

steel *n* **1** widely used strong hard alloy of iron and carbon. **2** quality of toughness. **3** steel weapon, esp. a sword. *vt* toughen; strengthen. **steel oneself** prepare oneself (to do something difficult or unpleasant). **steely** *adj* **1** of or like steel. **2** unwavering.

steep[1] *adj* **1** rising or sloping sharply; precipitous. **2** exorbitant; outrageous. **steeply** *adv*. **steepness** *n*. **steepen** *vi* become steep(er).

steep[2] *vt* soak thoroughly; immerse.

steeple *n* spire. **steeplechase** *n* horse race in which ditches, fences, etc., must be jumped.

steer *vt* guide; direct the course of (a vehicle, etc.). *vi* manoeuvre; guide. **steer clear of** keep away from.

stem[1] *n* **1** stalk of a plant. **2** anything resembling a stalk, such as the shaft of a pipe or wine glass. **3** unchanging part of a word to which inflexions are added. *v* (-mm-) **stem from** arise out of.

stem[2] (-mm-) *vt* stop the flow of; plug.

stencil *n* sheet of card, paper, or metal in which patterns or lettering have been cut in order to transfer the design to a further sheet or sheets. *vt* (-ll-) use or apply with a stencil.

Sten gun *n* lightweight machine gun.

step *n* **1** movement made by lifting the foot;

pace. **2** manner of walking, dancing, etc. **3** single section of a flight of stairs. **4** single grade or stage on a scale. **5** short distance. **step by step** gradually. **take steps (to)** begin to control; initiate action (on). ~*vi* (-pp-) move by steps; walk. **step on 1** trample on; walk on or rest the foot on. **2** *inf* accelerate; go fast. **step up** increase; intensify activity. **step-ladder** *n* folding ladder with wide flat rungs.

stepbrother *n* son of one's stepmother or stepfather by another marriage.

stepdaughter *n* daughter of one's spouse by another marriage.

stepfather *n* man married by one's mother after the death or divorce of one's father.

stepmother *n* woman married by one's father after the death or divorce of one's mother.

stepsister *n* daughter of one's stepmother or stepfather by another marriage.

stepson *n* son of one's spouse by another marriage.

stereo *adj* short for **stereophonic.** *n* apparatus for reproducing stereophonic sound. **stereophonic** *adj* (of music, etc.) recorded through separate microphones and relayed through separate loudspeakers to give an impression of natural distribution of sound.

stereotype *n* **1** conventionalized idea, conception, or person that lacks variation or individuality. **2** solid metal printing plate cast from a mould made from movable type.

sterile *adj* **1** free from live bacteria. **2** unable to produce offspring, seeds, or crops; barren; unproductive. **sterility** *n*. **sterilize** *vt* **1** destroy bacteria in. **2** render incapable of producing offspring, seeds, or crops. **sterilization** *n*.

sterling *adj* **1** relating to British money. **2** (of silver) conforming to a special standard. **3** valuable; reliable; excellent. *n* British money.

stern[1] *adj* strict; severe; grim. **sternly** *adv*. **sternness** *n*.

stern[2] *n* **1** back section of a ship or aircraft. **2** rear; rump.

stethoscope *n* medical instrument for listening to the sounds of the body.

stew *vt* cook by long slow boiling or simmering. *n* dish, usually of meat, cooked by stewing.

steward *n* **1** person organizing the catering, seating, and sleeping arrangements, esp. on a ship; passenger attendant. **2** estate or household manager; organizer or helper at a public function, etc. **stewardess** *n* female attendant on a ship or airliner.

stick[1] *v* (stuck) *vt* **1** join or attach by using glue, paste, nails, pins, etc. **2** pierce; prod; thrust. **3** put or place carelessly or absent-mindedly. *vi* **1** become fixed, attached, or jammed; wedge. **2** remain close to. **stick out 1** protrude; jut. **2** be conspicuous. **stick to** concentrate on for a length of time; adhere to. **stick up for** defend or support (a person, one's rights, etc.). **sticky** *adj* **1** tending to stick. **2** covered with glue, paste, etc. **3** *inf* awkward; tricky.

stick[2] *n* **1** wooden rod; thin detached branch; staff or cane. **2** rod used in certain sports. **3** anything resembling a stick in shape.

stiff *adj* **1** difficult to move, bend, or twist; rigid; not flexible. **2** (of persons) not moving easily; formal; not at ease socially. **3** strong. **4** (of prices) high. **stiff upper lip** stoicism. ~*n sl* corpse. **stiffly** *adv*. **stiffness** *n*. **stiffen** *vt,vi* make or become stiff. **stiffening** *n* substance used to stiffen something.

stifle *vt* **1** suffocate; choke. **2** suppress; put down. *vi* **1** die from suffocation; choke. **2** have a suffocating impression.

stigma *n* **1** mark or sign of disgrace; social blot. **2** that part of a flower that receives pollen. **stigmata** *pl n* marks of Christ's crucifixion. **stigmatize** *vt* denounce; brand.

stile *n* permanent set of steps or railings for climbing over a hedge, fence, etc.

still[1] *adv* **1** even now; yet. **2** even more. *conj* in spite of that. *adj* **1** quiet; hushed; calm; not agitated. **2** not fizzy. *vt* calm; subdue. *n* single photograph taken from a film. **stillborn** *adj* **1** born dead. **2** (of ideas, etc.) conceived but not put into practice. **still life** *n* painting or photograph of inanimate things.

still[2] *n* apparatus for distilling liquids by vaporizing and condensing.

stilt *n* **1** one of a pair of poles with platforms for the feet for walking above the ground. **2** supporting pole or pillar for a house, pier, etc.

stilted *adj* stiff; artificial; pompous.

stimulate *vt* **1** persuade; encourage; arouse. **2** inspire; excite mental activity in. **3** increase. **stimulation** *n*. **stimulant** *n* **1** anything, esp. a drink or drug, that produces extra mental or physical activity. **2** stimulus; spur. **stimulus** *n, pl* **stimuli** ('stimjulai) something that encourages, persuades, spurs on, or excites a response.

sting *vt,vi* (stung) **1** hurt by piercing the skin and secreting poison. **2** feel or cause to feel a piercing pain. **3** hurt (a person's feelings). **4** *sl* extort money (from), esp. by overcharging. *n* **1** act of or pain from stinging. **2** part of an insect, fish, or plant that causes a sting.

stink *vi* (stank *or* stunk; stunk) **1** smell disgusting or offensive. **2** *inf* (of a situation) be offensive or unpleasant. *n* disgusting smell. **stinker** *n* offensive person or thing.

stint *n* fixed amount; quota (of work). *vt* give small amounts to reluctantly; be ungenerous towards.

stipulate *vt,vi* insist (on) as a condition of agreement; require. **stipulation** *n*.

stir *v* (-rr-) *vt* **1** move or agitate (a mixture) with a spoon, etc. **2** move (slightly). **3** rouse; incite. *vi* move; become active. *n* **1** stirring movement. **2** disturbance; sensation.

stirrup *n* hooped metal footrest hanging either side of a horse's saddle.

stitch *n* **1** one unit in a row of sewing or knitting. **2** particular kind of stitch. **3** loop of thread used in surgery to close a wound, etc. **4** *inf* piercing pain in one's side. *vt,vi* sew using stitches.

stoat *n* small fur-covered mammal similar to but larger than a weasel.

stock *n* **1** store or supply of goods. **2** persons, animals, etc., having a common ancestor. **3** livestock. **4** unspecified number of shares. **5** liquid derived by cooking meat, bones, etc., in water. **6** flower having purple or white scented flowers. *vt* keep in supply; store. **stockbreeding** *n* breeding and rearing of livestock. **stockbroker** *n* person whc deals professionally in stocks and shares. **stock exchange** *n* place or association for the buying and selling of stocks and shares. **stockpile** *n* store set aside for future use. *vt,vi* build a stockpile (of). **stocktaking** *n* making of an inventory of goods or assets in a shop or business.

stocking *n* tight-fitting nylon, woollen, or cotton covering for the leg and foot.

stodge *n inf* heavy not easily digestible food. **stodgy** *adj* thick and heavy; unpalatable; turgid.

stoical *adj* bearing suffering without showing pain or emotion; being resigned to one's lot. **stoically** *adv*. **stoicism** *n*.

stoke *vt,vi* tend and pile fuel into (a fire or furnace).

stole[1] *v pt* of **steal.**

stole[2] *n* woven or knitted shawl, scarf, or fur collar worn round the shoulders.

stolen *v pp* of **steal.**

stomach *n* **1** principal digestive organ lying between the gullet and the intestines. **2** appetite. *vt* **1** digest. **2** bear; tolerate.

stone *n* **1** hard compact rock material, used in building, etc. **2** lump of rock. **3** jewel. **4** hard-shelled part of certain fruit. **5** anything resembling a stone or made of stone. **6** unit of weight equal to 14 pounds (6.3 kilograms). *adj* made of stone. *vt* **1** throw stones at. **2** remove stones from. **stony** *adj* **1** made of, covered with, or like stone(s). **2** hostile; cold. **stony broke** completely penniless.

stood *v pt* and *pp* of **stand.**

stool *n* **1** backless seat for one person; footstool. **2** solid excreta.

stoop *vt,vi* bend (one's head and body) forward and down. *vi* lower oneself morally; demean oneself. *n* **1** act of stooping. **2** habitually bent posture.

stop *v* (-pp-) *vt,vi* cease; bring or come to an end; halt. *vt* **1** discontinue; cut off; prevent. **2** prevent the passage of air, liquid, etc., through; block; plug. **stop off** call (at); visit. ~*n* **1** halt; end; finish. **2** place at which a bus, train, etc., stops to let passengers enter or leave. **3** full stop. **stopgap** *n* temporary measure or substitute in an emergency, etc. **stoppage** *n* **1** act of stopping; state of being stopped. **2** obstruction. **3** cessation of work. **stopper** *n* **1** person or thing that stops. **2** plug for a bottle or vessel. *vt* close with a stopper. **stopwatch** *n* watch that can be stopped and restarted for timing races, etc.

store *n* **1** stock set aside for future use; reserve supply; accumulation. **2** shop with several departments. **3** place where stock is kept. **in store 1** expected to happen. **2** set aside. **set store by** value greatly. ~*vt* make a store of. **store up** reserve for a future occasion; stock up. **storage** *n* keeping of stocks of goods for future use.

storey *n* floor or level of a building.

stork *n* large long-legged long-billed wading bird.

storm *n* **1** weather condition including a strong wind and often rain and thunder. **2** sudden outburst of noise, feelings, etc. **storm in a teacup** a lot of fuss over something unimportant. **take by storm 1** capture (a fortress) by a sudden massed attack. **2** bowl over; captivate. ~*vt* attack and capture suddenly. *vi* rage. **stormy** *adj* violent; tempestuous; relating to or portending a storm.

story *n* **1** tale; short narrative. **2** plot of a novel, etc. **3** *inf* lie; fib.

stout *adj* **1** fat; portly. **2** strong; sturdy. **3** brave. *n* strong dark ale. **stoutly** *adv*. **stoutness** *n*.

stove *n* device for cooking or heating, using gas, electricity, paraffin, etc.

stow *vt* put away; store. **stowaway** *n* person who hides on a ship or aircraft in order to avoid paying the fare.

straddle *vt,vi* stand or sit with one leg on either side (of); stand or sit astride.

straggle *vi* **1** sprawl; be scattered. **2** fall behind the main group; continue in small irregular groups.

straight *adj* **1** not crooked or curved. **2** direct. **3** rigid or erect. **4** honest; correct. *adv* **1** directly; in a straight line. **2** honestly. **straight away** immediately. **straighten** *vt,vi* make or become straight. **straighten out 1** make straight. **2** sort out or deal with (a problem). **straightforward** *adj* **1** uncomplicated; not difficult. **2** honest; open.

strain[1] *vt,vi* harm by stretching, exerting force, etc.; stress. *vt* **1** filter (a liquid). **2** make tense; demand excessive effort of. *n* tension; stress; act or instance of straining; demand.

strain[2] *n* **1** breed. **2** hereditary trait or tendency.

strand[1] *n* single thread from a wire, rope, etc.

strand[2] *vt,vi* run aground; beach. **stranded** *adj* abandoned; cut off; left helpless. ~*n* beach; shore.

strange *adj* **1** odd; peculiar. **2** unfamiliar; unusual; extraordinary. **3** foreign. **strangely** *adv* **strangeness** *n*. **stranger** *n* person foreign to or not familiar with a particular place, area, or society.

strangle *vt* kill by throttling. **strangler** *n*. **stranglehold** *n* **1** choking grip. **2** force that suppresses freedom of movement or growth.

strap *n* thin strip, esp. of leather and with a buckle, for holding objects together. *vt* (-pp-) **1** bind with a strap. **2** beat with a strap.

strategy *n* overall plan of attack or campaign, esp. military; set of tactics. **strategic** *adj* relating to or important to an overall strategy.

stratum *n, pl* **strata** ('strɑːtə) *or* **stratums 1** layer of rock. **2** level of society.

straw *n* **1** single dried stem of grain. **2** such stems used as a material for baskets, mats, etc., for packing, or as bedding for cattle, etc. **3** narrow tube of paper or plastic used for drinking. **the last straw** a final blow that makes a situation no longer tolerable.

strawberry *n* creeping plant bearing soft reddish edible fruit.

stray *vi* wander; digress; err; go astray. *n* homeless animal or child. *adj* strayed; lost; scattered.

streak *n* **1** narrow irregular stripe (of colour, etc.). **2** flash (of lightning). **3** slight surprising tendency or trace. *vt* mark with streaks. *vi* **1** dash. **2** *inf* run naked in public in order to amuse or shock. **streaky** *adj*. **streakiness** *n*.

stream *n* **1** flow (of water, blood, etc.); current. **2** brook. **3** educational division according to ability. *vi* **1** flow in a steady stream; pour out. **2** (of hair, a flag, etc.) wave in the air. *vt* divide (children) into educational groups according to ability. **streamline** *vt* **1** design (cars, aircraft, etc.) in a smooth narrow shape to give minimum air resistance. **2** remove inefficient areas from an operation or process.

street *n* road with houses along one or both sides. **streets ahead** wholly superior. **up one's street** in one's line or area of interest.

strength *n* **1** quality of being strong; power; force. **2** support; aid. **3** effectiveness. **4** potency; degree of concentration. **on the strength of** based on, relying on. **strengthen** *vt,vi* make or become strong(er).

strenuous *adj* vigorous; diligent; energetic. **strenuously** *adv*. **strenuousness** *n*.

stress *n* **1** anxiety or distress caused by pressure or tension. **2** importance; weight; emphasis. **3** emphasis put on a word or syllable. **4** deforming force applied to an object. *vt* emphasize; put the stress on.

stretch *vt* pull or push out; extend; pull taut. *vi* **1** extend. **2** be elastic. **3** flex one's muscles. *n* **1** act of stretching. **2** expanse. **3** continuous period of time. **4** *sl* term of imprisonment. **stretcher** *n* framework covered in canvas, etc., and used for transporting the sick or injured.

strict *adj* **1** accurate; precisely defined. **2** stern;

severe; requiring complete obedience. **strictly** *adv.* **strictness** *n.*

stride *n* long step. **take in one's stride** cope with easily and without worrying. ~*vt,vi* (strode; stridden) walk (over) in strides.

strident *adj* harsh; grating.

strike *v* (struck) *vt* **1** hit; touch violently; collide with; beat. **2** light (a match). **3** occur to; remind; seem to. **4** reach suddenly or unexpectedly. *vt,vi* chime. *vi* **1** attack. **2** collide. **3** take part in a strike. **strike out 1** delete; cross out. **2** embark on a new venture. **strike up** begin; set up; establish. ~*n* **1** stoppage of work by employees in support of a claim, etc. **2** discovery of oil, etc.

string *n* **1** twine or cord used for tying, binding, etc. **2** string-like object, such as a tendon or fibre. **3** taut cord of wire, catgut, etc., fitted to a musical instrument and producing a note when caused to vibrate. **4** linked series; chain; line. **strings** *pl n* stringed instruments of an orchestra. **no strings attached** with no restricting factors or conditions. **pull strings** use influence in order to better oneself. ~*vt* (strung) fit strings to; thread. **string along** keep happy with false promises. **string out 1** spread out over a long area. **2** make (something) last a long time.

stringent *adj* strict; harsh; rigorous. **stringency** *n.* **stringently** *adv.*

strip[1] *v* (-pp-) *vt* **1** remove (the covering, outer layer, or clothes) from; lay bare. **2** take (an engine, etc.) apart. *vi* remove one's clothes. **striptease** *n* cabaret act in which the performer seductively removes clothing piece by piece.

strip[2] *n* narrow band; long piece. **strip cartoon** cartoon made up of a sequence of drawings.

stripe *n* **1** band of contrasting colour or texture. **2** band worn to show military rank. **striped** *adj* marked with stripes.

strive *vi* (strove; striven) try hard; endeavour; labour (to do something).

strode *v pt* of **stride.**

stroke[1] *n* **1** hit; blow. **2** single controlled movement in sports such as tennis, golf, etc. **3** style of swimming. **4** individual mark made by a brush or pen. **5** one of a series of movements. **6** apoplexy; damage to the brain's blood supply causing paralysis. **7** oarsman facing the cox. **8** chime of a clock.

stroke[2] *vt* caress with the hand; smooth. *n* act of stroking.

stroll *vi* walk for pleasure; saunter. *n* leisurely walk.

strong *adj* **1** physically powerful; forceful; difficult to break down, overcome, capture, or injure. **2** sound; healthy; vigorous. **3** positive; persuasive; drastic; effective; convincing. **4** concentrated; intense. *adv* **going strong** doing well; flourishing. **strongly** *adv.* **stronghold** *n* **1** fortress; garrison. **2** area where something prevails or has gained control. **strong-minded** having a powerful will; able to resist temptation.

struck *v pt* and *pp* of **strike.**

structure *n* **1** way in which things are put together; internal organization; make-up. **2** something constructed, esp. a building. *vt* give structure or form to; organize. **structural** *adj.* **structurally** *adv.*

struggle *vi* **1** fight hand to hand; wrestle; grapple. **2** labour; make great efforts; endeavour. *n* fight; strenuous effort.

strum *vt,vi* (-mm-) play (a stringed instrument) idly; sound a few chords (on).

strung *v pt* and *pp* of **string.** *adj* **highly strung** very nervous or tense.

strut[1] *vi* (-tt-) walk proudly to show off; swagger. *n* pompous gait.

strut[2] *n* supporting bar of wood, iron, etc., slat; rung.

stub *n* piece left after something has been used or worn down, esp. a cigarette end or counterfoil of a ticket or cheque. *vt* (-bb-) accidentally strike (one's foot or toe) against. **stub out** crush and extinguish (a cigarette).

stubborn *adj* obstinate; difficult to persuade or influence; strong-willed. **stubbornly** *adv.* **stubbornness** *n.*

stuck *v pt* and *pp* of **stick** .

stud[1] *n* **1** ornamental heavy-headed nail or peg; flat knob. **2** button-like device for fastening collars or fronts to shirts. **3** threaded pin or bolt. *vt* (-dd-) **1** put studs into. **2** dot or cover (with jewels, stars, etc.).

stud[2] *n* **1** establishment for breeding pedigree animals, esp. horses. **2** horse or group of horses kept for breeding.

student *n* person who studies, esp. one following a course at a college or institute of further education.

studio *n* **1** artist's or craftsman's workroom. **2**

place where broadcasts, recordings, or films are made. **studio couch** sofa that doubles as a bed.

studious *adj* **1** hard-working; fond of studying. **2** deliberate.

study *vt* **1** examine closely; peer at. **2** give special attention to; learn about; devote oneself to (a particular subject). *vi* follow a course of instruction, devote oneself to learning from books. *n* **1** act or process of studying; learning. **2** book, etc., produced by study. **3** room intended for study, reading, etc. **studied** *adj* deliberate; intentional; carefully considered; elaborately executed.

stuff *n* any type of material or substance. *vt* **1** cram full; overfill. **2** fill with stuffing. *vi* overeat. **stuffing** *n* **1** material with which objects are stuffed. **2** seasoned filling for meat, poultry, vegetables, etc.

stuffy *adj* **1** close; poorly-ventilated; oppressive. **2** *inf* prim and proper; easily shocked. **stuffily** *adv*. **stuffiness** *n*.

stumble *vi* trip and lose one's balance. **stumble on** *or* **across** discover by chance; come across. ~*n* act of stumbling. **stumbling block** obstacle; something that causes hesitation or doubt.

stump *n* **1** portion remaining after the main part of a limb or tree has been removed. **2** one of the three posts of a cricket wicket. *vt inf* puzzle; outwit. *vi* walk slowly and heavily. **stump up** *inf* produce or come up with (money).

stun *vt* (-nn-) **1** knock senseless, make unconscious. **2** amaze or shock. **stunning** *adj inf* extremely attractive.

stung *v pt* and *pp* of **sting.**

stunk *v pt* and *pp* of **stink.**

stunt[1] *vt* impede the growth or development of.

stunt[2] *n* dangerous, sensational, or acrobatic feat; anything done to attract attention or publicity. **stunt man** *n* person employed to perform dangerous feats in films or for entertainment.

stupid *adj* foolish; silly; not clever, dim-witted. **stupidity** *n*. **stupidly** *adv*.

sturdy *adj* strong; stout; solid. **sturdily** *adv*. **sturdiness** *n*.

sturgeon *n* large edible fish whose roe is eaten as caviar.

stutter *n* speech impediment causing hesitation or constant repetition of a word or syllable; stammer. *vt,vi* speak or say with a stutter.

sty[1] *n* pen for pigs.

sty[2] *n* small inflamed swelling on an eyelid.

style *n* **1** characteristic manner or fashion, esp. of practising a particular art, craft, or sport. **2** fashion; mode. **3** elegance; luxury; grandeur. **4** form; kind; sort. **5** title; mode of address. *vt* fashion or shape (hair, clothes, etc.). **stylist** *n*. **stylistic** *adj* relating to artistic style. **stylish** *adj* fashionable; smart.

stylus *n* **1** sapphire or diamond point used as a gramophone needle. **2** pointed writing or engraving instrument.

subconscious *n* area of one's mind, memory, and personality of which one is not aware. *adj* unconscious; stemming from the subconscious. **subconsciously** *adv*.

subcontract *n* (sʌbˈkɔntrækt) agreement assigning part of the work specified in a contract to another party. *vt,vi* (ˈsʌbkəntrækt) make a subcontract (regarding). **subcontractor** *n* person accepting a subcontract.

subcutaneous *adj* situated or introduced beneath the skin.

subdue *vt* suppress; put down; quieten.

subject *n* (ˈsʌbdʒikt) **1** something dealt with; object of study, analysis, discussion, examination, etc.; topic. **2** citizen under the authority of a state or ruler. **3** grammatical term for word(s) about which something is predicated or for the noun or pronoun acting as the doer of the verb in a sentence. **4** central musical theme of a composition. **subject to** *adj* **1** liable or prone to. **2** owing allegiance to. **3** conditional; dependent. *adv* conditionally. ~*vt* (səbˈdʒekt) **1** force to experience or undergo. **2** bring under the control (of). **subjection** *n*. **subjective** *adj* **1** influenced by or arising from personal feelings rather than external evidence. **2** (in grammar) of the subject. **subjectively** *adv*.

sublime *adj* **1** of great moral or spiritual worth; majestic; awe-inspiring; supreme. **2** utter; extreme. *n* anything majestic or inspiring awe. *vt,vi* change directly from a solid to a gas. **sublimely** *adv*.

submachine gun *n* lightweight automatic gun

submarine *n* vessel that can operate underwater. *adj* relating to or intended for use below water level.

submerge *vt* place under water; flood; cover

with liquid. *vi* dip or go under water. **submergence** *or* **submersion** *n*.

submit *vt,vi* (-tt-) **1** surrender; yield. **2** put forward for consideration; suggest. **submit to** give in to; allow oneself to be under the control of. **submission** *n* **1** act of submitting. **2** suggestion. **submissive** *adj* timid and yielding.

subnormal *adj* mentally handicapped; below average intelligence.

subordinate *adj* (sə'bɔːdinit) **1** junior; inferior in rank, position, or importance. **2** (in grammar) subsidiary; dependent on a main clause. *n* (sə'bɔːdinit) person in an inferior position or rank. *vt* (sə'bɔːdineit) **1** reduce to a lower rank or position; assign to a lesser place. **2** subdue. **subordination** *n*.

subscribe *vt,vi* pledge a regular sum of money (to). *vi* **subscribe to 1** agree to buy (a magazine, etc.) regularly. **2** approve of; agree with. **subscriber** *n*. **subscription** *n* **1** act of subscribing. **2** amount subscribed. **3** regular monetary contribution.

subsequent *adj* later; following or coming afterwards. **subsequently** *adv*.

subservient *adj* **1** showing exaggerated feelings of humility; obsequious. **2** serving an end; useful as a means. **subservience** *n*.

subside *vi* **1** sink in, collapse. **2** die down; decrease. **subsidence** *n*.

subsidiary *adj* supporting, supplementary; secondary. *n* thing that is subsidiary, esp. a company that is part of a group.

subsidy *n* state grant for an industry, cultural organization, etc.; official financial assistance. **subsidize** *vt* support with a subsidy; assist financially.

substance *n* **1** stuff; matter; material. **2** chief part; importance; essence; gist. **3** worth; value; foundation. **substantial** *adj* **1** ample; large; considerable. **2** solid; well-established; wealthy. **substantially** *adv*. **substantiate** *vt* provide proof of (a claim, charge, etc.); establish; show to be true.

substitute *vt* put (one person or thing) in place of another. *vi* serve as. *n* person or thing substituted. **substitution** *n*.

subtitle *n* **1** title, often explanatory, subsidiary to the main one. **2** caption translating dialogue in a foreign film. *vt* provide a subtitle for.

subtle *adj* **1** delicate; slight; not gross; hard to detect or perceive. **2** ingenious; perceptive; complex. **subtlety** *n*. **subtly** *adv*.

subtract *vt* take (an amount) away from; deduct. **subtraction** *n*.

suburb *n* residential area on the outskirts of a town or city. **suburban** *adj* **1** conventional; narrow-minded. **2** relating to a suburb.

subway *n* **1** underground passage enabling pedestrians to cross a busy road. **2** *US* underground railway.

succeed *vi* achieve one's purpose; be able; manage. *vt* come after; follow and take the place or position of.

success *n* **1** achievement of one's purpose. **2** achievement of fame and wealth. **3** triumph; anything that succeeds. **successful** *adj*. **successfully** *adv*.

succession *n* **1** series of things coming one after another. **2** act or process of succeeding to a title or position. **successive** *adj* happening one after another or in sequence. **successively** *adv*. **successor** *n* person taking over the position or rank of another.

succulent *adj* **1** juicy. **2** fleshy-leaved, as a cactus. **succulence** *n*. **succulently** *adv*.

succumb *vi* **1** yield or give in, esp. to powerful persuasion. **2** die.

such *adj* **1** of a particular kind. **2** so much or so many. *pron* **1** those who or that which. **2** the same. **as such 1** by or in itself. **2** in that role or capacity. **such as** for example; like. ~*adv* this or that amount of. **suchlike** *pron* things of a similar sort. *adj* similar; of that sort.

suck *vt,vi* draw (liquid) into the mouth by action of the lips and tongue. *vi* **1** draw milk (from a mother's breast, an udder, etc.). **2** absorb; draw up (liquid). **3** hold in the mouth and lick. **4** make sucking actions. *n* act of sucking. **sucker** *n* **1** person that sucks. **2** *sl* person easily deceived. **3** device or organ, usually disc-shaped, that sticks to surfaces by suction. **4** shoot growing from the root of a plant.

suckle *vt,vi* give or suck milk from the breast.

suction *n* **1** action or process of sucking. **2** force causing a flow of liquid or gas or the adhesion of two surfaces.

sudden *adj* unexpected; happening quickly or without warning. *n* **all of a sudden** unexpectedly. **suddenly** *adv*. **suddenness** *n*.

suds *pl n* froth on the surface of soapy water; lather.

sue *vt,vi* take legal action (against). **sue for** beg; petition (for).

suede *n* soft leather with a velvety surface.

suet *n* hard fat found round the kidneys of sheep and cattle.

suffer *vt,vi* **1** endure; undergo mental or physical pain. **2** bear; tolerate. **suffer from** be ill, usually periodically, with. **suffering** *n* mental or physical pain; anguish.

sufficient *adj* enough; adequate for the purpose. **sufficiency** *n*. **sufficiently** *adv*.

suffix *n* letter(s) or syllable(s) put at the end of a word to change its part of speech, meaning, or grammatical inflexion.

suffocate *vt* kill by preventing or restricting breathing; smother. *vi* suffer restriction of one's breathing; die through lack of air; stifle. **suffocation** *n*.

sugar *n* sweet crystalline white or brown carbohydrate obtained from plants such as sugar cane or sugar beet. *vt* sweeten or coat with sugar. **sugary** *adj*. **sugar beet** *n* plant from the roots of which sugar is obtained. **sugar cane** *n* tall tropical grass from the canes of which sugar is obtained.

suggest *vt,vi* **1** propose; submit for consideration. **2** imply; intimate. **3** evoke, bring to mind; make (a person) think of. **suggestible** *adj* easily persuaded by suggestion. **suggestion** *n* **1** proposal; act of suggesting. **2** hint; trace. **3** implication. **4** production of an idea through association. **suggestive** *adj* **1** provoking thoughts (of). **2** having sexual overtones or implications.

suicide *n* **1** act of intentionally killing oneself **2** person who has committed suicide. **3** action likely to ruin oneself or one's interests. **suicidal** *adj*.

suit *vt* **1** be convenient for; be acceptable to; satisfy. **2** (of clothes, colours, etc.) look attractive on or with. **3** be or make appropriate. **4** equip, adapt. *n* **1** matching jacket and trousers or skirt. **2** matching set or series, esp. of playing cards. **3** court case involving a claim. **4** wooing. **follow suit** copy; follow the example. **suitable** *adj* appropriate; proper; fitting. **suitably** *adv*. **suitability** *n*. **suitor** *n* **1** one who courts a woman. **2** petitioner. **suitcase** *n* portable case for luggage.

suite *n* **1** set of rooms. **2** set of furniture designed for one room. **3** group of attendants; retinue. **4** musical work of several connected movements, esp. based on dance forms.

sulk *vi* show offence or resentment by refusing to speak or cooperate. *n* act of sulking. **sulky** *adj* glumly withdrawn; sullen. **sulkily** *adv*. **sulkiness** *n*.

sullen *adj* silently unfriendly or uncooperative; morose and resentful; gloomy. **sullenly** *adv*. **sullenness** *n*.

sulphur *n* yellow nonmetallic element, used in making sulphuric acid. **sulphurous** *adj*.

sultan *n* Moslem ruler, esp. the head of the Turkish empire.

sultana *n* **1** sweet seedless raisin. **2** wife, mother, or daughter of a sultan.

sultry *adj* **1** hot and humid. **2** sexually exciting; voluptuous.

sum *n* **1** result obtained from addition; total or whole. **2** amount of money. **3** simple arithmetical problem. *vt* (-mm-) find the sum of. **sum up** make a summary; review; appraise; judge. **summary** *n* review of the main points; précis. *adj* hasty and unceremonious. **summarily** *adv*. **summarize** *vt* make a summary of.

summer *n* season of the year between spring and autumn. **summery** *adj* characteristic or suggestive of summer.

summit *n* **1** highest point; peak. **2** zenith; highest point, esp. of a career. **summit conference** *n* high level discussion(s) between governments.

summon *vt* demand the presence of; call forth; call upon. **summons** *n* order to appear, esp. in court. ~*vt* issue a summons to.

sumptuous *adj* lavish; luxurious. **sumptuously** *adv*.

sun *n* star about which the earth rotates and from which it receives heat and light. *v* (-nn-) **sun oneself** expose one's body to the sun's warmth. **sunflower** *n* tall plant with large yellow flowers. **sunglasses** *pl n* spectacles with tinted lenses for protection from the sun's rays. **sunny** *adj* **1** exposed to the sun; full of or characterized by sunshine. **2** cheerful. **sunrise** *n* **1** daily appearance of the sun above the eastern horizon. **2** time when this occurs. **sunset** *n* **1** daily disappearance of the sun below the western horizon. **2** time when this occurs. **sunshine** *n also* **sunlight** light and warmth received from the sun.

Sunday *n* first day of the week; day of Christian worship.
sundry *adj* various; miscellaneous. **sundries** *pl n* miscellaneous articles; extras.
sung *v pp* of **sing.**
sunk *v pt* and *pp* of **sink. sunken** *adj* **1** situated below the surface; lying underwater; hollowed into the ground or floor. **2** fallen in.
super *adj inf* splendid; wonderful; first-rate.
superannuation *n* retirement pension. **superannuated** *adj* obsolete; out of date; antiquated.
superb *adj* excellent; splendid. **superbly** *adv.*
superficial *adj* shallow; perfunctory; of or on the surface; not probing or thorough. **superficiality** *n.* **superficially** *adv.*
superfluous (su:ˈpə:fluəs) *adj* more than is wanted; unnecessary; left over. **superfluity** *n.* **superfluously** *adv.*
superhuman *adj* greater or more intense than seems humanly possible.
superimpose *vt* place (something) on top of something else.
superintendent *n* **1** official in charge of an institution, department, building, etc. **2** high-ranking police officer. **superintend** *vt* supervise; direct.
superior *adj* **1** greater; higher; better. **2** excellent; of high quality; high-ranking. **3** disdainful; conceited; indifferent. *n* person above one in rank or status. **superiority** *n.*
supermarket *n* large self-service food store.
supernatural *adj* **1** existing outside or beyond the laws of nature; magical; ghostly. **2** unnatural. *n* **the supernatural** supernatural creatures and happenings.
supersonic *adj* travelling faster than sound.
superstition *n* irrational or uninformed belief or fear, esp. in or of the supernatural or magic. **superstitious** *adj.* **superstitiously** *adv.*
supervise *vt,vi* **1** direct (work and workers); control. **2** act as a tutor (to). **supervision** *n.* **supervisor** *n.*
supper *n* light evening meal.
supple *adj* easily bent or manipulated; physically agile; flexible. **suppleness** *n.*
supplement *n* (ˈsʌplimənt) **1** something added to complete or extend something else. **2** additional section of a book, newspaper, etc. *vt* (ˈsʌpliment) add to; make supplements to. **supplementary** *adj.*
supply *vt* **1** provide; keep provided with. **2** fulfil; satisfy. *n* **1** stock; amount stored; something supplied. **2** availability or production of goods, esp. in relation to demand. **supplies** *pl n* stored goods; provisions.
support *vt* **1** hold up; bear the weight of. **2** back; stand up for; favour the cause of; assist. **3** maintain financially; provide for. **4** tolerate. *n* **1** act of supporting. **2** person or thing that supports. **supporting** *adj* secondary; not principal.
suppose *vt,vi* imagine; be inclined to think; assume. **supposition** *n.* **supposed** *adj* presumed. **supposed to** expected or obliged to. **supposedly** *adv* said or thought to be.
suppress *vt* **1** put down; crush. **2** keep concealed; withhold; stifle. **suppression** *n.* **suppressive** *adj.*
supreme *adj* most powerful; absolute; highest; greatest. **supremely** *adv.* **supremacy** *n* state of being supreme; dominance.
surcharge *n* extra amount added to the main bill, total, or cost. *vt* **1** impose a surcharge. **2** overload.
sure *adj* **1** convinced; having no doubt; confident. **2** certain; inevitable. **3** reliable; proven. **make sure (of) 1** satisfy oneself (about); check. **2** make certain. ~*interj inf* certainly! of course! **surely** *adv* **1** in a sure way. **2** certainly; without doubt. **surety** *n* **1** pledge; guarantee; guarantor. **2** certainty.
surf *n* foam made by waves breaking along the shoreline; breakers. *vi* engage in surfing. **surfing** *n* sport of riding large waves while balancing on a board.
surface *n* **1** topmost or outer covering, layer, or edge. **2** outward appearance. *vt* provide with a surface; improve the surface (of). *vi* rise to the surface; emerge.
surfeit *n* excessive or superfluous amount; overabundance; excess, esp. of food consumed.
surge *vi* drive or press forward in a rush or flood. *n* surging action; gush; swell; onrush.
surgeon *n* **1** doctor who performs medical operations. **2** military or police doctor. **surgery** *n* **1** medical treatment involving operations. **2** doctor's consulting-room; hours for visiting a doctor. **surgical** *adj* used in or relating to surgery.
surly *adj* bad-tempered and unhelpful; sullen.
surmount *vt* overcome (an obstacle or problem);

climb over. *vt,vi* be above; place on top of. **surmountable** *adj*.

surname *n* hereditary family name.

surpass *vt* excel; outdo; exceed; transcend. **surpassing** *adj* extraordinary.

surplus *n* **1** excess amount. **2** portion that remains after needs have been supplied, expenses subtracted, etc. *adj* extra; left over; no longer needed.

surprise *vt* **1** astonish; amaze. **2** take unawares. *n* **1** something unexpected. **2** amazement; astonishment. **surprised** *adj* revealing or expressing surprise. **surprising** *adj* causing surprise. **surprisingly** *adv*.

surrender *vt,vi* yield; give in; give up; abandon. *n* act of surrendering.

surreptitious *adj* done clandestinely; furtive; deliberately concealed. **surreptitiously** *adv*. **surreptitiousness** *n*.

surround *vt* encircle; extend right round; crowd around. **surrounding** *adj* situated around or nearby. **surroundings** *pl n* environment; objects or area immediately surrounding one.

survey *vt* (sə'vei) **1** scan; look over carefully. **2** measure and record the area, elevations, and other geographical features of a piece of land. **3** make a detailed inspection of the condition of a building, etc. *n* ('sə:vei) **1** act or process of surveying. **2** review; analysis. **3** surveyor's report. **surveying** *n* study or practice of surveying land. **surveyor** *n* person employed to survey areas of land or buildings.

survive *vt,vi* continue to exist (following); come through; outlive. **survival** *n*. **survivor** *n*.

susceptible *adj* **1** prone (to); easily affected or influenced (by). **2** easily stricken by emotion; sensitive. **susceptibility** *n* **1** quality of being susceptible to. **2** weakness (for).

suspect *vt,vi* (sə'spekt) **1** believe to be true without proof; have a feeling (about); suppose. **2** be doubtful about. **3** think (a person) guilty of. *n* ('sʌspekt) person thought to have committed a crime, etc. *adj* ('sʌspekt) dubious; arousing suspicion.

suspend *vt* **1** hang (one object from another); hang from above. **2** postpone; defer; delay; keep unresolved. **3** remove temporarily from office, etc.; withdraw (someone's privileges). **suspension** *n* **1** act of suspending; condition of being suspended. **2** postponement; temporary dismissal. **3** mixture consisting of one substance dispersed in small particles in another. **suspension bridge** *n* bridge suspended from steel cables hung between two towers.

suspense *n* feeling of tension; state of uncertainty.

suspicion *n* **1** act of suspecting; doubt or mistrust. **2** hint; trace; vague idea. **suspicious** *adj* **1** dubious; likely to cause suspicion. **2** mistrustful; doubtful; likely to suspect. **suspiciously** *adv*.

sustain *vt* **1** keep alive; maintain. **2** support; hold up. **3** endure; suffer; bear. **4** give strength to. **sustenance** *n* nourishment; food.

swab *n* **1** piece of cotton wool, etc., used in medicine to absorb liquid, blood, etc., or to take specimens. **2** mop; cloth used for washing floors, etc. *vt* (-bb-) mop up; wash down.

swagger *vi* strut about; show off; behave conceitedly. *n* swaggering walk or manner.

swallow[1] *vt,vi* **1** take into the stomach through the throat; gulp. **2** *inf* believe or accept (something unlikely). **swallow up** consume; engulf. ~*n* act of swallowing.

swallow[2] *n* small migratory bird with a forked tail.

swam *v pt* of **swim.**

swamp *n* permanently waterlogged ground, often overgrown. *vt* **1** drench with water; fill with water and sink. **2** overwhelm; flood. **swampy** *adj*.

swan *n* large long-necked water-bird. **swansong** final appearance; last work or contribution.

swank *vi* boast; show off. *n* **1** person who swanks. **2** act of swanking. **swanky** *adj*.

swap *vt,vi* (-pp-) *also* **swop** *inf* exchange (one thing for another). *n* **1** act of exchanging. **2** thing exchanged.

swarm *n* **1** dense mass of insects, esp. bees. **2** large crowd or throng. *vi* **1** flock or surge; be crowded (with). **2** (of bees) leave the hive in a swarm with a new queen.

swat *vt* (-tt-) strike or slap (an insect, etc.) with the hand, a newspaper, etc. *n* sharp slap.

sway *vt,vi* **1** swing, move, or bend to and fro; lean to one side. **2** persuade; influence. *n* **1** act of swaying. **2** rule; power. **hold sway** rule (over); be in control; dominate.

swear *vi* (swore; sworn) **1** use obscene or insulting language; utter curses or oaths. **2** declare or promise solemnly; make a binding legal promise or oath. **swear by 1** take an oath on (a sacred object, etc.). **2** rely on absolutely. **swearword** *n* socially unacceptable word; profane or obscene word.

sweat *n* **1** moisture secreted from the pores of the skin; perspiration. **2** *inf* hard work; trouble. *vi* **1** exude sweat; perspire. **2** *inf* work hard; labour.

sweater *n* woollen garment covering chest, back, and arms; jersey; jumper; pullover.

swede *n* pale orange root vegetable related to the turnip.

sweep *vi,vt* (swept) **1** clean or clear with a broom, brush, etc. **2** proceed or move rapidly (through). **3** extend; curve. *n* **1** sweeping movement. **2** person who cleans chimneys. **sweeper** *n.*

sweet *adj* **1** tasting sugary; not sour. **2** kind, likeable; charming; cute. *n* **1** any type of small confection made principally from sugar. **2** pudding; dessert. **sweetly** *adv.* **sweetness** *n.* **sweeten** *vt* **1** make sweet(er). **2** make more acceptable. **sweetheart** *n* person who loves and is loved in return; darling. **sweet pea** *n* climbing garden plant with sweet-smelling flowers.

swell *vt,vi* (swelled; swollen) expand; bulge out; increase in size, volume, etc. *n* **1** act of swelling. **2** waves; action of waves when not breaking. **3** gradual increase in sound. **swelling** *n* **1** act of swelling. **2** something swollen, esp. a bruised or infected area of the body. **swollen-headed** *adj* conceited.

swerve *vi* make a sudden or abrupt sideways turn. *n* act of swerving.

swift *adj* speedy; rapid; prompt. *n* small widely distributed bird capable of fast sustained flight. **swiftly** *adv.*

swig *inf vt,vi* (-gg-) swallow; take gulps (from). *n* draught; gulp.

swill *vt,vi* **1** drink large quantities (of). **2** wash or slop down. *n* liquid food for animals, esp. pigs.

swim *v* (swam; swum) *vi* **1** move in or under water by movement of the body, limbs, tail, or fins, etc. **2** float; drift; appear to swim. **3** feel dizzy; swirl. *vt* cross by swimming. *n* act or period of swimming.

swindle *vt,vi* obtain by fraud; cheat; exploit unfairly. *n* instance of swindling. **swindler** *n.*

swine *n, pl* **swine 1** pig. **2** brutish or beastly person.

swing *vt,vi* (swung) **1** move; sway; rock back and forth. **2** whirl about. **3** veer; turn. **swing round** turn suddenly in a sweeping movement. ~*n* **1** swinging movement or action. **2** seat suspended on ropes, etc., on which a person can swing himself.

swipe *n* lunging blow. *vt,vi* **1** make a swipe (at). **2** *inf* seize; steal.

swirl *vi* move round in a slow whirl, eddy, or series of curves. *n* **1** swirling action. **2** eddy; whirl.

swish *n* whistling sound as of a thin rod swung through the air; rustle; hiss. *vi,vt* make a swishing sound (with).

switch *vt,vi* exchange; transfer; shift; make a change. **switch on/off** turn on/off (an electric appliance, etc.). ~*n* **1** act of switching. **2** device for turning an electrical appliance, etc., on or off. **3** thin flexible cane or whip. **switchboard** *n* device fitted with many switches, esp. one used for relaying telephone calls.

swivel *vt,vi* (-ll-) turn (round) on a pivot. *n* device for joining two objects to allow one to move independently of the other.

swollen *v pp* of **swell.**

swoop *vt,vi* plunge or sweep down (on), as of a bird of prey, esp. to attack or carry off. *n* act of swooping.

swop *vt,vi,n* swap.

sword *n* weapon with a long pointed blade set in a handle. **swordfish** *n* edible marine fish with a long pointed jaw resembling a sword. **swordsman** *n* person skilled in the use of a sword.

swore *v pt* of **swear.**

sworn *v pp* of **swear.**

swot *vt,vi* (-tt-) *inf* study hard, esp. for an examination. *n* person who swots.

swum *v pp* of **swim.**

swung *v pt* and *pp* of **swing.**

sycamore *n* any of various kinds of deciduous tree having large indented leaves.

syllable *n* word or part of a word uttered as a single unit of sound.

syllabus *n, pl* **syllabuses** *or* **syllabi** ('siləbai) outline of work to be studied; summary of a course.

symbol *n* sign or object that represents something else, esp. something abstract. **symbolic** *adj.* **symbolically** *adv.* **symbolism** *n* the use of symbols to express abstract concepts, esp. in the arts. **symbolize** *vt* represent; stand for; act as a symbol of

symmetry *n* harmonious balance between parts; regularity or correspondence of a pattern within a whole. **symmetrical** *adj.*

sympathy *n* quality of feeling for people's suffering or understanding their attitude; compassion; understanding. **sympathetic** *adj* **1** having sympathy. **2** understanding; congenial. **sympathetically** *adv.* **sympathize** *vi* share a person's feelings, esp. during suffering; have understanding; show sympathy. **sympathizer** *n* one who approves of or sanctions a cause, political party, etc., without being a member or an active supporter.

symphony *n* major orchestral composition in three or more movements.

symptom *n* **1** physical or mental change indicative of or due to a malfunction. **2** any sign indicative of a change, disorder, or condition. **symptomatic** *adj.*

synagogue *n* place of worship and instruction for members of the Jewish religion.

synchronize *vt,vi* work, operate, or occur at the same time or in harmony. **synchronization** *n.* **synchronous** *adj.*

syndicate *n* **1** association of people carrying out a business or joining in an enterprise. **2** agency that sells articles, etc., to several newspapers for simultaneous publication. *vt* publish through a syndicate.

syndrome *n* combination of symptoms or signs indicating a certain condition or disorder.

synopsis *n, pl* **synopses** (si'nɔpsi:z) brief summary, précis, or outline, esp. of the plot of a novel, play, etc.

synthesis *n, pl* **syntheses** ('sinθəsi:z) combination or fusing of parts into a whole; whole thus formed. **synthetic** *adj* **1** artificial; false, man-made. **2** produced by or relating to a synthesis. **synthesize** *vt.*

syphilis *n* serious contagious type of venereal disease. **syphilitic** *adj.*

syringe *n* device for sucking in liquid and/or forcing it out in a spray or jet, esp. one used for injecting fluid into the body. *vt* clean out or spray using a syringe.

syrup *n* thick solution of sugar and water or juice; treacle. **syrupy** *adj.*

system *n* **1** group of coordinating parts forming a whole. **2** carefully organized set of related ideas or procedures. **systematic** *adj* methodical; regular; following a system

T

tab *n* small flap or strip of cloth, paper, etc. **keep tabs on** keep a check or watch on

tabby *adj* (of cats) brown or grey with dark stripes or blotches. *n* tabby cat.

table *n* **1** piece of furniture with a flat top and legs or supports, usually high enough to sit at. **2** organized list, chart, index, etc. **turn the tables on** place in an inferior or losing position. ~*vt* put forward for future discussion. **tablespoon** *n* large spoon used for serving food. **table tennis** *n* game played with round bats and a small light ball on a table fitted with a low net.

tablet *n* **1** pill. **2** inscribed stone slab or plaque. **3** cake (of soap).

taboo *n also* **tabu** act, object, or word that is forbidden in a particular society or religion. *adj* forbidden.

tack *n* **1** large-headed short nail for fastening things. **2** direction taken by a sailing ship according to the angle of the wind. **3** method of approach; course of action. *vt* **1** fasten with tacks. **2** sew together with loose temporary stitching; gather together loosely. *vi* steer a course along a different tack.

tackle *n* **1** gear or equipment, esp. for fishing. **2** set of ropes used in a pulley system. **3** (in rugby football) act of seizing a player's legs so that he will give up the ball. **4** attempt to get the ball from another player in football. *vt* **1** attempt or attack (something difficult). **2** approach or deal with (a difficult or unwilling person, situation, etc.). **3** perform a tackle on in football.

tact *n* sensitivity to other people's feelings or to situations that require delicate and discreet handling. **tactful** *adj.* **tactfully** *adv*

tactic *n* manoeuvre, act directed towards a goal. **tactics** *pl n* strategy, plan of action. **tactical** *adj.* **tactically** *adv.*

tadpole *n* completely aquatic stage in a frog's or toad's life during which the legs develop and the tail and gills disappear

taffeta *n* strong stiff satin-like cloth

tag *n* small label or indentity disc *vt* (-gg-) label;

identify. **tag along** accompany; go along (with).

tail *n* **1** end part of an animal's body that is an elongation of the backbone. **2** back or end part, section, or projection. **turn tail** flee; run away. ~*vt,vi* **1** follow and observe (a person's actions), esp. without being noticed. **2** take the tail from. **tail off** gradually diminish or deteriorate. **tails** *s n* side of a coin not bearing the sovereign's head.

tailor *n* **1** person employed to make garments which require careful fitting, esp. those for men. **2** person selling men's clothes. *vt,vi* **1** make and fit (suits, etc.). **2** adapt; alter to suit individual needs.

taint *n* trace of some defect, infection, corrupting influence, etc. *vt* infect; stain; poison; spoil.

take *vt* (took; taken) **1** receive or accept (something offered). **2** bring into one's possession; help oneself to; remove. **3** accompany to a particular destination. **4** capture; seize. **5** grasp; grip; hold. **6** eat, drink, or swallow (medicine, tablets, etc.). **7** steal. **8** select; use. **9** transmit; transport; convey. **10** keep a record of. **11** last; be the time required for. **12** require; be necessary for. **13** have accommodation for. **14** regard; consider. **15** subtract; deduct. **16** study. **take in** deceive; swindle. **take off 1** remove. **2** become airborne. **3** impersonate; mimic. **take on** accept as a duty or commitment. **take out 1** extract; delete. **2** escort. **3** acquire (a licence, insurance, etc.). **take over** assume control. **take to** find pleasure in; develop a liking or skill for. **take up** pursue; adopt; become involved in. **take-off** *n* **1** act of jumping or lifting off the ground. **2** satirical imitation. **take-over** *n* act of taking over and assuming control, esp. of a business, government, etc. **takings** *pl n* money obtained in the course of business during a particular period.

talcum powder *n* very fine scented body powder.

tale *n* story; narrative; legend. **tell tales 1** report another's misdoings. **2** tell lies.

talent *n* ability; skill; special gift or aptitude.

talk *vi,vt* **1** communicate by means of speech. **2** discuss; express by speaking. **3** chatter; gossip. *n* **1** manner of speaking. **2** speech or brief lecture. **3** gossip. **talkative** *adj* tending to talk a lot; chatty.

tall *adj* large in height; not small. **tall order** difficult commission. **tall story** *or* **tale** *n* unlikely or exaggerated account or story.

tally *vi* correspond; agree. *vt* add up; reckon. *n* **1** reckoning; score; bill. **2** notched stick for recording numbers.

talon *n* claw, esp. of a bird of prey.

tambourine *n* small shallow drum with metal discs, which clink when shaken.

tame *adj* **1** (of animals) not wild; not aggressive towards or frightened of humans. **2** unexciting; unadventurous. *vt* make tame.

tamper *vi* interfere; meddle.

tan *n,adj* light brown. *n* skin browned by the sun. *vt,vi* (-nn-) **1** make or go brown. **2** turn (hides) into leather.

tang *n* sharp taste.

tangent *n* straight line that touches but does not intersect a curve. **go off at a tangent** digress; change the subject or line of thought. **tangential** *adj* **1** relating to tangents. **2** connected but irrelevant.

tangerine *n* type of small sweet orange.

tangible *adj* **1** able to be touched. **2** visible; factual; real.

tangle *n* muddle; confused web of knots; intricate mass. *vt,vi* make into a tangle; muddle.

tango *n* Latin-American ballroom dance.

tank *n* **1** large container for keeping or storing liquids. **2** large armour-plated military vehicle.

tankard *n* large mug with a handle, used esp for beer.

tanker *n* ship or lorry built for carrying liquids in bulk.

tantalize *vt* tease by offering or presenting something desirable that cannot be attained.

tantrum *n* hysterical fit of bad temper.

tap[1] *vt,vi* (-pp-) strike a quick gentle blow (on). *n* tapping action or sound. **tap dancing** *n* style of dancing involving complicated heel and toe tapping steps.

tap[2] *n* device with a screw and washer for controlling the flow of liquid from a pipe or container. **on tap** constantly available. ~*vt* (-pp-) **1** sap; drain off; extract. **2** fit a bugging device to (a telephone, etc.) so as to intercept or overhear calls.

tape *n* **1** strip of flexible resistant material for binding, mending, etc. **2** length of tape stretched across the finishing line of a race track or cut symbolically to open a fête, etc. **3** strip of plastic magnetized recording tape. *vt* **1**

bind or stick together with tape. **2** record on tape. **tape-measure** *n* length of tape marked off with measurements; flexible rule. **tape-recorder** *n* device for recording sound on magnetic tape.

taper *vt,vi* make or become gradually thinner at one end; tail off. *n* very thin candle.

tapestry *n* heavy fabric having a picture or design woven by hand in coloured threads.

tar *n* thick black sticky coal-based substance used in road building, wood preserving, etc. *vt,vi* (-rr-) cover with tar.

target *n* **1** object or person to be aimed at or attacked. **2** goal or objective.

tariff *n* **1** tax or list of taxes levied on imported goods. **2** fixed schedule of charges or prices.

tarnish *vt,vi* spoil the shine or lustre (of). *n* loss of shine or lustre.

tart[1] *adj* **1** sharp to the taste; acid. **2** sarcastic.

tart[2] *n* **1** small pie or flan with a sweet filling. **2** *sl* prostitute.

tartan *n* woollen plaid fabric in different patterns and colours corresponding to those of various Highland Scottish clans.

task *n* particular job or piece of work; chore. **take to task** reprove; censure.

tassel *n* ornamental knot with a bunch of loose threads.

taste *vt,vi* **1** sense the flavour (of) with one's tongue. **2** try; have a short experience of. **3** have the flavour (of). *n* **1** flavour. **2** sense by which one perceives flavour. **3** ability to make aesthetic judgment; discernment. **4** fineness or elegance of style, manners, etc. **5** particular preference. **6** small amount; trace; hint. **tasteful** *adj* elegant; fitting. **tasteless** *adj* **1** not strongly flavoured; insipid. **2** not tasteful; tactless. **tasty** *adj* good to eat.

tattoo[1] *vt* permanently mark (the skin) by putting indelible stains into pricked designs. *n* design made by tattooing.

tattoo[2] *n* **1** military entertainment involving marching and music, usually at night. **2** signal sounded on a drum or bugle recalling soldiers to their quarters for the night. **3** continuous drumming.

taught *v pt* and *pp* of **teach.**

taunt *vt* jeer at; provoke; tease. *n* jeer; insulting remark.

Taurus *n* second sign of the zodiac, represented by the Bull.

taut *adj* tightly stretched; having no slack; tense. **tautness** *n*.

tavern *n* public house; inn.

tax *n* **1** money demanded by law to be paid according to income, assets, goods purchased or imported, etc. **2** difficult or onerous obligation, demand, etc.; burden. *vt* **1** impose a tax on. **2** put a burden on; strain. **taxation** *n* system of imposing taxes or the amount of tax payable.

taxi *n* car with a driver for public hire. *vi* (of aircraft) move along the ground on landing or before take-off. *vt* cause (an aircraft) to taxi.

tea *n* **1** evergreen shrub grown in East Asia for its pungent leaves. **2** drink made from infusing dried tea leaves in boiling water. **3** meal between lunch and supper at which tea is drunk. **tea-cloth** *n also* **tea-towel** cloth for drying dishes.

teach *vt,vi* (taught) instruct; give lessons (in); show (a person) how to do something. **teacher** *n*. **teaching** *n* **1** ability to teach; knowledge or practice of teaching. **2** set of doctrines.

teak *n* large tree found in SE Asia with hard orange-brown wood, used for furniture, etc.

team *n* **1** group of people working together, esp. in order to compete against others. **2** group of horses, dogs, etc., pulling together. *v* **team up with** join with in order to pool resources and work in harmony.

tear[1] (tiə) *n also* **teardrop** drop of salty liquid that falls from the eye. **tearful** *adj* **1** liable to cry. **2** sad. **tear-gas** *n* type of gas that makes the eyes water, used to disperse rioting crowds, etc.

tear[2] (tɛə) *v* (tore; torn) *vt,vi* divide; split; rip. *vi* hurry; rush. **tear down** pull down; destroy. **tear off** **1** pull or pluck off, esp. violently. **2** *inf* do in a great hurry. **tear up** **1** divide into small pieces, strips, etc. **2** pull up; destroy. ~*n* torn hole; slit.

tease *vt,vi* **1** torment by joking; mock; make fun of. **2** draw out; comb out; disentangle. *n* person given to teasing others.

teat *n* **1** nipple. **2** feeding nipple on a baby's bottle.

technical *adj* **1** relating to a technique, method, or skill. **2** relating to specialized industrial or mechanical skills and crafts or to technology. **technically** *adv*.

technician *n* person skilled in the technical

processes of a particular craft, science, or industry.

technique *n* 1 method of performing some skill; system of practical procedures. 2 practical skill.

technology *n* 1 application of scientific ideas to industry or commerce. 2 methods and equipment so used. **technological** *adj*. **technologist** *n*.

tedious *adj* 1 boring; monotonous. 2 tiresome. **tediously** *adv*. **tedium** *n*.

tee *n* 1 small peg that supports a golf ball for the first stroke at each hole. 2 elevated area from which this stroke is played. *v* **tee off** 1 drive the ball from the tee. 2 start.

teenager *n* person aged between 13 and 19; adolescent.

teeth *n pl* of **tooth. get one's teeth into** begin to cope with or tackle seriously. **teethe** *vi* (esp. of babies) produce teeth.

teetotal *adj* refusing to drink or serve alcoholic drinks. **teetotaller** *n* teetotal person.

telegram *n* message transmitted by telegraph.

telegraph *n* method of or apparatus for transmitting messages using radio signals or electric impulses sent along wires. *vt,vi* send a telegram to. **telegraphy** *n*.

telepathy *n* human communication through scientifically inexplicable channels; mind-reading. **telepathic** *adj*.

telephone *n* system or apparatus for verbal communication over a distance, usually using electric impulses sent back and forth along a wire. *vt,vi* call or talk to by telephone; phone. **telephonist** *n* operator of a telephone switchboard.

telescope *n* 1 optical instrument using lenses or mirrors to magnify distant objects. 2 instrument, esp. one using radio or light waves, to study astronomical bodies. *vt,vi* make or become shorter, compressed, or crushed. **telescopic** *adj*.

television *n* 1 process of or apparatus for using high-frequency radio waves to transmit and receive visual images with accompanying sound. 2 radio broadcasts received on a television. **televise** *vt,vi* record or broadcast by means of television.

telex *n* telegraph service or apparatus for transmitting printed messages.

tell *v* (told) *vt,vi* inform; let know. *vt* 1 relate; recount; express in words; describe. 2 order; instruct. 3 disclose; reveal; confess. *vi* reveal secrets; inform against someone. **can tell** be able to discover, understand, distinguish, etc. **tell off** scold. **telltale** *adj* betraying; serving to reveal something hidden. *n* person given to informing on others.

temper *n* 1 state of mind; mood. 2 angry fit; rage; tendency to become angry. *vt* 1 modify; moderate; alleviate. 2 strengthen (metal) by sudden changes of temperature.

temperament *n* nature; disposition; person's style of thinking and behaviour. **temperamental** *adj* 1 given to violent changes of mood; excitable. 2 unreliable.

temperate *adj* 1 mild in temperature. 2 moderate; restrained; even-tempered.

temperature *n* 1 measured or approximate degree of hotness of something. 2 fever.

tempestuous *adj* stormy; violent.

temple[1] *n* 1 place of worship dedicated to a particular deity. 2 sacred place.

temple[2] *n* flat area on either side of the forehead.

tempo *n* speed at which a conductor or performer chooses to play a piece of music.

temporal *adj* existing in or limited by time; not spiritual; earthly. **temporally** *adv*.

temporary *adj* intended to be used for a short time; not permanent; passing. **temp** *n inf* person not employed on a permanent basis. **temporarily** *adv*.

tempt *vt* persuade or induce (a person) to try or do something undesirable; attract; seduce; influence. **temptation** *n*.

ten *n* 1 number equal to one plus nine. 2 group of ten persons, things, etc. 3 *also* **ten o'clock** ten hours after noon or midnight. *adj* amounting to ten.

tenacious *adj* holding or sticking firmly; stubbornly persisting. **tenaciously** *adv*. **tenacity** *n*.

tenant *n* person who occupies a house, flat, farm, etc., for payment of rent. **tenancy** *n* state of being a tenant or the period during which this occurs.

tend[1] *vt* look after; care for.

tend[2] *vi* be inclined or likely (to); have the effect of. **tendency** *n*.

tender[1] *adj* 1 soft; delicate; not hardy. 2 gentle, loving; compassionate. 3 painful when touched; sensitive. 4 easily chewed. 5 youthfully innocent; vulnerable. **tenderly** *adv*. **ten-**

derness *n.* **tender-hearted** *adj* easily moved to pity. **tenderize** *vt,vi* make (food) soft and easy to chew.

tender[2] *vt,vi* offer for acceptance or settlement. *n* offer of goods or services at a fixed rate.

tendon *n* band or sheet of fibrous tissue by which muscle is attached to bone.

tendril *n* threadlike shoot of a plant enabling it to cling to a support while climbing.

tenement *n* **1** rented room or flat in a block, esp. one in a poor quarter of a city. **2** property held by a tenant.

tennis *n* game for two or four players played by hitting a ball over a net with rackets.

tenor *n* **1** general meaning; tone; direction. **2** instrument or male voice with a range between that of baritone and alto.

tense[1] *adj* **1** anxious; in suspense; overwrought. **2** taut; strained; stretched. *vt* make tense. **tensely** *adv.* **tenseness** *n.* **tensile** *adj* able to be stretched. **tension** *n* **1** stretching or state of being stretched or strained. **2** excitement; suspense. **3** anxiety or unease caused by suppressed emotion.

tense[2] *n* form of a verb indicating the time of action.

tent *n* canvas portable shelter for camping, etc.

tentacle *n* slender flexible organ of various invertebrates, used for feeding, grasping, etc.

tentative *adj* **1** hesitating; cautious. **2** provisional.

tenth *adj* coming between ninth and eleventh. *n* **1** tenth person, object, etc. **2** one of ten equal parts; one divided by ten. *adv* after the ninth.

tenuous *adj* **1** thin; slender; flimsy. **2** subtle; weak.

tenure *n* holding of land or office.

tepid *adj* **1** slightly warm; lukewarm. **2** unenthusiastic.

term *n* **1** period of time for which something occurs or is in force, as a period of teaching in a college, school, etc. **2** word used in specialized field. **3** end of pregnancy. **terms** *pl n* **1** conditions of an agreement, bargain, etc. **2** relationships between people. **come to terms** form an agreement; reconcile. **in terms of** as expressed by. ~*vt* define (something) as; call.

terminology *n* set of terms specific to any particular field of study. **terminological** *adj.*

terminate *vt,vi* bring or come to an end. **termination** *n.* **terminal** *adj* of, at, or marking an end or limit; final. *n* **1** end of a transport route. **2** either end of an open electrical circuit. **terminally** *adv.*

terminus *n, pl* **termini** ('tə:minai) *or* **terminuses** **1** boundary points; final point reached. **2** end of a railway, airline, or bus route.

terrace *n* **1** raised bank or walk in a garden. **2** flat area cut into a slope, often for crop cultivation. **3** balcony; flat rooftop. **4** row of similar adjoined houses.

terrestrial *adj* **1** of or on earth; earthly. **2** living or growing on land rather than in the sea or air.

terrible *adj* **1** causing terror; appalling; very bad. **2** *inf* excessive; outstanding. **terribly** *adv.*

terrier *n* small dog of various breeds originally used in hunting out animals underground.

terrific *adj* **1** frighteningly large; instilling terror. **2** *inf* amazingly good; enjoyable. **terrifically** *adv.*

terrify *vt* cause terror in; frighten.

territory *n* area regarded as owned by the state or a social group or individual or animal. **territorial** *adj.* **territorially** *adv.*

terror *n* **1** extreme fear. **2** anything causing fear or dread. **3** *inf* nuisance; troublesome person. **terrorist** *n* person employing organized violence and intimidation to obtain political objectives. **terrorism** *n.* **terrorize** *vt* manipulate by inspiring terror.

terse *adj* concise; curt

Terylene *n Tdmk* type of synthetic fibre used as textile yarn.

test *n* any critical trial or examination to determine the merit or nature of something. *vt* conduct a test on; examine. **test case** *n* legal case that establishes a precedent. **test match** *n* international cricket match. **test-tube** *n* glass tube used in conducting chemical experiments.

testament *n* **1** one of the two major divisions of the Bible (the Old Testament and the New Testament). **2** act of testifying, as to religious faith. **3** (in law) will.

testicle *n* one of two glands in males producing sperm and male sex hormones.

testify *vi,vt* bear witness; affirm; give evidence.

testimony *n* evidence; proof; declaration. **testimonial** *n* **1** written testimony of character.

2 gift presented as a tribute or token of respect.

tether *n* rope or chain by which an animal is secured. **at the end of one's tether** at the end of one's patience or ability to withstand. ~*vt* fasten with a tether; tie.

text *n* **1** main section of written or printed words of a book as distinguished from illustrations, the index, etc. **2** passage from the Bible. **textual** *adj*. **textbook** *n* book used as a standard source for a particular course of study.

textile *n* woven fabric or cloth.

texture *n* **1** surface, arrangement of strands, etc., of a material, esp. as perceived by the sense of touch. **2** quality, esp. of music.

than *conj* **1** expressing the second stage of a comparison. **2** expressing an alternative after *rather, sooner,* etc.

thank *vt* **1** express gratitude to. **2** blame. **thankful** *adj*. **thankless** *adj*. **thanks** *pl n, interj* expression of gratitude, relief, etc.

that *adj* relating to the person or thing specified, esp. one further away than or different from another. *pron* **1** the particular person or thing so specified. **2** who(m) or which. *adv* so; to such an extent. *conj* introducing a noun clause. **that's that** there is no more to be said or done.

thatch *n* arrangement of straw, reeds, etc., used as a roof covering. *vt,vi* cover with a thatch.

thaw *vt,vi* **1** melt after being frozen. **2** make or become less hostile, frigid, etc. *n* period or process during which snow or ice melts.

the *def art* preceding a noun. *adv* used for emphasis or to express a comparative amount or extent.

theatre *n* **1** building in which plays, operas, etc., are performed. **2** lecture hall. **3** *also* **operating theatre** room equipped for carrying out surgery **4** drama. **5** business of working in or for a theatre. **theatrical** *adj*.

theft *n* crime of stealing another's property.

their *adj* belonging to them. **theirs** *pron* those things belonging to them.

them *pron* those people or things. **themselves** *r pron* **1** their own selves. **2** their normal selves.

theme *n* **1** main idea or concept with which a work of art, discussion, etc., is concerned; topic. **2** recurring melody.

then *adv* **1** at the particular time referred to. **2** immediately afterwards; next. **3** in that case. *adj* functioning at that time. *n* that time.

theology *n* study of religion and the nature of God. **theological** *adj*. **theologian** *n*.

theorem *n* statement that is to be proved by logical reasoning.

theory *n* **1** system or formula as an explanation of a particular phenomenon. **2** body of abstract ideas or principles, esp. as distinguished from practice. **theoretical** *adj*. **theoretically** *adv*. **theorize** *vi* speculate; formulate a theory.

therapy *n* course of treatment designed to cure various disorders of the body or mind. **therapeutic** *adj*. **therapist** *n*.

there *adv* **1** in, to, at, or towards that place. **2** at that point. *pron* used with forms of *be, can,* etc., to introduce a sentence or clause. *n* that position. *interj* expression of consolation, victory, pride, etc. **thereabouts** *adv also* **thereabout** in that approximate place or position. **thereafter** *adv* after that time; from then on. **thereby** *adv* thus; by those means. **therefore** *adv* so; consequently; for that reason. **thereupon** *adv* at which point; after which.

thermal *adj* of or relating to heat. *n* rising current of warm air.

thermodynamics *n* study of the relationships between work, heat, and other forms of energy.

thermometer *n* any instrument used to measure temperature.

thermonuclear *adj* involving fusion of two atomic nuclei, with consequent production of large amounts of heat. **thermonuclear bomb** *n* hydrogen bomb.

Thermos flask *n also* **Thermos** *Tdmk* container with double walls enclosing a vacuum to prevent heat transfer, used for keeping food or drink hot or cold.

thermostat *n* automatic device to maintain a room, enclosure, etc., at a constant temperature. **thermostatic** *adj*. **thermostatically** *adv*.

these *adj* form of **this** used with a plural noun.

thesis *n, pl* **theses** ('θiːsiːz) **1** original work submitted by a candidate for an academic degree. **2** hypothesis; proposition.

they *pron* **1** two or more persons or things when used as the subject in a sentence or clause. **2** people in general.

thick *adj* **1** relatively deep, wide, or fat; not thin. **2** measured by width or diameter. **3** densely layered, arranged, etc. **4** not watery or runny. **5** *inf* stupid. **6** having a broad accent. **a bit thick** unfair; unreasonable. **through thick and thin** throughout both good and bad periods. *adv also* **thickly** so as to be thick. **thickness** *n*. **thicken** *vt,vi* make or become thick(er). **thick-skinned** *adj* **1** insensitive, esp. to criticism. **2** having a thick hide or outer layer.

thief *n, pl* **thieves** person committing theft. **thieve** *vt,vi* commit theft; steal.

thigh *n* that part of the leg above the knee.

thimble *n* small cap worn over the fingertip whilst sewing.

thin *adj* **1** relatively narrow; not thick. **2** slim; slender; not fat. **3** not densely layered, arranged, etc.; sparse. **4** watery or runny. **5** lacking depth of quality; not rich. *adv also* **thinly** so as to be thin. *vt,vi* (-nn-) **1** make or become thin(ner). **2** dilute. **thinness** *n*. **thin-skinned** *adj* sensitive, esp. to criticism.

thing *n* **1** inanimate object; entity. **2** course or action; act; deed. **3** person or animal, esp. when referred to with affection, sympathy, etc. **have a thing about** be preoccupied with. **the thing** fashionable trend. **things** *pl n* **1** possessions. **2** points; matters; ideas. **3** conditions or circumstances.

think *v* (thought) *vi* use one's mind or power of reason. *vt,vi* **1** believe; consider. **2** be aware (of); regard. **think about 1** reflect or ponder on. **2** *also* **think of** have an opinion of. **think of 1** bring to mind; imagine or remember. **2** plan; anticipate; consider. ~*n inf* concentrated effort to examine or analyse an idea, suggestion, etc.

third *adj* coming between second and fourth in sequence. *n* **1** third person, object, etc. **2** one of three equal parts; one divided by three. **3** gear above second on a motor vehicle. *adv* **1** after the second. **2** *also* **thirdly** as a third point. **third party** *n* person only marginally involved in a case or affair. **third person** *n* category of pronouns or verbs other than the person speaking or addressed. **third rate** *adj also* **third-class** of a very poor standard; mediocre.

thirst *n* **1** desire for water or other liquids. **2** craving; yearning. *vi* have a thirst (for). **thirsty** *adj*.

thirteen *n* **1** number that is three more than ten. **2** thirteen things or people. *adj* amounting to thirteen. **thirteenth** *adj,adv,n*.

thirty *n* **1** number equal to three times ten. **2** thirty things or people. *adj* amounting to thirty. **thirtieth** *adj,adv,n*.

this *adj* relating to the person or thing specified, esp. one closer than or different from another. *pron* the particular person or thing so specified. *adv* to a specified extent.

thistle *n* plant with a purple flower and prickly leaves.

thong *n* thin strip of leather used in a whip, as a fastening, etc.

thorax *n, pl* **thoraxes** *or* **thoraces** ('θɔːrəsiːz) **1** part of the body containing the heart, lungs, etc.; chest. **2** part of an insect bearing the wings and legs.

thorn *n* **1** sharp woody point occurring on a stem or leaf. **2** bush, esp the hawthorn, having thorns. **thorny** *adj* **1** having thorns. **2** difficult to solve.

thorough *adj* **1** completed carefully and painstakingly; meticulous. **2** utter; absolute. **thoroughly** *adv*. **thoroughness** *n*. **thoroughbred** *n* animal of a pure breed; pedigree. *adj* relating to such an animal. **thoroughfare** *n* **1** road or street. **2** access; passage.

those *adj* form of **that** used with a plural noun.

though *conj* in spite of the fact that; although. **as though** as if. ~*adv* nevertheless; on the other hand.

thought *v pt* of **think.** *n* **1** idea, notion, concept, etc., produced by thinking. **2** act or process of thinking. **3** attention; consideration. **4** body of ideas relating to a particular period, movement, etc. **thoughtful** *adj* **1** considerate. **2** engaged in thought. **thoughtfully** *adv*. **thoughtfulness** *n*. **thoughtless** *adj* tactless; careless; inconsiderate. **thoughtlessly** *adv*. **thoughtlessness** *n*.

thousand *n* **1** number equal to ten times one hundred. **2** thousand people or things. **thousands** *pl n* huge number. *adj* amounting to a thousand. **thousandth** *adj,adv,n*.

thrash *vt* **1** flog; whip; beat. **2** defeat overwhelmingly. *vi* make a violent movement with the arms or legs, esp. in water. **thrash out** settle by debate or intense discussion. ~*n* beating; violent blow.

thread *n* **1** strand of cotton, yarn, wool, etc. **2** spiral groove of a screw, bolt, etc. **3** central idea running through a story, argument, etc. *vt* **1** pass (a thread) through (a needle). **2** make (a way) through (obstacles, etc.). **threadbare** *adj* **1** worn; having no pile or nap. **2** shabby; poor.

threat *n* **1** statement or indication of future harm, injury, etc. **2** person or thing likely to cause harm, injury, etc.; danger. **threaten** *vt,vi* make threats (to); be a threat (to); menace.

three *n* **1** number equal to one plus two. **2** group of three persons, things, etc. **3** *also* **three o'clock** three hours after noon or midnight. *adj* amounting to three. **three-dimensional** *adj also* **3-D** having three dimensions; solid or apparently solid. **threesome** *n* group of three; trio.

thresh *vt,vi* beat or shake (corn) so as to separate the grain from the husks. **thresher** *n* person or machine that threshes.

threshold *n* **1** slab or board placed at a doorway or entrance. **2** starting point or verge. **3** point at which a stimulus produces an observable effect.

threw *v pt of* **throw.**

thrift *n* economic or careful use of resources. **thrifty** *adj.*

thrill *n* **1** tingle of excitement; flush of enthusiasm; intense emotion or sensation. **2** event causing this. *vt,vi* cause or experience a thrill. **thriller** *n* book, film, etc., arousing strong excitement and suspense.

thrive *vi* **1** grow healthily and well. **2** prosper.

throat *n* **1** front of the neck. **2** passage connecting the mouth and stomach. **3** narrow part, passage, or opening. **cut one's throat** pursue a disastrous course. **jump down someone's throat** attack verbally with sudden vehemence. **ram down someone's throat** assert or force upon without allowing response. **throaty** *adj* hoarse, as if with a sore throat.

throb *vi* (-bb-) beat strongly and rhythmically. *n* strong pulsating beat.

throne *n* **1** monarch's, pope's, or bishop's seat. **2** sovereign power.

throng *n* crowd; mass of people. *vi,vt* form or fill with a throng.

throttle *n* valve that regulates an engine's fuel supply. *vt* **1** choke; strangle. **2** regulate or restrict (power supply).

through *prep* **1** along the length of; from one end to the other of. **2** in one side and out of the other side of. **3** during; from the beginning to the end of. **4** via. **5** with the influence of; by the means or agency of. **6** because of. *adv* **1** from one side or end to another. **2** from start to finish. **3** throughout; completely. **4** no longer functioning or successful. **throughout** *prep* right through; during the whole of. *adv* in every part.

throw *v* (threw; thrown) *vt,vi* **1** send (a missile) through the air. **2** toss; fling. *vt* **1** baffle; perplex; confuse; take aback. **2** place in a particular situation. **throw away** discard as useless; reject; get rid of. **throw out 1** eject; remove by force. **2** expel; dismiss. **throw up 1** vomit. **2** produce unexpectedly. **3** leave or reject (a job). ~*n* **1** act of throwing. **2** toss; pitch.

thrush *n* songbird with brown plumage and speckled underparts.

thrust *vt,vi* **1** push with force. **2** stab; pierce **3** force (a situation) upon (someone). *n* **1** violent lunge or push. **2** force of the propulsion of an engine. **3** *inf* ruthless drive to succeed.

thud *n* dull heavy sound of impact. *vi* (-dd-) make such a sound.

thumb *n* **1** short thick digit of the human hand. **2** corresponding digit in other mammals. **rule of thumb** practical method based on experience. **under the thumb of** under (someone's) control. ~*vt* **1** mark or touch with the thumb. **2** use the thumb as a signal, esp. as a hitch-hiker.

thump *n* **1** dull heavy blow. **2** sound made by such a blow. *vt,vi* strike; pound; beat.

thunder *n* loud rumbling noise caused by movement of air after lightning. *vi,vt* **1** make a sound like thunder; roar. **2** speak loudly and angrily. **thunderous** *adj.* **thunderstorm** *n* thunder and lightning accompanied by heavy rain.

Thursday *n* fifth day of the week.

thus *adv* **1** in the meantime. **2** to this extent or degree. **3** therefore.

thwart *vt* prevent; frustrate.

thyme (taim) *n* fragrant herb with a minty odour.

thyroid *n also* **thyroid gland** gland whose hormones regulate metabolism and growth.

tiara *n* jewelled head ornament worn by women.

tick[1] *n* **1** light tapping or clicking noise of a watch, clock, etc. **2** mark or symbol used to indicate approval or acknowledgment of having been noted. *vi* make a ticking sound. *vt* mark with a tick. **tick off** rebuke; scold. **tick over** (of an engine) idle.

tick[2] *n* any of a number of parasites of warm-blooded animals.

ticket *n* **1** card or slip indicating right to entry, service, etc. **2** price label. **3** slip issued for any of certain motoring offences.

tickle *vt* **1** touch lightly so as to cause laughter, pleasure, etc. **2** amuse; please. *vi* tingle; be the location of an itching sensation. *n* itching sensation. **ticklish** *adj* **1** susceptible or sensitive to tickling. **2** precarious; difficult to handle.

tide *n* **1** twice daily movement of the sea caused by the gravitational pull of the moon. **2** turning point in time. *v* **tide over** enable to cope until help or relief comes. **tidal** *adj*.

tidy *adj* neat; orderly. *vt,vi* make tidy. **tidily** *adv*. **tidiness** *n*.

tie *v* (tying) *vt* **1** fasten with a knot, bow, etc. **2** bind or secure with string, rope, etc. **3** restrict the freedom or mobility of. *vi* **1** fasten. **2** obtain an equal score or number of marks as someone else; draw. *n* **1** fastening such as string or rope. **2** obligation; restriction of freedom, etc.; commitment. **3** draw; equal score. **4** shaped piece of material worn with a shirt, fastened in a large knot at the throat.

tier *n* **1** row (of seats, etc.) above and slightly behind another or others. **2** level; layer.

tiger *n* Asiatic feline mammal with a yellow and black striped coat.

tight *adj* **1** taut; not loose. **2** fitting snugly; constricting. **3** compact. **4** strict; hard. **5** *inf also* **tight-fisted** stingy; mean; miserly. **6** *inf* drunk. **tightly** *adv*. **tightness** *n*. **tighten** *vt,vi* make or become tight(er). **tightrope** *n* taut rope or wire on which an acrobat performs. **tights** *pl n* close fitting sheer garment covering the lower part of the body, legs, and feet.

tile *n* thin flat slab used for covering roofs, floors, etc. *vt* cover with tiles.

till[1] *prep* until.

till[2] *n* box or receptacle into which money is put behind the sales counter in a shop, etc.

till[3] *vt* cultivate or work (land). **tillable** *adj*.

tiller *n* lever attached to a rudder.

tilt *vi,vt* incline; slant; lean. *n* slope; inclination.

timber *n* wood cut into planks for use in building. *vt* provide with timber.

time *n* **1** system that relates successive events, occurrences, or changes in terms of the past, present, or future. **2** measurement by means of a clock. **3** period; age. **4** period for which something lasts; duration. **5** tempo. **6** instance; moment. **7** experience of an event, emotion, etc. **8** leisure; freedom from other tasks or duties. **9** period allotted or taken to complete something. **10** occasion. **from time to time** occasionally. **in time** not late or overdue. **on time** at precisely the time fixed; punctual. ~*vt* **1** keep a record of (the amount of time needed or taken). **2** fix the time of. **time bomb** *n* bomb detonated by a timing device. **timekeeper** *n* person or mechanism that records time. **timely** *adj* happening at a fortunate or suitable time. **times** *prep* multiplied by. *pl n* period; era. **timetable** *n* schedule of times of events, arrivals, departures, etc.

timid *adj* easily frightened; shy. **timidity** *n*. **timidly** *adv*.

timpani *pl n* kettledrums.

tin *n* **1** soft silvery metal. **2** container for food, etc., made of iron and plated with tin. *vt* (-nn-) **1** cover with tin. **2** preserve (food) in airtight containers.

tinge *vt* colour faintly. *n* **1** faint colour or tint. **2** small trace; hint.

tingle *vi* experience a prickling or mildly vibrating sensation. *n* prickling feeling; mild vibration.

tinker *n* itinerant craftsman who mends or sells pots and pans. *vi* **1** work as a tinker. **2** work in a haphazard fashion. **3** meddle; interfere (with).

tinkle *n* light metallic bell-like sound. *vi,vt* make or produce such a sound.

tinsel *n* ornamental string of glittering metal threads used as a festive decoration.

tint *n* **1** shade of a colour produced by mixture with white. **2** dye; pigment. *vt* give a tint to; colour; dye.

tiny *adj* very small; minute.

tip[1] *n* end; extremity, esp. of anything tapering to a point. **tiptoe** *vi* walk very quietly. *n* **on tiptoe** standing or walking on the balls of the feet; straining to reach up.

tip[2] *v* (-pp-) *vt,vi* lean or tilt to one side. *vt* **1** pour out or dump by tipping the container. **2**

touch or raise (one's hat). **tip over** topple; overturn. ~*n* place where rubbish is dumped.

tip[3] *n* **1** extra payment in appreciation of services rendered. **2** useful hint or advice. *vt,vi* (-pp-) give a tip (to) **tip off** give a tip-off to. **tip-off** *n* advance warning or confirmation of advantage to the recipient.

tipsy *adj* inebriated; tight; slightly drunk.

tired *adj* **1** weary; suffering from fatigue; sleepy. **2** bored; fed up; no longer interested. **tire** *vt,vi* make or become tired. **tireless** *adj* unwearying. **tiresome** *adj* wearying; trying; irritating.

tissue *n* **1** finely woven thin paper. **2** substance consisting of cells forming the structure of plants and animals.

tithe *n* (formerly) tenth part of agricultural produce, levied as a tax.

title *n* **1** name by which a person or thing may be distinguished. **2** heading by which a novel, play, etc., is known. **3** position or mode of address, esp. of a member of the nobility. **4** legal right to possess something.

to *prep* **1** in the direction of. **2** as far as. **3** into the state of. **4** giving the result of. **5** near or in contact with. **6** in comparison with. **7** with the extent of. **8** conforming with. **9** for use with or on. **10** in the opinion of. **11** until. **12** into the possession of. **13** used before the infinitive form of a verb. *adv.* **1** fixed; closed. **2** into consciousness. **to and fro** alternately backwards and forwards. **to-do** *n* fuss; bother; commotion.

toad *n* **1** small tailless greenish-brown amphibian with a dry warty skin. **2** unpleasant person. **toadstool** *n* umbrella-shaped fungus living on dead organic matter.

toast[1] *n* slice of bread browned by heat on each side. *vt,vi* crisp; brown under heat.

toast[2] *vt* drink to the health of (a person, etc.). *n* drink in honour of a person, country, etc., or words proposing such a drink.

tobacco *n* **1** tall annual plant with large broad leaves. **2** cured leaves of this plant used in cigarettes, cigars, etc. **tobacconist** *n* person or shop selling tobacco.

toboggan *n* small sledge used on snow slopes for winter sport. *vi* ride on a toboggan.

today *n* this present day. *adv* **1** now; on this very day. **2** nowadays; at the present time.

toddle *vi* walk with an unsteady uneven gait, as a child learning to walk. **toddle along** *inf* go at an easy unhurried pace. **toddler** *n* child between the ages of one and three approximately, who is beginning to walk.

toe *n* **1** digit of the foot. **2** part of a shoe, stocking, etc., covering this. *v* **toe the line** obey; do as one is told. **toenail** *n* nail covering the toe.

toffee *n* sweet made of boiled sugar. **toffee-apple** *n* apple coated in toffee. **toffee-nosed** *adj sl* snobbish; conceited.

together *adv* **1** in close proximity. **2** in the company of one or more other persons. **3** simultaneously; at the same time.

toil *vi* **1** work hard and long. **2** proceed slowly and with difficulty. *n* labour; hard work.

toilet *n* **1** process of washing, combing one's hair, etc. **2** lavatory; W.C. **toilet water** *n* dilute solution of perfume.

token *n* **1** something used to represent or serve as a substitute. **2** symbol; gesture. **3** small gift; memento. **4** metal or plastic voucher used in place of money. *adj* **1** serving as a token. **2** in name only; having little practical effect.

told *v pp* and *pt* of **tell.**

tolerate *vt* allow; permit; endure. **tolerable** *adj* bearable. **tolerably** *adv* moderately; to a certain extent. **tolerance** *n* **1** *also* **toleration** forbearance; fair-mindedness; freedom from bigotry. **2** degree to which something can withstand specified conditions, etc.

toll[1] *n* **1** payment exacted for use of a bridge, road, etc., in certain circumstances. **2** price paid; number or amount sacrificed.

toll[2] *vt,vi* ring or cause to ring with slow heavy strokes.

tomato *n, pl* **tomatoes** juicy red fruit usually served as a vegetable with seasoning.

tomb *n* place where the dead are buried or laid out in a hollow chamber.

tomorrow *n* **1** the day after today. **2** the future. *adv* on the day after today.

ton *n* measure of weight equivalent to 2240 pounds (approx. 1016 kilograms).

tone *n* **1** quality of a musical note. **2** pure musical note. **3** manner of speaking, writing, etc., indicating attitude or emotion. **4** general physical or moral condition. **5** shade of colour; tint. *v* **tone down** reduce; soften; calm. **tonal** *adj.* **tonality** *n* system of musical keys, esp. in traditional Western music.

tongs *pl n* instrument consisting of two hinged arms for grasping objects.

tongue *n* **1** flexible organ in the mouth used in eating and in forming speech. **2** language; method or tone of speaking. **3** anything shaped like a tongue. **tongue in cheek** insincerely or ironically. **tongue-tied** *adj* **1** suffering from a speech defect. **2** speechless; inarticulate. **tongue-twister** *n* phrase or sentence that is difficult to pronounce because of unusual sound combinations.

tonic *n* **1** medicine used to stimulate and invigorate. **2** anything with this effect. **3** key on which a musical work is primarily based.

tonight *n* the night of the present day. *adv* on this night or evening.

tonsils *pl n* pair of oval-shaped organs situated on each side of the back of the throat. **tonsillitis** *n* enlargement or inflammation of the tonsils due to infection.

too *adv* **1** also; in addition; as well. **2** to an excessive extent.

took *v pt* of **take.**

tool *n* **1** instrument used in making or doing something; implement. **2** person used to serve another's purpose. **3** useful device; means. *vt,vi* use a tool (on).

tooth *n, pl* **teeth** **1** hard projection in the jaws of humans and most vertebrates, used for biting, chewing, etc. **2** any similar projection, as on a comb. **toothbrush** *n* brush used for cleaning the teeth.

top[1] *n* **1** highest point; peak. **2** upper part. **3** highest position. **4** cap or cover of a bottle, jar, box, etc. **blow one's top** lose one's temper. ~*adj* best; highest. *vt* (-pp-) **1** take the top off. **2** cover or form the top of. **3** surpass. **top up** add extra liquid to so as to fill. **top hat** *n* tall cylindrical hat worn by men on formal occasions. **top-heavy** *adj* **1** disproportionately heavier or thicker above than below and thus unstable. **2** with too much emphasis on certain parts. **topmost** *adj* highest. **topsoil** *n* uppermost and most fertile layer of the earth's crust.

top[2] *n* small shaped object made to balance by spinning on a point, used esp. as a toy.

topic *n* subject; theme. **topical** *adj* of current interest.

topography *n* detailed geographical description or representation of the features of an area.

topple *vi,vt* fall or cause to fall over; overturn. *vt* overthrow; depose.

topsy-turvy *adj,adv* **1** upside down. **2** confused; muddled.

torch *n* **1** burning material held on a stick. **2** device carried by hand for giving light, usually operated by a battery.

tore *v pt* of **tear**.

torment *n* ('tɔːment) severe mental or physical distress; anguish. *vt* (tɔː'ment) **1** torture; distress. **2** pester; harass.

torn *v pp* of **tear**.

tornado *n, pl* **tornadoes** *or* **tornados** violent storm of short duration with a characteristic rotating movement and funnel-shaped cloud.

torpedo *n, pl* **torpedoes** self-propelled missile carried by a submarine for use against ships. *vt* hit with or as if with a torpedo.

torrent *n* **1** rapidly flowing stream of large quantities of water. **2** any copious rapid flow, as of words, abuse, etc. **torrential** *adj.*

torso *n* trunk of the human body.

tortoise *n* slow-moving reptile with a bony shell and scaly head and legs.

tortuous *adj* **1** twisting; winding; snakelike. **2** devious; unnecessarily complicated.

torture *n* **1** severe pain inflicted as a punishment or method of persuasion. **2** any extreme physical or mental distress. *vt* **1** inflict torture on. **2** cause extreme agony, pain, or distress in. **torturous** *adj.*

Tory *n* supporter of the Conservative party. *adj* belonging or relating to this party.

toss *vt* **1** throw into the air. **2** move (the head, hair, etc.) upwards with a jerk. *vt,vi* **1** move about or up and down quickly and in an irregular manner; pitch; jerk. **2** move restlessly, as in sleep. **3** *also* **toss up** spin (a coin) in the air to decide something. **toss off** finish quickly. ~*n* act of tossing or being tossed.

tot[1] *n* **1** small child. **2** small measure of alcoholic liquor.

tot[2] *v* **tot up** (-tt-) add up; count.

total *n* **1** complete whole as compared with a part. **2** final figure obtained by addition. *adj* **1** complete; final. **2** absolute; unrestrained. *vt,vi* (-ll-) add up (to).

totalitarian *adj* (of a government) characterized by absolute authority; allowing no opposition. **totalitarianism** *n.*

totem *n* object, esp. an animal, regarded as having special significance for a clan, tribe, etc. **totem-pole** *n* carved post used as a totem by North American Indians.

totter *vi* **1** walk unsteadily. **2** be in a precarious state.

touch *vt,vi* **1** bring or come into contact with. **2** bring the hand into contact with; feel. **3** *also* **touch (up)on** allude to; mention in passing. *vt* **1** affect; influence. **2** deal with; be associated with. **3** *sl* borrow money from. *n* **1** sense by which objects in contact with the body are felt. **2** act of touching, esp. a light brush or blow. **3** small amount of something. **4** knack; ability. **5** *sl* act of borrowing money or the person borrowed from. **in touch 1** aware. **2** having correspondence or contact (with). **touched** *adj* **1** emotionally moved. **2** slightly mad. **touching** *adj* producing pity or sympathy; moving. **touchy** *adj* easily offended.

tough *adj* **1** strong; hard-wearing. **2** hardy; robust; capable of suffering hardship. **3** (of food) difficult to chew. **4** stubborn; uncompromising. **5** difficult. **6** vicious; rough. *n* ruffian; lout. **toughness** *n*. **toughen** *vt* make tough(er); strengthen.

toupee *n* small patch of false hair worn to cover a bald spot.

tour *n* journey through several places, usually for sightseeing. *vt,vi* make a tour (through). **tourism** *n* business catering for the needs of tourists. **tourist** *n* person, esp. a holidaymaker, visiting a city, foreign country, etc.

tournament *n* **1** medieval contest between armed horsemen. **2** organized competition involving several matches, as in tennis, chess, etc.

tow *vt* pull along behind, as with a rope. *n* act of towing.

towards *prep also* **toward 1** in the direction of. **2** close to; in the vicinity of. **3** as a contribution to.

towel *n* cloth or paper for drying things. **throw in the towel** surrender; concede. ~*vt,vi* (-ll-) dry with a towel. **towelling** *n* type of absorbent cloth used for towels.

tower *n* tall cylindrical or square-shaped construction, forming part of a church, castle, etc. **tower of strength** strong reliable person. **in an ivory tower** insulated from reality. ~*vi* rise up to great heights. **tower above** *or* **over 1** be much higher than. **2** be greatly superior to.

town *n* **1** group of houses, shops, etc., larger than a village and smaller than a city. **2** inhabitants of a town. **go to town** act in a wholehearted or unrestrained manner. **town clerk** *n* official in charge of civic records. **town hall** *n* public building used as the administrative centre of a town.

toxic *adj* poisonous.

toy *n* **1** plaything of a child. **2** trifle; something treated lightly. *adj* **1** relating to or like a toy. **2** (esp. of a dog) bred specially to be smaller in size than average. *v* **toy with 1** play or trifle with. **2** consider; ponder about.

trace *vt* **1** follow (a track, path, etc.). **2** discover or find by careful searching. **3** copy by overlaying a transparent sheet and marking the lines. **4** draw; sketch. *n* **1** trail; track. **2** sign showing former presence of something. **3** small amount; vestige.

track *n* **1** mark or marks left by the passage of something; trail. **2** path. **3** path designed for guiding something, as in a railway. **4** course on which races are held. **5** series of metal plates fitted instead of wheels to vehicles such as tractors, tanks, etc. *vt,vi* follow the track of. **track down** find by searching. **tracksuit** *n* loose-fitting garment fastened at the neck wrists, and ankles, worn by athletes in training.

tract[1] *n* **1** large area of water or land; expanse **2** bodily structure or system serving a specialized function. **3** bundle of nerve fibres

tract[2] *n* treatise or pamphlet.

tractor *n* vehicle with large wheels or tracks, for use esp. on farms.

trade *n* **1** business; commerce. **2** interchange of goods and money on an agreed basis. **3** skilled manual craft. *vt,vi* exchange for money or other goods; barter. *vi* engage in a business **trade in** give in part exchange for something **trade on** exploit. **trader** *n*. **trademark** *n* **1** mark or name registered by a manufacturer for a product. **2** characteristic trait. **tradesman** *n pl* **-men 1** person engaged in trade, esp a small shopkeeper. **2** skilled worker. **trade union** *n* association of people engaged in the same trade pledged to protect standards of wages, working conditions, etc.

tradition *n* beliefs and practices passed down from earlier generations. **traditional** *adj* **traditionally** *adv*.

traffic *n* **1** motor vehicles using a road. **2** movement of ships, aircraft, etc. **3** trade commerce. *vi* (-ck-) trade (in), esp. illicitly.

tragedy *n* **1** prose or drama with an inevitable unhappy ending. **2** sad event; great misfortune. **tragic** *adj* **1** in the style of a tragedy. **2** sad; moving; calamitous. **tragically** *adv*.

trail *n* track left behind by a person, animal, or thing. *vt* **1** drag or pull behind. **2** track; pursue. **3** hang loosely. *vi* **1** walk wearily with lagging steps. **2** hang or grow downwards. **trailer** *n* **1** vehicle attached to and pulled by another. **2** series of short extracts used to advertise a film.

train *n* **1** number of railway carriages or wagons coupled together and drawn by an engine. **2** succession of things, persons, or events. **3** part of a gown or robe trailing behind. *vt* **1** impart skill or knowledge to. **2** teach (an animal) to obey commands or perform tricks. **3** encourage (plants) to grow as required. **4** point (a gun, camera, etc.) at. *vi* **1** receive instruction. **2** exercise regularly to increase fitness. **trainee** *n*. **trainer** *n*.

traipse *vi* trudge; follow a long or circuitous route; wander about aimlessly; trek. *n* long tiring walk or journey.

traitor *n* person who betrays a trust, esp. one who commits treason. **traitorous** *adj*.

tram *n* passenger car running on a metal track on a road. **tramlines** *pl n* **1** tracks on which trams run. **2** parallel lines on a tennis court marking the boundaries of the singles court.

tramp *vi* walk with heavy tread. *vi,vt* walk (a certain distance), as for recreation. *n* **1** itinerant vagrant living by casual work or begging. **2** sound of someone tramping. **3** walk, esp. a long recreational walk.

trample *vt,vi* tread under foot; crush with the feet.

trampoline *n* gymnasium apparatus consisting of a sheet attached to a framework by springs, used for jumping, performing somersaults, etc. *vi* exercise on a trampoline.

trance *n* dreamlike semi-conscious state produced by hypnotism, drugs, etc.

tranquil *adj* calm; peaceful; unruffled. **tranquillity** *n*. **tranquillize** *vt* make tranquil; calm down. **tranquillizer** *n* drug used to reduce anxiety.

transact *vt,vi* perform; carry out (something, esp. a business deal). **transaction** *n*.

transatlantic *adj* **1** across or beyond the Atlantic Ocean. **2** relating to North America.

transcend *vt,vi* excel; surpass; exceed. **transcendent** *adj*. **transcendental** *adj* of or connected with the philosophy of seeking after truth by exploring the inner self. **transcendentalism** *n*.

transcribe *vt* copy out in writing. **transcription** *n*.

transfer *vt,vi* (træns'fə:) (-rr-) **1** move from one place to another. **2** change from one position, job, responsibility, etc., to another. **3** make over (power, responsibility, etc.) to another. *n* ('trænsfə:) **1** act of transferring. **2** prepared design or picture on paper that can be transferred to another surface.

transform *vt,vi* change in character, nature, shape, etc. **transformation** *n*.

transfusion *n* transfer of blood from one person to another or injection of other fluids to make up loss of blood. **transfuse** *vt* give a transfusion of.

transient *adj* transitory.

transistor *n* small electronic component made of certain solid materials. **transistorized** *adj* (of a piece of electronic equipment) using transistors rather than valves.

transit *n* **1** act of crossing or being conveyed from one place to another. **2** act of moving across. **transition** *n* **1** change from one place or set of circumstances or conditions to another. **2** process of continuous change or development. **transitory** *adj* changing; of limited duration.

transitive *adj* designating a verb that takes a direct object.

translate *vt,vi* **1** express in another language. **2** interpret; explain the meaning of. **translation** *n*. **translator** *n*.

translucent *adj* allowing light to pass through but not allowing a clear image of an object to be seen.

transmit *vt* (-tt-) **1** send across; pass on; communicate. **2** act as a condition or medium for. **transmission** *n*. **transmitter** *n* device used to broadcast radio or television signals.

transparent *adj* **1** transmitting rays of light; clear. **2** easily seen or detected. **transparently** *adv*. **transparency** *n* **1** quality of being transparent. **2** transparent photographic print projected or viewed by transmitted light.

transplant *vt* (træns'pla:nt) **1** dig up and plant elsewhere. **2** transfer (living tissue or an organ) from one person to another. *n* ('trænsplɑ:nt) act of transplanting or something transplanted.

transport *n* ('trænspɔ:t) **1** means of conveying a person or thing from one place to another. **2** vehicle used for this purpose. *vt* (træn'spɔ:t) **1** carry; move from one place to another. **2** carry away, as with emotion.

transpose *vt* **1** cause to exchange positions. **2** rewrite (music) in a different key. **transposition** *n*.

trap *n* **1** device for catching an animal. **2** trick to place someone in an unfavourable position. **3** hazard; pitfall. **4** device to prevent passage of gas, impurities, etc. **5** light open horse-drawn carriage. **6** stall from which greyhounds are released for a race. **7** *also* **trap door** door in a floor or ceiling. *vt* (-pp-) catch or remove by means of a trap. **trapper** *n* person who traps animals for fur.

trapeze *n* apparatus used by gymnasts or acrobats, consisting of two suspended ropes carrying a horizontal crossbar.

trash *n* **1** rubbish; refuse. **2** anything considered worthless or shoddy.

trauma *n* violent emotional shock or experience. **traumatic** *adj*.

travel *v* (-ll-) *vi* **1** go on a journey; make a trip. **2** go abroad frequently or regularly. **3** move; proceed. **4** move from place to place selling goods. *vt* cover (a specified distance).- **traveller** *n* **1** person who travels. **2** person employed to travel in goods; travelling salesman. **travels** *pl n* trips or journeys, esp. abroad.

traverse *vt,vi* cross from one side or corner to another. *n* act of crossing over or through.

trawl *n* large net pulled behind a boat to catch fish. *vi,vt* catch (fish) with a trawl. **trawler** *n* fishing boat equipped with a trawl.

tray *n* flat piece of wood, metal, etc., often with a raised edge, for carrying objects.

treacherous *adj* **1** deceitful; betraying a trust. **2** dangerous; hazardous. **treachery** *n*.

treacle *n* thick sticky syrup obtained by refining sugar.

tread *v* (trod; trod *or* trodden) *vi,vt* put the foot down on (something) or apply pressure to (something) with the foot. *vi* walk. *vt* **1** walk on (a path, road, etc.). **2** mark a floor with (mud, dirt, etc.) carried on the feet. **tread on 1** oppress. **2** crush; stamp out. ~*n* **1** act or manner of treading. **2** part of a tyre that makes contact with the ground, usually having a patterned surface to improve the grip. **3** horizontal part of a step.

treason *n* disloyalty to a sovereign or the state.

treasure *n* object or collection of objects of value. *vt* value or regard greatly; cherish. **treasurer** *n* person in charge of funds of a society, group, etc. **treasury** *n* storehouse for treasure. **the Treasury** government department responsible for finance.

treat *vt* **1** deal with; handle. **2** prescribe medicine or medical care for. **3** act towards or regard. **4** buy something for. **5** act upon; apply a process to. *n* **1** entertainment or a gift paid for by someone else. **2** something producing joy or pleasure. **treatment** *n* **1** act or manner of treating a person or thing. **2** course of medical care.

treaty *n* formal agreement between nations.

treble *vt,vi* multiply or be multiplied by three. *n* soprano or a voice or instrument in this range. *adj* threefold; multiplied by three.

tree *n* perennial plant with a thick trunk of wood topped by branches and leaves.

trek *vi* (-kk-) make a long slow journey, esp. through difficult country. *n* journey of this kind.

trellis *n* framework of criss-crossed bars used as a plant support, decorative screen, etc.

tremble *vi* **1** shake or quiver, as from cold, fear, etc. **2** be afraid. **3** vibrate. *n* act or an instance of trembling.

tremendous *adj* **1** overpowering; astonishing. **2** *inf* great; considerable. **tremendously** *adv*.

tremor *n* trembling; shaking; quivering.

trench *n* **1** narrow ditch dug in the ground. **2** ditch with soil parapets, used by soldiers during battle. *vi,vt* dig a trench (in).

trend *n* **1** movement or tendency in a particular direction. **2** *inf* fashion. **trendy** *adj inf* up-to-date; fashionable.

trespass *vi* **1** intrude upon private property without permission. **2** encroach upon. *n* act of trespassing. **trespasser** *n*.

trestle *n* structure consisting of a beam with hinged legs, used to support a plank, table top, etc.

trial *n* **1** test; experiment. **2** trying experience; hardship. **3** formal inquiry in court.

triangle *n* **1** plane figure bounded by three straight lines. **2** steel musical instrument of this shape sounded by striking with a small rod. **triangular** *adj.*

tribe *n* **1** group of people, usually primitive, with a common ancestry, culture, etc. **2** group of related animals or plants. **tribal** *adj.*

tribunal *n* **1** court of justice. **2** board or group appointed to settle any matter in dispute.

tributary *n* small river flowing into a larger one.

tribute *n* **1** payment in money or kind made by one ruler or country to another as an act or submission. **2** mark or expression of respect.

trick *n* **1** action or device intended to deceive. **2** skill; knack. **3** prank; joke. **4** cards played in one round. *vt,vi* deceive; delude; cheat. **trickery** *n.* **tricky** *adj* **1** crafty; deceitful. **2** difficult; complicated.

tricycle *n* vehicle with three wheels propelled with pedals.

trifle *n* **1** small object. **2** matter of little value or importance. **3** cold dessert sweet consisting of layers of cream, custard, fruit, and sponge. *v* **trifle with** act insincerely towards.

trigger *n* **1** device releasing the spring mechanism of a gun. **2** any device that sets off or initiates something. *vt also* **trigger off** set off; cause; initiate.

trill *n* high-pitched vibrating sound. *vi,vt* utter or sing with a trill.

trim *vt* (-mm-) **1** make neat or tidy, as by clipping. **2** cut away (superfluous material) from. *adj* **1** neat; tidy. **2** smart; in good condition. *n* **1** correct condition; good order. **2** act of trimming, esp. the hair. **trimmings** *pl n* additional decoration or garnish.

trio *n* group of three, esp. three singers or musicians.

trip *n* **1** journey; excursion. **2** stumble or fall. **3** mistake; slip. **4** sudden starting of a mechanism. *v* (-pp-) *vi,vt* **1** stumble or cause to stumble. **2** make or cause to make a mistake. **3** release (a mechanism) or (of a mechanism) be released. *vi* dance; skip.

tripe *n* **1** white lining of the stomach of a ruminant, used for food. **2** *sl* rubbish; worthless material.

triple *adj* **1** three times as great, threefold. **2** of three parts or kinds. *n* anything that is a group of three. *vt,vi* multiply or be multiplied by three. **triplet** *n* **1** one of three children born at the same birth. **2** any one of a group of three.

tripod *n* stand with three legs, for supporting a camera, etc.

trite *adj* commonplace; hackneyed.

triumph *n* **1** victory. **2** notable achievement; great success. *vi* **1** gain a victory; win. **2** achieve great success. **3** rejoice in something; exult. **triumphant** *adj* **1** victorious. **2** exultant.

trivial *adj* insignificant; of no account. **triviality** *n.*

trod *v pt* and a *pp* of **tread. trodden** *v* a *pp* of **tread.**

trolley *n* **1** small hand-drawn wheeled vehicle for carrying goods, dishes, etc. **2** wheel on the end of a pole running on an overhead cable, used to draw electric current to drive a bus (trolleybus) or tram.

trombone *n* long brass instrument, usually having a moving slide to control the notes. **trombonist** *n.*

troop *n* **1** body of soldiers. **2** group of people or animals. *vi* march or proceed in a group. **troops** *pl n* soldiers.

trophy *n* memento of a victory; prize; award.

tropic *n* one of two lines of latitude, either 23°28' north (tropic of Cancer) or 23°28' south (tropic of Capricorn) of the equator. **tropical** *adj* relating to the tropics. **tropics** *pl n* region between these lines of latitude.

trot *n* **1** pace between walking and running. **2** pace of horses with diagonal pairs of legs moving together. *vi* (-tt-) move with a trot. **trot out** produce; introduce. **trotter** *n* **1** horse bred for trotting. **2** foot of a pig or certain other animals.

trouble *n* **1** disturbance; uneasiness. **2** affliction; distress. **3** person or thing causing trouble or worry. **4** care; pains; effort. *vt* afflict; annoy; inconvenience. *vi* take pains; bother; make an effort

trough (trɔf) *n* **1** long narrow vessel holding food or drink for animals. **2** area of low barometric pressure.

troupe *n* group of performers.

trousers *pl n* garment designed to cover the legs and lower part of the body.

trout *n, pl* **trout** *or* **trouts** brownish speckled edible fish of the salmon family.

trowel *n* **1** flat-bladed tool with a pointed tip, used to spread mortar. **2** hand tool used by gardeners. *vt* (-ll-) use a trowel on.

truant *n* child absenting himself from school without permission. **truancy** *n.*

truce *n* temporary cessation of hostilities by mutual agreement.

truck *n* strong vehicle for carrying heavy loads.

trudge *vi* walk wearily. *n* long or tiring walk.

true *adj* **1** relating to truth; in accordance with facts; not false. **2** legitimate; rightful. **3** real; genuine. **4** exact; precise; correct. **5** faithful; reliable. **truly** *adv* **1** sincerely; honestly; truthfully. **2** really; absolutely.

trump *n* card of a suit ranking above the others for the duration of a game or round. *vt,vi* defeat by playing a trump.

trumpet *n* long funnel-shaped brass wind instrument, usually having three valves. *vi* make a loud noise similar to that of a trumpet. **trumpeter** *n*.

truncheon *n* short wooden club used esp. by policemen.

trundle *vt,vi* roll along or propel on or as if on wheels or castors.

trunk *n* **1** large strong box with a hinged lid for storing or transporting goods. **2** main stem of a tree. **3** human body, excluding the head and limbs; torso. **4** main telephone line. **5** long flexible snout of an elephant. **trunk call** *n* long distance call on a main telephone line.

trust *n* **1** belief in someone's honesty or something's reliability. **2** responsibility. **3** good faith. **4** association of companies combining for trade. **hold in trust** take legal charge for benefit of another. ~*vt,vi* place or have trust (in). **trustee** *n* person holding property or money in trust for another. **trustworthy** *adj* deserving of trust; reliable; dependable.

truth *n* fact, statement, or concept that is known to be true or can be verified. **truthful** *adj* given to speaking the truth. **truthfully** *adv*.

try *vt,vi* **1** attempt or make an effort to do (something). **2** test, as by experiment. *vt* **1** irritate; strain. **2** subject to a trial. **try on** put (a garment) on to test the fit. ~*n* **1** attempt; effort. **2** score of four points in rugby made by grounding the ball behind the opponent's line.

tsar *n also* **czar** Russian emperor.

T-shirt *n* short-sleeved shirt without buttons or collar.

tub *n* **1** small barrel. **2** bath, esp. one filled by hand. **tubby** *adj* shaped like a tub; chubby; rotund.

tuba *n* large low-pitched brass instrument.

tube *n* **1** long hollow cylinder. **2** narrow flexible container for toothpaste, etc. **the Tube** London's underground railway. **tubular** *adj*.

tuber *n* thick underground stem of certain plants on which buds are formed at or below ground level.

tuberculosis *n* disease produced by bacteria attacking body tissues, esp. the respiratory tract.

tuck *vt,vi* **1** fold under. **2** push or fit into a small space. **3** draw (the legs or arms) in close to the body. **4** make folds in (a material). **tuck in** eat heartily. ~*n* **1** small fold sewn into a garment. **2** position in which the knees are drawn up close to the chest.

Tuesday *n* third day of the week.

tuft *n* bunch of strands, hairs, etc.

tug *vt,vi* (-gg-) pull sharply or with force. *n* **1** act of tugging. **2** small boat used to tow larger boats. **tug-of-war** *n, pl* **tugs-of-war** sporting contest between two teams, each holding one end of a rope and trying to pull the other over a line between them.

tuition *n* instruction; teaching.

tulip *n* bulb producing a brightly coloured bell-shaped flower on a single upright stem.

tumble *vi,vt* **1** fall or cause to fall; topple. **2** move in an ungainly manner. **3** roll or toss about. **4** decrease or lose value sharply. *n* fall. **tumbler** *n* **1** acrobat who performs somersaults, etc. **2** stemless drinking glass.

tummy *n inf* stomach.

tumour *n* local swelling from a benign or malignant growth.

tumult ('tju:mʌlt) *n* noisy or violent disturbance, as of a crowd; uproar. **tumultuous** *adj*.

tuna *n also* **tunny** large ocean fish of the mackerel family with pinkish edible flesh.

tune *n* **1** sequence of musical notes forming a melody. **2** piece of music, song, etc. **out of/in tune** having the incorrect/correct pitch. **out of/in tune with** unsympathetic/sympathetic to. ~*vt* **1** adjust (a musical instrument) so as to obtain the correct pitch. **2** adjust (a radio, etc.) so as to obtain the correct setting. **3** adjust (a car engine) to improve performance. **tune in** adjust a radio to receive a particular programme. **tune up** (of an orchestra) check instruments to ensure that they are in tune before performing. **tuneful** *adj* melodious. **tunefully** *adv*. **tuning fork** *n* device with two prongs, which produce a sound of a set pitch when vibrated.

tunic *n* loose-fitting kneelength garment.
tunnel *n* underground passage. *vi,vt* (-ll-) make a tunnel (through).
turban *n* **1** headdress consisting of a long scarf wound around a cap, traditionally worn by men in parts of N Africa, India, etc. **2** woman's hat resembling this.
turbine *n* engine in which a wheel is turned by the direct force of steam, water, etc.
turbulent *adj* **1** restless; disturbed; tumultuous. **2** (of liquids) not flowing smoothly; agitated. **turbulence** *n*.
tureen (tju'ri:n) *n* large dish from which soup is served.
turf *n, pl* **turves** *or* **turfs** **1** ground covered with short close-growing springy grass. **2** single piece of grass and soil cut from the ground. **the turf** horseracing. ~*vt* cover with turf. **turf accountant** *n* bookmaker; person who takes legal bets on horseraces.
turkey *n* large domesticated bird used for food.
turmoil *n* state of confusion or anarchy; turbulence.
turn *vt,vi* **1** rotate; move around; spin. **2** face or cause to face a different direction. **3** go around (a corner). **4** move in a different direction. **5** change (into a specified state or condition); transform. *vt* **1** move (a page) over so as to display the other side. **2** dig or plough (the soil). **3** shape on a lathe. **4** reach (a specified age). *vi* **1** become sour, rancid, etc. **2** change colour. **turn away** send away; refuse. **turn down 1** refuse. **2** reduce the volume or intensity of. **3** fold down. **turn in 1** hand in; deliver. **2** go to bed. **3** finish; give up. **turn off 1** branch off; deviate. **2** cause to stop operating. **3** *sl* repel; disgust. **turn on 1** cause to operate. **2** produce automatically. **3** *sl* arouse; attract. **4** attack without warning. **5** *sl* initiate, esp. into the use of drugs. **turn out 1** stop (a light, gas burner, etc.) operating. **2** produce; make. **3** expel. **4** become; develop into. **5** assemble; gather. **6** dress; array. **7** clear out the contents of. **turn over 1** move so as to reverse top and bottom; shift position. **2** start (an engine). **3** deliver; hand over. **4** (of an engine) function correctly. **5** handle (a specified amount of stock or money) in a business. **turn tail** run away; flee. **turn to** have recourse to; seek help from. **turn up 1** appear; attend. **2** be found or discovered as if by chance. **3** increase the volume or intensity of. **4** point upwards. ~*n* **1** act or instance of turning. **2** one of a number of successive periods during which different people have the right or responsibility of doing something. **3** short spell of work, etc. **4** distinctive style. **5** something done to affect someone. **6** need; requirement. **7** *inf* shock; surprise. **8** short walk. **at every turn** on all occasions; in all directions. **to a turn** perfectly. **turn-off** *n* road branching off from a main road. **turnout** *n* **1** group of people appearing at a gathering. **2** output. **3** style in which someone is dressed or something is equipped. **4** act of clearing out the contents of something. **turnover** *n* **1** small pastry containing fruit or jam. **2** amount handled, produced, used, etc., during a specified period. **turntable** *n* **1** revolving circular table of a record player. **2** revolving platform for turning a locomotive. **turnup** *n* **1** cloth folded up at the bottom of a trouser leg. **2** chance occurrence.
turnip *n* vegetable having a rounded purplish edible root.
turpentine *n also inf* **turps** oily resin of several types of conifers, used in mixing paints.
turquoise *n* opaque greenish-blue stone. *adj,n* blue-green.
turret *n* **1** small round or square tower attached to a larger building. **2** revolving structure for a gun on a ship, tank, etc.
turtle *n* large marine reptile similar to a tortoise.
turves *n a pl of* **turf.**
tusk *n* long pointed tooth of an elephant, walrus, etc., protruding from the closed mouth.
tussle *vi,n* struggle; scuffle; fight.
tutor *n* **1** private teacher. **2** university teacher in charge of the studies of individual students or small groups. **tutorial** *n* teaching session run by a university tutor.
twang *n* resonant sound of the type produced by plucking a string. *vi,vt* produce a twang.
tweed *n* rough woollen fabric made from interwoven colours, used esp. for clothing.
tweezers *pl n* small metal tongs, used to lift small objects or pull out splinters, hairs, etc.
twelve *n* **1** number equal to one plus eleven. **2** group of twelve people, things, etc. **3** *also* **twelve o'clock** noon or midnight. *adj* amounting to twelve. **twelfth** *adj* coming between eleventh and thirteenth in sequence. *adv* after the eleventh. *n* **1** twelfth person, thing, etc. **2**

one of twelve equal parts; one divided by twelve.

twenty *n* **1** number equal to twice ten. **2** twenty things or people. *adj* amounting to twenty. **twentieth** *adj,adv,n*

twice *adv* **1** two times. **2** multiplied by two. **3** on two occasions. **4** doubly; two times as much or many.

twiddle *vt,vi* twirl; turn to and fro; fidget (with).

twig *n* small shoot of a branch of a tree or bush. *vt* (-gg-) *inf* catch the significance of.

twilight *n* evening light as the sun is setting; dusk.

twin *n* **1** one of two children born at one birth. **2** one of any identical or closely related pair. *adj* relating to a twin or pair. *vt* (-nn-) bring together as a couple or pair; match exactly.

twine *n* string made up of twisted strands. *vt,vi* wind; coil; entwine.

twinge *n* **1** sudden shooting pain. **2** sudden pang as of conscience, regret, etc.

twinkle *vi* **1** sparkle; glitter; flash intermittently. **2** move lightly and rapidly. *n* single flash; gleam.

twirl *vt,vi* revolve or cause to revolve; turn in rapid circles. *n* single rapid turn or flourish.

twist *vt,vi* **1** alter in shape by a rotating or screwing motion; wrench; contort. **2** wind or twine. *vt* **1** alter or misinterpret the meaning of. **2** *inf* deceive; cheat. *vi* **1** rotate or turn sharply. **2** writhe. *n* **1** twisting movement; turn; rotation. **2** anything twisted, as in a spiral. **3** unexpected turn of events.

twitch *vt,vi* **1** make spasmodic or convulsive muscle movements. **2** pull; jerk; pluck. *n* act of twitching; jerk.

twitter *vi,vt* chirp; produce a continuous chattering sound. *vi* tremble.

two *n* **1** number equal to one plus one. **2** group of two persons, things, etc. **3** *also* **two o'clock** two hours after noon or midnight. *adj* amounting to two. **two-faced** *adj* hypocritical; deceitful. **twosome** *n* **1** pair; couple, esp. when exclusive of others. **2** game with two players. **two-way** *adj* **1** operating in two directions. **2** reciprocal; of mutual benefit.

tycoon *n* wealthy powerful businessman.

type *n* **1** kind; sort. **2** class; category. **3** block of material carrying relief characters for printing. **4** printed characters considered collectively. *vt,vi* use a typewriter (for). *vt* assign to a type; classify. **typecast** *vt* (-cast) cast (an actor) in a part similar to parts he has played before. **typewriter** *n* machine for printing characters on paper, operated by pressing keys, which strike an ink-impregnated ribbon. **typical** *adj* **1** characteristic; normal or average. **2** showing the essential properties of a category. **typically** *adv*. **typify** *vt* represent; be typical of. **typist** *n* person who uses a typewriter, esp. a person employed to type.

typhoid *n* *also* **typhoid fever** infectious intestinal disease caused by bacilli growing in contaminated food or water.

typhoon *n* violent cyclonic storm occurring in the W Pacific Ocean.

tyrant *n* harsh ruler or master; despot. **tyranny** *n*. **tyrannical** *adj*. **tyrannize** *vt* treat tyrannically; terrorize.

tyre *n* solid or air-filled rubber tube held round the circumference of a vehicle wheel.

U

ubiquitous *adj* present everywhere. **ubiquity** *n*.

udder *n* external organ of cows, goats, etc., through which milk is secreted.

ugly *adj* **1** unpleasant to look at; repulsive; offensive. **2** threatening; angry. **ugliness** *n*.

ukulele *n* four-stringed instrument resembling but smaller than a guitar.

ulcer *n* open sore on the skin or an internal membrane, which is slow to heal.

ulterior *adj* **1** further away in time or space; distant. **2** not disclosed; deep-seated.

ultimate *adj* **1** last; final. **2** most desirable or significant. *n* **1** basis; final stage. **2** best; greatest; most desirable. **ultimately** *adv* eventually; in the end. **ultimatum** *n* final proposal of terms whose rejection will cancel further negotiations; deadline.

ultraviolet *n* invisible radiation having wavelengths between that of violet light and x-rays.

umbrella *n* portable collapsible object used as protection against rain or sun.

umpire *n* impartial person who enforces rules and settles disputes in cricket, tennis, etc. *vt,vi* act as umpire (for).

umpteen *adj inf* large number of; countless.

unaccompanied *adj* **1** alone. **2** singing or playing without instrumental accompaniment.

unanimous *adj* having the support and agreement of all concerned. **unanimity** *n*. **unanimously** *adv*.
unarmed *adj* without weapons.
unavoidable *adj* inevitable.
unaware *adj* ignorant; not aware. **unawares** *adv* by surprise; without warning or previous knowledge.
unbalanced *adj* not sane; mentally disturbed.
unbearable *adj* intolerable; beyond endurance. **unbearably** *adv*.
unbend *vt,vi* (-bent) **1** straighten. **2** *inf* relax or become relaxed, friendly, etc. **unbending** *adj* **1** stiff; rigid. **2** stubborn; formal.
unbutton *vt,vi* **1** undo the buttons (of). **2** *inf* unbend.
uncalled-for *adj* unwarranted; out of place; gratuitously rude.
uncanny *adj* weird; strange; irrational.
uncertain *adv* doubtful; undecided; variable; unpredictable. **uncertainty** *n*.
uncle *n* brother of one's father or mother; aunt's husband.
uncomfortable *adj* **1** not comfortable. **2** uneasy; awkward; embarrassing.
unconscious *adj* **1** unaware; unintentional. **2** having lost consciousness; insensible; in a faint, coma, etc. *n* part of the mind concerned with instincts, impulses, repressed feelings, etc., not normally accessible to the conscious mind. **unconsciously** *adv*.
unconventional *adj* not conforming; bizarre; eccentric.
uncouth *adj* ill-mannered; awkward; boorish.
uncut *adj* **1** entire; not abridged. **2** natural; unpolished and without facets.
undecided *adj* uncertain; hesitant; in two minds.
undeniable *adj* definite; obviously true. **undeniably** *adv*.
under *prep* **1** below the surface of; beneath; in a lower position than. **2** covered or concealed by. **3** lower in rank than; inferior to. **4** less in price or value than. **5** with the classification of. **6** in; according to. **7** influenced by; subject to. *adv* **1** in or to a lower or inferior place or position. **2** younger than. **3** less than. *adj* lower; low; inferior.
underclothes *pl n* underwear.
undercoat *n* coat of paint below the top or final coat. *vt* apply an undercoat to.
undercover *adj* secret; disguised.
undercut (-tt-; -cut) *vt,vi* sell at lower prices than competitors.
underdeveloped *adj* **1** not fully developed; developing; of unrealized potential. **2** primitive; backward.
underdone *adj* lightly cooked; rare.
underestimate *vt* (ʌndər'estimeit) estimate at too low a value; underrate. *n* (ʌndər'estimət) estimate that is too low.
underfoot *adv* **1** under the feet; on the ground. **2** in a subservient position.
undergo *vt* (-goes; -went; -gone) experience; submit oneself to; endure; suffer.
undergraduate *n* student who has not yet taken a degree.
underground *adj,adv* **1** below ground level. **2** secret; hidden. *n* **1** secret political resistance movement. **2** underground railway.
undergrowth *n* shrubs and plants growing under trees in a wood, etc.
underhand *adj* sly; dishonest; furtive. *adv* secretly; fraudulently.
underline *vt* **1** draw a line under. **2** stress; emphasize.
undermine *vt* **1** tunnel beneath; wear away. **2** destroy or weaken by subtle or insidious methods.
underneath *adv,prep* below; beneath; lower than. *n* lower part.
underpants *pl n* man's undergarment covering the waist to the thighs.
underpass *n* road or path crossing underneath another road, a railway, etc.; subway.
underrate *vt* underestimate; rate too low.
understand *v* (-stood) *vt,vi* know or grasp the meaning (of); comprehend; realize. *vt* **1** infer; believe. **2** sympathize with; tolerate. **understanding** *n* **1** sympathy. **2** comprehension; intelligence. **3** agreement; pact. *adj* sympathetic; wise.
understatement *n* expression with less force or completeness than merited or expected. **understate** *vt* express by understatement; minimize.
understudy *n* actor or actress prepared to take another's part when necessary. *vt* be ready to act as understudy to; learn a part as understudy.
undertake *vt* (-took; -taken) commit oneself (to); attempt to; accept; promise. **undertaker** *n* person who arranges funerals. **undertaking** *n* **1** task; venture. **2** promise.

undertone *n* **1** low, suppressed, or hidden tone of voice or feeling. **2** pale or subdued colour.

undervalue *vt* place too low a value on.

underwear *n* clothing worn under outer clothing, next to the skin; underclothes.

underweight *adj* of less than average or required weight.

underwent *v pt* of **undergo.**

underworld *n* **1** place of departed spirits. **2** section of society controlled by criminals, gangsters, etc.

underwrite *vt* (-wrote; written) accept liability; insure; guarantee. **underwriter** *n.*

undesirable *adj* not desirable; unpleasant; offensive.

undo *v* (-does; -did; -done) *vt,vi* open; loosen; unfasten. *vt* **1** cancel; reverse. **2** ruin the reputation of.

undoubted *adj* certain; sure **undoubtedly** *adv.*

undress *vt,vi* remove the clothes (of). *n* state of being naked or partly clothed.

undue *adj* excessive; unnecessary. **unduly** *adv.*

undulate *vi* move in a wavelike or rolling manner. **undulation** *n*

unearth *vt* dig up; uncover; reveal; bring to light. **unearthly** *adj* **1** ethereal; supernatural; uncanny. **2** ridiculous; unreasonable.

uneasy *adj* anxious; apprehensive; uncomfortable; awkward. **uneasily** *adv.*

unemployed *adj* **1** out of work. **2** not in use. *n* those without jobs. **unemployment** *n.* **unemployment benefit** *n* regular payments made to the unemployed; dole.

unequal *adj* not equal, similar, or uniform; not evenly balanced. **unequal to** lacking necessary strength, ability, etc., to. **unequalled** *adj* supreme; without rivals. **unequally** *adv.*

uneven *adj* **1** not level or straight; rough. **2** not uniform or well balanced; patchy. **3** odd; not divisible by two. **unevenly** *adv.*

unfailing *adj* dependable; continuous; certain.

unfair *adj* not fair; unjust; dishonest. **unfairly** *adv.* **unfairness** *n.*

unfaithful *adj* **1** not faithful; disloyal. **2** adulterous. **3** inaccurate; unreliable.

unfamiliar *adj* strange; not known or experienced. **unfamiliar with** having little knowledge of.

unfit *adj* **1** not fit; unhealthy. **2** unsuitable; incapable; not worthy.

unfold *vt,vi* **1** spread or open out. **2** reveal or be revealed; relate; develop.

unfortunate *adj* unlucky; unsuccessful; undesirable; regrettable. **unfortunately** *adv.*

ungainly *adj* awkward; gauche; clumsy.

unhappy *adj* **1** not happy; sad; miserable. **2** unfortunate; unlucky. **3** tactless. **unhappily** *adv.* **unhappiness** *n.*

unhealthy *adj* **1** not healthy; sick; diseased; abnormal. **2** threatening physical, mental, or moral damage; harmful.

unicorn *n* fabulous animal resembling a white horse with a single horn projecting from its forehead.

uniform *adj* exactly similar in appearance, quality, degree, etc.; unvarying; regular. *n* distinctive outfit worn by all members of a school, nursing staff, police force, etc. **uniformity** *n.* **uniformly** *adv.*

unify *vt,vi* make or become one; unite. **unification** *n.*

unilateral *adj* one-sided; of, affecting, or carried out by one side only.

uninterested *adj* not interested; bored. **uninteresting** *adj* arousing no interest; dull.

union *n* **1** act or condition of becoming united or joined together. **2** association or confederation of people, companies, countries, etc., formed for the common good. **3** trade union. **Union Jack** *n* national flag of Great Britain, combining the crosses of the patron saints Andrew, Patrick, and George.

unique *adj* **1** single; sole. **2** unequalled; remarkable. **uniquely** *adv.* **uniqueness** *n.*

unison *n* **in unison 1** sounding or speaking the same notes or words simultaneously. **2** in agreement.

unit *n* **1** single item; undivided entity. **2** standard amount such as the metre or second, by which a physical quantity, such as length or time, may be measured. **3** small part of a larger scheme, organization, etc. **4** apparatus; mechanical assembly; functional system.

unite *vt,vi* **1** join together; combine; cooperate. **2** unify; come or bring to agreement. **unity** *n* **1** state of being united; amalgamation; continuity; harmonious agreement. **2** the number one.

universe *n* **1** whole system of matter, energy, and space, including the earth, planets, stars, and galaxies. **2** field of human experience. **universal** *adj* **1** relating to all mankind, to nature, or to every member of a specific group. **2** widespread; general; applicable to most situations, conditions, etc.

university *n* institution of higher education empowered to confer degrees and having research facilities.

unkempt *adj* not cared for; neglected; untidy; messy.

unkind *adj* not kind; inconsiderate; hurtful. **unkindly** *adv*. **unkindness** *n*.

unknown *adj* not known, recognized, or identified. *n* unknown thing, state, etc.

unlawful *adj* against the law; illegal.

unless *conj* except on condition or under the circumstances that.

unlike *adj* not like; dissimilar; different. *prep* not like; not typical of.

unlikely *adj* not likely; improbable.

unload *vi,vt* remove a load (from). *vt* sell in bulk.

unlucky *adj* not successful; unfortunate; bringing misfortune or failure.

unnatural *adj* **1** not natural; artificial; unusual; abnormal; forced. **2** wicked; vile.

unnecessary *adj* not necessary; superfluous.

unofficial *adj* not official or confirmed; informal. **unofficially** *adv*.

unorthodox *adj* not orthodox; unconventional.

unpack *vt,vi* remove (items) from a case, box, package, etc.

unpleasant *adj* not pleasant; nasty; impolite; disagreeable. **unpleasantly** *adv*. **unpleasantness** *n*.

unravel *v* (-ll-) *vt* **1** disentangle; undo a piece of knitting. **2** sort out; straighten. *vi* become unravelled.

unreasonable *adj* not guided by reason; not justified; excessive; illogical.

unrest *n* state of discontent; disturbance; anxiety.

unruly *adj* difficult to control; not disciplined; wild; disorderly.

unscrew *vt* **1** unfasten or loosen by turning a screw. **2** loosen or detach by rotating. *vi* become unscrewed.

unsettle *vt* disturb; make uncertain or insecure; upset.

unsightly *adj* unpleasant to look at; ugly.

unsound *adj* not stable or reliable.

unstable *adj* **1** not firm or reliable, esp. mentally or emotionally. **2** decomposing spontaneously; radioactive. **3** readily decomposing into other chemicals.

unsteady *adj* not steady or firm; rocky; precarious. **unsteadily** *adv*.

untidy *adj* not tidy; disordered; slovenly. *vt* make untidy; mess up. **untidily** *adv*. **untidiness** *n*.

untie *vt* (-tying) unfasten; undo (a knot).

until *prep* during the time preceding; up to the time of. *conj* up to the time or stage that. **not...until** only...when.

untrue *adj* **1** not true; incorrect; false. **2** unfaithful. **3** diverging from a standard, rule, etc. **untruth** *n* lie; falsehood. **untruthful** *adj* **1** given to lying. **2** untrue.

unusual *adj* not usual or common; strange; remarkable. **unusually** *adv*.

unwarranted *adj* uncalled for; unnecessary.

unwell *adj* sick; ill.

unwieldy *adj* difficult to handle or use; awkward; clumsy; cumbersome.

unwind *vt,vi* (-wound) **1** unroll; uncoil; slacken; untangle. **2** relax; calm down.

unworldly *adj* **1** unearthly; spiritual. **2** not sophisticated; not materialist.

unworthy *adj* not worthy or deserving; lacking merit. **unworthily** *adv*.

unwrap *vt* (-pp-) remove the wrapping from.

up *adv* **1** in or to a higher position; further away from the ground. **2** in or to a higher status or rank. **3** into a hotter condition. **4** into a more intense emotional state. **5** no longer in bed. **6** so as to be equal to. **be up to 1** be the responsibility of. **2** be secretly engaged in. **up against** involved in a struggle with; face to face with. **up to date 1** modern; fashionable; current. **2** complete up to the present time; not in arrears. ~*prep* **1** to a higher position on. **2** further along. **3** to a place level with. *adj* moving or directed towards the top or north. *n* **ups and downs** fluctuations; alternate good and bad periods. ~*v* (-pp-) *vi* rise; get or stand up. *vt* make larger; increase or raise.

upbringing *n* education and rearing of children.

upheaval *n* great disturbance; commotion; eruption.

uphill *adj* **1** going or sloping upwards. **2** very difficult and exhausting. *adv* upwards; towards higher ground.

uphold *vt* (-held) maintain or defend against opposition; sustain.

upholstery *n* **1** coverings, padding, springs,

etc., of chairs, sofas, etc. **2** business, trade, or skill of upholstering. **upholster** *vt,vi* provide or work with upholstery. **upholsterer** *n*.

upkeep *n* **1** maintenance; keeping in good condition. **2** cost of maintenance.

uplift *vt* **1** elevate; raise. **2** raise spiritually, morally, etc.; exalt. *n* **1** raising; elevation. **2** improvement; encouragement; enlightenment. **3** moment of joy.

upon *prep* on; on top of.

upper *adj* **1** higher in position, rank, status, etc. **2** further upstream or inland. **upper hand** position of control. ~*n* upper part of a shoe, boot, etc., above the sole. **on one's uppers** reduced to desperate poverty. **uppermost** *adj* highest in position, power, etc. *adv* in the highest position, rank, etc.

upright *adj* **1** vertical; erect. **2** honest; worthy; righteous. *adv* vertically. *n* **1** vertical post, beam, etc. **2** *also* **upright piano** piano with vertical strings.

uproar *n* **1** loud clamorous noise. **2** angry protest. **uproarious** *adj* **1** hilarious. **2** accompanied by uproar; tumultuous. **uproariously** *adv*.

uprising *n* revolt; rebellion.

uproot *vt* **1** dig up by the roots. **2** displace or remove from native surroundings. **3** destroy.

upset (-tt-; -set) *vt,vi* **1** overturn; knock or be knocked over; spill. **2** distress; disturb; confuse. **3** make or become ill. *n* **1** act of upsetting. **2** quarrel; disturbance. *adj* **1** annoyed; unhappy; disturbed. **2** overturned. **3** ill; sick.

upshot *n* consequence; outcome.

upside down *adj* **1** turned over completely; inverted. **2** confused; chaotic. *adv* in an upside down position or fashion.

upstairs *adv* up the stairs; to, in, or on a higher level. *n* upper part or floor.

upstream *adv,adj* against the current of a river; nearer or towards the source.

upward *adj* facing or moving towards a higher place, level, etc. **upwards** *adv* **1** to or towards a higher place, level, etc. **2** onwards; further along a scale. **upwards of** more than.

uranium *n* radioactive metallic element, used in nuclear reactors.

Uranus *n* outer giant planet lying between Saturn and Neptune.

urban *adj* relating to a town or city.

urbane *adj* sophisticated; suave; refined.

urge *vt* **1** entreat; plead with; press; strongly advise. **2** drive or force forward. *n* impulse; strong tendency; yearning. **urgent** *adj* pressing; demanding immediate action or attention. **urgency** *n*. **urgently** *adv*.

urine *n* fluid containing waste products excreted by the kidneys that is stored in the bladder before being discharged from the body. **urinate** *vi* discharge urine. **urination** *n*.

urn *n* **1** large metal container for heating and dispensing tea, etc. **2** vase or vessel, esp. for holding the ashes of a dead person.

us *pron* form of **we** when used as the object.

use *vt* (ju:z) **1** employ; put to some purpose. **2** handle; treat. **3** exploit. **4** expend; consume. *v aux* **used to** expressing past habits or regular occurrences. **use up** finish; exhaust. **used to** *adj* accustomed to; in the habit of. ~*n* (ju:s) **1** act of using; state of being used; usage. **2** right of using. **3** need; purpose; point of using. **4** custom; familiar practice. **usage** *n* manner of use; employment; treatment. **useful** *adj* of use; convenient; serviceable; helpful. **usefully** *adv*. **usefulness** *n*. **useless** *adj* of no use or help; incompetent; hopeless.

usher *n* **1** person employed to show people to their seats. **2** minor official at a law court, parliament, etc. *vt* **1** act as usher to; escort; lead in or to. **2** precede; herald. **usherette** *n* female usher in a cinema, theatre, etc.

usual *adj* habitual; customary; ordinary. **usually** *adv*.

usurp *vt* oust or take forcibly; seize without legal authority. **usurper** *n*.

utensil *n* tool or implement, esp. used in cookery.

uterus *n* womb; organ in female mammals where an embryo develops.

utility *n* **1** usefulness. **2** something useful or practical. **3** *also* **public utility** public service, such as the railway or electricity supply. **utilize** *vt* make practical or worthwhile use of.

utmost *adj also* **uttermost** furthest; outermost; maximum; most extreme. *n* greatest possible amount, degree, extent, etc.; best.

utter[1] *vt,vi* give audible voice to; say or speak.

utter[2] *adj* extreme; complete; total; absolute. **utterly** *adv*.

V

vacant *adj* **1** empty; unoccupied; not in use. **2** blank; stupid. **vacantly** *adv*. **vacancy** *n* **1** position, job, etc., that is not yet filled. **2** stupidity; blankness. **vacate** *vt* make empty; leave. **vacation** *n* holiday period for universities, law courts, etc.

vaccinate *vt* produce immunity against a specific disease by inoculating with vaccine. **vaccination** *n*. **vaccine** *n* dead microorganisms used in vaccination to produce immunity by stimulating antibody production.

vacillate *vi* **1** oscillate; fluctuate. **2** waver; hesitate; prevaricate. **vacillation** *n*.

vacuum *n* **1** space devoid of air or containing air or other gas at very low pressure. **2** feeling of emptiness. **vacuum cleaner** *n* equipment for removing dust, etc., by suction. **vacuum flask** *n* container in which the contents are kept at constant temperature by means of the insulating effect of the vacuum between its two walls.

vagina (vəˈdʒainə) *n* passage from an exterior orifice to the uterus in female mammals. **vaginal** *adj*.

vagrant *n* person with no fixed abode or job; tramp. *adj* wandering; unsettled; erratic. **vagrancy** *n*.

vague *adj* lacking precision or clarity; uncertain; indefinite. **vaguely** *adv*. **vagueness** *n*.

vain *adj* **1** conceited; excessively proud of one's appearance, possessions, etc. **2** useless; futile; worthless; empty. **in vain** to no purpose. **vainly** *adv*

valiant *adj* brave; strong; heroic. **valiantly** *adv*.

valid *adj* based on truth; logically sound; having legal force. **validity** *n*. **validate** *vt* confirm; make valid. **validation** *n*.

valley *n* **1** trough between hills, often containing a river. **2** land area drained by a river.

value *n* **1** worth; market price; fair equivalent. **2** quality that makes something estimable, desirable, or useful. **3** degree of this quality. *vt* **1** assess the value of; assign a value to. **2** esteem; prize. **valuable** *adj* **1** of great worth; costing much money. **2** very useful; having admirable qualities, etc. *n* article of high value.

valve *n* **1** device or structure that seals, opens, or regulates fluid flow, usually in one direction. **2** electronic device in which current flows in one direction only, used esp. to amplify signals. **3** device on some brass instruments by which the tube length and hence pitch may be varied.

vampire *n* creature of folklore that rises by night from the grave to suck the blood of humans.

van *n* **1** covered motor vehicle for transporting or delivering goods. **2** railway wagon for luggage, goods, etc.

vandal *n* person who deliberately destroys or spoils something of value. **vandalism** *n*. **vandalize** *vt* destroy by vandalism.

vanilla *n* flavouring obtained from the bean of a tropical climbing orchid.

vanish *vi* disappear; become invisible; cease to exist.

vanity *n* **1** exaggerated opinion of oneself; conceit; excessive pride. **2** worthlessness; futility.

vapour *n* **1** moisture in the air, seen as mist, smoke, clouds, etc. **2** substance in a gaseous state, esp. when its temperature is below its boiling point. **vaporize** *vt,vi* turn into or become a vapour.

variable *adj* liable to change; not constant; inconsistent; unreliable. *n* something that can change value, etc.

variant *adj* showing discrepancy or difference; varying. *n also* **variance** different form of the same thing; variation; deviation.

variation *n* **1** change; modification. **2** departure from a standard type or norm.

variety *n* **1** state or quality of having many forms or versions; diversity; versatility. **2** different form or version of something. **3** assorted collection. **4** theatrical presentation of assorted turns.

various *adj* several; of different kinds; displaying variety. **variously** *adv*.

varnish *n* **1** oil-based solution that dries to provide a hard glossy skin. **2** glossy surface so produced. **3** superficial attractiveness. *vt* **1** coat with varnish. **2** conceal under superficial gloss.

vary *vt* make different; alter; diversify, modify. *vi* become different or altered; disagree; deviate.

vase *n* ornamental container, often used for holding flowers.

vasectomy *n* sterilization of men by surgical cutting of the spermatic duct.

vast *adj* boundless; immense; exceedingly great. **vastly** *adv*. **vastness** *n*.

vat *n* large vessel or cask for holding or storing liquids.

Vatican *n* **1** palace and principal residence and administrative centre of the Pope, in Rome. **2** Papal authority.

vault[1] *vi,vt* spring; leap over, esp. with the aid of the hands or a pole. *n* act of vaulting.

vault[2] *n* **1** underground room, often a burial chamber. **2** arched roof or ceiling. **3** strongroom in which valuables may be safely stored. **vaulted** *adj* arched. ~*vt,vi* cover with, construct, or curve like a vault.

veal *n* calf's flesh, prepared as food.

veer *vi,vt* change direction or course; swing round.

vegetable *n* **1** plant having various parts that may be used for food. **2** *inf* person entirely dependent on others due to loss of mental faculties, etc.

vegetarian *n* person who eats no meat but only vegetable foods and sometimes fish, eggs, and dairy produce. **vegetarianism** *n*.

vegetation *n* plants in a mass; plant life. **vegetate** *vi* lead a boring, empty, inactive life.

vehement *adj* marked by strong feelings; forceful; passionate; emphatic. **vehemence** *n*. **vehemently** *adv*.

vehicle *n* **1** means of transport or communication; conveyance. **2** medium for conveying or expressing ideas, etc. **vehicular** *adj*.

veil *n* **1** covering for a woman's head or face. **2** something flat that covers or conceals. *vt* cover with a veil; conceal; disguise.

vein *n* **1** vessel conducting oxygen-depleted blood to the heart. **2** fluid-conducting vessel in plant leaves. **3** fine tube in the framework of an insect's wing. **4** streak in marble, wood, etc. **5** trait in a person's character.

velocity *n* speed; rate of change of position; rate of motion.

velvet *n* **1** silk, cotton, or nylon fabric with soft thick pile on one surface. **2** soft smooth surface or covering.

vendetta *n* private feud; rivalry.

veneer *n* **1** thin layer of wood, plastic, etc., bonded to a surface. **2** superficial covering. *vt* cover with veneer.

venerate *vt* worship; have great respect or reverence for. **veneration** *n*.

venereal disease *n* disease transmitted by sexual intercourse.

vengeance *n* infliction of injury in return for injury suffered; revenge. **with a vengeance** thoroughly. **vengeful** *adj* vindictive; desiring revenge.

venison *n* deer's flesh prepared as food.

venom *n* **1** poison, esp. that of a snake. **2** spite. **venomous** *adj*.

vent *n* narrow opening or outlet; ventilating duct. **give vent to** allow free expression of. ~*vt* give expression to.

ventilate *vt* **1** allow free passage of air into; drive stale or foul air out. **2** expose to public examination and discussion. **ventilation** *n*.

venture *n* hazardous or speculative course of action; attempt. *vt* **1** risk. **2** dare to put forward. *vi also* **venture out** brave the dangers of something.

Venus *n* conspicuous bright planet, lying between Mercury and the earth.

veranda *n also* **verandah** covered terrace along the outside of a house.

verb *n* word expressing action, occurrence, or existence. **verbal** *adj*. **verbally** *adv*. **verbatim** *adj* word for word. **verbiage** *n* excess of words. **verbose** *adj* using an excessive number of words. **verbosity** *n*.

verdict *n* conclusion of a jury; decision.

verge *n* **1** limit; boundary; edge; margin. **2** grass border. *v* **verge on** approach; border on.

verger *n* person acting as an official attendant and usher in a church.

verify *vt* ascertain or confirm the truth of. **verifiable** *adj*. **verification** *n*.

vermin *pl n* **1** animals, esp. rodents, that are destructive or dangerous to man. **2** obnoxious people; scum.

vermouth *n* white wine flavoured with aromatic herbs.

vernacular *n* **1** spoken language or dialect of a people. **2** jargon or idiom.

versatile *adj* capable of many activities or uses; adapting readily. **versatility** *n*.

verse *n* **1** subsection of a poem; stanza. **2** metrical composition of a line of poetry. **3** poetry as opposed to prose. **4** unit into which chapters of the Bible are divided. **versed** *adj* acquainted with; skilled in.

version *n* one of a number of possible accounts, renderings, or interpretations.

vertebrate *n* animal having a backbone. *adj* having a backbone.
vertex *n, pl* **vertexes** *or* **vertices** ('vɜːtisiːz) apex; topmost point; meeting point of two intersecting lines.
vertical *adj* **1** upright; at right angles to the horizon. **2** extending at right angles from a surface; directly above or overhead. *n* vertical line or position. **vertically** *adv*.
verve *n* vigour; zest.
very *adv* used to add emphasis to an adjective. *adj* used with a noun to give emphasis to a quality inherent in the meaning of the noun.
vessel *n* **1** container or receptacle, esp. for a liquid. **2** ship or boat, usually large. **3** tube for conducting fluid in animals or plants.
vest *n* undergarment covering the upper half of the body. *vt* invest, confer on, or endow with (rights, property, etc.). **vest in** place in the control of.
vestige *n* faint trace or hint of proof, evidence, etc.
vestment *n* ceremonial garment as worn by clergy.
vestry *n* room in or attached to a church where vestments and church documents are kept.
vet *n* short for **veterinary surgeon.** *vt* (-tt-) examine; check.
veteran *n* **1** person with great or long experience in something. **2** old and experienced soldier. **veteran car** *n* old car constructed before 1905 or sometimes before 1919.
veterinary surgeon *n also* **vet** person having specialized medical training in the treatment of sick or injured animals.
veto *vt* forbid absolutely; withhold assent; reject. *n, pl* **vetoes 1** right to veto, esp. the passing of a law. **2** act of vetoing.
vex *vt* distress; tease; annoy; agitate. **vexation** *n*.
via *prep* through; by way of.
viable *adj* **1** capable of sustaining existence. **2** capable of being effected, validated, etc.; feasible; workable. **viability** *n*.
viaduct *n* structure bridging a valley, etc., bearing a road or railway.
vibrate *vt,vi* **1** move rapidly to and fro, oscillate; quiver. **2** resound; resonate. **vibration** *n*.
vicar *n* clergyman of a parish having the same spiritual status as a rector. **vicarage** *n* residence of a vicar.
vicarious *adj* deriving one's own pain, pleasure, etc., from another's experiences. **vicariously** *adv*.
vice[1] *n* evil practice or trait; wickedness; immorality; bad habit.
vice[2] *n* adjustable tool for gripping an object that is being worked on.
vice-chancellor *n* active head of a university.
vice-president *n* president's immediate deputy.
vice versa *adv* conversely.
vicinity *n* surrounding or adjacent area; neighbourhood; proximity.
vicious *adj* wicked; cruel; violent; harsh; spiteful. **viciously** *adv*. **viciousness** *n*.
victim *n* object of attack; person suffering from an accident or from ill treatment by others. **victimize** *vt* make a victim of. **victimization** *n*.
victory *n* defeat of an enemy; success in a contest or struggle. **victor** *n* person gaining victory; winner. **victorious** *adj*.
video-tape *n* magnetic tape on which television programmes, films, etc., may be recorded for subsequent transmission.
view *n* **1** act of seeing or observing; examination; inspection. **2** prospect of the surrounding countryside, etc. **3** range or field of vision. **4** mental attitude; opinion. **5** survey. **6** intention. **in view of** considering. ~*vt,vi* watch, esp a film or television; inspect; judge. **viewer** *n*. **view-finder** *n* device in a camera through which the area to be photographed can be established.
vigil *n* act of or time spent keeping watch, esp. at night. **vigilance** *n* alertness; watchfulness. **vigilant** *adj*.
vigour *n* energy; power; strength; forcefulness; good health. **vigorous** *adj*. **vigorously** *adv*.
vile *adj* **1** disgusting; despicable. **2** abominable; shameful; sinful. **3** unpleasant; objectionable. **vilify** *vt* speak ill of; abuse. **vilification** *n*.
villa *n* luxurious house, esp. one by the sea or in the country.
village *n* **1** group of rural dwellings with a smaller population than that of a town. **2** inhabitants of a village. **villager** *n*.
villain *n* **1** wicked person; scoundrel; evil-doer. **2** character whose evil is central to the plot in a story, play, etc. **villainous** *adj*.
vindictive *adj* vengeful; spiteful. **vindictively** *adv*.
vine *n* woody climbing plant, esp. one bearing grapes. **vineyard** *n* plantation of grapevines.

vinegar *n* sour-tasting acidic liquid used for pickling, as a seasoning, etc.

vintage *n* **1** age as an indication of quality. **2** time of origin. **3** harvesting or harvest of grapes and the making of wine. **4** wine obtained from grapes grown in a specified year, esp. one of good quality. *adj* **1** old and of good quality. **2** dated. **vintage car** *n* old car, esp. one built between 1919 and 1930.

vinyl *adj* containing an organic group of atoms that form the basis of many plastic and resins.

viola *n* four-stringed instrument resembling but slightly larger than a violin.

violate *vt* **1** do violence to; abuse; defile; treat disrespectfully. **2** rape or assault. **3** disregard or break (a rule, promise, etc.). **violation** *n*.

violence *n* **1** assault; use of excessive unrestrained force. **2** great force; intensity; fervour. **violent** *adj* **1** impetuously forceful; overwhelmingly vehement. **2** using or needing great physical strength. **violently** *adv*.

violet *n* **1** small purple spring flower. **2** spectral colour of a bluish-purple hue. *adj* of a violet colour.

violin *n* musical instrument having a hollow wooden waisted body and four strings, played with a bow. **violinist** *n*.

viper *n* small venomous snake; adder.

virgin *n* person, esp. a woman, who has never had sexual intercourse. *adj* **1** *also* **virginal** pure; chaste. **2** in the original condition; untouched; not yet used, cultivated, etc. **virginity** *n*.

Virgo *n* sixth sign of the zodiac, represented by the Virgin.

virile *adj* sexually potent; displaying traditional masculine characteristics. **virility** *n*.

virtual *adj* existing in effect or essence, but not in fact. **virtually** *adv* in effect; practically.

virtue *n* **1** goodness; moral excellence. **2** chastity; sexual purity. **by virtue of** by reason of; on the grounds of. **virtuous** *adj*.

virus *n* microorganism causing various infectious diseases. **viral** *adj*.

visa *n* stamp or endorsement on a passport permitting the bearer to enter a particular country.

viscount ('vaikaunt) *n* nobleman ranking between a baron and an earl in the British peerage. **viscountess** *n* wife or widow of a viscount.

viscous *adj* thick; sticky; slow to flow. **viscosity** *n*.

visible *adj* **1** capable of being seen. **2** apparent; obvious. **visibility** *n* **1** state of being visible. **2** clearness of the atmosphere; range of vision.

vision *n* **1** act or power of seeing; sight; range of sight. **2** beautiful person or object. **3** mystical experience or prophetic dream. **4** imagination; foresight.

visit *vt,vi* go or come to see for pleasure, business, etc.; call (on). *n* act of visiting; call. **visitor** *n*.

visual *adj* of or by sight; capable of being seen; visible. **visually** *adv*. **visualize** *vt* form a clear mental image of.

vital *adj* **1** necessary to or sustaining life; living. **2** lively. **3** very important; essential. **vitality** *n* strength; vigour; energy. **vitally** *adv* critically.

vitamin *n* substance found in food and essential in small quantities to health.

vivacious *adj* lively; sprightly; full of vitality. **vivaciously** *adv*. **vivacity** *n*.

vivid *adj* **1** very bright; intense. **2** graphic; distinct; clear. **3** vigorous; lively. **vividly** *adv*.

vivisection *n* practice of performing surgical operations on living animals, esp. for medical research.

vixen *n* female fox.

vocabulary *n* **1** total number of words used or understood by a person, group, etc., or contained in a language. **2** listing of words or phrases given with meanings, translations, etc.

vocal *adj* **1** relating to or produced by the voice. **2** readily disposed to express opinions; outspoken. **vocalist** *n* singer. **vocal cords** *pl n* vibrating membranes in the larynx that are responsible for vocal production.

vocation *n* **1** course of action or occupation to which a person feels called by God, duty, or conscience. **2** profession or occupation, esp. when viewed as a career. **vocational** *adj*.

vodka *n* traditional Russian alcoholic drink distilled from rye or potatoes.

voice *n* **1** sound produced by the vocal cords. **2** tone, quality, etc., of a voice; person's characteristic speech sounds. **3** musical sound of a singing voice. **4** faculty of speech or singing. **5** expression of opinion. *vt* express.

void *adj* **1** empty; vacant. **2** not binding; null; invalid. *vt* make empty, invalid, or ineffective.

n **1** empty space. **2** painful awareness of a lack of something or someone.

volatile *adj* **1** changeable; lively but unstable. **2** readily forming a vapour.

volcano *n, pl* **volcanoes** *or* **volcanos** outlet in the earth's crust for erupting subterranean matter (lava, rocks, dust, and gases), which forms into a conical mountain. **volcanic** *adj.*

vole *n* small rodent resembling a rat.

volition *n* power or exercise of the will.

volley *n* **1** series of things discharged simultaneously or rapidly. **2** return of a ball in cricket, tennis, etc., before it bounces. *vt,vi* **1** return (a ball) before it bounces. **2** discharge in a volley.

volt *n* unit for measuring voltage. **voltage** *n* force producing an electric current in a circuit.

volume *n* **1** measure of the space occupied by or enclosed inside something; quantity; amount. **2** intensity of sound. **3** book; one of a series of books forming one work. **voluminous** *adj* **1** sufficient to fill many volumes. **2** ample; large.

voluntary *adj* **1** done willingly or by one's own choice or desire; not compulsory. **2** given or offered for no payment; supported by donations. **voluntarily** *adv.* **volunteer** *vi,vt* freely offer (oneself, one's help, etc.) for something; enlist for service without compulsion. *n* person who makes a voluntary offer or enlists voluntarily.

voluptuous *adj* full of or suggesting sensual pleasure; alluring; provocative. **voluptuously** *adv.*

vomit *vi,vt* eject the contents of the stomach through the mouth. *n* **1** matter ejected. **2** act of vomiting.

voodoo *n* religious cult, esp. of Negroes in Haiti, involving belief in spirits, who possess the worshippers, and other rituals.

vote *n* **1** indication of preference or opinion; formal decision. **2** right to express such. **3** act of voting. *vt* **1** determine, decide on, or elect by a vote or general opinion. **2** *inf* suggest. *vi* express one's preference, etc., by a vote. **voter** *n.*

vouch *vi also* **vouch for** guarantee; confirm; bear witness to. **voucher** *n* **1** written evidence supporting a claim. **2** ticket acting as a substitute for cash.

vow *n* solemn promise; pledge. **take vows** enter and commit oneself to a religious order. ~*vt,vi* make a vow (that); solemnly promise (to).

vowel *n* speech sound represented by the letters a, e, i, o, u, or a combination of these.

voyage *n* journey of some distance, esp. by water. *vi* make a voyage.

vulgar *adj* **1** lacking in taste; crude; coarse; unrefined. **2** of the common people. **vulgarity** *n.*

vulnerable *adj* open to attack or injury; easily hurt. **vulnerability** *n.*

vulture *n* **1** large predatory bird, feeding mainly on dead flesh. **2** person who preys on others.

vulva *n, pl* **vulvae** ('vʌlvai) *or* **vulvas** external female genitals.

W

wad *n* **1** mass of soft material. **2** bundle; roll. *vt,vi* (-dd-) pack, pad, or stuff with a wad. **wadding** *n* material for padding, packing, etc.

waddle *vi* take short 'eps, swaying from side to side. *n* swaying walk.

wade *vi* **1** step forward through water, mud, etc. **2** progress with difficulty; labour. *vt* cross by wading.

wafer *n* **1** thin light crisp biscuit. **2** thin disc of bread or biscuit used in the Eucharist.

waft *vi,vt* convey or cause to move smoothly through the air, over water, etc. *n* **1** whiff or scent carried through the air. **2** rush of air.

wag *vt,vi* (-gg-) move or cause to move from side to side or up and down. *n* act of wagging.

wage *n* rate of pay for a job, manual work, etc. *vt* engage in; carry on. **wager** *n,vt,vi* bet; stake. **wages** *pl n* payment for a job; earnings.

waggle *vt,vi,n* wag.

wagon *n* four-wheeled vehicle, such as a cart or open lorry.

wail *vi* lament; moan, express grief in long plaintive cries. *n* cry of grief.

waist *n* **1** narrowest part of the human body between the ribs and hips. **2** *also* **waistband** part of a garment covering the waist. **3** narrow middle part of an object, such as a violin. **waistcoat** *n* sleeveless close-fitting garment covering the chest and back. **waistline** *n* **1** junction of the skirt and bodice of a garment. **2** level of or length around a waist.

wait *vt,vi* defer action; remain in the same place

(until, for, etc.); delay or be delayed. *vi* act as a waiter or waitress. *n* act or period of waiting. **lie in wait** prepare an ambush. **waiter** *n* male person employed to serve meals and wait at table in restaurants, etc. **waitress** *f n.*

waive *vt* refrain from insisting on, claiming, or enforcing; defer.

wake[1] *vi,vt* (woke; woken) *also* **wake up** disturb or be disturbed from sleep or inactivity; arouse; excite. *n* vigil beside a corpse before the funeral. **waken** *vt,vi* rouse or be roused; wake.

wake[2] *n* **1** disturbed water waves produced by a moving boat, etc. **2** disturbed track left by a hurricane, etc.

walk *vi* **1** move, pass through, or travel to on foot at a moderate pace. **2** stroll; ramble; hike. *vt* **1** pass through, pace, or traverse on foot. **2** cause to walk; accompany. **walk out** *v* **1** go on strike. **2** leave or abandon as a protest. **walkout** *n* industrial strike. **walk out on** *inf* abandon; desert. **walk over** *v* **1** beat or win easily. **2** *inf* take advantage of. **walkover** *n* easy victory; unopposed win. ~*n* **1** act or manner of walking. **2** leisurely excursion. **3** path; route.

wall *n* **1** upright construction of brick, stone, etc., forming part of a room or building, marking a boundary, etc. **2** containing surface or membrane. **3** barrier. *vt* surround, divide, fortify with, or confine within a wall. **wallflower** *n* **1** cultivated plant with fragrant yellow, brown, or red flowers. **2** *inf* spectator at an essentially participatory event. **wallpaper** *n* paper, usually decorated, for pasting to a wall or ceiling. *vt,vi* cover with wallpaper.

wallet *n* folding case for bank notes, etc.

wallop *inf vt,vi* beat soundly; thrash. *n* heavy blow.

wallow *vi* **1** indulge or delight (in). **2** roll about in mud, etc. *n* act of wallowing.

walnut *n* tree yielding highly esteemed hardwood for furniture, etc., and a nut with a wrinkled shell and edible kernel.

walrus *n* amphibious mammal related to the seal, having two long tusks.

waltz *n* **1** dance in three-four time performed in pairs. **2** music for this dance or having this rhythm. *vi* dance the waltz.

wand *n* slender and supple stick used as symbol of power or authority.

wander *vi* **1** roam without purpose or plan; stroll; meander. **2** deviate from the line of argument. **3** become delirious; talk incoherently. *n* ramble. **wanderer** *n.* **wanderlust** *n* urge to travel.

wane *vi* diminish in observed size, esp. after a peak; decrease; decline. *n* act of waning.

wangle *inf vt,vi* manipulate to suit oneself; use craft or irregular means to achieve ends. *n* act or instance of wangling.

want *vt* feel a need for; long for. *vt,vi* need; desire. **want for** lack. ~*n* **1** something wanted. **2** lack; shortage. **in want** destitute; requiring help.

war *n* **1** armed conflict between nations, groups of people, etc. **2** bitter conflict; hostility. *vi* (-rr-) make war; fight. **warfare** *n* act or process of waging war. **warlike** *adj* **1** hostile; belligerent. **2** military.

warble *vi,vt* sing with trills. *vi* produce a quavering note. *n* sound of such singing.

ward *n* **1** hospital room with beds for patients. **2** area of a city, borough, etc., for administrative purposes. **3** minor entrusted to the care of a guardian or a court of law. **ward off** protect against. **warden** *n* **1** guardian; guard; custodian. **2** superintendent or head of certain colleges and schools. **warder** *n* person in charge of prisoners in a gaol. **wardress** *f n.*

wardrobe *n* **1** cupboard in which clothes are kept. **2** range and extent of clothing or costumes of an individual or theatrical group.

warehouse *n* building used for storage of goods before their sale, distribution, etc. **wares** *pl n* goods for sale.

warm *adj* **1** having or maintaining a pleasant temperature; moderately hot. **2** affectionate; kind. **3** enthusiastic; passionate; lively. **4** red, yellow, or orange coloured. **5** near to discovery, guessing, etc. *vt,vi* **1** *also* **warm up** raise or be raised to medium temperature. **2** make or become livelier or happier. **warm to** become enthusiastic about or friendly towards. ~*n* process of warming. **warm up** **1** make receptive to a performance on television, etc. **2** exercise before a sporting contest. **3** run until operating conditions are achieved. *n* **warm-up** process of warming up. **warmly** *adv.* **warmth** *n.* **warm-blooded** *adj* able to maintain a constant body temperature. **warm-hearted** *adj* generous; sympathetic; kindly.

warn *vt,vi* **1** give an indication of approaching

danger, adverse results, etc.; threaten. **2** advise against or in advance. **warning** *n* indication of a likely course of events or state of affairs; caution.

warp *vt,vi* **1** twist or cause to twist out of shape; distort. **2** make or become full of misconceptions; pervert. *n* **1** threads running along the length of woven material. **2** distortion of wood, etc., caused by heat, damp, etc.

warrant *n* **1** authorization, esp. for police to make an arrest, search property, etc. **2** guarantee. *vt* authorize; guarantee. *vt,vi* declare; affirm. **warrant officer** *n* officer in the armed services holding a rank, authorized by warrant, between commissioned and non-commissioned officers.

warren *n* **1** interconnecting underground tunnels inhabited by rabbits. **2** overcrowded living quarters.

warrior *n* man who is skilled in or experienced in warfare or fighting.

wart *n* horny protuberance on the skin. **warty** *adj*.

wary *adj* cautious; careful of deception or danger. **warily** *adv*. **wariness** *n*.

was *v* 1st and 3rd person form of **be** in the past tense.

wash *vt,vi* make or become clean using water and usually soap. *vt* **1** remove with soap and water. **2** flow over. **3** cover with a thin layer of paint, etc. *vi inf* bear examination. **wash away** move or remove by the force of water. ~*n* **1** act of washing. **2** collection of articles for washing. **3** flow or wake of water. **4** medical lotion. **washing** *n* clothes, etc., washed or to be washed. **wash-out** *n inf* total failure.

washer *n* flat ring under a bolt head or nut to distribute pressure or provide a seal.

wasp *n* winged stinging insect, usually with black and yellow stripes on its body.

waste *vt* use carelessly; squander. **waste away** deteriorate in health; dwindle. ~*n* **1** misuse; neglect; act of wasting. **2** something squandered, neglected, discarded, worthless, superfluous, etc. **3** rubbish. **wasteful** *adj* causing or tending to waste.

watch *vt,vi* **1** look (at) or observe carefully or closely. **2** wait attentively (for); keep a lookout (for). **3** guard. *vi* keep guard or vigil. *n* **1** small mechanism, worn esp. on the wrist, registering the passage of time. **2** act or instance of watching; period of vigil. **3** person or persons performing this duty. **watchdog** *n* dog kept for guarding property. **watchful** *adj* vigilant; awake.

water *n* colourless liquid that consists of hydrogen and oxygen and forms ice below its freezing point and steam above its boiling point. **2** impure water, as found in rivers, oceans, etc. **3** large expanse of water. **4** solution of something in water. *vt* **1** supply or add water to; make wet. **2** irrigate. **3** dilute. *vi* **1** (of the mouth) secrete saliva at the sight of food. **2** (of the eyes) secrete tears.

watercolour *n* **1** painting in water-soluble pigments. **2** those pigments.

watercress *n* freshwater plant with edible leaves.

waterfall *n* precipitous descent of water in a river course.

watering-can *n* vessel with a handle, spout, and nozzle for watering plants, etc.

water lily *n* aquatic plant whose large leaves and showy flowers float on the surface of water.

waterlogged *adj* saturated with water.

watermelon *n* melon plant bearing large edible fruit with reddish watery flesh.

waterproof *adj* not allowing water through. *n* waterproof garment; raincoat. *vt* make waterproof.

water-ski *vi* travel over the surface of water on skis holding a rope pulled by a speedboat. *n* ski used for this purpose. **water-skier** *n*.

watertight *adj* **1** impervious to water. **2** irrefutable; allowing no points of dispute.

waterworks *n* **1** establishment for supplying water to a community. **2** *sl* shedding of tears. **3** *sl* urinary system.

watery *adj* **1** of, like, or containing water. **2** weak; pale; insipid.

watt *n* unit of electrical, mechanical, and thermal power.

wave *n* **1** undulation on the surface of a liquid, esp. the sea. **2** any undulation, as in the hair. **3** oscillating disturbances by which radio energy, sound energy, light energy, etc., is carried through air or some other medium. **4** surge of events, emotions, people, etc. **5** to-and-fro movement of the hand expressing greeting, etc. *vt,vi* move or cause to move to and fro. *vi* greet or signal by a wave. *vt* **1** direct by a wave. **2** set waves in (hair).

waveband *n* range of wavelengths used in radio transmission. **wavelength** *n* distance between two successive peaks of an energy wave. **wavy** *adj* undulating; full of waves; swaying to and fro.

waver *vi* **1** be unsteady. **2** oscillate; vary. **3** hesitate; falter.

wax[1] *n* solid or viscous insoluble natural substance that softens at low temperatures. *vt* smear or rub with wax. **waxy** *adj.*

wax[2] *vi* become larger or apparently larger; increase.

way *n* **1** route; direction; path. **2** progress; distance; journey. **3** manner; style; method; characteristic behaviour, etc. **4** condition; state. **by the way** incidentally. **give way (to)** **1** yield. **2** stop for. **in a way** in certain respects. **in the way** impeding progress. **out of the way** **1** so as not to obstruct. **2** unusual. **3** not easily accessible. **under way** in progress; in motion. **wayside** *n* edge of a road or route.

waylay *vt* **1** intercept so as to attack; ambush. **2** detain in order to speak with.

wayward *adj* wilful; capricious; selfish.

we *pron* used as the subject to refer to oneself and another person or all other people including oneself.

weak *adj* **1** not strong; frail. **2** very diluted; insipid. **3** below expected standard. **4** lacking moral, mental, or political strength. **weakly** *adv.* **weakness** *n.* **weaken** *vt, vi* make or become weaker; reduce or be diminished in stature, strength, or resolve. **weak-kneed** *adj* lacking resolution or firmness; timid. **weakling** *n* person or animal that gives way easily or lacks strength. **weak-minded** *adj* **1** mentally deficient. **2** lacking resolution; easily persuaded. **weak-willed** *adj* easily deterred, dissuaded, or distracted.

wealth *n* **1** aggregate of valuable property; affluence; riches. **2** abundance. **wealthy** *adj.*

weapon *n* object, device, or other means used for attack or defence or to injure another.

wear *v* (wore; worn) *vt* **1** be dressed in; have on. **2** carry; bear; display; present. *vt,vi* **1** produce or be produced by constant rubbing, long use, etc.; impair or deteriorate. **2** reduce or be reduced to a certain condition. *n* **1** act of wearing. **2** clothing. **3** damage; wastage caused by use. **4** lasting quality. **wearable** *adj.*

weary *adj* **1** tired; reduced in strength or patience. **2** tedious; causing or caused by fatigue. *vt,vi* make or become tired or impatient. **wearily** *adv.* **weariness** *n.*

weasel *n* **1** small nimble carnivorous animal with a long slender brownish body. **2** treacherous, furtive, or sharp-featured person.

weather *n* local current atmospheric conditions of temperature, humidity, cloudiness, rainfall, wind, etc. *vt* come safely through. *vt,vi* expose or be exposed to the air or the weather.

weave *v* (wove *or* weaved; woven *or* weaved) *vt,vi* **1** interlace by passing threads alternately below and above other threads. **2** make fabric in this way. **3** create or move by winding in and out. *vt* **1** construct; fabricate. **2** introduce; combine. *n* texture or pattern of a woven fabric. **weaver** *n.*

web *n* **1** something woven. **2** fine filmy net spun by a spider to trap its prey. **3** membrane between the digits of a bat, duck, etc. **webbed** *adj.*

wedding *n* marriage ceremony.

wedge *n* **1** piece of solid material tapering towards one end. **2** anything of this shape. *vt* **1** fix firmly by positioning a wedge. **2** split; force apart. *vt,vi* squeeze or be squeezed into a space.

Wednesday *n* fourth day of the week.

weed *n* **1** wild prolific plant, esp. one growing where it is not wanted by man. **2** *inf* person of puny stature. **3** *sl* tobacco; cigarette. *vt,vi* remove weeds from (ground).

week *n* **1** period of seven days, usually from Sunday to Saturday. **2** working days of the week. **weekday** *n* any day of the week except Sunday and usually Saturday. **weekend** *n* period from Friday night to Sunday night.

weep *v* (wept) *vi,vt* **1** shed tears of sorrow, joy, etc; grieve (for). **2** exude moisture. *n* act of grieving or crying.

weft *n* threads running across the width of woven material.

weigh *vt* **1** ascertain the weight of. **2** compare against; counterbalance. **3** have a weight of **4** estimate weight by holding or balancing in the hands. **5** consider carefully. **6** draw in an anchor. *vi* **1** have weight; be heavy. **2** be considered important or to have value. **weigh down** press down; oppress. **weigh out** measure by weight. ~*n* process of weighing.

weighbridge *n* machine for weighing vehicles and their loads.

weight *n* **1** heaviness. **2** standardized piece of metal used for weighing. **3** force by which a mass is attracted by gravity to the earth. **4** anything heavy or oppressive. **5** power; impressiveness; significance. *vt* load with a weight. **weighty** *adj*. **weight-lifting** *n* sport consisting of competitive attempts at lifting increasingly heavier weights.

weird *adj* odd; uncanny; unreal. **weirdly** *adv*.

welcome *n* cordial greeting or reception. *adj* agreeable; giving pleasure; gladly received; willingly permitted. **make welcome** treat hospitably. ~*vt* greet cordially; be glad of.

weld *vt* join (metals, plastics, etc.) by applying heat or pressure; unite. *vt,vi* bring or be brought together. *n* welded joint or union.

welfare *n* **1** well-being; state or condition of life; freedom from want, sickness, or ignorance. **2** work or plans to improve people's welfare.

well[1] *n* **1** underground source of water; spring. **2** deep sunken shaft through which oil, water, gas, etc., may be extracted. *vi* pour forth; flow; gush.

well[2] *adv* **1** satisfactorily; correctly; thoroughly. **2** intimately. **3** clearly; easily. **4** with reason or consideration. **5** fully; abundantly. **6** generously; kindly; with care. **as well** also; too; in addition. *adj* **1** healthy. **2** right; favourable; satisfactory. *interj* expression of surprise, etc. **well-being** *n* state of good health, happiness, etc.; good. **well-bred** *adj* of good stock; properly reared; having good manners, etc. **well-built** *adj* of generous proportions and stature. **well-known** *adj* celebrated; famous; notorious. **well-off** *adj* rich; fortunate. **well-spoken** *adj* **1** speaking with a sociably acceptable accent. **2** spoken fittingly or appropriately. **well-worn** *adj* **1** thoroughly used. **2** trite; hackneyed.

wellington *n also* **wellington boot** knee-length footwear, esp. of rubber.

went *v pt* of **go.**

wept *v pt* and *pp* of **weep.**

were *v* **1** 2nd person singular and 1st, 2nd, and 3rd person plural form of **be** in the past tense. **2** form of **be** in the subjunctive.

west *n* **1** one of the four cardinal points of the compass situated to the rear of a person facing the sunrise. **2** part of a country, area, etc., lying towards the west. *adj also* **western** of, in, or facing the west. *adv,adj also* **westerly 1** towards the west. **2** (of winds) from the west. **western** *n* story, film, etc., taking place in the American West during pioneering times. **westerner** *n*. **westward** *adj* facing or moving towards the west. **westwards** *adv* in the direction of the west.

wet *adj* **1** covered or saturated with liquid; not yet dry. **2** rainy. **3** *inf* sentimental; feeble; lacking spirit; naive. *vt* (-tt-) make wet. *n* rain; moisture; dampness. **wetness** *n*.

whack *vt* strike; hit. *n* **1** sharp blow or the sound of this. **2** *inf* share. **whacked** *adj inf* exhausted. **whacking** *n* beating. *adj inf* very large.

whale *n* very large marine mammal that breathes through a blowhole on its head. *vi* hunt whales.

wharf *n, pl* **wharves** *or* **wharfs** landing-stage for mooring, loading, and unloading boats. *vt,vi* **1** berth. **2** unload (cargo).

what *adj,pron* used as an interrogative to request further information. *adj* that which. *interj* exclamation of surprise, dismay, etc. **whatever** *pron* **1** anything or all that. **2** what. *adj,pron* whichever; no matter which. *adj* at all.

wheat *n* cereal grass or its grain used for flour to make bread, etc.

wheedle *vt,vi* persuade by devious means; cajole.

wheel *n* **1** circular frame attached by radial supports to a central axis around which it rotates, used to aid movement, transportation, etc. **2** thing of similar shape or function. *vt,vi* **1** move on wheels; push along. **2** change direction; pivot. **wheelbarrow** *n* barrow supported on one wheel in front and two legs behind, which may be lifted by two handles. **wheelchair** *n* chair on two wheels, used by invalids, etc.

wheeze *vi* breathe with difficulty, making a rattling or hissing sound. *n* **1** sound of difficult breathing. **2** *inf* ruse; clever scheme; dodge.

whelk *n* edible marine mollusc with a snail-like shell.

when *adv* **1** at what time. **2** in or during which period. *conj* at the time that. *pron* from or until what time. **whenever** *conj,adv* at any or whatever time that. *adv* when.

where *adv* **1** in, at, or to what or which place or position. **2** from which place. *conj* to or in the place or situation that. **whereabouts** *adv* in what place; near where. *n* place where something or someone is located or hidden. **whereas** *conj* but; though; while. **whereby** *adv* by which means. **whereupon** *conj,adv* at which point. **wherever** *conj,adv* in or to any or whatever place that. *adv* where.

whether *conj* used to introduce an indirect question, esp implying an alternative or choice and sometimes substitutable by 'if'.

which *adj,pron* used as an interrogative to request further information, esp so as to distinguish between things. *pron* used to introduce a relative clause when referring to inanimate objects. **whichever** *adj,pron* **1** any one(s) that. **2** no matter which.

whiff *n* **1** puff; gust. **2** slight smell. *vt,vi* **1** puff. **2** smell.

while *conj also* **whilst** as long as; during the time that; at the same time as; although. *n* space of time. *v* **while away** spend or pass idly.

whim *n* caprice; fancy. **whimsical** *adj* capricious; fanciful.

whimper *n* feeble cry, whine. *vi* utter a whimper; plaintively moan or whine.

whine *n* **1** wailing high-pitched cry or note. **2** undignified complaint. *vi,vt* make or utter in a whine.

whip *v* (-pp-) *vt* **1** beat with a lash to punish or cause (a horse, etc.) to move forward. **2** whisk into froth. *vi* move or act quickly. **whip out** produce suddenly. ~*n* **1** lash on a handle for whipping. **2** stroke of a lash. **3** person responsible for a political party's discipline. **4** call on members to vote according to party policy. **5** confection of whipped ingredients. **whip-round** *n* informal collection of money for a present, etc.

whippet *n* thin long-legged dog similar to a greyhound.

whir *vi* (-rr-) move rapidly with a buzzing sound.

whirl *vi,vt* **1** move or cause to move in a circle; spin very fast. **2** move away quickly. *vi* swing round quickly. *n* **1** rapid circular movement; rush; agitation. **2** state of bewilderment. **whirlpool** *n* circular current of water. **whirlwind** *n* moving spiral of air into which surrounding air can be drawn.

whisk *vt* **1** move or remove swiftly and lightly; brush, swing, or toss briskly. **2** beat lightly introducing air so as to make froth. *vi* move or pass quickly. *n* **1** rapid sweeping motion. **2** light stiff brush. **3** instrument for beating eggs, etc.

whisker *n* **1** firm sensitive hair at the side of an animal's mouth. **2** hairs on a person's upper lip or side of the face.

whisky *n* alcoholic drink, distilled esp from malted barley.

whisper *vi,vt* **1** speak in very low tones; murmur. **2** converse in secret. *vi* spread rumours. *n* **1** soft speech; murmur; rustle. **2** hint; rumour.

whist *n* card game played in pairs.

whistle *vi* make a shrill sound by forcing breath through almost sealed lips or teeth, or air through a crack, etc. *vt* use this method for rendering a tune. *n* **1** sound of whistling. **2** device making a similar sound.

white *n* **1** colour of fresh snow, having no hue. **2** something coloured or characteristically white. *adj* **1** of the colour white or nearly white; pale, colourless. **2** pure, unblemished. **White** *n* person with a pale skin colour, esp. a European. *adj* having skin colour of Europeans. **whiten** *vt* make white. *vi* grow pale. **whitewash** *n* substance for whitening walls, etc. *vt* **1** cover with whitewash. **2** *inf* gloss over; conceal (errors, faults, etc.).

whiting *n* marine food fish.

Whitsun *n* **1** *also* **Whit Sunday** seventh Sunday after Easter when the Christian Church celebrates Pentecost, the inspiration of the disciples by the Holy Spirit. **2** week following Whit Sunday.

whiz *vi,vt* (-zz-) **1** move quickly, making a buzzing whirring sound. **2** *inf* move or go rapidly. *n* buzzing sound.

who *pron* **1** what or which person. **2** used to introduce a relative clause when referring to a person or people. **whoever** *pron* **1** anyone at all that. **2** no matter who. **3** who.

whole *adj* complete; total; undamaged, healthy. *adv* in a complete or unbroken piece. *n* entire or undivided thing; total of all parts. **wholehearted** *adj* sincerely and enthusiastically felt, done, etc. **wholeheartedly** *adv*. **wholesale** *n* sale of goods in bulk rather than retail selling. *adj* **1** relating to sales in bulk. **2** large-scale; indiscriminate. *adv* on a wholesale basis. **wholesome** *adj* **1** containing good value. **2** healthy in body, mind, morals, etc. **3**

conducive to such. **wholly** *adv* completely; altogether.

whom *pron* form of **who** as the object.

whooping cough *n* infectious disease characterized by bouts of coughing, respiratory difficulties, etc.

whore (hɔː) *n* female prostitute.

whose *pron* belonging to whom; of whom or which.

why *adv,conj* for what reason; from what cause.

wick *n* stringlike cord that burns in a candle.

wicked *adj* **1** sinful; evil; extremely bad. **2** mischievous; roguish. **wickedly** *adv*. **wickedness** *n*.

wickerwork *n* craft of making furniture, etc., from twisted twigs or branches, or the objects so made.

wicket *n* **1** three pointed stumps with two bails resting on top, at which the bowler aims in a game of cricket. **2** strip of turf between two wickets. **3** batsman or batsman's turn. **4** small gate or door. **wicketkeeper** *n*.

wide *adj* **1** broad; of considerable dimension from side to side. **2** roomy; extensive; including much. *adv* **1** to the full extent. **2** widely. **widely** *adv* over a large area or extent; considerably; spreading far from. **widen** *vt,vi* make or grow wide(r). **widespread** *adj* found over a considerable area; distributed far.

widow *n* woman whose husband has died and who has not remarried. **widower** *m n*.

width *n* **1** distance or measurement between sides. **2** state of being wide.

wield *vt* hold and use; possess; exercise.

wife *n, pl* **wives** female partner in a marriage; married woman. **wifely** *adj*.

wig *n* hairpiece for the whole head made of artificial or real hair.

wiggle *vt,vi* move or cause to move to and fro jerkily. *n* wiggling movement.

wigwam *n* light conical dwelling used by North American Indians.

wild *adj* **1** uncivilized; undomesticated or uncultivated. **2** uncontrolled; boisterous; extremely excited or angry. **3** untidy; dishevelled. **4** lacking judgment; random; erratic; fantastic. **wildly** *adv*. **wildness** *n*. **wildlife** *n* animals, birds, plants, etc., that are undomesticated and live in their natural habitat.

wilderness *n* large desolate area; uncultivated and uninhabited region.

wilful *adj* headstrong; obstinately self-willed. **wilfully** *adv*.

will[1] *v aux* **1** used to form the future tense. **2** used to emphasize an intention. **3** used to express willingness or ability. **4** used to express probability or likelihood.

will[2] *n* **1** faculty by which decisions are made. **2** conscious choice; intention; inclination; moral strength. **3** intended distribution of one's property at death. **4** legal document expressing this. *vt,vi* **1** bequeath in a will. **2** compel by using the will; desire. **willpower** *n* strength of mind; firmess; control.

willing *adj* without reluctance; in agreement; eager; cooperative. **willingly** *adv*. **willingness** *n*.

willow *n* tree with slender pliant branches and long slender leaves, often found near rivers. **willowy** *adj* flexible; graceful; slender.

wilt *vt,vi* droop, as through lack of moisture, energy, etc.; fade.

win *v* (-nn-; won) *vi* reach a goal, esp. before anyone else; come first. *vt* secure or gain by effort or contest; obtain by gambling. **win over** persuade. ~*n* act of winning; victory; success. **winner** *n*.

wince *vi* draw back; flinch. *n* involuntary movement resulting from pain, etc.

winch *n* hauling or hoisting machine consisting of a drum on a rotating axle.

wind[1] (wind) *n* **1** current of air usually moving with speed. **2** gas produced in the alimentary canal. **3** empty meaningless words. **4** wind instruments in an orchestra. **5** *inf* hint; suggestion. **get/put the wind up** become frightened or alarmed/frighten or alarm. **in the wind** about to happen. ~*vt* cause to be short of breath. **windbag** *n* **1** *sl* person who talks a lot but says little of interest. **2** bag in bagpipes from which air can be squeezed to maintain a continuous sound. **windfall** *n* **1** fruit blown off a tree. **2** unexpected good fortune, often a receipt of money. **wind instrument** *n* musical instrument played by blowing or using an air current. **windmill** *n* mill with rotating sails driven by wind power. **windpipe** *n* passage between the mouth and lungs through which breath is inhaled or exhaled. **windscreen** *n* protective plate of glass in front of a vehicle. **windswept** *adj* exposed to or disordered by wind. **windy** *adj* like, characterized by, or exposed to wind.

wind[2] (waind) *v* (wound) *vt* **1** turn; twist; **2** *also* **wind up** tighten the spring of (a watch, etc.) by turning something. **3** make into a ball; coil. *vi* change direction constantly; meander.

windlass *n* machine with a revolving cylinder for hauling or hoisting. *vt* hoist by means of a windlass.

window *n* **1** opening in a wall, etc., to let in air and light. **2** frame of a window or the glass in it. **window-dressing** *n* **1** displaying of goods in a shop window. **2** art of doing this. **3** skill in emphasizing the best features of something. **window-shop** *vi* (-pp-) scrutinize goods in shop windows without buying.

wine *n* alcoholic drink made from fermented grape juice or sometimes from other fruits.

wing *n* **1** limb or organ by which a bird, insect, etc., flies. **2** similarly shaped structure on an aeroplane. **3** any side structure, as of a building or stage. **4** player on the extreme right or left of the forward line in football, etc. **wing-commander** *n* airforce officer similar in rank to lieutenant colonel or naval commander. **wingspan** *n* length from tip to tip of wings.

wink *vi,vt* **1** rapidly shut and open (one or both eyes), often to convey complicity, etc. *n* act or instance of winking.

winkle *n* edible shellfish. *v* **winkle out** extract with difficulty.

winter *n* coldest season of the year. *adj* of, like, happening, used, or sown in winter. *vi* spend the winter (in). *vt* feed and shelter (animals) through winter. **wintry** *adj.*

wipe *vt* clean or dry by drawing a cloth over or rubbing lightly. **wipe out** obliterate. ~*n* act of wiping; clean; rub.

wire *n* **1** flexible strand or rod of metal or a group of strands plaited or twisted together. **2** insulated wire for carrying an electric current. **3** *inf* telegram. *vt* join, fasten, support, protect, equip, etc., with wire. *vi* telegraph. **wireless** *n* radio. **wiry** *adj* sinewy; tough

wise *adj* **1** having knowledge, perception, or judgment; clever. **2** sensible; discreet. **3** *sl* knowing the whole situation; warned about. **wisdom** *n.* **wisely** *adv.*

wish *vt* **1** desire; long for. **2** request; want. *vt,vi* express or have a desire for *n* **1** desire. **2** thing desired. **wishful** *adj* desirous; hoping.

wisp *n* **1** thin strand or streak of something. **2** small bundle of straw, hay, etc.

wisteria *n* climbing plant with blue flowers hanging in clusters.

wistful *adj* yearning, with little hope of satisfaction; thoughtful. **wistfully** *adv.*

wit *n* **1** ability to think quickly and pertinently and say clever amusing things. **2** person with this ability. **3** *also* **wits** intelligence; resourcefulness.

witch *n* **1** woman believed to have supernatural powers through contact with evil spirits. **2** ugly malevolent woman. **witchcraft** *n* craft or practice of supernatural powers for evil purposes.

with *prep* **1** in the company of. **2** by means of; using. **3** bearing; possessing. **4** displaying; showing. **5** in relation to. **6** among; in the midst of. **7** at the same time as.

withdraw *v* (-drew; -drawn) *vi* draw back or away; retire. *vt* take out; take back; retract; remove. **withdrawal** *n.* **withdrawn** *adj* unsociable; very reserved.

wither *vi,vt* shrivel; dry (up); fade; decay. **withering** *adj* crushingly sarcastic.

withhold *vt* (-held) keep from; hold back; restrain; refuse to grant.

within *adv* inside; internally; indoors. *prep* **1** not out of or beyond. **2** in; inside; to the inner part of.

without *adv* outside. *prep* **1** outside. **2** not having; free from; in the absence of. **3** beyond the limits of. *conj* unless; but.

withstand *vt* (-stood) maintain; endure; oppose successfully.

witness *n* **1** person who is present and perceives a fact or event. **2** person who gives evidence, esp. in court. **3** person who attests another's signature. *vt,vi* give testimony; observe personally; act as witness. **witness box** *n* place in a lawcourt where witnesses give evidence.

witty *adj* capable of verbal wit; amusing. **wittily** *adv.*

wives *n pl* of **wife.**

wizard *n* **1** man having supernatural powers; magician. **2** ingenious person; expert. **wizardry** *n.*

wobble *vi* **1** move unsteadily; rock; shake; tremble. **2** be uncertain; vacillate. *n* unsteady motion. **wobbly** *adj.*

woke *v pt* of **wake. woken** *v pp* of **wake.**

wolf *n, pl* **wolves** **1** gregarious carnivorous predatory animal of the dog family. **2** person who is greedy and cunning. **cry wolf** raise a false alarm. ~*vt also* **wolf down** eat rapidly and ravenously.

woman *n, pl* **women 1** adult female human being. **2** women collectively. **womanhood** *n.* **womanly** *adj.*

womb *n* uterus.

won *v pt* and *pp* of **win.**

wonder *n* **1** emotion of delighted surprise and admiration. **2** object or person that excites this. **no wonder** not surprising(ly). **work wonders** achieve great results. ~*vt,vi* **1** be curious or seek to find out (about). **2** doubt. **3** marvel (at). **wonderful** *adj* **1** amazing. **2** *inf* very good; marvellous. **wonderfully** *adv.*

wonky *adj sl* unsound; shaky; not right or well.

wood *n* **1** collection of growing trees and other plants over an extensive area. **2** hard fibrous material in the trunks and branches of trees, used as a building material, in furniture, etc. **woody** *adj.* **wooden** *adj* **1** made of wood. **2** stiff; clumsy. **3** showing no emotion. **4** stupid; insensible. **woodpecker** *n* bird with a chisel-like bill, which it uses for drilling the bark of trees for insects. **woodwind** *n* section of an orchestra containing wind instruments with the exception of brass instruments. **woodwork** *n* anything made of wood; carpentry. **woodworm** *n* **1** larva of certain beetles laid in, boring through, and eating wood. **2** resulting damage in wooden furniture, etc.

wool *n* **1** hair-covering of sheep and other animals. **2** yarn spun from this. **3** garment, etc., made from the yarn. **woollen** *adj* made from wool. *n also* **woollens** woollen cloth or garments. **woolly** *adj* **1** made of or like wool. **2** lacking clearness or precision. *n* jersey.

word *n* **1** unit of spoken language or a written symbol of this, expressive of some object, idea, or relation. **2** brief conversation; remark. **3** news; message. **4** decree; promise; recommendation. **have words** argue. **in a word** in short. ~*vt* express in words; phrase. **wordy** *adj* using too many words. **word-perfect** *adj* memorized accurately.

wore *v pt* of **wear.**

work *n* **1** effort exerted in purposeful activity; expenditure of energy. **2** task; occupation for gain; employment. **3** product of one's efforts; creation. **4** place of employment or where activity takes place. *vt* **1** bring into action; effect. **2** handle; shape. *vi* **1** labour; expend energy; be occupied; be employed (at or in). **2** behave in a desired way when started; operate; function. **worked up** *adj* angry; excited. **work out** solve; develop. **working class** *n* workers, usually implying those in manual work. **workman** *n, pl* **-men** labourer; skilled manual worker. **workmanlike** *adj* efficient; of a high standard. **workmanship** *n* level of competence or skill in a product. **workshop** *n* place where goods are made, manual work is carried on, etc.

world *n* **1** universe; all that exists. **2** earth and its inhabitants; part of the earth. **3** mankind; public; society. **4** present state of existence; public life; sphere of interest or activity; environment. **5** materialistic standards or system; secular life. **6** large amount or quantity. **worldly** *adj* **1** familiar with public life and the ways of society. **2** adhering to materialistic standards; not idealistic or religious. **worldliness** *n.* **worldwide** *adj* extending over or applying to the whole planet.

worm *n* **1** long slender usually limbless invertebrate animal, esp. an earthworm. **2** internal parasite. *vt* wriggle; squirm; make (one's way) slowly or secretly; extract insidiously.

worn *v pp* of **wear.** *adj* **1** well used; long used; exhausted. **2** worried; haggard.

worry *vi* be anxious; fret. *vt* make anxious; disturb; pester; harass; be a trouble to. *n* **1** act of worrying. **2** cause of this.

worse *adj* less good; poorer in health; more inferior or severe in condition or circumstances. *adv* in a worse way; with more severity. **worsen** *vt,vi* make or become worse.

worship *v* (-pp-) *vt* **1** accord religious honour and supreme esteem to. **2** adore; idolize. *vi* attend religious worship. *n* **1** act of worshipping; religious service. **2** adoration; devotion.

worst *adj* of the extreme degree of badness. *adv* in the worst way. *n* worst part, state, etc.; least good part. *vt* get an advantage over; defeat.

worth *adj* **1** having a value of. **2** deserving; justifying. *n* intrinsic value; value in money; merit. **worthwhile** *adj* warranting the time, effort, etc; sufficiently important. **worthy** *adj* of sufficient merit; deserving; commendable. **worthily** *adv*.

would *v aux* form of **will**[1] in the past tense, conditional, or subjunctive.

wound[1] *vt,vi* (wu:nd) hurt; injure. *n* injury.

wound[2] *v* (waund) *pt* and *pp* of **wind**[2].

wove a *pt* of **weave. woven** a *pp* of **weave.**

wrangle *vi* argue; dispute doggedly. *n* angry dispute.

wrap *vt* (-pp-) cover; fold round or together; wind; envelop in. *vi* **1** enfold. **2** package. *n* **1** covering, such as a shawl or rug. **2** single turn or fold.

wreath *n* **1** arrangement, often circular, of intertwined leaves and flowers, often in memory of a deceased person; garland. **2** wisp or curl of smoke or vapour. **wreathe** *vt,vi* twist; entwine; interweave.

wreck *vt* ruin; damage or destroy; sabotage. *n* **1** ship that has foundered or sunk. **2** broken or damaged remains after a disaster; destruction. **3** person enfeebled mentally or physically. **wreckage** *n* **1** act of wrecking. **2** remains of a wrecked thing or person.

wren *n* small brown songbird with short erect tail.

wrench *vt* pull sharply and with a twist; force by violence; sprain; distort. *vi* undergo violent pulling, tugging, or twisting. *n* **1** act of wrenching; twist; sprain. **2** difficult parting; pain at parting. **3** adjustable spanner.

wrestle *vi,vt* struggle to overcome. *vi* contend in an organized fight by holding and throwing, without punching. *n* bout of wrestling, struggle. **wrestler** *n*. **wrestling** *n*.

wretch *n* **1** miserable unfortunate person. **2** worthless despicable person. **wretched** *adj* **1** miserable; dismal. **2** of poor quality; contemptible.

wriggle *vi,vt* squirm or make short twisting movements. **wriggle into/out of** *inf* insinuate oneself deviously into or extricate oneself out of. *n* act, motion, or shape of wriggling movement.

wring *v* (wrung) *vt,vi* twist and squeeze out moisture (from). *vt* **1** twist. **2** clasp in anguish. **3** grip in a friendly manner. **4** extract. *n* act of wringing.

wrinkle *n* small ridge or furrow on a surface; crease. *vt,vi* crease.

wrist *n* **1** joint between the hand and lower arm. **2** part of a garment covering this. **wristwatch** *n* watch worn at the wrist.

writ *n* legal or formal document summoning or requiring a person to take some course of action.

write *v* (wrote; written) *vt,vi* **1** mark letters, words, numbers, etc., usually on paper, to communicate ideas, thoughts, etc. **2** correspond (with) by letter. **3** be an author (of) *vt* state in a letter, book, etc. **write down** *or* **out** put in writing. **write off** consider a loss or failure. **write-off** *n* complete loss or failure; wreck. **write up** describe or bring up to date in writing. **write-up** *n* written account in a newspaper, etc., of a book, film, etc.; review. **writing** *n* **1** written work, book, etc. **2** act of writing. **3** style of handwriting.

writhe *vi* **1** twist or roll about as if suffering pain, squirm. **2** suffer mentally.

wrong *adj* **1** not correct, accurate, or true; mistaken. **2** wicked; unjust. **3** not suitable; not wanted. *n* injustice; wrong action. **in the wrong** mistaken. *adv also* **wrongly** in a wrong way. **get wrong 1** misunderstand. **2** produce an incorrect answer. ~*vt* do injustice or harm to; think ill of unjustifiably. **wrongdoing** *n* improper, illegal, or immoral action. **wrongdoer** *n*.

wrought iron *adj* malleable pure iron, often drawn out into decorative shapes.

wry *adj* **1** twisted; contorted. **2** ironical; dryly humorous. **wryly** *adv*

X

xenophobia *n* irrational fear or hatred of foreigners or things foreign or strange.

xerography *n* copying process in which images are produced using electrically charged surfaces.

Xerox *n Tdmk* process or machine employing xerography.

Xmas *n* Christmas

X-ray *n* **1** wave of radiation of considerable energy that can penetrate matter, used esp. in medical diagnosis and treatment. **2** image, esp. of bone structure, produced on film sensitive to X-rays. *vt,vi* irradiate with X-rays.

xylophone *n* musical instrument consisting of a graduated series of wooden bars struck by wooden hammers.

Y

yacht *n* light sailing vessel for racing, cruising, etc. *vi* sail in a yacht. **yachtsman** *n, pl* **-men** person who keeps or sails a yacht.

yank *vt,vi* pull sharply; jerk. *n* sharp tug.

yap *n* short sharp high-pitched bark; yelp. *vi* (-pp-) **1** bark in yaps. **2** *inf* chatter stupidly or at length.

yard[1] *n* **1** unit of length, equivalent to 0.91 metres (three feet). **2** piece of material of this length. **yardstick** *n* **1** graduated stick, one yard long, used for measuring. **2** any standard used for comparison.

yard[2] *n* enclosed area, usually adjoining a building and having a hard surface.

yarn *n* **1** continuous thread made from twisted fibres of wool, cotton, synthetic materials, etc. **2** story spun out to some length. *vi* tell stories.

yawn *vi* **1** breathe in through a wide open mouth, usually as a result of tiredness or boredom. **2** be open wide. *n* act of yawning.

year *n* **1** *also* **calender year** period of time of 365 days (or 366 in a leap year) from Jan 1 to Dec 31. **2** period of twelve months. **3** period of time (365.256 days) taken by the earth to complete one orbit of the sun. **yearly** *adj,adv.*

yearn *vi* **1** have a great longing; crave. **2** feel pity or tenderness. **yearning** *n.*

yeast *n* fungus or a preparation of this fungus, used in brewing and for raising bread.

yell *vi,vt* scream; shout loudly. *n* scream of anger, pain, or excitement; loud cry.

yellow *n* spectral colour, as that of gold or a daffodil. *adj* **1** of the colour yellow. **2** *inf* cowardly.

yelp *n* short sharp cry of pain, surprise, or excitement, esp. by a dog. *vi* utter a yelp.

yes *adv,interj* expression of affirmation, consent, etc. *n* affirmative reply.

yesterday *n* day before today. *adv* **1** on or during yesterday. **2** not long ago.

yet *adv* **1** up to that or this time. **2** now; at this moment. **3** still; even. *conj* but; nevertheless; however.

yew *n* coniferous tree with dark needle-shaped leaves and red cones.

yield *vt* **1** produce; supply. **2** give up under pressure; concede. *vi* submit; give way under pressure; comply. *n* amount yielded; product.

yodel *vi,vt* (-ll-) alternate in singing between a normal and falsetto voice. *n* song in this style. **yodeller** *n.*

yoga *n* philosophy and practice of type of oriental meditation. **yogi** *n* person who practises yoga.

yoghurt *n also* **yogurt, yoghourt** thickly clotted milk curdled by bacteria.

yoke *n* **1** wooden neckpiece holding together two draught oxen. **2** something resembling this. **3** fitted part of a garment, esp. for the chest and shoulders. **4** oppressive force; slavery. **5** bond of union. *vt* put a yoke on; join together.

yolk *n* yellow centre of an egg.

yonder *adv* over there. *adj* distant but in sight.

you *pron* **1** used to refer to one or more persons addressed directly, excluding the speaker. **2** people in general; one.

young *adj* having lived a relatively short time; undeveloped; immature; not old. *pl n* young people; offspring. **youngster** *n* young person or animal.

your *adj* belonging to you. **yours** *pron* something or someone that belongs to or is associated with you. **yourself** *r pron, pl* **-selves 1** of your own self. **2** your normal self.

youth *n* **1** age between childhood and adulthood; early life. **2** quality or condition of being young, inexperienced, etc. **3** young man. **4** young people collectively. **youthful** *adj* fresh; vigorous; optimistic; buoyant.

Z

zeal *n* enthusiasm; fervour; passionate ardour.

zebra *n* black-and-white striped animal of the horse family, originating in Africa. **zebra crossing** *n* black-and-white striped path used by pedestrians to cross a road.

zero *n* nought; nothing; nil; figure 0; point separating positive and negative values or quantities, as on a temperature scale.

zest *n* **1** gusto; keen interest; obvious enjoyment. **2** anything that gives added zest.

zigzag *n* **1** line that forms a series of sharp alternately right and left turns. **2** something having this form. *vt,vi* (-gg-) move or cause to move along such a line.

zinc *n* hard bluish-white metal, used esp. in alloys and in galvanizing iron.

zip *n* **1** interlocking fastener for openings in clothes. **2** whizzing sound. **3** energy; vigour. *v* (-pp-) *vt also* **zip up.** fasten with a zip. *vi* **1** hurry or rush (through, etc.). **2** move with a whizzing sound.

zither *n* musical instrument consisting of numerous strings stretched over a wooden frame.

zodiac *n* belt or zone of the heavens divided into twelve parts, each accorded a sign, in which the paths of the sun, moon, and planets appear to lie.

zone *n* area; region; belt; characteristic or distinctive section, as of the earth. *vt* divide into or mark with zones.

zoo *n* enclosure where wild animals are kept for display to the public, for breeding, etc.

zoology *n* scientific study of animals and animal life. **zoological** *adj.* **zoologist** *n.*

zoom *vi,vt* produce a loud buzzing noise. *vi* move or rise rapidly.

THESAURUS
OF ENGLISH WORDS

Introduction

A thesaurus is a book of words arranged according to ideas. You use it when you can think of an idea but cannot find the exact word to express it or when you have a word in mind that isn't close enough to the one you really want. This is where a thesaurus comes in: it gives words in lists according to the ideas they stand for.

This thesaurus covers the central part of the vocabulary of English – the 'core' of the language we all use most of the time – and groups this under 990 categories, each representing a different idea. It does not include highly technical words, but does reflect the fact that the English language used today is becoming more colloquial. By looking up a word in the index and referring to one of the categories in the book you will find a list of words with a similar meaning and you will then be able to choose the one you want.

The first thesaurus was written by Peter Mark Roget (1779–1869), and published in 1852. Its full original title was *The Thesaurus of English Words and Phrases Classified and Arranged so as to Facilitate the Expression of Ideas and Assist in Literary Composition.* It has since been published in many editions and the concept has been taken over and used for other languages. Many changes have been made in writing this thesaurus: categories have been re-ordered, many have been given more intelligible names, and there is a thorough coverage of new words that have entered the language. A large number of older words and phrases have been rejected as no longer used.

This thesaurus is written for those who use language – those who speak and write English and want to use a variety of words, for those who solve crosswords, and for those who just like browsing through its pages to pore over the richness of the language. After all, the word 'thesaurus' itself comes from the Greek word for 'treasure', and we hope that something of the deep resources of the language will be discovered in these pages.

M. H. Manser

How to use this thesaurus

Imagine that you have a word in mind, let us say, 'beautiful'. You have used this word already and don't want to use it again, or you want something more expressive. The first thing to do is to look up this word – 'beautiful' – in the index. The index is arranged in alphabetical order. Every entry in the index consists of a word or words, a part of speech, and a number or numbers. Parts of speech have been abbreviated as follows: *n.* = noun; *adj.* = adjective; *vb.* = verb; *adv.* = adverb; *prep.* = preposition. The numbers refer to categories. The entry for 'beautiful' looks like this:

beautiful *adj.* 844

If you turn to category **844** in the main part of the book and look under the appropriate part of speech – here *adj.* – you will find a list of alternative words that you can use: beautiful, attractive, good-looking, . . . Some of the entries in the index have numbers printed in a darker, bold type. These show the main references for particular words.

The words listed have slightly different meanings from each other. If you are not familiar with a word it would therefore be advisable to look up the word in a good modern dictionary before using it. Otherwise you may risk using the word in the wrong context. Two further abbreviations are used. Informal or colloquial words are marked as (*inf.*) and slang words (*sl.*). At the end of many entries there are cross-references to other categories (e.g. see also **56, 112**). These can usefully be followed up to find further lists of related words. You should also consult the words given at the other parts of speech in an entry, as some words there may suggest others to you.

If you look at the adjacent categories, too, you will find further help or perhaps the possibility of using a word meaning something opposite, e.g., the categories **534 resolution, 535 perseverance, 536 irresolution.**

A list of the 990 categories is given after the index and you can check that the number of the category you are looking up is the one you want.

Plan of categories

I Abstract relations

A Existence	**1 – 8**
B Relation	**9 – 25**
C Quantity	**26 – 78**
D Order	**79–106**
E Time	**107–141**
F Change	**142–154**
G Causation	**155–181**

II Space

A Space in general	**182–193**
B Dimension	**194–241**
C Form	**242–265**
D Motion	**266–326**

III Matter

A Matter in general	**327–331**
B Inorganic matter	**332–365**
C Organic matter	**366–381**

IV Intellect

1 Formation of ideas

A Intellectual operations in general	**382–387**
B Preliminary conditions and operations	**388–400**
C Materials for reasoning	**401–409**
D Reasoning processes	**410–414**
E Results of reasoning	**415–440**
F Extension of thought	**441–447**
G Creative thought	**448–449**

2 Communication of ideas

A Nature of ideas communicated	**450–457**
B Modes of communication	**458–481**
C Means of communicating ideas	**482–529**

V Volition

1 Individual volition

A Volition in general	**530–551**
B Prospective volition	**552–608**
C Voluntary action	**609–632**
D Antagonism	**633–658**
E Results of action	**659–666**

2 Intersocial volition

A General 667–689

B Special 690–697

C Conditional 698–704

D Possessive relations 705–750

VI Affections

A Affections in general 751–757

B Sensation 758–826

C Personal 827–881

D Sympathetic 882–914

E Moral 915–965

F Religion 966–990

Thesaurus

I Abstract Relations

A Existence

1 existence

n. existence, being, essence, self-existence, reality, actuality, presence; subsistence, givenness, historicity, factuality; actualization, creating, becoming, potentiality, possibility; ontology, existentialism, metaphysics, realism.

fact, truth, *fait accompli*, real thing, entity, vital principle.

adj. existing, being, in being, in existence, afoot, given, uncreated; ontological, metaphysical; extant, living, current, present, standing, surviving; subsisting, subsistent, obtaining, prevailing, prevalent; real, actual, true, authentic, genuine, mere, objective; essential, substantial, substantive, self-existing, self-existent, intrinsic, factual.

vb. be, exist, have being, live, breathe, abide, remain, stay, prevail, be so, be the case; subsist, obtain; consist in, inhere in, reside in; stand, find itself, lie, be situated, be found; occur, take place, happen, continue, go on, endure, last.

adv. actually, really, in fact, in reality.

2 non-existence

n. non-existence, inexistence, non-being, nonentity, nothingness, nullity, nihility, neverness; vacuum, vacuity, emptiness, void, blank; extinction, destruction, abolition, obsolescence.

adj. non-existent, void, vacuous, blank; extinct, dead, obsolete, vanished; unreal, wrong, untrue, false, specious, imaginary, fictitious, hypothetical, groundless, unfounded.

vb. come to nothing, pass away, die, vanish, disappear, dematerialize, evaporate, dissolve; bring to nothing, nullify, destroy, abolish, kill.

3 material existence

n. materiality, substantiality, actuality, essentiality, reality, objectivity, substantivity, corporeity, corporality, concreteness, solidity, tangibility.

substance, thing, body, solid, stuff, matter, entity, flesh and blood (*inf.*).

adj. material, substantial, actual, solid, corporeal, objective, substantive, concrete, physical, real, natural; visible, tangible.

see also 327

4 non-material existence

n. immateriality, insubstantiality, inessentiality, intangibility.

shadow, token, dream, vision, apparition, spirit, illusion, optical illusion, mirage, breath, mist, vapour, wisp.

adj. immaterial, insubstantial, abstract, intangible, imponderable, airy, vaporous, ethereal, spiritual, ghostly, spectral, bodiless, disembodied, visionary, shadowy, vague.

see also 328

5 being according to internal form

n. intrinsicality, inherence, inwardness, internality, essentiality, immanence.

essence, substance, basis, being, soul, fundamental, principle, quality, quintessence, essential, heart, core, character, nature, constitution, structure, make-up, bearing, framework, frame; attribute, element, aspect, quality, feature, manner, temper, temperament, mood, humour, disposition, personality, particularity, idiosyncrasy, endowment, heredity, gene.

adj. intrinsic, essential, inherent, inward, central, fundamental, immanent, implicit, internal, original, integral, innate, distinctive, specific, characteristic, particular, peculiar, unique; native, genetic, hereditary, inborn, congenital, ancestral.

vb. inhere, be intrinsic; internalize.

see also 223, 224

6 being according to external form

n. extrinsicality, externality, objectivity, outwardness, transcendence, projection, extrapolation; accessory, external.

adj. extrinsic, external, objective, transcendent, exterior, outward, extraneous, foreign, independent, additional, outside.

vb. be extrinsic, transcend, surpass; make extrinsic, objectify, project, extend, extrapolate.

see also 222, 825

7 absolute state

n. state, standing, condition, station, status, case, position, stand, rank, class, degree, estate, style, fashion, mode, aspect, facet, posture, attitude.

8 circumstance

n. circumstance, circumstances, situation, environment, surroundings, setting, background, backdrop, *milieu*, context, how the land lies, ambience, atmosphere, climate; conditions, factors, details, items, features, particulars, requirements, necessities; cause, reason, motives, grounds.

adj. circumstantial, modal, surrounding, environmental, contextual, incidental, background, contingent; detailed, itemized, particular.

adv. under the circumstances, this being the case, incidentally, under these conditions, in the event of.

B Relation

9 relation

n. relation, relatedness, association, relationship, arrangement; connection, link, dependence, involvement, implication, bearing; relativity, correspondence, analogy, correlation; relevance, suitability, appositeness.

adj. relative, related, connected, involved, arranged, linked, bearing upon, concerning, belonging, appertaining; reciprocal, mutual; analogous, comparable; relevant, suitable, apposite, appropriate, proper, applicable, pertinent.

vb. be related to, concern, refer to, touch upon, bear upon, deal with, treat, have to do with, apply, hold true for, be a factor in; relate, associate, link, refer; correspond to, be analogous to; belong, pertain.

adv., prep. concerning, regarding, as regards, on, about, with reference to, with respect to, on the subject of, in the matter of, à propos, re, in re.

10 absence of relation

n. irrelation, dissociation, unrelatedness, non-involvement, independence, arbitrariness; disproportion, difference, misfit, irreconcilability, irrelevance, unsuitability, inconsequence.

adj. unrelated, independent, unconcerned, uninvolved, unconnected, inappropriate, incongruent; isolated, arbitrary, free, unallied, unilateral; irrelevant, unsuitable, inapplicable, inapposite, inconsequential.

vb. be unrelated to, have no relation with, not concern, have no bearing upon, have nothing to do with, not be one's business.

adv. by the way, incidentally.

11 kindred relations

n. consanguinity, blood relationship, blood, ties of blood, kinship, kindred, relations, relatives, kith and kin; ancestry, parentage, antecedents, forbears, patrimony, heritage, lineage; descent, descendants; affiliation; children, offspring, issue, progeny; sibling, brother, sister, twin, cousin, uncle, aunt, nephew, niece, parent, father, mother; kinsman, clansman, fellow, compatriot; family, matriarch, patriarch, fatherhood, paternity, motherhood, maternity, brotherhood, fraternity, sisterhood, sorority; in laws; household, one's folks (*inf.*), home, family circle; race, stock, generation, strain, breed, line, side, clan, tribe, stirps.

adj. related, akin, kindred, consanguineous; parental, maternal, paternal, brotherly, fraternal, sisterly, sororal, cousinly, avuncular; collateral, allied; ethnic, racial, minority, tribal.

vb. be related to, be akin, generate, adopt, affiliate.

12 correlation

n. correlation, relation, correspondence, mutuality, reciprocity, interchange, interrelation, interdependence, interaction, interplay, exchange, alternation, equivalence.

adj. correlative, reciprocal, reciprocating, mutual, relative, corresponding, equivalent, interchangeable.

vb. correlate, interrelate, interconnect, interplay, interact, reciprocate, correspond, alternate.

adv. correlatively, mutually, reciprocally, alternately.

13 identity

n. identity, identicalness, oneness, sameness, selfsameness, equality, unity, homogeneity, uniformity, invariability, interchangeability.

adj. same, identical, one, very, constant, invariable, unchangeable, unvarying, homogeneous; like, alike, indistinguishable; equivalent, duplicate, equal, twin.

vb. be identical, coincide, coalesce, equate; not distinguish, not know from Adam.

14 absolute difference

n. contrariety, inequality, inequity, contrariness, oppositeness, adverseness; incompatibility, irreconcilability; contradiction, inconsistency, polarity, antithesis.

adj. contrary, different, contrasting, inconsistent, contradictory, mutually exclusive, opposite, reverse, diametrical, adverse, opposing.

vb. be contrary, differ, contrast, contradict, oppose, go against the grain; clash.

adv. on the other hand, on the contrary, contrariwise, conversely, in the opposite way.

15 variance

n. variance, difference, variation, unlikeness, heterogeneity, diversity; disparity, deviation, divergence, deflection, discrepancy, disagreement; differentiation, discrimination.

variant, irregularity, special case.

adj. different, unlike, unidentical, dissimilar, variable, changeable, varying, variant; heterogeneous, diverse, indiscriminate; changed, modified; contrasting, incongruous, contrary, deviating, divergent, disparate, incompatible.

vb. differ, vary, change, modify; diverge, deviate; differentiate, discriminate, distinguish.

16 uniformity

n. uniformity, homogeneity, constancy, sameness, invariability, stability, regularity; symmetry, evenness, unity, congruity; conformity; monotony, routine, ritual, standardization, stereotype.

adj. uniform, homogeneous, same, consistent, invariable, steady, stable, regular, symmetrical, even, unchanging, unvarying; monotonous, routine, standardized, stereotyped.

vb. be uniform, accord, conform; make uniform, characterize, standardize, normalize, level, smooth.

17 non-uniformity

n. non-uniformity, heterogeneity, inconstancy, variability, diversity, instability, irregularity, asymmetry, unevenness, disunity, incongruity.

adj. non-uniform, heterogeneous, inconsistent, variable, diversified, motley, unsteady, irregular, asymmetrical, uneven, changing, varying, incongruous.

18 similarity

n. similarity, likeness, resemblance, affinity, analogy, similitude; disguise, camouflage; correlation, comparison, equivalent, correspondence; counterpart.

adj. similar, like, alike, resembling, twin, analogous, *à la*, equivalent, typical, representative; lifelike, realistic, faithful, true, exact, simulating, imitative; camouflaged, disguised, mock.

vb. be similar, look like, seem, pass for, take after, approximate; liken, assimilate to, imitate; answer to the description of.

19 dissimilarity

n. dissimilarity, difference, unlikeness, dissimulation, diversity, disparity; variety, variation.

adj. dissimilar, different, unlike, disparate, incongruent; atypical; unrealistic, inexact.

vb. be unlike, differ from, bear no resemblance, have nothing in common with.

20 imitation

n. imitation, imitativeness, copying, representation, portrayal, mimicry, impersonation, caricature, parody; simulation, patterning; likeness, replica, reflection, portrait, echo, copy, reprint, facsimile, counterpart; translation, paraphrase, interpretation; cribbing, plagiarism; counterfeit, forgery, fake, sham.

imitator, simulator, ape, copycat (*inf.*), parrot, conformist, sheep, mimic, impersonator; translator, paraphraser, interpreter; plagiarist; forger, counterfeiter, faker.

adj. imitative, apish, parrot-like, counterfeit, pseudo-, sham, fake, mock, phoney (*sl.*); modelled on, based on.

vb. imitate, emulate, portray, depict, represent, simulate, do likewise, take after, follow suit, take a leaf out of someone's book; parrot, take off (*inf.*), send up (*inf.*), mimic, parody, caricature; repeat, mirror; pretend, disguise; copy, quote, reproduce, paraphrase, translate; crib, plagiarize; counterfeit, fake.

21 non-imitation

n. originality, creation, creativeness, inventiveness, ingenuity, independence, newness, novelty, individuality, authenticity, genuineness; real thing.

adj. unimitative, uncopied, underived, authentic, primary, genuine, creative, inventive, original, independent, first hand, incomparable, unique, rare, exceptional.

22 copy

n. copy, reprint, facsimile, reproduction, transcript, translation, paraphrase, interpretation, crib, forgery; semblance; study, representation, portrait, echo; parody, caricature, travesty; counterpart, duplicate, replica, reflection, likeness, impression, dummy, cast, tracing, model, transfer; analogue, correlate.

23 prototype

n. prototype, archetype, type, primitive form, original; precedent, first occurrence; principle, basis, standard, pattern, frame of reference, criterion; blueprint, design, plan, example, instance, illustration; dummy, mock-up; model, poser, sitter, mannequin; die, stamp, mould, shell, negative, plate, mint.

vb. be an example, set an example; act as a mould; model for, sit, pose; typify, exemplify.

24 agreement

n. agreement, understanding, harmony, unity, integration, uniformity, unanimity, consensus, unison, accord, concord, correspondence, concurrence, consonance; coincidence, congruity; reconciliation, sympathy; treaty, contract.

adj. agreeing, like-minded, unanimous, agreed, corresponding, conforming, concurrent, coinciding, concerted, harmonious, unifying, consonant, concurring, united, collective, undisputed, in step, in concert, of one accord, with one voice, sympathetic, reconcilable, compatible, consistent.

vb. agree, concur, assent, accord, tally, harmonize, match, reconcile, coincide, correspond, fit in with, dovetail, square with, synchronize, adapt, adjust, go hand in hand with, say yes to, see eye to eye, get along with, get on with, click (*inf.*), hit it off (*inf.*); keep in with (*inf.*), keep on the right side of (*inf.*).

see also **643, 699**

25 disagreement

n. disagreement, discord, misunderstanding, division, tension, dissidence, argument, dispute, contention, quarrel, disunion, dissension, strife; discrepancy, dissonance, dissimilarity, disparity, incongruence.

adj. disagreeing, differing, disputing, contradictory, inconsistent, incongruous, out of character, disproportionate, at odds, at variance, at loggerheads, out of step; hostile, inimical, factious, dissenting, non-conformist.

vb. disagree, object, not accept, say no to, speak against, contradict, defy, reject; oppose, fight, quarrel, dispute, come into conflict with, come up against; not conform, be contrary to.

see also **642**

C Quantity

26 quantity

n. quantity, amount, number, sum, extent, scope, expanse, size, dimensions, measure; length, breadth, width, height, depth, volume, capacity, area; mass, bulk, weight; mouthful, handful, spoonful, dose, portion, lot, batch, deal, whole, heaps (*inf.*), masses (*inf.*), load (*inf.*), abundance, profusion, greatness, magnitude, largeness.

adj. quantitative, quantified, measured, some, any.

vb. quantify, measure.

see also 32

27 relative quantity

n. degree, level, grade, point, stage, measure, rate, proportion, ratio, scale, measure, standard, comparison, criterion; extent, scope, range, intensity, frequency, size, speed, shade, nuance, tint; gradation, graduation, calibration, measurement.

adj. graded, graduated, calibrated, measured, scaled, comparative, proportional, relative; gradual, tapering, shading off, fading.

vb. graduate, grade, measure, calibrate; compare, rank, classify; taper off, shade off, fade, narrow, reduce, lessen, thin out.

adv. gradually, in stages, little by little, step by step.

28 equality

n. equality, parity, uniformity, sameness, equivalence, equalization, equation, adjustment, equilibrium, balance, symmetry, steadiness, synonymity, six of one and half a dozen of the other (*inf.*), six and two threes (*inf.*).

equivalent, draw, tie, dead heat, stalemate, no decision; counterpart, opposite number, equal, complement, twin, double, peer; synonym.

adj. equal, equivalent, equilateral, regular, symmetrical, fifty-fifty, on equal terms, even, level, flush, parallel, reciprocal, uniform, comparable, commensurate, proportionate, coextensive, tantamount, synonymous.

vb. be equal, agree with, coincide, suffice, rank with, match, rival, meet, touch, live up to, measure up to, come up to, be the equivalent of, keep pace with, come to the same thing, go halves; tie, draw, balance.

equalize, make equal, adjust, square.

29 inequality

n. inequality, disparity, non-uniformity, unlikeness, disproportion, dissimilarity, deviation, divergence, dissemblance, inferiority, shortcoming, deficiency; unevenness, imbalance, lopsidedness, unsteadiness.

adj. unequal, disparate, non-uniform, uneven, odd, inferior, deficient, insufficient, inadequate; disproportionate, lopsided, top-heavy, crooked, overbalanced.

vb. be unequal, outclass, outstrip, have the advantage, fall short of, not come up to, not hold a candle to (*inf.*).

30 mean

n. average, mean, golden mean, medium, happy medium, median, balance, norm, par, middle term, middle point, midpoint, centre, halfway, middle, compromise.

adj. mean, average, median, middle, grey, intermediate, halfway, lukewarm, middling, fair to middling, medium; typical; mediocre, run of the mill.

vb. average out, take the average, split the difference, strike a balance, go halfway.

31 compensation

n. compensation, weighting, equalization, balance, counterbalance, ballast, allowance, amends, costs, damages, remuneration, reimbursement, indemnification, indemnity, reparation, restitution, recompense, repayment, refund, offset, satisfaction, atonement, requital.

adj. compensatory, indemnificatory, restitutory, balancing.

vb. compensate, make amends, balance, neutralize, equalize, counterbalance, counteract, overcompensate, pay costs, indemnify, remunerate, recompense, reimburse, redeem, refund, recoup, satisfy, make up for, make reparation, allow for, set off, offset, take back.

32 greatness

n. greatness, largeness, bigness, vastness, enormity, immenseness, magnitude, size, bulk; spaciousness; might, mightiness, power, strength, intensity; amplitude, fullness, plenitude.

great quantity, profusion, abundance, masses, lots, quantities, oodles (*inf.*), stacks (*inf.*); excess, redundance, superfluity, superabundance.

adj. big, large, great, considerable, numerous, massive, enormous, vast, colossal, huge, sizeable; tall, lofty, high, towering; strong, mighty, powerful, energetic; ample, plentiful, abundant, profuse, plenteous, copious; noble, sublime, high, stately, exalted; remarkable, notable, unspeakable; extensive, far-reaching, widespread, prevalent, sweeping, universal, worldwide; marvellous, exceptional, surpassing, wonderful, overwhelming, unbelievable, stupendous, astounding.

vb. be great, be big, be large; mount, soar, tower, exceed, rise above, transcend.

adv. enormously, vastly, highly, on a big scale, in a big way; heavily, strongly, mightily, powerfully, actively; greatly, very, much, in a great measure, extremely, exceedingly, considerably; plenteously, plentifully, abundantly, immeasurably, unspeakably, ineffably, awfully (*inf.*), tremendously; excessively, inordinately, immoderately; unbelievably, exceptionally.

see also 75

33 smallness

n. smallness, littleness, tininess, diminutiveness, minuteness; shortness, slightness, slenderness; meagreness, scantiness, paucity, scarcity, fewness, sparseness, rareness.

small quantity, dash, trace, *soupçon*, shade, morsel, crumb, iota, jot, tittle; point, dot, spot, fleck, speck, grain, atom, particle, modicum, chip, flake, shred, bit, rag, fragment, trifle.

adj. small, little, diminutive, minimal, infinitesimal, imperceptible, tiny, minute, miniature; slim, slender, thin, slight, scanty, meagre, insufficient, few, sparse, rare, inconsiderable, minor, trifling; modest, poor, pitiful.

adv. slightly, little, to a small extent, faintly, on a small scale, in a small way; humbly, modestly; scarcely, hardly, barely, pitifully.

see also 76

34 superiority

n. superiority, supremacy, dominance, transcendence, excellence, perfection, nobility, sublimity, eminence, pre-eminence; advantage, privilege, prerogative, favour, upper hand, head start, start.

superior, better, elder, master, overlord, chief, boss, management, senior, top dog (*inf.*).

adj. superior, eminent, upper, higher, greater, major; better, preferred, surpassing, exceeding; supreme, pre-eminent, greatest; first, chief, principal, main, capital, leading, mainline, cardinal, paramount; best, excellent, superlative, first-class, matchless, unrivalled, unsurpassed, beyond compare.

vb. be superior, rise above, tower, transcend, exceed, excel, surpass, eclipse, top, cap, overshadow, outmatch, get the better of, lord it over; prevail, predominate; have the advantage, have the edge on (*inf.*).

adv. eminently, superlatively, prominently, above all, *par excellence*, principally, especially, particularly.

35 inferiority

n. inferiority, deficiency, imperfection, shortcoming; mediocrity, poorness; lowliness, subordination, subjection, back seat (*inf.*).

inferior, subordinate, servant, slave, junior, auxiliary, accessory, workers, poor relation, underdog (*inf.*).

adj. inferior, low, lower, junior, minor, lesser, subordinate, secondary, accessory, auxiliary, ancillary, unclassified; lowly, humble, menial, subject, obedient; deficient, mediocre, substandard, imperfect, worse, worst, common, below par, not a patch on (*inf.*).

vb. be inferior, fall short of, not come up to, not compare with, not come near, want, lack, not hold a candle to (*inf.*); take a back seat (*inf.*).

see also 571

36 increase

n. increase, rise, augmentation, growth, progression, development, spread, proliferation, build-up, prolongation, extension, expansion, enlargement, escalation, magnification, heightening, swelling, incorporation, merger, cumulative effect, snowball (*inf.*).

adj. increasing, rising, growing, progressing, developing, proliferating, expanding, escalating, enlarging, intensifying, cumulative, crescent.

vb. increase, grow, rise, gain; thrive, flourish; multiply, enlarge, magnify, amplify, aggrandize; develop, escalate, boost, build, build up, expand, swell, add, compound, upsurge, strengthen, intensify, accumulate, accrue, snowball (*inf.*); prolong, lengthen, broaden, widen, thicken, deepen, heighten; enhance; exacerbate, aggravate.

37 decrease

n. decrease, decline, fall, drop, reduction, wane, restriction, restraint, curtailment, paring, pruning, squeeze; fade-out, regression, depression, depreciation, shortening.

adj. decreasing, falling, declining, reducing, dwindling, fading, on the wane.

vb. decrease, lessen, fall, drop, diminish, moderate, subside, decline, abate, recede, dwindle, wane, shrink, ebb, drain away, tail off; peter out, taper off; deteriorate; reduce, restrain, limit, check, curb, curtail, cut back, economize, consume, use up, shorten, trim, squeeze, compress, erode, dilute, quell.

38 numeration

n. numeration, numbering, enumeration, counting, count, census, figuring, reckoning, calculation, computation; mathematics, arithmetic, algebra, geometry, trigonometry, calculus, analysis; addition, subtraction, multiplication, division; statistics, figures, data, tables, measurements; abacus, ready reckoner, computer, electronic brain, microprocessor, calculator; addent, subtrahend, product, quotient.

adj. numerable, countable, calculable, computable, statistical, numbered, mathematical, arithmetical, algebraical, geometrical, analytical.

vb. number, count, tell, score, tally, cast, enumerate, poll; calculate, add, total, subtract, multiply, divide, compute, figure, work out, reckon, estimate; inventorize, list; classify; measure.

39 number

n. number, numeral, figure, digit, cipher, integer, whole number, prime number, symbol, character, sign, notation; function, variable, expression, formula; fraction, denominator, numerator, decimal, power, root.

adj. numerical, arithmetical, even, odd, prime, whole, positive, negative, rational, irrational, transcendental, exponential, integral, digital, decimal, binary; multiple, reciprocal, fractional.

40 addition

n. addition, summation, total; increase, enlargement, annexation, accession, accretion, accruing, supplement; prefixion, suffixion, affixation.

adj. additional, additive, adopted, extra, new, further, added, fresh, other, extraneous, accessory, auxiliary, supplementary.

vb. add, add up, sum, total; append, annex, attach, tack on, clap on (*inf.*), slap on (*inf.*), join, insert, contribute, supplement, increase, accumulate; accrue; affix, suffix, prefix, infix.

adv. in addition, moreover, furthermore, further, besides, as well, also, additionally, extra, and, too, over and above, in conjunction with.

41 thing added

n. adjunct, addition, attachment, fixture, extension, accretion, accession, accessory, appurtenance, increment, rise, interest, bonus, contribution, supplement; qualification, rider; annexe, wing; *addendum*, appendix, appendage, postscript, note; prefix, suffix, infix.

42 subtraction

n. subtraction, deduction, removal, withdrawal, curtailment, reduction, decrease, outback, deletion, discount; amputation; abbreviation.

vb. subtract, deduct, take away, detract from, remove, exclude, withdraw, withhold, cut back; unload, unpack; shorten, abbreviate, delete; sever, amputate.

adv., prep. minus, without, with the exception of, bar, excepting, save.

43 thing subtracted

n. deduction, decrement, cut, decrease, reduction, rebate, discount, allowance, credit, depreciation, remission, forfeit, write-off; loss, shortcoming, defect.

44 remainder

n. remainder, rest, remnant, vestige, remains, residue, relic, hangover; result; balance, surplus, excess, margin; left-overs, waste, garbage, rejects, salvage, debris, sediment, dregs, slag, scum, leavings, clippings, crumbs, pairings, trimmings, castoffs.

adj. remaining, left, left over, over, residual, surviving; outstanding, carried over; surplus, unused, spare, to spare, superfluous; outcast.

45 mixture

n. mixture, mingling, combination, fusion, infusion, amalgamation, merger, integration; adulteration, transfusion.

blend, compound, composite, composition, conglomeration, amalgam, alloy, tincture, admixture; medley, miscellany, patchwork, pastiche, jumble, tangle, pot-pourri, *mélange*, mishmash, gallimaufry; hybrid, mongrel.

adj. mixed, composite, fused, merged, combined, united, amalgamated, half-and-half; stirred, blended, heterogeneous, adulterated, hybrid, mongrel; miscellaneous, assorted, motley, varied, jumbled, hotch-potch.

vb. mix, mix up, join, fuse, alloy, merge, combine, unite, amalgamate, conjoin, mingle, intermingle, stir, transfuse, shake, scramble; adulterate, water down; jumble; be mixed, permeate, infect, infiltrate; interbreed, cross with.

46 freedom from mixture

n. simpleness, purity, homogeneity, simplicity, plainness, purification, sifting, elimination.

adj. simple, pure, clean, clear, plain, uniform, absolute, homogeneous, uncomplicated, unadulterated, unqualified; mere, only, sheer.

vb. simplify, purify, unmix, unscramble, disentangle, eliminate, sift, winnow.

47 junction

n. junction, joining, connection, union, reunion, contact, tying, fastening, coupling, merging, fusion, bonding, marriage, concatenation; assemblage, structure, tie-up.

adj. joined, connected, linked, coupled, allied, married, wed, attached, fixed, secure, tied, hooked, stuck, firm, fast, close, rooted; tight, inextricable, inseparable; united, together, whole.

vb. join, attach, fix, stick on, affix, bolt, nail, screw; connect, link, make contact, span, bridge; put together, merge, fuse, combine, marry, juxtapose, cement; secure, tie, hook, couple, fasten, bind, splice, yoke, harness, knit, string, tether, clamp, clinch, twist; assemble, confederate, band together; dovetail, fit, set; unite, become one, meet, converge; unify, associate, ally with.

48 separation

n. separation, disconnection, dissociation, disjoining, detachment, segregation, disunion, disengagement, removal, withdrawal, dislocation, dismemberment, severance, division, cut, parting, divorce; dissolution, disintegration, break-up, dissection, breakdown, analysis; rupture, fracture, cleavage; burst, puncture, blowout.

adj. disjoined, discontinuous, unattached, unconnected; separable, detachable, divisible; apart, distinct, discrete, detached, divorced, isolated, alone, broken, fractured, in pieces, interrupted, torn, rent, cut, split, dismembered.

vb. separate, part, disunite, detach, disengage, break away, set apart, keep apart, disconnect, partition, demarcate, hive off, divide, subdivide, dissociate, divorce, isolate; disintegrate, decompose; fracture, rupture, break, fragment; unravel, disentangle; uncouple, unhitch, dislocate, unbind, loose, free, set free, release; tear, undo, rend; cut, dissect, hew, fell, reap, dice, chop, snip, slit, split, burst, puncture, sever, saw, chip, dissect, behead, carve; distribute, disperse; diverge; decollate.

49 bond

n. bond, link, connection, channel, passage, bridge; line, cable, string, rope, cord, chain, thread, ribbon, band, bandage, ligature, strip, girdle, belt, harness, lace, braid, tie, plait; knot, fastening, zip, hook, hook and eye, nut, bolt, screw, clasp, coupling; joint, junction, nexus, node, weld, seam, splice, swivel, hinge; adhesive, fixative, glue, paste, cement, epoxy, sticky tape.

50 coherence

n. coherence, cohesion, cohesiveness, consistency, adhesiveness; continuity, attachment, solidarity, inseparability, indivisibility.

adj. cohesive, adhesive, sticky, clinging, tenacious; inseparable, indivisible, inextricable, close, compact, solid.

vb. cohere, hold, hold fast, hold together; congregate; fit tight; adhere, stick, cleave, cling, fasten, unite, glue, gum, paste, weld, solder; hug, embrace, grasp, clasp, grip, clinch.

see also **332**

51 incoherence

n. incoherence, non-coherence, non-adhesion, separability, divisibility, looseness, laxity.

adj. non-adhesive, slippery, loose, disconnected, lax, runny, inconsistent.

vb. unstick, unglue, detach, disjoin, disunite, peel off; come unstuck, fall apart, shake.

52 combination

n. combination, coalescence, fusion, mixture, synthesis, amalgamation, merger, integration, union, incorporation, embodiment, association, affiliation.

adj. combined, linked, integrated, connected, synchronized, harmonious, unified.

vb. combine, join, link, integrate, fuse, put together, merge, consolidate, unify, compound, group, incorporate, embody, coalesce, amalgamate; mix, blend, absorb; harmonize, synchronize; affiliate, cooperate, work together; kill two birds with one stone; make the best of both worlds, have one's cake and eat it.

see also **639**

53 decomposition

n. decomposition, resolution, dissolution, analysis, breakdown, disintegration; decentralization; destruction; decay, putrefaction, corrosion, rottenness, putrescence, mould, rot, blight, mildew.

adj. decomposed, rotten, off, bad, rancid.

vb. decompose, resolve, break down, analyse, reduce, simplify, dissolve, dissect, atomize; decentralize, disband; disintegrate, break up; degenerate, waste away, decay, erode, corrode, rust, rot.

see also **588**

54 whole

n. wholeness, completeness, entirety, totality, unity, comprehensivity, inclusiveness, panorama, catch-all; all, everyone, everybody, everything, total, whole, aggregate, sum, ensemble.

adj. whole, all, every, entire, full, complete, single, integral, total, universal, aggregate, gross, outright, inclusive, undivided, indivisible, inseparable, indissoluble; comprehensive, all-inclusive, all-embracing, sweeping, extensive, widespread, far-reaching, omnibus, wholesale, indiscriminate, blanket, catch-all, compendious, encyclopedic; intact, solid, perfect, safe, good, unbroken, undamaged, unblemished, unimpaired, flawless.

adv. wholly, entirely, completely,

altogether, a hundred per cent, all in all.

55 part

n. part, portion, share, cut, division, section, sector, segment, compartment, department, class, group, family, branch; genus, phylum; piece, fragment, bit, scrap; detail; splinter, sliver, chip, chunk, lump, wedge, slice; instalment, part payment, foretaste, down-payment, deposit; excerpt, extract; constituent, component, factor, element, member, ingredient, integral part; aspect, facet, feature.

adj. in parts, fragmentary, broken, in bits and pieces, defective; partial, incomplete, half-finished; constituent, integral, inherent, built-in, inclusive.

vb. part, divide, separate, allot, share.

adv. partly, piecemeal, in part, bit by bit.

see also **73, 717**

56 completeness

n. completeness, wholeness, fullness, plenitude, saturation, one's fill, replenishment, refill; entirety, universality, comprehensivity, nothing lacking, nothing to add, integration; perfection, integrity, soundness; last touch, finish.

adj. complete, full, utter, entire, whole, plenary, all, gross, replete; comprehensive, exhaustive; absolute, extreme, thorough, thoroughgoing, radical, sweeping, wholesale, unqualified, unconditional; integral, perfect; abounding, profuse, brimful, saturated, swamped, drowned, sated, laden.

vb. be complete, come to maturity, culminate; overflow, bulge; make complete, consummate, add, perfect; conclude, fulfil; fill, replenish, top up, soak, overwhelm, saturate, swamp, drown; cloy, glut, gorge, sate, cram, pack, stuff.

adv. completely, wholly, entirely, fully, utterly, perfectly, altogether, quite, undividedly, exclusively, absolutely, out and out; hook, line, and sinker; with a vengeance, from beginning to end.

see also **659**

57 incompleteness

n. incompleteness, defectiveness, deficiency, shortcoming, deficit, shortage, shortfall, omission, defect, want, need, lack, break, decrease.

adj. incomplete, defective, imperfect, deficient, short, lacking, not enough, sparing, depleted; superficial, unfinished, half-done, under construction, in preparation, in progress; imperfect, sketchy, meagre, skimpy, scrappy, rough.

vb. be incomplete, lack, want.

adv. incompletely, partially, imperfectly, inadequately.

see also **660**

58 composition

n. composition, constitution, organization, make-up; nature, character, condition, quality, personality; design, pattern; compilation.

vb. constitute, compose, form, make up, comprise, consist, comprehend, include, incorporate, belong to, be a component of; arrange, mix, organize, systematize, construct, compile, assemble, devise, design, plan, write.

59 unity

n. unity, oneness, wholeness, homogeneity, unification, integration, uniqueness, singularity, individuality, singleness, isolation, solitude, indivisibility.

unit, item, bit, piece, one, point,

entity, whole, entirety; assembly, system.

adj. one, singular, individual, peculiar, specific, special; sole, single, only, unique, unprecedented, unequalled, *sui generis*, indivisible; lone, alone, lonely, lonesome, homeless, rootless, on one's own, single-handed, unaccompanied.

60 accompaniment

n. accompaniment, togetherness, concomitance, coexistence, society, association, partnership, cooperation, fellowship.

concomitant, accessory, adjunct, attachment, appendage, belongings, appurtenance, attendant, complement; satellite; *sine qua non;* coincidence; consequence.

adj. accompanying, concomitant, coexistent, attendant, accessory, connected, related, associated, belonging, attending, coincidental, incidental, ancillary; contemporary, concurrent, synchronous, simultaneous; symptomatic; united.

vb. accompany, be found with, exist with, happen with, coexist, belong, characterize, coincide, be connected with, go hand in hand, go together, be related, follow.

adv. together, hand in hand, collectively.

61 duality

n. duality, dualism, doubleness, double-sidedness; two, deuce, pair, couple, couplet, twosome, tandem.

adj. dual, duple, dualistic, binary, both, twin, paired, duplex, bilateral, bipartite, bipartisan, bi-.

vb. pair, couple, match, mate, dualize; combine.

62 duplication

n. duplication, doubling, reduplication, repetition, iteration, encore, copy.

adj. double, duplicate, twofold, twin, second.

vb. double, repeat, twin, duplicate, reduplicate, copy.

adv. twice, again, once more.

63 bisection

n. bisection, halving, forking, bifurcation; half, hemisphere, dichotomy; dividing line, equator.

adj. bisected, half, bifurcated, semi-, demi-, hemi-.

vb. bisect, halve, cut in two, divide, split, sunder, bifurcate; go halves; diverge, fork.

64 triality

n. triality, trinity; three, triad, threesome, trio, triplet, trilogy, triangle.

adj. three, tertiary, tripartite, trilateral, triangular, triplex, triform, tri-; triune.

65 triplication

n. triplication, triplicity, hat trick.

adj. treble, threefold, triplicate, third.

vb. treble, triple, triplicate.

66 trisection

n. trisection, tripartition, third, trichotomy.

vb. trisect, cut in three.

67 quaternity

n. quaternity; four, tetrad; square, quadrilateral, quadrangle; quartet, foursome, quadruplet, tetragon.

adj. four, quaternary, quaternal; quadratic, biquadratic, square, quadrilateral, quadri-, tetra-.

68 quadruplication

n. quadruplication, quadruplicity.

adj. fourfold, quadruplicate, fourth, quadruple.

vb. quadruple, quadruplicate.

69 quadrisection

n. quadrisection, quadripartition; fourth, quarter, quart.

vb. quadrisect, quarter, cut in four.

70 five and over

n. five, fiver, pentad, quintuplet, pentagon, quintet, quincunx, Pentateuch; six, half a dozen, hexad, sextuplet, hexagon, sextet; seven, heptad, septuplet, heptagon, septet; eight, octad, octagon, octet, octave; nine, ennead, nonagon, enneagon, nonet; ten, decade, decagon; double figures; eleven, endecagon; twelve, dozen, dodecagon; thirteen, baker's dozen; teens; twenty, score; hundred, century, centenary; three figures, treble figures; gross; thousand, grand, millenium; ten thousand, myriad; million; billion; trillion.

adj. five, quintuple; six, sextuple; seven, septuple; eight, octuple; ten, decimal; twelve, duodecimal; -fold.

71 multisection

n. multisection, quinquesection.

vb. multisect, quinquesect.

72 plurality

n. plurality, plural, number, multiplicity, variety, abundance, some; majority.

adj. plural, pluralistic, pluralistical, multiple, many, some, numerous; more.

73 fraction

n. fraction, fragment, part, section, portion, segment.

adj. fractional, partial, fragmentary, constituent, sectional.

see also 55, 717

74 zero

n. zero, nil, nought; nothingness, nullity, void; nothing, none, no one, nobody; no score, duck, love.

adj. zero, null, not one.

75 multitude

n. multitude, numerosity, multiplicity; great amount, quantity, lot; great number, hundreds, thousands, myriads, millions; crowd, mob, army, throng, flock, legion, host, posse; plenty, a great deal, abundance, profusion, bonanza (*inf.*); majority, main part, mass, bulk, main emphasis, weight.

adj. many, not a few, several, considerable, numerous, manifold, countless, legion; much, sufficient, enough, ample, galore (*inf.*); profuse, abundant, overflowing, prevalent, plentiful; crowded, populous, peopled; dense, teeming with, alive with, thick.

vb. be many, crowd with, throng with, flock, mass, swarm with, teem with, crawl with; overflow with; pack, stuff; outnumber.

76 fewness

n. fewness, paucity, scarcity, sparseness, thinness, rarity; a few, handful, smattering, sprinkling; remnant, minority, insufficiency, absence, lack.

adj. few, not many, sparse, scant, thin, inconsiderable, negligible, infrequent, few and far between.

vb. diminish, reduce, lessen; lack, need.

77 repetition

n. repetition, recurrence, repetitiveness, reappearance; reproduction, copy, duplication; renewal, resumption; reiteration, rehearsal, recapitulation.

repeat, encore, replay; reprint, reissue, rehash.

adj. repeated, reiterated, restated, reworded, retold; reproduced, remade, redone, copied; repetitious, repetitive, boring.

vb. repeat, reiterate, restate, reword, retell, iterate; recite, say after, echo; rehearse, go over, take it from the top (*inf.*); recapitulate; redo, remake, renew, rework, remodel; rehash, revive; reissue, republish, copy; reoccur, reappear.

adv. again, over again, anew; ditto, encore; repeatedly.

78 infinity

n. infinity, endlessness, limitlessness; eternity; infinitude, perpetuity.

adj. infinite, immense, vast, untold, boundless, endless, immeasurable, unexhaustible, interminable; countless, numberless, unnumbered; eternal, perpetual.

vb. go on and on, know no bounds.

adv. infinitely, *ad infinitum*, without end.

D Order

79 order

n. order, organization, arrangement, array, state of order; tidiness, orderliness, neatness; method, pattern, regularity, system; uniformity, routine, habit; discipline.

adj. orderly, organized, methodical, systematic, regular, harmonious; under control, businesslike; neat, tidy, shipshape, well-ordered.

vb. order, organize, harmonize; take shape, fall into place.

adv. in order, all right, all correct, O.K., orderly, systematically, methodically.

80 disorder

n. disorder, disarrangement, muddle, clutter, mess, disarray, disharmony, disorderliness, untidiness; chaos, crisis; confusion, disturbance, shambles, Bedlam, mix-up.

turmoil, tumult, turbulence, agitation, to-do, ferment, storm, upheaval, *mêlée*, *fracas*, uproar, hullabaloo, frenzy, row, riot; anarchy, unruliness.

adj. orderless, out of order, unorganized, disorganized, in disarray, out of order, untidy; unsystematic, unmethodical, irregular, non-uniform; incoherent, muddled, confused, mixed up (*inf.*), disconnected; chaotic; tumultuous, turbulent; anarchical, lawless.

adv. confusedly, anyhow, irregularly, in disorder, higgledy-piggledy, upside down.

81 arrangement

n. arrangement, ordering, reduction to order, composition, preparation, organization, reorganization, regulation, marshalling, disposal, distribution; plan, method, system.

adj. arranged, well-arranged, ordered, organized, well-organized, methodical, regular, systematic, well-regulated, classified, sorted; coordinated, connected, disposed; disciplined; disentangled, unravelled, straightened out.

vb. arrange, plan, prepare, compose, put in order, set in order, reduce to order, array, dispose; assign, set, establish, formulate, coordinate, line up, regulate, marshal, range; organize, systematize, standardize, formalize, coordinate, connect; collocate; classify, pattern; disentangle, unravel, untwist, uncoil, straighten out; put one's own house in order.

82 disarrangement

n. disarrangement, derangement, disorganization, dishevelment, discomposure; irregularity, tangle, entanglement.

adj. disarranged, discomposed, disorganized, disorderly.

vb. disturb, disorganize, disorder, jumble, shuffle, mix up, muddle, derange, upset, unsettle; agitate, disconcert, discompose; ruffle, dishevel; confuse, perturb, confound, trouble; disperse, scatter; destroy, disrupt, dislocate; disband; overturn, overthrow; stir up, put the cat among the pigeons (*inf.*).

83 list

n. list, enumeration, classification, record, register, catalogue, directory, file; statement, schedule, agenda, table; roll, roll-call; roster, rota; enrolment; inventory, stock list, checklist; programme, prospectus, syllabus, synopsis; index, table of contents, bibliography, thesaurus, dictionary, glossary, lexicon.

vb. list, enumerate, catalogue, itemize, classify; enter, register, book, inscribe, record, file, log; enrol, enlist, matriculate; schedule.

84 precedence

n. precedence, antecedence, priority, precedency, previousness; coming before, anteriority; pre-eminence, precedent, preference, superiority.

adj. preceding, precedent, antecedent, anterior; previous, earlier, former, foregoing, prior, aforementioned.

vb. come before, go before, go ahead, precede, have precedence, take precedence; lead, be in front, head, place before; herald, pioneer, forerun, blaze the trail (*inf.*), clear the way, show the way, set the fashion; preface, introduce, prelude, preamble, usher in.

adv. before, in advance, above.

85 sequence

n. sequence, going after, following, placement, succession; successiveness, consequence; order, series, progression, set, string, row, chain, train, flow, concatenation.

adj. following, succeeding, ensuing, resulting, subsequent, successive, consequent; next, later, posterior; sequential, consecutive, serial; connected.

vb. come after, go after, go behind; ensue, follow, result; place after, append; succeed, come next, supersede, displace, supplant, become heir to.

adv. after, afterwards, behind, subsequently.

86 precursor

n. precursor, predecessor; pioneer, herald, vanguard, scout, pathfinder, forerunner, harbinger; parent, ancestor, forbear.

precedent, antecedent; prelude, preliminary, introduction, prologue, foreword, preface, exordium, prolegomena, preamble; prefix; authoritative example; preparation.

adj. precursory, preliminary, prefatory, introductory; exploratory, preparatory.

87 sequel

n. sequel, consequence, effect, result, end, issue, outcome, upshot, aftermath; after-effect, by-product, spin-off; inference, deduction, conclusion; afterthought, second thoughts; follow-up; continuation, tail, tailpiece, supplement, postscript, epilogue, appendage; suffix.

88 beginning

n. beginning, start, commencement, outset, onset, outbreak; foundation, establishment, origination, invention, birth, origin, genesis, cause, source, root, spring; infancy, primitiveness, youth; starting-point, square one.

inauguration, initiation, début, coming out, unveiling, *première*, opening, inception.

preliminaries, introduction, prelude, foreword, preface; rudiments, first principles, ABC, primer, basics.

adj. beginning, first, starting, initial, maiden; introductory, precursory, opening, inaugural; foundational, elementary, fundamental, basic, rudimentary; original, embryonic, primitive.

vb. begin, start, commence, go ahead, make a beginning, make a start, kick off (*inf.*); come into existence, arise, break out, burst forth, rise, be born, see the light of day; make one's début, come out; undertake, do, set about, tackle, enter upon, set in motion, start up, get under way, start the ball rolling, activate; take the first step, break the ice; begin again, go back to square one (*inf.*).

initiate, conceive, introduce, found, establish, institute, inaugurate, open, originate, invent.

adv. initially, in the first place, first, *ab initio*, at the outset, to begin with, for a kick-off (*inf.*).

see also **605**

89 end

n. end, conclusion, close, termination, ending, finish, stop, cessation, completion, closure, adjournment, dissolution; expiration, death, decease, demise; retirement; finale, swan song, last word, death blow, curtains (*inf.*), *finis*, end of the line (*inf.*).

extreme, extremity, terminus, terminal, furthest point, achievement; consummation, perfection, culmination, climax, *dénouement;* goal, limit. point, boundary, top, peak, summit, head, bottom, base, tail; postscript, epilogue, appendage.

adj. ending, final, last, ultimate, terminal, concluding, consummate, ended, settled, concluded; extreme.

vb. end, finish, stop, conclude, terminate, cease, discontinue, desist, refrain, come to an end; expire, breathe one's last, die; run out, run its course, come to a close, draw to a close, break off; settle, determine, bring to an end, put an end to, dispose of, suspend, postpone, cancel, bring to a standstill, arrest, quell; switch off, wind up; end up.

adv. finally, lastly, at last, in conclusion, ultimately.

see also **144**

90 middle

n. middle, midpoint, centre, middle distance, equidistance, halfway house; pivot, heart, kernel, core; focus, focal point; average, mean, median; midst, thick of things.

adj. middle, centre, central, mid, equidistant, halfway, medial, intermediate; focal; mean, average; moderate, neutral, compromising.

adv. in the middle, midway, halfway, in between.

91 continuity

n. continuity, continuousness, consecutiveness, progression, continuance, one thing after another, constancy, flow, succession, endlessness, perpetuation, perpetuity; routine, daily round, monotony; sequence, queue, crocodile, procession, march, cortège, column, train, suite, retinue, single file, tail, tailback.

adj. continuous, consecutive, running, serial, successive, progressive, constant, endless, perpetual, sustained, persisting, unbroken, uninterrupted; regular.

vb. continue, carry on, maintain, sustain, remain, succeed, follow in a line; file, march, parade, queue; endure.

adv. continuously, in succession, successively, in file, in train.

92 discontinuity

n. discontinuity, disconnectedness, disjunction; interruption, intervention, break, interval, intermission, pause, breather, rest, stop-over; gap, missing link.

adj. discontinuous, disconnected, unconnected, interrupted, broken; intermittent, irregular, infrequent, few and far between; spasmodic, jerky, uneven, desultory.

vb. discontinue, break, interrupt, pause, stop over; disconnect.

adv. at intervals, irregularly, in fits and starts, discontinuously.

see also 200

93 position in a series

n. term, serial position, order, rank, grade, station, position, situation, status, standing, footing, level, tier, rung, degree.

94 assemblage

n. assemblage, bringing together, juxtaposition, mobilization.

gathering, assembly, association, collection, company, society; circle, clique; meeting, reception, party; council, committee, conference, congress, commission, convention, congregation, convocation, symposium.

group, body, mass, crowd, throng, mob, crush, huddle, band, gang, troop, horde; team, cast, crew, squad; swarm, colony, herd, flock, pack, brood, shoal, school; set, cluster, bunch, lot, batch, bundle.

adj. gathered, assembled, met, convened; crowded, dense, swarming.

vb. gather, assemble, meet, come together, associate, congregate, converge, rendezvous; group, crowd, throng, rally, flock in, pour in; swarm, huddle, bunch; accumulate, pile up, amass; collect, bring together, call up, summon, convene, muster, round up.

95 dispersion

n. dispersion, dispersal, scattering, dissemination, broadcasting, dissipation, diffusion, divergence, decentralization.

adj. dispersed, scattered.

vb. disperse, scatter; disseminate, broadcast, sow, seed; sprinkle, strew, spread, dissipate; separate, divide; shed, distribute, propagate, dispense, dole out, dispel, diffuse, decentralize, disband; evaporate; sprawl, diverge.

96 focus

n. focus, focal point, centre; meeting place, forum, market, club, rendezvous; heart, hub, centre of interest, headquarters, nerve centre; Mecca, promised land.

vb. focus, converge, concentrate, centre, attract, draw attention.

see also 224

97 class

n. class, sort, kind, type, category, section, division, group, grouping, department, branch; mark, brand, make; strain, breed, line, family, genus, species, phylum, caste; hierarchy, rank.

classification, categorization, specification, taxonomy, systematization, list.

adj. classificatory, taxonomic.

vb. class, sort, classify, categorize, hierarchize, rank, grade, group, divide.

98 inclusion

n. inclusion, admission, reception, incorporation, embodiment, composition.

adj. inclusive, comprehensive, all-inclusive, all-embracing, overall, wholesale, sweeping.

vb. include, admit, incorporate, embody, comprehend, comprise, consist of, constitute, contain, involve, take in, entail, embrace, enclose, subsume.

99 exclusion

n. exclusion, exclusiveness; omission, rejection, ejection; prohibition, boycott, embargo, blockade; eviction, dismissal, suspension, expulsion, excommunication, ostracism, segregation, apartheid; bar, ban, closed shop, lock-out.

adj. exclusive, restrictive, segregated, prohibitive.

vb. exclude, omit, leave out, remove, eliminate, except, disregard; disqualify, reject, dismiss, suspend, deport, banish, expel, excommunicate, send to Coventry, ostracize; feel left out, feel out of things; restrict, forbid, prohibit, bar, segregate, ban, black, blacklist, boycott; prevent, preclude, obviate.

prep. except, excluding, apart from, save, bar.

100 extraneousness

n. extraneousness, foreignness; outsider, foreigner, alien, stranger, immigrant, expatriot, migrant, emigrant, refugee; newcomer, guest, visitor; squatter, interloper, invader.

adj. extraneous, extrinsic, external, outward, outside; foreign, alien, strange, immigrant; exotic, imported, borrowed, adopted, introduced, naturalized; alienated, estranged.

101 generality

n. generality, universality; ubiquity; broadness; generalization, abstraction, observation, simplification, overview; average man, man in the street, everybody, every mother's son (*inf.*), all the world and his wife (*inf.*).

adj. general, overall, universal, global, catholic; worldwide, international, cosmopolitan; typical, representative, generic; broad, wide; comprehensive, widespread, ubiquitous, blanket, average.

vb. be general, prevail, predominate; generalize, expand, broaden; conclude, infer.

102 speciality

n. speciality, particularity, originality, individuality, peculiarity, distinctiveness, uniqueness, idiosyncrasy, characteristic.

particulars, specifications, details, minutiae.

adj. special, particular, peculiar, especial, distinct, unique, original, *sui generis*, individual, individualistic, characteristic, idiosyncractic; specific, precise.

vb. specify, define, particularize, itemize, designate, enumerate, go into detail; single out, isolate, put one's finger on (*inf.*).

103 rule

n. rule, regulation, law, direction,

instruction, ordinance, code, order, precept, norm, principle, maxim, proposition, formula, guide, criterion, model, standard, procedure, system, convention.

adj. regulated, normative, prescriptive; legislative; formulaic, conventional.

see also **626, 954**

104 diversity

n. diversity, variation, variousness, heterogeneity, multiformity, variability, difference; medley, mixture, variety, miscellany.

adj. diverse, diversified, various, manifold, heterogeneous, multifarious, motley, irregular; different, disparate, variable, changeable.

see also **45**

105 conformity

n. conformity, correspondence, congruity, consistency, coincidence, compatibility, agreement, affinity, resemblance, similarity, adjustment, acclimatization.

conformist, conventionalist, traditionalist, loyalist, conservative.

adj. conforming, agreeing, harmonious, corresponding, appropriate, applicable, consonant; similar, resembling, well-matched, conformable, adaptable, adjustable, compatible, consistent.

vb. conform, comply, agree, accord; accommodate, adapt, adjust, fit, suit, integrate, bend, square, accustom, acclimatize, harmonize, reconcile; follow, obey, observe, fall into line, toe the line, adhere to.

106 unconformity

n. unconformity, difference, contrast, dissimilarity, disagreement, inconsistency, incongruity, incompatibility; nonconformity, unorthodoxy, heresy, schism; eccentricity, peculiarity, unconventionality, abnormality, irregularity.

nonconformist, dissenter, rebel, angry young man, separatist, demonstrator, maverick; eccentric, crank; homosexual, queer (*sl.*), gay (*sl.*), lesbian.

adj. unconformable, different, dissimilar, inconsistent, incongruous, incompatible, inappropriate, inapplicable; nonconformist, unorthodox; heretical, dissident, unconventional, eccentric, peculiar, abnormal, irregular, unusual, unfamiliar.

E Time

107 time

n. time, duration, continuance, extent, life, span, season, date.

adj. temporal; dated.

vb. elapse, pass; continue, last; spend time, employ, fill, occupy oneself, use, what do with oneself, while away, idle, fritter, squander; happen, occur, transpire.

adv., prep. during, when, while, whilst, in the course of, throughout, in the process of; meanwhile, in the meantime, in the interim.

see also **109**

108 absence of time

n. timelessness, neverness, nothingness, eternity.

adv. never, at no time, never again, nevermore.

109 period

n. period, era, epoch, time, season, interval, phase, age, generation; term, span, spell, stint, stretch; cycle; second, minute, hour, day, week, fortnight, month, year, leap year, decade, decennium, jubilee, centenary, millenium, aeon.

adj. periodic, seasonal, recurring, recurrent, cyclic, regular.

110 course of time

n. course of time, lapse of time.

vb. elapse, pass, lapse; flow, proceed, run, fly.

see also **109**

111 contingent duration

adv., prep. as long as, provisionally, for the present, for the time being.

112 long duration

n. lifetime, ages, eternity, month of Sundays (*inf.*), prolongation, permanence; endurance.

adj. long-term, long-standing, long-lasting, abiding, lasting, durable, permanent; enduring, steadfast, unyielding, persistent, surviving.

vb. last, endure, continue, stay, persist, remain, abide, never end, prevail, persevere; survive, outlive, outlast, outstay, live on, linger.

113 short duration

n. transience, ephemerality, evanescence, impermanence; brief period, flash in the pan (*inf.*), nine days' wonder (*inf.*).

adj. transient, transitory, brief, temporary, quick, short, short-term, momentary, short-lived; fading, passing, fleeting, cursory, ephemeral, evanescent, impermanent, perishable, before one can say Jack Robinson (*inf.*).

vb. be transient, pass, pass away, fly, fleet, flit, fade, vanish, disappear.

114 endless duration

n. perpetuity, endlessness, eternity, infinity, everlastingness, timelessness, immortality, constancy, endurance.

adj. perpetual, eternal, endless, interminable, continual, unceasing, incessant, unremitting, infinite everlasting, enduring, around-the-clock, timeless, ageless, immortal, incorruptible, imperishable; perennial.

vb. perpetuate, immortalize, eternalize, preserve, keep alive; never end, go on forever.

adv. always, forever, on and on, perpetually.

115 point of time

n. instantaneousness, suddenness, abruptness; instant, second, moment, flash, jiffy (*inf.*), twinkling, point of time.

adj. instantaneous, immediate, spontaneous, sudden, abrupt, prompt, punctual.

adv. instantaneously, instantly, immediately, at once, directly, forthwith, without delay, promptly, suddenly, abruptly, at the drop of a hat, on the spur of the moment.

116 chronometry

n. chronometry, horology, chronology, timing, timekeeping, dendrochronology; date, day, time; local time, summer time, daylight saving.

timepiece, timekeeper, chronometer, clock, alarm clock, digital clock, watch, wristwatch, digital watch, stopwatch, hour-glass, sun-dial, egg-timer; time-signal, pips, siren, hooter; calendar, schedule, timetable, diary, journal, register, almanac, chronicle, annals, log, memoirs.

adj. chronological, horological, temporal, horometrical, chronometrical.

vb. time, date; put the clocks back, put the clocks forward, set the alarm, wind up, keep time, gain, lose; clock in, clock out.

117 anachronism

n. anachronism, wrong date, misdating, mistiming, parachronism, prochronism.

adj. anachronistic, misdated, undated; early, beforehand; late, overdue.

vb. misdate, antedate, predate, postdate.

118 priority

n. priority, antecedence, anteriority, previousness; pre-existence, preoccurrence; precedent, antecedent, foretaste, preview.

adj. prior, earlier, before, preceding, previous, anterior, past, antecedent, ahead of; pre-existing; one-time, ex-, retired, former; foregoing, abovementioned, above, aforesaid.

vb. go before, come before, precede, forerun, antecede, herald.

see also **84, 124**

119 posteriority

n. posteriority, succession, subsequence; sequel, follower, successor.

adj. following, subsequent, later, after, coming after, next, posterior; designate, elect, to-be; consequential, resulting.

vb. come after, go after, succeed, ensue, follow, result.

see also **85, 123**

120 present time

n. contemporaneity; present time, present moment, present, the time being, this day and age, modern times, today.

adj. present, contemporary, modern, current, present-day, latest, newest, actual, contemporaneous, existent.

adv. now, at present, at the moment, today, nowadays, right now, at this moment in time.

121 different time

n. different time, not now, other time.

adv. not now, yesterday, earlier, tomorrow, later, sometime, sooner or later, at one time or other, at a different time.

122 synchronism

n. synchronism, simultaneousness, coexistence, concurrence, coincidence, contemporaneity; same age; contemporary, own generation, peers, fellows, year, class, set.

adj. synchronous, contemporary, concurrent, coincident, coexistent, simultaneous, contemporaneous; accompanying.

vb. synchronize, coexist, exist together, coincide; accompany.

adv. at the same time, simultaneously, concurrently, in phrase, in step.

123 future

n. futurity, future, tomorrow, time to come; prospect, fate; the shape of things to come; afterlife, world to come, next world, hereafter.

adj. future, later, coming, to come, approaching, unfolding, at hand; prospective, designate; imminent, impending; likely, expected, inevitable.

vb. lie in the future, be near, draw near, approach; impend, threaten.

adv. tomorrow, in the future, in the course of time, hereafter.

124 past

n. past, history, antiquity, prehistory, archaism; retrospection, memory; olden times, yesterday good old days (*inf.*).

adj. past, historical, ancient, prehis

toric, primitive, proto-; gone, bygone, lost, forgotten, no more; former, late, old, once, one-time, ex-, retired, sometime, erstwhile.

vb. be past, have run its course, have had its day (*inf.*), be a thing of the past.

adv. yesterday, formerly, in the past, ago, of old.

125 newness

n. newness, modernity, renovation, modernization, novelty, innovation.

fad, craze, passing fancy, vogue, fashion, the latest thing (*inf.*), all the rage (*inf.*), the last word (*inf.*), the in-thing (*inf.*); innovator, pioneer, leader, futurist, trendsetter, pacesetter, *avant-garde*, upstart, fledgling.

adj. modern, new, novel, current, topical, recent, original; contemporary, present-day, up-to-the-minute, up-to-date, brand-new, just out, hot off the press (*inf.*); newfangled (*inf.*); untraditional, in fashion, in vogue, stylish, chic, smart, modish, trendy (*inf.*), in (*inf.*), *à la mode, avant-garde;* advanced, forward-looking, progressive, ultra-modern, streamlined, futuristic, space-age; convenient, automatic, electronic; fresh, virgin, budding, inexperienced.

vb. modernize, bring up to date, adapt, renew, reissue, republish, refurbish, renovate, streamline, update; innovate.

adv. recently, newly, lately, afresh, anew, of late.

126 oldness

n. oldness, antiquity; obsolescence, extinction, decay, deterioration, decline; maturity, ripeness; tradition, footsteps; old age, senility, infirmity.

adj. old, archaic, prehistoric, antique, ancient, primitive, primeval, aboriginal, extinct; time-worn, time-honoured, venerable, forgotten, antediluvian, distant, former, unrecorded, of earliest time; old-fashioned, antiquated, obsolete, obsolescent, outmoded, discarded, disused, unstylish, *passé*, out of date, old hat (*inf.*), out of fashion, behind the times, anachronistic, dated, outdated; traditional, handed down, established, customary, Victorian; dilapidated, secondhand, used, decrepit, decayed, faded; patched, mended, in holes, rusty, motheaten.

see also 30

127 morning; spring; summer

n. morning, morn, a.m., sunrise, dawn, daybreak, break of day, cockcrow, the small hours, forenoon, matin, matins, aurora; noon, midday, meridian; spring, springtime, springtide, flowering, budding; summer, summertime, summertide, midsummer, Indian summer, St. Luke's summer, St. Martin's summer.

adj. morning; spring, springlike, vernal; summer, summery, aestival.

128 evening; autumn; winter

n. p.m., afternoon, evening, eventide, eve, evensong, vesper, vespers; sunset, sundown, twilight, dusk, dimness, half-light, gloaming, curfew, night, nightfall, nighttime; midnight, witching time of night, dead of night; autumn, fall, harvest; winter, wintertime, wintertide, midwinter.

adj. afternoon, vespertine, evening; crepuscular; night, nocturnal; autumn, autumnal; wintry, winter, brumous.

129 youth

n. youth, youthfulness, young blood, juniority, juvenility; infancy, tender age, childhood, adolescence, puberty, pubescence, boyhood, girlhood, school-going age, teens, boyishness, girlishness, next generation; freshness, salad days, awkward age, growing pains, younger generation, immaturity, inexperience, callowness, greenness, prime, spring, springtime; minority, wardship, nonage, pupilage.

adj. young, youthful, boyish, girlish, childlike, teenage, adolescent, pubescent, in one's teens; formative, budding, flowering, unwrinkled, ageless, tender, developing; childish, unripe, green, callow, awkward, raw, unfledged, immature, inexperienced, puerile, juvenile; minor, under-age, infant, younger, minor, junior, youngest.

see also **131**

130 age

n. age, oldness, old age, senility, second childhood, senescence, seniority, dotage, infirmity; middle age, middle years, older generation; responsibility, experience, wisdom, maturity, caution.

adj. old, aged, elderly, advanced in years, senile, senescent, matured, seasoned, grey, balding, wrinkled, toothless; superannuated; inactive, infirm, debilitated, feeble, enfeebled, doddery, decrepit, moribund, dying, with one foot in the grave; experienced, qualified, expert, respected, venerable; major, senior, older, elder, oldest, eldest, first-born.

vb. age, grow old, decline, progress, advance in years, have seen better days, show one's age; superannuate; mellow, develop, mature.

see also **132**

131 infant

n. baby, babe, infant, suckling, mite, toddler, tot, bairn; child, youngster, kid, brat (*sl.*); young person, juvenile, pupil, schoolchild, minor, teenager, adolescent, student; boy, schoolboy, lad, junior, master; young man, youth, stripling, fellow; girl, schoolgirl, young lady, lass, miss.

adj. baby, newborn, childlike; infantile, babyish, childish, puerile, juvenile; boyish, girlish; adolescent, youthful, teenage, pubescent; immature, naive, innocent, spontaneous.

132 veteran

n. old person, elder, senior, retired person, old age pensioner, senior citizen, dependant; veteran, patriarch, old hand (*inf.*), old timer (*inf.*), grand old man, elder statesman; old woman, matriarch.

133 adulthood

n. adulthood, years of discretion, manhood, womanhood, maturity, age of majority, majority.

adult, grown-up, man, woman.

adj. adult, grown-up, manly, womanly, mature, responsible; marriageable.

vb. come of age, grow up, attain majority; mature.

see also **380, 381**

134 earliness

n. earliness, primitiveness, anticipation, presentiment, recency, immediacy, punctuality, promptness, promptitude, prematurity; foresight, hunch; early riser, early bird (*inf.*).

adj. early, prior, previous, recent, primitive; new, fresh, budding; premature, in advance, precocious, preceding, anticipatory, preparatory, advanced, prevenient; immediate, precipitant, speedy; imminent; punctual, prompt, timely, on time, sharp.

vb. be early, anticipate, foresee,

forestall, prepare for; precede, take precedence, get a head start, pre-empt, jump the queue.

135 lateness

n. lateness, belatedness, tardiness, retardation, slowness, dilatoriness, backwardness; late hour, high time, last minute; delay, deferment, postponement, adjournment, discontinuation, suspension, procrastination, cooling-off period, moratorium, respite, days of grace, stay, reprieve, remission, wait and see, filibuster; slow starter, late riser.

adj. late, advanced, tardy, dilatory; too late, overdue, belated, delayed, behind, behindhand; last-minute; unready, unpunctual.

vb. be late, stay up, burn the midnight oil; tarry, be slow, linger, saunter, dawdle, dally, shilly-shally; delay, defer, postpone, procrastinate, retard, stay, adjourn, put off, suspend, withhold, hold back, wait and see, play for time; filibuster; put in cold storage, mothball (*inf.*), put in mothballs (*inf.*), put on ice (*inf.*), shelve.

136 timeliness

n. timeliness, opportuneness, opportunism, expediency, fortuity.

opportunity, chance, occasion, right time; crisis, emergency, turning point, dilemma, eleventh hour, nick of time, moment of truth, hour of decision.

adj. opportune, fortuitous, timely, well-timed, punctual, on time, propitious, auspicious, providential, suitable, expedient, advantageous, convenient; critical, crucial, decisive, momentous, significant, key, urgent.

vb. grasp the opportunity, use to the full, take advantage of, cash in on, exploit, capitalize, make capital out of, opportunize, play on, profit by; hang in the balance.

see also **577, 915**

137 untimeliness

n. untimeliness, inopportuneness, inexpediency, mistiming; disturbance, interruption, intrusion.

adj. mistimed, ill-timed, untimely, unpunctual, too early, premature, too late; wrong, ill-chosen, improper, untoward, unseemly, intrusive, interrupting, disturbing, inconvenient, disadvantageous, unsuitable, inappropriate, unseasonable, unfavourable, inopportune, inauspicious.

vb. mistime; interrupt, disturb, intrude, break in on (*inf.*); miss an opportunity, let an opportunity slip, miss the boat, fail to exploit.

see also **578, 916**

138 frequency

n. frequency, recurrence, reoccurrence, regularity, constancy, oftenness.

adj. frequent, regular, recurrent, successive, reiterated, rhythmic; common, commonplace, customary, not rare, familiar, habitual, general, expected, usual, periodic; incessant, non-stop, perennial, constant, monotonous, continual, steady.

vb. recur, repeat; go on, continue, occur regularly.

adv. often, frequently, usually, generally, as a rule, commonly, regularly, repeatedly; sometimes, now and again, occasionally, at times, from time to time.

see also **140**

139 infrequency

n. infrequency, rarity, uncommonness, scarcity, intermittence, unpredictability, irregularity.

adj. infrequent, occasional, rare, sparse, scarce, few, few and far between, scanty, sporadic, meagre, precious; unique, single, individual; uncommon, unusual, bizarre; intermittent; casual, chance, incidental.

adv. infrequently, scarcely, hardly, hardly ever, occasionally, uncommonly, now and then, rarely, seldom.

see also 141

140 regularity

n. regularity, recurrence, periodicity, repetition, frequency; stabilization, evenness, steadiness, constancy; timing, phasing, alternation, oscillation; current, wave, rota, cycle, rotation, swing, circuit, pulsation, beat, rhythm, pulse; routine, daily round; anniversary, birthday, commemoration.

adj. periodical, regular, routine, periodic, systematic, methodical, organized, steady, constant, uniform, serial, cyclic, rotational, pulsating, rhythmic, alternating.

vb. recur, repeat, reiterate, come round again, alternate, undulate, regulate, revolve, throb, beat, pulsate, swing.

adv. periodically, systematically, regularly, at regular intervals, like clockwork; hourly, daily, weekly, monthly, annually.

see also 138

141 irregularity

n. irregularity, fitfulness, jerkiness, unsteadiness, inconstancy, unevenness, variability; jerk, fits and starts, spasm, stop, break, bump.

adj. irregular, sporadic, off and on, fitful, jerky, spasmodic, irregular, uneven; unsteady, shaky; inconstant, random, fluctuating, faltering, wavering, flickering; capricious, changeable, casual.

vb. fluctuate, come and go.

see also 139

F Change

142 change

n. change, variation, alteration, modification, adjustment, qualification, transformation, refinement, evolution, alternation; fluctuation, wavering, modulation; exchange, transference, substitution, mutation, permutation, conversion; transition, diversion, deviation; renewal, innovation, novelty, reconstruction, improvisation, reformation, revision, rearrangement, reorganization, readjustment, metamorphosis, vicissitude, transmutation; deterioration, withdrawal, removal.

modifier, changer, converter, transformer, catalyst, agitator, leaven, adapter.

adj. variable, varying, changeable, modifiable, qualifiable, alternating, inconstant, mutable, plastic, transformable, movable, mobile.

vb. change, alter, vary, modify, qualify, transform, adapt, adjust, improvise; exchange, transfer, substitute; turn, shift, veer; convert, commute; renew, revise, rearrange, reorganize, reform, translate, reconstruct, renovate; refine, moderate, temper; evolve; alternate, fluctuate, waver, modulate.

143 permanence

n. permanence, constancy, invariability, continuity, steadiness, stability; immobility, solidness, consistency; durability, endurance; conservatism, *status quo*, traditionalist, conservative, reactionary, die-hard, stick-in-the-mud.

adj. permanent, immovable, unchangeable, changeless, certain, fixed, uninterrupted, unchanging, continual, constant, lasting; enduring, unwavering, abiding; stable, unremitting; strong, robust, firm, steady, steadfast; conservative, traditional, unprogressive, reactionary, conventional; obstinate, stubborn.

vb. stay, remain, abide, persist; stabilize, maintain, preserve, uphold, sustain, support.

144 cessation

n. cessation, discontinuation, discontinuance, expiration, termination, conclusion.

stop, halt, standstill, closure, interruption, suspense, lapse; industrial action, stoppage, shut-down, strike, go-slow, work-to-rule, sit-in, walkout, unofficial strike, wildcat strike, general strike, lock-out; deadlock, confrontation; ceasefire, armistice, truce; rest, pause, holiday, vacation, respite, lull, breathing space, remission, recess; intermission, interlude, interval, interim, interregnum.

vb. cease, terminate, stop, discontinue, desist, refrain, finish, knock off (*inf.*), break up, quit, shut down, close down, shut up shop, call it a day (*inf.*); pack it in (*inf.*), knock it off (*sl.*); halt, check, restrain, put a stop to, arrest, stall, interrupt; strike, down tools, come out, go out, walk out, lock out, picket, boycott; pause, break, take five (*inf.*), rest, relax, let up (*inf.*); fizzle out (*inf*).

see also **89**

145 continuance

n. continuance, continuation, perpetuation, maintenance, persistence, duration, prolongation.

adj. continual, uninterrupted, unbroken, connected, steady, constant, unceasing, incessant, ceaseless, sustained, inexhaustible.

vb. continue, carry on, keep on, go on, maintain, sustain, uphold, keep at it; stay, remain, last, survive, abide; endure, progress, persist, persevere, stay the course.

see also **535**

146 conversion

n. conversion, convertibility, processing, development, change-over, transformation, alteration; regeneration, new birth, rebirth, evangelization; convert, disciple, follower, believer, proselyte, catechumen.

adj. converted, altered, changed, transformed; regenerate, born again.

vb. convert, turn into, alter, transform, transmute; evangelize, proselytize, save, redeem; camouflage, disguise, mask, hide, conceal, obscure; remodel, improve, mend, reconstruct, reshape, reform, mould, metamorphose.

see also **142**

147 reversion

n. reversion, return, regress, regression, reaction, rebound, flashback, boomerang, recoil, backfire, backlash; restoration, restitution, re-establishment, reconditioning, refreshment, rejuvenation, recovery, reopening; atavism, throwback; resurrection, renewal, revival, comeback; reversal, *volte-face*, about-turn, backsliding, apostasy, lapse, relapse.

adj. reverted; atavistic; apostate, degenerate.

vb. revert, go back, return, turn

back, reverse; recur, reappear, restore, restitute, reinstate, replace; recoil, rebound; regress, retrogress, throw back; backslide, fall away, lapse, relapse, degenerate.

148 revolution

n. revolution, disaster, *débâcle*, explosion, eruption; *coup*, shake-up, overthrow, upheaval, revolt, rebellion, insurrection, anarchy, plot, subversion.

radical, revolutionary, extremist, fanatic, demonstrator, agitator, rebel, anarchist, guerrilla, freedom fighter, insurrectionist, traitor.

adj. revolutionary, radical, progressive, extreme, thorough, deep, complete, rabid; earth-shaking, catastrophic, cataclysmic, shattering; militant, rebellious, revolting, anarchistic, insurgent, underground, subversive, seditious.

vb. revolutionize, subvert, overthrow, upset, shake up; rise up, revolt.

149 substitution

n. substitution, exchange, transference, alternation, commutation, shift, shuffle, switch, rearrangement, transposition, vicariousness.

substitute, transfer, alternative, replacement, understudy, proxy, ghostwriter, locum, reserve, stand-in, standby, relief; deputy, agent, delegate; double, dummy, stopgap, makeshift; scapegoat, whipping boy.

adj. substitutional, alternative, vicarious, reserve, provisional, temporary, makeshift; dummy, mock, imitation.

vb. substitute, exchange, transfer, replace, commute, transpose, shuffle, shift, switch, act for, stand in for, cover for, fill in, relieve, fill in for, put in the place of, ghost, double for, serve in one's stead; take it out on (*inf.*), work off.

adv. instead, in the place of, in lieu.

150 interchange

n. interchange, exchange, transfer, reciprocation, swap, mutuality, interrelation, interchangeability, tit for tat; barter, trade, commerce, correspondence, give and take (*inf.*).

adj. in exchange, mutual, reciprocal, reciprocating, interchangeable, commutable.

vb. interchange, exchange, swap, commute, interact, trade, barter, correspond; give and take (*inf.*).

151 changeableness

n. changeableness, changeability, variability, mutability, irregularity, instability, inconstancy, mobility, fluctuation, vacillation, wavering; fickleness, indecision, unreliability, erraticness, waywardness.

adj. changeable, variable, irregular, inconstant, mobile, vacillating, wavering, fluctuating, volatile, many-sided, versatile, flexible, malleable, adaptable, plastic, unstable, unsteady, protean; fickle, flighty, indecisive, fidgety, capricious, unreliable, erratic, wayward.

vb. vary, range, mutate, chop and change, waver, shift, vacillate, fluctuate, variegate, differ, depart, diverge, dissent.

152 stability

n. stability, immutability, invariability, firmness, permanence, constancy, irreversibility, immobility, immovableness, solidity; regularity; reliability, resoluteness, endurance; stabilization, equilibrium, balance, homeostasis.

fixture, establishment, constant,

invariant; rock, pillar; stabilizer, ballast, counterbalance, counterweight, sandbags.

adj. unchangeable, invariable, changeless, stable, constant, steady, immovable, immobile, stationary; unwavering, inflexible, unadaptable; resolute, reliable, steadfast; stereotyped, uniform; fixed, fast, set, sure, established, entrenched, inveterate.

vb. stabilize, fix, set, steady, secure, sustain, support, fasten; balance; establish, entrench, anchor, transfix.

see also 535

153 present events

n. eventuality, incidence; event, occurrence, incident, episode, happening, situation, circumstance, development, chance, proceeding, transaction, phenomenon, adventure, experience, triumph, celebration; affair, matter, concern; predicament, accident, misadventure, misfortune, mishap, calamity, emergency, catastrophe.

adj. happening, current, present, afloat, in the air, in the wind, about, prevailing.

vb. happen, take place, occur, come about, follow, ensue, arrive, transpire, fall on, befall, arise, come up, turn up, crop up; be realized, come off, turn out, feel, undergo, experience, meet.

154 future events

n. prospect, outlook, forecast, prediction, approach, promise; fate, destiny; imminence, threat, menace.

adj. impending, approaching, coming, near, close, forthcoming, imminent; threatening, brewing, ominous, certain, inevitable, inescapable, unavoidable, fateful, destined, fated; in prospect, in store, to come, in the offing, on the horizon.

vb. impend, approach, draw on, near, advance, hover, be in store; loom, threaten, hang over, overshadow, menace; forecast, prognosticate; anticipate, expect.

see also 902

G Causation

155 cause

n. causation, causality, origination, motivation, authorship.

cause, origin, source, root, spring, foundation, seed; beginning, birth, derivation, nativity, genesis; means, basis, grounds, ground, agent, occasion, influence, mainspring, determinant, antecedent; first cause, prime mover, producer, creator, author, originator, inventor, discoverer, founder; motive, inducement, activation; factor, element, rudiment, principle; reason, explanation.

adj. causal, original, determinant; basic, fundamental, primary, radical, initial.

vb. cause, make, create, produce, originate, effect, determine, bring about, provoke, generate, evoke, elicit, induce, call forth, give rise to, arouse, occasion, motivate, suggest, influence, lead to; conduce, contribute to, involve.

156 effect

n. effect, result, consequence, end, outcome, upshot, issue, product; consummation, after-effect, aftermath, repercussion, wake, reaction, backlash, sequel, fruit, harvest, emanation; by-product, spin-off.

adj. caused, consequent, consequential, resultant, resulting, following, ensuing, subsequent, derivative.

vb. result, follow, ensue, spring from,

proceed from, derive from, emanate from, originate in; become of, come of.

157 assignment of cause

n. assignment, attribution, imputation, reference, ascription; association; explanation, theory, hypothesis, rationale.

adj. attributable, assignable, referable, imputable, derivable, culpable; linked, associated; explanatory.

vb. attribute, assign, ascribe, impute, refer, charge, blame, trace, credit with, derive from, lay at; connect, associate, link; explain, account for, solve.

158 chance

n. chance, fortuity, randomness, unpredictability; odds, risk-taking, probability; fate, lot, fortune, luck, good luck, bad luck, pot luck; fluke (*inf.*), gamble.

adj. casual, chance, accidental, coincidental, fortuitous, random, haphazard, unthinking, hit-or-miss, aimless, fluky (*inf.*); unmotivated, inexplicable, unintentional.

vb. chance, fall to one's lot; chance upon, stumble on, venture, happen on, gamble, risk; stand a chance.

adv. by chance, by accident, unexpectedly, unintentionally, fortuitously, randomly, casually, perchance.

see also 553

159 power

n. power, potency, might, strength, energy, vigour, life, liveliness, dynamism; dominance, domination, omnipotence; sway, control, teeth, muscle, influence; ability, capability, skill, potentiality, competence, efficiency, capacity, faculty, efficacy; force, potential, thrust, pressure, horsepower, steam, electricity, juice (*sl.*), gas, nuclear power, solar energy, hydro-electricity; power station, grid, pylon.

adj. powerful, mighty, energetic, vigorous, strong, lively, dynamic, empowered, forceful, dominant, potent; omnipotent, almighty; able, capable, up to (*inf.*), equal to, potential, competent, efficient, effective.

vb. be able, be up to (*inf.*), be capable of, lie in one's power; be powerful, perform, operate, accomplish; empower, confer, enable, power, charge, invest, arm, strengthen, electrify.

see also 161

160 impotence

n. impotence, lifelessness, powerlessness, ineffectuality, ineffectivity, helplessness; inability, incapability, incompetence; unproductiveness, infertility, barrenness; eunuch, gelding.

adj. powerless, unenergetic, unable, incapable, incompetent, inefficient, ineffective, inadequate, disabled, incapacitated, inept; infirm, helpless, unprotected, defenceless; spineless, nerveless, feeble; impotent, sterilized, sterile, barren, infertile, frigid.

vb. not be able, cannot, not find it in oneself to; disable, impair, exhaust, wear down, run down, incapacitate, disarm, unman, paralyze, put out of action, throw a spanner in the works; disqualify, invalidate; castrate, emasculate, spay, geld.

161 strength

n. strength, might, energy, vigour, force, vitality, toughness, stamina, hardness, brawn, muscle; invincibility.

adj. strong, mighty, powerful, forceful, energetic, firm; unyielding, unresisting, persistent; brawny, muscular, stout, hardy, tough, robust, stalwart, strapping, burly, beefy, big, solid, hefty, virile, athletic; secure, durable.

vb. strengthen, fortify, confirm, reinforce, establish, substantiate, empower, energize, stimulate, build up, brace, refresh, invigorate.

see also 535, 537

162 weakness

n. weakness, feebleness, frailty, faintness, fragility, flimsiness, delicacy, tenderness; infirmity, debility; effeminacy, femininity.

weakling, coward, cry-baby, sissy (*sl.*), pansy (*sl.*).

adj. weak, powerless, helpless, delicate, puny, frail; fragile, flimsy, brittle, insubstantial, makeshift, unsteady; effeminate, womanly; weak-minded, spineless, anaemic (*inf.*), faint-hearted, insipid, diluted, wishy-washy (*inf.*); worn, rotten, decrepit.

vb. faint, sicken, languish, crumble, decline; weaken, exhaust, enfeeble, impoverish, debilitate, enervate, disable, handicap; dilute, water down, blunt, sap; fade, give way, fizzle out (*inf.*).

163 production

n. production, productivity, output, performance, through-put; foundation, manufacture, establishment, construction, fabrication, processing; propagation, generation, procreation, fertility, reproduction, breeding, copulation.

product, creation, work, article, piece, goods, merchandise, handiwork, fruit, harvest, produce, yield, result, opus; edifice, building, structure, erection, invention, concoction, brain-child (*inf.*), baby (*sl.*), thing (*sl.*).

adj. productive, generative, creative, manufacturing; fruitful, rich, prolific, fertile; pregnant, expecting, with child, with young, in the family way (*inf.*), in the club (*sl.*).

vb. produce, create, make, manufacture, put together, make up, fabricate, construct, build; devise, compose; furnish, effect, perform, return, render, provide; invent, concoct, cook up; carve, chisel; yield, blossom, flower; reproduce, generate, procreate, propagate, multiply, conceive, beget, breed.

164 destruction

n. destruction, annihilation, elimination, liquidation, extirpation, disintegration, demolition, eradication, obliteration, nullification, abolition, dissolution, suppression; slaughter; waste, overthrow, subversion, desolation, havoc, wreckage, sabotage, ruin, ravage, downfall, collapse, ruination.

adj. destructive, hurtful, troublesome, harmful, detrimental, ruinous, deadly, fatal, lethal, poisonous, venomous, toxic, internecine, shattering, annihilative.

vb. destroy, terminate, nullify, abolish, suppress, eradicate, wipe out, blot out, obliterate, wipe off the face of the earth, dissolve; annihilate, eliminate, liquidize, extirpate, exterminate, atomize, pulverize, decimate, decapitate; demolish, break, dismantle, knock down, pull down; crush, overthrow, overturn; blitz, bombard, smash, shatter, mutilate, undo; damage, lay waste, devastate, raze, plunder, ruin, pillage, ravage, despoil, sack.

be destroyed, perish, disintegrate, deteriorate, decay, crumble, go to rack and ruin.

165 reproduction

n. reproduction, reconstruction.

remaking, renovation, reforming; regeneration, resurrection; rediscovery, revival, renaissance; duplication, reduplication, reprinting.

adj. reproductive, regenerative, renascent.

vb. reproduce, reconstruct, rebuild, remake, redo, refashion, remould, reform, renovate, renew, revive, rediscover, regenerate, repeat; propagate, multiply; proliferate, duplicate, reprint, copy.

166 producer

n. producer, creator, maker, instigator, mover, manufacturer, constructor, builder, architect, composer, author, writer, originator, inventor, discoverer.

167 destroyer

n. destroyer, breaker; anarchist, terrorist, desperado, gunman, murderer; disrupter, ravager, vandal, defacer, wrecker, iconoclast, nihilist, abolitionist.

plague, pestilence, moth, locust, erosion, rust, cancer, poison, virus, fungus, mildew, blight; demolition expert, demolisher.

see also **370**

168 productiveness

n. productiveness, productivity, generative capacity; prolificness, fruitfulness, fertility, proliferation, fecundity; lushness, luxuriance, exuberance, profusion, richness, abundance, wealth, plenty, horn of plenty, cornucopia, bounty, plethora, hotbed, warren; prosperity, boom.

adj. productive, fruitful, prolific, profuse, fertile, rich, fecund; bounteous, spawning, abundant, plenty, copious, lush, luxurious, fulsome, exuberant, booming; prosperous, wealthy.

vb. be fruitful, blossom, prosper, thrive, flourish, proliferate, grow, swarm.

see also **163**

169 unproductiveness

n. unproductiveness, stagnation, unprofitability, incapacity, barrenness, desolateness, infertility; sterilization, contraception; slump, recession, depression, austerity.

adj. unproductive, unprofitable, fruitless, profitless; desolate, barren, poor, unfruitful; ineffectual, ineffective; infertile, unbearing, sterilized, sterile, impotent, frigid, childless, celibate.

vb. stagnate, vegetate, fail; exhaust; castrate, emasculate, spay, geld.

170 parenthood

n. parenthood, ancestry, origin, genealogy, parentage, line, lineage; fatherhood, paternity; parent, progenitor, procreator, begetter; father, dad, daddy, pop (*sl.*); motherhood, maternity; mother, mum, mummy.

adj. generative, procreative, life-giving; ancestral, genealogical; family, familial; parental, paternal, fatherly, maternal, motherly.

171 offspring

n. offspring, issue, progeny, posterity; lineage, generation, next generation; adoption; descent, sonship, filiation; family, child, son, daughter; heir, descendant; bastard.

adj. descended, familiar, lineal; filial, daughterly; bastard, illegitimate; adopted.

172 operation

n. operation, agency, action, execution, application, performance, running, management, conduct, function, process, instrumentality, means.

adj. operative, active, functioning, in operation, in action, in force; live, running, working, effective; executive, operational, functional, agential.

vb. operate, function, work, go, move, run; act, behave, perform, handle; produce, bring about.

see also **564, 565**

173 vigour

n. vigour, energy, power, dynamism, vehemence, strength, lustiness, élan, dash, verve, vitality, get-up-and-go (*inf.*), go (*inf.*), zest, pep, bounce, zip; drive, push, thrust, enterprise, initiative, aggression.

stimulant, invigorator, activator, incentive, stimulus, fillip, pick-me-up, catalyst, booster, drug, shot.

adj. vigorous, powerful, potent, dynamic, strong, vehement, intense, lively, brisk, energetic; enterprising; aggressive, pushy (*inf.*), self-assertive; stimulating, invigorating, activating.

vb. invigorate, energize, activate, strengthen, fortify, reinforce, stimulate, animate, enliven, vitalize, drive, push, intensify.

see also **159, 161**

174 inertness

n. inertness, inertia, inactivity, motionlessness, lifelessness, immobility, dullness, passivity, indolence, idleness, lethargy, listlessness.

adj. inert, lifeless, immobile, motionless, dead, inactive, idle, languid, torpid, lethargic, listless, indolent, passive, slow, still, pacific, dull, sluggish, dormant.

vb. slumber, languish, idle, stagnate, vegetate.

see also **267**

175 violence

n. violence, force, boisterousness, turbulence, destructiveness; outburst, outbreak, uproar, explosion, eruption, disruption, clash, clammer, assault, onslaught; disorder, disturbance, turmoil, ferment, fury, frenzy, tumult; storm, blizzard, gale, hurricane, tornado, thunderstorm, hailstorm, cloudburst, tempest.

savage, barbarian, brute, beast, monster, animal, maniac, fiend, terrorist, bully, ruffian.

adj. violent, extreme, severe; vehement, forceful, boisterous, turbulent; rough, raging, wild, stormy, furious, outrageous, rampageous, destructive; aggressive; brutal, brutish, savage, fierce, barbarous.

vb. run wild, rush, mob; erupt, explode, blast, break out; roar, fume, boil, seethe; incite, stir up, whip up, lash; force, coerce; provoke.

176 moderation

n. moderation, assuagement, alleviation, pacification, placating, soothing; reduction; gentleness, calmness, mildness; control.

moderator, balm, consolation, relief, cure, tranquillizer, restraint.

adj. moderate, modest, reasonable; calm, gentle, tranquil; restrained, temperate.

vb. be moderate, be at peace, keep a low profile; keep a happy medium; moderate, restrain, temper, alleviate, reduce, decrease, abate, tone down, cushion, soften the blow, mitigate, mollify, soothe, relieve, console, assuage, pacify, placate, still, quieten; relax, let up.

177 influence

n. influence, weight, dominance,

power, control, force, pressure, sway, authority, pull (*inf.*); significance; prestige, reputation.

adj. influential, weighty, dominant, powerful, forceful, controlling, prevailing, authoritative, important, significant, momentous; prominent, reputable.

vb. influence, determine, affect, convince, persuade, sway, compel, turn, dominate, govern, control, lobby, bring pressure to bear, put pressure on, carry weight with, pull strings (*inf.*), get in with (*inf.*).

see also **420**.

178 tendency

n. tendency, trend, direction, bent, drift, aim; tenor, thrust, spirit; inclination, bias, leaning, propensity, proneness, predisposition, predilection, penchant, fondness, liking, preference, weakness, proclivity.

adj. tending, conducive, predisposed.

vb. tend, lean, incline, drift, predispose, point to, aim, gravitate towards.

179 liability

n. liability, liableness, susceptibility, amenability; subjection, responsibility.

adj. liable, apt, inclined, disposed, prone, likely to, subject to; answerable, responsible, amenable.

vb. be liable, run the risk of, incur, fall on, be subject to, succumb to, fall prey to, expose oneself to, lay oneself open to.

180 concurrence

n. concurrence, collaboration, cooperation, partnership, working together, joint action; union, concert.

adj. concurrent, combined, allied, united, joint, cooperative; mutual.

vb. concur, cooperate, collaborate, work together, unite, combine; agree, harmonize, accord.

see also **639**

181 counteraction

n. counteraction, opposition, polarity, antagonism, contradiction; retroaction, offsetting, neutralization; friction, resistance, drag, counterweight, cross-current, countermeasure; antidote, cure, medicine, relief, preventive, antibiotic, injection.

adj. counter, counteractive, neutralizing, retarding.

vb. counteract, work against, militate against, run counter to; neutralize, cancel out, invalidate, hinder, prevent, frustrate; interfere, oppose, contradict; drag; counterbalance, countervail.

II Space

A Space in general

182 indefinite space

n. space, expanse, extent, expansion, span, area, surface; range, scope, compass, reach, sweep, stretch, gamut, spread; room, open space, clearance, elbow-room, breathing space, latitude, margin, leeway.

adj. spatial; spacious, ample, extensive, roomy, capacious, vast, expansive, deep, broad, wide, long, far-reaching, widespread.

vb. reach, extend, spread, stretch, sweep, flow, range, encompass, span; open, expand, widen.

183 definite space

n. region, area, district, zone; patch, section, sector, quarter, square.

territory, country, state, kingdom,

realm, principality, duchy, province, county, shire, community, city, capital, centre, borough, town, village, hamlet; constituency, ward; diocese, parish; conurbation, metropolitan county, metropolitan district, metropolis, suburb, suburbia; locality, surroundings, environment, neighbourhood, environs, locale, milieu.

adj. territorial, regional; provincial, local, municipal, urban, suburban, rural; parochial, insular.

184 limited space

n. place, spot, position, point, stand, locus, corner; enclosure, field, compound, pen, close, sty, pound, paddock, plot, zone, square, quadrangle, yard, patio, precinct; niche, groove, socket.

185 situation

n. situation, position, location, station, setting, site, place, scene, scenery; whereabouts, bearings.

adj. situated, located, placed, positioned, sited, set, situate.

vb. be situated, be, be found, lie, be there, stand, sit, be located.

186 location

n. location, position, site, place, seat, station, locus, stand, scene, placing, placement, emplacement; encampment, mooring, lodging.

adj. located, positioned, entrenched, installed, settled, encamped.

vb. locate, position, establish, determine, set, place, unearth, discover, search out, come across, find; park, encamp, set up, install, settle, entrench, camp, moor, lodge.

187 displacement

n. displacement, dislocation, derangement, misplacement, shift, unloading, unpacking; loss, mislaying.

adj. displaced, disturbed; dislocated, uprooted, homeless, rootless; out of place, uncomfortable.

vb. displace, disarrange, disturb, confuse; dislodge, dislocate, disestablish, unseat, uproot, unsettle, derail; shift, move, remove, replace, transpose, transport; discharge, unload, unpack, extract, withdraw, evacuate, vacate; misplace, lose, mislay; feel out of place.

188 presence

n. presence, attendance, participation; occupancy, residence, inhabitance, habitation; ubiquity, omnipresence.

adj. present, in attendance, attendant, resident; available, at one's disposal, at hand, ready, on call, on tap.

vb. be present, be there, be, be around, kick around (*inf.*); attend, visit; haunt, hang around (*inf.*), frequent; live, inhabit, occupy, reside; appear, make an appearance, turn up, show up (*inf.*), present oneself.

189 absence

n. absence, disappearance, non-appearance; absenteeism, non-attendance, truancy, defection, desertion; non-residence, inexistence; emptiness, vacuity, vacuum, bareness, void, loss, vacancy; lack, need, deficiency.

adj. absent, not here, away, missing, lost, out, not in, elsewhere, not at home, moved, removed, vanished, disappeared; wanting, lacking, minus, unavailable, omitted; empty, vacant, bare, vacuous, unoccupied, uninhabited.

vb. be absent, stay away, be missing, lack, want; absent oneself, take no part in, play truant, play hooky (*sl.*), take French leave.

190 inhabitant

n. inhabitant, native, national; citizen, resident, house-dweller, householder; tenant, lodger, paying guest, incumbent, boarder, occupier, squatter; tax-payer, commuter, voter; city-dweller, townsman, town-dweller, suburbanite; denizen; population, populace.

settler, colonist, pioneer; immigrant, foreigner, guest worker; aborigine, autochthon, primitive, ancient.

adj. native, vernacular, common, popular, national, indigenous, domestic, home, local, domesticated, naturalized, aboriginal.

191 habitation

n. habitation, abode, habitat, accommodation, dwelling, residence, residency, domicile, establishment.

house, address; mansion, country house, hall, lodge, grange, manor, castle, villa, chalet, cottage, bungalow; flat, apartment, suite, maisonette, pad (*sl.*), penthouse, bedsitter, block of flats, tenement, mews, skyscraper, high-rise flats; shelter, hut, shanty; home, fireside, hearth, homestead; lodgings, rooms, quarters, billet, berth, barrack, camp, digs (*inf.*), diggings (*inf.*).

inn, hotel, guest house, boarding house, bed and breakfast, hostel, motel, pension; public house, pub (*inf.*), local (*inf.*), tavern, hostelry, club; bar.

restaurant, café, cafeteria, snack bar, buffet, canteen, refreshment room, tea-room, teashop, coffee-bar, ice-cream parlour, take-away; pull-up.

vb. live, dwell, inhabit, people, populate; settle, colonize; reside, abide, stay, visit, sojourn, stop (*inf.*); settle down, take up residence, put down roots; occupy, rent, lodge, keep, squat.

192 contents

n. contents, items, pieces, ingredients, parts, elements, constituents, components; equipment, material, implements, accessories, articles; load, cargo, freight, stuffing.

vb. load, charge, store, freight, ship, weight, pile, mass, take on, pack.

193 container

n. container, receptacle, holder, cover, envelope; depository, reservoir; packet, package, parcel; bag, sack, purse, wallet, pouch, case, suitcase, trunk, briefcase, grip; box, carton, tin, can, chest, coffer, locker, capsule, canister, crate, bin, hopper, bunker, granary, basket, hamper, pannier; pot, jug, glass, beaker, cup, bucket, pail, bowl, plate, vessel, jar, pitcher, urn, basin, boat, crock, vase; bottle, flask, flagon; cauldron, vat; cistern.

B Dimensions

194 size

n. size, proportions, dimension, measurement, distance, area, extent, mass, weight, volume, capacity; largeness, greatness, hugeness, bigness, enormity, vastness, amplitude, immensity, capaciousness, solidness, bulkiness, corpulence, plumpness, obesity, fleshiness, stoutness.

giant, monster, colossus, leviathan, whale.

adj. big, large, great, huge, enormous, vast, jumbo; fat, obese, stout, plump, podgy, corpulent, fleshy, beefy. pot-bellied; overgrown, larger-than-life; bulky, heavy, solid.

see also 32

195 littleness

n. littleness, shortness, smallness, minuteness, tininess, slightness, scantiness, exiguity, diminutiveness, brevity.

dwarf, pigmy, midge, midget; atom, particle; reduction, miniature.

adj. little, small, tiny, slight, miniature, limited, puny; dwarfed, stunted, squat, dumpy; minute, microscopic, diminutive, atomic, infinitesimal, wee.

see also 33

196 expansion

n. expansion, increase, growth, spread, enlargement, augmentation, extension, supplementation, reinforcement, development, escalation, elaboration, amplification, intensification; dilation; inflation.

adj. expanded, expansive, dilated, stretched, swollen, tumescent.

vb. expand, grow, spread, increase, develop, boost, enlarge, blow up, extend, augment, supplement, reinforce, escalate, elaborate, amplify, intensify, magnify; dilate, distend, let out, gather, swell, bloat, stretch, protract, inflate.

197 contraction

n. contraction, reduction, lessening, decrease, shortening, abridgment, curtailment, compression, confinement, narrowing; shrinkage, constriction, recession, deflation; compressor, roller, constrictor.

adj. contracted, shrunken, shrivelled, astringent, wizened.

vb. contract, weaken, lessen, reduce, decrease, decline, abate, subside, dwindle; curtail, abridge, shorten; shrink, shrivel, wrinkle; constrict, confine, compress, squeeze, pinch, nip.

198 distance

n. distance, length, reach, extent, range, space, way, mileage; horizon, skyline, background; farness, remoteness, back of beyond, world's end, outpost, foreign parts, outskirts, limit; aloofness, reserve.

adj. distant, far, far-away, far-flung, far-off, furthest, farthest, furthermost, long-distance, long-range, out of range, out of sight, ultimate, hindmost; remote, inaccessible, out-of-the-way, God-forsaken; unapproachable, aloof.

vb. distance, outstrip, outpace, outrun, outspeed; keep one's distance, keep out of the way of.

adv. far, away, at a distance, to the ends of the earth, to the back of beyond; out of reach, out of range, out of bounds.

199 nearness

n. closeness, proximity, vicinity; adjacency, juxtaposition, contiguity.

near place, foreground, neighbourhood, locality; close quarters, close range, short step, stone's throw, earshot, spitting distance, hair's breadth.

adj. near, close, nearest, nearby; local, neighbouring; adjacent, adjoining, next; short-distance, short-range; intimate.

vb. be near, approach, approximate; adjoin, abut, connect, border, neighbour; juxtapose.

adv. nearby, in the neighbourhood, locally; at close quarters, at hand, close at hand; within hearing, within range, within earshot.

nearly, almost, approximately, virtually, practically, nigh; tantamount to, to all intents and purposes, substantially, in effect, all but.

200 interval
n. interval, space, separation, clearance, margin, leeway, gap, hole, ditch, cleft, break, crack, chink, rift, fault, passage, pass, gorge, ravine, gulf, chasm, valley, leap, interstice.
vb. space, keep apart, separate, split, intervene, interspace.

201 contact
n. contact, juxtaposition, contiguity, tangency, junction, connection, meeting, touching.
adj. contiguous, in contact, tangential.
vb. contact, touch, meet, brush, graze, kiss; adjoin, abut, border; juxtapose, bring together; unify.

202 length
n. length, space, measure, span, reach, extent; line, mark, stroke, strip, row, file, string, channel; longness, linearity, longimetry, linear measure; lengthening, extension, prolongation, elongation.
adj. long, lengthy, extensive; high, tall, lofty; lengthened, extended, outstretched, elongated, stretching, drawn out, long drawn out, protracted, enlarged; interminable, limitless, boundless, unending.
vb. be long, stretch out; lengthen, extend, stretch, elongate, draw out, prolong, spin out, protract, enlarge, expand.

203 shortness
n. shortness, briefness, brevity, abridgment, curtailment, reduction, shortening.
adj. short, small, low, slight, tiny, little, stunted, dwarf, compact, square, stunted, dumpy, stubby, chunky, thickset; curt, concise, succinct, terse.
vb. shorten, abbreviate, abridge, condense, abstract, summarize, telescope, epitomize, concentrate, boil down; curtail, cut back, truncate, slash; contract, reduce; cut down, shave, prune, shear, trim, strip, clip, nip, pare, whittle, crop, stunt.

204 breadth; thickness
n. breadth, broadness, width, wideness, expanse, latitude, amplitude; bore, calibre, diameter, girth; thickness, plumpness, density, solidity, crassitude; bulk, mess, body.
adj. broad, wide, extended, large, spacious, extensive, roomy, bulky, massive, full, thick, thickset, stout, compact, squat, dumpy, chunky, stubby.
vb. broaden, widen, thicken, fatten.

205 narrowness; thinness
n. narrowness, confinement, restriction, contraction, thinness, slimness, emaciation, leanness, tenuity, shallowness, delicacy; neck, strait, narrows, bottleneck.
adj. narrow, confined, limited, restrained, close; thin, slender, slim, meagre, lanky, lean, threadlike, fine, delicate, skinny, scraggy, weedy, emaciated, bony, spindly, flimsy; wasted, withered, haggard, shrivelled, wizened.
vb. make narrow, taper, confine, straiten; make thin, attenuate, compress; slim, reduce weight, lose weight, take off weight, diet, go on a diet, bant, watch one's weight, starve; shrink, contract.

206 layer
n. layer, stratum, thickness, bed, course, band, substratum, fold, overlap, overlay; row, tier, level, class, zone, storey, floor; coat, coating, ply, seam, laminate, lamina, sheet, slab,

foil, panel, slate, plate, scale, flake, squama; lamination, stratification.

adj. layered, laminated, laminate, flaky, scaly, squamous, laminar, lamellar, lamellate, lamelliform, lamellose, laminose.

vb. laminate, layer, overlay, overlap, cover, stratify, scale, flake; veneer.

207 filament

n. filament, wire, thread, cord, strand, string, rope, cable, twine, twist, wisp, lock, shred, hair, whisker, fibre, tendril, eyelash, gossamer; sinew, tendon; strip, tape, band, ribbon, belt, sash, bandage, scarf, strap.

adj. fibrous, threadlike, wiry, stringy, hairy, capillary, sinewy, tendinous.

208 height

n. height, elevation, altitude; loftiness, highness, tallness, stature; uplands, hill, mountain, rise, slope, escarpment, fell, moor; tower, spire, steeple, mast, skyscraper, pillar, column; summit, top.

adj. high, giant, towering, soaring, elevated, sky-high; multi-storey, high-rise; tall, lanky; eminent, distinguished, sublime, exalted, lofty.

vb. tower, soar, extend above, mount, look over, look out on, overlook, command, dominate, overshadow.

adv. high, up, aloft.

209 lowness

n. lowness, depression, netherness, debasement; lowlands, valley, hollow; depths, floor.

adj. low, low-lying, depressed, sunken, nether; squat, crouched; underlying; lesser, inferior.

vb. be low, lie low, crouch, squat, grovel; lower, depress, debase, sink.

adv. under, underneath, beneath, below, down; underfoot, underground.

210 depth

n. depth, lowness, profundity; drop, depression, bottom, abyss, gorge, pit, space, charm, hollow, trench, mine, chamber, ravine; deeps.

adj. deep, low, profound; deep-seated, deep-rooted; bottomless, fathomless; sunken, buried, immersed; submerged, underwater, deep-sea; subterranean, underground; yawning, gaping.

vb. deepen, hollow, dig, excavate, scrape out, sink, plunge.

adv. deeply, out of one's depth.

211 shallowness

n. shallowness, superficiality; shallow, shoal; covering, veneer, gloss, façade, surface.

adj. shallow, superficial, surface, skin-deep; cosmetic; light, inconsiderable, cursory, slight.

vb. skim, brush, touch on, scratch the surface.

212 summit

n. summit, top, peak, apex, zenith, pinnacle, tip, vertex, acme; consummation, maximum, limit, climax; crown, head, crest, brow, cap, spire.

adj. top, topmost, uppermost, highest, maximal, tip-top; apical, acmic, zenithal; head, capital.

vb. crown, top, tip, head, cap; culminate.

213 base

n. base, root, foundation, support, prop, stand, stay, pier, rest, bottom, basement, floor, basin, substratum, bed, channel, ground, understructure, shaft, substratum, groundwork; foot, toe, pedestal.

adj. bottom, undermost, fundamental, basic, underlying.

214 being vertical

n. verticality, uprightness, perpendicularity, erectness, plumbness, straightness, sheerness; steep, cliff, precipice.

adj. vertical, perpendicular, upright, erect, upstanding, plumb, on end, straight up; steep.

vb. be vertical, stick up, rise; make vertical, erect, raise, elevate.

215 being horizontal

n. horizontality, planeness, flatness, evenness; level, plane.

adj. horizontal, plane, level, even, flush; prostrate, prone, supine, recumbent.

vb. be horizontal, lie down, recline, repose; flatten, level, even out, smooth, plane, squash, prostrate, roll out, straighten.

216 hanging

n. pendency, suspension, hanging; pendant, locket, earring; curtain, hangings; pendulum, stalactite.

adj. hanging, suspended, pendent, dangling, drooping, swaying, pendulous, stalactitic, overhanging.

vb. hang, suspend, fall, hover, float, poise, dangle, drape; droop, sag, swing, sway, oscillate, flap.

217 support

n. support, sustenance, maintenance, reinforcement, back-up; supporter, guide, backing, stiffener, strengthener, sustainer; foundation, base, carriage, bearing, undercarriage, underframe, chassis, bogie, truck; stilt, stay, mainstay, buttress, pole, post, prop, stake, boom, column, pillar, corner-stone, pier, pile, timber, brace, beam, rafter, girder, strut, joist; breakwater, pier, wall; splint, crutch, truss; back, rest, headrest, backrest, backbone; wedge, chock; pivot, lever, hinge, axis, fulcrum; stand, board, table, seat, saddle, cushion, pillow; shelf, ledge, rack; backer, provider, patron.

adj. supporting, sustaining.

vb. support, hold up, prop, sustain, maintain, carry, bear, keep up; bolster, shore, brace, stay, truss, underpin, undergird, back, buoy up, shoulder; uphold, establish, promote, advance, further, encourage, confirm, strengthen, corroborate, back up, stand by, stick by (*inf.*), stand up for, stand behind, stick up for (*inf.*).

see also **636**

218 parallelism

n. parallelism, equidistance, coextension; likeness, correspondence, similarity, affinity; parallelogram; parallelopiped.

adj. parallel, equidistant, not meeting, not converging, coextensive; corresponding, similar, uniform.

vb. parallel, correspond, be equal; match, equate, compare.

219 being oblique

n. obliqueness, obliquity, skewness, curvature, asymmetry; curve, bend, twist, squint, divergence, diagonal; slope, inclination, slide, acclivity, decline, declivity.

adj. oblique, inclined, leaning, angled, skew, askew, skew-whiff (*inf.*), asymmetrical, awry, crooked, askance; sloping, upward, acclivitous, downward, declivitous; divergent, sideways, slanted, bent, curved, twisted, contorted; cross-wise, diagonal, transverse.

vb. incline, lean, slope, tilt, angle, bend, curve, twist, warp; diverge, deviate, slant.

220 inversion

n. inversion, transposition, reversion, reversal; palindrome, about-turn, *volte-face*; upset, capsizal, somersault.

adj. inverted, inverse, opposite, upside-down, back-to-front, topsy-turvy.

vb. invert, transpose, rearrange, exchange, reverse, revert, put the cart before the horse (*inf.*); turn over, overturn, overthrow, turn upside down, stand on its head, tip, topple, tilt, capsize, keel over, somersault; turn inside out.

221 crossing

n. crossing, junction, intersection, confluence, crossroads, crossover; cross, crux, crucifix, cruciform, swastika; network, system, intercommunication; wickerwork, lattice, grid, grill, web, net, netting, mesh, textile, fabric, weave, loom, plait.

vb. cross, intersect, interlink, cut, pass across, mesh, weave, loom, knit, sew, plait, twist, interlace, spin, twine, intertwine, interlock, tangle, entangle.

222 being exterior

n. exteriority, extraneousness, externality, outwardness; outside, exterior, surface, top, front, face, appearance, façade, covering.

adj. exterior, outside, external, outward, outer, outermost, outlying; extrinsic, foreign.

vb. be outside; externalize, extrapolate, project, objectify, embody.

see also **825**

223 being interior

n. interiority, internality, inwardness; inside, interior; substance, contents, heart, centre, soul.

adj. interior, inside, internal, inward, inner, innermost; intrinsic, inborn, innate; central, integral; inland.

vb. be inside; internalize.

see also **5, 224**

224 centrality

n. centrality, centralization; centre, middle, bull's eye; focus, concentration, convergence; nucleus, core, heart, hub, nub, gist, kernel, marrow, pith.

adj. central, centre, middle, inner, focal, pivotal.

vb. centre, centralize, concentrate, focus, converge, draw, attract.

see also **96**

225 covering

n. covering, superimposition, cover, lid, flap, box, wrapping; ceiling, roof, shelter, dome, awning, tent, marquee, tarpaulin, canopy, mask, hood, shade, film, blind, umbrella, parasol, sunshade, sheath; sheet, blanket, robe, carpet, rug, mat; coating, varnish, paint, veneer, lacquer, glaze, enamel, wash, polish, stain, distemper, gloss; skin, peel, shell, rind, coat, husk, hull, pod, jacket, integument, tegument.

adj. covered, sheltered, hooded, wrapped, enveloped, veiled, varnished, painted, surfaced.

vb. cover, put on, lay over, protect, shield, shelter, wrap, envelop, enshroud, enclose, veil, superimpose, superpose; roof, carpet, pave, paper; coat, surface, varnish, paint, plate, gloss, glaze, spray, veneer, wax; mask, hide, conceal.

226 lining

n. lining, insulation, interlining; inner surface, inside; filling, stuffing, wadding, padding, quilting, inlay.

vb. line, insulate, interline, inlay,

stuff, wad, pad, fill, quilt, reinforce, overlay, face, encrust.

227 dressing

n. dressing, toilet; dress, clothing, wardrobe, outfit, vesture, garb, gear, guise, raiment, apparel, attire; clothes, garment, vestment, costume, suit, dress; uniform, livery.

adj. dressed, well-dressed, dressed-up, clad.

vb. dress, clothe, turn out, deck out (*inf.*), equip, fit out; wear, have on, be dressed in; put on, get dressed, don, slip on, throw on, assume; dress up, get dressed up, smarten oneself up; change into; wrap up.

228 undressing

n. undressing, divestment; bareness, undress, nakedness, nudism, nudity, naturism, *déshabillé*, stripping, strip-tease; nude, nudist, naturist; baldness, alopecia, shaving, tonsure.

adj. bare, exposed, unveiled, uncovered, unprotected; revealing, *décolleté*; undressed, naked, nude, stark naked, stripped, in one's birthday suit (*inf.*), in the altogether (*inf.*), starkers (*sl.*); bald, hairless, bald-headed, balding, shaven, tonsured, shining, smooth; threadbare, denuded.

vb. uncover, expose, unveil, reveal; remove, take off, cast off; undress, unclothe, strip, disrobe, divest; pluck, peel, pare, shed, bare, skin, flay, scalp, shell, stone, excoriate, decorticate; denude, ravage.

229 being around

n. environment, ambience, circumstances, surroundings; circumjacence; scene, *milieu*, background, setting, habitat, situation; atmosphere, climate; environs, suburbs, vicinity.

adj. environmental, ambient, surrounding, background, situational.

vb. surround, circle, enclose, close in, envelop, girdle, encompass.

adv., prep. around, about.

see also **8**

230 being between

n. interposition, intermediacy, intercurrence, intervention, interruption, interjection, interpolation; mediation, intercession; partition, wall, watershed, fence, hurdle; insert, inset, wedge.

adj. intermediary, intermediate, intervening.

vb. place between, mediate, interpose; insert, intersperse; interrupt, interject, intervene.

prep. between, among.

see also **653**

231 circumscription

n. circumscription, encircling, circumnavigation; limitation, demarcation, boundary, restriction.

vb. circumscribe, encircle, ring, encompass, surround, circumambulate, circumnavigate, circumvent; surround; limit, restrict, bound, mark off, confine.

232 outline

n. outline, perimeter, periphery, outside, circumference, circuit, border, boundary, contour; sketch, skeleton, silhouette, profile, framework, tracing, delineation.

vb. outline, sketch, trace, delineate.

233 edge

n. edge, extremity, end, limit, verge; border, frontier, boundary; threshold, brink, brim, rim, side, corner, point, tip, margin, skirt; edging, skirting, fringe, hem.

vb. border, verge, edge, skirt; rim, hem, margin, fringe.

234 enclosure

n. enclosure, confinement; envelope, wrapping; area, ground, pitch, arena; plot, court, yard, garden, park; cell, prison, dungeon, den; pen, cage, pound, aviary, coop, warren.

fence, wire, wall, hedge, fencing, paling, rail, railing, balustrade, barrier, ditch, moat, trench, ha-ha.

vb. enclose, envelop, wrap, enfold, confine, contain, blockade, shut in, shut up, lock up, fence, impound, hedge in, hem in; package, parcel; bottle; jail, imprison.

235 limit

n. limit, end, utmost, extremity, destination, terminus, conclusion; limitation, delimitation, restriction, definition, control; hurdle, barrier, frontier, boundary, border, borderline; threshold, upper limit, ceiling; demarcation line, mark, fringe, edge.

adj. limited, set, defined.

vb. limit, set, settle, define, delimit, demarcate, bound, confine, restrict, draw the line at, curb.

236 front

n. front, frontage, exterior, façade, anterior, foreground, face, head, forehead, vanguard, front line; visage, countenance, physiognomy; semblance.

adj. front, forward, fore, foremost, frontal, frontmost, head, obverse, anterior, leading, advance.

vb. face, front, look out on, border; head, lead; meet, confront, encounter, come face to face with.

adv. in advance, ahead; in the foreground.

237 rear

n. rear, back, tail, end, reverse, posterior, backside, bottom, dorsum; wake, rearguard; background, hinterland, backstage.

adj. rear, back, hind, tail, posterior, after, terminal, final, bottom, dorsal, backmost, hindmost, rearmost, background, backstage.

vb. be behind, follow, back on to; bring up the rear.

adv. at the rear, behind, in the background.

238 sidedness

n. sidedness, laterality; juxtaposition, adjacency; side, hand, flank, shoulder.

adj. side, lateral, sidelong, sidewise, sideways, flanking; adjacent.

vb. be side by side, flank, skirt; juxtapose.

adv. laterally, sideways, abreast, alongside, side by side.

239 being opposite

n. opposition, contraposition, polarity; opposite, converse, reverse, contrary, contrast, contradiction, antipode, antipole.

adj. opposite, contrary, opposing, contradictory.

vb. be opposite, oppose, confront, face.

adv., prep. opposite, over against, facing, *vis à vis.*

240 right side

n. right-handedness, dexterity, dextrality; right, right hand; right-hander, dextral; starboard.

adj. right, right-hand, right-handed, off, offside, dextral, dextrorse.

241 left side

n. left-handedness, sinistrality; left, left hand; left-hander, sinistral; port.

adj. left, left-hand, left-handed, near-side, sinistrorse.

C Form

242 form

n. form, shape, style, look, appearance, fashion, design, outline, profile, contour; structure, construction, formation; morphology.

adj. formed, shaped, developed; formative, impressionable, plastic, mouldable.

vb. form, make, create, fashion, pattern, model, mould; cast, stamp, impress, carve, cut; arrange, construct, build, assemble; take shape, develop, express, grow, materialize.

243 absence of form

n. formlessness, shapelessness, amorphism, fuzziness; chaos, liquid; fluid.

adj. formless, shapeless, amorphous; vague, unclear, indistinct, blurred, fuzzy; indeterminate, indefinite; chaotic, misshapen, unshapely, deformed.

244 symmetry

n. symmetry, regularity, conformity, proportion, equality, evenness, balance, harmony, arrangement, order; shapeliness.

adj. symmetrical, balanced, even, proportioned, harmonious, shapely, regular, well-proportioned.

245 asymmetry

n. asymmetry, disproportion, lopsidedness, irregularity, distortion, contortion, twist, deformity, malformation.

adj. asymmetrical, disproportionate, irregular, misproportioned, uneven, unshapely, grotesque, ugly, hideous, distorted, deformed, malformed, disfigured, crippled, mangled, hunchbacked, crooked, awry, askew.

vb. distort, contort, twist, pervert, deform, misshape, disfigure, buckle, cripple; writhe, scowl, grimace.

see also 845

246 angular form

n. angularity, pointedness, serration; angle, crotch, elbow, fork, corner, point, zigzag; right angle, acute angle, obtuse angle, reflex angle; triangle; quadrilateral, parallelogram, rhomboid, rectangle, oblong, square, diamond, lozenge, rhombus, rhomb, polygon, pentagon, hexagon, heptagon, octagon, nonagon, enneagon, decagon, endecagon, dodecagon; polyhedron, cube, tetrahedron, pyramid, prism, wedge.

adj. angular, pointed, sharp-cornered, scraggy, jagged, serrated, zigzag, wedge-shaped, cuneiform, cuneate; triangular, rectangular, multilateral.

vb. angle, bend, intersect, serrate, zigzag.

see also 259

247 curved form

n. curvature, bending, flexion, flexure, arcuation; curve, bend, sweep, bow, curl, camber, arc, chord, arcade, rainbow, arch, crook, trajectory; catenary, parabola, hyperbola, circle, ellipse, epicycle; crescent, half-moon, lune, lunula, meniscus, lens, lunate.

adj. curved, bent, rounded, arched, vaulted, crescent, lunate.

vb. curve, turn, arch, bow, curl, crook, buckle, twist, warp, flex; waver, meander, swerve, deviate, veer.

248 straight form

n. straightness, rectilinearity; verticality, perpendicularity; horizontality; bee-line.

adj. straight, even, level, direct; upright, vertical, perpendicular, erect; horizontal; unbroken, uninterrupted.

vb. straighten, order, make straight; untwist, unbend, uncoil, disentangle, unravel, uncurl, unfold.

adv. in a straight line, as the crow flies.

249 round form

n. rotundity, roundness; round, globe, sphere, orb, ball, marble, balloon, bubble, drop, droplet, globule; cylinder, barrel, roll, drum.

adj. round, rotund, rounded, spherical, globular, orbicular, globe-shaped, globoid, globose, cylindrical.

vb. round, ball, roll, coil up.

250 simple circularity

n. circularity, roundness; circle, orbit, circuit, ring, loop, halo, crown, corona, aureola, circus, bowl, hoop, quoit, wheel, disc, equator; ellipse, oval, egg; band, belt, wreath, garland; circumference, perimeter, rim, periphery.

adj. round, circular, cyclic, orbicular; oval, elliptical.

vb. encircle, go round; make round.

see also 322

251 complex circularity

n. convolution, intricacy, twisting, sinuosity, torsion; coil, turn, twine, twist, plait, kink, loop, spiral, helix, screw, curl, tendril, scroll.

adj. convoluted, intricate, involved; winding, spiral, coiled, helical, flexuous, sinuous, tortuous; serpentine, snake-like; meandering, undulating, wavy.

vb. turn, wind, curl, loop, twist, twirl, fold, twine, plait, intertwine, entwine, sinuate, wrinkle, contort, wreathe; crimp, ripple; meander, undulate; wriggle, squirm, wiggle.

252 convexity

n. convexity, protuberance, bulginess, outgrowth.

swelling, growth, bump, hump, lump, ridge, protuberance, rising, bulge; tumour, cancer, corn, boil, inflammation, carbuncle, bunion, wart, pimple, bulb; dome, cupola, vault.

adj. convex, arched, raised, curved, bent; bulbous, swollen, bloated; bulging, swelling, excrescent, tumescent, tumid.

vb. swell, bulge, rise, project, protrude, jut.

253 prominence

n. prominence, salience; projection, protuberance, protrusion, extension, spur, spit, promontory, tongue, headland, relief; leader, figure-head, model, example.

adj. prominent, conspicuous, protuberant, extended, jutting, protruding, projecting, salient, obtrusive.

vb. protrude, extend, jut, project, stand out, stick out.

254 concavity

n. concavity, hollowness; hollow, hole, aperture, opening, depression; pit, abyss, mine, shaft, well, trench; corner, niche, recess, alcove, indentation, pocket; valley, dale, bowl, drop, gulf, basin, glen, ravine, crevasse, fissure, crater, gorge, canyon, gully, chasm; dip, dent, dimple; cave, burrow, cavern, grotto, furrow, covert, warren, pothole; excavation, tunnel, passage, retreat, dug-out, dig (*inf.*).

adj. concave, hollow, depressed, excavated, sunken, carved out, indented.

vb. hollow out, excavate, dig, spade,

gouge, delve, mine, tunnel, bore; indent, depress; cave in, fall in, collapse.

255 sharpness

n. sharpness, acuteness; point, tip, prick, thorn, sting, spike, nail, pin, needle, fork, prong; barb, thorn, bramble, prickle, brier, spine; tooth, edge, scissors, shears, knife.

adj. sharp, acute, pointed, fine, keen, cutting, biting, piercing, incisive, trenchant; spiked, spiky, spiny, prickly, thorny, needle-pointed, barbed; pronged, tapered, tapering, acuminate.

vb. be sharp, prick, sting, taper; sharpen, grind, edge, file, hone, whet, strop; barb, point; puncture.

256 bluntness

n. bluntness, obtuseness, flatness.

adj. blunt, unsharpened, unpointed, dull, unsharp, obtuse; toothless.

vb. blunt, dull, take the edge off, round, turn, obtund; be blunt, not cut.

257 smoothness

n. smoothness, flatness, levelness, regularity; stillness, glossiness, silkiness; glass, ice, marble; gloss, varnish, polish, finish.

adj. smooth, flat, plane, level, even, uniform, steady, stable, continuous; quiet, still, sleek, polished, glossy, glassy, lustrous, silky, soft, slippery, oily.

vb. smooth, even, level, plane, scrape, shave, flatten, iron, sand, file, press; polish, shine, burnish, glaze, gloss, varnish; glide, slide, float, skim, drift, stream.

258 roughness

n. roughness, asperity, unevenness, coarseness, harshness, bumpiness, brokenness, irregularity, jaggedness, corrugation.

adj. rough, uneven, coarse, harsh, bumpy, broken, jagged, rugged, choppy, ruffled; bristly, prickly, hairy, hirsute.

vb. roughen, coarsen, break, notch, serrate, crumple, ruffle.

259 notch

n. notch, indentation, cut, zigzag, cleft, trench, trough, gouge, saw, nick, incision, depression, serration.

adj. notched, jagged, saw-toothed, serrated.

vb. notch, serrate, cut, tooth, cog, indent, nick.

260 fold

n. fold, gather, pleat, lapel, overlap, tuck; crease, crimp, wrinkle, corrugation, turn.

adj. folded, gathered, creased, wrinkled, corrugated, pleated, puckered, overlapping.

vb. fold, double, crease, lap, overlap, plicate, pleat, curl, crimp, wrinkle, ruffle, pucker, gather, corrugate.

261 furrow

n. furrow, groove, slit, slot, trench, rut, gouge, moat, channel, canal, ditch, gutter; corrugation.

adj. furrowed, grooved, ribbed, fluted, corrugated, ridged.

vb. furrow, groove, slot, flute, corrugate, channel, plough.

262 opening

n. opening, aperture, orifice, hole, gap, hollow, slit, perforation, slot, break; mouth, throat, gullet; outlet, vent; window, porthole; door, doorway, gate, exit, entrance, hatch, hatchway, channel, passage.

adj. open, unlocked, unfastened, unsealed; clear, accessible; ajar, gaping, wide, yawning; torn, rent.

vb. open, unlock, unbolt, unbar,

unfasten, undo; clear, admit, free, loosen; expose, reveal, unfold; gape, yawn.

see also 264, 462

263 closure

n. closure, occlusion, stoppage, blockage, obstruction.

adj. closed, unopened, shut, fastened, bolted, blocked, sealed.

vb. close, shut, lock, fasten, bar, bolt.

see also 265

264 perforator

n. perforator, sponge, sieve, strainer, colander; borer, awl, gimlet, drill, lancet, needle, pin, punch; perforation, porosity.

adj. perforated, porous, pervious, permeable, penetrable, spongy, absorbent, holey.

vb. cut, perforate, pierce, prick, slit, puncture, crack, stick, inject, drill, stab, lance, spear, spike, skewer, impale, bore, mine, tunnel; hole, riddle.

265 stopper

n. stopper, plug, cork, bung, tap, valve, stopcock, wedge, rammer, stuffing, filling, stopping.

adj. stopped up, blocked, obstructed, sealed, impenetrable, impervious, watertight.

vb. block, obstruct, blockade, stop, choke, clog, stuff, ram, fill, dam, seal, cork, plug, bung, occlude, obturate.

D Motion

266 motion

n. motion, mobility, movableness, movement, action, activity, unrest, restlessness, move, passage, progress, advance, ascension, descension; velocity, speed.

adj. moving, in motion, transitional, movable, mobile, restless, nomadic.

vb. move, go, run, progress, proceed; push, impel, stir, set in motion, activate, propel.

267 rest

n. rest, immobility, motionlessness, cessation, stillness, standstill, stop; discontinuance, interval, pause; silence, calm; quiet, calmness, peace, tranquillity.

adj. quiet, peaceful, still, quiescent, asleep; immovable, immobile, motionless, unruffled, peaceful, placid, serene.

vb. rest, stand still, pause, halt, stop, cease; not stir, keep quiet; still, soften, quiesce, relax, lull, becalm, hush.

see also 174

268 transference

n. transference, transferal, conveyance, movement, removal, shift, relay, conduct, remittance, dispatch, delivery, hand-over; transport, transportation, transit, carriage, shipment, trans-shipment, haulage, freight, consignment.

adj. transferable, transmittable, transmissible, conveyable, movable, portable.

vb. transfer, move, remove, conduct, carry, take, convey, shift; send, direct, remit, relay, dispatch, forward, deliver, hand over, consign; ship, cart, truck, haul, load, post, mail; convoy, escort; import, export; transmit, communicate; relocate, transplant; ply, shuttle.

see also 714

269 land travel

n. travel, tourism, touring, sightseeing, globe-trotting, roaming; journey, tour, trip, outing, expedition, excursion, day out, picnic; pilgrimage;

venture, adventure; visit, sojourn; exploration, quest, safari.

walk, step, pace, stride, gait, march; stroll, hike, jaunt, saunter, amble, ramble, wayfaring, tramp; promenade, constitutional, perambulation; peregrinations, wanderings.

riding, horse-riding, horsemanship, horse-racing, equestrianism, show-jumping, dressage; cycling, spin, ride; drive; driving, motoring; itinerary, route, course, circuit, direction, map.

adj. journeying, travelling, visiting; peripatetic.

vb. travel, journey, tour, rove, visit, cruise, explore, traverse; walk, step, pace, march, tread, amble, ramble, wander, hike, trek, stroll, ambulate, perambulate, promenade; gad about (*inf.*), gallivant about (*inf.*); ride, cycle, bike (*inf.*); drive, motor.

270 traveller

n. traveller, tourist, sightseer, globetrotter, holiday-maker, daytripper, visitor, voyager, explorer, adventurer; itinerant, wanderer, roamer, pedlar, vagabond, vagrant, tramp, hobo; migrant, emigrant, immigrant, refugee, gypsy, nomad, bedouin.

pedestrian, walker, foot-passenger, hiker, trekker, rambler, pilgrim, wayfarer, runner, athlete; rider, horse-rider, jockey, show-jumper, hitch-hiker; passenger, commuter, season-ticket holder; motorist, driver.

271 water travel

n. navigation, sailing, cruising, circumnavigation; seamanship, seafaring, exploration; voyage, cruise; water sports, aquatics, sailing, yachting, boating, rowing, canoeing, swimming, diving, surfing.

adj. navigational, sailing, nautical, naval, marine, maritime.

vb. sail, cruise, voyage, ply, run, ferry; set sail; launch, cast off; navigate, steer, pilot, make for, head for, set a course; drop anchor, moor; swim, bathe, dive, dip, paddle, wade, surf, water-ski.

272 mariner

n. mariner, sailor, seaman, seafarer, pilot, boatman, marine, crew, captain, boatswain, navigator, helmsman.

273 air travel

n. air travel, aeronautics, aviation, flying, gliding, flight.

pilot, airman, aviator, flier, aeronaut.

adj. flying; aerial, aeronautical, aerodynamic.

vb. fly, pilot, taxi, take off, climb, rise, soar, zoom; spin, loop, roll; glide, dive, dart, shoot; plunge, plummet; parachute, bail out; touch down, land, come down, crash-land; talk down.

274 space travel

n. space travel, astronautics, cosmonautics; countdown, space flight, space walk; grand tour; re-entry, splashdown.

astronaut, spaceman, cosmonaut, space traveller.

adj. astronautical, cosmonautic, cosmonautical.

vb. take off, orbit, splash down.

275 carrier

n. carrier, bearer, porter, messenger, runner; basket, bag, container; horse, packhorse, llama, beast of burden.

vb. carry, transport, move, convey, transfer, bear.

276 vehicle

n. vehicle, conveyance; cycle, bike bicycle, pushbike (*sl.*), velocipede, tandem, tricycle; moped, scooter, motor scooter, motorcycle, motorbike; car, automobile, motor, saloon, sports car, G. T., coupé, hard-top, convertible, hatchback, estate car, station wagon, shooting-brake, minibus; taxi, taxicab, minicab, cab, hackney carriage, rickshaw; bus, coach, motor bus, tram, trolley-bus; van, lorry, pick-up, dump truck; train, underground, rapid transit; engine, locomotive, diesel locomotive, electric locomotive, steam engine.

cart, trolley, pram, barrow, trailer; carriage, wagon, buggy, trap, gig, hansom.

adj. vehicular, locomotive, wheeled.

277 ship

n. ship, boat, vessel, craft; motorboat, steamer, steamboat, steamship, freighter, barge, lighter, packet, ferry, mail-ship, tanker, supertanker, liner; pilot, tug, launch; destroyer, warship, frigate, battleship, aircraft carrier, submarine; sailing ship, clipper, yacht, rowing boat, paddle boat, canoe, kayak, gondola, junk, galleon.

adj. nautical, marine, maritime, naval, seagoing, seaworthy.

278 aircraft

n. aircraft, aeroplane, plane, airliner, jet, jumbo jet, turbo-prop, shuttle, glider, bomber, seaplane; hovercraft, hydrofoil, helicopter; airship, balloon, Zeppelin.

adj. aviational, aeronautical.

279 spaceship

n. spaceship, spacecraft, capsule, module, space shuttle, space probe; space station, satellite, sputnik; flying saucer, UFO; rocket.

280 velocity

n. velocity, speed, quickness, rapidity, hurry, haste, rush, expedition, celerity; acceleration, hastening, quickening, speeding up, spurt, burst, charge.

adj. quick, fast, speedy, brisk, swift; nimble, agile, deft, spirited; light-footed, prompt, expeditious.

vb. go fast, speed, hurry, hasten, quicken, race, tear, fly, dash, rush, run, sprint, dart, whiz, zip, pelt, bomb, run like mad, go all out, do a ton (*sl.*), go full pelt (*inf.*); accelerate, go faster, speed up, spurt, put on speed, step on it (*inf.*), put one's foot down (*inf.*), get a move on (*inf.*), get one's skates on (*inf.*), make it snappy (*inf.*); overtake, gain on, catch up, reach, pass, overhaul, go after, outstrip, outpace, outdistance, capture, beat; run for dear life.

adv. fast, quickly, speedily, swiftly, at full speed, flat out, at full pelt.

see also **613**

281 slowness

n. slowness, sluggishness, lethargy, apathy, hesitation, reluctance; deceleration, retardation, slackening, delay, go-slow, brake, curb, restraint.

slowcoach, tortoise, snail, dawdler, lingerer, loiterer, loafer, idler.

adj. slow, slow-moving, dawdling, lingering; sluggish, listless, lethargic, apathetic, inactive, leisurely, hesitant, reluctant.

vb. go slowly, idle, stroll, saunter, dawdle, linger, tarry, take one's time, loiter, loaf, crawl, inch, falter, limp, hobble, shuffle, plod; decelerate, slow down, reduce speed, slacken, relax, let up, ease off, delay, retard, brake, put on the brakes; curb.

282 impulse

n. impulse, thrust, impetus, charge, rush, drive, pressure, momentum, impulsion; bump, shove, shock, jolt, impact, brunt, clash, crash, collision, pile-up, smash-up; hit, knock, rap, blow, smack.

vb. impel, push, drive, press, propel, move, set in motion, activate, get going, start; collide, crash, run into, bump into, smash, dash, meet, encounter, touch, impinge, clash, butt, bump, jog, shove, jolt, force, scrape, jar.

hit, strike, beat, smite; tap, rap, jab; slap, thump, clout, smack, pummel, thrash, whip, whack, wallop (*sl.*), sock, clap, box, punch, club, cudgel; hammer, pound, bash, slosh (*sl.*), flail; bang, knock, bruise; kick, knee.

283 recoil

n. recoil, reaction, rebound, spring, bounce, repercussion, echo, reverberation, boomerang, backlash, rebuff, answer, reply.

vb. recoil, react, respond, rebound, bounce, spring, kick back, backfire, echo, reverberate; shrink from, draw back, pull back, wince, flinch.

284 direction

n. direction, bearing, orientation, point of the compass, cardinal point, north, south, east, west; destination, aim, object, intention; tendency, thrust, tenor; outlook, standpoint, point of view.

vb. orientate oneself, take one's bearings, locate; direct, signpost, lead, aim for, go for, head for, make for, point to, steer; tend.

adv. towards, in the direction of, via, heading for, on the way to.

285 deviation

n. deviation, misdirection, disorientation, deflection, divergence, turning, departure, diversion, detour; digression, tangent; irregularity, deterioration.

adj. deviating, aberrant, deviant, divergent, misguided, mistaken, lost; tangential, off-beam.

vb. deviate, deflect, swerve, bend, wander, stray, err, depart from, veer, shift, lose one's bearings, get lost, turn aside; disorientate, misdirect; digress, get sidetracked, go off the point, go off at a tangent.

286 precedence

n. precedence, priority, leading, heading, vanguard.

vb. precede, go before, come first, take precedence, herald, go in advance, lead, lead the way, head, take the lead.

adv. in advance, ahead, before.

see also **84, 118**

287 following

n. following, succession; follower, disciple, hanger-on, attendant, dependant, adherent, supporter, recruit.

vb. follow, go after, come after, ensue, succeed, attend, wait on; shadow, chase, pursue, track, tail (*sl.*), dog; lag behind, trail.

see also **85, 119**

288 progression

n. progression, progress, advance, headway, gain; development, growth, furtherance, advancement, improvement.

adj. forward, progressive, tolerant, broad-minded, forward-looking, enterprising; ongoing.

vb. progress, advance, proceed, move on, forge ahead, press on, strive forward, push ahead, make progress, make headway, gain ground, never look back (*inf.*); further, promote, develop, grow, evolve, become, mature, improve, move with the times.

adv. forward, onward, on, in progress.

289 regression
n. regression, retreat, withdrawal, retirement, return; regress, retrogression, reversal; departure, escape; about-turn, *volte-face*, about-face, U-turn.
adj. backward, backward-looking, reactionary, narrow-minded, reverse, retrograde, retrogressive.
vb. go backwards, regress, recede, retire, back out, withdraw, retreat, draw back, secede, fall back, lose ground; retrogress; go back on one's word, turn around.

290 propulsion
n. propulsion, impulsion, impetus, drive, push, thrust, pressure; missile, projectile, bullet, shell, torpedo, arrow, dart, propellant, shot.
vb. propel, push, move, impel, drive, direct, thrust, press, shove; launch, throw, cast, pitch, toss, chuck (*inf.*); shoot, discharge.

291 pulling
n. pulling, traction, drawing, tow, haul; tug, tractor, traction engine, draught animal; trailer, caravan, train.
vb. pull, draw, haul, drag, heave, tow, tug, take in tow; attract, magnetize; trail.

292 approach
n. approach, advance, arrival, coming; nearness, approximation.
adj. approaching, nearing, forthcoming, coming, looming, drawing near; accessible, get-at-able, approachable, obtainable, available, attainable, convenient, at one's disposal.
vb. approach, draw near, come near, advance, come forward, come into sight, close in on, sidle up to, loom up; approximate, verge on, near.

293 retreat
n. retreat, recession, withdrawal, departure, escape, retirement, removal, evacuation, flight.
vb. retreat, recede, withdraw, back out, depart, run away, fall back, evacuate, escape, retire, remove; fade, die away, sink.

294 attraction
n. attraction, drawing power, gravitation, affinity, pull, draw, influence; magnet, gravity, bait, lure, decoy.
adj. attracting, appealing, magnetic, charismatic.
vb. attract, pull, drag, draw, bring; interest, fascinate.
see also 547

295 repulsion
n. repulsion, rebuff, snub, beating off, dismissal.
adj. repulsive, offensive, repelling.
vb. repel, repulse, drive back, put to flight, beat off, hold off, push back, throw off, turn away, drive away; dismiss, send packing; rebuff, snub; resist.
see also 892

296 convergence
n. convergence, concurrence, confluence, concentration, confrontation, collision course, focalization; union, meeting, encounter.
adj. convergent, concurrent, converging.
vb. converge, come together, focalize, unite, gather, concentrate, meet, tend, narrow the gap, come to a point.

297 divergence
n. divergence, radiation, ramification; fork, bifurcation; fan, spoke, ray.

adj. divergent, deviating, radiating; centrifugal.

vb. diverge, radiate, branch, fork, bifurcate, diffuse, spread, fan out, disperse, scatter, ramify, divaricate.

298 arrival

n. arrival, coming, approach, entrance, entry, appearance, emergence; start, onset; reaching, attainment; return, homecoming; landing, touchdown, disembarkation, alighting, dismounting, docking, mooring.

destination, goal, terminus, journey's end, objective, resting place, harbour, port, dock, berth, landing place, airport.

vb. arrive, come, reach, get to, enter, approach, appear, show up (*inf.*), turn up, return, come home; land, touch down, disembark, alight, dismount, get down, set foot on, dock, moor, drop anchor.

299 departure

n. departure, going, leaving, setting out, exit, withdrawing, abandonment, removal, retreat, flight, take-off, embarkation, sailing; leave-taking, parting, separating, farewell, send-off, dismissal, valediction, parting shot, *congé*; exodus; emigration.

vb. depart, go, leave, move, quit, retire, withdraw, evacuate, go away, take one's leave, make tracks, set out, start out, be off, push off (*inf.*), push along (*inf.*), shove off (*sl.*); rush off, run away, beat it (*sl.*), scram (*sl.*).

300 entrance

n. entrance, entry, ingress, incoming, induction, initiation, immigration; admittance, admission; introduction, influx, intrusion, infiltration, incursion, penetration, invasion, raid.

vb. enter, come in, step in, go in, set foot in, make one's way into, visit, drop in; intrude, invade, trespass, gatecrash; force into, break in; wriggle in, worm in; insert, put in, admit, introduce, implant, penetrate, infiltrate, percolate.

301 emergence

n. emergence, egress, outflow, emanation, issue, discharge, outflow, effluence, flow; escape, gush, spout, welling, oozing, outpour, leakage, seepage, eruption, secretion.

vb. emerge, go out, come out, come out into the open; emit, eject, discharge, expel, flow out, run out, effuse, give out, exhale, send forth, pour out, gush, spurt, shoot, secrete, seep, erupt, squirt; bleed, leak, empty, weep; exude, ooze.

see also 312

302 reception

n. reception, admission, admittance, acceptance, receptivity; access, welcome, open arms, hospitality, registration, enlistment, enrolment; initiation, baptism, barmitzvah; incorporation, assimilation, absorption, digestion.

adj. admissible, acceptable, receivable; suitable; receptive, sympathetic.

vb. admit, receive, accept, take in; allow in, accommodate, welcome, make welcome; initiate, baptize, introduce, induct, install; assimilate, incorporate, swallow, absorb, digest.

see also 716

303 ejection

n. ejection, expulsion, eviction, removal, elimination; dismissal, discharge, sack (*inf.*), push (*sl.*), deportation, exile, banishment, extradition;

ejector, bouncer (*sl.*), chucker-out; nausea, sickness, vomiting.

vb. eject, emit, expel, remove, exclude, eliminate, eradicate, wipe out, evict; dismiss, get rid of, dispose of, discharge, sack (*inf.*); depart, exile, banish, extradite, relegate; urinate, excrete; be sick, vomit, bring up (*inf.*), throw up (*inf.*), spew, retch, heave.

304 eating; drinking

n. eating, ingestion, nourishment, feeding, nutrition, consuming, partaking; feasting, devouring, banqueting; digestion, chewing, mastication; drinking, imbibation, potation; gastronomy, epicurism, gourmandise, gluttony.

eater, partaker, consumer, nibbler, chewer, glutton; drinker, sipper, drunkard; connoisseur, gourmet, gourmand, epicure.

vb. eat, consume, feed on, partake; chew, masticate, champ; bite, digest, swallow; gorge, gobble, bolt, put away (*inf.*), eat up, tuck into (*inf.*), polish off (*inf.*), devour, dispose of; breakfast, lunch, sup; eat out, dine out, wine and dine, feast, banquet, gourmandize; stuff, eat one's fill.

nourish, feed, satisfy, provide, maintain, nurture, strengthen, sustain, tend, gratify; suckle, breast-feed, give suck, nurse.

drink, gulp, take in, imbibe, wash down (*inf.*); tipple, guzzle.

305 provisions

n. provisions, food, stores, sustenance, stock, foodstuffs, groceries, subsistence, rations, board; fodder, feed, pasture, pasturage, roughage, provender; portion, helping, share, slice, quota, division, ration; larder, pantry, refrigerator, freezer.

306 food

n. food, meat and drink, foodstuffs, edibles, comestibles, provisions, nutrition, aliment, nutriment, cooking, grub (*sl.*), tuck (*sl.*); victuals, pabulum, viands; delicacy, delicatessen, luxury, delight.

portion, mouthful, piece, bite, morsel, spoonful.

meal, refreshment, fare; repast, refection; breakfast, brunch, elevenses, lunch, luncheon, packed lunch, tea, afternoon tea, high tea, dinner, supper; snack, sandwich, bite, nibble, buffet, tiffin; feast, banquet, orgy, blow-out (*inf.*), beanfeast, beano (*sl.*); picnic, barbecue; menu, bill of fare, table, cover, spread; dish, course, hors-d'oeuvre, appetizer, soup, broth, pottage, aperitif, entrée, main course, sweet, dessert, afters (*inf.*), pudding, savoury.

meat, flesh, game, poultry, fowl; egg; flour, starch; fish, sea-food; milk product, butter, cream, cheese; oil, fat, grease, blubber, margarine, vegetable fat, vegetable oil; bread, staff of life, loaf, roll; pastry, patisserie, biscuit, wafer, cracker, cake; fruit, soft fruit, berry, jam, conserve, spread, extract, jelly, gelatin; vegetable, herb, edible root, greens, tuber, root; cereal, grain; nut, dried fruit, seed, stone, kernel, pip; sweet, confectionery, sweetmeat, confections; cookery, cuisine, catering, domestic science, home economics.

adj. edible, eatable, comestible, digestible, nutritious, delicious, succulent, palatable, appetizing, satisfying, tempting, scrumptious (*inf.*); culinary; prandial, pre-prandial, post-prandial.

vb. cook, prepare, fix, heat up, warm up; simmer, steam, boil, coddle; stew, casserole, braise; bake, roast, spit; grill, barbecue, broil; fry, sauté, sizzle; poach, scramble; toast, crisp, dry; curry, fricassee; dice, mince; lard, baste.

307 condiment

n. condiment, flavouring, seasoning, additive, sauce, relish, herb, plant, pickle, salt, pepper, mustard.

vb. season, flavour, spice, salt, pepper, bring out the flavour.

308 tobacco

n. tobacco, nicotine, snuff, cigarette, cigar, pipe.

vb. smoke, smoke a pipe, inhale, puff, draw, suck; take snuff.

309 drink

n. drink, beverage, potion, liquid, fluid, juice, sap, whey; infusion, decoction; soft drink, water, milk, tea, coffee, thirst-quencher, nightcap; alcoholic drink, beer, wine, champagne, toast, cocktail; sip, gulp, drop; draught, dram.

310 excretion

n. excretion, urination, evacuation, voiding, discharge, secretion, defecation, expulsion, ejection, excrement, exudation; faeces, excreta; waterworks (*sl.*); urine; bowel movement, diarrhoea, dysentry; offal, dung, droppings, manure; ordure, stool; smegma; perspiration, sweat.

adj. excretive, excretory, secretory; faecal.

vb. excrete, expel, defecate, discharge, evacuate, urinate, secrete, pass, spend a penny, go to the lavatory, be excused.

311 insertion

n. insertion, injection, infusion, introduction, insinuation.

vb. insert, put in, inject, infuse, introduce, interpolate, include, insinuate, pour in, impregnate, stick in, throw in; force in, drag in (*inf.*), embed, install, fix, implant, bury, sink, immerse.

312 extraction

n. extraction, removal, withdrawal, expulsion, discharge, ejection, extrication, pulling; quarrying, mining; scoop, digger, chisel, extractor, gouge, excavator, dredger.

vb. extract, remove, withdraw, pull out, draw out, pluck, wrench, extricate, cut out, extort, dislodge, uproot, displace, lever out; quarry, mine, excavate, dredge, gouge, chisel; get money out of a stone (*inf.*).

313 passage

n. passage, crossing, journey, trek, voyage; way, thoroughfare, traffic, flow; traffic control, traffic regulation, rule of the road, highway code.

vb. pass, cross, traverse, go through, penetrate, emerge, proceed, drive, weave, thread, ford, span.

314 overstepping

n. overstepping, overrunning, infestation, invasion; transcendence; encroachment, violation, transgression.

vb. go beyond, overstep, encroach, go too far, exceed the limit, overrun, overshoot; invade, infest, plague, swarm, ravage; excel, surpass, outdo, transcend, rise above, eclipse; outdistance, outstrip; trespass, violate, infringe, transgress.

315 shortcoming

n. shortcoming, inadequacy, imperfection, falling short; loss, deficit, shortfall, shortage, dearth, default; need, lack, requirement, deficiency, fault, weakness, lapse, weak point; privation, destitution.

adj. short, deficient, missing, lacking, inadequate, not up to scratch; imperfect, incomplete.

vb. fall short, come short, be deficient, fail, need, miss, lack; lag behind, lose ground; collapse, come to nothing.

316 ascent

n. ascent, ascension, climbing, rise, mount, lift, jump, surge, towering, soaring; ladder, step-ladder, steps, stairs, staircase, escalator, moving staircase, travelator, lift, elevator; hill, mountain, acclivity.

adj. ascending, rising, upward.

vb. ascend, go up, rise, tower, soar, rocket, surge, grow, sprout; take off; climb, mount, scale, surmount, progress, top, scale, conquer, scramble, clamber, creep, work one's way up.

317 descent

n. descent, drop, fall, lapse, swoop, sinking, plunge, downfall, tumble; slump, recession, reduction, declination; subsidence, landslide, hole, cave, chasm.

adj. descending, downward.

vb. descend, go down, fall, drop, subside, decline, swoop, plunge, slump, sink, droop, land, come down, touch down; parachute; crash-land; splash down; topple, push over; tumble, overbalance, lose one's balance, stumble, capsize, turn over, tilt, lurch.

318 elevation

n. elevation, lift, raising, erection; exaltation, ennoblement, sublimation.

adj. raised, lifted, elevated, high, aerial, tall, erect, upstanding, upraised; exalted, noble, sublime, lofty.

vb. lift, elevate, raise, pick up, pull up, help up, uplift, hoist, heave, erect; support, prop; leaven; boost; glorify, heighten, enhance, exalt.

get up, stand up, get to one's feet, arise; jump up, spring to one's feet.

319 depression

n. depression, lowering, dip; hole, cavity; curtsy, bow, genuflexion; debasement.

adj. depressed; smoothed, even; sitting, sedentary, settled, inactive; prostrate.

vb. depress, lower, press, squash; settle, sink, dip, sag, droop, decline; push down, bring low, ground; fell, cut down, chop down, topple, pull down, demolish, raze to the ground.

drop, let fall, shed, loosen, release, let go, spill; fall, drip, dribble, leak, ooze, seep, drain, permeate, percolate, filter.

sit down, be seated, squat, crouch, kneel, genuflect; perch, roost; bend over, stoop, incline, hunch, bow, curtsy.

320 leap

n. leap, jump, dance, spring, vault, bound, hop, rise, pounce, hurdle, leapfrog, saltation.

adj. lively, frisky, saltatory.

vb. leap, jump, spring, vault, dance, hop, bounce, skip, leapfrog, surge, rise.

321 plunge

n. plunge, jump, rush, dive, drop, fall, plummet, leap, pitch, dip, swoop; ducking, immersion, submergence.

vb. plunge, dive, dip, jump, fall, pounce, cast down; duck, submerge, immerse, drown, souse, dunk; go down, sink, go under; splash down; crash-land; go to the bottom.

322 circulation

n. circulation, circumnavigation; spiral; compass, lap, course, circuit, loop, round trip, orbit, ambit, full circle; by-pass, ring road, detour, diversion.

vb. circle, circulate, go around, revolve around, circumnavigate, circumscribe, circumambulate, lap, tour, ring, gird, wind; by-pass.

see also **250**

323 rotation

n. rotation, revolution, turn, circle, spin, cycle, roll, circuit, whirl, twirl, gyration, pirouette; spiral, orbit; whirlpool, eddy, whirlwind, cyclone, tornado, vortex.

adj. rotary, gyratory, rotating, revolving.

vb. rotate, revolve, twist, circle, circulate, spin, cycle, roll, whirl, twirl, loop, swing, spiral; swivel, pivot; swirl, eddy; pirouette.

324 evolution

n. evolution, development, growth, unfolding, unfurling; disentanglement; evolutionism, Darwinism; missing link.

adj. evolving, evolutionary.

vb. evolve, develop, grow, emerge; advance, progress, mature; unfold, open out, unfurl, unroll, unwind, uncurl, uncover, unwrap; unravel, disentangle, free, release, straighten.

325 oscillation

n. oscillation, fluctuation, vacillation, wavering, undulation, quiver, shake, swing, lurch, roll; vibration, tremor, thunder; faltering, hesitancy, uncertainty.

pulse, pulsation, throb, beat, drumming, pound, surge, palpitation, flutter, ripple, wave; earthquake, seismology.

pendulum, oscillator, vibrator, shuttle, see-saw, cradle, rocking-chair, rocking-horse.

adj. oscillating, fluctuating, throbbing, pulsatory; seismic; vacillating, hesitant, undecided, irresolute.

vb. oscillate, alternate, fluctuate, vacillate, vibrate, pulse, throb, beat, pound, surge, flutter, wave, waver, undulate, librate; nod, swing, sway, see-saw, wobble, totter, lurch, roll, rock, quake, quiver, teeter, zigzag; ebb and flow, back and fill; hesitate, falter.

adv. back and forth, to and fro, up and down, from side to side.

326 agitation

n. agitation, disturbance, vibration; jar, jolt, jog, bump, bounce; shudder, quake, tremble, wobble, tremor, jerk; shakes, jitters (*inf.*), shivers, heebie-jeebies (*sl.*), butterflies (*inf.*), apprehension; fit, convulsion, spasm, palsy, seizure, fever, attack, stroke; itch, twitch.

confusion, tumult, turmoil, turbulence; excitation, melodrama, emotion, commotion, fuss, bother, flap (*inf.*), dither (*inf.*), tizzy (*sl.*).

adj. agitated, shaking, unsteady, wavering, shaky, tremulous; jelly-like, itchy, twitching, nervous, apprehensive, jittery (*inf.*).

vb. shake, tremble, vibrate, quiver, quake, shiver, chatter, shudder, palpitate, flap, toss, flutter, totter, wobble, stagger; itch, twitch; twinkle, flicker, glimmer, sparkle.

agitate, sway, rock, swing, beat, disturb, jolt, jar, jerk, bounce; convulse, seize, throw a fit; go out of control.

III Matter

A Matter in general

327 materiality

n. materiality, substantiality, concreteness, corporeality, corporality, tangibility; materialism, Marxism, dialectical materialism.

matter, body, material, stuff, mass, flesh and blood, flesh; thing, object, something, article, commodity, item, being; element, atom, molecule; component, part, ingredient, factor.

adj. material, substantial; corporeal, bodily; physical, concrete, tangible, real, objective, somatic; materialistic, unspiritual, worldly, mundane.

vb. materialize, realize, become real, take form, become flesh, take flesh, objectify, substantialize.

328 immateriality

n. immateriality, insubstantiality, dematerialization, intangibility, disembodiment; spirituality, otherworldliness; shadow, ghost.

adj. immaterial, incorporeal, insubstantial, bodiless, disembodied, intangible, ethereal, shadowy, ghostly, unreal; otherworldly, spiritual.

vb. dematerialize, disintegrate, disembody; spiritualize.

329 universe

n. universe, creation, space, outer space, cosmos, galaxy; world, earth, sphere, globe, orb, nature; heavenly body, celestial body, planet, planetoid, asteroid, moon, satellite, falling star, shooting star, meteor, meteorite, star, sun, constellation, nebula, quasar, pulsar, black hole; heavens, firmament, vault; atmosphere, air, ether, sky, night sky; astronomy, astrophysics, stargazing; observatory, planetarium, telescope; astrology, horoscope, signs of the Zodiac; cosmology, cosmogony, cosmography, geography; map, atlas.

adj. universal, cosmic, galactic; terrestrial, earthly, worldly, mundane; heavenly, celestial, empyrean; extraterrestrial, planetary, solar, astral, lunar; astronomical; geographical.

330 weight

n. gravity, gravitation, attraction; weight, heaviness, pressure, force, mass, bulk; ballast, load, freight, sinker, counterweight, paperweight, stone, rock, sandbags, anchor, plumb; burden.

balance, scales, weighing machine, weighbridge.

adj. heavy, weighty, ponderous, bulky, cumbersome, top-heavy; burdensome, oppressive, troublesome.

vb. weigh, balance, poise, measure, put on the scales, counterpoise, counterbalance; weigh down, weight, load, overload; burden, overwhelm, saddle.

331 lightness

n. lightness, levity, weightlessness, imponderability; buoy, cork; leaven, lightener, ferment, yeast.

adj. light, insubstantial; underweight; weightless; feathery, dainty, airy, fluffy; gentle, delicate, soft; floatable, buoyant, unsinkable; lightweight, summerweight; small, portable.

vb. be light, float, surface, swim; levitate, defy gravity; lighten, raise, ferment; unburden, take off, remove, unload, disencumber, jettison.

B Inorganic matter

332 density

n. density, solidity, thickness, compactness, concreteness, heaviness, concentration, congestion, substantiality; incompressibility, impenetrability, impermeability; consolidation, crystallization, coagulation, solidification, thickening, stiffening; mass, solid, body, substance, lump, conglomerate.

adj. dense, solid, thick, compact, close, heavy, impenetrable, impermeable, condensed, compressed; clotted, curdled; frozen; indivisible, insoluble.

vb. solidify, thicken, coagulate, freeze, clot, fix, crystallize, harden, stiffen, set, congeal, jell (*inf.*), curdle; petrify, ossify; compress, condense, compact.

see also **50**

333 rarity

n. rarity, thinness, fineness; low pressure, vacuum, emptiness; rarefaction, attenuation.

adj. rare, thin, light, rarefied, fine, attenuated, airy, ethereal; weak, tenuous, sparse, shrill, flimsy, fragile, insubstantial, subtle; empty, void.

vb. rarefy, lessen, reduce pressure, purify, refine, thin, attenuate.

334 hardness

n. hardness, stiffness, firmness, toughness, rigidity, solidity, impenetrability, inflexibility; hardening, stiffening.

adj. hard, solid, thick, dense, compact; rigid, firm, stiff, taut, tight; tough, unyielding, unbreakable, impenetrable, unbending, inflexible, inelastic, unmalleable, impermeable.

vb. harden, toughen, strengthen, set, stiffen, temper; concentrate, consolidate, solidify, crystallize, freeze, coagulate, congeal, fossilize, ossify, petrify, starch.

see also **537**

335 softness

n. softness, penetrability, flexibility, plasticity, tractability, suppleness, pliancy, litheness; looseness, laxity.

adj. soft, smooth, fluffy, spongy, mellow; gentle, delicate; flimsy, limp; tender, pliant, flexible, plastic, elastic, supple, pliable, lithe, limber, mouldable.

vb. soften, ease, modify, temper, tenderize; subdue, assuage, mollify, appease; knead, mash; give, yield, relax, relent.

336 elasticity

n. elasticity, flexibility, pliability, springiness, spring, bounce, resilience, buoyancy; stretch, extensibility, tensility.

adj. elastic, flexible, pliant, resilient, buoyant; stretching, extensile, tensile.

vb. stretch; spring, bounce.

337 toughness

n. toughness, durability, strength, tenacity, cohesion; bone, gristle, cartilage.

adj. tough, durable, hard, firm, solid, robust, strong, stiff, enduring, unbreakable, tenacious; impervious, unyielding, resistant; fibrous, gristly, sinewy.

vb. toughen, strengthen, stiffen, harden.

338 brittleness

n. brittleness, frailty, fragility, delicacy.

adj. brittle, delicate, frail; breakable, fragile; crispy, crumbly; flimsy, frangible; shaky, unsteady; friable.

vb. break, break easily, split, snap,

shatter, fragment, burst, fall to pieces, splinter, crumble.

see also 48

339 texture

n. texture, pattern, weave, organization, composition, constitution, make-up, form, structure; feel, sense, taste, shape, mould, fibre, fabric, web, weft, tissue.

adj. structural, organizational, constructional. tectonic; textural, granular.

340 powderiness

n. powderiness, pulverulence; crumbling, pulverization; powder, dust, grain, particle, granule, crumb, flake, pollen.

adj. powdery, fine, granulated, pulverized, pulverulent; dusty; impalpable; crumbling, friable.

vb. grind, crush, pulverize, granulate, pound, beat, grate, scrape, crunch, crumble, atomize.

341 friction

n. friction, rubbing, abrasion, erosion, wearing away, grinding, filing, irritation; massage, polishing; stroke.

adj. frictional, abrasive, rubbing.

vb. rub, abrade, scour, grate, graze, rasp, chafe, grind, file, scrape, scrub; wear away, erode; polish, shine, smooth, massage; burnish; brush, clean, wipe.

342 lubrication

n. lubrication, anointment, unction; lubricant, grease, oil, wax, fat, ointment, cream, lotion, balm, salve, unguent; petrol, juice (*sl.*).

vb. lubricate, grease, oil, cream, daub, smear, coat, rub, anoint.

343 fluidity

n. fluidity, liquidity, wateriness, juiciness, solubility, dilution; fluid, liquid, liquor, vapour, solution, solvent, drink, flow.

adj. fluid, liquid, running, flowing, molten, liquefied, watery, juicy, liquescent.

vb. flow, run, pour, stream, swell; liquefy.

344 gaseity

n. gaseity, gaseousness, vaporousness, aeration; gas, vapour, steam, fume, air, smoke, fluid.

adj. gaseous, vaporous, vapory, gassy, gas-like, steaming, aeriform, airy, light, windy, volatile.

vb. gasify, aerate.

345 liquefaction

n. liquefaction, solubility, dissolution, thawing; solvent, dissolvent.

adj. runny, molten, liquefied, melted, thawed, disintegrated; liquefacient, soluble.

vb. liquefy, dissolve, melt, run, thaw, defrost, fuse, flux, condense, fluidify, fluidize, deliquesce, disintegrate.

346 vaporization

n. vaporization, evaporation, condensation, sublimation, gasification, volatization, distillation; vapour, moisture, exhalation, mist, smoke, sublimate.

adj. vaporous, steaming, steamy, gassy, volatile.

vb. vaporize, evaporate, sublimate, distil, diffuse, dissipate, gasify, exhale smoke, fume, steam.

347 water

n. water, liquid, rain, wet, dampness; ice, steam, water vapour.

adj. watery, aquatic, aqueous,

hydrated, liquid, fluid, wet, moist, hydrous, aqua-, hydro-.

see also 349

348 air

n. air, oxygen, fresh air; airing, exposure, ventilation, air conditioning, aeration; atmosphere, stratosphere, ozone, ether, sky; pneumatics, aerodynamics.

weather, climate, elements; meteorology, forecasting.

adj. airy, aerial; exposed, ventilated, open, aerated; draughty, breezy, windy; pneumatic, aero-; metereological.

vb. air, aerate, ventilate, open, refresh, freshen, cool, aerify, purify, fan.

see also 359

349 moisture

n. moisture, humidity, dampness, wetness, precipitation; drip, damp, dew, rain, wet; moistening, saturation, wettening, humidification.

adj. moist, damp, wet, humid, muggy, dank, misty; saturated, soaked, sodden, waterlogged, awash, drowned, drenched, wet through, like a drowned rat.

vb. moisten, dampen, wet, humidify; sprinkle, dabble, shower, dip, sponge, splash; saturate, drench, soak, bathe, souse, steep, stream, seep, sog; duck, immerse, submerge; waterlog, drown, flood, swamp, inundate, deluge.

350 dryness

n. dryness, aridity, aridness, parchedness, desiccation, dehydration; thirst, drought.

adj. dry, arid, parched, unmoistened, rainless, sapless, evaporated; barren, desert, dusty, baked, scorched, bleached; dried, dehydrated, thirsty; waterproof, rainproof, watertight.

vb. dry, dehydrate, freeze-dry, drip-dry; desiccate, parch, bake, scorch, torrefy; air, evaporate; shrivel, wither; soak up, absorb.

351 ocean

n. ocean, sea, deep, brine, high seas; oceanography.

adj. oceanic, marine, maritime, pelagic; oceanographical.

352 land

n. land, terrain, *terra firma*, mainland, continent; inland, interior; peninsula, neck, isthmus; ground, soil, earth, gravel, sand, rock, pebble; fields, pasture; shore, beach, seaside, strand, bank, coastline, seaboard.

adj. terrestrial, earthy; inland, interior, landlocked, central; coastal, seaside, littoral, riverside, riparian.

353 gulf

n. gulf, inlet, bay, estuary, bight, mouth, harbour, lagoon, sound, fiord, firth, loch, strait, narrows, arm, kyle; cove, cave.

354 lake

n. lake, tarn, loch, lagoon, pool, pond, creek, mere, inland sea, reservoir, basin; puddle.

355 marsh

n. marsh, fen, swamp, mire, bog, quagmire, quicksand, morass, slough, moor, mud.

adj. marshy, soft, fenny, swampy, boggy, wet, waterlogged, squelchy, slushy, muddy, miry, paludal.

356 plain

n. plain, expanse, open country, flat, lowland, champaign, grassland; meadow, field, grass, pasture; steppe, prairie, savannah, pampa, llano; moor, moorland, common, heath, wold; upland, plateau, tableland, downs; tundra, veld.

357 island

n. island, isle, islet, holm, eyot, ait, archipelago; reef, atoll, ridge, sandbank, cay, key.

358 water in motion

n. river, watercourse, waterway, tributary, branch, fork, effluent; stream, brook, rivulet, beck, runnel, rill, runlet, bourn, creek.

tide, current, flow, course, undercurrent; spring, fountain, spout, gush, rush, jet, outpouring, uprising; whirlpool, eddy, vortex, swirl, maelstrom; wash, backwash.

wave, billow, swell, roller, surge, crest, ripple, undulation, breaker, tidal wave, white-caps, white horses; waterfall, cataract, fall, shoot, cascade, torrent, rapids, weir.

rain, rainfall, precipitation, drizzle, shower, downpour, thunderstorm, cloudburst, flood, deluge, inundation, monsoon; mist.

adj. runny, streaming; rainy, moist, wet, showery, cloudy, thundery, stormy; torrential.

vb. flow, run, stream, sweep, rush; gush, well, spurt, squirt, jet, spout, issue, flood, inundate; wave, undulate, billow, swell, ripple, ebb; swirl, eddy, surge, roll, whirl, tumble; dash, break, splash; drop, drip, seep, leak, trickle, dribble, gurgle; spill, overflow, spew, exude; fall, cascade; drain, empty, clear, tap, expel, deplete, decant, bleed.

rain, pour, patter, spit, drizzle, shower.

359 air in motion

n. wind, draught, current, breeze, whisk, whiff, puff, flutter, waft, zephyr; gust, blast, flurry, flaw; gale, storm, squall, blizzard, whirlwind, cyclone, typhoon, tornado, hurricane, tempest; trade wind, mistral, föhn.

breathing, respiration, inhalation, expiration, exhalation, afflatus; breath, gasp, sigh, pant, cough, sneeze, wheeze.

adj. windy, open, exposed, fresh, blustery, squally, gusty, stormy, tempestuous; draughty, well-ventilated; wheezy, asthmatic.

vb. blow, breeze, whiff, waft, flutter, flap, buffet, sweep, whisk, fling; blast, rush, roar, howl, wail, stream, whirl; breathe, respire, inhale, exhale, expire, puff, pant, gasp; sigh; cough, sneeze, wheeze; pump, inflate, blow up, swell, fill.

360 water channel

n. conduit, channel, way, passage, bed, ditch, trench, trough, moat; course, canal, aqueduct; tunnel, pipe, pipeline, tube, main, duct, culvert; spout, tap, funnel, siphon; drain, drainpipe, gutter, sewer; flume, gully, cloaca.

361 air-pipe

n. air-pipe, shaft, tube; vent, chimney, flue, ventilator.

362 semiliquidity

n. semiliquidity, viscosity, glutinousness, stickiness, adhesiveness; semiliquid, glue, paste, size, colloid, emulsion, syrup.

adj. semiliquid, semifluid, gelatinous, viscous, viscid, glutinous, coagulated, slimy, syrupy, creamy, sticky, tacky, slushy, gummy, colloid.

363 bubble; cloud

n. bubble, globule, sac, froth, foam, spray, surf, spume; fizz, head; lather, suds; effervescence, fermentation, bubbling.

cloud, haze, haziness, mist, fog, smog, pea-souper (*inf.*), film.

adj. bubbly, foaming, bubbling, soapy, effervescent, sparkling, fizzy, spumous, spumy; cloudy, overcast, dull, grey, unclear, murky, gloomy, dim, misty, hazy, foggy, nebulous.

vb. effervesce, bubble, boil, fizz, foam, ferment.

364 pulpiness

n. pulpiness, sponginess, softness, succulence; pulp, mash, sponge, paste, pap, mulch, mush, jelly, dough, batter, poultice.

adj. pulpy, mushy, doughy, soggy, spongy, pulpous, ripe, fleshy, succulent; thick, smooth.

vb. pulp, mash, crush.

365 unctuousness

n. unctuousness, oiliness, greasiness; oil, fat, grease, blubber; unction, oil, unguent, embrocation, salve, nard, ointment, lubricant, balm, emollient, remedy, cream; resin, gum, pitch, varnish, lacquer, shellac, asphalt, bitumen.

adj. unctuous, oily, greasy, fatty, unguent, creamy.

vb. grease, oil, lubricate; resin, varnish; anoint.

C Organic matter

366 animate matter

n. creation, nature, animals, plants, fauna, flora; creature, organism, cell, protoplasm; biology, natural history, nature study, ecology, genetics, evolution, biochemistry, anatomy, physiology, botany, zoology.

adj. animate, organic, biological.

367 inorganic matter

n. mineral, rock, deposit, ore, metal, coal; geology, mineralogy, metallurgy.

adj. inorganic, inanimate, mineral, metallurgical.

368 life

n. life, existence, being; organism, human, body, creature, man, person, individual, personage, mortal.

soul, spirit, life-blood, breath, heart; élan, verve; vivification, animation, liveliness, vigour, vitality, force, energy.

adj. living, alive, surviving, in the flesh, vital; lively, animated, vigorous, vivacious, forceful, energetic, spirited, alive and kicking, active.

vb. live, exist, be, have life, breathe, respire; move, subsist; be spared, survive.

be born, come to life, come into the world, see the light; bear, beget, conceive, give birth to, bring to life.

vivify, quicken, animate, reanimate, vitalize, enliven, revive, breathe life into.

369 death

n. death, mortality; decease, dying, passing, departure, end, expiration, exit, extinction, parting, separation, release, homecall; loss, bereavement; fatality; demise, dissolution.

last hour, death bed, last breath, swan-song; death list, death toll, casualty list; obituary; the dead, departed, deceased, ancestors, forefathers, those gone before.

adj. mortal, sick, perishing, deathly, moribund, at death's door, on one's last legs; dead, deceased, departed, late, lamented; lifeless, breathless; defunct, extinct, cold, extinguished, terminated, ended, exterminated, lost.

vb. die, depart, go, expire, pass away, give up the ghost, breathe one's last, go the way of all flesh, be taken, kick the bucket (*sl.*); perish, succumb, come to nothing, be no more; be killed, lose one's life; push up daisies (*inf.*).

370 killing

n. killing, slaying, slaughter, destruction, assassination, murder, homicide, manslaughter; bloodshed, carnage, massacre, genocide, butchery, holocaust, liquidation, extermination, annihilation, decimation; shooting, knifing, lynching, poisoning, execution, hanging, strangulation, electrocution, crucifixion, burning, drowning, vivisection; euthanasia, mercy killing; abortion; suicide, self-destruction, hara-kiri, kamikaze.

killer, murderer, assassin, slayer, butcher, cut-throat, poisoner, strangler; gunman, terrorist, gangster, homicidal maniac; hangman, executioner.

adj. killing, lethal, fatal, mortal, deadly, destructive; homicidal, murderous, internecine; suicidal.

vb. kill, murder, slay, destroy, take life, put to death, bump off (*sl.*), knock off (*sl.*), do in (*sl.*), do away with (*inf.*), slaughter, assassinate, massacre, butcher, mow down (*inf.*), gun down (*inf.*), liquidate, annihilate, decimate, exterminate; execute, behead, guillotine, decapitate; shoot, gun, knife, hang, lynch; poison; strangle, suffocate, choke, asphyxiate; put to sleep (*inf.*), put down, put away.

kill oneself, commit suicide, take one's life, do oneself in (*sl.*), blow one's brains out, shoot oneself, cut one's throat.

371 corpse

n. corpse, remains, body, carcass, skeleton, relics, ashes, dust, mummy, cadaver, stiff (*sl.*).

adj. cadaverous, corpse-like, deathlike, deathly, pale.

372 burial

n. burial, funeral, interment, entombment, sepulture; cremation, incineration; embalment, mummification.

burial service, funeral rites, last rites, mourning, obsequies; requiem, elegy, last post, knell, passing bell; epitaph, obituary, in memoriam, RIP; coffin, urn, sarcophagus, pall, mummy case.

mortuary, morgue; undertaker, funeral director; gravestone, headstone, tombstone, monument, memorial; tomb, grave, sepulchre, vault, crypt, mausoleum, barrow; burial ground, graveyard, churchyard, God's acre, cemetery, catacomb, necropolis; pyre, crematorium; war memorial, cenotaph; exhumation, disinterment.

adj. buried, interred; funereal, funeral, mourning, mournful, sad.

vb. bury, inter, inhume, entomb, enshrine, embalm, lay out, lay to rest, sepulture; cremate; exhume, disinter, unearth.

373 animality; animal

n. animality, fauna, zoology; animal, creature, beast, vertebrate, invertebrate; quadruped, biped, man; mammal, marsupial; carnivore, herbivore, omnivore; fish, amphibian, mollusc, crustacean; bird, fowl, bird of prey, waterfowl; insect; reptile; cattle, herd, livestock, poultry, game; pet, domestic animal; rodent, vermin, parasite.

adj. animal, zoological, mammalian; piscine, fishy, amphibian; avian.

374 vegetability; plant

n. vegetability, vegetation, botany;

plant, shrub; plantation, shrubbery, undergrowth, corn, grain, cereal, crop, field; flower, bloom, bud, petal, blossom; flower-bed, garden; foliage; foliation, leafage; grass, pasture, verdure, sod, turf, lawn; herb; weed; tree, sapling, scion; branch, limb, bough, twig, sprig, spray, shoot, stem, stalk, leaf; wood, forest, bush, jungle; copse, spinney, coppice, woodland, thicket, covert, arboretum; forestry, dendrology, conservation; seed, root, bulb.

adj. vegetal, vegetative, botanical, horticultural, floral, verdant, grassy, weedy, arboreal.

375 zoology

n. zoology, life science, anthropology, anatomy, physiology, ichthyology, ornithology, bird-watching, entomology, embryology, taxonomy.

adj. zoological, ornithological.

376 botany

n. botany, plant science, horticulture, ecology, phytology.

adj. botanical, horticultural.

377 management of animals

n. animal husbandry, breeding, stockbreeding, grazing, taming, domestication.

farm, ranch, homestead; fishery, aquarium; zoo, zoological gardens; veterinary science, vet; shepherd, herdsman, herd, cattleherd, cowherd.

vb. keep, husband, breed, rear, raise, herd, drive, ranch, farm, tend, shepherd; feed, fodder, graze, fatten, market; shear, chip, fleece; milk; tame, domesticate, train; groom.

378 agriculture

n. agriculture, farming, cultivation, horticulture, gardening, growing, crop raising, husbandry; strip farming, rotation crops, contour ploughing; landscape gardening.

farm, ranch, homestead, holding, smallholding, grange; kibbutz; farmland, meadow, grassland, farmstead, estate, croft, enclosure, land, field, soil, patch, plot, allotment, plantation; garden, orchard, nursery; greenhouse, vineyard, arboretum.

farmer, husbandman, agriculturalist, cultivator, tiller, planter, grower, rancher, homesteadman, peasant, serf, hiredman, labourer, farmhand; gardener, nurseryman, horticulturalist, landscape gardener.

adj. agrarian, farming, agricultural, rustic, rural, peasant; horticultural, garden.

vb. cultivate, till; fertilize, manure; water, irrigate; dig, plough, harrow; seed, sow, broadcast, disseminate, plant, drill, bed, transplant; weed, hoe; graft; harvest, reap, gather in, glean, winnow, thresh, mow, cut, scythe, bind, stack, pick, pluck.

379 mankind

n. mankind, humanity, human race, human beings, populace, population, the world, flesh; person, man, human being, individual, creature, mortal, body, earthling, *homo sapiens*, Adam, anthropoid; people, public, folk.

society, community, civilization, politics; nation, state, body politic, nationality, statehood; chauvinism, nationalism, imperialism; anthropology, social anthropology, ethnology, sociology.

adj. human, mortal; individual, personal; social, civilized; political, national, state, general, public, civil, federal, social, communal, societal, civic; nationalistic, chauvinist, racialist.

380 male

n. male, man, gentleman, sir; chap, fellow, guy (*sl.*), bloke (*inf.*), boy; virility, masculinity, manliness, manhood.

male animal, cock, drake, gander, dog, tom-cat, hart, stag, stallion, billy-goat, ox, bull; gelding.

adj. male, masculine; manly, virile; gentlemanly.

381 female

n. female, woman, lady, girl; madam, miss; fair sex, weaker sex; femininity, womanliness, girlishness, womanhood; feminism, women's lib; effeminacy; womankind.

female animal, hen, duck, goose, bitch, she-dog, filly, ewe, sow, hind, doe, mare, nanny-goat, cow.

adj. female, feminine, girlish, womanly, lady-like; effeminate.

IV Intellect

1 Formation of ideas

A Intellectual operations in general

382 intellect

n. intellect, mind, brain, consciousness, mentality, intelligence, intellectuality, instinct, faculties; perception, conception, capacity, judgment, understanding, reasoning, genius, wisdom; psychology, behaviourism; psychiatry, psychotherapy.

soul, spirit, psyche, heart, individuality, personality, conscience, self, ego, id, superego, unconscious, subconscious.

adj. mental, intellectual, conceptional, abstract, perceptual, critical, rational, conscious, cognitive, cerebral, intelligent; psychological, psychic, subconscious, subliminal; spiritual.

vb. conceive, cognize, perceive, reason, judge; realize, sense, mark, note.

see also 434

383 absence of intellect

n. unintellectuality, unintelligence, imbecility, stupidity, shallowness, mindlessness, brainlessness.

adj. unintellectual, unintelligent, empty-headed, mindless, brainless.

see also 435

384 thought

n. thought, cogitation, concentration, brain-work; reflection, meditation, rumination, contemplation, thoughtfulness, brooding, pondering, absorption, preoccupation, deliberation; consideration, perception, appreciation, discernment, observation, reasoning, concluding.

adj. thoughtful, pensive, contemplative, reflective, studious; absorbed, engrossed, wrapped up in, dreamy; introspective; discerning, penetrating, intellectual.

vb. think, cogitate, consider, give thought to, concentrate, reflect, meditate, deliberate, ponder, muse, ruminate, contemplate, brood, turn over in one's mind, mull, study, examine, bear in mind, put on one's thinking cap (*inf.*), have on one's mind, take it into one's head (*inf.*); esteem, appraise, weigh up; philosophize, reconsider.

occur to, come to mind, strike, suggest itself, enter one's head.

385 absence of thought

n. thoughtlessness, irrationality, incomprehensibility, folly, senselessness, ignorance, inattention, inconsideration, carelessness, neglect.

adj. thoughtless, irrational, unreasoning, incomprehensible, foolish, blank, vacant, switched off (*inf.*).

vb. not think about, ignore, forget, dismiss, get off one's mind, get out of one's mind, get out of one's head; think no more of, not give another thought to, not give a second thought, not enter one's head.

386 idea

n. idea, notion, concept, conception, thought, mental impression, image, impression; conjecture, fancy, guess, theory, hypothesis, postulate; observation, opinion, assessment, plan.

see also **420**

387 topic

n. topic, subject, problem, matter, question; argument, theme, burden, concern, thesis, proposition, thrust, *leitmotif*, issue, point, point in question, moot point.

B Preliminary conditions and operations

388 curiosity

n. curiosity, interest, concern, regard; thirst, quest, desire, eagerness, inclination; inquisitiveness, intrusiveness, nosiness (*sl.*), prying.

questioner; busy-body, snoop, intruder, meddler, Nosy Parker (*sl.*); gossip, backbiter, chatterbox, scandalmonger.

adj. curious, interested, concerned, into (*inf.*), questioning; inquisitive, searching, poking, scrutinizing; intrusive, prying, snooping, meddlesome, nosy (*sl.*).

vb. enquire, question, investigate, seek; show interest, be into (*inf.*), have a thing about (*inf.*); intrude, pry, snoop, meddle, gossip, chatter, backbite.

389 incuriosity

n. incuriosity, apathy, dislike, disinclination.

adj. incurious, unconcerned, inattentive, apathetic, indifferent, uninquisitive, uninterested, bored.

vb. ignore, disregard, be blind to, dismiss, take no interest in, not care less.

390 attention

n. attention, regard, notice, observation, inspection; consideration, study, attentiveness; assiduousness, diligence; mindfulness, heed, heedfulness, vigilance; concentration, preoccupation.

adj. attentive, mindful; heeding, wary, vigilant; considerate, observant; studious, assiduous, diligent.

vb. pay attention, listen, catch, give heed to, observe, notice, take notice, mind, heed, look to, regard, note, take into account; consider, study, inspect, examine, mark, scrutinize, concentrate on; drink in (*inf.*), lap up (*inf.*), hang on someone's every word; lose oneself in; keep one's ear to the ground (*inf.*); attract, draw, pull, focus.

391 inattention

n. inattention, carelessness, inconsideration, unconcern, heedlessness, thoughtlessness; slackness, indolence; neglect, disregard; indifference, coolness, coldness, detachment; absent-mindedness, wandering.

adj. inattentive, careless, inconsiderate, thoughtless, heedless, unobservant; negligent, indifferent, cool, cold, detached; absent-minded, distracted.

vb. be inattentive, dream, day-dream, let one's mind wander; not catch, miss, disregard, overlook, neglect; go in one ear and out the other; distract, divert, draw away, turn away, call away, detract, attract from, beguile; upset, disconcert.

392 care

n. care, concern, regard, thought, heed, consideration, solicitude, thoughtfulness, pains; carefulness, scrupulousness, prudence, judiciousness, wisdom; watchfulness, vigilance, alertness; forethought, precaution, caution.

exactness, particularity, thoroughness, meticulousness, neatness, fastidiousness, conscientiousness; economy, conservation, frugality, management, husbandry, stewardship.

oversight, direction, surveillance, supervision, inspection, protection, guarding.

adj. careful, concerned, thoughtful, considerate, courteous, kind, solicitous; prudent, judicious, wise, discreet, unobtrusive, self-possessed, watchful, sober, alert, awake, circumspect, vigilant; diplomatic, politic.

thorough, rigorous, particular, precise, exact, exacting, discriminating, conscientious, meticulous, punctilious, scrupulous; neat, tidy, fussy, finicky; pedantic, fastidious, religious; assiduous, diligent, painstaking, dependable, faithful; economical, sparing, frugal, thrifty, stingy (*inf.*).

vb. be careful, mind, heed, tend, look after, take care of; watch, observe; superintend, supervise, direct, manage, stand over; baby-sit, chaperon; keep vigil; keep tabs on, follow up, protect, support, guard.

393 neglect

n. neglect, carelessness, unconcern, disregard, inconsideration, negligence, neglectfulness, apathy, indifference, omission, dereliction, failure, procrastination; imprudence, rashness, hastiness.

adj. negligent, careless, inconsiderate, unthinking, thoughtless, unmindful, forgetful, oblivious; remiss, lax, inattentive; lackadaisical, imprudent, unguarded, hasty, rash, unwary, reckless, unheeding, injudicious, unwise; apathetic, indifferent, casual, slipshod, lazy; wasteful, extravagant, immoderate.

vb. neglect, omit, miss, forget, dismiss, reject, leave undone, lose sight of, evade, gloss over, skip, skimp; disregard, ignore, overlook, not look at, pass over, make light of, brush aside, laugh off, pooh-pooh, shut one's eyes to, give the go-by, turn a blind eye to.

see also 920

394 enquiry

n. enquiry, inquiry, examination, investigation, study, analysis, search, probe, quest, perusal; checking, scrutiny, review, inspection; question, query, request, invitation, petition, challenge, feeler; experiment, quiz, test, exam, viva, questionnaire; interrogation, interview, dialogue, cross-examination, grilling, catechism.

questioner, examiner, enquirer, interrogator, interviewer, researcher, investigator, canvasser, pollster.

adj. inquiring, inquisitive, curious, nosy (*sl.*); exploratory, fact-finding.

vb. enquire, ask, put a question, pose, put it to; call upon, request, invite, challenge, charge, bid, petition, canvass; question, interrogate, quiz, cross-examine, interview, grill; seek, look for, search, hunt, turn inside out, peruse; sniff out (*inf.*), smell out; investigate, examine, study, inspect, analyse, probe, scrutinize, check, review, monitor; try, hear; pry, snoop, spy.

395 answer

n. answer, reply, response, acknowledgement; comeback, feedback, rebuttal, rejoinder, retort; repartee, backchat, retaliation.

answerer, replier, correspondent, examinee, candidate.

adj. answering, responsive.

vb. answer, reply, respond, come back to, write back, acknowledge, remark, rejoin, retort, answer back, rebut.

396 experiment

n. experiment, test, research; observation, analysis, inspection, operation, diagnosis, exercise; check, verification, proof, sifting; rehearsal, practice run, trial run, test case, pilot, pilot scheme; feeler, probe; speculation, guess, conjecture, trial and error, hit and miss, shot in the dark, hypothesis; sounding board, guinea pig.

researcher, research worker, scientist, boffin (*sl.*), back-room boy, experimenter, experimentalist, speculator.

adj. experimental, hypothetical; tentative, trial, provisional, temporary, probationary, preliminary, preparatory, unproved, speculative, trial, test.

vb. experiment, investigate, study, examine, scrutinize, explore, research, search, sound out, prove; analyse, diagnose; check, verify, prove; guess, speculate, hypothesize; put out a feeler, see which way the wind is blowing, spy out the land.

397 comparison

n. comparison, juxtaposition; weighing, estimation, measurement; relation, connection, association, balance, match, parallel, parallelism, correspondence, equation; identification, resemblance, similarity, likening, analogy, illustration, example, picture, metaphor, simile, allegory; contrast, opposition.

vb. compare, juxtapose, parallel, draw a parallel between, put side by side; measure, weigh, confront, collate; liken, relate, associate, link, balance, match, equate; contrast, oppose, separate.

398 discrimination

n. discrimination, discernment, acumen, astuteness, keenness, shrewdness, penetration; distinction, nicety, differentiation; diagnosis, appreciation, critique, judgment, sense, sensitivity, tact, feel, refinement, taste, selection, choice.

adj. discriminating, careful, selective, particular, exacting, choosy (*inf.*), judicious, tactful, discerning, perceptive, sensitive, critical, tasteful, refined.

vb. discriminate, differentiate, discern, tell apart, tell from, distinguish; compare and contrast; choose, pick carefully, select, separate, set apart.

399 indiscrimination

n. indiscrimination, uncriticalness, insensitiveness, tastelessness.

adj. indiscriminate, undiscriminating, unselective, uncritical, undiscerning, careless; mixed, blanket, promiscuous; random, haphazard; aimless, chaotic, confused.

vb. not discriminate, draw no distinction, disregard differences, lump together; confuse, confound, mix, muddle, jumble together.

400 measurement

n. measurement, mensuration; quantification; estimation, determination, computation, calculation, assessment, evaluation, reckoning; graduation, calibration; measure, dimension, distance, degree, pitch, time; size, length, depth, height, width, breadth, thickness; area; mass, weight, density, volume, capacity, pressure, intensity, speed, strength, calibre, viscosity; quantity, magnitude, range, extent; amplitude, frequency, ratio, diameter, radius; temperature.

meter, gauge, scale, rule, ruler, tape-measure, slide-rule, calculator, computer; scales, balance, mark, grade, step, point, limit, standard, criterion; weights and measures, imperial system, avoirdupois, apothecary, troy, metric system, SI unit; metrication.

adj. mensural, dimensional; measurable, assessable, calculable, computable.

vb. measure, quantify, estimate, compute, assess, count, reckon, determine, evaluate, appraise, calculate, survey; gauge, calibrate, graduate; take a reading; level, square; survey, map; average; check; go metric, metricate.

C Materials for reasoning

401 evidence

n. evidence, fact, clue, reason, justification, explanation, grounds, data, case; support, foundation, backing; sign, indication, trace; document, documentation, information; testimony, witness, statement, plea, assertion, allegation, attestation, exhibit, reference, affidavit; confirmation, corroboration.

adj. suggestive, indicative, symptomatic, corroborative, supporting.

vb. evidence, show, suggest, indicate, evince, illustrate, demonstrate, document, manifest, imply; confirm, verify, support, substantiate, attest, corroborate; testify, bear witness to, witness, affirm; speak for itself (*inf.*), speak volumes (*inf.*).

see also **413**

402 counter-evidence

n. counter-evidence, counterclaim, defence, rebuttal, answer, reply.

adj. rebutting, defending, conflicting; uncorroborative, countervailing; contradictory, contrary, answering, replying.

vb. weigh against, contradict, rebut, refute, squash, deny; be contrary to; cancel out.

see also **414**

403 qualification

n. qualification, modification, limitation, restriction; proviso, exception, reservation; allowance.

adj. qualifying, qualificatory, provisional, contingent, conditional, mitigating, extenuating.

vb. qualify, modify, adjust; limit, restrict, restrain, moderate, mitigate, lessen, temper; condition, colour, make exceptions, exempt, allow for, make allowances for.

see also **700**

404 possibility

n. possibility, potentiality, practicability, feasibility, plausibility, reasonableness, virtuality.

adj. possible, likely, probable; virtual, potential; able, capable, viable, feasible, plausible, practical, practicable, available, attainable, within reach, obtainable, within the bounds of possibility; conceivable, thinkable, imaginable, credible.

vb. be possible, can, may, might, stand a chance; make possible, enable, admit of.

see also **406**

405 impossibility

n. impossibility, impracticability, unavailability, inaccessibility; unreasonableness, no hope, hopelessness, no chance.

adj. impossible, unbelievable, inconceivable, umimaginable, unthinkable; prohibited; insoluble, difficult; unable, implausible, unpracticable, unavailable, insurmountable, insuperable, inaccessible, unobtainable, out of the question, beyond the bounds of possibility.

vb. be impossible, defy possibilities; not dream of (*inf.*); make impossible, exclude.

adv. no way (*inf.*).

see also **407**

406 probability

n. probability, likelihood, likeliness, expectation; prospect, promise, chance, possibility, good chance, hope, opportunity.

adj. probable, likely, expected; reasonable, presumable, on the cards, supposable; promised, well-founded, seeming; feasible, practicable, workable, plausible, credible.

vb. be probable, may well happen, show signs of; make likely, increase the chances of, hope for.

adv. probably, likely, no doubt, in all probability, quite possibly, most likely, to be expected, to be supposed, as likely as not, everything being equal.

407 improbability

n. improbability, unlikelihood, implausibility, inconceivableness, unreasonableness; rarity, infrequency; bare possibility, million to one chance.

adj. improbable, unlikely, unexpected, unreasonable, impracticable, unworkable, implausible, unbelievable, hardly possible, unheard of, doubtful, dubious, questionable; absurd, extraordinary.

vb. be improbable, probably not happen.

408 certainty

n. certainty, certitude; conviction, assurance; reliance, confidence, trust; truth, accuracy, genuineness; dogmatism; unambiguity, conclusiveness; necessity, inevitability, inexorability.

foregone conclusion, safe bet, sure thing (*inf.*), dead cert (*sl.*).

adj. certain, settled, decided, final, definite; absolute, sure, conclusive, solid, irrefutable, indubitable, indisputable, unquestionable, unmistakable, incontrovertible, unassailable, undisputed; reliable, unfailing, unshakable, inerrant, infallible, sound, authoritative, unerring, trustworthy; unambiguous, unequivocal, incontestable; unconditional; ascertained, certified, verified, attested, confirmed, ratified; self-evident, axiomatic.

vb. make certain, guarantee, authenticate, certify, check, confirm, test, prove, verify, corroborate, ratify; ensure, secure, settle, attest, endorse, clinch; commit, engage, take sides; seal, sign, shake hands.

adv. certainly, without doubt, of

course, definitely, at all events, sure thing (*inf.*); in the bag (*inf.*).

409 uncertainty

n. uncertainty, incertitude; unreliability, questionableness, unpredictability, untrustworthiness, ambiguity; vagueness, obscurity; inconclusiveness, indeterminateness, improbability, unlikelihood.

doubt, disbelief, unbelief, suspicion, misgiving, scepticism, agnosticism, faithlessness, doubtfulness, incredulity; indecision, equivocalness, wavering, hesitancy, suspense; perplexity, bewilderment; puzzle, problem, maze, dilemma, quandary, enigma; fog, haziness; anybody's guess.

adj. uncertain, doubtful, undecided; unsure, inconclusive, ambiguous, vague, unclear, indeterminate, unpredictable, unlikely, possible; risky, chancy, insecure; haphazard, random, casual; questionable, unreliable, fallible, erring; shakable, precarious; puzzling, perplexing.

controversial, open, debatable, contentious, problematical, moot; uncertified, unverified, unattested, unconfirmed, unratified.

doubting, unbelieving, suspicious, sceptical, faithless, distrustful, agnostic.

vb. be uncertain, doubt, flounder, grope, fumble; suspect, smell a rat; not know where one stands, not know which way to turn; sit on the fence, waver; fall between two stools; puzzle, bewilder, perplex.

adv. in the air, in question, open to question.

D Reasoning processes

410 reasoning

n. reasoning, rationalizing; judgment, argumentation; reason, rationality, logic, rationalism; thinking, brainwork, cogitation, knowing, realizing; insight, discernment, acumen, penetration, understanding, comprehension, grasp; reflection, deliberation; concluding.

conclusion, inference, deduction, induction, derivation; syllogism; problem, proposition, premise, postulate, thesis, theorem.

discussion, conversation, exchange, dialogue, interview, disputation, argument, dispute, debate, controversy, symposium; apolegetics.

adj. rational, reasoning, logical, sound, rationalistic, reasonable; thoughtful, deliberate, collected; arguing, discursive, controversial, polemical; argumentative.

vb. reason, argue, discuss, converse, dispute, talk about, explain; defend, justify, plead, make out a case, support, contend; philosophize; conclude, put two and two together (*inf.*), deduce, infer, derive, syllogize; be reasonable, add up (*inf.*), make sense, hold water.

411 intuition

n. intuition, instinct, sentiment, feeling, sense; insight, inspiration, extra-sensory perception, ESP, sixth sense; automatic reaction, reflex action, hunch, presentiment, premonition, impression.

adj. intuitive, instinctive; involuntary, reflex, automatic, mechanical, unthinking; spontaneous, inspired, impulsive.

vb. feel, sense, feel in one's bones,

guess, just know, have a funny feeling, have the feeling, follow one's nose.

412 false reasoning

n. sophistry, irrationality, unreasonableness, unsoundness, invalidity; delusion, deceit, deception, erroneousness, speciousness, evasion.

fallacy, sophism, ambiguity, solecism, illogicality, paralogism; inconsistency, *non sequitur*, contradiction; circular argument, vicious circle; misinterpretation; miscalculation; preconception; perversion, prejudice, deviation, aberration.

adj. sophistic, fallacious, illogical, specious, inconsistent, loose, contradictory, ambiguous, solecistic; irrational, unreasonable, unsound, untenable, inconsistent, invalid, deceptive, erroneous, heretical.

vb. reason falsely, evade the issue, beat about the bush, miss the point, beg the question; cavil.

413 demonstration

n. demonstration, proof, verification, justification, establishment, affirmation, validation, corroboration; averment; explanation, elucidation, interpretation, illustration; exhibition, presentation, display.

adj. demonstrative; demonstrated, clear, evident, conclusive, certain, decisive; established, concluded, upheld, valid; demonstrable, verifiable, deducible, inferable.

vb. demonstrate, prove, show, verify, make evident, establish, confirm, substantiate, bear out, affirm, authenticate, attest, validate, test, check; declare, testify, witness, document; have a case; settle, determine; justify; explain, illustrate, describe; manifest, exhibit, display.

414 disproof

n. disproof, confutation, refutation, invalidation, rebuttal, contradiction, denial; upset; exposure; clincher.

adj. disproved, confuted, invalidated; shown up, exposed; contradicted.

vb. disprove, prove false, rebut, invalidate, repudiate, contradict, deny; contend, debate, argue, oppose, dispute; show up (*inf.*), discredit, expose; overthrow, overturn, defeat, finish, confound, overwhelm, crush, floor, silence; knock the bottom out of (*inf.*), cut the ground from under one's feet, get the better of.

E Results of reasoning

415 judgment

n. judgment, consideration, contemplation, appraisal, examination, review, weighing, sifting, assessment, estimation, appreciation, evaluation, determination; adjudication, arbitration; report, opinion, view, belief, idea, decree, decision, finding, recommendation, pronouncement, verdict, ruling, resolution.

judge, assessor, examiner, valuer, surveyor, adjudicator, arbitrator, referee, umpire.

adj. judicial, judicious; critical; unprejudiced, unbiased.

vb. judge, consider, contemplate, size up (*inf.*), examine, review, appraise, survey, analyse, weigh, sift, assess, evaluate, estimate, appreciate; decide, conclude, find, recommend, pronounce, rule, decree, settle, adjudicate, arbitrate.

416 misjudgment

n. misjudgment, miscalculation, misconception, misunderstanding, misinterpretation, distortion, overestimation, preconception; underestimation; prejudice, bias; narrow-mindedness, pettiness, narrowness, bigotry.

adj. misjudging, wrong; uncritical, unrealistic; injudicious, unwise, ill-judged; partial, unfair, one-sided, biased, prejudiced, intolerant; narrow-minded, petty, mean, narrow, short-sighted, bigoted, insular.

vb. misjudge, miscalculate, misconceive, misconstrue, misapprehend, misunderstand, bark up the wrong tree (*inf.*); undervalue, overvalue, overrate; prejudge, presume, suppose, preconceive, jump to conclusions; prejudice, bias, jaundice, twist, sway, warp, influence.

see also **916**

417 overestimation

n. overestimation, overvaluation, overrating, exaggeration, overstatement; optimism.

adj. overestimated, exaggerated.

vb. overestimate, exaggerate, overvalue, overrate; maximize, emphasize, make a mountain out of a molehill, make too much of, paint in glowing colours.

see also **481**

418 underestimation

n. underestimation, undervaluation, understatement, minimization; pessimism.

adj. underestimated, understated; deprecatory; modest.

vb. underestimate, underplay, play down, underrate, understate, minimize; depreciate, disparage, slight; make light of, not do justice to, think too little of.

419 discovery

n. discovery, finding, disclosure, uncovering; manifestation, revelation; detection, identification, catching; invention; exploration.

adj. on the right track, near, close, warm (*inf.*).

vb. discover, find, hit upon; realize, see, perceive, understand, become aware of, get wise to, get on to, twig (*inf.*); meet, come across, happen upon; expose, disclose, detect, spot, lay bare, reveal, uncover, unearth, bring to light, run to earth (*inf.*), run to ground (*inf.*), track down; catch in the act, catch red-handed.

420 belief

n. belief, credence, trust, acceptance, faith, credit; reliance, dependence, conviction, confidence, persuasion; certainty, surety, assurance, hope; admission, confession, avowal.

creed, doctrine, dogma, credo, revelation; tenet, canon, principle; articles of faith, catechism.

opinion, thought, view, sentiment, idea, notion, conception, impression, assumption; attitude, way of thinking; point of view, position, outlook, angle, stand, stance.

adj. believing, accepting, reliant, dependent, convinced, persuaded, certain, confident; believable, credible, tenable, plausible, trustworthy, reliable, unfailing.

vb. believe, accept, hold, trust, depend, rely, be convicted of, be persuaded of, take at one's word, take on trust, take one's word for; think, consider, regard as, suppose, presume, surmise, fancy, assume, deem, conclude; come round to, change one's views, be converted; have faith in, be a believer, profess, confess.

convince, persuade, bring round, prove, argue, assure, satisfy, make realize, bring home to; teach; captivate, have a way with (*inf.*).

see also 854

421 unbelief

n. unbelief, disbelief, doubt, uncertainty, incredulity, scepticism, misgiving, suspicion, mistrust, distrust, qualm, hesitation, reservation, apprehension, irresolution; faithlessness, rejection; agnosticism, atheism.

adj. unbelieving, disbelieving, doubting, questioning, sceptical, distrusting, incredulous; unbelievable, untenable, unreliable, doubtful, dubious, suspicious, questionable, implausible.

vb. disbelieve, doubt, hesitate, waver, not believe, give no credence to, lack confidence in, set no store by; mistrust, suspect, question, challenge.

422 gullibility

n. gullibility, credulity, simpleness, unsophistication.

adj. gullible, credulous, trusting, unsuspecting, simple, naive, unsophisticated, inexperienced, guileless, simple, green.

vb. be gullible, fall for (*inf.*), be easily persuaded.

423 incredulity

n. incredulity, suspicion, scepticism; sophistication.

adj. incredulous, unbelieving, sceptical, unresponsive, ungullible, sophisticated.

vb. refuse to believe, distrust, doubt; reject, turn a deaf ear to.

see also 421

424 assent

n. assent, affirmative, yes; approval, agreement, acceptance, support, approbation; authorization, permission, consent, empowering, legalization, authority, sanction, guarantee, warrant, authentication, ratification, endorsement, affirmation, go-ahead (*inf.*), green light (*inf.*), nod (*sl.*).

like-mindedness, unanimity, consensus, general agreement; supporter, follower, assenter, signer, subscriber, ratifier, signatory, aye.

adj. assenting, acquiescent; approved, accepted, voted, carried, passed; unanimous, of one mind.

vb. assent, say yes to, agree, concur, affirm, accept, support, subscribe to, approve, vote for, pass, rubber-stamp (*inf.*), put up with (*inf.*), go along with, tolerate, stand for (*inf.*), bear, endure, acquiesce; acknowledge, admit, concede, grant, yield, recognize, defer to.

authorize, grant permission, empower, legalize, ratify, sign, endorse, authenticate, seal.

425 dissent

n. dissent, disapproval, disagreement, dissidence, disapprobation; difference, variance, discord, dissension, protest, controversy, vendetta, animosity, division; non-conformity; non-acceptance, withdrawal, secession; objection, reservation, negative, no.

dissenter, objector, protester, rebel, non-conformist, caviller; interrupter, heckler; separatist; recusant.

adj. dissident, disagreeing, differing; protesting, objecting.

vb. dissent, disagree, disapprove, differ, agree to differ, protest, object, oppose, challenge, heckle, shout down, take exception; reject, refuse, contradict; withdraw, secede.

426 knowledge

n. knowledge, knowing, awareness, consciousness, recognition, realization, understanding, grasp, cognition; intelligence, education, instruction, learning, erudition, scholarship, culture, bookishness; accomplishments, attainments; facts, information, encyclopedia; expertise, know-how, skill, proficiency; wisdom, maturity, experience.

adj. knowing, conscious, mindful, aware, cognizant; discerning, perceptive; acquainted, familiar, well versed in, well grounded in, *au fait;* clever, intelligent, informed, instructed, trained, knowledgeable, educated, well-taught, well-read, learned, erudite, scholarly, cultured, intellectual; mature, wise, experienced.

known, widely known, common, proverbial, commonplace, household name, hackneyed; infamous, notorious.

vb. know, realize, understand, grasp, see, perceive, realize, apprehend, be aware of, discern, appreciate, recognize; experience; be well-informed, be well up on, be into (*inf.*), know backwards, know inside out, know like the back of one's hand.

see also **434, 460**

427 ignorance

n. ignorance, unawareness, unconsciousness, unknowingness, nescience; unenlightenment, incomprehension, darkness, fog, haziness, vagueness; inexperience, immaturity, greenness, naivety, simplicity, empty-headedness, stupidity; unlearnedness, unintellectuality, illiteracy; unskilfulness, awkwardness.

smattering, shallowness; unknown, unknown quantity, unexplored ground, virgin territory, mystery, closed book, sealed book.

adj. ignorant, unaware, unknowing; unmindful, unconscious, disregarding; inexperienced, immature, green, inept, simple, stupid, thick, dense; unenlightened, in the dark, unfamiliar with, not conversant, a stranger to, none the wiser; untaught, illiterate, uneducated, untrained, backward, unscholarly, unlearned, uncultivated, unread, uncultured, Philistine, unintellectual; unknown, untold, unseen, mysterious, secret, undiscovered, virgin, uncharted.

vb. not know, be ignorant, be in the dark, not have any idea, not have the foggiest idea (*inf.*); pass (*inf.*).

see also **435**

428 student

n. student, scholar, schoolchild, learner, disciple; philosopher, scientist, researcher, expert, man of letters, wise man, savant, sage; professor, don, teacher, doctor; bookworm, intellectual, egghead (*inf.*); genius, brain, know-all, mine of information, walking encyclopedia.

see also **473, 474**

429 ignoramus

n. ignoramus, know-nothing, dunce, fool, blockhead; greenhorn, raw recruit, babe, simpleton.

see also **437**

430 truth

n. truth, fact, reality, the case, gospel truth, plain truth, real thing, real McCoy (*inf.*).

trueness, verity, correctness, exactitude, accuracy, precision, perfection, rectitude, faithfulness, sincerity, honesty; authenticity, infallibility, genuineness, validity.

adj. true, truthful, veracious, real,

right, factual, correct, objective, actual; historical; genuine, authentic, original, official, veritable; unadulterated, unmixed; attested, valid, guaranteed; undisputed, conclusive, final; accurate, exact, precise, faithful, infallible; sincere, honest, upright.

vb. be true, be the case· ring true; hit the nail on the head (*inf.*); come true, come about, happen, occur.

see also **476**

431 error

n. error, mistake, fault, blunder, failure, fall, flaw, lapse, omission, lie, untruth, wrong, deviation, sin; *faux pas*, slip, slip-up (*inf.*); misjudgment, misunderstanding, misconception, inaccuracy, mismanagement; misprint, literal; bloomer (*sl.*), clanger (*sl.*), howler (*sl.*).

erroneousness, falsity, inaccurateness, inexactness.

adj. wrong, incorrect, unreal, untrue; unauthentic, unoriginal, spurious; inaccurate, inexact, imprecise; erroneous, mistaken, lying, untruthful, in error; unfaithful, disloyal, deceitful, corrupt, unsound; deceptive, fallacious, misleading, pretended, sham, counterfeit, faked, mocked; misunderstood; fallible.

vb. go wrong, make a mistake, err, blunder, slip up (*inf.*), bungle; be wrong, be mistaken; misconceive, misunderstand; not hold water, fall down, fall to the ground; mislead, lead astray, lead up the garden path (*inf.*), pervert, deceive, trick, hoax.

see also **477, 478**

432 maxim

n. maxim, proverb, saying, truth, text, dictum, motto, slogan, watchword, moral, aphorism, adage, axiom; banality, truism, platitude, commonplace, cliché; epigram, witticism.

adj. aphoristic, proverbial, epigrammatic; brief, concise, pithy, terse; trite, commonplace.

433 absurdity

n. absurdity, ridiculousness, ludicrousness, outrageousness, folly, silliness, stupidity, nonsense; spoonerism, malapropism; jest, trick, practical joke, prank, farce, buffoonery, clowning, wildness; extravaganza.

adj. absurd, ridiculous, crazy, farcical, nonsensical, senseless, inane, wild, foolish, silly, stupid, bizarre, extravagant, fantastic.

vb. be absurd, talk nonsense, fool around; play tricks.

see also **451**

434 intelligence; wisdom

n. intelligence, understanding, brightness, cleverness, brilliance; genius, talent, brains, grey matter, intellect, sense, common sense, wit.

wisdom, experience, erudition, sagacity, sapience; shrewdness, discernment, judgment, acumen, insight, perspicacity, sharpness, acuteness, penetration, prudence, foresight.

adj. intelligent, clever, bright, brilliant, able, knowledgeable; wise, sagacious, shrewd, prudent, knowing, contemplative, reasoning, thoughtful, sober, sensible, judicious, circumspect, discreet, considerate, astute, perceptive, perspicacious, far-sighted, discerning, quick, acute, sharp, penetrating, keen, discriminating, having one's wits about one, not born yesterday (*inf.*).

vb. be wise, understand, discern; have one's head screwed on the right way (*inf.*).

see also **426**

435 unintelligence; folly

n. unintelligence, stupidity, dullness, slowness, heaviness; foolishness, folly, weakness, shallowness, silliness, simplicity, childishness, puerility, imbecility; imprudence, short-sightedness, indiscretion.

adj. unintelligent, unthinking, unreasoning; stupid, dull, slow, weak, shallow, superficial, vacant, simple, dumb, thick, dense, empty-headed, slow-witted, feeble-minded, simple-minded, weak-minded, half-witted, blockish, oafish, feather-brained, doltish; foolish, crazy, silly, insane, inane, idiotic, imbecile, puerile, childish; backward, retarded, handicapped, subnormal, deprived; unwise, imprudent, short-sighted, undiscerning.

vb. be foolish, act the fool, fool around, lark about (*inf.*).

see also **427**

436 sage

n. sage, wise man, man of learning, savant, pundit, expert, doctor, scholar, master, great thinker, authority, oracle, elder statesman, connoisseur, luminary; wiseacre, know-all, sciolist.

see also **428, 473**

437 fool

n. fool, simpleton, dunce, idiot, ignoramus, scatterbrain, half-wit, fathead, thickhead, blockhead, nitwit, nincompoop, moron, cretin, imbecile, numskull, bore, dolt, ass, buffoon, chump (*sl.*), lout, oaf, ninny, jerk (*sl.*), twit (*sl.*).

see also **429, 630**

438 sanity

n. sanity, saneness, balance, normality, clearmindedness, lucidity, wholesomeness, *mens sana*, rationality, reason.

adj. sane, normal, sound-minded, healthy-minded, sound, right-minded, sober, lucid, in one's right mind, self-possessed, all there (*inf.*).

439 insanity

n. insanity, insaneness, madness, lunacy; imbecility, cretinism, idiocy; phobia, mania, craze, passion, obsession, infatuation, fixation, compulsion; mental illness, nervous breakdown, nervous disorder; nervousness, nerves; hysteria, frenzy, fever, attack, fit, rage; peculiarity, eccentricity, abnormality, oddity.

adj. insane, mad, unsound, unbalanced, crazy, deranged, confused, demented, rabid, berserk, out of one's mind, off one's head, off one's rocker (*sl.*); obsessed, infatuated; frenzied, wild, raging, furious; eccentric, odd, cranky, peculiar.

vb. be mad, wander, ramble; go mad, lose one's sanity, take leave of one's senses, go out of one's mind, crack up (*inf.*), go off one's rocker (*sl.*); madden, drive mad, unbalance.

440 madman

n. madman, lunatic, mental case, loony (*sl.*), bedlamite; maniac, psychopath, psychotic, paranoid, hysteric, neurotic, manic-depressive, melancholic, hypochondriac, kleptomaniac; imbecile, idiot, moron, cretin, mongol; fool, crank, nut (*sl.*), eccentric, freak, weirdo (*inf.*), crackpot (*inf.*).

F Extension of thought

441 memory

n. memory, recollection, reminiscence, retrospection, recall, review, flashback, afterthought, hindsight, reconsideration, reflection, thought; retention, good memory, photographic memory, *déjà vu*.

memorandum, memo, reminder, record, note, jotting, scribble, mark; notes, summary, agenda, minutes; mnemonic, aid to memory; souvenir, memento, token, keepsake, relic, trinket; testimonial, memorial, monument, trophy, commemoration; warning, advice, suggestion, hint; prompt, prompter; memoirs, reminiscences, recollections, memories, memorabilia; diary, journal, album, scrapbook, notebook.

adj. remembered, recalled, retained, unforgotten, fresh, vivid; half-remembered, at the back of one's mind; reminiscent, reminding, evocative; memorable, unforgettable, indelibly fixed on one's mind; commemorative, memorial.

vb. remember, recollect, recall, bring to mind, be reminded of, think of, not forget; review, retrace, go back, flash back, look back, turn one's thoughts back, reminisce, call up, revive, rake up the past, drag up (*inf.*), dredge up (*inf.*); recognize, identify, know again, make out.

come to mind, ring a bell, stay in the memory, never be forgotten, haunt, recur, penetrate, stay in one's mind, not leave one's thoughts, not get out of one's mind.

memorize, learn, commit to memory, know by heart, learn by rote, master, impress, retain, fix in the mind; keep always, hold dear, treasure, cherish, commemorate, enshrine in the memory, keep the memory alive.

remind, prompt, suggest, hint, bring back, make one think of, jog one's memory, refresh one's memory; warn, throw the book at (*inf.*).

442 oblivion

n. oblivion, forgetfulness, unmindfulness, absent-mindedness, amnesia, memory like a sieve, loss of memory, blankness, complete blank, mental block; insensibleness, indifference, carelessness.

adj. forgotten, unremembered, lost, out of one's mind, clean forgotten, unrecalled, unretained, in one ear and out the other; out of sight, out of mind; almost remembered, on the tip of one's tongue.

oblivious, forgetful, unmindful, heedless, inattentive, preoccupied, distracted, absent-minded.

vb. forget, fail to remember, have no recollection, put out of one's mind, have a short memory, think no more of, not give another thought, one's memory be a blank, escape one; be forgotten, sink into oblivion, fade from one's memory.

443 expectation

n. expectation, expectancy, looking forward, contemplation, anticipation, prospect, outlook; confidence, trust, hope, high hopes; preparedness; suspense, apprehension, pessimism.

adj. expectant, waiting, in anticipation, looking forward to, in suspense, on tenterhooks, itching, on edge, with bated breath; hoping, hopeful, confident; eager, watchful, vigilant, prepared; apprehensive, pessimistic.

expected, awaited, anticipated, foreseen, predicted, prophesied, longed for, looked for; on the cards, prospective.

vb. expect, look forward to, promise oneself, hope for, anticipate, contemplate, foresee, long for, bargain for (*inf.*), predict, prophesy, forecast, see coming, take for granted; wait for, await, bide one's time, mark time, hold one's breath, be in suspense; rely on, bank on, count on; be expected, lead one to expect, not put it past (*inf.*), be just like one.

444 non-expectation

n. inexpectation, unpreparedness, unexpectedness; surprise, shock, start, jolt, blow, bombshell, bolt from the blue, thunderbolt; turn-up for the book (*sl.*).

adj. unexpected, unforeseen, sudden, surprising, astonishing, staggering; unheralded, unpredicted, uncontemplated; unheard of, not thought of; more than one bargained for, not on the cards, without warning, out of the blue.

surprised, startled, thunderstruck, off one's guard, unready, unprepared, caught napping.

vb. not expect, not bargain for; surprise, take by surprise, catch unawares, catch in the act, catch red-handed, make one jump, startle, astonish, bowl over (*inf.*), knock down with a feather; come unexpectedly, turn up.

445 disappointment

n. disappointment, foiling, bafflement; discouragement, despondency, dissatisfaction, unfulfilment, discontent, frustration, disillusionment, regret, distress, displeasure.

bad news, setback, adversity, defeat, failure, anti-climax, miscarriage, let-down (*inf.*).

adj. disappointed, discouraged, dissatisfied, thwarted, baffled, unsuccessful, defeated, foiled, let-down (*inf.*), disconcerted, depressed, frustrated, disillusioned, full of regrets, despondent; disappointing, unsatisfactory, inadequate, insufficient, not up to expectations.

vb. disappoint, fail, let down (*inf.*), thwart, foil, baffle; come short of, dash one's hopes, not come up to expectations, leave much to be desired; frustrate, disconcert, disillusion, dissatisfy, let the side down (*inf.*).

446 foresight

n. foresight, second sight, foresightedness, anticipation; forethought, premeditation, preconsideration, preconception.

adj. foreseeing, foresighted, looking ahead, anticipatory.

vb. foresee, prophesy, forecast, anticipate; see ahead, look into the future, have a premonition, feel in one's bones.

447 prediction

n. prediction, forecast, foretelling, prophecy, prognostication, prognosis, foresight, forethought, foreknowledge, precognition, prescience, prevision; augury, divination, vaticination, astrology, clairvoyancy, soothsaying, fortune-telling, crystal-gazing, palmistry, casting lots; parapsychology, extrasensory perception; telepathy, telesthesia.

omen, sign, indication, symptom, portent, clue, hint, auspice, writing on the wall; warning, forewarning, foreboding, presentiment; guess, estimate, conjecture, budget; foretoken; presage; horoscope, fortune; herald, harbinger.

oracle, forecaster, prognosticator, prophet, prophetess, seer; fortune-teller, soothsayer, clairvoyant, augur, diviner, palmist, astrologer, crystal-gazer, gipsy; witch, wizard, medium; sibyl, haruspex; thought-reader, mind-reader, telepath, parapsychologist; weatherman, meteorologist.

adj. predicting, predictive, prognostic, divinatory, clairvoyant, portentous, significant; auspicious, favourable; ominous, foreboding; psychic, second-sighted; supernatural, paranormal, parapsychological; predictable, foreseen, expected, likely; divinable.

vb. predict, forecast, prognosticate, foresee, foretell, prophesy, vaticinate; forewarn; promise; bode, forebode, betoken, portend, foreshadow, presage; divine, augur, tell the future, tell fortunes, cast lots, read one's hand, read one's palm, read tea leaves.

see also 984

G Creative thought

448 supposition

n. supposition, guesswork, speculation, theorizing, postulation.

guess, surmise, notion, fancy, conjecture, inkling, hint, intimation, shrewd idea, vague idea, sneaking suspicion, rough guess, wild guess, shot in the dark.

premise, presupposition, postulate, proposition; inference, deduction, conclusion; thesis, hypothesis, working hypothesis, theory.

theorist, scientist, theorizer, academic, thinker, speculator, backroom boy, boffin (*sl.*).

adj. suppositional, unproved, tentative, speculative, conjectural, hypothetical, theoretical; supposed, assumed, presupposed, presumed, reputed, alleged, postulated, putative.

vb. suppose, believe, imagine, think, fancy, deem, guess, venture a guess, conjecture, speculate, estimate, divine, surmise, suspect, gather, assume, presume, presuppose; postulate, posit; infer, imply, deduce, theorize.

449 imagination

n. imagination, inventiveness, creativity, originality, visualization; fantasy, diversion, whimsy, daydreaming, castle-building, pipe-dreaming, wishful thinking, escapism; utopia, paradise, world of fantasy, cloud-cuckoo land, dream world.

idea, figment of the imagination, invention, notion, fancy, whim, caprice, vagary, chimera, will-o'-the-wisp, vision, appearance, day-dream, castles in the air, romance, flight of fancy, dream, nightmare.

visionary, prophet, seer, idealist, escapist, Quixote, dreamer, day-dreamer.

adj. imaginative, inventive, creative, resourceful, inspired, visionary, idealistic, with one's head in the clouds, quixotic, impractical, unrealistic; imaginary, fanciful, fantastic, capricious, whimsical, chimerical, dream-like, ideal, utopian, fictitious, pretended, make-believe, illusory, fabulous.

vb. imagine, picture, conjure up, envisage, conceive, suppose, visualize; invent, create, make up, think of, devise, fabricate, coin, hatch; dream, muse, fancy, fantasize, idealize, romanticize, build castles in the air, day-dream, pretend, make believe.

2 Communication of ideas

A Nature of ideas communicated

450 meaning

n. meaning, sense, significance, interpretation, implication, explanation; intent, aim, import, drift, tenor, thrust, purport; substance, essence, content.

meaningfulness, expressiveness; signification, connotation, denotation, reference, referendum, definition; unambiguity, equivalence, synonymity; synonym, related word.

adj. meaningful, significant, indicative, expressive, suggestive, evocative; substantial, pithy, full of meaning, pregnant; unambiguous; literal, verbal, word for word, verbatim, exact, faithful, true; semantic, linguistic.

vb. mean, signify, designate, refer to, drive at (*inf.*), denote, connote, indicate, symbolize, suggest, express, convey, declare, state, assert, spell; intimate, hint, betoken, bode, purport, import; imply, involve, speak of, touch on, point to.

451 meaninglessness

n. meaninglessness, senselessness, inexpressiveness, expressionlessness, nonsensicalness; misinterpretation, illogicality, ambiguity.

nonsense, balderdash, rubbish, twaddle, blather, rot (*sl.*), poppycock (*sl.*), trash, inanity, drivel, bunkum, prattle, baloney (*sl.*), bunk (*sl.*), ballyhoo, piffle (*sl.*); hot air (*sl.*), empty talk, humbug; cliché, truism, platitude.

adj. meaningless, insignificant, unindicative, inexpressive, unevocative; insubstantial, empty, void, vacant, blank; irrelevant, unimportant; senseless, aimless, purposeless; vague, ambiguous, tautological; trite, trivial, absurd, nonsensical, foolish; unintended, misinterpreted.

vb. be meaningless, mean nothing; talk nonsense, babble, prattle, blather, twaddle; talk through one's hat (*sl.*).

452 intelligibility

n. intelligibility, comprehensibility; recognizability, cognizability; lucidity, clarity, transparency; precision, plainness, explicitness, unambiguousness; readability, legibility, decipherability; audibility; plain speech; plain English.

adj. intelligible, comprehensible, understandable; clear, obvious, lucid, precise, plain, explicit, clear-cut, distinct, unambiguous, unequivocal; simple, straightforward, popular, made simple, for the beginner, made easy, without tears, for the million; recognizable, readable, legible, decipherable; audible.

vb. understand, apprehend, comprehend, grasp, follow, take in, figure out (*inf.*), catch on (*inf.*), get the meaning of, get the hang of (*inf.*), twig (*inf.*); fathom, penetrate, get to the bottom of, read between the lines, get the idea, get the gist of; know, have knowledge of, realize, perceive, appreciate; discern, distinguish, make out (*inf.*), work out (*inf.*); conceive, be aware of, recognize, sense, be conscious of.

be intelligible, make sense, be clear, click (*sl.*); make clear, put in plain English, put in words of one syllable.

see also **502**

453 unintelligibility

n. unintelligibility, incomprehensibility, meaninglessness, unrecognizability, unsearchableness, impenetrability; unclearness, obscurity, illegibility, ambiguity, indecipherability, unreadability; inaudibility; gibberish, incoherence, double Dutch, Greek; puzzle, mystery, enigma, sealed book, closed book.

adj. unintelligible, incomprehensible, meaningless, beyond one's comprehension; indistinct, vague, indefinite, hazy, inexact, ill-defined, loose, unclear, ambiguous, equivocal; incoherent, mixed up; obscure, puzzling, hard, complicated, intricate, profound, academic, over one's head, abstruse, recondite; concealed, mysterious, hidden, enigmatic, esoteric; illegible, indecipherable, unreadable; inaudible; unrecognizable, impenetrable, unsearchable, inexplicable; inscrutable, unfathomable, unutterable, ineffable.

vb. not understand, not have the first idea, not get the hang of (*inf.*), not make head or tail of, be baffled, be beyond one, get hold of the wrong end of the stick (*inf.*); be unintelligible, talk above someone's head; not make sense, escape one, be all Greek to one.

see also **503**

454 ambiguity

n. ambiguity, equivocalness; vagueness, uncertainty; ambivalence, equivocation, incongruity, inconsistency, prevarication; play on words, pun, *double entendre.*

adj. ambiguous, ambivalent, equivocal, uncertain, vague, vacillating, prevaricating; two-edged, backhanded; incongruous.

vb. cut both ways; play on words, pun; quibble, equivocate, prevaricate.

455 figure of speech

n. figure of speech, metaphor, transference, figurativeness; symbolism, imagery; rhetoric; comparison, simile, likeness, allegory, trope, fable, parable, allusion, personification; euphemism, irony, satire; understatement; onomatopoeia.

adj. figurative, metaphorical, extended, transferred, allusive; rhetorical; symbolic; comparative, allegorical, parabolic; euphemistic, euphuistic, ironical, satirical.

456 interpretation

n. interpretation, explanation, exposition, commentary, elucidation, clarification, illumination, explication; background, reason; analysis, diagnosis, review, criticism, critique, survey, investigation, appraisal, evaluation; significance, importance; annotation, note, comment; example, illustration, instance.

translation, equivalent, dynamic equivalent, paraphrase, rendering, rendition, adaptation, rewording, restatement, gloss, transcription, transliteration, version, reading.

interpreter, commentator, reviewer, critic, analyst, exponent, writer, editor, annotator, expositor, preacher, exegete; translator, linguist, polyglot; hermeneutics, exegetics, homiletics.

adj. interpretive, explanatory, expository, explicatory; analytical, diagnostic, critical, evaluatory; defining, descriptive, illuminating, discursive, exegetical; exemplary, illustrative; editorial, glossarial; literal, faithful, word-for-word; free, rough.

vb. interpret, explain, account for, give reasons for, give reasons why, make sense of; expound, lay bare the meaning, give an account of, state the significance of, read between the lines; make clear, elucidate, make plain, clarify, illuminate, throw light on, cast light on; simplify, expand on, emphasize; demonstrate, illustrate, exemplify, show by example; set forth, reveal, expose, lay bare, unfold, spell out.

translate, render, put in other words, put into, reword, restate, rephrase, paraphrase; transliterate, transcribe; decipher, decode, crack, solve; annotate, comment on, remark on, edit, gloss.

457 misinterpretation

n. misinterpretation, misreckoning, misconception, misunderstanding, misconstruction, falsification, distortion, perversion, delusion, error, mistake; mistranslation.

vb. misinterpret, misunderstand, get hold of the wrong end of the stick (*inf.*), misquote, falsify, distort, pervert, read into, misconstrue, not give a true account of, give a false impression of.

see also **453**

B Modes of communication

458 manifestation

n. manifestation, revelation, showing, demonstration, disclosure, expression, presentation, exhibition; publishing, telling, announcement; divulgence, betrayal.

appearance, vision, apparition; exhibit, show, layout, example, specimen, showpiece; parade, procession, pageant; evidence, sign, miracle, theophany.

adj. manifest, apparent, clear, visible, perceptible, observable, obvious, patent, open, evident, self-evident, unmistakable, crystal-clear, staring one in the face, written all over one, express, explicit, conspicuous, noticeable, prominent, bold, striking, pronounced, flagrant, glaring, salient.

vb. manifest, appear, reveal, show, disclose, express; present, produce, publish, tell, announce, proclaim, betray, divulge, demonstrate, exemplify, indicate, show signs of, evince; make manifest, make plain, lay bare, expose, show forth; display, exhibit, set out, uncover, unfold, unmask, parade; promote, publicize.

see also **462, 823**

459 latency

n. latency, secrecy, subtlety, dormancy; insidiousness; undercurrent, implication, suggestion, hint, allusion, connotation, inference, more than meets the eye, snake in the grass.

adj. latent, hidden, veiled, dormant, quiescent, lurking, subtle, insidious, beneath the surface, between the lines, underlying, undercover; underdeveloped, potential, possible; implied, inherent, inferred, suggested, intimated, hinted, supposed, tacit, understood, unmentioned, unspoken, unexpressed; suggestive, indicative, provocative.

vb. be latent, be beneath the surface, lurk, lie low; imply, indicate, infer, suggest, mean, intimate, hint, insinuate, involve, provoke, entail.

see also **461**

460 information

n. information, knowledge, facts, info (*inf.*), gen (*sl.*), low-down (*sl.*); briefing, run-down (*inf.*); proof, evidence, notes, details, results, figures, tables, statistics, data; intelligence; news, message, report, notice, communication, notification, declaration, presentation, proclamation, broadcast, transmission; narration, account, description, story, tale, paper; tidings, discovery, revelation, enlightenment; dispatch, release, hand-out, announcement; telephone call, telex, telegram, cable, wire, teletext.

hint, mention, advice, aside, wink, whisper, word in one's ear, tip-off (*inf.*), warning, intimation, suspicion, glimmer, indication, suggestion.

informant, spokesman, narrator, story-teller, messenger, newsman, reporter, authority, announcer, broadcaster, correspondent, journalist; dispatcher, courier, herald, emissary, envoy, ambassador, carrier; guidebook, manual, chart, itinerary, map, timetable.

informer, spy, secret agent, observer, wire tapper, snoop, grass (*sl.*), squealer (*sl.*); gossip, tell-tale, eavesdropper, newsmonger, tattler, scandalmonger.

adj. informative, instructive, enlightening, educational, enriching, newsy (*inf.*), chatty (*inf.*), communicative.

vb. inform, speak, say, tell, notify, let know, communicate, give the facts, put over, put across, get across, get over, present, give to understand, convey, declare, announce, express, proclaim; relate, narrate, recite, report, describe, set forth, make known, let in on, tip off (*inf.*), have a word in someone's ear; enlighten, put in the picture; broadcast, spread the news, circulate, disseminate, promulgate; telephone, ring, call, telex, cable, wire; report back, debrief (*inf.*).

bring up to date, fill in on (*inf.*); keep up with, keep tabs on (*inf.*), keep track of, keep one's finger on the pulse, keep up to date, keep posted; hint, suggest, get at, insinuate, intimate, advise, warn; tell on, inform on, betray, grass on (*sl.*), squeal (*sl.*).

see also **464, 597**

461 concealment

n. concealment, covering, hiding, confinement, burying, secretion; suppression, evasion; seclusion, privacy, isolation, solitude; camouflage, disguise, shroud, veil, curtain, screen, mask, cloak, purdah; cabal.

adj. concealed, hidden, out of sight, behind the scenes, covered, eclipsed, buried, obscured, unseen, unexposed; disguised, camouflaged, incognito; furtive, stealthy, secret, hush-hush, clandestine, underhand, sly.

vb. conceal, hide, cover, bury, suppress, screen, cloak, shroud, veil, curtain, evade, withhold, pull the wool over someone's eyes (*inf.*), keep secret, lie low, keep in the dark, keep under one's hat (*inf.*), sweep under the carpet (*inf.*), secrete; cloud, obscure, envelop, ensconce, camouflage, disguise, dissemble; confine, store, harbour, cache, shelter, stash (*inf.*); close, seal, lock.

sneak, prowl, creep, lurk, steal, slink.

see also **463, 466, 826**

462 disclosure

n. disclosure, exposure, opening, uncovering, revelation, apocalypse; show-down; betrayal, manifestation, give-away; acknowledgement, admission.

adj. disclosed, uncovered, exposed, conspicuous, open; indicative, betraying, tell-tale.

vb. disclose, reveal, give away, expose, divulge, lay open, lay bare, make plain, uncover, unfold, unveil, unfurl, unmask, take the wraps off; not contain oneself for, bring into the open; declare, make known, spit it out (*inf.*); put one's cards on the table, nail one's colours to the mast, show one's colours; open up (*inf.*), unburden oneself, unbosom, confide, get out of one's system (*inf.*), get off one's chest (*inf.*); come out of one's shell.

confess, admit, acknowledge, concede, grant, own up (*inf.*), come clean, avow, plead guilty, make a clean breast of; one's sins will find one out.

betray, not keep a secret, blurt out, let on, let out, blabber, leak, let the cat out of the bag (*inf.*), spill the beans, come out with, talk out of turn, give the game away.

see also **458, 460**

463 hiding

n. hiding, deceit, faking, deception; hiding place, hide-out, hidey-hole, refuge, retreat, covert, den, shelter.

disguise, camouflage, mask, blind, masquerade, cloak, cover, veil, guise, façade, envelope, shade, blackout, masking; ambush, snare, trap, pitfall, net, noose.

vb. ambush, trap, ensnare, waylay, lay in wait, set a trap for, decoy.

see also **459, 801**

464 publication

n. publication, announcement, communication, revelation, disclosure, notification, proclamation, declaration, promulgation, broadcasting, dissemination.

broadcast; book, booklet; newspaper, periodical, magazine, journal; publicity, promotion, canvassing, advertisement, poster, sign, bill, placard, notice, broadsheet, leaflet, folder, brochure, pamphlet, circular, hand-out, handbill, flysheet, blurb, plug (*inf.*).

adj. published, in print, available, obtainable, in circulation; current, public.

vb. publish, issue, bring out, put into circulation, print, distribute; reissue, reprint; be published, come out, circulate, get around.

make known, announce, notify, proclaim, declare, pronounce, impart, send forth, communicate, reveal, disclose, spread, broadcast, diffuse, pass the word round, put about, blazon, promulgate, disseminate; publicize, promote, advertise, canvass, circularize, sell, plug (*inf.*), tell the world.

465 news

n. news, tidings, information, facts, events, current affairs; headlines, front-page news, stop press, newsflash, scoop, sensation; description, account, report, story, bulletin, message, release, communiqué, press release, announcement, hand-out, dispatch.

rumour, gossip, hearsay, scandal, whisper, popular report, fabrication, tale, chit-chat; grapevine, bush telegraph.

vb. report, tell, broadcast, publish, circulate, spread; make news, hit the headlines.

466 secret

n. secret, mystery, puzzle, riddle, brain-teaser, enigma, arcanum; code, cipher, cryptogram, hieroglyph; confidence; skeleton in the cupboard; suppression, blackout, censure.

adj. secret, strange, mysterious, hidden, unknown, puzzling, mystical, cryptic, enigmatic; private, confidential, classified, top secret, hush-hush; secretive, reticent, taciturn; secluded.

vb. keep secret, keep to oneself, not tell, hide, conceal, keep mum (*inf.*), suppress, stifle, sit on (*inf.*), hush up, censor.

adv. in secret, in private, confidentially, under one's breath, between ourselves; between you, me, and the bedpost.

see also **461**

467 messenger

n. messenger, dispatcher, dispatch bearer, carrier, courier, runner, crier, bearer, office-boy, message-boy, errand-boy, page-boy, buttons; spokesman, intermediary, go-between, ambassador, envoy, emissary, internuncio; herald, forerunner, precursor, harbinger, trumpet; minister, angel, prophet.

post, mail, correspondence; post office; telecommunications, telephony, telegraphy; broadcasting, radio, transistor, wireless, television, the box; telephone, phone, receiver; radio set, two-way radio, intercom (*inf.*), pocket radio, walkie-talkie, field radio; telegram, wire, cable, cablegram, telegraph; teleprinter, telex, teletext, semaphore, flag, beacon, smoke-signal.

468 affirmation

n. affirmation, assertion, statement, declaration, proposition, profession, pronouncement, explanation, answer, report, observation, expression, formulation; admission, acknowledgement, attestation, avowal; agreement, ratification, endorsement.

swearing, asseveration; oath, vow, testimony, sworn statement, affidavit, promise, contract, pledge.

adj. affirmative, assertive, affirmatory, declarative; emphatic, strong, forceful, dogmatic, positive, assured, solemn, sworn, on oath.

vb. affirm, assert, state, declare, profess, pronounce, express, explain, maintain, contend, submit, asseverate, aver; confirm, endorse, ratify; admit, acknowledge; emphasize, stress, underline, highlight, impress, urge, reinforce, rub in (*inf.*), make much of, plug; speak out, have one's say, put one's foot down (*inf.*); swear, vow, promise, pledge, testify, attest, assure, guarantee, vouch; swear in, put on oath, charge, adjure.

see also **514, 698**

469 negation

n. negation, denial, contradiction, repudiation, refusal, renunciation, disclaimer, disavowel; abnegation, recusance.

adj. negative, denying, contrary, contradictory, disavowing, recusant, repugnant.

vb. negate, deny, belie, give the lie to, contradict, contravene, gainsay, renounce, repudiate, disown, disavow, disclaim, abjure, abnegate; refuse, reject; cancel, nullify, invalidate.

see also **694**

470 teaching

n. teaching, education, pedagogy, pedagogics, didactics; instruction, training, study, schooling, direction, guidance, tuition, tutoring, coaching, tutelage; preparation, discipline, cultivation, enlightenment, edification; indoctrination, brainwashing, inculcation, conditioning, propagandism, proselytism; spoon-feeding.

course, curriculum, class, lesson, lecture, talk; catechism, sermon; homework, prep (*inf.*), assignment, exercise, task, work.

adj. educational, informative, instructive, enlightening, edifying; academic, pedagogical, didactic, scholastic.

vb. teach, educate, instruct, impart, inform, acquaint, familiarize, direct, guide, discipline, advise, counsel; convince, explain; prepare, initiate; school, coach, cram, prime, put through the mill (*inf.*); enlighten, edify; cultivate, nurture, train, exercise, practise, groom, drill, ground, bring up, foster, rear, breed, lick into shape (*inf.*); indoctrinate, inculcate, din into, force down someone's throat, ram down someone's throat (*inf.*), instill, imbue, condition; proselytize; catechize; hold classes, lecture, hold forth, expound, preach, sermonize, moralize.

471 misdirection

n. misdirection, misguidance, misinstruction, misteaching, misrepresentation, falsification, perversion, mistake, error, blind leading the blind.

vb. misdirect, misinform, mislead, misrepresent, pervert, distort, deceive.

472 learning

n. learning, knowledge, scholarship, training, erudition, lore; self-improvement, self-education, self-instruction; attainments, study, reading, application, studiousness, industry; lesson, class, course, classwork, homework, prep (*inf.*), assignment; revision, refresher course.

adj. knowledgeable, academic, studious, well-read, learned, industrious, scholarly, erudite; self-taught, self-instructed, self-made.

vb. learn, acquire, pick up, attain; experience, understand, grasp, discover, appreciate; master, become familiar with, get off pat (*inf.*), get the hang of (*inf.*); memorize, learn by heart; study, read, go into, go in for, specialize; absorb, assimilate, digest, drink in, imbibe; read up on, revise, review, refresh oneself, cram, prepare, get up, brush up, improve; pore over, bury oneself in; contemplate; burn the midnight oil; browse, scan, thumb through, flick through (*inf.*), dip into; improve one's mind, teach oneself; study under, sit at the feet of.

see also **426**

473 teacher

n. teacher, educator, advisor, guide, counsellor; school-teacher, headmaster, principal, head; professor, lecturer, don, reader, fellow, doctor, dean; tutor, instructor, pedagogue, coach, trainer, guru, governess.

see also **436**

474 learner

n. learner, pupil, scholar, student, schoolchild; undergraduate, fresher, freshman, graduate, postgraduate; swot, bookworm; follower, disciple, adherent; apprentice, trainee, probationer, novice, beginner, recruit, newcomer, tyro; class, set, form, grade, stream.

see also **428**

475 place of learning

n. school; nursery, kindergarten, crèche; college, polytechnic, university, academy, institute, institution, seminary, varsity (*inf.*), *conservatoire*, *lycée*, *gymnasium;* classroom, schoolroom, study, lecture theatre, auditorium; library, carrel.

476 truthfulness

n. truthfulness, veracity, integrity, frankness, openness, candour, straightforwardness, forthrightness; accuracy, honesty, reliability, sincerity, uprightness, guilelessness, impartiality.

adj. truthful, veracious, sincere, guileless, impartial; frank, open, candid, unreserved, plain, direct, straight, straightforward, forthright, blunt, ingenuous.

vb. be truthful, not lie; speak plainly, tell someone straight, not hesitate, make no bones about, speak one's mind, paint in its true colours, call a spade a spade, tell all; not to put too fine a point on it (*inf.*).

see also **430, 508**

477 falsehood

n. falsehood, fraudulence, falsification, fabrication, inaccuracy, deception, dishonesty, lying, mendacity, perjury; misrepresentation, distortion, perversion; double dealing, two-facedness, duplicity, hypocrisy, insincerity, guile; mockery, pretence, make-believe, façade.

adj. false, lying, untruthful, mendacious; fabricated, inaccurate, misrepresented, distorted, put on (*inf.*), make-believe, counterfeit, bogus, pretended, fake, invented, spurious; fraudulent, dishonest, insincere, hypocritical; double-dealing, two-faced; roguish, corrupt, oily, smooth, disingenuous, perfidious.

vb. falsify, lie, fib, exaggerate, understate, tell a white lie, bear false witness, perjure oneself, forswear; prevaricate, equivocate; deceive, mislead, misrepresent, distort, manipulate, doctor, adulterate, make up, invent, concoct, construct, contrive, fabricate, hatch, get up (*inf.*), trump up, spin a yarn; fake, counterfeit, forge; feign, put on (*inf.*), put on a brave face, go through the motions, play, pretend, make believe, sham, simulate, dissemble; laugh off (*inf.*).

see also **431**

478 deception

n. deception, misleading, deceit, misrepresentation, cheating, trickery, craftiness, treachery, fraudulence, dishonesty; lying, guile, furtiveness, beguilement, betrayal, treason; hoax, crying wolf, delusion, self-deception, wishful thinking, hallucination, illusion.

trick, dodge, ruse, trap, artifice, stratagem, subterfuge; fraud, swindle, fiddle, rip-off (*sl.*), bamboozle (*inf.*), skulduggery (*inf.*), underhand dealing, sharp practice, sleight of hand, legerdemain.

adj. deceiving, deceptive, illusory, false, sham, fake, fraudulent, dishonest, underhand, behind someone's back, furtive, treacherous, crafty, wily, cunning, shifty.

vb. deceive, mislead, delude, fool, trick, trap, trip up, catch, entrap, ensnare, hoodwink, beguile, dupe, pull the wool over someone's eyes (*inf.*); outwit, outmanoeuvre; go behind someone's back.

cheat, trick, defraud, swindle, fleece, rip off (*sl.*), bamboozle (*inf.*), chisel (*sl.*), cozen; go down (*inf.*), diddle (*sl.*), cross (*sl.*), double-cross, pull a fast one (*sl.*), stack the cards against, put one over on (*inf.*), victimize; take advantage of, get the better of, take for a ride (*inf.*); hoax, cry wolf; play a joke on, kid (*sl.*), pull someone's leg, have on (*inf.*); trifle with, cajole; betray, commit treason.

479 dupe

n. dupe, fool, victim, sucker (*sl.*), sitting duck, simpleton, greenhorn, gull.

480 deceiver

n. deceiver, beguiler, dodger, trickster, swindler, crook, cheat, rogue, impostor, con man (*sl.*), phoney (*sl.*), wolf in sheep's clothing, charlatan, chisel (*sl.*), knave, cozener, sharper; hypocrite, actor, dissembler, Tartuffe; liar, fibber, story-teller; betrayer, traitor, quisling, rat (*sl.*), informer, double-crosser, victimizer; underground, fifth columnist, saboteur, terrorist.

481 exaggeration

n. exaggeration, overstatement, extravagance, hyperbole, misrepresentation, misjudgment, stretching; storm in a teacup, much ado about nothing, stretch of the imagination, fantasy, tall story.

adj. exaggerated, extravagant, preposterous, fabulous, hyperbolic, excessive, superlative, overdone, out of all proportion, coloured, high-falutin, boastful, bombastic.

vb. exaggerate, overstate, overestimate, overplay, hyperbolize, make too much of, overdo, strain, misrepresent; amplify, enlarge, magnify, emphasize, highlight, maximize, heighten, intensify, aggravate; colour, embroider; make a mountain out of a molehill, stretch a point, lay it on thick, pile it on (*inf.*), out-herod Herod.

see also **417**

C Means of communicating ideas

482 indication

n. indication, calling, identification, designation, symbolization, signification; sign, badge, emblem, figure, design, symbol, representation, type, token, logo; colophon, flag, banner, pennant, standard, ensign, colours, pendant, bunting, streamer, Union Jack, Stars and Stripes; coat of arms, crest, insignia, medal, regalia.

label, ticket, name, card, notice, bill, stub, counterfoil, docket, form, voucher, counter, chip, tab, tag; indicator, marker, pointer, needle, arrow, index, gauge; stamp, seal, imprint, impression, fingerprint, footprint; signature, autograph, initials, monogram.

signal, gesticulation, gesture; wink, nod, wave, call, shout, whistle, nudge; alarm, siren, hooter, bell; light, beacon.

evidence, hint, suggestion, note, explanation, proof, clue, intimation, symptom, hallmark.

adj. indicative, suggestive, symptomatic, symbolic, typical, representative.

vb. indicate, call, mean, signify; identify, designate, show, name, specify, appoint, assign, symbolize, point to; manifest, express, imply, bear the marks of, evince, intimate, denote, betoken; mark, point, gauge, brand, score, scratch, spot.

label, tag, docket, tab, earmark; stamp, seal, print, punch, impress, emboss, emblazon; sign, initial, autograph; annotate, number, letter, paginate.

gesticulate, gesture, signal, motion, wave, beckon, wink, nod, hoot, ring, shout, whistle, nudge.

483 record

n. record, register, catalogue, account, document, report, statement; brief, memo, memorandum, note; newspaper, bulletin, gazette, almanac; diary, journal, log; certificate, ticket; archives, public records, proceedings, minutes, annals, chronicle, scroll, inscription, manuscript; tape-recording, photograph, film, videotape.

souvenir, memento; relic, mark, trace, remains, evidence; trail, footprint, impression, scent; wash, wake; monument, testimony, witness, memorial, statue, column, cenotaph, remembrance, testimonial, mausoleum, shrine.

adj. recorded, documented, noted, reported.

vb. record, note, mark, report,

account, write down, take down, jot down; register, write in, enter, fill in, insert, inscribe, enrol, matriculate; document, list, catalogue, minute, chronicle; tape, tape-record, photograph, film.

adv. on record, in black and white, in writing, on the books.

484 recorder

n. recorder, registrar, secretary, clerk, accountant; diarist, chronicler, annalist, historian, biographer, journalist, archivist, scribe, amanuensis.

tape-recorder, stereo-recorder, cassette-recorder, video-recorder; record, disc.

485 obliteration

n. obliteration, deletion, erasure, effacement, blotting out, eradication, cancellation, expunction; eraser, rubber, sponge, duster.

vb. obliterate, wipe out, rub off, delete, efface, erase, blot out, black out, strike out, write out, leave no traces, remove, iron out, raze, cancel, expunge.

486 representation

n. representation, description, depiction, illustration, portrayal, exemplification, enactment, personification; reproduction, copy, imitation, image, likeness; picture, sketch, diagram, chart, map, model; art, painting, sculpture; photography, photograph, photo, snapshot, slide, transparency.

adj. representative, characteristic, typical, illustrative.

vb. represent, stand for, stand in the place of, serve as; render, realize, draw, depict, describe, portray, illustrate, picture, reproduce, delineate; reflect, mirror; exemplify, typify, embody, symbolize; designate, express.

487 misrepresentation

n. misrepresentation, distortion, perversion, twisting, falsification, exaggeration, understatement; caricature, parody, travesty, burlesque, counterfeit; misinterpretation.

vb. misrepresent, distort, twist, garble, warp, pervert, falsify, caricature, parody, give the wrong impression; misinterpret, misstate.

488 painting

n. painting, art, graphics, fine art; picture, illustration, mural, depiction, canvas, fresco, wall-painting, collage; work, study, sketch, drawing, outline, silhouette, cartoon, representation, copy, composition, likeness; abstract painting, landscape, portrait, self-portrait, still-life; watercolour, oil painting, miniature, masterpiece, old master.

technique, treatment, design, pattern, atmosphere, tone, shadow, values, perspective.

adj. graphic, visual, pictorial, picturesque, scenic.

vb. paint, portray, depict, compose, illustrate, draw, sketch, design, represent, copy, crayon, pencil, silhouette, ink, shade, tint, limn.

489 sculpture

n. sculpture, carving, stone-carving, cutting, casting, moulding; ceramics, pottery; statue, bust, cast, embossment, relief, marble, plaque, cameo; figure, representation, image.

adj. carved, sculptured, glyptic, glyphic.

vb. sculpture, sculpt, carve, chisel, cut, hew, shape, fashion, model, mould, emboss, cast.

490 engraving

n. engraving, etching, carving, chiselling, incising, printing, photogravure, lithography; inscription, print, lithograph, block, woodcut, linocut, plate.

vb. engrave, etch, inscribe, cut, carve, chisel, incise, chase, print, impress, stamp.

491 artist

n. artist, creator, composer, painter, designer, draughtsman, architect, drawer, sketcher, cartoonist, photographer, cameraman; sculptor, carver, modeller, statuary, lapidary; potter, ceramist; engraver, etcher, lithographer, printer, typographer.

492 language

n. language, communication, speech, tongue, talk, style, diction, parlance; utterance, expression, voice, articulation; idiom, dialect, provincialism, *patois,* jargon, pidgin, *koine, lingua franca;* mother tongue, vernacular, common speech, British English, American English, Standard English, Queen's English, Received Pronunciation; artificial language, world language, Esperanto; Babel, confusion of tongues.

linguistics, grammar, syntax, semantics, phonetics, phonology, historical linguistics, comparative linguistics, etymology, philology, dialectology, lexicography; linguist, polyglot, philologist, grammarian, lexicographer.

adj. linguistic, lingual, grammatical, standard, current, vernacular, idiomatic.

see also **514**

493 letter

n. letter, symbol, consonant, vowel; capital, upper case, large letter, majuscule; small letter, lower case, minuscule; rune, cuneiform, hieroglyph; syllable, character, ideogram, pictogram; alphabet, ABC; orthography, spelling, spelling-pronunciation.

adj. literal, alphabetical, orthographic, syllabic.

vb. spell, letter, form letters; syllabify.

494 word

n. word, expression, term, name, designation, vocable, sound, syllable, utterance, phrase, construction, locution; neologism, slang, colloquialism, jargon, provincialism, cliché, vogue word, catch phrase, slogan; archaism; root, derivative, derivation; synonym, antonym, homonym.

vocabulary, lexicon, wordlist, dictionary, glossary, thesaurus, concordance, index; lexicology, lexicography, etymology, terminology.

adj. verbal, literal, lexical, lexicographical.

495 neologism

n. neologism, new word, new usage, coinage, neology; formation, translation, loan-word, borrowing, calque, portmanteau, blend, hybrid; corruption, barbarism, nonce word; cliché, vogue word, slang, vulgarism, argot, cant, colloquialism, informal usage, journalese, Americanism, Anglicism, Briticism.

adj. newly-coined, newfangled, colloquial, informal, slang, foreign, borrowed, translated, nonce, vogue.

496 nomenclature

n. nomenclature, naming, calling, appellation, designation, identification, terminology, classification.

name, title; Christian name, first name, given name, forename; surname, last name, family name, signature; sign, style, label, tag; nomen, denomination; nickname, description, epithet.

adj. nominal, titular; named, known as.

vb. name, call, designate, identify, specify, term, title, dub, label, tag, style; classify, characterize, describe, define, nominate, denominate; christen, baptize; be known as, be called, go by the name of, go under the name of.

497 misnomer

n. misnomer, misnaming, malapropism; nickname, pet name, pen name, pseudonym, fictitious name, assumed name, alias, *nom de plume*, stage name, sobriquet, *nom de guerre*.

anonymity, namelessness; what's-its-name, thinggamy (*inf.*), thingumabob (*inf.*), what-d'you-call-it, so-and-so, A. N. Other, Mr. X.

adj. misnamed, in name only, professed, pretended, pseudo-, quasi-, self-styled, so-called, *soi-disant;* anonymous, unknown, unidentified, nameless, unknown.

vb. misname, nickname, dub, mislabel, mistake.

498 phrase

n. phrase, clause, sentence, group of words; idiom, figure of speech; expression, utterance, locution; slogan, maxim, saying, formula, cliché.

vb. phrase, word, reword, express, state, put into words, formulate, verbalize.

499 grammar

n. grammar, usage, syntax, word order, sentence structure, analysis, parsing; inflection, case-ending, morphology, accidence.

part of speech, noun, substantive, proper noun, collective noun, mass noun, count noun, case, gender, number, declension; pronoun; verb, participle, gerund, copula, infinitive, split infinitive, person, tense, active, passive, conjugation; adjective, qualifier, modifier, comparative, superlative, comparison; adverb, particle; preposition; interjection; conjunction; article, definite article, indefinite article, determiner; subject, predicate; affix, prefix, suffix, infix.

adj. grammatical, syntactic, correct, proper, well-formed, acceptable, appropriate.

vb. parse, analyse, inflect, conjugate, decline.

500 solecism

n. solecism, ungrammaticalness, bad grammar, misusage, mistake, error, barbarism, blunder; mispronunciation, slip of the tongue; malapropism, spoonerism, cacology, catachresis.

adj. ungrammatical, incorrect, solecistic; slovenly, slipshod, loose; inappropriate, unacceptable, badly-formed.

vb. use bad grammar, make a mistake, murder the language.

see also **511**

501 style

n. style, manner, characteristics, presentation; command, fluency, mastery, skill; manner of speaking, diction, phrasing, phraseology, wording, composition, writing; usage, mode of expression, expression, vocabulary, word-power, parlance, choice of words, way of putting it, feeling for words, *sprachgefühl;* mannerism, idiosyncrasy, intonation.

see also **510, 514**

502 lucidity

n. lucidity, clearness, clarity, perspicuity, transparency, unambiguousness, intelligibility, directness, plain speech, simplicity, exactness, precision.

adj. lucid, clear, perspicuous, unambiguous, distinct, obvious, direct, plain, intelligible, explicit, easily understood, limpid, pellucid.

see also **452, 802**

503 obscurity

n. obscurity, imperspicuity, vagueness, opaqueness, ambiguity, imprecision, unintelligibility, complexity, abstruseness.

adj. obscure, cloudy, blurred, fuzzy, vague, unclear, imperspicuous, imprecise, indistinct, ambiguous, unintelligible, incomprehensible, complicated, involved, intricate, abstruse.

see also **453, 803**

504 conciseness

n. conciseness, succinctness, brevity, terseness, curtness, pithiness, laconism; contraction, ellipsis.

adj. concise, brief, succinct, condensed, compressed, shortened, short, precise, pithy, terse, compact, summary, laconic, sententious; elliptic, telegraphic.

vb. be concise, condense, compress, shorten, abridge, abbreviate, summarize, come to the point, put in a nutshell.

adv. in short, in brief, in a nutshell, to the point, to cut a long story short.

505 diffuseness

n. diffuseness, profuseness, abundance; wordiness, verbosity, discursiveness; digression, departure, deviation, excursus; tautology, redundancy, verbiage, repetition, padding, circumlocution, periphrasis, pleonasm.

adj. diffuse, discursive, wordy, lengthy, long-winded, verbose, tedious, rambling, digressive, redundant, repetitious, protracted, prolix, pleonastic, roundabout, periphrastic, circumlocutory.

vb. amplify, enlarge on, develop, expatiate; digress, ramble, wander, deviate, go off at a tangent, go off the subject, get off the point, get sidetracked, beat about the bush (*inf.*); go on and on, talk at length, repeat oneself.

see also **516**

506 vigour

n. vigour, power, strength, intensity, force, effectiveness, forcefulness, urgency, piquancy; sparkle, spirit, punch (*sl.*), fervour, vehemence, verve, animation, vitality, fire, glow, warmth.

adj. vigorous, powerful, strong, forceful, trenchant, incisive, bold, tough, lively, inspired, sparkling, racy, fervent, vehement, insistent, impassioned, fiery, ardent, passionate, persuasive; vivid, graphic; pointed.

see also **173, 755**

507 feebleness

n. feebleness, weakness, faintness, frailty, flaccidity, enfeeblement, pauperism, barrenness, lifelessness.

adj. feeble, weak, faint, frail, thin, poor, limp, lifeless, flaccid, insipid, meagre, scant, slight, shallow, diluted, wishy-washy, uninspired, stale, flat, tame, forced.

see also **162**

508 plainness

n. plainness, simplicity, plain speech, naturalness, straightforwardness, modesty, unpretentiousness, severity.

adj. plain, simple, natural, unaffected, artless, naive, straightforward, modest, ordinary, undramatic, severe, restrained, unadorned, unpretentious, unsophisticated, common, homely, homespun, unimaginative, matter-of-fact; direct, frank, open, blunt.

vb. speak plainly, call a spade a spade, come straight to the point.

see also **476**

509 ornament

n. ornamentation, adornment, embellishment, elaboration, enrichment, enhancement, decoration, embroidery, floweriness.

ornament, colour, frills, rhetoric, metaphor, euphemism, verbosity, grandiloquence, bombast, fustian.

adj. ornate, adorned, embellished, grand, rich, lofty, elaborate, lavish, grandiose; vivid, dazzling, scintillating; fancy, extravagant, pretentious, showy, flashy, loud, flaunting, boastful, big, high-falutin, high-flown, big-sounding, magniloquent; rhetorical, voluble, pompous, flowery, euphemistic, euphuistic, grandiloquent.

vb. embellish, adorn, enrich, colour; talk big, lay it on (*inf.*).

see also **846**

510 elegance

n. elegance, tastefulness, style, grace, graciousness, dignity, beauty, correctness, refinement, propriety, polish, finish; harmony, balance, proportion, rhythm; artificiality, affectation.

adj. elegant, tasteful, gracious, graceful, dignified, artistic, delicate, refined, pure, stylized, polished; proper, appropriate, happy, well-expressed, right, correct, felicitous, seemly; harmonious, balanced, well-proportioned, well-turned, mellifluous; affected, artificial.

see also **848**

511 inelegance

n. inelegance, tastelessness, bad taste, gracelessness, impropriety; barbarism, coarseness, vulgarity; incorrectness, stiltedness, formality, awkwardness, clumsiness.

adj. inelegant, tasteless, graceless, unseemly, improper, incorrect, laboured, stilted, forced, heavy, stiff, formal, ponderous, clumsy, awkward, inappropriate; coarse, crude, vulgar, rude, uncouth.

see also **849**

512 voice

n. voice, sound, speech, language, utterance; vocal organs, vocal chords, tongue, lips, larynx, lungs, breath; articulation, pronunciation, vocalization, enunciation, delivery, inflection, intonation, pitch, rhythm, tone, accent, timbre, stress, emphasis; vowel, consonant, phoneme; phonetics.

adj. vocal, expressed, uttered, spoken, oral, lingual, vocalic, phonetic, voiced, sonant, sounded; clear, distinct, articulate.

vb. voice, speak, express, sound, pronounce, utter, articulate, get one's tongue round, vocalize, enunciate; nasalize, palatalize, aspirate; roll, trill, burr; stress, emphasize.

513 muteness

n. muteness, aphonia, voicelessness, inarticulation, dumbness, silence.

adj. mute, voiceless, speechless, tongueless, unsounded, unvoiced, unvocal, surd, inarticulate, tongue-tied, dumb, silent, mum, inaudible.

vb. mute, silence, dumbfound, strike dumb, still, soften, deaden, muffle, suppress, smother.

see also **517, 779**

514 speech

n. speech, language, talk, discourse, utterance, articulation, expression, pronunciation, communication; eloquence, fluency, expressiveness, facility, vivacity, style, poise, delivery, rhetoric, vigour, force, gift of the gab (*inf.*).

speaker, talker, conversationalist; public speaker, orator, lecturer, after-dinner speaker, expositor, rhetorician, declaimer, preacher; spokesman, mouthpiece.

adj. speaking, talking, verbal, oral; articulating; eloquent, fluent, voluble, expressive, forceful, meaningful.

vb. speak, say, talk; vocalize, pronounce, voice, enunciate; express, utter, tell, affirm, converse, communicate, chat; repeat, rattle off, trot out (*inf.*).

address, discuss, lecture, teach, instruct, plead, argue, make a speech, give a talk, deliver a lecture, have the floor, hold forth, preach, speechify (*inf.*), rant, spout.

see also **468, 516**

515 imperfect speech

n. imperfect speech, speech defect, aphasia, impediment, stammer, stutter, faltering, hesitation, mispronunciation, lisp, twang, nasalization, drawl.

adj. inarticulate, indistinct, throaty, shaking, stuttering, stammering, hesitant.

vb. stammer, stutter, hesitate, pause, falter, stumble, lisp, drawl, slur, speak through one's nose, mispronounce, mumble, mutter, garble, swallow one's words.

516 talkativeness

n. talkativeness, gift of the gab (*inf.*), loquacity, garrulity, verbosity, long-windedness.

chatter, chat, jabber, babble, prattle, blather, prittle-prattle (*inf.*), chit-chat, idle talk, chinwag (*sl.*), palaver, small talk; nonsense, drive, twaddle, hot air (*sl.*), yap (*inf.*), yackety-yack (*sl.*); gossip, scandal.

chatterbox, prattler, jabberer, tattler, windbag (*inf.*), gasbag (*sl.*); gossip, muckraker (*inf.*).

adj. talkative, chatty, voluble, loquacious, garrulous; chattering, babbling; glib, eloquent, fluent; long-winded, verbose; gossipy.

vb. chat, keep on, go on about (*inf.*), chatter, talk idly, waffle, ramble on; babble, jabber, prattle, gabble, yackety-yack (*sl.*), yack (*sl.*), yap (*inf.*); gossip, tell tales.

see also **505**

517 taciturnity

n. taciturnity, reserve, reticence, silence, uncommunicativeness, no comment, curtness, brusqueness; modesty, hesitance.

adj. taciturn, reserved, reticent, silent, dumb, mute, quiet, uncommunicative, secretive, tight-lipped, close-lipped, mum, restrained, hesitant, modest, retiring; curt, brusque, laconic; aloof, distant.

vb. say nothing, refuse to comment, keep quiet, keep one's mouth shut, hold one's tongue, save one's breath; stand aloof.

see also **779**

518 address

n. address, speech, talk, lecture, oration, discourse, reading, recitation, recital, exhortation, paper, pep talk (*sl.*), spiel (*sl.*), appeal, invocation, homily, sermon, allocution; harangue, tirade, declamation.

inaugural address, opening; greeting, salutation; farewell address, goodbye, valediction.

oratory, rhetoric, speech-making,

public speaking, elocution, preaching, homiletics.

519 conversation

n. conversation, chat, talk, discussion, interview, exchange of views, interchange, expression, repartee, colloquy, interlocution; chatter, chitchat, prattle; *tête-à-tête*, heart-to-heart.

conference, debate, dialogue, consultation, conflab (*inf.*), powwow, summit conference, summit, congress, symposium, convention, seminar, parley, council, audience, hearing.

vb. converse, chat, discuss, hold a conversation, communicate, counsel, confer, exchange views, debate, negotiate, put one's heads together, confabulate.

520 monologue

n. monologue, soliloquy, monody; apostrophe, aside.

vb. soliloquize, talk to oneself.

521 writing

n. writing, script, lettering, calligraphy, stroke, flourish; handwriting, hand, fist, longhand; graphology, chirography; mark, scribble, scrawl; transcription, inscription, printing, copying, shorthand, stenography, typing; correspondence, letter-writing; journalism, reporting.

written matter, copy, work, composition, document, paper, manuscript, transcript, typescript, parchment, scroll.

writer, calligrapher, scribe, copyist, transcriber, secretary, stenographer, typist; author, novelist, journalist.

adj. written, graphic, in writing, handwritten, in black and white, roman, italic.

vb. write, pen, compose, prepare, draft, write out, report, document, write down, record, put pen to paper; scribble, scrawl; transcribe, inscribe, copy, engrave, print, type.

522 printing

n. printing, typography; composition, typesetting; publishing; print, impression, stamp, page, sheet, copy, printed matter; type, lead, leading, rule, letter, fount, space; galley, proof, slip, bromide.

printer, typographer, typesetter, compositor; proofreader, reader; copy editor.

adj. printed, in print, typographical.

vb. print, impress, imprint, stamp, engrave; compose, set type, set up; run off, go to press, put to bed; publish, issue, bring out.

523 correspondence

n. correspondence, communication, exchange of letters, post, mail; letter, postcard, note, message, report, missive, dispatch, epistle, chit, acknowledgement, reply, answer; business letter, love letter, valentine, fan letter, poison pen letter, chain letter, round robin, circular; address, destination.

correspondent, letter-writer, penfriend, pen-pal (*inf.*), addressee, recipient.

adj. epistolary, postal.

vb. correspond, write to, communicate, exchange letters, drop a line, send, post, mail, dispatch.

524 book

n. book, publication, work, volume, tome, copy, text, manuscript, bestseller, paperback, hardback, booklet, edition, reprint, offprint; study book, course book, textbook, set book, primer, workbook; reader, companion volume, selected readings; complete works, omnibus edition.

magazine, periodical, journal, review, gazette; back number, back issue.

reference book, encyclopedia, cyclopedia, handbook, manual, dictionary, bible, guidebook; index, concordance; bibliography, reading list.

library, collection of books, lending library, public library, mobile library, inter-library loan.

writer, author, novelist, biographer, essayist, reporter, ghost-writer, hack; editor, publisher, reviewer, critic; man of letters, man of learning, bookworm, scholar, book-collector, bibliophile.

525 description

n. description, account, report, statement, record, summary, information, explanation, characterization, specification; portrayal, sketch, portrait, representation, illustration, picture, image, profile; narrative, story, tale, yarn, anecdote, saga, epic; fiction, myth, legend, fairy-tale, fairy story, fantasy, fable, parable, allegory; plot, story-line, subject, argument.

narrator, reciter, story-teller, novelist, raconteur, anecdotist, fabricator.

adj. descriptive, narrative, expressive; graphic, vivid, true-to-life, lifelike, telling, detailed, pictorial; fictional, made-up, legendary, mythical, fabulous, parabolic, allegorical.

vb. describe, portray, sketch, set forth, represent, outline, trace, illustrate, picture, draw, paint, imagine, delineate, characterize, define, specify, mark out, express; account, report, state, record, explain, summarize; narrate, tell, recount, relate, recite, rehearse.

526 dissertation

n. dissertation, essay, paper, composition, commentary, exposition, thesis, treatise, monograph, discourse, disquisition; survey, review, analysis, examination, enquiry, investigation, study, discussion, story, comment, write-up, critique.

essayist, expositor, commentator; critic, reviewer.

vb. discuss, treat, handle, concern, deal with, consider, comment; analyse, survey, examine, explain, interpret; review, criticize, write up.

527 compendium

n. compendium, summary, resumé, precis, abridgment, abstract, summing up, syllabus, survey, outline, synopsis, skeleton, reduction, analysis, conspectus, epitome; core, essence; digest, miscellany, anthology, selections, readings.

adj. compendious, concise, brief, succinct, abbreviated.

vb. summarize, sum up, abstract, abridge, condense, reduce, shorten, digest, outline, survey; boil down to.

528 poetry; prose

n. poetry, song, rhyme, poem, verse, stanza, sonnet, ode, lyric, idyll, epic, ballad, jingle, limerick; chorus, refrain; prosody, versification, scansion, rhythm, metre, stress, beat, foot; prose, writing, literature, composition, story.

poet, writer, composer, versifier, poet laureate, bard, minstrel, troubadour.

adj. poetic, rhythmic, lyrical, idyllic, tuneful.

vb. poetize, sing, versify; rhyme, scan; write, conceive, imagine, compose.

529 drama

n. theatre, the stage; hall, opera

house, cinema, playhouse; play, drama, show, opera, melodrama, tragicomedy, tragedy, comedy, farce, slapstick, pantomime, mime, variety, cabaret, pageant, revue, spectacle, carnival; presentation, appearance, exhibition, production; dramatics, stagecraft, showmanship, acting, performance, histrionics.

actor, actress, performer, player, role, part, character, Thespian, lead, star, understudy, extra; cast, characters, *dramatis personae*.

adj. dramatic, theatrical; impressive, spectacular.

vb. dramatize, direct, produce, present, stage, produce, put on, perform, enact, play.

V Volition

1 Individual volition

A Volition in general

530 will

n. will, volition, intention, resolution, power, mind, conviction, determination, willpower, choice, free will, discretion, conation; desire, wish, inclination.

adj. volitional, willing, minded, voluntary, free, intentional, wilful, deliberate, wished, premeditated, conative.

vb. will, wish, want, desire, incline, choose, resolve, make a decision, decide, make up one's mind, determine, purpose, see fit, take it into one's head to (*inf.*), have one's own way; conclude, come to the conclusion.

adv. at will, at pleasure, as one thinks, of one's own accord.

531 necessity

n. necessity, compulsion, obligation; inevitability, unavoidability, certainty, inexorableness, inescapableness; determinism, predestination, foreordination, fatalism; involuntariness, spontaneity, reflex action, instinct, intuition.

no choice, no alternative, Hobson's choice, six of one and half a dozen of the other; must (*inf.*), essential, prerequisite; fate, the inevitable, whatever will be shall be, *che sara, sara*.

adj. necessary, inevitable, unavoidable, inescapable, inexorable, certain, sure, foreordained, predetermined, destined, predestined, irresistible; essential, indispensable, imperative; compulsory, obligatory; deterministic, fatalistic; involuntary, unintentional, instinctive, unconscious, automatic, reflex, mechanical.

vb. necessitate, compel, oblique, constrain, force, dictate; destine, foreordain; need, require, cry out for.

adv. of necessity, necessarily, inevitably, certainly, willy-nilly.

532 willingness

n. willingness, readiness, disposition, inclination, compliance; eagerness, enthusiasm, zeal, earnestness.

adj. willing, prepared, ready, disposed, inclined, game, desirous, compliant, eager, enthusiastic, zealous; voluntary, uninvited, unasked, unprompted.

vb. be willing, like to, want, desire, choose, feel like, show willing (*inf.*), be inclined towards; volunteer, take on the responsibility, offer oneself; be eager, enthuse, jump at, leap at, lean over backwards (*inf.*), fall over oneself to (*inf.*); gush over, go overboard about (*inf.*), go to town on (*inf.*).

adv. willingly, gladly, eagerly, readily; voluntarily, of one's own accord; off one's own bat.

see also **611**

533 unwillingness

n. unwillingness, disinclination, unreadiness, hesitation, reluctance, scruple, qualm, aversion, demur; non-cooperation, protest, abstention.

adj. unwilling, unready, disinclined, reluctant, hesitant, averse, opposed, loath, not in the mood, unenthusiastic, indifferent, half-hearted.

vb. be unwilling, not feel like, not want to, would rather not, refuse, hesitate, hold back, balk at, shirk, demur, fight shy of, shy away, shrink, dodge, evade; force oneself.

adv. unwillingly, without enthusiasm, against one's will, against one's better judgment, under protest, grudgingly.

see also **612**

534 resolution

n. resolution, determination, resolve, certainty, persistence, constancy, doggedness, conviction, perseverance, boldness, tenacity, fortitude, steadfastness; firmness, willpower, strength of will, mettle; self-control, self-reliance, self-possession.

adj. resolute, determined, steadfast, firm, steady, strong, certain, serious, strong-willed, iron-willed, inflexible, bold, persistent, tenacious, constant, dogged; single-minded, wholehearted, committed, decided; unyielding, unhesitating, unflinching, unwavering, unswerving, unbending.

vb. be resolute, determine, resolve, decide, be bent on; have one's heart set upon, stand fast, take one's stand, hold one's ground, not give in, stick to one's guns, stand no nonsense, put one's foot down; take the bull by the horns; commit oneself, dedicate, put one's heart and soul into.

535 perseverance

n. perseverance, tenacity, steadfastness, firmness, persistence, continuance, constancy, endurance, indefatigability, undauntedness, doggedness; stamina, guts (*inf.*), staying power, backbone, stickability (*sl.*), moral fibre, stiff upper lip.

stayer, bulldog.

adj. persevering, persistent, determined, tenacious, steadfast, constant, steady, firm, unmoved, undaunted, indefatigable, untiring, obstinate, enduring, continuing; diligent, industrious, assiduous.

vb. persevere, remain, persist, endure, continue to the end, go on, carry on, have what it takes, keep at it, keep going (*inf.*), stick at it (*inf.*), soldier on, plod (*inf.*), plug away (*inf.*), slog away, see it through (*inf.*), stick it out (*inf.*); stick out for, hold out for; hold a job down (*inf.*).

536 irresolution

n. irresolution, indecision, vacillation, wavering, fluctuation; inconstancy, hesitation, fickleness, instability.

adj. irresolute, indecisive, undecided, fluctuating, wavering, vacillating, fickle, hesitant, in two minds, unstable, infirm, inconstant, changeable.

vb. be irresolute, vacillate, waver, fluctuate, hesitate, falter, shilly-shally.

537 obstinacy

n. obstinacy, stubbornness, inflexibility, rigidity, tenacity, hardness, relentlessness, obduracy, intransigence, intractableness; bigotry, dogmatism, narrow-mindedness, intolerance, fanaticism.

dogmatist, bigot, fanatic, die-hard, mule, intransigent; pedant, stickler.

adj. obstinate, stubborn, inflexible, tenacious, uncompromising, intransigent, unyielding, unrelenting, hardened, hard, intractable, headstrong, self-willed, set in one's ways; stiff-necked, pig-headed, recalcitrant, refractory, obdurate, pertinacious; dogmatic.

vb. be obstinate, not give in, stick to one's guns; resist, oppose, dig one's heels in.

see also **534, 535**

538 change of mind

n. change of mind, second thoughts, afterthought, change of heart, *volte-face*, repentance; retraction, withdrawal, backing out, reversal, abandonment, desertion, defection, renunciation, recantation; tergiversation, backsliding, apostasy.

turncoat, time-server, rat, renegade, traitor, deserter, apostate.

adj. fickle, irresolute, unfaithful, inconstant.

vb. change one's mind, have second thoughts, think beter of, change one's tune; take back, withdraw, back out, back down, climb down (*inf.*), disown, deny, retract, revoke, recant, disclaim; nullify; trim; apologize, eat humble pie, eat one's words; fall away, apostasize.

539 caprice

n. caprice, whim, fancy, vagary, notion, quirk, prank, crotchet, freak, craze, whimsy, whim-wham, flash; jest, witticism; capriciousness, whimsicality; fickleness, inconstancy.

adj. capricious, whimsical, fanciful, inconstant, fickle, changeable, flighty, frivolous, freakish, crotchety, unpredictable, erratic, fitful.

540 choice

n. choice, option, decision, determination, selection, adoption; alternative, preference, substitute.

vote, ballot, poll, election, representation, referendum, plebiscite; suffrage, franchise; voter, elector, electorate, constituency, ward.

adj. optional, elective, selective, discretional, discriminating, choosy (*inf.*), fastidious; electoral, voting.

vb. choose, pick, decide on, opt, adopt, sort, prefer, take up, go for, plump for (*inf.*), like, fancy, favour, appoint, co-opt, elect, nominate, commit oneself; separate, select, isolate, segregate, cull, glean, sift, winnow, divide the sheep from the goats, separate the wheat from the chaff; weigh, judge, discriminate, make up one's mind; vote, cast votes, poll, ballot, draw lots, vote in, return.

541 absence of choice

n. no choice, Hobson's choice, first come first served; impartiality, neutrality, no preference, indifference; abstention, don't know.

adj. choiceless, neutral, impartial, disinterested, unbiased, indifferent.

vb. be neutral, abstain, not commit oneself, sit on the fence, not take sides.

542 rejection

n. rejection, dismissal, repudiation, denial, refusal, renunciation, rebuff, disownment, disapproval, exclusion, expulsion.

adj. rejected, repudiated, excluded, renounced, spurned.

vb. reject, not accept, dismiss, exclude, repudiate, renounce, deny, refuse, disapprove, rebuff, spurn, decline, disown, disclaim, despise, turn up one's nose at (*inf.*), expel, jettison, discard, brush aside, have nothing to do with, turn one's back on, laugh in someone's face (*inf.*).

see also **556, 694**

543 predetermination

n. predetermination, predestination, preordination, inevitability, necessity, finality; prediction, forecast; doom, fate; premeditation, predeliberation, foregone conclusion.

adj. predetermined, planned, proposed, designed, fixed, deliberate.

vb. predetermine, foreordain, predestine, appoint, destine, predestinate; predict, forecast, foretell, determine beforehand; premeditate, preconceive.

544 spontaneity

n. spontaneity, spur of the moment; improvisation, extemporization; involuntariness, reflex action; impetuosity, impulsiveness, hastiness, suddenness, rashness; impulse buying.

adj. spontaneous, impulsive, unpremeditated, unthinking, unconsidered; involuntary, automatic, instinctive, reflex; extempore, impromptu, improvised, ad lib (*inf.*); hasty, sudden, rash, precipitate; casual, offhand, throwaway.

vb. act impulsively; blurt out, say the first thing that comes into one's mind; improvise, extemporize, ad lib (*inf.*), play by ear.

adv. on impulse, on the spur of the moment, impulsively, rashly, instinctively, automatically.

see also **613, 859**

545 habit

n. habit, custom, mode, practice, wont, usage, fashion, style, rule, procedure; tendency, propensity, bent, disposition, predisposition, weakness, bias, penchant, second nature, instinct; routine, ritual, rut, groove, treadmill, regularity; convention, precedent, tradition, etiquette, protocol, the done thing; conditioning, accustoming, adaptation, familiarization, training, acclimatization.

addict, habitué, fiend, creature of habit, devotee, client, patron, regular (*inf.*).

adj. usual, customary, normal, common, general, accepted, expected, prevalent, current, conventional, orthodox, established; habitual, frequent, regular, routine, stereotyped; mechanical, seasoned, inveterate; confirmed, ingrained, deep-seated; besetting, clinging, persistent; accustomed, used to, adapted.

vb. accustom, get used to, take to, adapt, adjust, accommodate, condition, train, familiarize, orientate, acclimatize, harden, season, inure, habituate; catch on.

be wont to, be in the habit of, make a practice of.

adv. usually, as is usual, generally.

546 absence of habit

n. disuse, unaccustomedness, desuetude; cessation, relinquishment; decay, neglect, deterioration.

adj. unused, unaccustomed, not used to, not in the habit of; unskilled, inexperienced.

vb. break a habit, abandon, neglect, relinquish, discard, discontinue, rid

oneself of, throw off, wean from; not get used to, not take to; not catch on.
see also **607**

547 motive

n. motive, cause, reason, purpose, ground, basis, spring, spur, impetus, urge, prod, goad, carrot, lure, bait; influence, stimulus, incentive, inspiration, prompting, instigation; persuasion, inducement, coaxing, cajolery, wheedling; charm, attraction, glamour; enticement, temptation, bribery.

motivator, instigator, prompter, animator, coaxer, wheedler; pressure group, lobby, lobbyist.

adj. motivating, persuasive, convincing, impelling, forceful; provocative, stimulating, rousing; fascinating, alluring, charming, captivating, enthralling; enticing, tantalizing.

vb. motivate, cause, inspire, stimulate, prompt, instigate, insist, induce, drive, push, egg on, spur, urge, prod, goad; provoke, elicit, call forth, evoke; influence, encourage, support; persuade, sway, prevail on, talk into, win over, wear down resistance, brainwash (*inf.*), twist round one's little finger (*inf.*), pull strings; coax, cajole, wheedle; captivate, fascinate, charm, attract, interest, entice, tempt, tantalize, beguile, enrapture; lobby, put pressure on; bribe, buy, get at (*inf.*), oil, corrupt.

548 dissuasion

n. dissuasion, discouragement, hindrance, deterrent, disincentive, damper, restraint, cold water, wet blanket; spoilsport, killjoy.

adj. dissuasive, discouraging.

vb. dissuade, deter, hinder, prevent, advise against, discourage, talk out of, wean from, dampen, stifle, disparage, pour cold water on.

549 pretext

n. pretext, excuse, plea, apology, justification, pretence, gesture, show, guise, veil, cloak, mask, appearance, alibi.

adj. ostensible, alleged, specious.

vb. allege, pretend, claim, profess, excuse; apologize, make excuses, bluff.

550 good

n. good, benefit, gain, profit, success, advantage, service, boon, windfall, godsend, pennies from heaven, providence, blessing, good turn; well-being, welfare, prosperity, fortune, happiness, weal; improvement, betterment, edification, progress.

adj. good, beneficial, advantageous, helpful, useful, edifying.

see also **899, 935**

551 evil

n. evil, misfortune, ill, harm, ruin, nuisance, disadvantage, bane, accident, tragedy, disaster, catastrophe, calamity, affliction, trial, crying shame, raw deal; foul play, wrong, injury, pain, anguish, hurt; wickedness, corruption.

adj. evil, bad, wicked; unfortunate, ill, tragic, catastrophic, disastrous, painful, distressing, hurtful.

see also **900, 936**

B Prospective volition

552 intention

n. intention, purpose, aim, intent, meaning; goal, object, end, objective, mark, destination, target; plan, design, idea, proposal; dream, desire, aspiration, expectation, ambition.

adj. intended, designed, planned, proposed, deliberate; intending, purposeful, teleological.

vb. intend, aim, go for, attempt, try for, pursue; plan, propose, project, design, purpose, mean; dream, expect, hope, aspire, have designs on (*inf.*); consider, think about, contemplate, study, have in mind, have in view, calculate, work out, decide, determine, resolve.

553 chance

n. chance, randomness, uncertainty, fortuity; fate, fortune, luck, coincidence, fluke, toss-up (*inf.*); speculation, venture, risk, hazard; bet, gamble, wager, stake, flutter, draw, lottery.

speculator, gambler, better, backer, punter; bookmaker, turf accountant, bookie (*inf.*).

adj. chance, lucky, fortuitous, unintentional, haphazard, aimless, random, risky, hazardous, touch-and-go.

vb. chance, risk, venture, hazard, speculate, gamble, bet, wager, back.

see also **158**

554 pursuit

n. pursuit, hunt, chase, race, pursuance, quest, search, tracking; hunter, chaser, pursuer, seeker, quester, follower.

adj. pursuing, following.

vb. pursue, look for, search, follow up, seek, quest, prosecute; hunt, go after, chase, give chase, hound, tail, trail, stalk, shadow, track, sniff out (*inf.*), smell out, dog.

prep. after, in pursuit of, on the track of.

555 avoidance

n. avoidance, evasion, escape, flight, withdrawal, retreat, shunning, abstinence, circumvention; shirker, fugitive, runaway, absconder, eloper, deserter, refugee, truant.

adj. avoiding, evasive, elusive.

vb. avoid, escape, evade, elude, keep away, keep off, boycott; flee, shrink, flinch; get out of, shun, shirk, dodge, flunk, turn away, duck, hedge; steer clear of, keep one's distance, take no part in, leave alone, not get involved in, disregard, give the go-by; abstain, refrain; retreat, withdraw.

556 relinquishment

n. relinquishment, abandonment, giving up, surrender, renunciation, discontinuance, withdrawal, desertion, quitting.

vb. relinquish, abandon, give up, renounce, forgo, abdicate, waive, surrender, throw in the towel; turn over to, turn in; leave, quit, withdraw, back out, go back on, retreat, secede, forsake; discontinue, break with, break off with, drop, let go, throw away, cast off, discard, part with, shed, desert, chuck (*inf.*), ditch, jilt; leave in the lurch, have done with (*inf.*), walk out on (*inf.*).

see also **542, 713**

557 business

n. business, affairs, dealings, trade; job, employment, post, appointment, position, situation, engagement, incumbency; vocation, calling, pursuit, occupation, profession, line of business, speciality, *métier*, craft; career, life-work, life, mission; work, task, undertaking, activity, assignment, affair, concern; function, office, role, capacity, responsibility, duty, charge, commission, terms of reference, scope, area, field, realm, province, portfolio.

adj. businesslike, efficient, professional, official, prompt; busy, tied up with (*inf.*).

vb. employ, occupy, appoint, select, recruit, engage, contract, take on, give a job to, commission, enlist, hire, rope in (*inf.*), take on the payroll; work, undertake, be busy, be occupied with, be engaged on, be about.

558 plan

n. plan, scheme, project, design, programme, proposal, schedule; scope, outline, sketch; method, procedure, guidelines, principles; policy, course of action, strategy; representation, chart; master-plan, long-range plan; blueprint, draft, rough draft, pilot scheme, dummy run; plot, conspiracy, intrigue, cabal, little game (*inf.*).

planner, director, designer, organizer, architect, engineer, administrator; conspirer, plotter, schemer.

adj. planned, projected, prospective, on the drawing board, procedural.

vb. plan, design, work out, draw up, organize, arrange, propose, devise, create, dream up (*inf.*), frame, undertake, proceed, outline, sketch, draft; forecast, project, think ahead, phase; scheme, plot, conspire, concoct, hatch.

559 way

n. way, manner, fashion; method, means, procedure, process; tactics, measures, steps; direction, passage, entrance, access, approach, route, itinerary, course.

path, track, footpath, walk; road, street, avenue, lane, drive, crescent, close, alley, terrace, park, garden, green, hill, grove, boulevard, square, place, court, circus, arcade, piazza, market, mall, embankment; ring-road, by-pass, arterial road, motorway, dual carriageway, clearway, primary route, trunk road, highway.

railway, underground, tube; main line, branch line, feeder.

560 mid-course

n. centre, mean, middle course, middle of the road, half-way house.

adj. middle, central, medial, neutral, middle-of-the-road, unextreme, moderate, intermediate, midway, half-way.

561 circuit

n. circuit, detour, by-pass, roundabout way; digression, deviation.

adj. circuitous, roundabout, indirect, out-of-the-way.

see also **250**

562 requirement

n. requirement, requisite, stipulation, need, want, demand; condition; essential, imperative, necessity, must (*inf.*), desideratum; needfulness, obligation, compulsion, indispensability, emergency, urgency, matter of life and death, essentiality.

adj. necessary, essential, imperative, indispensable, vital, needful, urgent; wanted, in demand.

vb. require, need, want, wish; lack, be in need of, miss; demand, call for, ask, invite, cry out for; necessitate, force, compel.

563 instrumentality

n. instrumentality, mediation, subservience, intervention; help, aid, assistance, agency, medium, vehicle, intermediary, organ.

adj. instrumental, intermediate, conducive, assisting, subsidiary, auxiliary, subservient, contributory, helpful; effective.

vb. be instrumental, help, aid, mediate.

see also **172**

564 means

n. means, wherewithal, resources, ways and means, equipment, supplies, assets, reserves, provisions; power, potential; factor, agent, medium, channel, organization.

vb. find the means, provide, equip, supply.

565 instrument

n. instrument, implement, apparatus, equipment, appliance, gadget, device, invention, contrivance, contraption; machine, mechanism, machinery, engine; tool, utensil; computer, robot, automaton.

adj. instrumental, mechanical, automatic.

566 materials

n. materials, resources, supplies, assets, means, wherewithal, stuff, raw materials.

567 store

n. store, collection, accumulation, heap, pile, stack, load, mass, stock, hoard, bulk, deposit, bundle; crop, harvest; hoard, treasure, reserves, savings, nest-egg; backlog; fountain, well, spring, gold-mine, reservoir; abundance, profusion, fullness.

storage, safekeeping; warehouse, stockroom, storeroom, depot, depository; library, museum, archives.

adj. stored, accumulated, saved, kept.

vb. store, keep, put away, put aside, put by, stow away, stash away (*inf.*); accumulate, pile up, heap, stack, amass, bulk, bundle, stockpile, lay in; collect, save, deposit, invest, hoard, salt away (*inf.*); harvest, gather; put by for a rainy day.

adv. aside, in store, in reserve, in stock.

568 provision

n. provision, equipment, supply, furnishings, fittings, fixtures, reserve, store, facilities, belongings, accessories, accompaniments, outfit, paraphernalia, apparatus, appliance; catering, purveying.

adj. provided, furnished, equipped, well-equipped.

vb. provide, equip, supply, furnish, fit, prepare, rig, dress, assemble, deck; give, afford, lend, invest, endow; maintain, stock, cater; supplement, complement; replenish, fill up.

569 waste

n. waste, ruin, decay, devastation, desolation, dilapidation, deterioration, erosion, wear and tear, loss, exhaustion, depletion, decline; consumption, disuse, misuse, squandering, uselessness, dissipation; extravagance, wastefulness, prodigality; excess.

adj. wasteful, extravagant, prodigal, squandering, spendthrift; wasted, squandered, depleted, worthless.

vb. waste, consume, expend, eat up, eat away, exhaust, reduce, deplete, empty, drain, devour, dissipate; squander, lavish, abuse; destroy, erode, decay, dry up, dwindle, wither, run dry, wear out; be of no avail, come to nothing.

570 sufficiency

n. sufficiency, adequacy, enough to go on with; right amount.

adj. sufficient, adequate, enough, satisfactory, acceptable; plenty, abundant, generous, liberal, full, complete, replete.

vb. be sufficient, suffice, be enough, avail, do, comply with, qualify, fill the bill, come up to, live up to, satisfy requirements, make the grade, prove acceptable; lick into shape (*inf.*).

571 insufficiency

n. insufficiency, inadequacy, deficiency, scarcity, meagreness, scantiness, slightness, poverty, paucity, dearth, lack.

adj. insufficient, inadequate, not enough, unacceptable, meagre, thin, slight, scanty, poor, bankrupt, sparing, unsatisfactory, wanting, lacking, missing, failing, disappointing; miserly, parsimonious.

vb. be insufficient, not come up to, fall short, come short, fail, want, need, lack, require.

prep. without, in want of, short of.

see also 35

572 excess

n. excess, redundance; exorbitance, inordinacy, superfluity, oversufficiency, abundance, plenty, lavishness, plethora, profusion, glut, surfeit, surplus, over-supply, saturation, exuberance, superabundance, inundation, flood, deluge, torrent, avalanche, bounty, bonanza, cornucopia, congestion; enough and to spare, more than enough; luxury, extravagance, too much of a good thing.

adj. excessive, inordinate, exorbitant, extravagant, immoderate, unreasonable, saturated, plentiful, superfluous, overfull, congested, surplus, redundant, to spare, extra; plenty, abundant.

vb. abound, teem, swarm; overdo; saturate, glut, inundate, flood, overwhelm, choke, drench.

573 importance

n. importance, significance, consequence; seriousness, gravity; substance, matter, weight, moment, import; prominence, eminence; be-all and end-all, priority, urgency.

adj. important, significant, momentous, decisive, critical, relevant, consequential, crucial, considerable, valuable; great, extensive; serious, grave, weighty, ponderous, heavy, solemn; famous, well-known, eminent, notable, distinguished, prominent, impressive, imposing, influential, illustrious, extraordinary, outstanding, exceptional, top-notch (*inf.*), heavyweight (*inf.*), mainline (*inf.*); basic, essential, fundamental; chief, main, primary, principal, foremost, leading, paramount, salient.

vb. be important, carry weight, influence, matter, deserve attention; make important, emphasize, underline, stress; value, prize, set great store by, think much of.

574 unimportance

n. unimportance, insignificance, triviality, worthlessness, immateriality, paltriness, irrelevance; red herring, trifle, nothing to speak of, nothing to write home about, nonentity, drop in the ocean.

adj. unimportant, insignificant, immaterial, worthless, inconsequential, irrelevant, trivial, worthless, paltry, petty, trifling, inconsiderable, slight, common, ordinary, superficial.

vb. be unimportant, not matter; play second fiddle, make light of, play down, make nothing of.

575 utility

n. utility, usefulness; utilization, employment, helpfulness, efficacy; suitability, applicability, practicability, serviceableness.

advantage, benefit, profit, worth, value, merit; service, application, convenience.

adj. useful, valuable, beneficial, profitable, advantageous, suitable, practicable, convenient, helpful, handy, available, applicable; utilitarian, functional, sensible, pragmatic.

vb. be useful, help, serve a purpose, perform a function, come in handy; profit, benefit, stand one in good stead, avail.

use, employ, have the use of, exploit, exercise, utilize, take advantage of, turn to, take up, adopt, practise, apply, avail oneself of; handle, operate; spend, consume.

see also **606**

576 inutility

n. inutility, uselessness, worthlessness, fruitlessness, ineffectiveness, unsuitability, impracticability; futility, hopelessness, vanity.

lost labour, waste of time, wild-goose chase; dead wood; waste, refuse, rubbish, waste-product, litter, dregs, dust, muck.

adj. useless, of no use, worthless, purposeless, futile, vain, pointless, empty, ineffective, incompetent, counter-productive; thankless, unrewarding; unusable, unsuitable, impracticable, inconvenient, unhelpful, disadvantageous, unavailable; out of order, broken down, inoperative; unnecessary, uncalled for.

vb. be useless, be of no help, come to nothing; flog a dead horse, labour in vain, have no future, beat the air.

577 expedience

n. expedience, suitability, appropriateness, fitness, rightness, advisability, propriety, desirability, advantageousness, usefulness.

adj. expedient, advantageous, suitable, fitting, appropriate, apposite, desirable, advisable, seemly; practical, useful, convenient; wise, politic.

vb. suit, fit; help, do, benefit.

see also **136, 915**

578 inexpedience

n. inexpedience, unsuitability, inappropriateness, inadvisability, undesirability, unfitness, impropriety, inconvenience, disadvantage, prejudice.

adj. inexpedient, unsuitable, inappropriate, undesirable, inadvisable, unfitting, unseemly, unwise, inopportune, imprudent, unfavourable, detrimental, disadvantageous, inconvenient.

vb. not do, not help; inconvenience, put out, embarrass, bother, trouble, hinder.

see also **137, 916**

579 goodness

n. goodness, excellence, fineness, greatness, magnificence, superiority; quality, value, price, worth, merit.

top people, elite, cream, pick of the bunch, salt of the earth, treasure, gem, one in a million, champion, corker (*sl.*).

adj. good, excellent, fine, great, superb, splendid, magnificent, marvellous, wonderful, attractive, lovely; masterly, skilled, competent; praiseworthy, commendable; admirable, desirable, enticing, surprising, astonishing; super, terrific, out of this world (*inf.*), cool (*sl.*), neat (*sl.*), magic (*sl.*).

best, first-class, first-rate, optimum, premium, prime, highest, supreme, superlative, A-1, top-notch (*inf.*), tops; exceptional, incomparable, surpassing, incredible, unbelievable, excelling, exemplary; choice, select, exquisite, superior, capital (*inf.*); valuable, priceless, inestimable.

fair, pretty good, not bad, all right, O.K., passable, tolerable, adequate, middling, fair to middling.

vb. be good, have value, have quality; do good, benefit, help, edify.

see also **550, 844**

580 badness

n. badness, nastiness, wickedness, vileness, foulness; inferiority, unsatisfactoriness, mediocrity; bane, ill wind, woe, spanner in the works, fly in the ointment.

adj. bad, wrong, awful, nasty, terrible, horrid, horrible; inferior, imperfect, defective, worthless, poor, second-rate, below average, deficient, unsatisfactory, mediocre, ordinary, unwholesome, shoddy, trashy, crummy (*sl.*), shabby; lousy (*sl.*), rotten; pitiful, contemptible, paltry.

harmful, damaging, detrimental, hurtful, destructive, fatal, deadly, corrupting, poisonous, corroding, toxic, venomous, subversive.

vb. be bad, have no value; do bad, harm, injure, hurt, wound, ruin, destroy, corrupt, subvert; vex, trouble, wrong.

see also **551**

581 perfection

n. perfection, excellence, impeccability, faultlessness, stainlessness; maturity, completion, culmination, consummation.

ideal, standard, model, paragon, summit, ultimate, height, acme; showpiece, masterpiece, *pièce de résistance*.

adj. perfect, faultless, pure, flawless, impeccable, immaculate, untainted, unblemished, untarnished, stainless, spotless, unstained, uncontaminated, unadulterated, irreproachable, beyond compare, brilliant; supreme, ideal.

whole, sound, complete, entire, finished, developed, fulfilled, completed, accomplished, consummate.

vb. perfect, develop, complete, finish, bring to fruition, get down to a fine art, consummate.

582 imperfection

n. imperfection, impurity, defectiveness, inadequacy, immaturity; disfigurement, defacement, deformity, discoloration.

blemish, flaw, stain; fault, mistake, defect, lack, drawback, snag, loophole, weak spot, weak link in the chain.

adj. imperfect, flawed, defective, deficient, malformed, distorted, tainted, adulterated, blemished, damaged, injured, impaired.

incomplete, unfinished, unsound, uneven, unsatisfactory, faulty, inadequate, fallible.

vb. be imperfect, show faults, fall short, not come up to, be found wanting.

see also **847**

583 cleanness

n. cleanness, cleanliness, pureness, spotlessness, whiteness; neatness, tidiness, orderliness, trimness; cleaning, washing, scrubbing, scouring, sprinkling; sterilization, disinfection; cleansing, purification, purgation, ablution.

adj. clean, tidy, neat; immaculate, white, spotless, stainless, untarnished, unblemished, unstained, unsullied, unpolluted, unsoiled, dirtless, spick and span, starched, laundered, polished; germ-free.

vb. clean, tidy, clear; wash, lather, shampoo; bathe, scrub, scour, sponge, mop, swab; brush, sweep; freshen, ventilate; disinfect, fumigate; sterilize, pasteurize; launder, starch, iron; cleanse, purify, sprinkle, purge, expurgate.

584 uncleanness

n. uncleanness, impurity, untidiness, disorderliness, muckiness, filthiness, pollution, defilement.

dirt, filth, spot, stain, smear, smudge, blot, muck, grime, grease, slime; squalor.

adj. unclean, dirty, soiled, polluted, tarnished, sullied, spotted, smeared, daubed, smudged, besmirched; filthy, grimy, greasy, muddy, sooty; squalid, foul, mucky; contaminated, decayed, rotten, rancid, putrid; sloppy, untidy, messy, slovenly, dishevelled, bedraggled, unkempt, like something the cat brought in (*inf.*), unwashed; defiled, unrefined, unpurified.

vb. be dirty, rust, decay, rot, collect dust; dirty, soil, sully, tarnish, daub, bedaub, smudge, blot, pollute, foul; mess up, untidy; corrupt, defile, debase, taint, contaminate, infect.

585 health

n. health, wholeness, soundness, healthfulness, healthiness, salubrity, wholesomeness, balance, vitality; sanity; fitness, strength, well-being, good health, rosy cheeks.

hygiene, sanitation, public health, cleanliness.

adj. healthy, well, sound, whole, wholesome, fit, strong, robust, vigorous, energetic, hale, hearty; all right, rosy-cheeked, flourishing, never feeling better, in fine fettle, in good shape, fighting fit.

healthful, invigorating, stimulating, bracing, beneficial, salubrious; nutritious, nourishing, body-building, restorative, therapeutic, corrective; good for one, what the doctor ordered; hygienic, sanitary.

vb. be healthy, flourish, feel fine; be good for.

586 ill health

n. ill health, poor health, bad health, frailty, weakness, infirmity, invalidity, unhealthiness, indisposition.

illness, disease, ailment, malady, sickness, complaint, disability, affliction, condition, disorder, breakdown, collapse, relapse; fever, infection, virus (*inf.*), bug (*sl.*), pain; bout, spell; stroke, fit, attack, seizure, spasm, convulsions.

lack of hygiene, insalubrity, uncleanliness, contagiousness, infectiousness.

adj. ill, unwell, ailing, weak, unhealthy, poorly, frail, infirm, sick; suffering, down with, indisposed, disabled; drooping, languishing, declining, bedridden, laid up, confined; run down, exhausted; under the weather (*inf.*), out of sorts, seedy (*inf.*), groggy (*inf.*).

unhygienic, insanitary, polluted, bad for, insalubrious; infectious, contagious, endemic; poisonous, toxic, deadly.

vb. be ill, be down with, suffer; fall ill, catch, become ill with, contract, go down with, get, be stricken with; show symptoms of, sicken for; waste away, droop, languish; be bad for, disagree with.

587 improvement

n. improvement, betterment, change, advance, development, refinement, progress, reformation, face-lift, amelioration; enrichment, promotion, furtherance, reform, modernization; revision, correction, amendment.

adj. improved, corrected, amended, revised, reformed, touched up; progressive, reformatory.

vb. improve, develop, further, better, reorganize, promote, reform, straighten out, mend, ameliorate; revise, update, upgrade, correct, rectify; polish, refine, enrich; decorate, beautify, touch up, refurbish; progress, make progress, get better, advance, profit; pick up, come on, rally; pull one's socks up (*inf.*); mellow, mature.

see also **288**

588 deterioration

n. deterioration, impairment, degeneration, decay, rotting, decomposition, erosion, rust; dilapidation, ruin, collapse, decadence, disintegration; impoverishment, adulteration, defilement, corruption, spoiling, detriment, pollution; retrogression; damage, injury, wound, lesion, cut, gash, sore, bruise.

adj. deteriorated, impaired, spoiled, decadent, ruined; damaged, harmed, desolate, ravaged, plundered, robbed, marred, mutilated; decayed, decomposed, rotten, putrified, foul, putrid; worn away, wasting away, emaciated, depleted; ramshackle, tumbledown.

vb. deteriorate, worsen, degenerate, decay, decline, slide, fall, slump, sink, go downhill, fall away, depreciate; go bad, rot, wither, crumble, the rot set in (*inf.*); wither, shrivel; spoil; go to pieces, break up, decompose, fade away, waste away, die; collapse, break down, founder, go to wrack and ruin, go to the dogs (*inf.*), go to pot (*inf.*); go off the rails (*inf.*).

impair, pervert, ruin, corrupt, distort; lower, pull down, reduce, degrade, dehumanize, adulterate, defile, deprave, infect, contaminate; eat away, erode, corrode.

harm, damage, injure, wound, savage, cripple, lame; maltreat, misuse; disgrace, dishonour, discredit; exacerbate, aggravate; hold against (*inf.*), count against; confuse, mess up (*inf.*).

589 restoration

n. restoration, healing, cure, recovery, convalescence, recuperation; renovation, repair, reconditioning, refurbishing, reconstruction, remaking; rehabilitation, re-establishment, resumption, reinstatement, return, getting back to normal; reparation, restitution, amends; reclamation, salvage, rescue.

revival, renewal, reawakening, reinvigoration, resuscitation, rebirth, regeneration, resurrection, renaissance, resurgence, rejuvenation; Indian summer, face-lift, new look, comeback.

adj. restored, repaired, re-established, back to normal; restorative, corrective, remedial, recuperative, therapeutic, soothing, curative.

vb. restore, rebuild, reconstruct, remodel, refashion, reorganize, recondition, reform, remake, revamp, renovate, modernize; repair, mend, fix; refurbish, touch up; darn, patch, sew.

put right, correct, rectify, amend, redress; return, recompense, refund, make amends, make restitution, reinstate, put back, reinstall, re-establish, resume, return to normal; reclaim, salvage, rescue, retrieve, redeem.

revive, refresh, renew, recreate, reanimate, regenerate, resurrect, resuscitate, rejuvenate, reawaken, revitaiize, rekindle.

cure, heal, treat, minister to, nurse, rehabilitate, put on one's feet again.

be restored, recover, convalesce, recuperate, get well, get better, fall on one's feet (*inf.*), pick up, rally, pull through, gain strength, get back into circulation (*inf.*); come up smiling (*inf.*).

see also **618**

590 relapse

n. relapse, return, reversion, retrogression, regression; deterioration, declension; apostasy.

vb. relapse, regress, retrogress, deteriorate, degenerate, sink back, slip back, revert, suffer, relapse; backslide, fall from grace, apostasize.

see also **289**

591 remedy

n. remedy, cure, relief, assistance, treatment, medication; medicine, medicament, preparation, prescription, pharmaceutical, drug; mixture, dose, potion, linctus; pill, tablet, capsule, lozenge; vaccine, injection, inoculation, jab (*inf.*), shot (*inf.*); lotion, ointment, balm salve; tonic, pick-me-up, stimulant, restorative, refresher, tranquillizer. sedative; panacea, cure-all, elixir; operation, surgery.

adj. remedial, therapeutic, healing, medicinal, corrective, curative, restorative.

vb. remedy, cure, heal, restore; treat, attend, practise; relieve, support, help, mitigate, soothe, palliate; send for the doctor, send to hospital, dial 999, hospitalize, operate; undergo treatment, take pills, take one's medicine.

592 bane

n. bane, curse, plague, evil, scourge, affliction, trial, cross, thorn in the flesh; pain in the neck (*inf.*); weakness, besetting sin; poison, venom, virus; blight, mildew, rust, mould, rot, fungus, gangrene, cancer.

adj. baneful, evil, pestilent; deadly, poisonous, venomous; harmful, destructive.

593 safety

n. safety, security, surety, impregnability, invulnerability, immunity; protection, defence, safekeeping, custody, guardianship, supervision, care; law and order.

protector, guard, defender; custodian, warden, curator, keeper, trustee; life-guard, bodyguard, guardian; patrol, lookout, scout, night watchman, watchdog, vigilante, sentry, policeman.

adj. safe, secure, impregnable, invulnerable, unassailable; protected, guarded, safeguarded, defended, shielded, sheltered; unharmed, unhurt, safe and sound, unscathed; waterproof, bulletproof.

vb. make safe, safeguard, protect, keep, guard, defend, shelter, screen, shield, harbour; supervise, care for, mind, look after, take charge of, keep an eye on, attend to, take under one's wing; keep order, patrol, police, be on the lookout, keep vigil, keep cave (*sl.*); hide, lie low, go to earth.

adv. out of danger, in the clear, out of harm's way, in safe hands, under one's wing, under lock and key.

see also **595**

594 danger

n. danger, peril, risk, hazard, jeopardy; menace, threat; dangerousness, perilousness, riskiness, insecurity, precariousness, vulnerability, exposure, openness, helplessness; weak spot.

adj. dangerous, perilous, hazardous, risky, insecure, precarious, alarming, unsafe, treacherous, slippery, shaky, unstable; unsheltered, unshielded, vulnerable, exposed, open, naked, unfortified; menacing, threatening, ominous; critical, serious, delicate, explosive.

vb. endanger, jeopardize, put in jeopardy, expose, lay open to, risk, run the risk of, render liable to, court disaster, tempt providence.

595 refuge

n. refuge, shelter, sanctuary, asylum, retreat; home, ivory tower, port, harbour, haven; den, lair, nest, covert; castle, fortress, stronghold; safeguard, protection, defence; cover, screen, shade, shield, umbrella, wind-break; escape, way out, recourse, last resort.

see also **593, 646**

596 pitfall

n. pitfall, trap, snare, ambush, booby-trap; reef, rock, sandbank, quicksand, undercurrent; danger spot, black spot, trouble spot; trouble-maker, wrecker, snake in the grass.

597 warning

n. warning, caution, lesson, example, advice, counsel, caveat; alert, hint, intimation, admonition, tip-off (*inf.*), early warning, writing on the wall, symptom, sign, omen, augury; foreboding, premonition; notice, indication, notification; call, cry, shout.

adj. warning, cautionary, advisory, instructive.

vb. warn, caution, advise, alert, admonish, counsel, encourage, exhort, hint, prompt, suggest; forewarn, tip off (*inf.*); notify, inform, give notice, apprise.

see also **460**

598 indication of danger

n. alarm, alert, bell, alarm bell, fire alarm; siren, horn, fog-horn, klaxon, tocsin; light, red light, warning light; red alert; SOS, distress signal; beacon; war-cry, drum-beat; false alarm, hoax, scare.

vb. give the alarm, raise the alarm, dial 999, alert, put on the alert; cry wolf.

599 preservation

n. preservation, protection, maintenance, saving, keeping, conservation; storage, canning, freezing, refrigeration, dehydration.

adj. preservative, protective; preserved, kept, intact, protected; fresh, well-preserved.

vb. preserve, maintain, keep, protect, look after; conserve, keep fresh, bottle, can, tin, season, cure, salt, dry, smoke, freeze, refrigerate, freeze-dry, dehydrate, pickle, spice, marinade; embalm, mummify.

600 escape

n. escape, flight, departure, getaway; evasion, avoidance, abdication, desertion, disappearance; freedom, release, deliverance, rescue; retreat, withdrawal; narrow escape, close shave, near miss, near thing.

exit, way out, overflow, vent, waste-pipe, exhaust, leak, leakage, life-line, loophole.

escaper, runaway, truant, dodger, fugitive, refugee.

adj. escaped, free, out, at large, at liberty, missing, wanted.

vb. escape, flee, take flight, abscond, leave, depart, break loose, break out, decamp, free, get clear of, get away with, make one's getaway, make oneself scarce, give the slip, slip through one's fingers, elude, avoid, evade, elope, play truant; emerge, issue, burst out.

see also **921**

601 deliverance

n. deliverance, saving, rescue, release, freeing, liberation, relief; extrication, unbinding, loosening, disentanglement; ransom, forgiveness, pardon; remission, discharge, acquittal, reprieve, exoneration; emancipation, affranchisement, manumission.

vb. deliver, rescue, release, free, discharge, relieve; remit, acquit, let off (*inf.*), exonerate; extricate, loosen, untie; emancipate, liberate; salvage, retrieve; save, redeem, ransom, pardon, forgive.

see also **680**, **911**

602 preparation

n. preparation, plan, step, arrangement; outline, draft, scheme, foundation, groundwork, spadework; rehearsal, practice, training, dummy run; approach, run-up (*inf.*); preparedness, readiness, fitness, experience, all systems go (*inf.*); red alert.

adj. preparatory, introductory, initial; prepared, ready, alert, waiting, on call, standing by, all set; experienced, skilled, qualified, versed, seasoned, broken in.

ready-made, prefabricated, ready-mixed, treated; frozen, pre-cooked, processed, dehydrated, ready-to-eat, oven-ready, instant; off-the-peg.

vb. prepare, get ready, arrange, plan, make preparations; settle, decide; adapt, adjust, fit, equip, supply, deck out, fit out, provide; take steps, take measures; practise, rehearse, train, study, hold in readiness; clear the decks, lay the foundations, prepare the ground, pave the way, smooth the way, blaze a trail, do the groundwork, do one's homework, break the ice.

see also **558**

603 non-preparation

n. non-preparation, unpreparedness, lack of training, inexperience; immaturity, rawness, naivety.

adj. unprepared, unready, napping, surprised, taken aback, unguarded, off one's guard, with one's pants down (*sl.*); unorganized, makeshift, hasty, rush (*inf.*); thoughtless; inexperienced, unskilled, uninstructed, untrained, unqualified, unequipped; new, naive, raw, immature; undeveloped, half-baked; backward, developing; fallow, virgin.

vb. be unprepared, be taken unawares, be caught napping; not plan, make no provision for; improvise.

604 attempt

n. attempt, try, effort, trial, experiment, endeavour, essay, undertaking, enterprise, venture.

adj. experimental, probationary, tentative, trial.

vb. attempt, try, have a try, make an effort, endeavour, venture, seek, aim for, strive, contend, risk, aspire, contest, have a go, lift a finger, put oneself out, have a crack at (*inf.*), have a shot at (*inf.*), have a stab at (*inf.*).

605 undertaking

n. undertaking, enterprise, project, plan, programme, cause, pursuit, campaign, operation, exercise, venture, exploit, feat; occupation, business, job, task, work, concern, matter in hand, proposition, engagement, commitment, obligation.

adj. enterprising, adventurous, venturesome, daring, go-ahead, pioneering, progressive, up-and-coming; ambitious, aspiring.

vb. undertake, engage in, go in for, do, take part in, participate in, devote oneself to; manage, engage, promise, contract; take upon oneself, put one's hand to, commit oneself to, take on, assume, shoulder, bear the burden of, tackle, embark on, enter upon, get down to (*inf.*), launch into, plunge into, commence, begin, start, set to, broach, set about; get down to business, get one's teeth into (*inf.*), take the bit between the teeth (*inf.*), get down to brass tacks (*inf.*), get to grips with.

adv. in hand, under control, in order.

see also **88**

606 use

n. use, usage, application, practice, exercise, employment, management, conduct, realization, adoption, conversion, treatment, handling, performance, control; method, technique; utility, usefulness.

adj. used, applied, utilized, adopted, accepted, practised; in use, in service, in force; old, second-hand.

vb. use, employ, apply, utilize, put to use, put into service; realize, adopt, draw on, take advantage of; adapt, convert, relate, bring to bear, resort to, have recourse to, fall back on; manage, conduct, deal with, treat, handle; exploit, use to the full, get the most out of, cash in on (*inf.*), capitalize, get the benefit of.

see also **575**

607 disuse

n. disuse, non-use, discontinuance, suspension, abolition, rejection, relinquishment, abandonment, unemployment, abeyance; obsolescence.

adj. disused, neglected, abandoned, idle, abolished, deserted, derelict; unused, unemployed, unspent; out of order, out of service, inactive; extra, spare.

vb. disuse, suspend, abolish, put aside, have done with, reject, get rid of, throw out, jettison, discard, scrap, throw on the scrap-heap, neglect, abandon, desert, relinquish.

608 misuse

n. misuse, abuse, misapplication, misemployment, mishandling, mismanagement, misappropriation; perversion, debasement, degradation, prostitution, desecration, defilement, profanation, pollution; outrage, violation; error, mistake.

vb. misuse, abuse, mistreat, ill-treat, maltreat, mishandle, misemploy, misappropriate; pervert, prostitute, debase, desecrate, defile, violate, deprave, profane; wrong, insult, injure, hurt, harm, malign; squander, waste.

C Voluntary action

609 action

n. action, doing, execution, commission, operation, management, handling.

act, deed, thing, work, job, activity, feat, exploit; performance, achievement, undertaking, accomplishment; move, step, measure; blow, stroke.

doer, performer, worker, workman; instrument.

adj. doing, in operation, in process, operative.

vb. act, do, conduct, operate, work, function.

achieve, accomplish, complete, fulfil, carry out, bring about, execute, realize, effect, perform, dispose of, commit, transact, put into effect, put into action, put into operation.

take action, take steps, do something about, specialize in, concern oneself with, make it one's business, go in for; persist, persevere, keep going.

see also **611, 615**

610 inaction

n. inaction, rest, waiting, inertia, suspension, abeyance; laissez-faire, dormancy, neglect, stagnation.

adj. inoperative, idle, unemployed; suspended, in abeyance.

vb. not act, wait, pause, hang fire, bide one's time, twiddle one's thumbs, hold your horses (*inf.*); wait and see, do nothing, abstain, refrain; leave alone, have nothing to do with, let sleeping dogs lie.

see also **612**

611 activity

n. activity, liveliness, agility, nimbleness, alertness, alacrity, readiness, keenness, eagerness; energy, life, vigour, spirit, verve, zest, dynamism, enthusiasm, get-up-and-go (*inf.*); hurry, bustle, flurry, rush, commotion, rat-race.

industry, diligence, assiduousness, perseverance, resolution, determination, application, concentration; enterprise, initiative; activism, militancy, aggressiveness.

busy person, enthusiast, zealot, activist, fanatic, militant, live wire.

adj. active, lively, energetic, dynamic; busy, hard at it, eventful, bustling, dashing, raring to go; alert, agile, nimble, sharp, spry, wire, alive; restless, fidgety.

enthusiastic, keen, zealous; pushy (*inf.*), ambitious, aggressive, forceful, activist, militant, go-ahead, enterprising; industrious, diligent, hardworking, studious.

vb. be active, be busy, rush around, bustle about, have one's hands full, have a finger in every pie; have many irons in the fire; busy oneself in, stir oneself, rouse onself; persevere, keep going, keep at it; work hard, not have a moment to spare, never stop, overwork, overdo it, have no time to call one's own.

see also **532, 609**

612 inactivity

n. inactivity, stillness, inertia; lethargy, slackness, sluggishness, torpor, lifelessness, listlessness; apathy, indifference, carelessness; idleness, laziness, indolence, sloth.

fatigue, tiredness, weariness, sleepiness; sleep, slumber, rest, doze, nod, snooze, shut-eye, catnap, forty winks, siesta, repose, dormancy; breather, pause, holiday, vacation.

lazy person, idler, loafer (*inf.*), good-for-nothing, lazy-bones, bum (*sl.*), tramp, sluggard, wastrel, parasite, sponger.

adj. inactive, still, stable; unemployed, unoccupied, fallow, barren; idle, lazy, slothful, indolent, lethargic, slack, sluggish, listless, torpid, languid; unadventurous, unenterprising, stay-at-home; apathetic, indifferent, uninterested.

tired, weary, drowsy, sleepy, fatigued, somnolent, dormant; exhausted, run down, overworked, worn out, washed out, drooping, faint, weak, stale.

vb. be inactive, rest, relax, pause, bide one's time; drift, vegetate, stagnate.

idle, loaf about (*inf.*), mooch about (*sl.*), loiter about, hang about (*inf.*), bum around (*sl.*); dilly-dally, shilly-shally, languish; kill time, waste time, while away the time.

sleep, slumber, doze, drowse, snooze, take a nap, nod off, have forty winks, yawn, dream; go to bed, turn in, kip down (*sl.*), hit the sack (*sl.*).

see also **533, 617, 841**

613 haste

n. haste, rush, hurry, scramble, scurry, flurry, hurly-burly; dash, spirit, spurt, run, burst, sprint, bolt, race;

hurriedness, hastiness, urgency, promptness, precipitation, rashness, impulsiveness, impetuosity.

adj. hasty, quick, fast, swift, speedy, hurried, dashing; impetuous, impulsive, rash, inconsiderate, reckless, foolhardy, precipitate, headlong, impatient.

vb. hasten, quicken, speed up, accelerate, expedite, dispatch, stimulate, fillip, urge, goad, whip, incite, push through, rush through, railroad through (*inf.*).

rush, sprint, spurt, scurry, scuttle, dash, bustle, zoom, tear, bomb (*inf.*), go all out (*inf.*), step on it (*inf.*).

see also **280, 544, 859**

614 leisure

n. leisure, free time, spare time, time off, recreation, relaxation, rest, respite, breather, break, pause, lull, recess; holiday, leave, leave of absence, vacation, sabbatical, furlough, home leave.

adj. leisurely, resting, unoccupied.

vb. have time to spare, be off, take one's ease, relax, rest.

adv. off, off duty, on holiday; at leisure, at one's convenience, at an early opportunity.

see also **281, 840**

615 exertion

n. exertion, effort, panic, trouble, toil, labour, work, travail, strife, strain, tension, elbow grease, drudgery; hard work, handful (*inf.*), uphill task, sweat (*sl.*), drudge.

adj. laborious, arduous, hard, difficult, strenuous, onerous, painstaking, gruelling, punishing, uphill, backbreaking.

vb. exert oneself, try, attempt; take pains, work, labour, fight, toil, contend, struggle, strive, sweat blood; knuckle down (*inf.*), get down to it (*inf.*), buckle down (*inf.*); drudge, grind, plod (*inf.*), plug away (*inf.*), slog away, sweat one's guts out (*sl.*); make heavy weather of, make a meal of; put oneself out, do one's best, do one's utmost, go to all lengths, go all out, leave no stone unturned, move heaven and earth, pull out all the stops (*inf.*); overdo it, have one's work cut out.

see also **535, 611**

616 repose

n. repose, rest, relaxation, inaction; breather, break, pause, coffee-break, tea-break, lunch-break, lunch-hour, rest period; day of rest, Sabbath, Lord's Day; ease, quiet, quietness, tranquillity.

adj. restful, tranquil, quiet, calm, peaceful; sabbatical.

vb. rest, be quiet, stop, halt; take a rest, take it easy, let up, ease off, slow down, stretch one's legs, have a break; get away from it all (*inf.*).

see also **610, 618**

617 fatigue

n. fatigue, tiredness, weariness; sleepiness, heaviness, drowsiness, doziness, somnolence; faintness, weakness. exhaustion, collapse, staleness, jadedness; lassitude, languor.

adj. tired, weary, exhausted, run down, fagged out (*inf.*), worn out, ready to drop (*inf.*), dog-tired, dead beat, all in, whacked (*inf.*); heavy, dozy (*inf.*), drowsy, sleepy; weak, faint, dropping, haggard; washed out, drained, stale, jaded.

vb. be tired, drop, collapse, flag, jade, peg out (*inf.*), flake out (*sl.*); faint, pass out (*inf.*), lose consciousness; work too hard, overdo it.

weary, tire, fatigue, wear out,

exhaust, take it out of (*inf.*), fag out (*inf.*), strain; bore.

see also **612, 841**

618 refreshment

n. refreshment, enlivenment, invigoration, recovery, restoration, convalescence, recuperation, relief.

adj. refreshing, restoring, invigorating, exhilarating, bracing, stimulating, arousing; refreshed, invigorated, like a new man.

vb. refresh, restore, arouse, revive, enliven, animate, strengthen, stimulate, invigorate, renew, reawaken, bring round, give new life to, energize, improve, relieve, resuscitate, vivify; encourage, cheer.

recover, recuperate, pick up, perk up, recharge one's batteries, get one's breath back.

see also **589, 616**

619 agent

n. agent, doer, actor, performer, participant, instrument, medium, practitioner, executor; worker, workman, operator, mechanic, labourer, operative, craftsman, skilled worker; apprentice; hack, drudge, slave, fag.

workforce, employees, staff, personnel, labour, payroll, manpower, resources.

620 workshop

n. workshop, workplace, establishment, installation, institution, plant, factory, works, foundry, yard; shop, house, office, bureau, branch, station, laboratory; firm, company, concern, industry.

621 conduct

n. conduct, behaviour, manner, deportment, demeanour, air, carriage, bearing, posture, attitude, comportment, mien, delivery, appearance, guise; guidance, control, oversight, supervision, superintendence, execution, government, management, organization; strategy, tactics, policy, campaign, programme.

adj. behavioural; tactical, strategical.

vb. behave, act, conduct; acquit oneself, bear oneself, comport onself, pose, appear, seem; behave oneself, mind one's manners, mind one's P's and Q's, be on one's best behaviour; manage, guide, supervise, direct, regulate, administer.

622 management

n. management, conduct, guidance, direction, control, order, charge, power, execution, government, organization, administration, decision making, handling, regulation, legislation, jurisdiction; oversight, supervision, superintendence, surveillance, com mand, authority, leadership; stewardship, husbandry, housekeeping, economics.

adj. directive, managerial, controlling, supervisory; executive, administrative, governmental, gubernatorial, legislative; official, bureaucratic.

vb. manage, conduct, run, guide, direct, lead, control, regulate, order, govern, command, steer, point the way, decide; handle, execute, administer, organize, legislate; supervise, superintend; steward.

623 director

n. manager, director, controller, leader, executive, governor, politician, minister, legislator, commander; dictator; superintendent, supervisor, inspector, overseer, foreman; steward; administrator, official, bureaucrat, functionary, secretary; guide, organizer.

see also **34, 675**

624 advice

n. advice, suggestion, opinion, view, counsel, guidance, encouragement, information, instruction, recommendation; warning, admonition, criticism, dissuasion; caution, notice; notification.

advisor, counsellor, right-hand man, friend, confidant, teacher, informant, helper, consultant; think-tank.

adj. advisory, consultative.

vb. advise, guide, direct, tell, have a word with, suggest; exhort, urge, prompt, encourage, persuade, recommend, counsel; warn, admonish, dissuade; inform, notify, acquaint.

consult, ask, discuss, talk over, seek the opinion of, seek advice, turn to, confide in.

625 council

n. council, cabinet, committee, government, parliament, board, directorate, board of governors; congress, conference, assembly, convention, synod, convocation, diet; panel, forum, brains trust.

councillor, minister, member of parliament, back-bencher, parliamentarian, statesman, senator, congressman; delegate, representative, officer.

626 precept

n. precept, maxim, command, direction, instruction, prescription, principle, law, statute, commandment, rule; canon, doctrine, law, charge, mandate, injunction, edict; formula, recipe.

see also **103, 954**

627 skill

n. skill, capability, proficiency, competence, skilfulness, expertness, ability, aptitude, talent, gift, genius, endowment, flaw, strong point, forte, what it takes, knack; experience, practice, training, qualifications, expertise, know-how, judgment; adeptness, deftness, adroitness, facility.

adj. skilful, capable, able, proficient, competent, effective, clever; experienced, trained, qualified, fit, suited, cut out for (*inf.*), accomplished, well-versed, expert, veteran; gifted, endowed; handy, adept, deft, adroit, agile, dexterous; all-round, versatile; enterprising, inventive.

vb. be good at, shine at, have what it takes; be expert, know backwards, know the ropes (*inf.*), know the ins and outs (*inf.*).

628 unskilfulness

n. unskilfulness, inability, ineptitude, inexperience, greenness, weak point, incompetence, inefficiency, mismanagement; awkwardness, clumsiness; botch-up, hash, mess, cock-up (*inf.*).

adj. unskilful, inexperienced, uneducated, unqualified, incompetent, amateur, unsuited, unused to, lay, amateurish, unprofessional, do-it-yourself, scratch; butterfingers; awkward, clumsy, heavy-handed, bungling, maladroit; impracticable, home-made, Heath Robinson; unwieldy, cumbersome, bulky.

vb. be no good at (*inf.*), spoil, bungle, ruin, botch, mismanage, mishandle, make a mess of, make a hash of, mess up (*inf.*), louse up (*sl.*), screw up (*sl.*), cock up (*sl.*), put one's foot in it; misfire.

629 expert

n. expert, master, adept, proficient,

handyman, Jack-of-all-trades, man of many parts, man of many talents; professional, authority, specialist, scholar, genius, whizz-kid (*inf.*), veteran, old hand; man of the world.

see also **436**

630 bungler

n. bungler, fumbler, botcher, muddler, dunce, idiot, blockhead, scatterbrain, ignoramus; butterfingers; beginner, novice, greenhorn; amateur, layman; lout, lubber.

see also **437**

631 cunning

n. cunning, craftiness, intrigue, deceit, guile, artfulness, craft, subtlety, slyness, wiliness, cleverness, shrewdness, chicanery, finesse.

stratagem, artifice, trick, deception, plot, scheme, ruse, wile, dodge, trap, little game (*inf.*), con (*sl.*), hoax, fabrication, double-dealing, casuistry.

artful dodger, hypocrite, fraud, cheat, plotter, con-man (*sl.*), trickster, slippery customer (*inf.*), smooth talker (*inf.*).

adj. cunning, shrewd, crafty, artful, sly, wily, deceptive, subtle, dishonest, fraudulent, unscrupulous, underhand, shifty, smart, shady, smooth, slippery, sharp, clever (*inf.*), too clever by half (*inf.*).

vb. be cunning, trick, deceive, fraud, cheat, trap, hoax, con (*sl.*), plot, scheme, contrive, pull a fast one (*sl.*), put one over on (*inf.*), put one across (*inf.*), outwit, get the better of.

632 artlessness

n. artlessness, simplicity, innocence, naivety, simple-mindedness, guilelessness, ingenuousness; child, babe.

adj. artless, innocent, simple, naive, simple-minded, guileless, unaffected, natural, uncomplicated, straightforward, ingenuous, childlike, unsophisticated, genuine, frank, open, candid, forthright.

vb. be natural, wear one's heart on one's sleeve; speak one's mind, not mince words.

D Antagonism

633 difficulty

n. difficulty, problem, headache trouble, tall order, handful, heavy going; dilemma, predicament, quandary, strait, plight, embarrassment, fix, pickle (*inf.*), scrape, tight spot (*inf.*), hole (*sl.*); hardship, arduousness, laboriousness, troublesomeness; perplexity.

adj. difficult, hard, tough, laborious, arduous, uphill, strenuous; awkward, burdensome, trying, troublesome, bothersome, wearisome; unclear, obscure, knotty, thorny, baffling, perplexing, complicated, intricate.

vb. be in difficulties, flounder, have a hard time, strike a bad patch, make heavy weather of, make a meal of, not keep one's head above water; get into difficulty, get into hot water; put one's foot in it (*inf.*); beset, trouble, harm, disconcert, discourage, inconvenience, embarrass; baffle, perplex, put on the spot (*inf.*).

adv. in deep water, in difficulty, on the horns of a dilemma, in a quandary, in a spot, in hot water, in trouble.

see also **615, 635**

634 ease

n. ease, facility, straightforwardness; child's play, plain sailing, piece of cake (*inf.*), nothing to it (*inf.*), walk-over (*inf.*), push-over (*inf.*), cinch (*sl.*).

adj. easy, simple, cushy (*inf.*), manageable, facile; obvious, apparent; pleasant, comfortable; clear, uncomplicated; effortless.

vb. be easy, require no effort, present no difficulties, give no trouble, run smoothly, go like clockwork; take in one's stride.

ease, facilitate, smooth the way, free, relieve, rid, get rid of, lighten, release, disentangle; take a weight off someone's mind (*inf.*).

635 hindrance

n. hindrance, impedance, intervention, interruption; restriction, prohibition, restraint, check, blockage; retardation, curb, arrest, drag; inconvenience, hitch, setback, hold-up, bottleneck, catch, snag, spanner in the works (*inf.*), encumbrance, chain, menacle.

obstacle, obstruction, barrier, impediment, interference, stumbling-block, barricade, hurdle, bar, impasse, cul de sac.

adj. hindering, restraining, preventive.

vb. hinder, prevent, thwart, frustrate, hamper, trammel; stop, check, restrain, foil, confine, retard, arrest; deter, prohibit, restrict, bar, forbid, encumber, burden, chain, fetter, shackle; interfere, meddle; obstruct, block, impede, barricade; spoil, gum up the works (*sl.*).

see also **633, 665**

636 aid

n. aid, help, assistance; helping hand, leg up; encouragement, comfort, relief, succour, alleviation, mitigation; favour, benevolence, service; advice, backing, guidance.

financial aid, giving, support, maintenance, charity; compensation, allowance, grant, subsidy, benefit, stipend, honorarium, expenses; patronage, sponsorship, promotion, advancement.

adj. helpful, beneficial, assisting; auxiliary.

vb. help, aid, assist, cooperate; encourage, stand by, back up, sustain, bolster, relieve, comfort, succour, save, rescue, abet; lend a hand, play one's part; befriend, advise, serve, minister to, take under one's wing.

patronize, finance, support, keep, maintain, promote, subsidize, foster, shoulder, sponsor, sanction.

see also **217, 639**

637 opposition

n. opposition, antagonism, confrontation, repugnance, defiance, hostility, abhorrence, aversion, incompatibility, polarity; dislike, dissension, contradiction.

adj. opposing, antagonistic, defiant; hostile.

vb. oppose, counter, conflict with, fly in the face of, run counter to; confront, fight, combat, hinder, obstruct, thwart; object, dispute, contradict; resist, defy; deny, not have any part in, part company with, disapprove, disagree.

see also **648, 883**

638 opponent

n. opponent, antagonist, adversary, enemy, foe, the opposition, competitor, challenger, candidate, entrant, rival, contestant.

see also **883**

639 cooperation

n. cooperation, collaboration, participation, partnership, fellowship, brotherhood, harmony; give and take, teamwork, solidarity; amalgamation, merger, fusion, affiliation, membership; help, assistance.

adj. cooperative, collaborative, participatory; associated.

vb. cooperate, collaborate, give and take, help each other out, play ball with; contribute, help.

join, combine, unite, merge, club together, affiliate, join forces, pool together, pool resources, stand together, stick together (*inf.*), pull together; share, take part in, participate, throw in one's lot, go along with, team up with, take sides; gang up against (*inf.*); put one's heads together (*inf.*).

see also **180, 709**

640 auxiliary

n. auxiliary, helper, assistant, aid, ancillary, collaborator, helping hand, partner, associate, colleague, fellow-worker, co-worker, team-mate, sidekick (*inf.*); accomplice, confederate; friend, companion, ally, comrade; follower, adherent, disciple; hanger-on; patron, backer, supporter; right-hand man, stalwart, tower of strength.

see also **636**

641 party

n. party, group, movement, organization, society, band, body; council, congress, alliance, association, confederation, federation, league, coalition, union; community, fellowship, brotherhood; company, firm, establishment, concern, cooperative, cartel, syndicate.

faction, sect, denomination, tradition, splinter-group, clique, coterie, inner circle.

adj. federal, allied, confederate, cooperative; exclusive, cliquish, partisan, sectarian.

vb. join, enrol, become a member of, affiliate, subscribe; associate with, side with.

642 discord

n. discord, dissension, trouble, difference, disagreement, misunderstanding, cross purposes, variance, ill feeling, tension, friction; divisiveness, troublesomeness, quarrelsomeness, rivalry.

dispute, quarrel, row, fight, argument, squabble, bickering, tiff, vendetta, feud; schism, split, rift, parting of the ways.

adj. discordant, disagreeing, divisive; contradictory; quarrelsome, troublesome, violent, factious, pugnacious, harsh, uncooperative, bolshie (*sl.*).

vb. differ, clash, conflict, dissent; fall out with, part company with; break up.

dispute, contend, fight, struggle, strive, come to blows, complain, object, argue, disagree; quarrel, wrangle, squabble, bicker; have a bone to pick with, have words with, take issue with; look for trouble (*inf.*), ask for it (*inf.*), rub up the wrong way (*inf.*), tread on someone's toes.

adv. at loggerheads, at odds, at variance, at sixes and sevens, not on speaking terms.

see also **25, 893**

643 concord

n. concord, agreement, harmony, conformity, understanding, consonance, rapport, goodwill, friendship, amity, concert, accord, consensus, unanimity, unity, *détente, rapprochement*, entente, entente cordiale.

adj. agreeing, harmonious, friendly.

peaceful, amicable, reconciled, unanimous, united.

vb. agree, get on with, get along with, hit it off (*inf.*), see eye to eye, be at one with; come to an understanding.

see also **24, 699**

644 defiance

n. defiance, disobedience, rebellion, insubordination, insolence, obstinacy; mutiny, revolt, revolution; challenge, dare.

adj. defiant, bold, daring, proud; unruly, rebellious, disobedient, insubordinate; independent, lawless, anarchistic, militant.

vb. defy, confront, brave, challenge, dare, fling down the gauntlet, call one's bluff; resist, disobey, oppose, disregard, flout, spurn, laugh at, scorn, taunt; rebel, revolt, insult, protest, kick against, kick against the pricks.

see also **648**

645 attack

n. attack, assault, onslaught, aggression, advance, charge, push, thrust, drive, outbreak, outburst, raid, offensive, storm, skirmish, foray, sally, sortie; invasion, intrusion, inroad, incursion, encroachment; siege, barrage, bombardment, blitz; mugging, rape.

attacker, aggressor, assailant, fighter, raider, stormer, invader, enemy, intruder, sniper, ravager; mugger, rapist.

adj. attacking, assaulting, aggressive.

vb. attack, assault, advance, charge, rush, push, thrust, assail, fight; raid, invade, storm, sally, sortie, foray; intrude, encroach; besiege, lay siege to, blockade; ravage, lay waste; fire, shoot, snipe; bomb, bombard; beat up, do over (*sl.*), smash somone's face in (*inf.*), mug, rob, rape.

646 defence

n. defence, protection, guarding, security; fortification, castle, fort, fortress, stronghold, keep, bastion, citadel, garrison; trenches, ditch, moat; embankment, rampart, battlement, earthworks; armour.

defender, guard, watch, sentry; protector, champion.

adj. defended, guarded, safe; defensive, armed, watchful.

vb. defend, protect, guard, keep, keep safe, safeguard, secure, shield, shelter, screen; withstand, beat off, ward off, fend off, drive back, take evasive action; spring to someone's defence; strengthen, reinforce, fortify; arm, cover, camouflage.

see also **593**

647 retaliation

n. retaliation, reprisal, revenge, reaction, backlash, counterattack, counterinsurgence, second-strike capability; measure for measure, an eye for an eye, tit for tat, just deserts; requital, repayment, vengeance, punishment, retribution; recrimination; retort, riposte.

adj. retaliatory, retributive, reciprocal.

vb. retaliate, hit back, strike back, fight back, get back (*inf.*), defend oneself; requite, avenge, revenge, punish, return, repay, vindicate, pay back, settle up, get square, get one's own back, give tit for tat, get even with; reciprocate, return the compliment, give someone a dose of his own medicine; retort, counter, recriminate.

see also **912**

648 resistance

n. resistance, withstanding, defence, stand, check; steadfastness, renitence.

adj. resisting, recalcitrant, hard-hearted.

vb. resist, withstand, not give in, not submit, repel, stand up to, not take lying down, stand fast; stay, defend, hold off, oppose, prevent, thwart, foil, frustrate, obstruct, attack; counteract, neutralize; endure, suffer, tolerate; persevere, hold out, stick it out (*inf.*); maintain, take one's stand, stand one's ground, stick one's heels in (*inf.*), stick to one's guns, hold one's own.

see also **535, 644**

649 contest

n. contest, engagement, fight, battle, war, encounter, confrontation, action, skirmish, feud, *mêlée*, set-to, tussle, scrap (*sl.*), brush, affray, altercation; duel, joust, warfare, hostilities; conflict, strife, struggle, bloodshed, onslaught, carnage.

game, match, event, rally, race, challenge; competition, round, tournament; sport, recreation.

adj. contending, contestant; competitive.

vb. contend, fight, oppose, combat, confront, challenge, encounter, engage in battle, campaign, battle, brush with, dispute, strive, struggle, scrap (*sl.*), set to, take on, tussle, joust, assert oneself; compete, contest, race, vie with.

see also **651, 655**

650 peace

n. peace, absence of hostilities, armistice, truce, treaty; pacification, conciliation, reconciliation, love, friendship, agreement, harmony, accord; cold war, peaceful coexistence.

adj. peaceful, quiet, tranquil; bloodless, nonaggressive; pacifist; appeasing, conciliatory, peace-making.

see also **24, 652**

651 war

n. war, hostilities, combat, fighting, warfare, attack, battle, campaign, operation, mission, action, contention.

aggressiveness, warlikeness, belligerence, militancy, warmongering, pugnacity.

adj. warlike, aggressive, militant, pugnacious, belligerent, martial, threatening, contentious, warmongering, unfriendly, bellicose, up in arms, on the warpath; fighting, warring.

vb. wage war, engage in hostilities, attack, invade, contend, strive; declare war, go to war; mobilize, call up, recruit, enlist, conscript, muster.

see also **645, 649**

652 pacification

n. pacification, peace-making, appeasement, conciliation, reconciliation, reparation, satisfaction, assuagement, alleviation, mollification, soothing, calming; propitiation, atonement.

peace-offering, sacrifice, placation, gift; white flag, olive branch.

adj. pacificatory, placatory, propitiatory; irenic.

vb. pacify, conciliate; appease, satisfy, sacrifice, atone, propitiate; quiet, calm, still, moderate, quell, soften, alleviate, assuage, mollify, placate, tranquillize; reconcile, harmonize, bring together, bring to terms, settle one's differences, accommodate; make peace, bury the hatchet; make it up, shake hands.

see also **650**

653 mediation

n. mediation, arbitration, interposition, intervention, shuttle diplomacy.

mediator, arbitrator, go-between, intermediary, arbiter, negotiator, peace-maker, trouble-shooter, intercessor, third party; judge, referee, umpire; adjudicator, assessor; neutral, independent.

adj. mediatory, intercessory.

vb. mediate, arbitrate, negotiate, reconcile, hear both sides, intercede, interpose, intervene; judge, umpire, rule; interfere, meddle.

see also **230**

654 submission

n. submission, yielding, obedience; acquiescence, resignation, deference; submissiveness, docility, meekness, humility, passivity.

adj. submissive, obedient; compliant, amenable, tractable, mouldable; resigned, subdued; acquiescent, reconciled, patient; docile, humble, lowly, tame.

vb. submit, give in, yield, surrender, capitulate, resign, relinquish, give up, throw in the towel, admit defeat.

obey, defer, bow to, comply, acquiesce; take the line of least resistance.

see also **673, 679**

655 combatant

n. combatant, fighter, contender, opponent, serviceman, soldier, conscript, recruit, pressed man; casual, irregular; mercenary, hireling; warrior, veteran.

armed forces, services, troops, forces, military force, army, infantry, cavalry, artillery; navy, air force; unit, group, division, section, squad, troop, patrol; party; task force; formation, column, line, array.

656 non-combatant

n. non-combatant, pacifist, conscientious objector, neutral, dove, flower people, conchie (*sl.*); peace-maker.

657 arms

n. arms, weapons, armament, munitions; armour, mail, panoply; small arms, firearm, gun; revolver, rifle, shotgun, machine gun, automatic; cannon, mortar; bazooka; hand-grenade bomb, explsoive, dynamite, gunpowder; atomic bomb, hydrogen bomb, H-bomb, neutron bomb; armoury, arsenal; ballistics.

658 arena

n. arena, battlefield, battleground, scene of action, field of action, theatre of war, trenches, front; field, ground, centre, scene, sphere, track, court, course; stadium, gymnasium, playground, campus, coliseum, amphitheatre, circus, forum, pit.

E Results of action

659 completion

n. completion, finish, end, conclusion, achievement, performance, accomplishment, fulfilment, perfection, realization, execution.

finishing touch, crown, *coup de grâce;* last straw, limit (*sl.*).

adj. complete, finished, accomplished, fulfilled, perfect, entire, whole; conclusive, final, last.

vb. complete, finish, end, conclude, terminate; achieve, perform, carry out, implement, bring off (*inf.*), pull off (*inf.*), succeed; knock off (*inf.*), polish off (*inf.*), wrap up (*inf.*); get over with (*inf.*), get over and done with (*inf.*); accomplish, work out, hammer out, see through, go through with, realize, effect, fulfil, discharge, settle; be resolved, things work out, perfect, consummate, ripen, mature; culminate, come to a head.

see also **56, 609**

660 non-completion

n. non-completion, failure, non-performance, neglect, defeat; fault, blemish, deficiency, defect.

adj. uncompleted, failed, neglected, incomplete, half-done, partial, imperfect, deficient.

vb. not complete, leave undone, neglect, miss, fail, drop out, leave, not stay the course.

see also 57, 582

661 success

n. success, completion, achievement, attainment, accomplishment; successfulness, happy ending, favourable outcome, prosperous issue; triumph, victory, conquest, push-over (*inf.*), walk-over (*inf.*); breakthrough, advance, progress; prosperity, luck, happiness, bed of roses; success story, hit, smash hit (*sl.*).

winner, victor, champion, hero, title-holder, conqueror.

adj. successful, winning, victorious, triumphant, champion, in the lead, unbeaten, invincible; beneficial, advantageous; fruitful, prosperous, fortunate, thriving, flourishing.

vb. succeed, make a success of, achieve, attain, accomplish, reach, complete, fulfil, obtain, get, capture, gain, pull off (*inf.*), bring off (*inf.*); be successful, come off (*inf.*), do the trick (*inf.*); advance, get on, make it (*inf.*), make a go of (*inf.*), make a breakthrough, proceed, progress, benefit, reap, profit, prosper, flourish, thrive, prevail, score a hit, hit the jackpot.

win, beat, conquer, defeat, get the better of, gain the upper hand, clobber (*sl.*), overcome, ride out the storm, crush, overwhelm, win hands down, walk away with (*inf.*), come out on top (*inf.*), come off with flying colours; survive, get by, hang on.

662 failure

n. failure, misadventure, breakdown, collapse, fiasco, disaster, débâcle, disappointment, flop (*inf.*), wash-out (*inf.*); defeat, overthrow, downfall, ruin, landslide; unsuccessfulness, ineffectiveness, defectiveness; neglect, omission, shortcoming; no-go (*inf.*), wild goose chase, utter defeat, clobbering (*sl.*), rout.

loser, underdog, has-been (*inf.*), also-ran (*inf.*), non-starter, dud.

adj. unsuccessful, futile, vain, useless, fruitless, profitless; unfortunate, disastrous; inadequate, ineffective, abortive; overthrown, defeated, fallen, outmatched, thwarted, frustrated, foiled, pipped at the post, outvoted.

vb. fail, go amiss, fall down, let one down; abandon, neglect, miss; thwart, frustrate; fall short, break down, fall through (*inf.*), miscarry, come to nothing, flounder, falter, go on the rocks, flop (*inf.*), fizzle out (*inf.*); lose, be defeated, suffer defeat, go down, go under; bark up the wrong tree (*inf.*), not get to first base (*inf.*); get no change out of (*inf.*).

663 trophy

n. trophy, prize, reward, award, honour, medal, badge, cup, memorial, decoration, ribbon, order, crown, palm, laurel, accolade, mention, citation; consolation prize, booby prize, wooden spoon.

booty, loot, spoil, plunder, premium, capture.

see also 724

664 prosperity

n. prosperity, good fortune, happiness, welfare, well-being, successfulness, luckiness, affluence, wealth, riches, luxury, benefits, blessings; golden age, good old days, heyday, boom, bed of roses, halcyon days, summer.

adj. prosperous, flourishing, thriving, successful, well-to-do, well-off, comfortable, rich, auspicious; up-and-coming, born with a silver spoon in one's mouth; golden, glorious, cloudless, sunny, halcyon.

vb. prosper, thrive, flourish, increase, blossom, be successful, fare well, turn out well; get on in the world, make one's mark, be rich, make a fortune; Fortune smile upon.

see also 661

665 adversity

n. adversity, misfortune, trouble, hardship, unluckiness, bad luck, hard times, bad patch, ill wind, deep water, difficulty, misadventure, unhappiness; disaster, distress, catastrophe, crisis, calamity, burden, pressure, affliction, blight, curse, plague, scourge.

adj. adverse, unfavourable, hostile, unfriendly, sinister; disastrous, catastrophic; afflicted, troubled, wretched, stricken; unfortunate, unlucky, unhappy, ill-starred, ill-fated, down on one's luck, in a bad way, in the wars.

vb. be in trouble, hit a bad patch, be in for it (*inf.*), have a hard time of it, feel the pinch, fall on hard times, decline, sink, stew in one's own juice, go under, get out of one's depth, fall flat on one's face (*inf.*), fall by the wayside.

see also 633

666 mediocrity

n. mediocrity, commonness, ordinariness, averageness, passableness, tolerableness.

adj. mediocre, average, ordinary, indifferent, middling, fair, poor, feeble, common, commonplace, dull, monotonous, stale, insipid, wishy-washy, tolerable, fair-to-middling, passable, humdrum, run of the mill, so-so, nothing to write home about, much of a muchness,

vb. make do, just exist, struggle along, muddle through, scrape through, manage somehow, get by, just keep one's head above water, stagnate, vegetate.

2 Intersocial volition

A General

667 authority

n. authority, power, control, right, prerogative, command, rule, sway; dominion, sovereignty, ascendancy, upper hand, supreme authority, last word; influence, prestige, power behind the throne, arm of the law.

government, democracy, *vox populi*, officialdom, bureaucracy, administration, establishment, them, powers that be; open government, devolution.

adj. authoritative, commanding, dominant, lawful, powerful, sovereign; in office, in power; official, executive, administrative, bureaucratic, governmental, democratic, gubernatorial, political.

vb. rule, govern, control, direct, dominate, lord it over, domineer, command, sway, reign; assume control, take over, take the reins, have power, rule the roost; authorize, empower, back, devolve, decentralize.

see also 671

668 laxity

n. laxity, slackness, looseness, flexibility; anarchy, lawlessness, mob rule, disorder, chaos, turmoil.

adj. lax, slack, loose, remiss, soft, flabby, relaxed, flexible; anarchic, uncontrolled, lawless, chaotic, rebellious.

vb. be lax, tolerate, not enforce, stretch a point; misrule, misgovern; give a free hand to, give free rein to; take the law into one's own hands, do what is right in one's own eyes.

see also **670**

669 severity

n. severity, strictness, austerity, firmness, rigidity, inflexibility, rigour; hardness, cruelty; firm hand, strong hand, heavy hand, rod of iron, tight rein, pound of flesh, letter of the law.

tyranny, oppression, despotism, fascism; tyrant, dictator, despot, autocrat, taskmaster, authoritarian, disciplinarian.

adj. severe, stern, strict, harsh, hard, austere, extreme, puritanical; firm, rigid, unbending, inflexible, immovable, unchanging; rigorous, exacting, uncompromising, stringent; grim, cruel, forbidding; unfeeling, hard-hearted; tyrannical, overbearing, domineering, despotic, totalitarian, authoritarian, oppressive, heavy-handed.

vb. be severe, be hard on, discipline, come down on (*inf.*), deal harshly with, insist, crack down on (*inf.*), clamp down on (*inf.*), put one's foot down (*inf.*), keep a tight rein on, rule with an iron hand, domineer, lord it over, dominate, oppress, tyrannize.

see also **963**

670 lenience

n. lenience, softness, tolerance, mildness, forbearance; mercy, clemency, forgiveness, pardon; kindness, compassion, favour.

adj. lenient, soft, gentle, mild, kind, compassionate, loving, soft-hearted, tender, sympathetic, easy-going; tolerant, forbearing, long-suffering; merciful, forgiving, clement.

vb. be lenient, go easy on, spare the rod; pass over, forbear, refrain; forgive, pardon; tolerate, bear.

671 command

n. command, direction, rule, charge, ordinance, mandate, directive, dictate, injunction, behest; bidding, call, summons; decree, ruling, law, act, fiat, canon, edict, bull, proclamation; writ, warrant, subpoena; demand, claim, request, requirement; final demand, ultimatum.

adj. commanding, powerful, authoritative.

vb. command, rule, direct, dictate, order, charge, decree, proclaim, ordain; lay down, prescribe; demand, claim, request, ask, require, exact; bid, call, summon, invite, send for.

see also **667, 954**

672 disobedience

n. disobedience, violation, disregard, neglect, non-observance, infringement, transgression, sin; misbehaviour, naughtiness; waywardness, stubbornness, insubordination, defiance, intractableness, unruliness; mutiny, revolt, rebellion, revolution, desertion, riot, insurgence.

rebel, revolutionary, radical, anarchist, reactionary, extremist, insurrectionist, insurgent, rioter, terrorist, mutineer, deserter; trouble-maker, brawler.

adj. disobedient, insubordinate; naughty, misbehaving; defiant, refractory, unsubmissive, disloyal, rebellious, intractable, unruly, lawless, uncontrollable, obstreperous; stubborn, wayward, insolent; revolutionary, mutinous, riotous, anarchistic, dissident, factious, insurgent.

vb. disobey, defy, fly in the face of, disregard, neglect, ignore, pay no attention to, not heed, violate, infringe, transgress, sin, break rules; misbehave; revolt, rebel, mutiny.

673 obedience

n. obedience, submission, compliance, loyalty, devotion, faithfulness, fidelity, constancy; meekness, docility.

adj. obedient, submissive, complaisant; law-abiding, well-behaved, good; devoted, loyal, faithful, respectful, dutiful, subservient, docile, acquiescent; round one's little finger (*inf.*), at one's beck and call, on a string, henpecked.

vb. obey, submit, do, keep, observe, follow, pay attention to, bow to, heed, comply, fulfil, agree, behave, do what one is told, do one's duty, do what is expected of one.

see also **654, 679**

674 compulsion

n. compulsion, force, drive, necessity, need, obligation, pressure, constraint, coercion, violence, strong arm, duress; urgency; conscription.

adj. compelling, compulsive, necessary, driving, pressing, coercive, unavoidable, irresistible, compulsory, urgent.

vb. compel, force, drive, coerce, constrain, impel, dictate, necessitate, oblige, require, urge, bring pressure to bear on, inflict.

675 master

n. master, mistress, chief, leader, head, superior, principal, lord; director, manager, supervisor, boss, management, overseer, authority, officer, official, mayor, mayoress; governor, governess, ruler, president, executive, sovereign, king, queen, prince, princess, emperor, empress, regent; captain, commander, lieutenant; big Chief (*sl.*), bigwig.

see also **34, 623**

676 servant

n. servant, dependant, assistant, right-hand man, subordinate, employee, worker, staff, personnel; slave, serf, vassal, captive, bondman, fag; orderly, menial; drudge, hack; chauffeur, butler, domestic, housekeeper, maid, nurse; porter, janitor, doorman; steward, stewardess, waiter, waitress, barman, barmaid; charwoman, cleaner.

adj. serving, ministering, attending, helping.

vb. serve, work for, be in the employment of, minister, aid, help, wait upon, care for, look after, nurse, mother; attend, do for (*inf.*).

677 sign of authority

n. badge of office, insignia, symbol, emblem, livery, uniform, regalia, rod, sceptre, mace, crown, staff, wand, rod, sword, stripe, decoration, flag.

678 freedom

n. freedom, liberty, independence, autonomy, democracy, self-determination; freedom of choice, free will; immunity, exemption, privilege, *carte blanche*, blank cheque, unrestraint; range, scope, play, field, room, leeway, latitude, opportunity, full play, free rein, elbow room.

adj. free, released, liberated, freed, at liberty, at large, let out, scot free; clear, extricated, unshackled, unfettered, unattached, unengaged, unconfined, unimpeded, unhindered, unrestrained; independent, autonomous, self-governing, democratic, enfranchised.

vb. free, have a free hand, have the run of; be independent, please onself, do as one wishes, fend for oneself, stand on one's own two feet, go it alone.

see also **680**

679 subjection

n. subjection, subservience, servitude, dependence, subordination, inferiority; allegiance, service; bondage, slavery, serfdom, servility, thrall.

adj. subject, dependent, subordinate, submissive, inferior, junior, accessory, subsidiary, satellite, auxiliary; accountable, answerable, liable, contingent.

vb. subject, enslave, dominate, subordinate, master, rule, hold captive, conquer, tame, subdue, subjugate, hold under one's thumb; repress, suppress, sit on.

be subject to, depend on, lean on; be at the mercy of, serve.

see also **35**

680 liberation

n. liberation, release, discharge, deliverance, rescue; extrication, disengagement, unravelling, loosing, unfettering, loosening, untying; emancipation, enfranchisement, manumission.

adj. freed, liberated, released, loose.

vb. liberate, free, release, discharge, deliver, save, rescue, set at liberty, restore, let out; extricate, loose, remove fetters, unfetter, untie, remove, unbind, undo, cut loose, disengage, unravel, let slip; ransom, pardon, dismiss, acquit; emancipate, enfranchise; shake off, free oneself of, get rid of, lose.

see also **601, 961**

681 restraint

n. restraint, control, constraint, discipline, self-control, self-discipline, self-restraint, reticence, reserve, caution; repression.

restriction, limitation, barrier, check, hindrance, impediment, obstacle, block, bar, curb, blockade, embargo, ban, veto; curfew; closed shop; censorship, news blackout; monopoly, cartel, protectionism.

custody, detention, imprisonment, confinement, impounding; chain, bond, irons, fetter, shackle.

adj. restraining, restrictive, controlling, limiting, strict, narrow, repressive; restrained, under control, in check, controlled, disciplined, reserved, cautious, calm, reticent, withdrawn, repressed, pent-up, bottled-up.

in custody, under arrest, imprisoned, detained, confined, in prison, in detention, behind bars, inside (*sl.*), in jug (*sl.*), in clink (*sl.*).

vb. restrain, control, limit, govern, check, arrest, curb, keep in check, hold back, narrow; discipline, bridle; repress, suppress, keep back, bottle up, muzzle, gag, subdue, quell, quash; hinder, impede, restrict, hamper; control oneself, pull oneself together, take a grip on oneself (*inf.*), sort oneself out (*inf.*), get organized.

take into custody, apprehend, help police with their inquiries, run in, turn in (*inf.*), turn over to, pick up, arrest, convict, take prisoner; imprison, detain, confine, put into prison, put away (*inf.*), shut up, lock up, put behind bars, intern, impound; tie, bind, chain, fetter, manacle.

682 prison

n. prison, gaol, jail, lock-up, nick (*sl.*), clink (*sl.*), jug (*sl.*), maximum-security prison, police station; cell, cage, guardroom; dungeon; detention camp, internment camp, concentration camp; Borstal, detention centre, approved home, remand centre.

683 keeper

n. keeper, custodian, warden, curator, attendant, official, guard; caretaker, porter, janitor, concierge, housekeeper, gatekeeper; watchman, lookout, patrol, scout; baby-sitter, governess, nurse, nanny, guardian; escort, bodyguard; gamekeeper, ranger; jailer, warder, prison governor, screw (*sl.*).

see also **593**

684 prisoner

n. prisoner, convict, culprit, con (*sl.*), inmate, star, gaolbird, young offender, captive, prisoner of war, internee; defendant, the accused, detainee; criminal, rogue.

see also **906, 940**

685 vicarious authority

n. commission, delegation, deputation, representation, authorization, committal, trusteeship; appointment, nomination, assignment; mission, embassy, envoy, legation, agency; devolution, decentralization; inauguration, installation, investiture, induction, ordination, coronation; accession.

trust, charge, mandate, authority, warrant; task, duty, errand, employment.

adj. commissioned, delegated, vicarious, deputed.

vb. commission, delegate, appoint, empower, grant authority to, authorize, charge, commit, assign, entrust; devolve, decentralize; name, nominate; inaugurate, invest, induct, ordain, install, place, establish; crown, enthrone; employ, engage, hire, contract.

represent, deputize, act on behalf of, stand in for.

686 annulment

n. annulment, cancellation, abrogation, dissolution, revocation, retraction, invalidation, nullification, reversal, repeal, abolition, countermand.

dismissal, removal, displacement, the sack (*inf.*), the boot (*sl.*), the push (*sl.*); retirement, lay-off, redundancy, natural wastage; deposal, dethronement, impeachment.

demotion, downgrading, degradation.

adj. annulled, cancelled, null and void; rained off, abandoned, postponed.

vb. annul, cancel, abolish, repeal, revoke, dissolve, rescind, quash, render void, nullify, invalidate; refute, counteract, reverse, repudiate, countermand.

dismiss, oust, overthrow, unseat, remove from office, discharge, depose, dethrone, displace, suspend, sack, fire, give the push to (*sl.*), give the boot to (*sl.*), give papers to, show the door to, strike off the register, write out, pension off; relieve, replace, recall; impeach, unfrock; demote, degrade, downgrade.

687 resignation

n. resignation, abdication, retirement, relinquishment, renunciation, withdrawal, departure, leaving, surrender, desertion; pension, golden handshake, leaving gift, leaving present, gratuity, superannuation.

adj. resignatory; retired, former,

previous, outgoing, one-time, sometime, emeritus.

vb. resign, quit, leave, depart, vacate office, relinquish, abandon, step down, stand down, stand aside, retire, abdicate, give up office, walk out of, hand in one's notice, tender one's resignation, hand in one's papers.

688 consignee

n. consignee, delegate, representative, substitute, deputy; trustee, executor, nominee, proxy; intermediary, middleman, negotiator, broker; committee, board, panel, group, organization, deputation, cabinet, decision maker.

ambassador, envoy, commissioner, delegation, emissary, diplomat, consul, attaché, plenipotentiary, nuncio; embassy, consulate, mission.

see also **619, 689**

689 deputy

n. deputy, assistant, second-in-command, right-hand man; delegate, substitute, representative, proxy, surrogate, stand-in, agent, proxy, vicar; ambassador, commissioner; spokesman, mouthpiece.

adj. deputy, deputizing, vice, pro, acting.

vb. deputize, substitute, represent, stand in for, act on behalf of.

B Special

690 permission

n. permission, liberty, leave, freedom, consent; authorization, legalization, confirmation, endorsement, affirmation, sanction; authority, permit, grant, charter, licence, certificate, concession, allowance; pass, passport, visa, password; letter of commendation; go-ahead, green light (*inf.*), all-clear, clearance, nod; free hand, free rein, *carte blanche*, blank cheque.

adj. permitting, allowing; tolerant, lenient, permissive; permitted, granted, allowed, authorized, approved.

vb. permit, let, allow, grant, give permission; consent, approve, favour, have no objections; authorize, warrant, legalize, sanction, certify, charter, franchise, license; give the go-ahead, give the green light (*inf.*), give clearance, rubber-stamp (*inf.*); tolerate, concede, bear, suffer.

691 prohibition

n. prohibition, forbiddance, obstruction, suppression, repression, refusal, interdiction, injunction, disallowance, countermand, ban, veto, embargo, boycott, taboo.

adj. prohibiting, forbidding; prohibitive, excessive, restrictive; prohibited, forbidden, illegal, illicit, unlawful, taboo, impermissible.

vb. prohibit, forbid, refuse, withhold, deny, disallow, prevent, hinder, hamper, preclude, restrain, interdict; ban, veto, boycott, say no to, debar, exclude, shut out; obstruct, oppose, suppress, repress, restrict, stop, halt.

692 consent

n. consent, acceptance, agreement, allowance, permission, approval, assent, concurrence, acquiescence, compliance.

adj. consenting, agreeable, willing, acquiescent.

vb. consent, accept, allow, agree, approve, assent, say yes to, be in favour of, concur, acquiesce, accede; concede, grant, yield, acknowledge, vouchsafe.

see also **690**

693 offer

n. offer, tender, bid, submission; approach, advance, overture; proposal, proposition, presentation, suggestion.

adj. on offer, available, for sale, advertised.

vb. offer, hold out, present, suggest, propose, submit, extend, move, put forward, put forth, tender, bid, approach; make overtures, make advances; lay at one's feet, sacrifice, proffer.

volunteer, offer oneself, come forward, stand for.

694 refusal

n. refusal, rejection, denial, declension; rebuff, snub, slap in the face, insult; veto, ban, exclusion.

adj. refusing, unwilling, uncompliant, resisting, hard-hearted, reluctant.

vb. refuse, reject, not want, decline, resist, ignore, turn down, say no to, not hear of, exclude, disallow, shun, repudiate, repel, spurn, rebuff, scorn, snub, repulse, turn one's back on, turn a deaf ear to, set one's face against, wash one's hands of, harden one's heart against; slam the door in someone's face (*inf.*); withhold, deny, hold back.

see also **469, 542**

695 request

n. request, call, petition, invitation, bid, application, demand, appeal, plea, address; inquiry, question; offer, proposal, proposition; prayer, entreaty, intercession, invocation, supplication; importunity, urgency.

adj. requesting, petitioning, supplicatory, imprecatory, invocatory, prayerful, begging, on bended knees; urgent, importunate, persistent, clamorous.

vb. request, call, ask, express a wish, apply for, summon, demand, implore, beseech, beg, appeal, entreat, pray, call on, petition, crave, plead, adjure; inquire, invite.

urge, ply, press, persist, pester, bother, coax, clamour.

canvass, solicit, importune, tout, hawk; appeal for money, pass the hat round (*inf.*), have a whip-round (*inf.*), make a collection.

696 protest

n. protest, deprecation, disapproval, objection, complaint, dissent, expostulation, remonstrance.

demonstration, demo (*inf.*), rally, sit-in, mass meeting, march, protest march, strike, hunger strike.

adj. protesting, deprecatory, expostulatory, remonstrative.

vb. protest, depreciate, speak against, lodge a protest, ask not to, disapprove, object, disagree, oppose, criticize, demur, remonstrate, expostulate; groan, jeer, murmur, heckle, sneer; demonstrate, march, strike, go on strike, picket.

see also **144**

697 petitioner

n. petitioner, supplicant, suppliant, applicant, claimant, candidate, bidder; inquirer, advertiser; lobby, lobbyist, pressure group, canvasser, hawker, tout, pedlar, vendor; beggar, scrounger, cadger, sponger, loafer, idler, vagabond, tramp, down-and-out.

C Conditional

698 promise

n. promise, covenant, pledge, contract, pact, undertaking, commitment, consent, word, vow, word of honour; gentleman's agreement.

engagement, betrothal; fiancée, fiancé, intended (*inf.*).

adj. promised, committed, pledged, bound; engaged, betrothed.

vb. promise, agree, undertake, commit, declare, covenant, pledge, contract, consent, vow, swear; warrant, guarantee; bind onself, give one's word, pledge one's honour; become engaged, betrothe.

699 contract

n. contract, agreement, covenant, undertaking, pact, concordat, promise, pledge, understanding, arrangement, settlement, transaction, bargain, deal (*inf.*); negotiation, compromise, give and take; treaty, convention, alliance, league, charter, entente; gentleman's agreement.

adj. contractual, conventional, promissory.

vb. contract, agree, covenant, undertake, pledge, promise, arrange, bargain, deal, negotiate, hammer out, stipulate; sign, sign on the dotted line, agree on terms, settle, come to an agreement, accept an offer, shake on it (*inf.*); ratify, confirm.

see also **24, 643**

700 conditions

n. conditions, terms, provisions, specifications, frame of reference, strings, proviso, contingencies, arrangements, limitations, restrictions, reservations, exceptions, escape clause, *sine qua non*.

adj. conditional, provisional, contingent, with strings attached, granted on certain terms, dependent on, subject to.

vb. negotiate, discuss; propose conditions, postulate, stipulate, attach strings, insist on, impose.

see also **403**

701 security

n. security, surety, warranty, covenant, bond, promise, pledge, earnest, token, certainty; deposit, caution money, money in advance, forfeit, stake, insurance, bail, pawn, mortgage, collateral; liability, responsibility; hostage, captive, prisoner.

adj. guaranteed, pledged, pawned, on deposit.

vb. give security, guarantee, pledge, sign for, insure, assure, underwrite, mortgage, stake, pawn; give bail, go bail; stand surety, bail out; stand for, back.

702 observance

n. observance, attention, performance, doing, carrying out, keeping, heeding, practice; obedience, compliance, devotion.

adj. observant, practising, professing; diligent, conscientious; exact, scrupulous, pedantic; dependable, responsible; loyal, faithful, devoted, obedient.

vb. observe, heed, keep, do, carry out, follow, adhere to, perform, discharge, practise, adopt, conform to, fulfil, comply; keep on the right side of the law; hold fast, stand by, embrace, profess, give allegiance to, be loyal to.

703 non-observance

n. non-observance, neglect, disregard, omission; breaking, infringement, violation, transgression, trespass, breach, sin; disobedience, disloyalty, infidelity; inattention, carelessness, indifference, irresponsibility.

adj. non-observant, negligent,

careless, indifferent; unfaithful, disobedient.

vb. not observe, not practise, not keep; break, disobey, violate, infringe, transgress, breach, contravene; neglect, disregard, omit; break faith, be faithless.

704 compromise

n. compromise, bargaining, agreement, understanding, settlement; give and take, concessions, mutual concessions; middle course, middle ground, half-way house; composition; *modus vivendi.*

vb. compromise, make concessions, give and take, meet half-way, go fifty-fifty, steer a middle course, split the differences; negotiate, come to an agreement, come to an understanding, reconcile, settle, adjust, agree to differ.

D Possessive relations

705 acquisition

n. acquisition, getting, obtainment, procuration; recovery, retrieval, redemption.

gain, benefit, advantage, reward, income, earnings, wages, salary, grant, profit, receipts, proceeds, emolument; collection, gathering, produce, output, yield, fruit, harvest, crop; addition, accrual, accumulation.

adj. obtainable, available; acquisitive, hoarding, grasping.

profitable, fruitful, productive, advantageous, worthwhile, lucrative, paying its way, remunerative.

vb. acquire, get, obtain, take possession of, make one's own, appropriate, lay hold of, procure; force from, grab, seize, capture, pocket, secure, draw, tap; gain, accept, receive, make, collect, earn, benefit, win, accumulate; gather, harvest, glean, reap.

get back, recover, retrieve, regain, redeem.

buy, purchase; profit, capitalize on, cash in on (*inf.*); inherit, come into, be left.

see also **716**

706 loss

n. loss, mislaying, misplacement; dispossession, deprivation, forfeiture, want, bereavement; insolvency, bankruptcy.

adj. lost, missing, misplaced, mislaid, nowhere to be found, hidden, obscured, vanished, strayed, gone; lacking, wanting, deprived of, bereft; overdrawn, insolvent, bankrupt; unprofitable, disadvantageous, wasted, irretrievable, desperate, hopeless, futile.

vb. lose, mislay, misplace, not find; let slip, drop, miss, fail, forfeit; deprive, displace; waste, squander; incur losses, go bankrupt.

707 possession

n. possession, ownership, occupancy, residence, tenancy, tenure; possessorship, proprietorship; hold, mastery, grasp, control, custody; purchase.

adj. possessing, having, owning; possessive, exclusive, monopolistic, selfish; possessed, owned, purchased, enjoyed, in possession of.

vb. possess, own, have, hold, keep, retain, grasp, occupy, control, maintain, use, boast of, enjoy; have title to, have rights to, have claim upon; monopolize, hog (*inf.*), have all to oneself, corner; include, comprise, contain; belong, appertain.

708 non-possession

n. non-possession, loss, deprivation, surrender of rights; lease; no man's land.

adj. not owning, lacking; destitute, poor, impoverished, penniless; unowned, unoccupied, unpossessed, unattached, free, ownerless, virgin, unclaimed, lost, independent, unbound.

see also **706**

709 joint possession

n. joint possession, co-ownership, cooperation, participation, partnership, sharing; socialism, communism, public ownership, nationalization, worker participation, profit-sharing; community, cooperative, collective, kibbutz; joint fund, kitty, pool; share, portion.

participator, partner, member, partaker, shareholder, worker-director.

adj. cooperative, joint, participatory, common, communal, profit-sharing; involved, committed, dedicated, connected with.

vb. participate, share, cooperate, join, take part in, partake, go halves.

see also **639**

710 possessor

n. possessor, owner, holder, master, partner; buyer, purchaser; occupant, occupier, tenant, resident, lodger, lessee, landlord, landlady, landowner, landholder, proprietor, proprietress; heir, heiress, inheritor.

711 property

n. property, land, assets, resources, means, goods, riches, wealth, valuables, inheritance, capital, investment, equity, land, holding, estate.

belongings, equipment, paraphernalia, things, trappings, fixtures, furniture, furnishings, goods and chattels; appurtenances, accoutrements; personal effects, luggage, baggage; burden, encumbrance, impedimenta.

712 retention

n. retention, holding, keeping; hold, grasp, clench, clinch, grip, hug, embrace, clasp; confinement, stranglehold, tight grip, straitjacket.

adj. retentive, holding; retained, held, kept.

vb. retain, hold, keep, keep hold of, grasp, clench, grip, clinch, clasp, clutch, embrace, hug, squeeze, press; cling to, stick to, fasten on, secure, hold fast; contain, restrain, enclose, confine; maintain, preserve; cherish, nurture, harbour; detain, reserve, withhold.

713 non-retention

n. relinquishment, abandonment, renunciation, disposal; exemption, dispensation, release; divorce, dissolution.

adj. abandoned, thrown away, rejected, marooned.

vb. not retain, relinquish, abandon, renounce, let go, part with, dispose of, discard, throw away, jettison, release; waive, lift restrictions, derestrict, exempt.

see also **556, 921**

714 transfer

n. transference, conveyancing, assignation; changeover, change of hands; devolution, delegation; exchange, conversion, interchange; sale, lease; bequest, endowment, legacy.

adj. transferable, negotiable, interchangeable, exchangeable; transferred, made over.

vb. convey, transfer, sell, sign,

consign, assign, change over, deliver, make over; entrust, commit; exchange, convert; devolve, delegate, decentralize; bequeath, will, make a will, pass on, hand down.

see also **268**

715 giving

n. giving, bestowal, conferral, granting, imparting, delivery.

gift, present, donation, grant, award, presentation, prize; allowance, subsidy, aid, assistance; tip, gratuity; bounty, largesse, windfall; leaving present, golden handshake; charity, hand-out, alms; bequest, legacy; blessing, favour, grace, mercy.

sacrifice, offering, worship, dedication, consecration; offering, collection, offertory.

giver, donor, contributor.

adj. giving, charitable, generous, liberal, sacrificial; given, free.

vb. give, donate, grant, award, present, contribute, render, remit, convey, supply, furnish, provide, afford, dispense, hand out, dole out, distribute, administer, deal out, mete out, subsidize, give towards; bestow, confer, endow, invest with, impart, communicate; expend, spend, lavish; offer, sacrifice.

716 receiving

n. receiving, reception, acquisition, acceptance, admission, collection; receipts, proceeds, dues, monies, toll.

recipient, receiver, beneficiary; object, target, victim, guinea pig; customer, client; trustee, payee, addressee, earner; heir, heiress.

adj. receiving, receptive, welcoming, hospitable, sensitive.

vb. receive, accept, admit, be given, get, gain, acquire, collect, obtain, draw, take in, derive, come by, attract, come in for, be on the receiving end; take up, levy, charge; be received, accrue, come in, fall to one.

see also **302, 705**

717 apportionment

n. apportionment, allotment, sharing, division, distribution, dealing, rationing.

portion, share, allocation, section, piece, part, fraction, fragment; helping, serving, slice, ration; proportion, quota, allowance; cut (*sl.*), split, parcel, lot.

vb. apportion, allot, distribute, divide, share out, hand out, dole out, dish out (*inf.*), farm out, parcel out, deal, assign, dispose, administer, give away, dispense, ration.

see also **55**

718 lending

n. lending; loan, advance, mortgage, allowance, credit, investment, credit card, credit account, hire purchase, never-never (*inf.*).

bank, building society, pawnbroker, pop-shop (*sl.*); banker, bank manager, lender, financier, money-lender, creditor; usurer, shark, angel (*sl.*), Shylock.

vb. lend, let out, allow to borrow, trust with, entrust, hire out, let, lease, charter; loan, finance, support, back, advance, grant, lend on security, put out at interest, give credit, risk.

719 borrowing

n. borrowing, rental, hire, loan; assumption; appropriation, adoption, importation; imitation, copy.

vb. borrow, rent, hire, lease, charter; take on tick (*inf.*), raise money, pawn, cadge; touch for (*sl.*); obtain, use, adopt.

720 taking

n. taking, possession, acceptance, appropriation, requisition; seizure, grab, capture; kidnapping, abduction; dispossession, deprivation, extortion, confiscation; recovery, retrieval.

taker, possessor; seizer, grabber, raider; kidnapper, abductor.

adj. taking, grasping, greedy, rapacious, extortionate, ravenous.

vb. take, possess, accept, receive, get, obtain, win, gain; seize, lay hold of, appropriate, take for oneself, acquire, avail oneself of, adopt, assume; grip, clasp; catch, apprehend, grasp; grab, trap, snatch, capture, raid; take away, steal, kidnap, abduct; confiscate, commandeer; recover, retrieve; take from, remove, deprive of, divest of, dispossess, extort, strip, disinherit.

see also **722**

721 restitution

n. restitution, restoration, return, giving back, reinstatement; retrieval, recovery, repossession, repatriation; recompense, repayment, refund, amends, compensation, reimbursement, remuneration, reparation, indemnification, redemption, satisfaction.

adj. restitutive, restoring, compensatory, redemptive.

vb. restore, return, give back, reinstate, reinstall; rehabilitate, repair; recover, get back, retrieve, recoup, regain, retake, reclaim.

make restitution, refund, make amends, reimburse, repay, compensate, indemnify, redeem, ransom.

see also **589**

722 stealing

n. stealing, theft, larceny, robbery, burglary, house-breaking, shop-lifting; vandalism, looting, pilfering, ransacking, pillage, plunder, sacking; hijacking, skyjacking (*inf.*); kidnapping, abduction; hold-up, stick-up (*inf.*), mugging (*inf.*), hit-and-run-raid, smash-and-grab-raid, job (*sl.*); embezzlement, misappropriation, extortion, fraud.

adj. thieving, light-fingered.

vb. steal, take, burgle, thieve, rob, remove, go off with, get away with, make off with, run off with, seize, pilfer, pick-pocket, pinch (*sl.*), nick (*sl.*), filch, fleece, nobble (*sl.*), knock off (*sl.*), rip off (*sl.*), screw (*sl.*), shop-lift, purloin; abduct, kidnap, mug (*inf.*), hijack, skyjack; embezzle, misappropriate, defraud, swindle, cheat, fiddle, peculate, smuggle; loot, rifle, sack, raid, ransack, plunder, pillage.

be stolen, fall off the back of a lorry (*inf.*).

723 thief

n. thief, robber, stealer; burglar, house-breaker, shop-lifter, mugger, attacker; pilferer, pick-pocket; hijacker, skyjacker (*inf.*), highwayman; safe-blower, safe-cracker; kidnapper, abductor; plunderer, looter; embezzler, swindler, cheater, fiddler; crook, rogue, thug, smuggler, pirate.

see also **684**

724 booty

n. booty, prize, haul, loot, swag (*sl.*), takings, plunder, spoil, winnings, stolen goods, goods fallen off the back of a lorry (*inf.*), capture, premium, contraband, prey.

725 business

n. business, trade, commerce, business affairs, traffic; negotiations, bargaining, transactions, marketing, buying and selling; barter, exchange, swap (*inf.*).

adj. business, trading, commercial, mercantile.

vb. transact business, trade, traffic, deal in, handle, market, buy and sell; negotiate, bargain; exchange, barter, swap (*inf.*).

726 purchase

n. purchase, buying, obtaining, acquisition; shopping, payment, investment, marketing.

buyer, purchaser, consumer, shopper, customer, patron, client, clientele, custom, market, patronage.

vb. purchase, buy, get, obtain, gain, acquire; go shopping, pay for, invest, exchange, bargain, sign; patronize; go window-shopping, buy back, redeem.

727 sale

n. sale, disposal, selling, marketing, trading; clearance, sell-out; bazaar, jumble sale, rummage sale; auction, public sale; sales talk, salesmanship, high-pressure salesmanship, sales patter, promotion, advertising.

seller, vendor, retailer, shopkeeper, shop assistant, salesman, commercial traveller, sales rep.

adj. saleable, marketable, in demand; available, on the market.

vb. sell, dispose, market, flog (*sl.*), retail, trade, dump, vend; ask, demand; transfer, transact, exchange; peddle, hawk; reduce prices, sell off; auction, come under the hammer.

728 trader

n. trader, dealer, retailer, shopkeeper, tradesman, middleman, wholesaler, exporter, importer, shipper, trafficker, merchant; businessman, industrialist, capitalist, manager, financier, entrepreneur, tycoon, stockbroker, speculator.

pedlar, hawker, tinker, huckster; tout; rag-and-bone man.

729 merchandise

n. merchandise, commodities, stock, wares, articles, goods, property, product, possessions; things, stuff; line, supplies; consumer goods, consumer durables.

730 market

n. market, mart, square, mall, arcade, shopping centre, shopping precinct, exchange, emporium; shop, store, supermarket, department store, multiple, chain store, boutique, hypermarket; kiosk, stand, stall, booth, barrow, bazaar; place of business, premises, concern, establishment.

731 money

n. money, currency, legal tender, cash, bank notes, bread (*sl.*), dough (*sl.*), lolly (*sl.*); change, small change; cheque, credit card, hire purchase; pay, salary, wages, pocket money, pin money; sum, amount, balance; funds, credit, finance, reserves, capital, wealth, wherewithal.

adj. monetary, pecuniary, financial.

vb. mint, coin, issue, monetize, put in circulation; withdraw, remove from circulation, call in, demonetize.

732 treasury

n. treasury, bank, exchequer, repository, coffer, vault, strongroom, depository, safe, cash box; cash register, till; money-box, piggy bank; wallet, purse, bag.

733 treasurer

n. treasurer, receiver, cashier, banker, purser, bursar, paymaster, accountant, teller, steward, trustee.

734 wealth

n. wealth, riches, money, affluence, luxury, opulence, prosperity, fortune, money to burn; profits, assets, means, resources.

rich man, millionaire, moneybags, man of means, capitalist.

adj. rich, wealthy, affluent, prosperous, luxurious, well-off, in the money, well-to-do, well provided for, made of money (*inf.*), rolling in it (*inf.*).

vb. get rich, make a fortune, come into money, line one's pocket; live comfortably, afford, bear the expense of, make both ends meet.

735 poverty

n. poverty, impoverishment, poorness; destitution, scarcity, privation, penury, pennilessness, pauperism, indigence, insolvency; beggary, mendicancy; poor man, pauper, beggar.

adj. poor, needy, destitute, underprivileged, distressed; impecunious, poverty-stricken, penniless, hard up, broke (*inf.*), bankrupt, insolvent; begging, mendicant; starving, hungry, empty-handed, down-and-out.

vb. be poor, find it hard going, live from hand to mouth, starve; impoverish, ruin, eat out of house and home.

736 credit

n. credit, trust, reliability; loan, account, credit account, credit card; creditor, mortgagee.

vb. credit, charge, charge to an account, credit one's account; give credit, defer payment, lend.

737 debt

n. debt, liability, obligation, claim, commitment, indebtedness, due, duty; debts, bills, amount due, amount owing, accounts outstanding, score, deficit, arrears.

debtor, borrower, purchaser, buyer, mortgagor.

adj. indebted, liable, answerable, responsible, committed, under obligation; owing, in debt, overdrawn, in the red; unpaid, due, outstanding, payable, unsettled, in arrears, overdue.

vb. be in debt, owe, be under obligation, overdraw, run up a bill, fall into debt, be in Queer Street (*sl.*).

738 payment

n. payment, remittance; settlement, clearance, reckoning; recompense, restitution, compensation, reimbursement, refund, subsidy; deposit, instalment, down payment, first payment.

pay, wages, salary, earnings, remuneration, emolument; fee, stipend, allowance, expenses, honorarium; pay packet, pay slip; payroll.

adj. paying, remunerative, not owing; paid, discharged, out of debt.

vb. pay, make payment for; repay, reward, remunerate; settle, discharge, defray, meet, bear the cost of, foot the bill; recompense, reimburse, compensate, recoup, refund; subsidize; pay on the nail; contribute, chip in (*inf.*), fork out (*inf.*), cough up (*sl.*); spend, expend; stand, treat.

739 non-payment

n. non-payment, failure to pay, default, bankruptcy, insolvency, liquidation, crash, ruin; overdraft, overdrawn account; debts.

non-payer, defaulter, bankrupt, lame duck; embezzler.

adj. non-paying, defaulting, insolvent, bankrupt, failed, ruined, on the rocks (*inf.*), bust (*inf.*), liquidated.

vb. not pay, default, fall into arrears, go bankrupt, go into liquidation, go to the wall, fold up (*inf.*), fail, be wound up, go bust (*inf.*), crash, go under; write off; bankrupt, ruin, wind up, put in the hands of a receiver, liquidate.

740 expenditure

n. expenditure, outlay, payment, disbursement, spending, costs, expenses, outgoings, investment.

vb. spend, expend, pay, pay out, lay out, invest, foot the bill; exhaust, discharge, consume; squander, waste, lavish.

741 income

n. income, receipts, revenue, returns, earnings, salary, wages, profit, assets, proceeds, dividends, gains, takings, turn-over, box-office receipts, gate-money.

receipt, acknowledgement, slip, voucher, record.

742 accounts

n. accounts, bookkeeping; account, bill, invoice, reckoning, statement, balance sheet; ledger, log, cash-book; budget.

accountant, chartered accountant, auditor, bookkeeper, actuary, cashier.

adj. accounting, budgetary.

vb. account, keep the books, enter, debit, credit, balance; budget; cook the books (*inf.*), falsify, fiddle (*sl.*).

743 price

n. price, cost, expense, amount, charge, toll, fee, fare; rent, rental, hire charge; value, face value, worth; evaluation, valuation, estimate, quotation.

taxation, tax, duty, levy, tariff, inland revenue; excise, custom, impost, tribute, dues; rates, rateable value, assessment.

price control, price freeze, austerity, squeeze; cost of living, price index; price tag, label, ticket.

adj. priced, marked, charged, valued, worth.

vb. price, value, charge, assess, estimate, put a price on, reckon, rate; demand, ask; reduce, mark down; increase, mark up.

cost, be worth, go for, sell for, fetch, come to, amount to.

tax, exact, levy, put a tax on, raise taxes; pay taxes.

744 discount

n. discount, reduction, rebate, allowance, deduction, cut, subtraction, remission, concession; depreciation; subsidy.

vb. reduce, lower, rebate, deduct, cut, take off, knock off, subtract, allow; depreciate.

745 dearness

n. dearness, expensiveness, expense, costliness; exorbitance, excessiveness, extravagance.

adj. dear, expensive, costly, high-priced, pricey (*inf.*); exorbitant, too high, overpriced, excessive, prohibitive, extortionate, immoderate, unreasonable, extravagant, lavish, steep (*inf.*), stiff (*inf.*).

vb. be dear, cost a lot, cost a pretty penny (*inf.*); go up, increase, revalue; overcharge, exploit, bleed, fleece, extort.

746 cheapness

n. cheapness, inexpensiveness, competitiveness, reasonableness; bargain, good value, good buy.

adj. cheap, inexpensive, low-priced, moderate, reasonable, fair, peanuts (*sl.*).

family-sized, economy-sized, economy, bargain, standard; reduced, cut-price, half-price, marked down, dirt cheap.

free, gratuitous, for nothing, without charge, complimentary, gratis, on the house, for love.

vb. be cheap, get one's money's worth; fall in price, decrease, cheapen, depreciate, mark down, devalue.

747 liberality

n. liberality, generosity, benevolence, bounteousness, bounty, largesse; kindness, giving, charity, hospitality, cordiality.

adj. liberal, generous, big-hearted, open-handed, bountiful, lavish, unsparing, unstinting, munificent; kind, benevolent, unselfish, charitable, beneficient.

vb. be liberal, give generously, lavish, heap upon, spare no expense, go beyond what one can afford.

748 economy

n. economy, thrift, care, prudence, housekeeping, stewardship, management, frugality, husbandry, providence; parsimony, stinginess; saving; retrenchment.

adj. economical, economizing, careful, prudent, good, saving, thrifty, frugal, sparing; stingy, mean; convenient, time-saving, labour-saving.

vb. economize, cut back, keep costs down, cut costs, cut corners, tighten one's belt (*inf.*), make ends meet, live within one's means; manage, steward, husband, save, conserve.

749 extravagance

n. extravagance, wastefulness, squandering, prodigality, lavishness, immoderateness; money to burn, shopping spree, spending spree, no thought of tommorow; prodigal, wastrel, spendthrift, squanderer.

adj. extravagant, wasteful, squandering, prodigal, lavish, over-generous, immoderate, exorbitant, reckless, careless, profligate.

vb. waste, squander, throw away, have money to burn, spend money like water, hang the expense, blow (*sl.*), blue (*sl.*); fritter away, dissipate; go too far, overdo it.

750 parsimony

n. parsimony, parsimoniousness, stinginess, scrimping, niggardliness, penny-pinching, cheese-paring, meanness, miserliness, penuriousness; niggard, miser, screw; greed, avarice, covetousness, avidity, voracity, gluttony.

adj. parsimonious, stingy, niggardly, miserly, mean, tight-fisted, close-fisted, penny-pinching, scrimping; sparing, chary,

greedy, avaricious, voracious, possessive, acquisitive, grasping, grabby (*inf.*), itchy (*inf.*), rapacious, covetous, avid.

vb. be parsimonious, scrimp, stint, skimp; over-economize; be greedy, always want more.

VI Affections

A Affections in general

751 affections

n. affections, qualities, character, nature, make-up; personality, psyche, heart, soul, breast, inner self; temperament, disposition, spirit, temper, mood, state of mind, frame of mind, humour; tendency, inclination, bent, bias.

adj. affected, characterized, formed,

moulded, disposed, inclined, predisposed.

see also 5, 58

752 feeling

n. feeling, emotion, affection, sentiment, passion; experience, sense, impression, consciousness, sensation, perception, sympathy, warmth, tenderness, sensitivity, empathy; fervour, ardour, enthusiasm.

adj. feeling, emotional, sentimental, romantic, passionate, fervent, intense, impassioned, dramatic, burning, earnest, moving, tender; felt, experienced, heart-felt, thrilled, moved, affected, touched.

vb. feel, sense, experience, go through, enjoy, suffer, undergo, bear, endure.

move, affect, touch, stir, impress, excite, influence, quicken, touch one's heart, touch to the quick; appreciate, respond; thrill, tingle.

753 sensitivity

n. sensitivity, sensibility, susceptibility, awareness, consciousness, responsiveness, excitability.

five senses, sight, hearing, smell, taste, touch; sixth sense, intuition, feminine intuition; extra-sensory perception.

adj. sensitive, aware, conscious of, alive to, awake to, susceptible, impressionable, receptive, sensible; sensory, sentient.

raw, tender, bare, sore, bruised, delicate, painful, oversensitive, hypersensitive; exposed, open, vulnerable.

754 insensitivity

n. insensitivity, insensibility, unawareness, unresponsiveness, inexcitability, impassivness; apathy, indifference, lethargy, aloofness, coldness; hypnosis, numbness, paralysis; dream, trance, coma, stupor; hardness of heart, callousness; stoic, ascetic; iceberg.

adj. insensitive, insusceptible, unimpressionable, unresponsive, inexcitable, unmoved, unaffected, unaware, unconscious, dead to, blind to, oblivious to, lost to, insensible; lethargic, dull, unenthusiastic, apathetic, indifferent, cool, aloof; unfeeling, unemotional, passionless, unresponsive, frigid, cold, numb, paralyzed; blank, poker-faced, dead pan, expressionless; thick-skinned, hard-hearted, callous, cold-blooded.

vb. deaden, numb, paralyze, stupefy, stun, harden, sear, blunt, dull, drug; turn off (*inf.*), switch off (*inf*); be unaffected, leave cold.

755 excitation

n. excitation, stimulation, activation, animation, inspiration, quickening; incitement, provocation, agitation, excitement; captivation, fascination, interest.

adj. exciting, stimulating, inspiring, moving, sparkling, exhilarating, thrilling, delightful; captivating, fascinating, interesting, absorbing, gripping, stirring, tantalizing, compelling, impressive, dramatic, sensational.

vb. excite, stimulate, arouse, activate, move, stir, work up, whip up, incite, influence, affect, provoke, awaken, touch, interest, animate, quicken, inspire; inflame, intensify, kindle, fire, light up; electrify, galvanize, energize.

absorb, fascinate, attract attention, impress, intrigue; tantalize, tease, anger, cause a stir; catch one's attention, come home, arrest, compel, engage; make one's mouth water, whet the appetite; knock for six (*inf.*), take one's breath away; delight, thrill, exhilarate, turn on (*inf.*), switch on (*inf.*).

see also 756, 829

756 excitability

n. excitability, impetuousness, boisterousness, instability, emotionalism, restlessness, agitation, irritability, intolerance.

excitement, exhilaration, thrill, ecstasy, transport; rage, fury, outburst, agony; hysterics, delirium; fuss, big song and dance (*inf.*), hullabaloo, tizzy (*sl.*), tiz-woz (*sl.*), dither (*inf.*), fluster, stew (*inf.*), to-do.

adj. excited, moved, stirred, inspired, thrilled, quickened, enthusiastic, eager, impressed, delighted, pleased, happy, joyful, touched.

excitable, sensitive, highly-strung, nervous, easily excited, emotional; impulsive, quick-tempered, impetuous; moody, temperamental; impatient, irritable, touchy, edgy, jumpy, jittery, restless, fidgety; tense, uptight, all worked up (*inf.*), keyed up, a bundle of nerves (*inf.*); distraught, beside onself; mad, fuming, raging.

vb. be excited, thrill; let oneself go, get carried away, abandon oneself, freak out (*sl.*); tingle, glow, palpitate, pant; tremble, quiver, shake.

get excited, work oneself up; feet, flap (*inf.*), shuffle, fuss; rage, fume, explode, flare up, boil over (*inf.*).

see also 755

757 inexcitability

n. inexcitability, imperturbability, stability, composure, calmness, coolness, level-headedness, even temper, steadiness; peace of mind, serenity, tranquillity; self-possession, self-control, self-restraint, self-assurance; detachment, aloofness; stoicism.

patience, endurance, forbearance, long-suffering, submission, humility, meekness, resignation.

adj. inexcitable, calm, cool, composed, collected, self-possessed, dispassionate, imperturbable, unflappable (*inf.*), unruffled, immovable, stable, level-headed, even-tempered, easygoing, moderate, sedate, serene, tranquil, placid, inoffensive, mild, phlegmatic; patient, forbearing, uncomplaining, meek, submissive, philosophic, stoical; detached, aloof, disinterested, spiritless, nonchalant, blasé, casual.

vb. keep calm, keep one's temper, keep one's cool (*sl.*), keep one's shirt on (*sl.*), not bat an eyelid; calm down, compose oneself, control oneself, relax, take hold of oneself, pull oneself together, cool it (*sl.*), simmer down (*inf.*), cool off.

bear, tolerate, endure, put up with, stomach (*inf.*), stick it out (*inf.*), swallow, brook, resign oneself to, grin and bear it, submit to, make the best of.

B Sensation

758 touch

n. touch, feeling, contact, tactility; feel, touching, stroking, massage, manipulation; tickle, titillation, itching, scratching, pricking, stinging, shivers.

adj. tactile, tactual, tangible, touchable, palpable.

vb. touch, feel, press, squeeze, stroke, rub, finger, paw, smooth, caress, fondle, massage, manipulate, lick, kiss; tap, pat, hit, strike; explore, feel for, grope, fumble; grasp, grip, grab, grapple, clasp, clutch; tickle, titillate, itch; graze, scratch, prick, sting.

759 heat

n. heat, hotness, warmth, tepidity; temperature, thermometer; thermostat, hot weather, summer, heatwave, scorcher (*inf.*), dog days; fire, blaze, glow, light, sparkle, flicker, conflagration; ardour, fervour, zeal, passion, intensity.

adj. thermal; hot, very warm, torrid, parched; burning, fiery, blazing, ignited, lit, alight, on fire, in flames, glowing, incandescent, smoking; heated, molten; sweltering, baking, scorching, sizzling, scalding, grilling, roasting; tropical, humid, sticky, close, sultry, muggy, stifling, oppressive; warm, tepid, lukewarm; temperate, mild, fair, sunny, summery; bright, clear; intense, fervent, vehement, passionate, ardent, excited.

vb. be hot, burn, flame, burst into flames, catch fire, flare up, flicker, glow; smoke, fume, reek, smoulder, smother, suffocate; cook, boil, scald, seethe, fry, sizzle, roast, parch, scorch, bake, swelter.

760 cold

n. cold, coldness, chilliness, frigidity, frozenness, iciness, frostiness, congelation; chill, nip, shivers, shivering; cold snap, arctic conditions; ice, icicle, glacier, iceberg, black ice; frost, rime, hoar-frost; hail, hailstorm; snow, snowflake, snowdrift, snowstorm, blizzard, avalanche, sleet, slush.

adj. cryoscopic, cold, cool, chilly, fresh, crisp, brisk, nippy, frigid; piercing, biting, cutting, numbing, stinging; raw, sharp, keen; wintry, brumal, bleak, Siberian, arctic, polar; freezing, icy, gelid, frosty, hoary.

vb. be cold, freeze, shiver, shudder, quiver; chatter.

761 heating

n. heating, warming; combustion, burning, incineration, flaming, kindling, ignition, scorching, incandescence.

adj. heating, warming, calefactory; combustible, flammable; glowing, incandescent.

vb. heat, warm, heat up, reheat, put on the fire; ignite, kindle, set fire to, strike a light, put a match to, touch off; burn, scorch, consume, scald, incinerate, reduce to ashes, cremate; fire, smelt; thaw, defrost, de-ice, unfreeze, melt, liquefy; insulate.

762 refrigeration; incombustibility

n. refrigeration, cooling, chilling, freezing, glaciation, glacification.

incombustibility, non-flammability; asbestos, safety curtain.

adj. cooled, chilled; frozen, icy.

incombustible, non-flammable, fireproof.

vb. refrigerate, cool, chill, make cold, freeze, deep-freeze, ice, frost, congeal, glaciate.

extinguish, put out, blow out, quench, stifle, smother, damp, choke, snuff, douse, drown.

763 furnace

n. furnace, boiler, kiln, stove, cooker, oven; incinerator; crematorium; fire, heater, radiator; hearth, fireplace, fireside, grate, hob.

764 refrigerator

n. refrigerator, fridge, freezer, deepfreeze, icebox, icepack, cool-bag, coolbox, cooling apparatus, cold storage; air-conditioner, fan, ventilator.

765 fuel

n. fuel, combustible; coal, coke, charcoal, briquette, wood, log, gas, oil, petrol, electricity, juice (*sl.*), hydroelectricity, nuclear power, solar energy.

match, lighter, firelighter, fuse, touch-paper, vesta, detonator, torch, firebrand, tinder, flint.

adj. combustible, flammable, explosive.

vb. fuel, fire, power; feed, stoke.

766 thermometer

n. thermometer, calorimeter, thermostat, mercury, clinical thermometer, pyrometer, thermocouple, thermopile, thermograph; Fahrenheit, centigrade, Celsius, Réamur, kelvin; degree.

767 taste

n. taste, flavour, relish, savour, smack, sapor; tang, after-taste; tongue, palate, taste buds; gustation.

adj. tasty, palatable, delicious, appetizing, gustatory.

vb. taste, relish, enjoy, eat, smack one's lips; try, sample, sip; taste of, savour of.

768 tastelessness

n. tastelessness, insipidity, flavourlessness, dullness, flatness, staleness.

adj. tasteless, unsavoury, insipid, flavourless, dull, flat, bland, stale, wishy-washy, unseasoned, unspiced, plastic (*inf.*), uninteresting.

see also 507, 843

769 pungency

n. pungency, piquancy, sharpness, keenness, spiciness, tanginess; zest, bite, edge, tang, kick (*inf.*), zing (*sl.*), punch (*sl.*).

adj. pungent, sharp, piquant, penetrating, poignant, strong, tangy, racy; spiced, curried, hot; tart, sour, bitter.

see also 307

770 savouriness

n. savouriness, palatability, deliciousness, tastiness, richness, lusciousness.

delicacy, luxury, treat, rarity, delight, titbit, dainty, *bonne bouche*, chef's special, dish fit for a king; caviar; ambrosia, nectar.

adj. palatable, delicious, savoury, tasty, nice, dainty, delightful, choice, rich, luscious, delectable, exquisite, heavenly (*inf.*), scrumptious (*inf.*), yummy (*inf.*); fit for a king, fit for the gods; well done, done to a turn.

appetizing, mouth-watering, tempting, inviting, enticing, tantalizing, moreish (*inf.*).

vb. taste good; enjoy, like, relish, savour, appreciate.

771 unsavouriness

n. unsavouriness, unpalatability, unpleasantness, flavourlessness; bread and water, bitter pill, yuk (*sl.*).

adj. tasteless, flavourless, bland, dull, inedible; undrinkable; underdone; gone off; yukky (*sl.*); uninteresting, unappealing, unappetizing, uninviting, disagreeable, horrible, revolting.

vb. nauseate, disgust, turn one's stomach; disagree with, turn off (*inf.*); dislike, loathe.

772 sweetness

n. sweetness, sweetening, sugariness; sweet, sweetener, sugar, honey, molasses, syrup, treacle, saccharin.

adj. sweet, sweetened, sugared; sugary, saccharine, sirupy, rich, luscious, delicious; sticky; bitter-sweet, sweet-and-sour.

vb. sweeten, make sweet, sugar; dulcify.

773 sourness

n. sourness, acidity, bitterness, sharpness; acid, vinegar, gall, wormwood.

adj. sour, acid, tart, bitter, caustic, cutting, pungent, sharp, biting, dry; acidulous, vinegary, acetous; unsweetened, unsugared, unripe.

vb. sour, turn sour, set one's teeth on edge; ferment, curdle, tartarize.

774 odour

n. odour, smell, scent, trace, trail, exhalation, emanation, effluvium; fragrance; stench.

sense of smell, smelling, olfaction, detection.

adj. smelling, scented, odorous; strong, pungent, redolent; olfactory.

vb. smell, smell of, give out, give off, emit, scent, exhale; sniff, whiff, detect, perceive, smell out.

see also **776, 777**

775 inodorousness

n. inodorousness, no smell; deodorization, ventilation, fumigation; deodorant, deodorizer; fumigant, fumigator, cleanser.

adj. inodorous, odourless, unscented, scentless.

vb. deodorize, fumigate, aerate, clean, purify.

776 fragrance

n. fragrance, aroma, bouquet, scent, perfume, spice, balm.

adj. fragrant, aromatic, scented, perfumed, spicy, sweet-scented, sweet-smelling, redolent, odoriferous, odorous, ambrosial.

vb. smell, scent, be fragrant; scent, perfume, embalm.

777 stench

n. stench, smell, stink, fetor, reek, fume, mephitis, miasma; foulness, uncleanness, smelliness, mustiness, rancidity; B.O. (*inf.*), body odour; skunk, polecat; stink-bomb.

adj. smelly, stinking, foul, unclean, fetid, strong-smelling, foul-smelling, nasty, vile, repulsive, offensive, rank, noxious, noisome; stale, musty, rancid, putrid, decaying, high, putrescent.

vb. smell, stink, reek, smell to high heaven (*inf.*).

778 sound

n. sound, noise, vibration, resonance, report, reverberation, echo, ringing; loudness, softness; note, level, accent, cadence, tenor, intonation, tone, timbre; acoustics, phonetics.

adj. sounding, heard, audible, distinct, within earshot; loud, resonant, sonorous; auditory, acoustic, phonetic.

vb. sound, make a noise, give out, emit, produce; hear, listen.

see also **795**

779 silence

n. silence, inaudibility, quietness, stillness, noiselessness; peace, quiet, still, hush; loss of signal, blackout, news blackout, security blackout, censorship.

adj. silent, inaudible, noiseless, hushed, quiet, still, soundless, unuttered, unspoken, unvoiced; soundproof.

vb. silence, hush, quiet, still, calm, muffle, reduce to silence, mute, stifle; subdue, deaden, repress, tone down, put the lid on.

see also **513, 517**

780 loudness

n. loudness, noisiness, audibility, rowdiness; noise, racket, roar, boom, blast, swell, din, clamour, tumult, outcry, uproar, hubbub, hullabaloo, pandemonium.

adj. loud, noisy, clamorous, vociferous, loud-mouthed; boisterous, rumbustious, rowdy, obstreperous; thundering, deafening, ringing, booming, ear-splitting, resounding, piercing, blaring, crashing, stentorian, enough to wake the dead.

vb. be loud, boom, roar, thunder, fulminate, resound, bellow, blare, peal, crash, rattle, deafen, be unable to hear oneself think.

781 faintness

n. faintness, softness, inaudibility; whisper, breath, undertone, murmur, mutter, sigh, rustle, ripple, hum.

adj. faint, soft, quiet, hushed, inaudible; indistinct, stifled, muted, muffled, deadened, subdued; feeble, weak, low, distant, muttering.

vb. whisper, speak softly, murmur, mutter, sigh, hum, rustle, purr, creak, squeak.

782 sudden and violent sound

n. bang, blast, shot, report, boom, detonation, eruption, explosion; thud, whack, knock, slap, tap, rap, snap; crash, crackle; shout, cry, yelp.

vb. crash, crack, knock, slap, smack, whack, tap, rap, snap; click; plop, plonk, thud; thunder, boom, detonate, bang, pop, slam, burst, explode, blow up, set off.

783 repeated and prolonged sound

n. roll, clang, clatter; rattle, rustle; chuckle, cackle; whistle, hum, whirr, purr, buzz, strum; throb.

vb. roll, clang, clatter; rattle, rustle; ripple, swish, hum, drone, whirr, purr, buzz, strum, whistle, trill; thump, throb, palpitate, tick, beat, pound, patter; chime, peal, toll; chuckle, cackle; rumble, grumble, growl.

784 resonance

n. resonance, vibration, tintinnabulation; ringing, clanging, echo, resounding, thunder, boom; chime, bell, gong, jingle, tinkle.

adj. resonant, vibrant, reverberating, loud, echoing, ringing, clanging, chiming, deep-sounding.

vb. resound, reverberate, boom, vibrate, echo, re-echo, ring, gong, chime, tinkle, jingle, clang, whirr, buzz, drone, whine, purr, hum.

785 non-resonance

n. non-resonance, thud, bump, plop, plump, thump, plonk, clonk, clunk.

adj. non-resonant, deadened, muffled, dead, heavy, dull.

vb. thud, bump, plonk, plump, plop, thump, clonk, clunk; muffle, stifle, dull, damp, deaden.

786 hissing sound

n. hiss, hissing, sibilance, buzz, swish, rustle, whirr, whistle, splash, squelch, whoosh, zip.

adj. hissing, sibilant.

vb. buzz, hiss, swish, rustle, whistle, splash, whoosh, zip, fizz, whiz, whirr, squelch, sizzle, sneeze, wheeze, effervesce, sibilate.

787 harsh sound

n. harshness, hoarseness, gruffness, discord, dissonance, cacophony; shrillness, whistle, croak, squawk, squeal, screech, shriek.

adj. strident, shrill, high-pitched, piercing, sharp, penetrating; squealing, creaking, grating, scratchy, tinny, metallic; clanging, clashing, screeching, jarring, discordant, dissonant; hoarse, gruff, harsh, raucous, loud, husky, throaty, guttural, dry.

vb. clang, clatter, clunk, crash, bang, clash, jangle; croak, quack, squawk, caw, cluck; saw, grind; shrill, whistle, shriek, screech, scream, squeal, yelp, squeak, creak; grate, rasp, irritate, jar, set one's teeth on edge, get on one's nerves.

788 human sound

n. cry, exclamation, utterance, shout, call, noise, shouting, clamour, outcry; scream, shriek, yell, moan, groan, wail, bellow, howl, whimper.

adj. clamorous, noisy, loud, yelling, vociferous.

vb. cry, exclaim, call, speak, utter, shout, scream, yell, shriek, screech, squeal, squeak, caterwaul, bawl, bellow, hoot, vociferate, whoop, hoop, hollo; groan, moan, complain, howl, wail, whine, whimper, sob.

cheer, chant, clamour, support; shout down, hiss, boo, ridicule, disapprove, censure.

789 animal sound

n. call, cry, ululation, barking.

vb. cry, yelp, yap, squeal, squawk; cackle, cluck, quack; caw, crow; screech, croak; coo, cuckoo; gobble, gaggle; chuckle, chirp, chirrup, cheep; tweet, twitter, whistle, pipe, trill, sing, warble; purr, miaow, mew, caterwaul; hum, drone, buzz; bark, bay, howl, woof, roar, bellow, bell; grunt, snort, snap, growl, snarl, whine, oink; neigh, bray, whinny; bleat, baa; moo, low.

790 melody

n. melody, melodiousness, tunefulness, concord, consonance, euphony, harmony, unison, accord, concert, music, blending.

adj. melodious, musical, euphonic, tuneful, rhythmical, melodic, lyrical, harmonious, in tune, accordant; sweet-sounding, dulcet, soothing, pleasing, mellow, soft, rich; catchy, memorable, singable, popular.

791 discord

n. discord, discordance, unmelodiousness, inharmoniousness, dissonance, atonality; noise, din, racket, cacophony.

adj. discordant, dissonant, atonal, unmelodious, inharmonious, unmusical, untuneful, out of tune, off key, flat, sharp; cacophonous, clashing, jarring, grating.

792 music

n. music, composition, work, opus, piece; arrangement, adaptation, setting, transcription, orchestration, instrumentation; incidental music, background music, accompaniment; record, recording; concert, recital.

classical music, chamber music, light music, country and western, folk music, pop music, electronic music, jazz, blues, reggae, punk, rock, soul, ragtime.

symphony, concerto, suite; overture, prelude; sonata; ballet, dance; opera, operetta; song, air, solo, hymn, strain; tune, chorus, refrain, round; duo, trio, quartet; passage, movement, phrase.

adj. musical, tuneful, pleasing; vocal, choral; scored, arranged, adapted.

vb. compose, write, set to music, arrange, score; perform, render, play, make music, interpret; sing, chant, croon; listen.

793 musician

n. musician, artist, player, performer, virtuoso, soloist, instrumentalist, concert artist; singer, vocalist, chorister, bard, minstrel, artiste, choir, chorus, singing group; orchestra, band, ensemble, symphony orchestra, chamber orchestra; group; dancer, ballerina; composer.

794 musical instrument

n. musical instrument, brass, woodwind, stringed instruments, percussion; record player, gramophone, stereo, hi-fi, music centre, stereogram, juke-box; record, disc, single, LP; tape-recorder, cassette-recorder; recording tape.

795 hearing

n. hearing, sense of hearing; good hearing, an ear for; earshot, range, carrying distance, sound; listening, auscultation; eavesdropping, wire-tapping.

listener, hearer, auditor, witness; eavesdropper, wire-tapper, peeping Tom; audience, auditorium; audition, interview, reception.

adj. auditory, hearing, auricular.

vb. hear, listen to, catch, take in, pick up, lend an ear, be all ears, give a hearing to, hark; attend to, pay attention to; perceive, detect, get wind of; overhear, listen in, eavesdrop, tap, bug.

796 deafness

n. deafness, inaudibility, deaf-and-dumbness, deaf-mutism; lip reading, deaf-and-dumb alphabet, deaf-and-dumb language, dactylology.

adj. deaf, hard of hearing, stone-deaf, deaf-and-dumb, deaf-mute; deafening, stunning, ear-splitting; deaf to, unaware of.

vb. deafen, stun.

797 light

n. light, illumination, lighting, radiance, brilliance, splendour, brightness, clearness, lightness; luminosity, phosphorescence.

beam, ray, gleam, shaft, streak, laser, pencil, stream, glint, chink; flash, streak, blaze, flame, flare, glow, spark, sparkle, twinkle, flicker, glimmer, glitter, dazzle, shimmer; glare, gloss, shine, lustre; polish, reflection; daylight, sunshine; sunrise, daybreak, dawn.

adj. luminous, light, bright, clear, shining, brilliant, beaming, glowing, glittering, sparkling, gleaming, dazzling; shiny, glossy, sheeny; illuminated, lighted, lit; cloudless.

vb. shine, burn, glow, blaze, glitter, glimmer, glisten, gleam, sparkle, dazzle, blind; flash, shimmer, flicker, twinkle, scintillate, blink, flare, beam; dance, play, reflect, glare.

illuminate, switch on, lighten, brighten, enlighten, dawn, shed light on, light up, irradiate; polish, burnish.

798 darkness

n. darkness, dark, night, nightfall, Cimmerian gloom, blackness, blackout, eclipse, shade, shadow, umbra, penumbra, adumbration, obscuration; gloom, sombreness.

adj. dark, unlit, unlighted, unilluminated; black, starless, dull, overcast, cloudy; indistinct, obscure, shady, nebulous, shaded, shadowy; tenebrous, obfuscous; dismal, gloomy, sombre, dreary, bleak, desolate, murky, dim.

vb. darken, blacken, black out, switch off, cover, eclipse, obscure, overshadow, becloud, place in shadow, cast a shadow over, obfuscate, adumbrate.

799 dimness

n. dimness, murkiness, shadiness, obscurity; dusk, twilight, half-light, gloaming, gloom.

adj. dim, dull, faint, vague, indistinct, obscure, blurred, opaque, fading, evanescent; grey, cloudy, foggy, hazy, misty, shadowy, gloomy.

vb. dim, dull, fade out, blur, obscure, shade, becloud, cloud over, dull, vanish, wane, evanesce.

800 source of light

n. light, luminary, sun, moon, planet, star, halo, aurora, corona, nimbus; meteor, shooting star; lightning, flash; fireworks.

lamp, torch, bulb, spotlight, searchlight, flashlight, floodlight, headlamp, side-light, indicator; neon light, fluorescent tube, strobe light, lantern; beacon, lighthouse.

candle, wick, spill, taper, wax; match, flame, flare; coal, ember, brand.

801 shade

n. shade, covering, veil, shield, screen, blind, curtain, shutter, drape; sunglasses, blinkers, goggles; visor, hood; shelter, awning, canopy; umbrella, parasol.

adj. shady; screened.

vb. shade, cover, veil, screen, shield, shelter, protect, curtain, blinker.

see also **463, 593**

802 transparency

n. transparency, clearness, glassiness, vitreosity, translucence, lucidity.

adj. transparent, translucent, clear, see-through, revealing, unobstructed, glassy, vitreous, crystal, lucid, diaphanous, pellucid, limpid.

vb. be transparent, see through, show, show through.

see also **502**

803 opacity

n. opacity, opaqueness, cloudiness, murkiness, obscurity, darkness; smoke, mist, cloud, film.

adj. opaque, non-transparent, absorbing light, impervious, dark, unclear, smoky, misty, cloudy, muddy, blurred, filmy, dull, murky, dim, darkened, turbid.

vb. make opaque, devitrify, obscure, darken, cloud, smoke, obstruct one's vision.

see also **503**

804 semitransparency

n. semitransparency, translucence, pearliness, milkiness; smoked glass, frosted glass, opal glass; dark glasses, sunglasses.

adj. semitransparent, semitranslucid, semiopaque, frosted, pearly, smoked, milky.

805 colour

n. colour, hue, shade, tinge, tone, dash, touch, tint, tincture, cast; paint, pigment, dye, wash, stain, lake; prism, spectrum; glow, brilliance, warmth, intensity; coloration, colouring, pigmentation, complexion, chromatism.

adj. coloured, chromatic, tinted, tinged, touched, dyed, painted, stained; constant, fast.

colourful, bright, warm, glowing, intense, strong, deep, rich, brilliant; garish, glaring, gaudy, loud, showy, flashy, lurid, harsh, clashing, painful.

soft, pastel, subdued, refined, tender, delicate, matt; faded, dingy, dull, drab, cold, uninviting.

vb. colour, shade, tinge, paint, touch up, stain, wash, coat, put on, lay on; contrast, set off, throw into relief; clash, not go with, conflict, grate.

806 absence of colour

n. colourlessness, achromatism, discoloration, fading, paleness, dullness, dimness, faintness, flatness; anaemia, sallowness, whitening, bleaching.

adj. colourless, hueless, toneless, lacklustre, dull, lifeless, cold, dim, faint, weak; faded, washed out, pale, pallid, sallow, ashen, white, anaemic, pasty; transparent.

vb. fade, lose colour, lose brightness, bleach, blanch, wash out, whiten, drain, turn pale, discolour, grow dim, etiolate.

807 white

n. white, whiteness, whitishness, lightness, fairness, paleness; milkiness, chalkiness, silveriness, snowiness.

adj. white, fair, light, blonde, hoary; snowy, snow-white, frosted, milky, lactescent, chalky, silvery, pearly, ivory, albescent; whitish, cream, off-white; pale, ashen, anaemic, sallow, wan; clean, spotless, pure.

vb. whiten, whitewash, bleach, blanch, snow; clean, purify.

808 black

n. black, blackness, darkness, inkiness, sootiness.

adj. black, blackish; jet-black, pitch-black, coal-black; inky, sooty, stained; dark, murky; sable, swarthy.

vb. blacken, ink, ink in, darken, shade.

809 grey

n. grey, greyness, dinginess, drabness, dusk, shade.

adj. grey, greyish, shaded, dull, drab, dingy, sombre, neutral; dusty, smoky; silver-haired, hoary; speckled, pepper-and-salt.

810 brown

n. brown, tan, beige, mahogany.

adj. brown, brownish, beige, khaki, maroon, auburn, buff, bronze, copper, chocolate, coffee, rust-coloured, reddish-brown, bay, chestnut, russet, sepia, ochre, hazel.

811 red

n. red, redness, blush, glow, colour, cochineal, carmine.

adj. red, reddish, ruddy, scarlet, crimson, vermilion, ruby, cherry-red, blood-red, coral, brick-red, maroon, rust, magenta, russet, auburn, pink, salmon-pink, rosy; glowing, warm; blushing, embarrassed, burning.

vb. redden, blush; glow, flush.

812 green

n. green, verdure; lawn, turf.

adj. green, greenish, grassy, verdant, leafy, lime, emerald, sage, olive, beryl, blue-green, aquamarine, sea-green, pea-green; bilious, sickly, pale; fresh, unripe.

813 yellow

n. yellow, cream, tan, lemon; buttercup, daffodil, crocus, jasmine.

adj. yellow, yellowish, cream, saffron, sand, gold, golden, buff, tan, khaki, light-brown; sallow, bilious, jaundiced.

814 purple

n. purple; violet, pansy, lavender.

adj. purple, purplish, reddish-blue, bluish-red, violet, indigo, mauve, lilac, lavender, plum-coloured.

815 blue

n. blue, sky, azure, indigo.

adj. blue, bluish, turquoise, azure, royal blue, navy blue; sapphire, sky-blue, indigo.

816 orange

n. orange, tangerine, apricot, peach, mandarin, carrot, salmon, coral.

adj. orange, orangey, reddish-yellow, gold, old gold, copper, bronze, brass, ginger.

817 variegation

n. variegation, diversification, diversity, motley, spectrum, rainbow, kaleidoscope; chequerwork, tartan, mosaic, parquetry, marquetry.

adj. variegated, kaleidoscopic, many-coloured, multi-coloured; spotted, mottled, motley, patched, piebald, pied, dappled, speckled, freckled; striped, streaked, checked.

vb. diversify, variegate, chequer, checker; stud, mottle, spatter, dapple, speckle, stipple, streak, strip.

818 vision

n. vision, sight, eyesight, perception, recognition; observation, inspection, scrutiny, investigation, notice, once-over (*inf.*); bird's eye view, survey, panorama, overview.

look, view, regard, glance, glimpse, eye; squint, peep, peek; leer; wink, twinkle.

viewpoint, standpoint, position, outlook, perspective, attitude; look-out, observation point, watch-tower, gallery, grandstand.

adj. visual, ocular, opthalmic, optical; observant; watchful, vigilant.

vb. see, look at, view, watch, look on, observe, perceive, discern, recognize, notice, catch sight of, set eyes on, eye; glance, glimpse, catch a glimpse of, peep; blink, wink, twinkle; gaze, gape, stare, fix one's eyes on; leer, ogle, glare, glower.

scrutinize, investigate, survey, inspect; scan, look through, look over, flick through (*inf.*), thumb through (*inf.*).

819 blindness

n. blindness, sightlessness, colour-blindness, night-blindness, snow-blindness; blind spot, blind side, failing, mote in one's eye.

adj. blind, sightless, unseeing, eyeless, colour-blind; blinded, blindfold, blinkered, hoodwinked, in the dark.

vb. be blind, lose one's sight, strike blind, put someone's eyes out; obscure, hide, mask, screen, blindfold, blinker, hoodwink.

820 imperfect vision

n. imperfect vision, partial vision; shortsightedness, myopia; longsightedness, presbyopia; double vision; colour-blindness; squint, strabism, cross-eye, astigmatism, conjunctivitis, cataract.

adj. dim-sighted, purblind, half-blind; shortsighted, myopic; long-sighted, presbyopic; colour-blind, astigmatic, cross-eyed, squinting, strabismic.

vb. see double, squint, screw up one's eyes, see blurred.

821 spectator

n. spectator, viewer, onlooker, observer, watcher, eye-witness, bystander, passer-by, looker-on, beholder; sightseer; peeper, peeping Tom; spy, snoop, meddler.

spectators, crowd, public, supporters, fans, followers, turn-out, audience.

822 optical instrument

n. glasses, spectacles, bifocals, goggles, specs (*inf.*), contact lenses, monocle, eye-glasses, lorgnette, pince-nez; binoculars, opera glasses, field glasses, telescope; microscope, magnifying glass, lens; camera; mirror, looking glass, reflector, glass, speculum.

823 visibility

n. visibility, perceptibility, clarity, distinctness, plainness, prominence, conspicuousness.

adj. visible, apparent, in view, in sight, observable, perceptible, noticeable, before one's very eyes; evident, clear, plain, obvious, patent; prominent, conspicuous, pronounced, standing out; unmistakable, glaring; open, exposed; distinct, well-defined, definite, clear-cut.

vb. show, show through, show itself, manifest itself, be revealed, come into sight, come into view; stand out, stand out a mile (*inf.*), stick out like a sore thumb (*sl.*), hit in the face, leap to the eye.

see also **458, 825**

824 invisibility

n. invisibility, concealment, seclusion, latency, obscurity, indistinctness, imperceptibility, indefiniteness, vagueness, indiscernibility, cloudiness, darkness, haziness, fuzziness.

adj. invisible, imperceptible, indiscernible; hidden, out of sight, concealed, obscure; inconspicuous; indistinct, unclear, ill-defined, vague; intangible, unseen, spiritual; cloudy, nebulous, shadowy, mysterious, hazy, blurred, fuzzy.

see also **461, 826**

825 appearance

n. appearance, look, aspect, feature, shape, form, outline, profile, face; condition, presentation, expression; posture, pose, bearing; mien, countenance, manner, behaviour; externals, appearances, outward show, first impression, face value.

phenomenon, spectacle, display, exhibition, show, demonstration, scene, parade, pageant.

adj. apparent, visible, manifest; seeming, ostensible, supposed, specious, plausible, alleged, outward, superficial, external, to look at (*inf.*).

vb. appear, look, seem, show, take the form of; emerge, arise, come into view, be revealed, turn up, show up, put in an appearance, crop up (*inf.*), pop up (*inf.*), occur, happen, present itself, express itself, manifest itself, materialize, come to light, come into the picture, come onto the horizon, see the light of day.

adv. apparently, to all appearances, superficially, at first sight, on the face of it, for show, to all intents and purposes.

see also **222, 458, 823**

826 disappearance

n. disappearance, vanishing, fading, fade-out, evanescence, evaporation, dematerialization; departure, retirement, flight, escape, removal, withdrawal, loss.

adj. disappearing, fading, evanescent; disappeared, vanished, missing.

vb. disappear, vanish, fade, evaporate, dematerialize, dissolve; pass out of sight, leave no trace, disappear into thin air, go up in smoke, vanish from sight, be eclipsed, be swallowed up, be lost to view.

go away, depart, remove, withdraw, retire, escape, flee; cease, be no more, die, perish, sink.

see also **824**

C Personal

827 pleasure

n. pleasure, joy, happiness, gladness, delight, enjoyment, satisfaction, fulfilment; serenity.

enchantment, bewitchment, exultation, relish, gusto, zest, glee, cheer, thrill, kick (*inf.*), ecstasy, elation, bliss, rapture, euphoria, transport; luxury, ease, convenience, comfort, paradise, bed of roses, golden age, halcyon days, lap of luxury.

gratification, indulgence, self-indulgence, revelry, hedonism, sensuousness, sensuality, sexuality.

adj. pleasant, satisfying, enjoyable, delightful, exciting, adorable, welcome; comfortable, snug, cosy, homely, comfy (*inf.*), congenial, convenient, palatial, luxurious; gratifying, pleasurable, sensuous, bodily, physical, hedonistic, voluptuous, self-indulgent, carnal.

happy, pleased, joyful, glad, delighted, joyous, satisfied; thrilled, excited, tickled pink (*inf.*), exhilarated, starry-eyed, bubbling over, in the seventh heaven; smiling, laughing, genial, convivial, delirious; merry, in good spirits, cheery, jolly, blithe, gladsome, blissful; overjoyed, ecstatic, in ecstasies, enraptured, in raptures enthusiastic, carried away; peaceful, contented, at peace.

vb. enjoy, like, take delight in, derive pleasure from, rejoice in, love, fancy, be keen on, appreciate, relish, revel in, get a kick out of (*inf.*), rave about (*inf.*), enjoy oneself, have a good time, tread on air.

see also **829, 836, 840**

828 pain

n. pain, hurt, distress, discomfort, affliction, anguish, misery, agony, shock, blow, injury, suffering, unhappiness, sorrow, grief, sadness, regret, melancholy, despair, broken heart, weeping, wretchedness, tribulation, trial, ordeal, torment, torture, martyrdom, crucifixion, hell; bereavement, sense of loss, mourning, grieving; ache, twinge, pang, spasm, stitch, wound, sting, burn, illness, sickness.

worry, anxiety, heartache, vexation, fretting, uneasiness, discontent, disquiet, dissatisfaction; problem, care, burden.

sufferer, victim, prey, scapegoat, wretch, guinea pig.

adj. painful, hurtful, tormenting, excruciating, suffering, writhing, agonizing, harrowing; unpleasant, extreme, sharp, severe, grievous, sore, sensitive.

unfortunate, unhappy, sad, miserable, troubled, afflicted, heavy-laden, burdened, anxious, worried, vexed, uneasy; sorrowful, weeping, mournful, wretched, cut up (*inf.*), heart-broken.

vb. undergo, suffer, go through, bear, endure, put up with (*inf.*), persevere; ache, smart, throb, sting, burn; be tender, be sore, be bruised; regret, despair, mourn, weep.

see also **830**

829 pleasurableness

n. pleasurableness, pleasantness, niceness, enjoyableness, loveliness; charm, fascination, glamour, prestige, attractiveness, winsomeness, allurement.

delight, treat, surprise, amusement, fun, gift, joy, honeymoon, benefit, refreshment, titbit, feast, banquet, manna.

adj. pleasant, nice, enjoyable, agreeable, pleasing, lovely, charming, fascinating, attractive, beautiful, picturesque; glamorous, prestigious, appealing, enchanting, winsome, luring, seductive; delightful, exquisite, delicious, luscious, tasty.

vb. please, satisfy, delight, gladden, rejoice, thrill, gratify; turn on (*inf.*), turn on to (*inf.*), switch on (*inf.*), stimulate, excite; interest; attract, charm, enchant, enthrall, captivate, bewitch, enrapture; amuse, tickle, titillate.

see also **755, 827**

830 painfulness

n. painfulness, hurtfulness, unpleasantness, bitterness, disagreeableness; sorrow, pain, disappointment, irritation, annoyance, nuisance, difficulty, problem, care, burden, trouble, load, cross, concern, nightmare, bitter cup, bitter pill; embarrassment.

adj. unpleasant, disagreeable, bothersome, upsetting, disturbing, troublesome, annoying, irritating, trying, tiresome; distressing, awful, grim, shocking, appalling, tragic, extreme, dreadful.

vb. hurt, grieve, injure, wound, afflict, pain; distress, worry, trouble, outrage, bother, upset, disturb, annoy, irritate, vex, needle; torment, harass, pester, tease, pick on (*inf.*), have it in for (*inf.*); harrow, agonize, excruciate, crucify, martyr, torture, obsess, haunt, plague; lose sleep over (*inf.*); discomfort, put out, inconvenience.

see also **828, 893**

831 content

n. content, contentment, peace, peace of mind, happiness, satisfaction; self-satisfaction, complacency; ease, rest, comfort, serenity, solace.

adj. contented, content, pleased, peaceful, satisfied, happy, carefree, without cares, uncomplaining.

vb. be content, be satisfied, sit pretty, have one's wishes granted, have all that one could wish for, have nothing to worry about, have nothing to complain of, can't complain.

satisfy, gratify, indulge, suffice; go down well, put at ease; appease, reconcile.

832 discontent

n. discontent, dissatisfaction, unhappiness, sadness, depression, resentment, regret, unrest, uneasiness, tension, strain; grudge, chip on one's shoulder.

complainer, grumbler, fault-finder, grouch; reactionary, radical, protester, angry young man.

adj. discontented, unhappy, uneasy, restless, disgruntled, dissatisfied, cheesed off (*sl.*), browned off; grumbling, complaining, critical, hyper-critical, hard to please, never satisfied.

vb. be discontented, grumble, criticize, find fault, go on about, pick holes in (*inf.*), speak out against, moan; dissatisfy, disappoint, disconcert, disgruntle, discourage, dishearten.

833 regret

n. regret, sorrow, misgiving, compunction, scruple, qualm, pang of conscience, apology, repentance, change of heart, contrition, penitence, self-reproach, remorse, soul-searching.

adj. regretful, apologetic, penitent, humble, sorry, remorseful, contrite, repentant, broken, conscience-stricken.

vb. regret, apologize, be sorry for, cry over, repent, humble oneself, admit, own up, grieve, weep over, mourn, bewail, bemoan; rue.

834 relief

n. relief, alleviation, mitigation, assuagement; help, aid, comfort, consolation, relaxation, ease, load off one's mind; remedy, cure.

adj. relieving, easing, comforting, consoling, consolatory, soothing, comfortable, breathing easily.

vb. relieve, alleviate, mitigate, ease, soften, comfort, cushion, assuage, soothe, lighten, ease the strain, console, cheer up.

be relieved, feel better, recover; heave a sigh of relief, breathe again.

see also **176**

835 aggravation

n. aggravation, exacerbation, worsening, heightening, intensification, sharpening, deepening, strengthening, inflammation; annoyance, irritation, exasperation.

adj. aggravated, worsened, made worse, not improved.

vb. aggravate, worsen, exacerbate, make things worse, complicate, increase, magnify, multiply, heighten, intensify, deepen, go from bad to worse, get worse and worse; annoy, irritate.

836 cheerfulness

n. cheerfulness, good humour, happiness, gladness, joy; high spirits, vitality, animation, sparkle, liveliness, jollity, merriment, mirth, gaiety, glee; laughter, fun and games; light-heartedness, levity, breeziness; stoicism, stiff upper lip.

adj. cheerful, glad, happy, joyful; genial, animated, lively, in good humour, sparkling, vivacious, exuberant, full of beans (*inf.*), in high spirits, high-spirited, on top of the world, jolly, merry, gay, jovial, jocular, playful, sporty; light-hearted, perky, chirpy, breezy, carefree, debonair.

cheering, heartening, encouraging, inspiring, heartwarming.

vb. cheer, gladden, cheer up, perk up (*inf.*); brighten, encourage, comfort; enliven, animate, inspire; uplift, raise the spirits, warm the heart.

be cheerful, take heart, snap out of it (*inf.*); persevere, keep smiling (*inf.*), grin and bear it, keep one's chin up (*inf.*), keep a stiff upper lip, keep one's end up (*inf.*).

see also **827, 838**

837 dejection; seriousness

n. dejection, despondency, melancholy, sorrow, sadness, grief, depression, despair, gloom, misery, heaviness of spirit, low spirits, blues, dumps, doldrums, mopes, *weltschmerz.*

seriousness, earnestness, solemnity, gravity, sedateness, sobriety, coolness; dead pan (*inf.*), straight face.

adj. dejected, unhappy, despondent, downcast, sad, sorrowful, down-hearted, depressed, low, troubled, desolate, dispirited, broken-hearted, crushed, heart-broken, upset, cut up (*inf.*), discouraged, crestfallen, blue, down, moping, down in the mouth, down in the dumps, in the doldrums (*inf.*), out of sorts; melancholy, world-weary, careworn; gloomy, miserable, dismal, forlorn, doleful, wretched, cheerless, dull; suicidal, despairing.

serious, earnest, grave, sober, solemn; thoughtful, pensive; stern, strict; straight-faced, dead pan (*inf.*), expressionless.

vb. be dejected, lose heart; regret, grieve, mourn, sorrow; fret, brood, mope; languish, droop, wilt, pull a long face, beat one's breast.

sadden, oppress, break a person's heart, cut up (*inf.*), discourage, deject, depress, unnerve, dismay, demoralize, get down (*inf.*); cast down; drive to drink (*inf.*); dampen, pour cold water on.

be serious, keep a straight face, take life seriously, not see the joke.

see also **828, 839**

838 rejoicing

n. rejoicing, happiness, celebration, congratulation, jubilation, exultation, revelry, festivity, merrymaking, mirth, thanksgiving; cheers, shouts, hurrahs, applause; laughter, laugh, chuckle, chortle, giggle, snigger, cackle, titter, roar, guffaw; smile, grin, smirk, beam.

adj. rejoicing, jubilant, elated, exultant, rollicking.

vb. rejoice, be happy, sing for joy, leap for joy, dance, exult, celebrate, revel, have a party; clap one's hands, applaud, say thankyou to, congratulate.

laugh, chuckle, chortle, guffaw, giggle, titter, snigger; burst out laughing, roar, fall about laughing, double up with laughter, be convulsed with laughter, split one's sides, roll in the aisles (*inf.*), be in stitches (*inf.*); smile, beam, smirk, grin, twinkle; laugh at, ridicule, poke fun at, deride.

see also **840, 842**

839 lamentation

n. lamentation, mourning, grief, sorrow, weeping, sobbing, tears, waterworks (*sl.*); cry, weep, good cry, sob, bawl, wail, whimper; lament, elegy, requiem, dirge, funeral oration.

adj. lamenting, sad, mournful; weeping, sobbing, in tears, tearful.

vb. lament, grieve, sorrow; cry, weep, burst into tears, break down, dissolve into tears, shed tears, turn on the waterworks (*sl.*), sob, cry one's eyes out (*inf.*), sob one's heart out (*inf.*), blubber, snivel, whimper, whine, howl, bawl, wail.

see also **837**

840 amusement

n. amusement, pleasure, fun, good time; leisure; hobby, pastime, diversion, relaxation, entertainment, recreation, sport, play, game; television, radio, cinema, concert, theatre; meal, picnic, party, barbecue, banquet, feast; fete, fair, carnival, gala, fiesta, festivity; holiday, excursion, outing, pleasure trip, jaunt.

adj. entertaining, amusing, engaging, diverting, pleasant, witty; amused, entertained.

vb. amuse, entertain, delight, cheer, enliven, brighten up.

amuse oneself, enjoy oneself, relax, play games, go out, have fun, have a good time, let off steam (*inf.*), have a ball (*sl.*), let one's hair down (*inf.*), live it up (*inf.*), whoop it up (*inf.*), paint the town red (*sl.*), carouse, revel.

see also **614, 827, 842**

841 weariness

n. weariness, tiredness, exhaustion, fatigue, lassitude; tedium, boredom, apathy, listlessness, world-weariness, ennui, monotony, sameness, humdrum, the same old thing (*inf.*).

misery, wet blanket, drip; pain in the neck.

adj. wearisome, tiresome; tedious, boring, uninteresting, uninspiring, heavy, monotonous, dreary, flat, stale, repetitious, repetitive, soporofic; tired, weary, exhausted, drowsy, jaded, worn out.

vb. weary, fatigue, tire, tire out, send to sleep, bore, exhaust, depress, leave cold; flag, droop.

see also **612, 617, 843**

842 wit

n. wit, wittiness, humour, joking, fun; jocularity, whimsicality, facetiousness, flippancy, drollery.

joke, witticism, repartee, pun, play on words, quip, jest, Spoonerism, *double entendre*, whimsy, sally, wisecrack, gag, funny story, shaggy-dog story, chestnut, aphorism, epigram; satire, sarcasm, irony; banter, burlesque, badinage.

humorist, comedian, joker, wag, life and soul of the party, jester, clown, buffoon, satirist.

adj. witty, humorous, funny, amusing, jocular, quick-witted, whimsical, quick, keen, lively, nimble; waggish; clownish; teasing, bantering.

vb. be witty, crack a joke, joke, jest, pun, bring the house down (*inf.*), sparkle, scintillate; tease, pull a person's leg, banter, rib (*inf.*), rag (*sl.*), make fun of, ridicule, kid (*sl.*).

843 dullness

n. dullness, heaviness, tediousness, mediocrity, insipidity, colourlessness, drabness, dreariness, tameness, flatness, dryness, stuffiness, slowness; familiarity, triteness, banality.

adj. dull, heavy, ponderous, tedious, boring, uninteresting, dry, stuffy, stodgy, sluggish, mediocre, flat, uninspired, lifeless, dead, drab, dreary, gloomy; long-winded, prosaic; conventional, stereotyped, common, commonplace, trite, banal, pointless.

844 beauty

n. beauty, elegance, attractiveness, good looks, loveliness, prettiness, fairness, handsomeness, shapeliness, pulchritude; glamour, grace, charm, appeal; magnificence, gloriousness, splendour, brilliance; beautification, face-lift, hair-dressing, adornment; cosmetics, make-up; plastic surgery.

good looker, smasher (*inf.*), stunner (*inf.*), belle, raving beauty, peach (*sl.*), pin-up (*inf.*), dream, Venus; ornament, masterpiece, showpiece.

adj. beautiful, attractive, good-looking, lovely, pretty, swell (*inf.*), smashing (*inf.*), glamorous, fair, handsome, appealing, pleasing, sightly, graceful, elegant, refined, comely, charming; shapely, well-formed, well-proportioned.

splendid, magnificent, brilliant, wonderful, glorious, marvellous, gorgeous, grand, fine, resplendent, excellent, impressive, exquisite.

vb. beautify, improve the appearance of, pretty up (*inf.*), doll up (*inf.*), tart up (*sl.*), dress up (*inf.*), adorn, decorate, ornament, trim, embellish.

see also **579, 846**

845 ugliness

n. ugliness, hideousness, unloveliness, uncomeliness, inelegance, disfigurement, offensiveness; mutilation, deformity, distortion.

eyesore, defacement, horror, mess, blemish, blot, graffiti, slum.

adj. ugly, hideous, inelegant, unbecoming, unprepossessing; frightful, horrid, shocking, offensive; unlovely, unseemly, uncomely; disfigured, deformed, misshapen, monstrous, grotesque.

vb. make ugly, disfigure, deface, distort, mutilate.

see also **245**

846 ornamentation

n. ornamentation, decoration, adornment, embellishment, enhancement, trimming, frill, foil; embroidery, needlework; illumination, lettering, illustration; jewellery, jewel, gem, stone, precious stone; tinsel, ribbon, lace, gilt, tassel, bunting.

adj. ornamental, decorative, adorning, embellishing, garnishing, cosmetic; florid, dressy, ornate, fancy, gaudy, garish.

vb. decorate, adorn, beautify, enhance, brighten up, embellish, garnish, embroider, deck, bedeck, gild, festoon, array, set off.

see also **509, 844**

847 blemish

n. blemish, defect, flaw, stain, smudge, blot, blur, taint, daub, spot, speck, smirch, blotch, tarnish, rust, stigma, dent, impurity, disfigurement, deformity.

adj. blemished, spoilt, disfigured, defective, imperfect.

vb. blemish, stain, smudge, blot, daub, smear, smirch, tarnish, sully, soil, spoil, mar, damage, deface, disfigure.

see also **582, 845**

848 good taste

n. good taste, refinement, tastefulness, elegance, grace, polish; discrimination, good judgment, culture, sophistication; decorum, decency, soberness, seemliness, properness, restraint, simplicity, delicacy, daintiness.

good judge, connoisseur, expert, critic, gourmand, *bon vivant.*

adj. tasteful, in good taste, refined, polished, elegant, dignified, graceful, delicate; decent, sober, becoming, seemly, proper, simple, aesthetic; cultured, discriminating, sophisticated, cultivated.

see also **510**

849 bad taste

n. bad taste, tastelessness; vulgarity, coarseness, rudeness, barbarism; pretension, artificiality; showiness, gaudiness; ugliness, unloveliness, hideousness; dowdiness, unfashionableness; cad, bounder (*sl.*).

adj. tasteless, in bad taste, unrefined, unpolished; vulgar, coarse, rude, gross, crass, uncouth; pretentious, artificial, florid, ostentatious, flashy, showy; inelegant, ugly, unsightly, unlovely; dull, tawdry, shoddy, low, common, plebeian.

see also **511**

850 fashion

n. fashion, style, mode, trend; new look, latest style, the latest; fad, craze, rage, all the rage, the last word; society, high society, set, right people; upper cut, upper crust.

adj. fashionable, stylish, trendy, latest, in fashion, in vogue, in (*inf.*), all the rage (*inf.*), modern, up-to-the-minute.

vb. catch on (*inf.*), become popular, grow in popularity, find favour; jump on the bandwagon (*inf.*), follow the crowd.

851 ridiculousness

n. ridiculousness, ludicrousness, funniness, outrageousness, absurdity.

adj. ridiculous, funny, comic, droll, amusing, hilarious, farcical, whimsical, side-splitting, too funny for words, rich, priceless (*sl.*), killing (*sl.*), absurd, ludicrous, preposterous, outrageous, fantastic.

vb. be ridiculous; laugh; bring the house down (*inf.*); play the fool, look silly.

see also **853**

852 affectation

n. affectation, pretentiousness, pretense; artificiality, unnaturalness; show, sham, foppery, put-on (*sl.*), play-acting, front, façade, act, airs, airs and graces.

pretender, actor; play-actor; charlatan, impostor, humbug, dandy, fop.

adj. affected, pretentious, put-on, tongue in cheek, pretended, assumed, artificial, unnatural, theatrical; showy, for effect; awkward; superficial, shallow, hollow; insincere.

vb. be affected, pretend, assume, put on, feign, simulate, act out the part of, pose, fake, sham, go through the motions of; talk big; put up a front.

853 ridicule

n. ridicule, mockery, contempt, scorn, disdain, derision, sneering, jeering, scoffing; satire, parody, caricature, burlesque; irony, sarcasm.

laughing-stock, target, victim, butt, dupe, fool.

adj. derisory, contemptuous; scoffing; ironical.

vb. ridicule, mock, laugh at, deride, sneer, jeer, scoff, revile, gibe; boo, hiss, hoot; pour scorn on, run down, make fun of, pull a person's leg; banter, taunt; laugh on the other side of one's face (*inf.*); parody, caricature, satirize.

see also **924**

854 hope

n. hope, faith, trust, reliance, confidence, assurance; promise; expectation, anticipation; aspiration, dream, vision, pipe-dream, desire, wish, longing, yearning, ambition; optimism, cheerfulness, high hopes; false optimism, wishful thinking, pious hopes, fool's paradise.

hoper, aspirant, competitor, candidate, optimist, idealist.

adj. hoping, trusting, expecting, hopeful, assured, expectant, optimistic, relying on, confident, sanguine, bold, fearless, ambitious; promising, auspicious, favourable.

vb. hope, trust, believe, have faith in, rely, rest on, depend, lean on, bank on, rest assured, expect, anticipate; aspire, dream, wish, desire, long for, yearn for, contemplate; look on the bright side, see things through rose-coloured spectacles.

raise one's hopes, inspire, promise, lead one to expect, have the makings of, show signs of promise, bid fair, bode well.

see also **420, 836**

855 hopelessness

n. hopelessness, despair, desperation, despondency; irrevocability, irredeemability; defeatism, pessimism; pessimist, Job's comforter.

adj. hopeless, irrevocable, irredeemable, incurable, irreversible, beyond hope, vain, to no avail, futile; unfortunate, bad, disastrous, impossible, helpless, lost, gone; pessimistic, defeatist.

vb. despair, lose heart, give up hope, abandon all hope, give up; dash one's hopes.

see also **837**

856 fear

n. fear, fright, terror, horror, dread, scare, tremor, panic, despair, alarm, blue funk (*sl.*), consternation, awe, trepidation; timidity, fearfulness, timorousness.

anxiety, hesitation, worry, concern, uneasiness; nervousness, apprehension, cold feet, butterflies (*inf.*), nerves, jitters (*inf.*), willies (*sl.*), heebie jeebies (*sl.*), cold sweat.

adj. afraid, frightened, terrified, dreading, scared, scared stiff, shocked, in awe, trembling, panicking, panic-stricken, startled, petrified, shrinking.

uneasy, worrying, anxious, troubled, bothered, disturbed, hesitant, timid, shy, timorous, cautious; nervous, apprehensive, fidgety, jittery (*inf.*), jumpy, edgy, on edge, tense.

terrible, frightful, awful, dreadful, horrifying, ghastly, atrocious, frightening, terrifying, appalling, harrowing, traumatic, inconceivable; disturbing, disquieting.

vb. fear, be afraid, panic; dread, shake, quiver, quake, cringe, tremble, shudder, one's knees be knocking, be scared out of one's wits, break out in a cold sweat; funk, shrink, flinch; go to pieces, crack up (*inf.*), break down.

frighten, scare, terrify, shock, startle, make one jump; intimidate; give cause for alarm, appal, petrify, frighten out of one's wits, make one's hair stand on end, make one's blood run cold; put the fear of God into (*inf.*); disturb, trouble, bother, concern, dismay, daunt, disquiet, unnerve, worry, torment.

see also **858**

857 courage

n. courage, valour, bravery, fearlessness, boldness, intrepidity, audacity, daring, fortitude; pluck, mettle, heart, backbone, guts (*inf.*), what it takes, stamina, staying power, spunk (*inf.*), grit (*inf.*); Dutch courage; gallantry, chivalry, heroism, prowess, manliness, self-reliance, resolution, determination, firmness, strength; enterprise, initiative.

brave person, hero, heroine, stalwart.

adj. courageous, brave, valiant, bold, confident, fearless, intrepid, audacious, daring, dauntless, undaunted, unflinching; determined, resolute, strong, tough; plucky, heroic, chivalrous, gallant; game; enterprising, adventuresome.

vb. be courageous, have what it takes; keep one's chin up (*inf.*); face, brave, encounter, confront, handle, look in the face, face up to, meet face to face, take the bull by the horns; have the nerve to; make a stand, risk.

pluck up courage, take heart, summon, muster, nerve oneself.

hearten, encourage, strengthen, fortify, inspire, assure, boost.

see also **534, 535**

858 cowardice

n. cowardice, cowardliness, faint-heartedness, weakness, shrinking, funk, cold feet, weak knees, yellow streak; fear, apprehension; shyness, timidity.

coward, scaredy-cat (*inf.*), cry-baby; deserter, shirker, slacker; poltroon, dastard, sneak.

adj. cowardly, craven, faint-hearted, timid, shy, weak, weak-kneed, scared, lily-livered, yellow (*inf.*), chicken (*sl.*); dastardly, pusillanimous.

vb. lose one's courage, get cold feet, back out, chicken out (*inf.*), funk, shrink, quail, show the white feather.

859 rashness

n. rashness, temerity, imprudence, impulsiveness; hurriedness, overhastiness, carelessness, recklessness, foolhardiness; indiscretion; daring, presumption; flippancy, levity; daredevil, harum-scarum (*inf.*).

adj. rash, impulsive, impetuous, hurried, sudden, precipitous, overhasty, premature, breakneck, headlong, frenzied, furious; reckless, foolhardy, careless, thoughtless, imprudent, inconsiderate; headstrong, unthinking, heedless; wild, brash, ill-considered.

vb. be rash, stick one's neck out (*inf.*), jump to conclusions, rush to conclusions, play with fire, burn one's fingers, court danger, court disaster, ask for trouble (*inf.*), ask for it (*inf.*), fools rush in where angels fear to tread, throw caution to the winds, tempt providence.

see also 544, 613

860 caution

n. caution, prudence, cautiousness, care, heed, alertness, vigilance, wariness, suspicion; discretion, circumspection, deliberation, forethought, precaution, presence of mind, foresight.

adj. cautious, watchful, wary, circumspect, careful, prudent, vigilant.

vb. be cautious, play safe, take precautions, take care, look out, provide for, look before one leaps, watch one's step.

861 desire

n. desire, wish, need, want; liking, fondness, fancy, weakness, predilection, inclination, urge, aspiration, ambition; ardour, longing, yearning, pining; nostalgia, homesickness; craze, frenzy, lust, covetousness.

hunger, thirst, ravenousness, craving, voracity, relish, appetite, famine, drought.

adj. desiring, wanting, wishing, liking, desirous, fond, inclined, partial, longing, yearning, pining, itching (*inf.*), dying; eager, keen, crazy, mad, keen, craving; covetous.

hungry, greedy, ravenous, starving, famished, voracious, dry, parched; unsatisfied; peckish (*inf.*).

vb. desire, want, wish, need; like, be fond of, enjoy, choose, fancy, take a fancy to, incline towards, love, take to, be sweet on, have a soft spot for, go for in a big way, set one's heart on (*inf.*), set one's sights on, prize, esteem; aspire, dream; long for, crave, yearn, pine, hanker, make one's mouth water, lust, covet; relish.

be hungry, hunger, starve, famish; be thirsty, be dry, thirst.

see also 889

862 dislike

n. dislike, distaste, disinclination, dissatisfaction; hate, hatred, loathing, aversion, repugnance.

adj. disliking, disinclined, averse to, loath to, fed up with, allergic, squeamish.

disliked, objectionable, repugnant, loathsome, abhorrent, abominable, disagreeable, unpopular.

vb. dislike, not feel like, not care for, hate, loathe, detest, not take kindly to, have nothing to do with, avoid, turn up one's nose at (*inf.*), not go for, not stomach.

see also 892

863 indifference

n. indifference, unconcern, apathy, coldness, insensitivity, neutrality; half-heartedness, lukewarmness; unambitiousness.

adj. indifferent, cold, neutral; lukewarm, half-hearted; unconcerned, impassive, dispassionate, unresponsive, unmoved, uninvolved, lackadaisical, listless, inattentive; isolated, uncommunicative.

vb. be indifferent, not mind, not care, not care less, not give a damn (*inf.*), take no interest in, not matter, be all the same to, leave one cold; take it or leave it.

see also 754

864 fastidiousness

n. fastidiousness, fussiness, meticulousness, scrupulousness, punctiliousness, pedantry, conscientiousness; perfectionism, idealism.

perfectionist, idealist, stickler, purist, pedant; fuss-pot (*inf.*).

adj. fastidious, particular, exact, precise, meticulous, exacting, scrupulous, rigorous, choosy (*inf.*), discriminating, selective, squeamish, finicky, pernickety (*inf.*), overscrupulous, overparticular, overprecise, hypercritical; hard to please; pedantic; delicate, nice.

vb. be fastidious, fuss, be hard to please, split hairs, pick and choose; make a fuss about, make a song and dance about (*inf.*).

865 satiety

n. satiety, repletion, saturation, fill, surfeit, glut, plethora, jadedness, too much of a good thing.

adj. sated, satiated, replete, gorged, glutted, cloyed, overfull, overflowing; full, satisfied.

vb. satiate, fill, surfeit, glut, gorge, stuff, cloy, overfill, overfeed, satisfy, gratify; have one's fill, have enough.

866 wonder

n. wonder, surprise, amazement, awe, astonishment, bewilderment, fascination, stupefaction, incredulity.

sensation, miracle, sign, phenomenon, portent, spectacle, freak, marvel, drama, the unbelievable, prodigy, curiosity, oddity, rarity, something to write home about.

adj. surprising, amazing, astonishing, marvellous, fantastic, unbelievable, incredible, dramatic, remarkable, sensational, phenomenal, miraculous, stupendous, unprecedented, unparalleled, extraordinary, unusual, freakish, unique.

surprised, amazed, astonished, lost in wonder, bewildered, flabbergasted, spellbound, speechless, dumbfounded, thunderstruck, aghast.

vb. wonder, marvel, be surprised, be amazed, be taken aback, stare, gape, not believe, not get over.

amaze, astonish, surprise, bewilder, stupefy, dumbfound, flabbergast, overwhelm, take one's breath away.

867 absence of wonder

n. non-wonder, blankness; expectation; ordinariness, just as one thought, nothing much to write home about.

adj. unastonishing, expected, common, ordinary, usual; unamazed, unsurprised, unimpressed.

vb. not wonder, not be surprised, not bat an eyelid, not turn a hair; expect, take for granted, presume.

868 repute

n. repute, good standing, reputation, name, good name, renown, character, credit, respectability, reliability, trustworthiness, dependability; respect, favour, prestige, honour, glory, regard, kudos (*inf.*); fame, distinction, eminence, prominence, popularity; greatness, dignity, superiority, exaltation, majesty; rank, position, station, status.

big name, somebody, celebrity, star, dignitary, VIP, bigwig, big shot (*sl.*), grand old man.

adj. reputable, respectable, reliable, trustworthy, dependable, respected, well thought of, esteemed, acclaimed; renowned, of renown, famous, popular, celebrated, notable, leading, well-known; prestigious, honourable, distinguished, illustrious, eminent, prominent.

dignified, noble, great, grand, superior, high, exalted, elevated, sublime, majestic.

vb. be somebody, have a name, leave one's mark, make a name for oneself, go down in history.

honour, regard, respect, esteem, hold in high regard, admire, revere, praise, worship; exalt, glorify, crown, enthrone, ennoble, knight, immortalize.

869 disrepute

n. disrepute, disfavour, dishonour, ill-repute, bad name, bad character, unreliability, poor reputation; notoriety, infamy; disgrace, disrespect, reproach, shame, humiliation, degradation, abasement, ignominy, contempt.

scandal, gossip, backbiting, slander, calumny, defamation; slur, slight, insult, stain, stigma, brand, blot.

adj. disreputable, dishonourable, discreditable, ignominious; humiliating, lowering, degrading; notorious, infamous; shady, questionable; disgraceful, scandalous, shameful, outrageous, shocking, contemptible, despicable, corrupt, offensive, flagrant, base, mean, low, shabby, shoddy.

disgraced, humiliated, unable to show one's face.

undistinguished, obscure, unknown, unheard of, unrenowned.

vb. disgrace oneself, lose one's reputation, lose face, lapse from grace, fall from grace, fade; condescend, stoop, descend, lower oneself.

put to shame, disgrace, discredit, dishonour, expose, mock, show up; ridicule, embarrass, humiliate, humble; debase, degrade, snub, confound, unfrock; stain, tarnish, smear, sully, blot; take down a peg or two (*inf.*), cut down to size (*inf.*), drag through the mire (*inf.*).

870 nobility

n. nobility, dignity, grandeur, greatness, distinction, eminence; rank, descent, birth, blood, high birth, blue blood; royalty, majesty, court; aristocracy, gentry, landed gentry, peerage, ruling class, privileged class, elite, gentility; society, high society, upper classes, upper ten thousand, upper crust (*inf.*), higher-ups (*inf.*).

nobleman; peer, peeress; archbishop; duke, duchess; marquis, marchioness; earl; count, countess; viscount, viscountess; bishop; baron, baroness; lord, lady; baronet; knight, dame; life peer; dowager.

adj. noble, dignified, grand, great, magnificent, lofty, imposing, distinguished; royal, majestic, monarchic, regal, reigning, princely; aristocratic, courtly, titled, lordly; highborn, of gentle birth, born in the purple.

871 common people

n. commonalty, common people, commons; people, the masses, general public, rank and file, grass roots; bourgeoisie, middle class; working class, lower class, have-nots, underdogs, proletariat; rabble, crowd, herd, riffraff, *hoi polloi*, ragtag and bobtail, the great unwashed, scum, dregs.

commoner, plebeian, citizen, civilian, man in the street, Mr. Average; countryman, rustic, yokel, country bumpkin, peasant, serf.

adj. common, plebeian, bourgeois, ordinary, average, lowly, humble, of low estate, mean, ignoble; rustic.

872 title

n. title, name, designation; courtesy title, handle (*inf.*), honorific; order, privilege, honour; decoration, ribbon, medal, crest, emblem.

873 pride

n. pride, self-respect, self-regard, self-esteem, dignity, self-love; conceit, vanity, haughtiness, vainglory; self-exaltation, self-glorification; ego-trip; arrogance, insolence.

proud person, bighead (*inf.*), swank (*inf.*), boaster, bragger.

adj. self-respecting, pleased with oneself, self-assured, self-satisfied; dignified, lofty, stately, elevated, high-falutin; egotistic, conceited, bigheaded (*inf.*), patronizing.

vb. be proud, hold one's head high; take pride in, pride oneself on, glory in, boast.

see also **875**

874 humility

n. humility, humbleness, self-abasement, self-effacement; submission, obedience, meekness, lowliness, modesty, subservience, subjection; unobtrusiveness.

humiliation; abasement; mortification; come-down (*inf.*), let-down (*inf.*), deflation, crushing, shame.

adj. humble, lowly, meek, submissive, modest, self-effacing, subservient, servile; unassuming, unpretentious; humiliated, humbled, let down (*inf.*), deflated, squashed, crushed, crestfallen, chastened; embarrassed, ashamed.

vb. humble oneself, submit, obey; condescend, stoop, deign; eat humble pie, come down from one's high horse; be humiliated, not dare show one's face, feel small, feel squashed.

humiliate, humble, shame, embarrass, deflate, crush, squash, let down (*inf.*), bring low, put to shame, disconcert, make one feel small, take down a peg or two (*inf.*), teach one his place, reduce to tears.

see also **881**

875 vanity

n. vanity, conceit, self-importance, self-glorification, egotism, vainglory, self-applause, boastfulness; self-worship, narcissism; show, ostentation, exhibitionism; futility, emptiness, uselessness.

egotist, show-off, exhibitionist, know-all, smart aleck (*inf.*), toffee-nose (*sl.*), Narcissus.

adj. vain, conceited, haughty, self-centred, self-important, self-glorifying, self-applauding, full of oneself, boastful, cocky, swollen-headed, stuck up (*inf.*), puffed up, too big for one's boots (*sl.*), swanky (*inf.*), snooty (*inf.*), high and mighty (*inf.*), pompous, arrogant, insolent, supercilious, pretentious, snobbish, toffee-nose (*sl.*), standoffish; showy, exhibitionist.

vb. be vain, be puffed up, get too big for one's boots (*sl.*), have a high opinion of oneself, think too much of oneself, come the high and mighty with (*inf.*), know it all, boast, show off; turn up one's nose at (*inf.*); go to one's head, puff up.

see also **879**

876 modesty; shyness

n. modesty, unassumingness, unpretentiousness, unobtrusiveness, restraint, meekness, retiring nature; chastity, purity, virtue.

shyness, timidity, bashfulness, reserve, reticence, coyness; inhibition, nervousness.

adj. modest, retiring, restrained, meek, unassuming, unobtrusive, diffident, shrinking; restrained, tasteful, undecorated; chaste, pure, innocent.

shy, timid, bashful, quiet, reserved, coy, reticent, reluctant, backward, inhibited, secretive, demure, proper; blushing, embarrassed, red.

vb. hold back, hide one's face, keep in the background, take a back seat, hide one's light under a bushel, retire into one's shell; blush, go red.

877 ostentation

n. ostentation, exhibitionism, showiness, pretension; pomp, pompousness, magnificence, splendour, grandeur, majesty, pageantry; blatancy, flagrancy, flashiness, gaudiness, loudness; flourish, parade, fuss, splurge, showing off; bravado, histrionics, theatricality, sensationalism, effect, showmanship; exhibitionist, show-off, showman.

adj. ostentatious, showing off, proud, pompous, grandiose, extravagant, bombastic, high-flown, fancy, jazzy, showy, garish, gaudy, flashy, flamboyant, flaunting, blatant, flagrant, obtrusive, conspicuous, loud, screaming; spectacular, sensational, theatrical, histrionic, for effect, for show.

vb. show off, flaunt, parade, flourish, splurge, play to the gallery, do for show, make an exhibition of oneself, give oneself airs; sensationalize.

878 celebration

n. celebration, commemoration, honouring, keeping, observance; anniversary, jubilee, birthday, red-letter day, centenary, bicentenary, tercentenary; ceremonial; solemnization; ceremony, function, occasion, festive occasion, do (*inf.*); clapping, applause, praise, acclaim, cheers, hurrahs, cries, ovation, standing ovation, salute.

adj. celebrative, commemorative, anniversary, congratulatory, ceremonial, festive.

vb. celebrate, commemorate, observe, keep, remember, honour, congratulate, crown; throw a party, make merry, kill the fatted calf.

879 boasting

n. boasting, self-glory, self-glorification; boast, brag, empty talk, big talk, hot air, bombast, bluster, braggadocio, gasconade.

boaster, big mouth, swank (*inf.*), gas-bag (*sl.*), braggart, Gascon.

adj. boastful, bragging, big-mouthed, pretentious, inflated, self-glorifying, vaunting.

vb. boast, vaunt, brag, show off, talk big, bounce, exaggerate; blow one's own trumpet, have a high opinion of oneself, pat oneself on the back, congratulate oneself, flatter oneself.

880 insolence

n. insolence, rudeness, boldness, audacity, effrontery, impudence, impertinence, arrogance, presumption, forwardness, shamelessness, officiousness, sauciness, defiance, lip (*sl.*), cheek, nerve (*inf.*), sauce, brass.

upstart, wise guy (*sl.*), pup.

adj. insolent, impudent, impertinent, arrogant, high-handed, disrespectful, insulting, rude, offensive, officious, outrageous, defiant, cheeky, saucy, uppity (*inf.*); presumptious, forward.

vb. be insolent, have the cheek, have a nerve (*inf.*), get fresh, come the high and mighty with (*inf.*), get on one's high horse (*inf.*), throw one's weight about (*inf.*); give lip (*sl.*), brazen it out, answer back, presume, take for granted.

881 servility

n. servility, obsequiousness, menality, sycophancy, toadyism; sycophant, toady, back-scratcher, yes-man, sponger, parasite, hanger-on, boot-licker.

adj. servile, menial, beggarly, slavish, subservient, obsequious, cringing, toadyish, boot-licking, ingratiating, fawning, grovelling, snivelling.

vb. be servile, suck up to (*sl.*), crawl (*inf.*), grovel, go down on one's knees, lick the boots of, ingratiate oneself with, toady, fawn, curry favour; flatter.

D Sympathetic

882 friendship

n. friendship, companionship, amity, comradeship, fraternity, intimacy, familiarity; friendliness, affection, amicability, sociability, good terms, neighbourliness, understanding, compatibility, matiness, warmth, cordiality.

friend, companion, mate, pal, chum, buddy, comrade; boy-friend, girlfriend; acquaintance, neighbour; close friend, best friend, bosom friend, confidant, intimate.

adj. friendly, close, familiar, intimate, inseparable, confiding; faithful, loyal, devoted, true, trusted, staunch, firm; amicable, sympathetic, compatible, sociable, affectionate, warmhearted, brotherly, matey, pally; kind, benevolent.

vb. be friendly, know, be acquainted with, be on good terms with; befriend, get to know, make friends with, get in with (*inf.*), get pally with, chum up with, break the ice; go out with (*inf.*), go with, knock about with (*inf.*), go around with, keep company with, go together, see (*inf.*), run after (*inf.*), go after (*inf.*), chase, try to get, take out, accompany, court, woo, make advances; be just good friends.

see also **889**

883 enmity

n. enmity, hostility, inimicality; antipathy, unfriendliness; hatred, antagonism, dislike, repugnance, animosity; ill-feeling, hard feelings; separation, estrangement, alienation; bitterness, acrimony, coolness.

enemy, foe, antagonist, opponent, adversary, arch-enemy, invader; public enemy; rival, informer.

adj. inimical, hostile, antagonistic, unfriendly, ill-disposed, opposed; irreconcilable, alienated, estranged; at odds, at daggers drawn, at loggerheads, not on speaking terms, on bad terms; cool, cold, chilly, uncordial; opposite, contrary, conflicting; quarrelsome, unsympathetic, grudging, resentful.

vb. be opposed to, differ, be at odds with, conflict, clash; antagonize, provoke, alienate, estrange.

see also **637, 638**

884 sociability

n. sociability, geniality, friendliness, cordiality, gregariousness, conviviality, affability, hospitality, open house, social intercourse.

party, social, get-together, ball, meeting, reunion, rendezvous, reception, at home, soirée; visit, call, appointment, engagement, date, interview, stay; arrangement.

visitor, dropper-in, guest, caller; mixer, good mixer, life and soul of the party; gate-crasher, uninvited guest.

adj. sociable, friendly, genial, cordial, affable, gregarious, neighbourly, hospitable.

vb. be sociable, invite, welcome, receive, entertain, throw a party; keep open house; visit, drop in on, look in, call by.

885 unsociability

n. unsociability, unfriendliness, uncommunicativeness, shyness; distance, unapproachability, aloofness; seclusion, privacy, separateness, isolation, retirement, withdrawal, solitariness, loneliness; backwater, back of beyond, backwoods, refuge, retreat, cloister, ivory tower, shell, desert island.

recluse, hermit, monk, anchorite, backwoodsman; loner, stay-at-home; outcast, castaway; refugee, evacuee; outlaw, bandit; orphan, leper.

adj. unsociable, unfriendly, distant, shy, uncommunicative, unapproachable, aloof, stand-offish, antisocial, inhospitable; lonesome, solitary, lonely, friendless, desolate, retiring, withdrawn; secluded, forsaken, isolated, rustic, out-of-the-way, remote, God-forsaken, unexplored, uninhabited, deserted.

vb. be unsociable, stand aloof, keep oneself to oneself, keep one's distance, go into seclusion, shut oneself up, retire into one's shell; seclude, exclude, expel, excommunicate, repel, cold-shoulder, keep at arm's length, keep at bay, beat off.

886 courtesy

n. courtesy, thoughtfulness, consideration, politeness, manners, good manners, civility, culture, refinement, breeding, gentility, respect, kindness, friendliness, generosity, gallantry, chivalry; condescension, flattery, oiliness.

good turn, favour, compliment; greeting, handshake, smile, embrace, hug, kiss.

adj. courteous, polite, well-mannered, civil, amiable, affable, thoughtful, considerate, kind, friendly, generous, obliging; cultivated, cultured, refined, polished, well-bred; politic, diplomatic; gentlemanly, ladylike; gallant, chivalrous; condescending, obsequious, ingratiating, patronizing.

vb. be courteous, behave oneself, mind one's P's and Q's, be on one's best behaviour; give one's regards, give one's compliments, send best wishes, pay one's respects, compliment; greet, welcome, hail, exchange greetings, hold out one's hand, shake hands, smile, wave, hug, embrace, kiss.

887 discourtesy

n. discourtesy, impoliteness, bad manners, misbehaviour, incivility, ill breeding; disrespect, impudence, unfriendliness, brusqueness; meanness, nastiness, unpleasantness, rudeness, vulgarity, boorishness, coarseness, grossness, shamelessness.

adj. discourteous, impolite, bad-mannered, uncivil, uncultured, unrefined, unbecoming, misbehaved, ungentlemanly, rude, unfriendly, unkind, ungracious, unpleasant, nasty, obstreperous, disrespectful, offensive, crude, coarse, vulgar, shameless; loutish, rowdy, disorderly, boorish; thoughtless, careless, inconsiderate, tactless, gauche, outspoken; brusque, abrupt, curt, offhand, rough, gruff, surly, difficult; audacious, brash; cheeky, high-handed.

vb. be rude, insult, affront, outrage; give the cold shoudler; irritate, annoy, shout down, interrupt; snub, disregard, ignore.

888 congratulation

n. congratulation, felicitation, best wishes, compliments, happy returns; applause, appreciation, bouquet, praise, acknowledgement, toast.

adj. congratulatory, complimentary.

vb. congratulate, compliment, felicitate, pay one's respects, offer one's congratulations, salute, praise, honour, acclaim, sound the praises of, appreciate, admire, adulate; toast, celebrate; mob.

889 love

n. love, fondness, affection, attachment, devotion, adoration; passion, Eros, ardour, amorousness, lust, infatuation, crush (*sl.*), pash (*sl.*); first love, calf-love, puppy love; emotion, sentiment; attractiveness, charm, winsomeness, appeal, sex-appeal, fascination; love affair, affair, romance, liaison, relationship, flirtation, amour, eternal triangle.

lover, admirer, suitor, wooer, boyfriend, girl-friend, date (*inf.*), steady (*inf.*), blind date; Romeo, Juliet, fiancé, fiancée; mistress; cohabitant.

adj. loving, fond, affectionate, devoted, adoring, attached; emotional, sentimental, tender, soft; yearning, longing, passionate, ardent, amorous, glowing.

enamoured, attracted, enchanted, fascinated, caught, charmed, captivated, enraptured, taken with, sweet on, keen on, infatuated, gone on, crazy, wild, mad, smitten, in love, head over heels in love.

lovable, winsome, attractive, charming, appealing, captivating, irresistible, dear; loved, beloved, cherished.

vb. love, like, be fond of, care for, delight in, adore, fancy; treasure, hold dear, take to one's heart (*inf.*), admire, regard, cherish, appreciate, esteem, value, prize; be in love, dote on, be enraptured by; fall in love, fall for, be crazy about, have it bad (*inf.*); lose one's heart to, have a crush on, be swept off one's feet (*inf.*), be infatuated with; long, yearn; copulate, have intercourse, make love to, have sex with (*inf.*), sleep with (*inf.*), sleep together (*inf.*), go to bed with, have it off with (*sl.*); live with, live together, cohabit, live in sin (*inf.*).

attract, appeal, fascinate, captivate, charm, enchant, allure, draw, rouse, enrapture, infatuate, sweep off one's feet (*inf.*).

see also **861, 882**

890 endearment

n. endearment, affection, attachment, fondness, love, soft nothings, embrace, kiss, cuddle, stroke, fondling, petting, necking (*sl.*); courtship, courting, wooing, pass, advance, dating, flirtation, amorous intentions; loveletter, Valentine; proposal, offer of marriage, engagement.

vb. woo, court, go out with (*inf.*), run after (*inf.*), pursue, chase, date, pay attentions to, make overtures, make advances, make passes, make eyes at (*inf*), ogle, flirt; propose, pop the question (*inf.*).

be fond of, cherish; embrace, hug, clasp, draw close, snuggle, kiss, cuddle; stroke, fondle, caress, pat, pet, neck, smooch (*inf.*).

see also **882**

891 darling; favourite

n. darling, dear, love, beloved, dearest, sweetheart, angel, pet, sweet, sweetie (*inf.*), sweetie-pie (*inf.*), sugar (*inf.*), honey (*inf.*), precious (*inf.*), treasure (*inf.*), jewel (*inf.*); favourite, mother's darling, teacher's pet, blue-eyed boy, apple of one's eye.

892 hate

n. hate, hatred, dislike, antipathy, aversion, loathing, abhorrence, repugnance, repulsion, disgust, scorn, detestation, nasty look.

anathema, abomination, menace, pest, *bête noire*, bitter pill.

adj. detestable, hateful, odious, abominable, abhorrent, loathsome, accursed, offensive, repugnant, disgusting, revolting, repulsive, vile; averse to, hostile, antagonistic.

vb. hate, dislike, loathe, abhor, detest, abominate, denounce, condemn, object to, spurn, spit upon, curse, reject, have it in for (*inf.*).

offend, rub up the wrong way, repel, disgust, shock, alienate, estrange, antagonize, make one's blood run cold.

see also **295**, **862**

893 resentment; anger

n. resentment, bitterness, hurt, soreness, malice, grudge, bone to pick; sore point.

anger, indignation, displeasure, antagonism; rage, fury, wrath, vehemence, passion, vexation, exasperation, annoyance, impatience, ire; bad temper, outburst, fit, tantrum, huff, tiff, quarrel, argument, fight.

adj. resentful, indignant, sore, hurt, grudging, bitter, embittered, with a chip on one's shoulder, acrimonious.

angry, cross, irate, furious, raging, fiery, mad (*inf.*), hopping mad (*inf.*), fuming, displeased; antagonized, enraged, exasperated, infuriated, annoyed, irritated, peeved (*sl.*), impatient, irritable, ratty (*sl.*), shirty (*sl.*), provoked, affronted, riled, vexed, worked up, het up (*inf.*), up in arms, in a huff, hot under the collar, foaming at the mouth (*inf.*).

vb. resent, feel bitter towards, take umbrage, take exception, be insulted, bear a grudge, bear malice, have a bone to pick.

get angry, get cross, lose one's temper, blow one's top (*inf.*), hit the roof (*inf.*), fly off the handle (*inf.*), blow up (*inf.*), explode; get worked up, get het up (*inf.*), get hot under the collar, go up the wall (*inf.*), go off the deep end (*inf.*).

be angry, burn, roar, rage, rant and rave, fume, storm, boil, seethe, foam at the mouth (*inf.*); snap, bite someone's head off (*inf.*), jump down someone's throat (*inf.*); criticize, nag, get at.

anger, enrage, incense, infuriate, madden, antagonize, exasperate, provoke, bother, harass, vex, annoy, incite, irritate, needle, nettle, rankle, rile, stir, get someone's back up (*inf.*), get someone's blood up, make one's blood boil, send up the wall, rub up the wrong way (*inf.*), tread on someone's toes (*inf.*), get on someone's nerves, get under someone's skin, get someone's goat (*sl.*), upset, ruffle, discompose, put out.

see also **642**

894 irritability

n. irritability, sensitivity, nervousness, uneasiness, exasperation, impatience, touchiness, bad temper.

adj. irritable, sensitive, susceptible, touchy, oversensitive, prickly, edgy, short-tempered, ratty (*sl.*), shirty (*sl.*), uptight, gruff, grumpy; nervous, anxious, jumpy, jittery (*inf.*); temperamental, moody; irritated, annoyed, needled, riled, rankled, nettled, rubbed up the wrong way, with a chip on one's shoulder; irascible, choleric, querulous, cantankerous.

895 sullenness

n. sullenness, moroseness, glumness, moodiness, unsociability, sourness, bad temper, gruffness, spleen; frown, scowl, grimace, sneer, dirty look (*inf.*), wry face.

adj. sullen, morose, glum, silent,

unsociable; moody, surly, grouchy, churlish, sulky, cross, mopish, ill-humoured, ill-natured, disagreeable, sour, mournful, saturnine; scowling, frowning; gloomy, dismal, sad, dim, dark, cheerless, sombre.

vb. scowl, frown, grimace, make a face, pull a face, glower, growl, sulk, grouch, mope, sneer.

896 marriage

n. marriage, matrimony, wedlock, conjugality, union, match, alliance, marriage tie, marriage bed; wedding, pledging, ceremony, nuptials, espousals; church wedding, civil marriage, registry-office wedding; elopement, abduction; shotgun wedding; reception, wedding breakfast, party, dance; honeymoon, consummation.

man and wife, bride and groom, bridal pair, newlyweds, honeymooners; partner, spouse, mate; husband, man; wife, helpmeet, better half (*inf.*), the missus (*sl.*).

adj. matrimonial, marital, nuptial, conjugal, married, wed, united, matched; newly-wed; honeymooning, going-away, marriageable, eligible, suitable, of marriageable age.

vb. marry, get married, wed, espouse, take to oneself, lead to the altar, plight one's troth, become one, get hitched (*sl.*), get spliced (*sl.*), make an honest woman of (*inf.*); honeymoon, go away, consummate; run away, leave home, elope; join, unite, pronounce man and wife, marry, give in marriage, give away; marry into, marry out of; marry off, match, matchmake, find a match for, find a mate for; catch, find, hook (*sl.*).

see also **889**

897 celibacy

n. celibacy, singleness, bachelorhood, virginity, spinsterhood; celibate, bachelor, confirmed bachelor; spinster, bachelor girl, old maid, virgin.

adj. celibate, single, unmarried, unwed, not the marrying kind; eligible, unattached, free; virgin.

898 divorce; widowhood

n. divorce, separation, annulment, dissolution, decree nisi, desertion; breakdown of marriage.

widowhood; survivor, widow, dowager, relict; widower; grass widow, golf widow.

adj. divorced, parted, separated, living apart.

vb. divorce, get a divorce, annul, cancel, put asunder, sue for a divorce, desert, split up (*inf.*), separate, live apart; widow, bereave; leave, survive.

899 benevolence

n. benevolence, kindness, helpfulness, thoughtfulness, kindheartedness, graciousness, courtesy, charity, altruism, philanthropy, fellow-feeling, the golden rule; service, good deed, good turn, aid, relief, favour, benefit, alms.

kind person, good Samaritan, good neighbour, altruist, humanitarian, do-gooder, philanthropist, heart of gold.

adj. kind, benevolent, charitable, helpful, careful, thoughtful, well-meaning, well-intentioned, well-meant, gracious, good, pleasant, generous, obliging, neighbourly, kindhearted, warm-hearted, compassionate, sympathetic, unselfish, altruistic, humanitarian, philanthropic; merciful, pitying.

vb. be kind, help, do a good turn, do a favour, benefit, support, encourage, comfort, relieve, bless, mean well, wish well, do as one would be done by, bend over backwards to help.

see also **550, 905, 935**

900 malevolence

n. malevolence, unkindness, hate, animosity, malice, malignity, spite, bitterness, acrimony; cruelty, inhumanity, wickedness, ruthlessness, relentlessness, harshness, severity, callousness; tyranny, oppression, despotism, intolerance; brutality, beastliness, savagery, barbarousness, brutishness, monstrousness.

ill, harm, misfortune, mischief, blow, outrage, foul play, catastrophe, disaster, atrocity, torture.

adj. unkind, unfriendly, unloving, uncharitable, stepmotherly, inconsiderate, thoughtless; spiteful, malicious, catty, hateful, resentful, bitter, acrimonious, caustic.

cruel, malevolent, malicious, inhuman, wicked, harsh, severe, relentless, fierce, savage, barbarous, brutal, beastly; pitiless, unmerciful, intolerant, ruthless, cold, callous, hardhearted, oppressive, despotic, devilish, diabolical.

vb. be malevolent, hurt, harm, abuse, maltreat, damage, injure, oppress, tyrannize, not tolerate, persecute, torture, torment, victimize, have it in for (*inf.*), take it out on (*inf.*).

see also **551, 906, 936**

901 curse

n. curse, malediction, denunciation, execration, abuse, vilification, vituperation, scurrility; profanity, swearing, oath, imprecation, expletive, swearword, naughty word, bad language, blasphemy, sacrilege, profanation.

adj. maledictory, imprecatory, damnatory; abusive, scurrilous, profane, sacrilegious, blasphemous, blue, naughty, indecent, obscene.

vb. curse, wish on (*inf.*), invoke, summon, call down on; abuse, defame, denounce, pour abuse, call names, revile, vituperate, vilify, damn; swear, swear like a trooper, blaspheme.

902 threat

n. threat, menace, warning, intimidation, blackmail; writing on the wall, danger signal, distress signal; threatening, commination.

adj. threatening, menacing, intimidating, frightening; ominous, imminent.

vb. threaten, menace, intimidate, blackmail, frighten, scare, torment, bully, push around (*inf.*), order about (*inf.*); be brewing, loom, be imminent.

see also **154**

903 philanthropy

n. philanthropy, humanitarianism, utilitarianism, altruism, social conscience; welfare state, social services; patriotism, love of one's country, loyalty, public spirit; nationalism, chauvinism; internationalism.

philanthropist, humanitarian, dogooder; idealist, altruist, visionary, man with a vision, missionary; patriot, lover of one's country, loyalist, nationalist, chauvinist; internationalist, citizen of the world, cosmopolitan.

adj. philanthropic, humanitarian, humane, kind, altruistic, patriotic; chauvinistic; public-spirited, reforming.

vb. have a social conscience, be public-spirited, show public spirit; love one's country.

904 misanthropy

n. misanthropy, selfishness, egotism, cynicism, unsociability, incivism;

misanthrope, man-hater, misogynist, woman-hater, cynic, egoist.

adj. misanthropic, antisocial, unsocial, unsociable, inhuman, cynical; unpatriotic.

see also **885**

905 benefactor

n. benefactor, benefactress, helper, good neighbour, do-gooder, giver, donor, contributor; protector, guard, watch, champion, guardian; patron, supporter, backer; rescuer, deliverer, liberator, redeemer; angel, guardian angel.

see also **640**

906 evildoer

n. evildoer, wrongdoer, troublemaker, mischief-maker; criminal, lawbreaker, offender, transgressor, sinner, public enemy; crook, villain, rogue; thief, gangster, con man (*inf.*); murderer, assassin; ruffian, thug, hooligan, layabout (*inf.*), nasty piece of work (*inf.*); beast, brute, monster, vampire, viper.

see also **684, 723, 940**

907 pity

n. pity, compassion, goodness, kindliness, benevolence, understanding, charity; tenderness, soft-heartedness, warm-heartedness; condolence, sympathy, commiseration, fellow feeling, comfort, solace, consolation; mercy, favour, grace, clemency, forbearance, forgiveness, second chance.

adj. pitying, compassionate, kind, tender, gentle, lenient; merciful, gracious, clement, forbearing, forgiving, generous; sympathetic, consoling, commiserating, comforting, sorry; pitiful, pitiable.

vb. pity, show mercy, take pity on, pardon, spare, forgive, reprieve, give a second chance; relent, relax, repent; put out of one's misery.

sympathize, feel for, feel with, put oneself in someone's shoes, be understanding, express sympathy, commiserate, share another's sorrow, grieve with, weep for, love, console, comfort, support, uphold, encourage, sit by, put one's arm round.

908 pitilessness

n. pitilessness, ruthlessness, mercilessness, relentlessness, cruelty, heartlessness, callousness, hardness of heart; letter of the law, pound of flesh.

adj. pitiless, unpitying, unmerciful, merciless, relentless, unrelenting, unforgiving, barbarous, tyrannical, vindictive, revengeful; rough, harsh, severe; cruel, brutal, savage; cold, unsympathetic, unfeeling, unmoved, inflexible; hard-hearted, stony-hearted, cold-blooded.

vb. show no pity, stop at nothing (*inf.*), harden one's heart, turn a deaf ear to, give no quarter, exact one's pound of flesh; one's heart bleed for (*inf.*).

909 gratitude

n. gratitude, thankfulness, appreciation, gratefulness, sense of obligation; thanks, thank-you, acknowledgement, response, recognition, praise, tribute, vote of thanks, honour, credit; blessing, grace, prayer, benediction; bread-and-butter letter; reward, trip; leaving-present.

adj. grateful, thankful, appreciative, responsive; indebted, obliged, much obliged; pleased, gratified, overwhelmed.

vb. thank, say thank you, show one's gratitude, respond, appreciate, show one's appreciation, acknowledge, recognize, praise, pay a tribute to, never forget, applaud; reward, tip; give thanks, say grace, return thanks.

910 ingratitude

n. ingratitude, ungratefulness, lack of appreciation, thanklessness, no sense of obligation; thoughtlessness, rudeness.

adj. ungrateful, unappreciative, unmindful, forgetful, rude; thankless, unrewarding, unprofitable, worthless; unthanked, unacknowledged, unrewarded.

vb. be ungrateful, not thank, take for granted, presume upon.

911 forgiveness

n. forgiveness, pardon, free pardon, absolution; remission, acquittal, release, discharge; exoneration, exculpation; justification, reconciliation, redemption, atonement; reprieve, amnesty, indemnity; grace, mercy, patience, forbearance.

adj. forgiven, pardoned, excused, absolved, let off, acquitted, free, not guilty, released, reinstated, reconciled, restored, taken back, welcomed home; redeemed, justified, adopted.

vb. forgive, pardon, excuse, remit, reprieve, clear, absolve, discharge, acquit, free, declare not guilty, let off (*inf.*), let go; let pass, disregard, ignore, shut one's eyes to, grant amnesty to; show mercy, tolerate, forbear; redeem, reconcile, justify; purge, blot one's sins out, wipe the slate clean; bury the hatchet, make it up, kiss and make up; forgive and forget, let bygones be bygones.

see also **921, 961**

912 revenge

n. revenge, vengeance, requital, reprisal, retaliation; vindictiveness, spitefulness, rancour; avenger, vindicator.

adj. revengeful, vengeant, spiteful, retaliatory, unrelenting, rancorous, unappeasable, implacable.

vb. avenge, take revenge, take vengeance, requite, vindicate, retaliate, get even with, get one's own back.

see also **647**

913 jealousy

n. jealousy, resentment, intolerance, distrust, suspicion, green eye, green-eyed monster; rivalry, unfaithfulness, hostility; vigilance, watchfulness, possessiveness.

adj. jealous, green-eyed, resentful, distrustful, suspicious, vigilant, watchful, possessive.

914 envy

n. envy, covetousness, resentment.
adj. envious, covetous, jealous.
vb. envy, covet, lust after, desire, crave, hanker; grudge, begrudge.

E Moral

915 right

n. right, justice, rightfulness, lawfulness, legality, legitimacy, fairness, equity, impartiality, poetic justice; suitability, reasonableness, fittingness; the right thing, what is right, the proper thing, square deal, fair play.

adj. right, correct, precise, true, valid, accurate; appropriate, proper, suitable, apt, fit, on the right track; fair, honest, upright, righteous, just, rightful, lawful, legitimate, equitable, impartial, objective, unprejudiced, unbiased, disinterested, dispassionate, straightforward, plain; fair and square, straight, fair-minded, sporting.

vb. be just, play the game, try to be

fair, do justice to, do the right thing, give the Devil his due.

see also **577**

916 wrong

n. wrong, wrongness, injustice, wrongfulness, inequity, unfairness, partiality, partisanship, prejudice, bias, favouritism; foul play, raw deal, irregularity; grievance, injury; preferential treatment, discrimination, reverse discrimination, nepotism.

adj. wrong, unjust, wrongful, unreasonable, unfair, inequitable, partial, biased, prejudiced, partisan, uneven, unbalanced; below the belt, not cricket (*inf.*), unsportsmanlike; erroneous, imprecise, inaccurate, on the wrong track, at fault; injurious, harmful; wicked, sinful; unsuitable, unfitting, inappropriate, improper; unjustifiable, inexcusable, unforgivable; inadmissible, illegal, illicit, illegitimate.

vb. do wrong, break the law, wrong, hurt, injure, harm, treat unfairly, maltreat, cheat; discriminate, favour, prefer, show preference, be biased, show partiality; not play the game properly, not play fair, hit below the belt.

see also **416, 578**

917 dueness

n. dueness, due; deserts, comeuppance, just deserts, merits; right, human rights, rights of man, women's rights; dues, fees, levy, contribution; reward, compensation; punishment; privilege, responsibility, prerogative.

adj. due, owing, payable, overdue, outstanding, unpaid, unsettled, in arrears, chargeable; deserved, well-deserved, merited, worthy, just, warranted, entitled, deserving, worthy, needy, rightful, meritorious.

vb. be due, become due, mature, deserve, merit, have the right to, be entitled to; be worthy of, warrant, expect, earn, claim, lay claim to; demand one's rights; have it coming to one (*inf.*), have only oneself to thank, serve someone right.

918 undueness

n. undueness, unfittingness; presumption, assumption, overstepping, arrogation, violation, encroachment; dispossession, disentitlement, forfeiture, disfranchisement.

adj. undue, undeserved, unmerited, unwarranted, uncalled for, improper, unnecessary, immoderate; unworthy, unjust, unfair, undeserving; unentitled, unprivileged.

vb. have no right to, presume, venture, overstep, assume, usurp, violate, not be entitled to, take liberties; not expect; disqualify; invalidate, disentitle, disfranchise.

919 duty

n. duty, obligation, liability, responsibility, burden, onus; accountability; engagement, commitment, pledge, contract, debt; call of duty, sense of duty, moral obligation, conscience, still small voice; loyalty, faithfulness, allegiance.

adj. incumbent, up to one, behoving; obliged, duty-bound, under obligation; liable, responsible, answerable, subject to, accountable; obligatory, binding, compulsory, necessary; dutiful, obedient, submissive, tractable, compliant.

vb. be one's duty, be the duty of, should, ought, had better, behove; be responsible for, rest with, devolve on, rest on the shoulders of, fall to, fall to one's lot; accept responsiblity, commit oneself; do one's duty, do what is expected of one, perform, fulfil, acquit oneself well, meet one's obligations; impose a duty, call upon, enjoin, look to; oblige, bind, saddle with, put under obligation.

920 neglect of duty

n. neglect, disregard, omission, evasion, non-observance, dereliction, negligence; carelessness, slackness, remissness, slovenliness; absence, absenteeism, truancy; defection, desertion, mutiny; disloyalty, unfaithfulness.

adj. negligent, inattentive, careless, slack, undutiful; disloyal, unfaithful; rebellious, mutinous.

vb. neglect, fail, break, violate; pass over, let slip, let go, omit, ignore, evade, shirk; defer, postpone, procrastinate; suspend, discard, dismiss; rebel, mutiny; absent oneself, play truant; let someone down, not trouble oneself.

see also **393**

921 exemption

n. exemption, immunity, privilege; freedom, liberation, release, dispensation, exception, absolution; permission, leave; lifting of restrictions; escape-clause.

adj. exempt, free, clear, non-liable, not subject to, not chargeable; immune, privileged; unaffected, unrestrained, uncontrolled, unbound, unrestricted; outside.

vb. exempt, free, clear, release, acquit, discharge; lift restrictions; shrug off, pass the buck (*inf.*); be exempt, be free, enjoy immunity, get away with murder (*inf.*).

see also **680, 961**

922 respect

n. respect, regard, honour, esteem, appreciation, favour, admiration, recognition, high opinion, high regard, deference, liking, love; praise, reverence, veneration, awe, worship; respects, bow, curtsy, salute, greeting, salutation.

adj. respectful, deferential, courteous, polite, admiring, showing respect for; attentive, reverential; on one's knees, prostrate.

respected, highly regarded, valued, appreciated, esteemed, honoured, time-honoured, important, well thought of.

vb. respect, regard highly, think well of, think a great deal of, have a high opinion of, admire, take off one's hat to (*inf.*), value, appreciate, honour, hold dear; praise, extol, revere, worship; pay one's respects, bow, kneel, curtsy, welcome, greet; scrape, grovel; keep in with (*inf.*), keep on the right side of; stand in awe of.

command respect, impress, overawe, awe, stun, overwhelm, humble.

923 disrespect

n. disrespect, discourtesy, impoliteness, irreverence, dishonour, low opinion, low regard; insult, affront, offence, humiliation, slight, snub, rebuff, slap in the face, backhanded compliment.

adj. disrespectful, discourteous, impolite, irreverent, dishonourable, insulting, offensive, slighting, cutting, humiliating, rude, scornful, impertinent, depreciating, pejorative.

vb. have no respect for, show disrespect for, have a low opinion of, have no time for, underrate, dishonour, offend, insult, affront, slight, snub, rebuff, scorn, despise, look down on (*inf.*), humiliate, interrupt.

924 contempt

n. contempt, scorn, disdain, ridicule, mocking, derision, disrespect, disdainfulness, contemptuousness, scornful-ness, snobbishness, haughtiness; sneer, slight, scoff, cold shoulder.

adj. contemptuous, disdainful, scornful, disrespectful, haughty, supercilious, insolent, snooty, snobbish; contemptible, mean, poor, base, worthless, shameful, despicable, beneath contempt.

vb. despise, disdain, spurn, scorn, pour scorn on, turn one's nose up at (*inf.*), sneer at, mock, laugh at, ridicule, deride; pity, look down on (*inf.*), look down one's nose at (*inf.*); disregard, cut dead; avoid, shun, steer clear of; cheapen, belittle, pooh-pooh, not care a fig for.

see also 853

925 approval

n. approval, recognition, acknowledgement; satisfaction; agreement, permission, sanction, adoption, acceptance; admiration, esteem, credit, honour; compliment, bouquet, commendation, citation, write-up; praise, glorification; applause, clapping, ovation, acclaim.

adj. approving, favourable, complimentary, commendatory, laudatory; approvable, commendable, laudable, praiseworthy, creditable, acceptable; approved, popular, praised, uncensored.

vb. approve, recognize, acknowledge; agree, give permission, allow, sanction; accept, adopt, favour; not reject, not sniff at; praise, admire, esteem, compliment, commend, speak well of, write up, crack up (*inf.*), take off one's hat to (*inf.*), give full marks to, must hand it to (*inf.*); find no fault with, have nothing but praises for; sing the praises of, rave about (*inf.*); clap, applaud, cheer, acclaim, hail, give a big hand to.

926 disapproval

n. disapproval, disagreement, non-acceptance, objection, criticism, complaint, opposition, rejection, contradiction, denunciation, censure, fault-finding, reprehension, judgment, blame, reproach, sneer, taunt.

rebuke, reprimand, reproof, admonition, talking to, telling off, lecture, piece of one's mind; brickbat; dissatisfaction, discontent, displeasure.

adj. disapproving, critical, hostile, reproachful, sneering, taunting, reproving, chiding, censorious, condemnatory, defamatory; niggling, fault-finding; unfavourable, uncomplimentary, disparaging; shocked, not amused.

objectionable, blameworthy, reprehensible, not good enough, in person's bad books, not all it is cracked up to be (*inf.*).

vb. disapprove, disagree, not accept, not think much of, not hold with, hold no brief for, frown on; run down, disparage, belittle; object to, oppose, contradict; boo, hiss; blame, reproach, incriminate; snub, taunt, sneer.

criticize, complain, denounce, find fault with, pick holes; reprehend, reprove, rebuke, reprimand, admonish, upbraid, judge, knock (*sl.*), slam (*sl.*), condemn, censure, punish, put someone in his place; tell off, talk to, tick off (*inf.*), speak to, lecture, have words with (*inf.*), dress down (*inf.*), dust down (*inf.*), tear off a strip (*sl.*), chide, scold, take to task, rap over the knuckles (*inf.*), haul over the coals (*inf.*); give a piece of one's mind to, give a person what for (*sl.*).

927 flattery

n. flattery, adulation, compliment,

soft soap (*inf.*), eyewash (*sl.*), false praise, insincerity, obsequiousness, fawning, cajolery, wheedling.

flatterer, cajoler, wheedler, hypocrite, toady,

adj. flattering, adulatory, blandishing, complimentary, over-complimentary, unctuous, ingratiating, insincere, smooth, smarmy (*inf.*).

vb. flatter, butter up (*inf.*), suck up to (*sl.*), soft-soap (*inf.*), cajole, wheedle, inveigle; lay it on thick (*inf.*), lay it on with a trowel (*inf.*).

see also **881**

928 disparagement

n. disparagement, depreciation, detraction, degradation, debasement, vilification, discrediting, belittling; defilement, denigration, smear campaign, whispering campaign, muckraking, mud-slinging, backbiting; slander, libel, calumny, defamation; aspersion, slur, smear, insinuation, innuendo, scandal, gossip.

disparager, critic, slanderer, libeller, backbiter, scandal-monger, muckraker, mud-slinger; mocker, scoffer, cynic, satirist.

adj. disparaging, deprecatory, derogatory, pejorative, denigratory, slanderous, libellous, defamatory, slighting; cynical.

vb. disparage, depreciate, belittle. play down, run down (*inf.*), decry. discredit, cut down to size (*inf.*); denounce, denigrate, blacken; attack, cast aspersions on; criticize, revile, defame, vilify, malign, slight, slur, tarnish, defile, sully, knock (*sl.*), smear; slander, libel; hound; deride, scoff, mock, ridicule.

929 vindication

n. vindication, justification, establishment, support, plea, defence, excuse, extenuation; ground, right, basis; exoneration, exculpation.

adj. vindicating, justifying, excusing; extenuating; justifiable, arguable, defensible, plausible.

vb. vindicate, justify, establish, support, bear out, uphold, confirm, show, prove, demonstrate, maintain, defend, give grounds for; absolve, acquit, clear, exonerate, excuse, make excuses for, make allowances for.

930 accusation

n. accusation, indictment, prosecution, arraignment, impeachment, charge, censure, incrimination, insinuation, slur, exposé, complaint, denunciation, smear, blame, allegation, action, case; frame-up (*inf.*), put-up job.

accuser, plaintiff, prosecutor.

adj. accusing, denunciatory, incriminating, defamatory.

vb. accuse, censure, charge, bring charges, prefer charges, arrest, arraign, impeach, indict, impute, complain, bring a complaint, find fault with, blame, pin blame on, denounce, incriminate, implicate, involve, reprove, slur, attack, recriminate, slander, libel; point the finger at; frame (*sl.*), trump up, concoct, invent, fabricate, construct, bear false witness.

931 probity

n. probity, uprightness, rectitude, honesty, integrity, fidelity, faithfulness, loyalty, morality, goodness, virtue, reliability, conscientiousness, truthfulness, character, principles, high principles.

adj. honourable, upright, moral, right, fair, good, straight, square, virtuous, honest, law-abiding, reputable, reliable, trustworthy, dependable, conscientious, faithful, loyal, straightforward, sincere, frank, candid, principled, scrupulous.

see also **935, 951**

932 improbity

n. improbity, dishonesty, immorality, badness, evil, wickedness, criminality, corruption; cunning, guile; disloyalty, faithlessness, double-dealing, double-crossing, sell-out, duplicity, betrayal, defection, treason, treachery, perfidy, foul play, trick, prank.

adj. dishonest, immoral, bad, wicked, corrupt, evil, criminal, fraudulent; unscrupulous, unprincipled, disreputable; unreliable, undependable, faithless; betraying, treacherous, perfidious, insidious, two-faced, insincere, deceitful, double-dealing; underhand, sly, crafty, devious, shady, dubious, suspicious, questionable, fishy (*sl.*).

vb. be dishonest, lie, cheat, swindle, deceive, betray, double-cross, sell out (*inf.*), two-time (*sl.*).

see also **936, 952**

933 disinterestedness

n. disinterestedness, impartiality, indifference, non-involvement, unconcern, detachment, objectivity, neutrality; selflessness, self-sacrifice, self-denial.

adj. disinterested, impartial, indifferent, unconcerned, unbiased, unprejudiced, dispassionate, objective, fair, unselfish, selfless, self-denying, self-sacrificing, self-effacing, self-forgetful; generous, liberal, magnanimous.

934 selfishness

n. selfishness, self-indulgence, greed, meanness, narrowness; self-worship, narcissism, egoism, vanity, self-interest, self-seeking.

self-seeker, egoist, individualist, time-server, narcissist, number one.

adj. selfish, self-centred, self-indulgent, greedy, miserly, mean, narrow; wrapped up in oneself, self-absorbed, self-seeking, egoistic.

vb. be selfish, look after number one.

935 virtue

n. virtue, morality, goodness, uprightness, righteousness, narrow way, sanctity, rectitude; honesty, temperance, kindness, excellence; quality, character, integrity; purity, chastity, innocence; ethics, morals.

adj. virtuous, moral, good, upright, righteous, holy, saintly, angelic; honest, kind, excellent, worthy, proper; perfect, irreproachable, unblemished, immaculate, impeccable; chaste, pure, innocent.

vb. be good, behave oneself, acquit oneself well, keep to the straight and narrow; set a good example.

see also **931, 951**

936 vice

n. vice, wickedness, corruption, iniquity, evil, immorality, perversity, baseness, meanness, malignity, malevolence, grossness, wantonness; degeneration, deterioration; unrighteousness, transgression, ungodliness; bad habit, besetting sin, failing, weakness, fault.

adj. wicked, evil, bad, corrupt, immoral, wayward, dissolute, perverse, gross, wanton, base, mean, malevolent, perverted, depraved, degenerate, irreligious, sinful, unrighteous, ungodly, unregenerate.

offensive, shocking, outrageous, scandalous, atrocious, abominable, heinous, repugnant, monstrous, unforgivable.

vb. err, stray, fall, lapse, degenerate, transgress, go off the rails (*inf.*); make wicked, corrupt, demoralize, defile, lead astray.

see also **932, 952**

937 innocence

n. innocence, guiltlessness, blamelessness, inculpability, irreproachability, faultlessness, integrity, probity, uprightness, perfection, purity, impeccability; clear conscience, clean hands, clean slate.

adj. innocent, not guilty, above suspicion, in the clear, pure, clean, spotless, unsoiled, untainted, undefiled, blameless, irreproachable, faultless, upright, perfect, impeccable; unoffending, simple, unsophisticated, inexperienced, guileless.

vb. be innocent, have a clear conscience, have nothing to confess.

938 guilt

n. guilt, blame, culpability; responsibility, liability, answerability; criminality, sinfulness; bad conscience, guilty conscience.

crime, offence, transgression, trespass, misdeed, sin, misdemeanour, misconduct, misbehaviour, error, fault, lapse, slip.

adj. guilty, wrong, at fault, offending, to blame, culpable, reproachable; blamed, condemned, judged, incriminated; red-handed, caught in the act.

939 good person

n. good person, good example, model, standard, pattern, ideal, paragon; one in a million, salt of the earth, last word, ultimate; saint, angel, hero, pillar; perfect gentleman; good fellow, good sort, good egg, sport (*sl.*).

see also **905**

940 bad person

n. bad person, wrongdoer, evildoer, sinner, transgressor; reprobate; scoundrel, wretch, villain, miscreant, rogue, rascal, blackguard, knave; bully, scallywag, scamp, scapegrace; wastrel, bum (*sl.*), idler, loafer, prodigal, beggar, tramp; ugly customer, nasty piece of work (*inf.*), bad lot, bad egg; good-for-nothing, ne'er-do-well, black sheep; criminal, crook, liar, cheat, traitor, impostor; rat, louse (*sl.*), worm.

941 penitence

n. penitence, repentance, change of heart, confession, contrition; sorrow, regret, remorse; sackcloth and ashes, hair shirt; penitent, convert, prodigal son.

adj. penitent, repentant, confessing, humble, contrite, conscience-stricken, convicted; regretful, sorry, compunctious, apologetic, full of regrets.

vb. repent, confess, acknowledge, plead guilty, humble oneself, own up, admit; feel shame, deplore; be penitent, be sorry, regret, apologize; turn from sin, see the light, be converted.

942 impenitence

n. impenitence, hardness of heart, heart of stone, seared conscience, obduracy; no regrets; hardened sinner.

adj. impenitent, unrepentant, uncontrite; hard, insensitive, callous, stubborn, obdurate, unashamed, incorrigible, irredeemable; dead, lost.

vb. be impenitent, have no regrets, show no remorse; harden one's heart.

943 atonement

n. atonement, satisfaction, amends

apology, redress, compensation, indemnity, retribution, requital, repayment, restitution, reparation.

propitiation, reconciliation, sacrifice, offering; substitute, representative; scapegoat; expiation; penance; purgatory.

adj. atoning, satisfying, indemnificatory, compensatory; propitiatory, reconciliatory, sacrificial, redemptive; substitutionary, representative, vicarious.

vb. atone, make amends, redress, compensate, indemnify, requite, repay; apologize; propitiate, reconcile, appease, satisfy, redeem.

944 temperance

n. temperance, moderation, abstemiousness, restraint, self-restraint, self-control, self-discipline; self-denial, abstinence, teetotalism; abstainer, total abstainer, teetotaller.

adj. temperate, moderate, restrained, disciplined, careful; self-denying, self-controlled, abstinent; continent; sparing, frugal, plain; abstemious, sober.

vb. be temperate, exercise self-control, control oneself, deny oneself, abstain, refrain; know when to stop, know when one has had enough.

945 intemperance

n. intemperance, excess, extravagance, inordinateness, self-indulgence; sensuality, voluptuousness, carnality, flesh; luxury, high living; dissipation, debauchery; hedonism, epicureanism.

adj. intemperate, immoderate, unrestrained, inordinate, excessive, self-indulgent; sensual, sensuous, voluptuous, carnal, bodily, fleshly, gluttonous, debauched; high-living, pleasure-loving, epicurean, hedonistic.

vb. be intemperate, indulge oneself, have one's fling, sow one's wild oats, paint the town red (*sl.*), not know when to stop, overeat, drink too much.

946 ascetism

n. ascetism, austerity, abstinence, abstemiousness, mortification, plain living.

ascetic, self-denier, recluse, hermit, anchorite, stylite; fakir, dervish, flagellant.

adj. ascetic, austere, plain, severe, rigid, stern, abstemious, puritanical, rigorous.

947 fasting

n. fasting, abstinence, hunger, starvation; fast, bread and water, short commons, diet, slimming; fast-day, Lent, Ramadan.

adj. fasting, abstinent, abstaining, starving, hungry, unfed, famished, Lenten.

vb. fast, eat nothing, go hungry, starve, famish; go on hunger strike; diet, reduce weight, slim, take off weight.

948 gluttony

n. gluttony, greed, voracity, rapacity, unsatiability, intemperance, excess, indulgence.

glutton, pig (*inf.*), guzzler, hog, greedy-guts (*sl.*); gourmand, epicure.

adj. greedy, gluttonous, ravenous, devouring, guzzling.

vb. overeat, stuff oneself, make a pig of oneself (*inf.*), eat like a horse, devour, guzzle, gobble, gulp down, bolt down; eat out of house and home.

949 soberness

n. soberness, sobriety, temperance, abstinence, teetotalism, prohibition.

sober person, abstainer, teetotaller, total abstainer, prohibitionist, Band of Hope, Temperance League.

adj. sober, temperate, abstinent, teetotal, on the wagon (*sl.*), off drink, clear-headed, in one's right mind, in possession of one's senses, unintoxicated, stone-cold sober, dry.

vb. be sober, not drink, sign the pledge; hold one's drink, have a good head for drink; sober up, sleep it off (*inf.*).

950 drunkenness

n. drunkenness, intoxication, inebriety, insobriety, intemperance; alcoholism, dipsomania; a drop too much, tipsiness; drinking-bout, pub-crawl, party, celebration, orgy; pink elephants; hangover, head, headache.

drunkard, drinker, heavy drinker, hard drinker, tippler, boozer, alcoholic, drunk (*sl.*).

adj. drunk, intoxicated, inebriated, under the influence, tipsy, befuddled; on the bottle; happy, high, lit up (*inf.*); seeing double, glassy-eyed; groggy; the worse for drink, sloshed (*sl.*), tight (*inf.*), stoned (*sl.*), blotto (*sl.*), canned (*sl.*), sozzled (*sl.*), plastered (*sl.*), under the table.

vb. drink, booze, guzzle, tipple, wet one's whistle (*inf.*), hit the bottle, drink like a fish, drown one's sorrows; be merry, be tipsy, have a drop too much, have one over the eight; be drunk, have more than one can hold, see double, get stoned out of one's mind (*sl.*); intoxicate, inebriate, go to one's head.

951 purity

n. purity, cleanness, cleanliness, whiteness; sinlessness, perfection; untaintedness, unsulliedness, spotlessness, immaculateness.

morality, chastity, virtue, decency, abstemiousness, virginity; prudery, primness, prudishness, overmodesty, false modesty, squeamishness; prude, prig, old maid.

adj. pure, clean, perfect, sinless; unsullied, untainted, spotless, undefiled, unadulterated, uncontaminated; decent, demure, abstemious; edifying; chaste, virtuous; continent, celibate, virgin, platonic; prudish, prim, squeamish, shockable, narrow, strict, Victorian, puritanical, strait-laced, old-maidish; simple, innocent, guileless, artless; inexperienced.

see also **931, 935**

952 impurity

n. impurity, uncleanness, sinfulness, imperfection, taintedness, sulliedness, contamination, pollution, adulteration.

immorality, unchastity, indecency, looseness of morals, permissive society; lewdness, prurience, profligacy, incontinence, lechery, wantonness, licentiousness, dissoluteness, salaciousness, lasciviousness; lust, sensuality, eroticism; obscenity, filth, dirt, smut, pornography; free love, promiscuity, adultery, wife-swapping (*inf.*), sleeping around (*inf.*), fornication, unfaithfulness, infidelity, affair, relationship, liaison, eternal triangle; seduction, rape, assault, violation, defilement; prostitution, street-walking, harlotry, whoredom; homosexuality, lesbianism, sodomy, incest.

adj. impure, unclean, imperfect, tainted, sullied, contaminated, polluted, adulterated; immoral, unchaste, indecent, loose, slack, of loose morals, easy, fast, wild, promiscuous, of easy virtue, permissive; lewd, profligate, lecherous, licentious, lascivious, wanton, dissolute, salacious, debauched; sensual, erotic; vulgar, coarse, risqué, spicy; obscene, filthy, dirty, smutty, lurid, sexy, pornographic, blue, unprintable, unexpurgated; homosexual, gay (*sl.*), queer (*sl.*), lesbian; extramarital, unlawful, illicit, adulterous, incestuous.

vb. be impure, commit adultery, fornicate, sleep around (*inf.*); seduce, take advantage of (*inf.*), rape, assault, violate; go on the streets, walk the streets, prostitute, adulterate, contaminate; sully, taint, pollute.

see also **932, 936**

953 libertine

n. libertine, profligate, Don Juan, rake, womanizer, lecher, adulterer, seducer, rapist, fornicator; homosexual, homo (*inf.*), queer (*sl.*), gay (*sl.*), fairy (*sl.*), pansy (*inf.*), nancy (*sl.*), butch (*sl.*), transvestite, pervert; lesbian.

adultress, woman of easy virtue, loose woman, flirt, tart (*sl.*), slut, pick-up (*inf.*); mistress; prostitute, pro, call-girl, fallen woman, whore, harlot, street-walker, hustler (*sl.*).

954 legality

n. legality, legitimacy, lawfulness, permissibility, validity, constitutionality; legislation, law-giving, law-making, authorization, codification, sanction, enactment; right, authority, justice; jurisprudence.

law, statute, decree, ordinance, act, edict, order, code, regulation, rule, by-law, constitution.

adj. legal, legitimate, lawful, right, just; constitutional; permissible, permitted, valid, sanctioned, codified, authorized, prescribed, within the law, statutory; jurisprudential, nomothetic.

vb. legalize, permit, authorize, sanction, approve, validate, establish, enforce, pass, license, charter, empower; legislate.

see also **103, 626**

955 illegality

n. illegality, unlawfulness, unconstitutionality, miscarriage of justice, injustice; law-breaking, violation, transgression, trespass, contravention, encroachment, infringement, offence, wrong, crime.

lawlessness, antinomianism, irresponsibility, terrorism, anarchism, mob rule, chaos, disorder, breakdown of law and order.

illegitimacy, bastardy; bastard, illegitimate child, natural child, love child.

adj. illegal, unlawful, illicit, forbidden, prohibited, banned, unauthorized, wrong, against the law, outside the law; stolen, black-market, smuggled, contraband; lawless, wild, chaotic, anarchic, irresponsible; illegitimate, bastard, natural, born out of wedlock, born on the wrong side of the blanket, born without benefit of clergy (*inf.*).

vb. break the law, disobey, commit, violate, transgress, contravene, infringe; take the law into one's own hands, be a law unto oneself; nullify, abrogate, void, annul, cancel.

956 jurisdiction

n. jurisdiction, authority, control, direction, supervision; right, power, responsibility, capacity, competence; executive, corporation, administration; domain, extent, scope, range, territory.

police, police force, constabulary; police officer, policeman, constable, officer, copper (*sl.*), cop (*sl.*), rozzer (*sl.*), fuzz (*sl.*); traffic warden, meter maid.

adj. jurisdictional, judiciary, competent, responsible, judicial, executive.

vb. administer, preside, direct, supervise; judge; police, keep order, control.

957 tribunal

n. tribunal, court, assizes, session, bench, bar; judgment seat, mercy seat, throne; dock, witness-box; courthouse.

958 judge

n. judge, justice, J.P., recorder, magistrate, stipendiary, beak (*sl.*); judiciary; marshal; jury, panel, tribunal; juror, juryman, jurywoman, foreman.

see also **653, 960**

959 lawyer

n. lawyer, legal practitioner; the bar, legal profession; defender, counsel, barrister, advocate, bencher; legal adviser, attorney, procurator, solicitor; prosecution; notary, commissioner for oaths; legist, jurist, jurisconsult; pettifogger.

vb. practise law, plead; be called to the bar, take silk; argue, defend, advocate; allege, prosecute.

960 lawsuit

n. lawsuit, case, suit, action, legal proceedings, hearing, indictment; litigation, judicature; summons, writ, subpoena; affidavit, bill; pleadings, argument, prosecution, cross-examination, defence, plea, summing-up; verdict, finding, decision, ruling, pronouncement, sentence, decree, award, precedent; appeal; litigant, party, suitor, plaintiff, defendant.

vb. go to law, prosecute, sue, litigate, bring an action against, bring to trial, file a claim; try, hear, give a hearing to, judge, arbitrate, adjudicate; rest one's case; sum up; rule, find, pronounce, declare, return a verdict, bring in a verdict, pass sentence, sentence, convict, acquit.

961 acquittal

n. acquittal, discharge, reprieve, release, remission, pardon, clearance, dismissal, exoneration, exculpation; innocence; suspended sentence.

adj. acquitted, not guilty, clear, discharged, released, set free, liberated, justified; forgiven.

vb. acquit, declare not guilty, discharge, pardon, absolve, forgive, clear, dismiss, grant remission, reprieve, release, set free, let off (*inf.*), exempt; exonerate, exculpate; justify, vindicate; save, rescue, redeem.

see also **601, 921**

962 condemnation

n. condemnation, denunciation, conviction.

adj. condemnatory, damnatory.

vb. condemn, find guilty, sentence, pass sentence on, judge, convict, punish, doom, damn, curse; proscribe, denounce, criticize, find fault with, blame, rebuke.

963 punishment

n. punishment, reproof, discipline, chastisement, correction, reprimand, retribution; penalty, imposition, fine, damages, costs, compensation; exile, banishment; hard labour; bread and water.

corporal punishment, slap, rap, cuff, blow, clout; capital punishment, death sentence, execution, decapitation, beheading, hanging, electrocution, strangling, strangulation, poisoning, crucifixion, impalement, drowning; torture; slaughter, genocide, mass murder, massacre, annihilation.

punisher; executioner, hangman, firing squad; inquisition.

adj. punitive, penal, castigatory, disciplinary, corrective.

vb. punish, reprove, discipline, chastise, correct, sentence, take to task, admonish, rebuke, reprimand, dress down (*inf.*), come down on like a ton of bricks (*inf.*), crack down on (*inf.*); make an example of; retaliate, get one's revenge, get even with.

expel, exile, banish, deport, transport, outlaw, isolate, send to Coventry; imprison, jail; penalize, fine, endorse one's licence.

strike, hit, slap, rap over the knuckles, box on the ears; flog, whip, beat, thrash, scourge, flay; spank, give a good hiding (*inf.*), thrash the living daylights out of (*sl.*), lick (*sl.*), tan (*sl.*), belt, strap, clout, wallop (*sl.*), cane, whack (*inf.*).

kill, put to death, shoot, execute, behead, guillotine, decapitate; hang, lynch; hang, draw, and quarter; crucify, impale; electrocute, gas; strangle; burn at the stake; drown; poison; slaughter, annihilate, massacre; torture, martyr, put on the rack, break on the wheel, tar and feather.

be punished, suffer, pay the penalty, get one's just deserts, have it coming, deserve; face the music, take the rap.

see also **926**

964 means of punishment

n. scourge, birch, whip, lash, belt, cane, rod, stick, switch, cat-o'-nine-tails; pillory, stocks, ducking stool, whipping post; torture chamber, rack, wheel, screw, water torture; axe, guillotine; block, scaffold; cross, stake; gallows, gibbet, noose, rope; electric chair, gas chamber, death chamber; condemned cell.

965 reward

n. reward, pay, payment, compensation, recompense, remuneration, reimbursement, reparation, redress; allowance, expenses, honorarium; tip, gratuity; prize, award, trophy, bonus, premium, bounty, accolade, guerdon.

adj. rewarding, remunerative, compensatory; profitable, advantageous, worthwhile; charitable, liberal, generous, open-handed, unsparing.

vb. reward, pay, recompense, reimburse, redress, compensate; award, recognize, pay tribute, present, give, bestow, confer, grant, thank.

see also **663, 715**

F Religious

966 divinity

n. divinity, divineness, deity, godhead; God, Spirit, Supreme Being, Creator, prime mover, Providence.

adj. divine, spiritual; godlike, godly; heavenly, celestial, sublime; transcendent, immanent, self-existent; eternal, everlasting, immortal; almighty, omnipotent, all-powerful, infinite, supreme; omniscient, all-knowing; just, merciful, gracious, loving, personal.

967 God

n. God; Trinity; Father, Lord, Yahweh, Jehovah, Almighty, King of Kings; Son of God, Jesus Christ, Son of Man, Immanuel, Word, Messiah, Saviour, Redeemer; Holy Spirit, Holy Ghost, Comforter, Paraclete.

god, goddess, object of worship; idol, false god; golden calf; pantheon; numen; totem, fetish; mumbo-jumbo.

supreme deity, Zeus, Jupiter; goddess of women and marriage, Hera, Juno; goddess of crops, Demeter,

Ceres; god of the sun, Phoebus, god of music, medicine, and poetry, Apollo; god of war, Ares, Mars; god of commerce, eloquence, and cunning, Hermes, Mercury; god of the sea, Poseidon, Neptune; god of metal-working, Hephaestus, Vulcan; god of wine and revelry, Dionysus, Bacchus; god of the underworld, Hades, Pluto, Dis; god of agriculture, Kronos, Saturn; god of love, Eros, Cupid; goddess of love and beauty, Aphrodite, Venus; goddess of the moon and hunting, Artemis, Diana; goddess of wisdom, Athena, Minerva; god of the countryside, Pan, Faunus.

Allah; Brahma, Atman, Vishnu, Shiva; Buddha.

968 good spirit

n. good spirit, angel, ministering spirit, seraph, cherub, host, principalities, authorities, powers, thrones, dominions; archangel.

adj. angelic, ministering, heavenly, celestial.

969 evil spirit

n. devil, Satan, fallen angel, father of lies, Beelzebub, prince of this world, prince of darkness; demon, evil spirit, unclean spirit, powers of darkness; imp, fiend, vampire; adversary.

adj. satanic, devilish, diabolic, diabolical, wicked.

see also **984**

970 mythical being

n. fairy, spirit, elf, brownie, goblin, hob, bogle, body, kobold, hobgoblin, dryad, pixie, gnome, peri; sprite, genie, jinnee; nymph; wood-nymph, hamadryad; mountain-nymph, oread; water-nymph, naiad; sea-nymph, nereid; siren, mermaid, water-spirit, water-elf, nix, nixie, kelpie; imp, puck, leprechaun, gremlin, urchin; changeling; sylph; dwarf, troll.

adj. fairy, mythical, imaginary, fabulous; elfin, elfish, impish.

971 ghost

n. ghost, spectre, spook (*inf.*), apparition, vision, phantom, phantasm, appearance, shade, presence, poltergeist, wraith, *doppelgänger*, double, fetch, visitant, spirit, departed spirit, zombie.

adj. ghostly, spooky (*inf.*), supernatural, evil, haunted, eerie, weird, uncanny, phantom.

vb. haunt, visit, walk, return from the dead.

972 heaven

n. heaven, paradise, bliss, glory, kingdom of heaven, Abraham's bosom, heavenly city, next world, world to come, eternal rest, kingdom-come (*sl.*), happy hunting ground, Elysium; rapture, resurrection, translation, ascension, glorification.

adj. heavenly, celestial, blessed, glorious, glorified, empyrean.

973 hell

n. hell, perdition, underworld, lower world, nether regions, bottomless pit, abyss, inferno, everlasting fire, lake of fire and brimstone, place of the lost, place of torment, pandemonium, Sheol, Gehenna.

adj. hellish, infernal.

974 religion

n. religion, belief, faith, dogma, teaching, doctrine, creed, tenet, revelation, articles of faith, confession; theology.

deism, theism, monotheism, polytheism, pantheism; animism; gnosticism.

Christianity, Judaism; Islam,

Buddhism, Hinduism, Brahmanism, Taoism, Confucianism.

teacher; prophet, apostle; preacher, lay-preacher, exponent, interpreter, commentator, evangelist, missionary.

adj. religious, spiritual, divine, holy, sacred; theological, doctrinal; devout, godly, believing, practising, faithful, regenerate, converted.

see also **980**

975 irreligion

n. irreligion, ungodliness, godlessness, unholiness, unspirituality, wickedness, sinfulness; idolatry, heathenism, paganism; atheism, unbelief; disbelief, scepticism, doubt, agnosticism; heresy, antichristianity; rationalism, free thinking, materialism.

unbeliever, atheist; agnostic, doubter, sceptic, doubting Thomas; idolater; heathen, pagan; infidel, heretic, dissenter.

adj. irreligious, ungodly, godless, wicked, sinful, idolatrous, heathen, pagan; unbelieving, atheistic; heretical, unorthodox; disbelieving, sceptical, agnostic; materialistic, secular, worldy, profane; unregenerate, unconverted, lost, damned.

see also **981**

976 revelation

n. revelation, disclosure; inspiration, afflatus, prophecy, vision; signs, foreshadowing; Scripture, Bible, Word of God, canon; Talmud, Torah, Ten Commandments; Law, Gospel.

Koran, Vedas.

adj. revelational, inspirational, inspired, revealed, prophetic, biblical, scriptural, canonical; evangelical; authoritative.

977 orthodoxy

n. orthodoxy, soundness, faithfulness, strictness, truth, adherence, observance.

the Church, body of Christ, Church invisible, Church militant, Church triumphant, Christendom; believer, true believer, Christian, practising Christian, church member, the saints, the faithful.

adj. orthodox, sound, correct, right, pure, true, faithful; evangelical, conservative, strict, literal, fundamentalist; practising, believing.

978 heresy

n. heresy, heterodoxy; divergence, aberration, distortion, perversion, unorthodoxy, unauthenticity, apostasy, infidelity.

adj. heretical, heterodox, divergent, different, unorthodox, unsound, unscriptural, unbiblical.

979 sectarianism

n. sectarianism, partisanship, schismatism, separatism; denominationalism; party-spirit.

sect, schism, split, section, faction, division, branch; denomination, communion, tradition; off-shoot, secession; sectarian, party-man, seceder, dissident, non-conformist, rebel.

adj. sectarian, partisan, schismatic, party-minded; denominational; dissident, non-conformist; separatist, secessionist, break-away; exclusive.

980 piety

n. piety, devoutness; devotion, single-mindedness; trust, faith; loyalty, submission, dedication, commitment, faithfulness, adherence, perseverance, allegiance, zeal, ardour, earnestness; adoration, worship, reverence, fear, awe, prayerfulness; holiness, sanctity, consecration, godliness, saintliness, humility, spirituality.

saint, believer, convert, man of prayer, man of God; follower, disciple, pilgrim; pietist.

adj. pious, devout, devoted, faithful, loyal, dedicated, committed, single-minded, zealous, earnest; believing, practising, holy, godly, saintly, spiritual, sanctified, consecrated, other-worldly, humble, meek.

vb. be pious, repent and believe, have faith, trust, fear God; keep the faith, persevere; worship, pray; sanctify, consecrate, make holy, dedicate, hallow.

981 impiety

n. impiety, godlessness, irreverence, unrighteousness, unholiness, sinfulness, disobedience; worldliness; blasphemy, sacrilege, desecration, defilement, violation.

hypocrisy, sanctimoniousness, false piety, self-righteousness, religiosity, formalism, hallowness, churchianity (*inf.*), religious show, façade, lip service, cant.

sinner, blasphemer; scoffer, mocker; materialist, worldling; hypocrite, Pharisee, scribe.

adj. impious, irreligious, ungodly, godless, irreverent, unholy, unrighteous, sinful, wicked, disobedient; unbelieving, atheistic, agnostic, non-practising; unhallowed, unsanctified, unregenerate, hardened; blasphemous, sacrilegious, profane; sanctimonious, hypocritical, pharasaical, false, deceitful, insincere, dishonest.

vb. be impious, sin, blaspheme; desecrate, profane, pay lip service.

982 worship

n. worship, honour, reverence, praise, adoration, exaltation, homage, veneration; service, devotions; prayer, private devotion, quiet time, meditation; confession; thanksgiving, grace; supplication, request, entreaty, appeal, petition, intercession, rogation; hymn, song, psalm, chant, anthem, canticle, chorus.

worshipper, church-goer, Christian, communicant; supplicant, petitioner, intercessor, man of prayer; congregation, church, flock, assembly.

adj. worshipping, devoted, reverent, religious, devout, prayerful, on one's knees, supplicant; worshipful, reverential, solemn, holy, serious, dignified, sublime, majestic, glorious.

vb. worship, adore, praise, glorify, bless, exalt, honour, magnify, revere, venerate, pay homage to, laud, bow down, humble oneself; idolize; pray to, seek; confess; thank, give thanks, ask, invoke, entreat, petition, implore, intercede, say one's prayers, beseech; sing; meditate, contemplate, consider, reflect.

see also 977

983 idolatry

n. idolatry, idolism, idol worship, irreligion, heathenism, paganism, fetishism, demonism, devil-worship, hero-worship, iconolatry, image-worship, mumbo-jumbo; idolization, deification, apotheosis.

idol, false god, image, graven image, icon, statue, golden calf, totem, fetish.

idolater, idolizer, pagan, heathen, image-maker.

adj. idolatrous, heathen, pagan, idol-worshipping.

vb. idolatrize, idolize, worship, enshrine, deify; sing the praises of, put on a pedestal, admire, dote on, treasure.

984 sorcery

n. sorcery, magic, superstition, witchcraft, diabolism, black magic, occultism, cabbala, exorcism, divination; miracle-working, thaumaturgy; spell, incantation, bewitchment, enchantment, influence, possession, trance, hocus-pocus, mumbo-jumbo, open sesame, abracadabra; charm, amulet, talisman, mascot, fetish, good-luck charm.

spiritism, spiritualism, spirit communication; séance, sitting; ouija board, planchette, automatic writing; levitation.

sorcerer, wizard, witch, enchanter, spell-binder, magician, conjurer; soothsayer, clairvoyant; astrologer; shaman, witch-doctor, medicine-man; voodoo; thaumaturgist, miracle-worker; diviner; exorcist; occultist, necromancer, spiritualist.

adj. sorcerous, devilish, diabolical, occult, necromantic; spell-binding; magical, supernatural, weird, uncanny, eerie; charmed, bewitched, enchanted; mystic, esoteric, transcendental.

vb. divine, conjure; wave a wand; exorcise, lay ghosts; call up spirits; bewitch, enchant, charm, fascinate, mesmerize, obsess, possess, put under a curse; hold a séance; go into a trance; materialize, dematerialize.

see also **447**

985 churchdom

n. churchdom, Christendom, the church, ministry; call, vocation; office, holy orders; pastorship, pastorate, priesthood, clerical order, cure of souls, spiritual guidance, pastoral case, service, preaching, administration of the sacraments, prayer; fellowship communion.

adj. ecclesiastical, ministerial, pastoral, cleric, priestly, sacerdotal.

vb. call, ordain, consecrate, present, nominate; take holy orders.

986 clergyman

n. clergyman, servant of God, shepherd; pastor, preacher, minister, incumbent, priest, vicar, parson, rector; curate, chaplain, cleric, padre, father, reverend; abbot, prelate, bishop, archbishop, prior, dean, archdeacon, canon, primate, Pope; metropolitan, patriarch, cardinal; monk, friar; nun, sister; rabbi, teacher.

adj. clerical, ordained.

vb. be ordained, enter the ministry.

987 laity

n. laity, layman, lay people, parish, congregation, church, fold, flock, assembly, church member, parishioner, brethren; elder, deacon; lay-preacher, lay-reader.

adj. lay, unordained, non-clerical, secular, temporal, oi the world, civil, profane, unholy, unconsecrated, unsacred.

vb. laicize, secularize, deconsecrate.

988 religious service

n. ceremony, ordinance, rite, ritual, custom, institution, observance; order, form, litany; administration, celebration, officiation.

service, divine worship, service of worship, morning service, matins, evening service, evensong, vespers, compline, fellowship, prayer meeting, Bible Study, Sunday School; Holy Communion, Lord's Supper, mass, Eucharist; baptism.

adj. ritual, ceremonial, customary, formal, liturgical.

vb. observe, keep, celebrate, minister, administer, officate, perform, dedicate, bless, pray, baptize, worship; encourage, share, fellowship.

989 vestment

n. vestment, cloth, clerical dress, canonicals, robes, surplice, gown, mantle, cassock, rochet, chasuble, cape, hood; mitre, staff, crook, crosier.

990 church building

n. church, chapel, sanctuary, house of prayer, house of God, Lord's house, bethel, kirk, tabernacle; mission, house-church, meeting-house; cathedral, minster, abbey; monastery, priory, friary, convent, nunnery; synagogue; mosque, shrine, temple.

Index

index does not list every word or phrase in the main part of the book. In particular, many ds derived from other related words, e.g. adverbs ending in *-ly* derived from adjectives, have excluded. If you want to look up a word that is not in the index, you should therefore look up vord closest to it, and refer to the categories in the main part of the book, looking at the part of ch of the word you originally wanted. Further, a reference to a particular entry does not ssarily mean that the word looked up will appear at that entry – but since you are interested in r words related to this one, the fact that it does not occur at the entry is of no consequence.

umbers printed in darker, bold type show the main categories for the particular words. The s of the categories are also printed in the bolder typeface. For further help on finding the word want, see the section 'How to use this thesaurus' at the front of the book.

Index

A

A-1 *adj.* 579
abacus *n.* 38
abandon *vb.* 546, 556, 607, 687, 713
abasement *n.* 869, 874
abate *vb.* 37, 176, 197
abbey *n.* 990
abbot *n.* 986
abbreviate *vb.* 203, 504, 527
ABC *n.* 88, 493
abdicate *vb.* 556, 687
abduct *vb.* 720, 722
aberrant *adj.* 285
aberration *n.* 412, 978
abet *vb.* 636
abeyance *n.* 607, 610
abhorrence *n.* 637, 892
abhorrent *adj.* 862, 892
abide *vb.* 112, 143, 145, 191
able *adj.* 159, 434, 627
ablution *n.* 583
abnormality *n.* 106, 439
abode *n.* 191
abolish *vb.* 2, 164, 607, 686
abolitionist *n.* 167
abominable *adj.* 862, 892, 936
abomination *n.* 892
aborigine *n.* 190
abortion *n.* 370
abortive *adj.* 662
abound *vb.* 572
about *adv., prep.* 9, 229
about-turn *n.* 147, 220, 289
above *adj.* 118; *adv.* 84
above-mentioned *adj.* 118
abracadabra *n.* 984
abrade *vb.* 341
abreast *adv.* 238
abridge *vb.* 197, 203, 504, 527
abrogation *n.* 686
abrupt *adj.* 115, 887
abscond *vb.* 600
absence *n.* 76, 189
absence of choice *n.* 541
absence of colour *n.* 806
absence of form *n.* 243
absence of habit *n.* 546
absence of intellect *n.* 383
absence of relation *n.* 10
absence of thought *n.* 385
absence of time *n.* 108
absence of wonder *n.* 867
absent *adj.* 189
absenteeism *n.* 189, 920
absent-minded *adj.* 391, 442
absolute *adj.* 46, 56, 408
absolute difference *n.* 14
absolutely *adv.* 56
absolute state *n.* 7
absolution *n.* 911, 921
absorb *vb.* 302, 350, 472
absorbed *adj.* 384
absorbent *adj.* 264
absorbing *adj.* 755
absorption *n.* 302, 384
abstain *vb.* 541, 555, 610, 944
abstainer *n.* 944, 949
abstaining *adj.* 947
abstemious *adj.* 944, 946, 951
abstinence *n.* 555, 944, 946, 947, 949
abstract *n.* 527; *adj.* 4, 382; *vb.* 203, 527
abstraction *n.* 101
abstruse *adj.* 453, 503
absurdity *n.* 433, 451, 851
abundance *n.* 26, 32, 75, 168, 572
abuse *n.* 608, 901; *vb.* 569, 608, 900, 901
abusive *adj.* 901
abut *vb.* 199, 201
abyss *n.* 210, 254, 973
academic *n.* 448; *adj.* 453, 470, 472
academy *n.* 475
accede *vb.* 692
accelerate *vb.* 280, 613
accent *n.* 512, 778
accept *vb.* 420, 424, 692, 716, 925
acceptable *adj.* 302, 499, 570, 925
accepted *adj.* 424, 545, 606
access *n.* 302, 559
accessible *adj.* 262, 292
accession *n.* 40, 41
accessories *n.* 192, 568
accessory *n.* 6, 35, 41, 60; *adj.* 35, 40, 60, 679
accident *n.* 153, 551
accidental *adj.* 158
acclaim *n.* 878, 925; *vb.* 888, 925
acclaimed *adj.* 868
acclimatize *vb.* 105, 545
acclivity *n.* 219, 316

accolade *n.* 663, 965
accommodate *vb.* 105, 302, 545, 652
accommodation *n.* 191
accompaniment *n.* **60**, 792
accompany *vb.* 60, 122, 882
accomplice *n.* 640
accomplish *vb.* 159, 609, 659, 661
accomplished *adj.* 581, 627, 659
accomplishment *n.* 609, 659, 661
accord *n.* 24, 643; *vb.* 16, 24, 105, 180
account *n.* (description) 460, 465, 483, 525; (money) 736, 742; *vb.* (describe) 157, 456, 483, 525; (pay) 742
accountable *adj.* 679, 919
accountant *n.* 733, 742
accounts *n.* **742**
accretion *n.* 40, 41
accrue *vb.* 36, 40, 705, 716
accumulate *vb.* 36, 40, 94, 567, 705
accurate *adj.* 430, 476, 915
accursed *adj.* 892
accusation *n.* **930**
accuse *vb.* 930
accustom *vb.* 105, 545
ache *n.* 828; *vb.* 828
achieve *vb.* 609, 659, 661
achievement *n.* 89, 609, 659, 661
achromatism *n.* 806
acid *n.* 773; *adj.* 773
acknowledge *vb.* 395, 424, 468, 692, 909, 925, 941
acme *n.* 212, 581
acoustics *n.* 778
acquaintance *n.* 882
acquiesce *vb.* 424, 654, 673, 692
acquire *vb.* 472, 705, 716, 720, 726
acquisition *n.* **705**, 716, 726
acquisitive *adj.* 705, **750**
acquit *vb.* 601, 680, 911, 921, 961
acquit oneself well *vb.* 919, 935
acquittal *n.* 601, 911, **961**
acrimonious *adj.* 893, **900**
act *n.* 609, 852, 954; *vb.* 172, 529, **609**, 621
acting *n.* 529; *adj.* 689
action *n.* 172, 266, **609**, 651, 960
activate *vb.* 88, 266, 282
active *adj.* 172, 368, 611
activism *n.* 611
activist *n.* 611; *adj.* 611
activity *n.* 266, 557, 609, **611**
actor *n.* 529, 619
actress *n.* 529
actual *adj.* 1, 3, 120, 430
actuary *n.* 742
acumen *n.* 434
acute *adj.* 255, 434
acute angle *n.* 246
adage *n.* 432
Adam *n.* 379
adapt *vb.* 24, 105, 125, 142, 602, 606
adaptable *adj.* 105, 151
adaptation *n.* 456, 545, 792
add *vb.* 36, **40**
addendum *n.* 41
addict *n.* 545
addition *n.* 38, **40**, 41, 705
additional *adj.* 6, 40
additive *n.* 307
address *n.* 191, **518**, 523, 695; *vb.* 514
addressee *n.* 523, 716
adept *n.* 629; *adj.* 627
adequate *adj.* **570**, 579
adhere *vb.* 50
adherent *n.* 474, 640
adhesive *n.* 49; *adj.* 50
ad infinitum *adv.* 78
adjacent *adj.* 199, 238
adjective *n.* 499
adjoin *vb.* 199, 201
adjournment *n.* 89, 135
adjudicate *vb.* 415, 960
adjudicator *n.* 415, 653
adjunct *n.* 41, 60
adjure *vb.* 468, 695
adjust *vb.* 24, 105, 142, 403, 704
ad lib *adj.* 544; *vb.* 544
administer *vb.* 621, **622**, 956, 988
administration *n.* 622, 667, 956
administrator *n.* 558, 623
admirable *adj.* 579
admire *vb.* 868, 888, **922**, 925
admissible *adj.* 302
admission *n.* 98, 300, 302, 420, 462, 468, 716
admit *vb.* 98, 262, 300, 302, 424, 462, 468, 716, 833
admit defeat *vb.* 654
admonish *vb.* 597, 624, 926, 963
adolescent *n.* 131; *adj.* 129, 131
adopt *vb.* 540, 575, 606, 702, 720
adopted *adj.* 40, 100, 171, 606

adoption *n.* 171, 540, 606
adorable *adj.* 827
adore *vb.* 889, 982
adorn *vb.* 509, 844, 846
adroit *adj.* 627
adulation *n.* 927
adult *n.* 133; *adj.* 133
adulterate *vb.* 45, 477, 582, 952
adulterer *n.* 953
adultery *n.* 952
adulthood *n.* 133
adumbrate *vb.* 798
advance *n.* **288**, 292, 587, 645, 693, 718, 890; *adj.* 236; *vb.* **288**, 292, 587, 645, 661, 718
advanced *adj.* 125
advantage *n.* 34, 550, 575
advantageous *adj.* 550, 575, 577, 661, 965
adventure *n.* 153, 269
adventurer *n.* 270
adventurous *adj.* 605
adverb *n.* 499
adversary *n.* 638, 883, 969
adverse *adj.* 14, 665
adversity *n.* 445, 665
advertisement *n.* 464
advertising *n.* 727
advice *n.* 460, 597, 624, 636
advisable *adj.* 577
advise *vb.* 460, 597, 624, 636
advisor *n.* 473, 624
advisory *adj.* 597, 624
advocate *n.* 959; *vb.* 959
aerate *vb.* 344, 348, 775
aerial *adj.* 273, 318, 348
aerodynamics *n.* 348
aeronautical *adj.* 273, 278
aeronautics *n.* 273
aeroplane *n.* 278
aesthetic *adj.* 848
affable *adj.* 884
affair *n.* 153, 557, 889, 952
affect *vb.* 177, 752, 755
affectation *n.* 510, **852**
affected *adj.* 510, 751, 752, 852
affection *n.* 752, 882, 889, 890
affections *n.* **751**
affidavit *n.* 401, 468, 960
affiliate *vb.* 11, 52, 639, 641
affinity *n.* 18, 105, 218, 294
affirm *vb.* 401, 413, 424, 468, 514
affirmation *n.* 413, 424, 468, 690
affirmative *n.* 424; *adj.* 468
affix *n.* 499; *vb.* 40, 47
afflict *vb.* 830
affliction *n.* 551, 586, 592, 665, 828
affluence *n.* 664, 734
afford *vb.* 568, 715, 734
affront *n.* 923; *vb.* 887, 923
affronted *adj.* 893
afloat *adj.* 153
aforementioned *adj.* 84
afraid *adj.* 856
after *adj.* 119; *adv.* 85
after-effect *n.* 87, 156
afterlife *n.* 123
aftermath *n.* 87, 156
afternoon *n.* 128
afterthought *n.* 87, 441, 538
afterwards *adv.* 85
again *adv.* 62, 77
age *n.* 109, **130**; *vb.* 130
aged *adj.* 130
ageless *adj.* 114, 129
agency *n.* 172, 563, 685
agenda *n.* 83, 441
agent *n.* 149, 155, 564, 619, 689
aggravation *n.* 835
aggregate *n.* 54; *adj.* 54
aggressive *adj.* 173, 175, 645, 651
aggressor *n.* 645
aghast *vb adj.* 866
agile *adj.* 280, 611, 627
agitation *n.* 80, **326**, 755, 756
agitator *n.* 142, 148
agnostic *n.* 975; *adj.* 409, 975, 981
agnosticism *n.* 409, 421, 975
ago *adv.* 124
agonize *vb.* 830
agonizing *adj.* 828
agony *n.* 756, 828
agrarian *adj.* 378
agree *vb.* 24, 105, 180, 424, 692, 925
agreeable *adj.* 692, 829
agreed *adj.* 24
agreement *n.* **24**, 105, 424, 643, 650, 692, 699, 704, 925
agriculture *n.* **378**
ahead *adv.* 236, 286
ahead of *adj.* 118
aid *n.* 563, **636**, 640, 834, 899; *vb.* 563, 636
ailment *n.* 586
aim *n.* 178, 284, 450, 552; *vb.* 178, 284, 552
aimless *adj.* 158, 399, 451, 553
air *n.* 329, 344, **348**, 621, 792; *vb.* 348, 350
air conditioning *n.* 348
aircraft *n.* 278
airing *n.* 348
air in motion *n.* **359**
airman *n.* 273
air-pipe *n.* **361**

airport n. 298
airs n. 852
air travel n. 273
airy adj. 4, 331, 333, 344, 348
ajar adj. 262
akin adj. 11
alacrity n. 611
alarm n. 482, 598, 856
alarming adj. 594
album n. 441
alcoholism n. 950
alcove n. 254
alert n. 597, 598; adj. 392, 602, 611; vb. 597, 598
algebra n. 38
alias n. 497
alibi n. 549
alien n. 100; adj. 100
alienate vb. 883, 892
alight adj. 759; vb. 298
alike adj. 13, 18
alive adj. 368, 611, 753
all n. 54; adj. 54, 56
Allah n. 967
allegation n. 401, 930
allege vb. 549, 959
alleged adj. 448, 549, 825
allegiance n. 679, 919, 980
allegory n. 397, 455, 525
all-embracing adj. 54, 98
allergic adj. 862
alleviate vb. 176, 652, 834
alley n. 559
alliance n. 641, 699, 896
allied adj. 11, 47, 180, 641
all-inclusive adj. 54, 98
allocation n. 717
allot vb. 55, 717
allotment n. 378, 717
allow vb. 690, 692, 744, 925
allowance n. 31, 690, 715, 717, 718, 738, 744, 965
allow for vb. 31, 403
alloy n. 45; vb. 45
all right adj. 579, 585; adv. 79
all-round adj. 627
allure vb. 547, 829, 889
allusion n. 455, 459
ally n. 640
ally with vb. 47
almanac n. 116, 483
Almighty n. 967
almighty adj. 159, 966
almost adv. 199
alms n. 715, 899
aloft adv. 208
alone adj. 48, 59
alongside adv. 238
aloof adj. 198, 517, 754, 757, 885
alphabet n. 493
also adv. 40
alter vb. 142, 146
alternate vb. 12, 140, 142, 325
alternative n. 149, 540; adj. 149
altitude n. 208
altogether adv. 54, 56
altruistic adj. 899, 903
always adv. 114
amalgamate vb. 45, 52
amass vb. 94, 567
amateur n. 630; adj. 628
amaze vb. 866
ambassador n. 460, 467, 688, 689
ambience n. 8, 229
ambiguity n. 409, 412, 451, 453, 454, 503
ambition n. 552, 854, 861
ambitious adj. 605, 611, 854
ambivalent adj. 454
amble n. 269; vb. 269
ambrosia n. 770
ambulate vb. 269
ambush n. 463, 596; vb. 463
amelioration n. 587
amenable adj. 179, 654
amend vb. 589
amendment n. 587
amends n. 31, 589, 721, 943
amiable adj. 886
amicable adj. 643, 882
amity n. 643, 882
amnesia n. 442
amnesty n. 911
among prep. 230
amorous adj. 889
amorphous adj. 243
amount n. 26, 731, 743; vb. 743
amphibian n. 373; adj. 373
amphitheatre n. 658
ample adj. 32, 75, 182
amplify vb. 36, 196, 481, 505
amplitude n. 32, 194, 204, 400
amputate vb. 42
amulet n. 984
amuse vb. 829, 840
amusement n. 829, 840
amusing adj. 840, 842, 851
anachronism n. 117
anachronistic adj. 117, 126
anaemic adj. 162, 806, 807
analogy n. 9, 18, 397
analysis n. 38, 48, 53, 394, 396
analyst n. 456
analytical adj. 38, 456

anarchist *n.* 148, 167, 672
anarchistic *adj.* 148, 644, 672
anarchy *n.* 80, 148, 668
anathema *n.* 892
anatomy *n.* 366, 375
ancestor *n.* 11, 86
anchor *n.* 330; *vb.* 152
ancient *adj.* 124, 126
ancillary *n.* 640; *adj.* 35, 60
and *adv.* 40
anecdote *n.* 525
anew *adv.* 77, 125
angel *n.* 467, 891, 905, 939, 968
angelic *adj.* 935, 968
anger *n.* 893; *vb.* 755, 893
angle *n.* 246, 420; *vb.* 219, 246
angry *adj.* 893
anguish *n.* 551, 828
angular form *n.* 246
animal *n.* 175, 373, *adj.* 373
animality *n.* 373
animal sound *n.* 789
animate *adj.* 366; *vb.* 173, 368, 618, 755, 836
animate matter *n.* 366
animism *n.* 974
animosity *n.* 425, 883, 900
annals *n.* 116, 483
annex *vb.* 40
annexe *n.* 41
annihilate *vb.* 164, 370, 963
anniversary *n.* 140, 878; *adj.* 878
annotate *vb.* 456, 482
announce *vb.* 458, 460, 464
announcement *n.* 458, 460, 464, 465
announcer *n.* 460
annoy *vb.* 830, 835, 887, 893
annoyed *adj.* 893, 894
annually *adv.* 140
annulment *n.* 686, 898
anoint *vb.* 342, 365
anonymous *adj.* 497
answer *n.* 283, 395, 402, 468, 523; *vb.* 395
answerable *adj.* 179, 679, 737, 919
answer back *vb.* 395, 880
antagonism *n.* 181, 637, 883, 892, 893
antagonist *n.* 638, 883
antagonistic *adj.* 637, 883, 892
antecede *vb.* 118
antecedent *n.* 86, 118, 155; *adj.* 84, 118
antedate *vb.* 117
antediluvian *adj.* 126
anterior *n.* 236; *adj.* 84, 118, 236
anthem *n.* 982
anthology *n.* 527
anthropoid *n.* 379
anthropology *n.* 375, 379
anticipate *vb.* 134, 154, 443, 446, 854
anti-climax *n.* 445
antidote *n.* 181
antinomianism *n.* 955
antiquated *adj.* 126
antique *adj.* 126
antiquity *n.* 124, 126
antisocial *adj.* 885, 904
anxious *adj.* 828, 856, 894
any *adj.* 26
anyhow *adv.* 80
apart *adj.* 48
apartheid *n.* 99
apartment *n.* 191
apathy *n.* 281, 389, 393, 612, 754, 841, 863
ape *n.* 20
aperitif *n.* 306
aperture *n.* 254, 262
aphasia *n.* 515
apocalypse *n.* 462
apolegetics *n.* 410
apologetic *adj.* 833, 941
apologize *vb.* 538, 549, 833, 941, 943
apology *n.* 549, 833, 943
apostasy *n.* 147, 538, 590, 978
apostle *n.* 974
appal *vb.* 856
appalling *adj.* 830, 856
apparatus *n.* 565, 568
apparent *adj.* 458, 634, 823, 825
apparently *adv.* 825
apparition *n.* 4, 458, 971
appeal *n.* 518, 695, 960; *vb.* 695, 829
appear *vb.* 188, 298, 458, 621, 825
appearance *n.* 222, 242, 298, 458, 621, 825
appease *vb.* 335, 652, 831, 943
append *vb.* 40, 85
appendage *n.* 41, 60, 87, 89
appendix *n.* 41
appertain *vb.* 707
appertaining *adj.* 9
appetite *n.* 861
appetizer *n.* 306
appetizing *adj.* 306, 767, 770
applause *n.* 838, 878, 888, 909, 925
appliance *n.* 565, 568
applicable *adj.* 9, 105, 575
applicant *n.* 697
application *n.* 172, 472, 575, 606, 611, 695

apply *vb.* 9, 575, 606, 695
appoint *vb.* 540, 557, 685
appointment *n.* 557, 685, 884
apportionment *n.* 717
apposite *adj.* 9, 577
appraise *vb.* 384, 400, 415
appreciate *vb.* 415, 770, 827, 888, 889, 909, 922
appreciative *adj.* 909
apprehend *vb.* 426, 452, 681, 720
apprehensive *adj.* 326, 443, 856
apprentice *n.* 474, 619
apprise *vb.* 597
approach *n.* 154, 292, 298, 559, 602, 693; *vb.* 123, 154, 199, 292, 298, 693
approachable *adj.* 292
appropriate *adj.* 105, 499, 510, 577, 915; *vb.* 705, 720
approval *n.* 424, 690, 692, 925, 954
approximate *vb.* 18, 199, 292
approximately *adv.* 199
apricot *n.* 816
apt *adj.* 179, 915
aptitude *n.* 627
aquarium *n.* 377
aquatic *adj.* 347
aquatics *n.* 271
aqueduct *n.* 360
arbiter *n.* 653
arbitrary *adj.* 10
arbitrate *vb.* 415, 653, 960
arc *n.* 247
arcade *n.* 247, 559, 730
arch *n.* 247; *vb.* 247, 252
archaic *adj.* 126
archaism *n.* 124, 494
archbishop *n.* 870, 986
archetype *n.* 23
architect *n.* 166, 491, 558
archives *n.* 483, 567
archivist *n.* 484
arctic *adj.* 760
ardent *adj.* 506, 759, 889
ardour *n.* 752, 759, 861, 889, 980
arduous *adj.* 615, 633
area *n.* 26, 182, 183, 194, 234, 400, 557
arena *n.* 234, 658
arguable *adj.* 929
argue *vb.* 410, 414, 420, 514, 642, 959
argument *n.* 25, 387, 410, 525, 642, 893, 960
argumentative *adj.* 410
arid *adj.* 350
arise *vb.* 88, 153, 318, 825
aristocracy *n.* 870
arithmetic *n.* 38
arm *n.* 353; *vb.* 159, 646
armistice *n.* 144, 650
armour *n.* 646, 657
arms *n.* 657
army *n.* 75, 655
aroma *n.* 776
around *adv., prep.* 229
arouse *vb.* 155, 618, 755
arraign *vb.* 930
arrange *vb.* 58, 81, 242, 558, 602, 699, 792
arrangement *n.* 9, 79, 81, 244, 602, 699, 792, 884
array *n.* 79, 655; *vb.* 81, 846
arrears *n.* 737
arrest *n.* 635; *vb.* 89, 144, 635, 681, 681, 755, 930
arrival *n.* 292, 298
arrive *vb.* 153, 298
arrogant *adj.* 875, 880
arrow *n.* 290, 482
arsenal *n.* 657
art *n.* 486, 488
artful *adj.* 631
article *n.* 163, 327, 499
articles *n.* 192, 729
articulate *adj.* 512; *vb.* 512
artifice *n.* 478, 631
artificial *adj.* 510, 849, 852
artillery *n.* 655
artist *n.* 491, 793
artistic *adj.* 510
artlessness *n.* 508, 632, 951
asbestos *n.* 762
ascend *vb.* 316
ascent *n.* 316
ascertained *adj.* 408
ascetism *n.* 946
ascribe *vb.* 157
ashamed *adj.* 874
ashen *adj.* 806, 807
aside *n.* 460, 520; *adv.* 567
ask *vb.* 394, 695
askance *adj.* 219
askew *adj.* 219, 245
asleep *adj.* 267
as long as *adv., prep.* 111
aspect *n.* 5, 7, 55, 825
aspersion *n.* 928
asphalt *n.* 365
asphyxiate *vb.* 370
aspirate *vb.* 512
aspire *vb.* 552, 604, 854, 861
aspiring *adj.* 605
ass *n.* 437
assail *vb.* 645
assassin *n.* 370, 906
assassinate *vb.* 370
assault *n.* 175, 645, 952; *vb.* 645, 952

assemblage *n.* 47, 94
assemble *vb.* 47, 58, 94, 242, 568
assembly *n.* 59, 94, 625, 982, 987
assent *n.* 424, 692; *vb.* 24, 424, 692
assert *vb.* 450, 468
assert oneself *vb.* 649
assess *vb.* 400, 415, 743
assessor *n.* 415, 653
assets *n.* 564, 566, 711, 734, 741
asseverate *vb.* 468
assiduous *adj.* 390, 392, 535
assign *vb.* 685, 714, 717
assignable *adj.* 157
assignment *n.* 470, 557
assignment of cause *n.* 157
assimilate *vb.* 302, 472
assist *vb.* 636
assistance *n.* 563, 636, 639
assistant *n.* 640, 676, 689
assizes *n.* 957
associate *n.* 640; *vb.* 9, 47, 94, 157, 397
associated *adj.* 60, 157, 639
association *n.* 52, 60, 397, 641
assorted *adj.* 45
assuage *vb.* 176, 652, 834
assume *vb.* 448, 720, 852
assumption *n.* 420, 918
assurance *n.* 408, 420, 854
assure *vb.* 420, 468, 701, 857
asthmatic *adj.* 359
astigmatism *n.* 820
astonish *vb.* 444, 866
astonishing *adj.* 444, 579, 866
astrologer *n.* 447, 984
astrology *n.* 329, 447
astronaut *n.* 274
astronomy *n.* 329
astute *adj.* 434
asylum *n.* 595
asymmetry *n.* 17, 219, 245
atavism *n.* 147
at hand *adj.* 123, 188; *adv.* 199
atheism *n.* 421, 975
atheist *n.* 975
athlete *n.* 270
athletic *adj.* 161
at home *n.* 884
atlas *n.* 329
at last *adv.* 89
atmosphere *n.* 8, 229, 329, 348, 488
atoll *n.* 357
atom *n.* 33, 195, 327
atomic *adj.* 195
atomic bomb *n.* 657
atomize *vb.* 53, 164, 340
atonal *adj.* 791
at once *adv.* 115
atonement *n.* 31, 652, 911, 943
atrocious *adj.* 856, 936
atrocity *n.* 900
attach *vb.* 40, 47
attaché *n.* 688
attached *adj.* 47, 889
attachment *n.* 41, 50, 60, 889, 890
attack *n.* 326, 439, 586, 645, 651; *vb.* 645, 648, 651, 928, 930
attacker *n.* 645, 723
attain *vb.* 472, 661
attainable *adj.* 292, 404
attainments *n.* 426, 472
attempt *n.* 604; *vb.* 552, 604, 615
attend *vb.* 188, 287, 591, 676
attendant *n.* 60, 287, 683; *adj.* 60, 188
attending *adj.* 60, 676
attend to *vb.* 593, 795
attention *n.* 390, 702
attentive *adj.* 390, 922
attenuate *vb.* 205, 333
attest *vb.* 401, 408, 413, 468
attested *adj.* 408, 430
at the same time *adv.* 122
attire *n.* 227
attitude *n.* 7, 420, 621, 818
attorney *n.* 959
attract *vb.* 224, 291, 294, 390, 547, 889
attract attention *vb.* 755
attraction *n.* 294, 330, 547
attractive *adj.* 579, 829, 844, 889
attributable *adj.* 157
attribute *n.* 5; *vb.* 157
atypical *adj.* 19
auburn *adj.* 810, 811
auction *n.* 727; *vb.* 727
audacious *adj.* 857, 887
audacity *n.* 857, 880
audible *adj.* 452, 778
audience *n.* 519, 795, 821
audition *n.* 795
auditorium *n.* 475, 795
augment *vb.* 36, 196
augur *n.* 447; *vb.* 447
augury *n.* 447, 597
aunt *n.* 11
aurora *n.* 127, 800
auspicious *adj.* 136, 447, 664, 854
austere *adj.* 669, 946
austerity *n.* 169, 669, 743, 946

authentic *adj.* 21, 430
authenticate *vb.* 408, 413, 424
author *n.* 155, 166, 521, 524
authoritarian *n.* 669; *adj.* 669
authoritative *adj.* 177, 408, 667, 671, 976
authority *n.* 177, 436, 629, 667, 675, 685, 690, 956
authorize *vb.* 424, 667, 685, 690, 954
autocrat *n.* 669
autograph *n.* 482; *vb.* 482
automatic *adj.* 125, 411, 531, 544, 565
automaton *n.* 565
automobile *n.* 276
autonomous *adj.* 678
autumn *n.* 128; *adj.* 128
auxiliary *n.* 35, 640; *adj.* 35, 40, 563, 636, 679
avail *vb.* 570, 575, 720
available *adj.* 188, 404, 464, 575, 705, 727
avalanche *n.* 572, 760
avant-garde *n.* 125; *adj.* 125
avarice *n.* 750
avenge *vb.* 647, 912
avenger *n.* 912
avenue *n.* 559
aver *vb.* 468
average *n.* 30, 90, 871; *adj.* 30, 90, 101, 666, 871; *vb.* 30, 400
averse *adj.* 533, 637, 862, 892
aviary *n.* 234
aviation *n.* 273
avid *adj.* 750
avoid *vb.* 555, 600, 862, 924
avoidance *n.* 555, 600
avow *vb.* 462
avowal *n.* 420, 468
avuncular *adj.* 11
await *vb.* 443
awake *adj.* 392, 753
award *n.* 663, 715, 960, 965; *vb.* 715, 965
aware *adj.* 426, 753
awash *adj.* 349
away *adj.* 189; *adv.* 198
awe *n.* 856, 866, 922, 980
awful *adj.* 580, 830, 856
awfully *adv.* 32
awkward *adj.* 129, 511, 628, 633, 852
awl *n.* 264
awning *n.* 225, 801
awry *adj.* 219, 245
axe *n.* 964
axiom *n.* 432
axiomatic *adj.* 408
axis *n.* 217
azure *n.* 815; *adj.* 815

B

baa *vb.* 789
babble *vb.* 451, 516
babe *n.* 131, 429, 632
Babel *n.* 492
baby *n.* 131, 163; *adj.* 131
babyish *adj.* 131
baby-sit *vb.* 392
baby-sitter *n.* 683
bachelor *n.* 897
back *n.* 217, 237; *adj.* 237; *vb.* 217, 553, 667, 701, 718
back and forth *adv.* 325
back-bencher *n.* 625
backbiting *n.* 869, 928
backbone *n.* 217, 535, 857
back-breaking *adj.* 615
back down *vb.* 538
backer *n.* 217, 553, 640, 905
backfire *n.* 147; *vb.* 283
background *n.* 8, 198, 229, 237, 456
backhanded *adj.* 454
back-handed compliment *n.* 923
backing *n.* 217, 401, 636
backlash *n.* 147, 156, 283, 647
backlog *n.* 567
back of beyond *n.* 198, 885
back on to *vb.* 237
back out *vb.* 289, 293, 538, 556, 858
backrest *n.* 217
backside *n.* 237
backslide *vb.* 147, 590
backsliding *n.* 147, 538
backstage *n.* 237
back-to-front *adj.* 220
back up *vb.* 217, 636
backward *adj.* 289, 427, 435, 603, 876
backwardness *n.* 135
backwash *n.* 358
backwoods *n.* 885
bad *adj.* 53, 551, 580, 855, 932, 936
badge *n.* 482, 663
badge of office *n.* 677
bad luck *n.* 158, 665
bad-mannered *adj.* 887
badness *n.* 580, 932
bad news *n.* 445
bad person *n.* 940
bad taste *n.* 511, 849
bad temper *n.* 893, 894, 895
baffle *vb.* 445, 633
bag *n.* 193, 275, 732
baggage *n.* 711
bail out *vb.* 273, 701
bait *n.* 294, 547
bake *vb.* 306, 350, 759

balance n. 28, 31, 44, 152, 244, 330, 400, 731; vb. 28, 31, 152, 330, 397, 742
balance sheet n. 742
bald adj. 228
balderdash n. 451
balk at vb. 533
ball n. 249, 884
ballad n. 528
ballast n. 31, 152, 330
ballerina n. 793
ballet n. 792
ballistics n. 657
balloon n. 249, 278
ballot n. 540
ballyhoo n. 451
balm n. 176, 342, 365, 591, 776
balustrade n. 234
bamboozle vb. 478
ban n. 99, 681, 691, 694; vb. 99, 691
banality n. 432, 843
band n. 49, 94, 207, 250, 641, 793; vb. 47
bandage n. 49, 207
bandit n. 885
bane n. 551, 580, 592
bang n. 782; vb. 282, 782, 787
banish vb. 99, 303, 963
bank n. 352, 718, 732
banker n. 718, 733
bank on vb. 443, 854
bankrupt adj. 571, 706, 735, 739; vb. 739
banner n. 482
banquet n. 306, 829, 840; vb. 304
banter vb. 842, 853
baptism n. 302, 988
baptize vb. 302, 496, 988
bar n. (inn) 191; (restraint) 681; (tribunal) 957; vb. 99, 263, 635; prep. 42, 99
barb n. 255; vb. 255
barbarian n. 175
barbarism n. 495, 500, 511, 849
barbarous adj. 175, 900, 908
barbecue n. 306, 840
bard n. 528, 793
bare adj. 189, 228, 753; vb. 228
barely adv. 33
bargain n. 699, 746; vb. 699, 725, 726
bargain for vb. 443
bargaining n. 704, 725
barge n. 277
bark vb. 789
barman n. 676
baron n. 870
barrack n. 191
barrage n. 645
barrel n. 249
barren adj. 160, 169, 350, 612
barricade n. 635; vb. 635
barrier n. 234, 235, 635, 681
barrister n. 959
barrow n. 276, 372, 730
barter n. 150, 725; vb. 150, 725
base n. 89, 213, 217; adj. 869, 924, 936
basement n. 213
bash vb. 282
bashful adj. 876
basic adj. 88, 155, 213, 573
basin n. 193, 213, 254, 354
basis n. 23, 155, 547
basket n. 193, 275
bastard n. 171, 955
baste vb. 306
bastion n. 646
batch n. 26, 94
bathe vb. 271, 349, 583
battle n. 649, 651
battleground n. 658
battlement n. 646
battleship n. 277
bawl vb. 788, 839
bay n. 353; adj. 810; vb. 789
bazaar n. 727, 730
be vb. 1, 185, 188, 368
beach n. 352
beacon n. 467, 482, 598, 800
beaker n. 193
be-all and end-all n. 573
beam n. 217, 797, 838; vb. 797, 838
beanfeast n. 306
bear vb. 217, 275, 368, 828
bearer n. 275, 467
bearing n. 9, 217, 284, 621, 825
bearings n. 185
bear in mind vb. 384
bear malice vb. 893
bear out vb. 413, 929
bear upon vb. 9
bear witness to vb. 401
beast n. 175, 373, 906
beastly adj. 900
beast of burden n. 275
beat n. 140, 325, 528; vb. 140, 282, 325, 340, 661, 783, 963
beat about the bush vb. 412, 505
beat off vb. 295, 646, 885
beat one's breast vb. 837
beat up vb. 645
beautiful adj. 844
beautify vb. 587, 844, 846
beauty n. 510, 844
becalm vb. 267
beck n. 358

beckon *vb.* 482
becloud *vb.* 798, 799
become *vb.* 1, 142, 288
become of *vb.* 156
becoming *n.* 1; *adj.* 848
bed *n.* 206, 213, 360; *vb.* 378
bed and breakfast *n.* 191
bedaub *vb.* 584
bedeck *vb.* 846
Bedlam *n.* 80
bedlamite *n.* 440
bed of roses *n.* 661, 664, 827
bedouin *n.* 270
bedraggled *adj.* 584
bed-ridden *adj.* 586
be drunk *vb.* 950
be dry *vb.* 861
bedsitter *n.* 191
beefy *adj.* 161, 194
bee-line *n.* 248
Beelzebub *n.* 969
beer *n.* 309
be excited *vb.* 756
be excused *vb.* 310
befall *vb.* 153
before *adj.* 118; *adv.* 84, 286
beforehand *adj.* 117
be found *vb.* 1, 185
befriend *vb.* 636, 882
befuddled *adj.* 950
beg *vb.* 695
beget *vb.* 163, 368
begetter *n.* 170
beggar *n.* 697, 735, 940
beggarly *adj.* 881
begin *vb.* 88, 605
begin again *vb.* 88
beginner *n.* 474, 630
beginning *n.* **88**, 155
begrudge *vb.* 914
beg the question *vb.* 412
beguile *vb.* 391, 478, 547
beguiler *n.* 480
behave oneself *vb.* 621, 886, 935
behead *vb.* 48, 370, 963
behest *n.* 671
behind *adj.* 135; *adv.* 85, 237
behind bars *adj.* 681
behindhand *adj.* 135
behind someone's back *adj.* 478
behind the scenes *adj.* 461
behind the times *adj.* 126
beholder *n.* 821
behove *vb.* 919
beige *n.* 810; *adj.* 810
being *n.* **1**, 5, 327, 368; *adj.* 1
being according to external form *n.* **6**
being according to internal form *n.* **5**
being around *n.* **229**
being between *n.* **230**
being exterior *n.* **222**
being horizontal *n.* **215**
being interior *n.* **223**
being oblique *n.* **219**
being opposite *n.* **239**
being vertical *n.* **214**
belated *adj.* 135
belie *vb.* 469
belief *n.* 415, **420**, 974
believable *adj.* 420
believe *vb.* **420**, 448, 854
believer *n.* 146, 977, 980
believing *adj.* 420, 974, 977, 980
belittle *vb.* 924, 926, 928
bell *n.* 482, 598, 784; *vb.* 789
belle *n.* 844
belligerent *adj.* 651
bellow *vb.* 780, 788, 789
belong *vb.* 9, 58, 60, 202, 707
belonging *adj.* 9, 60
belongings *n.* 60, 568, 711
beloved *n.* 891; *adj.* 889
below *adv.* 209
below average *adj.* 580
below par *adj.* 35
below the belt *adj.* 916
belt *n.* 49, 207, 250, 964; *vb.* 963
bemoan *vb.* 833
bench *n.* 957
bencher *n.* 959
bend *n.* 219, 247; *vb.* 105, 219, 246, 285
bend over *vb.* 319
bend over backwards to help *vb.* 899
beneath *adv.* 209
beneath contempt *adj.* 924
beneath the surface *adj.* 459
benediction *n.* 909
benefactor *n.* 905
beneficial *adj.* 550, 575, 585, 636, 661
beneficiary *n.* 716
beneficient *adj.* 747
benefit *n.* 550, 575, 636, 705, 829, 899; *vb.* 575, 577, 579, 661, 705, 899
benevolence *n.* 636, 747, **899**, 907
bent *n.* 178, 545, 751; *adj.* 219, 247, 252
bequeath *vb.* 714
bequest *n.* 714, 715
bereave *vb.* 898
bereavement *n.* 369, 706, 828
bereft *adj.* 706
berry *n.* 306
berserk *adj.* 439
berth *n.* 191, 298

beryl adj. 812
beseech vb. 695, 982
beset vb. 633
besetting adj. 545
besetting sin n. 592, 936
beside onself adj. 756
besides adv. 40
besiege vb. 645
be situated vb. 1, 185
besmirched adj. 584
best adj. 34, 579
best friend n. 882
bestow vb. 715, 965
bestseller n. 524
best wishes n. 888
be subject to vb. 179, 679
bet n. 553; vb. 553
bête noire n. 892
be the duty of vb. 919
bethel n. 990
betoken vb. 447, 450, 482
betray vb. 458, 462, 478, 932
betrayer n. 480
betrothal n. 698
betrothed adj. 698
better n. 34, 553; adj. 34; vb. 587
better half n. 896
betterment n. 550, 587
between prep. 230
between ourselves adv. 466
between the lines adj. 459
be up to vb. 159
beverage n. 309
bewail vb. 833
bewilder vb. 409, 866
bewitch vb. 829, 984
bewitched adj. 984
be worth vb. 743
beyond compare adj. 34, 581
beyond hope adj. 855
bi- adj. 61
bias n. 178, 416, 545, 751, 916; vb. 416
biased adj. 416, 916
Bible n. 524, 976
biblical adj. 976
bibliography n. 83, 524
bicker vb. 642
bicycle n. 276
bid n. 693, 695; vb. 394, 671, 693
bidder n. 697
bide one's time vb. 443, 610, 612
bifurcate vb. 63, 297
big adj. 32, 161, 194, 509
bigheaded adj. 873
big-hearted adj. 747
big-mouthed adj. 879
big name n. 868
bigot n. 537
bigoted adj. 416
big-sounding adj. 509
big talk n. 879
bigwig n. 675, 868
bike n. 276; vb. 269
bilateral adj. 61
bilious adj. 812, 813
bill n. 464, 482, 742, 960
billet n. 191
billion n. 70
bill of fare n. 306
billow vb. 358
billy-goat n. 380
bin n. 193
binary adj. 39, 61
bind vb. 47, 378, 681, 698, 919
binding adj. 919
binoculars n. 822
biographer n. 484, 524
biology n. 366
bipartite adj. 61
birch n. 964
bird n. 373
bird's eye view n. 818
bird-watching n. 375
birth n. 88, 155, 870
birthday n. 140, 878
biscuit n. 306
bisection n. 63
bishop n. 870, 986
bit n. 33, 55, 59
bit by bit adv. 55
bitch n. 381
bite n. 306, 306, 769; vb. 304
bite someone's head off vb. 893
biting adj. 255, 760, 773
bitter adj. 769, 773, 893, 900
bitter-sweet adj. 772
bitumen n. 365
bizarre adj. 139, 433
blabber vb. 462
black n. 808; adj. 798, 808; vb. 99
blacken vb. 798, 808, 928
blackguard n. 940
black hole n. 329
blackish adj. 808
blacklist vb. 99
black magic n. 984
blackmail n. 902; vb. 902
black-market adj. 955
black out vb. 485, 798
blackout n. 463, 466, 779, 798
black sheep n. 940
black spot n. 596
blame n. 926, 930, 938; vb. 157, 926, 930, 962
blameless adj. 937
blameworthy adj. 926
blanch vb. 806, 807
bland adj. 768, 771
blank n. 2; adj. 2, 385, 451, 754
blank cheque n. 678, 690
blanket n. 225; adj. 54, 101, 399
blankness n. 442, 867

blare *vb.* 780
blasé *adj.* 757
blaspheme *vb.* 901, 981
blast *n.* 359, 780, 782; *vb.* 175, 359
blatant *adj.* 877
blather *n.* 451, 516; *vb.* 451
blaze *n.* 759, 797; *vb.* 797
blazon *vb.* 464
bleach *vb.* 806, 807
bleached *adj.* 350
bleak *adj.* 760, 798
bleat *vb.* 789
bleed *vb.* 301, 358, 745
blemish *n.* 582, 660, 845, 847; *vb.* 847
blend *n.* 45, 495; *vb.* 52
bless *vb.* 899, 982, 988
blessed *adj.* 972
blessing *n.* 550, 715, 909
blessings *n.* 664
blight *n.* 53, 167, 592, 665
blind *n.* 225, 463, 801; *adj.* 754, 819; *vb.* 797
blinded *adj.* 819
blindfold *adj.* 819; *vb.* 819
blindness *n.* 819
blind spot *n.* 819
blink *vb.* 797, 818
blinker *vb.* 801, 819
blinkers *n.* 801
bliss *n.* 827, 972
blithe *adj.* 827
blitz *n.* 645; *vb.* 164
blizzard *n.* 175, 359, 760
bloat *vb.* 196
bloated *adj.* 252
block *n.* 490, 681, 964; *vb.* 263, 265, 635
blockade *n.* 99, 681; *vb.* 234, 265, 645
blockage *n.* 263, 635
blockhead *n.* 429, 437, 630
blonde *adj.* 807
blood *n.* 11, 870
blood relationship *n.* 11
bloodshed *n.* 370, 649
bloom *n.* 374
bloomer *n.* 431
blossom *n.* 374; *vb.* 163, 168, 664
blot *n.* 584, 845, 847, 869; *vb.* 584, 847, 869
blotch *n.* 847
blot out *vb.* 164, 485, 911
blow *n.* 282, 444, 609, 828, 900, 963; *vb.* 359, 749
blowout *n.* 48, 306
blow up *vb.* 196, 359, 782, 893
blubber *n.* 306, 365; *vb.* 839
blue *n.* 815; *adj.* 815, 837, 901, 952
blue blood *n.* 870
blue-eyed boy *n.* 891
blueprint *n.* 23, 558
blues *n.* 792, 837
bluff *vb.* 549
blunder *n.* 431, 500; *vb.* 431
blunt *adj.* 256, 476, 508; *vb.* 162, 256, 754
bluntness *n.* 256
blur *n.* 847; *vb.* 799
blurb *n.* 464
blurred *adj.* 243, 503, 799, 803, 824
blurt out *vb.* 462, 544
blush *n.* 811; *vb.* 811, 876
bluster *n.* 879
blustery *adj.* 359
board *n.* 217, 305, 625, 688
boarder *n.* 190
boast *n.* 879; *vb.* 873, 875, 879
boaster *n.* 873, 879
boastful *adj.* 481, 509, 875, 879
boasting *n.* 879
boat *n.* 193, 277
bode *vb.* 447, 450
bode well *vb.* 854
bodiless *adj.* 4, 328
bodily *adj.* 327, 827, 945
body *n.* 3, 327, 368, 371
body-building *adj.* 585
bodyguard *n.* 593, 683
body odour *n.* 777
boffin *n.* 396, 448
bog *n.* 355
bogie *n.* 217
bogus *adj.* 477
boil *n.* 252; *vb.* 175, 306, 363, 759, 893
boil down *vb.* 203, 527
boiler *n.* 763
boil over *vb.* 756
boisterous *adj.* 175, 756, 780
bold *adj.* 458, 506, 534, 644, 854, 857
boldness *n.* 534, 857, 880
bolshie *adj.* 642
bolster *vb.* 217, 636
bolt *n.* 49, 613; *vb.* 47, 263, 304
bolt down *vb.* 948
bomb *n.* 657; *vb.* 280, 613, 645
bombard *vb.* 164, 645
bombast *n.* 509, 879
bombastic *adj.* 481, 877
bomber *n.* 278
bombshell *n.* 444
bonanza *n.* 75, 572
bond *n.* 49, 681, 701
bondage *n.* 679
bone *n.* 337
bone to pick *n.* 893

bonus *n.* 41, 965
boo *vb.* 788, 853, 926
booby prize *n.* 663
booby-trap *n.* 596
book *n.* 464, 524; *vb.* 83
bookishness *n.* 426
bookkeeping *n.* 742
booklet *n.* 464, 524
bookmaker *n.* 553
bookworm *n.* 428, 474, 524
boom *n.* 168, 217, 664, 780, 782, 784; *vb.* 780, 782, 784
boomerang *n.* 147, 283
boon *n.* 550
boorish *adj.* 887
boost *vb.* 36, 196, 318, 857
booster *n.* 173
booth *n.* 730
booty *n.* 663, 724
booze *vb.* 950
boozer *n.* 950
border *n.* 232, 233, 235; *vb.* 199, 201, 233, 236
bore *n.* 204, 437; *vb.* 254, 264, 617, 841
boredom *n.* 841
borer *n.* 264
boring *adj.* 77, 841, 843
borough *n.* 183
borrow *vb.* 719
borrowed *adj.* 100, 495
borrower *n.* 737
borrowing *n.* 495, 719
boss *n.* 34, 675
botany *n.* 366, 374, 376
botch *vb.* 628
both *adj.* 61
bother *n.* 326; *vb.* 578, 695, 830, 856, 893
bothered *adj.* 856
bothersome *adj.* 633, 830
bottle *n.* 193; *vb.* 234, 599
bottleneck *n.* 205, 635
bottle up *vb.* 681
bottom *n.* 89, 210, 213, 237; *adj.* 213, 237
bottomless *adj.* 210
bough *n.* 374
bounce *n.* 173, 283, 326, 336; *vb.* 283, 320, 326, 336, 879
bouncer *n.* 303
bound *n.* 320; *vb.* 231, 235
boundary *n.* 89, 231, 232, 233, 235
boundless *adj.* 78, 202
bounteous *adj.* 168, 747
bounty *n.* 168, 572, 715, 747, 965
bouquet *n.* 776, 888, 925
bourgeois *adj.* 871
bout *n.* 586
boutique *n.* 730
bow *n.* 247, 319, 922; *vb.* 247, 319, 654, 673, 922
bow down *vb.* 982
bowl *n.* 193, 250, 254
bowl over *vb.* 444
box *n.* 193, 225; *vb.* 282, 963
boy *n.* 131, 380
boycott *n.* 99, 691; *vb.* 99, 144, 555, 691
boy-friend *n.* 882, 889
brace *n.* 217; *vb.* 161, 217
bracing *adj.* 585, 618
brag *vb.* 879
braid *n.* 49
brain *n.* 382, 428
brain-child *n.* 163
brainwash *vb.* 470, 547
braise *vb.* 306
brake *n.* 281; *vb.* 281
bramble *n.* 255
branch *n.* 55, 97, 358, 374, 620, 979; *vb.* 297
brand *n.* 97, 800, 869; *vb.* 482
brand-new *adj.* 125
brash *adj.* 859, 887
brass *n.* 794, 880; *adj.* 816
brat *n.* 131
brave *adj.* 857; *vb.* 644, 857
brawler *n.* 672
brawn *n.* 161
brawny *adj.* 161
bray *vb.* 789
brazen it out *vb.* 880
breach *n.* 703; *vb.* 703
bread *n.* 306
breadth *n.* 26, 204, 400
break *n.* 92, 200, 262, 614, 616; *vb.* 48, 92, 144, 164, 338, 703, 920
breakable *adj.* 338
break-away *adj.* 979
break down *vb.* 53, 588, 662, 839, 856
breakdown *n.* 48, 53, 586, 662
breaker *n.* 167, 358
breakfast *n.* 306
break in *vb.* 300
break in on *vb.* 137
breakneck *adj.* 859
break off *vb.* 89
break out *vb.* 88, 175, 600
break the law *vb.* 916, 955
breakthrough *n.* 661
break up *vb.* 53, 144, 588, 642
breakwater *n.* 217
break with *vb.* 556
breath *n.* 4, 359, 368, 512, 781
breathe *vb.* 359, 368
breather *n.* 92, 612, 614, 616
breathing space *n.* 144, 182

breathless *adj.* 369
breed *n.* 11, 97; *vb.* 163, 377, 470
breeding *n.* 377, 886
breeze *n.* 359
breezy *adj.* 348, 836
brevity *n.* 195, 203, 504
brewing *adj.* 154
bribe *vb.* 547
brickbat *n.* 926
bride *n.* 896
bridge *n.* 49; *vb.* 47
bridle *vb.* 681
brief *n.* 483; *adj.* 113, 203, 432, 504, 527
briefcase *n.* 193
briefing *n.* 460
brier *n.* 255
bright *adj.* 434, 759, 797, 805
brighten *vb.* 797, 836
brighten up *vb.* 840, 846
brilliant *adj.* 434, 581, 797, 805, 844
brim *n.* 233
brine *n.* 351
bring *vb.* 294
bring about *vb.* 155, 172, 609
bring back *vb.* 441
bring out *vb.* 464, 522
bring round *vb.* 420, 618
bring together *vb.* 94, 201, 652
bring to mind *vb.* 441
bring up *vb.* 303, 470
brink *n.* 233
brisk *adj.* 173, 280, 760
bristly *adj.* 258
brittleness *n.* 162, 338
broach *vb.* 605
broad *adj.* 101, 182, 204
broadcast *n.* 460, 464; *vb.* 95, 378, 460, 464, 465
broadcaster *n.* 460
broaden *vb.* 36, 101, 204
broad-minded *adj.* 288
brochure *n.* 464
broil *vb.* 306
broke *adj.* 735
broken *adj.* 833
broken down *adj.* 576
broken-hearted *adj.* 837
broken in *adj.* 602
broker *n.* 688
bronze *adj.* 810, 816
brood *n.* 94; *vb.* 384, 837
brook *n.* 358; *vb.* 757
broth *n.* 306
brother *n.* 11, 987
brotherhood *n.* 11, 639, 641
brow *n.* 212
brown *n.* 810; *adj.* 810
browned off *adj.* 832
browse *vb.* 472
bruise *n.* 588; *vb.* 282
bruised *adj.* 753
brunt *n.* 282
brush *n.* 649; *vb.* 201, 211, 341, 583, 649
brush aside *vb.* 393, 542
brush up *vb.* 472
brusque *adj.* 517, 887
brutal *adj.* 175, 900, 908
brute *n.* 175, 906
brutishness *n.* 900
bubble *n.* 249, 363; *vb.* 363
bubbling over *adj.* 827
bucket *n.* 193
buckle *vb.* 245, 247
buckle down *vb.* 615
bud *n.* 374
Buddha *n.* 967
Buddhism *n.* 974
budding *adj.* 125, 129, 134
buddy *n.* 882
budget *n.* 447, 742; *vb.* 742
buff *adj.* 810, 813
buffet *n.* 191, 306; *vb.* 359
buffoon *n.* 437, 842
buffoonery *n.* 433
bug *n.* 586; *vb.* 795
buggy *n.* 276
build *vb.* 36, 163, 242
builder *n.* 166
building *n.* 163
building society *n.* 718
build up *vb.* 36, 161
built-in *adj.* 55
bulb *n.* 252, 374, 800
bulbous *adj.* 252
bulge *n.* 252; *vb.* 56, 252
bulk *n.* 32, 75, 204, 330, 567
bulkiness *n.* 194
bull *n.* 380, 671
bulldog *n.* 535
bullet *n.* 290
bulletin *n.* 465, 483
bulletproof *adj.* 593
bull's eye *n.* 224
bully *n.* 175, 940; *vb.* 902
bump *n.* 141, 252, 282, 326, 785; *vb.* 282, 785
bunch *n.* 94
bundle *n.* 94, 567; *vb.* 567
bung *n.* 265; *vb.* 265
bungalow *n.* 191
bungle *vb.* 431, 628
bungler *n.* 630
bunion *n.* 252
bunk *n.* 451
bunker *n.* 193
bunting *n.* 482, 846
buoy *n.* 331
buoyant *adj.* 331, 336
burden *n.* 387, 665, 828, 919; *vb.* 330, 635

burdensome *adj.* 330, 633
bureau *n.* 620
bureaucracy *n.* 667
bureaucrat *n.* 623
bureaucratic *adj.* 622, 667
burglar *n.* 723
burglary *n.* 722
burial *n.* 372
buried *adj.* 210, 372, 461
burlesque *n.* 487, 842, 853
burly *adj.* 161
burn *n.* 828; *vb.* 759, 761, 797, 828, 893
burning *n.* 370, 761; *adj.* 752, 759, 811
burnish *vb.* 257, 341, 797
burr *vb.* 512
burrow *n.* 254
bursar *n.* 733
burst *n.* 48, 280, 613; *vb.* 48, 338, 782
burst forth *vb.* 88
burst into flames *vb.* 759
burst into tears *vb.* 839
burst out *vb.* 600
bury *vb.* 311, 372, 461, 472
bus *n.* 276
bush *n.* 374
business *n.* 557, 605, 725
businesslike *adj.* 79, 557
businessman *n.* 728
bust *n.* 489; *adj.* 739
bustle *n.* 611; *vb.* 611, 613
busy *adj.* 557, 611
busy-body *n.* 388
butcher *n.* 370; *vb.* 370
butler *n.* 676
butt *n.* 853; *vb.* 282
butter *n.* 306
buttercup *n.* 813
butterfingers *n.* 630; *adj.* 628
butterflies *n.* 326, 856
butter up *vb.* 927
buttress *n.* 217
buy *vb.* 547, 705, 726
buyer *n.* 710, 726, 737
buzz *n.* 783, 786; *vb.* 783, 784, 786, 789
by accident *adv.* 158
by chance *adv.* 158
bygone *adj.* 124
by-law *n.* 954
by-pass *n.* 322, 559, 561; *vb.* 322
by-product *n.* 87, 156
bystander *n.* 821
by the way *adv.* 10

C

cab *n.* 276
cabal *n.* 461, 558
cabaret *n.* 529
cabinet *n.* 625, 688
cable *n.* 49, 207, 460, 467; *vb.* 460
cackle *n.* 783, 838; *vb.* 783, 789
cacophony *n.* 787, 791
cad *n.* 849
cadge *vb.* 719
cadger *n.* 697
café *n.* 191
cage *n.* 234, 682
cajole *vb.* 478, 547, 927
cajoler *n.* 927
cake *n.* 306
calamity *n.* 153, 551, 665
calculate *vb.* 38, 400, 552
calculation *n.* 38, 400
calculator *n.* 38, 400
calculus *n.* 38
calendar *n.* 116
calibrate *vb.* 27, 400
calibre *n.* 204, 400
call *n.* 788, 789, 884; *vb.* 482, 496, 788
call away *vb.* 391
call by *vb.* 884
caller *n.* 884
call for *vb.* 562
call forth *vb.* 155, 547
call-girl *n.* 953
calligraphy *n.* 521
call in *vb.* 731
calling *n.* 557
call of duty *n.* 919
call on *vb.* 695
callous *adj.* 754, 900, 942
callow *adj.* 129
call up *vb.* 94, 441, 651
call upon *vb.* 394, 919
calm *n.* 267; *adj.* 176, 616, 681, 757; *vb.* 652, 779
calm down *vb.* 757
calque *n.* 495
calumny *n.* 869, 928
camber *n.* 247
cameo *n.* 489
camera *n.* 822
cameraman *n.* 491
camouflage *n.* 18, 461, 463; *vb.* 146, 461, 646
camp *n.* 191; *vb.* 186
campaign *n.* 605, 621, 651; *vb.* 649
campus *n.* 658
can *n.* 193; *vb.* 404, 599
canal *n.* 261, 360
cancel *vb.* 485, 686, 955
cancel out *vb.* 181, 402
cancer *n.* 167, 252, 592
candid *adj.* 476, 632, 931
candidate *n.* 395, 638, 697, 854
candle *n.* 800

candour *n.* 476
cane *n.* 964; *vb.* 963
canister *n.* 193
cannon *n.* 657
canoe *n.* 277
canoeing *n.* 271
canon *n.* 420, 626, 671, 976, 986
canonical *adj.* 976
canonicals *n.* 989
canopy *n.* 225, 801
cant *n.* 495, 981
cantankerous *adj.* 894
canteen *n.* 191
canticle *n.* 982
canvas *n.* 488
canvass *vb.* 394, 464, 695
canvasser *n.* 394, 697
canyon *n.* 254
cap *n.* 212; *vb.* 34, 212
capable *adj.* 159, 404, 627
capacious *adj.* 182, 194
capacity *n.* 26, 159, 194
cape *n.* 989
capillary *adj.* 207
capital *n.* 493, 711, 731; *adj.* 34, 212, 579
capitalist *n.* 728, 734
capitalize *vb.* 136, 606, 705
capital punishment *n.* 963
capitulate *vb.* 654
caprice *n.* 449, 539
capricious *adj.* 141, 151, 449, 539
capsize *vb.* 220, 317
capsule *n.* 193, 279, 591
captain *n.* 272, 675
captivate *vb.* 420, 547, 829, 889
captivation *n.* 755
captive *n.* 676, 684, 701
capture *n.* 663, 720, 724; *vb.* 705, 720
car *n.* 276
caravan *n.* 291
carcass *n.* 371
card *n.* 482
cardinal *n.* 986; *adj.* 34
cardinal point *n.* 284
care *n.* (carefulness) 392, 860; (worry) 828, 830; *vb.* 593, 676, 889
career *n.* 557
carefree *adj.* 831, 836
careful *adj.* 392, 398, 748, 860
careless *adj.* 391, 393, 703, 749, 859, 920
caress *vb.* 758, 890
caretaker *n.* 683
cargo *n.* 192
caricature *n.* 20, 22, 487, 853; *vb.* 20, 487, 853
carnage *n.* 370, 649
carnal *adj.* 827, 945
carnival *n.* 529, 840
carnivore *n.* 373
carouse *vb.* 840
carpet *n.* 225
carrel *n.* 475
carriage *n.* 217, 268, 276, 621
carried away *adj.* 827
carrier *n.* 275, 460, 467
carrot *n.* 547, 816
carry *vb.* 217, 268, 275
carry on *vb.* 91, 145, 535
carry out *vb.* 609, 659, 702
cart *n.* 276; *vb.* 268
carte blanche *n.* 678, 690
cartel *n.* 641, 681
cartilage *n.* 337
carton *n.* 193
cartoon *n.* 488
cartoonist *n.* 491
carve *vb.* 48, 163, 242, 489, 490
carver *n.* 491
cascade *n.* 358; *vb.* 358
case *n.* 7, 193, 401, 499, 930, 960
cash *n.* 731
cash-book *n.* 742
cash box *n.* 732
cashier *n.* 733, 742
cash in on *vb.* 136, 606, 705
cash register *n.* 732
casserole *vb.* 306
cassette-recorder *n.* 484, 794
cassock *n.* 989
cast *n.* 22, 94, 489, 529; *vb.* 242, 489
castaway *n.* 885
cast down *vb.* 321, 837
caste *n.* 97
castle *n.* 191, 595, 646
castles in the air *n.* 449
cast lots *vb.* 447
cast off *vb.* 228, 271, 556
castoffs *n.* 44
castrate *vb.* 160, 169
casual *n.* 655; *adj.* 139, 158, 393, 409
casuistry *n.* 631
catacomb *n.* 372
catalogue *n.* 83, 483; *vb.* 83, 483
catalyst *n.* 142, 173
cataract *n.* 358, 820
catastrophe *n.* 153, 551, 665, 900
catastrophic *adj.* 148, 551, 665
catch *n.* 635; *vb.* 478, 720, 795
catch-all *n.* 54; *adj.* 54
catch in the act *vb.* 419, 444, 938
catch on *vb.* 452, 545, 850
catch sight of *vb.* 818
catch up *vb.* 280
catchy *adj.* 790

catechism *n.* 420, 470
categorize *vb.* 97
category *n.* 97
catenary *n.* 247
cater *vb.* 568
catering *n.* 306, 568
cathedral *n.* 990
catholic *adj.* 101
cattle *n.* 373
cattleherd *n.* 377
catty *adj.* 900
cauldron *n.* 193
causal *adj.* 155
causation *n.* 155
cause *n.* 155, 547, 605; *vb.* 155, 547
caustic *adj.* 773, 900
caution *n.* 392, 597, 624, 860; *vb.* 597
cautionary *adj.* 597
cautious *adj.* 681, 856, 860
cavalry *n.* 655
cave *n.* 254, 317, 353
caveat *n.* 597
cave in *vb.* 254
cavity *n.* 319
caw *vb.* 787, 789
cease *vb.* 89, 144, 267, 826
ceasefire *n.* 144
ceaseless *adj.* 145
ceiling *n.* 225, 235
celebrate *vb.* 838, 878, 888, 988
celebrated *adj.* 868
celebration *n.* 838, 878
celebrity *n.* 868
celestial *adj.* 329, 966, 968, 972
celestial body *n.* 329
celibacy *n.* 897
celibate *n.* 897; *adj.* 169, 897, 951
cell *n.* 234, 366, 682
cement *n.* 49; *vb.* 47
cemetery *n.* 372
cenotaph *n.* 372, 483
censor *vb.* 466
censorious *adj.* 926
censorship *n.* 681, 779
censure *n.* 466, 926, 930; *vb.* 926, 930
census *n.* 38
centenary *n.* 70, 109, 878
central *adj.* 5, 90, 223, 224
centrality *n.* 224
centralize *vb.* 224
centre *n.* 90, 96, 183, 560; *adj.* 90, 224; *vb.* 96, 224
centrifugal *adj.* 297
century *n.* 70
ceramics *n.* 489
ceramist *n.* 491
cereal *n.* 306, 374
ceremonial *adj.* 878, 988
ceremony *n.* 878, 896, 988
certain *adj.* 408, 413, 420, 531, 534
certainly *adv.* 408, 531
certainty *n.* 408, 420, 531, 534
certificate *n.* 483, 690
certified *adj.* 408
certify *vb.* 408, 690
cessation *n.* 89, 144, 267
chafe *vb.* 341
chain *n.* 49, 85, 635, 681; *vb.* 635, 681
chalet *n.* 191
chalky *adj.* 807
challenge *n.* 394, 644, 649; *vb.* 394, 425, 644, 649
challenger *n.* 638
chamber *n.* 210
champ *vb.* 304
champagne *n.* 309
champion *n.* 579, 646, 661, 905; *adj.* 661
chance *n.* 158, 406, 553; *adj.* 139, 553; *vb.* 158, 553
chance upon *vb.* 158
chancy *adj.* 409
change *n.* 142, 731; *vb.* 15, 142
changeable *adj.* 15, 142, 151, 536, 539
changeableness *n.* 151
change of mind *n.* 538
change over *vb.* 714
channel *n.* 261, 262, 360, 564; *vb.* 261
chant *n.* 982; *vb.* 788, 792
chaos *n.* 80, 243, 668, 955
chap *n.* 380
chapel *n.* 990
chaperon *vb.* 392
chaplain *n.* 986
character *n.* 5, 58, 493, 529, 751, 868, 931
characteristic *n.* 102; *adj.* 5, 102, 486
characterize *vb.* 525
charcoal *n.* 765
charge *n.* 557, 622, 626, 645, 671, 685, 743, 930; *vb.* 159, 645, 671, 685, 736, 743, 930
charismatic *adj.* 294
charitable *adj.* 715, 747, 899, 965
charity *n.* 636, 715, 747, 899, 907
charlatan *n.* 480, 852
charm *n.* 547, 829, 844, 889, 984; *vb.* 547, 829, 889, 984
charming *adj.* 547, 829, 844, 889
chart *n.* 460, 486, 558
charter *n.* 690, 699; *vb.* 690, 718, 719, 954
charwoman *n.* 676
chary *adj.* 750

chase *n.* 554; *vb.* 287, 490, 554, 882, 890
chaser *n.* 554
chasm *n.* 200, 254, 317
chassis *n.* 217
chaste *adj.* 876, 935, 951
chastened *adj.* 874
chastise *vb.* 963
chat *n.* 516, 519; *vb.* 514, 516, 519
chatter *n.* 516, 519; *vb.* 326, 388, 516, 760
chatterbox *n.* 388, 516
chatty *adj.* 460, 516
chauffeur *n.* 676
chauvinist *n.* 903; *adj.* 379
cheap *adj.* 746
cheapen *vb.* 746, 924
cheapness *n.* 746
cheat *n.* 480, 631, 940; *vb.* 478, 631, 722, 916, 932
cheater *n.* 723
check *n.* 396, 635, 648, 681; *vb.* 37, 144, 394, 396, 408, 413, 635, 681
checker *vb.* 817
checklist *n.* 83
cheeky *adj.* 880, 887
cheer *n.* 827; *vb.* 618, 788, 834, 836, 840, 925
cheerfulness *n.* 836, 854
cheerless *adj.* 837, 895
cheers *n.* 838, 878
cheese *n.* 306
cheesed off *adj.* 832
cheese-paring *n.* 750
cheque *n.* 731
chequer *vb.* 817
cherish *vb.* 441, 712, 889, 890
cherub *n.* 968
chest *n.* 193
chestnut *n.* 842; *adj.* 810
chew *vb.* 304
chicanery *n.* 631
chicken *adj.* 858
chicken out *vb.* 858
chide *vb.* 926
chief *n.* 34, 675; *adj.* 34, 573
child *n.* 11, 131, 171
childhood *n.* 129
childish *adj.* 129, 131, 435
childless *adj.* 169
childlike *adj.* 129, 131, 632
chill *n.* 760; *vb.* 762
chilly *adj.* 760, 883
chime *n.* 784; *vb.* 783, 784
chimney *n.* 361
chink *n.* 200, 797
chip *n.* 33, 55, 482; *vb.* 48, 377
chip in *vb.* 738
chip on one's shoulder *n.* 832
chirp *vb.* 789
chirpy *adj.* 836
chirrup *vb.* 789
chisel *n.* 312, 480; *vb.* 163, 312, 478, 489, 490
chit *n.* 523
chit-chat *n.* 465, 516, 519
chivalry *n.* 857, 886
chocolate *adj.* 810
choice *n.* 398, 530, 540; *adj.* 579, 770
choiceless *adj.* 541
choir *n.* 793
choke *vb.* 265, 370, 572, 762
choleric *adj.* 894
choose *vb.* 398, 530, 532, 540, 861
choosy *adj.* 398, 540, 864
chop *vb.* 48, 319
chop and change *vb.* 151
choppy *adj.* 258
choral *adj.* 792
chord *n.* 247
chorister *n.* 793
chortle *vb.* 838
chorus *n.* 528, 792, 793, 982
christen *vb.* 496
Christendom *n.* 977, 985
Christian *n.* 977, 982
Christianity *n.* 974
chromatic *adj.* 805
chronicle *n.* 116, 483; *vb.* 483
chronicler *n.* 484
chronological *adj.* 116
chronometer *n.* 116
chronometry *n.* 116
chuck *vb.* 290, 556
chuckle *n.* 783, 838; *vb.* 783, 789, 838
chum *n.* 882
chunky *adj.* 203, 204
church *n.* 977, 982, 985, 987, 990
church building *n.* 990
churchdom *n.* 985
church-goer *n.* 982
church member *n.* 977, 987
churchyard *n.* 372
churlish *adj.* 895
cigar *n.* 308
cigarette *n.* 308
cinema *n.* 529, 840
cipher *n.* 39, 466
circle *n.* 94, 247, 250, 323; *vb.* 229, 322, 323
circuit *n.* 140, 232, 250, 269, 322, 323, 561
circular *n.* 464, 523; *adj.* 250
circulate *vb.* 322, 323, 460
circulation *n.* 322
circumambulate *vb.* 231, 322

circumference *n.* 232, 250
circumlocution *n.* 505
circumscription *n.* 231
circumspect *adj.* 392, 434, 860
circumstance *n.* 8, 153
circumstances *n.* 8, 229
circumstantial *adj.* 8
circumvent *vb.* 231, 555
circus *n.* 250, 559, 658
cistern *n.* 193
citadel *n.* 646
citation *n.* 663, 925
citizen *n.* 190, 871
city *n.* 183
city-dweller *n.* 190
civic *adj.* 379
civil *adj.* 379, 886, 987
civilian *n.* 871
civility *n.* 886
civilization *n.* 379
civilized *adj.* 379
clad *adj.* 227
claim *n.* 671, 737; *vb.* 549, 671, 917
claimant *n.* 697
clairvoyant *n.* 447, 984
clamber *vb.* 316
clammer *n.* 175
clamorous *adj.* 695, 780, 788
clamour *n.* 780, 788; *vb.* 695, 788
clamp *vb.* 47
clamp down on *vb.* 669
clan *n.* 11
clandestine *adj.* 461
clang *n.* 783; *vb.* 783, 784, 787
clanger *n.* 431
clanging *n.* 784; *adj.* 784, 787
clap *vb.* 282, 838, 878, 925
clarify *vb.* 456
clarity *n.* 452, 502, 823
clash *n.* 175, 282; *vb.* 14, 282, 642, 787, 791, 805, 883
clasp *n.* 49, 712; *vb.* 50, 712, 720, 758, 890
class *n.* 7, 55, 97, 122, 206, 470, 472, 474; *vb.* 97
classified *adj.* 81, 466
classify *vb.* 81, 83, 97, 496
classroom *n.* 475
clatter *vb.* 783, 787
clause *n.* 498
clean *adj.* 46, 583, 937, 951; *vb.* 341, 583, 775, 807
cleaner *n.* 676
cleanliness *n.* 583, 585, 951
cleanness *n.* 583, 951
cleanse *vb.* 583
cleanser *n.* 775
clear *adj.* 46, 413, 452, 458, 502, 512, 678, 797, 802, 823, 921; *vb.* 320, 583, 921, 961
clearance *n.* 182, 200, 690, 727
clear-cut *adj.* 452, 823
clear-headed *adj.* 949
clearmindedness *n.* 438
cleavage *n.* 48
cleave *vb.* 48, 50
cleft *n.* 200, 259
clemency *n.* 670, 907
clergyman *n.* 986
cleric *n.* 986; *adj.* 985
clerical *adj.* 986
clerical dress *n.* 989
clerk *n.* 484
clever *adj.* 426, 434, 627, 631
cliché *n.* 495, 498
click *vb.* 24, 452, 782
client *n.* 545, 716, 726
cliff *n.* 214
climate *n.* 8, 229, 348
climax *n.* 89, 212
climb *vb.* 273, 316
climb down *vb.* 538
clinch *n.* 712; *vb.* 47, 50, 408, 712
clincher *n.* 414
cling *vb.* 50, 712
clip *vb.* 203
clipper *n.* 277
clippings *n.* 44
clique *n.* 94, 641
cloak *n.* 461, 463, 549; *vb.* 461
clock *n.* 116
clog *vb.* 265
cloister *n.* 885
clonk *n.* 785; *vb.* 785
close *n.* 89, 184, 559; *adj.* 47, 50, 154, 199, 419, 759, 882; *vb.* 144, 263, 461
closed book *n.* 427, 453
closed shop *n.* 99, 681
close-fisted *adj.* 750
close friend *n.* 882
close in on *vb.* 292
close-lipped *adj.* 517
close shave *n.* 600
closure *n.* 89, 144, 263
clot *vb.* 332
cloth *n.* 989
clothe *vb.* 227
clothes *n.* 227
cloud *n.* 363, 803; *vb.* 461, 799, 803
cloudburst *n.* 175, 358
cloudless *adj.* 664, 797
cloudy *adj.* 358, 363, 503, 799, 803, 824
clout *n.* 963; *vb.* 282, 963
clown *n.* 842
clowning *n.* 433
cloy *vb.* 56, 865
club *n.* 96, 191; *vb.* 282, 639
cluck *vb.* 787, 789
clue *n.* 401, 447, 482
clumsy *adj.* 511, 628

cluster *n.* 94
clutch *vb.* 712, 758
clutter *n.* 80
coach *n.* 276, 473; *vb.* 470
coagulate *vb.* 332, 334
coagulated *adj.* 362
coal *n.* 367, 765, 800
coalesce *vb.* 13, 52
coalition *n.* 641
coarse *adj.* 258, 511, 849, 887, 952
coastline *n.* 352
coat *n.* 206, 225; *vb.* 225, 342, 805
coating *n.* 206, 225
coat of arms *n.* 482
coax *vb.* 547, 695
cock *n.* 380
cocktail *n.* 309
cock-up *n.* 628
cocky *adj.* 875
coddle *vb.* 306
code *n.* 103, 466, 954
codification *n.* 954
coerce *vb.* 175, 674
coexist *vb.* 60, 122
coextensive *adj.* 28, 218
coffee *n.* 309; *adj.* 810
coffee-bar *n.* 191
coffee-break *n.* 616
coffer *n.* 193, 732
coffin *n.* 372
cog *vb.* 259
cogitation *n.* 384, 410
cognition *n.* 426
cognitive *adj.* 382
cognizability *n.* 452
cognizant *adj.* 426
cohabit *vb.* 889
cohabitant *n.* 889
cohere *vb.* 50
coherence *n.* 50, 337
cohesive *adj.* 50
coil *n.* 251; *vb.* 249
coin *vb.* 449, 731
coinage *n.* 495
coincide *vb.* 13, 24, 28, 60, 122
coincidence *n.* 24, 60, 105, 122, 553
coincidental *adj.* 60, 158
coke *n.* 765
cold *n.* 760; *adj.* 754, 760, 806, 863
cold-blooded *adj.* 754, 908
cold feet *n.* 856, 858
cold shoulder *n.* 924; *vb.* 885
cold war *n.* 650
coliseum *n.* 658
collaborate *vb.* 180, 639
collaborator *n.* 640
collage *n.* 488
collapse *n.* 164, 588, 617, 662; *vb.* 254, 588, 617
collate *vb.* 397
collateral *n.* 701; *adj.* 11
colleague *n.* 640
collect *vb.* 94, 567, 705, 716
collective *n.* 709; *adj.* 24
collectively *adv.* 60
college *n.* 475
collide *vb.* 282
collision course *n.* 296
colloid *n.* 362; *adj.* 362
colloquial *adj.* 495
colloquialism *n.* 494, 495
colonist *n.* 190
colonize *vb.* 191
colony *n.* 94
coloration *n.* 805
colossal *adj.* 32
colour *n.* 509, 805, 811; *vb.* 403, 509, 805
colour-blind *adj.* 819, 820
colourful *adj.* 805
colourlessness *n.* 806, 843
colours *n.* 482
column *n.* 91, 208, 217
coma *n.* 754
combat *n.* 651; *vb.* 637, 649
combatant *n.* 655
combination *n.* 45, 52
combine *vb.* 45, 47, 52, 639
combustible *n.* 765; *adj.* 761, 765
combustion *n.* 761
come *vb.* 298
come about *vb.* 153, 430
come across *vb.* 186, 419
come after *vb.* 85, 119, 287
comeback *n.* 147, 395, 589
come back to *vb.* 395
come before *vb.* 84, 118
come by *vb.* 716
come clean *vb.* 462
comedian *n.* 842
come down *vb.* 273, 317
come-down *n.* 874
come down on *vb.* 669, 963
comedy *n.* 529
come first *vb.* 286
come forward *vb.* 292, 693
come home *vb.* 298, 755
come in *vb.* 300, 716
come into *vb.* 705
come into conflict with *vb.* 25
come into sight *vb.* 292, 823
come into view *vb.* 823, 825
comely *adj.* 844

come near *vb.* 292
come next *vb.* 85
come of *vb.* 156
come of age *vb.* 133
come off *vb.* 153, 661
come on *vb.* 587
come out *vb.* 88, 144, 301, 464
come out with *vb.* 462
come round again *vb.* 140
come round to *vb.* 420
come short *vb.* 315, 445, 571
comestible *adj.* 306
comet *n.* 329
come to *vb.* 743
come to a head *vb.* 659
come to an agreement *vb.* 699, 704
come to an end *vb.* 89
come to blows *vb.* 642
come together *vb.* 94, 296
come to life *vb.* 368
come to light *vb.* 825
come to mind *vb.* 384, 441
come to nothing *vb.* 2, 315, 369, 576, 662
come to the point *vb.* 504
come up *vb.* 153
come up against *vb.* 25
come up to *vb.* 28, 570
comfort *n.* 636, 834; *vb.* 636, 834, 836, 899, 907
comfortable *adj.* 634, 664, 827, 834
comforting *adj.* 834, 907
comic *adj.* 851
coming *n.* 292, 298; *adj.* 123, 154
coming out *n.* 88
command *n.* 501, 622, 626, 667, 671; *vb.* 208, 622, 667, 671
commandeer *vb.* 720
commander *n.* 623, 675
commanding *adj.* 667, 671
commandment *n.* 626
commemorate *vb.* 441, 878
commemorative *adj.* 441, 878
commence *vb.* 88, 605
commend *vb.* 925
commendable *adj.* 579, 925
commensurate *adj.* 28
comment *n.* 456, 526; *vb.* 456, 526
commentary *n.* 456, 526
commentator *n.* 456, 526, 974
commerce *n.* 150, 725
commercial *adj.* 725
commercial traveller *n.* 727
commiserate *vb.* 907
commission *n.* 94, 557, 609, 685; *vb.* 557, 685
commissioner *n.* 688, 689
commissioner for oaths *n.* 959
commit *vb.* 609, 685, 698, 714
commit adultery *vb.* 952
commitment *n.* 605, 698, 737, 919, 980
commit oneself *vb.* 534, 540, 605, 919
commit suicide *vb.* 370
committed *adj.* 534, 698, 737, 980
committee *n.* 94, 625, 688
commodities *n.* 729
commodity *n.* 327
common *n.* 356; *adj.* 35, 138, 508, 666, 709, 843, 867
commoner *n.* 871
commonly *adv.* 138
common people *n.* 871
commonplace *n.* 432; *adj.* 138, 666, 843
common sense *n.* 434
commotion *n.* 326, 611
communal *adj.* 379, 709
communicant *n.* 982
communicate *vb.* 460, 464, 514, 519, 523
communication *n.* 460, 464, 492, 514, 523
communicative *adj.* 460
communion *n.* 979
communiqué *n.* 465
communism *n.* 709
community *n.* 183, 379, 641, 709
commutable *adj.* 150
commutation *n.* 149
commute *vb.* 142, 149, 150
commuter *n.* 190, 270
compact *adj.* 50, 203, 204, 332, 334, 504; *vb.* 332
companion *n.* 640, 882
company *n.* 94, 620, 641
comparable *adj.* 28
comparative *adj.* 27, 455
compare *vb.* 27, 218, 397
comparison *n.* 18, 27, 397, 455, 499
compartment *n.* 55
compass *n.* 182, 322
compassion *n.* 670, 907
compassionate *adj.* 670, 899, 907
compatible *adj.* 24, 105, 882
compatriot *n.* 11

compel *vb.* 177, 531, 562, 674, 755
compelling *adj.* 674, 755
compendious *adj.* 54, 527
compendium *n.* 527
compensation *n.* 31, 721, 738, 917, 965
compensatory *adj.* 31, 721, 943, 965
compete *vb.* 649
competence *n.* 159, 627, 956
competent *adj.* 159, 579, 627, 956
competition *n.* 649
competitive *adj.* 649
competitor *n.* 638, 854
compile *vb.* 58
complacency *n.* 831
complain *vb.* 642, 788, 832, 926, 930
complainer *n.* 832
complaint *n.* 586, 696, 926, 930
complement *n.* 28, 60
complete *adj.* 54, 56, 581, 659; *vb.* 581, 609, 659, 661
completely *adv.* 54, 56
completeness *n.* 54, 56
completion *n.* 89, 581, 659, 661
complex circularity *n.* 251
complexion *n.* 805
complexity *n.* 503
compliance *n.* 532, 673, 692, 702
compliant *adj.* 532, 654, 919
complicate *vb.* 835
complicated *adj.* 453, 503, 633
compliment *n.* 886, 888, 925, 927; *vb.* 886, 888, 925
comply *vb.* 105, 570, 654, 673, 702
component *n.* 55, 192, 327
compose *vb.* 58, 81, 163, 521, 528, 792
composed *adj.* 757
composer *n.* 166, 491, 528, 793
composite *adj.* 45
composition *n.* 45, 58, 81, 339, 488, 521, 522, 526, 528, 792
compositor *n.* 522
composure *n.* 757
compound *n.* 45, 184; *vb.* 36, 52
comprehend *vb.* 58, 98, 452
comprehensible *adj.* 452
comprehension *n.* 410, 452
comprehensive *adj.* 54, 56, 98, 101
compress *vb.* 37, 197, 205, 332, 504
compressed *adj.* 332, 504
compressor *n.* 197
comprise *vb.* 58, 98
compromise *n.* 30, 699, 704; *vb.* 704
compulsion *n.* 439, 531, 562, 674
compulsive *adj.* 674
compulsory *adj.* 531, 674, 919
compunction *n.* 833
compunctious *adj.* 941
compute *vb.* 38, 400
computer *n.* 38, 400, 565
comrade *n.* 640, 882
con *n.* 631, 684; *vb.* 631
concatenation *n.* 47, 85
concavity *n.* 254
conceal *vb.* 225, 461, 466
concealment *n.* 461, 824
concede *vb.* 424, 462, 690, 692
conceited *adj.* 873, 875
conceivable *adj.* 404
conceive *vb.* 88, 163, 368, 382, 449
concentrate *vb.* 96, 296, 334, 384, 390
concentration *n.* 296, 332, 384, 390, 611
concept *n.* 386
conception *n.* 382, 386, 420
concern *n.* 387, 392, 557, 605, 620; *vb.* 9, 526, 609, 856
concerned *adj.* 388, 392
concerning *adv.*, *prep.* 9
concert *n.* 180, 643, 790, 792, 840
concerto *n.* 792
concession *n.* 690, 704, 744
conciliation *n.* 650, 652
concise *adj.* 203, 432, 504, 527
conciseness *n.* 504
conclude *vb.* 56, 89, 410, 530
conclusion *n.* 89, 144, 235, 410, 659
conclusive *adj.* 408, 413, 430, 659
concoct *vb.* 163, 477, 558, 930
concomitant *n.* 60; *adj.* 60
concord *n.* 24, 643, 790
concordance *n.* 494, 524
concordat *n.* 699
concrete *adj.* 3, 327, 332

concur *vb.* 24, 180, 424, 692
concurrence *n.* 24, 180, 296, 692
concurrent *adj.* 24, 60, 122, 180, 296
condemn *vb.* 892, 926, 962
condemnation *n.* 962
condemned *adj.* 938
condemned cell *n.* 964
condensation *n.* 346
condense *vb.* 203, 332, 345, 504, 527
condescend *vb.* 869, 874, 886
condiment *n.* 307
condition *n.* 7, 562, 825; *vb.* 470, 545
conditional *adj.* 403, 700
conditioning *n.* 470, 545
conditions *n.* 8, 700
condolence *n.* 907
conduce *vb.* 155
conducive *adj.* 178, 563
conduct *n.* 172, 606, 621, 622; *vb.* 268, 606, 609, 621, 622
conduit *n.* 360
confectionery *n.* 306
confederate *n.* 640; *adj.* 641; *vb.* 47
confederation *n.* 641
confer *vb.* 159, 519, 715, 965
conference *n.* 94, 519, 625
confess *vb.* 420, 462, 941, 982
confession *n.* 420, 941, 974, 982
confidant *n.* 624, 882
confide *vb.* 462, 624
confidence *n.* 408, 420, 443, 466, 854
confident *adj.* 420, 443, 854, 857
confidential *adj.* 466
confine *vb.* 205, 234, 681, 712
confirm *vb.* 401, 408, 413, 468, 699, 929
confiscate *vb.* 720
conflict *n.* 649; *vb.* 637, 642, 805, 883
confluence *n.* 221, 296
conform *vb.* 16, 24, 105, 702
conformist *n.* 20, 105
conformity *n.* 16, 105, 244, 643
confound *vb.* 82, 399, 414, 869
confront *vb.* 239, 637, 644, 649
confrontation *n.* 637, 649
confuse *vb.* 82, 187, 399
confused *adj.* 80, 399, 439
confusedly *adv.* 80
confusion *n.* 80, 326
confuted *adj.* 414
congeal *vb.* 332, 334, 762
congelation *n.* 760
congenial *adj.* 827
congenital *adj.* 5
congestion *n.* 332, 572
conglomerate *n.* 332
conglomeration *n.* 45
congratulate *vb.* 838, 878, 888
congratulate oneself *vb.* 879
congratulation *n.* 838, 888
congregate *vb.* 50, 94
congregation *n.* 94, 982, 987
congress *n.* 94, 519, 625, 641
congressman *n.* 625
congruity *n.* 16, 24, 105
conjecture *n.* 386, 396, 447, 448; *vb.* 448
conjugal *adj.* 896
conjugate *vb.* 499
conjunction *n.* 499
conjunctivitis *n.* 820
conjure *vb.* 449, 984
conjurer *n.* 984
con man *n.* 480, 631, 906
connect *vb.* 47, 81
connected *adj.* 9, 47, 52, 60, 81
connection *n.* 9, 47, 49, 201
connoisseur *n.* 304, 436, 848
connotation *n.* 450, 459
conquer *vb.* 316, 661, 679
conqueror *n.* 661
conscience *n.* 382, 919
conscience-stricken *adj.* 833, 941
conscientiousness *n.* 392, 864, 931
conscious *adj.* 382, 426, 753
conscript *n.* 655; *vb.* 651
conscription *n.* 674
consecrate *vb.* 980, 985
consecration *n.* 715, 980
consecutive *adj.* 85, 91
consensus *n.* 24, 424, 643
consent *n.* 424, 690, 692, 698; *vb.* 690, 692, 698
consequence *n.* 60, 85, 87, 156, 573
consequent *adj.* 85, 156
consequential *adj.* 119, 156, 573
conservation *n.* 374, 392, 599

conservatism n. 143
conservative n. 105, 143; adj. 143, 977
conserve n. 306; vb. 599, 748
consider vb. 384, 390, 415, 420, 526, 982
considerable adj. 32, 75, 573
considerate adj. 390, 392, 434, 886
consideration n. 384, 390, 392, 415, 886
consign vb. 268, 714
consignee n. 688
consignment n. 268
consist vb. 1, 58, 98
consistency n. 50, 105, 143
consistent adj. 16, 24, 105
consolation n. 176, 834, 907
consolation prize n. 663
console vb. 176, 834, 907
consolidate vb. 52, 334
consolidation n. 332
consonance n. 24, 643, 790
consonant n. 493, 512; adj. 24, 105
conspicuous adj. 253, 458, 462, 823, 877
conspiracy n. 558
conspire vb. 558
conspirer n. 558
constable n. 956
constancy n. 16, 91, 114, 140, 143, 152, 535
constant n. 152; adj. 91, 140, 143, 145, 152, 535
constellation n. 329
consternation n. 856
constituency n. 183, 540
constituent n. 55, 192; adj. 55, 73
constitute vb. 58, 98
constitution n. 5, 58, 339, 954
constitutional n. 269; adj. 954
constrain vb. 531, 674
constraint n. 674, 681
constrict vb. 197
construct vb. 58, 163, 242, 477, 930
construction n. 163, 242, 494
constructor n. 166
consul n. 688
consult vb. 624
consultant n. 624
consultation n. 519
consultative adj. 624
consume vb. 304, 569, 575, 740, 761
consumer n. 304, 726
consummate adj. 89, 581; vb. 56, 581, 659, 896
consummation n. 89, 156, 212, 581, 896
consumption n. 569
contact n. 47, 201, 758; vb. 201
contagious adj. 586
contain vb. 98, 234, 707, 712
container n. 193, 275
contaminate vb. 584, 588, 952
contemplate vb. 384, 415, 552
contemplative adj. 384, 434
contemporaneous adj. 120, 122
contemporary n. 122; adj. 60, 120, 122, 125
contempt n. 853, 869, 924
contemptible adj. 580, 869, 924
contemptuous adj. 853, 924
contend vb. 414, 615, 649, 651
contender n. 655
content n. 450, 831; adj. 831
contented adj. 827, 831
contentious adj. 409, 651
contents n. 192, 223
contest n. 649; vb. 604, 649
contestant n. 638; adj. 649
context n. 8
contiguity n. 199, 201
continent n. 352; adj. 944, 951
contingencies n. 700
contingent adj. 8, 403, 679, 700
contingent duration n. 111
continual adj. 114, 138, 143, 145
continuance n. 91, 107, 145, 535
continue vb. 91, 107, 112, 138, 145, 535
continuity n. 50, 91, 143
continuous adj. 91, 257
contort vb. 245, 251
contour n. 232, 242
contraband n. 724; adj. 955
contraception n. 169
contract n. 24, 468, 698, 699, 919; vb. 197, 203, 205 557, 698, 699
contraction n. 197, 205, 504
contractual adj. 699
contradict vb. 14, 25,

181, 402, 414, 425, 469, 637
contradiction n. 14, 181, 239, 412, 414, 469, 637
contraption n. 565
contrary n. 239; adj. 14, 15, 239, 402, 469, 883
contrast n. 106, 239, 397; vb. 14, 397, 805
contravene vb. 469, 703, 955
contribute vb. 40, 155, 639, 715, 738
contribution n. 41, 917
contributor n. 715, 905
contributory adj. 563
contrite adj. 833, 941
contrivance n. 565
contrive vb. 477, 631
control n. 159, 177, 235, 622, 667, 681, 707, 956; vb. 177, 622, 667, 681, 707, 956
controller n. 623
control oneself vb. 681, 757, 944
controversial adj. 409, 410
conurbation n. 183
convalescence n. 589, 618
convene vb. 94
convenience n. 575, 827
convenient adj. 136, 575, 577, 748
convent n. 990
convention n. 94, 103, 519, 545, 625, 699
conventional adj. 103, 143, 545, 699, 843
converge vb. 47, 94, 96, 224, 296
convergence n. 224, 296
conversation n. 410, 519
converse n. 239; vb. 410, 514, 519
conversely adv. 14
conversion n. 142, 146, 606, 714
convert n. 146, 941, 980; vb. 142, 146, 606, 714
convexity n. 252
convey vb. 268, 275, 450, 460, 714, 715
conveyance n. 268, 276
conveyancing n. 714
convict n. 684; vb. 681, 960, 962
convicted adj. 941
conviction n. 408, 420, 530, 534, 962
convince vb. 177, 420, 470
convincing adj. 547
convivial adj. 827
conviviality n. 884
convocation n. 94, 625
convolution n. 251
convoy vb. 268
convulsion n. 326, 586
coo vb. 789
cook vb. 306, 759
cooker n. 763
cookery n. 306
cook up vb. 163
cool adj. 391, 579, 754, 757, 760, 883; vb. 348, 762
cooling apparatus n. 764
cooling-off period n. 135
coolness n. 391, 757, 837, 883
cooperate vb. 52, 180, 636, 639, 709
cooperation n. 60, 180, 639, 709
cooperative n. 641, 709; adj. 180, 639, 641, 709
co-opt vb. 540
coordinate vb. 81, 81
coordinated adj. 81
co-ownership n. 709
cop n. 956
copious adj. 32, 168
copper n. 956; adj. 810, 816
copse n. 374
copulate vb. 889
copy n. 20, 22, 62, 77, 486, 488, 521, 522, 524; vb. 20, 62, 77, 165, 488, 521
copyist n. 521
coral n. 816; adj. 811
cord n. 49, 207
cordial adj. 884
cordiality n. 747, 882, 884
core n. 5, 90, 224, 527
cork n. 265, 331; vb. 265
corn n. 252, 374
corner n. 184, 233, 246, 254; vb. 707
corner-stone n. 217
cornucopia n. 168, 572
corona n. 250, 800
coronation n. 685
corporality n. 3, 327
corporal punishment n. 963
corporation n. 956
corpse n. 371
corpulent adj. 194
correct adj. 430, 499, 510, 915, 977; vb. 587, 589, 963
correction n. 587, 963
corrective adj. 585, 589, 591, 963
correlate n. 22; vb. 12
correlation n. 9, 12, 18
correspond vb. 12, 24, 150, 218, 523
correspondence n. 9,

12, 18, 24, 105, 397, 521, 523
correspondent *n.* 395, 460, 523
corroborate *vb.* 217, 401, 408
corroborative *adj.* 401
corrode *vb.* 588
corrosion *n.* 53
corrugate *vb.* 260, 261
corrupt *adj.* 431, 477, 869, 932, 936; *vb.* 547, 580, 584, 588, 936
corruption *n.* 495, 551, 588, 932, 936
cosmetic *adj.* 211, 846
cosmetics *n.* 844
cosmic *adj.* 329
cosmology *n.* 329
cosmonaut *n.* 274
cosmopolitan *n.* 903; *adj.* 101
cosmos *n.* 329
cost *n.* 743; *vb.* 743
costly *adj.* 745
costs *n.* 31, 740, 963
costume *n.* 227
cosy *adj.* 827
cottage *n.* 191
cough *n.* 359; *vb.* 359
cough up *vb.* 738
council *n.* 94, 519, 625, 641
councillor *n.* 625
counsel *n.* 597, 624, 959; *vb.* 470, 519, 597, 624
counsellor *n.* 473, 624
count *n.* 38, 870; *vb.* 38, 400
countable *adj.* 38
count against *vb.* 588
countdown *n.* 274
countenance *n.* 236, 825
counter *n.* 482; *adj.* 181; *vb.* 637, 647
counteract *vb.* 31, 181, 648, 686
counteraction *n.* 181
counterattack *n.* 647
counterbalance *n.* 31, 152; *vb.* 31, 181, 330
counter-evidence *n.* 402
counterfeit *n.* 20, 487; *adj.* 20, 431, 477; *vb.* 20, 477
counterfoil *n.* 482
countermand *n.* 686, 691; *vb.* 686
countermeasure *n.* 181
counterpart *n.* 18, 20, 22, 28
counterpoise *vb.* 330
counter-productive *adj.* 576
counterweight *n.* 152, 181, 330
countless *adj.* 75, 78
count on *vb.* 443
country *n.* 183
countryman *n.* 871
county *n.* 183
coup *n.* 148
coup de grâce *n.* 659
coupé *n.* 276
couple *n.* 61; *vb.* 47, 61
couplet *n.* 61
coupling *n.* 47, 49
courage *n.* 857
courier *n.* 460, 467
course *n.* 269, 306, 358, 360, 470, 559
course of action *n.* 558
course of time *n.* 110
court *n.* 234, 559, 658, 870, 957; *vb.* 882, 890
court danger *vb.* 859
courteous *adj.* 392, 886, 922
courtesy *n.* 886, 899
courtship *n.* 890
cousin *n.* 11
cove *n.* 353
covenant *n.* 698, 699, 701; *vb.* 698, 699
cover *n.* 193, 225, 306, 463, 595; *vb.* 206, 225, 461, 646, 798, 801
cover for *vb.* 149
covering *n.* 211, 222, 225, 461, 801
covert *n.* 254, 374, 463, 595
covet *vb.* 861, 914
covetous *adj.* 750, 861, 914
covetousness *n.* 750, 861, 914
cow *n.* 381
coward *n.* 162, 858
cowardice *n.* 858
cowardly *adj.* 858
co-worker *n.* 640
coy *adj.* 876
crack *n.* 200; *vb.* 264, 456, 782
crack down on *vb.* 669, 963
cracker *n.* 306
crackle *n.* 782
crack up *vb.* 439, 856, 925
cradle *n.* 325
craft *n.* 277, 557, 631
craftsman *n.* 619
crafty *adj.* 478, 631, 932
cram *vb.* 56, 470, 472
crank *n.* 106, 440
cranky *adj.* 439
crash *n.* 282, 739, 782; *vb.* 282, 739, 780, 782, 787
crash-land *vb.* 273, 317, 321
crass *adj.* 849
crate *n.* 193
crater *n.* 254
crave *vb.* 695, 861, 914
craven *adj.* 858
craving *n.* 861
crawl *vb.* 281, 881

crawl with *vb.* 75
crayon *vb.* 488
craze *n.* 125, 439, 539, 850, 861
crazy *adj.* 433, 435, 439, 861, 889
creak *vb.* 781, 787
cream *n.* 306, 342, 365, 579, 813; *adj.* 807, 813; *vb.* 342
creamy *adj.* 362, 365
crease *n.* 260; *vb.* 260
create *vb.* 155, 163, 242, 449, 558
creation *n.* 21, 163, 329, 366
creative *adj.* 21, 163, 449
creator *n.* 155, 166, 491, 966
creature *n.* 366, 368, 373, 379
crèche *n.* 475
credence *n.* 420
credible *adj.* 404, 406, 420
credit *n.* 420, 718, 731, 736, 868, 909, 925; *vb.* 736, 742
creditable *adj.* 925
credit card *n.* 718, 731, 736
creditor *n.* 718, 736
credulous *adj.* 422
creed *n.* 420, 974
creek *n.* 354, 358
creep *vb.* 316, 461
cremate *vb.* 372, 761
cremation *n.* 372
crematorium *n.* 372, 763
crescent *n.* 247, 559; *adj.* 36, 247
crest *n.* 212, 358, 482, 872
crestfallen *adj.* 837, 874
cretin *n.* 437, 440
crevasse *n.* 254
crew *n.* 94, 272
crib *n.* 22; *vb.* 20
crier *n.* 467
crime *n.* 938, 955
criminal *n.* 684, 906, 940; *adj.* 932
criminality *n.* 932, 938
crimp *n.* 260; *vb.* 251, 260
crimson *adj.* 811
cringe *vb.* 856
cringing *adj.* 881
cripple *vb.* 245, 588
crisis *n.* 80, 136, 665
crisp *adj.* 760; *vb.* 306
crispy *adj.* 338
criterion *n.* 23, 27, 103, 400
critic *n.* 456, 524, 526, 848, 928
critical *adj.* 136, 382, 398, 415, 573, 594, 926
criticism *n.* 456, 624, 926
criticize *vb.* 696, 832, 893, 926, 962
critique *n.* 398, 456, 526
croak *vb.* 787, 789
crocodile *n.* 91
crocus *n.* 813
croft *n.* 378
crook *n.* 247, 480, 723, 906, 940, 989; *vb.* 247
crooked *adj.* 29, 219, 245
crop *n.* 374, 567, 705; *vb.* 203
crop up *vb.* 153, 825
cross *n.* 221, 592, 830, 964; *adj.* 893, 895; *vb.* 45, 221, 313, 478
cross-examination *n.* 394, 960
cross-eyed *adj.* 820
crossing *n.* 221, 313
cross purposes *n.* 642
crotchety *adj.* 539
crouch *vb.* 209, 319
crow *vb.* 789
crowd *n.* 75, 94, 821, 871; *vb.* 75, 94
crown *n.* 212, 250, 659, 663, 677; *vb.* 212, 685, 868, 878
crucial *adj.* 136, 573
crucifix *n.* 221
crucifixion *n.* 370, 828, 963
crucify *vb.* 830, 963
crude *adj.* 511, 887
cruel *adj.* 669, 900, 908
cruise *n.* 271; *vb.* 269, 271
crumb *n.* 33, 340
crumble *vb.* 162, 164, 338, 340, 588
crumple *vb.* 258
crunch *vb.* 340
crush *n.* 94, 889; *vb.* 164, 340, 364, 414, 661, 874
crushed *adj.* 837, 874
crushing *n.* 874
crustacean *n.* 373
crutch *n.* 217
crux *n.* 221
cry *n.* 597, 782, 788, 789, 839; *vb.* 788, 789, 833, 839
cry-baby *n.* 162, 858
cry out for *vb.* 531, 562
cry over *vb.* 833
cryptic *adj.* 466
crystal *adj.* 802
crystal-clear *adj.* 458
crystallize *vb.* 332, 334
cry wolf *vb.* 478, 598
cube *n.* 246
cuckoo *vb.* 789
cuddle *vb.* 890
cudgel *vb.* 282
cuff *n.* 963
cuisine *n.* 306
cul de sac *n.* 635
culinary *adj.* 306
cull *vb.* 540

culminate *vb.* 56, 212, 659
culmination *n.* 89, 581
culpable *adj.* 157, 938
culprit *n.* 684
cultivate *vb.* 378, 470
cultivated *adj.* 848, 886
cultivator *n.* 378
culture *n.* 426, 848, 886
cultured *adj.* 426, 848, 886
culvert *n.* 360
cumbersome *adj.* 330, 628
cumulative *adj.* 36
cuneiform *n.* 493; *adj.* 246
cunning *n.* 631, 932; *adj.* 478, 631
cup *n.* 193, 663
curate *n.* 986
curative *adj.* 589, 591
curator *n.* 593, 683
curb *n.* 281, 635, 681; *vb.* 37, 235, 281, 681
curdle *vb.* 332, 773
cure *n.* 176, 181, 589, 591, 834; *vb.* 589, 591, 599
curfew *n.* 128, 681
curiosity *n.* 388, 866
curious *adj.* 388, 394
curl *n.* 247, 251; *vb.* 247, 251, 260
currency *n.* 731
current *n.* 140, 358, 359; *adj.* 120, 125, 153, 464, 492, 545
current affairs *n.* 465
curriculum *n.* 470
curried *adj.* 769
curry *vb.* 306
curry favour *vb.* 881
curse *n.* 592, 665, 901; *vb.* 892, 901, 962
cursory *adj.* 113, 211
curt *adj.* 203, 504, 517, 887
curtail *vb.* 37, 197, 203
curtain *n.* 216, 461, 801
curtsy *n.* 319, 922; *vb.* 319, 922
curve *n.* 219, 247; *vb.* 219, 247
curved form *n.* 247
cushion *n.* 217; *vb.* 176, 834
custodian *n.* 593, 683
custody *n.* 593, 681, 707
custom *n.* 545, 726, 743, 988
customary *adj.* 126, 138, 545, 988
customer *n.* 716, 726
cut *n.* 43, 55, 259, 717, 744; *vb.* 48, 259, 264, 490, 744
cut back *vb.* 37, 42, 203, 748
cut down *vb.* 203, 319
cut out *vb.* 312
cut out for *adj.* 627
cut-price *adj.* 746
cut-throat *n.* 370
cutting *adj.* 255, 760, 773, 923
cut up *adj.* 828, 837; *vb.* 837
cycle *n.* 109, 140, 276, 323; *vb.* 269, 323
cyclic *adj.* 109, 140, 250
cycling *n.* 269
cyclone *n.* 323, 359
cyclopedia *n.* 524
cylinder *n.* 249
cylindrical *adj.* 249
cynic *n.* 904, 928
cynical *adj.* 904, 928
cynicism *n.* 904

D

dabble *vb.* 349
dad *n.* 170
daffodil *n.* 813
daily *adv.* 140
dainty *n.* 770, 848; *adj.* 331, 770
dally *vb.* 135
dam *vb.* 265
damage *n.* 588; *vb.* 164, 582, 588, 847
damages *n.* 31, 963
damaging *adj.* 580
damn *vb.* 901, 962
damned *adj.* 975
damp *n.* 349; *adj.* 349; *vb.* 762
dampen *vb.* 349, 548, 837
dampness *n.* 347, 349
dance *n.* 792, *vb.* 320, 838
dancer *n.* 793
dandy *n.* 852
danger *n.* 594
dangerous *adj.* 594
dangle *vb.* 216
dank *adj.* 349
dapple *vb.* 817
dare *n.* 644; *vb.* 644
daredevil *n.* 859
daring *n.* 857, 859; *adj.* 644, 857
dark *n.* 798; *adj.* 798, 803, 808
darken *vb.* 798, 803, 808
darkness *n.* 427, 798, 803, 808
darling *n.* 891
darn *vb.* 589
dart *n.* 290; *vb.* 273, 280
dash *n.* 33, 173, 613; *vb.* 280, 282, 613
dashing *adj.* 611, 613
dastardly *adj.* 858
data *n.* 38, 401, 460
date *n.* 107, 116, 884; *vb.* 116
dated *adj.* 107, 126

daub *n.* 847; *vb.* 342, 584, 847
daughter *n.* 171
daunt *vb.* 856
dauntless *adj.* 857
dawdle *vb.* 135, 281
dawn *n.* 127, 797; *vb.* 797
day *n.* 109, 116
daybreak *n.* 127, 797
day-dream *n.* 449; *vb.* 391, 449
daylight *n.* 797
dazzle *n.* 797; *vb.* 797
dazzling *adj.* 509, 797
deacon *n.* 987
dead *adj.* 2, 174, 369, 754, 785, 843
deaden *vb.* 513, 754, 779, 785
deadlock *n.* 144
deadly *adj.* 164, 370, 580, 586, 592
deaf *adj.* 796
deafen *vb.* 780, 796
deafening *adj.* 780, 796
deafness *n.* 796
deal *n.* 26, 699; *vb.* 9, 526, 606, 699, 717, 725
dealer *n.* 728
dealings *n.* 557
deal out *vb.* 715
dean *n.* 986
dear *n.* 891; *adj.* 745, 889
dearness *n.* 745
dearth *n.* 315, 571
death *n.* 89, 369
death chamber *n.* 964
deathly *adj.* 369, 371
death sentence *n.* 963
débâcle *n.* 148, 662
debar *vb.* 691
debase *vb.* 209, 584, 608, 869
debasement *n.* 209, 319, 608, 928
debatable *adj.* 409
debate *n.* 410, 519; *vb.* 414, 519
debauched *adj.* 945, 952
debilitate *vb.* 162
debility *n.* 162
debit *vb.* 742
debonair *adj.* 836
debrief *vb.* 460
debris *n.* 44
debt *n.* 737, 919
debts *n.* 737, 739
début *n.* 88
decade *n.* 70, 109
decadent *adj.* 588
decamp *vb.* 600
decant *vb.* 358
decapitate *vb.* 164, 370, 963
decay *n.* 53, 126, 588; *vb.* 53, 164, 588
decaying *adj.* 777
deceased *n.* 369; *adj.* 369
deceit *n.* 412, 463, 478, 631
deceitful *adj.* 431, 932, 981
deceive *vb.* 431, 471, 477, 478, 631, 932
deceiver *n.* 480
deceleration *n.* 281
decent *adj.* 848, 951
decentralize *vb.* 53, 95, 667, 714
deception *n.* 463, 477, 478, 631
deceptive *adj.* 431, 478, 631
decide *vb.* 415, 530, 534, 552, 622
decided *adj.* 408, 534
decimal *n.* 39; *adj.* 39, 70
decimate *vb.* 164, 370
decipher *vb.* 456
decipherable *adj.* 452
decision *n.* 415, 540, 960
decisive *adj.* 136, 413, 573
deck *vb.* 227, 568, 602, 846
declaim *vb.* 468
declaimer *n.* 514
declaration *n.* 460, 464, 468
declare *vb.* 413, 450, 460, 462, 468, 651, 698, 960, 961
declension *n.* 37, 499, 694
decline *n.* 37, 126, 219, 317, *vb.* 37, 130, 162, 197, 317, 319, 499, 542, 588
declining *adj.* 37, 586
decode *vb.* 456
decollate *vb.* 48
decompose *vb.* 48, 53, 588
decomposition *n.* 53, 588
deconsecrate *vb.* 987
decorate *vb.* 587, 844, 846
decoration *n.* 509, 663, 677, 846, 872
decorum *n.* 848
decoy *n.* 294; *vb.* 463
decrease *n.* 37, 42, 43, 57, 197; *vb.* 37, 176, 197, 746
decree *n.* 415, 671, 898, 954, 960; *vb.* 415, 671
decrepit *adj.* 126, 130, 162
decry *vb.* 928
dedicate *vb.* 534, 980, 988
dedicated *adj.* 709, 980
dedication *n.* 715, 980
deduce *vb.* 410, 448
deduction *n.* 42, 43, 87, 410, 744
deed *n.* 609
deem *vb.* 420, 448

deep *n.* 351; *adj.* 148, 182, 210, 805
deepen *vb.* 36, 210, 835
deep-freeze *n.* 764; *vb.* 762
deep-seated *adj.* 210, 545
deface *vb.* 845, 847
defamation *n.* 869, 928
defamatory *adj.* 926, 928, 930
default *n.* 315, 739; *vb.* 739
defeat *n.* 445, 660, 662; *vb.* 414, 661
defeatist *adj.* 855
defecate *vb.* 310
defect *n.* 43, 57, 582, 660, 662, 847
defection *n.* 189, 538, 920, 932
defective *adj.* 55, 57, 580, 582, 847
defence *n.* 402, 593, 595, 646, 648, 929, 960
defenceless *adj.* 160
defend *vb.* 410, 593, 646, 647, 648, 929, 959
defendant *n.* 684, 960
defer *vb.* 135, 424, 654, 920
deference *n.* 654, 922
defiance *n.* 637, 644, 672, 880
deficiency *n.* 29, 35, 57, 189, 315, 571, 660
deficient *adj.* 29, 35, 57, 315, 582, 660
deficit *n.* 57, 315, 737
defile *vb.* 584, 588, 608, 928, 936
defilement *n.* 584, 588, 608, 928
define *vb.* 102, 235, 496, 525
defining *adj.* 456
definite *adj.* 408, 823
definite article *n.* 499
definite space *n.* 183
definition *n.* 235, 450
deflate *vb.* 874
deflated *adj.* 874
deflation *n.* 197, 874
deflect *vb.* 285
deformed *adj.* 243, 245, 845
deformity *n.* 245, 582, 845, 847
defraud *vb.* 478, 722
defrost *vb.* 345, 761
deft *adj.* 280, 627
defunct *adj.* 369
defy *vb.* 25, 331, 637, 644, 672
degenerate *n.* 940; *adj.* 147, 936; *vb.* 53, 147, 588, 590, 936
degradation *n.* 608, 686, 869, 928
degrade *vb.* 588, 686, 869
degree *n.* 7, 27, 93, 400, 766
dehydrate *vb.* 350, 599
de-ice *vb.* 761
deification *n.* 983
deign *vb.* 874
deism *n.* 974
deity *n.* 966
déjà vu *n.* 441
dejection *n.* 837
delay *n.* 135, 281; *vb.* 135, 281
delegate *n.* 149, 625, 688, 689; *vb.* 685, 714
delete *vb.* 42, 485
deliberate *adj.* 410, 530, 543, 552; *vb.* 384
deliberation *n.* 384, 410, 860
delicacy *n.* 162, 205, 306, 338, 770, 848
delicate *n.* 753; *adj.* 162, 205, 331, 338, 510, 594, 735, 848, 864
delicatessen *n.* 306
delicious *adj.* 306, 767, 770, 772, 829
delight *n.* 306, 770, 827, 829; *vb.* 755, 829, 840, 889
delighted *adj.* 756, 827
delightful *adj.* 755, 770, 827, 829
delineate *vb.* 232, 486, 525
delirious *adj.* 827
delirium *n.* 756
deliver *vb.* 268, 601, 680, 714
deliverance *n.* 600, 601, 680
delivery *n.* 268, 512, 514, 621, 715
delude *vb.* 478
deluge *n.* 358, 572; *vb.* 349
delusion *n.* 412, 457, 478
demand *n.* 562, 671, 695; *vb.* 562, 671, 695, 727, 743
demarcation *n.* 48, 231, 235
dematerialize *vb.* 2, 328, 826, 984
demeanour *n.* 621
demented *adj.* 439
demise *n.* 89, 369
democracy *n.* 667, 678
demolish *vb.* 164, 319
demolition *n.* 164
demon *n.* 969
demonism *n.* 983
demonstrate *vb.* 401, 413, 456, 458, 696
demonstration *n.* 413, 458, 696, 825
demonstrator *n.* 106, 148
demoralize *vb.* 837, 936
demote *vb.* 686
demur *n.* 533; *vb.* 533, 696

demure *adj.* 876, 951
den *n.* 234, 463, 595
dendrochronology *n.* 116
denial *n.* 414, 469, 542, 694
denigrate *vb.* 928
denomination *n.* 496, 641, 979
denominational *adj.* 979
denominator *n.* 39
denote *vb.* 450, 482
dénouement *n.* 89
denounce *vb.* 892, 928, 930, 962
dense *adj.* 75, 332, 334, 435
density *n.* 204, 332, 400
dent *n.* 254, 847
denude *vb.* 228
denunciation *n.* 901, 926, 930, 962
deny *vb.* 402, 414, 469, 542, 637, 691, 694, 944
deodorant *n.* 775
depart *vb.* 151, 285, 293, 299, 600, 687, 826
department *n.* 55, 97
departure *n.* 285, 293, 299, 369, 600, 687, 826
depend *vb.* 420, 679, 854
dependable *adj.* 392, 702, 868, 931
dependant *n.* 132, 287, 676
dependence *n.* 9, 420, 679
dependent *adj.* 420, 679, 700
depict *vb.* 20, 486, 488
deplete *vb.* 358, 569
depleted *adj.* 57, 569, 588
deplore *vb.* 941
deport *vb.* 99, 963
deposit *n.* 55, 367, 567, 701, 738; *vb.* 567
depository *n.* 193, 567, 732
depot *n.* 567
deprave *vb.* 588, 608
depreciate *vb.* 696, 744, 746, 928
depreciation *n.* 37, 43, 744, 928
depress *vb.* 209, 254, 319, 837, 841
depression *n.* 37, 169, 209, 210, 254, 259, 319, 837
deprive *vb.* 706, 720
deprived *adj.* 435, 706
depth *n.* 26, 209, 210, 400
deputation *n.* 685, 688
deputize *vb.* 685, 689
deputy *n.* 149, 688, 689; *adj.* 689
derail *vb.* 187
deranged *adj.* 439
derelict *adj.* 607
dereliction *n.* 393, 920
deride *vb.* 838, 853, 924, 928
derivation *n.* 155, 410, 494
derivative *n.* 494; *adj.* 156
derive *vb.* 156, 157, 410, 716
derogatory *adj.* 928
descend *vb.* 317, 869
descendant *n.* 11, 171
descent *n.* 11, 171, 317, 870
describe *vb.* 413, 460, 496, 525
description *n.* 460, 465, 486, 496, 525
descriptive *adj.* 456, 525
desecrate *vb.* 608, 981
desert *adj.* 350; *vb.* 556, 607, 898
deserter *n.* 538, 555, 672, 858
desertion *n.* 189, 556, 600, 672, 898, 920
deserts *n.* 917
deserve *vb.* 573, 917, 963
desiccate *vb.* 350
design *n.* 23, 58, 242, 482, 488, 552, 558; *vb.* 58, 488, 543, 552, 558
designate *adj.* 119, 123; *vb.* 102, 450, 482, 486, 496
designer *n.* 491, 558
desirable *adj.* 577, 579
desire *n.* 388, 530, 552, 854, 861; *vb.* 530, 532, 854, 861, 914
desist *vb.* 89, 144
desolate *adj.* 169, 588, 837
desolation *n.* 164, 569
despair *n.* 828, 837, 855, 856; *vb.* 828, 855
desperate *adj.* 706
desperation *n.* 855
despise *vb.* 542, 923, 924
despondency *n.* 445, 837, 855
despotism *n.* 669, 900
dessert *n.* 306
destination *n.* 235, 284, 298, 552
destined *adj.* 154, 531, 543
destiny *n.* 154
destitute *adj.* 708, 735
destroy *vb.* 82, 164, 370, 569
destroyer *n.* 167, 277
destruction *n.* 2, 53, 164, 370
destructive *adj.* 164, 175, 370, 580

detach *vb.* 48, 51
detached *adj.* 48, 391, 757
detachment *n.* 48, 391, 757, 933
detail *n.* 8, 55, 460
detailed *adj.* 8, 525
detain *vb.* 681, 712
detect *vb.* 419, 774, 795
détente *n.* 643
detention *n.* 681
deter *vb.* 548, 635
deteriorate *vb.* 37, 164, 588, 590
deterioration *n.* 126, 142, 569, 588, 590
determination *n.* 400, 415, 530, 534, 540, 857
determine *vb.* 89, 155, 177, 400, 413, 530, 534, 543, 552
determined *adj.* 534, 535, 857
determinism *n.* 531
deterrent *n.* 548
detest *vb.* 862, 892
detonate *vb.* 782
detonator *n.* 765
detour *n.* 285, 322, 561
detract *vb.* 42, 391
detriment *n.* 580, 588
detrimental *adj.* 164, 578, 580
devastate *vb.* 164
devastation *n.* 569
develop *vb.* 36, 196, 242, 288, 324, 587
developing *adj.* 36, 129, 603
development *n.* 36, 153, 196, 288, 324, 587
deviate *vb.* 15, 219, 247, 285, 505
deviation *n.* 15, 29, 142, 285, 431
device *n.* 565
devil *n.* 969, 984
devilish *adj.* 900, 969, 984
devious *adj.* 932
devise *vb.* 58, 163, 449, 558
devolution *n.* 667, 685, 714
devolve *vb.* 667, 685, 714, 919
devoted *adj.* 673, 702, 882, 889, 982
devotee *n.* 545
devote oneself to *vb.* 605
devotion *n.* 673, 702, 889, 980
devour *vb.* 304, 569, 948
devout *adj.* 974, 980, 982
dew *n.* 349
dexterity *n.* 240
dexterous *adj.* 627
diabolical *adj.* 900, 969, 984
diabolism *n.* 984
diagnosis *n.* 396, 398, 456
diagonal *n.* 219; *adj.* 219
diagram *n.* 486
dial 999 *vb.* 591, 598
dialect *n.* 492
dialectical materialism *n.* 327
dialogue *n.* 394, 410, 519
diameter *n.* 204, 400
diametrical *adj.* 14
diamond *n.* 246
diarrhoea *n.* 310
diary *n.* 116, 441, 483
dice *vb.* 48, 306
dichotomy *n.* 63
dictate *n.* 671; *vb.* 531, 671, 674
dictator *n.* 623, 669
dictionary *n.* 83, 494, 524
didactic *adj.* 470
die *n.* 23; *vb.* 2, 89, 293, 369, 588, 826
die-hard *n.* 143, 537
diet *n.* 625, 947; *vb.* 205, 947
differ *vb.* 14, 15, 19, 151, 425, 642
difference *n.* 10, 15, 19, 104, 106, 425, 642
different *adj.* 14, 15, 19, 104, 106
differentiate *vb.* 15, 398,
different time *n.* 121
differing *adj.* 25, 425
difficult *adj.* 405, 615, 633, 887
difficulty *n.* 633, 665, 830
diffuse *adj.* 505; *vb.* 95, 297, 346, 464
diffuseness *n.* 505
dig *n.* 254; *vb.* 210, 254, 378
digest *n.* 527; *vb.* 304, 472, 527
digestible *adj.* 306
digger *n.* 312
digit *n.* 39
dignified *adj.* 510, 848, 868, 870, 873, 982
dignity *n.* 510, 868, 870, 873
dig one's heels in *vb.* 537
digression *n.* 285, 505, 561
digs *n.* 191
dilapidated *adj.* 126
dilapidation *n.* 569, 588
dilated *adj.* 196
dilatory *adj.* 135
dilemma *n.* 136, 409, 633
diligent *adj.* 390, 392, 535, 611, 702

dilute *vb.* 37, 162
diluted *adj.* 162, 507
dim *adj.* 798, **799**, 806, 820, 895; *vb.* 799
dimension *n.* 26, 194, 400
diminish *vb.* 37, 76
diminutive *adj.* 33, 195
dimness *n.* 128, **799**, 806
dimple *n.* 254
din *n.* 780, 791
dine out *vb.* 304
dingy *adj.* 805, 809
dinner *n.* 306
diocese *n.* 183
dip *n.* 254, 319, 321; *vb.* 319, 321, 349
diplomat *n.* 688
diplomatic *adj.* 392, 886
dipsomania *n.* 950
direct *adj.* 248, 476, 502, 508; *vb.* **284**, 290, 470, 529, 622, 624, 667, 671, 956
direction *n.* 103, 178, 269, **284**, 392, 470, 559, 622, 626, 671, 956
directive *n.* 671; *adj.* 622
director *n.* 558, 623, 675
directory *n.* 83
dirge *n.* 839
dirt *n.* 584, 952
dirty *adj.* 584, 952; *vb.* 584
disable *vb.* 160, 162
disabled *adj.* 160, 586
disadvantage *n.* 551, 578
disadvantageous *adj.* 137, 576, 578
disagree *vb.* **25**, 425, 586, 637, 642, 696, 771, 926
disagreeable *adj.* 771, 830, 862, 895
disagreeing *adj.* 25, 425, 642
disagreement *n.* 15, 25, 106, 425, 642, 926
disallow *vb.* 691, 694
disappear *vb.* 2, 113, 826
disappearance *n.* 189, 600, **826**
disappeared *adj.* 189, 826
disappoint *vb.* 445, 832
disappointing *adj.* 445, 571
disappointment *n.* **445**, 662, 830
disapproval *n.* 425, 542, 696, **926**
disapprove *vb.* 425, 542, 637, 696, **926**
disarm *vb.* 160
disarrangement *n.* 80, **82**
disaster *n.* 551, 662, 665, 900
disastrous *adj.* 551, 662, 665, 855
disband *vb.* 53, 82, 95
disbelief *n.* 409, 421, 975
disbelieving *adj.* 421, 975
disc *n.* 250, 484, 794
discard *vb.* 542, 556, 607, 713
discarded *adj.* 126
discern *vb.* 398, 426, 434, 818
discerning *adj.* 384, 398, 426, 434
discharge *n.* 301, 303, 310, 680, 911, 961; *vb.* 290, 301, 303, 310, 601, 680, 738, 740, 911, 921, 961
disciple *n.* 146, 287, 428, 474
disciplinarian *n.* 669
discipline *n.* 79, 470, 681, 963; *vb.* 470, 669, 681, 963
disciplined *adj.* 81, 681, 944
disclaim *vb.* 469, 538, 542
disclosure *n.* 419, 458, **462**, 464, 976
discoloration *n.* 582, 806
discomfort *n.* 828; *vb.* 830
disconcert *vb.* 82, 391, 445, 832
disconnect *vb.* 48, 92
disconnected *adj.* 51, 80, 92
discontent *n.* 445, 828, **832**, 926
discontinue *vb.* 89, 92, 144, 546, 556
discontinuity *n.* **92**
discord *n.* 25, 425, **642**, 787, **791**
discount *n.* 42, 43, 744
discourage *vb.* 548, 633, 832, 837
discourse *n.* 514, 518, 526
discourteous *adj.* **887**, 923
discourtesy *n.* **887**, 923
discover *vb.* 186, 419, 472
discoverer *n.* 155, 166
discovery *n.* **419**, 460
discredit *vb.* 414, 588, 869, 928
discreet *adj.* 392, 434
discrepancy *n.* 15, 25
discrete *adj.* 48
discretion *n.* 530, 860
discriminate *vb.* 15, 398, 540, 916

discriminating *adj.* 392, 398, 434, 540, 848, 864
discrimination *n.* 15, 398, 848, 916
discuss *vb.* 410, 514, 519, 526, 624, 700
disdain *n.* 853, 924; *vb.* 924
disease *n.* 586
disembark *vb.* 298
disembodied *adj.* 4, 328
disentangle *vb.* 46, 48, 81, 248
disfigure *vb.* 245, 845, 847
disfigurement *n.* 582, 845, 847
disfranchise *vb.* 918
disgrace *n.* 869; *vb.* 588, 869
disgraceful *adj.* 869
disgruntle *vb.* 832
disgruntled *adj.* 832
disguise *n.* 18, 461, 463; *vb.* 20, 146, 461
disgust *n.* 892; *vb.* 771, 892
dish *n.* 306
dishearten *vb.* 832
dishevel *vb.* 82
dishevelled *adj.* 584
dishonest *adj.* 477, 478, 631, 932
dishonour *n.* 869, 923; *vb.* 588, 869, 923
dish out *vb.* 717
disillusion *vb.* 445
disinclination *n.* 389, 533, 862
disinfect *vb.* 583
disingenuous *adj.* 477
disinherit *vb.* 720
disintegrate *vb.* 48, 53, 164, 328
disintegration *n.* 48, 53, 164, 588
disinter *vb.* 372
disinterested *adj.* 541, 757, 915, 933
disinterestedness *n.* 933
dislike *n.* 637, 862, 883, 892; *vb.* 771, 862, 892
dislocate *vb.* 48, 82, 187
dislodge *vb.* 187, 312
disloyal *adj.* 431, 672, 920
disloyalty *n.* 703, 920, 932
dismal *adj.* 798, 837, 895
dismantle *vb.* 164
dismay *vb.* 837, 856
dismembered *adj.* 48
dismiss *vb.* 99, 295, 303, 389, 542, 686, 920, 961
dismount *vb.* 298
disobedience *n.* 644, 672, 703, 981
disobey *vb.* 644, 672, 703, 955
disorder *n.* 80, 175, 584, 586, 668, 955; *vb.* 82
disorderly *adj.* 82, 887
disorganized *adj.* 80, 82
disorientate *vb.* 285
disown *vb.* 469, 538, 542
disparage *vb.* 418, 548, 926, 928
disparagement *n.* 928
disparate *adj.* 15, 19, 29, 104
dispassionate *adj.* 757, 863, 915, 933
dispatch *n.* 268, 460, 465, 523; *vb.* 268, 523, 613
dispatch bearer *n.* 467
dispel *vb.* 95
dispensation *n.* 713, 921
dispense *vb.* 95, 715, 717
disperse *vb.* 48, 82, 95, 297
dispersion *n.* 95
dispirited *adj.* 837
displace *vb.* 85, 187, 312, 706
displacement *n.* 187, 686
display *n.* 413, 825; *vb.* 413, 458
displeasure *n.* 445, 893, 926
disposal *n.* 81, 713, 727
dispose *vb.* 81, 717
disposed *adj.* 81, 179, 532, 751
dispose of *vb.* 89, 303, 609, 713, 717
disposition *n.* 5, 532, 545, 751
dispossession *n.* 706, 720, 918
disproof *n.* 414
disproportion *n.* 10, 29, 245
disproportionate *adj.* 25, 29, 245
disprove *vb.* 414
dispute *n.* 25, 410, 642; *vb.* 25, 410, 414, 637, 642, 649
disqualify *vb.* 99, 160, 918
disquiet *n.* 828; *vb.* 856
disregard *n.* 391, 393, 672, 703, 920; *vb.* 99, 389, 391, 393, 555, 644, 672, 703, 887, 924
disreputable *adj.* 869, 932
disrepute *n.* 869
disrespect *n.* 869, 887, 923, 924
disrespectful *adj.* 880, 887, 923, 924
disrupt *vb.* 82
disruption *n.* 175
dissatisfaction *n.* 445, 828, 832, 862, 926
dissect *vb.* 48, 53

dissemble *vb.* 461, 477
disseminate *vb.* 95, 378, 460, 464
dissension *n.* 25, 425, 637, 642
dissent *n.* 425, 696; *vb.* 151, 425, 642
dissenter *n.* 106, 425, 975
dissertation *n.* 526
dissident *n.* 979; *adj.* 106, 425, 672, 979
dissimilarity *n.* 19, 25, 29, 106
dissimulation *n.* 19
dissipate *vb.* 95, 346, 569, 749
dissipation *n.* 95, 569, 945
dissociation *n.* 10, 48
dissolute *adj.* 936, 952
dissolution *n.* 48, 53, 164, 345, 369, 686, 898
dissolve *vb.* 2, 53, 164, 345, 686, 826
dissonance *n.* 25, 787, 791
dissuade *vb.* 548, 624
dissuasion *n.* 548, 624
distance *n.* 194, 198, 400, 885; *vb.* 198
distant *adj.* 198, 517, 781, 885
distaste *n.* 862
distemper *n.* 225
distend *vb.* 196
distil *vb.* 346
distinct *adj.* 48, 102, 452, 512, 778, 823
distinction *n.* 398, 868, 870
distinctive *adj.* 5
distinguish *vb.* 15, 398, 452
distinguished *adj.* 208, 573, 868, 870
distort *vb.* 245, 457, 471, 477, 487, 588, 845
distorted *adj.* 245, 477, 582
distortion *n.* 245, 416, 457, 477, 487, 845
distracted *adj.* 391, 442
distraught *adj.* 756
distress *n.* 445, 665, 828; *vb.* 830
distressed *adj.* 735
distressing *adj.* 551, 830
distress signal *n.* 598, 902
distribute *vb.* 95, 464, 715, 717
distribution *n.* 81, 717
district *n.* 183
distrust *n.* 421, 913; *vb.* 423
disturb *vb.* 82, 137, 187, 326, 856
disturbance *n.* 80, 137, 175, 326
disunite *vb.* 48, 51
disunity *n.* 17
disuse *n.* 546, 569, 607; *vb.* 607
ditch *n.* 261, 360, 646; *vb.* 556
dither *n.* 326, 756
ditto *adv.* 77
dive *n.* 321; *vb.* 271, 273, 321
diverge *vb.* 15, 48, 95, 151, 219, 297
divergence *n.* 285, 297
divergent *adj.* 15, 219, 285, 297, 978
diverse *adj.* 15, 104
diversified *adj.* 17, 104
diversify *vb.* 817
diversion *n.* 142, 285, 449, 840
diversity *n.* 15, 17, 19, 104, 817
divert *vb.* 391
diverting *adj.* 840
divest *vb.* 228, 720
divide *vb.* 38, 48, 55, 63, 95, 97, 717
dividends *n.* 741
divination *n.* 447, 984
divine *adj.* 966, 974; *vb.* 447, 448, 984
divinity *n.* 966
divisibility *n.* 51
division *n.* 25, 38, 48, 55, 97, 425, 655, 717
divisive *adj.* 642
divorce *n.* 48, 713, 898; *vb.* 48, 898
divulge *vb.* 458, 462
do *n.* 878; *vb.* 570, 577, 605, 609, 673, 702
do away with *vb.* 370
docile *adj.* 654, 673
dock *n.* 298, 957; *vb.* 298
docket *n.* 482; *vb.* 482
doctor *n.* 428, 436, 473; *vb.* 477
doctrine *n.* 420, 626, 974
document *n.* 401, 483, 521; *vb.* 401, 483, 521
dodge *n.* 478, 631; *vb.* 533, 555
dodger *n.* 480, 600
doe *n.* 381
doer *n.* 609, 619
dog *n.* 380; *vb.* 287, 554
doggedness *n.* 534, 535
dogma *n.* 420, 974
dogmatic *adj.* 468, 537
do-gooder *n.* 899, 903, 905
do in *vb.* 370
doing *n.* 609, 702; *adj.* 609
do-it-yourself *adj.* 628
doldrums *n.* 837
doleful *adj.* 837
dole out *vb.* 95, 715, 717
doll up *vb.* 844
doltish *adj.* 435

domain *n.* 956
dome *n.* 225, 252
domestic *n.* 676; *adj.* 190
domestic animal *n.* 373
domesticate *vb.* 377
domesticated *adj.* 190
domestic science *n.* 306
domicile *n.* 191
dominance *n.* 34, 159, 177
dominant *adj.* 159, 177, 667
dominate *vb.* 177, 208, 667, 669, 679
domineer *vb.* 667, 669
dominion *n.* 667
don *n.* 428, 473; *vb.* 227
donate *vb.* 715
donor *n.* 715, 905
doom *n.* 543; *vb.* 962
door *n.* 262
doorman *n.* 676
do over *vb.* 645
dormancy *n.* 459, 610, 612
dorsal *adj.* 237
dose *n.* 26, 591
dot *n.* 33
dotage *n.* 130
dote on *vb.* 889, 983
double *n.* 28, 149, 971; *adj.* 62; *vb.* 62, 149, 260
double-cross *vb.* 478, 932
double dealing *n.* 477, 631, 932; *adj.* 477, 932
double entendre *n.* 454, 842
double-sidedness *n.* 61
doubt *n.* 409, 421, 975; *vb.* 409, 421, 423
doubtful *adj.* 407, 409, 421
dough *n.* 364, 731
douse *vb.* 762
dove *n.* 656
dovetail *vb.* 24, 47
dowager *n.* 870, 898
dowdiness *n.* 849
down *adj.* 837; *adv.* 209
down-and-out *n.* 697; *adj.* 735
downcast *adj.* 837
downfall *n.* 164, 317, 662
downgrade *vb.* 686
down-hearted *adj.* 837
down-payment *n.* 55, 738
downpour *n.* 358
downward *adj.* 219, 317
doze *n.* 612, 617; *vb.* 612
dozen *n.* 70
drab *adj.* 805, 809, 843
draft *n.* 558, 602; *vb.* 521, 558
drag *n.* 181, 635; *vb.* 181, 291, 294
drag up *vb.* 441
drain *n.* 360; *vb.* 319, 358, 569, 806
drained *adj.* 617
drake *n.* 380
dram *n.* 309
drama *n.* 529, 866
dramatic *adj.* 529, 752, 755, 866
dramatis personae *n.* 529
drape *n.* 801; *vb.* 216
draught *n.* 309, 359
draught animal *n.* 291
draughtsman *n.* 491
draughty *adj.* 348, 359
draw *n.* 28, 294, 553; *vb.* 28, 291, 294, 308, 312, 390, 486, 488, 525, 705, 889
drawback *n.* 582
drawer *n.* 491
drawing *n.* 291, 488
drawl *n.* 515; *vb.* 515
draw up *vb.* 558
dread *n.* 856; *vb.* 856
dreadful *adj.* 830, 856
dream *n.* 4, 449, 552, 854; *vb.* 391, 449, 552, 612, 854, 861
dream up *vb.* 558
dreamy *adj.* 384
dreary *adj.* 798, 841, 843
dredge *vb.* 312
dredge up *vb.* 441
dregs *n.* 44, 576, 871
drench *vb.* 349, 572
dress *n.* 227; *vb.* 227, 568, 844
dressage *n.* 269
dress down *vb.* 926, 963
dressing *n.* 227
dribble *vb.* 319, 358
dried *adj.* 350
drift *n.* 178, 450; *vb.* 178, 257, 612
drill *n.* 264; *vb.* 264, 378, 470
drink *n.* 309, 343; *vb.* 304, 950
drinker *n.* 304, 950
drink in *vb.* 390, 472
drinking *n.* 304
drip *n.* 349, 841; *vb.* 319, 358
drip-dry *vb.* 350
drive *n.* 173, 269, 282, 290, 559, 645, 674; *vb.* 173, 269, 282, 290, 295, 377, 547, 674
drive at *vb.* 450
drivel *n.* 451
driver *n.* 270
driving *n.* 269; *adj.* 674
drizzle *n.* 358; *vb.* 358
droll *adj.* 851
drone *vb.* 783, 784, 789
droop *vb.* 216, 317, 319, 837, 841
drop *n.* 37, 210, 249, 254, 309, 317, 321; *vb.*

37, 317, 319, 358, 556, 617, 706
drop anchor *vb.* 271, 298
drop in *vb.* 300
drop out *vb.* 660
droppings *n.* 310
drought *n.* 350, 861
drown *vb.* 321, 349, 370, 963
drowsy *adj.* 612, 617, 841
drudge *n.* 615, 619, 676; *vb.* 615
drug *n.* 173, 591; *vb.* 754
drum *n.* 249
drumming *n.* 325
drunk *n.* 950; *adj.* 950
drunkard *n.* 304, 950
dry *adj.* 350, 773, 787, 843, 949; *vb.* 306, 350
dryness *n.* 350, 843
dualism *n.* 61
duality *n.* 61
dub *vb.* 496, 497
dubious *adj.* 407, 421, 932
duchess *n.* 870
duchy *n.* 183
duck *n.* 74, 381; *vb.* 321, 349, 555
duct *n.* 360
dud *n.* 662
due *n.* 737, 917; *adj.* 737, 917
duel *n.* 649
dueness *n.* 917
dues *n.* 716, 743, 917
dug-out *n.* 254
duke *n.* 870
dull *adj.* 174, 256, 435, 666, 754, 768, 771, 785, 798, 799, 806, 843; *vb.* 256, 754, 785, 799
dullness *n.* 174, 435, 768, 806, 843
dumb *adj.* 435, 513, 517
dumbfound *vb.* 513, 866
dummy *n.* 22, 23, 149; *adj.* 149
dump *vb.* 727
dumpy *adj.* 195, 203, 204
dunce *n.* 429, 437, 630
dung *n.* 310
dungeon *n.* 234, 682
duo *n.* 792
dupe *n.* 479, 853; *vb.* 478
duple *adj.* 61
duplicate *n.* 22; *adj.* 13, 62; *vb.* 62, 165
duplication *n.* 62, 77, 165
duplicity *n.* 477, 932
durability *n.* 143, 337
durable *adj.* 112, 161, 337
duration *n.* 107, 145
duress *n.* 674
during *adv., prep.* 107
dusk *n.* 128, 799, 809
dust *n.* 340, 371, 576
duster *n.* 485
dusty *adj.* 340, 350, 584, 809
dutiful *adj.* 673, 919
duty *n.* 557, 685, 737, 743, 919
dwarf *n.* 195, 970; *adj.* 203
dwell *vb.* 191
dwindle *vb.* 37, 197, 569
dye *n.* 805
dying *n.* 369; *adj.* 130, 861
dynamic *adj.* 159, 173, 611
dynamite *n.* 657
dysentry *n.* 310

E

eager *adj.* 443, 532, 756, 861
earl *n.* 870
earlier *adj.* 84, 118; *adv.* 121
earliness *n.* 134
early *adj.* 117, 134
early warning *n.* 597
earmark *vb.* 482
earn *vb.* 705, 917
earner *n.* 716
earnest *n.* 701; *adj.* 532, 752, 837
earnings *n.* 705, 738, 741
earring *n.* 216
earshot *n.* 199, 795
earth *n.* 329, 352
earthquake *n.* 325
earthworks *n.* 646
earthy *adj.* 352
ease *n.* 616, 634, 827, 831, 834; *vb.* 335, 634, 834
ease off *vb.* 281, 616
east *n.* 284
easy *adj.* 634, 952
easy-going *adj.* 670, 757
eat *vb.* 304, 569, 767
eat away *vb.* 569, 588
eating *n.* 304
eavesdropping *n.* 460, 795
ebb *vb.* 37, 358
eccentric *n.* 106, 440; *adj.* 106, 439
ecclesiastical *adj.* 985
echo *n.* 22, 283, 778, 784; *vb.* 77, 283, 784
eclipse *n.* 798; *vb.* 34, 314, 461, 798
ecology *n.* 366, 376
economical *adj.* 392, 748
economics *n.* 622

economize vb. 37, 748
economy n. 392, 748; adj. 746
ecstasy n. 756, 827
eddy n. 323, 358; vb. 323, 358
edge n. 233, 235, 255, 769; vb. 233, 255
edgy adj. 756, 856, 894
edible adj. 306
edict n. 626, 671, 954
edifice n. 163
edify vb. 470, 550, 579
edit vb. 456
edition n. 524
editor n. 456, 524
educate vb. 470
educated adj. 426
education n. 426, 470
educational adj. 460, 470
eerie adj. 971, 984
efface vb. 485
effect n. 87, 156, 877; vb. 155, 163, 609, 659
effective adj. 159, 172, 563, 627
effeminate adj. 162, 381
effervesce vb. 363, 786
efficacy n. 159, 575
efficient adj. 159, 557
effluent n. 301, 358
effort n. 604, 615
effortless adj. 634
effrontery n. 880
egg n. 250, 306
egg-timer n. 116
ego n. 382
egoist n. 904, 934
egotism n. 875, 904
ego-trip n. 873
eight n. 70; adj. 70
eject vb. 301, 303
ejection n. 99, 303, 310, 312
elaborate adj. 509; vb. 196
elapse vb. 107, 110
elasticity n. 336
elated adj. 756, 827, 838
elbow n. 246
elder n. 34, 132, 987; adj. 130
eldest adj. 130
elect adj. 119; vb. 540
election n. 540
electorate n. 540
electric chair n. 964
electricity n. 159, 765
electrify vb. 159, 755
electrocute vb. 370, 963
electronic adj. 125
elegance n. 510, 844, 848
elegy n. 372, 839
element n. 5, 55, 155, 327
elementary adj. 88
elements n. 192, 348
elevated adj. 208, 318, 868, 873
elevation n. 208, 318
elevator n. 316
eleven n. 70
elevenses n. 306
eleventh hour n. 136
elf n. 970
elicit vb. 155, 547
eligible adj. 896, 897
eliminate vb. 46, 99, 164, 303
elite n. 579, 870
elixir n. 591
ellipse n. 247, 250
ellipsis n. 504
elliptic adj. 504
elocution n. 518
elongated adj. 202
elope vb. 600, 896
eloquent adj. 514, 516
elsewhere adj. 189
elucidate vb. 413, 456
elude vb. 555, 600
emaciated adj. 205, 588
emanation n. 156, 301, 774
emancipation n. 601, 680
emasculate vb. 160, 169
embalm vb. 372, 599, 776
embankment n. 559, 646
embargo n. 99, 681, 691
embarkation n. 299
embark on vb. 605
embarrass vb. 578, 633, 869, 874
embarrassed adj. 811, 830, 874, 876
embassy n. 685, 688
embed vb. 311
embellish vb. 509, 844, 846
ember n. 800
embezzle vb. 722
embezzler n. 723, 739
embittered adj. 893
emblazon vb. 482
emblem n. 482, 677, 872
embody vb. 52, 98, 222, 486
emboss vb. 482, 489
embrace n. 886, 890; vb. 50, 98, 702, 886, 890
embrocation n. 365
embroider vb. 481, 509, 846
embryology n. 375, 376
embryonic adj. 88
emerald adj. 812
emerge vb. 301, 313, 324, 600, 825
emergence n. 298, 301
emergency n. 136, 153, 562
emigrant n. 100, 270
emigration n. 299
eminent adj. 34, 208, 573, 868, 870
emissary n. 460, 467, 688

emit *vb.* 301, 303, 774, 778
emollient *n.* 365
emolument *n.* 705, 738
emotion *n.* 326, 752, 756, 889
empathy *n.* 752
emperor *n.* 675
emphasize *vb.* 417, 456, 468, 481, 512, 573
employ *vb.* 107, 557, 575, 606, 685
employee *n.* 619, 676
emporium *n.* 730
empower *vb.* 159, 161, 667, 685, 954
emptiness *n.* 2, 189, 333, 875
empty *adj.* 189, 333, 451; *vb.* 301, 358, 569
empty-handed *adj.* 735
empty-headed *adj.* 383, 427, 435
emulate *vb.* 20
emulsion *n.* 362
enable *vb.* 159, 404
enact *vb.* 529
enactment *n.* 486, 954
enamel *n.* 225
enamoured *adj.* 889
encampment *n.* 186
enchant *vb.* 827, 829, 889, 984
encircle *vb.* 231, 250
enclose *vb.* 98, 225, 229, 234
enclosure *n.* 184, 234, 378
encompass *vb.* 182, 229, 231
encore *n.* 62, 77; *adv.* 77
encounter *n.* 296, 649; *vb.* 649, 857
encourage *vb.* 217, 547, 618, 624, 636, 836, 857, 907
encroachment *n.* 314, 645, 918, 955
encrust *vb.* 226
encumbrance *n.* 635, 711
encyclopedia *n.* 426, 524
end *n.* 89, 156, 235, 237, 369, 552, 659; *vb.* 89, 659
endanger *vb.* 594
endearment *n.* 890
endeavour *n.* 604; *vb.* 604
endemic *adj.* 586
endless *adj.* 78, 91, 114
endless duration *n.* 114
endorsement *n.* 408, 424, 468, 690, 963
endow *vb.* 568, 715
endowment *n.* 5, 627, 714
endurance *n.* 112, 114, 143, 152, 337, 535, 757
endure *vb.* 91, 112, 145, 535, 648, 752, 757, 828
enemy *n.* 638, 645, 883
energetic *adj.* 32, 159, 161, 173, 368, 585, 611
energize *vb.* 161, 173, 618, 755
energy *n.* 159, 161, 173, 368, 611
enfeeble *vb.* 130, 162, 507
enforce *vb.* 954
enfranchise *vb.* 678, 680
engage *vb.* 557, 605
engaged *adj.* 698
engage in battle *vb.* 649, 651
engagement *n.* 557, 605, 649, 698, 890
engine *n.* 276, 565
engineer *n.* 558
engrave *vb.* 490, 521, 522
engraver *n.* 491
engraving *n.* 490
engrossed *adj.* 384
enhance *vb.* 36, 318, 509, 846
enigma *n.* 409, 453, 466
enjoy *vb.* 752, 770, 827, 861
enjoyable *adj.* 827, 829
enjoy immunity *vb.* 921
enjoy oneself *vb.* 827, 840
enlarge *vb.* 36, 40, 196, 202, 505
enlighten *vb.* 460, 470, 797
enlist *vb.* 83, 302, 557, 651
enliven *vb.* 173, 368, 618, 836, 840
enmity *n.* 883
ennoble *vb.* 318, 868, 870
ennui *n.* 841
enormous *adj.* 32, 194
enough *adj.* 75, 570
enquire *vb.* 388, 394
enquiry *n.* 394, 526
enrage *vb.* 893
enrapture *vb.* 547, 827, 829, 889
enrich *vb.* 509, 587
enrol *vb.* 83, 483, 641
ensconce *vb.* 461
ensemble *n.* 54, 793
enshrine *vb.* 372, 983
enshroud *vb.* 225
ensign *n.* 482
enslave *vb.* 679
ensnare *vb.* 463, 478
ensue *vb.* 85, 119, 153, 156, 287
ensure *vb.* 408
entail *vb.* 98, 459
entangle *vb.* 82, 221
entente *n.* 643, 699
enter *vb.* 298, 300, 483, 742

enterprise *n.* 173, 288, 604, 605, 611, 627, 857
entertain *vb.* 840, 884
enter upon *vb.* 88, 605
enthralling *adj.* 547, 829, 866
enthrone *vb.* 685, 868
enthusiasm *n.* 532, 611, 752
enthusiastic *adj.* 532, 611, 756, 827
entice *vb.* 547, 770
entire *adj.* 54, 56, 581, 659
entirety *n.* 54, 56, 59
entitled *adj.* 917
entity *n.* 1, 3, 59
entomb *vb.* 372
entomology *n.* 375
entrance *n.* 262, 298, 300, 559
entrant *n.* 638
entrap *vb.* 478
entreat *vb.* 695, 982
entrée *n.* 306
entrench *vb.* 152, 186
entrepreneur *n.* 728
entrust *vb.* 685, 714, 718
entry *n.* 298, 300
entwine *vb.* 251
enumerate *vb.* 38, 83, 102
enunciate *vb.* 512, 514
envelop *vb.* 225, 229, 234, 461
envelope *n.* 193, 234
envious *adj.* 914
environment *n.* 8, 183, 229
envisage *vb.* 449
envoy *n.* 460, 467, 685, 688
envy *n.* 914; *vb.* 914
ephemeral *adj.* 113
epic *n.* 525, 528
epicure *n.* 304, 945, 948
epigram *n.* 432, 842
epilogue *n.* 87, 89
episode *n.* 153
epistle *n.* 523
epitaph *n.* 372
epithet *n.* 496
epitome *n.* 527
epitomize *vb.* 203
epoch *n.* 109
equal *n.* 28; *adj.* 13, 28, 159
equality *n.* 13, 28, 244
equalize *vb.* 28, 31
equate *vb.* 13, 218, 397
equation *n.* 28, 397
equator *n.* 63, 250
equestrianism *n.* 269
equidistant *adj.* 90, 218
equilibrium *n.* 28, 152
equip *vb.* 227, 564, 568, 602
equipment *n.* 568, 711
equity *n.* 711, 915
equivalence *n.* 12, 28, 450
equivalent *n.* 18, 28, 456; *adj.* 12, 13, 18, 28
equivocal *adj.* 409, 453, 454
equivocate *vb.* 454, 477
era *n.* 109
eradicate *vb.* 164, 303, 485
erase *vb.* 485
erect *adj.* 214, 248, 318; *vb.* 214, 318
erection *n.* 163, 318
erode *vb.* 37, 53, 164, 341, 569, 588
Eros *n.* 889, 967
erotic *adj.* 952
err *vb.* 285, 431, 936
errand *n.* 685
errand-boy *n.* 467
erratic *adj.* 151, 539
erring *adj.* 409
erroneous *adj.* 412, 431, 916
error *n.* 431, 457, 471
erudite *adj.* 426, 472
eruption *n.* 148, 175, 301, 782
escalate *vb.* 36, 196
escalator *n.* 316
escape *n.* 293, 301, 555, 595, 600, 826; *vb.* 293, 555, 600, 826
escapism *n.* 449
escarpment *n.* 208
escort *n.* 683; *vb.* 268
esoteric *adj.* 453, 984
especial *adj.* 34, 102
Esperanto *n.* 492
espouse *vb.* 896
essay *n.* 526, 604
essence *n.* 1, 5, 450
essential *n.* 5, 531, 562; *adj.* 1, 5, 531, 562, 573
establish *vb.* 81, 88, 152, 161, 413, 685, 929, 954
established *adj.* 126, 152, 413, 545
establishment *n.* 88, 152, 191, 413, 620, 641, 667, 730
estate *n.* 7, 378, 711
esteem *n.* 922, 925; *vb.* 384, 861, 868, 889, 925
estimate *n.* 447, 743; *vb.* 38, 400, 415, 448, 743
estrange *vb.* 883, 892
estuary *n.* 353
etcher *n.* 491
etching *n.* 490
eternal *adj.* 78, 114, 966
eternity *n.* 78, 108, 112, 114
ethereal *adj.* 4, 328, 333
ethics *n.* 935
ethnic *adj.* 11, 379
etiquette *n.* 545
etymology *n.* 492, 494
Eucharist *n.* 988
eunuch *n.* 160
euphemism *n.* 455, 509

euphoria *n.* 827
euthanasia *n.* 370
evacuate *vb.* 293, 299, 310, 600
evacuee *n.* 885
evade *vb.* 393, 412, 533, 555, 600, 920
evaluation *n.* 400, 415, 456, 743
evanescent *adj.* 113, 799, 826
evangelical *adj.* 976, 977
evangelist *n.* 974
evangelize *vb.* 146
evaporate *vb.* 2, 95, 346, 350, 826
even *adj.* 16, 28, 39, 140, 244, 248, 257; *vb.* 215, 257
evening *n.* 128; *adj.* 128
event *n.* 153, 465, 649
eventful *adj.* 611
eventuality *n.* 153
everlasting *adj.* 114, 966
every *adj.* 54
everybody *n.* 54, 101
everything *n.* 54
eviction *n.* 99, 303
evidence *n.* 401, 458, 460, 482, 483; *vb.* 401
evident *adj.* 413, 458, 823
evil *n.* 551, 592, 932, 936; *adj.* 551, 592, 932, 936
evildoer *n.* 906, 940
evil spirit *n.* 969
evocative *adj.* 441, 450
evoke *vb.* 155, 547
evolution *n.* 142, 288, 324, 366
ewe *n.* 381
ex- *adj.* 118, 124
exacerbate *vb.* 36, 588, 835
exact *adj.* 392, 430, 864; *vb.* 671, 743
exacting *adj.* 392, 398, 669, 864
exactness *n.* 392, 502
exaggeration *n.* 417, 477, 481, 487, 879
exalt *vb.* 318, 868, 982
exalted *adj.* 32, 208, 318, 868
examination *n.* 394, 415, 526
examine *vb.* 384, 390, 394, 396, 415, 526
examinee *n.* 395
example *n.* 23, 597
exasperation *n.* 835, 893, 894
excavate *vb.* 210, 254, 312
exceed *vb.* 32, 34, 314
excel *vb.* 34, 314
excellence *n.* 34, 579, 581, 935
excellent *adj.* 34, 579, 844, 935
except *vb.* 99; *prep.* 99
excepting *adv., prep.* 42
exception *n.* 403, 921
exceptional *adj.* 21, 32, 573, 579
excerpt *n.* 55
excess *n.* 44, 569, 572, 945, 948
excessive *adj.* 481, 572, 691, 745, 945
exchange *n.* 142, 149, 150, 410, 714, 725, 730; *vb.* 142, 149, 150, 714, 725
exchequer *n.* 732
excise *n.* 743
excitability *n.* 753, 756
excitation *n.* 326, 755
excite *vb.* 752, 755, 829
excited *adj.* 756, 759, 827
exclaim *vb.* 788
exclude *vb.* 42, 99, 542, 691, 694
exclusion *n.* 99, 542, 694
exclusive *adj.* 99, 641, 707, 979
exclusively *adv.* 56
excommunicate *vb.* 99, 885
excrement *n.* 310
excrescent *adj.* 252
excrete *vb.* 303, 310
excretion *n.* 310
excruciating *adj.* 828
excursion *n.* 269, 840
excuse *n.* 549, 929; *vb.* 549, 911, 929
execration *n.* 901
execution *n.* 172, 370, 609, 621, 963
executive *n.* 623, 675, 956; *adj.* 172, 622, 667, 956
executor *n.* 619, 688
exegetical *adj.* 456
exemplary *adj.* 456, 579
exemplify *vb.* 23, 456, 458, 486
exempt *adj.* 921; *vb.* 403, 713, 921, 961
exemption *n.* 678, 713, 921
exercise *n.* 396, 470, 605, 606; *vb.* 470, 575
exercise self-control *vb.* 944
exertion *n.* 615
exert oneself *vb.* 615
exhale *vb.* 301, 346, 359, 774
exhaust *n.* 600; *vb.* 162, 169, 569, 617, 841
exhaustive *adj.* 56
exhibit *n.* 401, 458; *vb.* 413, 458
exhibition *n.* 413, 458, 529

exhibitionist *n.* 875, 877; *adj.* 875
exhilarate *vb.* 618, 755, 827
exhilaration *n.* 756
exhort *vb.* 518, 597, 624
exhume *vb.* 372
exile *n.* 303, 963; *vb.* 303, 963
existence *n.* 1, 368
existent *adj.* 120
existentialism *n.* 1
exit *n.* 262, 299, 369, 600
exodus *n.* 299
exonerate *vb.* 601, 911, 929, 961
exorbitant *adj.* 572, 745, 749
exorcise *vb.* 984
exotic *adj.* 100
expand *vb.* 36, 196
expand on *vb.* 456
expanse *n.* 26, 182, 204, 356
expansion *n.* 36, 182, 196
expatriot *n.* 100
expect *vb.* 154, 443, 552, 854
expectation *n.* 406, 443, 552, 854, 867
expected *adj.* 123, 138, 406, 443, 447, 545, 867
expecting *adj.* 163, 854
expedience *n.* 136, 577
expedite *vb.* 613
expedition *n.* 269, 280
expel *vb.* 99, 301, 303, 310, 542, 885, 963
expend *vb.* 569, 715, 738, 740
expenditure *n.* 740
expense *n.* 743, 745
expenses *n.* 636, 738, 740, 965
experience *n.* 130, 153, 426, 434, 602, 627, 752; *vb.* 153, 426, 472, 752
experiment *n.* 394, 396, 604; *vb.* 396
expert *n.* 428, 436, 629, 848; *adj.* 130, 627
expertise *n.* 426, 627
expiation *n.* 943
expiration *n.* 89, 144, 359, 369
explain *vb.* 157, 410, 413, 456, 470, 525, 526
explanation *n.* 155, 157, 413, 450, 456, 525
expletive *n.* 901
explicit *adj.* 452, 458, 502
explode *vb.* 175, 756, 782, 893
exploit *n.* 605, 609; *vb.* 136, 575, 606, 745
exploration *n.* 269, 271, 419
exploratory *adj.* 86, 394
explore *vb.* 269, 396, 758
explorer *n.* 270
explosive *n.* 657; *adj.* 594, 765
exponent *n.* 456, 974
exponential *adj.* 39
export *vb.* 268
exporter *n.* 728
expose *vb.* 228, 262, 414, 419, 458, 462
exposed *adj.* 228, 348, 414, 462, 753, 823
expose oneself to *vb.* 179
expositor *n.* 456, 514, 526
expostulate *vb.* 696
expound *vb.* 456, 470
express *adj.* 458; *vb.* 242, 450, 458, 460, 514, 525
expression *n.* 242, 458, 468, 492, 494, 498, 825
expressionless *adj.* 451, 754, 843
expulsion *n.* 99, 303, 310, 312, 542
expunge *vb.* 485
expurgate *vb.* 583
exquisite *adj.* 579, 770, 829, 844
extant *adj.* 1
extemporize *vb.* 544
extend *vb.* 6, 182, 196, 202, 208, 253, 693
extended *adj.* 202, 204, 253, 455
extension *n.* 36, 41, 196, 202, 253
extensive *adj.* 32, 54, 182, 202
extent *n.* 26, 27, 107, 182, 194, 198, 202, 400, 956
extenuating *adj.* 403, 929
exterior *n.* 222, 236; *adj.* 6, 222
exterminate *vb.* 164, 369, 370
external *n.* 6; *adj.* 6, 100, 222, 825
extinct *adj.* 2, 126, 369
extinguish *vb.* 164, 369, 762
extol *vb.* 922
extort *vb.* 312, 720, 722, 745
extra *n.* 529; *adj.* 40, 572, 607; *adv.* 40
extract *n.* 55, 306; *vb.* 187, 312
extraction *n.* 312
extradite *vb.* 303
extramarital *adj.* 952
extraneousness *n.* 6, 40, 100, 222
extraordinary *adj.* 407, 573, 866
extrapolate *vb.* 6, 222

extra-sensory perception *n.* 411, 447, 753
extraterrestrial *adj.* 329
extravagance *n.* 481, 569, 572, 745, 749, 945
extravagant *adj.* 481, 509, 569, 572, 745, 749, 877
extreme *n.* 89; *adj.* 89, 148, 175, 669, 828, 830
extremely *adv.* 32
extremist *n.* 148, 672
extremity *n.* 89, 233, 235
extricate *vb.* 312, 601, 678, 680
extrinsic *adj.* 6, 100, 222
exuberant *adj.* 168, 572, 836
exudation *n.* 310
exude *vb.* 301, 358
exultation *n.* 827, 838
eye *n.* 818; *vb.* 818
eye for an eye *n.* 647
eyelash *n.* 207
eyesight *n.* 818
eyesore *n.* 845
eye-witness *n.* 821

F

fable *n.* 455, 525
fabric *n.* 221, 339
fabrication *n.* 163, 465, 477, 631
fabulous *adj.* 449, 481, 525, 970
façade *n.* 211, 222, 236, 477, 852
face *n.* 222, 236, 825; *vb.* 226, 239, 857
face-lift *n.* 587, 589, 844
facet *n.* 7, 55
facetiousness *n.* 842
face value *n.* 743, 825
facility *n.* 514, 568, 627, 634
facsimile *n.* 20, 22
fact *n.* 1, 401, 426, 430, 460
fact-finding *adj.* 394
faction *n.* 641, 979
factious *adj.* 25, 642, 672
factor *n.* 8, 55, 155, 327
factory *n.* 620
factual *adj.* 1, 430
faculties *n.* 382
faculty *n.* 159
fad *n.* 125, 850
fade *vb.* 162, 588, 806, 826
fade out *vb.* 799
faeces *n.* 310
failing *n.* 819, 936
failure *n.* 315, 393, 431, 445, 571, 660, 662
faint *vb.* 162, 617
faint-hearted *adj.* 162, 858
faintness *n.* 162, 507, 617, 781, 799, 806
fair *n.* 840; *adj.* (average) 30, 666; (of weather) 759; (whitish) 807; (good-looking) 844; (just) 915, 931, 933
fairy *n.* 953, 970
fairy story *n.* 525
faith *n.* 420, 854, 974, 980
faithful *adj.* 430, 456, 673, 702, 882, 977
faithless *adj.* 409, 421
fake *n.* 20; *adj.* 20, 477, 478; *vb.* 20, 477, 852
fall *n.* 37, 317, 321, 358; *vb.* 37, 317, 321, 588, 936
fallacy *n.* 412, 431
fall apart *vb.* 51
fall away *vb.* 538, 588
fall back *vb.* 289, 293
fall back on *vb.* 606
fall down *vb.* 431, 662
fallen *adj.* 662
fallen angel *n.* 969
fallen woman *n.* 953
fall for *vb.* 422, 889
fallible *adj.* 431, 582
fall ill *vb.* 586
fall in *vb.* 254
falling star *n.* 329
fall in love *vb.* 889
fall on *vb.* 153, 179
fallow *adj.* 603, 612
fall short *vb.* 29, 35, 315, 571, 582, 662
fall through *vb.* 662
fall to *vb.* 716, 919
false *adj.* 2, 477, 478
falsehood *n.* 431, 477
false reasoning *n.* 412
falsification *n.* 457, 471, 477, 487
falter *vb.* 325, 515, 536, 662
fame *n.* 868
familiar *adj.* 138, 426, 545, 882
familiarize *vb.* 470, 545
family *n.* 11, 55, 97, 171
famished *adj.* 861, 947
famous *adj.* 573, 868
fan *n.* 764; *vb.* 348
fanatic *n.* 148, 537, 611
fanciful *adj.* 449, 539
fancy *n.* 448, 449, 539, 861; *adj.* 509, 846; *vb.* 448, 449, 540, 861, 889
fan out *vb.* 297
fantastic *adj.* 433, 449, 851, 866
fantasy *n.* 449, 481
far *adj.* 198
farce *n.* 433, 529, 851
fare *n.* 306, 743
farewell *n.* 299
far-flung *adj.* 198

farm *n.* 377, 378; *vb.* 377
farm out *vb.* 717
far-reaching *adj.* 32, 182
far-sighted *adj.* 434
farthest *adj.* 198
fascinate *vb.* 294, 547, 755, 889
fascinating *adj.* 547, 755, 829
fascism *n.* 669
fashion *n.* 125, 242, 545, 559, 850
fast *n.* 947; *adj.* 280, 613, 805; *vb.* 947; *adv.* 280
fasten *vb.* 47, 50, 152, 263
fastidiousness *n.* 392, 540, 864
fasting *n.* 947; *adj.* 947
fat *n.* 306; *adj.* 194
fatal *adj.* 164, 369, 370
fatalism *n.* 531
fate *n.* 123, 154, 158, 531, 543, 553
fat-head *n.* 437
father *n.* 11, 170
fathom *vb.* 452
fathomless *adj.* 210
fatigue *n.* 617, 841
fatten *vb.* 204, 377
fatty *adj.* 365
fault *n.* 200, 315, 431, 582
faultless *adj.* 581, 937
faulty *adj.* 582
fauna *n.* 366, 373
faux pas *n.* 431
favour *n.* 636, 670, 715, 886, 899, 907, 922; *vb.* 540, 925
favourable *adj.* 854, 925
favourite *n.* 891
favouritism *n.* 916
fawning *n.* 927; *adj.* 881
fear *n.* 856, 858, 980; *vb.* 856
fearless *adj.* 857
feasible *adj.* 404, 406
feast *n.* 306; *vb.* 304
feat *n.* 605, 609
feathery *adj.* 331
feature *n.* 5, 8, 55, 825
fecundity *n.* 168
federal *adj.* 379, 641
federation *n.* 641
fed up with *adj.* 862
fee *n.* 738, 743, 917
feeble-minded *adj.* 435
feebleness *n.* 160, 162, 507, 666, 781
feed *vb.* 304, 377
feedback *n.* 395
feeder *n.* 559
feel *n.* 339, 398, 758; *vb.* 411, 752, 758
feel better *vb.* 834
feeler *n.* 394, 396
feel for *vb.* 758, 907
feeling *n.* 411, 752, 758; *adj.* 752
feel like *vb.* 532
feel small *vb.* 874
fees *n.* 917
feign *vb.* 477, 852
felicitate *vb.* 888
felicitous *adj.* 510
fell *n.* 208; *vb.* 48
fellow *n.* 11, 122, 131, 380, 473
fellow-feeling *n.* 899, 907
fellowship *n.* 60, 639, 641, 988; *vb.* 988
fellow-worker *n.* 640
female *n.* 381; *adj.* 381
femininity *n.* 162, 381
feminism *n.* 381
fen *n.* 355
fence *n.* 230, 234
fend for oneself *vb.* 678
fend off *vb.* 646
ferment *n.* 80, 175; *vb.* 331, 363, 773
ferry *n.* 277; *vb.* 271
fertile *adj.* 163, 168
fertilize *vb.* 378
fervour *n.* 506, 752, 759
festive *adj.* 878
festivity *n.* 838, 840
festoon *vb.* 846
fetch *vb.* 705, 718, 743
fete *n.* 840
fetid *adj.* 777
fetish *n.* 967, 983, 984
fetter *n.* 681; *vb.* 635, 681
feud *n.* 642, 649
fever *n.* 326, 439, 586
few *adj.* 33, 76, 139
fewness *n.* 33, 76
fiancée *n.* 698, 889
fiasco *n.* 662
fib *vb.* 477
fibber *n.* 480
fibre *n.* 207, 339
fibrous *adj.* 337
fickle *adj.* 151, 536, 538, 539
fiction *n.* 525
fictitious *adj.* 2, 449
fiddle *n.* 478; *vb.* 722, 742
fidelity *n.* 673, 931
fidgety *adj.* 151, 611, 756, 856
field *n.* 184, 352, 356, 378, 557, 658
fiend *n.* 175, 969
fierce *adj.* 175, 900
fiery *adj.* 506, 759, 893
fiesta *n.* 840
fifth columnist *n.* 480
fight *n.* 642, 649, 651; *vb.* 25, 615, 637, 642, 645, 649
fight back *vb.* 647
fighter *n.* 645, 655
figurative *adj.* 455
figure *n.* 39, 489; *vb.* 38

figure-head n. 253
figure of speech n. 455, 498
figure out vb. 452
filament n. 207
filch vb. 722
file n. 83, 202; vb. 83, 91, 255, 257, 341
filial adj. 171
filibuster n. 135; vb. 135
fill n. 865; vb. 56, 107, 265, 865
fill in vb. 149, 460, 483
fillip n. 173; vb. 613
fill up vb. 568
filly n. 381
film n. 225, 363, 483, 803; vb. 483
filter vb. 319
filth n. 584, 952
final adj. 89, 237, 408, 659
finality n. 543
finance n. 731; vb. 636, 718
financier n. 718, 728
find vb. 415, 419, 960
find fault with vb. 832, 926, 930, 962
fine n. 963; adj. 205, 255, 333, 340, 579, 844; vb. 963
finesse n. 631
finger vb. 758
fingerprint n. 482
finicky adj. 392, 864
finish n. 56, 89, 257, 510, 659; vb. 89, 144, 414, 581, 659
fiord n. 353
fire n. 506, 759, 763; vb. 645, 686, 755, 761, 765
firearm n. 657
fireproof adj. 762
fireside n. 191, 763
fireworks n. 800
firing squad n. 963
firm n. 620, 641; adj. 143, 152, 161, 334, 337, 534, 535, 669
first adj. 34, 88
first-class adj. 34, 579
first hand adj. 21
firth n. 353
fish n. 306, 373
fishy adj. 373, 932
fissure n. 254
fit n. 326, 439, 586, 893; adj. 585, 915; vb. 47, 105, 568, 602
fitful adj. 141, 539
fit in with vb. 24
fit out vb. 227, 602
fitting adj. 577, 915
fittings n. 568
five and over n. 70
fix n. 633; vb. 47, 152, 311, 589
fixation n. 439
fixative n. 49
fixed adj. 47, 143, 152, 543
fixtures n. 152, 568, 711
fizz n. 363; vb. 363, 786
fizzle out vb. 144, 162, 662
flabbergasted adj. 866
flabby adj. 668
flaccid adj. 507
flag n. 467, 482, 677; vb. 617, 841
flagellant n. 946
flagon n. 193
flagrant adj. 458, 877
flail vb. 282
flake n. 33, 206, 340; vb. 206
flake out vb. 617
flamboyant adj. 877
flame n. 797, 800; vb. 759
flammable adj. 761, 765
flank n. 238; vb. 238
flap n. 225, 326; vb. 216, 326, 359, 756
flare n. 797, 800; vb. 756, 797
flash n. 115, 539, 797, 800; vb. 797
flashback n. 147, 441
flashlight n. 800
flashy adj. 509, 805, 849, 877
flask n. 193
flat n. 191, 356; adj. 215, 257, 768, 791, 843
flat out adv. 280
flattery n. 881, 886, 927
flaunt vb. 877
flavour n. 767; vb. 307
flavourless adj. 768, 771
flaw n. 431, 582, 847
flawless adj. 54, 581
flay vb. 228, 963
fleck n. 33
fledgling n. 125
flee vb. 555, 600, 826
fleece vb. 377, 478, 722
fleeting adj. 113
flesh n. 306, 327, 379
flesh and blood n. 3, 327
fleshly adj. 945
fleshy adj. 194, 364
flex vb. 247
flexible adj. 151, 335, 336, 668
flexuous adj. 251
flicker vb. 326, 759, 797
flickering adj. 141
flick through vb. 472, 818
flight n. 273, 293, 299, 555, 600, 826
flighty adj. 151, 539
flimsy adj. 162, 205, 335, 338
flinch vb. 283, 555, 856
fling vb. 359
flint n. 765
flippancy n. 842
flirt n. 953; vb. 890

flirtation *n.* 889, 890
flit *vb.* 113
float *vb.* 216, 257, 331
flock *n.* 75, 94, 982, 987; *vb.* 75, 94
flog *vb.* 963
flood *n.* 358, 572; *vb.* 349, 358, 572
floodlight *n.* 800
floor *n.* 206, 209, 213
flop *n.* 662
flora *n.* 366
floral *adj.* 374
florid *adj.* 846, 849
flounder *vb.* 409, 633, 662
flourish *n.* 877; *vb.* 36, 168, 585, 661, 664, 877
flout *vb.* 644
flow *n.* 85, 91, 301, 313, 343, 358
flower *n.* 374; *vb.* 163
flowering *n.* 127; *adj.* 129
flowery *adj.* 509
fluctuate *vb.* 141, 142, 151, 325, 536
flue *n.* 361
fluency *n.* 501, 514, 516
fluffy *adj.* 331, 335
fluid *n.* 243, 309, 343; *adj.* 343, 347
fluidity *n.* 343, 345
fluke *n.* 158, 553
flurry *n.* 359, 611, 613
flush *adj.* 28, 215; *vb.* 811
fluster *n.* 756
fluted *adj.* 261
flutter *vb.* 325, 326, 359
flux *vb.* 345
fly *vb.* 110, 113, 273, 280
foam *n.* 363; *vb.* 363, 893
focal *adj.* 90, 96, 224
focalize *vb.* 296
focus *n.* 90, 96, 224; *vb.* 96, 224, 390
fodder *n.* 305; *vb.* 377
foe *n.* 638, 883
fog *n.* 363, 409, 427, 799
foil *vb.* 445, 635, 648, 662
fold *n.* 206, 260; *vb.* 251, 260, 739
foliage *n.* 374
folk *n.* 379
follow *vb.* 85, 105, 119, 237, 287, 452, 673, 702
follower *n.* 119, 287, 424, 474, 554, 640, 821
following *n.* 85, 287; *adj.* 85, 119, 156, 554
follow up *vb.* 392, 554
follow-up *n.* 87
folly *n.* 385, 433, 435
fond *adj.* 861, 889
fondle *vb.* 758, 890
fondness *n.* 861, 889, 890
food *n.* 305, 306
fool *n.* 429, 437, 440, 479; *vb.* 478
fool around *vb.* 433, 435
foolhardy *adj.* 613, 859
foolish *adj.* 385, 433, 435, 451
foot *n.* 213, 528
footing *n.* 93
footpath *n.* 559
footprint *n.* 482, 483
fop *n.* 852
foray *n.* 645
forbearance *n.* 670, 757, 907, 911
forbears *n.* 11, 86
forbid *vb.* 99, 635, 691, 955
forbidding *adj.* 669, 691
force *n.* 159, 161, 175, 177, 506, 674; *vb.* 175, 282, 531, 562, 674
forced *adj.* 507, 511
force in *vb.* 300, 311
force oneself *vb.* 533
forces *n.* 655
ford *vb.* 313
fore *adj.* 236
foreboding *n.* 447, 597; *adj.* 447
forecast *n.* 154, 348, 447; *vb.* 154, 443, 446, 447, 558
foregoing *adj.* 84, 118
foreground *n.* 199, 236
foreign *adj.* 100, 222
foreknowledge *n.* 447
foreman *n.* 623, 958
foremost *adj.* 236, 573
foreordain *vb.* 531, 543
forerun *vb.* 84, 118
forerunner *n.* 86, 467
foresee *vb.* 443, 446, 447
foreshadow *vb.* 447, 976
foresight *n.* 134, 434, 446, 447, 860
forest *n.* 374
forestall *vb.* 134
foretaste *n.* 55, 118
foretell *vb.* 447, 543
forethought *n.* 392, 446, 447, 860
forever *adv.* 114
forewarn *vb.* 447, 597
foreword *n.* 86, 88
forfeit *n.* 43, 701; *vb.* 706
forge *vb.* 477
forge ahead *vb.* 288
forgery *n.* 20, 22
forget *vb.* 385, 393, 442
forgiveness *n.* 601, 670, 907, 911
forgo *vb.* 556
forgotten *adj.* 124, 126, 442
fork *n.* 246, 255, 297, 358; *vb.* 63, 297
fork out *vb.* 738

forlorn *adj.* 837
form *n.* 242, 339, 474, 482, 825; *vb.* 58, 242
formal *adj.* 511, 988
formalism *n.* 981
formalize *vb.* 81
formation *n.* 242, 655
formative *adj.* 129, 242
former *adj.* 84, 118, 124, 126
formless *adj.* 243
formula *n.* 39, 103, 498, 626
formulate *vb.* 81, 468, 498
fornicate *vb.* 952
fornicator *n.* 953
forsake *vb.* 556
forswear *vb.* 477
forte *n.* 627
forthcoming *adj.* 154, 292
forthright *adj.* 476, 632
forthwith *adv.* 115
fortification *n.* 646
fortify *vb.* 161, 173, 646, 857
fortitude *n.* 534, 857
fortress *n.* 595, 646
fortuitous *adj.* 136, 158, 553
fortunate *adj.* 661
fortune *n.* 158, 447, 550, 553, 734
forum *n.* 96, 625, 658
forward *adj.* 236, 288, 880; *vb.* 268; *adv.* 288
forward-looking *adj.* 125, 288
fossilize *vb.* 334
foster *vb.* 470, 636
foul *adj.* 584, 777; *vb.* 584
foul play *n.* 551, 900, 916, 932
found *vb.* 88
foundation *n.* 88, 155, 213, 217, 401, 602
founder *n.* 155; *vb.* 588
foundry *n.* 620
fountain *n.* 358, 567
four *n.* 67; *adj.* 67
fourfold *adj.* 68
fowl *n.* 306, 373
fracas *n.* 80
fraction *n.* 39, 73, 717
fracture *n.* 48; *vb.* 48
fragile *adj.* 162, 338
fragment *n.* 33, 55, 73, 717; *vb.* 48, 338
fragrance *n.* 774, 776
frail *adj.* 162, 338, 507, 586
frame *n.* 5; *vb.* 558, 930
frame of mind *n.* 751
frame of reference *n.* 700
framework *n.* 5, 232
franchise *n.* 540; *vb.* 690
frangible *adj.* 338
frank *adj.* 476, 508, 632, 931
fraternity *n.* 11, 882
fraud *n.* 478, 631, 722
fraudulent *adj.* 477, 478, 631, 932
freak *n.* 440, 539, 866
freckled *adj.* 817
free *adj.* 10, 530, 600, 678, 708, 715, 897, 911; *vb.* 48, 600, 601, 678, 680, 921
freedom *n.* 600, 678, 690, 921
freedom from mixture *n.* 46
free thinking *n.* 975
free time *n.* 614
free will *n.* 530, 678
freeze *vb.* 332, 334, 599, 760, 762
freight *n.* 192, 268
frenzied *adj.* 439, 859
frenzy *n.* 80, 175, 439, 861
frequency *n.* 27, 138, 140, 400
frequent *adj.* 138, 545; *vb.* 188
fresh *adj.* 125, 359, 599, 760
freshen *vb.* 348, 583
fret *vb.* 837
fretting *n.* 828
friable *adj.* 338, 340
friar *n.* 986
friary *n.* 990
friction *n.* 181, 341, 642
fridge *n.* 764
friend *n.* 640, 882
friendless *adj.* 885
friendly *adj.* 643, 882, 884, 886
friendship *n.* 643, 650, 882
frighten *vb.* 856, 902
frightful *adj.* 845
frigid *adj.* 160, 169, 754, 760
frill *n.* 509, 846
fringe *n.* 233, 235
frisky *adj.* 320
fritter away *vb.* 749
frivolous *adj.* 539
front *n.* 222, 236, 658, 852; *adj.* 236
frontier *n.* 233, 235
frost *n.* 760; *vb.* 762
frosted *adj.* 804, 807
froth *n.* 363
frown *n.* 895; *vb.* 895
frown on *vb.* 926
frozen *adj.* 332, 760, 762
frugal *adj.* 392, 748, 944
fruit *n.* 156, 163, 306
fruitful *adj.* 163, 168, 661
fruitless *adj.* 169, 576, 662
frustrate *vb.* 181, 445, 635, 648, 662
fry *vb.* 306, 759

fuel *n.* 765; *vb.* 765
fugitive *n.* 555, 600
fulcrum *n.* 217
fulfil *vb.* 56, 659, 661, 673, 702
fulfilment *n.* 659, 827
full *adj.* 54, 56, 204, 570, 865
fullness *n.* 32, 56, 567
fulminate *vb.* 780
fulsome *adj.* 168
fumble *vb.* 409, 758
fumbler *n.* 630
fume *n.* 344, 777; *vb.* 175, 346, 756, 759, 893
fumigate *vb.* 583, 775
fun *n.* 829, 836, 840, 842
function *n.* 39, 172, 557, 878; *vb.* 172, 609
functional *adj.* 172, 575
functionary *n.* 623
fundamental *adj.* 5, 88, 155, 213, 573
fundamentalist *adj.* 977
funds *n.* 731
funeral *n.* 372
fungus *n.* 167, 592
funk *n.* 858; *vb.* 856, 858
funny *adj.* 842, 851
furious *adj.* 175, 893
furlough *n.* 614
furnace *n.* 763
furnish *vb.* 163, 568, 715
furniture *n.* 711
furrow *n.* 254, 261
further *adj.* 40; *vb.* 217 288, 587; *adv.* 40
furthest *adj.* 89, 198
furtive *adj.* 461, 478
fury *n.* 175, 756, 893
fuse *n.* 765; *vb.* 45, 47, 52, 345
fusion *n.* 45, 47, 52, 639
fuss *n.* 326, 756, 877; *vb.* 756, 864
fussy *adj.* 392, 864
futile *adj.* 576, 662, 855
future *n.* 123; *adj.* 123
future events *n.* 154
futuristic *adj.* 125
fuzzy *adj.* 243, 503, 824

G

gabble *vb.* 516
gad about *vb.* 269
gadget *n.* 565
gag *n.* 842; *vb.* 681
gaiety *n.* 836
gain *n.* 288, 550, 705; *vb.* 36, 116, 705, 720
gala *n.* 840
galaxy *n.* 329
gale *n.* 175, 359
gallant *adj.* 857, 886
gallery *n.* 818
galley *n.* 522
gallivant about *vb.* 269
gallows *n.* 964
galore *adj.* 75
galvanize *vb.* 755
gamble *n.* 158, 553; *vb.* 158, 553
gambler *n.* 553
game *n.* 306, 373, 649, 840; *adj.* 532, 857
gamekeeper *n.* 683
gamut *n.* 182
gang *n.* 94
gangster *n.* 370, 906
gang up against *vb.* 639
gaol *n.* 682
gap *n.* 92, 200, 262
gape *vb.* 262, 818, 866
garb *n.* 227
garbage *n.* 44
garble *vb.* 487, 515
garden *n.* 234, 374, 378
gardener *n.* 378
garish *adj.* 805, 846, 877
garment *n.* 227
garnish *vb.* 846
garrison *n.* 646
garrulous *adj.* 516
gas *n.* 159, 344, 765; *vb.* 963
gaseity *n.* 344
gash *n.* 588
gasify *vb.* 344, 346
gasp *n.* 359; *vb.* 359
gastronomy *n.* 304
gate *n.* 262
gatecrash *vb.* 300
gate-crasher *n.* 884
gather *n.* 260; *vb.* 94, 196, 260, 296, 448, 567
gaudy *adj.* 805, 846, 877
gauge *n.* 400, 482; *vb.* 400, 482
gay *n.* 106, 953; *adj.* 836, 952
gaze *vb.* 818
gazette *n.* 483, 524
gear *n.* 227
geld *vb.* 160, 169
gem *n.* 579, 846
gene *n.* 5
genealogy *n.* 170
general *adj.* 101
generality *n.* 101
generalize *vb.* 101
generally *adv.* 138, 545
generate *vb.* 11, 155, 163
generation *n.* 11, 109, 163, 171
generative *adj.* 163, 170
generic *adj.* 101
generosity *n.* 747, 886
generous *adj.* 715, 747, 899, 965
genetics *n.* 366
genial *adj.* 827, 836, 884
genius *n.* 382, 428, 434, 627, 629
genocide *n.* 370, 963
gentle *adj.* 176, 670, 907
gentleman *n.* 380
gentlemanly *adj.* 380, 886

gentleman's agreement *n.* 698, 699
gentry *n.* 870
genuine *adj.* 1, 21, 430, 632
geography *n.* 329
geology *n.* 367
geometry *n.* 38
gesticulate *vb.* 482
gesture *n.* 482, 549; *vb.* 482
get *vb.* 705, 716, 720, 726
get across *vb.* 460
get along with *vb.* 24, 643
get around *vb.* 464
get at *vb.* 460, 547, 893
get-at-able *adj.* 292
getaway *n.* 600
get away with /*vb.* 600, 722, 921
get back *vb.* 647, 705, 721
get by *vb.* 661, 666
get down *vb.* 298, 837
get down to *vb.* 605
get dressed *vb.* 227
get even with *vb.* 647, 912, 963
get in with *vb.* 177, 882
get on *vb.* 661, 664
get one's own back *vb.* 647, 912
get on one's nerves *vb.* 787, 893
get on with *vb.* 24, 643
get over *vb.* 460, 659
get ready *vb.* 602
get rid of *vb.* 303, 607, 634, 680
get the hang of *vb.* 452, 472
get to *vb.* 298
get-together *n.* 884
get up *vb.* 318, 472, 477
get-up-and-go *n.* 173, 611
get used to *vb.* 545
get well *vb.* 589
ghastly *adj.* 856
ghost *n.* 328, 971
ghostly *adj.* 4, 328, 971
ghost-writer *n.* 149, 524
giant *n.* 194; *adj.* 208
gibberish *n.* 453
gibe *vb.* 853
gift *n.* 627, 652, 715, 829
gifted *adj.* 627
gift of the gab *n.* 514, 516
giggle *vb.* 838
gild *vb.* 846
ginger *adj.* 816
gipsy *n.* 447
gird *vb.* 322
girder *n.* 217
girdle *n.* 49; *vb.* 229
girl *n.* 131, 381
girl-friend *n.* 882, 889
girth *n.* 204
gist *n.* 224
give *vb.* 335, 568, 715, 965
give and take *n.* 150, 639, 704
give away *vb.* 462, 717, 896
give in *vb.* 654
given *adj.* 1, 715
give off *vb.* 301, 774
give out *vb.* 301, 774, 778
giver *n.* 715, 905
give up *vb.* 556, 654, 855
give up office *vb.* 687
give way *vb.* 162
giving *n.* 636, 715, 747
glaciate *vb.* 762
glacier *n.* 760
glad *adj.* 827, 836
gladden *vb.* 829, 836
gladly *adv.* 532
glamorous *adj.* 829, 844
glamour *n.* 547, 829, 844
glance *n.* 818; *vb.* 818
glare *n.* 797; *vb.* 797, 818
glaring *adj.* 458, 805, 823
glass *n.* 193, 257, 822
glasses *n.* 822
glassy *adj.* 257, 802
glaze *n.* 225; *vb.* 225, 369, 257
gleam *n.* 797; *vb.* 797
glean *vb.* 378, 540, 705
glee *n.* 827, 836
glib *adj.* 516
glide *vb.* 257, 273
glider *n.* 278
glimmer *n.* 460, 797; *vb.* 326, 797
glimpse *n.* 818; *vb.* 818
glint *n.* 797
glisten *vb.* 797
glitter *n.* 797; *vb.* 797
global *adj.* 101
globe *n.* 249, 329
globe-trotter *n.* 270
globule *n.* 249, 363
gloom *n.* 798, 799, 837
gloomy *adj.* 798, 799, 837, 843, 895
glorification *n.* 925, 972
glorify *vb.* 318, 868, 982
glorious *adj.* 664, 972, 982
glory *n.* 868, 972; *vb.* 873
gloss *n.* 211, 225, 257, 456, 797; *vb.* 225, 257, 456
glossary *n.* 83, 494
gloss over *vb.* 393
glossy *adj.* 257, 797
glow *n.* 759, 797, 805; *vb.* 759, 797, 811
glue *n.* 49, 362; *vb.* 50
glum *adj.* 895
glut *n.* 572, 865

glutton *n.* 304, 948
gluttony *n.* 304, 750, 945, 948
gnome *n.* 970
go *vb.* 172, 266, 299
goad *vb.* 547, 613
go after *vb.* 85, 119, 287, 554, 882
go-ahead *n.* 424, 690; *adj.* 605, 611
goal *n.* 89, 298, 552
go along with *vb.* 424, 639
go around *vb.* 322
go around with *vb.* 882
go away *vb.* 299, 826, 896
go back *vb.* 147, 289, 441
go back on *vb.* 556
go bad *vb.* 588
gobble *vb.* 304, 789, 948
go before *vb.* 84, 118, 286
go behind *vb.* 85
go-between *n.* 467, 653
go beyond *vb.* 314
goblin *n.* 970
God *n.* 966, 967
goddess *n.* 967
God-forsaken *adj.* 198, 885
godhead *n.* 966
godless *adj.* 975, 981
godly *adj.* 966, 974, 980
go down *vb.* 317, 321, 586, 662
godsend *n.* 550
go for *vb.* 284, 540, 552, 743, 861
goggles *n.* 801, 822
go in *vb.* 300
go in for *vb.* 472, 605
go into *vb.* 394, 472
go it alone *vb.* 678
gold *adj.* 813, 816
golden *adj.* 664, 813
golden age *n.* 664, 827
golden calf *n.* 967, 983
golden handshake *n.* 687, 715
golden rule *n.* 899
gold-mine *n.* 567
go mad *vb.* 439
gondola *n.* 277
gone *adj.* 124, 706, 855
gone off *adj.* 771
gone on *adj.* 889
gong *n.* 784
good *n.* 550; *adj.* 550, 579, 585, 673, 899, 931
goodbye *n.* 518
good deed *n.* 899
good example *n.* 939
good-for-nothing *n.* 612, 940
good health *n.* 585
good humour *n.* 836
good-looking *adj.* 844
good luck *n.* 158
good manners *n.* 886
good memory *n.* 441
good name *n.* 868
good neighbour *n.* 899, 905
goodness *n.* 579, 907, 931, 935
good person *n.* 939
goods *n.* 163, 711, 729
good spirit *n.* 968
good taste *n.* 848
good time *n.* 840
good turn *n.* 550, 886, 899
goodwill *n.* 643
go off at a tangent *vb.* 285, 505
go off with *vb.* 722
go on *vb.* 1, 138, 145, 535
go on about *vb.* 516, 832
go on strike *vb.* 696
goose *n.* 381
go out *vb.* 144, 301
go out of control *vb.* 326
go out with *vb.* 882, 890
go over *vb.* 77
gorge *n.* 200, 210, 254; *vb.* 56, 304, 865
gorgeous *adj.* 844
go round *vb.* 250
go shopping *vb.* 726
go-slow *n.* 144, 281
gospel *n.* 430, 976
gossamer *n.* 207
gossip *n.* 388, 516, 516, 869, 928; *vb.* 388, 516
go through *vb.* 313, 752, 828
go through the motions *vb.* 477, 852
go through with *vb.* 659
go together *vb.* 60, 882
go to law *vb.* 960
go to pieces *vb.* 588, 856
go to press *vb.* 522
go to the bottom *vb.* 321
gouge *n.* 259, 261, 312; *vb.* 254, 312
go under *vb.* 321, 662, 665, 739
go up *vb.* 316, 745
gourmand *n.* 304, 848, 948
gourmandise *n.* 304
gourmet *n.* 304
govern *vb.* 177, 622, 667, 681
governess *n.* 473, 675, 683
government *n.* 621, 622, 625, 667
governmental *adj.* 622, 667
governor *n.* 623, 675
go with *vb.* 24, 60, 882
go wrong *vb.* 431
grab *vb.* 705, 720, 758

grace *n.* 844, 848, 907, 911
graceful *adj.* 510, 844, 848
gracious *adj.* 510, 899, 907, 966
gradation *n.* 27
grade *n.* 27, 93, 400, 474; *vb.* 27, 97
gradual *adj.* 27
graduate *n.* 474; *vb.* 27, 400
graft *vb.* 378
grain *n.* 33, 306, 340, 374
grammar *n.* 492, 499
grammarian *n.* 492
grammatical *adj.* 492, 499
granary *n.* 193
grand *adj.* 509, 844, 868, 870
grandeur *n.* 870, 877
grandiloquent *adj.* 509
grandiose *adj.* 509, 877
grandstand *n.* 818
grange *n.* 191, 378
grant *n.* 636, 715; *vb.* 424, 690, 692, 715
grant permission *vb.* 424
granular *adj.* 339
granulate *vb.* 340
granule *n.* 340
grapevine *n.* 465
graphic *adj.* 488, 506, 521, 525
graphics *n.* 488
grapple *vb.* 758
grasp *n.* 410, 707, 712; *vb.* 50, 426, 452, 472, 707, 712, 720, 758
grasping *adj.* 705, 720, 750
grass *n.* 356, 374, 460
grassland *n.* 356, 378
grassy *adj.* 374, 812
grate *n.* 763; *vb.* 341, 787, 805
grateful *adj.* 909
gratify *vb.* 829, 831, 865
grating *adj.* 787, 791
gratitude *n.* 909
gratuity *n.* 715, 965
grave *n.* 372; *adj.* 573, 837
graven image *n.* 983
gravestone *n.* 372
gravitate towards *vb.* 178
gravity *n.* 294, 330, 573, 837
graze *vb.* 201, 341, 377, 758
grease *n.* 306, 342, 365, 584; *vb.* 342, 365
greasy *adj.* 365, 584
great *adj.* 32, 573, 579, 868, 870
greater *adj.* 34
greatness *n.* 26, 32, 194, 579, 868, 870
greedy *adj.* 720, 750, 861, 934, 948
greedy-guts *n.* 948
green *n.* 559, 812; *adj.* 129, 422, 427, 812, 913
greenhorn *n.* 429, 479, 630
greenhouse *n.* 378
greet *vb.* 886, 922
greeting *n.* 518, 886, 922
gregarious *adj.* 884
gremlin *n.* 970
grey *n.* 809; *adj.* 30, 130, 363, 799, 809
grey matter *n.* 434
grid *n.* 159, 221
grief *n.* 828, 837, 839
grievance *n.* 916
grieve *vb.* 830, 833, 837, 839
grill *n.* 221; *vb.* 306, 394, 759
grim *adj.* 669, 830
grimace *n.* 895; *vb.* 245, 895
grimy *adj.* 584
grin *n.* 838; *vb.* 838
grin and bear it *vb.* 757, 836
grind *vb.* 341, 615, 787
grip *n.* 193, 712; *vb.* 50, 712, 720, 758
gripping *adj.* 755
gristle *n.* 337
groan *n.* 788; *vb.* 696, 788
groceries *n.* 305
groggy *adj.* 586, 950
groom *vb.* 377, 470
groove *n.* 184, 261, 545; *vb.* 261
grope *vb.* 409, 758
gross *n.* 70; *adj.* 54, 56, 849, 936
grotesque *adj.* 245, 845
grotto *n.* 254
grouch *n.* 832; *vb.* 895
ground *n.* (reason) 155, 401, 547, 929; (land) 213, 352, 658; *vb.* 319, 470
groundwork *n.* 213, 602
group *n.* 55, 94, 97, 641, 793; *vb.* 52, 94, 97
grovel *vb.* 209, 881, 922
grow *vb.* 36, 168, 196, 242, 288, 316, 324
growl *vb.* 783, 789, 895
grown-up *n.* 133; *adj.* 133
growth *n.* 36, 196, 252, 288, 324
grow up *vb.* 133
grudge *n.* 832, 893; *vb.* 914
grudgingly *adv.* 533
gruelling *adj.* 615
gruff *adj.* 787, 887, 894
grumble *vb.* 783, 832
grumbler *n.* 832

grumpy adj. 894
grunt vb. 789
guarantee n. 424; vb. 408, 468, 698, 701
guard n. 593, 646, 683; vb. 392, 593, 646
guardian n. 593, 683, 905
guardroom n. 682
guerdon n. 965
guerrilla n. 148
guess n. 386, 396, 447, 448; vb. 396, 411, 448
guest n. 100, 884
guffaw vb. 838
guidance n. 470, 624
guide n. 103, 217, 473, 623; vb. 470, 621, 622, 624
guidebook n. 460, 524
guile n. 477, 478, 631, 932
guileless adj. 422, 476, 632, 937, 951
guillotine n. 964; vb. 370, 963
guilt n. 938
guilty adj. 938
guinea pig n. 396, 716, 828
guise n. 227, 463, 549
gulf n. 200, 254, 353
gullibility n. 422
gully n. 254, 360
gulp n. 309; vb. 304, 948
gum n. 365; vb. 50
gun n. 657; vb. 370
gunman n. 167, 370
gunpowder n. 657
gurgle vb. 358
guru n. 473
gush vb. 301, 358, 532
gust n. 359
gusto n. 827
gusty adj. 359
guts n. 535, 857
gutter n. 261, 360
guzzle vb. 304, 948, 950
gypsy n. 270
gyration n. 323

H

habit n. 79, 138, 545
habitat n. 191, 229
habitation n. 188, 191
hack n. 524, 619, 676
hackneyed adj. 426
haggard adj. 205, 617
hail n. 760; vb. 886, 925
hair n. 207
hair-dressing n. 844
hairless adj. 228
hairy adj. 207, 258
halcyon days n. 664, 827
hale adj. 585
half n. 63; adj. 63
half a dozen n. 70
half-and-half adj. 45
half-done adj. 55, 57, 660
half-hearted adj. 533, 863
half-price adj. 746
half-remembered adj. 441
halfway n. 30, 704; adj. 30, 90, 560; adv. 90
half-wit n. 437
half-witted adj. 435
hall n. 191, 529
hallmark n. 482
hallow vb. 980
hallucination n. 478
halo n. 250, 800
halt n. 144; vb. 144, 267, 691
halve vb. 63
hamlet n. 183
hammer vb. 282
hammer out vb. 659, 699
hamper n. 193; vb. 635, 681, 691
hand n. 238, 521
handbook n. 524
hand down vb. 714
handful n. 26, 76, 633
handicap vb. 162
hand in one's notice vb. 687
handiwork n. 163
handle n. 872; vb. 172, 606, 609, 622, 725
hand out vb. 715, 717
hand-out n. 464, 465, 715
hand over vb. 268
handshake n. 886
handsome adj. 844
handwriting n. 521
handy adj. 575, 627
handyman n. 629
hang vb. 216, 370, 963
hang around vb. 188, 612
hanger-on n. 287, 640, 881
hanging n. 216, 370, 963
hangman n. 370, 963
hangover n. 44, 950
hanker vb. 861, 914
haphazard adj. 158, 399, 409, 553
happen vb. 1, 107, 153, 825
happening n. 153
happiness n. 550, 661, 664, 831, 836
happy adj. 827, 831, 836, 950
happy medium n. 30
happy returns n. 888
harangue n. 518
harass vb. 830, 893
harbour n. 298, 353, 595; vb. 461, 593, 712
hard adj. 334, 337, 537, 633, 669, 942

harden *vb.* 332, 334, 337, 754
hardened *adj.* 537, 942
hard-hearted *adj.* 648, 754, 908
hard labour *n.* 963
hardly *adv.* 33, 139
hardness *n.* 334, 537, 633, 669, 754
hardship *n.* 633, 665, 735
hard-working *adj.* 611, 615
hardy *adj.* 161
harlot *n.* 953
harm *n.* 551, 900; *vb.* 580, 608, 900, 916
harmful *adj.* 164, 580, 592, 916
harmonious *adj.* 24, 79, 105, 244, 643, 790
harmony *n.* 24, 244, 510, 643, 650, 790
harness *n.* 49; *vb.* 47
harrow *vb.* 378, 830
harrowing *adj.* 828, 856
harsh *adj.* 258, 642, 669, 787, 900, 908
harsh sound *n.* 787
harvest *n.* 128, 163, 567; *vb.* 378, 567
haste *n.* 280, 613
hasty *adj.* 393, 544, 603, 613
hatch *n.* 262; *vb.* 449, 477, 558
hatchway *n.* 262
hate *n.* 862, 892, 900; *vb.* 862, 892
hatred *n.* 862, 883, 892
haughty *adj.* 873, 875, 924
haul *n.* 291, 724; *vb.* 268, 291
haunt *vb.* 188, 441, 830, 971
have *vb.* 707
have a go *vb.* 604
have fun *vb.* 840
have in mind *vb.* 552
have it in for *vb.* 892, 900
haven *n.* 595
have nothing to do with *vb.* 10, 542, 862
have no time for *vb.* 923
have-nots *n.* 871
have on *vb.* 227, 478
have one's own way *vb.* 530
have one's say *vb.* 468
have on one's mind *vb.* 384
havoc *n.* 164
hawk *vb.* 695, 727
hawker *n.* 697, 728
hazard *n.* 553, 594; *vb.* 553
hazel *adj.* 810
hazy *adj.* 363, 799, 824
H-bomb *n.* 657
head *n.* 89, 236, 675; *vb.* 212, 236, 284, 286
headache *n.* 633, 950
headlines *n.* 465
headlong *adj.* 613, 859
headmaster *n.* 473
headquarters *n.* 96
head start *n.* 34
headstone *n.* 372
headstrong *adj.* 537, 859
headway *n.* 288
heal *vb.* 589, 591
health *n.* 585
heap *n.* 567; *vb.* 567, 747
hear *vb.* 778, 795, 960
hearing *n.* 795, 960
hearsay *n.* 465
heart *n.* 223, 224, 368, 751, 857
heart-broken *adj.* 828, 837
heartening *adj.* 836, 857
hearth *n.* 191, 763
heartlessness *n.* 908
heart-to-heart *n.* 519
heartwarming *adj.* 836
hearty *adj.* 585
heat *n.* 759, 763; *vb.* 306, 761
heath *n.* 356
heathen *n.* 975, 983
heating *n.* 761
heatwave *n.* 759
heave *vb.* 291, 303, 318, 834
heaven *n.* 329, 972
heavenly *adj.* 770, 966, 972
heavy *adj.* 330, 332, 511, 573, 617, 841
heavy drinker *n.* 950
heavy-handed *adj.* 628, 669
heavy-laden *adj.* 828
heavyweight *adj.* 573
heckle *vb.* 425, 696
hedge *n.* 234; *vb.* 555
hedonistic *adj.* 827, 945
heed *n.* 390, 392, 860; *vb.* 390, 392, 673, 702
heedless *adj.* 391, 442, 859
hefty *adj.* 161
height *n.* 26, 208, 400, 581
heighten *vb.* 36, 318, 481, 835
heinous *adj.* 936
heir *n.* 171, 710, 716
helicopter *n.* 278
helix *n.* 251
hell *n.* 828, 973
helmsman *n.* 272
help *n.* 563, 636, 639, 834; *vb.* 563, 575, 577, 636, 639, 676
helper *n.* 624, 640, 905
helpful *adj.* 550, 575, 636
helping *n.* 305, 717

helpless *adj.* 160, 162, 855
hem *n.* 233; *vb.* 233
hem in *vb.* 234
hemisphere *n.* 63
hen *n.* 381
henpecked *adj.* 673
herald *n.* 86, 467; *vb.* 118, 286
herb *n.* 306, 307, 374
herbivore *n.* 373
herd *n.* 94, 373, 377, 871; *vb.* 377
hereafter *n.* 123; *adv.* 123
hereditary *adj.* 5
heresy *n.* 106, 975, 978
heretical *adj.* 106, 412, 975, 978
heritage *n.* 11
hermit *n.* 885, 946
hero *n.* 661, 857, 939
heroic *adj.* 857
hesitant *adj.* 515, 533, 536, 856
hesitate *vb.* 325, 409, 421, 515, 533, 536
heterodox *adj.* 978
heterogeneous *adj.* 15, 17, 45, 104
hew *vb.* 48, 489
hexagon *n.* 70, 246
heyday *n.* 664
hidden *adj.* 453, 459, 461, 466, 824
hide *vb.* 225, 461, 466, 593
hideous *adj.* 245, 845
hide-out *n.* 463
hiding *n.* 461, 463
hierarchy *n.* 97
hi-fi *n.* 794
high *adj.* 32, 208, 318, 777, 868
high birth *n.* 870
highest *adj.* 212, 579
high-flown *adj.* 509, 877
high-handed *adj.* 880, 887
high hopes *n.* 443, 854
highlight *vb.* 468, 481
high living *n.* 945
highly-strung *adj.* 756
high opinion *n.* 922
high-pitched *adj.* 787
high principles *n.* 931
high-rise *adj.* 208
high spirits *n.* 836
high tea *n.* 306
high time *n.* 135
highway *n.* 559
highway code *n.* 313
highwayman *n.* 723
hijack *vb.* 722
hijacker *n.* 723
hike *n.* 269; *vb.* 269
hiker *n.* 270
hilarious *adj.* 851
hill *n.* 208, 316, 559
hind *n.* 381; *adj.* 237
hinder *vb.* 181, 548, 635, 637, 681
hindmost *adj.* 198, 237
hindrance *n.* 548, 635, 681
hindsight *n.* 441
hinge *n.* 49, 217
hint *n.* 459, 460, 482; *vb.* 459, 460
hire *vb.* 557, 685, 719
hire out *vb.* 718
hire purchase *n.* 718, 731
hiss *vb.* 786, 788, 853, 926
hissing sound *n.* 786
historian *n.* 484
historical *adj.* 124, 430
history *n.* 124
histrionics *n.* 529, 877
hit *n.* 282, 661; *vb.* 282, 758, 963
hit and miss *n.* 396
hit back *vb.* 647
hitch *n.* 635
hitch-hiker *n.* 270
hit it off *vb.* 24, 643
hit-or-miss *adj.* 158
hit upon *vb.* 419
hive off *vb.* 48
hoard *n.* 567; *vb.* 567
hoarse *adj.* 787
hoary *adj.* 126, 807, 809
hoax *n.* 478, 598, 631; *vb.* 478, 631
hob *n.* 763, 970
hobble *vb.* 281
hobby *n.* 840
hoe *vb.* 378
hog *n.* 948; *vb.* 707
hoist *vb.* 318
hold *n.* 707, 712; *vb.* 50, 420, 707, 712
hold against *vb.* 588
hold back *vb.* 533, 681, 694, 876
hold dear *vb.* 441, 889, 922
holder *n.* 193, 710
hold forth *vb.* 470, 514
holding *n.* 378, 711, 712
hold off *vb.* 295, 648
hold one's breath *vb.* 443
hold out *vb.* 648, 693
hold out for *vb.* 535
hold up *vb.* 135, 217, 635
hold-up *n.* 635, 722
hold water *vb.* 410
hole *n.* 254, 262, 319; *vb.* 264
holiday *n.* 144, 612, 614, 840
holiday-maker *n.* 270
hollow *n.* 210, 254, 262; *adj.* 254, 852; *vb.* 210, 254
holocaust *n.* 370
holy *adj.* 935, 974, 980, 982
Holy Communion *n.* 988

holy orders *n.* 985
Holy Spirit *n.* 967
homage *n.* 982
home *n.* 11, 191, 595; *adj.* 190
homecoming *n.* 298
homeless *adj.* 59, 187
homely *adj.* 508, 827
home-made *adj.* 628
homesickness *n.* 861
homestead *n.* 191, 377, 378
homework *n.* 470, 472
homicide *n.* 370
homogeneity *n.* 13, 16, 46, 59
homo sapiens *n.* 379
homosexual *n.* 106, 953; *adj.* 952
honest *adj.* 430, 476, 915, 931
honey *n.* 772, 891
honeymoon *n.* 829, 896; *vb.* 896
honour *n.* 663, 868, 872, 909, 922, 982; *vb.* 868, 878, 922, 982
honourable *adj.* 868, 931
hood *n.* 225, 801, 989
hooded *adj.* 225
hoodwink *vb.* 478, 819
hook *n.* 49; *vb.* 47, 896
hooligan *n.* 906
hoop *n.* 250; *vb.* 788
hoot *vb.* 482, 788, 853
hooter *n.* 116, 482
hop *n.* 320; *vb.* 320
hope *n.* 406, 420, 443, 854; *vb.* 406, 443, 552, 854
hopeful *adj.* 443, 854
hopelessness *n.* 405, 576, 855
horizon *n.* 198
horizontal *adj.* 215, 248
horn *n.* 598
horn of plenty *n.* 168
horology *n.* 116
horoscope *n.* 329, 447
horrible *adj.* 580, 771
horrid *adj.* 580, 845
horrifying *adj.* 856
horror *n.* 845, 856
horse *n.* 275
horsemanship *n.* 269
horse-power *n.* 159
horse-racing *n.* 269
horse-rider *n.* 270
horticultural *adj.* 374, 376, 378
hospitable *adj.* 716, 884
hospitality *n.* 302, 747, 884
host *n.* 75, 968
hostage *n.* 701
hostel *n.* 191
hostile *adj.* 637, 665, 883, 892
hostilities *n.* 649, 651
hot *adj.* 759, 769
hotel *n.* 191
hour *n.* 109
hour-glass *n.* 116
hourly *adv.* 140
house *n.* 191, 620
household *n.* 11; *adj.* 426
householder *n.* 190
housekeeper *n.* 676, 683
housekeeping *n.* 622, 748
hover *vb.* 154, 216
hovercraft *n.* 278
howl *vb.* 359, 788, 789, 839
hub *n.* 96, 224
huddle *n.* 94; *vb.* 94
hue *n.* 805
hug *n.* 712, 886; *vb.* 50, 712, 886, 890
huge *adj.* 32, 194
hull *n.* 225
hum *n.* *vb.* 781, 783, 784, 789
human *n.* 368; *adj.* 379
human being *n.* 379
humane *adj.* 903
humanitarian *adj.* 899, 903
humanity *n.* 379
human rights *n.* 917
human sound *n.* 788
humble *adj.* 35, 654, 833, 871, 874, 941, 980; *vb.* 869, 874, 922
humble oneself *vb.* 833, 874, 941, 982
humid *adj.* 349, 759
humiliate *vb.* 869, 874, 923
humility *n.* 654, 874, 980
humorous *adj.* 842
humour *n.* 5, 751, 842
hump *n.* 252
hunch *n.* 134, 411; *vb.* 319
hunchbacked *adj.* 245
hundred *n.* 70
hunger *n.* 861, 947; *vb.* 861
hunger strike *n.* 696
hungry *adj.* 735, 861, 947
hunt *n.* 554; *vb.* 394, 554
hurdle *n.* 230, 235, 320, 635
hurricane *n.* 175, 359
hurried *adj.* 613, 859
hurry *n.* 280, 611, 613; *vb.* 280, 613
hurt *n.* 828; *adj.* 893; *vb.* 580, 608, 830, 900, 916
hurtful *adj.* 164, 551, 580, 828, 830
husband *n.* 896; *vb.* 377, 748
husbandry *n.* 378, 622, 748

hush *n.* 779, 781; *vb.* 267, 779
hush-hush *adj.* 461, 466
hush up *vb.* 466
husk *n.* 225
husky *adj.* 787
hut *n.* 191
hybrid *n.* 45, 495
hydrated *adj.* 347
hydro- *adj.* 347
hydro-electricity *n.* 159, 765
hydrogen bomb *n.* 657
hygienic *adj.* 585
hymn *n.* 792, 982
hyperbole *n.* 481
hyper-critical *adj.* 832, 864
hyper-sensitive *adj.* 753
hypnosis *n.* 754
hypochondriac *n.* 440
hypocrisy *n.* 477, 981
hypocrite *n.* 480, 631
hypothesis *n.* 157, 386, 396, 448
hypothetical *adj.* 2, 396, 448
hysteria *n.* 439, 756
hysteric *n.* 440

I

ice *n.* 347, 760; *vb.* 762
iceberg *n.* 754, 760
icon *n.* 983
icy *adj.* 760, 762
idea *n.* 386, 415, 420, 449, 552
ideal *n.* 581, 939; *adj.* 449, 581
idealist *n.* 449, 864, 903
identical *adj.* 13
identification *n.* 397, 419, 482, 496
identify *vb.* 482, 496
identity *n.* 13
idiom *n.* 492, 498
idiosyncractic *adj.* 102
idiosyncrasy *n.* 5, 102, 501
idiot *n.* 437, 440, 630
idiotic *adj.* 435
idle *adj.* 174, 610, 612; *vb.* 107, 174, 281, 612
idler *n.* 281, 612, 940
idol *n.* 967, 983
idolatry *n.* 975, 983
idolize *vb.* 982, 983
idyllic *adj.* 528
ignite *vb.* 761
ignited *adj.* 759
ignoble *adj.* 871
ignominious *adj.* 869
ignoramus *n.* 429, 437, 630
ignorance *n.* 385, 427
ignorant *adj.* 427
ignore *vb.* 385, 389, 393, 672, 694, 887, 911
ill *n.* 551, 900; *adj.* 586
illegal *adj.* 691, 916, 955
illegality *n.* 955
illegible *adj.* 453
illegitimate *adj.* 171, 916, 955
ill feeling *n.* 642, 883
ill health *n.* 586
ill-humoured *adj.* 895
illicit *adj.* 691, 916, 952, 955
illiterate *adj.* 427
illness *n.* 586, 828
illogical *adj.* 412, 451
illuminate *vb.* 456, 797
illusion *n.* 4, 449, 478
illustrate *vb.* 413, 456, 486, 488, 525
illustration *n.* 23, 397, 413, 456, 486, 488, 525
illustrative *adj.* 456, 486
illustrious *adj.* 573, 868
image *n.* 386, 486, 489, 525, 983
imagery *n.* 455
imaginable *adj.* 404
imaginary *adj.* 2, 449, 970
imagination *n.* 449
imagine *vb.* 448, 449
imbecile *n.* 437, 440; *adj.* 435
imbecility *n.* 383, 435, 439
imitate *vb.* 18, 20
imitation *n.* 20, 486, 719; *adj.* 149
immaculate *adj.* 581, 583, 935
immanent *adj.* 5, 966
immateriality *n.* 4, 328, 574
immaturity *n.* 129, 427, 582, 603
immeasurable *adj.* 78
immediate *adj.* 115, 134
immensity *n.* 194
immerse *vb.* 311, 321, 349
immersed *adj.* 210
immigrant *n.* 100, 190, 270; *adj.* 100
immigration *n.* 300
imminent *adj.* 123, 134, 154, 902
immobile *adj.* 152, 174, 267
immoderate *adj.* 32, 393, 572, 749, 918, 945
immoral *adj.* 932, 936, 952
immortal *adj.* 114, 966
immortalize *vb.* 114, 868
immovable *adj.* 143, 152, 267, 669, 757
immunity *n.* 593, 678, 921
immutability *n.* 152
imp *n.* 969, 970
impact *n.* 282
impair *vb.* 160, 588

impale vb. 264, 963
impart vb. 464, 470, 715
impartial adj. 476, 541, 915, 933
impassioned adj. 506, 752
impassive adj. 863
impatient adj. 613, 756, 893
impeach vb. 686, 930
impeccable adj. 581, 935, 937
impede vb. 635, 681
impediment n. 515, 635, 681
impel vb. 266, 282, 290, 674
impend vb. 123, 154
impenetrable adj. 265, 332, 334, 453
impenitence n. 942
imperative n. 562; adj. 531, 562
imperceptible adj. 33, 824
imperfect adj. 35, 57, 315, 582, 847, 952
imperfection n. 35, 315, 582, 952
imperfect speech n. 515
imperfect vision n. 820
imperialism n. 379
imperishable adj. 114
impermeable adj. 332, 334
impersonation n. 20
impertinent adj. 880, 923
imperturbable adj. 757
impervious adj. 265, 337, 803
impetuous adj. 613, 756, 859
impetus n. 282, 290, 547
impiety n. 981
impinge vb. 282
implacable adj. 912
implant vb. 300, 311
implausible adj. 405, 407, 421
implement n. 192, 565; vb. 659
implicate vb. 930
implication n. 450, 459
implicit adj. 5
implore vb. 695, 982
imply vb. 401, 448, 450, 459, 482
impolite adj. 887, 923
imponderability n. 4, 331
import n. 450, 573; vb. 268, 450
importance n. 456, 573
important adj. 177, 573, 922
importer n. 728
importunity n. 695
impose vb. 700, 919
imposing adj. 573, 870
imposition n. 963
impossibility n. 405
impostor n. 480, 852, 940
impotence n. 160, 169
impoverish vb. 162, 735
impracticable adj. 407, 576, 628
impractical adj. 449
imprecatory adj. 695, 901
imprecise adj. 431, 503, 916
impregnable adj. 593
impregnate vb. 311
impress vb. 242, 441, 468, 482, 490, 522, 752, 755, 922
impression n. 22, 386, 411, 420, 482, 483, 522, 752
impressionable adj. 242, 753
impressive adj. 529, 573, 755, 844
imprint n. 482; vb. 522
imprison vb. 234, 681, 963
improbability n. 407, 409
improbity n. 932
improper adj. 137, 511, 916, 918
improve vb. 288, 472, 587, 618
improvement n. 288, 550, 587
improvise vb. 142, 544, 603
imprudent adj. 393, 435, 859
impudent adj. 880, 887
impulse n. 282
impulsive adj. 411, 544, 613, 756, 859
impurity n. 582, 584, 847, 952
impute vb. 157, 930
inability n. 160, 628
inaccessible adj. 198, 405
inaccurate adj. 431, 477, 916
inaction n. 610, 616
inactive adj. 174, 281, 607, 612
inactivity n. 174, 612
inadequate adj. 315, 571, 582, 662
in advance adj. 134; adv. 84, 236, 286
inadvisable adj. 578
inane adj. 433, 435
inanimate adj. 367
inanity n. 451
inapplicable adj. 10, 106
inappropriate adj. 10, 106, 137, 500, 511, 578
in arrears adj. 737, 917
inarticulate adj. 513, 515

inattention *n.* 385, 391, 703
inattentive *adj.* 389, 391, 393, 442, 863
inaudibility *n.* 453, 779, 781, 796
inaugural *adj.* 88
inaugurate *vb.* 88, 685
inauspicious *adj.* 137
inborn *adj.* 5, 223
incandescent *adj.* 761
incantation *n.* 984
incapable *adj.* 160
incapacitate *vb.* 160
incapacity *n.* 169
incense *vb.* 893
incentive *n.* 173, 547
incessant *adj.* 114, 138, 145
incest *n.* 952
inch *vb.* 281
incident *n.* 153
incidental *adj.* 8, 60, 139
incineration *n.* 372, 761
incinerator *n.* 763
incise *vb.* 490
incision *n.* 259
incisive *adj.* 255, 506
incite *vb.* 175, 755, 893
inclination *n.* 178, 219, 532, 861
incline *vb.* 178, 219, 319, 530, 861
include *vb.* 58, 98
inclusion *n.* 98
inclusive *adj.* 54, 55, 98
incoherence *n.* 51, 453
incoherent *adj.* 80, 453
incombustibility *n.* 762
income *n.* 705, 741
incomparable *adj.* 21, 579
incompatibility *n.* 14, 106, 637
incompetent *adj.* 160, 576, 628
incomplete *adj.* 55, 57, 315, 582, 660
incompleteness *n.* 57
incomprehensible *adj.* 385, 453, 503
incomprehension *n.* 427
incompressibility *n.* 332
inconceivable *adj.* 405, 856
inconclusive *adj.* 409
incongruence *n.* 25
incongruent *adj.* 10, 19
incongruous *adj.* 15, 17, 25, 106
inconsequential *adj.* 10, 574
inconsiderable *adj.* 33, 574
inconsiderate *adj.* 391, 393, 887, 900
inconsistent *adj.* 14, 17, 25, 51, 106, 412
inconspicuous *adj.* 824
inconstant *adj.* 142, 151, 536, 538, 539
incontinence *n.* 952
incontrovertible *adj.* 408
inconvenience *n.* 578, 635; *vb.* 578, 633, 830
inconvenient *adj.* 137, 576, 578
incorporate *vb.* 52, 58, 98, 302
incorrect *adj.* 431, 500, 511
incorrigible *adj.* 942
incorruptible *adj.* 114
increase *n.* 36, 40, 196; *vb.* 36, 40, 196, 664, 745
incredible *adj.* 579, 866
incredulity *n.* 409, 421, 423, 866
increment *n.* 41
incriminate *vb.* 926, 930
incumbency *n.* 557
incumbent *n.* 190, 986; *adj.* 919
incur *vb.* 179
incurable *adj.* 855
incuriosity *n.* 389
incursion *n.* 300, 645
indebted *adj.* 737, 909
indecent *adj.* 901, 952
indecipherable *adj.* 453
indecision *n.* 151, 409, 536
indefinite *adj.* 243, 453
indefinite space *n.* 182
indemnification *n.* 31, 721
indemnify *vb.* 31, 721, 943
indent *vb.* 254, 259
independent *n.* 653; *adj.* 10, 644, 678
indeterminate *adj.* 243, 409
index *n.* 83, 482, 494, 524
indicate *vb.* 401, 450, 458, 482
indication *n.* 401, 447, 460, 482, 597
indication of danger *n.* 598
indicative *adj.* 401, 450, 482
indicator *n.* 482, 800
indictment *n.* 930, 960
indifference *n.* 391, 393, 541, 612, 754, 863, 933
indifferent *adj.* 389, 391, 393, 533, 541, 612, 666, 754, 863, 933
indigenous *adj.* 190
indignant *adj.* 893
indigo *n.* 815; *adj.* 814, 815
indirect *adj.* 561
indiscernible *adj.* 824

indiscretion *n.* 435. 859
indiscriminate *adj.* 15. 54, 399
indiscrimination *n.* 399
indispensable *adj.* 531, 562
indisputable *adj.* 408
indissoluble *adj.* 54
indistinct *adj.* 243, 503, 515, 781, 799, 824
indistinguishable *adj.* 13
individual *n.* 368, 379; *adj.* 59, 102, 139, 379
individualist *n.* 934
indivisibility *n.* 50, 59
indivisible *adj.* 50, 54, 59, 332
indoctrinate *vb.* 470
indolent *adj.* 174, 612
indubitable *adj.* 408
induction *n.* 300, 410, 685
indulge *vb.* 831, 945
indulgence *n.* 827, 948
industrialist *n.* 728
industrious *adj.* 472, 535, 611
industry *n.* 472, 611, 620
inebriated *adj.* 950
inedible *adj.* 771
ineffable *adj.* 453
ineffably *adv.* 32
ineffective *adj.* 160, 169, 576, 662
inefficient *adj.* 160, 628
inelegance *n.* 511, 845, 849
inept *adj.* 160, 427, 628
inequality *n.* 14, 29
inequity *n.* 14, 916
inerrant *adj.* 408
inertia *n.* 174, 610, 612
inertness *n.* 174
inescapable *adj.* 154, 531
inevitable *adj.* 123, 154, 408, 531, 543
inexact *adj.* 19, 431, 453
inexcitability *n.* 754, 757
inexcusable *adj.* 916
inexhaustible *adj.* 145
inexpedience *n.* 137, 578
inexpensive *adj.* 746
inexperience *n.* 129, 427, 603, 628
inexperienced *adj.* 125, 129, 422, 546, 628, 937
inexplicable *adj.* 158, 453
infallible *adj.* 408, 430
infamous *adj.* 426, 869
infancy *n.* 88, 129
infant *n.* 131; *adj.* 129
infantry *n.* 655
infatuated *adj.* 439, 889
infatuation *n.* 439, 889
infect *vb.* 45, 584, 588
infection *n.* 586
infectious *adj.* 586
infer *vb.* 101, 410, 448, 459
inferable *adj.* 413
inference *n.* 410, 448, 459
inferiority *n.* 29, 35, 580, 679
infernal *adj.* 973
inferno *n.* 973
infertile *adj.* 160, 169
infest *vb.* 314
infidel *n.* 975
infidelity *n.* 703, 952, 978
infiltrate *vb.* 45, 300
infinite *adj.* 78, 114
infinitely *adv.* 78
infinitesimal *adj.* 33, 195
infinity *n.* 78, 114
infirm *adj.* 130, 160, 586
infirmity *n.* 126, 130, 162, 586
inflammation *n.* 252, 835
inflate *vb.* 196, 359
inflated *adj.* 879
inflation *n.* 196
inflect *vb.* 499
inflection *n.* 499, 512
inflexible *adj.* 152, 334, 537, 908
inflict *vb.* 674
influence *n.* 155, 159, 177, 294, 547; *vb.* 155, 177, 547, 573, 755
influential *adj.* 177, 573
influx *n.* 300
in force *adj.* 172, 606
inform *vb.* 460, 470, 597, 624
informal *adj.* 495
informant *n.* 460, 624
information *n.* 401, 426, 460, 465, 525, 624
informative *adj.* 460, 470
informed *adj.* 426
informer *n.* 460, 480, 883
infrequency *n.* 139, 407
infringement *n.* 672, 703, 955
infuriate *vb.* 893
infusion *n.* 309, 311
ingenuity *n.* 21
ingenuous *adj.* 476, 632
ingratiating *adj.* 881, 886, 927
ingratitude *n.* 910
ingredient *n.* 55, 192, 327
inhabit *vb.* 188, 191
inhabitant *n.* 190
inhale *vb.* 308, 359
inharmonious *adj.* 791
inhere *vb.* 5
inherent *adj.* 5, 55, 459
inherit *vb.* 705

inheritance *n.* 711
inheritor *n.* 710
inhibition *n.* 876
inhuman *adj.* 900, 904
inimical *adj.* 25, 883
iniquity *n.* 936
initial *adj.* 88, 155, 602; *vb.* 482
initiation *n.* 88, 300, 302, 470
initiative *n.* 173, 611, 857
inject *vb.* 264, 311
injection *n.* 181, 311, 591
injudicious *adj.* 393, 416
injunction *n.* 626, 671, 691
injure *vb.* 580, 588, 608, 830, 900, 916
injured *adj.* 582
injury *n.* 551, 588, 828, 916
injustice *n.* 916, 955
ink *vb.* 488, 808
inkling *n.* 448
inland *n.* 352; *adj.* 223, 352
inland revenue *n.* 743
inlay *n.* 226; *vb.* 226
inlet *n.* 353
in lieu *adv.* 149
in love *adj.* 889
inmate *n.* 684
in memoriam *n.* 372
inn *n.* 191
innate *adj.* 5, 223
inner *adj.* 223, 224
innermost *adj.* 223
inner self *n.* 751
innocence *n.* 632, 935, 937, 961
innocent *adj.* 632, 935, 937, 951
innovation *n.* 125, 142
innuendo *n.* 928
inoculation *n.* 591
inodorousness *n.* 775
inoffensive *adj.* 757
in operation *adj.* 172, 609
inoperative *adj.* 576, 610
inopportune *adj.* 137, 578
in order *adv.* 79, 605
inordinate *adj.* 572, 945
inordinately *adv.* 32
inorganic matter *n.* 367
in part *adv.* 55
in progress *adj.* 57; *adv.* 288
inquire *vb.* 695
inquirer *n.* 697
inquiry *n.* 394, 695
inquisition *n.* 963
inquisitive *adj.* 388, 394
inroad *n.* 645
insalubrious *adj.* 586
insane *adj.* 435, 439
insanitary *adj.* 586
insanity *n.* 439
inscription *n.* 483, 490, 521
inscrutable *adj.* 453
insect *n.* 373
insecure *adj.* 409, 594
insensible *adj.* 754
insensitive *adj.* 754, 942
insensitivity *n.* 754, 863
inseparable *adj.* 47, 50, 54, 882
insert *n.* 230; *vb.* 40, 230, 311, 483
insertion *n.* 311
inside *n.* 223, 226; *adj.* 223, 681
insidious *adj.* 459, 932
insight *n.* 410, 411, 434
insignia *n.* 482, 677
insignificant *adj.* 451, 574
insincere *adj.* 477, 852, 927, 932, 981
insinuate *vb.* 311, 459, 460
insinuation *n.* 311, 928, 930
insipid *adj.* 162, 507, 666, 768, 843
insist *vb.* 547, 669, 700
insistent *adj.* 506
insobriety *n.* 950
insolence *n.* 644, 672, 873, 880, 924
insoluble *adj.* 332, 405
insolvent *adj.* 706, 735, 739
inspect *vb.* 390, 394, 818
inspection *n.* 390, 392, 394, 396, 818
inspector *n.* 623
inspiration *n.* 411, 755, 976
inspire *vb.* 547, 755, 836, 854, 857
inspired *adj.* 411, 449, 506, 756, 976
instability *n.* 17, 151, 536, 756
install *vb.* 186, 302, 311, 685
installation *n.* 620, 685
instalment *n.* 55, 738
instance *n.* 23, 456
instant *n.* 115; *adj.* 602
instantaneous *adj.* 115
instantly *adv.* 115
instead *adv.* 149
instigate *vb.* 547
instigator *n.* 166, 547
instill *vb.* 470
instinct *n.* 382, 411, 531, 545
instinctive *adj.* 411, 531, 544
institute *n.* 475; *vb.* 88
institution *n.* 475, 620, 988
in store *adj.* 154; *adv.* 567

instruct *vb.* 470, 514
instructed *adj.* 426
instruction *n.* 103, 426, 470, 624, 626
instructive *adj.* 460, 470, 597
instructor *n.* 473
instrument *n.* 565, 609, 619
instrumental *adj.* 563, 565
instrumentalist *n.* 793
instrumentality *n.* 172, 563
insubordinate *adj.* 644, 672
insubstantial *adj.* 4, 328, 331, 333, 451
insufficiency *n.* 315, 571
insular *adj.* 183, 416
insulate *vb.* 226, 761
insult *n.* 869, 923; *vb.* 644, 887, 923
insulting *adj.* 880, 923
insuperable *adj.* 405
insurance *n.* 701
insurgence *n.* 672
insurgent *n.* 672; *adj.* 148, 672
insurmountable *adj.* 405
insurrection *n.* 148
insurrectionist *n.* 148, 672
insusceptible *adj.* 754
intact *adj.* 54, 599
intangible *adj.* 4, 328, 824
integer *n.* 39
integral *adj.* 5, 39, 54, 55, 56, 223
integrate *vb.* 52, 105
integration *n.* 24, 45, 52, 56, 59
integrity *n.* 56, 476, 931, 935, 937
intellect *n.* 382, 434
intellectual *n.* 428; *adj.* 382, 384, 426
intelligence *n.* 382, 426, 434, 460
intelligent *adj.* 382, 426, 434
intelligibility *n.* 452, 502
intemperance *n.* 945, 948, 950
intend *vb.* 552
intended *n.* 698; *adj.* 552
intense *adj.* 173, 752, 759, 805
intensification *n.* 196, 835
intensify *vb.* 36, 173, 196, 481, 835
intensity *n.* 27, 32, 506, 759, 805
intention *n.* 284, 530, 552
intentional *adj.* 530
interact *vb.* 12, 150
intercession *n.* 230, 653, 695, 982
intercessor *n.* 653, 982
interchange *n.* 12, 150, 519, 714; *vb.* 150
interdiction *n.* 691
interest *n.* 41, 388, 755; *vb.* 294, 547, 755, 829
interested *adj.* 388
interesting *adj.* 755
interfere *vb.* 181, 635, 653
interior *n.* 223, 352; *adj.* 223, 352
interjection *n.* 230, 499
interlude *n.* 144
intermediary *n.* 653; *adj.* 230
intermediate *adj.* 30, 90, 230, 560, 563
interminable *adj.* 78, 114, 202
intermingle *vb.* 45
intermission *n.* 92, 144
intermittent *adj.* 92, 139
internal *adj.* 5, 223
international *adj.* 101
internationalism *n.* 903
internecine *adj.* 164, 370
internee *n.* 684
internment camp *n.* 682
interplay *n.* 12; *vb.* 12
interpose *vb.* 230, 653
interpret *vb.* 456
interpretation *n.* 450, 456
interpreter *n.* 456, 974
interrogate *vb.* 394
interrupt *vb.* 92, 137, 144, 230, 887, 923
interruption *n.* 92, 230
intersect *vb.* 221, 246
intersperse *vb.* 230
interval *n.* 92, 109, 144, 200, 267
intervention *n.* 92, 230, 563, 635, 653
interview *n.* 394, 410, 519, 884; *vb.* 394
interviewer *n.* 394
intimacy *n.* 882
intimate *n.* 882; *adj.* 199, 882; *vb.* 450, 459, 460, 482
intimation *n.* 448, 460, 482, 597
intimidate *vb.* 856, 902
intolerance *n.* 537, 900
intonation *n.* 501, 512, 778
intoxicate *vb.* 950
intractable *adj.* 537, 672
intransigent *adj.* 537
intrepid *adj.* 857
intricate *adj.* 251, 453, 503, 633
intrigue *n.* 558, 631; *vb.* 755

intrinsic *adj.* 1, 5, 223
introduce *vb.* 84, 88, 300, 302, 311
introductory *adj.* 86, 88, 602
introspective *adj.* 384
intrude *vb.* 137, 300, 388, 645
intruder *n.* 388, 645
intrusive *adj.* 137, 388
intuition *n.* 411, 531, 753
inundate *vb.* 349, 358, 572
in use *adj.* 606
inutility *n.* 576
invade *vb.* 314, 645, 651
invader *n.* 100, 645, 883
invalid *adj.* 412, 586
invalidate *vb.* 414, 469, 686
invariability *n.* 13, 16, 143, 152
invasion *n.* 300, 314, 645
inveigle *vb.* 927
invent *vb.* 163, 449, 477, 930
invention *n.* 88, 163, 419, 449
inventive *adj.* 21, 449, 627
inventor *n.* 155, 166
inventory *n.* 83
inversion *n.* 220
invertebrate *n.* 373
invest *vb.* 159, 568, 715, 726, 740
investigate *vb.* 388, 394, 396, 818
investigation *n.* 394, 526, 818
investigator *n.* 394
investiture *n.* 685
investment *n.* 718, 726, 740
inveterate *adj.* 152, 545
in view *adj.* 823
invigorate *vb.* 161, 173, 618
invigorating *adj.* 173, 585, 618
invincible *adj.* 161, 661
invisibility *n.* 824
invitation *n.* 394, 695
invite *vb.* 562, 695, 884
invocation *n.* 518, 695
invoice *n.* 742
invoke *vb.* 901, 982
involuntary *adj.* 411, 531, 544
involve *vb.* 9, 98, 155, 450
involved *adj.* 9, 251, 503, 709
inward *adj.* 5, 223
iota *n.* 33
irate *adj.* 893
iron *vb.* 257, 583
ironical *adj.* 455, 853
iron out *vb.* 485
irony *n.* 455, 842, 853
irrational *adj.* 39, 385, 412
irreconcilability *n.* 10, 14
irreconcilable *adj.* 883
irredeemable *adj.* 855, 942
irrefutable *adj.* 408
irregular *adj.* 17, 80, 92, 104, 106, 141, 151, 245
irregularity *n.* 17, 106, 141, 151, 245, 258, 285, 916
irrelevant *adj.* 10, 451, 574
irreligion *n.* 975, 983
irreligious *adj.* 936, 975, 981
irreproachable *adj.* 581, 935, 937
irresistible *adj.* 531, 674, 889
irresolution *n.* 421, 536, 538
irresponsible *adj.* 955
irretrievable *adj.* 706
irreverent *adj.* 923, 981
irreversibility *n.* 152, 855
irrevocable *adj.* 855
irrigate *vb.* 378
irritability *n.* 756, 893, 894
irritate *vb.* 830, 835, 893
irritation *n.* 341, 830, 835
Islam *n.* 974
island *n.* 357
isolate *vb.* 48, 102
isolated *adj.* 885
isolation *n.* 59, 461, 885
issue *n.* 11, 87, 156, 171, 301, 387; *vb.* 358, 464, 522, 600, 731
italic *adj.* 521
itch *vb.* 326, 758
itching *adj.* 443, 861
item *n.* 59, 192, 327
itinerant *n.* 270
itinerary *n.* 269, 460, 559
ivory *adj.* 807
ivory tower *n.* 595, 885

J

jab *n.* 591; *vb.* 282
jacket *n.* 225
jaded *adj.* 617, 841, 865
jagged *adj.* 246, 258, 259
jail *n.* 682; *vb.* 234, 963
jailer *n.* 683
jam *n.* 306
jangle *vb.* 787
janitor *n.* 676, 683
jar *n.* 193, 326; *vb.* 282, 326, 787, 791
jargon *n.* 492, 494

jaundice *vb.* 416, 813
jaunt *n.* 269, 840
jazz *n.* 792
jealousy *n.* **913**, 914
jeer *vb.* 696, 853
jell *vb.* 332
jelly *n.* 306, 364
jeopardize *vb.* 594
jerk *n.* 92, 141, 326, 437; *vb.* 326
jest *n.* 433, 539, 842; *vb.* 842
jet *n.* 278, 358; *vb.* 358
jettison *vb.* 331, 542, 607, 713
jewel *n.* 846, 891
jilt *vb.* 556
jittery *adj.* 326, 756, 856, 894
job *n.* 557, 605, 609, 722
jockey *n.* 270
jocular *adj.* 836, 842
jog *n.* 326; *vb.* 282, 441
join *vb.* 40, 45, 47, 52, 639, 709
joint *n.* 49; *adj.* 180, 709
joint possession *n.* **709**
joke *n.* 842; *vb.* 842
jolly *adj.* 827, 836
jolt *n.* 282, 326, 444; *vb.* 282, 326
jot *n.* 33
jot down *vb.* 441, 483
journal *n.* 116, 441, 464, 483, 524
journalist *n.* 460, 484, 521
journey *n.* 269, 313; *vb.* 269
jovial *adj.* 836
joy *n.* 827, 829, 836
J.P. *n.* 958
jubilant *adj.* 838
jubilee *n.* 109, 878
Judaism *n.* 974
judge *n.* 415, 653, **958**; *vb.* 382, 415, 540, 653, 956, 960
judgment *n.* 382, 398, 410, **415**, 434, 627, 926
judicious *adj.* 392, 398, 415, 434
jug *n.* 193, 682
juice *n.* 309, 343
jumble *n.* 45; *vb.* 45, 82, 399
jump *n.* 316, 320, 321; *vb.* 320, 321
jump at *vb.* 532
jump the queue *vb.* 134
jumpy *adj.* 756, 856, 894
junction *n.* 47, 49, 201, 221
jungle *n.* 374
junior *n.* 35, 131; *adj.* 35, 129, 679
junk *n.* 277
jurisdiction *n.* 622, **956**
jurisprudence *n.* 954
jurist *n.* 959
juror *n.* 958
jury *n.* 958
just *adj.* 915, 917, 954, 966
just deserts *n.* 647, 917
justice *n.* 915, 954, 958
justification *n.* 401, 413, 549, 911, 929
justify *vb.* 410, 413, 911, 929, 961
jut *vb.* 252, 253
juvenile *n.* 131; *adj.* 129, 131
juxtaposition *n.* 94, 199, 201, 238, 397

K

kaleidoscope *n.* 817
keel over *vb.* 220
keen *adj.* 255, 434, 611, 760, 842, 861
keenness *n.* 611
keen on *adj.* 889
keep *n.* 646; *vb.* 377, 567, 593, 599, 673, 702, 707, 712
keep apart *vb.* 48, 200
keep away *vb.* 198, 555, 885
keep back *vb.* 681
keeper *n.* 593, 683
keep in with *vb.* 24, 922
keep off *vb.* 555
keep on *vb.* 145, 516
keep one's temper *vb.* 757
keep order *vb.* 593, 956
keepsake *n.* 441
keep up *vb.* 217, 460
kernel *n.* 90, 224, 306
key *n.* 357; *adj.* 136
keyed up *adj.* 756
kick *n.* 769, 827; *vb.* 282
kick against *vb.* 644
kid *n.* 131; *vb.* 478, 842
kidnap *vb.* 720, 722
kidnapper *n.* 720, 723
kill *vb.* 370, 963
killing *n.* **370**; *adj.* 370, 851
killjoy *n.* 548
kill time *vb.* 612
kiln *n.* 763
kind *n.* 97; *adj.* 882, 886, 899, 903, 935
kindergarten *n.* 475
kindhearted *adj.* 899
kindle *vb.* 755, 761
kindness *n.* 670, 747, 886, 899, 935
kindred relations *n.* **11**
king *n.* 675
kingdom *n.* 183
kingdom of heaven *n.* 972
kink *n.* 251
kinship *n.* 11
kiosk *n.* 730
kip down *vb.* 612

kiss n. 886, 890; vb. 758, 886, 890
kitty n. 709
kleptomaniac n. 440
knack n. 627
knead vb. 335
kneel vb. 319, 922
knell n. 372
knife n. 255; vb. 370
knight n. 870; vb. 868
knit vb. 47, 221
knock n. 282, 782; vb. 282, 782, 926, 928
knock down vb. 164
knock off vb. 144, 370, 659, 722, 744
knot n. 49
know vb. 426, 452, 882
know-all n. 428, 436, 875
know-how n. 426, 627
knowing n. 410, 426; adj. 426, 434
knowledge n. 426, 460, 472
knowledgeable adj. 426, 434, 472
knuckle down vb. 615
Koran n. 976

L

label n. 482, 496, 743; vb. 482, 496
laboratory n. 620
laborious adj. 615, 633
labour n. 615, 619; vb. 615
laboured adj. 511
labourer n. 378, 619
lace n. 49, 846
lack n. 57, 76, 189, 315, 571, 582, 706, 708; vb. 35, 57, 76, 189, 562, 571
lacklustre adj. 806
laconic adj. 504, 517
lacquer n. 225, 365
lactescent adj. 807
lad n. 131
ladder n. 316
laden adj. 56
lady n. 381, 870
lady-like adj. 381, 886
lag behind vb. 287, 315
lagoon n. 353, 354
laid up adj. 586
lair n. 595
laissez-faire n. 610
laity n. 987
lake n. 354, 805
lame vb. 588
lamellar adj. 206
lament n. 839; vb. 839
lamentation n. 839
lamina n. 206
laminate n. 206; adj. 206; vb. 206
lamp n. 800
lance vb. 264
lancet n. 264
land n. 352, 378, 711, 711; vb. 273, 298, 317
landed gentry n. 870
landlady n. 710
landlord n. 710
landscape n. 488
landscape gardener n. 378
landslide n. 317, 662
land travel n. 269
lane n. 559
language n. 492, 512, 514
languish vb. 162, 174, 586, 612, 617, 837
lanky adj. 205, 208
lantern n. 800
lap n. 322; vb. 260, 322
lapel n. 260
lapidary n. 491
lapse n. 110, 144, 147, 315, 431, 938; vb. 110, 147, 869, 936
lap up vb. 390
larceny n. 722
lard vb. 306
larder n. 305
large adj. 26, 32, 194, 204
largesse n. 715, 747
lark about vb. 435
larynx n. 512
lascivious adj. 952
laser n. 797
lash n. 964; vb. 175
lass n. 131
lassitude n. 617, 841
last adj. 89, 659; vb. 107, 112, 143, 145
last-minute adj. 135
last resort n. 595
last rites n. 372
last straw n. 659
last word n. 89, 667, 939
late adj. 117, 124, 135, 369
lately adv. 125
latency n. 459, 824
lateness n. 135
later adj. 85, 119, 123; adv. 121
lateral adj. 238
latest adj. 120, 850
lather n. 363; vb. 583
latitude n. 182, 204, 678
lattice n. 221
laud vb. 982
laudable adj. 925
laugh n. 838; vb. 644, 827, 838, 851, 853, 924
laugh off vb. 393, 477
launch n. 277; vb. 271, 290
launch into vb. 605
launder vb. 583
laurel n. 663
lavender n. 814; adj. 814
lavish adj. 509, 745,

747, 749; vb. 569, 740, 747
law n. 103, 626, 671, 954, 976
lawful adj. 667, 915, 954
lawless adj. 80, 644, 668, 672, 955
lawn n. 374, 812
lawsuit n. 960
lawyer n. 959
laxity n. 51, 335, 393, 668
lay adj. 628, 987
layabout n. 906
lay at vb. 157, 693
lay bare vb. 419, 456, 458, 462
lay claim to vb. 917
lay down vb. 671
layer n. 206; vb. 206
lay hold of vb. 705, 720
lay in wait vb. 463
lay it on vb. 481, 509, 927
layman n. 630, 987
lay-off n. 686
lay on vb. 805
lay out vb. 372, 740
lay-preacher n. 974, 987
lay siege to vb. 645
lay waste vb. 164, 645
lazy adj. 393, 612
lead n. 286, 529; vb. 34, 84, 236, 284, 286, 573, 622
lead astray vb. 431, 936
leader n. 125, 253, 623, 675
leading n. (printing) 522
lead to vb. 155
leaf n. 374, 812
leaflet n. 464
league n. 641, 699
leak n. 600; vb. (escape) 301, 358; (disclosure) 462
lean adj. 205; vb. (tend) 178; (incline) 219
lean on vb. 679, 854
leap n. 200, 320, 321; vb. 320
leapfrog n. 320; vb. 320
leap year n. 109
learn vb. 441, 472
learner n. 428, 474
learning n. 426, 472
lease n. 708, 714; vb. 718, 719
leave n. 614, 690, 921; vb. 299, 556, 600, 660, 687
leave alone vb. 555, 610
leaven n. 142, 331; vb. 318
leave of absence n. 614
leave out vb. 99
leave-taking n. 299
leave undone vb. 393, 660
leavings n. 44
lechery n. 952, 953
lecture n. 470, 518, 926; vb. 470, 514, 926
lecturer n. 473, 514
lecture theatre n. 475
ledge n. 217
ledger n. 742
leer n. 818; vb. 818
leeway n. 182, 200, 678
left n. 241; adj. 44, 241
legacy n. 714, 715
legal adviser n. 959
legality n. 915, 954
legalize vb. 424, 690, 954
legal proceedings n. 960
legal tender n. 731
legation n. 685
legend n. 525
legerdemain n. 478
legible adj. 452
legion n. 75; adj. 75
legislation n. 622, 954
legislative adj. 103, 622
legislator n. 623
legist n. 959
legitimacy n. 915, 954
leisure n. 614, 840
leisurely adj. 281, 614
leitmotif n. 387
lemon n. 813
lend vb. 568, 718, 736
lending n. 718
length n. 26, 198, 202, 400
lengthen vb. 36, 202
lengthy adj. 202, 505
lenience n. 670
lenient adj. 670, 690, 907
lens n. 247, 822
Lent n. 947
leper n. 885
leprechaun n. 970
lesbian n. 106, 953; adj. 952
lesion n. 588
lessee n. 710
lessen vb. 37, 76, 197, 333, 403
lesser adj. 35, 209
lesson n. 470, 472, 597
let vb. 690, 718
let down vb. 445, 874
let fall vb. 319
let go vb. 556, 713
lethal adj. 164, 370
lethargy n. 174, 281, 612, 754
let off vb. 601, 911, 961
let on vb. 462
let out vb. 196, 462, 680, 718
let pass vb. 911
let slip vb. 680, 706, 920
letter n. 493, 522, 523; vb. 482, 493
lettering n. 521, 846

letter of the law *n.* 669, 908
let up *vb.* 144, 176, 281, 616
level *n.* 27, 93, 206, 215; *adj.* 28, 215, 248, 257; *vb.* 16, 257, 400
level-headed *adj.* 757
lever *n.* 217
leviathan *n.* 194
levitation *n.* 331, 984
levity *n.* 331, 836, 859
levy *n.* 743, 917; *vb.* 716, 743
lewdness *n.* 952
lexical *adj.* 494
lexicography *n.* 492, 494
lexicology *n.* 494
lexicon *n.* 83, 494
liability *n.* 179, 701, 737, 919, 938
liaison *n.* 889, 952
liar *n.* 480, 940
libel *n.* 928; *vb.* 928, 930
liberal *adj.* 570, 715, 747, 965
liberated *adj.* 678, 680, 961
liberation *n.* 601, 680, 921
liberator *n.* 905
libertine *n.* 953
liberty *n.* 678, 690
library *n.* 475, 524, 567
librate *vb.* 325
licence *n.* 690
license *vb.* 690, 954
licentiousness *n.* 952
lick *vb.* 758, 963
lick into shape *vb.* 470, 570
lid *n.* 225
lie *n.* 431; *vb.* 185, 477, 932
lie down *vb.* 215
lie low *vb.* 209, 459, 461, 593
lieutenant *n.* 675
life *n.* 107, 159, 368, 557, 611
life-blood *n.* 368
life-giving *adj.* 170
life-guard *n.* 593
lifeless *adj.* 174, 369, 507, 612, 843
lifelike *adj.* 18, 525
life-line *n.* 600
life peer *n.* 870
life science *n.* 375
lifetime *n.* 112
life-work *n.* 557
lift *n.* 316, 318; *vb.* 318
lift restrictions *vb.* 713, 921
ligature *n.* 49
light *n.* 797, 800; *adj.* (not heavy) 331, 333, 344; (of colour) 797, 807
lighted *adj.* 797
lighten *vb.* 634, 797, 834
lighter *n.* 277, 765
light-hearted *adj.* 836
lighthouse *n.* 800
lighting *n.* 797
light music *n.* 792
lightness *n.* 331, 797, 807
lightning *n.* 800
light up *vb.* 755, 797
like *adj.* 13, 18; *vb.* 540, 770, 827, 861, 889
like clockwork *adv.* 140
likely *adj.* 123, 404, 406, 447; *adv.* 406
likely to *adj.* 179
like-minded *adj.* 24, 424
liken *vb.* 18, 397
likeness *n.* 18, 20, 22, 486, 488
like to *vb.* 532
liking *n.* 178, 861, 922
lilac *adj.* 814
lily-livered *adj.* 858
limb *n.* 374
limber *adj.* 335
lime *adj.* 812
limerick *n.* 528
limit *n.* 89, 233, 235, 400, 659; *vb.* 231, 235, 403, 681
limitation *n.* 231, 235, 403, 681
limitations *n.* 700
limited *adj.* 195, 205, 235
limited space *n.* 184
limitless *adj.* 78, 202
limp *adj.* 335, 507; *vb.* 281
limpid *adj.* 502, 802
line *n.* 11, 170, 202, 655, 729; *vb.* 81, 226
lineage *n.* 11, 170, 171
lineal *adj.* 171
linearity *n.* 202
liner *n.* 277
linger *vb.* 112, 135, 281
lingua franca *n.* 492
linguist *n.* 456, 492
linguistic *adj.* 450, 492
lining *n.* 226
link *n.* 9, 49; *vb.* 9, 47, 52, 157, 397
lip reading *n.* 796
lip service *n.* 981
liquefaction *n.* 345
liquefied *adj.* 343, 345
liquefy *vb.* 343, 345, 761
liquescent *adj.* 343
liquid *n.* 309, 343, 347; *adj.* 343, 347
liquidate *vb.* 164, 370, 739
liquidize *vb.* 164
liquor *n.* 343
lisp *n.* 515; *vb.* 515

list *n.* 83, 97; *vb.* 38, 83, 483
listen *vb.* 390, 778, 792, 795
listless *adj.* 174, 281, 612, 863
lit *adj.* 759, 797
litany *n.* 988
literal *n.* 431; *adj.* 456, 493, 494, 977
literature *n.* 528
lithe *adj.* 335
lithographer *n.* 491
lithography *n.* 490
litigation *n.* 960
litter *n.* 576
little *adj.* 33, 195, 203; *adv.* 33
little by little *adv.* 27
liturgical *adj.* 988
live *adj.* 172; *vb.* 1, 188, 191, 368
live apart *vb.* 898
live comfortably *vb.* 734
lively *adj.* 173, 368, 506, 611, 836
livery *n.* 227, 677
livestock *n.* 373
live together *vb.* 889
live up to *vb.* 28, 570
live wire *n.* 611
live with *vb.* 889
llama *n.* 275
llano *n.* 356
load *n.* 26, 192, 330, 830; *vb.* 192, 268, 330
loaf about *vb.* 612
loafer *n.* 281, 612, 697, 940
loan *n.* 718, 719, 736; *vb.* 718
loan-word *n.* 495
loath *adj.* 533
loathe *vb.* 771, 862, 892
loathsome *adj.* 862, 892
lobby *n.* 547, 697; *vb.* 177, 547
local *n.* 191; *adj.* 183, 190, 199
locality *n.* 183, 199
locate *vb.* 186, 284
location *n.* 185, 186
loch *n.* 353, 354
lock *n.* 207; *vb.* 263, 461
locker *n.* 193
locket *n.* 216
lock out *vb.* 144
lock-out *n.* 99, 144
lock up *vb.* 234, 681
lock-up *n.* 682
locomotive *n.* 276; *adj.* 276
locust *n.* 167
lodge *n.* 191; *vb.* 186, 191
lodger *n.* 190, 710
lodging *n.* 186
lodgings *n.* 191
loftiness *n.* 208
lofty *adj.* 208, 318, 870
log *n.* 116, 483, 742, 765; *vb.* 83
logic *n.* 410
logo *n.* 482
loiter *vb.* 281, 612
lone *adj.* 59
loneliness *n.* 59, 885
long *adj.* 182, 202; *vb.* 443, 854, 861, 889
long-distance *adj.* 198
long duration *n.* 112
longhand *n.* 521
longing *n.* 854, 861; *adj.* 861, 889
long-lasting *adj.* 112
longness *n.* 202
long-range *adj.* 198
longsighted *adj.* 820
long-standing *adj.* 112
long-suffering *n.* 757; *adj.* 670
long-term *adj.* 112
long-winded *adj.* 505, 516, 843
look *n.* 242, 818, 825; *vb.* 818, 825
look after *vb.* 392, 593, 599, 676
look back *vb.* 441
look down on *vb.* 923, 924
looker-on *n.* 821
look for *vb.* 394, 554
look forward to *vb.* 443
look in *vb.* 884
looking glass *n.* 822
look like *vb.* 18
look out *vb.* 860
lookout *n.* 593, 683, 818
look out on *vb.* 208, 236
look over *vb.* 208, 818
look through *vb.* 818
look to *vb.* 390, 919
loom *n.* 221; *vb.* 154, 221, 292, 902
loop *n.* 250, 251, 322; *vb.* 251, 273, 323
loophole *n.* 582, 600
loose *adj.* 335, 453, 500, 668, 680, 952; *vb.* 48, 680
loosen *vb.* 262, 319, 601
loot *n.* 663, 724; *vb.* 722
lopsidedness *n.* 29, 245
loquacious *adj.* 516
lord *n.* 675, 870, 967
lord it over *vb.* 34, 667, 669
Lord's Day *n.* 616
Lord's Supper *n.* 988
lore *n.* 472
lorgnette *n.* 822
lorry *n.* 276
lose *vb.* 116, 187, 662, 706
lose consciousness *vb.* 617
lose face *vb.* 869
lose ground *vb.* 289, 315
lose heart *vb.* 837, 855

loser *n.* 662
lose weight *vb.* 205
loss *n.* 43, 189, 369, 569, 706
lot *n.* (many) 26, 32, 75, 94; (fate) 158; (apportionment) 717
lotion *n.* 342, 591
lottery *n.* 553
loud *adj.* 778, 780, 787, 788, 805, 877
loudness *n.* 778, 780, 877
louse *n.* 940
louse up *vb.* 628
lousy *adj.* 580
lout *n.* 437, 630
love *n.* 650, 889, 890, 891, 922; *vb.* 827, 861, 889
love affair *n.* 889
love child *n.* 955
love letter *n.* 523, 890
lovely *adj.* 579, 829, 844
lover *n.* 889
loving *adj.* 670, 889, 966
low *adj.* 35, 209, 210, 781, 837, 849, 869; *vb.* 789
lower *adj.* 35; *vb.* 209, 319, 588, 744
lower class *n.* 871
lowland *n.* 356
lowlands *n.* 209
lowly *adj.* 35, 654, 871, 874
low-lying *adj.* 209
lowness *n.* 209, 210
low opinion *n.* 923
low-priced *adj.* 746
low regard *n.* 923
low spirits *n.* 837
loyalist *n.* 105, 903
loyalty *n.* 673, 702, 919, 931
lozenge *n.* 246, 591
LP *n.* 794
lubber *n.* 630
lubricate *vb.* 342, 365
lubrication *n.* 342
lucidity *n.* 438, 452, 502, 802
luck *n.* 158, 553, 661, 664
lucrative *adj.* 705
ludicrous *adj.* 433, 851
luggage *n.* 711
lukewarm *adj.* 30, 759, 863
lull *n.* 144, 614; *vb.* 267
luminary *n.* 436, 800
luminous *adj.* 797
lump *n.* 55, 252, 332
lump together *vb.* 399
lunacy *n.* 439
lunar *adj.* 329
lunate *n.* 247; *adj.* 247
lunatic *n.* 440
lunch *n.* 306; *vb.* 304
lunch-break *n.* 616
lunch-hour *n.* 616
lune *n.* 247
lungs *n.* 512
lurch *n.* 325; *vb.* 317, 325
lure *n.* 294, 547
lurid *adj.* 805, 952
luring *adj.* 829
lurk *vb.* 459, 461
luscious *adj.* 770, 772, 829
lushness *n.* 168
lust *n.* 861, 889, 952; *vb.* 861, 914
lustiness *n.* 173
lustre *n.* 257, 797
luxurious *adj.* 168, 734, 827
luxury *n.* 572, 664, 734, 747, 827, 945
lynch *vb.* 370, 963
lyric *n.* 528
lyrical *adj.* 528, 790

M

mace *n.* 677
machinery *n.* 565
mad *adj.* 439, 756, 861, 889, 893
madam *n.* 381
madden *vb.* 439, 893
made-up *adj.* 525
madman *n.* 440
madness *n.* 439
magazine *n.* 464, 524
magic *n.* 984; *adj.* 579
magistrate *n.* 958
magnanimous *adj.* 933
magnetic *adj.* 294
magnetize *vb.* 291
magnification *n.* 36
magnificent *adj.* 579, 844, 870
magnify *vb.* 36, 196, 481, 835, 982
magnifying glass *n.* 822
magnitude *n.* 26, 32, 400
maid *n.* 676
maiden *n.* 897; *adj.* 88
mail *n.* 467, 523, 657; *vb.* 268, 523
main *n.* 360; *adj.* 34, 573
mainland *n.* 352
maintain *vb.* 91, 143, 145, 217, 304, 468, 568, 599, 636, 712, 929
majesty *n.* 868, 870, 877
major *adj.* 34, 130
majority *n.* 72, 75, 133
make *n.* 97; *vb.* 155, 163, 242, 705
make advances *vb.* 882, 890
make a face *vb.* 895
make a fortune *vb.* 664, 734
make a go of *vb.* 661

make amends vb. 31, 589, 721, 943
make a mess of vb. 628
make a mistake vb. 431, 500
make an example of vb. 963
make a noise vb. 778
make a speech vb. 514
make-believe n. 477; adj. 449, 477
make certain vb. 408
make clear vb. 452, 456
make do vb. 149, 606, 666
make exceptions vb. 403
make excuses vb. 549
make eyes at vb. 890
make for vb. 271, 284
make friends with vb. 882
make fun of vb. 842, 853
make headway vb. 288
make it vb. 661
make it up vb. 652, 911
make known vb. 460, 462, 464
make light of vb. 393, 418, 574
make love to vb. 889
make nothing of vb. 574
make off with vb. 722
make one jump vb. 444, 856
make one think of vb. 441
make out vb. 288, 441, 452
make over vb. 714
make passes vb. 890
make peace vb. 652
make plain vb. 456, 458, 462
make possible vb. 404
make preparations vb. 602
make progress vb. 288, 587
maker n. 166, 967
make sense vb. 410, 452, 456
makeshift adj. 149, 162, 603
make the best of vb. 757
make too much of vb. 417, 481
make up vb. 58, 163, 449, 477
make-up n. 5, 58, 339, 751, 844
make up for vb. 31
make up one's mind vb. 530, 540
malady n. 586
malapropism n. 433, 497, 500
male n. 380; adj. 380
malevolence n. 900, 936
malformed adj. 245, 582
malice n. 893, 900
malign vb. 608, 900, 928, 936
malleable adj. 151
maltreat vb. 588, 608, 900, 916
mammal n. 373
man n. 133, 368, 373, 379, 380
manage vb. 392, 605, 606, 621, 622, 661, 666, 748
manageable adj. 634
management n. 392, 606, 609, 621, 622, 675
management of animals n. 377
manager n. 623, 675, 728
manage to vb. 661
mandate n. 626, 671, 685
mangled adj. 245
manhood n. 133, 380
mania n. 439
maniac n. 175, 440
manifest adj. 458, 825; vb. 401, 413, 458, 482, 823, 825
manifestation n. 419, 458, 462
manipulate vb. 477, 758
mankind n. 379
manliness n. 380, 857
manner n. 501, 559, 621, 825
mannerism n. 501
manners n. 886
man of learning n. 428, 436, 524
man of many talents n. 629
man of means n. 734
man of the world n. 629
manor n. 191
manpower n. 619
mansion n. 191
manslaughter n. 370
manual n. 460, 524
manufacture n. 163; vb. 163
manufacturer n. 166
manure n. 310; vb. 378
manuscript n. 483, 521, 524
many adj. 72, 75
many-coloured adj. 817
many-sided adj. 151
map n. 269, 460, 486; vb. 400
mar vb. 847
march vb. 91, 269, 696
mare n. 381
margarine n. 306
margin n. 44, 182, 200, 233; vb. 233
marine n. 272; adj. 271, 277, 351

mariner *n.* 272
marital *adj.* 896
maritime *adj.* 271, 277, 351
mark *n.* 97, 202, 235, 400, 441, 483, 521, 522; *vb.* 382, 390, 482, 483
mark down *vb.* 743, 746
marker *n.* 482
market *n.* 96, 559, 726, 730; *vb.* 377, 725, 727
mark up *vb.* 743
maroon *adj.* 810, 811
marooned *adj.* 713
marquee *n.* 225
marquis *n.* 870
marred *adj.* 588
marriage *n.* 47, 896
marrow *n.* 224
marry *vb.* 47, 896
marsh *n.* 355
marshal *n.* 958; *vb.* 81
marsupial *n.* 373
martial *adj.* 651
martyr *n.* 980; *vb.* 830, 963
martyrdom *n.* 828
marvel *n.* 866; *vb.* 866
marvellous *adj.* 32, 579, 844, 866
Marxism *n.* 327
mascot *n.* 984
masculine *adj.* 380
mash *vb.* 335, 364
mask *n.* 225, 461, 463, 549; *vb.* 146, 225, 819
mass *n.* 26, 75, 94, 194, 327, 330, 332, 567, 988; *vb.* 75, 192
massacre *n.* 370, 963
massage *vb.* 341, 758
masses *n.* 26, 32, 871
massive *adj.* 32, 204
mast *n.* 208
master *n.* 34, 131, 436, 629, 675; *vb.* 441, 472, 679
masterly *adj.* 579
masterpiece *n.* 488, 581, 844
master-plan *n.* 558
mastery *n.* 501, 707
masticate *vb.* 304
mat *n.* 225
match *n.* 397, 649, 765, 800, 896; *vb.* 24, 28, 61, 218, 397, 896
matchless *adj.* 34
mate *n.* 882, 896; *vb.* 61, 889
material *n.* 192, 327; *adj.* 3, 327
material existence *n.* 3
materialist *n.* 981
materialistic *adj.* 327, 975
materiality *n.* 3, 327
materialize *vb.* 242, 327, 825, 984
materials *n.* 566
maternal *adj.* 11, 170
mathematics *n.* 38
matriculate *vb.* 83, 483
matt *adj.* 805
matter *n.* 3, 153, 327, 387, 573; *vb.* 573
matter in hand *n.* 605
matter-of-fact *adj.* 508
matter of life and death *n.* 562
mature *adj.* 133, 426; *vb.* 130, 133, 288, 324, 587, 659
maturity *n.* 126, 130, 133, 581
mauve *adj.* 814
maxim *n.* 103, 432, 498, 626
maximize *vb.* 417, 481
maximum *n.* 212
mayor *n.* 675
maze *n.* 409
meadow *n.* 356, 378
meagre *adj.* 33, 57, 205, 507, 571
meal *n.* 306, 840
mean *n.* 30, 90, 560; *adj.* (average) 30, 90; (stingy) 748, 750; (disreputable) 869, 871, 924, 936; (selfish) 934; *vb.* 450, 459, 482, 552
meander *vb.* 247, 251
meaning *n.* 450, 552
meaningful *adj.* 450, 514
meaninglessness *n.* 451, 453
meanness *n.* 750, 887, 934, 936
means *n.* 155, 172, 559, 564, 566, 711, 734
means of punishment *n.* 964
meanwhile *adv., prep.* 107
measure *n.* 26, 27, 400, 559, 609; *vb.* 26, 27, 330, 397, 400
measure for measure *n.* 647
measurement *n.* 27, 194, 397, 400
meat *n.* 306
Mecca *n.* 96
mechanic *n.* 619
mechanical *adj.* 411, 531, 545, 565
mechanism *n.* 565
medal *n.* 482, 663, 872
meddle *vb.* 388, 635, 653
meddler *n.* 388, 821
medial *adj.* 90, 560
median *n.* 30, 90
mediation *n.* 230, 563, 653
mediator *n.* 653
medicine *n.* 181, 591
mediocre *adj.* 30, 35, 580, 666, 843
mediocrity *n.* 35, 580, 666, 843
meditate *vb.* 384, 982

medium *n.* 30, 447, 563, 564, 619; *adj.* 30
medley *n.* 45, 104
meekness *n.* 654, 673, 757, 874, 876
meet *vb.* 94, 153, 201, 296, 419
meet half-way *vb.* 704
meeting *n.* 94, 201, 296, 884
meeting place *n.* 96
melancholy *n.* 828, 837; *adj.* 837
mellow *adj.* 335, 790; *vb.* 130, 587
melodious *adj.* 790
melodrama *n.* 326, 529
melody *n.* 790
melt *vb.* 345, 761
member *n.* 55, 709
member of parliament *n.* 625
membership *n.* 639
memo *n.* 441, 483
memoirs *n.* 116, 441
memorable *adj.* 441, 790
memorial *n.* 372, 441, 483, 663; *adj.* 441
memorize *vb.* 441, 472
memory *n.* 124, 441
menace *n.* 154, 594, 892, 902; *vb.* 154, 902
mend *vb.* 146, 587, 589
menial *n.* 676; *adj.* 35, 881
meniscus *n.* 247
mensuration *n.* 400
mental *adj.* 382
mental block *n.* 442
mental illness *n.* 439
mention *n.* 460, 663; *vb.* 460, 514
menu *n.* 306
mercantile *adj.* 725
mercenary *n.* 655
merchandise *n.* 163, 729
merchant *n.* 728
merciful *adj.* 670, 899, 907, 966
merciless *adj.* 908
mercury *n.* 766, 967
mercy *n.* 670, 715, 907, 911
mere *n.* 354; *adj.* 1, 46
merge *vb.* 45, 47, 52, 639
merger *n.* 36, 45, 52, 639
meridian *n.* 127
merit *n.* 575, 579, 917; *vb.* 917
mermaid *n.* 970
merry *adj.* 827, 836
merrymaking *n.* 838
mesh *n.* 221; *vb.* 221
mesmerize *vb.* 984
mess *n.* 80, 204, 628, 845
message *n.* 460, 465, 523
messenger *n.* 275, 460, 467
Messiah *n.* 967
mess up *vb.* 584, 588, 628
messy *adj.* 584
metal *n.* 367
metallic *adj.* 787
metallurgy *n.* 367
metamorphosis *n.* 142
metaphor *n.* 397, 455, 509
metaphysics *n.* 1
meteor *n.* 329, 800
meteorologist *n.* 447
meteorology *n.* 348
mete out *vb.* 715
meter *n.* 400
method *n.* 79, 81, 558, 559, 606
methodical *adj.* 79, 81, 140
meticulous *adj.* 392, 864
metre *n.* 528
metric system *n.* 400
metropolis *n.* 183
metropolitan *n.* 986
mettle *n.* 534, 857
mew *vb.* 789
miaow *vb.* 789
microscope *n.* 822
microscopic *adj.* 195
mid *adj.* 90
mid-course *n.* 560
midday *n.* 127
middle *n.* 30, 90, 224; *adj.* 30, 90, 224, 560
middle age *n.* 130
middle class *n.* 871
middleman *n.* 688, 728
middle of the road *adj.* 560
middling *adj.* 30, 579, 666
midget *n.* 195
midnight *n.* 128
midpoint *n.* 30, 90
midsummer *n.* 127
midway *adj.* 560; *adv.* 90
midwinter *n.* 128
mien *n.* 621, 825
might *n.* 32, 159, 161
mighty *adj.* 32, 159, 161
migrant *n.* 100, 270
mild *adj.* 176, 670, 757, 759
mildew *n.* 53, 167, 592
mileage *n.* 198
milieu *n.* 8, 183, 229
militant *n.* 611; *adj.* 148, 611, 644, 651
militate against *vb.* 181
milk *n.* 309; *vb.* 377
milk product *n.* 306
milky *adj.* 804, 807
millenium *n.* 70, 109
million *n.* 70
millionaire *n.* 734
mime *n.* 529
mimic *n.* 20; *vb.* 20

mince *vb.* 306
mind *n.* 382, 530; *vb.* 390, 392, 593
mindful *adj.* 390, 426
mindless *adj.* 383
mind-reader *n.* 447
mine *n.* 210, 254; *vb.* 254, 264, 312
mineral *n.* 367
mingle *vb.* 45
miniature *n.* 195, 488; *adj.* 33, 195
minibus *n.* 276
minimal *adj.* 33
minimize *vb.* 418
mining *n.* 312
minister *n.* 467, 623, 625, 986; *vb.* 589, 636, 676, 988
ministerial *adj.* 985
ministry *n.* 985
minor *n.* 131; *adj.* 33, 35, 129
minority *n.* 76, 129; *adj.* 11
minstrel *n.* 528, 793
mint *n.* 23; *vb.* 731
minus *adj.* 189; *adv., prep.* 42
minute *n.* 109; *adj.* 33, 195; *vb.* 483
minutes *n.* 441, 483
minutiae *n.* 102
miracle *n.* 458, 866
miracle-working *n.* 984
miraculous *adj.* 866
mirage *n.* 4
mire *n.* 355
mirror *n.* 822; *vb.* 20, 486
mirth *n.* 836, 838
misadventure *n.* 153, 662, 665
misanthropy *n.* 904
misapprehend *vb.* 416
misappropriation *n.* 608, 722
misbehaviour *n.* 672, 887, 938
miscalculation *n.* 412, 416
miscarriage *n.* 445
miscarriage of justice *n.* 955
miscarry *vb.* 662
miscellany *n.* 45, 104, 527
mischief *n.* 900
mischief-maker *n.* 906
misconception *n.* 416, 431, 457
misconduct *n.* 938
misconstrue *vb.* 416, 457
misdate *vb.* 117
misdemeanour *n.* 938
misdirection *n.* 285, 471
misemployment *n.* 608
miser *n.* 750
miserable *adj.* 828, 837
miserly *adj.* 571, 750, 934
misery *n.* 828, 837, 841
misfire *vb.* 628
misfit *n.* 10
misfortune *n.* 153, 551, 665, 900
misgiving *n.* 409, 421, 833
misgovern *vb.* 668
misguidance *n.* 471
misguided *adj.* 285
mishandle *vb.* 608, 628
mishap *n.* 153
mishmash *n.* 45
misinform *vb.* 471
misinstruction *n.* 471
misinterpretation *n.* 412, 416, 451, 457, 487
misjudgment *n.* 416, 431, 481
mislay *vb.* 187, 706
mislead *vb.* 431, 471, 477, 478
mismanagement *n.* 431, 608, 628
misnomer *n.* 497
misogynist *n.* 904
misplace *vb.* 187, 706
misprint *n.* 431
mispronunciation *n.* 500, 515
misquote *vb.* 457
misrepresentation *n.* 471, 477, 478, 481, 487
miss *n.* 131, 381; *vb.* 137, 315, 391, 393, 660, 662, 706
misshapen *adj.* 243, 245, 845
missile *n.* 290
missing *adj.* 189, 315, 571, 600, 706, 826
missing link *n.* 92, 324
mission *n.* 557, 651, 685, 688, 990
missionary *n.* 903, 974
mist *n.* 4, 346, 358, 363, 803
mistake *n.* 431, 457, 471, 500, 582, 608; *vb.* 497
mistaken *adj.* 285, 431
mistiming *n.* 117, 137
mistranslation *n.* 457
mistreat *vb.* 608
mistress *n.* 675, 889, 953
mistrust *n.* 421; *vb.* 421
misty *adj.* 349, 363, 799, 803
misunderstanding *n.* 25, 416, 431, 457, 642
misusage *n.* 500
misuse *n.* 569, 608; *vb.* 588, 608
mite *n.* 131
mitigate *vb.* 176, 403, 591, 834
mitigation *n.* 636, 834
mitre *n.* 989

mix *vb.* 45, 52, 58, 82, 399
mixed up *adj.* 80, 453
mixer *n.* 884
mixture *n.* 45, 52, 104, 591
mix-up *n.* 80
mnemonic *n.* 441
moan *vb.* 788, 832
moat *n.* 234, 261, 360, 646
mob *n.* 75, 94; *vb.* 175, 888
mobile *adj.* 142, 151, 266
mobilization *n.* 94, 651
mob rule *n.* 668, 955
mock *adj.* 18, 20, 149; *vb.* 853, 869, 924, 928
mocker *n.* 928, 981
mockery *n.* 477, 853
mock-up *n.* 23
modal *adj.* 8
mode *n.* 7, 545, 850
model *n.* 22, 486, 581, 939; *vb.* 23, 242, 489
modeller *n.* 491
moderate *adj.* 176, 560, 746, 757, 944; *vb.* 142, 176, 403, 652
moderation *n.* 176, 944
modern *adj.* 120, 125, 850
modernization *n.* 125, 587, 589
modest *adj.* 33, 176, 418, 508, 517, 874, 876
modesty *n.* 508, 517, 874, 876
modify *vb.* 15, 142, 335, 403
modulation *n.* 142
module *n.* 279
moist *adj.* 347, 349, 358
moisten *vb.* 349
moisture *n.* 346, 349
molecule *n.* 327
mollify *vb.* 176, 335, 652
molten *adj.* 343, 345, 759
moment *n.* 115, 573
momentary *adj.* 113
momentous *adj.* 136, 177, 573
momentum *n.* 282
monarchic *adj.* 870
monastery *n.* 990
money *n.* 731, 734
money-lender *n.* 718
mongol *n.* 440
mongrel *n.* 45; *adj.* 45
monitor *vb.* 394
monk *n.* 885, 986
monocle *n.* 822
monograph *n.* 526
monologue *n.* 520
monopolize *vb.* 707
monopoly *n.* 681
monotony *n.* 16, 91, 841
monsoon *n.* 358
monster *n.* 175, 194, 906
monstrous *adj.* 845, 936
month *n.* 109
monthly *adv.* 140
monument *n.* 372, 441, 483
moo *vb.* 789
mooch about *vb.* 612
mood *n.* 5, 751
moody *adj.* 756, 894, 895
moon *n.* 329, 800
moor *n.* 208, 355, 356; *vb.* 186, 271, 298
moot *adj.* 409
moot point *n.* 387
mop *vb.* 583
mope *vb.* 837, 895
moral *n.* 432; *adj.* 931, 935
moralize *vb.* 470
moral obligation *n.* 919
moratorium *n.* 135
more *adj.* 72
moreish *adj.* 770
moreover *adv.* 40
more than enough *n.* 572
morgue *n.* 372
moribund *adj.* 130, 369
morning *n.* 127; *adj.* 127
moron *n.* 437, 440
moroseness *n.* 895
morphology *n.* 242, 499
morsel *n.* 33, 306
mortal *n.* 368, 379; *adj.* 369, 370, 379
mortgage *n.* 701, 718
mortgagee *n.* 736
mortgagor *n.* 737
mortification *n.* 874, 946
mortuary *n.* 372
mosaic *n.* 817
mosque *n.* 990
motel *n.* 191
moth *n.* 167
mothball *vb.* 135
moth-eaten *adj.* 126
mother *n.* 11, 170; *vb.* 676
motion *n.* 266; *vb.* 482
motionless *adj.* 174, 267
motivate *vb.* 155, 547
motivator *n.* 547
motive *n.* 8, 155, 547
motley *adj.* 17, 45, 104, 817
motor *n.* 276; *vb.* 269
motorcycle *n.* 276
motoring *n.* 269
motorist *n.* 270
motorway *n.* 559
mottled *adj.* 817
motto *n.* 432
mould *n.* 23, 53, 339, 592; *vb.* 146, 242, 489

mouldable *adj.* 242, 335, 654
mount *n.* 316; *vb.* 32, 208, 316
mountain *n.* 208, 316
mourn *vb.* 828, 833, 837
mournful *adj.* 372, 828, 839, 895
mouth *n.* 262, 353
mouthful *n.* 26, 306
mouthpiece *n.* 514, 689
mouth-watering *adj.* 770
movable *adj.* 142, 266, 268
move *n.* 266, 609; *vb.* 172, 187, 266, 268, 282, 290, 299, 693, 752, 755
moved *adj.* 189, 752, 756
movement *n.* 266, 268, 641, 792
move on *vb.* 288
mover *n.* 166
moving *adj.* 752, 755
mow *vb.* 378
mow down *vb.* 370
Mr. X *n.* 497
much *adj.* 75; *adv.* 32
muck *n.* 576, 584
muckraker *n.* 516, 928
mucky *adj.* 584
mud *n.* 355
muddle *n.* 80; *vb.* 82, 399
muddler *n.* 630
muddle through *vb.* 666
muddy *adj.* 355, 584, 803
mud-slinging *n.* 928
muffle *vb.* 513, 779, 785
muffled *adj.* 781, 785
mugging *n.* 645, 722
muggy *adj.* 349, 759
mulch *n.* 364
mule *n.* 537
mull *vb.* 384
multi-coloured *adj.* 817
multifarious *adj.* 104
multilateral *adj.* 246
multiple *n.* 730; *adj.* 39, 72
multiplication *n.* 38
multiplicity *n.* 72, 75
multiply *vb.* 36, 38, 163, 165, 835
multisection *n.* 71
multi-storey *adj.* 208
multitude *n.* 75
mum *n.* 170; *adj.* 513, 517
mumble *vb.* 515
mumbo-jumbo *n.* 967, 983, 984
mummify *vb.* 372, 599
mundane *adj.* 327, 329
municipal *adj.* 183
munificent *adj.* 747
munitions *n.* 657
mural *n.* 488
murder *n.* 370; *vb.* 370
murderer *n.* 167, 370, 906
murky *adj.* 363, 798, 803, 808
murmur *n.* 781; *vb.* 696, 781
muscle *n.* 159, 161
muse *vb.* 384, 449
museum *n.* 567
mush *n.* 364
music *n.* 790, 792
musical instrument *n.* 794
musician *n.* 793
must *n.* 531, 562
mustard *n.* 307
muster *vb.* 94, 651, 857
musty *adj.* 777
mutability *n.* 151
mutation *n.* 142
mute *adj.* 513, 517, 781; *vb.* 513, 779
muteness *n.* 513
mutilate *vb.* 164, 845
mutineer *n.* 672
mutiny *n.* 644, 672, 920; *vb.* 672, 920
mutter *n.* 781; *vb.* 515, 781
mutual *adj.* 9, 12, 150, 180
muzzle *vb.* 681
myriads *n.* 75
mystery *n.* 427, 453, 466
mystic *adj.* 984
myth *n.* 525
mythical being *n.* 970

N

nag *vb.* 893
nail *n.* 255; *vb.* 47
naive *adj.* 131, 422, 632
naked *adj.* 228, 594
name *n.* 482, 494, 496, 868, 872; *vb.* 482, 496
nanny *n.* 683
nanny-goat *n.* 381
nap *n.* 612
narcissism *n.* 875, 934
narrate *vb.* 460, 525
narrative *n.* 525; *adj.* 525
narrow *adj.* 205, 416, 681, 934; *vb.* 27, 681
narrow-mindedness *n.* 416, 537
narrowness *n.* 205, 416, 934
narrows *n.* 205, 353
nasalization *n.* 515
nasty *adj.* 580, 777, 887
nation *n.* 379
national *n.* 190; *adj.* 190, 379
nationality *n.* 379
nationalization *n.* 709
native *n.* 190; *adj.* 5, 190

nativity *n.* 155
natural *adj.* 3, 508, 632, 955
natural history *n.* 366
naturalized *adj.* 100, 190
nature *n.* 5, 58, 329, 366, 751
naturism *n.* 228
naughty *adj.* 672, 901
nausea *n.* 303
nautical *adj.* 271, 277
naval *adj.* 271, 277
navigate *vb.* 271
navy *n.* 655
near *adj.* 154, 199, 419; *vb.* 154, 292
nearby *adj.* 199; *adv.* 199
nearly *adv.* 199
nearness *n.* **199**, 292
nearside *adj.* 241
neat *adj.* 79, 392, 579, 583
nebula *n.* 329
nebulous *adj.* 363, 798, 824
necessary *adj.* 531, 562, 674, 919
necessities *n.* 8
necessity *n.* 408, 531, 543, 562, 674
neck *n.* 205, 352; *vb.* 890
nectar *n.* 770
need *n.* 57, 189, 315, 562, 674, 861; *vb.* 76, 315, 531, 562, 571, 861
needle *n.* 255, 264, 482; *vb.* 830, 893
needlework *n.* 846
needy *adj.* 735, 917
negation *n.* 469
negative *n.* 23, 425; *adj.* 39, 469
neglect *n.* 385, 391, **393**, 546, 610, 660, 662, 672, 703, **920**; *vb.* 391, 393, 546, 607, 660, 662, 672, 703, 920
negligent *adj.* 391, 393, 703, 920
negligible *adj.* 76
negotiable *adj.* 714
negotiate *vb.* 519, 653, 700, 704, 725
neigh *vb.* 789
neighbour *n.* 882
neighbourhood *n.* 183, 199
neighbouring *adj.* 199
neighbourly *adj.* 884, 899
neologism *n.* 494, 495
nephew *n.* 11
nerve *n.* 880
nerveless *adj.* 160
nerves *n.* 439, 856
nervous *adj.* 326, 756, 856, 894
nervousness *n.* 439, 856, 876, 894
nest *n.* 595
net *n.* 221, 463
nether *adj.* 209
netting *n.* 221
network *n.* 221
neurotic *n.* 440
neutral *n.* 653, 656; *adj.* 90, 541, 560, 863
neutrality *n.* 541, 863, 933
neutralize *vb.* 31, 181, 648
never *adv.* 108
new *adj.* 40, 125, 134, 603
newborn *adj.* 131
newcomer *n.* 100, 474
newest *adj.* 120
newly *adv.* 125
newly-wed *adj.* 896
newness *n.* 21, 125
news *n.* 460, 465
newspaper *n.* 464, 483
next *adj.* 85, 119, 199
nibble *n.* 304, 306
nice *adj.* 770, 829, 864
niche *n.* 184, 254
nick *n.* 259, 682; *vb.* 259, 722
nickname *n.* 496, 497; *vb.* 497
nicotine *n.* 308
niece *n.* 11
niggardly *adj.* 750
nigh *adv.* 199
night *n.* 128, 798; *adj.* 128
nightfall *n.* 128, 798
nightmare *n.* 449, 830
nihilist *n.* 167
nil *n.* 74
nimble *adj.* 280, 611, 842
nimbus *n.* 800
nine *n.* 70
nip *n.* 760; *vb.* 197, 203
no *n.* 425
nobility *n.* 34, **870**
noble *adj.* 32, 318, 868, 870
nobody *n.* 74
nocturnal *adj.* 128
nod *n.* 424, 482, 612, 690; *vb.* 325, 482
node *n.* 49
nod off *vb.* 612
noise *n.* 778, 780, 788, 791
noiseless *adj.* 779
noisome *adj.* 777
nomad *n.* 270
nomadic *adj.* 266
nom de plume *n.* 497
nomenclature *n.* 496
nominal *adj.* 496
nominate *vb.* 496, 540, 685, 985
nominee *n.* 688
non-acceptance *n.* 425, 926
non-adhesive *adj.* 51
non aggressive *adj.* 650

nonce *adj.* 495
nonchalant *adj.* 757
non-combatant *n.* 656
non-completion *n.* 660
nonconformist *n.* 106, 425, 979; *adj.* 25, 106, 979
none *n.* 74
nonentity *n.* 2, 574
non-existence *n.* 2
non-expectation *n.* 444
non-flammable *adj.* 762
non-imitation *n.* 21
non-material existence *n.* 4
non-observance *n.* 672, 703, 920
non-payment *n.* 739
non-possession *n.* 708
non-preparation *n.* 603
non-resonance *n.* 785
non-retention *n.* 713
nonsense *n.* 433, 451, 516
non sequitur *n.* 412
non-starter *n.* 662
non-stop *adj.* 138
non-uniformity *n.* 17, 29
noon *n.* 127
no one *n.* 74
noose *n.* 463, 964
norm *n.* 30, 103
normal *adj.* 438, 545
normalize *vb.* 16
normative *adj.* 103
north *n.* 284
nostalgia *n.* 861
nosy *adj.* 388, 394
notable *adj.* 32, 573, 868
notary *n.* 959
notation *n.* 39
notch *n.* 259; *vb.* 258, 259
note *n.* 41, 441, 456, 460, 482, 483, 523, 778; *vb.* 382, 390, 483
nothing *n.* 74
notice *n.* 390, 460, 464, 482, 597, 624, 818; *vb.* 390, 818
noticeable *adj.* 458, 823
notify *vb.* 460, 464, 597, 624
notion *n.* 386, 420, 448, 449
notorious *adj.* 426, 869
nought *n.* 74
noun *n.* 499
nourish *vb.* 304
nourishing *adj.* 585
novel *n.* 525; *adj.* 125
novelist *n.* 521, 524, 525
novelty *n.* 21, 125, 142
novice *n.* 474, 630
now *adv.* 120
nowadays *adv.* 120
no way *adv.* 405
noxious *adj.* 777
nuance *n.* 27
nucleus *n.* 224
nude *n.* 228; *adj.* 228
nudge *n.* 482; *vb.* 482
nuisance *n.* 551, 830
null *adj.* 74
nullify *vb.* 2, 164, 469, 686
numb *adj.* 754; *vb.* 754
number *n.* 26, 39, 72, 499; *vb.* 38, 482
numbering *n.* 38
numbing *adj.* 760
numeral *n.* 39
numeration *n.* 38
numerous *adj.* 32, 72, 75
nun *n.* 986
nunnery *n.* 990
nuptial *adj.* 896
nurse *n.* 676, 683; *vb.* 304, 589, 676
nursery *n.* 378, 475
nurture *vb.* 304, 470, 712
nut *n.* 49, 306, 440
nutrition *n.* 304, 306
nutritious *adj.* 306, 585
nymph *n.* 970

O

oaf *n.* 437
oafish *adj.* 435
oath *n.* 468, 901
obdurate *adj.* 537, 942
obedience *n.* 654, 673, 702, 874
obedient *adj.* 654, 673, 702, 919
obesity *n.* 194
obey *vb.* 105, 654, 673, 874
obituary *n.* 369, 372
object *n.* 327, 552, 716; *vb.* 25, 425, 637, 642, 696, 892, 926
objection *n.* 425, 696, 926
objectionable *adj.* 862, 926
objective *n.* 298, 552; *adj.* 3, 6, 327, 430, 933
obligation *n.* 531, 562, 605, 674, 737, 919
oblige *vb.* 674, 919
obliged *adj.* 909, 919
obliging *adj.* 886, 899
oblique *adj.* 219; *vb.* 531
obliteration *n.* 164, 485
oblivion *n.* 442
oblivious *adj.* 393, 442, 754
oblong *n.* 246
obscene *adj.* 901, 952
obscure *adj.* 453, 503, 798, 799, 824; *vb.* 461, 798, 799
obscurity *n.* 453, 503, 799, 803, 824

obsequious *adj.* 881, 886
observable *adj.* 458, 823
observance *n.* **702**, 878, 977, 988
observant *adj.* 390, 702, 818
observation *n.* 101, 384, 386, 390, 396, 818
observatory *n.* 329
observe *vb.* 105, 390, 392, 673, 702, 818, 878, 988
observer *n.* 460, 821
obsess *vb.* 830, 984
obsessed *adj.* 439
obsolete *adj.* 2, 126
obstacle *n.* 635, 681
obstinacy *n.* 537, 644
obstinate *adj.* 143, 535, 537
obstruct *vb.* 265, 635, 637, 648, 691
obtain *vb.* 1, 661, 705, 716, 720, 726
obtainable *adj.* 292, 404, 464, 705
obtrusive *adj.* 253, 877
obtuse *adj.* 256
obtuse angle *n.* 246
obvious *adj.* 452, 458, 502, 634, 823
occasion *n.* 136, 155, 878; *vb.* 155
occasionally *adv.* 138, 139
occult *adj.* 984
occupancy *n.* 188, 707
occupation *n.* 557, 605
occupier *n.* 190, 710
occupy *vb.* 107, 188, 191, 557, 707
occur *vb.* 1, 107, 153, 384, 430, 825
ocean *n.* **351**
octagon *n.* 70, 246
octave *n.* 70
octet *n.* 70
odd *adj.* 29, 39, 439
oddity *n.* 439, 866
odds *n.* 158
ode *n.* 528
odious *adj.* 892
odorous *adj.* 774, 776
odour *n.* 774
of course *adv.* 408
off *adj.* 53, 240; *adv.* 614
offal *n.* 310
offence *n.* 923, 938, 955
offend *vb.* 892, 923
offender *n.* 906
offensive *n.* 645; *adj.* 295, 777, 845, 869, 880, 887, 892, 923, 936
offer *n.* **693**, 695; *vb.* 532, 693, 715
offering *n.* 715, 943
offertory *n.* 715
offhand *adj.* 544, 887
office *n.* 557, 620, 985
office-boy *n.* 467
officer *n.* 625, 675, 956
official *n.* 623, 675, 683; *adj.* 430, 557, 622, 667
officious *adj.* 880
offset *n.* 31; *vb.* 31
off-shoot *n.* 979
offside *adj.* 240
offspring *n.* 11, **171**
often *adv.* 138
ogle *vb.* 818, 890
oil *n.* 306, 342, 365, 765; *vb.* 342, 365, 547
oiliness *n.* 365, 886
oily *adj.* 257, 365, 477
ointment *n.* 342, 365, 591
O.K. *adj.* 579; *adv.* 79
old *adj.* 124, 126, 130, 606
old-fashioned *adj.* 126
old maid *n.* 897, 951
old master *n.* 488
oldness *n.* **126**, 130
olive *adj.* 812
olive branch *n.* 652
omen *n.* 447, 597
ominous *adj.* 154, 447, 594, 902
omission *n.* 57, 99, 393, 431, 662, 703, 920
omitted *adj.* 189
omnibus *n.* 524; *adj.* 54
omnipotent *adj.* 159, 966
on *adv.* 288; *adv., prep.* 9
on and on *adv.* 114
once *adj.* 124
one *n.* 59; *adj.* 13, 59
on edge *adj.* 443, 856
on end *adj.* 214
oneness *n.* 13, 59
onerous *adj.* 615
one-sided *adj.* 416
one-time *adj.* 118, 124, 687
ongoing *adj.* 288
onlooker *n.* 821
only *adj.* 46, 59
onomatopoeia *n.* 455
onset *n.* 88, 298
onslaught *n.* 175, 645, 649
on time *adj.* 134, 136
ontological *adj.* 1
onus *n.* 919
onward *adv.* 288
ooze *vb.* 301, 319
opacity *n.* 803
opal glass *n.* 804
opaque *adj.* 799, 803
open *adj.* 262, 348, 409, 458, 462, 476, 508, 632, 753, 823; *vb.* 88, 182, 262, 348
open-handed *adj.* 747, 965
opening *n.* 88, 254, 262, 462, 518; *adj.* 88
openness *n.* 476, 594
open up *vb.* 462

opera *n.* 529, 792
opera glasses *n.* 822
operate *vb.* 159, 172, 575, 591, 609
operation *n.* 172, 396, 591, 605, 609, 651
operative *n.* 619; *adj.* 172, 609
ophthalmic *adj.* 818
opinion *n.* 386, 415, 420, 624
opponent *n.* 638, 655, 883
opportune *adj.* 136
opportunity *n.* 136, 406, 678
oppose *vb.* 14, 25, 181, 239, 414, 425, 637, 644, 648, 649, 696, 926
opposed *adj.* 533, 883
opposite *n.* 239; *adj.* 14, 220, 239, 883; *adv., prep.* 239
opposition *n.* 181, 239, 397, 637, 926
oppress *vb.* 669, 837, 900
oppressive *adj.* 330, 669, 759, 900
opt *vb.* 540
optical *adj.* 818
optical illusion *n.* 4
optical instrument *n.* 822
optimism *n.* 417, 854
optimum *adj.* 579
option *n.* 540
opulence *n.* 734
opus *n.* 163, 792
oracle *n.* 436, 447
oral *adj.* 512, 514
orange *n.* 816; *adj.* 816
oration *n.* 518
orator *n.* 514
orb *n.* 249, 329
orbit *n.* 250, 322, 323; *vb.* 274
orchard *n.* 378
orchestra *n.* 793
ordain *vb.* 671, 685, 985
ordeal *n.* 828
order *n.* 79, 81, 85, 93, 103, 622, 663, 872; *vb.* 79, 248, 622, 671, 902
orderliness *n.* 79, 583
orderly *n.* 676; *adj.* 79; *adv.* 79
ordinance *n.* 103, 671, 954, 988
ordinary *adj.* 508, 574, 580, 666, 867, 871
ordure *n.* 310
ore *n.* 367
organ *n.* 563
organic *adj.* 366
organism *n.* 366, 368
organization *n.* 58, 79, 81, 564, 622, 641
organize *vb.* 58, 79, 81, 558, 622
organizer *n.* 558, 623
orgy *n.* 306, 950
orientate *vb.* 284, 545
orifice *n.* 262
origin *n.* 88, 155, 170
original *n.* 23; *adj.* 21, 88, 102, 125, 155, 430
originality *n.* 21, 102, 449
ornament *n.* 509, 844; *vb.* 844
ornamentation *n.* 509, 846
ornate *adj.* 509, 846
ornithology *n.* 375
orphan *n.* 885
orthodox *adj.* 545, 977
orthodoxy *n.* 977
orthography *n.* 493
oscillation *n.* 140, 325
ostentation *n.* 875, 877
ostracize *vb.* 99
other *adj.* 40
otherworldly *adj.* 328, 980
ought *vb.* 919
oust *vb.* 686
out *adj.* 189, 600
outbreak *n.* 88, 175, 645
outburst *n.* 175, 645, 756, 893
outcast *n.* 885; *adj.* 44
outclass *vb.* 29
outcome *n.* 87, 156
outcry *n.* 780, 788
outdated *adj.* 126
outdistance *vb.* 280, 314
outdo *vb.* 314
outer *adj.* 222
outer space *n.* 329
outfit *n.* 227, 568
outflow *n.* 301, 301
outgoing *adj.* 687
outgoings *n.* 740
outgrowth *n.* 252
outing *n.* 269, 840
outlast *vb.* 112
outlaw *n.* 885; *vb.* 963
outlay *n.* 740
outlet *n.* 262
outline *n.* 232, 242, 488, 558, 602, 825; *vb.* 232, 525, 558
outlive *vb.* 112
outlook *n.* 154, 284, 420, 443
outlying *adj.* 222
outmanoeuvre *vb.* 478
outmatch *vb.* 34
outmoded *adj.* 126
outnumber *vb.* 75
out of date *adj.* 126
outpace *vb.* 198, 280
outpost *n.* 198
outpour *n.* 301
output *n.* 163, 705
outrage *n.* 608, 900; *vb.* 830, 887
outrageous *adj.* 175, 433, 851, 869, 880, 936
outright *adj.* 54
outrun *vb.* 198
outset *n.* 88

outside *n.* 222, 232; *adj.* 6, 100, 222, 921
outskirts *n.* 198
outspeed *vb.* 198
outspoken *adj.* 887
outstanding *adj.* 44, 573, 737, 917
outstay *vb.* 112
outstretched *adj.* 202
outstrip *vb.* 29, 198, 280, 314
outward *adj.* 6, 100, 222, 825
outwit *vb.* 478, 631
oval *n.* 250; *adj.* 250
ovation *n.* 878, 925
oven *n.* 763
over *adj.* 44
over again *adv.* 77
over against *adv., prep.* 239
overall *adj.* 98, 101
over and above *adv.* 40
overawe *vb.* 922
overbalance *vb.* 317
overbearing *adj.* 669
overcast *adj.* 363, 798
overcharge *vb.* 745
overcome *vb.* 661
overcompensate *vb.* 31
overdo *vb.* 481, 572, 611, 615, 617
overdraft *n.* 739
overdrawn *adj.* 706, 737
overdue *adj.* 117, 135, 737, 917
overeat *vb.* 945, 948
overestimation *n.* 416, 417
overfeed *vb.* 865
overfill *vb.* 865
overflow *n.* 600; *vb.* 56, 358
overflowing *adj.* 75, 865
over-generous *adj.* 749
overgrown *adj.* 194
overhanging *adj.* 216
overhaul *vb.* 280
overhear *vb.* 795
overjoyed *adj.* 827
overlap *n.* 206, 260; *vb.* 206, 260
overlay *n.* 206; *vb.* 206, 226
overload *vb.* 330
overlook *vb.* 208, 391, 393
overlord *n.* 34
overplay *vb.* 481
overrate *vb.* 416, 417
overrun *vb.* 314
overseer *n.* 623, 675
oversensitive *adj.* 753, 894
overshadow *vb.* 34, 154, 208, 798
overshoot *vb.* 314
oversight *n.* 392, 621, 622
overstatement *n.* 417, 481
overstepping *n.* 314, 918
overtake *vb.* 280
overthrow *n.* 148, 164, 662; *vb.* 148, 164, 220, 414, 686
overture *n.* 693, 792
overturn *vb.* 82, 164, 220, 414
overvalue *vb.* 416, 417
overwhelm *vb.* 414, 572, 661, 866, 922
overwhelming *adj.* 32
overwork *vb.* 611
owe *vb.* 737
owing *adj.* 737, 917
own *vb.* 707
owner *n.* 710
ownership *n.* 707
own up *vb.* 462, 833, 941
ox *n.* 380
oxygen *n.* 348
ozone *n.* 348

P

pace *n.* 269; *vb.* 269
pacesetter *n.* 125
pacification *n.* 176, 650, 652
pacifist *n.* 656; *adj.* 650
pack *n.* 94; *vb.* 56, 75, 192
package *n.* 193; *vb.* 234
packet *n.* 193, 277
pact *n.* 698, 699
pad *vb.* 226
padding *n.* 226, 505
paddle *vb.* 271
paddock *n.* 184
padre *n.* 986
pagan *n.* 975, 983
page *n.* 467, 522
pageant *n.* 458, 529, 825
pageantry *n.* 877
pail *n.* 193
pain *n.* 551, 586, 828, 830; *vb.* 830
painful *adj.* 551, 753, 805, 828
painfulness *n.* 830
pain in the neck *n.* 592, 841
pains *n.* 392
painstaking *adj.* 392, 615
paint *n.* 225, 805; *vb.* 225, 488, 525, 805
painter *n.* 491
painting *n.* 486, 488
pair *n.* 61; *vb.* 61
pal *n.* 882
palatable *adj.* 306, 767, 770
palatalize *vb.* 512
palate *n.* 767
palatial *adj.* 827

palaver *n.* 516
pale *adj.* 371, 806, 807, 812
palindrome *n.* 220
paling *n.* 234
pall *n.* 372
palliate *vb.* 591
pallid *adj.* 806
pally *adj.* 882
palm *n.* 663
palmist *n.* 447
palpable *adj.* 758
palpitate *vb.* 326, 756, 783
palpitation *n.* 325
palsy *n.* 326
paltry *adj.* 574, 580
pampa *n.* 356
pamphlet *n.* 464
panacea *n.* 591
pandemonium *n.* 780, 973
panel *n.* 206, 625, 688, 958
pang *n.* 828, 833
panic *n.* 615, 856; *vb.* 856
pannier *n.* 193
panoply *n.* 657
panorama *n.* 54, 818
pansy *n.* 162, 814, 953
pant *n.* 359; *vb.* 359, 756
pantheism *n.* 974
pantheon *n.* 967
pantomime *n.* 529
pantry *n.* 305
pap *n.* 364
paper *n.* 460, 518, 521, 526; *vb.* 225
paperback *n.* 524
par *n.* 30
parable *n.* 455, 525
parabola *n.* 247
parabolic *adj.* 455, 525
parachute *vb.* 273, 317
parade *n.* 458, 825, 877; *vb.* 91, 458, 877
paradise *n.* 449, 827, 972
paragon *n.* 581, 939
parallel *n.* 397; *adj.* 28, 218; *vb.* 218, 397
parallelism *n.* 218, 397
parallelogram *n.* 218, 246
paralysis *n.* 754
paralyze *vb.* 160, 754
paramount *adj.* 34, 573
paranoid *n.* 440
paranormal *adj.* 447
paraphernalia *n.* 568, 711
paraphrase *vb.* 20, 456
parapsychology *n.* 447
parasite *n.* 373, 612, 881
parasol *n.* 225, 801
parcel *n.* 193, 717; *vb.* 234, 717
parch *vb.* 350, 759
parchment *n.* 521
pardon *vb.* 601, 670, 680, 907, 911, 961
pare *vb.* 203, 228
parent *n.* 11, 86, 170
parenthood *n.* 170
parish *n.* 183, 987
parishioner *n.* 987
parity *n.* 28
park *n.* 234, 559; *vb.* 186
parliament *n.* 625
parochial *adj.* 183
parody *n.* 20, 487, 853
parrot *n.* 20; *vb.* 20
parse *vb.* 499
parsimony *n.* 748, 750
parson *n.* 986
part *n.* 55, 73, 327, 529, 717; *vb.* 48, 55, 637, 642, 898
partake *vb.* 304, 709
partial *adj.* 55, 73, 660, 861, 916
participant *n.* 619, 709
participate *vb.* 605, 639, 709
participation *n.* 188, 639, 709
participle *n.* 499
particle *n.* 33, 195, 340, 499
particular *adj.* 5, 8, 102, 392, 398, 864
particularize *vb.* 102
particularly *adv.* 34
parting *n.* 48, 299, 369, 642
partisan *adj.* 641, 916, 979
partition *n.* 230; *vb.* 48
partly *adv.* 55
partner *n.* 640, 709, 710, 896
partnership *n.* 60, 180, 639, 709
part of speech *n.* 499
part with *vb.* 556, 713
party *n.* 94, 641, 655, 840, 884, 896, 950, 960
party-minded *adj.* 979
pass *n.* 200, 690, 890; *vb.* 107, 110, 310, 313, 424, 427, 954
passable *adj.* 579, 666
passage *n.* 200, 262, 266, 313, 360, 559, 792
pass away *vb.* 369
passé *adj.* 126
passenger *n.* 270
passer-by *n.* 821
pass for *vb.* 18
passing *n.* 369
passion *n.* 752, 889, 893
passionate *adj.* 506, 752, 759, 889
passive *n.* 499; *adj.* 174
pass on *vb.* 714
pass out *vb.* 617
pass over *vb.* 393, 670, 920
passport *n.* 690
pass sentence *vb.* 960

password *n.* 690
past *n.* 124; *adj.* 118, 124
paste *n.* 49, 362, 364; *vb.* 50
pastel *adj.* 805
pasteurize *vb.* 583
pastime *n.* 840
pastor *n.* 986
pastry *n.* 306
pasturage *n.* 305
pasture *n.* 305, 352, 356, 374
pasty *adj.* 806
pat *vb.* 758, 890
patch *n.* 183, 378; *vb.* 589
patched *adj.* 126, 817
patent *adj.* 458, 823
paternal *adj.* 11, 170
path *n.* 559
patience *n.* 757, 911
patient *adj.* 654, 757
patio *n.* 184
patisserie *n.* 306
patriarch *n.* 11, 132, 986
patrimony *n.* 11
patriotic *adj.* 903
patrol *n.* 593, 655, 683; *vb.* 593
patron *n.* 217, 545, 640, 726, 905
patronage *n.* 636, 726
patronize *vb.* 636, 726
patronizing *adj.* 873, 886
patter *vb.* 358, 783
pattern *n.* 23, 58, 79, 339, 488; *vb.* 81
pauper *n.* 735
pause *n.* 92, 144, 267, 612, 614, 616; *vb.* 92, 144, 267, 610, 612
pave *vb.* 225
paw *vb.* 758
pawn *n.* 701; *vb.* 701, 719
pawnbroker *n.* 718
pay *n.* 731, 738, 965; *vb.* 726, 738, 740, 965
payable *adj.* 737, 917
pay attention *vb.* 390
pay back *vb.* 647
payee *n.* 716
paymaster *n.* 733
payment *n.* 726, 738, 740, 965
payroll *n.* 619, 738
peace *n.* 267, 650, 779, 831
peaceful *adj.* 267, 616, 643, 650, 831
peace-maker *n.* 653, 656
peace-offering *n.* 652
peace of mind *n.* 757, 831
peach *n.* 816, 844
peak *n.* 89, 212
peal *vb.* 780, 783
pearly *adj.* 804, 807
peasant *n.* 378, 871; *adj.* 378
pebble *n.* 352
peculiar *adj.* 102, 106, 439
pedagogics *n.* 470
pedagogy *n.* 470
pedant *n.* 537, 864
pedantic *adj.* 392, 702, 864
peddle *vb.* 727
pedestal *n.* 213
pedestrian *n.* 270
pedlar *n.* 270, 697, 728
peek *n.* 818
peel *n.* 225; *vb.* 228
peel off *vb.* 51
peep *n.* 818; *vb.* 818
Peeping Tom *n.* 795, 821
peer *n.* 28, 122, 870
peg out *vb.* 617
pejorative *adj.* 923, 928
pellucid *adj.* 502, 802
pelt *vb.* 280
pen *n.* 184, 234; *vb.* 521
penalty *n.* 963
penance *n.* 943
penchant *n.* 178, 545
pencil *n.* 797; *vb.* 488
pendant *n.* 216, 482
pendulum *n.* 216, 325
penetrability *n.* 335
penetrate *vb.* 300, 313, 441, 452
penetrating *adj.* 384, 434, 769, 787
penetration *n.* 300, 434
pen-friend *n.* 523
peninsula *n.* 352
penitence *n.* 833, 941
pennant *n.* 482
penniless *adj.* 708, 735
penny-pinching *n.* 750; *adj.* 750
pen-pal *n.* 523
pension *n.* 191, 687
pension off *vb.* 686
pensive *adj.* 384, 837
pentagon *n.* 70, 246
pent-up *adj.* 681
penumbra *n.* 798
people *n.* 379, 871; *vb.* 191
pep *n.* 173
pepper *n.* 307; *vb.* 307
perceive *vb.* 382, 419, 426, 452, 795, 818
perceptible *adj.* 458, 823
perception *n.* 382, 384, 752, 818
perceptive *adj.* 398, 426, 434
perch *vb.* 319
percolate *vb.* 300, 319
percussion *n.* 794
perennial *adj.* 114, 138
perfect *adj.* 581, 659, 937, 951; *vb.* 56, 581, 659

perfection *n.* 581, 659, 937, 951
perfectionist *n.* 864
perforation *n.* 262, 264
perforator *n.* 264
perform *vb.* 163, 172, 529, 609, 659, 702, 792, 919, 988
performance *n.* 163, 172, 529, 609, 659, 702
performer *n.* 529, 609, 619, 793
perfume *n.* 776; *vb.* 776
peril *n.* 594
perimeter *n.* 232, 250
period *n.* 109
periodic *adj.* 109, 138, 140
periodical *n.* 464, 524; *adj.* 140
peripatetic *adj.* 269
periphery *n.* 232, 250
periphrastic *adj.* 505
perish *vb.* 164, 369, 826
perishable *adj.* 113
perjury *n.* 477
perk up *vb.* 618, 836
permanence *n.* 112, 143, 152
permeable *adj.* 264
permeate *vb.* 45, 319
permissible *adj.* 954
permission *n.* 424, 690, 692, 921, 925
permissive society *n.* 952
permit *n.* 690; *vb.* 690, 954
permutation *n.* 142
pernickety *adj.* 864
perpendicular *adj.* 214, 248
perpetual *adj.* 78, 91, 114
perpetuate *vb.* 114
perpetuation *n.* 91, 145
perpetuity *n.* 78, 91, 114
perplex *vb.* 409, 633
perplexing *adj.* 409, 633
persecute *vb.* 900
perseverance *n.* 534, 535, 611, 980
persevere *vb.* 145, 535, 611, 648, 980
persist *vb.* 112, 143, 145, 535, 695
persistence *n.* 145, 534, 535
person *n.* 368, 379, 499
personal *adj.* 379, 966
personal effects *n.* 711
personality *n.* 5, 58, 382, 751
personification *n.* 455, 486
personnel *n.* 619, 676
perspective *n.* 488, 818
perspicacity *n.* 434
perspicuity *n.* 502
perspiration *n.* 310
persuade *vb.* 177, 420, 547, 624
persuasion *n.* 420, 547
perturb *vb.* 82
peruse *vb.* 394
perverse *adj.* 936
perversion *n.* 412, 457, 471, 477, 487, 608, 978
perversity *n.* 936
pervert *n.* 953; *vb.* 431, 457, 487, 588, 608
perverted *adj.* 936
pessimism *n.* 418, 443, 855
pest *n.* 892
pester *vb.* 695, 830
pestilence *n.* 167
pestilent *adj.* 592
pet *n.* 373, 891; *vb.* 890
petal *n.* 374
peter out *vb.* 37
petition *n.* 394, 695, 982; *vb.* 394, 695, 982
petitioner *n.* 697, 982
petrify *vb.* 332, 334, 856
petrol *n.* 342, 765
petty *adj.* 416, 574
phantom *n.* 971; *adj.* 971
Pharisee *n.* 981
pharmaceutical *n.* 591
phase *n.* 109; *vb.* 558
phasing *n.* 140
phenomenal *adj.* 866
phenomenon *n.* 153, 825, 866
philanthropy *n.* 899, 903
philosopher *n.* 428
philosophic *adj.* 757
philosophize *vb.* 384, 410
phlegmatic *adj.* 757
phobia *n.* 439
phoneme *n.* 512
phonetics *n.* 492, 512, 778
phoney *n.* 480; *adj.* 20
phosphorescence *n.* 797
photograph *n.* 483, 486; *vb.* 483
photographer *n.* 491
photography *n.* 486
phrase *n.* 494, 498, 792; *vb.* 498
phraseology *n.* 501
physical *adj.* 3, 327, 827
physiognomy *n.* 236
physiology *n.* 366, 375
piazza *n.* 559
pick *vb.* 378, 398, 540
picket *vb.* 144, 696
pickle *n.* 307, 633; *vb.* 599
pick-me-up *n.* 173, 591
pick on *vb.* 830
pick-pocket *n.* 723; *vb.* 722
pick up *vb.* 318, 472, 587, 589, 618
picnic *n.* 269, 306, 840
pictogram *n.* 493

pictorial *adj.* 488, 525
picture *n.* 397, 486, 488, 525; *vb.* 449, 486, 525
picturesque *adj.* 488, 829
piece *n.* 55, 59, 306, 717, 792
pièce de résistance *n.* 581
piecemeal *adv.* 55
pier *n.* 213, 217
pierce *vb.* 264
piercing *adj.* 255, 760, 780, 787
piety *n.* 980
pig *n.* 948
pigment *n.* 805
pigmy *n.* 195
pile *n.* 217, 567; *vb.* 192
pile-up *n.* 282
pile up *vb.* 94, 567
pilfer *vb.* 722
pilferer *n.* 723
pilgrim *n.* 270, 980
pilgrimage *n.* 269
pill *n.* 591
pillage *n.* 722; *vb.* 164, 722
pillar *n.* 152, 208, 217, 939
pillow *n.* 217
pilot *n.* 272, 273, 277, 396; *vb.* 271, 273
pilot scheme *n.* 396, 558
pimple *n.* 252
pin *n.* 255, 264
pinch *vb.* 197, 722
pine *vb.* 861
pink *adj.* 811
pinnacle *n.* 212
pin-up *n.* 844
pioneer *n.* 86, 125, 190; *vb.* 84
pious *adj.* 980
pip *n.* 306
pipe *n.* 308, 360; *vb.* 789
pipe-dreaming *n.* 449, 854
pipeline *n.* 360
piquancy *n.* 506, 769
pirate *n.* 723
pirouette *n.* 323; *vb.* 323
pit *n.* 210, 254, 658
pitch *n.* 234, 321, 365, 400, 512; *vb.* 290
pitfall *n.* 463, 596
pith *n.* 224
pithy *adj.* 432, 450, 504
pitiable *adj.* 907
pitiful *adj.* 33, 580, 907
pitilessness *n.* 908
pity *n.* 907; *vb.* 907, 924
pivot *n.* 90, 217; *vb.* 323
pivotal *adj.* 224
pixie *n.* 970
placard *n.* 464
placate *vb.* 176, 652
place *n.* 184, 185, 186, 559; *vb.* 186
placement *n.* 85, 186
place of business *n.* 730
place of learning *n.* 475
placid *adj.* 267, 757
plagiarize *vb.* 20
plague *n.* 167, 592, 665; *vb.* 314, 830
plain *n.* 356; *adj.* 46, 452, 476, 502, 508, 823
plain living *n.* 946
plainness *n.* 46, 452, 508, 823
plain speech *n.* 452, 502, 508
plaintiff *n.* 930, 960
plait *n.* 49, 221, 251; *vb.* 221, 251
plan *n.* 23, 81, 386, 552, 558, 602, 605; *vb.* 58, 81, 552, 558, 602
plane *n.* 215, 278; *vb.* 215, 257
planet *n.* 329, 800
planetarium *n.* 329
planned *adj.* 543, 552, 558
plant *n.* 307, 374, 620; *vb.* 378
plantation *n.* 374, 378
planter *n.* 378
plants *n.* 366
plaque *n.* 489
plastic *adj.* 142, 151, 242, 335, 768
plastic surgery *n.* 844
plate *n.* 23, 193, 206, 490; *vb.* 225
plateau *n.* 356
platitude *n.* 432, 451
platonic *adj.* 951
plausible *adj.* 404, 406, 420, 825, 929
play *n.* 529, 678, 840; *vb.* 477, 529, 792, 797
play-acting *n.* 852
play down *vb.* 418, 574, 928
player *n.* 529, 793
playful *adj.* 836
play games *vb.* 840
playground *n.* 658
playhouse *n.* 529
play on words *n.* 454, 842
plea *n.* 401, 549, 695, 929, 960
plead *vb.* 410, 514, 695, 959
plead guilty *vb.* 462, 941
pleadings *n.* 960
pleasant *adj.* 827, 829, 840
please *vb.* 829
pleased *adj.* 756, 827, 831, 909
pleased with oneself *adj.* 873
please onself *vb.* 678
pleasing *adj.* 790, 792, 829, 844
pleasurableness *n.* 829

pleasure *n.* 827, 840
pleasure trip *n.* 840
pleat *n.* 260; *vb.* 260
plebeian *n.* 871; *adj.* 849, 871
plebiscite *n.* 540
pledge *n.* 468, 698, 699, 701, 919; *vb.* 468, 698, 699, 701
plenary *adj.* 56
plenipotentiary *n.* 688
plenitude *n.* 32, 56
plentiful *adj.* 32, 75, 572
plenty *n.* 75, 168, 572; *adj.* 168, 570, 572
plethora *n.* 168, 572, 865
pliable *adj.* 335
pliant *adj.* 335, 336
plight *n.* 633
plight one's troth *vb.* 896
plod *vb.* 281, 535, 615
plonk *vb.* 782, 785
plop *n.* 785; *vb.* 782, 785
plot *n.* 148, 184, 234, 378, 525, 558, 631; *vb.* 558, 631
plough *vb.* 261, 378
pluck *n.* 857; *vb.* 228, 312, 378
pluck up courage *vb.* 857
plucky *adj.* 857
plug *n.* 265, 464; *vb.* 265, 464, 468
plug away *vb.* 535, 615
plumb *n.* 330; *adj.* 214
plummet *n.* 321; *vb.* 273
plump *n.* 785; *adj.* 194, 204; *vb.* 540, 785
plunder *n.* 663, 722, 724; *vb.* 164, 722
plunderer *n.* 723
plunge *n.* 317, 321; *vb.* 210, 273, 317, 321, 605
plural *n.* 72; *adj.* 72
plurality *n.* 72
ply *n.* 206; *vb.* 268, 271, 695
pneumatic *adj.* 348
poach *vb.* 306
pocket *n.* 254; *vb.* 705
pocket money *n.* 731
pod *n.* 225
podgy *adj.* 194
poem *n.* 528
poet *n.* 528
poetic justice *n.* 915
poet laureate *n.* 528
poetry *n.* 528
poignant *adj.* 769
point *n.* 184, 233, 246, 255, 387, 400; *vb.* 178, 255, 284, 482
pointer *n.* 482
pointless *adj.* 576, 843
point of time *n.* 115
point of view *n.* 284, 420
poise *n.* 514; *vb.* 216, 330
poison *n.* 167, 592; *vb.* 370, 963
poisoner *n.* 370
poisonous *adj.* 164, 580, 586, 592
poke fun at *vb.* 838
poker-faced *adj.* 754
polar *adj.* 760
polarity *n.* 14, 181, 239, 637
pole *n.* 217
polemical *adj.* 410
police *n.* 956; *vb.* 593, 956
policeman *n.* 593, 956
police station *n.* 682
policy *n.* 558, 621
polish *n.* 225, 257, 510, 797, 848; *vb.* 257, 341, 587, 797
polished *adj.* 257, 510, 583, 848, 886
polish off *vb.* 304, 659
polite *adj.* 886, 922
politic *adj.* 392, 577, 886
political *adj.* 379, 667
politician *n.* 623
politics *n.* 379
poll *n.* 540; *vb.* 38, 540
pollen *n.* 340
pollster *n.* 394
pollution *n.* 584, 588, 608, 952
poltergeist *n.* 971
polygon *n.* 246
polytechnic *n.* 475
pomp *n.* 877
pompous *adj.* 509, 875, 877
pond *n.* 354
ponder *vb.* 384
ponderous *adj.* 330, 511, 573, 843
pooh-pooh *vb.* 393, 924
pool *n.* 354, 709; *vb.* 639
poor *adj.* 169, 507, 571, 666, 735
poorly *adj.* 586
pop *n.* 170; *vb.* 782
Pope *n.* 986
pop music *n.* 792
popular *adj.* 190, 868, 925
populate *vb.* 191
population *n.* 190, 379
pop up *vb.* 825
pore over *vb.* 472
pornography *n.* 952
porous *adj.* 264
port *n.* 241, 298, 595
portable *adj.* 268, 331
portentous *adj.* 447
porter *n.* 275, 676, 683
portfolio *n.* 557
porthole *n.* 262
portion *n.* 55, 73, 305, 306, 717

portrait *n.* 20, 22, 488, 525
portray *vb.* 20, 486, 488, 525
portrayal *n.* 20, 486, 525
pose *n.* 825; *vb.* 23, 394, 621, 852
position *n.* 7, 93, 184, 185, 186, 420, 557; *vb.* 186
position in a series *n.* 93
positive *adj.* 39, 468
possess *vb.* 707, 720, 984
possession *n.* 707, 720, 729, 984
possessive *adj.* 707, 750, 913
possessor *n.* 710, 720
possibility *n.* 404, 406
possible *adj.* 404, 409, 459
post *n.* 217, 467, 523, 557; *vb.* 268, 523
postdate *vb.* 117
poster *n.* 464
posterior *n.* 237; *adj.* 85, 119, 237
posteriority *n.* 119
posterity *n.* 171
postgraduate *n.* 474
post office *n.* 467
postpone *vb.* 89, 135, 920
postscript *n.* 41, 87, 89
postulate *n.* 386, 410, 448; *vb.* 448, 700
posture *n.* 7, 621, 825
pot *n.* 193
pot-bellied *adj.* 194
potent *adj.* 159, 173
potential *n.* 159, 564; *adj.* 159, 404, 459
pothole *n.* 254
potion *n.* 309, 591
pot luck *n.* 158
potter *n.* 491
pottery *n.* 489
pouch *n.* 193
poultry *n.* 306, 373
pounce *n.* 320; *vb.* 321
pound *n.* 184, 234, 325; *vb.* 282, 325, 340, 783
pound of flesh *n.* 669, 908
pour *vb.* 343, 358
pour out *vb.* 301
poverty *n.* 571, 735
powder *n.* 340
powderiness *n.* 340
power *n.* 159, 173, 177, 506, 530, 564, 622, 667; *vb.* 159, 765
powerful *adj.* 159, 161, 173, 177, 506, 667, 671
powerless *adj.* 160, 162
power station *n.* 159
practicable *adj.* 404, 406, 575
practical *adj.* 404, 577
practical joke *n.* 433
practically *adv.* 199
practice *n.* 396, 545, 602, 627, 702
practise *vb.* 470, 591, 602, 702
practised *adj.* 606
practising *adj.* 702, 974, 977, 980
practitioner *n.* 619
pragmatic *adj.* 575
prairie *n.* 356
praise *n.* 909, 922, 925, 982; *vb.* 868, 909, 922, 925, 982
praiseworthy *adj.* 579, 925
pram *n.* 276
prank *n.* 433, 539, 932
prattle *vb.* 451, 516
pray *vb.* 695, 980, 982, 988
prayer *n.* 695, 909, 982, 985, 988
prayerful *adj.* 695, 980, 982
preach *vb.* 470, 514
preacher *n.* 456, 514, 974, 986
preaching *n.* 518, 985
preamble *n.* 86; *vb.* 84
precarious *adj.* 409, 594
precaution *n.* 392, 860
precede *vb.* 84, 118, 134, 286
precedence *n.* 84, 286
precedent *n.* 23, 84, 86, 118, 545, 960; *adj.* 84
preceding *adj.* 84, 118, 134
precept *n.* 103, 626
precinct *n.* 184
precious *adj.* 139
precious stone *n.* 846
precipice *n.* 214
precipitate *adj.* 544, 613
precipitation *n.* 349, 358, 613
precipitous *adj.* 859
precis *n.* 527
precise *adj.* 392, 504, 864
preclude *vb.* 99, 691
precocious *adj.* 134
preconception *n.* 412, 416, 446
precursor *n.* 86, 467
predate *vb.* 117
predecessor *n.* 86
predestination *n.* 531, 543
predetermination *n.* 543
predicament *n.* 153, 633
predict *vb.* 443, 447, 543
predictable *adj.* 447
prediction *n.* 154, 447, 543
predilection *n.* 178, 861

predisposed *adj.* 178, 751
predisposition *n.* 178, 545
predominate *vb.* 34, 101
pre-eminent *adj.* 34
pre-empt *vb.* 134
pre-existence *n.* 118
prefabricated *adj.* 602
preface *n.* 86, 88; *vb.* 84
prefer *vb.* 540, 916
preference *n.* 84, 178, 540
prefix *n.* 41, 86, 499; *vb.* 40
pregnant *adj.* 163, 450
prehistoric *adj.* 124, 126
prejudge *vb.* 416
prejudice *n.* 412, 416, 578, 916
preliminary *n.* 86, 88; *adj.* 86, 396
prelude *n.* 86, 88, 792; *vb.* 84
premature *adj.* 134, 137, 859
premeditated *adj.* 530, 543
première *n.* 88
premise *n.* 410, 448
premises *n.* 730
premium *n.* 663, 724, 965; *adj.* 579
premonition *n.* 411, 597
preoccupation *n.* 384, 390
preoccupied *adj.* 442
prep *n.* 470, 472
preparation *n.* 81, 86, 470, 591, 602
preparatory *adj.* 86, 396, 602
prepare *vb.* 81, 306, 470, 521, 568, 602
prepared *adj.* 443, 532, 602
preposition *n.* 499
preposterous *adj.* 481, 851
prerequisite *n.* 531
prerogative *n.* 34, 667, 917
prescribe *vb.* 671
prescribed *adj.* 954
prescription *n.* 591, 626
prescriptive *adj.* 103
presence *n.* 188, 971
presence of mind *n.* 860
present *n.* 120, 715; *adj.* 1, 120, 153, 188; *vb.* 460, 529, 693, 715, 825, 965
presentation *n.* 413, 458, 460, 501, 529, 693, 715, 825
present-day *adj.* 120, 125
present events *n.* 153
present time *n.* 120
preservation *n.* 599
preserve *vb.* 599, 712
preside *vb.* 956
president *n.* 675
press *vb.* 257, 282, 290, 319, 695, 712, 758
pressed man *n.* 655
pressing *adj.* 674
pressure *n.* 159, 177, 282, 290, 330, 665, 674
pressure group *n.* 547, 697
prestige *n.* 177, 667, 829, 868
prestigious *adj.* 829, 868
presumable *adj.* 406
presume *vb.* 416, 420, 448, 867, 880, 910, 918
presuppose *vb.* 448
pretend *vb.* 20, 449, 477, 549, 852
pretender *n.* 852
pretentious *adj.* 509, 849, 852, 875, 877, 879
pretext *n.* 549
pretty *adj.* 844
prevail *vb.* 1, 34, 101, 112, 661
prevail on *vb.* 547
prevalent *adj.* 32, 75, 545
prevaricate *vb.* 454, 477
prevent *vb.* 99, 181, 548, 635, 648, 691
preview *n.* 118
previous *adj.* 84, 118, 134, 687
prey *n.* 724, 828
price *n.* 579, 743; *vb.* 743
priceless *adj.* 579, 851
prick *vb.* 255, 264, 758
prickly *adj.* 255, 258, 894
pride *n.* 873
pride oneself on *vb.* 873
priest *n.* 986
prig *n.* 951
prim *adj.* 951
primary *adj.* 21, 155, 573
primate *n.* 986
prime *n.* 129; *adj.* 39, 579; *vb.* 470
prime mover *n.* 155, 966
primer *n.* 88, 524
primitive *n.* 190; *adj.* 88, 124, 126, 134
prince *n.* 675
princely *adj.* 870
princess *n.* 675
principal *n.* 473, 675; *adj.* 34, 573
principality *n.* 183
principle *n.* 5, 23, 103, 155, 420, 626
principles *n.* 558, 931
print *n.* 490, 522; *vb.* 464, 482, 490, 521, 522

printer n. 491, 522
printing n. 490, 521, 522
prior n. 986; adj. 84, 118, 134
priority n. 84, 118, 286, 573
priory n. 990
prism n. 246, 805
prison n. 234, 682
prisoner n. 684, 701
privacy n. 461, 885
private adj. 466
privilege n. 34, 678, 872, 917, 921
prize n. 663, 715, 724, 965; vb. 573, 861, 889
pro n. 953; adj. 689
probability n. 158, 406
probable adj. 404, 406
probationary adj. 396, 604
probationer n. 474
probe n. 394, 396; vb. 394
probity n. 931, 937
problem n. 387, 409, 410, 633, 828, 830
problematical adj. 409
procedure n. 103, 545, 558, 559
proceed vb. 110, 266, 288, 313, 558, 661
proceedings n. 483
proceeds n. 705, 716, 741
process n. 172, 559
processed adj. 602
processing n. 146, 163
procession n. 91, 458
proclaim vb. 458, 460, 464, 671
procrastinate vb. 135, 920
procreation n. 163
procuration n. 705
procure vb. 705
prod n. 547; vb. 547
prodigal n. 749, 940; adj. 569, 749
prodigality n. 569, 749
prodigal son n. 941
prodigy n. 866
produce n. 163, 705; vb. 155, 163, 172, 458, 529
producer n. 155, 166
product n. 38, 156, 163, 729
production n. 163, 529
productive adj. 163, 168, 705
productiveness n. 168
profanation n. 608, 901
profane adj. 901, 975, 981, 987; vb. 608, 981
profess vb. 420, 468, 549, 702
profession n. 468, 557
professional n. 629; adj. 557
professor n. 428, 473
proffer vb. 693
proficiency n. 426, 627
proficient n. 629; adj. 627
profile n. 232, 242, 525, 825
profit n. 550, 575, 705, 734, 741; vb. 136, 575, 587, 661, 705
profitable adj. 575, 705, 965
profitless adj. 169, 662
profit-sharing n. 709; adj. 709
profligate n. 953; adj. 749, 952
profound adj. 210, 453
profuse adj. 32, 56, 75, 168, 505
profusion n. 26, 32, 75, 168, 567, 572
prognosis n. 447
prognosticate vb. 154, 447
programme n. 83, 558, 605, 621
progress n. 266, 288, 550, 587, 661; vb. 130, 145, 266, 288, 324, 587, 661
progression n. 36, 85, 91, 288
progressive adj. 91, 125, 148, 288, 587, 605
prohibit vb. 99, 635, 691
prohibition n. 99, 635, 691, 949
prohibitive adj. 99, 691, 745
project n. 558, 605; vb. 6, 222, 252, 253, 552, 558
projectile n. 290
projection n. 6, 253
prolegomena n. 86
proletariat n. 871
proliferate vb. 36, 165, 168
prolific adj. 163, 168
prolix adj. 505
prologue n. 86
prolongation n. 36, 112, 145, 202
promenade n. 269
prominence n. 253, 573, 823, 868
prominent adj. 177, 253, 458, 573, 823, 868
promiscuous adj. 399, 952
promise n. 698, 699, 701, 854; vb. 698, 699, 854
promised adj. 406, 698
promised land n. 96
promontory n. 253
promote vb. 217, 288, 458, 464, 587, 636
promotion n. 464, 587, 636, 727
prompt adj. 115, 134,

280, 557; *vb.* 441, 547, 597, 624
prompter *n.* 441, 547
promptly *adv.* 115
promulgate *vb.* 460, 464
prone *adj.* 178, 179, 215
prong *n.* 255
pronoun *n.* 499
pronounce *vb.* 415, 464, 468, 512, 514, 960
pronounced *adj.* 458, 823
pronouncement *n.* 415, 468, 960
pronunciation *n.* 512, 514
proof *n.* 396, 413, 460, 482, 522
proofreader *n.* 522
prop *n.* 213, 217; *vb.* 217, 318
propagandism *n.* 470
propagate *vb.* 95, 163, 165
propel *vb.* 266, 282, 290
propellant *n.* 290
propensity *n.* 178, 545
proper *adj.* 499, 510, 848, 876, 915, 935
proper noun *n.* 499
property *n.* 711, 729
prophecy *n.* 447, 976
prophesy *vb.* 443, 446, 447
prophet *n.* 447, 449, 467, 974
prophetic *adj.* 976
propitiation *n.* 652, 943
propitious *adj.* 136
proportion *n.* 27, 244, 510, 717
proportions *n.* 194
proposal *n.* 552, 558, 693, 695, 890
proposition *n.* 103, 410, 448, 468, 605, 693, 695
proprietor *n.* 710
propriety *n.* 510, 577
propulsion *n.* 290
prosaic *adj.* 843
proscribe *vb.* 962
prose *n.* 528
prosecution *n.* 930, 959, 960
prosecutor *n.* 930
proselytize *vb.* 146, 470
prosody *n.* 528
prospect *n.* 123, 154, 406, 443
prospective *adj.* 123, 443, 558
prospectus *n.* 83
prosperity *n.* 168, 550, 661, 664, 734
prostitute *n.* 953; *vb.* 608, 952
prostrate *adj.* 215, 319, 922; *vb.* 215
protect *vb.* 225, 392, 593, 599, 646, 801
protection *n.* 392, 593, 595, 599, 646
protectionism *n.* 681
protector *n.* 593, 646, 905
protest *n.* 425, 533, 696; *vb.* 425, 644, 696
protester *n.* 425, 832
protocol *n.* 545
prototype *n.* 23
protract *vb.* 196, 202
protrude *vb.* 252, 253
protuberance *n.* 252, 253
proud *adj.* 644, 877
prove *vb.* 396, 396, 408, 413, 420, 929
proverb *n.* 432
proverbial *adj.* 426, 432
provide *vb.* 163, 304, 564, 568, 602, 715
providence *n.* 550, 748, 966
providential *adj.* 136
province *n.* 183, 557
provincial *adj.* 183
provincialism *n.* 492, 494
provision *n.* 568
provisional *adj.* 149, 396, 403, 700
provisionally *adv.*, *prep.* 111
provisions *n.* 305, 306, 564, 700
proviso *n.* 403, 700
provocation *n.* 755
provocative *adj.* 459, 547
provoke *vb.* 155, 459, 547, 755, 883, 893
prowess *n.* 857
prowl *vb.* 461
proximity *n.* 199
proxy *n.* 149, 688, 689, 689
prudent *adj.* 392, 434, 748, 860
prudish *adj.* 951
prune *vb.* 203
pry *vb.* 388, 394
psalm *n.* 982
pseudo- *adj.* 20, 497
pseudonym *n.* 497
psyche *n.* 382, 751
psychiatry *n.* 382
psychic *adj.* 328, 382, 447
psychology *n.* 382
psychopath *n.* 440
psychotherapy *n.* 382
psychotic *n.* 440
pub *n.* 191
puberty *n.* 129
public *n.* 379, 821; *adj.* 379, 464
publication *n.* 464, 524
public house *n.* 191
publicity *n.* 464
publicize *vb.* 458, 464
public records *n.* 483
public-spirited *adj.* 903

publish *vb.* 458, 464, 465, 522
publisher *n.* 524
publishing *n.* 458, 522
puck *n.* 970
pucker *vb.* 260
pudding *n.* 306
puddle *n.* 354
puerile *adj.* 129, 131, 435
puff *n.* 359; *vb.* 308, 359
puff up *vb.* 875
pugnacious *adj.* 642, 651
pull *n.* 177, 294; *vb.* 291, 294, 390
pull a person's leg *vb.* 478, 842, 853
pull down *vb.* 164, 319, 588
pulling *n.* **291**, 312
pull off *vb.* 659, 661
pull oneself together *vb.* 681, 757
pull one's socks up *vb.* 587
pull out *vb.* 312
pull through *vb.* 589
pull together *vb.* 639
pull up *vb.* 318
pull-up *n.* 191
pulp *n.* 364; *vb.* 364
pulpiness *n.* 364
pulsar *n.* 329
pulsate *vb.* 140
pulsation *n.* 140, 325
pulse *n.* 140, 325; *vb.* 325
pulverize *vb.* 164, 340
pummel *vb.* 282
pump *vb.* 359
pun *n.* 454, 842
punch *n.* 264, 506, 769; *vb.* 282, 482
punctiliousness *n.* 392, 864
punctual *adj.* 115, 134, 136
puncture *n.* 48; *vb.* 48, 255, 264
pungency *n.* 769
pungent *adj.* 769, 773, 774
punish *vb.* 647, 926, 962, 963
punishment *n.* 647, 917, 963
punk *n.* 792
puny *adj.* 162, 195
pup *n.* 880
pupil *n.* 131, 474
purchase *n.* 707, **726**; *vb.* 705, 726
purchaser *n.* 710, 726, 737
purdah *n.* 461
pure *adj.* 46, 581, 583, 935, 937, **951**, 977
purgatory *n.* 943
purge *vb.* 583, 911
purify *vb.* 46, 333, 348, 583, 775, 807
purist *n.* 864
puritanical *adj.* 669, 946, 951
purity *n.* 46, 876, 935, 937, **951**
purloin *vb.* 722
purple *n.* **814**; *adj.* 814
purport *n.* 450; *vb.* 450
purpose *n.* 547, 552; *vb.* 530, 552
purposeful *adj.* 552
purposeless *adj.* 451, 576
purr *vb.* 781, 783, 784, 789
purse *n.* 193, 732
purser *n.* 733
pursue *vb.* 287, 552, 554, 890
pursuer *n.* 554
pursuit *n.* **554**, 557, 605
push *n.* 303, 645; *vb.* 282, **290**, 547, 645
push ahead *vb.* 288
push along *vb.* 299
push around *vb.* 902
push back *vb.* 295
push down *vb.* 319
push off *vb.* 299
push-over *n.* 634, 661
pushy *adj.* 173, 611
put *vb.* 186
put about *vb.* 464
put across *vb.* 460
put aside *vb.* 567, 607
put a stop to *vb.* 144
put asunder *vb.* 898
putative *adj.* 448
put away *vb.* 304, 370, 567, 681
put back *vb.* 589
put by *vb.* 567
put down *vb.* 370
put forward *vb.* 693
put in *vb.* 300, 311
put into *vb.* 456
put into action *vb.* 609
put it to *vb.* 394
put off *vb.* 135
put on *vb.* 225, 227, 477, 529 805, 852
put-on *n.* 852; *adj.* 477, 852
put on a brave face *vb.* 477
put oneself out *vb.* 604, 615
put out *vb.* 578, 762, 830, 893
put over *vb.* 460
putrefaction *n.* 53, 777
putrid *adj.* 584, 588, 777
put right *vb.* 589
put together *vb.* 47, 52, 163
put up *vb.* 191
put-up job *n.* 930
put up with *vb.* 424, 757, 828
puzzle *n.* 409, 453, 466; *vb.* 409

pylon *n.* 159
pyramid *n.* 246
pyre *n.* 372

Q

quack *vb.* 787, 789
quadrangle *n.* 67, 184
quadratic *adj.* 67
quadrilateral *n.* 67, 246
quadrisection *n.* 69
quadruped *n.* 373
quadruple *adj.* 68; *vb.* 68
quadruplet *n.* 67
quadruplication *n.* 68
quagmire *n.* 355
quail *vb.* 858
quake *n.* 326; *vb.* 325, 326, 856
qualification *n.* 41, 142, 403
qualifications *n.* 627
qualified *adj.* 130, 602, 627
qualify *vb.* 142, 403, 570
quality *n.* 5, 58, 579, 935
qualm *n.* 421, 533, 833
quandary *n.* 409, 633
quantify *vb.* 26, 400
quantitative *adj.* 26
quantity *n.* 26, 32, 75, 400
quarrel *n.* 25, 642, 893; *vb.* 25, 642
quarrelsome *adj.* 642, 883
quarry *vb.* 312
quart *n.* 69
quarter *n.* 69, 183; *vb.* 69
quartet *n.* 67, 792
quasar *n.* 329
quash *vb.* 681, 686
quasi- *adj.* 497
quaternity *n.* 67
queen *n.* 675
Queen's English *n.* 492
queer *n.* 106, 953; *adj.* 952
quell *vb.* 37, 89, 652, 681
quench *vb.* 762
query *n.* 394
quest *n.* 269, 388, 394, 554; *vb.* 554
question *n.* 387, 394, 695; *vb.* 388, 394, 421
questionable *adj.* 407, 409, 421, 869, 932
questioner *n.* 388, 394
questionnaire *n.* 394
queue *n.* 91; *vb.* 91
quibble *vb.* 454
quick *adj.* 280, 434, 613, 842
quicken *vb.* 280, 368, 613, 752, 755
quicksand *n.* 355, 596
quick-tempered *adj.* 756
quick-witted *adj.* 842
quiescent *adj.* 267, 459
quiet *n.* 267, 616, 779; *adj.* 517, 616, 650, 779, 781, 876; *vb.* 652, 779
quieten *vb.* 176
quiet time *n.* 982
quilt *vb.* 226
quintessence *n.* 5
quintet *n.* 70
quintuple *adj.* 70
quintuplet *n.* 70
quip *n.* 842
quirk *n.* 539
quisling *n.* 480
quit *vb.* 299, 556, 687
quite *adv.* 56
quiver *n.* 325; *vb.* 325, 326, 756, 760, 856
Quixote *n.* 449
quiz *n.* 394; *vb.* 394
quoit *n.* 250
quota *n.* 305, 717
quotation *n.* 743
quote *vb.* 20
quotient *n.* 38

R

rabbi *n.* 986
rabble *n.* 871
rabid *adj.* 148, 439
race *n.* 11, 554, 613, 649; *vb.* 280, 649
racialist *adj.* 379
rack *n.* 217, 964
racket *n.* 780, 791
raconteur *n.* 525
racy *adj.* 506, 769
radiate *vb.* 297
radiation *n.* 297
radiator *n.* 763
radical *n.* 148, 672, 832; *adj.* 56, 148, 155
radio *n.* 467, 840
radius *n.* 400
rafter *n.* 217
rag *n.* 33; *vb.* 842
rage *n.* 439, 756, 850, 893; *vb.* 756, 893
ragtime *n.* 792
raid *n.* 300, 645; *vb.* 645, 720, 722
rail *n.* 234
railing *n.* 234
railway *n.* 559
rain *n.* 347, 349, 358; *vb.* 358
rainbow *n.* 247, 817
rainfall *n.* 358
rainproof *adj.* 350
raise *vb.* 214, 318, 331, 377
rake *n.* 953
rally *n.* 649, 696; *vb.* 94, 587, 589
ram *vb.* 265

Ramadan *n.* 947
ramble *n.* 269; *vb.* 269, 439, 505
rambler *n.* 270
rambling *adj.* 505
ramification *n.* 297
rampart *n.* 646
ramshackle *adj.* 588
ranch *n.* 377, 378
rancid *adj.* 53, 584, 777
rancorous *adj.* 912
random *adj.* 141, 158, 399, 409, 553
range *n.* 27, 182, 198, 400, 678, 795, 956; *vb.* 81, 182
ranger *n.* 683
rank *n.* 7, 93, 97, 870; *adj.* 777; *vb.* 27, 97
rankle *vb.* 893
ransack *vb.* 722
ransom *n.* 601; *vb.* 601, 680, 721
rant *vb.* 514
rap *n.* 282, 782, 963; *vb.* 282, 782
rape *vb.* 645, 952
rapidity *n.* 280
rapids *n.* 358
rapist *n.* 645, 953
rapport *n.* 643
rapprochement *n.* 643
rapture *n.* 827, 972
rare *adj.* 21, 33, 139, 333
rarefied *adj.* 333
rarely *adv.* 139
rarity *n.* 76, 139, 333, 770
rascal *n.* 940
rashness *n.* 393, 544, 613, 859
rasp *vb.* 341, 787
rat *n.* 480, 538, 940
rate *n.* 27; *vb.* 743
rates *n.* 743
ratify *vb.* 408, 424, 468, 699
ratio *n.* 27, 400
ration *n.* 305, 717; *vb.* 717
rational *adj.* 39, 382, 410
rationale *n.* 157
rationalism *n.* 410, 975
rationality *n.* 410, 438
rat-race *n.* 611
rattle *n.* 783; *vb.* 780, 783
raucous *adj.* 787
ravage *n.* 164; *vb.* 164, 228, 314, 645
ravaged *adj.* 588
rave *vb.* 439, 827, 925
ravenous *adj.* 720, 861, 948
ravine *n.* 200, 210, 254
raw *adj.* 129, 603, 753, 760
raw deal *n.* 551, 916
raw materials *n.* 566
ray *n.* 297, 797
raze *vb.* 164, 319, 485
re *adv., prep.* 9
reach *n.* 182, 198, 202; *vb.* 182, 280, 298, 661
reaction *n.* 147, 156, 283, 647
reactionary *n.* 143, 672, 832; *adj.* 143, 289
read *vb.* 456, 472, 482
readable *adj.* 452
reader *n.* 473, 522, 524
reading *n.* 456, 472, 518
read into *vb.* 457
readjustment *n.* 142
ready *adj.* 188, 532, 602
ready reckoner *n.* 38
real *adj.* 1, 3, 327, 430
realistic *adj.* 18
realize *vb.* 327, 382, 419, 426, 452, 486, 659
really *adv.* 1
realm *n.* 183, 557
reanimate *vb.* 368, 589
reap *vb.* 48, 378, 661, 705
reappear *vb.* 77, 147
rear *n.* 237; *adj.* 237; *vb.* 377, 470
rearguard *n.* 237
rearrange *vb.* 142, 220
reason *n.* 8, 155, 401, 410, 438, 456, 547; *vb.* 382, 410
reasonable *adj.* 176, 406, 410, 746
reasoning *n.* 382, 384, 410; *adj.* 410, 434
reawaken *vb.* 589, 618
rebate *n.* 43, 744; *vb.* 744
rebel *n.* 106, 148, 425, 672; *vb.* 644, 672
rebellion *n.* 148, 644, 672
rebellious *adj.* 148, 644, 668, 672
rebirth *n.* 146, 589
rebound *n.* 147, 283; *vb.* 147, 283
rebuff *n.* 283, 295, 542, 694, 923; *vb.* 295, 542, 694, 923
rebuild *vb.* 165, 589
rebuke *n.* 926; *vb.* 926, 962, 963
rebuttal *n.* 395, 402, 414
recalcitrant *adj.* 537, 648
recall *n.* 441; *vb.* 441, 686
recantation *n.* 538
recapitulate *vb.* 77
recede *vb.* 37, 289, 293
receipts *n.* 705, 716, 741
receive *vb.* 302, 705, 716, 720, 884
receiver *n.* 467, 716, 733
receiving *n.* 716; *adj.* 716
recency *n.* 134

recent adj. 125, 134
receptacle n. 193
reception n. 94, 98, 302, 716, 795, 884, 896
receptive adj. 302, 716, 753
recess n. 144, 254, 614
recession n. 169, 197, 293, 317
recipe n. 626
recipient n. 523, 716
reciprocal adj. 9, 12, 28, 39, 150, 647
recital n. 518, 792
recite vb. 77, 460, 525
reckless adj. 393, 613, 749, 859
reckon vb. 38, 400, 743
reckoning n. 38, 400, 738, 742
reclaim vb. 589, 721
recline vb. 215
recluse n. 885, 946
recognition n. 426, 818, 909, 925
recognize vb. 426, 441, 452, 818, 909, 925
recoil n. 147, 283; vb. 147, 283
recollect vb. 441
recommend vb. 415, 624
recompense n. 31, 721, 738, 965; vb. 31, 589, 738, 965
reconcile vb. 24, 105, 652, 653, 704, 831, 911, 943
reconciled adj. 643, 654, 911
reconciliation n. 24, 650, 652, 911, 943
recondite adj. 453
reconditioning n. 147, 589
reconsider vb. 384
reconsideration n. 441
reconstruct vb. 142, 146, 165, 589
record n. 83, 441, 483, 484, 525, 792, 794; vb. 83, 483, 525
recorder n. 484, 958
recount vb. 525
recoup vb. 31, 721, 738
recourse n. 595
recover vb. 589, 618, 720, 721, 834
recovery n. 147, 589, 618, 705, 720, 721
recreation n. 614, 649, 840
recriminate vb. 647, 930
recruit n. 287, 474, 655; vb. 557, 651
rectangle n. 246
rectify vb. 587, 589
rector n. 986
recuperate vb. 589, 618
recur vb. 77, 138, 140, 441
recurrent adj. 109, 138
red n. 811; adj. 811, 876
redeem vb. 31, 146, 601, 721, 726, 911, 943
redeemer n. 905, 967
rediscover vb. 165
red-letter day n. 878
redress n. 943, 965; vb. 589, 943, 965
reduce vb. 37, 76, 197, 203, 588, 743, 744
reduction n. 37, 42, 195, 197, 527, 744
redundancy n. 505, 686
redundant adj. 505, 572
reduplication n. 62, 165
re-echo vb. 784
reef n. 357, 596
reek n. 777; vb. 759, 777
re-entry n. 274
re-establish vb. 589
refer vb. 9, 157, 450
referee n. 415, 653
reference n. 157, 401, 450
reference book n. 524
referendum n. 450, 540
refill n. 56
refine vb. 142, 333, 587
refined adj. 398, 510, 805, 844, 848, 886
reflect vb. 384, 486, 797, 982
reflection n. 22, 384, 441, 797
reflector n. 822
reflex adj. 411, 531, 544
reform n. 587; vb. 142, 146, 587, 589
reforming n. 165; adj. 903
refractory adj. 537, 672
refrain n. 528, 792; vb. 89, 144, 555, 610, 944
refresh vb. 161, 348, 472, 589, 618
refresher n. 591
refreshment n. 147, 306, 618, 829
refresh one's memory vb. 441
refrigeration n. 599, 762
refrigerator n. 305, 764
refuge n. 463, 595, 885
refugee n. 270, 600, 885
refund n. 31, 721, 738; vb. 31, 589, 721, 738
refurbish vb. 125, 587, 589
refusal n. 469, 542, 691, 694
refuse n. 576; vb. 425, 469, 533, 542, 691, 694
refutation n. 414
refute vb. 402, 686
regain vb. 705, 721
regal adj. 870
regalia n. 482, 677
regard n. 388, 390, 392,

868, 922; *vb.* 390, 420, 868, 889
regarding *adv., prep.* 9
regenerate *adj.* 146, 974; *vb.* 165, 589
regent *n.* 675
reggae *n.* 792
region *n.* 183
register *n.* 83, 116, 302, 483; *vb.* 83, 483
registrar *n.* 484
regress *n.* 147, 289; *vb.* 147, 289, 590
regression *n.* 37, 147, 289, 590
regret *n.* 445, 828, 832, 833; *vb.* 828, 833, 837, 941
regular *n.* 545; *adj.* 16, 79, 81, 91, 138, 140, 244, 545
regularity *n.* 16, 79, 138, 140, 244, 257, 545
regulate *vb.* 81, 140, 621, 622
regulation *n.* 81, 103, 622, 954
rehabilitate *vb.* 589, 721
rehearse *vb.* 77, 525, 602
reign *vb.* 667
reigning *adj.* 870
reimburse *vb.* 31, 721, 738, 965
reinforce *vb.* 161, 173, 226, 468, 646
reinforcement *n.* 196, 217
reinstate *vb.* 147, 589, 721
reissue *n.* 77; *vb.* 77, 125, 464
reiterate *vb.* 77, 140
reject *vb.* 25, 99, 393, 425, 469, 542, 694
rejection *n.* 99, 421, 542, 694, 926
rejects *n.* 44
rejoice *vb.* 829, 838
rejoicing *n.* 838
rejoin *vb.* 395
rejuvenation *n.* 147, 589
rekindle *vb.* 589
relapse *n.* 147, 586, 590; *vb.* 147, 590
relate *vb.* 9, 397, 460, 525
related *adj.* 9, 11, 60
relation *n.* 9, 11, 12, 397
relationship *n.* 9, 889, 952
relative *n.* 11; *adj.* 9, 12, 27
relative quantity *n.* 27
relax *vb.* 144, 176, 267, 335, 612, 614, 840, 907
relaxation *n.* 614, 616, 834, 840
relay *n.* 268; *vb.* 268
release *n.* 460, 465, 600, 601, 680, 713, 911, 921, 961; *vb.* 601, 634, 680, 713, 921, 961
relegate *vb.* 303
relent *vb.* 335, 907
relentless *adj.* 900, 908
relevant *adj.* 9, 573
reliable *adj.* 152, 408, 868, 931
reliance *n.* 408, 420, 854
relic *n.* 44, 371, 441, 483
relief *n.* 149, 176, 181, 253, 489, 591, 601, 618, 636, 834, 899
relieve *vb.* 149, 176, 591, 601, 618, 634, 636, 686, 834, 899
religion *n.* 974
religious *adj.* 392, 974, 982
religious service *n.* 988
relinquishment *n.* 546, 556, 607, 687, 713
relish *n.* 307, 767, 827, 861; *vb.* 767, 770, 827, 861
relocate *vb.* 268
reluctant *adj.* 281, 533, 694, 876
rely *vb.* 420, 443, 854
remain *vb.* 91, 112, 143, 145, 535
remainder *n.* 44
remains *n.* 44, 371, 483
remake *vb.* 77, 165, 589
remark *vb.* 395, 456
remarkable *adj.* 32, 866
remedy *n.* 365, 591, 834; *vb.* 591
remember *vb.* 441, 878
remembrance *n.* 483
remind *vb.* 441
reminiscences *n.* 441
reminiscent *adj.* 441
remiss *adj.* 393, 668
remission *n.* 43, 144, 601, 744, 911, 961
remit *vb.* 268, 601, 715, 911
remittance *n.* 268, 738
remnant *n.* 44, 76
remodel *vb.* 77, 146, 589
remonstrate *vb.* 696
remorse *n.* 833, 941
remote *adj.* 198, 885
remould *vb.* 165
removal *n.* 42, 48, 142, 268, 293, 299, 303, 312
remove *vb.* 42, 99, 187, 228, 268, 293, 303, 312, 485, 680, 720, 722, 826
remuneration *n.* 31, 721, 738, 965
remunerative *adj.* 705, 738, 965
renaissance *n.* 165, 589
rend *vb.* 48
render *vb.* 456, 486, 715, 792

rendezvous *n.* 96, 884; *vb.* 94
renegade *n.* 538
renew *vb.* 77, 125, 142, 165, 589
renounce *vb.* 469, 542, 556, 713
renovate *vb.* 125, 142, 165, 589
renown *n.* 868
rent *n.* 743; *adj.* 48, 262; *vb.* 191, 719
renunciation *n.* 469, 538, 542, 556, 713
reoccurrence *n.* 77, 138
reorganization *n.* 81, 142
reorganize *vb.* 142, 587, 589
repair *n.* 589; *vb.* 589, 721
reparation *n.* 31, 589, 721, 943, 965
repartee *n.* 395, 519, 842
repatriation *n.* 721
repay *vb.* 647, 721, 738, 943
repeal *n.* 686; *vb.* 686
repeat *n.* 77; *vb.* 20, 62, 77, 138, 140, 165
repeated and prolonged sound *n.* 783
repel *vb.* 295, 648, 885, 892
repent *vb.* 833, 907, 941
repercussion *n.* 156, 283
repetition *n.* 62, 77, 140, 505
repetitive *adj.* 77, 841
replace *vb.* 147, 149, 187, 686
replay *n.* 77
replenish *vb.* 56, 568
replete *adj.* 56, 570, 865
replica *n.* 20, 22
reply *n.* 283, 395, 402, 523; *vb.* 395
report *n.* 415, 460, 465, 468, 483, 523, 525, 778, 782; *vb.* 460, 465, 483, 521, 525
reporter *n.* 460, 524
repose *n.* 612, 616; *vb.* 215
repository *n.* 732
reprehensible *adj.* 926
represent *vb.* 20, 486, 488, 525, 685, 689
representation *n.* 20, 22, 486, 488, 489, 525, 558, 685
representative *n.* 625, 688, 689; *adj.* 18, 101, 482, 486
repress *vb.* 679, 681, 691, 779
reprieve *n.* 135, 601, 911, 961; *vb.* 907, 911, 961
reprimand *n.* 926, 963; *vb.* 926, 963
reprint *n.* 20, 22, 77, 524; *vb.* 165, 464
reprisal *n.* 647, 912
reproach *n.* 869, 926; *vb.* 926
reproduce *vb.* 20, 163, 165, 486
reproduction *n.* 22, 77, 163, 165, 486
reprove *vb.* 926, 930, 963
reptile *n.* 373
repudiate *vb.* 414, 469, 542, 686, 694
repugnance *n.* 637, 862, 883, 892
repugnant *adj.* 862, 892, 936
repulse *vb.* 295, 694
repulsion *n.* 295, 892
repulsive *adj.* 295, 777, 892
reputable *adj.* 177, 868, 931
reputation *n.* 177, 868
repute *n.* 868
request *n.* 394, 671, 695, 982; *vb.* 394, 671, 695
requiem *n.* 372, 839
require *vb.* 531, 562, 571, 671, 674
requirement *n.* 8, 315, 562, 671
requital *n.* 31, 647, 912, 943
rescue *n.* 589, 600, 601, 680; *vb.* 589, 601, 636, 680
research *n.* 396; *vb.* 396
researcher *n.* 394, 396, 428
resemblance *n.* 18, 105, 397
resentful *adj.* 883, 893, 900, 913
resentment *n.* 832, 893, 913, 914
reservation *n.* 403, 421, 425, 700
reserve *n.* 149, 198, 517, 568, 681, 876; *adj.* 149; *vb.* 712
reserves *n.* 564, 567, 731
reservoir *n.* 193, 354, 567
reside *vb.* 188, 191
residence *n.* 188, 191, 707
resident *n.* 190, 710; *adj.* 188
residual *adj.* 44
residue *n.* 44
resign *vb.* 654, 687
resignation *n.* 654, 687, 757
resilience *n.* 336
resin *n.* 365; *vb.* 365
resist *vb.* 295, 537, 637, 644, 648, 694

resistance *n.* 181, **648**
resistant *adj.* 337
resolute *adj.* 152, 534, 857
resolution *n.* 415, 530, **534**, 611, 857
resolve *n.* 534; *vb.* 53, 530, 534, 552
resonance *n.* 778, **784**
resort to *vb.* 606
resounding *n.* 784; *adj.* 780
resourceful *adj.* 449
resources *n.* 564, 566, 711, 734
respect *n.* 868, 886, **922**; *vb.* 868, 922
respectful *adj.* 673, 922
respiration *n.* 359
respite *n.* 135, 144, 614
respond *vb.* 283, 395, 752, 909
responsibility *n.* 179, 557, 701, 917, 919, 956
responsible *adj.* 133, 179, 702, 919, 956
responsive *adj.* 395, 909
rest *n.* 44, 92, 144, 213, 217, **267**, 610, 612, 614, 616; *vb.* 144, 267, 612, 614, 616
restate *vb.* 77, 456
restaurant *n.* 191
restitution *n.* 31, 147, 589, **721**, 738, 943
restless *adj.* 266, 611, 756, 832
restoration *n.* 147, **589**, 618, 721
restorative, *n.* 591; *adj.* 585, 589, 591
restore *vb.* 147, 589, 591, 618, 680, 721, 911
restrain *vb.* 37, 144, 176, 403, 635, **681**, 691
restrained *adj.* 176, 508, 517, 681, 876, 944
restraint *n.* 37, 176, 281, 548, 635, **681**, 876, 944
restrict *vb.* 99, 231, 235, 403, 635, 681, 691
restrictions *n.* 700
result *n.* 44, 87, 156, 163, 460; *vb.* 85, 119, 156
resumé *n.* 527; *vb.* 589
resumption *n.* 77, 589
resurgence *n.* 589
resurrection *n.* 147, 165, 589, 972
resuscitate *vb.* 589, 618
retail *vb.* 727
retailer *n.* 727, 728
retain *vb.* 441, 707, 712
retaliate *vb.* 647, 912, 963
retaliation *n.* 395, **647**, 912
retard *vb.* 135, 281, 635
retarded *adj.* 435
retch *vb.* 303
retention *n.* 441, **712**
reticent *adj.* 466, 517, 681, 876
retinue *n.* 91
retire *vb.* 289, 293, 299, 687
retired *adj.* 118, 124, 687
retirement *n.* 89, 293, 687, 826
retiring *adj.* 517, 876, 885
retort *n.* 395, 647; *vb.* 395, 647
retrace *vb.* 441
retraction *n.* 538, 686
retreat *n.* 289, **293**, 299, 463, 595, 600, 885; *vb.* 289, 293, 556
retribution *n.* 647, 943, 963
retrieve *vb.* 589, 601, 705, 720, 721
retrograde *adj.* 289
return *n.* 147, 289, 298, 721; *vb.* 147, 163, 298, 589, 647, 721
reunion *n.* 47, 884
revalue *vb.* 745
reveal *vb.* 228, 262, 419, 456, 458, 462
revealed *adj.* 976
revealing *adj.* 228, 802
revel *vb.* 827, 838, 840
revelation *n.* 419, 420, 458, 462, 464, 974, **976**
revenge *n.* 647, **912**; *vb.* 647
revengeful *adj.* 908, 912
revenue *n.* 741
reverberate *vb.* 283, 784
reverberation *n.* 283, 778
revere *vb.* 868, 922, 982
reverence *n.* 922, 980, 982
reverend *n.* 986
reversal *n.* 147, 220, 289, 538, 686
reverse *n.* 237, 239; *adj.* 14, 289; *vb.* 147, 220, 686
reversion *n.* 147, 220, 590
review *n.* 394, 415, 456, 524, 526; *vb.* 394, 415, 441, 472, 526
reviewer *n.* 456, 524, 526
revile *vb.* 853, 901, 928
revise *vb.* 142, 472, 587
revitalize *vb.* 589
revival *n.* 147, 165, 589
revive *vb.* 77, 165, 368, 441, 589, 618
revoke *vb.* 538, 686
revolt *n.* 148, 644, 672; *vb.* 148, 644, 672
revolting *adj.* 148, 771, 892

revolution *n.* 148, 323, 644, 672
revolve *vb.* 140, 323
revolver *n.* 657
revue *n.* 529
reward *n.* 663, 705, 909, 917, 965; *vb.* 738, 909, 965
reword *vb.* 77, 456, 498
rhetorical *adj.* 455, 509
rhetorician *n.* 514
rhombus *n.* 246
rhyme *n.* 528; *vb.* 528
rhythm *n.* 140, 510, 512, 528
rhythmical *adj.* 790
rib *vb.* 842
ribbon *n.* 49, 207, 663, 846, 872
rich *adj.* 163, 168, 509, 664, 734, 770, 772, 790, 805
riches *n.* 664, 711, 734
rickshaw *n.* 276
rid *vb.* 634
riddle *n.* 466; *vb.* 264
ride *n.* 269; *vb.* 269
rider *n.* 41, 270
ridge *n.* 252, 357
ridicule *n.* 853, 924; *vb.* 788, 842, 853, 869, 924, 928
ridiculousness *n.* 433, 851
riding *n.* 269
rifle *n.* 657; *vb.* 722
rift *n.* 200, 642
rig *vb.* 568
right *n.* 240, 667, 915, 917, 929, 954, 956; *adj.* 240, 430, 915, 931, 954, 977
right angle *n.* 246
righteous *adj.* 915, 935
right-hand man *n.* 624, 640, 676, 689
right side *n.* 240
rigid *adj.* 334, 669, 946
rigorous *adj.* 392, 669, 864, 946
rigour *n.* 669
riled *adj.* 893, 894
rim *n.* 233, 250; *vb.* 233
rind *n.* 225
ring *n.* 250; *vb.* 231, 322, 460, 482, 784
ringing *n.* 778, 784; *adj.* 780, 784
riot *n.* 80, 672
ripe *adj.* 364
ripen *vb.* 659
ripple *n.* 325, 358, 781; *vb.* 251, 358, 783
rise *n.* 36, 41, 208, 316, 320; *vb.* 32, 34, 36, 88, 214, 252, 273, 316, 320
risk *n.* 553, 594; *vb.* 158, 553, 594, 604, 718, 857
risqué *adj.* 952
rite *n.* 988
ritual *n.* 16, 545, 988; *adj.* 988
rival *n.* 638, 883; *vb.* 28
rivalry *n.* 642, 913
river *n.* 358
riverside *adj.* 352
road *n.* 559
roamer *n.* 270
roaming *n.* 269
roar *n.* 780, 838; *vb.* 175, 359, 780, 789, 838, 893
roast *vb.* 306, 759
rob *vb.* 645, 722
robber *n.* 723
robbery *n.* 722
robe *n.* 225
robes *n.* 989
robot *n.* 565
robust *adj.* 143, 161, 337, 585
rock *n.* 152, 330, 352, 367, 792; *vb.* 325, 326
rocket *n.* 279; *vb.* 316
rod *n.* 677, 677, 964
rodent *n.* 373
rogue *n.* 480, 723, 906, 940
roguish *adj.* 477
role *n.* 529, 557
roll *n.* 83, 249, 306, 323, 325, 783; *vb.* 249, 323, 325, 358, 783
roller *n.* 197, 358
roman *adj.* 521
romance *n.* 449, 889
romantic *adj.* 752
roof *n.* 225; *vb.* 225
room *n.* 182, 678
roomy *adj.* 182, 204
roost *vb.* 319
root *n.* 39, 88, 155, 213, 306, 374, 494
rooted *adj.* 47
rope *n.* 49, 207, 964
roster *n.* 83
rosy *adj.* 585, 811
rot *n.* 53, 451, 592; *vb.* 53, 584, 588
rota *n.* 83, 140
rotary *adj.* 323
rotate *vb.* 323
rotation *n.* 140, 323
rotten *adj.* 53, 162, 580, 584, 588
rotund *adj.* 249
rough *adj.* 57, 175, 258, 887, 908
roughage *n.* 305
roughness *n.* 258
round *n.* 249, 649, 792; *adj.* 249, 250; *vb.* 249, 256
roundabout *adj.* 505, 561
rounded *adj.* 247, 249
round form *n.* 249
rouse *vb.* 611, 889
rousing *adj.* 547
rout *n.* 662
route *n.* 269, 559
routine *n.* 16, 79, 91,

140, 545; *adj.* 16, 140, 545
rove *vb.* 269
row *n.* 85, 202, 206, 642
rowdy *adj.* 780, 887
rowing *n.* 271
royal *adj.* 870
rub *vb.* 341, 342, 758
rubber *n.* 485
rubbish *n.* 451, 576
rub in *vb.* 468
ruby *adj.* 811
rude *adj.* 511, 849, 880, 887, 910, 923
rudiment *n.* 155
rudimentary *adj.* 88
rue *vb.* 833
ruffian *n.* 175, 906
ruffle *vb.* 82, 258, 260, 893
rug *n.* 225
rugged *adj.* 258
ruin *n.* 164, 551, 569, 588, 662, 739; *vb.* 164, 588, 628, 735
rule *n.* 103, 400, 522, 626, 667, 671, 954; *vb.* 415, 653, 667, 671
ruler *n.* 400, 675
rumble *vb.* 783
ruminate *vb.* 384
rumour *n.* 465
run *n.* 613; *vb.* 110, 172, 266, 280, 343, 345, 358, 622
run away *vb.* 293, 299, 896
runaway *n.* 555, 600
run down *vb.* 160, 853, 926, 928
run-down *n.* 460; *adj.* 586, 612, 617
rung *n.* 93
run in *vb.* 681
run into *vb.* 282
runner *n.* 270, 275, 467
running *n.* 172; *adj.* 91, 172, 343
runny *adj.* 51, 345, 358
run off with *vb.* 722, 896
run out *vb.* 89, 301
rupture *n.* 48; *vb.* 48
rural *adj.* 183, 378
ruse *n.* 478, 631
rush *n.* 280, 282, 358, 611, 613; *adj.* 603; *vb.* 280, 358, 359, 613, 645
russet *adj.* 810, 811
rust *n.* 167, 588, 592, 847; *adj.* 810, 811; *vb.* 53, 584
rustic *n.* 871; *adj.* 378, 871, 885
rustle *n.* 781, 783, 786; *vb.* 781, 783, 786
rusty *adj.* 126, 810, 811
rut *n.* 261, 545
ruthless *adj.* 900

S

Sabbath *n.* 616
sabbatical *n.* 614; *adj.* 616
sable *adj.* 808
sabotage *n.* 164
saboteur *n.* 480
saccharin *n.* 772
sack *n.* 193, 303, 686; *vb.* 164, 303, 686, 722
sackcloth and ashes *n.* 941
sacred *adj.* 974
sacrifice *n.* 652, 715, 943; *vb.* 652, 693, 715
sacrilege *n.* 901, 981
sad *adj.* 828, 837, 839, 895
sadden *vb.* 837
saddle *n.* 217; *vb.* 330, 919
safari *n.* 269
safe *n.* 732; *adj.* 54, 593, 646
safe-blower *n.* 723
safeguard *n.* 595; *vb.* 593, 646
safekeeping *n.* 567, 593
safety *n.* 593
safety curtain *n.* 762
sag *vb.* 216, 319
saga *n.* 525
sage *n.* 428, 436
sail *vb.* 271
sailing *n.* 271, 299
sailing ship *n.* 277
sailor *n.* 272
saint *n.* 939, 977, 980
saintly *adj.* 935, 980
salacious *adj.* 952
salad days *n.* 129
salary *n.* 705, 731, 738, 741
sale *n.* 714, 727
salesman *n.* 727
sales talk *n.* 727
salient *adj.* 253, 458, 573
sallow *adj.* 806, 807, 813
sally *n.* 645, 842; *vb.* 645
salmon *n.* 811, 816
saloon *n.* 276
salt *n.* 307; *vb.* 307, 599
salt away *vb.* 567
salt of the earth *n.* 579, 939
salubrious *adj.* 585
salutation *n.* 518, 922
salute *n.* 878, 922; *vb.* 888
salvage *n.* 44, 589; *vb.* 589, 601
salve *n.* 342, 365, 591
same *adj.* 13, 16, 28
sample *vb.* 767
sanctify *vb.* 980
sanctimonious *adj.* 981

sanction *vb.* 690, 925, 954
sanctity *n.* 935, 980
sanctuary *n.* 595, 990
sand *n.* 352; *adj.* 813; *vb.* 257
sandbags *n.* 152, 330
sandbank *n.* 357, 596
sandwich *n.* 306
sane *adj.* 438
sanguine *adj.* 854
sanitation *n.* 585
sanity *n.* 438, 585
sap *n.* 309; *vb.* 162
sapling *n.* 374
sapphire *adj.* 815
sarcasm *n.* 842, 853
sarcophagus *n.* 372
sash *n.* 207
Satan *n.* 969
sated *adj.* 56, 865
satellite *n.* 60, 279, 329; *adj.* 679
satiety *n.* 865
satire *n.* 455, 842, 853
satirist *n.* 842, 928
satisfaction *n.* (pacification) 652, 721, 943; (enjoyment) 827, 831
satisfactory *adj.* 570
satisfied *adj.* 827, 831, 865
satisfy *vb.* (of food) 304, 865; (enjoy) 829, 831
satisfying *adj.* 306, 827, 943
saturation *n.* 56, 349, 572, 865
sauce *n.* 307, 880
saunter *n.* 269; *vb.* 135, 281
savage *n.* 175; *adj.* 175, 900, 908; *vb.* 588
save *vb.* 567, 601, 680, 748, 961
saving *n.* 567, 599, 601, 748
Saviour *n.* 967
savour *n.* 767; *vb.* 767, 770
savouriness *n.* 770
savoury *n.* 306; *adj.* 770
saw *n.* 259; *vb.* 48, 787
say *vb.* 460, 514
saying *n.* 432, 498
scaffold *n.* 964
scald *vb.* 759, 761
scale *n.* 27, 206, 400; *vb.* 206, 316
scales *n.* 330, 400
scallywag *n.* 940
scalp *vb.* 228
scamp *n.* 940
scan *vb.* 472, 528, 818
scandal *n.* 465, 516, 869, 928
scandalmonger *n.* 388, 460, 928
scandalous *adj.* 869, 936
scant *adj.* 76, 507
scanty *adj.* 33, 139, 571
scapegoat *n.* 149, 828, 943
scarce *adj.* 139
scarcity *n.* 33, 76, 139, 571, 735
scare *n.* 598, 856; *vb.* 856, 902
scared *adj.* 856, 858
scarf *n.* 207
scarlet *adj.* 811
scatter *vb.* 82, 95, 297
scene *n.* 185, 186, 658
scenery *n.* 185
scenic *adj.* 488
scent *n.* 483, 774, 776; *vb.* 774, 776
scented *adj.* 774, 776
sceptic *n.* 975
sceptical *adj.* 409, 421, 423, 975
sceptre *n.* 677
schedule *n.* 83, 116, 558; *vb.* 83
scheme *n.* 558, 602, 631; *vb.* 558, 631
schemer *n.* 558
schism *n.* 106, 642, 979
scholar *n.* 428, 436, 474, 524, 629
scholarly *adj.* 426, 472
scholarship *n.* 426, 472
school *n.* 94, 475; *vb.* 470
schoolchild *n.* 131, 428, 474
schooling *n.* 470
school-teacher *n.* 473
scientist *n.* 396, 428, 448
scintillate *vb.* 797, 842
scintillating *adj.* 509
scissors *n.* 255
scoff *n.* 924; *vb.* 853, 928
scoffer *n.* 928, 981
scold *vb.* 926
scoop *n.* 312, 465
scooter *n.* 276
scope *n.* 182, 557, 558, 678, 956
scorch *vb.* 350, 759, 761
scorcher *n.* 759
score *n.* 70, 737; *vb.* 38, 482, 792
scorn *n.* 853, 892, 924; *vb.* 644, 694, 923, 924
scornful *adj.* 923, 924
scoundrel *n.* 940
scour *vb.* 341, 583
scourge *n.* 592, 665, 964; *vb.* 963
scout *n.* 86, 593, 683
scowl *n.* 895; *vb.* 245, 895
scraggy *adj.* 205, 246
scram *vb.* 299
scramble *n.* 613; *vb.* 45, 306, 316
scrap *n.* 55, 649; *vb.* 607, 649
scrapbook *n.* 441

scrape n. 633; vb. 257, 341
scrape out vb. 210
scrape through vb. 666
scrappy adj. 57
scratch adj. 628; vb. 482, 758
scratch the surface vb. 211
scratchy adj. 787
scrawl n. 521; vb. 521
scream n. 788; vb. 787, 788
screech vb. 787, 788, 789
screen n. 461, 595, 801; vb. 461, 593, 646, 801
screw n. 49, 251
scribble n. 441, 521; vb. 521
scribe n. 484, 521, 981
script n. 521
Scripture n. 976
scroll n. 251, 483, 521
scrounger n. 697
scrub vb. 341, 583
scrumptious adj. 306, 770
scruple n. 533, 833
scrupulous adj. 392, 702, 864, 931
scrutinize vb. 390, 394, 396, 818
scrutiny n. 394, 818
sculptor n. 491
sculpture n. 486, 489; vb. 489
scum n. 44, 871
scurrilous adj. 901
scurry n. 613; vb. 613
scythe vb. 378
sea n. 351
seaboard n. 352
seafaring n. 271
sea-food n. 306
seagoing adj. 277
seal n. 482; vb. 265, 408, 424, 461, 482
sealed book n. 427, 453
seam n. 49, 206
seaman n. 272
séance n. 984
sear vb. 754
search vb. 394, 396, 554
searching adj. 388
searchlight n. 800
seared conscience n. 942
seaside n. 352; adj. 352
season n. 107, 109; vb. 307, 545, 599
seasoned adj. 130, 545, 602
seat n. 186, 217
secede vb. 289, 425, 556
secession n. 425, 979
secluded adj. 466, 885
seclusion n. 461, 824, 885
second n. 109, 115; adj. 62
secondary adj. 35
secondhand adj. 126, 606
second nature n. 545
second-rate adj. 580
second thoughts n. 87, 538
secrecy n. 459
secret n. 466; adj. 427, 461, 466
secret agent n. 460
secretary n. 484, 521, 623
secrete vb. 301, 310, 461
secretive adj. 466, 517, 876
sect n. 641, 979
sectarian n. 979; adj. 641, 979
sectarianism n. 979
section n. 55, 73, 97, 183, 717
sectional adj. 73
sector n. 55, 183
secular adj. 975, 987
secure adj. 47, 161, 593; vb. 47, 152, 408, 646, 705, 712
security n. 593, 646, 701
sedateness n. 757, 837
sedative n. 591
sedentary adj. 319
sediment n. 44
seditious adj. 148
seducer n. 953
seduction n. 952
seductive adj. 829
see vb. 419, 426, 818, 882
see ahead vb. 446
seed n. 155, 306, 374; vb. 95, 378
see double vb. 820, 950
seedy adj. 586
see fit vb. 530
see it through vb. 535
seek vb. 388, 394, 554, 604, 982
seem vb. 18, 621, 825
seeming adj. 406, 825
seemly adj. 510, 577, 848
seep vb. 301, 319, 349, 358
seer n. 447, 449
see-saw n. 325; vb. 325
seethe vb. 175, 759, 893
see through vb. 659, 802
segment n. 55, 73
segregate vb. 99, 540
segregation n. 48, 99
seismic adj. 325
seize vb. 326, 705, 720, 722
seizure n. 326, 586, 720
seldom adv. 139
select adj. 579; vb. 398, 540, 557
selection n. 398, 527, 540

selective adj. 398, 540, 864
self n. 382
self-abasement n. 874
self-assurance n. 757, 873
self-centred adj. 875, 934
self-control n. 534, 681, 757, 944
self-deception n. 478
self-denial n. 933, 944
self-destruction n. 370
self-determination n. 678
self-discipline n. 681, 944
self-effacing adj. 874, 933
self-esteem n. 873
self-evident adj. 408, 458
self-forgetful adj. 933
self-glory n. 879
self-important adj. 875
self-improvement n. 472
self-indulgent adj. 827, 934, 945
self-instruction n. 472
self-interest n. 934
selfishness n. 904, 934
selfless adj. 933
self-love n. 873
self-made adj. 472
self-portrait n. 488
self-possessed adj. 392, 438, 757
self-regard n. 873
self-reliance n. 534, 857
self-respect n. 873
self-sacrifice n. 933
selfsameness n. 13
self-satisfied adj. 831, 873
self-seeking n. 934; adj. 934
self-styled adj. 497
self-taught adj. 472
sell vb. 464, 714, 727
sell-out n. 727, 932
semantic adj. 450
semantics n. 492
semaphore n. 467
semblance n. 22, 236
semi- adj. 63
semiliquidity n. 362
seminar n. 519
seminary n. 475
semitransparency n. 804
senator n. 625
send vb. 268, 523
send for vb. 671
send forth vb. 301, 464
send-off n. 299
send up vb. 20
senility n. 126, 130
senior n. 34, 132; adj. 130
sensation n. 465, 752, 866
sensational adj. 755, 866, 877
sense n. 398, 411, 434, 450, 752; vb. 382, 411, 452, 752
senseless adj. 433, 451
sense of duty n. 919
sense of hearing n. 795
sense of smell n. 774
sensibility n. 753
sensible adj. 434, 575, 753
sensitive adj. 398, 716, 753, 756, 828, 894
sensitivity n. 398, 752, 753, 894
sensory adj. 753
sensual adj. 945, 952
sensuality n. 827, 945, 952
sentence n. 498, 960; vb. 960, 962, 963
sententious adj. 504
sentient adj. 753
sentiment n. 411, 420, 752, 889
sentimental adj. 752, 889
sentry n. 593, 646
separability n. 48, 51
separate vb. 48, 55, 95, 398, 540, 898
separation n. 48, 898
separatism n. 979
separatist n. 106, 425; adj. 979
sepia adj. 810
septet n. 70
sepulchre n. 372
sequel n. 87, 119, 156
sequence n. 85, 91
seraph n. 968
serenity n. 267, 757, 827, 831
serf n. 378, 676, 871
serfdom n. 679
serial adj. 85, 91, 140
serial position n. 93
series n. 85
serious adj. 534, 573, 594, 837, 982
seriousness n. 573, 837
sermon n. 470, 518
serrate vb. 246, 258, 259
servant n. 35, 676
serve vb. 636, 676, 679
serve as vb. 486
service n. 550, 575, 679, 982, 988
service of worship n. 988
services n. 655
servility n. 679, 881
serving n. 717
session n. 957
set n. 94, 474, 850; adj. 152, 185, 235; vb. 47, 81, 152, 186, 235, 332, 334
set about vb. 88, 605
set apart vb. 48, 398

setback n. 445, 635
set fire to vb. 761
set forth vb. 456, 460, 525
set free adj. 961; vb. 48, 961
set great store by vb. 573
set in motion vb. 88, 266, 282
set in order vb. 81
set no store by vb. 421
set off vb. 782, 805, 846
set one's heart on vb. 861
set one's teeth on edge vb. 773, 787
set out vb. 299, 458
set sail vb. 271
setting n. 8, 185, 229, 792
settle vb. 186, 191, 319, 408, 413, 652, 659, 699, 738
settle down vb. 191
settlement n. 699, 704, 738
settler n. 190
settle up vb. 647
set to vb. 605, 649
set up vb. 186, 522
seven n. 70; adj. 70
sever vb. 42, 48
several adj. 75
severe adj. 175, 508, 669, 828, 908, 946
severity n. 508, 669, 900
sew vb. 221, 589
sewer n. 360
sex-appeal n. 889
sextet n. 70
sexuality n. 827
sexy adj. 952
shabby adj. 580, 869
shackle n. 681; vb. 635
shade n. 225, 463, 595, 798, 801; vb. 799, 801
shadow n. 4, 328, 798; vb. 287, 554
shadowy adj. 4, 328, 798, 799, 824
shady adj. 631, 798, 801, 869, 932
shaft n. 213, 254, 361, 797
shake vb. 45, 51, 326, 756, 856
shake hands vb. 408, 652, 699, 886
shake off vb. 680
shake-up n. 148
shaky adj. 141, 326, 338, 594
shallow adj. 211, 435, 507, 852
shallowness n. 211, 383, 427, 435
sham n. 20, 852; adj. 20, 431, 478; vb. 477, 852
shambles n. 80
shame n. 869, 874; vb. 874
shameful adj. 869, 924
shameless adj. 887
shampoo vb. 583
shanty n. 191
shape n. 242, 339, 825; vb. 489
shapeless adj. 243
shapely adj. 244, 844
share n. 55, 305, 709, 717; vb. 55, 639, 709, 988
shareholder n. 709
share out vb. 717
sharing n. 709, 717
shark n. 718
sharp adj. 255, 434, 769, 773, 787, 791, 828
sharpen vb. 255
sharpness n. 255, 434, 769, 773
sharp practice n. 478
shatter vb. 164, 338
shattering adj. 148, 164
shave vb. 203, 257
shaving n. 228
shear vb. 203, 377
shears n. 255
sheath n. 225
shed vb. 95, 228, 319, 556
shed light on vb. 797
sheep n. 20
sheer adj. 46, 214
sheet n. 206, 225, 522
shelf n. 217
shell n. 23, 225, 290, 885; vb. 228
shellac n. 365
shelter n. 191, 225, 463, 595, 801; vb. 225, 461, 593, 646, 801
shelve vb. 135
Sheol n. 973
shepherd n. 377, 986
shield n. 595, 801; vb. 225, 593, 646, 801
shift n. 149, 187, 268; vb. 142, 149, 151, 187, 268, 285
shifty adj. 478, 631
shilly-shally vb. 135, 536, 612
shimmer n. 797; vb. 797
shine n. 797; vb. 257, 341, 797
shine at vb. 627
ship n. 277; vb. 192, 268
shipment n. 268
shipper n. 728
shirk vb. 533, 555, 920
shirker n. 555, 858
shirty adj. 893, 894
shiver vb. 326, 760
shoal n. 94, 211
shock n. 282, 444, 828; vb. 856, 892
shockable adj. 951
shocked adj. 856, 926

shocking *adj.* 830, 845, 869, 936
shoddy *adj.* 580, 849, 869
shoot *n.* 374; *vb.* 290, 370, 645, 963
shooting star *n.* 329, 800
shop *n.* 620, 730
shop assistant *n.* 727
shop-lifter *n.* 723
shop-lifting *n.* 722
shopper *n.* 726
shopping *n.* 726
shopping centre *n.* 730
shopping spree *n.* 749
shore *n.* 352; *vb.* 217
short *adj.* 57, 113, 203, 315, 504
shortage *n.* 57, 315
shortcoming *n.* 29, 35, 43, 57, 315, 662
short duration *n.* 113
shorten *vb.* 37, 42, 197, 203, 504, 527
shortfall *n.* 57, 315
shorthand *n.* 521
short-lived *adj.* 113
shortness *n.* 33, 195, 203
short-sighted *adj.* 416, 435, 820
short-sightedness *n.* 435, 820
short-tempered *adj.* 894
short-term *adj.* 113
shot *n.* 173, 290, 782
shoulder *n.* 238; *vb.* 217, 605, 636
shout *n.* 482, 597, 782, 788; *vb.* 482, 788
shout down *vb.* 425, 788, 887
shove *n.* 282; *vb.* 282, 290
show *n.* (manifestation) 458; (drama) 529; (vanity) 852, 875; *vb.* (be visible) 458, 802, 823, 825; (demonstrate) 413; (indicate) 482
show-down *n.* 462
shower *n.* 358; *vb.* 349, 358
show-jumper *n.* 270
show-jumping *n.* 269
showman *n.* 877
showmanship *n.* 529, 877
show off *vb.* 419, 875, 877, 879
show-off *n.* 875, 877
show one's colours *vb.* 462
showpiece *n.* 458, 581, 844
show through *vb.* 802, 823
show up *vb.* 188, 298, 414, 825, 869
show willing *vb.* 532
showy *adj.* 509, 852, 875, 877
shred *n.* 33, 207
shrewd *adj.* 434, 631
shrewd idea *n.* 448
shrewdness *n.* 398, 434, 631
shriek *n.* 787, 788
shrill *adj.* 333, 787; *vb.* 787
shrine *n.* 483, 990
shrink *vb.* 37, 197, 205, 283, 533, 555, 856, 858
shrivel *vb.* 197, 350, 588
shroud *vb.* 461
shrub *n.* 374
shrug off *vb.* 921
shudder *vb.* 326, 760, 856
shuffle *vb.* 82, 149, 281, 756
shun *vb.* 555, 694, 924
shut *vb.* 263
shut down *vb.* 144
shut-eye *n.* 612
shut in *vb.* 234
shut oneself up *vb.* 885
shut out *vb.* 691
shutter *n.* 801
shuttle *n.* 278, 325; *vb.* 268
shut up *vb.* 144, 234, 681
shy *adj.* 856, 858, 876, 885
shy away *vb.* 533
shyness *n.* 858, 876, 885
sibilant *adj.* 786
sick *adj.* 369, 586
sicken *vb.* 162, 586
sickly *adj.* 812
sickness *n.* 303, 586, 828
side *n.* 11, 233, 238
side by side *adv.* 238
sidedness *n.* 238
side-splitting *adj.* 851
sideways *adj.* 219, 238; *adv.* 238
side with *vb.* 641
sidle up to *vb.* 292
siege *n.* 645
siesta *n.* 612
sieve *n.* 264
sift *vb.* 46, 415, 540
sigh *vb.* 359, 781
sight *n.* 753, 818
sightly *adj.* 844
sightseeing *n.* 269
sightseer *n.* 270, 821
sign *n.* 401, 447, 458, 482, 597; *vb.* 424, 482, 699, 701, 714, 726
signal *n.* 482; *vb.* 482
signatory *n.* 424
signature *n.* 482, 496
significance *n.* 450, 456, 573
significant *adj.* 136, 450, 573
signify *vb.* 450, 482
sign of authority *n.* 677

signpost *vb.* 284
silence *n.* 267, 513, 517, 779; *vb.* 414, 513, 779
silent *adj.* 513, 517, 779, 895
silhouette *n.* 232, 488; *vb.* 488
silky *adj.* 257
silly *adj.* 433, 435
silver-haired *adj.* 809
silvery *adj.* 807
similarity *n.* 18, 105, 218, 397
simile *n.* 397, 455
simmer *vb.* 306
simmer down *vb.* 757
simple *adj.* (not mixed) 46; (gullible) 422, 632, 937, 951; (foolish) 427, 435; (easy to understand) 452, 502, 508; (easy) 634
simple circularity *n.* 250
simple-minded *adj.* 435, 632
simpleton *n.* 429, 437, 479
simplify *vb.* 46, 53, 456
simulate *vb.* 20, 477, 852
simultaneous *adj.* 60, 122
sin *n.* 431, 672, 703, 938; *vb.* 672, 981
sincere *adj.* 430, 476, 931
sine qua non *n.* 60, 700
sinew *n.* 207
sinful *adj.* 916, 936, 938, 952, 975, 981
sing *vb.* 528, 789, 792, 982
singer *n.* 793
single *adj.* 54, 59, 139, 897
single-minded *adj.* 534, 980
single out *vb.* 102
singular *adj.* 59
sinister *adj.* 665
sinistral *n.* 241
sink *vb.* 209, 210, 317, 319, 321, 588
sink back *vb.* 590
sinker *n.* 330
sinless *adj.* 951
sinner *n.* 906, 940, 981
sinuate *vb.* 251
sip *n.* 309; *vb.* 767
siphon *n.* 360
sir *n.* 380
siren *n.* 116, 482, 598, 970
sirupy *adj.* 772
sister *n.* 11, 986
sit *vb.* 23, 185
sit down *vb.* 319
site *n.* 185, 186
sit-in *n.* 144, 696
sit on *vb.* 466, 679
sit on the fence *vb.* 409, 541
sit pretty *vb.* 831
sitting *n.* 984
sitting duck *n.* 479
situation *n.* 8, 93, 153, 185, 229, 557
six *n.* 70; *adj.* 70
sixth sense *n.* 411, 753
size *n.* 26, 27, 32, 194, 362, 400
size up *vb.* 415
sizzle *vb.* 306, 759, 786
skeleton *n.* 232, 371, 527
sketch *n.* 232, 486, 488, 525, 558; *vb.* 232, 488, 525, 558
sketchy *adj.* 57
skew *adj.* 219
skewer *vb.* 264
skilful *adj.* 627
skill *n.* 159, 426, 501, 627
skilled *adj.* 579, 602
skilled worker *n.* 619, 629
skim *vb.* 211, 257
skimp *vb.* 393, 750
skimpy *adj.* 57
skin *n.* 225; *vb.* 228
skinny *adj.* 205
skip *vb.* 320, 393
skirmish *n.* 645, 649
skirt *n.* 233; *vb.* 233, 238
skunk *n.* 777
sky *n.* 329, 348, 815
skyjacking *n.* 722
skyline *n.* 198
skyscraper *n.* 191, 208
slab *n.* 206
slack *adj.* 391, 612, 668, 920, 952
slacken *vb.* 281
slacker *n.* 858
slag *n.* 44
slam *vb.* 782, 926
slander *n.* 869, 928; *vb.* 928, 930
slanderer *n.* 928
slang *n.* 494, 495; *adj.* 495
slant *vb.* 219
slap *n.* 782, 963; *vb.* 282, 782, 963
slap in the face *n.* 694, 923
slapstick *n.* 529
slash *vb.* 203
slate *n.* 206
slaughter *n.* 164, 370, 963; *vb.* 370, 963
slave *n.* 35, 619, 676
slavery *n.* 679
slavish *adj.* 881
slay *vb.* 370
sleek *adj.* 257
sleep *n.* 612; *vb.* 612
sleep around *vb.* 952
sleep together *vb.* 889
sleep with *vb.* 889
sleepy *adj.* 612, 617

sleet *n.* 760
sleight of hand *n.* 478
slender *adj.* 33, 205
slice *n.* 55, 305, 717
slide *n.* 219, 486; *vb.* 257, 588
slide-rule *n.* 400
slight *n.* 869, 923, 924; *adj.* 33, 195, 203, 571; *vb.* 418, 923, 928
slim *adj.* 33, 205; *vb.* 205, 947
slime *n.* 584
slimy *adj.* 362
slink *vb.* 461
slip *n.* 431, 500, 522, 741, 938
slip back *vb.* 590
slippery *adj.* 51, 257, 594, 631
slipshod *adj.* 393, 500
slip-up *n.* 431
slit *n.* 261, 262; *vb.* 48, 264
sliver *n.* 55
slogan *n.* 432, 494, 498
slog away *vb.* 535, 615
slope *n.* 208, 219; *vb.* 219
sloppy *adj.* 584
slot *n.* 261, 262; *vb.* 261
slothful *adj.* 612
slough *n.* 355
slovenly *adj.* 500, 584, 920
slow *adj.* 174, 281, 435; *vb.* 281, 616
slowcoach *n.* 281
slowness *n.* 135, 281, 435, 843
sluggard *n.* 612
sluggish *adj.* 174, 281, 612, 843
slum *n.* 845
slumber *vb.* 174, 612
slump *n.* 169, 317; *vb.* 317, 588
slur *n.* 869, 928, 930; *vb.* 515, 928, 930
slush *n.* 760
slushy *adj.* 355, 362
slut *n.* 953
sly *adj.* 461, 631, 932
smack *vb.* 282, 782
smack one's lips *vb.* 767
small *adj.* 33, 195, 203, 331
small arms *n.* 657
small change *n.* 731
smallholding *n.* 378
smallness *n.* 33, 195
small talk *n.* 516
smarmy *adj.* 927
smart *adj.* 125, 631; *vb.* 828
smart aleck *n.* 875
smash *vb.* 164, 282, 645
smash-and-grab-raid *n.* 722
smash hit *n.* 661
smash-up *n.* 282
smattering *n.* 76, 427
smear *n.* 584, 928, 930; *vb.* 342, 847, 869, 928
smell *n.* 753, 774, 777; *vb.* 774, 776, 777
smell out *vb.* 394, 554, 774
smelly *adj.* 777
smelt *vb.* 761
smile *n.* 838, 886; *vb.* 838, 886
smirch *n.* 847; *vb.* 847
smirk *n.* 838; *vb.* 838
smite *vb.* 282
smitten *adj.* 889
smog *n.* 363
smoke *n.* 344, 346, 803; *vb.* 308, 346, 599, 759, 803
smoke-signal *n.* 467
smoking *adj.* 759
smoky *adj.* 803, 809
smooth *adj.* 228, 257, 335, 364, 477, 631, 927; *vb.* 16, 215, 257, 341, 758
smoothness *n.* 257
smother *vb.* 513, 759, 762
smoulder *vb.* 759
smudge *vb.* 584, 847
smuggle *vb.* 722
smuggled *adj.* 955
smuggler *n.* 723
smut *n.* 952
snack *n.* 306
snack bar *n.* 191
snag *n.* 582, 635
snail *n.* 281
snake in the grass *n.* 459, 596
snake-like *adj.* 251
snap *vb.* 338, 782, 789, 893
snap out of it *vb.* 836
snapshot *n.* 486
snare *n.* 463, 596
snarl *vb.* 789
snatch *vb.* 720
sneak *n.* 858; *vb.* 461
sneer *n.* 895, 924, 926; *vb.* 696, 853, 895, 924, 926
sneeze *vb.* 359, 786
sniff *vb.* 774
sniff out *vb.* 394, 554
snigger *n.* 838; *vb.* 838
snip *vb.* 48
sniper *n.* 645
snivel *vb.* 839
snobbish *adj.* 875, 924
snoop *n.* 388, 460, 821; *vb.* 388, 394
snooty *adj.* 875, 924
snooze *n.* 612; *vb.* 612
snort *vb.* 789
snow *n.* 760; *vb.* 807
snowball *n.* 36; *vb.* 36
snowdrift *n.* 760
snowflake *n.* 760
snowstorm *n.* 760

snub *n.* 295, 694, 923; *vb.* 887, 923, 926
snuff *n.* 308; *vb.* 762
snug *adj.* 827
snuggle *vb.* 890
soak *vb.* 56, 349
soak up *vb.* 350
so-and-so *n.* 497
soapy *adj.* 363
soar *vb.* 32, 208, 273, 316
sob *n.* 839; *vb.* 788, 839
sober *adj.* 837, 848, 944, 949
soberness *n.* 848, 949
so-called *adj.* 497
sociability *n.* 882, 884
social *n.* 884; *adj.* 379
social conscience *n.* 903
socialism *n.* 709
social services *n.* 903
society *n.* 379, 641, 850, 870
sociology *n.* 379
socket *n.* 184
sod *n.* 374
sodden *adj.* 349
sodomy *n.* 952
soft *adj.* 257, 331, 335, 670, 781, 805, 889
soft drink *n.* 309
soften *vb.* 267, 335, 513, 652, 834
soft-hearted *adj.* 670, 907
softness *n.* 335, 364, 670, 778, 781
soft nothings *n.* 890
soft soap *n.* 927
sog *vb.* 349
soggy *adj.* 364
soi-disant *adj.* 497
soil *n.* 352, 378; *vb.* 584, 847
soirée *n.* 884
sojourn *n.* 269; *vb.* 191
solace *n.* 831, 907
solar *adj.* 329
solar energy *n.* 159, 765
solder *vb.* 50
soldier *n.* 655
soldier on *vb.* 535
sole *adj.* 59
solecism *n.* 412, 500
solemn *adj.* 468, 573, 837, 982
solicit *vb.* 695
solicitor *n.* 959
solicitous *adj.* 392
solid *n.* 3, 332; *adj.* 3, 50, 161, 332, 334, 337
solidarity *n.* 50, 639
solidify *vb.* 332, 334
solidity *n.* 3, 152, 204, 332, 334
soliloquize *vb.* 520
soliloquy *n.* 520
solitary *adj.* 885
solitude *n.* 59, 461
solo *n.* 792
soloist *n.* 793
soluble *adj.* 345
solution *n.* 343
solve *vb.* 157, 456
solvent *n.* 343, 345
sombre *adj.* 798, 809, 895
some *adj.* 26, 72
somebody *n.* 868
somersault *n.* 220; *vb.* 220
something *n.* 327
sometime *adj.* 124, 687; *adv.* 121
sometimes *adv.* 138
somnolence *n.* 612, 617
son *n.* 171
sonata *n.* 792
song *n.* 528, 792, 982
sonnet *n.* 528
sonorous *adj.* 778
soothe *vb.* 176, 591, 834
soothing *adj.* 589, 790, 834
soothsayer *n.* 447, 984
sooty *adj.* 584, 808
sophism *n.* 412
sophisticated *n.* 848; *adj.* 423, 848
sophistry *n.* 412
soporofic *adj.* 841
sorcery *n.* 984
sore *n.* 588; *adj.* 753, 828, 893
sore point *n.* 893
sorrow *n.* 828, 830, 833, 837, 839, 941; *vb.* 837, 839
sorry *adj.* 833, 907, 941
sort *n.* 97; *vb.* 97, 540
sortie *n.* 645; *vb.* 645
SOS *n.* 598
soul *n.* 223, 368, 382, 751
sound *n.* 353, 512, 778, 795; *adj.* 410, 438, 581, 585, 977; *vb.* 512, 778
sounding board *n.* 396
sound out *vb.* 396
soundproof *adj.* 779
soup *n.* 306
soupçon *n.* 33
sour *adj.* 769, 773, 895
source *n.* 88, 155
source of light *n.* 800
sourness *n.* 773, 895
souvenir *n.* 441, 483
sovereign *n.* 675; *adj.* 667
sow *n.* 381; *vb.* 95, 378
space *n.* 182, 198, 200, 202, 329
space-age *adj.* 125
spaceman *n.* 274
spaceship *n.* 279
space travel *n.* 274
space traveller *n.* 274
spacious *adj.* 32, 182, 204
spade *vb.* 254
spadework *n.* 602
span *n.* 109, 182, 202; *vb.* 47, 182, 313

spank *vb.* 963
spanner in the works *n.* 580, 635
spare *adj.* 44, 607; *vb.* 670, 907
spare time *n.* 614
sparing *adj.* 748, 750, 944
spark *n.* 797
sparkle *n.* 506, 759, 797, 836; *vb.* 326, 797, 842
sparse *adj.* 33, 76, 139, 333
spasm *n.* 141, 326, 586, 828
spasmodic *adj.* 92, 141
spatial *adj.* 182
spatter *vb.* 817
spay *vb.* 160, 169
speak *vb.* 460, 512, 514, 788
speak against *vb.* 25, 696
speaker *n.* 514
speak for itself *vb.* 401
speak one's mind *vb.* 476, 632
speak out *vb.* 468
speak out against *vb.* 832
speak volumes *vb.* 401
spear *vb.* 264
special *adj.* 59, 102
specialist *n.* 629
speciality *n.* 102, 557
specialize *vb.* 472, 609
species *n.* 97
specific *adj.* 5, 59, 102
specification *n.* 97, 525
specifications *n.* 102, 700
specify *vb.* 102, 482, 496, 525
specimen *n.* 458
specious *adj.* 412, 549, 825
speck *n.* 33, 847
speckle *vb.* 817
spectacle *n.* 529, 825, 866
spectacles *n.* 822
spectacular *adj.* 529, 877
spectator *n.* 821
spectre *n.* 971
spectrum *n.* 805, 817
speculation *n.* 396, 448, 553
speculator *n.* 396, 448, 553, 728
speech *n.* 492, 512, 514, 518
speech defect *n.* 515
speechless *adj.* 513, 866
speech-making *n.* 518
speed *n.* 27, 266, 280, 400; *vb.* 280
speed up *vb.* 280, 613
speedy *adj.* 134, 280, 613
spell *n.* 109, 586, 984; *vb.* 450, 493
spell-binder *n.* 984
spellbound *adj.* 866
spelling *n.* 493
spell out *vb.* 456
spend *vb.* 575, 715, 738, 740
spendthrift *n.* 749; *adj.* 569
spend time *vb.* 107
spew *vb.* 303, 358
sphere *n.* 249, 329, 658
spice *n.* 776; *vb.* 307, 599
spick and span *adj.* 583
spicy *adj.* 769, 776, 952
spike *n.* 255; *vb.* 264
spill *n.* 800; *vb.* 319, 358
spin *n.* 269, 323; *vb.* 221, 273, 323
spine *n.* 255
spineless *adj.* 160, 162
spinney *n.* 374
spin-off *n.* 87, 156
spin out *vb.* 202
spinster *n.* 897
spiral *n.* 251, 322, 323; *adj.* 251; *vb.* 323
spire *n.* 208, 212
spirit *n.* 4, 368, 382, 506, 611, 751, 966, 968, 969
spirited *adj.* 280, 368
spiritism *n.* 984
spiritless *adj.* 757
spiritual *adj.* 4, 328, 382, 966, 974, 980
spiritualist *n.* 984
spirituality *n.* 328, 980
spit *n.* 253; *vb.* 306, 358
spiteful *adj.* 900, 912
splash *n.* 786; *vb.* 349, 358, 786
splash down *vb.* 274, 317, 321
spleen *n.* 895
splendid *adj.* 579, 844
splendour *n.* 797, 844, 877
splice *n.* 49; *vb.* 47, 896
splint *n.* 217
splinter *n.* 55; *vb.* 338
splinter-group *n.* 641
split *n.* 642, 717, 979; *adj.* 48; *vb.* 48, 63, 200, 338
split hairs *vb.* 864
spoil *n.* 663, 724; *vb.* 588, 628, 635, 847
spoilsport *n.* 548
spoke *n.* 297
spokesman *n.* 460, 467, 514, 689
sponge *n.* 264, 364, 485; *vb.* 349, 583
sponger *n.* 612, 697, 881
spongy *adj.* 264, 335, 364
sponsor *vb.* 636
spontaneity *n.* 531, 544
spontaneous *adj.* 115, 131, 411, 544

spooky *adj.* 971
spoonerism *n.* 433, 500, 842
spoon-feeding *n.* 470
spoonful *n.* 26, 306
sporadic *adj.* 139, 141
sport *n.* 649, 840, 939
sporting *adj.* 915
spot *n.* 33, 184, 584, 847; *vb.* 419, 482
spotless *adj.* 581, 583, 807, 937, 951
spotlight *n.* 800
spotted *adj.* 584, 817
spouse *n.* 896
spout *n.* 301, 358, 360; *vb.* 358, 514
sprachgefühl *n.* 501
sprawl *vb.* 95
spray *n.* 363, 374; *vb.* 225
spread *n.* 36, 182, 196, 306; *vb.* 95, 182, 196, 297, 460
sprig *n.* 374
spring *n.* (season) 127; (cause) 155, 547; (recoil) 283, 336; (leap) 320; (water) 358; *adj.* 127; *vb.* 156, 283, 320, 336
sprinkle *vb.* 95, 349, 583
sprinkling *n.* 76, 583
sprint *n.* 613; *vb.* 280, 613
sprout *vb.* 316
spry *adj.* 611
spur *n.* 253, 547; *vb.* 547
spurious *adj.* 431, 477
spurn *vb.* 542, 644, 694, 892, 924
spur of the moment *n.* 544
spurt *vb.* 280, 301, 358, 613
sputnik *n.* 279
spy *n.* 460, 821; *vb.* 394, 396
squabble *n.* 642; *vb.* 642
squad *n.* 94, 655
squalid *adj.* 584
squall *n.* 359
squander *vb.* 107, 569, 608, 706, 740, 749
squanderer *n.* 749
square *n.* 67, 183, 184, 246, 730; *adj.* 67, 931; *vb.* 24, 28, 105, 400
square deal *n.* 915
square one *n.* 88
squash *vb.* 215, 319, 402, 874
squat *adj.* 195, 204, 209; *vb.* 191, 209, 319
squatter *n.* 100, 190
squawk *n.* 787; *vb.* 787, 789
squeak *vb.* 781, 787, 788
squeal *vb.* 460, 787, 788, 789
squealer *n.* 460
squeamish *adj.* 862, 864, 951
squeeze *n.* 37, 743; *vb.* 37, 197, 712, 758
squelch *vb.* 786
squelchy *adj.* 355
squint *n.* 219, 818, 820; *vb.* 820
squirm *vb.* 251
squirt *vb.* 301, 358
stab *vb.* 264
stability *n.* 16, 143, 152, 757
stabilizer *n.* 152
stable *adj.* 16, 143, 152, 257, 612, 757
stack *n.* 567; *vb.* 378, 567
stadium *n.* 658
staff *n.* 619, 676, 677, 989
stag *n.* 380
stage *n.* 27, 527; *vb.* 529
stagger *vb,* 326
staggering *adj.* 444
stagnate *vb.* 169, 174, 610, 666
stain *n.* 225, 582, 584, 805, 847, 869; *vb.* 805, 847, 869
stainless *adj.* 581, 583
staircase *n.* 316
stake *n.* 217, 553, 701, 964; *vb.* 701
stalactite *n.* 216
stale *adj.* 612, 617, 666, 768, 841
stalemate *n.* 28
stalk *n.* 374; *vb.* 554
stall *n.* 730; *vb.* 144
stallion *n.* 380
stalwart *n.* 640, 857; *adj.* 161
stamina *n.* 161, 535, 857
stammer *n.* 515; *vb.* 515
stamp *n.* 23, 482, 522; *vb.* 242, 482, 490, 522
stance *n.* 420
stand *n.* 7, 184, 186, 213, 217, 420, 648, 730; *vb.* 1, 185, 318, 738
standard *n.* 23, 27, 103, 400, 482, 531, 939; *adj.* 492, 746
standardize *vb.* 16, 81
stand by *vb.* 217, 636, 702
stand-by *n.* 149
stand down *vb.* 687
stand fast *vb.* 534, 648
stand for *vb.* 424, 486, 693, 701
stand-in *n.* 149, 689
stand in for *vb.* 149, 685, 689
standing *n.* 7, 93
stand-offish *adj.* 875, 885
stand out *vb.* 253, 823

standpoint *n.* 284, 818
standstill *n.* 144, 267
stand together *vb.* 639
stand up *vb.* 318
stand up for *vb.* 217
stand up to *vb.* 648
stanza *n.* 528
star *n.* 329, 529, 684, 800, 868
starboard *n.* 240
starch *n.* 306; *vb.* 334, 583
stare *vb.* 818, 866
starless *adj.* 798
start *n.* 34, 88, 298, 444; *vb.* 88, 282, 605
startle *vb.* 444, 856
start out *vb.* 299
starve *vb.* 205, 735, 861, 947
stash away *vb.* 567
state *n.* 7, 183, 379; *adj.* 379; *vb.* 468, 498, 525
statehood *n.* 379
stately *adj.* 32, 873
statement *n.* 83, 401 468, 483, 525, 742
statesman *n.* 625
station *n.* 7, 93, 185, 186, 620, 868
stationary *adj.* 152
statistics *n.* 38, 460
statue *n.* 483, 489, 983
stature *n.* 208
status *n.* 7, 93, 868
status quo *n.* 143
statute *n.* 626, 954
statutory *adj.* 954
staunch *adj.* 882
stay *n.* 135, 213, 217, 884; *vb.* (of time) 112, 135, 143, 145; (dwell) 191; (support) 217; (resist) 648
stay-at-home *n.* 885; *adj.* 612
stay away *vb.* 189
staying power *n.* 535, 857
stay up *vb.* 135
steadfast *adj.* 112, 143, 152, 534, 535
steady *n.* 889; *adj.* 16, 140, 143, 145, 152, 534, 535; *vb.* 152
steal *vb.* 461, 720, 722
stealing *n.* 722
stealthy *adj.* 461
steam *n.* 159, 344, 347; *vb.* 306, 346
steam engine *n.* 276
steamer *n.* 277
steep *adj.* 214, 745; *vb.* 349
steeple *n.* 208
steer *vb.* 271, 284, 622
steer clear of *vb.* 555, 924
stem *n* 374
stench *n.* 774, 777
stenography *n.* 521
step *n.* 269, 400, 602, 609; *vb.* 269
step by step *adv.* 27
step down *vb.* 687
step in *vb.* 300
stepmotherly *adj.* 900
step on it *vb.* 280, 613
steppe *n.* 356
steps *n.* 316, 559
stereogram *n.* 794
stereo-recorder *n.* 484
stereotyped *adj.* 16, 152, 545, 843
sterile *adj.* 160, 169
sterilization *n.* 169, 583
stern *adj.* 669, 837, 946
stew *n.* 756; *vb.* 306
steward *n.* 623, 676, 733; *vb.* 622, 748
stewardship *n.* 392, 622, 748
stick *n.* 964; *vb.* 47, 50, 264
stick by *vb.* 217
stick-in-the-mud *n.* 143
stick it out *vb.* 535, 648, 757
stickler *n.* 537, 864
stick one's heels in *vb.* 648
stick one's neck out *vb.* 859
stick out *vb.* 253, 823
stick out for *vb.* 535
stick to *vb.* 712
stick together *vb.* 639
stick to one's guns *vb.* 534, 537, 648
stick-up *n.* 722
stick up for *vb.* 217
sticky *adj.* 50, 362, 759, 772
stiff *n.* 371; *adj.* 334, 337, 511, 745
stiffen *vb.* 332, 334, 337
stiff-necked *adj.* 537
stiff upper lip *n.* 535, 836
stifle *vb.* 466, 548, 762, 779, 785
stifled *adj.* 781
stifling *adj.* 759
stigma *n.* 847, 869
still *adj.* 174, 257, 267, 612, 779; *vb.* 176, 267, 513, 652, 779
still-life *n.* 488
stilt *n.* 217
stilted *adj.* 511
stimulant *n.* 173, 591
stimulate *vb.* 173, 547, 618, 755, 829
stimulus *n.* 173, 547
sting *n.* 255, 828; *vb.* 255, 758, 828
stinginess *n.* 748, 750
stink *n.* 777; *vb.* 777
stint *n.* 109; *vb.* 750
stipend *n.* 636, 738
stipendiary *n.* 958
stipple *vb.* 817
stipulate *vb.* 699, 700

stipulation *n.* 562
stir *vb.* 45, 266, 752, 755, 893
stirring *adj.* 755
stir up *vb.* 82, 175
stitch *n.* 828
stock *n.* 11, 305, 567, 729; *vb.* 568
stockbreeding *n.* 377
stockbroker *n.* 728
stockpile *vb.* 567
stocks *n.* 964
stodgy *adj.* 843
stoic *n.* 754
stoical *adj.* 757
stoke *vb.* 765
stolen *adj.* 955
stolen goods *n.* 724
stomach *vb.* 757
stone *n.* 306, 330, 846; *vb.* 228
stone-carving *n.* 489
stone's throw *n.* 199
stool *n.* 310
stoop *vb.* 319, 869, 874
stop *n.* 89, 141, 144, 267; *vb.* (finish) 89, 144; (live) 191; (plug) 265; (of motion) 267, 616; (prevent) 635, 691
stop at nothing *vb.* 908
stopcock *n.* 265
stopgap *n.* 149
stop-over *n.* 92
stoppage *n.* 144, 263
stopper *n.* 265
stop press *n.* 465
stopwatch *n.* 116
storage *n.* 567, 599
store *n.* 567, 568, 730; *vb.* 192, 461, 567
stores *n.* 305
storey *n.* 206
storm *n.* 80, 175, 359, 645; *vb.* 645, 893
storm in a teacup *n.* 481
story *n.* 460, 465, 525, 526, 528
story-teller *n.* 460, 480, 525
stout *adj.* 161, 194, 204
stove *n.* 763
stow away *vb.* 567
straight *adj.* 248, 476, 915, 931
straighten *vb.* 215, 248, 324
straight face *n.* 837
straight form *n.* 248
straightforward *adj.* 452, 476, 508, 632, 915, 931
strain *n.* 11, 97, 615, 792, 832; *vb.* 481, 617
strainer *n.* 264
strait *n.* 205, 353, 633
straiten *vb.* 205
straitjacket *n.* 712
strait-laced *adj.* 951
strand *n.* 207, 352
strange *adj.* 100, 466
stranger *n.* 100
strangle *vb.* 370, 963
stranglehold *n.* 712
strap *n.* 207; *vb.* 963
strapping *adj.* 161
stratagem *n.* 478, 631
strategy *n.* 558, 621
stratify *vb.* 206
stratosphere *n.* 348
stratum *n.* 206
stray *vb.* 285, 936
strayed *adj.* 706
streak *n.* 797, 797; *vb.* 817
stream *n.* 358, 474, 797; *vb.* 257, 343, 349, 358, 359
streamer *n.* 482
streamlined *adj.* 125
street *n.* 559
street-walking *n.* 952
strength *n.* 32, 159, 161, 173, 337, 400, 506, 585, 857
strengthen *vb.* 36, 159, 161, 173, 217, 304, 334, 337, 646, 857
strengthener *n.* 217
strenuous *adj.* 615, 633
stress *n.* 512, 528; *vb.* 468, 512, 573
stretch *n.* 109, 182, 336; *vb.* 182, 196, 202, 336
stretch a point *vb.* 481, 668
stretch one's legs *vb.* 616
strew *vb.* 95
stricken *adj.* 665
strict *adj.* 669, 681, 837, 951, 977
stride *n.* 269
strife *n.* 25, 615, 649
strike *n.* 144, 696; *vb.* 144, 282, 384, 696, 758, 963
strike a bad patch *vb.* 633
strike back *vb.* 647
strike out *vb.* 485, 686
striking *adj.* 458
string *n.* 49, 85, 202, 207; *vb.* 47
stringed instruments *n.* 794
stringent *adj.* 669
strings *n.* 700, 794
stringy *adj.* 207
strip *n.* 49, 202, 207; *vb.* 203, 228, 720, 817
stripe *n.* 677
striped *adj.* 817
stripling *n.* 131
striptease *n.* 228
strive *vb.* 604, 615, 642, 649, 651
stroke *n.* 341, 586, 609; *vb.* 758, 890
stroll *n.* 269; *vb.* 269, 281

strong adj. 32, 159, **161**, 173, 337, 506, 534, 585, 769, 774
stronghold n. 595, 646
strong point n. 627
strongroom n. 732
strong-smelling adj. 777
strong-willed adj. 534
structure n. 5, 47, 163, 242, 339
struggle n. 649; vb. 615, 642, 649
strum n. 783; vb. 783
strut n. 217
stub n. 482
stubborn adj. 143, 537, 672, 942
stubby adj. 203, 204
stuck up adj. 875
stud vb. 817
student n. 131, **428**, 474
studious adj. 384, 390, 472, 611
study n. 390, 394, 472, 475, 488, 526; vb. 384, 390, 394, 472, 602
stuff n. 3, 327, 566, 729; vb. 56, 75, 226, 265, 304, 865, 948
stuffing n. 192, 226, 265
stuffy adj. 843
stumble vb. 317, 515
stumble on vb. 158
stumbling-block n. 635
stun vb. 754, 796, 922
stunner n. 844
stunted adj. 195, 203
stupefy vb. 754, 866
stupendous adj. 32, 866
stupid adj. 427, 433, 435
stupidity n. 383, 427, 433, 435
stupor n. 754
stutter n. 515; vb. 515
sty n. 184
style n. 242, 492, **501**, 510, 850; vb. 496
stylish adj. 125, 850
subconscious adj. 382
subdivide vb. 48
subdue vb. 335, 679, 681, 779
subdued adj. 654, 781, 805
subject n. 387, 499, 525; vb. 679
subjection n. 35, 179, 679, 874
subject to adj. 35, 179, 679, 700, 919
subjugate vb. 679
sublimation n. 318, 346
sublime adj. 32, 208, 318, 868, 966, 982
subliminal adj. 382
sublimity n. 34
submarine n. 277
submerge vb. 321, 349
submerged adj. 210
submission n. **654**, 673, 757, 874
submissive adj. 654, 673, 679, 757, 874
submit vb. 468, 654, 673, 693, 757, 874
subnormal adj. 435
subordinate n. 35, 676; adj. 35, 679; vb. 679
subpoena n. 671, 960
subscribe vb. 424, 641
subscriber n. 424
subsequent adj. 85, 119, 156
subservient adj. 563, 673, 679, 874, 881
subside vb. 37, 197, 317
subsidiary adj. 563, 679
subsidize vb. 636, 715, 738
subsidy n. 636, 715, 738, 744
subsist vb. 1, 368
subsistence n. 1, 305
substance n. 3, 5, 223, 332, 450, 573
substandard adj. 35
substantial adj. 1, 3, 327, 450
substantiate vb. 161, 401, 413
substitute n. 149, 540, 688, 699, 943; vb. 142, 149, 689
substitution n. 142, **149**
substratum n. 206, 213
subsume vb. 98
subterfuge n. 478
subterranean adj. 210
subtle adj. 333, 459, 631
subtraction n. 38, **42**, 744
suburb n. 183
suburban adj. 183
subversion n. 148, 164
subversive adj. 148, 580
subvert vb. 148, 580
succeed vb. 85, 119, 287, 659, **661**
success n. 550, **661**
successful adj. 661, 664
succession n. 85, 91, 119, 287
successor n. 119
succinct adj. 203, 504, 527
succour n. 636
succulence n. 364
succulent adj. 306, 364
succumb vb. 179, 369
suck vb. 308
sucker n. 479
suckle vb. 304
suckling n. 131
suck up to vb. 881, 927
sudden adj. 115, 444, 544, 859
sudden and violent sound n. **782**
suds n. 363
sue vb. 960

suffer *vb.* 586, 590, 648, 752, 828, 963
suffer defeat *vb.* 662
sufferer *n.* 828
suffice *vb.* 28, 570, 831
sufficiency *n.* 570
sufficient *adj.* 75, 570
suffix *n.* 41, 87, 499; *vb.* 40
suffocate *vb.* 370, 759
suffrage *n.* 540
sugar *n.* 772, 891; *vb.* 772
sugary *adj.* 772
suggest *vb.* 155, 401, 441, 450, 459, 460, 597, 624, 693
suggestion *n.* 441, 459, 460, 482, 624, 693
suggestive *adj.* 401, 450, 459, 482
suicide *n.* 370
sui generis *adj.* 59, 102
suit *n.* 227, 960; *vb.* 105, 577
suitable *adj.* 136, 302, 575, 577, 896, 915
suitcase *n.* 193
suite *n.* 91, 191, 792
suitor *n.* 889, 960
sulk *vb.* 895
sullenness *n.* 895
sullied *adj.* 584, 952
sully *vb.* 584, 847, 869, 928, 952
sultry *adj.* 759
sum *n.* 26, 54, 731; *vb.* 40
summarize *vb.* 203, 504, 525, 527
summary *n.* 441, 525, 527; *adj.* 504
summer *n.* 127, 664, 759; *adj.* 127
summer time *n.* 116, 127
summery *adj.* 127, 759
summing up *n.* 527, 960
summit *n.* 89, 208, 212, 519, 581
summon *vb.* 94, 671, 695, 857, 901
summons *n.* 671, 960
sum up *vb.* 527, 960
sun *n.* 329, 800
Sunday School *n.* 988
sunder *vb.* 63
sundown *n.* 128
sunglasses *n.* 801, 804
sunken *adj.* 209, 210, 254
sunny *adj.* 664, 759
sunrise *n.* 127, 797
sunset *n.* 128
sunshine *n.* 797
sup *vb.* 304
super *adj.* 579
superabundance *n.* 32, 572
superannuated *adj.* 130
superannuation *n.* 687
superb *adj.* 579
supercilious *adj.* 875, 924
superficial *adj.* 211, 435, 574, 825, 852
superfluity *n.* 32, 572
superimpose *vb.* 225
superintend *vb.* 392, 622
superintendent *n.* 623
superior *n.* 34, 675; *adj.* 34, 579, 868
superiority *n.* 34, 84, 579, 868
superlative *n.* 499; *adj.* 34, 481, 579
supermarket *n.* 730
supernatural *adj.* 447, 971, 984
superpose *vb.* 225
supersede *vb.* 85
superstition *n.* 984
supervision *n.* 392, 593, 621, 622, 956
supervisor *n.* 623, 675
supper *n.* 306
supplant *vb.* 85
supple *adj.* 335
supplement *n.* 40, 41, 87; *vb.* 40, 196, 568
supplementary *adj.* 40
supplicant *n.* 697, 982; *adj.* 982
supplication *n.* 695, 982
supplies *n.* 564, 566, 729
supply *n.* 568; *vb.* 564, 568, 602, 715
support *n.* 213, 217, 401, 424, 636, 929; *vb.* 152, 217, 392, 401, 410, 424, 636, 907
supporter *n.* 217, 287, 424, 640, 821, 905
suppose *vb.* 416, 420, 448, 449
supposed *adj.* 448, 459, 825
supposition *n.* 448
suppress *vb.* 164, 461, 466, 513, 679, 681, 691
supreme *adj.* 34, 579, 581, 667, 966
sure *adj.* 152, 408, 531
surety *n.* 420, 593, 701
surf *n.* 363; *vb.* 271
surface *n.* 182, 211, 222; *adj.* 211; *vb.* 225, 331
surfeit *n.* 572, 865; *vb.* 865
surge *vb.* 316, 320, 325, 358
surgery *n.* 591
surly *adj.* 887, 895
surmise *n.* 448; *vb.* 420, 448
surmount *vb.* 316
surname *n.* 496
surpass *vb.* 6, 34, 314
surpassing *adj.* 32, 34, 579
surplice *n.* 989
surplus *n.* 44, 572

surprise n. 444, 829, 866; vb. 444, 866
surrender n. 556, 687, 708; vb. 556, 654
surround vb. 229, 231, 231
surroundings n. 8, 183, 229
surveillance n. 392, 622
survey n. 456, 526, 527, 818; vb. 400, 415, 526, 527, 818
surveyor n. 415
survive vb. 112, 145, 368, 661, 898
surviving adj. 44, 112, 368
survivor n. 898
susceptibility n. 179, 753
susceptible adj. 753, 894
suspect vb. 409, 421, 448
suspend vb. 89, 99, 135, 216, 607, 686, 920
suspended sentence n. 961
suspense n. 144, 409, 443
suspension n. 99, 135, 216, 607, 610
suspicion n. 409, 421, 423, 460, 860, 913
sustain vb. 91, 143, 145, 152, 217, 304, 636
sustenance n. 217, 305
swab vb. 583
swag n. 724
swallow vb. 302, 304, 757
swamp n. 355; vb. 56, 349
swampy adj. 355
swank n. 873, 879
swan song n. 89, 369
swap vb. 150, 725
swarm n. 94; vb. 75, 94, 168, 314, 572
swarthy adj. 808
swastika n. 221
sway n. 159, 177, 667; vb. 177, 216, 325, 326, 547, 667
swear vb. 468, 698, 901
swearword n. 901
sweat n. 310, 615 vb. 615
sweep n. 182, 247; vb. 182, 358, 359, 583
sweeping adj. 32, 54, 56, 98
sweet n. 306, 772, 891; adj. 772, 776, 790, 889
sweeten vb. 772
sweetener n. 772
sweetheart n. 891
sweetmeat n. 306
sweetness n. 772
swell n. 358, 780; adj. 844; vb. 36, 196, 252, 343, 358, 359
swelter vb. 759
swerve vb. 247, 285
swift adj. 280, 613
swim vb. 271, 331
swindle n. 478; vb. 478, 722, 932
swindler n. 480, 723
swing n. 140, 325; vb. 140, 216, 323, 325, 326
swirl vb. 323, 358
swish vb. 783, 786
switch n. 149, 964; vb. 149
switched off adj. 385
switch off vb. 89, 754, 798
switch on vb. 755, 797, 829
swivel vb. 323
swollen adj. 196, 252
swollen-headed adj. 875
swoop n. 317, 321; vb. 317
sword n. 677
swot n. 474
sycophancy n. 881
syllable n. 493, 494
syllabus n. 83, 527
syllogism n. 410
symbol n. 482, 493, 677
symbolic adj. 455, 482
symbolism n. 455
symbolize vb. 450, 482, 486
symmetry n. 16, 28, 244
sympathetic adj. 24, 302, 670, 882, 899, 907
sympathize vb. 907
sympathy n. 24, 752, 907
symphony n. 792
symphony orchestra n. 793
symposium n. 94, 410, 519
symptom n. 447, 482, 597
symptomatic adj. 60, 401, 482
synagogue n. 990
synchronism n. 122
synchronize vb. 24, 52, 122
syndicate n. 641
synod n. 625
synonym n. 28, 450, 494
synopsis n. 83, 527
syntactic adj. 499
syntax n. 492, 499
synthesis n. 52
syrup n. 362, 772
system n. 59, 79, 81, 103, 221
systematic adj. 79, 81, 140
systematize vb. 58, 81, 97

T

tab *n.* 482; *vb.* 482
table *n.* 83, 217, 306
tablet *n.* 591
taboo *n.* 691; *adj.* 691
tacit *adj.* 459
taciturnity *n.* 517
tackle *vb.* 88, 605
tack on *vb.* 40
tacky *adj.* 362
tactful *adj.* 398
tactical *adj.* 621
tactics *n.* 559, 621
tactless *adj.* 887
tag *n.* 482, 496; *vb.* 482, 496
tail *n.* 87, 89, 91, 237; *adj.* 237; *vb.* 37, 287, 554
taint *n.* 847; *vb.* 584, 952
take *vb.* 268, 720, 722
take action *vb.* 609
take advantage of *vb.* 136, 478, 575, 606, 952
take after *vb.* 18, 20
take away *vb.* 42, 720
take back *vb.* 31, 538
take care *vb.* 860
take care of *vb.* 392
take charge of *vb.* 593
take exception *vb.* 425, 893
take for granted *vb.* 443, 867, 880, 910
take from *vb.* 720
take heart *vb.* 836, 857
take in *vb.* 98, 302, 304, 452, 716, 795
take into account *vb.* 390
take it out of *vb.* 617
take it out on *vb.* 149, 900
take liberties *vb.* 918
take life *vb.* 370
take measures *vb.* 602
take notice *vb.* 390
take off *vb.* 20, 228, 273, 744
take on *vb.* 557, 605, 649
take out *vb.* 882
take over *vb.* 667
take pains *vb.* 615
take part in *vb.* 605, 639, 709
take place *vb.* 1, 153
take precautions *vb.* 860
take sides *vb.* 408, 639
take steps *vb.* 602, 609
take to *vb.* 545, 861
take umbrage *vb.* 893
take up *vb.* 540, 575, 716
take upon oneself *vb.* 605
taking *n.* 720
takings *n.* 724, 741
tale *n.* 460, 465, 525
talent *n.* 434, 627
talisman *n.* 984
talk *n.* 470, 492, 514, 518, 519; *vb.* 514
talkativeness *n.* 516
talk down *vb.* 273
talker *n.* 514
talk into *vb.* 547
talk out of *vb.* 548
talk over *vb.* 624
tall *adj.* 32, 202, 208, 318
tally *vb.* 24, 38
tame *adj.* 507, 654; *vb.* 377, 679
tan *n.* 810, 813; *adj.* 813; *vb.* 963
tandem *n.* 61, 276
tang *n.* 767, 769
tangency *n.* 201
tangent *n.* 285
tangerine *n.* 816
tangible *adj.* 3, 327, 758
tangle *n.* 45, 82; *vb.* 221
tangy *adj.* 769
tanker *n.* 277
tantalize *vb.* 547, 755
tantamount *adj.* 28; *adv.* 199
tantrum *n.* 893
tap *n.* 265, 360, 782; *vb.* 282, 358, 758, 782
tape *n.* 207; *vb.* 483
tape-measure *n.* 400
taper *n.* 800; *vb.* 37, 205, 255
tape-recorder *n.* 484, 794
tape-recording *n.* 483
tardy *adj.* 135
target *n.* 552, 716, 853
tariff *n.* 743
tarnish *n.* 847; *vb.* 584, 847, 869, 928
tarpaulin *n.* 225
tarry *vb.* 135, 281
tart *adj.* 769, 773
tartan *n.* 817
tart up *vb.* 844
task *n.* 557, 605
tassel *n.* 846
taste *n.* 339, 398, 753, 767; *vb.* 767
tasteful *adj.* 398, 510, 848, 876
taste good *vb.* 770
tasteless *adj.* 511, 768, 771, 849
tastelessness *n.* 399, 511, 768, 771, 849
tasty *adj.* 767, 770, 829
taunt *n.* 926; *vb.* 644, 853, 926
taut *adj.* 334
tautological *adj.* 451
tautology *n.* 505
tavern *n.* 191
tawdry *adj.* 849
tax *n.* 743
taxi *n.* 276; *vb.* 273
taxonomy *n.* 97, 375

tea *n.* 306, 309
tea-break *n.* 616
teach *vb.* 420, 470
teacher *n.* 428, 473, 624, 974, 986
teaching *n.* 470
team *n.* 94
team-mate *n.* 640
team up with *vb.* 639
teamwork *n.* 639
tear *vb.* 48, 280, 613
tea-room *n.* 191
tears *n.* 839
tease *vb.* 755, 830, 842
technique *n.* 488, 606
tedious *adj.* 841, 843
teem *vb.* 75, 572
teenager *n.* 131
teens *n.* 70, 129
teeter *vb.* 325
teeth *n.* 159
teetotalism *n.* 944, 949
telecommunications *n.* 467
telegram *n.* 460, 467
telegraphic *adj.* 504
telepathy *n.* 447
telephone *n.* 467; *vb.* 460
telescope *n.* 329, 822; *vb.* 203
television *n.* 467, 840
tell *vb.* 38, 460, 465, 514, 525, 624
tell apart *vb.* 398
teller *n.* 733
tell fortunes *vb.* 447
telling *adj.* 525
tell off *vb.* 926
tell on *vb.* 460
tell-tale *n.* 460; *adj.* 462
tell tales *vb.* 516
tell the future *vb.* 447
temerity *n.* 859
temper *n.* 5, 751; *vb.* 142, 176, 334, 335, 403
temperament *n.* 5, 751
temperamental *adj.* 756, 894
temperance *n.* 935, 944, 949
temperate *adj.* 176, 759, 944, 949
temperature *n.* 400, 759
tempest *n.* 175, 359
tempestuous *adj.* 359
temple *n.* 990
temporal *adj.* 107, 116, 987
temporary *adj.* 113, 149, 396
tempt *vb.* 547
temptation *n.* 547
tempting *adj.* 306, 770
tempt providence *vb.* 594, 859
ten *n.* 70; *adj.* 70
tenable *adj.* 420
tenacious *adj.* 50, 337, 534, 535, 537
tenancy *n.* 707
tenant *n.* 190, 710
tend *vb.* 178, 284, 377, 392
tendency *n.* 178, 284, 545, 751
tender *n.* 693; *adj.* 129, 335, 670, 752, 753, 889; *vb.* 693
tenderize *vb.* 335
tendril *n.* 207, 251
tenement *n.* 191
tenet *n.* 420, 974
tenor *n.* 178, 284, 450, 778
tense *n.* 499; *adj.* 756, 856
tension *n.* 25, 615, 642, 832
tent *n.* 225
tentative *adj.* 396, 448, 604
tenuous *adj.* 333
tenure *n.* 707
tepid *adj.* 759
tergiversation *n.* 538
term *n.* 93, 109, 494; *vb.* 496
terminal *n.* 89; *adj.* 89, 237
terminate *vb.* 89, 144, 164, 659
terminology *n.* 494, 496
terminus *n.* 89, 235, 298
terms *n.* 700
terms of reference *n.* 557
terrace *n.* 559
terra firma *n.* 352
terrain *n.* 352
terrestrial *adj.* 329, 352
terrible *adj.* 580, 856
terrific *adj.* 579
terrify *vb.* 856
territory *n.* 183, 956
terror *n.* 856
terrorism *n.* 955
terrorist *n.* 167, 175, 370
terse *adj.* 203, 432, 504
test *n.* 394, 396; *vb.* 408, 413
testify *vb.* 401, 413, 468
testimonial *n.* 441, 483
testimony *n.* 401, 468, 483
tether *vb.* 47
text *n.* 432, 524
textbook *n.* 524
textile *n.* 221
textural *adj.* 339
texture *n.* 339
thank *vb.* 909, 965
thankful *adj.* 909
thankless *adj.* 576, 910
thanks *n.* 909
thanksgiving *n.* 838, 982
thaw *vb.* 345, 761
theatre *n.* 529, 840
theatrical *adj.* 529, 852, 877
theft *n.* 722

theism *n.* 974
theme *n.* 387
theology *n.* 974
theorem *n.* 410
theoretical *adj.* 448
theorist *n.* 448
theorize *vb.* 448
theory *n.* 157, 386, 448
therapeutic *adj.* 585, 589, 591
thermal *adj.* 759
thermometer *n.* 759, 766
thermostat *n.* 766
thesaurus *n.* 83, 494
thesis *n.* 387, 410, 448, 526
thick *adj.* 204, 332, 364, 435
thicken *vb.* 204, 332
thicket *n.* 374
thickness *n.* 204, 206, 332
thickset *adj.* 203, 204
thick-skinned *adj.* 754
thief *n.* 723, 906
thin *adj.* 33, 76, 205, 333, 507, 571; *vb.* 27, 333
thing *n.* 3, 163, 327, 609
thing added *n.* 41
thing subtracted *n.* 43
think *vb.* 384, 420, 448
thinkable *adj.* 404
think about *vb.* 552
think ahead *vb.* 558
thinker *n.* 448
think-tank *n.* 624
thinness *n.* 76, 205, 333
third *n.* 66; *adj.* 65
third party *n.* 653
thirst *n.* 350, 388, 861; *vb.* 861
thirst-quencher *n.* 309
thirsty *adj.* 350
thorn *n.* 255, 255
thorn in the flesh *n.* 592
thorny *adj.* 255, 633
thorough *adj.* 56, 148, 392
thoroughfare *n.* 313
thought *n.* 384, 386, 392, 420, 441
thoughtful *adj.* 384, 392, 410, 434, 837, 886
thoughtless *adj.* 385, 391, 393, 603, 859, 887, 900, 910
thousand *n.* 70
thrall *n.* 679
thrash *vb.* 282, 963
thread *n.* 49, 207; *vb.* 313
threadbare *adj.* 228
threadlike *adj.* 205, 207
threat *n.* 154, 594, 902
threatening *adj.* 154, 594, 651, 902
three *n.* 64; *adj.* 64
thresh *vb.* 378
threshold *n.* 233, 235
thrifty *adj.* 392, 748
thrill *n.* 756, 827; *vb.* 752, 755, 756, 829
thrive *vb.* 36, 168, 661, 664
throat *n.* 262
throaty *adj.* 515, 787
throb *n.* 325, 783; *vb.* 140, 325, 783, 828
throne *n.* 957
throng *n.* 75, 94; *vb.* 75, 94
throughout *adv., prep.* 107
throw *vb.* 290
throw away *vb.* 556, 713, 749
throwaway *adj.* 544
throw in *vb.* 311
throw in the towel *vb.* 556, 654
throw light on *vb.* 456
throw off *vb.* 295, 546
throw out *vb.* 607
throw up *vb.* 303
thrust *n.* 173, 178, 282, 290, 645; *vb.* 290, 645
thud *vb.* 782, 785
thug *n.* 723, 906
thumb through *vb.* 472, 818
thump *vb.* 282, 783, 785
thunder *n.* 325, 784; *vb.* 780, 782
thunderbolt *n.* 444
thunderstorm *n.* 175, 358
thunderstruck *adj.* 444, 866
thundery *adj.* 358
thwart *vb.* 445, 635, 637, 648, 662
tick *vb.* 783
ticket *n.* 482, 483, 743
tickle *vb.* 758, 829
tick off *vb.* 926
tide *n.* 358
tidy *adj.* 79, 392, 583; *vb.* 583
tie *n.* 28, 49; *vb.* 28, 47, 681
tier *n.* 93, 206
tie-up *n.* 47
tight *adj.* 47, 334, 950
tight-fisted *adj.* 750
tight-lipped *adj.* 517
till *n.* 732; *vb.* 378
tilt *vb.* 219, 220, 317
timber *n.* 217
timbre *n.* 512, 778
time *n.* 107, 109, 116, 400; *vb.* 116
time-honoured *adj.* 126, 922
timekeeping *n.* 116
timelessness *n.* 108, 114
timeliness *n.* 136
timepiece *n.* 116
time-saving *adj.* 748
time-server *n.* 538, 934
timetable *n.* 116, 460
timid *adj.* 856, 858, 876
timing *n.* 116, 140

timorous adj. 856
tin n. 193; vb. 599
tincture n. 45, 805
tinder n. 765
tinge n. 805; vb. 805
tingle vb. 752, 756
tininess n. 33, 195
tinker n. 728
tinkle n. 784
tinny adj. 787
tinsel n. 846
tint n. 27, 805; vb. 488
tinted adj. 805
tiny adj. 33, 195, 203
tip n. 212, 233, 255, 715, 965; vb. 212, 220, 909
tip-off n. 460, 597
tipple vb. 304, 950
tipsy adj. 950
tirade n. 518
tire vb. 617, 841
tired adj. 612, 617, 841
tiresome adj. 830, 841
tissue n. 339
titbit n. 770, 829
tit for tat n. 150, 647
titillate vb. 758, 829
title n. 496, 872
titled adj. 870
title-holder n. 661
titter n. 838
titular adj. 496
tizzy n. 326, 756
toady n. 881, 927; vb. 881
to and fro adv. 325
toast n. 309, 888; vb. 306, 888
tobacco n. 308
today n. 120
toddler n. 131
to-do n. 80, 756
toe n. 213
together adj. 47; adv. 60
togetherness n. 60
toil n. 615; vb. 615
toilet n. 227
token n. 4, 441, 482, 701
tolerable adj. 579, 666
tolerant adj. 288, 670, 690
tolerate vb. 670, 690, 911
toll n. 716, 743; vb. 783
tomb n. 372
tomorrow n. 123; adv. 121, 123
tone n. 488, 512, 778, 805
tone down vb. 176, 779
toneless adj. 806
tongue n. 253, 492, 512, 767
tongue in cheek adj. 852
tongue-tied adj. 513
tonic n. 591
tonsure n. 228
too adv. 40
tool n. 565
tooth n. 255; vb. 259
toothless adj. 130, 256
top n. 89, 208, 212, 222; adj. 212; vb. 34, 212, 316
top-heavy adj. 29, 330
topic n. 387
topical adj. 125
top-notch adj. 573, 579
topple vb. 220, 317, 319
topsy-turvy adj. 220
top up vb. 56
Torah n. 976
torch n. 765, 800
torment n. 828; vb. 830, 856, 900, 902
torn adj. 48, 262
tornado n. 175, 323, 359
torpedo n. 290
torpid adj. 174, 612
torrent n. 358, 572
torrential adj. 358
tortoise n. 281
tortuous adj. 251
torture n. 828, 900, 963; vb. 830, 900, 963
toss vb. 290, 326
toss-up n. 553
tot n. 131
total n. 40, 54; adj. 54; vb. 38, 40
totalitarian adj. 669
totality n. 54
totem n. 967, 983
totter vb. 325, 326
touch n. 753, 758, 805; vb. 201, 752, 755, 758
touch-and-go adj. 553
touch down vb. 273, 298, 317
touched adj. 752, 756
touch on vb. 211, 450
touch up vb. 587, 589, 805
touchy adj. 756, 894
tough adj. 161, 334, 337, 506, 633, 857
toughen vb. 334, 337
toughness n. 161, 334, 337
tour vb. 269, 322
tourism n. 269
tourist n. 270
tournament n. 649
tout n. 697, 728; vb. 695
tow vb. 291
towards adv. 284
tower n. 208; vb. 32, 34, 208, 316
towering adj. 32, 208
tower of strength n. 640
town n. 183
townsman n. 190
toxic adj. 164, 580, 586
trace n. 33, 401, 483, 774; vb. 157, 232, 525
tracing n. 22, 232
track n. 559, 658; vb. 287, 554
track down vb. 419
tractable adj. 654, 919
tractor n. 291

trade *n.* 150, 557, 725; *vb.* 150, 725, 727
trader *n.* 728
tradition *n.* 126, 545, 641, 979
traditional *adj.* 126, 143
traditionalist *n.* 105, 143
traffic *n.* 313, 725; *vb.* 725
trafficker *n.* 728
traffic warden *n.* 956
tragedy *n.* 529, 551
tragic *adj.* 551, 830
trail *n.* 483, 774; *vb.* 287, 291, 554
trailer *n* 276, 291
train *n.* 85, 91, 276, 291; *vb.* 377, 470, 545, 602
trained *adj.* 426, 627
trainee *n.* 474
trainer *n.* 473
training *n.* 470, 472, 545, 602, 627
traitor *n.* 148, 480, 538, 940
tramp *n.* 269, 270, 612, 697, 940
trance *n.* 754, 984
tranquil *adj.* 616, 757
tranquillize *vb.* 652
tranquillizer *n.* 176, 591
transact *vb.* 609, 727
transaction *n.* 153, 699, 725
transcend *vb.* 6, 32, 34, 314
transcribe *vb.* 456, 521
transcriber *n.* 521
transcript *n.* 22, 521
transcription *n.* 456, 521, 792
transfer *n.* 22, 149, 150, 714; *vb.* 142, 149, 268, 275, 714
transferable *adj.* 268, 714
transferal *n.* 268
transference *n.* 142, 149, 268, 455, 714
transfix *vb.* 152
transform *vb.* 142, 146
transformer *n.* 142
transfusion *n.* 45
transgression *n.* 672, 936, 955
transgressor *n.* 906, 940
transient *adj.* 113
transit *n.* 268
transition *n.* 142
transitional *adj.* 266
transitory *adj.* 113
translate *vb.* 20, 142, 456
translation *n.* 456, 495, 972
translator *n.* 456
transliterate *vb.* 456
translucent *adj.* 802, 804
transmission *n.* 460
transmit *vb.* 268
transmutation *n.* 142
transmute *vb.* 146
transparency *n.* 452, 486, 502, 802
transparent *adj.* 802, 806
transpire *vb.* 107, 153
transplant *vb.* 268, 378
transport *n.* 268, 756, 827; *vb.* 187, 275, 963
transpose *vb.* 149, 187, 220
transverse *adj.* 219
transvestite *n.* 953
trap *n.* 276, 463, 478, 596, 631; *vb.* 463, 478, 631, 720
trappings *n.* 711
trash *n.* 451
trashy *adj.* 580
traumatic *adj.* 856
travail *n.* 615
travel *vb.* 269
traveller *n.* 270
traverse *vb.* 269, 313
travesty *n.* 22, 487
treacherous *adj.* 478, 594, 932
treachery *n.* 478, 932
treacle *n.* 772
tread *vb.* 269
treason *n.* 478, 932
treasure *n.* 567, 579, 891; *vb.* 441, 889, 983
treasurer *n.* 733
treasury *n.* 732
treat *n.* 770, 829; *vb.* 526, 589, 591, 606, 738
treated *adj.* 602
treatise *n.* 526
treatment *n.* 488, 591, 606
treaty *n.* 24, 650, 699
treble *adj.* 65; *vb.* 65
tree *n.* 374
trek *n.* 313; *vb.* 269
tremble *vb.* 326, 756, 856
tremendously *adv.* 32
tremor *n.* 325, 326, 856
tremulous *adj.* 326
trench *n.* 210, 234, 254, 259, 261, 360
trenchant *adj.* 255, 506
trenches *n.* 646, 658
trend *n.* 178, 850
trepidation *n.* 856
trespass *n.* 703, 938, 955; *vb.* 300, 314
trial *n.* 551, 592, 604, 828; *adj.* 396, 396, 604
triality *n.* 64
triangle *n.* 64, 246
tribe *n.* 11
tribulation *n.* 828
tribunal *n.* 957, 958
tributary *n.* 358
tribute *n.* 743, 909
trick *n.* 433, 478, 631, 932; *vb.* 431, 478, 478, 631
trickery *n.* 478

trickle *vb.* 358
trickster *n.* 480, 631
trifle *n.* 33, 574; *vb.* 478
trigonometry *n.* 38
trill *vb.* 512, 783, 789
trim *vb.* 37, 203, 538, 844
trimming *n.* 846
trimmings *n.* 44
trimness *n.* 583
trinity *n.* 64, 967
trio *n.* 64, 792
trip *n.* 269, 909; *vb.* 478
triplication *n.* 65
trisection *n.* 66
trite *adj.* 432, 451, 843
triumph *n.* 153, 661
trivial *adj.* 451, 574
troll *n.* 970
trolley *n.* 276
troop *n.* 94, 655
trophy *n.* 441, 663, 965
tropical *adj.* 759
trot out *vb.* 514
troubadour *n.* 528
trouble *n.* 615, 633, 642, 665, 830; *vb.* 82, 578, 580, 633, 830, 856
troubled *adj.* 665, 828, 837, 856
trouble-maker *n.* 596, 672, 906
trouble-shooter *n.* 653
troublesome *adj.* 164, 330, 633, 642, 830
trouble spot *n.* 596
trough *n.* 259, 360
truancy *n.* 189, 920
truant *n.* 555, 600
truce *n.* 144, 650
truck *n.* 217; *vb.* 268
true *adj.* 1, 430, 450, 882, 915
true-to-life *adj.* 525
truism *n.* 432, 451
trump up *vb.* 477, 930
truncate *vb.* 203
trunk *n.* 193
truss *n.* 217
trust *n.* 408, 420, 443, 685, 736, 854; *vb.* 420, 854, 980
trustee *n.* 688, 733
trusteeship *n.* 685
trustworthy *adj.* 408, 420, 868, 931
truth *n.* 1, 408, 430, 432, 977
truthful *adj.* 430, 476
truthfulness *n.* 476, 931
try *n.* 604; *vb.* 604, 615, 767, 960
trying *adj.* 633, 830
tube *n.* 360, 361, 559
tuck *n.* 260, 306; *vb.* 304
tug *n.* 277, 291; *vb.* 291
tuition *n.* 470
tumble *vb.* 317, 358
tumid *adj.* 252
tumour *n.* 252
tumult *n.* 80, 175, 326, 780
tumultuous *adj.* 80
tundra *n.* 356
tune *n.* 792
tuneful *adj.* 528, 790, 792
tunnel *n.* 254, 360; *vb.* 254, 264
turbulence *n.* 80, 175, 326
turf *n.* 374, 812
turmoil *n.* 80, 175, 326, 668
turn *n.* 251, 260, 323; *vb.* 142, 177, 247, 251, 256
turn around *vb.* 289
turn aside *vb.* 285
turn away *vb.* 295, 391, 555
turn back *vb.* 147
turn down *vb.* 694
turn in *vb.* 556, 612, 681
turning *n.* 285
turning point *n.* 136
turn inside out *vb.* 220, 394
turn into *vb.* 146
turn off *vb.* 754, 771
turn on *vb.* 755, 829
turn out *vb.* 153, 227
turn-out *n.* 821
turn over *vb.* 220, 317
turn-over *n.* 741
turn to *vb.* 575, 624
turn up *vb.* 153, 188, 298, 444, 825
turn upside down *vb.* 220
turquoise *adj.* 815
tussle *n.* 649
tutor *n.* 473
twaddle *n.* 451, 516
twang *n.* 515
tweet *vb.* 789
twice *adv.* 62
twig *n.* 374; *vb.* 419, 452
twilight *n.* 128, 799
twin *n.* 11, 28; *adj.* 13, 18, 61, 62; *vb.* 62
twine *n.* 207, 251; *vb.* 221, 251
twinge *n.* 828
twinkle *n.* 797, 818; *vb.* 326, 797, 818, 838
twinkling *n.* 115
twirl *n.* 323; *vb.* 251, 323
twist *n.* 245, 251; *vb.* 219, 221, 245, 247, 251, 323
twitch *vb.* 326
twitter *vb.* 789
two *n.* 61
two-edged *adj.* 454
two-faced *adj.* 477, 932
two-time *vb.* 932
tycoon *n.* 728
type *n.* 23, 97, 482, 522; *vb.* 521
typescript *n.* 521

typhoon *n.* 359
typical *adj.* 18, 30, 101, 482, 486
typify *vb.* 23, 486
typist *n.* 521
typography *n.* 522
tyrannical *adj.* 669, 908
tyrannize *vb.* 669, 900
tyranny *n.* 669, 900
tyrant *n.* 669

U

ubiquitous *adj.* 101, 188
UFO *n.* 279
ugliness *n.* 245, 845, 849
ultimate *n.* 581, 939; *adj.* 89, 198
ultimatum *n.* 671
umbra *n.* 798
umbrella *n.* 225, 595, 801
umimaginable *adj.* 405
umpire *n.* 415, 653; *vb.* 653
unable *adj.* 160, 405
unacceptable *adj.* 500, 571
unaccompanied *adj.* 59
unaccustomed *adj.* 546
unacknowledged *adj.* 910
unadorned *adj.* 508
unadulterated *adj.* 46, 430, 581, 951
unadventurous *adj.* 612
unaffected *adj.* 508, 632, 754, 921
unamazed *adj.* 867
unambiguous *adj.* 408, 450, 452, 502
unambitiousness *n.* 863
unanimity *n.* 24, 424, 643
unappealing *adj.* 771
unappetizing *adj.* 771
unappreciative *adj.* 910
unapproachable *adj.* 198, 885
unashamed *adj.* 942
unasked *adj.* 532
unassailable *adj.* 408, 593
unassuming *adj.* 874, 876
unattached *adj.* 48, 678, 897
unattested *adj.* 409
unauthenticity *n.* 431, 978
unauthorized *adj.* 955
unavailable *adj.* 189, 405, 576
unavoidable *adj.* 154, 531, 674
unaware *adj.* 427, 754, 796
unbalanced *adj.* 439, 916
unbeaten *adj.* 661
unbecoming *adj.* 845, 887
unbelief *n.* 409, 421, 866, 975
unbending *adj.* 334, 534, 669
unbiased *adj.* 415, 541, 915, 933
unbind *vb.* 48, 601, 680
unblemished *adj.* 54, 581, 583, 935
unbolt *vb.* 262
unbosom *vb.* 462
unbound *adj.* 708, 921
unbreakable *adj.* 334, 337
unbroken *adj.* 54, 91, 145
unburden oneself *vb.* 462
uncanny *adj.* 971, 984
unceasing *adj.* 114, 145
uncertainty *n.* 325, 409, 421, 454, 553
uncertified *adj.* 409
unchangeable *adj.* 13, 143, 152
unchanging *adj.* 16, 143, 669
uncharitable *adj.* 900
uncharted *adj.* 427
unchaste *adj.* 952
unclassified *adj.* 35
uncle *n.* 11
uncleanness *n.* 584, 586, 777, 952
unclear *adj.* 409, 453, 503, 633, 803
uncoil *vb.* 81, 248
uncomfortable *adj.* 187
uncommon *adj.* 139
uncommunicative *adj.* 517, 863, 885
uncomplaining *adj.* 757, 831
uncompleted *adj.* 660
uncomplicated *adj.* 46, 632, 634
uncomplimentary *adj.* 926
uncompromising *adj.* 537, 669
unconcerned *adj.* 389, 391, 393, 863, 933
unconditional *adj.* 56, 408
unconfirmed *adj.* 409
unconformity *n.* 106
unconnected *adj.* 10, 48, 92
unconscious *n.* 382; *adj.* 427, 531, 754
unconsecrated *adj.* 987
unconsidered *adj.* 544
unconstitutionality *n.* 955
uncontrolled *adj.* 668, 672, 921
unconventional *adj.* 106

unconverted adj. 975
uncooperative adj. 642
uncouple vb. 48
uncouth adj. 511, 849
uncover vb. 419, 462
uncritical adj. 399, 416
unctuousness n. 365, 927
uncultured adj. 427, 887
uncurl vb. 248, 324
undamaged adj. 54
undated adj. 117
undaunted adj. 535, 857
undecided adj. 325, 409, 536
undefiled adj. 937, 951
undependable adj. 932
under adv. 209
undercarriage n. 217
undercover adj. 459
undercurrent n. 358, 459, 596
underdeveloped adj. 459
underdog n. 35, 662, 871
underdone adj. 771
underestimation n. 416, 418
underfoot adv. 209
underframe n. 217
undergo vb. 153, 752, 828
undergraduate n. 474
underground n. 276, 480, 559; adj. 148, 210; adv. 209
undergrowth n. 374
underhand adj. 461, 478, 631, 932
underline vb. 468, 573
underlying adj. 209, 213, 459
underneath adv. 209
underplay vb. 418
under-privileged adj. 735
underrate vb. 418, 923
understanding n. (knowledge) 382, 410, 426, 434; (agreement) 24, 643, 699, 704; (pity) 907
understate vb. 418, 477, 487
understood adj. 459
understudy n. 149, 529
undertaker n. 372
undertaking n. 557, 604, 605, 609, 698, 699
undertone n. 781
undervalue vb. 416, 418
underwater adj. 210
underworld n. 973
underwrite vb. 701
undeserved adj. 918
undesirable adj. 578
undeveloped adj. 603
undiscerning adj. 399, 435
undiscovered adj. 427
undiscriminating adj. 399
undisputed adj. 24, 408, 430
undistinguished adj. 869
undivided adj. 54, 56
undo vb. 48, 164, 262, 680
undress n. 228; vb. 228
undressing n. 228
undueness n. 918
undulate vb. 140, 251, 325, 358
unearth vb. 186, 372, 419
uneasy adj. 828, 832, 856
uneducated adj. 427, 628
unemotional adj. 754
unemployed adj. 607, 610, 612
unending adj. 202
unenterprising adj. 612
unenthusiastic adj. 533, 754
unequal adj. 29, 59
unequipped adj. 603
unequivocal adj. 408, 452
unerring adj. 408
uneven adj. 17, 29, 92, 141, 245, 258
unexpected adj. 158, 407, 444
unexplored adj. 885
unexpurgated adj. 952
unfailing adj. 408, 420
unfair adj. 416, 916, 918
unfaithful adj. 431, 538, 703, 920
unfamiliar adj. 106
unfashionableness n. 849
unfasten vb. 262
unfavourable adj. 137, 578, 665, 926
unfeeling adj. 669, 754, 908
unfinished adj. 57, 582
unfitting adj. 578, 916
unflinching adj. 534, 857
unfold vb. 262, 324, 458, 462
unforeseen adj. 444
unforgettable adj. 441
unforgivable adj. 916, 936
unforgiving adj. 908
unfortunate adj. 662, 665, 828
unfounded adj. 2
unfreeze vb. 761
unfriendly adj. 883, 885, 887, 900
unfrock vb. 686, 869
unfruitful adj. 169
unfurl vb. 324, 462
ungodly adj. 936, 975, 981

ungracious *adj.* 887
ungrammatical *adj.* 500
ungrateful *adj.* 910
unguarded *adj.* 393, 603
unguent *n.* 342, 365; *adj.* 365
unhallowed *adj.* 981
unhappy *adj.* 665, 828, 832, 837
unharmed *adj.* 593
unhealthy *adj.* 586
unheard of *adj.* 407, 444, 869
unheeding *adj.* 393
unhelpful *adj.* 576
unhesitating *adj.* 534
unhindered *adj.* 678
unhitch *vb.* 48
unholy *adj.* 975, 981
unhurt *adj.* 593
unhygienic *adj.* 586
unidentified *adj.* 497
uniform *n.* 227, 677; *adj.* 16, 46, 140, 152, 257
uniformity *n.* 13, 16, 24, 28, 79
unify *vb.* 47, 52, 59
unilateral *adj.* 10
unimaginative *adj.* 508
unimpaired *adj.* 54
unimpeded *adj.* 678
unimportance *n.* 451, 574
unimpressed *adj.* 867
uninhabited *adj.* 189, 885
uninspired *adj.* 507, 843
uninspiring *adj.* 841
unintelligibility *n.* 453, 503
unintended *adj.* 451
unintentional *adj.* 158, 531, 553
uninterested *adj.* 389, 612
uninteresting *adj.* 771, 841, 843
uninterrupted *adj.* 91, 143, 145
uninvited *adj.* 532
uninviting *adj.* 771, 805
uninvolved *adj.* 10, 863
union *n.* 47, 52, 180, 296, 641, 896
unique *adj.* 21, 59, 102
unison *n.* 24, 790
unit *n.* 59, 655
unite *vb.* 45, 47, 180, 296, 639, 896
unity *n.* 16, 54, 59, 643
universal *adj.* 32, 54, 56, 101, 329
universe *n.* 329
university *n.* 475
unjust *adj.* 916, 918
unjustifiable *adj.* 916
unkempt *adj.* 584
unkind *adj.* 887, 900
unknown *n.* 427; *adj.* 427, 466, 497
unlawful *adj.* 691, 952, 955
unlearned *adj.* 427
unlike *adj.* 15, 19
unlikely *adj.* 407, 409
unlit *adj.* 798
unload *vb.* 42, 187, 331
unlocked *adj.* 262
unlovely *adj.* 845, 849
unloving *adj.* 900
unlucky *adj.* 665
unman *vb.* 160
unmarried *adj.* 897
unmask *vb.* 458, 462
unmelodious *adj.* 791
unmentioned *adj.* 459
unmerited *adj.* 918
unmindful *adj.* 393, 427, 442, 910
unmistakable *adj.* 408, 458, 823
unmix *vb.* 46
unmixed *adj.* 430
unmotivated *adj.* 158
unmoved *adj.* 535, 754, 863, 908
unmusical *adj.* 791
unnatural *adj.* 852
unnecessary *adj.* 576, 918
unnerve *vb.* 837, 856
unobservant *adj.* 391
unobtainable *adj.* 405
unobtrusive *adj.* 876
unoccupied *adj.* 189, 612, 614, 708
unoffending *adj.* 937
unopened *adj.* 263
unorganized *adj.* 80, 603
unoriginal *adj.* 431
unorthodox *adj.* 106, 975, 978
unpack *vb.* 42, 187
unpaid *adj.* 737, 917
unparalleled *adj.* 866
unpatriotic *adj.* 904
unpitying *adj.* 908
unpleasant *adj.* 828, 830, 887
unpolished *adj.* 849
unpolluted *adj.* 583
unpopular *adj.* 862
unprecedented *adj.* 59, 866
unpredictable *adj.* 139, 158, 409, 539
unprejudiced *adj.* 415, 915, 933
unpremeditated *adj.* 544
unprepared *adj.* 444, 603
unprepossessing *adj.* 845
unpretentious *adj.* 508, 874
unprincipled *adj.* 932
unprivileged *adj.* 918
unproductiveness *n.* 160, 169
unprofessional *adj.* 628

unprofitable adj. 169, 706, 910
unprompted adj. 532
unprotected adj. 160, 228
unproved adj. 396, 448
unqualified adj. 46, 56, 603, 628
unravel vb. 48, 81, 248, 324, 680
unreadable adj. 453
unready adj. 135, 444, 533, 603
unreal adj. 2, 328, 431
unrealistic adj. 19, 416, 449
unreasonable adj. 407, 412, 572, 745, 916
unreasoning adj. 385, 435
unrecognizable adj. 453
unrecorded adj. 126
unrefined adj. 584, 849, 887
unrelated adj. 10
unrelenting adj. 537, 908, 912
unreliable adj. 151, 409, 421, 932
unremitting adj. 114, 143
unrepentant adj. 942
unreserved adj. 476
unresponsive adj. 423, 754, 754, 863
unrest n. 266, 832
unrestrained adj. 678, 921, 945
unrestricted adj. 921
unretained adj. 442
unrewarding adj. 576, 910
unripe adj. 129, 773, 812
unrivalled adj. 34
unroll vb. 324
unruffled adj. 267, 757
unruly adj. 644, 672
unsafe adj. 594
unsatisfactory adj. 445, 571, 580, 582
unsatisfied adj. 861
unsavouriness n. 771
unscathed adj. 593
unscholarly adj. 427
unscrupulous adj. 631, 932
unsearchable adj. 453
unseat vb. 187, 686
unseeing adj. 819
unseemly adj. 137, 511, 578, 845
unseen adj. 427, 461, 824
unselective adj. 399
unselfish adj. 747, 899, 933
unsettle vb. 82, 187
unsettled adj. 737, 917
unshakable adj. 408
unsightly adj. 849
unsinkable adj. 331
unskilfulness n. 427, 628
unskilled adj. 546, 603
unsociability n. 885, 895, 904
unsocial adj. 904
unsophisticated adj. 422, 508, 632, 937
unsound adj. 412, 431, 439, 582, 978
unspeakable adj. 32
unspiced adj. 768
unspirituality n. 327, 975
unspoken adj. 459, 779
unsportsmanlike adj. 916
unstable adj. 151, 536, 594
unsteady adj. 17, 141, 151, 162, 326
unstinting adj. 747
unsuccessful adj. 445, 662
unsuitable adj. 10, 137, 576, 578, 916
unsuited adj. 628
unsure adj. 409
unsurpassed adj. 34
unsuspecting adj. 422
unswerving adj. 534
unsympathetic adj. 883, 908
unsystematic adj. 80
untainted adj. 581, 937, 951
untarnished adj. 581, 583
untaught adj. 427
untenable adj. 412, 421
unthinkable adj. 405
unthinking adj. 158, 393, 411, 435, 544, 859
untidy adj. 80, 584; vb. 584
untie vb. 601, 680
untimeliness n. 137
untiring adj. 535
untold adj. 78, 427
untoward adj. 137
untrained adj. 427, 603
untrue adj. 2, 431
untruthful adj. 431, 477
untwist vb. 81, 248
unused adj. 44, 546, 607, 628
unusual adj. 106, 139, 866
unvarying adj. 13, 16
unveil vb. 228, 462
unverified adj. 409
unvoiced adj. 513, 779
unwary adj. 393
unwashed adj. 584
unwavering adj. 143, 152, 534
unwed adj. 897
unwell adj. 586
unwholesome adj. 580
unwieldy adj. 628
unwillingness n. 533
unwind vb. 324

unwise *adj.* 393, 416, 435, 578
unworthy *adj.* 918
unwrap *vb.* 324
unyielding *adj.* 112, 161, 334, 337, 534, 537
up *adv.* 208
update *vb.* 125, 587
upgrade *vb.* 587
upheaval *n.* 80, 148
uphill *adj.* 615, 633
uphold *vb.* 143, 145, 217, 929
upland *n.* 356
uplands *n.* 208
uplift *vb.* 318, 836
upper *adj.* 34
upper classes *n.* 870
uppermost *adj.* 212
upraised *adj.* 318
upright *adj.* 214, 248, 430, 915, 931, 935
uprising *n.* 358
uproar *n.* 80, 175, 780
uproot *vb.* 187, 312
upset *n.* 220, 414; *adj.* 837; *vb.* 82, 148, 830, 893
upshot *n.* 87, 156
upside-down *adj.* 220; *adv.* 80
upstanding *adj.* 214, 318
upstart *n.* 125, 880
upsurge *vb.* 36
uptight *adj.* 756, 894
up-to-date *adj.* 125
upward *adj.* 219, 316
urban *adj.* 183
urchin *n.* 970
urge *n.* 547, 861; *vb.* 468, 547, 613, 624, 674, 695
urgency *n.* 506, 562, 573, 613, 674, 695
urinate *vb.* 303, 310
urn *n.* 193, 372
usage *n.* 499, 501, 545, 606
use *n.* 606; *vb.* 575, 606, 707, 719
used *adj.* 126, 606
used to *adj.* 545
useful *adj.* 550, 575, 577
useless *adj.* 576, 662
usher in *vb.* 84
usual *adj.* 138, 545, 867
usurer *n.* 718
usurp *vb.* 918
utensil *n.* 565
utilitarian *adj.* 575
utilitarianism *n.* 903
utility *n.* 575, 606
utilize *vb.* 575, 606
utmost *n.* 235
utopia *n.* 449
utter *adj.* 56; *vb.* 512, 514, 788
utterance *n.* 492, 494, 498, 512, 514, 788

V

vacant *adj.* 189, 385, 435, 451
vacate *vb.* 187
vacation *n.* 144, 612, 614
vaccine *n.* 591
vacillate *vb.* 151, 325, 536
vacuity *n.* 2, 189
vacuum *n.* 2, 189, 333
vagabond *n.* 270, 697
vagrant *n.* 270
vague *adj.* 4, 243, 409, 454, 503, 799, 824
vain *adj.* 576, 662, 855, 875
valentine *n.* 523, 890
valiant *adj.* 857
valid *adj.* 413, 430, 915, 954
validate *vb.* 413, 954
validity *n.* 430, 954
valley *n.* 200, 209, 254
valour *n.* 857
valuable *adj.* 573, 575, 579
valuables *n.* 711
value *n.* 575, 579, 743; *vb.* 573, 743, 889, 922
valuer *n.* 415
valve *n.* 265
vampire *n.* 906, 969
van *n.* 276
vandal *n.* 167
vandalism *n.* 722
vanished *adj.* 2, 189, 706, 826
vanity *n.* 576, 873, 875, 934
vaporization *n.* 346
vaporous *adj.* 4, 344, 346
vapour *n.* 4, 343, 344, 346
variable *n.* 39; *adj.* 15, 17, 104, 142, 151
variance *n.* 15, 425, 642
variant *n.* 15; *adj.* 15
variation *n.* 15, 19, 104, 142
variegation *n.* 817
variety *n.* 19, 72, 104, 529
various *adj.* 104
varnish *vb.* 225, 257, 365
vary *vb.* 15, 142, 151
vase *n.* 193
vast *adj.* 32, 78, 182, 194
vastly *adv.* 32
vat *n.* 193
vault *n.* 252, 320, 329, 372, 732; *vb.* 320
vaulted *adj.* 247
vaunt *vb.* 879
veer *vb.* 142, 247, 285
vegetability *n.* 374

vegetable *n.* 306
vegetate *vb.* 169, 174, 612, 666
vegetation *n.* 374
vehement *adj.* 173, 175, 506, 759
vehicle *n.* 276, 563
veil *n.* 461, 463, 549, 801; *vb.* 225, 461, 801
veiled *adj.* 225, 459
velocity *n.* 266, 280
vendetta *n.* 425, 642
vendor *n.* 697, 727
veneer *n.* 211, 225; *vb.* 206, 225
venerable *adj.* 126, 130
venerate *vb.* 922, 982
vengeance *n.* 647, 912
venomous *adj.* 164, 580, 592
vent *n.* 262, 361, 600
ventilate *vb.* 348, 583
ventilation *n.* 348, 775
ventilator *n.* 361, 764
venture *n.* 269, 553, 604, 605; *vb.* 158, 553, 604, 918
veracity *n.* 476
verb *n.* 499
verbal *adj.* 450, 494, 514
verbalize *vb.* 498
verbose *adj.* 505, 516
verdict *n.* 415, 960
verge *n.* 233; *vb.* 233
verge on *vb.* 292
verify *vb.* 396, 401, 408, 413
veritable *adj.* 430
vermin *n.* 373
vernacular *n.* 492; *adj.* 190, 492
versatile *adj.* 151, 627
verse *n.* 528
versed *adj.* 602
version *n.* 456
vertebrate *n.* 373
vertical *adj.* 214, 248
verve *n.* 173, 368, 506, 611
very *adj.* 13; *adv.* 32
vespers *n.* 128, 988
vessel *n.* 193, 277
vestige *n.* 44
vestment *n.* 227, 989
vet *n.* 377
veteran *n.* 132, 629, 655; *adj.* 627
veterinary science *n.* 377
veto *n.* 681, 691, 694; *vb.* 691
vexed *adj.* 828, 893
via *adv.* 284
viable *adj.* 404
vibration *n.* 325, 326, 778, 784
vicar *n.* 689, 986
vicarious *adj.* 149, 685, 943
vicarious authority *n.* 685
vice *n.* 936; *adj.* 689
vicinity *n.* 199, 229
vicious circle *n.* 412
vicissitude *n.* 142
victim *n.* 479, 716, 828, 853
victimize *vb.* 478, 900
victor *n.* 661
Victorian *adj.* 126, 951
victorious *adj.* 661
victory *n.* 661
video-recorder *n.* 484
videotape *n.* 483
view *n.* 415, 420, 624, 818; *vb.* 818
viewer *n.* 821
vie with *vb.* 649
viewpoint *n.* 818
vigilant *adj.* 390, 392, 818, 860
vigilante *n.* 593
vigour *n.* 159, 161, 173, 368, 506, 585, 611
vile *adj.* 580, 777, 892
vilify *vb.* 901, 928
villa *n.* 191
village *n.* 183
villain *n.* 906, 940
vindicate *vb.* 647, 912, 929, 961
vindication *n.* 929
vindictive *adj.* 908, 912
vinegar *n.* 773
vineyard *n.* 378
violate *vb.* 314, 608, 672, 703, 920, 952, 955, 981
violence *n.* 175, 674
violent *adj.* 175, 642
violet *n.* 814; *adj.* 814
VIP *n.* 868
viper *n.* 906
virgin *n.* 897; *adj.* 125 427, 603, 897, 951
virgin territory *n.* 427
virile *adj.* 161, 380
virtual *adj.* 404
virtually *adv.* 199
virtue *n.* 876, 931, 935, 951
virtuoso *n.* 793
virtuous *adj.* 931, 935, 951
virus *n.* 167, 586, 592
visa *n.* 690
viscosity *n.* 362, 400
viscount *n.* 870
visibility *n.* 823
visible *adj.* 3, 458, 823, 825
vision *n.* 449, 458, 818, 854, 971, 976
visionary *n.* 449, 903; *adj.* 4, 449
visit *n.* 269, 884; *vb.* 188, 269, 300, 971
visitor *n.* 100, 270, 884
visual *adj.* 488, 818
visualize *vb.* 449
vital *adj.* 368, 562
vitality *n.* 161, 173, 368, 506, 585, 836

vitalize *vb.* 173, 368
vitreous *adj.* 802
vivacious *adj.* 368, 836
vivacity *n.* 514
vivid *adj.* 441, 506, 509, 525
vivisection *n.* 370
vocabulary *n.* 494, 501
vocal *adj.* 512, 792
vocalist *n.* 793
vocalize *vb.* 512, 514
vocation *n.* 557, 985
vociferous *adj.* 780, 788
vogue *n.* 125; *adj.* 495
voice *n.* 492, 512; *vb.* 512, 514
void *n.* 2, 74, 189; *adj.* 2, 333, 451; *vb.* 955
volatile *adj.* 151, 344, 346
volition *n.* 530
volte-face *n.* 147, 220, 289, 538
voluble *adj.* 509, 514, 516
volume *n.* 26, 194, 400, 524
voluntary *adj.* 530, 532
volunteer *vb.* 532, 693
voluptuous *adj.* 827, 945
vomit *vb.* 303
voodoo *n.* 984
voracity *n.* 750, 861, 948
vortex *n.* 323, 358
vote *n.* 540, 909; *vb.* 424, 540
voted *adj.* 424
voter *n.* 190, 540
vouch *vb.* 468
voucher *n.* 482, 741
vow *n.* 468, 698; *vb.* 468, 698
vowel *n.* 493, 512
voyage *n.* 271, 313; *vb.* 271
voyager *n.* 270
vulgar *adj.* 511, 849, 887, 952
vulnerable *adj.* 594, 753

W

wadding *n.* 226
wade *vb.* 271
wafer *n.* 306
waffle *vb.* 516
waft *vb.* 359
wag *n.* 842; *vb.* 325
wager *n.* 553
wages *n.* 731, 738, 741
wagon *n.* 276
wail *n.* 788, 839; *vb.* 788, 839
wait *vb.* 443, 610
wait and see *vb.* 135, 610
waiter *n.* 676
wait on *vb.* 287, 676
waive *vb.* 556, 713
wake *n.* 237
walk *n.* 269, 559; *vb.* 269
walk away with *vb.* 661
walker *n.* 270
walkie-talkie *n.* 467
walk out *vb.* 144, 556, 687
walkout *n.* 144
walk-over *n.* 634, 661
wall *n.* 217, 230, 234
wallet *n.* 193, 732
wallop *vb.* 282, 963
wan *adj.* 807
wand *n.* 677
wander *vb.* 269, 285, 505
wanderer *n.* 270
wandering *n.* 391
wane *n.* 37; *vb.* 37, 799
want *n.* 57, 562, 706, 861; *vb.* 57, 189, 530, 532, 562, 571, 861
wanted *adj.* 562, 600
wanton *adj.* 936, 952
war *n.* 649, 651
warble *vb.* 789
ward *n.* 183, 540
warden *n.* 593, 683
warder *n.* 683
ward off *vb.* 646
wardrobe *n.* 227
wardship *n.* 129
warehouse *n.* 567
wares *n.* 729
warfare *n.* 649, 651
warlike *adj.* 651
warm *adj.* 419, 759, 805; *vb.* 306, 761, 836
warm-hearted *adj.* 882, 899
warmth *n.* 506, 752, 759, 805, 882
warm up *vb.* 306
warning *n.* 447, 460, 597, 902; *adj.* 597
warp *vb.* 219, 247, 416, 487
warrant *n.* 424, 671, 685; *vb.* 690, 698, 917
warranty *n.* 701
warren *n.* 234, 254
warrior *n.* 655
wart *n.* 252
wary *adj.* 390, 860
wash *n.* 358, 805; *vb* 583, 805
washed out *adj.* 612, 617, 806
wash-out *n.* 662
waste *n.* 44, 164, 569 576; *vb.* 569, 608, 749
waste away *vb.* 53, 586 588
wasted *adj.* 205, 569
wasteful *adj.* 393, 569, 749
waste-pipe *n.* 600
waste time *vb.* 612
wastrel *n.* 612, 749, 940

watch *n.* 116, 646; *vb.* 392, 818
watchdog *n.* 593
watcher *n.* 821
watchful *adj.* 392, 443, 818, 860
watchman *n.* 683
watchword *n.* 432
water *n.* 309, 347; *vb.* 378
water channel *n.* 360
water down *vb.* 45, 162
waterfall *n.* 358
water in motion *n.* 358
waterlogged *adj.* 349, 355
waterproof *adj.* 350, 593
watershed *n.* 230
water sports *n.* 271
watertight *adj.* 265, 350
water travel *n.* 271
waterway *n.* 358
watery *adj.* 343, 347
wave *n.* 325, 358, 482; *vb.* 325, 482, 886
wavering *n.* 142, 151, 325, 409, 536; *adj.* 141, 151, 326, 536
wavy *adj.* 251
wax *n.* 342, 800; *vb.* 36, 225
way *n.* 198, 313, 559
wayfarer *n.* 270
way out *n.* 301, 600
wayward *adj.* 151, 672
weak *adj.* 162, 507, 586, 617, 628, 781, 858
weak-minded *adj.* 162, 435
weakness *n.* 162, 178, 315, 507, 586, 617, 858, 936
weak spot *n.* 582, 594
wealth *n.* 168, 664, 711, 731, 734
wean from *vb.* 546, 548
weapons *n.* 657
wear *vb.* 227
wear and tear *n.* 569
wear away *vb.* 341
wear down *vb.* 160, 547
weariness *n.* 612, 617, 841
wearisome *adj.* 633, 841
wear out *vb.* 569, 617
weather *n.* 348
weave *n.* 339; *vb.* 221, 313
web *n.* 221, 339
wed *adj.* 47; *vb.* 896
wedding *n.* 896
wedge *n.* 230, 246, 265
weed *n.* 374; *vb.* 378
weedy *adj.* 205
week *n.* 109
weep *vb.* 301, 833, 839, 907
weigh *vb.* 330, 397, 415
weight *n.* 26, 177, 194, 330, 400, 573; *vb.* 330
weighting *n.* 31
weightless *adj.* 331
weigh up *vb.* 384
weird *adj.* 971, 984
welcome *n.* 302; *adj.* 827; *vb.* 302, 884, 886
welcoming *adj.* 716
weld *n.* 49; *vb.* 50
welfare *n.* 550, 664
well *n.* 254, 567; *adj.* 585; *vb.* 301, 358
well-behaved *adj.* 673
well-being *n.* 550, 585, 664
well-dressed *adj.* 227
well-formed *adj.* 499, 844
well grounded *adj.* 426
well-meaning *adj.* 899
well-off *adj.* 664, 734
well-proportioned *adj.* 244, 510, 844
well-read *adj.* 426, 472
well thought of *adj.* 868, 922
well-turned *adj.* 510
well-versed *adj.* 426, 627
weltschmerz *n.* 837
west *n.* 284
wet *n.* 347, 349; *adj.* 347, 349; *vb.* 349
wet blanket *n.* 548, 841
whack *n.* 782; *vb.* 282, 782, 963
whacked *adj.* 617
whale *n.* 194
what's-its-name *n.* 497
wheedle *vb.* 547, 927
wheel *n.* 250
wheeled *adj.* 276
wheeze *vb.* 359, 786
when *adv., prep.* 107
whereabouts *n.* 185
wherewithal *n.* 564, 566
whet *vb.* 255, 755
while *adv., prep.* 107
while away *vb.* 107, 612
whim *n.* 449, 539
whimper *vb.* 788, 839
whimsical *adj.* 449, 539, 842, 851
whine *vb.* 784, 788, 789, 839
whip *n.* 964; *vb.* 282, 963
whip up *vb.* 175, 755
whirl *n.* 323; *vb.* 323, 358, 359
whirlpool *n.* 323, 358
whirlwind *n.* 323, 359
whirr *n.* 783, 786; *vb.* 783, 784, 786
whisk *n.* 359; *vb.* 359
whisper *n.* 460, 781; *vb.* 781
whistle *n.* 482, 786, 787; *vb.* 482, 786, 787, 789
white *n.* 807, 951; *adj.* 583, 806, 807

white flag *n.* 652
whittle *vb.* 203
whiz *vb.* 280, 786
whizz-kid *n.* 629
whole *n.* 26, 54, 59; *adj.* 39, 54, 56, 581, 585
wholehearted *adj.* 534
wholesale *adj.* 54, 56, 98
wholesome *adj.* 438, 585
whoop *vb.* 788, 840
whore *n.* 953
wicked *adj.* 551, 580, 900, 916, 932, 936, 981
wickerwork *n.* 221
wide *adj.* 101, 182, 204
widen *vb.* 36, 182, 204
widespread *adj.* 32, 54, 101, 182
widow *n.* 898; *vb.* 898
widowhood *n.* 898
width *n.* 26, 204, 400
wife *n.* 896
wiggle *vb.* 251
wild *adj.* 175, 433, 439, 859, 889
wilful *adj.* 530
will *n.* 530; *vb.* 530, 714
willies *n.* 856
willingness *n.* 532, 692
willpower *n.* 530, 534
wilt *vb.* 837
wily *adj.* 478, 631
win *vb.* 661, 705, 720
wince *vb.* 283
wind *n.* 359; *vb.* 251, 322
windfall *n.* 550, 715
window *n.* 262
wind up *vb.* 89, 116, 739
windy *adj.* 344, 348, 359
wine *n.* 309
wink *n.* 482, 818; *vb.* 482, 818
winner *n.* 661
winnings *n.* 724
winnow *vb.* 46, 48, 378
win over *vb.* 547
winsome *adj.* 829, 889
winter *n.* 128; *adj.* 128
wintry *adj.* 128, 760
wipe *vb.* 341
wipe out *vb.* 164, 485, 911
wire *n.* 207, 460, 467; *adj.* 611; *vb.* 460
wireless *n.* 467
wiry *adj.* 207
wisdom *n.* 382, 392, 426, 434
wisecrack *n.* 842
wish *n.* 530, 854, 861; *vb.* 530, 854, 861
wishful thinking *n.* 449, 478, 854
wishy-washy *adj.* 162, 507, 666, 768
wisp *n.* 4, 207
wit *n.* 434, 842
witchcraft *n.* 984
withdraw *vb.* 42, 289, 293, 299, 312, 538, 556, 600, 687, 731, 826
withdrawn *adj.* 681, 885
wither *vb.* 350, 588
withhold *vb.* 461, 694, 712
within hearing *adv.* 199
within reach *adj.* 404
without *adv., prep.* 42; *prep.* 571
with reference to *adv., prep.* 9
withstand *vb.* 646, 648
with strings attached *adj.* 700
with the exception of *adv., prep.* 42
with young *adj.* 163
witness *n.* 401, 483; *vb.* 401, 413
witty *adj.* 840, 842
wizard *n.* 447, 984
wizened *adj.* 197, 205
wobble *n.* 326; *vb.* 325, 326
woe *n.* 580
wold *n.* 356
woman *n.* 133, 381
woman-hater *n.* 904
womanizer *n.* 953
women's rights *n.* 917
wonder *n.* 866; *vb.* 866
wonderful *adj.* 32, 579, 844
wont *n.* 545
woo *vb.* 882, 889, 890
wood *n.* 374, 765
woodwind *n.* 794
word *n.* 494, 698; *vb.* 498
word for word *adj.* 450, 456
wording *n.* 501
Word of God *n.* 976
word order *n.* 499
wordy *adj.* 505
work *n.* 163, 488, 521, 524, 557, 605, 615, 792; *vb.* 172, 557, 615, 676
workable *adj.* 406
work against *vb.* 181
worked up *adj.* 893
worker *n.* 609, 619, 676
work off *vb.* 149
work oneself up *vb.* 756
work one's way up *vb.* 316
work out *vb.* 38, 452, 552, 558, 659
workshop *n.* 620
work together *vb.* 52, 180
work up *vb.* 755
world *n.* 329, 379
worldliness *n.* 327, 329, 981
world-weariness *n.* 837, 841
worldwide *adj.* 32, 101

worm in *vb.* 300
worn *adj.* 162, 588
worn out *adj.* 612, 617, 841
worried *adj.* 828
worry *n.* 828, 856; *vb.* 830, 856
worse *adj.* 35
worsen *vb.* 588, 835
worship *n.* 922, 980, **982**; *vb.* 922, 980, **982**, 983, 988
worth *n.* 575, 579, 743; *adj.* 743
worthless *adj.* 574, 576, 580, 924
worthwhile *adj.* 965
worthy *adj.* 917, 935
wound *n.* 588, 828; *vb.* 580, 588, 830
wraith *n.* 971
wrangle *vb.* 642
wrap *vb.* 225, 227, 234
wrapped up in *adj.* 384, 934
wrap up *vb.* 227, 659
wrath *n.* 893
wreath *n.* 250
wreathe *vb.* 251
wreckage *n.* 164
wrecker *n.* 167
wrench *vb.* 312
wretch *n.* 828, 940
wretched *adj.* 665, 828, 837
wriggle *vb.* 251, 300
wrinkle *n.* 260; *vb.* 197, 251, 260
wrinkled *adj.* 130, 260
writ *n.* 671, 960
write *vb.* 58, 483, **521**, 528
write off *vb.* 739
writer *n.* 456, 521, 524, 528
write to *vb.* 523
write up *vb.* 526, 925
writhe *vb.* 245, 251
writhing *adj.* 828
writing *n.* 501, **521**, 528
writing on the wall *n.* 447, 597, 902
wrong *n.* 431, 551, **916**, 955; *adj.* 137, 416, 431, 580, **916**, 938, 955; *vb.* 580, 608, 916
wrongdoer *n.* 906, 940

X,Y,Z

yacht *n.* 277
yap *n.* 516; *vb.* 516, 789
yard *n.* 184, 234, 620
yarn *n.* 207, 525
yawn *vb.* 262, 612
yawning *adj.* 210, 262
year *n.* 109, 122
yearning *n.* 854, 861; *adj.* 861, 889
yeast *n.* 331
yell *n.* 788; *vb.* 788
yellow *n.* **813**; *adj.* 813, 858
yelp *n.* 782; *vb.* 787, 789
yes *n.* 424
yes-man *n.* 881
yesterday *n.* 124; *adv.* 121, 124
yield *n.* 163, 705; *vb.* 163, 335, 424, 654, 692
yoke *vb.* 47
yokel *n.* 871
young *adj.* 129
youngster *n.* 131
youth *n.* 88, **129**, 131
zeal *n.* 532, 759, 980
zealot *n.* 611
zealous *adj.* 532, 611, 980
zenith *n.* 212
zephyr *n.* 359
zero *n.* 74; *adj.* 74
zest *n.* 173, 611, 769, 827
zigzag *n.* 246; *vb.* 246, 325
zip *n.* 49, 173; *vb.* 280
zombie *n.* 971
zone *n.* 183, 184, 206
zoo *n.* 377
zoology *n.* 366, 373, **375**
zoom *vb.* 273, 613

GUIDE TO ENGLISH USAGE

Introduction

Anyone who sets out to write *A Guide to English Usage* is faced with a formidable task. One dictionary defines 'usage' as 'the customary manner of using a language or any of its forms, especially standard practice in a given language.' This will serve very nicely as a definition, but it can be of only limited assistance to the compilers of a book on the subject. One of the chief difficulties confronting them is that usage is constantly changing. What may have been unacceptable twenty years ago is now standard English. There is nothing particularly surprising in this: the English language, like everything else in this world, is constantly evolving and twenty years is quite long enough for some slang terms and colloquialisms to achieve the status of respectability, and for others to alter their meaning or to fade away altogether.

However, there is a real problem in dealing with words or phrases which are in some sense 'borderline cases' and have not yet become universally acceptable either because they are new or are being used in a new way. Thus the authors are constantly faced with a choice. Do they accept or reject? Is it their function to tell people what they *ought* to say or to describe what they *do* say? How is the written language to be distinguished from the spoken language?

In the *Guide to English Usage* the authors have faced these dilemmas to the best of their ability. They have pointed out instances where what may be acceptable in speech is not yet so in more formal language. They have indicated where words or meanings have become so entrenched in the language that they must be tolerated, however regrettable this may be. They have fought rearguard actions to try and preserve useful distinctions of meaning where these were in danger of being lost and have provided a sturdy defence against slipshod expressions and the vague and woolly thinking behind the use of so many vogue words and clichés.

The chief aim of the *Guide to English Usage* is to help people to express themselves clearly and to communicate more easily in both speech and writing through a better understanding of the English language. Set out in alphabetical order for ease of reference, the *Guide* deals with a variety of topics. There are articles on punctuation showing the correct use of commas, quotation marks, semicolons, the apostrophe and others. Although it is in no sense a grammar book, it does deal with specific points of grammar where these may prove a source of difficulty and of course the aid of grammar is enlisted where necessary to point out the misuse of words – a frequent source of error. English spelling bristles with difficulties and a number of entries have been devoted to this particular problem. Special attention has also been paid to American spelling where this differs from British English. Words whose meanings are confused (and there are, unfortunately, a large number of these) are dealt with together so that the distinction between them can be clearly pointed out.

This book is intended to be a concise but comprehensive guide to good English, and every effort has been made to present the information it contains in the simplest possible terms and to illustrate it with examples wherever practicable. The authors hope that, with the *Guide*, they have made a useful contribution to the understanding of English, in which everybody will find something of value.

A

a, an Use *a* before all words beginning with a consonant except silent *h* and before all words beginning with vowels which are sounded like consonants:

A good boy, a harvest, a historical event, a hotel, a unifying factor, a European.

Use *an* before words beginning with a vowel or a silent *h*:

An apple, an energetic man, an hour, an honour.

The use of *a* or *an* before initial letters pronounced as letters depends on whether these have a consonant or vowel sound at the beginning:

A B.A., a D.F.C., an F.A. cup match, an SOS signal.

It was formerly quite common to use *an* before an unstressed syllable in certain words beginning with an *h*:

An hereditary peer, an habitual response.

Some speakers and writers still do so but it is no longer considered current usage.

A and *an* are sometimes wrongly introduced in certain comparative expressions preceded by *no*:

No easier a task, no more formidable an opponent.

In the above phrases both *a* and *an* should be omitted.

a-, an- This is a Greek prefix meaning 'not' or 'without' which should normally be attached only to words of Greek origin, e.g. *anarchy*. It has, however, occasionally been prefixed to Latin words, e.g. *amoral* and *asexual*.

abbreviations and contractions Abbreviations are usually followed by a full stop:

mi. (mile, miles), Jan. (January), Lat. (Latin).

But there is an increasing tendency to omit the full stop in contractions – shortened forms of words in which the first and last letters of the full word are shown:

Dr, Mr, St, ft (foot, feet).

The full stop is usually omitted after points of the compass:

N, E, S, W, SW, NNE.

But note that in most cases it is better to spell these out. It is usually omitted after the shortened forms used in metric units of measurement:

km, m, cm, mm, kg.

It is usually omitted after symbols used in chemistry and physics:

H (hydrogen), Mg (magnesium), F (Fahrenheit).

The full stop is left out in words which have become fully accepted as independent although they are abbreviations of other words:

bra(ssiere), disco(theque), pop(ular), pub(lic house).

The full stop is also frequently omitted from the abbreviated titles of organizations which are usually known by their initials, especially when the initials are commonly pronounced as a word:

BBC, NATO, UNESCO, GATT.

abetter, abettor The generally accepted spelling is *abetter*, although *abettor* is preferred in the legal sense of one who encourages the commission of a crime.

abide This has the past tense *abode* when used in its archaic sense of 'dwell' or 'stay'. However, *abide by* has *abided* in the past tense:

He abided by his decision.

ability, capacity Although there is generally some overlapping in the way these words are used, the following distinction should be made. *Ability* is the power to accomplish things, whether physical or mental, and the skill displayed in so doing:

He showed great ability as a chess player.

Capacity means the power to absorb and hold things, such as ideas, impressions or knowledge:

She was not very talented but had a great capacity for hard work.

abjure, adjure These two verbs can cause some confusion. *Abjure* means to renounce or repudiate:

He abjured his errors.

Adjure is to request earnestly and solemnly, often under oath:

The priest adjured him to consider carefully before abandoning his religious beliefs.

-able Adjectives ending in *-able* may be formed from any transitive verb and from some nouns. If the verb ends in a silent *-e* this is usually dropped in the adjective:

desirable, pleasurable, insurable, debatable.

However, if the mute or silent *-e* is preceded by a soft *c* or *g* it is retained:

serviceable, replaceable, changeable, manageable.

There are a number of exceptions to the rule that the *-e* should be dropped, especially when the verb has only one syllable, and the following are a sample of those about which no agreement has yet been reached:

blamable or blameable, ratable or rateable, salable or saleable.

Final consonants are usually doubled before *-able* when they are also doubled in the present participle of the verb:

deferrable (deferring), forgettable (forgetting), regrettable (regretting).

The following are some exceptions:

inferable (inferring), preferable (preferring), transferable (transferring).

When the verb ends in a *y* preceded by a consonant, the *y* becomes an *i*:

deniable, justifiable, reliable.

If there is a vowel before the *y*, the *y* is retained:

payable, enjoyable.

[See also *spelling*]

ablutions Most authorities still deplore the use of this word except in the context of specific religious ceremonial. Condemned as pompous or pedantic, it is best avoided unless being deliberately used facetiously.

abnormal, subnormal Anything which does not conform to the rule or standard or to what is accepted is *abnormal*:

Everyone noticed his abnormal behaviour.

Subnormal means below or inferior to the normal or average:

Temperatures in the Arctic are usually subnormal.

aboriginal This adjective is also used as the singular of the noun *aborigines*. The form *aborigine* is generally little employed.

about When giving distances, measurements, etc. *about* should be used only with round numbers:

about 30 feet long *not* about 30.25 feet long.

above As an adjective in *the above statement*, as a noun in *the above* or as an adverb in *the statement above*, this word has attracted some criticism from modern writers as being both pedantic and not altogether clear. However, provided it is not overworked it can still serve a useful function.

abrasive This is a vogue word which has become very popular in the past few years in the sense of 'irritating' or 'tending to annoy'. It is already less fashionable and the reader is advised not to use it.

abridgement, abridgment The first spelling is now the preferred one.

abrogate, arrogate Similarity in spelling occasionally causes these two verbs to be confused. To *abrogate* is to repeal or abolish:

The new king abrogated many of his predecessor's laws.

To *arrogate* (to oneself) is to claim or assume unjustly or unreasonably:

The president arrogated to himself the final decision in everything.

absolute terms There are certain adjectives, such as *infinite*, *unique*, *maximum*, *ultimate*, which express an absolute idea – there are no degrees of infiniteness. Consequently these adjectives must not be preceded by *more*, *most*, *very* or *less*, because they cannot have a comparative form.

abstract words The primary aim of the speaker or writer should be to make himself understood. Accordingly, the advice given by reputable grammarians over the years to avoid the abstract and use concrete words and expressions wherever possible remains as sound as ever it was.

abysmal, abyssal Both these words were formerly employed in much the same way, but their meanings are now quite distinct. *Abysmal* means 'measureless' or 'bottomless' and is generally used figuratively:

He showed abysmal ignorance of the subject.

Abyssal means 'belonging to the ocean depths below a certain level' and is used as a technical term:

The abyssal zone of the ocean.

academic This is a word whose original meaning of having to do with learning and scholarship or a place of learning has been overshadowed by its current and rather less agreeable connotation, i.e. of purely theoretical interest, impractical, or remote from everyday life.

accent marks In words reprinted from foreign languages which use the Roman alphabet any accent marks should be retained:

Liège, Malmö, San Sebastián, Košice.

It is better to avoid using accents in words from languages such as Russian, Arabic and Chinese which have to be transliterated into the Roman alphabet.

accept, except *Accept* means to take, receive or agree to:

He accepted their offer.

Except means to leave out or exclude:

Present company excepted.

acceptance, acceptation These words were formerly interchangeable in several of their meanings but are now quite distinct. *Acceptance* means the act of acceptance or a favourable reception:

His ready acceptance of the new position pleased everybody.

Acceptation means the usual or generally agreed sense:

The acceptation of this word is quite clear.

access, accession The most important distinction between these two words is that *access* means the possibility or opportunity of approaching or gaining admittance, whereas *accession* means actually arriving at or reaching. *Accession* is generally restricted to the meanings of 'coming into possession of a dignity or office', 'an increase' or 'something added'. *Access* has the additional sense of a sudden attack of illness or anger.

accessary, accessory Both as an adjective and as a noun *accessary* formerly carried the notion of complicity in a crime. *Accessory*, a more general word meaning, as a noun, 'an accompaniment', and, as an adjective, 'subsidiary', 'subordinate', has also largely taken over the meaning of *accessary*, thus blurring a useful distinction.

accommodation This word, beloved of local authorities, is much too frequently used in official communications to mean 'house' or 'flat', which are almost invariably preferable in all contexts.

accompanist, accompanyist *Accompanist* has now more or less completely replaced *accompanyist* in the sense of a musician who accompanies another player, although it is an unusual way of forming a noun from a verb. [See also *-ist*]

accord, account The prepositions used with the two phrases embodying these words are sometimes confused. The correct forms are *of one's own accord* and *on one's own account*.

achieve This means 'to bring to a successful end' and should not be used as a synonym for *get*, *reach* or *arrive at*.

acknowledgement, acknowledgment The first spelling is the preferred one.

acquaint This is always followed by *with*:

To acquaint someone with the facts.

It is, however, generally considered a rather stilted substitute for *inform* or *tell*.

acronym This is a word formed from the initial letters of other words such as *NATO*, *radar* and *UNESCO*. Such formations have become increasingly popular in recent years.

act as This means to take someone's place or to perform specific duties or functions on a particular occasion and should not be used as a more elaborate alternative to *is* or *are*:

He acted as spokesman for the company,

Not:

He acted as his company's representative for the northeastern region.

activate, actuate *Activate*, for long a rarely used word, has recently acquired fresh currency in scientific language and may be confused with *actuate*. *Activate* means to make active or to render radioactive:

To activate a catalyst.

Actuate means to cause to act, to prompt or motivate:

He was actuated by his own selfish desires.

adapt, adopt *Adapt* means to change or make suitable for a purpose:

The car has been adapted to carry heavy loads.

Adopt means to take and use as one's own:

They adopted the committee's recommendations entirely.

adaptation, adaption *Adaptation* is now the form in general use and *adaption* occurs only rarely.

addict, devotee An *addict* is a person who is physically dependent upon something:

A drug addict needs careful treatment.

A *devotee* is one who is strongly attracted to something and generally carries a favourable connotation:

He is a devotee of classical music.

adduce, deduce Confusion sometimes arises between these two words. *Adduce* means to bring forward in argument or to quote as conclusive evidence:

He adduced reasons to support his point of view.

Deduce means to draw as a conclusion from something known or assumed:

From the available evidence he deduced that the boy had been lying.

adhere, cohere *Adhere* means to stick fast to or to be strongly attached to a cause or belief:

To adhere to a political party.

Cohere means to hold or stick together or be united:

The particles of wet sand cohered to form a solid mass.

adherence, adhesion The chief distinction between these two words is that *adherence* is generally used figuratively. Its primary meaning is attachment to a cause or belief:

He was well known for his adherence to free speech.

Adhesion usually means the sticking of one thing to another:

The adhesion of newspaper to a wall.

It can, however, be used in the sense of *adherence* above.

adjacent, contiguous *Adjacent* means lying near or close, or adjoining:

A small field lay adjacent to the main road.

Contiguous has the more restricted sense of touching or being in close proximity to:

France is contiguous to Spain.

In practice the two words are virtually interchangeable in most of their meanings, but *adjacent* is much more commonly used.

adjective An adjective is a word which in some way modifies the meaning of a noun or pronoun, by describing, limiting or defining them. Adjectives may be used attributively, that is, they precede the noun they qualify:

a blue hat, every girl, my book.

Alternatively, they may be used predicatively, that is, after the verb *to be* and some other verbs:

She is angry, the dog is lively, he seems lonely.

adjectives, comparison of Adjectives of one syllable usually add *-er* and *-est* to make the comparative and superlative forms:

hard, harder, hardest; great, greater, greatest; nice, nicer, nicest.

Adjectives of two syllables which either have the stress on the second syllable or end in *-er*, *-le*, *-ow*, or *-y* take *-er* and *-est* to make the comparative and superlative forms:

polite, politer, politest; narrow, narrower, narrowest; able, abler, ablest; happy, happier, happiest.

Some other adjectives with two syllables which cannot readily be classified also take *-er* and *-est*. These include:

cruel, pleasant, quiet, stupid.

All other adjectives generally use *more* and *most* to form the comparative and superlative forms, although there are many exceptions.

adjectives, position of It is important to ensure that adjectives are placed immediately before the nouns they qualify in order to avoid any possibility of ambiguity. *Men's fashionable clothing* is preferable to *fashionable men's clothing*, since *fashionable* presumably applies to *clothing* and not to *men*.

adjectives, unnecessary It is better not to use adjectives which add nothing to the meaning of the noun they accompany. Phrases such as *grave crisis*, *serious emergency*, *definite decision* and *real danger* are to be avoided.

adjure see **abjure**

admission, admittance The use of *admittance* is now largely restricted to 'permission to enter', *admission* being employed in all senses.

admit *Admit of* meaning 'to leave room for', unlike *admit*, usually takes an impersonal noun as subject:

The problem admits of no other solution.

Admit to is now frequently used in answer to a charge:

He admitted to having stolen the watch.

However, correct usage still prefers *admit* without the addition of *to*.

adopt see **adapt**

adopted, adoptive The distinction between these two words is as follows. A child is described as being *adopted* by its new parents. They are referred to as the *adoptive* not *adopted* parents.

advance, advancement *Advance* means progress or moving forwards:

The advance of science.

Advancement means promotion, preferment or helping to move forwards:

The advancement of a cause dear to his heart.

advantage, vantage Both words mean a superior or favourable position, but *advantage* is generally used in a non-physical sense:

His good education gave him an advantage over all the other candidates.

Vantage may be used figuratively, but is more often employed in a purely literal sense:

He watched the battle from the vantage point of the hill top.

adventure, venture Both *adventure* and *venture* can be used to mean a hazardous or daring undertaking with an uncertain outcome. But whereas *adventure* is usually associated with danger and excitement in a physical sense, *venture* more often refers to a business enterprise or to commercial or financial speculation.

adventurous, venturesome These two words have supplanted *adventuresome* and *venturous* in current usage, but because of the similarity in spelling of all four of them the possibility of confusion remains.

adverb An *adverb* is a word which modifies a verb, an adjective or another adverb, altering in some way their meaning:

He spoke sharply. The weather was very hot. The water level rose extremely quickly.

The characteristic ending of the adverb is *-ly*, although a few common adverbs, such as *fast* and *hard*, have the same form as the adjective. There are, however, a number of adjectives which end in *-ly*, such as *lonely*, *holy* and *slovenly*. The addition of *-ly* to produce a form like *holily* is generally avoided by using a phrase such as *in a holy manner* or *in a slovenly fashion*.

adverbs, comparison of Most adverbs form their comparative and superlative forms by the addition of *more* and *most*, so as to avoid endings like *-lier*, *-liest*:

bravely, more bravely, most bravely; pleasantly, more pleasantly, most pleasantly.

Adverbs of only one syllable usually form their comparative and superlative forms by adding *-er* and *-est*.

late, later, latest; hard, harder, hardest; soon, sooner, soonest.

adverbs, unnecessary Just as superfluous adjectives are all too readily added to nouns, adjectives themselves are frequently adorned with unwanted adverbs. These include *absolutely*, *comparatively*, *relatively* and *vitally* and appear in such phrases as *absolutely essential* and *vitally important*.

adverse, averse These two words are quite similar in meaning. *Adverse* is 'antagonistic', 'hostile' or 'contrary', and, when used after a verb, can be followed only by *to*:

He was the victim of an adverse fate.
I am not adverse to your suggestion.

Averse means 'disinclined', 'opposed' or 'reluctant' and is usually followed by *to*, although some purists insist on using *from*:

He was by inclination averse to any kind of flattery.

-ae, -as see **Latin and French plurals**

aero-, air- The prefix *aero-* has been losing ground for some time to *air-* and is found only in *aeroplane* and *aerodrome*. *Air-* is now far more common, for example, *aircraft*, *airfield*, *airport*.

affect, effect Despite the similarity in their appearance these two words are completely different in meaning. *Affect* means to produce a change in or have an influence upon:

The loss of his children affected his health.

Effect means to bring about or accomplish:

His financial troubles did not prevent him from effecting his plans for sweeping changes.

Affect is all too frequently used instead of a more precise verb:

Work on the new building has been affected by bad weather.

It would have been better to use *hindered* or *delayed* in this context.

affinity There is some disagreement about what prepositions may be used after this word. Normally it is followed by *between* or *with*, but in modern usage *to* and *for* are becoming acceptable, *for* especially in scientific language.

afflict, inflict These two words are occasionally confused. *Afflict* means to distress with physical or mental pain:

She was afflicted with gout.

Inflict means to impose or lay on, invariably something which has to be endured or suffered:

A severe punishment was inflicted on the prisoner.

affront, effrontery An *affront* is an offensive act or a show of disrespect:

His conduct was an affront to the prime minister.

Effrontery means 'impudent boldness' or 'barefaced audacity'.

He had the effrontery to ask for a free ticket.

afraid This perfectly respectable word meaning 'feeling fear or apprehension or filled with concern or regret' has undergone an unwarranted extension of its original sense in such phrases as:

I am afraid that I can't come

or

I am afraid there are no oranges left.

It is best used only when there is real cause for concern or regret.

afterwards, afterward *Afterwards* is the only form of the adverb now found in British English. *Afterward* is the usual American form.

agenda This is a Latin word, the plural form of *agendum*, but in English it is always treated as a singular noun followed by a singular verb:

The agenda for the meeting has been drawn up.

aggravate Attempts by some grammarians to restrict the meaning of this word to 'make worse' or 'intensify' have been unsuccessful. Its popular sense of 'annoy' or 'irritate' is now firmly entrenched in the language.

agnostic, atheist Confusion sometimes arises between these two terms. An *agnostic* believes that nothing can be known about the existence of God and accordingly it cannot be proved or disproved. An *atheist* is one who denies or disbelieves the existence of God.

ago, since These two words are frequently but wrongly used together in sentences such as:

It is ten years ago since I last saw him.

Ago can be followed only by *that*, so the sentence must be recast in one of two following ways:

It was ten years ago that I last saw him.
It is ten years since I last saw him.

Alternatively it can be shortened to the following:

I last saw him ten years ago.

agree This is normally used as an intransitive verb followed by the prepositions *to*, *on*, or *with*. However, it has shown a tendency in recent years to discard its prepositions and appear as a transitive verb meaning 'to reach agreement about':

The board has agreed the price increase.

Despite protests from some quarters there seems every likelihood that this change will eventually win complete acceptance.

agreement of verbs Verbs must agree with their subject in number and person. Difficulties over whether verbs should be singular or plural sometimes arise in the following instances.

Collective nouns: These may be used with either a singular or a plural verb. The singular is more appropriate when the emphasis is on the body as a whole or a unit and the plural when the emphasis is on a collection of individuals:

The committee has agreed upon its programme.

The committee were divided about the merits of the scheme.

Words joined by and: These are almost invariably followed by a plural verb unless the linked words are very closely associated:

A boy and a girl were approaching the house,

but:

Bread and butter is his staple diet.

Words joined by with: If the subject is singular the verb must also be singular:

The chairman, together with the managing director, is coming.

Alternative subjects: *Either* and *neither* are always followed by a singular verb when there are two singular subjects:

Either the front door or the back door is sure to be open.

Neither business expertise nor a knowledge of printing techniques is essential.

If both alternatives are in the plural then the verb is plural:

Neither the soldiers nor their officers were fit for combat.

However, if one of the alternatives referred to is in the singular and the other in the plural, the verb may agree with the nearest subject, though it might be found preferable to rephrase the sentence:

Either the boy or his parents are supposed to attend.

Use of each: When *each* is the subject of a sentence it is followed by a singular verb:

Each of the boys was given a room for the night.

When it refers to a plural antecedent, however, it takes a plural verb:

They arrived early and were each given a ticket.

Use of none: This is usually followed by a singular verb when it means *no amount*, *no quantity*, *not one* or *no one*:

None of the jewellery is missing.

None of his friends was able to come.

When *none* means *no people* or *no things* the verb is generally in the plural:

Some of the lorries arrive late but none reach the depot after 8 pm.

agriculturalist, agriculturist Both forms are still perfectly acceptable English but *agriculturist* is gradually displacing the longer word.

aim This is usually followed by *at* when it means 'to strive' or 'to try', but is now being used more frequently with *to*. It is also followed by *to* when it means 'to intend':

We aim to start tomorrow.

akin This is usually followed by *to* but is occasionally found followed by *with*, a practice condemned by most authorities.

alarm, alarum Both forms were formerly employed without distinction of meaning but *alarum* has now been almost entirely displaced by *alarm* except in one or two set expressions.

albeit Meaning 'although' or 'notwithstanding', this conjunction was only quite recently considered an archaism, but has since received a fresh lease of life:

The army chose a strategic albeit inglorious retreat.

alibi In law this means a defence by an accused person that he was elsewhere at the time when a crime was committed. It is now frequently used to mean an 'excuse' or 'pretext', even by respectable writers, and this colloquial extension of meaning has crept into the definitions given in dictionaries. However deplorable this may be, there appears to be no way of stopping it.

alien As an adjective this was formerly used with the prepositions *from* and *to*. However, in recent years *from* has been almost entirely displaced by *to*.

allege This means 'to assert without proof, to plead in support of' or 'to urge as an excuse', and should not be used as a substitute for *assert* or *affirm*, which have a much more positive sense.

allegory This is the figurative or metaphorical treatment of one subject under the guise of another: the narrating of a story using a symbolic language, usually in order to expound some moral truth. [See also *metaphor*, *parable*, *simile*]

allergic The medical definition is 'physically hypersensitive to certain substances'. In colloquial speech it has been extended to mean having a dislike or aversion. It is better to avoid both *allergic* and its noun *allergy* wherever possible and to substitute phrases using more suitable words such as *dislike*, *antipathy* or *hostility*.

alliteration This is the repetition in a phrase or sentence of words beginning with the same letter or sound in order to create an effect, as in a line of verse or a television advertising jingle.

all of When *all* is used before a pronoun it must be followed by *of*:

all of them, all of us.

When it is followed by a noun the *of* is usually omitted in British English, but may be retained in American English, although frowned on by many American authorities:

all (of) the people, all (of) the girls at my school.

allow of The meaning of this phrase has become restricted to 'leave room for' in much the same way as *admit of*:

The rules do not allow of any exceptions.

all right, alright Although *alright* is commonly found it is not generally regarded as good usage. The only acceptable form is *all right*.

allusion, illusion An *allusion* is a passing or casual reference to something:

He made an allusion to the events of the previous day.

An *illusion* is something producing a false impression or a deceptive appearance:

He cherishes the illusion that everyone likes him.

alone *Not alone* is sometimes wrongly substituted for *not only*. This use of *alone* is now archaic and the word should be restricted to its various meanings as an adjective.

alternate, alternative These two adjectives have quite distinct meanings but are nevertheless frequently confused. *Alternate* means 'following each in succession', 'first one, then the other' or 'every other one in a series':

There will be alternate hot and cold spells.
The two men worked on alternate days.

There is also a verb *alternate* meaning 'to follow one another by turns'.

Alternative means 'affording a choice between one of two (or possibly more) things':

There is an alternative route through the mountains.

Alternative is unfortunately a vogue word which has acquired an extension of meaning and is sometimes used by the ignorant (and by those who should know better) to mean *new*, *revised* or *fresh*. Remember that *alternative* implies a choice.

The same distinctions apply to the adverbs *alternately* and *alternatively*.

They alternately walked and ran.
The journey could be made by steamer or alternatively by aircraft.

although see **though**

altogether, all together These two words are quite often wrongly substituted, the one for the other. *Altogether* means wholly, entirely, completely:

She did not altogether like the new dress.

All together means all at the same time or the same place:

The guests had assembled all together in the drawing room.

amatory, amorous There is some overlapping between the meanings of these two words, but in current usage it is possible to make the following distinction. *Amatory*, meaning expressing love, is frequently applied to something written:

The author of a book of amatory poetry.

Amorous is more frankly concerned with sexual desire:

No girl could resist his amorous approaches.

ambiguity This can arise in a number of ways and is generally the result of clumsy writing. In most cases the real meaning may be quite clear, but sometimes complete obscurity results. The following are some of the most frequent causes of ambiguity.

The incorrect positioning of a word or phrase:

No unnecessary force was used to put an end to the disturbance by the police.

He met his former girl friend out walking with his wife.

The use of words with a double meaning or more than one meaning:

The new secretary worked very happily under the export manager.

The misuse of punctuation:

The manager has only a very small team who are always busy.

This needs a comma after *team*. Otherwise it implies that most of the manager's subordinates do not have enough to do.

Confusion of pronouns: it is unfortunately all too easy to be ambiguous in the use of pronouns.

Mr Jones told Mr Brown that he was prepared to lend him the money, provided he received the guarantees which he had been promised.

It is quite impossible to be sure to whom the two *he's* in the second part of the sentence refer.

ambiguous, ambivalent *Ambiguous* means open to various interpretations or having a double meaning:

To their clear question he gave an ambiguous answer.

Ambivalent, which is a fashionable and much overworked word, is frequently and wrongly substituted for *ambiguous*. It means having mixed or conflicting feelings:

The older members of the staff were ambivalent in their attitude towards the new young manager.

amend, emend *Amend* means to improve or make better:

He was told to amend his ways.

Emend means to remove errors or to correct and is used only in connection with manuscripts or printed matter:

They emended the document to the best of their ability.

America, American These words are commonly used for 'The United States' and a 'citizen of the United States' respectively. Objections may be raised that the term *America* can also be used to cover all North America (*i.e.*, including Canada), and Central and South America. However, *America* and *American* have become so firmly established in their popular senses that nothing can be done to alter the position now.

American usage and spelling Much has been written about the influence of American English on British English. Some Americanisms are deplored as ugly or unnecessary, others seem somehow to fill a gap and to gain ready acceptance. A considerable number of words have in fact become so absorbed into British English that their transatlantic origins are quite forgotten. However, despite this continuous American invasion

British English remains stubbornly resistant in some areas and many words describing ordinary things remain quite different in both countries.

Some of the most important distinctions between British and American spelling are given below. A number of words ending in *-re* in British usage change this to *-er* in American usage:

theater, liter, scepter, somber, caliber, center.

But note British English *meter* (meaning 'instrument') and *filter*.

In American usage many words ending in *-our* in British English drop the *u* in these words and those derived from them:

behavior, behaviorism, candor, color, favor, favoritism, honor, humor, labor, rancor.

But note American *glamour* and the following which are correct in both British and American usage:

clangor, coloration, glamorous, glamorize, honorary, humorist, humorous, odorous, stupor, tremor, vaporize and vigorous.

There are also some differences in certain words containing *c* or *s*. British usage has *licence* and *practice* as nouns and *license* and *practise* as verbs. American usage has *license* and *practise* for both nouns and verbs. Note also the American *defense*, *offense* and *pretense*.

In some words ending in the suffixes *-ed*, *-ing*, *-er*, *-or*, etc., the final consonant before the suffix is left single where in British usage it would be doubled:

leveled, rivaled, libeling, traveler, carburetor, worshiping.

American usage tends to eliminate *a* and *o* from the combinations *ae* and *oe* when British English retains them:

anemia, anesthetic, diarrhea, maneuver, presidium, toxemia.

But note the American preference for the following spellings:

aeon, aesthete, aesthetic.

Other important words which are spelt differently in America are:

aluminum, appall, ax, catalog, caldron, check (British cheque), councilor, counselor, disk, enroll, font (printer's) fulfill, gelatin, glycerin, jewelry, mollusk, mold, molt, plow, program, prolog, skeptic, skillful, stanch, sulfur, tire, woolen.

amiable, amicable Both words are very similar in meaning. *Amiable* is used only when referring to people and means having a good-natured disposition:

He proved to be a most amiable companion.

Amicable means friendly or peaceable and refers to arrangements, settlements and attitudes.

They came to an amicable agreement.

amid, amidst Both words, which are identical in meaning, are falling into disuse, but *amid* is the more common form.

amok see **amuck**

among, amongst There is no real distinction between these two words. *Amongst* used to be found more frequently before words beginning with a vowel, but *among* is now almost invariably the preferred form. [See also *between*]

amoral, immoral *Amoral* means without moral quality or not concerned with morals, or having no moral standards, good or bad, by which one may be judged. *Immoral* means not conforming to a set of moral standards, wicked or evil.

amount, number *Amount* can only properly be used of a material or substance having mass or weight, in fact, anything which can be measured, and should never be applied to things which are divisible into individual units. *A large amount of sheep* is not acceptable and *number* should be substituted for *amount*. It is correctly used as follows:

A large amount of dress material.
A large amount of firewood.

amuck This form is now much more frequently met with than *amok*, and is to be preferred on all occasions.

anacoluthon This rather formidable-looking word describes a common phenomenon in which the structure or grammatical sequence of a sentence is broken:

Let me begin by expressing my thanks to those people who – but I shouldn't have been here in the first place.

analysis, synthesis *Analysis* is the separation of a whole into its constituent elements:

The grammatical analysis of a sentence.

Synthesis, the opposite of *analysis*, is the combination of parts to form a whole:

The production of rubber from petroleum by synthesis.

analyst, annalist There is sometimes a possibility of confusion between these two words. An *analyst* is a person who is skilled in analysis. An *annalist* is one who writes annals or chronicles.

ancient, antiquated, antique *Ancient* is invariably used to refer to a remote past:

The history of the ancient world.

Antiquated means grown old and ill adapted to present use:

An antiquated fire engine.

Antique means belonging to former times and does not, except when used facetiously, have the pejorative sense of *antiquated*:

A lover of antique furniture.

and This is used as a conjunction joining two parts of a sentence. Care must be taken to ensure that the words, phrases or clauses linked by *and* are of the same kind:

He played a fast game of tennis, enjoyed the company of pretty women and good conversation.

The insertion of *and* after *tennis* balances the two parts of the sentence:

He played a fast game of tennis, and enjoyed the company of pretty women and good conversation.

And is often used wrongly with *who* and *which*:

She was a girl of infinite tact and who knew when to keep quiet.

The *and* in the above sentence is unnecessary. The rule is that it can be used with *who* or *which* only if there is a relative clause in the first part of the sentence:

She was a girl whose tact was infinite and who knew when to keep quiet.

Despite widespread belief to the contrary, there is no reason why a sentence should not begin with *and*. Provided it is used with moderation, it can be stylistically very effective.

angry This is followed by *with* when the object of the anger is a person, but by *at* when it is caused by situations or events:

She was angry with her son because he arrived home late.
He was angry at the delay at the airport.

another For the distinction between *each other* and *one another* see *each other*.

antagonist, protagonist These two words are occasionally confused, although their meanings are quite distinct. An *antagonist* is one who is opposed to another in any kind of contest or fight. A *protagonist* is the leading character in a play or novel.

ante-, anti- Similarity in spelling may lead to some doubt about these two prefixes. *Ante-*, which comes from Latin, means 'before in space or time', and occurs in such words as *antecedent*, *anteroom*, and *antenatal*. *Anti-*, which comes from Greek, means 'against' or 'opposed to' and is much more commonly used than *ante*. Examples are:

anti-aircraft, anti-American, anticlimax, antifreeze.

anticipate The valiant efforts of those who have tried to prevent this word from being used simply as a synonym for *expect* or *foresee* have not, unfortunately, been very successful. However, it is better where possible to confine it to its basic meaning of 'to forestall an event' or 'to take action beforehand':

Foreknowledge of the enemy's plans enabled us to anticipate his every move.

A sentence like:

We are not anticipating any trouble

is better expressed as:

We are not expecting any trouble

unless you really mean to say you are not taking any preventive measures.

Anticipate is a case in which the Latin prefix *ante* has changed its *e* to an *i*.

antonym An *antonym* is a word opposed in meaning to another. Thus 'good' is the antonym of 'bad', and 'top' the antonym of 'bottom'. [See also *synonym*]

anyone, any one *Anyone* is a singular pronoun and is followed by a singular verb, pronoun or possessive adjective:

Anyone who takes time off risks losing his job.

It should be spelt as one word except when it singles out a particular person or item. In this instance *any* becomes an adjective and *one* a numeral:

Any one of these books will be suitable.
He has not informed any one of them.

aphorism A short meaningful saying embodying a general truth:

Manners makyth man.

[See also *axiom*]

apiary, aviary These words are occasionally confused. An *apiary* is a place where bees are kept. An *aviary* is for keeping birds.

apocope This is the cutting off of a final letter, sound or syllable of a word to form a new word, as *curio* from *curiosity* and *cinema* from *cinematograph*.

apology, apologia An *apology* is an expression of regret offered for some fault, failure, insult etc. It is, however, also used in the same sense as *apologia*, which is a formal defence or justification of a cause or doctrine.

apostrophe The apostrophe is used to show the omission of letters or figures:

can't (cannot), it's (it is), the early '20s.

The apostrophe is used with *s* to form the plurals of letters, numbers, symbols and words which do not have a plural form or are not easily recognizable as plurals with the addition of just an *s*:

1's, 2's, 5's, p's and q's, do's and don't's.

But note:

M.A.s, M.P.s, G.P.s.

The addition of an apostrophe and *s* is the regular way of forming the possessive case of nouns. In the singular the apostrophe is placed before the *s*:

The boy's book, his daughter's school.

In the plural the apostrophe is placed after the *s*:

His parents' car, the soldiers' uniforms.

When the noun itself already ends in an *s* (or an *s* sound), as in the case of personal names, add *'s*:

Thomas's car, Charles's shop, St. James's Square, Marx's theories, the Jones's Christmas party.

Note that ancient names (Classical or Biblical) ending in an *s* usually add only the apostrophe:

Moses' Law, Sophocles' stories, Xerxes' fleet.

Nouns which form their plural in some other way than by adding an *s*, add an apostrophe and an *s* in the possessive case:

The men's room, geese's wings.

The apostrophe is used after the *s* in phrases like the following involving expressions of time, which are treated as possessives:

Two weeks' time, a five days' journey, two months' holiday.

Do not use an apostrophe with the following personal pronouns:

Its (of it), hers, ours, theirs, yours.

The single exception is *one's*.

apposition This means the addition of a word or group of words to another as an explanation or description. In the sentence:

Gerald Smith, the new managing director, has arrived.

the new managing director is in apposition to *Gerald Smith*.

appraise, apprise *Appraise* means to estimate the worth of or evaluate:

The task of appraising the new candidates had begun.

Apprise means to inform or advise:

The prime minister has not yet been apprised of their decision.

Apprise is a rather formal, not to say pompous word, and one which good writers tend to avoid.

appreciate This undoubtedly useful word has various meanings including 'to form an estimate of the value of something' and 'to acknowledge gratefully'. However, it has in recent times been worked to death in contexts where such verbs as *understand*, *admit* and *realize*, would be far more suitable. In sentences like:

I appreciate that you have taken a lot of trouble

any of the verbs listed above would be preferable to *appreciate*.

apprehend, comprehend Although several of the meanings of *apprehend* are quite distinct from those of *comprehend*, these two words do overlap when they are used in the sense of 'understand'. *Apprehend* is to 'grasp the meaning of', and *comprehend* means to 'have complete understanding of the meaning or nature of something'.

appropriate As an adjective *appropriate* is in danger of being overworked. It is often used where such words as *suitable* or *fitting* would be just as acceptable.

approximate, approximately *Approximate* means 'nearly exact or equal' or 'approaching a great degree of accuracy'. It should not be used as a synonym of *rough* or *roughly* which imply a considerably lesser degree of accuracy. *Very approximately*, which has unfortunately come to mean no more than *very roughly*, should be avoided altogether.

a priori This means reasoning from cause to effect or from a general law to a particular instance without prior study or investigation.

apt, liable In some senses these words are very close and the one is often used where the other would be more suitable. *Apt* and *liable* both mean inclined, disposed or subject to, but *liable* contains a much stronger possibility of unpleasant or disagreeable consequences:

Problems are apt to occur. Serious shortages are liable to result.

Arab, Arabian, Arabic When used as adjectives, these words are now more or less distinct in meaning. *Arab* means 'belonging or pertaining to the Arabs', as in *Arab World*, *Arab statesmen*. *Arabian* is used specifically to mean 'belonging or pertaining to Arabia', as in *Arabian Desert*. *Arabic* refers to the language: *Arabic script*, *Arabic newspaper*, *Arabic numerals*.

arbiter, arbitrator These words are sometimes used indiscriminately but they do have important distinctions of meaning. An *arbiter* is a person who has the sole or absolute power to judge or determine:

The dictator became the arbiter of his country's destiny.

An *arbitrator* is a person chosen to decide a specific dispute:

The government appointed an arbitrator to settle the strike in the steel industry.

arbitrate, mediate *Arbitrate* means to decide a dispute as an arbitrator does. To *mediate* means to act as an intermediary between parties involved in a dispute.

archaism An *archaism* is a word or expression which was once current English, but is no longer acceptable as part of the living language. In the hands of an experienced writer archaisms may be used effectively, otherwise it is best to leave them alone.

aren't I Despite its illogical appearance this is the recognized colloquial interrogative form of *I am.* It is formed by analogy with *aren't you* and *aren't they* and replaces the earlier *an't I.*

arise, rise In the literal sense of 'to get up' or 'to come up' *arise* has been replaced by *rise.* It is used now to mean 'to come into being' or 'to originate' in an abstract sense:

A new problem has arisen.

around, round Although *around* is less frequently met with than *round* it appears in certain set phrases such as *all around us* and *sitting around the table.* It can also replace *about* in expressions of time such as *around five o'clock.*

arouse, rouse The distinction between these words is similar to that between *arise* and *rise. Rouse* means 'to bring out of a state of sleep' or 'to stir to action':

Her screams roused the sleeping children.

Arouse is generally (though not always) used in the figurative sense of 'to bring into being' or 'to give rise to':

His erratic behaviour aroused their suspicions.

arrogate see **abrogate**

artist, artiste An *artist* is one who practises the fine arts, in particular painting or sculpture. An *artiste* is one who performs in public, especially a singer or dancer on the stage or on television.

as This is a much overworked word and is frequently used where *because, while, since, for* or *when* would be more suitable. It also results in ambiguity:

He spotted the mistake as he was reading in his study.

This would be better expressed:

He spotted the mistake while he was reading in his study.

and

She felt tired as she was walking up the stairs.

It would be better to say:

She felt tired while she was walking up the stairs.

or:

She felt tired because she was walking up the stairs.

As sometimes appears in phrases like *equally as important, equally as cheap*. It is quite unnecessary and should be deleted. It is also superfluous in expressions like *as from* (a certain date) unless reference is made to past time.

When *as* is used to mean 'in the function, role or capacity of' it is important to ensure that it does not become unrelated to its proper subject:

As chairman of the company, you will all, I am sure, agree with me when I say . . .

Logically, although nonsensically, this means that the people referred to as 'you' are chairman of the company. It could be recast as follows:

You will all, I am sure, agree with me as chairman of the company . . .

Another cause of ambiguity with *as* is in expressions such as:

She hates him as much as you.

This can be put right either by saying:

She hates him as much as you do.

or:

She hates him as much as she does you.

ascendancy, ascendant These words have alternative but less common spellings *ascendency* and *ascendent*. Both *ascendancy* and *ascendant* mean a dominating or controlling influence, although *ascendant* has a specifically astrological connotation.

Asian, Asiatic It is advisable to use *Asian* rather than *Asiatic*, either as a noun or as an adjective. *Asiatic* was once more frequent but its unfortunate pejorative overtones make it generally unacceptable today.

assay, essay Neither of these verbs is now frequently used. *Assay* means 'to test or analyse', usually with reference to metals. *Essay* means 'to attempt' or 'to try'.

asset This has been condemned in some quarters as a poor substitute for *advantage* or *resource*, but it now seems to have firmly established itself in the language with the meaning of 'something useful' in addition to its other meanings.

assignation, assignment An *assignation* is an appointment to meet, especially an illicit meeting between lovers. *Assignment* is the transfer or handing over of something or the thing handed over.

assonance In poetry this is a substitute for rhyme where words with the same vowel sounds but with different consonants are used, such as *make* and *tame* or *dream* and *seen*.

assume, presume *Assume* has several meanings, but it is also used as a near synonym of *presume* in the sense of 'to suppose as a fact'. The difference is that *assume* is 'to take for granted' without any evidence, whereas *presume* implies a greater degree of certainty and the belief that something is true.

assurance This is a term used by insurance companies when dealing with life policies as opposed to insurance of property, but the general public does not normally make any distinction, using the term *insurance* on all occasions.

assure, ensure, insure Confusion can arise over the correct use of these verbs. *Assure* means to make confident or reassure, and to insure, especially against death. *Ensure* means to make sure or certain. *Insure* means to safeguard against loss or damage by paying insurance.

as to This phrase tends to appear rather frequently as a clumsy substitute for *about*:

We have no information as to his reliability.

Sometimes it occurs as a completely superfluous phrase:

Doubt has been expressed (as to) whether he is the right man for the job.

atheist see **agnostic**

attend see **tend**

aural, oral These words are usually pronounced in exactly the same way, which may lead to some difficulties in their use. *Aural* means pertaining to or perceived by the organs of hearing. *Oral* means uttered by, administered by or pertaining to the mouth.

autarchy, autarky Although pronounced identically, these two words have quite distinct meanings. *Autarchy* is absolute sovereignty or self-government. *Autarky* is a condition of self-sufficiency.

authentic, genuine There is frequent overlapping between these two words and some authorities make no distinction in meaning. *Authentic* is used particularly of documents and works of art, and implies that they are not false, or copies, and that they really represent what they claim to do.

authoress Feminine designations such as *authoress*, *poetess* and *sculptress* are now falling into disuse. Women writers have always shown much hostility to the word *authoress*, possibly because it has a somewhat pejorative nuance. *Author* should be used for both sexes without discrimination.

authoritarian, authoritative *Authoritarian* means favouring the principle of subjection to authority as opposed to that of individual freedom:

Authoritarian governments have always been more common than democratic ones.

Authoritative means having due authority or the sanction or weight of authority:

The prime minister issued an authoritative statement about the crisis.

Authoritative can also be used to mean 'peremptory' or 'dictatorial' and in this sense it approaches the meaning of *authoritarian*.

auxiliary verbs These are verbs which are used with other verbs to express distinctions between active and passive and in tense or mood. In the following examples the verbs in italics are auxiliaries:

She *has* made her bed. *Do* you think they *will* come? He *has* been knocked down by a car. I *do* not know the answer. They *may* decide otherwise. You *ought* to stay the night. She *can* come when she likes. He *must* decide quickly.

avail This verb can only be used in a restricted way, the normal construction being to *avail oneself of something*:

They availed themselves of the opportunity for a drive.

It should never be used in the passive as *be availed of*. *Avail* can also take a direct object, but this form is much rarer:

All their attempts availed them nothing.

availability This is a word much favoured in official writing and one which tends to produce obscurity or long-windedness in the construction of sentences.

The availability of these products is extremely limited, would be better expressed as:

These products are extremely scarce.

avenge, revenge It is not always easy to preserve a distinction between these two verbs. The main difference is that *avenge* and its noun *vengeance* are now usually restricted to the infliction of punishment as a means of achieving justice:

The murder was avenged when the criminal was brought to trial.

Revenge is generally used in the sense of retaliation for wrongs committed by the infliction of pain, emotional or real:

He was determined to revenge the insult he had received.

averse see **adverse**

avocation, vocation *Avocation* originally meant a hobby or something apart from one's regular work. It is now frequently used as an alternative to *vocation* to mean a regular occupation and is in danger of blurring a useful distinction in meaning.

await, wait The usual distinction between these verbs is that *await* is transitive, being followed by a direct object:

We are awaiting your instructions.

Wait is usually intransitive:

He waited for a train for more than two hours.

awake, wake These verbs, together with their alternative spellings *awaken* and *waken*, are often used interchangeably. *Awake* and *waken* are more formal than *wake* and are commonly employed in figurative senses:

To awaken to the realities of life.

Moreover, *awaken* and *waken* can be transitive and intransitive and are preferred in the passive mood:

She was awakened by the sound of gunfire.

Wake, however, remains the basic verb for expressing the idea of arousing from sleep and is the most frequently used of all four. It is also the only one which can be normally followed by *up*.

award, reward An *award* is in law a decision made by arbitrators on matters submitted to them and, by extension, something awarded. A *reward* is something given or received in return for a meritorious action or for services rendered.

axiom This is a universally accepted principle or rule or a recognized truth. [See also *aphorism*]

B

-b-, -bb- With a single-vowelled, single-syllabled word such as *snob*, the *b* is doubled when followed by a vowel, as in *snobbery*. If the *b* is preceded by two vowels, however, or a single vowel followed by an *r*, the *b* remains single:

boob, booby; curb, curbing.

bacillus see **Latin and French plurals**

back formation A word is sometimes created from another which is wrongly – or facetiously – taken to be its derivative. *Typewrite* from *typewriter* and *donate* from *donation*, now acceptable verbs, were probably first introduced ironically, but were later acknowledged as genuine verbs, from which it might be erroneously assumed the nouns had been formed.

Such words are continually being introduced into the language, condemned at first as incorrect or as slang, then later accepted through common usage.

background The dictionary definition, 'the ground or parts situated in the rear', has been extended to cover a variety of contexts so that this has become an overused vogue word. An example of its correct use is:

With his mother always in the background, the marriage was bound to fail.

However, in the instance:

The background of the quarrel was jealousy over a girl,

it would have been better to substitute 'cause', and a sentence such as:

With his background, he could reach the top of his profession

is ambiguous and therefore insufficiently precise. Unless the intended meaning is 'origins', either 'qualifications' or 'experience' would be preferable.

backlog Originally a U.S. term for the log at the back of a fire, it was brought into use as a metaphor meaning a stockpile held in reserve, and is now used almost exclusively in the sense of arrears, or an accumulation of work (such as correspondence) awaiting attention.

backward, backwards *Backward* can be used either as an adjective:

A backward country, the child is backward,

or as an adverb, especially in the United States:

To move backward.

Backwards can be used only as an adverb, and its use in the above example would be equally correct:

To move backwards.

bail out, bale out *To bail out* is usually applied to getting a person out of jail. For removing water from a boat *to bale out* is nowadays considered the preferable spelling, although some authorities contend that *to bail out* is more correct, derived as it is from the Old French *baille*, 'bucket'.

To bale out is also the term used for leaving an aircraft in a hurry.

balance There are dangers in using this word in its colloquial sense of 'the remainder' or 'the rest'. Strictly speaking, it should be applied only when there is a clear indication of comparison, as in this example, where the sums involved could be defined:

When the bills have been paid, the balance of the housekeeping money can be spent on clothes.

Just to say:

He works hard at the office every day, so the balance of his time is his own

is too vague a concept to be of value.

baleful, baneful Both words mean 'pernicious'; *baleful* is also 'full of menacing or malign influences', and *baneful* is 'destructive, poisonous'. It is important to stress that they are interchangeable only in the one sense.

ballad, ballade Both words mean a poem. A *ballad* is essentially of popular origin, simple in form with short stanzas, and often represented as a light, romantic song. The *ballade* is a poem of three eight- or ten-line stanzas with an identical rhyme scheme and an envoy or postscript, the same last line recurring in each stanza and envoy. It can also be a romantic musical composition for piano or orchestra.

balmy, barmy The word for mild, refreshing, soft or soothing is *balmy*. In its literal sense *barmy* means frothy or something containing barm, the yeast formed from fermentation. Figuratively, it is used to mean silly, stupid or mad:

He must be barmy if he thinks he can get away with it.

barbarian, barbaric, barbarous These adjectives have distinct places in everyday usage. *Barbarian* is the most neutral of the three and means rough and uncultured:

The barbarian tribes.

Barbaric describes something that might be done by or owned by a *barbarian*. Its connotations are simple, rustic, crude and unsophisticated but not necessarily violent, and imply amused tolerance rather than condemnation:

Those gaudy ties he wears display his barbaric tastes.

Barbarous, on the other hand, suggests cruelty and violence, the harsh side of barbarian behaviour, and is the antithesis of everything cultured and civilized:

The docking of dogs' tails is a barbarous practice.

baroque In an architectural context this word has a definite meaning, describing a style of architecture developed in 16th-century Italy with bold, contorted forms, heavy decoration and asymmetrical design. It is, however, often applied to other art forms such as music and literature, which has led to a blurring of meaning, since it is not always clear whether the writer is referring merely to the date or period of a work, or using the term in a metaphorical sense to indicate a florid, heavily ornate style.

barrage Originally this was used in the sense of 'curtain' or 'barrier', especially in a military context, 'a *barrage* of fire', or during the war when '*barrage* balloons' became a familiar sight, forming a layer or 'barrier' to keep aircraft at a height where anti-aircraft fire was most effective.
Extended use has brought this word to mean any overwhelming quantity, implying a density through which it is impossible to break, and also in an attacking sense instead of a defensive one, from which it is impossible to escape. Hence, in the following sentence:

After his speech, he faced a barrage of questions,

volley would be a more accurate substitute.

barrister, solicitor A *barrister* is allowed to plead at the bar of any court. A *solicitor* advises his clients and briefs the barrister, preparing the case for him to plead. He can also appear on behalf of his client in a lower court, but only a barrister may plead the case in a higher court.

basic, basically These are vogue words and very overworked ones. They may be quite meaningless, popped into sentences that would survive perfectly happily without them, or they may be used in place of 'fundamental' or 'fundamentally'.

Basically, it's a question of time.

It will remain a question of time with or without *basically*.

It is a basic fact that hedgehogs hibernate in winter.

Here again, the word is superfluous. Omitting *basic* renders the sentence simpler in style and no less informative. But in the following example:

His basic premise was accurate,

the word is used legitimately as an alternative to 'fundamental', since it serves to stress that the premise was the original one upon which ensuing argument was built and from which subsequent conclusions were drawn.

basis Often used by those who enjoy a roundabout way of speaking (see *periphrasis*).

He took a room on a temporary basis while searching for a house

is unnecessarily wordy. The straight adverb is better:

He took a room temporarily while searching for a house.

bathos, pathos *Bathos* is an anticlimax, a sudden leap from the sublime to the ridiculous. *Pathos* is the power of inspiring a feeling of pity or sadness. Confusion arises, however, because *bathos* can also mean a false pathos, or acute sentimentality.

because This is a word which is often misused *because* its purpose is not fully understood. In that sentence the word *because* is a positive link between effect and cause which no other word would provide so strongly. But in the next example:

The reason why he is late is because he missed the train

it is incorrectly used, since it merely repeats the meaning of 'the reason why'. The sentence should read:

The reason why he is late is *that* he missed the train.

Care must also be taken that it is not used in a way that appears ambiguous:

She did not go out that night because she knew he wouldn't like it.

Was it out of deference to his feelings that she refrained from going out, or did she deliberately stay in to annoy him? When the word is used the weight of the meaning should be borne in mind. By providing a strong link between cause and effect *because* implies greater emphasis on the reason for an action than either *for* or *since*, which treat the reason as subordinate to the main statement and not as the more important part of the sentence. For example, in the sentence:

He usually goes to a match on Saturdays, *because* he is keen on football

for might be a better substitute, and put the other way round:

Because he is keen on football, he usually goes to a match on Saturdays

since might well be preferable.

begin, commence, start Either *begin* or *start* is acceptable in daily use. In most contexts *begin* is perhaps preferable, being a little less suggestive of sudden movement.

Commence should be avoided except in a strictly formal, legal or business context. In daily use it is pompous and unnecessary and smacks of false genteelness.

behalf The idiom *on behalf of* means 'acting for', 'on the part of'.

I am speaking to you today on behalf of the candidate for whom you voted

means that the speaker is standing in or acting for the candidate in question. But

I am speaking on behalf of you all to support the candidate for whom you voted

is wrong if it is for the sake of the candidate the speaker is appearing and not the audience.

beholden The phrase is *beholden to*, not *beholding*, and it means 'indebted to'.

She is beholden to me for introducing her to the man she is going to marry.

behoves This is used only in an impersonal way, meaning 'to be necessary or proper for':

It behoves me to write to him.

It has come to be regarded as a somewhat pedantic expression and is better left alone.

belittle A word which tends to be overused, meaning 'to play down', 'minimize', 'to make small'. There are many other words such as *decry*, *depreciate*, *disparage* or *ridicule* which serve the same purpose with often stricter accuracy.

belly A fine old English word which, for the sake of euphemism, is invariably replaced by the less accurate 'stomach' or, worse, the nursery phrase 'tummy'. Perhaps the pendulum is about to swing the other way: *guts* is returning to daily use with a vigour that once belonged to *belly*.

below, beneath, under *Below* or *under* can in most cases replace *beneath*, except in certain figurative senses:

He considered it beneath his notice

and:

Her remarks were beneath contempt,

or in a poetic or literary context:

They sat holding hands beneath the stars; she sought shelter beneath the trees.

Below implies a comparison, 'lower than', whereas *under* suggests a close relationship, such as in:

The grass under her feet was damp.

Contrast this with:

The grass beneath her feet was damp

and it can be seen that the second example might be more appropriate in a literary context, the former is a factual, prosaic setting. But:

The grass below her feet was damp

presents an image of a pair of feet floating a little way above the ground, or at any rate poised on a steep bank at quite a different level.

beneficence, benevolence These words are apt to be confused. *Beneficence* is 'the act of doing good', 'active goodness or kindness', 'charity'. *Benevolence* is 'the desire to do good', 'goodwill or charitableness'. The first is concerned with the action, the second with the feelings surrounding it.

Thanks to the beneficence of the parish, the church roof was repaired

and:

His benevolence was an outstanding feature of his character.

bereaved, bereft The relationship between these words is close. *Bereft* is generally used with *of*:

Bereft of his senses; bereft of all he owned,

and implies a sudden withdrawal. *Bereaved* is used in a more emotional context, and tends to be a continuing condition:

The bereaved mother was at the graveside,

but it can also be used with *of* in the special sense, 'deprived of':

Bereaved of her children, she turned to go.

beside, besides Apart from its use in poetry, which sometimes cheats for the sake of rhyme, *beside* occurs only as a preposition meaning 'by the side of'.

Beside his brother, he looked very young.

The adverb *besides* means 'in addition to', 'moreover', 'otherwise':

Besides a successful husband, she has wealth and beauty too.

As a preposition it also means 'other than', 'except':

She has no other friend besides you.

between This preposition is often misused. For instance, a choice is made between one object *and* another, not *or* another. Like the word 'after', *between* takes the accusative case:

This secret is between you and me,

not *you and I*, which is just as wrong as saying *after I*. *Between* must link two objects, be they singular words or plural:

He had to choose between each one

is wrong – he cannot choose between 'each' one. The correct line would be:

He had to choose between each one and the next.

Nor is the following sentence correct:

To understand fully, he should read between each line.

It should be:

To understand fully, he should read between the lines.

It is sometimes believed that *between* cannot be used for linking more than two objects, and *among* is substituted. But:

There was agreement between the Chairman, his advisers and other members of the Board

is perfectly acceptable.

There was agreement among the Chairman, his advisers, and other members of the Board

is much less precise, and *among* blends uneasily with the singular *Chairman*.

beware If it is remembered that this means literally 'be wary of it is not hard to understand that it can be used only in an imperative sense and will, in most instances, be followed by *of*:

Beware of the dog (Be wary of the dog)

or:

Beware lest you fall (Be wary lest . . .)

biannual, biennial These words have distinct meanings. *Biannual* is twice a year; *biennial* means every two years.

bicentenary see **centenary**

bid Except in the context of an auction or a game of cards, to *bid* for something, the past tense of the verb is *bade* and the past participle *bidden*. But the noun, whose original meaning, an offer or the price of one, has now been extended to include an attempt to gain some purpose, is often exploited as a blanket term in headline use:

Prisoners' Bid for Freedom Fails,
and
Last Desperate Bid for Peace
and has consequently become devalued.

big, great, large Generally speaking, *big* or *large* imply size, *great* an extreme degree or extension of something. In a few contexts, however, the terms can be interchangeable.
A great man implies a man of high quality or degree compared with other men. *A big man* or *a large man* both convey physical size; colloquially, *big* in this context can also mean 'important':
He's a big man in his field.
Large is more often used than *big* in terms of quantity:
There were a large number of people waiting.
But in the sentence:
There was a large crowd waiting
big could just as well be substituted, since the concept of 'crowd' can be of a single object having a tangible size, as well as a collection of separate units, as in the first example.
There are occasions when *great* is used to convey size in place of *big* or *large*:
Take your great boots out of here
certainly suggests enormity of size, but it is being used ironically in the original sense of 'extreme degree of largeness', and not as a simple factual description.

billion There is an important difference between British and French, German or American usage of this word. In Britain a billion represents one million millions, an amount so vast it is really only of use in an astronomical context. Elsewhere the word means one thousand millions.

blame Most authorities recommend that the expression *blame* something *on* a person should be avoided as an unnecessary elaboration of to *blame* a person *for* something. More acceptable in formal writing would be *to put the blame on* someone *for* something.

blank verse The form in which most of Shakespeare's plays and Milton's *Paradise Lost* are written, consisting of unrhymed iambic pentameter verse. It can, however, be applied to any form of unrhymed verse.

blatant, flagrant 'Flauntingly obvious or undisguised, offensively conspicuous, brazen or barefaced' are some of the dictionary definitions of *blatant*:

He was caught out in a blatant lie.

Flagrant means glaring, notorious or scandalous:

He showed a flagrant disregard for the regulations.

Of the two, *flagrant* invites the greater condemnation.

bloom, blossom In their literal sense these words are close in meaning. A flower can either *bloom* or *blossom*, the apple tree may be in *bloom* or in *blossom* in spring, though *bloom* may imply a completion and *blossom* a state of progress. This is much more marked in a figurative sense, where to *blossom* suggests a development which culminates in a climax:

Under his tutelage, she has blossomed into a gifted artist

and to *bloom* implies that the peak of development has already been reached:

He was in the first bloom of youth.

In these examples the words are distinct and cannot be interchanged.

blueprint Literally, a photographic printing process giving a white print on a blue ground, and used chiefly for copying tracings. In extended use the word has been applied to any kind of plan, formula, design or master copy so that it is now a much overused jargon word. It is best confined to the world of the technical drawing office from which it came.

bogey, bogie, bogy *Bogey* is a term used in golf. It is also an alternative form of spelling for *bogy*, a hobgoblin or evil spirit.
Bogie is a low truck or trolley, especially the pivoted truck which bears the wheels beneath a railway wagon. This, too, is an alternative spelling for a hobgoblin or evil spirit.
Bogy is the usual spelling for a hobgoblin or evil spirit. The plural form of the word is *bogies.*

bona fide Though this is a adverb, meaning 'in good faith', it is more usually treated as an adjective:

He showed me a bona-fide certificate.

The *fides* in *bona fides* is a singular noun and not, as is sometimes supposed, a plural:

His bona fides was questionable.

born, borne *Born* is used only in connection with birth; *borne* is the usual past participle of the verb 'to bear':

He was borne out of the ring by two stalwarts in the corner.

It also occurs as a past participle in connection with birth when used in the active sense:

She has borne eleven children,

and in a passive sense only when followed by the preposition *by*:

The child was borne by a gipsy woman.

But not in the following examples:

She was born in America,

or:

She was born of poor parents.

both Some words and phrases should never be used with *both*. For example, in:

Both the captain as well as the crew were all at sea,

the phrase *as well as* makes *both* redundant and could either replace it:

As well as the captain the crew were all at sea

or the sentence could be altered to read:

Both the captain *and* his crew were all at sea.

Other words with which *both* is unnecessary are *equal*, *at once*, *alike* or *between*. In the examples:

He and his son are both alike in appearance,

She is both equally proud and elegant

the use of *both* is superfluous.

The placing of the word is also important:

He is both concerned with fighting for a cause and achieving justice

is incorrect. The word common to each part of the sentence which is linked by *both . . . and* should always appear before the link itself. In this case it is 'concerned':

He is concerned both with fighting for a cause and achieving justice.

Both implies two objects only, and it is not intended to refer to more. The following sentence is therefore incorrect:

Both John and Mary and Mary's brother went out to play.

However, in the sentence:

Both Adam and Eve and the serpent lived in the Garden of Eden,

both is here linking Adam and Eve as a single human unit and treating the serpent as a separate item. In such a case it would be permissible.

Though it is possible to say either *both of the girls* or *both the girls*, the *of* implies two separate units rather than a single entity, and is usually better omitted.

bottleneck As a metaphor, which is about the only purpose for which it is used, this can be a useful word, provided it is remembered that it represents a constriction and cannot therefore be worsened by enlarging, nor improved by reducing. It can be cleared or removed but neither cured nor solved.

bracket The word *bracket*, associated with mathematical formulae, is sometimes used figuratively to mean 'group' or 'class', an extended use which is euphemistic and dehumanizing:

Most of the pupils were from homes in the lower income bracket.

It should be avoided.

brackets Round brackets or parentheses are used to enclose material in the form of information, explanation, or definition which is additional to the main sentence and which is already complete without it.

Because of the severe conditions (there has been a serious drought in the area for several weeks) the annual flower show has been cancelled.

Punctuation marks such as commas are not used before the first bracket but where necessary may be inserted immediately after the closing bracket:

His pockets contained a grubby handkerchief, a return railway ticket (London to Leeds), and some loose change.

Only if the whole sentence is in brackets should the full stop be included inside:

The Queen reviewed her troops. (This is an annual ceremony.) After the event, Her Majesty returned to the Palace.

The use of square brackets occurs when alien material by another author is interpolated into a text, or there is a deliberate substitution of some words in the original. They are also used when a further parenthesis is required in a passage already enclosed in round brackets, and for mathematical formulae.

bravado, bravery *Bravado* is boasting, swaggering pretence; *bravery* is the real thing – courage or valour.

breakdown This word should never be used figuratively in its statistical sense if there is any possibility of it holding a literal meaning as well:

The breakdown of crime prevention must be brought to the attention of the Commissioner.

This does not necessarily mean that law and order no longer prevail, simply that statistics on the subject must be passed on.

brethren A plural form of *brother*, this is now archaic and used only occasionally, in an ecclesiastical context or in a few technical senses.

British, English It is important to distinguish whether the reference is meant in a wide or a narrow sense. *British* is correct applied to persons or things from Great Britain as a whole:

The British government, the British army, British nationality.

But if speaking of an individual it is better to be specific:

Robert Burns, the Scottish poet; the English novelist, Thomas Hardy.

It must be remembered that for any period before 1707 the term *British* did not exist in a political sense and only English, Scots, Irish or Welsh should be used.

broad, wide Though in many contexts these terms can be interchangeable, there is a distinct difference in meaning in some senses. *Wide* is chiefly concerned with the distance from one limit to the next, *broad* with the expanse of matter between them. In the example:

A broad river flowed between steep banks

the impression evoked is from a viewpoint somewhere in the middle, looking up- or downstream, of a big expanse of water with indeterminate limits. But in:

A wide river flowed between steep banks,

the impression is of a river viewed from the side, where the distance between one bank and the other is the predominant feature – the water between is hardly noticed.

With this analogy in mind the place of each word in various idioms and phrases may be seen. In the following examples:

Broad shoulders, broad leaves, broad outline, broad minded

a degree of expansiveness is being expressed, whether in an actual or a metaphorical sense. But in:

Wide eyes, wide open, giving something a wide berth,

it is the distance involved between the limits imposed that is important, not the area itself.

If the idea expressed is indeterminate, either word may be suitable.

broadcast Since the noun was evolved from the verb and not the other way round, the past tense and the past participle of the verb is *broadcast* and not *broadcasted.*

He broadcast for the first time

and:

The speech was broadcast on all wavelengths.

bulk The meaning of this word is 'magnitude in three dimensions', implying a mass of great size. It can be used figuratively in the sense of 'the greater part of' but it is better not to use it to express numbers, only size:

The bulk of the merchandise was sent on later

implies a weighty mass of some dimensions, but in:

The bulk of the crowd was prepared to wait

'majority' would be a better word to use.

burglar, burgle This is a good example of back formation(*q.v.*), where the verb *to burgle* has been formed from the noun.

burlesque, caricature The dictionary definition of *burlesque* is 'an artistic composition . . . which vulgarizes lofty material for the sake of laughter' and of *caricature* is 'a picture ludicrously exaggerating the defects and peculiarities of a person or things'. Both words are often used in a figurative sense, *burlesque* mostly in connection with acting or performance:

His attempt to conduct the meeting in an orderly manner was a burlesque of the real thing

and *caricature* with appearance and features:

When he left her at the door, his face was a caricature of a disappointed lover.

burn, burned, burnt Though either form of the verb is acceptable in the past tense or as a past participle, *burnt* is more often used in the transitive form, where there is an object:

He burnt his boats behind him

and *burned* when the verb is intransitive:

He burned with desire to possess the diamond.

The adjective is always *burnt*:

When the meal came out of the oven, it was like a burnt offering.

but Used as a conjunction joining two parts of a sentence, *but* implies a contrast with a contradictory element between the parts:

He wanted to go to the station but he did not know the way.

If the contradiction is removed, *but* is no longer relevant:

He wanted to go to the station but he knew the way

is incorrect: *and* would be the logical choice.

Care is needed in using a negative with the construction *but that*:

Who could be sure but that the whole deal was not a trick?

But that already implies a negative and therefore the *not* is redundant.

But what is a colloquialism which should be avoided in sentences such as:

She never goes away but what she returns with a cold.

What should be omitted.

Also superfluous is *however* when used with *but*:

All the world's a stage, but if that is true, however, some of the actors give pretty poor performances.

But may be used quite justifiably to begin a sentence in order to provide a contrast with one that has gone before. It is not true that conjunctions such as *but* and *and* should never be used in this position. However, care should be taken that the construction is not repeated later in the sentence:

But he is not the only one to know how the mechanism works, but the others are not such experts.

Assuming that the sentence is in contrast to one immediately preceding it, this would be better expressed as:

But he is not the only one to know how the mechanism works. The others, however, are not such experts.

by, bye Broadly speaking, *by* is the preposition and *bye* the noun, but there are variations of this general rule. *Bylaw* can be spelt *byelaw*, probably because the word is derived from *byrlaw*, and *bye-bye* comes from *goodbye*, a contracted form of 'God be with you'.

In well-established words the hyphen is usually omitted and the word is written as one, unless there is an awkward juxtaposition of vowels or there is more than one syllable:

byword, bylaw, byway,

but:

by-election, by-product.

C

-c-, -ck- When verbs ending in a *c* occur in the past tense or continuous present they usually take an additional *k* to retain the hard pronunciation:

Let us picnic in the woods,

but:

They were picnicking in the woods.

One exception to this rule is the verb *to arc*, which although pronounced with a hard *c* is spelt *arced*, *arcing*. *Arcked* and *arcking* are given as alternative spellings, but are seldom used.

cacao, coca, cocoa *Cacao* is a small evergreen tree of tropical America from the seeds of which cocoa and chocolate are derived. *Coca* is the name of two South American shrubs cultivated for the stimulating properties of their dried leaves, which contain cocaine and other alkaloids. *Cocoa* is the roasted, husked and ground seeds of the cacao tree. The powder is used as a beverage and manufactured into chocolate.

caesura A literary term in poetry, this is a break or sense pause in the middle of a metrical line. It may cut across the metrical pattern in order to correspond to the rhythm of natural speech.

café Although now naturalized into the English language, this French word should still be spelt and pronounced with an accented *é*.

can, may *Can* indicates a possibility; *may* is used in a permissive sense:

Sarah can go to the party by bus

means that the bus will enable Sarah to reach the party.

Sarah may go to the party by bus

means that Sarah has permission to go to the party by bus. Colloquially, *can* is sometimes used in a permissive sense:

Can I call tomorrow?

cannot, can not *Cannot* is the usual negative form unless there is a particular reason to stress the *not*, when the two words may be written separately. In a sentence such as:

The use of a dictionary can not only promote understanding but also provide instruction,

it can be seen that *not* is part of the correlating phrase *not only . . . but also* and it would therefore be incorrect to attach it to *can*.

can't This contraction of *cannot* is widely accepted in all but the most formal contexts. Such a negative should never be used in a phrase such as:

He can't hardly speak

since a negative is already implied. It should be:

He can hardly speak.

The phrase *can't seem to* is an awkward one and should be avoided:

I can't seem to raise any energy

would be better expressed as:

I seem unable to raise any energy

or:

I can't raise any energy.

canvas, canvass The noun *canvas* is 'a heavy cloth'; the verb to *canvass* is 'to solicit votes, subscriptions or opinions'. *Canvass* is also a noun meaning 'an examination, a close inspection, or scrutiny'.

capacity see **ability**

capitalization Capitals should be used sparingly, and it should be borne in mind that capitalization makes a word more limited in its reference. As a rough guide, an initial capital letter gives a word the quality of a proper name, such as Mary or John, and is usually employed in a specific rather than a general sense. Names of specific organizations should carry capitals, since these are, in their way, proper names:

The British Medical Association, Royal Academy of Dramatic Art, School of Slavonic Studies, London School of Journalism.

But if no specific organization is mentioned, and the reference is in general terms, then lower case lettering is correct:

Every country has its own medical association. Many of the universities have recently acquired a college of art, a school of journalism and a school of Slavonic studies.

In a religious context it is customary to treat specific denominations as proper names:

the Roman Catholic Church, the Orthodox Church, the Presbyterian Church,

but in a more general sense:

the Christian church, the parish church, the church at the bottom of the street

capital letters not required. When used in a general sense words such as *catholic* (meaning universal in extent), *orthodox*, *heaven*, *hell*, *the devil* and *paradise* remain in lower case, but the *Reformation* or the *Puritan* religious movement of the 16th century are treated as proper names since they are used in a specific sense. This is true, too, of the *Church* as opposed to the *State*, when giving these bodies the status of named authorities and not referring to them in a general sense such as in:

He was fully occupied in dealing with church and state matters which arose during his time in office.

Political parties are capitalized in the same way when specifically referred to as the *Conservative Party* (the *Conservatives*), the *Labour Party* (*Labour*), and the *Communist Party* (the *Communists*), but when used in a general sense the terms labour, communist and conservative do not need an initial capital.

Again, in a reference to the legislative body of the country, *Parliament* will have an initial capital, and so will the *Government*, meaning the one at present in power, but in a general context neither parliament nor the government – meaning *any* parliament, *any* government – require capital letters:

As to the next step, Parliament must decide; the Government is the only body in a position to judge the situation.

but:

It would require an act of parliament to convince that particular group of workers that the government was the proper authority to control the fund.

This differentiation between the general and the specific applies in most contexts. In titles, for example:

The Queen attended the state opening of Parliament,

but:

By the 16th century the king of England enjoyed absolute power with very little interference from parliament.

And:

The Duke of Bedford opened the fete. The Duke then made a speech,

but:

At dinner she was placed beside a duke of the realm.

There is some support for the custom of dropping the initial capital when only part of the title is used and in a historical context if titles occur frequently, even though the reference is specific. In the above example, for instance:

The Duke of Bedford opened the fete. The duke then made a speech,

this would be considered equally correct, as would:

The archbishop was applied to for permission to marry,

or:

The cathedral was built at Canterbury.

Such variation of the general rules is a matter of taste rather than correctness, but whichever style is adopted it is vital to be consistent within the same text.

Geographical directions in the nature of descriptive adjectives should be in lower case letters, but political or cultural boundaries which imply a proper name for a defined area require initial capitals:

He drove from west to east Africa and through to eastern Asia,

but:

South Africa, East Anglia and Northern Ireland are politically or geographically defined areas.

The North is preferred when referring to the North of England as a specific area; *north of the Wash*, however, is correct in its vaguer geographical sense. Mountains, straits and seas take capital initial letters if they are part of a proper name, such as:

the Straits of Dover, Mount Everest, the English Channel.

The Gulf of Mexico would subsequently be referred to as *the Gulf* – signifying not just any gulf – and the warm stream of water flowing from it across the Atlantic is known as the *Gulf Stream*.

To sum up: capitals are used for nouns placed in a specific context as proper names or titles. In some instances, only part of the title may be capitalized. Provided the writer is consistent, this can be a matter of choice, but it must be borne in mind that ambiguities can arise: *a company secretary* may mean something quite different from *a Company Secretary*, or even *a Company secretary*, and the decision must depend finally on the context.

carat, caret *Carat* is a unit of weight in gem stones, or a measurement of the purity of gold. *Caret* is an omission mark made in written or printed matter to indicate where further material is to be inserted.

carcase, carcass The dead body of an animal. Though both spelling forms are acceptable, *carcass* is to be preferred.

carousal, carousel *Carousal*, with the stress on the second syllable which is pronounced *ow*, means a noisy or drunken feast. *Carousel*, or *carrousel* which is the more acceptable spelling, is a merry-go-round or a tournament with horsemen manoeuvring in formation. The *ou* is pronounced *oo* and the stress is on the last syllable of the word.

case This has become a jargon word. A gift to the sloppy writer, it is frequently used unnecessarily to embroider an otherwise simple sentence:

John was eager to show his skill, but in the case of Mark, he was not so anxious to perform.

The simpler version:

John was eager to show his skill, but Mark was not so anxious to perform

is preferable. And the next example:

In the case of those who have passed the exam, no difficulties will be encountered

would be improved by:

Those who have passed the exam will encounter no difficulties.

But in the following sentences:

The court found there was a case to answer;
In case of illness, ring the doctor;
In a case like yours, I would be the first to complain,

the word has a legitimate place.

cask, casque A *cask* is a barrel-like container made of staves for holding liquids; a *casque* is a word for a helmet, chiefly used in poetry.

cast, caste *Cast* is the spelling of the noun associated with the verb meaning 'to throw'; an object made in a mould or particular pattern. *Caste* is a hereditary social group or rigid system of social distinction.

catachresis The misuse or strained use of words:

It was fortuitous that he was wearing a crash helmet when he fell off

is an example of *catachresis*. Fortuitous means 'accidental', not 'fortunate'.

category, class *Category* is often loosely used to mean *class*, but its definition is more precisely a classificatory division in any particular field of knowledge, especially in science or philosophy. The word *class* refers to a number of persons or things regarded as forming a group. For example:

> The domestic cat belongs to the category of flesh-eating mammals,

but:

> He joined the class for beginners.

catholic, Catholic The adjective *catholic* means universal in extent, involving all. *Catholic* originally described the whole of the Christian church, but it is now used in contrast to Protestant as a term applying to the Roman Catholic Church.

cause, reason A *cause* is a factor which produces an effect. A *reason* is the explanation or justification for a certain effect being produced. For example:

> Ice on the road was the cause of the car skidding,

but:

> The reason the car skidded was that he put his foot on the brake when the road was icy.

To say that a cause is *due to* something is repetitive, nor can it be said that a reason is *because* something has occurred:

> The cause of the breakdown was due to metal fatigue

is wrong. The sentence should either read:

> Metal fatigue was the cause of the breakdown

or:

> The breakdown was due to metal fatigue

And:

> The reason he made a mistake is because he was careless

is another example of tautology. The sentence should be:

> The reason he made a mistake is that he was careless,

or:

> He made a mistake because he was careless.

cavalcade, procession The precise meaning of *cavalcade* is 'a procession of persons on horseback or in horse-drawn carriages', but inevitably, with the advent of the motor car, the word has acquired an extended use to include motorized transport. As a result, it is often used loosely to apply to any kind of *procession* or pageant, and is in danger of being overworked.

cease *To cease fire*, *to cease trading* or *to cease operations* are a few of the phrases in which the word is still sometimes used, but except for some legal and official contexts it has in most cases been superseded by *stop*.

-cede, -ceed, -sede With a few exceptions, all words with this sound at the end are spelt *-cede*. Those which do not obey this rule are *proceed*, *succeed*, *exceed*, and *supersede*, the only one with an *s* instead of a *c*.

ceiling This word is often employed as a metaphor denoting the highest limits that can be reached – a harmless practice, provided it is remembered that a ceiling can be raised or lowered, but not swept aside, extended or increased.

cello Although an abbreviation for *violoncello*, it is so commonly used that it is no longer necessary to precede it with an apostrophe. The plural form of the word is *cellos*, without an *e*.

cement, concrete These words are not interchangeable. *Cement* is the mixture of clay and limestone which, when bound with water, forms an adhesive paste. It is an ingredient of *concrete*, which is formed by the addition of sand and broken stones and bound by water into a malleable consistency which can be set in a mould. *Cement* is also used as an adhesive between other materials, such as tiles or bricks.

censer, censor, censure A *censer* is a container in which incense is burned. A *censor* is an official who examines, and if necessary amends, written material for contravention of existing moral or political conditions, and *censure* is adverse or hostile criticism. The verb *to censor* is to perform the act of censorship, and *to censure* is to criticize or blame.

centenary, centennial Although both these words mean 'one hundred years' and can be interchangeable, the noun *centenary* is more often used in Britain and *centennial* in the United States. One advantage in using *centenary* is that *bicentenary* and *tercentenary* are also established terms. As adjectives, *bicentennial* and *centennial* are the preferred forms.

centre, middle The *centre* implies the central point or pivot of a circle, round which everything else revolves. The *middle* is a less precise term meaning a point or area at an equal distance between two limits. The *middle of the road* is not just one point but a continuous line equal in distance from each side, and the *middle of the room* implies an undefined area around the centre. *To centre round* or *around*, though commonly used phrases, are grammatically incorrect, and should be replaced by *centre on*, or *to be centred in*.

century The word *century* means 'one hundred years', and this always begins on the first year of any given century, so that the last year of that hundred years gives the century its name. Thus 1900 is the last year of the 19th century, and 1901 the first year of the 20th century.

ceremonial, ceremonious The noun *ceremonial* is a rite or ceremony, or a system of rites or ceremonies, and the adjective *ceremonial* pertains to these rites or ceremonies. *Ceremonious* is an adjective describing the observance of rites or ceremonies or formally polite behaviour. Broadly speaking, *ceremonial* is concerned with the ceremonies themselves, *ceremonious* with the people who practise them.

certainty, certitude *Certainty* is an assured fact; *certitude* is a sense of complete conviction. The first is concerned with fact, the second with feelings about the fact.

chance The verb *to chance* is giving way to *happen* in the same way as *cease* is being superseded by *stop*:

He chanced to come upon them standing by the bus stop

is more formal than:

He happened to come upon them standing by the bus stop,

and therefore sounds a little pedantic.

The noun *chance* is sometimes used when *opportunity* would be more appropriate:

It was a chance he knew he should not miss

would be more precise as:

It was an opportunity he knew he should not miss.

chancellery, chancery The *chancellery* is the position or the official residence of a chancellor; *chancery* is a division of the High Court of Justice.

change, alter *Change* has a wider application than *alter*, which implies a modification in one particular only. *Change* can mean a total substitution, or alteration in many respects at once:

He was persuaded to change his habits,

and:

He changed from an amiable, happy boy into a surly, morose adult.

But:

By shaving off his moustache he had altered his whole appearance

is an example of the more limited use of *altered*.

character The dictionary definition is 'the aggregate of qualities that distinguishes one person or thing from another', but this word is often made to stand in for 'kind', 'sort' and 'nature', or used unecessarily in a sentence where a simple adjective would do. For example:

This house is of a spacious character

means:

This house is of a spacious nature

but the simple way of saying this is:

This house is spacious.

charge Originally there was no ambiguity if it were said:

Children in charge of an adult may be admitted free.

But meanings change, and such a sentence now implies that the children are in full control of the adults. This may well be true, but it is probably not what is meant. The sentence should read:

Children in *the* charge of an adult may be admitted free,

for it is the adult who is normally *in charge of* the child.

childish, childlike Both words are defined as 'like or befitting a child', but *childish* is more often used in a slightly derogatory sense, meaning that certain behaviour is suitable only for a child, whereas *childlike* is a term implying admiration and stressing the freshness and innocence of childhood. Examples of the contexts in which these words might be used are:

Such a childish display of temper will achieve nothing,

and:

Her childlike simplicity appealed to all who came in contact with her.

Chinese, Chinaman *Chinese* is the term to use when referring to the Chinese people or the Chinese nation. *Chinamen*, like the slang terms *Chinee* and *Chink*, has a derogatory implication and should be avoided.

choice This word implies an alternative, but it is often loosely used, particularly in advertising copy, in a context which offers no choice at all:

Last opportunity to win the holiday of your choice!

and:

Choice vegetables, freshly picked.

But:

He offered her a choice of three alternatives

is an example of the correct use of the word.

chorale A simple hymn-like tune in slow tempo which is sung by choir and congregation. The emphasis is on the second syllable.

chord, cord *Chord* is a string of a musical instrument, or the sound produced by a combination of three or more harmonious notes struck simultaneously. It is also used figuratively in respect of feelings:

He struck a chord of sympathy in her heart,

and is a technical term in the fields of geometry, civil engineering and aeronautics. *Cord* is a string or small rope consisting of several strands twisted together.

Christian name, first name, forename There is a tendency today to prefer the terms *first name* or *forename* to *Christian name* on the grounds that the person referred to may well not be a Christian. At one time, when all children in the Western world were baptized into some branch of the Christian church, the term *Christian name* had a logical basis, even though many of the names given may have derived from classical or other pagan origins. It seems, however, to be a matter of personal preference rather than one of precept, since long-standing usage has given the term *Christian name* the widest possible application.

chronic A victim of misapplication, chronic is often wrongly used to mean 'severe' or 'deplorable':

The pains in my legs were chronic last night.

Its true meaning is 'of long-standing duration, inveterate or constant', as in:

She was a chronic invalid, and had been unable to walk for twenty years.

circumstances Both *in the circumstances* and *under the circumstances* are acceptable, and there are no grounds for believing that the latter phrase is less correct than the former.

city In general usage a *city* is a very large town, particularly one which is a centre of business and administration. In Britain, however, in its strict sense the word is applied only to those towns which have been appointed by royal charter. Often, though not necessarily, this refers to a cathedral town, which may be of quite a small size. The City of London, for instance, which is the centre of banking and insurance for the rest of the country, is only about a square mile in extent.

clad, clothed Though both words are the past tense and past participle of the verb *to clothe*, the older word, *clad*, cannot be used in so many contexts, but is limited to mean specific kinds of clothing:

He was clad in shining armour

is acceptable, but in:

He was fed and clothed and educated at very little cost to the state

the word *clothed* could not suitably be replaced by *clad*.

claim The meaning of this word, 'to demand as a right or due', has been extended colloquially to replace words such as 'assert', 'allege', 'declare', and 'say', and has lost much of its precision in the process:

He claimed he had seen the thief run off.

He could *allege* or *declare* or even *say*, he had seen the thief, with more accuracy. But:

As the sole survivor of that branch of the family he claimed the legacy

is an example of the word used in its proper context.

clarinet, clarionet Both forms are acceptable, but *clarinet* is now the preferred spelling. The stress is on the last syllable.

classic, classical Though in many contexts these words overlap in meaning, *classic* is more generally used to signify 'of the very first order', 'first class', and *classical*, 'in accordance with Greek and Roman models in literature or art, or later systems of principles modelled upon them'.
Though the term *classic* may be used to mean *classical*, as in:

The house was of classic proportions, with pillars supporting a high portico,

the word is often loosely applied in a variety of contexts in which *classical* could not be substituted and which are in no way connected with Greek or Roman perfection. For example:

It was a classic example of a petty official exceeding his powers,

and:

It was a classic case of whitewashing.

In these two examples 'typical' might be more apt. But in:

This book should become a classic

the allusion is close to the original meaning. Books that are *classics* are those of the highest order, such as might be compared with the models of literature of ancient Greece and Rome. However, music of a similar quality is referred to as *classical*, and the term is used in opposition to 'popular' or 'romantic', as well as applying to that of a particular period.

clause A *clause* is a group of words including a verb and its subject, together with any modifying adjectives or adverbs. If it can stand on its own, making a sentence complete in itself, it is known as a *main clause*. If it depends upon another part of the sentence for its meaning it is a *subordinate clause*.
A sentence can consist of two or more main clauses linked by a conjunction:

The wood was dense, but the trees were not very tall:

A subordinate clause is linked to the main part of the sentence by a relative pronoun or a subordinating conjunction:

My father, who is elderly, is giving up his home.

My father . . . is giving up his home is the main clause, and *who is elderly* is the subordinate clause, *who* being the relative pronoun.

Nero fiddled while Rome burned.

In this sentence *while* is the subordinating conjunction joining the subordinate part of the sentence to the main clause, *Nero fiddled*.

A *clause* is also the name given to each paragraph of a legal document, and each section of an act of parliament while in the preparatory stages.

clean, cleanse Though *clean* and *cleanse* both mean 'to make clean', or 'to remove dirt', *cleanse* should be used only figuratively in a moral, spiritual or ritualistic sense:

Cleansed of his sins, he felt able to return to the world.

The noun *cleanser* sometimes finds its way into advertising copy describing a proprietary brand of household cleaner. This, no doubt, is because it presents an image not just of cleanliness, but also of purity.

cleave There are two distinct meanings of this word. The first is 'to stick or adhere to', 'be attached or faithful to,' the past tense of which is *cleaved*:

He cleaved to his beliefs despite the conflicting evidence.

The second meaning is 'to part by a cutting blow', 'to sever, rend apart, or split'. The past tense is *cleft*, *cleaved* or *clove*, and the past participle *cloven* or *cleft*.

clench, clinch To *clench* is to grasp firmly or to grip: a fist, teeth or hands are *clenched*. To *clinch* is to secure, or fasten together, particularly a nail, by beating down the point. Boxers go into a *clinch*, when they have to be separated, and in a figurative sense a bargain is *clinched*.

clever This word is sometimes misused in the sense of being academically well qualified, erudite, or hard to understand. The true meaning of the word is 'having quick intelligence', 'mentally bright', 'showing adroitness or ingenuity'. For example:

> Thanks to a clever manoeuvre, he extricated himself from a difficult position.

In other words quick intelligence will usually result in academic achievement, but it is the sharp intelligence that the word *clever* relates to, not the result of it.

cliché A trite phrase which 'springs to mind', 'at the drop of a hat', 'in a nutshell' – there are three examples of clichés. Such phrases start life as apt metaphors in a given context but are then adopted by other writers and repeated so frequently and so mechanically that they quickly become overworked and often meaningless. Words, too, become fashionable and are often so ill used that they lose their purpose – 'democratic', 'significant', 'escalation' are examples of vogue words which have lost much of the force of their original meaning and have become trite clichés.

client, customer, patron A *client* is one who seeks professional advice, or who employs the services of a professional expert. A *customer* purchases goods from another, and a *patron* supports another by dealing with him as a *customer*. In the word *patron* there is an implication that he, as a *customer*, is doing the other a favour by 'patronizing' his establishment and buying goods or services from him.

climactic, climatic, climacteric *Climactic* is pertaining to or forming a climax. *Climatic* is relating to weather conditions, and *climacteric* means crucial, pertaining to a critical period, or a year in which important changes are said to occur.

close, shut Some authorities assert that *close* is a genteel euphemism for *shut*. In certain cases this may be true, but there are also specific implications in the two words. In some contexts *shut* signifies a more positive action than *close*, in which there is also a suggestion of enclosure or containment:

He got up and closed the door

implies a closing *in*.

He got up and shut the door

implies a shutting *out*.

clothe see **clad**

cockscomb, coxcomb *Cockscomb* is the comb of a cock, or the pointed cap of a jester which resembles it, and it is also the name of a plant. *Coxcomb* is the word for a conceited dandy.

cohere see **adhere**

coherence, cohesion Both *coherence* and *cohesion* mean the act or state of sticking together, but *coherence* is used more often in a figurative sense, as of thoughts or of verbal statements, whereas *cohesion* is applied to the uniting of objects or substances.

coiffeur, coiffure *Coiffeur* is a hairdresser; *coiffure* is a style of arranging or setting the hair. It can also mean a headdress or head covering.

collective nouns There are different types of *collective noun*. Those that apply to a series of articles collected together, such as luggage, cutlery, clothing and transport are treated as singular and take a singular verb:

The luggage was put on the train.

Some nouns are the same in the singular as the plural and take either a singular or a plural verb according to the sense:

The fish *are* rising

but:

My fish *is* delicious.

Group nouns, known as *nouns of multitude*, may take a singular or a plural verb according to the context. A singular verb is used if the emphasis is on the group acting as an individual unit. A plural verb is used if the emphasis is on the individuals who make up the group:

The jury *has* agreed upon its verdict

but:

The committee *were* unable to come to a decision.

Whichever form of the verb is used, it is most important to be consistent throughout the sentence:

The company *has* agreed that *they* will delay delivery

is incorrect. Either:

The company *has* agreed that *it* will delay delivery

or:

The company *have* agreed that *they* will delay delivery

are acceptable and, since in this context it (the company) is acting as a single unit, the singular version is to be preferred. In the same way, with other group words the choice of a singular or plural verb depends on whether the noun implies a single unit or several members of a group:

The rest of the cake *is* still to be eaten,

but:

The rest of the soldiers *were* forced to retreat.

Three-quarters of the building *is* completed,

but:

Two-thirds of the children *were* unable to read.

With the word *number* itself, *the number* is usually singular, but *a number* is plural:

The number of acts of terrorism *has* shown a steep increase,

but:

A number of students *are* taking part in the demonstration.

This is because in the second example 'a number of students' is a composite subject standing in the place of 'numerous students'. Similarly, in:

Three hundred miles is a long way to come for a funeral,

'a journey of' is implied at the beginning of the sentence, rendering 'three hundred miles' part of a composite subject which takes a singular verb.

collusion This must not be confused with *collaboration*, which has a friendly, benign ring to it. *Collusion* means conspiracy, or a secret agreement for a fraudulent purpose, and there is nothing friendly about it.

colon This punctuation mark is generally considered to be intermediate between the semicolon and the full stop in weight, but with the exception of certain contexts it is not very widely used today.

Its chief purpose is to form a relationship between a general statement and qualifying remarks which follow, each part of the sentence being complete in itself. Indeed, in many cases the colon could be replaced by a full stop with little loss of sense or meaning, though a difference would be seen in the balance of the text as a whole. For example:

He goes for long walks in all kinds of weather: this may account for the muddy condition of his shoes,

and:

Most people have some special dislikes in foods: for some it is stewed prunes, for others cabbage.

In both examples a full stop, though grammatically acceptable, would, by dividing the sentences into two, have separated the parts more drastically than the sense demanded. A semi-colon, too, would be a possible substitute, but it also tends to be divisive and would not provide the balancing link so effectively as the colon.

In a similar way a colon is used to introduce a list of items or examples (as in the present text). This is really just an extension of the role already described:

The company produces four types of motor vehicle: a sports car, a saloon, an estate car and a van,

and:

The procedure is as follows: dial 999 and ask for the police.

It is also used as an alternative to the comma when introducing direct speech:

He said: 'I come to bury Caesar, not to praise him.'

comedy, farce, burlesque *Comedy* is the comic element in a piece of drama, a play or film of humorous character. *Farce* stresses the outrageous absurdity of a comic situation or character, and *burlesque* is a caricature or vulgar treatment of ordinary material aimed at provoking laughter. In the United States *burlesque* has the specific sense of a theatrical entertainment of coarse and vulgar comedy and dancing.

comic, comical *Comic* describes the aim, or intention, of causing laughter; *comical* describes the effect. A *comic* actor is one who sets out to perform humorous roles; a *comical* actor is a man whose every word and gesture causes mirth, whether intended or not.

comma The chief function of a *comma* is to separate or set off different parts of a sentence. It should be used to avoid ambiguity, to achieve greater clarity and to prevent a sentence becoming unwieldy, but it should always be used sparingly. Too many commas hold up the flow of thought and are irritating to the reader. There are occasions when the use of a comma is obligatory, some when its use may be a matter of choice, and others where it should not be used at all.

A comma may be inserted between two main clauses linked by a co-ordinating conjunction such as *and* or *but*:

It has been exceptionally cold today, but rain is forecast for tomorrow.

The comma here is optional. If the two parts of the sentence are fairly short and closely related it is better to omit it.

It is also used to separate three or more clauses, words and phrases in a series:

She picked up her shopping bag, wheeled out the pram, and set off for the shops,

and:

She was so desperate for a cigarette she was quite prepared to beg, borrow or steal one.

In modern practice the comma is often omitted before the conjunction connecting the last two items, as in the second example. Whichever course is followed, it is important to be consistent.

Commas are used to separate individual adjectives modifying a noun provided they are not related, and could logically be linked by 'and':

She was a tall, thin, angular woman.

But:

She was a pretty little thing.

In this example 'little thing' is thought of as a single unit modified by the adjective 'pretty': *and* could not logically be inserted between 'pretty' and 'little', so a comma is not needed.

A comma is used following a phrase, clause or word introducing the main clause:

When the time came to go, he put on his coat.

Later, he called to see how she was.

One of its most important functions is to set off a phrase or clause in the middle of a sentence:

My brother, who lives in the city, is a keen photographer.

Here the commas are a form of parenthesis round a clause which is providing additional, but expendable, information about the subject. This is known as a non-restrictive clause: the main part of the sentence:

My brother . . . is a keen photographer

could very well stand on its own. It is important to ensure that both commas are used in such a sentence; as with brackets, the end of the parenthesis must be shown.

If, however, the same sentence is used without the commas the sense is changed:

My brother who lives in the city is a keen photographer.

This implies that I have more than one brother. *Who lives in the city* is a restrictive or defining clause distinguishing him from the others, and is therefore essential to the meaning of the sentence, so it must not be separated off by commas. Another example is as follows:

The doctor who was best known in the town was elected to the committee.

Without the commas this too is a restrictive clause. That doctor was elected because he was the one who was known best. But with commas inserted the sense is altered:

The doctor, who was best known in the town, was elected to the committee.

The clause is now non-restrictive, just providing incidental information about the doctor who had been elected to the committee and who happened to be better known in the town than anywhere else.

A comma is sometimes essential to a sentence in order to avoid ambiguity:

She jumped, the hedge producing unexpected prickles which penetrated her thick skirt.

A comma is not required in a list connected by conjunctions:

He is tall and slim and handsome,

and it should never be inserted between a subject and its verb, even in a long sentence:

The truth of the matter that we are considering in the light of the evidence put before us in court today, is that there is no justification for his behaviour.

The truth is the subject, *is* the verb, and there is no justification for the comma which separates them. It would be preferable to rewrite the sentence if it is felt to be too unwieldy.

commence see **begin**

commitment, committal *Commitment* is a pledge, or the state of being committed to something:

We have a firm commitment every Sunday to drive our neighbour to church.

In other contexts *committal* is often interchangeable, but it is also used in the special sense of committing an offence or of being committed to prison:

His committal to prison was endorsed by the court

and:

The committal of a crime is anti-social behaviour.

common, mutual *Common* is belonging equally to, or shared by two or more people, joint, united. *Mutual* is reciprocal, possessed or experienced by two people or more. On the whole, *common* has a wider application. *Mutual* tends to be thought of as a two-way activity, often restricted to two people.

Mutual should be avoided with words that already indicate reciprocity, as in *mutual agreement*.

Commonwealth of Nations A community bound together by a common allegiance to the British crown and recognizing the British monarch as its head, in which Britain is an equal partner with certain independent nations and their dependencies.

comparative, comparatively These words should be used only when there are two or more things to compare, and not as generalized modifiers of adjectives and adverbs:

He was comparatively slow in learning French.

Slow compared to what? *Fairly* or *rather* would be more suitable substitutes. But:

Of the total number of absentees, comparatively few had genuine excuses.

Here the word is appropriate, since the proportion of those with genuine excuses is being compared with the total number of absentees.

compare to, compare with To *compare* something *to* something else is figuratively to set them up beside each other in order to draw attention to their similarities. To *compare* something *with* something else is to set it against the other object in order to point out their dissimilarities, the implication usually being a derogatory one:

Describing his new girl friend, he compared her to Helen of Troy.

This is complimentary to the girl friend, but:

Compared with Helen, Susan is a non-starter in the beauty stakes

is placing Susan at a disadvantage.

With the verb *compare*, it is important to ensure that the comparison made is a possible one, that like is compared with like:

His work was badly done compared with his neighbour

should read:

His work was badly done compared with that of his neighbour

or:

His work was badly done compared with his neighbour's (work).

comparisons, false see **absolute terms**

compel, impel *Compel* means to force or drive, especially to a course of action. *Impel* also means to drive, or to urge forward, or to incite to action.

There is more strength in the word *compel*, suggesting coercive pressure from outside, whereas *impel* is used more often in a figurative sense, implying the internal pressure of feelings and strong motivation. In the example:

He was compelled to stand against the wall with his hands raised

there is the suggestion of physical force.

She felt impelled to volunteer for extra duty at Christmas.

Here, the driving force is self-motivated.

complacent, complaisant *Complacent* is pleased, especially with oneself, salf-satisfied; *complaisant* is obliging or compliant, agreeable.

complement, compliment *Complement* is that which completes or makes perfect: the full quantity or amount that completes anything, as with *a ship's complement*, meaning the officers and crew required to man a vessel. In grammar the term means a word or words used to complete a grammatical construction, as with an object following a verb:

The girl is tall

Tall is the complement: the sentence is unfinished without it. *Compliment* is an expression of praise or admiration.

complement, supplement A *complement* is that which completes something, and makes up the full quantity or amount. A *supplement* is something added to supply a deficiency and implies an addition to the whole, a reinforcement or extension:

I always give the dog a vitamin pill as a supplement to his rations.

complex sentence A *complex sentence* is one which contains a main clause and one or more dependent or subordinate clauses as well:

She took out a book which she had wanted to read for some time, having seen a review of it.

compound sentence This is a sentence containing two or more main clauses:

It was a brave thing to do and he did not hesitate to do it, but the outcome was quite unexpected.

comprehend see **apprehend**

comprehensible, comprehensive *Comprehensible* is intelligible, capable of being understood. *Comprehensive* is inclusive, having a wide mental grasp, comprehending much, of large scope:

She has a comprehensive knowledge of early English painting.

comprise, include, consist of *To comprise* means to be made up of, encompass, or to be composed of. *To include* means to contain or embrace parts or part of a whole, and *to consist of* means to be composed of, or to be made up of. *Comprise* implies a containment or embracing of all the parts of a whole; *include* suggests that only some of the parts are contained, while *consist of* means that the whole is made up of the sum of its constituent parts:

The course *comprises* the whole spectrum of book publishing, and *includes* illustration research, an important aspect of which *consists of* the selection and commissioning of artwork and photographs.

concave, convex *Concave* is curved outward like a hollow sphere. The opposite is *convex*, which means curved inward like a sphere viewed from the outside, and bulging in the middle. Both terms are applied especially to lenses and mirrors.

concise, succinct *Concise* means expressing a lot in a few words. *Succinct* also means expressing much in a few words, or characterized by brevity, and suggests compactness. With *concise* there is not a word to spare, and *succinct* implies economy in the choice of the words themselves.

condemn, contemn *Condemn* is to censure, or pronounce to be guilty, to compel or force into a certain state of action. *Contemn* is to view with contempt or treat disdainfully.

confidant(e), confident A *confidant* is someone to whom secrets are confided. The word, which is French, also has a feminine form, *confidante*.

Confident is having a strong belief or assurance about something: to be sure of oneself.

confide in, confide to To *confide in* someone is to entrust them with a secret. In the transitive form of the verb one *confides* or entrusts a secret *to* someone.

conjugal, connubial *Conjugal* is an adjective meaning concerning husband and wife. *Connubial* is to do with marriage, or the state of matrimony:

The husband insisted on his conjugal rights,

and:

For forty years they lived in a state of connubial bliss.

conjunction This is the term for a connecting word which joins two words, parts of a sentence or whole sentences together. There are two kinds of conjunction: co-ordinating and subordinating. The co-ordinating conjunctions – *and*, *but*, *or*, *for*, *yet* and *nor* – join words or groups of equal weight:

Horse and hounds.
He knew her name but he couldn't recall her face.

Some are called correlatives, because they are often closely linked:

Neither his wife *nor* his mother knew what to say.
She *not only* plays, *but also* sings.

It is important to ensure that these are correctly placed:

She *both* liked the pink dress *and* the brown one

is incorrect. The correlation is between the two colours:

She liked *both* the pink dress *and* the brown one.

Subordinate conjunctions join a main clause to a subordinate one. They may be of time (*as*, *since*, *before*, *when*), reason (*as*, *since*, *because*, *why*), condition (*though*, *if*, *unless*), purpose (*so*, *lest*, *that*) or comparison (*than*):

You must not climb the ladder lest you fall.
I do not know when I shall be back.
If you are going to the shops, you could buy me some butter.

In the last example, even though it is placed at the beginning of the sentence, the conjunction *if* still does its job of subordinating the clause.

connection, connexion Though both forms are admissible, the former is the more widely used, and is standard in American practice.
In connection with is another of those tiresome phrases frequently used in sloppy English to replace the simple preposition:

I want to speak to you in connection with the matter we discussed yesterday

means:

I want to speak to you about the matter we discussed yesterday.

It is simpler to say so.

connote, denote *Connote* means to signify, but also to imply, or to have associated meanings. *Denote* is to indicate, to be a sign of:

The bristly moustache and upright bearing denote his status as a sergeant; they connote a disciplinarian with a fanatical regard for conformity.

consecutive, successive *Consecutive* is following on in uninterrupted succession one behind the other. *Successive* is also following on one behind the other in order or sequence, but does not necessarily mean next to each other:

When picking the raffle tickets, he chose consecutive numbers. Successive attempts had been made to communicate with the hostages, and some of these had been successful.

consequent, consequential *Consequent* is following as a result, or as a logical conclusion, or logically consistent. *Consequential* is of the nature of a consequence, following as an effect or result. It also means self-important or pompous. *Consequent* is the word usually adopted in the sense of 'resulting':

His speech was deliberately provocative and the consequent uproar was only to be expected,

but *consequential* is correct in the special sense of *consequential damages* or *consequential loss insurance*, which means contingency loss and damage following as the indirect result of something, such as the necessity of taking hotel accommodation when a car has been incapacitated in an accident. In this sense it implies consistency with a result, but not the direct result itself.

consist of, consist in *To consist of* something means to be composed of, to be made up of a material:

Hadrian's Wall consists of nothing more than large stones piled on top of each other.

To consist in means to be contained in, to lie in, and is usually applied in an abstract sense when speaking of qualities:

Success in show jumping consists in acquiring a close understanding with your horse.

consistence, consistency *Consistency* is the form invariably used nowadays. Many dictionaries merely list *consistence* as an alternative.

constrain, restrain *Constrain* is to force, compel, oblige, or to confine forcibly. *Restrain* is to hold back from action, keep in check, keep under control:

She felt constrained to speak her mind and not even his pleading could restrain her.

constructive There is a tendency for this overworked word, the opposite of destructive, to be used solely as a meaningless cliché. *Constructive criticism* has become a euphemism for saying something unpleasant. A suggestion is still the contribution of an idea, whether it is termed *constructive* or not.

consult, consult with *To consult* is to seek counsel for, ask advice of or refer to someone for information. *To consult with* is to consider or deliberate as well as to confer with someone. It is an Americanism to apply the *with* form in the wider context as well. Such an expression should be left to the specific context of a conference in which a topic is deliberated.

contagious, infectious *Contagious* is communicable to others, carrying or spreading a disease. *Infectious* is causing or communicating infection, tending to spread from one to another. The difference between them is that *contagious* means contact by touch, whereas an *infectious* disease is spread by germs in the air that is breathed. Both terms are often used figuratively.

contemporary There is a danger that the true meaning of this word will soon be lost in the confusion of its misapplication. *Contemporary* means belonging to the same time. It can only be equated with 'modern', 'up to date' if that is the time which is under discussion:

I like contemporary furniture

is a perfectly valid statement in the context of the person talking, whenever that was. If, say, Henry VIII had made that remark, he would have been referring to the furniture of the Tudor period – that is, *contemporary* with him.

It was a production of *Romeo and Juliet* in contemporary dress

does not mean a production in modern dress, but in the clothes of Shakespeare's period. To say *they are contemporaries* is to describe two people of the same age group.

contemptible, contemptuous *Contemptible* is despicable, deserving of being held in contempt. *Contemptuous* means scornful, expressing contempt or disdain:

He regarded the suggestion contemptibly

is incorrect. He could regard it *contemptuously*, with contempt or scorn, because he thought it was a *contemptible* or despicable suggestion.

contiguous see **adjacent**

continual, continuous *Continual* is recurring with relentless regularity. *Continuous* is non-stop and unbroken. A telephone might be described as ringing *continually*, because of the number of calls received. Water from a burst pipe would pour through the ceiling in a *continuous* stream.

continuance, continuation, continuity *Continuance* and *continuation* both mean the act or fact of continuing. To continue, meaning the intransitive sense of to last or endure, is a *continuance* of an act; to continue an action, the transitive form of the verb, will produce a *continuation* of it. So:

I hope you will allow a continuance of my tenancy,

and:

The continuation of the serial will be published next week.

Continuity is the state of being continuous, and in a film-making context it has acquired the special sense of consistency.

converse, inverse The adjective *converse* is turned about, opposite or contrary in direction or action:

He is certainly not making money; in fact, the converse is true.

Inverse is reversed in position, direction or tendency, or turned upside down:

I shall announce the winners in inverse order. Third prize goes to...

contrary, converse, opposite *Contrary* is diametrically or mutually opposed; *converse* is turned about, opposite in action or direction; *opposite* is diametrically different, an antonym. With the phrase:

Each cat has nine lives,

a *contrary* statement would be:

Each cat does not have nine lives,

a *converse* statement would be:

Nine cats each have one life,

and the *opposite* is:

No cat has nine lives.

Opposite is contrary, but a *contrary* statement is not necessarily opposite: it will also include shades of lesser meanings.

copulative verb This is the grammatical term for a linking verb, tying the complement in to the subject of a sentence:

He *is* tall.
She has *grown* old.
He *seems* well.

correspond to, correspond with If an object is like something else, it *corresponds to* it. To *correspond with* somebody is to write them a letter.

co-respondent, correspondent A *co-respondent* is the third party in a divorce suit. A *correspondent* is one who writes a letter; also, in a journalistic context, a reporter who specializes in a given subject or area.

corporal, corporeal *Corporal* is of or belonging to the human body. *Corporeal* means bodily, of the nature of matter, as distinct from *spiritual.*

correlatives These are conjunctions that go in pairs: *either . . . or*, *not only . . . but also*, *both . . . and*. [See *conjunction*]

cost effectiveness The degree of stability measured by the relationship of costs over returns. This is one of the vogue words at present, more popular than helpful.

could, might *Could* suggests a greater degree of probablity than *might*:

If he had practised harder, he could have made the English team.

There may have been a possibility but hardly a probability about such a prediction. *Might* would be a better word. But:

You could get yourself killed, running across that busy road.

That is intended as a statement of probability. *Could* is therefore the correct choice.

council, counsel A *council* is a board or assembly of people convened for deliberation or advice; *counsel* is advice, an opinion or instruction given for directing the conduct of others.

A *councillor* is a member of a council or board; a *counsellor* is an advisor. In the United States it is the word for a lawyer:

He was elected to the Parish Council, where he proved to be a better counsellor than councillor. For though his counsel was sound enough he was never able to attend the meetings.

counter-productive A very popular vogue word meaning little more than 'unhelpful', but longer.

credence, credit Both words mean belief, but *credit* has many other meanings as well, such as trustworthiness, credibility, reputation, a source of commendation or honour:

She gave no credence to the rumours she had heard about him, but gave him credit for possessing sense enough to have remained an honest man.

credible, credulous, creditable *Credible* is capable of being believed, trustworthy; *credulous* is ready to believe anything; *creditable* is bringing credit, honour or esteem:

The child's story was quite credible and in keeping with the facts, though the old lady was credulous enough to believe anything. But on the whole he had behaved creditably, and made a good impression.

creole This is the term for someone of European descent who is a native of the West Indies or Spanish America.

crevasse, crevice Though similar, these words are not interchangeable. A *crevasse* is a deep cleft or fissure in a glacier. In the United States, it is also applied to a breach in a river bank or embankment. A *crevice* is a crack, rift or fissure in the ground.

crucial Decisive, critical, involving a final and supreme decision are the true meanings of this word, which is often carelessly employed to stand in for 'important'. Such an extended meaning can only have a weakening effect.

cultivated, cultured Literally, *cultivated* is that which is produced or improved by cultivation, such as a plant; figuratively, it means educated and refined. *Cultured* means artificially nurtured or grown, and is a term used especially in the context of scientific and laboratory work.
Figuratively, it means much the same as *cultivated* does in the figurative sense: enlightened, refined. The use of the term 'culture', applied to a race of people and their way of life, has influenced the way in which the adjective is used, and it is often applied in a broader sense than its counterpart *cultivated*:

He is a very cultivated man, interested in philosophy and literature, but then, of course, he comes from a cultured background.

curb, kerb A *curb* is something that restrains or checks, and is the name of the chin-strap or chain which is part of a certain type of horse's bit. It can also apply to the paved edging of a pavement or footpath, though in Britain (not the United States) for this meaning *kerb* is the usual spelling. *Kerb* is also applied to the framework round the top of a well and the fender of a hearth.

Czech, Czechoslovak A *Czech* is a Bohemian and a member of the most westerly branch of the Slavs comprising Bohemians, Moravians and Slovaks. A *Czechoslovak* is a citizen of Czechoslovakia and the word *Czechoslovak* embraces Bohemians, Moravians and Slovaks. *Czech* is, however, used loosely to cover all three groups.

D

-d-, -dd- Single-syllable words ending in *d* double it before suffixes beginning with a vowel if the *d* is preceded by a single short vowel:

bedding, laddie, sadden, maddest.

If, however, it is preceded by two vowels, an *n* or an *r* the *d* is not doubled:

feeding, guarded, loaded, moody, spending.

Words of more than one syllable behave in the same way as single-syllable words if their last syllable is stressed and is preceded by a single short vowel:

embedded, hagridden.

They do not double the *d* otherwise:

impending, rapidity, defended, avoidance.

dangling modifier see **unattached participle**

dare This is a verb with some peculiarities in its use. When it means 'to have the necessary courage or boldness' it has *dare* instead of *dares* as the third person singular in negative and interrogative sentences and also in sentences where the infinitive dependent upon *dare* is not preceded by *to* (although such sentences are usually either negative or interrogative):

He dare not go. How dare she say such a thing?

When *dare* means 'to challenge or provoke to action' the third person singular is *dares* and any dependent infinitive is preceded by *to*:

He dares me to confess everything to my father.

dare say This is usually written as two words and is nowadays almost invariably used only in the first person singular and the present tense.

dash It is advisable to use the dash with great caution. It is too often employed when some other kind of punctuation might have served the purpose much better. The dash can, however, be used legitimately, if sparingly, as follows.

Two dashes in a sentence show that the words enclosed between them are to be read parenthetically, separated off from the rest of the sentence:

His third novel – his last as it turned out – was a failure.

The dash is used in a sentence to explain or expand what immediately precedes it:

These were his greatest achievements – the founding of a successful company, the bringing of prosperity to a depressed region, and the establishment of a better relationship between management and workers.

The dash is used to add a final summing up to a sentence or to gather up the loose ends of a long sentence:

The resources of the Western world, its technological expertise, its capacity for long-term planning, the energy and dynamism of its leaders, its ability to adapt to changing circumstances – all these are at our disposal.

The dash is used to show a change of subject or to indicate that a sentence begun is to remain unfinished:

When he arrived home – but I'd better tell you what happened to his sister first.

data This is a Latin plural and is generally used with a plural verb in English:

The data available are inadequate.

However, there is a growing tendency to consider *data* as a collective noun grouping together individual objects and to attach a singular verb to it:

The data he has accumulated is sufficient for our purposes.

dates It is better to print dates in the sequence day – month – year, i.e., 15 July 1971, 19 December 1861, without commas and omitting *st*, *nd*, *rd* and *th* unless the day is given without the month:

Payment is due on the 10th of each month.
He arrived on 15 May and left on the 20th.

Note that if the sequence month – day – year is used the *st*, *nd*, *rd* or *th* should be included:

December 2nd 1959, October 23rd 1965.

When months have to be abbreviated, as for example in tables, use the following forms:

Jan., Feb., Aug., Sept., Oct., Nov., Dec.

Do not abbreviate March, April, May, June or July unless absolutely necessary for reasons of space.

The apostrophe is omitted in expressions such as 'the 1940s'.

For centuries and millenniums it is better to spell out the numbers:

The eighth century, the fourth millennium, the seventeenth century.

If consecutive four-figure dates fall within the same century the first two figures of the second date are usually omitted:

1820–25, 1914–18, 1730–1840.

Note: 'from 1940 to 1949' or 'during 1940–49' but not 'from 1940–49'.

When using *B.C.* remember that this always follows the figures:

500 B.C., 44 B.C.

A.D. always precedes the figures but it should be used only after one or more *B.C.* dates or to avoid ambiguity:

From 55 B.C. to A.D. 40.

de-, dis- These prefixes, which have a negative or privative force, are put at the beginning of words to create new ones with the opposite meaning. Many authorities have deplored the appearance of such words as *deactivate*, *derestrict*, *disincentive* and *disinflation*, but there is no doubt that they are capable of expressing precise shades of meaning which no other words can convey. The popularity of these prefixes does lead to some rather ugly formations, which, it must be hoped, will disappear in the course of time.

deal Although *a deal of* in the sense of 'a large amount' has been current English for over 200 years it is still considered a colloquialism by most authorities. It is better to say *a good deal* or *a great deal.*

debar, disbar There is some similarity in meaning between these two words, but in practice they are used quite differently. *Debar* means to exclude, prevent or prohibit (an action):

> The committee decided to debar from the club all members who had not paid their subscriptions.

Disbar is much more specific in its application, and means to expel from the legal profession or from the bar:

> Solicitors found guilty of corrupt practices were disbarred.

decided, decisive It is still possible, although increasingly difficult, to preserve a useful distinction between these two words. *Decided* means 'unquestionable, unmistakeable, resolute or determined':

> There is a decided air of importance about him.
> The new manager has a very decided manner.

Decisive means 'conclusive, bringing to an end' and is commonly used in phrases like *a decisive battle.* It is, however, beginning to encroach upon the meanings of *decided* in such expressions as *a decisive character*.

decimate This originally meant 'to kill one person in every ten' but has now been extended to cover the destruction in large numbers of people, animals and even crops. It should not, however, be used to mean the complete extermination of anything.

deduce see **adduce**

defective, deficient *Defective* means 'having a defect, faulty or imperfect':

> Several parts of the machine were defective.

Deficient is 'lacking in some element or characteristic, insufficient or inadequate' and, although its meaning approaches that of *defective*, it is generally possible to keep the two words distinct:

Their accommodation at the hotel was deficient in every respect.

defensible, defensive *Defensible* means 'capable of being protected or defended, justifiable, or capable of being defended in argument':

Their actions were considered defensible in view of the gravity of the situation.

Defensive means 'serving to defend or protect':

They built a defensive barrier around the camp.

definite, definitive These words are easily confused. *Definite* means 'clearly defined, precise or exact':

They were awaiting a definite reply to their question.

Definitive means 'conclusive or final':

Their offer is a definitive one and must be either accepted or rejected.

deism, theism The difference between these two words is that *deism* means belief in God based on the evidence of reason alone. *Theism* means belief in God which includes supernatural revelation.

delusion, illusion A *delusion* is a mistaken belief that something really exists and cannot be removed by an appeal to reason:

She suffered from the delusion that all her food was poisoned.

An *illusion* is a false mental image which may result from a misinterpretation of something real or from something imagined:

He was under the illusion that he was really quite popular.

demi-, semi- Both prefixes, which are Latin in origin, mean 'half', but *demi-* is found in only a handful of words such as *demigod*, *demijohn* and *demilune*. *Semi-* is much more common and is often used in the formation of new words.

denote see **connote**

depend This verb is normally followed by *on* or *upon*:

Children depend on their parents for support.

However, in colloquial speech and despite the opposition of some eminent authorities *depend* is frequently used without *on* or *upon*, provided it is preceded by *it*:

It depends what you mean by free speech.

dependant, dependent In English usage the noun, meaning 'someone who relies on others for support', ends in *-ant*. The adjective form 'relying on others for support, subordinate or subject to' ends in *-ent*. In American usage *dependent* serves as both noun and adjective.

depositary, depository A *depositary* is a person to whom something is given in trust. A *depository* is a place where something is stored for safekeeping.

deprecate, depreciate These verbs and their derivatives are quite frequently confused. *Deprecate* means 'to express disapproval of or protest against':

They strongly deprecated the use of force to settle the argument.

Depreciate means 'to reduce the value of, belittle' or 'to decline in value':

His shares have depreciated considerably since the stock market crisis.

derisive, derisory These two adjectives can be used interchangeably, but it is possible to make a distinction between them. Both have the sense of 'ridiculing, mocking, or expressing derision', but *derisory* has acquired the additional meaning of 'worthy of derision, causing derision, worthless or insignificant':

The management's offer was considered derisory by the union negotiators.

despatch see **dispatch**

devotee see **addict**

dialectal, dialectic, dialectical *Dialectal* means 'pertaining to or characteristic of a dialect'. *Dialectic* as a noun means 'logical discussion or argumentation', and its adjective can be either *dialectic* or *dialectical*.

dialogue, duologue A *dialogue* is a conversation between two or more people. A *duologue* is a conversation between two people only, especially as part of a dramatic performance.

dieresis This means the separate pronunciation of two adjacent vowels in a word and the term is also applied to the sign placed over them to indicate this separate pronunciation. It is rarely found in English, but is sometimes used in such words as *naïve* and *coöperate*, as well as in a few personal names like *Chloë*.

different There has long been much controversy over which preposition should follow *different*: *to* or *from*. All that can really be said on the subject is that *different from* is the established usage, but that *different to* is quite acceptable. *Different* is also occasionally found followed by *than*, but this particular construction is not to be recommended.

differentiate, distinguish The uses of these two verbs are very similar but not identical. *Differentiate* means to point out precisely and in some detail the differences between two things:

It is difficult to differentiate between one insect and another when they have so many attributes in common.

Distinguish means to recognize the characteristic features that mark out something as different, but without going into specific details:

It's not difficult to distinguish between a traffic warden and a policeman.

digraph, diphthong A *digraph* is a pair of letters which combine to represent a single speech sound such as *ch* in *chop* or *ea* in *seat*. *Diphthong* is a term used to describe a composite vowel sound made up of two single vowel sounds as *ei* in *rein* and *ou* in *loud*.

dilemma Its growing popularity has given this word an extension to its original meaning. It is better not to treat it as a synonym for *problem* or *difficulty*, but to restrict its use to describing a situation in which there is a choice between equally undesirable alternatives.

diminish, minimize *Diminish* means 'to make smaller, lessen, reduce, or decrease':

The use of drugs can help to diminish pain.

Minimize means 'to reduce to the smallest possible amount, belittle or underestimate':

Try not to minimize the risks of riding a motor-cycle.

diphthong see **digraph**

direct, directly It is better to keep the meanings of these two words separate when they are used as adverbs in order to avoid misunderstanding, although they tend to be interchangeable. Use *direct* to mean 'straight', 'without any detours':

It told him to go direct to the airport.

Use *directly* to mean 'at once' or 'immediately':

He promised he would be there directly.

Directly is also used as a conjunction meaning 'as soon as'.

discomfit, discomfort *Discomfit* is sometimes used mistakenly for *discomfort*. However, there is really no connection between the two words. *Discomfit*, which is now rather rare, means 'to defeat utterly or rout, frustrate or thwart'.

discreet, discrete Although these two adjectives are far apart in meaning their identical pronunciation and almost identical spelling can be the source of some confusion. *Discreet* means 'prudent, circumspect or cautious'. *Discrete* means 'detached from others, separate, or distinct'.

disinterested, uninterested The confusion between these two words is now so complete that it is difficult to keep them separate. *Disinterested* means 'impartial' or 'not influenced by personal motives':

> The committee issued a disinterested report, for they prided themselves on their impartiality.

Uninterested means 'having no interest in':

> The students were completely uninterested in what the lecturer had to say to them.

Disinterested is so frequently used by people who ought to know better to mean *uninterested* that those who are trying to preserve a useful distinction in meaning may feel that their task is a pretty hopeless one.

dispatch, despatch The form *dispatch* is still preferred to *despatch* when used as a noun or a verb.

dispersal, dispersion These two words are frequently used interchangeably but it is possible to distinguish between them. *Dispersal* means 'the act of scattering or dispersing':

> The dispersal of the mob was possible only after the arrival of police reinforcements.

Dispersion means 'the state of being dispersed' and refers to the condition after the dispersal has taken place:

> The widespread dispersion of the mob made it difficult for them to reassemble.

disposal, disposition Although some of the various meanings of these two words are quite distinct, there is some possibility of confusion. *Disposal* has the basic idea of getting rid of something by removing it from one place to another:

The disposal of the refugees was soon completed.

Disposition conveys rather the sense of placing or arranging according to a plan worked out beforehand:

The disposition of the property under the terms of the will.

dissimulate, simulate *Dissimulate* means 'to hide or conceal (something which one has)':

He dissimulated his fear with a show of bravado.

Simulate means 'to make a pretence of having (something which one has not)':

She simulated distress by pretending to cry.

dissociate This verb and its noun *dissociation* are now almost invariably preferred to the alternative forms *disassociate* and *disassociation*.

distinct, distinctive These adjectives are similar in meaning and the one is sometimes wrongly used for the other. *Distinct* means 'definite, unmistakeable, clear to the senses':

There was a distinct smell of gas in the bedroom.

Distinctive means 'characteristic, individual or distinguishing':

The distinctive cry of a hungry baby.

distrust, mistrust These verbs are frequently used interchangeably in the sense of 'to regard with doubt or suspicion' but *distrust* generally implies a much stronger degree of feeling than *mistrust*.

divers, diverse These were originally the same word but have now acquired quite separate meanings. *Divers*, which is rarely used except facetiously, means 'several' or 'sundry'. *Diverse* means 'of a different kind or of various kinds'.

do Apart from its basic meaning of performing an action, *do* is employed in several ways as an auxiliary verb.

It is used to avoid repeating another verb:

He came along past the church, as he did every morning.

In this instance *did* avoids the repetition of *came*, but care must be taken with *do* as a substitute verb. It cannot be used, for instance, to represent the verb *to be* or a verb in a compound tense:

She has read the same books as I have done.

Either substitute *read* for *done* or (better) delete *done*.

Anyone who has been here for twenty years as I have done.

Again either substitute *been* for *done* or delete *done*.

Do is also used to form the interrogative in direct questions:

Did you know he was lying? Do they expect her now?

Do is used in negative sentences with *not*.

I did not know you were here. She doesn't realize what has happened.

Finally *do* is used for emphasis:

I do know what you mean. Do please tell me at once.

donate This is a back formation from *donation*, which has achieved a certain popularity despite the disapproval of some authorities. In most cases it is better to use a simple word like *give*.

double comparatives and superlatives These may still be heard in the conversation of uneducated people, but despite the fact that Shakespeare made effective use of them, they are no longer acceptable English. Do not say *more easier* or *most sharpest*.

double entendre This is the accepted English form of the French *double entente* and has been for three hundred years. Attempts to establish the correct French form have so far proved futile.

double negatives English usage generally frowns upon double negatives, although in the past both Chaucer and Shakespeare used them to enrich the language of their poetry and plays. Expressions like *I never did nothing wrong* are not acceptable, but some double negatives do find their way into the speech of even educated people, especially in sentences like the following:

I shouldn't be surprised if it didn't rain.

Care must be taken to avoid double negatives with *scarcely* and *hardly*, in which the negative force is disguised:

It was impossible to believe hardly anything he said.

doubt The verb *doubt* is followed by *whether* or *if* when it forms part of a positive statement:

I doubt if he will accept. They doubt whether he will come.

When the statement is negative or forms a question, *doubt* is followed by *that*:

I do not doubt that he is right. Do you doubt that they can do it?

doubtful Like *doubt* the adjective *doubtful* is followed by *whether* or *if* when it forms part of a positive statement. When the statement is negative or forms a question it is followed by *that*:

We are not in the least doubtful that we shall succeed.

dower, dowry Originally the same word, *dower* and *dowry* have quite distinct meanings. *Dower* is the portion of a deceased husband's property allowed by law to his widow for life. *Dowry* is the money and goods brought by a woman to her husband on marriage.

draft, draught Both words have their origins in the verb *draw*, *draft* being a phonetic spelling of *draught*. In English usage *draft* can mean 'a drawing or sketch, a preliminary form of something written, a sum of money drawn on a bank'. *Draught* is 'a current of air, a drink, a team of animals used to pull a load'. In the United States *draft* is more widely used and covers some of the meanings listed under English *draught*.

drunk, drunken It is quite difficult to establish a rigid dividing line between the use of these two words. *Drunk* as an adjective is usually placed after the verb as in *he was drunk* but is now frequently found before the noun:

The street was littered with drunk soldiers.

Drunken is normally placed before the noun, as in *drunken dissipation*. One useful distinction is that *drunken* generally describes a permanent or habitual state and when used thus can be placed after the verb:

He was drunken in his habits.

Drunk usually refers to a temporary state as in *drunk and disorderly*.

dry When suffixes are added to this word the usual forms are *drier*, *driest*, *drying*, *drily* or *dryly*. *Dryer*, rather than *drier*, is now more common when referring to a machine for drying things.

due to This is not really an acceptable substitute for adverbial phrases like *owing to* or *because of*. *Due* is an adjective and should accompany a noun. The two following examples are correct:

His death was due to cancer. Errors due to carelessness are all too frequent.

The following example is incorrect:

Due to cancer he was unable to walk.

Unfortunately, the incorrect use of *due to* is rapidly establishing itself in English with the connivance of such official bodies as British Rail or the B.B.C.:

Due to adverse weather conditions ... Due to a technical fault ...

E

each When *each* is the subject of a sentence, either as a pronoun or as an adjective accompanying a noun, it takes a singular verb:

Each has got to pay his share.
Each child receives the same food.

When used as a pronoun with an antecedent it can be either singular or plural. If the antecedent is plural *each* is plural:

The soldiers each have a meal in the canteen.
We each take a small part in the play.

each other, one another Usage now appears to have discarded the rule that *each other* should be used when only two people are involved, *one another* being reserved for three or more. Thus the following is quite acceptable:

The six prisoners were told to help each other with their work.

Each other is treated as a compound word and may be used as the object or indirect object of a verb or preposition:

They dislike each other.
The children sent books to each other.

When the possessive case is used, the form is *each other's* not *each others'*:

They take in each other's washing.

However, the phrase cannot be used in combination when *other* is itself the subject of a verb:

They each knew what the other liked,

not:

They knew what each other liked.

earthen, earthly, earthy *Earthen* means 'composed of earth or of baked clay':

The archaeologists discovered earthen pots from the second millennium B.C.

Earthly means 'pertaining to earth, especially as opposed to heaven':

Not everyone considers this world to be an earthly paradise.

Earthy means 'of the nature of earth, worldly, coarse or unrefined':

His earthy views on the subject embarrassed his sophisticated guests.

easterly *Easterly* is most commonly used of winds in the sense of 'coming from the east'. It can, however, be used to mean 'situated towards the east', but implies previous movement in that direction:

The most easterly outpost of Roman civilization.

In other cases the usual adjectives are *east* or *eastern*.

easy, easily *Easily* is now the normal form of the adverb. *Easy* as an adverb is found in only a few phrases like *to go easy* and *take it easy*.

eatable, edible The main distinction between these two words is that *edible* refers to anything which may normally be eaten, as *an edible plant*. *Eatable* is used of something which is agreeable to the taste, although *edible* would not be wrong in this context:

The burnt porridge was barely eatable.

echelon This is another word whose growing popularity has led to an extension of its original meaning. It is used now to mean 'a level of command or organization' although its proper sense is 'a step-like or staggered formation of troops'.

economic, economical Economic means 'pertaining to economics or reasonably profitable, offering an adequate return': *economic laws*, *an economic rent*. *Economical* means 'avoiding waste or extravagance, thrifty':

Economical ways of budgeting household expenditure.

-ed verb endings see **-t and -ed verb endings**

educational, educative Both adjectives can be used virtually interchangeably, but *educational* is the more common and is applied to education generally: *an educational organization*, *an educational tour*. *Educative* tends to have a more restricted sense of 'serving to educate': *an educative work*.

effective, effectual, efficacious, efficient All these adjectives have similar meanings and all can have the sense of 'capable of producing an effect', but care must be taken to distinguish between them.

Effective means having the power to produce or producing an effect or bringing about a desired result:

At last effective measures are being taken to reduce the crime rate.

Effectual stresses that which actually produces the desired effect:

His conciliatory speech was effectual in ending the tension.

Efficacious means capable of achieving a certain aim and is applied particularly to remedies, treatments, etc.:

Modern drugs are much more efficacious in their treatment of illness.

Efficient refers to the expert use of knowledge, resources etc., to achieve results:

Really efficient managers are hard to find.

e.g., i.e. *E.g.* is a Latin abbreviation meaning 'for example'. It is often confused with *i.e.*, which means 'that is to say', and is used when what follows is an alternative way of saying what went before. The sentences show the correct use of both words:

There were several subjects for discussion, *e.g.* staff holidays, the works canteen, the annual outing.

The man was a palaeontologist, *i.e.* he studied forms of life which existed in previous geological periods.

egoism, egotism Both words are concerned with preoccupation with oneself. *Egoism*, the less common word, means the valuing of everything in accordance with one's own interests and the emphasizing of the importance of the self in relation to other things:

He considered his own egoism to be a philosophical doctrine.

Egotism is boastfulness and self-importance which implies disregard for other's opinions and feelings:

Her egotism angered even her friends.

either *Either* means 'one or other of two' and consequently cannot be used if more than two persons, groups or things are referred to, when it should be replaced by *any*:

either of the twins *but* any of the three boys.

Either is always followed by a singular verb:

Either of the girls has the right to leave.

either . . . or In phrases of this sort the *either* is frequently put in the wrong position. In the following sentence, for example, the *either* is misplaced:

They must either apologize or suffer the consequences.

Since *They must* forms part of the alternative offered by *either* the two words must be placed after it:

Either they must apologize or suffer the consequences.

This misplacement of *either* is common in conversation but should be avoided in writing.

The verb used with *either . . . or* should be singular if there are two singular subjects and plural if both the subjects are plural. However, if one of the subjects is in the singular and the other in the plural, the verb may agree with the nearest subject, but it is better to phrase the sentence so that the plural noun is nearest the verb, which will then be in the plural:

Either the boy or his brother has the book.
Either the mother or her children have to be present.

eke out The proper meaning of to *eke out* is to make something, of which there is only a small amount, go further by adding to it:

They eked out their scanty supply of food with other people's leftovers.

However, *eke out* has acquired an extension of meaning in the sense of 'to contrive to make' in such phrases as *to eke out a living*. This is deplored by some authorities, but seems to have established itself as acceptable usage.

elder, older The comparative adjective *elder* and its superlative form *eldest* are now used almost exclusively to denote priority of birth in a family: *my elder brother*, *my eldest sister*. *Elder* can also be employed as a noun to mean an older person, and survives in the phrase *elder statesman*. Otherwise, *older* and *oldest*, the normal comparative and superlative forms of *old*, are used to indicate someone or something of greater age.

elemental, elementary Although there is some slight overlapping between these two words, they are usually quite distinct in meaning. *Elemental* refers to the power, forces or phenomena of physical nature, especially the four elements of earth, water, air and fire:

The elemental violence of a thunderstorm.

Elementary means 'pertaining to rudiments or first principles':

The teaching of elementary arithmetic in schools.

elision This is the omission of a vowel, consonant or syllable in writing or pronunciation. It is most frequently found with pronouns, auxiliary verbs and in negative expressions:

I'm, let's, don't, they're, you've, shan't.

ellipsis *Ellipsis* is the omission from a sentence of a word or words which would complete the construction or clarify the sense. In the sentence:

The factory was shut and the workers dismissed,

the word *were* is omitted before *dismissed* but can be easily supplied from the context. Some authorities advise against the omission of any verbs necessary for completeness or clarity. The sentence:

Jane is beautiful but her friends ugly

is unacceptable on the grounds that the verb to be supplied after *friends* (*are*) is not the same as the one in the first clause (*is*). However, most authorities would agree on the necessity of not using a single form of the verb to be to do duty as both main verb and auxiliary verb:

The soldiers were in rags and spurned by the crowd.

The *were* omitted before *spurned* is an auxiliary verb and differs from its use as a main verb after soldiers. It should not, therefore, be left out.

Care must be taken over the omission of subordinate conjunctions like *that*, or relative pronouns like *who* and *which*, before dependent clauses. If there is any possibility of ambiguity or even clumsiness the conjunction or pronoun should be retained. The sentence:

Everybody realized he was a liar

is quite acceptable, but:

His decision was they should go ahead immediately

would read better with *that* inserted after *was*.

When using a verb with more than one auxiliary verb be sure that the auxiliary is repeated if necessary:

He can and will work

is quite correct, but:

The remedy which they can and are applying

must be rephrased as:

The remedy which they can apply and are applying.

else It is still sometimes considered an error to use *but* instead of *than* after *else*, so that the phrase *nothing else but a full-scale enquiry* should be *nothing else than a full-scale enquiry*. However, *nothing else but* seems well established in popular usage. The possessive forms are *anybody else's*, *somebody else's*, but when *else* is used with *who* there is some hesitation between *whose else* and *who else's*, although the latter form is now far more common.

elusive, illusory The meanings of these two adjectives are sometimes confused. *Elusive* means 'hard to grasp, express or define', and has the alternative form *elusory*:

Her poetry had an elusive quality about it.

Illusory means 'of the nature of an illusion, deceptive or unreal':

His apparent success in his job was proved illusory when he was forced to resign.

emend see **amend**

emigrant, immigrant An *emigrant* is one who leaves his own country in order to settle in another. An *immigrant* is one who arrives from another country. Thus an *emigrant* and an *immigrant* may be the same person seen at a different stage on his or her journey or from a different point of view.

emotive, emotional Both words can be used to mean 'exciting emotion' or 'appealing to the emotions'. However, in practice a sharp distinction is made between them. *Emotive* is restricted to 'causing emotion' and *emotional* to 'being affected by or expressing emotion'.

endemic, epidemic, pandemic *Endemic* applies to a disease which is peculiar to a particular people or locality. An *epidemic* disease is one which affects a large number of people in a locality, but is not permanently prevalent there. A *pandemic* disease is one which is prevalent throughout an entire region, such as a country or continent.

endorse Some authorities deplore the fact that *endorse* is now used to mean 'to express approval of', notably in the domain of advertising, but this sense does seem to have established itself and is recorded in the more modern dictionaries.

England, English These words are very rarely interchangeable with *(Great) Britain* and *British*, and doubts about their correct use are frequently a source of error and confusion. For English people *England* and *English* have a strong emotional appeal, similar to the feelings aroused in other part of the British Isles by *Scotland* and *Scots*, or *Wales* and *Welsh*. The majority of Englishmen, Welshmen and Scotsman prefer to be called this rather than the collective *Britons*. Moreover, *English* must be used when referring to *English* history and *English* literature. *England* has a patriotic ring to it and Englishmen use it on appropriate occasions even when they may actually be referring to the whole of Great Britain. [See also *British*]

enhance Care must be taken in the use of this verb. It cannot have a person as a direct object in the active form or as a subject in the passive form:

Success has enhanced his prestige

or:

His prestige has been enhanced by his success

are both correct. But one cannot say:

Success has enhanced him

or:

He has been enhanced by success.

enough, sufficient Both words mean 'adequate or equal to what is required'. *Enough* is a more flexible word and can be used as a noun, adjective or adverb, whereas *sufficient* is only an adjective. However, *enough* has its limitations as an adjective. We can say *a sufficient quantity* but not *an enough quantity*. Despite this, *enough* remains the more natural word on most occasions, and *sufficient* may sometimes appear as an over-refined alternative:

Do you have enough money?

is still preferable to:

Do you have sufficient money?

enquire, inquire The spelling *enquire* is now the more normal one in the sense of 'to seek information by questioning, to ask'. However, *inquire into* has the additional meaning of 'to investigate', which provides a useful distinction between these two verbs.

ensure see **assure**

envelop, envelope *Envelop* is the verb and *envelope* (with an extra *e*) is the noun.

epic This is a poetic composition in which a series of heroic events are dealt with as a continuous narrative in an elevated style. By extension it has been applied to a film or novel resembling an epic, and now is used loosely of any play, film or event which is in any way out of the ordinary.

epidemic see **endemic**

epigram This is a witty and pointed saying briefly expressed. The term is also applied to a short poem dealing with a single subject and usually ending with an amusing or ingenious turn of thought.

epigraph, epitaph An *epigraph* is an inscription, especially one on a public building. An *epitaph* is a commemorative inscription on a tomb.

epithet The original meaning is an adjective or other term applied to a person or thing in order to express an attribute. In 'Richard the Lion-Heart', 'Lion Heart' is an *epithet*. The word *epithet* has unfortunately now become a synonym for a term of abuse, which has tended to overshadow its original sense.

equable, equitable These adjectives may be a source of confusion since their meanings are in some respects quite close.

Equable means 'free from variations, uniform', 'tranquil, not easily disturbed': *an equable temperament*, *an equable climate*. *Equitable* means 'just and right, fair, reasonable': *an equitable decision*. It also refers to equity as opposed to common law.

equally A frequent mistake is to insert an unnecessary *as* after *equally*. One can say:

Her work was equally good

or:

Her work was as good,

but not:

Her work was equally as good.

Where there is a comparison *as* must stand alone and *equally* can neither accompany it nor replace it:

Good health is as (not *equally* as) important as good pay.

-er, -or The ending *-er* can be added to English verbs to denote one who does (something):

teacher, singer, fighter, buyer, winner.

The Latin ending *-or*, which has the same function as *-er*, tends to be added to verbs which are formed from Latin stems:

actor, confessor, creditor, protector.

Some words of Latin origin, however, end in *-er*:

deserter, dispenser, digester.

Other words can end in either *-er* or *-or*, sometimes with a slightly different meaning:

adapter, adaptor; conjurer, conjuror; resister, resistor.

eruption, irruption An *eruption* is 'a sudden and violent issuing forth, an outburst or a breaking out (of a rash, etc)'. An *irruption* is 'a breaking in', 'a violent incursion or invasion'.

escalate This now very popular verb was formed from the noun *escalator*. It means 'to increase in intensity or magnitude', and although it was not really an essential addition to the English language it appears to have established a firm position.

especially, specially The similarity in spelling and meaning of these adverbs has led to some doubt about their correct use. *Especially* means 'to an exceptional degree' and singles out what is prominent or pre-eminent:

The winter was especially severe that year.

Specially means 'for a specific purpose' or 'to a particular end':

This dress was made specially for her.

The distinction can no longer be observed in the adjectives, *especial* and *special*, since *special* is rapidly displacing *especial*, and even *especially* is losing ground to *specially*.

essay see **assay**

essential, necessary Both words apply to something which is indispensable for the fulfilment of a need. *Essential*, which is a much stronger word, means an absolutely vital condition:

Air is essential to mammals.

Necessary refers to that which is determined by natural laws or results inevitably from certain causes:

Food is necessary to life.

etc. This useful word, an abbreviation for the Latin *et cetera*, meaning 'and others', 'and so forth', is used to indicate that others of the same kind might have been mentioned but for shortage of space:

cats, dogs, horses, sheep, etc.

Etc. is usually preceded by a comma unless only one item has been mentioned before it. It is best not to use it in writing of a formal or literary kind.

ethic, ethical Both adjectives mean 'pertaining to or dealing with morals', but *ethical* is now the more common form, *ethic* being almost exclusively confined to grammar in the *ethic dative*, which refers to a person indirectly interested. In *shoot me a bird* 'me' is an ethic dative.

ethics, morals Both words are concerned with right and wrong and rules of conduct, but their various senses are distinct. *Ethics* is used to mean a system of moral principles, whereas *morals* are concerned with right and wrong in practice.
Ethics is also applied to standards of conduct and behaviour in business:

The ethics of the legal profession.

Morals refer to generally accepted standards of conduct in a society:

The morals of Western civilization.

Morals is also used especially to refer to behaviour in sexual matters. The distinction of meaning holds true for the adjectives *ethical* and *moral*, although here the differences are more blurred. [See also *amoral*]

euphemism, euphuism Although similar in spelling, these two words are entirely different in meaning. *Euphemism* is the substitution of a mild, inoffensive or indirect expression for a blunt one, such as 'mental disorder' for 'insanity' or 'pass away' for 'die'. *Euphuism*, a much rarer word, means an affected, artificial or ornate style of writing or speaking.

evasion, evasiveness *Evasion* means 'the act or practice of escaping something by trickery, an excuse, subterfuge':

An evasion of responsibilities.

Evasiveness is the quality of being evasive:

The evasiveness of his replies aroused our suspicions.

even The correct placing of the adverb *even* in a sentence is very important.

She did not ring on Tuesday

can yield four different meanings with the use of *even*:

Even she did not ring me on Tuesday (she was the most likely to do so).
She did not even ring me on Tuesday (this was the thing she was most likely to do).

She did not ring even me on Tuesday (I was the person she was most likely to ring).
She did not ring me even on Tuesday (this was the day on which she was most likely to ring).

eventuate It is better not to use this rather pompous word when a simpler one will do. *Take place*, *occur*, *happen*, and *come about* are all preferable.

-ever, ever The suffix *-ever* may be added to the words *who*, *which*, *what*, *where* and *how*, which are then written as one word: *whoever*, *whatever*:

Whatever you do try to be home early.

But when *ever* is used for emphasis after interrogative pronouns and adverbs, such as *who*? and *why*? it remains a separate word:

Who ever said that? Why ever didn't you tell me?

every day, everyday *Every day* is an adverbial phrase of time:

He goes to school every day.

everyday is an adjective:

An everyday occurrence, my everyday clothes.

every one, everyone, everybody When the meaning is 'every single one' with the stress on the separateness use the two words *every one*:

He spoke to all those present in the room and every one of them replied.

Every one is also used when referring to inanimate objects:

He wrote ten novels and every one of them was a best seller.

Everyone, when it refers to people who are not singled out, and *everybody* are written as one word. Like *every one* they are followed by a singular verb:

Everyone was cheering, everybody was shouting.

However, these words are in many ways felt to be plural. Although the following is recommended when a pronoun is involved:

Everyone is doing his best,

their best is frequently found, and in the sentence:

Everyone is doing their best, aren't they?

their best seems unavoidable.

evolve The basic meaning is 'to develop gradually by a natural process'. Popular usage has, however, made *evolve* a synonym for such words as *change*, *develop*, *plan* or *devise*, all of which are usually preferable.

except see **accept**

except, excepting *Except* is a preposition and is followed by a noun, pronoun or adverbial phrase:

Except the latecomers, except me, except in the north.

Excepting means the same as *except* and is used instead of it only after 'always', 'not' and 'without':

Not excepting the children, always excepting the pensioners.

exceptionable, exceptional *Exceptionable*, which is a much less common word than *exceptional*, means 'objectionable, open to objection', or 'to which exception may be taken':

We found his wild statements exceptionable.

Exceptional means 'unusual', 'extraordinary' or 'forming an exception':

He showed exceptional courage.

exclamation mark This is a punctuation mark (!) which is placed at the end of an interjection, an exclamatory word, or a phrase or sentence expressing strong emotion, or a wish:

Oh! Help! Heaven forbid! What a way to go! Don't be such a prude! If only we could!

The exclamation mark should be employed very sparingly if it is to be effective and it should not normally be used after an imperative:

Open your books. Shut the door.

Nor should it be used when a question mark is what is needed:

Why in heaven's name did you do that?

exhaustive, exhausting These adjectives are sometimes confused. *Exhaustive* means 'comprehensive', 'thorough':

He published an exhaustive study of Jane Austen.

Exhausting means 'using up or consuming fully', 'draining strength' or 'tiring out':

Digging coal is exhausting work.

explicit, implicit *Explicit* means 'clearly expressed', 'definite', or 'unequivocal':

He refused to do anything without explicit instructions.

Implicit means 'implied rather than openly stated', 'understood':

There was implicit consent in all his actions.

Implicit also means 'unreserved' or 'absolute':

He showed implicit faith in God.

extempore, impromptu Both words apply to something done without proper preparation in advance. *Extempore*, however, is generally used to describe a speech or performance unmemorized or delivered without notes: *an extempore lecture*.

Impromptu is applied to a speech or performance delivered without any preparation or notice:

Despite being called upon on the spur of the moment, he made an effective impromptu speech.

exterior, external These adjectives may be used in the same way but there are some important differences in usage. *Exterior* usually implies the existence of something similar or corresponding which is *interior* – an outer surface which has an inner surface:

The exterior decorations of the wall did not match the interior ones.

Exterior and *interior* can also be used as nouns.

External means 'belonging to the outside' and *internal* 'existing in the interior', but these words do not correspond to each other like *exterior* and *interior*. *External* can apply to things more remote and abstract than *exterior*, as in *the external world*, *external relations*, and, together with *internal*, can be used of medicines: *for external/internal use*.

F

facilitate To make a process less difficult or to help it forward. It is the action that is made easier, and not the one who carries it out who is assisted:

She moved her car to facilitate the parking of the lorry.

facility, faculty *Facility* is ease, advantage, freedom from difficulty, dexterity and also things that make a task easier:

She knitted her way through several sweaters with a facility born of long practice.

Faculty is an ability for a particular activity; an inherent capability of the body, or one of the powers of the mind such as reason, speech or memory:

He had a faculty for languages that was of great assistance in his travels.

factitious, fictitious *Factitious* is artificial, not spontaneous or natural, manufactured. *Fictitious* is counterfeit or false, created by the imagination; in reality, it may not exist at all. It is applied more often to a mental concept than a practical object, especially to products of the imagination.

factitive A grammatical term describing verbs such as 'make', 'render', 'consider', which take the complement of a noun or adjective in addition to the usual object:

I make him angry.
He found me a home.

factor This word is often overworked and widely applied in contexts where a more specific term would be preferable. Its meaning, 'one of the elements that contribute to a given result or have a certain effect', is so generally applicable that it has come to be adopted for every contingency:

One of the factors that make him outstanding is his ability to compromise.

Features would be a better substitute.

A key factor in any industrial dispute is the quality of labour relations.

Element or *constituent* are possible alternatives.

Let me outline for you some of the factors that led to this situation.

Circumstances might be a more accurate word in this context.

fallacy A *fallacy* is a deceptive or misleading belief or false notion. It is not a falsehood, which implies a deliberate act of deception, and cannot be used in its place:

He told her he was not married, but this turned out to be a fallacy

is therefore incorrect.

falseness, falsity, falsehood Both *falseness* and *falsity* express an untruth, a statement of a fact that is erroneous, or incorrectness, but *falseness* also implies treachery and deception, especially in a personal sense. *Falsehood* is a lie, an untrue idea or belief, or a false statement:

When truth is opposed to falsehood, only those in whom falseness resides will refuse to recognize the falsity of their position.

false scent A sentence that can be misunderstood on first reading might be described as providing a 'false scent':

The situation is grave as these figures show only a hint of the true position.

On first sight 'the situation is grave as these figures show' seems to be the complete sentence, but 'only a hint of the true position' makes it clear that the verb 'show' is intended to apply to 'hint' and not to the main clause, 'the situation is grave'. The sentence has therefore to be read twice before the sense becomes obvious.

farce see **comedy**

Far East The countries of East and South East Asia including China, Japan, Korea, the Malay Archipelago and Indochina make up the area known as the Far East.

farther, further Though these words are often used indiscriminately, *farther* is usually applied to a greater distance or space:

The moon is farther away than I thought.

Further is generally used to indicate a greater extent, quantity or time; it also means 'moreover':

We are further committed to implement the decision by the New Year.

fatal, fateful *Fatal* is causing death, destruction or ruin; figuratively, it means of momentous importance, implying doom:

The fatal event took place on Thursday.

Fateful is also of momentous importance, or controlled by irresistible destiny, but although it may be synonymous with *fatal* it may also mean a happy event of great consequence, not necessarily one with a deadly outcome:

At last the fateful day arrived when she walked down the aisle on her father's arm.

feasible The dictionary definition is given as 'capable of being done, effected or accomplished'. In many senses it can therefore be equated with *possible*, but there is a tendency to use it in all senses of *possible*, and of *probable* too, beyond its true capacity:

It is quite feasible that the shares he inherited when he came of age are now worth double.

In this example *feasible* is incorrect; either *possible* or *probable* should be substituted. But in the next example the word is correctly used:

He was convinced that an attempt to overthrow the government by force would be feasible.

female, feminine, womanly *Female* is both a noun and an adjective describing the sex of a plant, animal or human being. *Feminine* is an adjective only, qualifying the condition of being female, and applied only to human beings. *Womanly* is used primarily in opposition to *manly*, indicating possession of qualities that are especially feminine or, sometimes in contrast to girlish, meaning mature.

feminine forms The usual English feminine of nouns of occupation is formed by adding *-ess*:

Host, hostess; actor, actress; warder, wardress.

These particular examples are well entrenched in the English language, but the modern tendency is to avoid such differentiation between the sexes wherever possible, in keeping with the trend towards sex equality. For some occupational words that previously took a feminine form the male form now does duty for both: *sculptor*, *instructor* and *editor* are examples of this group. With other nouns such as doctors or teachers the term 'woman' is simply added to differentiate between them when necessary: *woman doctor*, *woman teacher*, *woman lawyer*.

ferment, foment As a noun a *ferment* is an agent that causes fermentation; figuratively, it means agitation, excitement. The verb means to inflame, agitate or excite. *Foment* is a verb only, meaning to promote the growth or development of, or to instigate or foster, especially in the sense of discord and rebellion. It also means to apply hot water and medication to a body:

The army was in a state of ferment. Rebels had infiltrated their ranks, fomenting discontent.

festal, festive Both words mean 'pertaining to a feast or festival', but *festive* also implies merriment and gaiety, and has come to be associated with such common phrases as 'festive occasion'.

few As a noun *a few* means a small number, *the few*, the minority, and *few*, the adjective, means 'not many':

A few stragglers were left; of these, few were properly clad.
The remaining few had one blanket between them.

fewer, less *Fewer* is correct when referring to numbers, *less* when meaning an amount or bulk quantity:

There are fewer people here than usual,

but:

There is less money about this Christmas.

In the example:

There were large numbers of French and Germans staying at the resort but less British than last year,

the word should be *fewer*.

fictional, fictitious *Fictional* means something that occurs only in fiction, created from the imagination. *Fictitious* is untrue, counterfeit or false.

finical, finicky There is no difference in meaning. Both words are adjectives meaning excessively fastidious or too fussy, but *finical* is the more literary word and *finicky* more frequently used in colloquial speech.

flammable see **inflammable**

flaunt, flout *To flaunt* is to parade or display something conspicuously or boldly. *To flout* is to mock or scoff at, treat with disdain or contempt:

She flaunted her newly won independence by going out of her way to flout every school rule.

flautist, flutist Both words mean one who plays a flute. *Flutist*, though the older word, is now used chiefly in the United States. In Britain *flautist* is the more usual term.

fleshly, fleshy *Fleshly* is pertaining to the flesh or body, and is generally used in the sense of worldly or physical as distinct from spiritual:

Let us set aside all fleshly temptations and concentrate on spiritual matters.

Fleshy means plump, fat, or consisting of flesh:

He was of medium build with thinning hair and a thick-set, fleshy neck.

flotsam and jetsam The phrase *flotsam and jetsam* means the debris thrown out from a ship which either floats on the water (*flotsam*)or is cast up on shore (*jetsam*). Figuratively, it is also applied to the outcasts of society.

following This word is often too easily used as a formal substitute for 'after'. There can be justification for this only when the meaning is fairly closely related to the participle of the verb *to follow*, implying a consequence of an event, such as in:

Following the declaration of martial law, a curfew was imposed.

It has little excuse for appearing in a sentence such as:

Following the talk by Professor Smith, we come to the main item of the programme.

And in:

Following a hunt by police in the London suburbs, a man was arrested in Putney

a false scent (*q.v.*) is created by a curiously circular sentence.

for-, fore- If the meaning intended is 'before', 'in front' or 'superior', the prefix to choose is *fore-*, as in *foreword*, *forecast*, *foreman*. The prefix *for-* comes from an Old Scottish word meaning 'away', 'off', 'to the uttermost', and implies a negative, prohibitive force, as in *forbid*, *forget*, *forlorn* or *forfeit*.

forbear, forebear Both forms are used for the noun meaning 'ancestor', but as *forbear* is also a verb meaning to desist or refrain from, it seems preferable to retain the *e* form for the noun. This usually occurs in the plural;

His forebears were of noble birth.

forceful, forcible *Forceful* means full of force, powerful, vigorous and effective:

He has such a forceful personality he can persuade the committee to vote whichever way he pleases,

and:

He put up a forceful argument.

Forcible means having force, or effected by force or violence:

He gained forcible entry by breaking the window.

forego, forgo *Forego* means to go before, to precede; *forgo* is to do without, abstain or refrain from.

foreign words and phrases These may be divided into three categories: those words and phrases that through common usage have become completely assimilated to the English language, in many cases losing their foreign identity and accents, such as *role*, *omelette*, *concerto*; those that are familiar through daily use, but nevertheless retain their original characteristics, such as *café*, *soufflé*, *protégé*, *au revoir*, and those that may be less familiar but which are sometimes used in a literary context, often by people whose knowledge of the language may be limited. In these cases it is particularly important to ensure that there is full understanding of the meaning of a word or phrase and that they are spelt correctly, with all accents present.

Two examples of common errors are:

I knew exactly where I was – it was a case of *déja vu*.

The word is *déjà* and must be shown with both accents. And in:

Do come back with us for supper. It will just be an *alfresco* meal as we won't reach home till midnight.

Alfresco means 'in the fresh air'; it does not mean 'casual'. Unless they are in such frequent use that they are accepted as part of the English language, as in the first two categories mentioned above, foreign words and phrases are usually indicated in italics.

On the whole, those in the third category are best avoided. Even if you are able to skirt round the pitfalls, their use may place your reader at a disadvantage and might suggest a tendency to show off.

for ever, forever *For ever* should always be written as two words. In the United States, however, the single word is acceptable.

former, latter These are rather clumsy terms restricted to a straight choice between two nouns. It is preferable to use *first*, *second* or *third*, or the *last mentioned*, or, where possible, to rephrase the sentence so that they are unnecessary:

Of the two participants, Mr Ellis and Mr Jones, the former was the taller, the latter the fatter.

A better construction would be:

Of the two participants, Mr Ellis was the taller and Mr Jones the fatter.

forward, forwards These words are often interchangeable but where *forward* is acceptable in most contexts, especially in phrases of time, *forwards* is limited in application. *Forward* is therefore the more widely used word:

It is designed to travel both backwards and forwards

is an example where *forwards* still holds its own, in a sentence indicating movement in a specific direction. But:

In March we move the clocks forward to summer time

is a sentence in which *forwards* could not be substituted.

fragile, frail Both words mean easily broken, but *fragile* implies a brittleness which may be shattered, such as that of glass, while *frail* suggests an inherent weakness, and is used especially of people in a medical sense:

His health was very frail.

Frail can also be used in an abstract sense meaning moral weakness.

full stop The full stop is the most final of the punctuation marks, indicating the end of a complete sentence. It is also sometimes used in place of commas or semi-colons to break up long sentences, or for a deliberate stylistic effect:

He was not in the mood for cheering. Quite the contrary.

And:

The moon, its beams glinting on the water, provided sufficient light for him to see the other man's pale face, tense as he stooped over his sinister task. And then he struck.

In addition the full stop is used after abbreviations except where these end with the same letter as the full word, when in modern usage the punctuation mark may be dispensed with. For example, Doctor James Smith becomes Dr James Smith, but the Reverend John Doe should be abbreviated as Rev. John Doe.

funeral, funereal *Funeral* is a noun which may sometimes be used as a noun adjective, as in:

The funeral arrangements were made by his wife.

Funereal is an adjective meaning pertaining to funerals or anything mournful, gloomy or dismal which might be suggestive of them:

Why did you choose such funereal colours for the hall?

fused participle This is the joining of a noun with a participle to form a single composite subject:

Maggie wearing trousers is an indication that women's lib. is here to stay.

It is a construction frowned on by many purists, but there seems a case for it in certain circumstances in idiomatic English, as in the above example where it is obviously intended as a humorous observation.

G

-g-, -gg- If another syllable is added to words ending in *-g*, the *g* is doubled when a single short vowel precedes it:

Bagged, jogging, bigger.

In most words where the *g* is preceded by a long vowel sound it is also followed by *e* or *ue*, as in *plague*, *league* or *rage*, in which case the *g* is not doubled.

Gallic, Gaelic *Gallic* is pertaining to the French, from Gaul, the ancient name of the region. *Gaelic* is the Celtic language of ancient Ireland and Scotland. As an adjective it means of or pertaining to the Gaels or their language.

Gallicisms The custom of using words of French origin in an anglicized form, or using an English word with an extended meaning borrowed from its French counterpart. [See also *foreign words and phrases*]

gaol, jail Both words mean a prison. Although in Britain both are equally acceptable and *gaol* is still in official use, *jail* is now the more common form. It is the normal spelling in the United States.

gap A term often used in journalism when describing a wide divergence, a rift or discrepancy. There is nothing wrong with this except when it is forgotten that a *gap* can only widen or narrow; it cannot expand or fall:

The gap in our understanding can be easily bridged by closer co-operation

is fine – it is an appropriate metaphor.

The gap between them was aggravated by pettifogging bureaucracy

is not. Aggravation is hardly a quality that can be ascribed to a *gap*.

gender A grammatical term of classification distinguishing the masculine, feminine and neuter categories.

genitive case A grammatical term meaning the possessive case. It can be expressed with *of* or with the use of an apostrophe *s*:

the tail of the dog, the dog's tail.

In general, the apostrophe *s* is confined to people or animals. With inanimate objects the *of* construction is customary, though many objects may take either form:

The car's headlights were bright

is as acceptable in colloquial speech as:

The headlights of the car were bright.

The post-genitive case means phrases such as:

A cousin of my wife's, a book of my father's, a friend of yours,

the last of which illustrates the use of the possessive pronoun. These do not take the apostrophe.

Your friend means a specific person. *A friend of yours* could mean any friend. [See also *apostrophe*]

genius, geniuses, genii *Genius* means the highest level of mental ability, a distinctive character, as of a nation, or a person who strongly influences another. The plural form is *geniuses*. It can also mean the guardian spirit of a place, or two mutually opposing spirits attending someone through life and hence any demon or spirit. In these senses the plural form is *genii*.

gentlemen This is no longer acceptable in a general context, suggesting as it does a 'we' and 'them' division. Put another way, all men are now considered 'gentlemen'. The old forms of class distinction are regarded as anachronisms. As a formal means of address, 'Ladies and Gentlemen', as a notice on a door, 'Gentlemen', and in speech when referring to another in front of him:

I think this gentleman was first,

the word is still correct. Otherwise 'man' or 'men' should always be used.

gerund This is the grammatical term for a verbal noun:

His *working* late was bad enough; what was worse was his *lying*.

When a *gerund* takes a subject, this is in the possessive case: hence the possessive pronoun *his* in the above example. Like a verb, it can be modified by an adverb, in this case *late*.

gibe, gybe, jibe At one time these words were interchangeable, but in modern usage *gibe* is confined to scoff or jeer, taunt or deride, and *gybe* is the nautical term meaning to shift from one side or the other when running before the wind. *Jibe* is an alternative form for both meanings.

gipsy, gypsy *Gipsy* is the usual spelling, although the *y* form is nearer the original meaning (Egyptian). It is more widely acceptable when in the plural *gypsies*.

glance, glimpse *To glance at* is to look quickly or briefly. *To glimpse* is to catch sight of quickly or briefly. The slight difference in meaning is that *glance* is used for the act of looking, *glimpse* for the result of that act. The nouns also correspond to this emphasis.

global At one time this word simply meant shaped like a globe. It has since come to be used as a synonym for world-wide, and hence in a figurative sense comprehensive, all-embracing.

glossary A glossary is a selective vocabulary in which specialized words, usually those of a technical nature, are listed and defined.

goodwill, good will, good-will *Goodwill* is benevolence or favour, especially in a commercial context:

The price offered for the business includes a valuation for goodwill.

When good intent or friendly disposition is meant, *good will* is the correct form:

I believe them to be men of good will.

The hyphenated *good-will* is applicable only in an adjectival phrase such as:

He made a good-will gesture.

Turned round, the sentence would read:

He made a gesture of good will.

got, gotten The use of *got* in a sentence is acceptable colloquial English but not necessarily good literary English. It is useful as an emphasizer, and as an adjunct in a sentence using the abbreviated 'I've' or 'he's':

He's got to go

is much more emphatic than:

He has to go

or:

He's to go,

which would be taken to mean:

He is to go.

But unless it is serving such a positive purpose, indiscriminate use of this word is not good style:

I got a new car

is the past tense, but is sometimes incorrectly used for the present:

I have (or I've) got a new car

is the present form often used in colloquial speech, though unnecessary. The straightforward:

I have a new car

is preferable, certainly in written English.

Too often *got* is used in place of another verb:

I got to London without difficulty.

I reached would be a better substitute.

Gotten is an acceptable word in the United States but not in Britain, except in the phrase *ill-gotten*.

gourmand, gourmet A *gourmand* is one who is fond of good eating and therefore, by implication, tending to greed. A *gourmet* is a connoisseur of good food and wine, an epicure. The first term is often used in a derogatory sense; the second is more complimentary.

grammar, linguistics, syntax *Grammar* may be defined as the features of a language considered systematically, the rules of a language as it is used. The word lacks the precision required today and in modern usage the term *linguistics* is employed to describe the science of language, covering every aspect of it: sounds, inflections, word formation, sentence structure, meaning and spelling. *Syntax*, the pattern or arrangement of words in a sentence showing their relationship to one another, is therefore a branch of linguistics.

gramophone Like *phonograph* (still acceptable in the United States) this word is rapidly becoming obsolete, having been replaced by *record player*. The latest term for it, often incorporating tape and cassette facilities, is *music centre*.

great see **big**

Great Britain The term *Great Britain* applies to England, Scotland and Wales, both in a geographical and in a political sense. The correct term for England, Scotland, Wales and Northern Ireland is the *United Kingdom of Great Britain and Northern Ireland*. The British Isles incorporates the Republic of Ireland as well, and is only a geographical term, not a political one.

Grecian, Greek *Grecian* has in almost all general senses been superseded by *Greek*. It may still be used for certain aspects of art and architecture, and in the special sense of a scholar of the Greek language.

griffin, griffon, gryphon A *griffin* is a mythical monster with an eagle's head and wings and a lion's legs. A *griffon* is a species of vulture, and also a breed of dog. *Gryphon* is an alternative spelling for *griffin.*

grisly, grizzly, grizzled *Grisly* is an adjective meaning gruesome or causing horror. Both *grizzly* and *grizzled* mean grey or grey-haired.

groin, groyne *Groin* is the fold in the body where the thigh joins the abdomen. It is also an alternative but less often used spelling for *groyne*, which is a small jetty built into the sea or river bank to prevent erosion.

guarantee, guaranty, guarantor *To guarantee* means to secure by giving or taking security for, to engage to do something, or to protect or indemnify. The noun means a promise that something is of specified quality, implying an assurance that defects will be put right. A *guaranty* is a pledge accepting responsibility for another's liabilities, or that which is presented as security. A *guarantor* is one who makes or gives a *guarantee* or *guaranty.*

guerrilla This is really a back formation (*q.v.*) from a type of warfare. It now means one who wages this kind of war, a member of a small, independent band of soldiers who harass the enemy by surprise raids.

H

habitable, inhabitable Both words mean 'able to be lived in'. *Habitable* is usually applied to buildings, houses, flats, etc:

Much work was necessary to make the flats habitable.

Inhabitable generally refers to much larger areas:

Desert regions are not usually inhabitable.

half This is followed by a verb in the singular when it refers to a singular noun or pronoun:

Half the town was destroyed.

If the noun or pronoun is plural, so is the verb:

Half of our men were absent.

When *half* is used as a prefix to adjectives, nouns and verbs it is generally hyphenated:

Half-holiday, half-pay, half-pint,

but a *half pint* of bitter. Sometimes it is written as one word:

Halftone, halfway.

hang, hanged, hung When the reference is to capital punishment the past tense and past participle are *hanged*:

The prisoner was hanged at dawn.

Otherwise *hung* is the correct form for the past tense and the past participle.

happen, occur These verbs are to a large extent interchangeable but the following differences should be noted.

Both refer to the taking place of an event, but *happen* is the more common word:

It all happened very quickly.

Occur is a more formal word and is usually more specific in its reference:

The incident occurred on the following day.

harangue, tirade Both words mean 'a long vehement speech', but a *harangue* is usually delivered before an audience:

His lengthy harangue was listened to in silence.

A *tirade* is a denunciation and may be intended for a single person only:

His tirade reduced the girl to tears.

harbour, haven, port All are names of places where ships may shelter. A *harbour* may be either natural or artificially built: *the new harbour on the south coast.* A *haven* suggests a natural harbour where ships may seek refuge from storms, etc. It is also used to mean any place of shelter and safety. A *port* is a place, usually a town with a harbour, where ships may load or unload, although it too can be used to mean a source of refuge: *any port in a storm.*

hard, hardly The usual form of the adverb in its various senses is *hard*:

To work hard, to look hard, frozen hard.

Hardly can be used instead of *hard* in some instances but is best avoided because of the possibility of confusion over its other meaning of 'scarcely' or 'barely'. Remember that when *hardly* is used in the sense of 'scarcely' it is followed by *when* and not *than*:

Hardly had we sat down when it began to rain.

harmony, melody Both words are used to mean a combination of sounds from voices or musical instruments, but there is a difference between them. The *harmony* is a simultaneous combination of notes to form chords. The *melody* is the combination of successive sounds to make up a tune.

have, had Care must be taken to avoid the trap of inserting an extra *have* in certain constructions: *had I have done* for *had I done*, *if she'd have known* for *if she'd known*, and *if I hadn't have seen* for *if I hadn't seen.*

healthy, healthful Both adjectives refer to what promotes good health. *Healthy*, which is the more common word, means both 'possessing health' and 'conducive to health': *a healthy body, a healthy climate.*

Healthful is applied mainly to what is conducive to health, wholesome or salutary: *a healthful diet.*

heir apparent, heir presumptive An *heir apparent* is one whose title cannot be made void by any birth. Thus, the eldest son of a reigning monarch is an *heir apparent*. An *heir presumptive* loses his title if an *heir apparent* is born. Consequently the younger brother of a reigning monarch may be *heir apparent* until such time as the monarch has a child.

help The verb *help* is frequently followed by an infinitive without *to*. This usage is quite common when the one who helps participates in the activity of the person who is being helped:

He helped me mend my garage door.

It is never wrong to insert *to* in such instances. *To* should always be included when *help* is separate from the action which follows:

His speech helped them to understand.

The speech did not actually take part in the effort of understanding. Try to avoid the construction *cannot help but* which wrongly combines *cannot help being* and *cannot but be. Cannot help being* is preferable:

He cannot help being untidy.

The use of *help* to mean 'to refrain from' or 'avoid' is illogical but is now firmly entrenched in the language:

The spectacle was so ridiculous that we couldn't help laughing.

heritage, inheritance Both words mean something inherited. *Heritage* is that which belongs to one by reason of birth or that which is bequeathed to a subsequent generation by an individual or by a society as a whole:

Our Victorian heritage.

Inheritance is the usual word for any property or possessions which are passed on to an heir:

He received a substantial inheritance from his grandparents.

hesitance, hesitancy, hesitation *Hesitance* is now a rarely used alternative spelling to *hesitancy*. *Hesitation* is the most common word and more or less interchangeable with *hesitancy*. The only real difference is that *hesitancy* may be said to be the characteristic tendency of a person which gives rise to the *hesitation*.

hiccup, hiccough *Hiccup* is the preferred form. The alternative, *hiccough*, is given in most dictionaries but is strongly condemned by some authorities.

high see **tall**

high, highly Both adverbs are in common use. *High* is more usual when reference is made to altitude, amount, or status:

The cranes were flying high.

To aim high in one's chosen profession

Highly means 'to a high degree' or 'with high appreciation':

A highly amusing episode, to speak highly of someone.

But it can be used with the meaning of *high* in such expressions as *highly placed*, *highly paid*.

Note that compounds with *high* take a hyphen, but those with *highly* (see above) do not: *high-fidelity*, *high-powered*.

historic, historical These words are frequently confused but their meanings are quite distinct. *Historic* means 'well-known or important in history':

Hastings was a historic battle.

Historical means 'concerned with or relating to history':

A historical novel, historical evidence.

hoard, horde These words are sometimes mixed up. A *hoard* is 'an accumulation of something for future use', as *a hoard of tinned food.* A *horde* is 'a great multitude of people, often an unruly one':

A horde of football fans ran into the arena.

Holland see **Netherlands**

homonym, homophone A *homonym* is a word which has the same spelling and usually the same pronunciation as another but a different meaning, such as *boil* (as water) and *boil* (a painful sore). A *homophone* is a word which has the same pronunciation as another, but a different spelling and meaning, such as *heir* and *air*, *feat* and *feet*. [See also *synonym*]

Hon. This is an abbreviation for both *honourable* and *honorary*. *Honourable* is a title prefixed to the Christian names of younger sons of earls and all children of viscounts and barons, to the names of certain High Court justices, and to some others. It is also used inside the House of Commons when one M.P. is referring to another. *Honorary* describes the unpaid holder of an office and is invariably abbreviated: *the hon. secretary*.

hopefully As the adverb formed from *hopeful*, *hopefully* means 'in a hopeful mood'. In recent years, however, it has acquired a new use which, though deplored by some authorities, has made its way into the dictionaries. *Hopefully* now has the additional sense of 'it is to be hoped':

Hopefully, we will finish work by tonight.

hotchpotch, hodgepodge Most dictionaries give both forms but the first is now the preferred spelling. The form *hotchpot* is a legal term, but even this has the alternative spelling *hotchpotch*.

how This is both an adverb and a conjunction, and care must be taken to avoid ambiguity when it is used as a conjunction. A sentence like:

They told me how they had managed to complete the job in four hours

may be a simple statement, in which case *how* should be replaced by *that* or omitted altogether. On the other hand if *how* means 'in what manner' or 'the way in which' it is perfectly acceptable.

however, how ever When *however* is used as a conjunction meaning 'nevertheless' or 'yet' it is separated by a comma or commas from the rest of the sentence which it modifies:

However, they decided to go at once.
They decided, however, to go at once.

When *however* is used as an adverb meaning 'to whatever extent or degree' or 'in whatever manner' it is not separated by a comma:

However hard he tried, he never succeeded.

As an interrogative adverb in direct and indirect questions it is written as two words and is used for emphasis:

How ever did you succeed in getting up so early?
We wondered how they ever managed to complete the job.

human, humane Both adjectives refer to what is characteristic of human beings, but their meanings are now quite separate. *Human* can refer to the good and bad in mankind: *human kindness*, *human weakness*, or to man as opposed to God: *human frailty*, *divine compassion*.

Humane, which was once interchangeable with *human*, is now restricted to the idea of being tender and compassionate towards the sufferings of others:

Humane treatment of the injured, humane feelings.

hyphens Much can be written about such a complicated subject as the use of hyphens. To hyphenate too much is as bad as to hyphenate too little. The following are some guidelines which the general reader may find useful.

The hyphen is normally used with a composite adjective:

a light-coloured suit, a poverty-stricken family.

It is not normally used to join an adverb to an adjective which it qualifies:

a tastefully furnished room, an ever increasing amount.

It is used with the adverbs *well*, *better*, *best*, *ill*, *worse* and *worst*, and any other adverbs which might not be recognized as such:

A well-known actor, an ill-advised move.

However, when the compound adjective or adverb plus adjective are used predicatively, *i.e.*, after the verb, the hyphen is omitted:

His suit is light coloured, the actor was well known, the move would be ill advised.

There are many compound words which hover uneasily between complete separation, a hyphenated form and one word:

pile driver, pile-driver; book-binder, bookbinder.

All that can be said is that the more commonly such a compound is used the more likely it is to be printed as one word:

bullfighting, watchmaker, doorkeeper.

Other compounds, originally printed as two words or hyphenated, have through frequent use become one word:

eyelid, blackbird, armchair, bedroom, electrostatic, thermonuclear.

Some compounds are still written with a hyphen in order to avoid an ugly combination of vowels and consonants, to make the pronunciation clear, or to distinguish between two different meanings:

micro-organism, anti-icing, damp-proof, re-emerge, re-cover (to cover again), re-form (to form again).

There is little consistency in the use of hyphens with prefixes. Some prefixes, like *all-*, *ex-*, *non-* and *self-* are normally hyphenated to the word with which they are compounded:

all-embracing, ex-serviceman, non-self-governing.

Others, like *anti-*, *co-*, *counter-*, *neo-*, *pan*, *pre-* and *post-* are normally joined to the main word unless this begins with a capital letter or produces an awkward combination of vowels:

antifreeze, coedition, neocolonialism, predecease, posthaste, Pan-American.

The prefixes *mis-* and *re-* are almost always spelt without a hyphen. The prefix *by-* may be spelt with or without a hyphen: *bypass*, *by-product*.

The following suffixes are usually hyphenated:

-all (know-all), -elect (president-elect), -odd (twenty-odd), -off (rake-off, spin-off), -to (lean-to).

The following suffixes do not generally require hyphens:

-down (showdown), -fold (fivefold), -goer (cinemagoer), -less (endless), -like (childlike), -over (takeover), -wise (lengthwise).

Note that *-like* usually has a hyphen when the word to which it is attached ends in an *l*, as in *snail-like*.

A hyphen is used in spelling out numbers between 21 and 99:

thirty-five, eighty-eight, two hundred and ninety-two.

It is also used in fractions:

one-third, two-fifths, three-quarters.

I

I The trap into which the unwary fall is to say 'you and I' or 'you and me' in the wrong context:

This piece of information is just intended for you and I

is wrong, and so is:

You and me had better leave it to the experts.

In the first example, the two pronouns are both objects of the preposition *for* and are therefore in the accusative case, so they should be *you and me*. In the second example both pronouns are the subjects of the sentence and are therefore in the nominative case, which means that *you and I* are the correct forms.

The simple way to decide is to strip away all but the bare essentials. It then becomes obvious that '. . . is for I' simply wouldn't do, nor would '. . . me had better leave'.

The idiomatic *It's me* is so widespread that it is generally acceptable, though most authorities recommend that in formal writing the correct form *It is I* should be used. However, given the nature of the words themselves it is highly unlikely that they would occur in a formal context. Nobody would ever say *It's I* in speech and so it would not appear in reported speech. The argument would seem, therefore, to be specious.

-ible The *-ible* suffix occurs in adjectives derived from Latin words ending in *-ibilis*, such as admissible, credible, collapsible, flexible, indigestible, legible, visible, and several others.

-ic, -ical Some of the adjectives ending in *-ic* and *-ical* have different meanings, such as *economic*, 'pertaining to the production and distribution of wealth' and *economical*, 'avoiding waste or extravagance'. Others, such as *poetic* and *poetical*, are interchangeable. In many instances the *-ic* form may also be a noun and when this is the case it is preferable to differentiate by using the *-ical* form for the adjective and to keep the *-ic* form for the noun.

-ics When referring to a subject suitable for study nouns ending in *-ics* are singular:

I am taking mathematics for my A levels, because it is my best subject.

But in a more generalized context they will take a plural verb:

Economics offer a gateway into politics, which are the best means of wielding influence in public life.

idiom The Greek word has been translated as 'a manifestation of the peculiar', and the dictionary definition is 'a form of expression peculiar to a language, especially one having a significance other than its literal one'. Idiomatic English is very much concerned with usage. It is English as it is spoken every day, and its conventions and phraseology have become established by practice. That is not to say that an idiom is necessarily ungrammatical. It may well be correct, but have taken a short cut. Or it is simply a colourful metaphor, apparently arbitrary and incapable of being literally interpreted. It is the idioms of a language that are so hard for a foreigner to learn:

Not a single flight was taking off – the weather had seen to that.

Not a single is an idiomatic way of saying 'no flight'. *The weather had seen to that*: how could the weather 'see' anything? Though seemingly quite illogical, the phrase *seen to* meaning 'accounted for' in such a context is a well-established idiom.

i.e. see **e.g.**

if, whether *If*, used in place of *whether*, can be ambiguous:

Let me know if you would like a lift to the station.

Does this mean that he should be contacted only if a lift is required?

Let me know whether you would like a lift to the station.

In this sentence it is clear that he should be informed whether a lift is required or not – it leaves no room for doubt.

if and when It is seldom necessary to use both *if and when* in a sentence:

We can expect a reduction in income tax if and when the Conservatives return to power.

In this sentence either *if* or *when* would be acceptable. The use of both together should be avoided.

ill, sick In general *ill* occurs only predicatively:

She was very ill.

If *sick* were substituted here it would mean she was vomiting. But in:

She was a very sick woman

ill could not take its place. *Sick* is the term used when speaking of a sick person, sick list, sick benefit, sick leave, and in idiomatic phrases such as *to go sick*. Though the general term is *ill health*, the word has also the secondary meaning of bad or evil, so that used in this context it is being equated with bad health. American usage is different. The two words are interchangeable, *ill* being used for the more serious complaints and *sick* for a simple ailment like a cold. *Ill* may also be used attributively: in the United States it is usual to speak of an *ill person*.

illegal, unlawful, illegitimate, illicit *Illegal* is against the law of the land. *Unlawful* may be against the law or what the law intends, but it can also apply to religious or moral laws. *Illegitimate* is outside the law, not in accordance with or sanctioned by law, often used with particular reference to birth out of wedlock. *Illicit* means not permitted or authorized, but this does not necessarily mean by law – it could simply be describing a breach of school rules.

illegible, unreadable *Illegible* refers to the quality of the handwriting or the printed words, which may be impossible to decipher. *Unreadable* refers to the contents of the text as a whole, which may be too technical, learned or ill conceived to be understood. Or just too boring. That which is *illegible* will, of course, be *unreadable*.

illicit, elicit These two words are sometimes confused because they sound alike. *Illicit* (see above) means not permitted or authorized. *Elicit* is to draw or bring out, or to evoke:

Perhaps his sister will be able to elicit the truth about his illicit activities.

illusion see **delusion**

illusory see **elusive**

image This is a vogue word which has become fashionable since the power of television has emphasized the need for politicians and moguls of industry to present themselves to the public in the best possible light. People in the public eye have become conscious of the *image* that they project, and the word has acquired a fresh significance.

imaginary, imaginative *Imaginary* is an image created in the imagination, having no existence in reality. *Imaginative* is having the faculty for creating such images or mental pictures:

Her work was highly imaginative, yet it was possible to believe in the existence of her imaginary characters.

imbue, infuse, instil *Imbue* is to impregnate or inspire. *Infuse* is to cause to penetrate. *Instil* is to infuse slowly into the mind or feelings, to insinuate. It is possible to *imbue* someone with something, such as enthusiasm, or enthusiasm can be *infused* into him, but he cannot be *infused* with it. Modern dictionaries give 'inspire with' as one of the definitions of *infuse*, an indication of the common loose usage of these two words.

Enthusiasm can also be *instilled into* a person. Again, he cannot be *instilled with* it:

> Joe was imbued with excitement. He tried to infuse some of his enthusiasm into Bob. But Bob remained indifferent, however hard Joe tried to instil some life into him.

immanent, imminent *Immanent* means remaining within, inherent, or taking place within the mind and having no effect outside it:

> The faculty of imagination is immanent to human progress.

It is a little-used word, occurring most frequently in a theological context.

Imminent means impending, or about to occur.

> The threat of a breakdown in negotiations was imminent.

immature, premature *Immature* is not fully developed. *Premature* is coming into existence or maturing too soon:

> Premature shoots are likely to be damaged by frost because they are immature.

immigrant see **emigrant**

immoral see **amoral**

immunity, impunity *Immunity* is exemption from any natural or usual liability, especially susceptibility to disease. It can also mean special privilege. *Impunity* is exemption from punishment or ill consequences.

impassable, impassible *Impassable* applies to that which cannot be passed over or through. *Impassible* is incapable of suffering pain or harm, or of displaying emotion. The word is seldom used, having been superseded by impassive.

impel, induce *Impel* is to drive or urge forward or to incite to action. *Induce* is to lead or move by persuasion or influence:

He felt impelled to take an active part in union affairs, believing that his example would induce others to follow.

imperative mood A grammatical term for the mood of command:

Stop! Raise your arms above your head. Now bend down and touch your toes.

Each of these commands is in the *imperative mood.*

imperial, imperious *Imperial* is of or pertaining to an empire, an emperor or empress, of a commanding quality or aspect, very fine or grand. *Imperious* is domineering, dictatorial or overbearing; also urgent or imperative. At one time the words were almost synonymous, stemming as they do from the same Latin word meaning 'commanding':

His imperious behaviour is an offensive reminder of the imperial circles in which he used to move.

implicit see **explicit**

imply, infer, insinuate *Imply* is to signify, indicate or suggest without expressly stating:

He implied that the bank knew the position from the beginning.

Infer is to draw a conclusion from, to derive by reasoning. It is therefore possible to *infer* that something is true by the evidence that has been *implied*:

It is reasonable to infer that the bank acted as they did because of what they knew.

To *insinuate* is to suggest or hint slyly, to instil something into someone's mind subtly by underhand means. It is even less explicit than to *imply*, and is often used in a derogatory sense:

He insinuated that the bank had not acted very creditably.

impractical, impracticable see **practicable**

impromptu see **extempore**

in-, un- As a rough guide, the negative prefix *in-* applies to Latin-based words and to most of those ending in *-ible* and *-ent*:

Inessential, inexact, incredible, ineligible, incoherent.

With some exceptions, such as *incapacitated*, words ending in *-ed* and *-ing* take the negative prefix *un-*.

in, at *In* is the more general term, *at* the preposition for the specific. When thinking of a place as a district or area *in* would be the preposition to choose:

I live in the village of Middleton,

meaning that I live within the area the village occupies. But to say:

I live at Middleton

means that I am identifying Middleton as a particular pinpoint on a map, a specific place at which I live within a wider area. Thus *in* a city, because it is a vague term implying a large district, but *at* No. 6 Acacia Avenue, a given point in that city. In the same way, I could be said to work *in* a department store (any department store) but *at* James Smith Ltd, a particular department store, *in* the sports department (anywhere in it) but *at* the sports counter, one specific place in the department.

inability, disability *Inability* is lack of ability, power or means, which may be a temporary condition:

His inability to pay should have been foreseen.

Disability is lack of power or ability due to a physical or mental defect, and is usually a situation of long standing. *Inability*, which means that someone has been rendered unable to fulfil an obligation, may be a result of a *disability*, a physical factor which impairs capacity to carry out such an obligation:

Because of his disability he could not travel by train, which accounts for his inability to attend the board meeting.

inapt, inept *Inapt* means not apt or fitted, without aptitude or capacity. *Inept* also means not apt or fitted. It is the term preferred when applied to what is unsuitable or out of place, and also implies clumsiness. *Inapt* is more usually confined to lack of aptitude or capacity.

incapable, unable Both words mean lacking ability or power to do something. The chief difference is that *incapable* is usually applied to a long-standing condition, *unable* to a specific situation:

He is incapable of expressing himself clearly, so it is not surprising that he was unable to make himself understood at the meeting.

incredible, incredulous *Incredible* is too extraordinary to be possible or that cannot be believed. *Incredulous* is sceptical, showing disbelief:

As she unfolded her incredible story, her audience became increasingly incredulous.

incubus, succubus An *incubus* is an imaginary demon who was supposed to have intercourse with sleeping women, and a *succubus* is a female demon who was supposed to have visited sleeping men. *Incubus* is the more familiar word, because it has come to mean anything that weighs oppressively on one like a nightmare.

inculcate, indoctrinate *Inculcate* is to impress on someone by repeated statement, to instil in or teach persistently. *Indoctrinate* is to instruct, especially in a doctrine, to imbue someone with information or principles.

It must be remembered that it is the ideas that are *inculcated* into a person, whereas the person is *indoctrinated* with the ideas:

From earliest childhood religious principles had been inculcated into her, so that she had become indoctrinated with the ethics of a rigid code of morality.

indicative mood This is the most important mood of English verbs. It is the mood of fact, a statement, as distinct from the imperative mood (command) or subjunctive (conditional):

Look! (*imperative*) I see a flying saucer (*indicative*), as clearly as if it were standing (*subjunctive*) where you are now.

indict, indite *Indict* is to accuse or charge with an offence or crime. *Indite*, a rarely used word, is to compose or write, especially a speech or poem. Both words are pronounced in the same way.

indifferent Originally this word meant 'impartial'. Other dictionary definitions are 'without interest or concern, apathetic, neutral in character, neither good nor bad'. From the last definition it has come to mean 'not very good', and this has supplanted the original meaning of 'impartial':

He was an indifferent judge of character and his opinion was often biased.

At one time such a sentence would have been nonsense, since an 'impartial' judge cannot be biased. Today it simply means that he was not a very good judge of character.

One is *indifferent to* a circumstance, not *for* it.

individual The proper use of this word is in contrasting a single person with a group:

The local bird society has supported our conservation efforts, though certain individuals have criticized our methods.

It is often used colloquially, however, as a term of contempt or facetiousness. The first can be detected in the tone of the above example, and the second is exemplified in:

Into the room walked an extraordinary individual. He was clad from head to foot in shining blue plastic and there were dangling antennae attached to his head.

indoor, indoors *Indoor* is the adjective:

Card playing is a pleasant indoor pastime,

and *indoors* the adverb, meaning in or into a house or building:

You will have to play indoors. It is raining hard outside,

or:

You will have to go indoors. It's raining quite hard now.

induction, deduction *Induction* is the process of drawing a general principle from certain specific facts. *Deduction* is assuming the truth of a specific fact because of a known set of general principles:

I have never come across a male tortoiseshell cat, so it seems a fair induction that tortoiseshell cats are generally female,

and:

Since tortoiseshell cats are invariably female, it would be an obvious deduction that the next tortoiseshell cat that I meet will be a female.

industrial, industrious *Industrial* is pertaining to industry or productive labour. *Industrious* is hard working or diligent. The first is applied to the processes of industry, the second to the people concerned with it.

ineffective, ineffectual see **effective**

infamous, notorious *Infamous* means detestable, shamefully bad, having an extremely bad reputation, but not necessarily widely known. *Notorious* is widely known for unfavourable reasons, but not necessarily evil ones. [See also *famous, notorious*]

infectious see **contagious**

infer see **imply**

infinitive The infinitive can be either the subject or the object of a sentence:

To understand (*subject*) is to believe (*object*).

It should not be used in a sentence where the gerund is clearly required:

The custom of shopkeepers to label their goods in decimal quantities can be very confusing.

The infinitive in this sentence should be replaced by *of labelling*. Equally incorrect is the 'dangling' infinitive:

To achieve a high record, concentration and determination are required.

Somebody must require them – 'concentration and determination' cannot achieve the record by themselves. The correct sentence should read:

To achieve a high record, *a man* requires (or *one* requires) concentration and determination.

[See also *split infinitive*]

inflammable, flammable, inflammatory *Inflammable* is capable of being set alight, combustible, (figuratively) excitable. *Flammable* means the same thing and is interchangeable, but *inflammable* is in more general use, especially in its combustible sense. *Inflammatory* means tending to inflame, kindling passion or anger, and is used almost entirely figuratively.

inflict see **afflict**

inform, information An overworked word, *inform* is too often employed as a formal way of saying 'tell', especially in commercial jargon:

I have to inform you that your licence has been withdrawn.

To inform someone *to* do something is not possible. He can be informed *that* he should or must do something, or he can be informed *of* an event.

For your information is another glib phrase. This is acceptable if it does indeed mean 'just for information – don't do anything', but it is often used as an officious way of passing on a directive:

For your information the form XYZ must be completed in triplicate by the end of January.

informant, informer An *informant* is one who informs or gives information. An *informer* also gives information, but the word is used more specifically to apply to someone who passes on incriminating evidence to a prosecuting officer. The information given by an *informant* is not necessarily about anyone else, though it may well be of an illicit character:

It is supposed to be a Cabinet secret, so I can't tell you the name of my informant.

ingenious, ingenuous *Ingenious* is having inventive faculty, skilful in contriving or constructing:

His plan for solving the city parking problems is very ingenious.

Ingenuous is free from restraint or dissimulation, artless or innocent:

Her open, ingenuous manner was the chief quality for which she was chosen.

Ingenuity is the noun for *ingenious*, and ingenuousness the noun for *ingenuous*.

inhabitable see **habitable**

inherent, innate *Inherent* is existing in something as a permanent and inseparable element:

A talent for mimicry is an inherent part of the comic's job.

Innate means inborn, existing from birth. It also means part of the essential character of something:

Because of her innate shyness she found it hard to communicate with the children.

inheritance see **heritage**

inhibit, prohibit *Inhibit* is to restrain, hinder or check:

He was inhibited from expressing himself too freely by the presence of several women.

Prohibit is to forbid by authority, to prevent or hinder:

It is prohibited to spit.

Although some of the meanings overlap, in general *prohibit* is much stronger than *inhibit* and presupposes the possibility of authority to enforce it.

inmost, innermost These words, both meaning situated farthest within or most intimate, are interchangeable, but *inmost* is the more usual choice, especially in the figurative sense.

innuendo In common usage *innuendo* is an indirect intimation, usually derogatory, about a person or thing. It also has the specific meaning in law of a parenthetic explanation in a pleading, and it is from this, the original definition, that the extended meaning in common use has evolved.
The plural is innuendoes.

in order that This construction should always be followed by 'may' or 'might':

He drove slowly in order that she might follow.

In this example the phrase serves to emphasize the purposefulness of the sentence '. . . *in order that she might* (be able to) *follow*', but in many instances the simpler construction *that* or *so that* is preferable:

They came early in order that they might get good seats

sounds a little pedantic.

They came early so that they could get good seats

is a more natural way of expressing it.

inquire see **enquire**

in so far This should always be written as three words, not one, but it is not a very desirable expression, and tends to lead to wordiness. It is usually better replaced by *although*, *except that* or *so far*:

He did not agree to the proposal, save in so far as he was prepared to make a few marginal concessions.

Although would be a better substitute here, replacing *save in so far as*.

insolate, insulate *Insolate* is to expose to the sun's rays, to treat by exposure to the sun. *Insulate* is to cover or surround something, especially an electric wire, with non-conducting material.

instinct, intuition *Instinct* is an inborn pattern of activity, innate impulse or natural inclination. Figuratively, it is a natural aptitude or gift for something:

Migrating birds find their way by instinct.

Intuition is direct perception of facts independently of any reasoning process:

How she knew you were coming I don't know – it must have been her feminine intuition.

institute, institution An *institute* is a society or organization for carrying on particular work, especially of an educational, literary or scientific nature:

Classes are held at the institute every evening of the week.

An *institution* is an organization or establishment for the promotion of a particular object. It is also an organized pattern of group behaviour or any established law or custom:

The institution of beating the bounds goes back to pagan times.

instructional, instructive *Instructional* is pertaining to the act of teaching or education. *Instructive* is also conveying instruction, knowledge or information, but whereas the emphasis of *instructional* is on the process of imparting the knowledge *instructive* deals more with the quality of the information imparted:

It was a very instructive lecture, but you would expect a high standard for an instructional course of this kind.

insure see **assure**

intelligent, intellectual *Intelligent* is having a good understanding or mental capacity, quick to grasp. *Intellectual* is appealing to or engaging the intellect. An *intelligent* person is not necessarily *intellectual*. He may have great mental capabilities and a quick understanding but be wholly uninterested in academic matters and things of the mind. Conversely, however, an *intellectual* person is likely to be *intelligent*, since without the capacity for understanding, mental exercise is unlikely to appeal to him:

> He is extremely intelligent, showing a quick grasp of essentials, but his intellectual commitment appears to be minimal: he prefers sport.

Intellectual has come to have a derogatory sense in social terms, implying a superiority to others who are not so occupied with things of the mind.

intense, intensive *Intense* is existing in a high degree, acute, strong or vehement, especially of feelings:

> His intense anxiety about his wife's safety is understandable.

Intensive means characterized by intensity, concentrated or thorough. It has special application to treatment in medicine and to increasing effectiveness in agriculture: *intensive treatment*, *intensive cultivation*. It is also applied to grammar, indicating expressions of emphasis or force, as *self* in *himself*.

inter-, intra- Both these prefixes occur in Latin words, *inter-* meaning 'between' or 'among', as in *interdenominational*, *interrupt*, *interfere*, and *intra-* indicating 'within', as in *intramural*, *intravenous*, *intracellular*.

interface A surface regarded as the common boundary of two bodies or spaces. It is becoming a vogue word increasingly in use as a metaphor, and as such is in danger of being overworked.

interject, interpolate, interpose *Interject* is to throw in abruptly between other things in a conversation:

I went shopping for new shoes today – by the way, there's a sale on at Marsh's – and managed to get just what I wanted.

Interpolate is to introduce new material between other things in a text or manuscript, especially deceptively or without authorization.

Interpose is to place something between, cause to intervene, or to put in a remark in the middle of a conversation:

They interposed a gauze curtain between the audience and the stage so you couldn't really see any details.

interjection A part of speech used to express delight, anger, surprise and other emotions. It is independent of the rest of the sentence, to which it bears no grammatical relation. Examples are:

Heavens! Rubbish! Good gracious!

in to, into When used as a straightforward preposition *into* is written as one word:

They opened the front door and went into the house.

But if the sense demands a separate adverb and preposition, it must be written as two words:

She took the post in to him as soon as he arrived.

This is also the case when *to* is attached to an infinitive:

He left the envelope in to be collected later.

intransitive and transitive verbs The term *intransitive* applies to those verbs that need no object; the action is confined to the subject alone:

He is sleeping.

The verb applies only to the subject *he*. It is not doing anything to anyone or anything else, and can stand alone.

A *transitive* verb is one that requires an object to complete its sense:

He opened the book

In this sentence the action moves from the subject *he* to the object *the book*. By itself the phrase *he opened* is meaningless without *the book*.

inverted commas see **quotation marks**

involve This has become a rather ineffective vogue word. Originally it could be defined as envelop or enfold, and it then came to mean implicate, especially in a crime, or to entangle (someone), to entail, include or contain. It is often used quite unnecessarily in a sentence which could stand equally well and more positively without it:

It is estimated that the work involved will take approximately ten days.

Here *involved* is quite superfluous.

In sloppy writing it is frequently chosen in place of a word with a more precise meaning:

Nothing can be countenanced which might involve labour problems at a later date.

It would be a more appropriate choice if *lead to* were substituted for *involve*. And in:

Snow was blocking many roads but the motorway was not involved,

affected would be preferable.

involve, entail *Entail* shares the meaning of include or contain with *involve*, but it also means to impose as a burden, and has a special legal sense of limiting inheritance to a specified line of heirs:

The estate was entailed, so she was unable to touch the capital.

inward, inwards *Inward* is the adjective describing something that is situated within, directed towards the inside or interior. It can also be an adverb, though this is less usual:

She stared out of the window, lost in inward thought.

Inwards, the adverb, can be equated with inwardly, and means towards the inside, as of a place or body, or in the mind or soul:

It was easy to identify his footprints, with the toes turned slightly inwards.

irony This is a mild form of humour in which the speaker says one thing but means an… …ometimes to the confusion of his listener:

> The Express Delivery servic… been extraordinarily generous. They have allowed me… …und of half the cost of postage of the parcel they didn't …

The speaker obviously considers th… …livery service anything but generous, and his enlightened …rs will recognize his *irony*.

Socratic irony is pretending ignorance i… …cussion in order to expose the weakness of the other's argum… *Dramatic irony* is the ignorance of the characters in a drama… …tuation when the audience knows more than they do:

> But Jemima, I love you and only you!

says the hero, but the audience has just watche… …im cavorting with another woman in the previous scene.

The idiomatic phrase *irony of fate*, which is much …erworked, refers to a twist of circumstances which renders an …ion futile or ridiculous.

-ist Some words offer the choice of ending in *-ist* or *-a…t*: for example, *educationist* or *educationalist* are both acceptab… On principle, unless there is a sound etymological reason for …sing *-alist*, the shorter form should be preferred: *horticulturist* rather than *horticulturalist*, and *agriculturist* rather than *agriculturalist*. In some cases, however, the longer version is firmly established in general use, for example *conversationalist* instead of *conversationist*.

italics This sloping typeface should be used judiciously in printed matter to emphasize or single out one word or short phrase which, for some reason, requires special attention in a sentence. Its effect is equivalent to underlining in handwriting or typescript. It may indicate a word which would be stressed vocally:

> He can't tell *me* what to do,

out the title of a book or
or contrast two words together inverted commas. It is also
play, taking the place of the ud phrases which have not yet
used to distinguish foreign wenglish language:
become fully assimilated to damaged his *amour-propre*.

Being reprimanded like thasis is to diminish the importance
To overuse the device of s will cause irritation to the reader.
of the rest of the text, a ictoria's habit of underlining lengthy
It is reminiscent of Qu
passages in her lette

its, it's *Its* is the ssive pronoun and, like *yours*, *hers* and *theirs*, does not an apostrophe before the *s*:

The bird flutte its wings and settled on the branch.

It's is the abbr ted form of *it is* or *it has*. Because the *i* has been omitted from and the *ha* from *has*, the apostrophe is necessary to indicate missing letters:

It's cold tside, but it's stopped raining.

-ize, -is For some verbs of Greek and Latin origin the French suffix e is preferred by many people to *-ize*: *realise* rather than *reali*z for example. But in American practice and in that of man respected authorities the *z* spelling is given preference. It must be remembered, however, that words which do not have Greek origins must retain the *s*, and many common verbs such as advertise, surprise, chastise, supervise, revise and televise come into this category.

J

Jacobean, Jacobin, Jacobite *Jacobean* describes anything belonging to the period of James I of England. A *Jacobin* was a member of a famous club of French revolutionaries started in 1789, and *Jacobite* was the name given to adherents of James II of England and his descendants after his overthrow in 1688.

jail see **gaol**

jargon, commercialese, journalese The proper meaning of *jargon* is a language peculiar to a particular trade or profession. But in extended use the word has come to be applied to any pretentious form of writing that uses a quantity of long words, euphemisms and cumbersome phrases, often quite meaningless, in an attempt to impress or lend weight to an ordinary sentence. *Commercialese* is commercial jargon, a peculiarly sterile form of it:

> We are in receipt of yours of the 14th inst. in respect of which we beg to inform you that we are expediting the matter as urgently as possible and we remain your obedient servants . . .

Journalese is journalist's jargon, particularly evident in headline copy:

> Councillor Presses Reform in Rate Probe

and:

> Gross Negligence Charges Minister.

This kind of verbal shorthand in which clichés play a prominent part occurs all too often in the body of the text.

jetsam see **flotsam and jetsam**

jocose, jocular Both words mean given to or characterized by joking, or facetious. Perhaps *jocose* is a little more ponderous than *jocular*, suggesting rather heavier humour, whereas *jocular* is humour in a lighter vein, almost waggish.

judg(e)ment Both spelling versions are acceptable, but *judgement* is the preferred form, in line with other words containing a mute *e*, such as *abridgement* and *acknowledgement*.

judicial, judicious *Judicial* pertains to judgement in a court of law or the administration of justice. *Judicious* means using or showing good judgement, wise or sensible.

junction, juncture *Junction* is the act of joining, a combination, or the state of being joined. It also has the special sense of a station where railway lines meet and cross. *Juncture* applies especially to a point in time, a critical moment being a critical *juncture*, though it can also mean the joining point of two bodies.

jurist, juror A *jurist* is one who professes the science of the law or who is versed in law. A *juror* is a member of a body of people sworn to deliver a verdict in a case.

just To say:

It is just exactly five o'clock

is an unnecessary repetition. Either *exactly* five o'clock or *just* five o'clock is quite sufficient.

The use of the word in such expressions as *I'm just fine*, meaning truly, positively, is an Americanism which is now acceptable in Britain as a colloquialism, but not in formal English. Otherwise it is a widely used adverb meaning only a moment before:

He has just gone,

or exactly, precisely, as in:

That is just what I meant.

juvenile, puerile *Juvenile* is young, or intended for young persons. *Puerile* means childishly foolish or trivial, an extension of its original meaning 'of or pertaining to a child or boy'.

K

kerb see **curb**

ketchup This is the accepted British spelling of this word, but in the United States it is sometimes spelt *catsup* or *catchup*.

kind It seems to be generally agreed that the phrase *those kind of things* is acceptable in colloquial speech but better avoided in written English. Ideally, the singular pronoun should be used with the singular noun *kind*, but since this can sound awkward – *that kind of things* – it is better to rephrase it as *things of that kind*, or keep the whole phrase singular, *that kind of thing*. Quite unacceptable in written English, though often used colloquially, is *kind of* used as an adverb:

He was kind of awkward.

kneeled, knelt Both forms are correct for the past tense and past participle.

knit *Knitted* is the past tense when applied to the weaving of fabric on knitting needles. In other senses, especially abstract ones, the past tense and past participle is *knit*:

The views they shared knit them even closer in a common bond.

kowtow, kotow Although *kotow* may be nearer the original Mandarin Chinese, *kowtow* is the more generally acceptable form of the word, with equal stress on both syllables.

L

-l-, -ll- When a verb ends in an *-l* preceded by a single vowel the *l* is doubled, regardless of stress, if another syllable is added:

channel, channelled; tunnel, tunnelling; revel, revelling.

An exception is *parallel*, *paralleled*.

The *l* remains single when preceded by two vowels or a vowel and a consonant:

reveal, revealing; curl, curling; boil, boiled.

The present or infinitive form may finish in a single or double *l*. As a general rule it is usually a *ll* if preceded by *a*, single if any other vowel precedes it:

enthrall but instil; recall but extol.

An exception is *appal*.

In nouns and adjectives the *l* is doubled when followed by *-er*, *-ed* or *-y*:

leveller, metalled, literally,

but not before *-ish*, *-ist*, *-ism*, or *-ment*:

existentialism, fulfilment, finalist, foolish.

Compound words often drop the second *l*, as in:

almost, already and skilful.

In American usage, unlike English, the *l* follows the normal rules of stress and is not doubled when the stress falls on the first syllable:

travel, traveler, traveled, traveling; level, leveler, leveled, leveling.

lacuna see **Latin and French plurals**

laden This is the past participle of the old word to *lade*, and is little used now except in such phrases as *a heavily laden lorry*. It has in most cases been superseded by *loaded*.

lady, woman As a term for differentiating sex, *woman* should be used in preference to *lady*, which is a genteelism to be avoided.

For example, *woman* doctor, *woman* barrister, and:

This job is not suitable for a woman.

An exception is made, however, if the person referred to is present, when *lady* is used as an expression of courtesy:

Would you let this lady through, please?

The term *lady* is little used now to describe a social category, carrying as it does snobbish implications which are unacceptable today. It may occasionally be employed to emphasize the superiority of a post such as a *lady housekeeper*, but is not recommended. However, when a group of women at a formal meeting are being addressed the term *Ladies* is still used as a courtesy.

lama, llama A *lama* is a Buddhist priest from Tibet. A *llama* is a South American mammal.

large see **big**

last, latest *Last*, meaning final, occurring or coming after all others, refers chiefly to position, though it can also mean final in time. *Latest* refers only to the most recent in time:

The last turn to appear was the best in the show,

and:

This is the latest fashion in Paris,

meaning that it is absolutely up to the minute, the most up to date.

late Care must be taken when using this word that it cannot be interpreted to mean 'dead':

The late editor of the paper was a man of strong principles

may mean either that he has moved to another job or that he has died. If it is intended to mean the former, it would be better to say *previous* in this context.

lath, lathe A *lath* is a thin strip of wood used with others to form the base for supporting tiles or plaster on a ceiling, wall or roof. A *lathe* is a machine used for wood- or metalwork.

Latin and French plurals In some words it is customary to retain the Latin forms for the plural. For example *species*, not specieses, *crises*, not crisises, and *emphases*, not emphasises. In others the choice is open. Both the English and the Latin forms are acceptable, and often the only criterion is the context in which they will appear. For a text of popular appeal the English form is preferable: *indexes* rather than *indices*, *formulas* rather than *formulae*, *radiuses* rather than *radii*, and *aquariums* rather than *aquaria*, but in a text intended for scientific or scholarly purposes the Latin forms would be preferred. Use the English plural in cases of doubt.

Not all words ending in *-us* should automatically take *i* in the plural. *Hippopotamuses* is the accepted plural and not hippopotami. We refer to the *buses* (omnibuses) running late, and not the busi. Like octopus, *hippopotamus* is from a Greek word, not Latin, and *omnibus* is the Latin dative plural, meaning literally 'for all'.

French words ending in *-eau* take the plural *-eaux*, though in almost all cases the anglicized form *-eaus* is also acceptable, and it is becoming increasingly common to see the *s* form preferred. Again, choice should depend on the context, and the degree of anglicization is based largely on the frequency with which the word is encountered in the English language:

beaux or beaus; tableaux or tableaus; plateaux or plateaus.

latter, former, last The *latter* should be used only in contrast with the *former* when the choice is between two items comparable in kind. These terms cannot be applied to just one noun simply in order to avoid repeating a word:

He plodded on steadily, making his way down a steep path. The latter was slippery with recent rain.

This is incorrect. *The latter* should be replaced by *This*.

To use these terms in respect of more than two choices is also wrong:

When Tom, Dick and Harry started to sing everyone stopped to listen. The former had a resonant, pleasing voice.

Who had a resonant voice, Tom or Dick?

Mary Ann went shopping on Friday. She bought a dress, a coat, two pairs of shoes and a handbag, the latter in real leather.

Last is the word that should have been here instead of *latter*, or alternatively *last-mentioned.*

As a general rule, it is preferable to avoid using the terms *former* and *latter* and instead to refer to *first* and *last.*

laudable, laudatory *Laudable* is praiseworthy, commendable:

It was a laudable piece of work.

Laudatory is expressing or containing praise:

The reviews were laudatory in their comments on the play.

lawful, legal *Lawful* is allowed by law, not contrary to law. *Legal* is established or authorized by law, connected or concerned with the law or its administration:

I don't know what the legal position is. He was carrying out his lawful business when the police arrested him.

Of the two words *lawful* is merely permissive, whereas *legal* is more positive. *Lawful* can also be applied to moral laws; *legal* refers only to the laws of the land.

lawyer, attorney, notary A *lawyer* conducts suits in court or gives legal advice and aid. Both a barrister and a solicitor are *lawyers.* An *attorney* is someone appointed or empowered by another to transact business for him. In the United States, however, the word is synonymous with *lawyer.* A *notary,* or (to use the full term) a *notary public,* is someone who attests to deeds or writings and certifies their authenticity, usually for the purpose of passing copies on abroad. [See also *barrister*]

lay, lie These verbs are probably mistreated more frequently than any others in the English language.

To *lay* is to put or place something in a prone position. It is a transitive verb: it must have an object:

Lay your cards out on the table.

In this sentence *your cards* is the object of the verb *lay*.

The present participle is *laying*:

He is laying his cards out on the table.

The past tense and past participle is *laid*:

He laid his cards out on the table,

and:

He has laid his cards out on the table.

Note the spelling, *laid*: no such word as *layed* exists.

To *lie* is to recline in a prone position. It is an intransitive verb: it does not take an object, but can stand alone:

In summer it is delightful to lie in the sun,

and:

Sometimes in summer I lie in the sun.

The present participle is *lying*:

In summer nothing is more delightful than lying in the sun,

and:

She has been lying in the sun, and now I am lying beside her.

The past tense is *lay*, and it is this which leads so often to confusion with the present tense of the transitive verb:

For much of the time last summer she lay in the sun.

The past participle is *lain*:

He has lain idle for quite long enough.

There are many idiomatic and colloquial phrases with special meanings using the transitive verb *to lay*: to lay in, lay off, lay out, lay siege to, lay waste, and lay down (your weapons, or some other possession). It will be seen that all these phrases require an object.

The verb *to lie*, meaning to tell an untruth, is quite a different word and is seldom confused. The past tense and past participle are *lied*, the present participle *lying*.

leading question This is a question which is so worded that it leads the recipient on to give the answer which the questioner wants. Contrary to belief, it does not mean a hostile or important or principal question but one so worded that it incorporates a strong suggestion, a device which is often attempted in a court of law:

> *Question:* You had at no time met the deceased in the week prior to his death, had you?
> *Answer:* No, sir.

The expression is loosely used to mean an unfair question or one difficult to answer.

leap The past tense and past participle may be either *leapt* or *leaped*. Both are correct, but on the whole *leapt* is the preferred form in Britain.

learn Both *learnt* and *learned* are acceptable as the past tense and past participle. However, since there is an adjective *learned*, it avoids confusion if *learnt* is chosen as the preferred form for the verb.

least *Least*, the superlative form of *less*, is used in phrases such as *at least* and *least of all*. There is occasionally confusion about whether *least of all* or *most of all* is appropriate, depending on the negative or positive quality of the sentence:

> I do not like the idea of a man calling at the door and asking questions, most of all a council official.

With the negative slant of this sentence the correct phrase should be *least of all*, since I would like even *less* the idea of a council official calling than any other man.

leastways, leastwise *Leastways* is a colloquialism unacceptable in formal speech or in writing. *Leastwise*, which is now almost obsolete, is no less colloquial.

legend, myth A *legend* is a story which has been handed down by tradition, and for which there is no firm basis in fact, though it may be popularly accepted as true. A *myth* is also a traditional story, but one which is invented, often in an attempt to explain natural phenomena in terms of supernatural beings. It is sometimes used figuratively to describe an untruth:

That story he told us about being offered a marvellous job was a complete myth.

legible see **readable**

legislation, legislature *Legislation* is the act of making laws. The *legislature* is the law-making body of a country or state, as Parliament is in Britain.

lengthways, lengthwise Either form is acceptable.

lengthy, long *Long* is of considerable or great extent either of time, scope or distance, and has a widespread application. *Lengthy* is used more specifically for the duration of a speech or the extent of a written text, and implies a degree of tedium.

-less Added to nouns, this suffix forms adjectives to indicate 'without' whatever the noun means:

hopeless (without hope), formless (without form), colourless (without colour).

In some cases the suffix is applied to verbs, as in *tireless*.

less see **fewer, less**

less, lesser Both *less* and *lesser* are in origin comparative forms of *little*. *Less* is an adverb (*less* easy, *less* complicated) and an adjective, when it can be employed both attributively and predicatively: *less butter is available* or *there is less*. *Lesser* can be used only as an attributive adjective:

A lesser evil; lesser troubles.

lessee, lessor The *lessee* is the person to whom a lease is granted and the *lessor* is the one who grants the lease.

lest The correct construction following *lest* is *should*:

The newspaper did not print his name and address lest he should be inundated with unwelcome callers.

The alternative is the pure subjunctive, now regarded as rather old-fashioned:

I always leave the light on, lest he be frightened by the dark.

let A common mistake is to use the wrong case for the personal pronoun in a construction such as:

Let you and I make up our differences.

This should be *let you and me*, since both pronouns are the objects of the verb *let*.

The phrase *let alone*, though frequently used, is a colloquial one:

I can't keep my present garden tidy, let alone one twice its size.

In a formal context *much less* would be a preferable phrase. It is also better to say *leave the child alone* rather than *let the child alone*, which is acceptable only as a colloquialism in informal speech. But *to let go* is as correct as *to leave go*.

letter forms The formalities with which business and other letters used to be presented have to a large extent been superseded by simple, direct formulas which are universally applicable. No longer is it deemed necessary for an official to sign himself 'I am, sir, your obedient servant', nor is it any longer customary to begin a business letter with 'We beg to acknowledge recepit of your favour of the 14th instant', though both examples may still be encountered.

Briefly, a formal letter between strangers should start with *Dear Sir* or *Dear Madam*, *Dear Sirs* or *Mesdames*, and end with *Yours faithfully* or *Yours truly*, though the former is to be preferred. In less formal letters the recipient can be addressed by name, *Dear*

Mr Smith, and the letter should end with *Yours sincerely*. This formula may be used even with strangers if a degree of friendliness is desired.

Letters to friends and acquaintances may start *Dear Mary* or *My dear Mary*, *Dear John* or *My dear John*. Older people still sometimes use the surname alone and address an acquaintance as *Dear Smith*, but this is now considered rather old fashioned and is no longer customary, especially between younger people.

Letters to friends and acquaintances may be ended *Yours ever*, *Yours affectionately* or, simply, *Yours*.

To summarize: if a letter begins *Dear Mr Smith* it should never end *Yours faithfully* but always *Yours sincerely*. Similarly, a *Dear Sir* letter should not end with the more intimate *Yours sincerely*, but should terminate in *Yours faithfully* or *Yours truly*.

Do not finish a letter with an unattached clause:

> Looking forward to an early reply,
> Yours faithfully.

If this formula is to be used it should include a verb:

> Looking forward to an early reply,
> I am
> Yours faithfully.

Better still, it should be rephrased into a complete sentence:

> I look forward to an early reply.
> Yours faithfully.

Formal invitations may be worded in the third person:

> Mr and Mrs John Smith request the pleasure of the company of Mr and Mrs Tom Jones at . . .

This demands a reply in exactly the same style:

> Mr and Mrs Tom Jones have pleasure in accepting the kind invitation of Mr and Mrs John Smith to . . .

and the rest of the wording can be copied from the original invitation. A refusal might be couched in the following terms:

> Mr and Mrs Tom Jones thank Mr and Mrs John Smith for their kind invitation to . . . but regret that they are unable to accept owing to a previous engagement.

Note that the third person pronoun should be used throughout and not *we* or *your*.

liable see **apt**

libel and slander Both words mean defamation of character. *Libel* is defamation in a form that is permanent such as the written or printed word, pictures or broadcast material. *Slander* is a malicious or defamatory statement or report in the form of speech only.
In bringing an action for *slander* proof must be offered that damage has actually been caused. There is no such obligation with *libel*, and to be able to prove the truth of the libel or establish that it was 'fair comment' is a good defence.

liberality, liberalism *Liberality* is generosity, the quality of giving freely. *Liberalism* describes liberal principles, especially in religion or politics, emphasizing freedom from tradition and authority. When applied to the principles of the Liberal party in politics, denoting a specific philosophy, *Liberalism* should be written with a capital *L*.

licence, license *Licence* is the noun, *to license* the verb. In the United States, however, *license* is the usual form for both the verb and the noun.

lifelong, livelong *Lifelong* means lasting a lifetime. *Livelong* means long to the full extent, whole or entire, and is used only in the expression *the livelong day*.

light The verb *to light* has two separate meanings: (1) to illuminate or ignite, and (2) to get down or descend, to come upon or fall on a place or person. The past tense and past participle for both verbs is either *lighted* or *lit*. Of the two, *lit* is the more usual form:

As soon as she entered the room her eyes lit upon the open book,

or:

I have lit the fire,

but *lighted* is the usual adjectival form:

Somebody dropped a lighted match.

lightening, lightning *Lightening* is the lessening of a weight, *lightning* the flash of light in the sky caused by electrical discharge.

like Colloquially, this word is often used as a conjunction in constructions such as:

The man was not qualified to teach mathematics like his predecessor was.

Though common in speech, this should be avoided in writing, the appropriate word *as* being substituted. In the United States this construction has been carried a step further to replace *as if*:

He ran down the road like he was chased by a thousand devils,

but in Britain this is regarded as a vulgarism.

Like is acceptable as a *prepositional adverb*:

He is behaving like a child,

but in:

Like the man before him, mathematics was his special subject

it is incorrect, for the two subjects compared are incompatible. *Mathematics* is not like *the man*. The sentence would be better rephrased:

Like the man before him, he specialized in mathematics.

This misrelationship is a common mistake of careless writing, not confined only to *like*.

Pronouns following *like* are in the accusative case, *like you and me*, not *like you and I*.

like (verb) A construction frequently encountered is *would like to*:

There is one passage in the article that I would like to change.

If the verb *like* is removed, the sentence is correct:

There is one passage . . . that I would change,

but with *like* included *should* is the correct form (see *shall*, *will*, *should*, *would*):

There is one passage in the article that I should like to change.

likely Only in dialect or archaic speech, especially in Scotland and Ireland, is *likely* found on its own without a qualifying *very*, *most* or *more*:

He will likely call tomorrow

sounds quaint to our ears and is not generally acceptable.

He will most likely call tomorrow

is quite correct.

limit, delimit To limit is to restrict by fixing limits or boundaries to something:

The extent of his pruning is limited by the height to which he can reach.

To *delimit* is to demarcate, to fix or mark the limits:

Let us delimit the distance he has to run with a white cross.

limited The meaning of this word has been extended beyond its proper province. Though not necessarily wrong, it is often used to stand in for other more suitable adjectives:

With limited resources the authority is limited to undertaking only a limited number of projects

could easily be written as:

With scarce resources the authority is restricted to undertaking only a few projects.

It is sometimes used as a euphemism to soften a much harsher meaning:

He is a man of limited means = he is poor.

The child was of limited intellect = he was backward.
The company's resources are limited = they're losing money.

This device has its uses, but can be overdone.

linage, lineage *Linage* is alignment, or the number of lines of written or printed matter. *Lineage*, which is pronounced as three syllables, is lineal descent from an ancestor.

lineament, liniment *Lineament* is a distinctive characteristic or feature of a face or body. *Liniment* is a liquid preparation for rubbing into the skin, especially in the treatment of bruises.

liqueur, liquor A *liqueur* is a strong, sweet alcoholic drink such as curaçao. *Liquor* refers to spirits such as brandy or whisky, though in the United States it may also apply to any alcoholic drink.

litany, liturgy A *litany* is a ceremonial form of prayer consisting of supplications with responses. *Liturgy* is a form of public worship, a particular arrangement of services.

literally This has become a word of emphasis which is all too often misapplied. It should never be used in a figurative sense, unless it is intended to indicate that what might be taken to be metaphorical is – *literally* – true:

I literally rolled about on the floor with laughter.

If this is really the case, the word is well used. If the speaker did not, in fact, lie down on the floor and roll over and over, the word should have no place in the sentence. But:

I literally screamed at him

carries the truth of hysteria and does its job of emphasis in the right place.

litotes This is a Greek word for the device by which an affirmative is expressed by the negative of its opposite, having the effect of a modest understatement. For example:

That's not a bad likeness, is it?

and:

She was not unattractive in a quiet sort of way,

meaning that she was rather fetching.

little, small Perhaps these words can best be differentiated by pairing them with their opposites, *big and little*, *large and small*, *much and little*. *Little* refers to size, duration or extent:

Little dog, little child, little time, little noise.

It is also widely used figuratively:

Little hope, little scope, little wonder,

and in these senses it contrasts with *much*, qualifying the amount or degree.

Small is a word of dimension, of limited size or quantity·

Small room, small size, small tree, small amount.

It too is used figuratively, and in some expressions overlaps with *little*:

Small thanks, small wonder, small consolation,

but on the whole each has its place in accepted idiomatic use.

loaded see **laden**

loan Once this word was in general use as a verb, but it was supplanted by *lend*. It survives in the United States, but in Britain it is not acceptable. *To lend* is the correct verb and *loan* is just the noun.

loath, loathe, loth *To loathe* is the verb meaning to feel hatred or intense aversion for. *Loath* is the adjective, meaning averse, unwilling or reluctant, and *loth* an alternative spelling, once the usual form but now less favoured than *loath*:

Although I always loathed the colour, I am rather loath to part with this dress, old though it is.

locality, location A *locality* is the geographical designation of a place, spot or district, without reference to the people or things in it. A *location* is a place of settlement or residence, or something occupied. The difference is largely in the association of people with the word *location*.

locate, find To *locate* is to discover the place of, to establish in a place or situation; to settle:

Can you locate the exact spot where the murder took place?

To *find* is to come upon by chance, or to recover something.

loose, loosen To *loose* is to free from restraint, to release:

If you loose his lead, he'll come to heel when you call.

To *loosen* is to slacken or relax, to make less tight. It is also sometimes used to signify undo or let go, but this is an extension of meaning which blurs the distinction between *loose* and *loosen* and should be avoided. It must, however, be borne in mind that *to loose* is only rarely encountered.

loose, lose These verbs are sometimes confused because of their similar spelling. The past and present participles of *loose* are *loosed* and *loosing*, and those of *lose* are *lost* and *losing*.

loud, loudly *Loud* is both an adjective and an adverb, and *loudly* is an adverb. *Loud* is usually used in reference to sound volume, though *loudly* also occurs in this context:

If you play it loud, the neighbours will hear.

Loudly is the form for the figurative sense of clamorous or vociferous:

He complained loudly when they cut off his allowance.

lustful, lusty *Lustful* is full of lust or passion. *Lusty* is characterized by healthy vigour, hearty.

luxuriant, luxurious *Luxuriant* is abundant in growth, producing abundantly. *Luxurious* is characterized by luxury or sumptuousness.

lyric, lyrical In poetry *lyric* is having the form and musical quality of a song and characterized by an ardent expression of feeling. Colloquially, *lyrics* mean the words of a song.
Lyrical is almost synonymous with *lyric*, but is also used more loosely to describe a general mood of euphoria:

She became quite lyrical in her praises.

M

-m-, -mm- Single-syllable words ending in *m* double it before suffixes beginning with a vowel if the *m* is preceded by a single vowel:

crammed, ramming, drummer, slimmest.

If it is preceded by two vowels or a vowel and an r the *m* is not doubled:

aiming, doomed, roomy, charming.

In words of more than one syllable the same rule applies as for single-syllable words if the last syllable is stressed:

overbrimming, undimmed.

Otherwise they do not double the *m*:

systematic, envenomed, ransoming, victimize, emblematic.

However, words ending in *-gram* do double the *m*:

diagrammatic, epigrammatic.

madam, madame *Madam* is the polite form of address for a woman. *Madame*, the French equivalent of the English *Mrs*, has the plural *mesdames*, which is still occasionally used in English as the plural of *madam*.

magic, magical Although the meanings of *magic* and *magical* are to a considerable extent interchangeable, a distinction can be made. *Magic* is almost exclusively concerned with the realm of the supernatural and is usually placed before the noun:

A magic carpet, a magic wand, magic forces.

Magical, on the other hand, is used mainly attributively (that is, following the verb) and tends to be employed more loosely to mean 'like magic':

The change was magical. The twilight appeared magical. A magical moment. A magical voice.

Mahomet, Mohammed *Mahomet* is the traditional English spelling of the name of the founder of Islam. In recent years this has been giving way to *Mohammed*, which has the merit of being closer in pronunciation to what the Arabs call him. The purists insist on *Mahammad* since the vowels *e* and *o* do not exist in Arabic, but *Mohammed* seems to be the most acceptable form for the time being. Similarly *Mohammedans* must now be preferred to *Mahometans*.

main clause In a sentence containing several clauses the main clause is the basic sentence, on which the other clauses depend, and which can stand by itself:

When they arrived, although it was blowing fiercely, the sun was shining brightly.

In the above sentence *the sun was shining brightly* is the main clause.

major This word has lost most of its original force as a comparative but is in danger of being overworked because of its popularity in some quarters. It is frequently used when such words as *chief*, *principal* or *important* would have been more suitable.

majority This has several senses and it is important to distinguish between them. First of all *majority* is used to mean most or the numerically greater part:

His work makes an appeal to the majority of mankind.

It should not, however, be used of something which is not divisible numerically. Do not say:

The majority of this book is unreadable.

Majority also means a group of voters in agreement forming more than half the total number:

The majority decided to go ahead with their reforms.

Finally *majority* is the number by which votes cast for the leading candidate exceed those cast for the next in line:

His majority was so small as to be barely useful.

In this use of *majority* it is always followed by a singular verb, but in the other examples listed above it may be followed by either a singular or plural verb. The verb is normally plural when it refers to a collection of individuals.

malapropism This is the misapplication or misuse of words which have a similar sound or spelling but are widely divergent in meaning, usually producing a comical result:

The patient was to have an explanatory (read *exploratory*) operation.

male, manly, masculine *Male* is always used with reference to sex, whether of human beings or other forms of life:

Male animals in herds protect the females.

Manly means possessing the noblest qualities to be found in man:

His manly show of defiance in the face of adversity was an inspiration to us.

Masculine refers to those qualities that are supposed to be characteristic of the male sex:

He was noted for his masculine enthusiasm for the outdoor life.

mandatary, mandatory When used as nouns both words mean a person holding a mandate, the first being the more common form. However, when used as an adjective *mandatory* means 'obligatory' or 'permitting no option':

Attendance at the union meeting is mandatory.

mankind *Mankind* is always followed by a verb in the singular:

Mankind has not tolerated such treatment in the past.

mannered *Well-mannered* and *ill-mannered* are preferred by some authorities to *good-mannered* and *bad-mannered*, but the latter two seem to be steadily gaining ground.

many a This phrase is always used with a singular verb, although *many* by itself always requires the plural:

Many a good man has been ruined in this way.

marginal This has become such a favourite with some writers, who use it to mean 'slight', 'slightest' or 'small', that it is in danger of losing its basic sense. *Marginal* means close to a border, edge or dividing line, and so uncertain. Thus it is correct to talk about *a marginal constituency*, whose voters are likely to choose their candidate by a narrow margin.

marquess, marquis Both spellings are acceptable, but *marquess* has now established itself as the most popular amongst the English nobility who hold that rank.

marry see **wed**

marten, martin The *marten* is a North American mammal. *Martin* is the name given to any of various swallows.

mask, masque A *mask* is a covering for the face, especially one worn as a disguise. A *masque* was in times past a form of entertainment consisting of pantomime, dancing and song. It can also be spelt *mask*.

massive This is another word which has unfortunately become rather too fashionable in its figurative sense. It is used where a whole host of other adjectives would be more suitable, including *huge*, *widespread*, *vigorous*, *intense* and *powerful*. Avoid it in such phrases as:

> A massive assault on the problems of the Third World

and find a more fitting alternative.

masterful, masterly At one time these words were very close in meaning and there is still some confusion about their correct use. *Masterful* means showing the qualities of a master or dominant person, authoritative or domineering:

> The prime minister showed a masterful disregard for his opponent's angry protests.

Masterly means showing a high degree of skill in the performance of any activity:

The young pianist gave a masterly display of his talents.

materialize This word has been much overworked in recent years. It has several useful meanings including 'to assume material form' or 'to make physically perceptible'. It should not be used as a substitute for *happen*, *occur* or *take place*.

mathematics There is some doubt whether this should be followed by a plural or singular verb. It is generally followed by a singular verb when it is thought of as a science:

Mathematics is an important item in the school curriculum.

The plural is frequently used when reference is made to someone's specific knowledge of the subject:

She is good at games but her mathematics are weak.

Even here, however, there is uncertainty and the verb after *mathematics* may be influenced by a following singular noun:

Mathematics is his weak point.

maunder, meander These words are often incorrectly taken to be alternative forms of each other. *Maunder* means 'to speak in a rambling, foolish or incoherent way'. *Meander* means 'to wander aimlessly' or 'to proceed by a winding or indirect course'.

maxim A *maxim* is the expression of a general truth, especially in relation to conduct. [See also *aphorism*]

maximize This is another word which has suffered from overexposure. It means 'to increase to the greatest possible amount', but is often used as a substitute for *increase*, *enlarge*, *heighten*, etc.

may, might *May* is an auxiliary verb which is used to express possibility, probability or permission:

I may be able to work on Friday (possibility or probability).

May I go to the cinema tonight? (permission).

It is important not to confuse *may* with *can*, which implies ability or power to do something, although in colloquial speech *can* is frequently substituted for *may* in the sense of permission. *Might* is the past tense of *may* and is used with the same meanings:

He said he might be able to work on Friday.
The child asked if she might go to the cinema.

When *may* is used in the past tense with a perfect infinitive, it implies that there is still a possibility of something being so:

The prisoner may have been captured.

However, if the sentence is changed to:

The prisoner might have been captured,

then the possibility of his being captured existed in the past but does so no longer.

maybe, may be This is finding increasing favour as a synonym for *perhaps*. When used as a verb it must be written as two words:

It may be that I shall have to stay late.

me The use of *me* instead of *I* in such expressions as *it's me* and *it was me* now appears to have been accepted by most authorities. However, when *it's me* is followed by a clause beginning with *who*, educated speakers tend to revert to *I*:

It was I who discovered that the lock was broken.

means When this signifies 'resources or income', it takes a plural verb:

My means are not sufficient for a holiday abroad.

When it means 'method' it can be either singular or plural:

They found a new means of communication.
Several means are being tried out.

meantime, meanwhile When these words are used as adverbs *meanwhile* is generally preferred. However, of the expressions *in the meanwhile* and *in the meantime* the latter is more common.

medieval, mediaeval The first spelling is now more usual, although many people still prefer *mediaeval*.

medium, mediums, media When *medium* is used to mean a person through whom some supernatural agency is manifested the plural is always *mediums*. In other senses of the word either *mediums* or *media* are acceptable, but *media* seems to be gaining ground, no doubt because of its status as a vogue word.

meet, meet with To *meet* generally means 'to come into contact with, to encounter, become acquainted with':

I met the new teacher at the station.

To *meet with* has the sense of 'to undergo, experience or be subject to':

His efforts to improve matters met with much criticism.

melted, molten *Melted* is the past participle of *melt*. *Molten*, which is an alternative form, is now used only as an adjective applied to substances which are considered hard to melt: *melted butter* but *molten metal*, *molten lead*.

mendacity, mendicity *Mendacity* means 'the practice of lying'. *Mendicity* is 'the practice or condition of being a beggar'.

mental, mentality Both these words have acquired perjorative meanings. The basic sense of *mental* is 'pertaining to the mind', but it also means 'foolish or mad', although this particular slang use appears to be dying out. *Mentality* has undergone a similar downgrading and is frequently employed in a derogatory sense to describe a certain kind of character or disposition:

He had the mentality of a man who was unable to think for himself.

metaphor A *metaphor* is a figure of speech in which a term or phrase is applied to something to which it cannot literally refer in order to suggest a resemblance. In such phrases as:

He proved to be a tower of strength, she spoke with tongue in cheek, he made an acid remark,

a man cannot literally be a tower nor a woman literally speak with her tongue in her cheek nor a remark be literally composed of acid. However, we accept such literary conventions because when properly used they enrich the language we speak and write. Pitfalls lie in employing the same metaphor too often, so that it becomes a cliché, such as *leave no stone unturned*, *grinding to a halt*, and many others. Another danger is the mixed metaphor, in which two or more images are confused, often with ludicrous results:

Now that we have buttered our bread we must lie on it.

There is also the hazard of moving from a literal meaning to a metaphorical one:

The even distribution of material has been made possible by the reduction of bottlenecks.

meticulous This means 'solicitous or finical about minute details'. Since it always implies excessive or undue care it should not be used as a synonym for such words as *careful*, *scrupulous* or *exact*, which have a more favourable connotation.

metre, meter These two words are sometimes the source of confusion. *Metre* is a basic unit of linear measurement now used in most countries. It is also used to mean 'a poetic measure or the arrangement of words in regularly patterned lines of verse'. When referring to linear measurement *metre* has the adjective *metric*. When it applies to verse the adjective is *metrical*. A *meter* is an instrument that measures and is frequently found in compound words like *thermometer*, *tachometer*, etc. This spelling is also used for the various poetic *metres*, as in *hexameter*, *pentameter*, etc.

Middle East This rather vague term was at one time used to describe lands as far east as Afghanistan, India, Tibet and Burma. It now tends to be confined to the countries at and beyond the eastern end of the Mediterranean, including Egypt, Syria and the Arabian Peninsula.

might see **may**

mileage, milage Some authorities claim that the *e* in *mileage* is an unnecessary one, since it does not affect the pronunciation. However, the spelling *mileage* is the preferred one in most dictionaries.

militate, mitigate *Militate* (*against*) means 'to work or operate against':

Unforeseen circumstances militated against the success of our plans.

Mitigate means 'to lessen, moderate or make less severe' but is quite frequently used by mistake for *militate*:

This unfortunate incident ought not to mitigate (read *militate*) against my chances of getting the job.

It is used correctly as follows:

Her gentle words successfully mitigated his anger.

million This is generally spelt without an *s* when it stands for a definite number:

Six million men; more than two million died.

When used vaguely to indicate a large amount, it usually adds an *s*:

Millions of times, thousands of millions of people.

The *s* is also used when *million* refers to money, even when a definite number is involved:

They estimated that the property was worth four millions.

minimal This means 'pertaining to the least possible or smallest'. It is a popular word and tends to be overworked, being frequently used where *slight* or *small* would be more suitable.

minimize see **diminish**

minimum This is another vogue word which is commonly misused. It means 'the least quantity or amount possible' and is often used where *a little* or *a small amount* would be more acceptable, as in:

The child gave only a minimum of trouble.

minority Like *majority* this occasionally causes some confusion. One meaning is 'the smaller part or number', or 'a number forming less than half the whole':

This film was appreciated only by a minority of those present.

Do not use *minority* to mean 'a few' or 'a very small number of' as in:

The police were called to investigate only a minority of cases.

Remember that a *minority* can be quite a large number, provided it is less than 50 per cent of a total. *Minority* is also used in the sense of a smaller group or party as opposed to a *majority*:

The minority on the council protested in vain against the new housing programme.

Minority may be followed by either a singular or plural verb, but the verb is usually plural when *minority* is considered as a collection of individuals:

A minority of the shareholders have strong objections.

mis- It is now normal practice not to hyphenate words made with this prefix, even when the word it is attached to already begins with an *s*:

misspell, misstatement.

misplaced modifiers These are words whose connection with the word they modify is not clear, thus leading to ambiguity. They include adverbs such as *only*, *nearly*, *hardly*, *scarcely*, *just*, *even* and *quite*. In a sentence like:

He only told her what he had seen

it is not clear what the speaker means. If he means

He told her what he had seen (and nothing else),

then the sentence should be recast as follows:

He told her only what he had seen.

[See also *only*]

Miss, Misses The correct plural of *Miss Brown* is the *Misses Brown*. However, although it may still be used on formal occasions the *Miss Browns* is now the usual plural.

mistrust see **distrust**

modifiers, dangling see **unattached participle**

Mohammed see **Mahomet**

momentary, momentous Despite similar spellings these adjectives have very different meanings. *Momentary* means 'lasting only very briefly':

He caught a momentary glimpse of a very beautiful woman.

Momentous means 'of great importance or having far-reaching consequences':

His decision was a momentous one for the future of the world.

monarchical, monarchic, monarchal *Monarchical* and *monarchic* are virtually interchangeable in their meaning 'of a monarch or characterized by monarchy', although *monarchical* is the much commoner form. *Monarchal* means 'befitting or having the status of a monarch' and carries an aura of pomp about it.

moneys, monies Both forms exist as the plural of *money* but *moneys* is the generally more acceptable form.

monogram, monograph A *monogram* is a character or device consisting of two or more letters combined or interlaced to make a design. A *monograph* is a treatise on a particular subject.

monologue, soliloquy Both words refer to a 'prolonged talk or discourse made by a single speaker'. However, whereas a *monologue* is usually intended to be heard, *soliloquy* means talking to oneself when alone or thinking out loud, regardless of whether anybody may be present. A *monologue* also means a form of dramatic entertainment by a single speaker.

moral, morale *Moral* means concerned with right conduct or the distinction between right and wrong:

It is impossible to ignore moral considerations in your treatment of people.

Morale, which is derived from a French word, *moral*, means the condition of mind which enables people to show courage, confidence or cheerfulness under difficult conditions:

He was amazed at the high morale of troops under fire.

morals see **ethics**

more The expression *more than one* is followed by a singular verb, despite being to all intents and purposes plural:

More than one boy was killed in the accident.

Otherwise verbs used with *more than* are in the plural:

More than ten men are involved in the plot.

Be careful not to try and form comparisons using *more* with adjectives which are already comparative such as *more prettier*, or with adjectives which cannot take a comparative form, such as *more superior*, *more unique* or *more perfect*.

mortgagor, mortgagee These words are often mixed up. The *mortgagor* is the person who mortgages his property, *i.e.*, the one who pledges his property in order to receive the loan. The *mortgagee* is the person to whom the property is mortgaged, *i.e.*, the one who lends money on the security of an estate.

Moslem, Muslim *Moslem*, the more traditional English spelling, is being displaced by *Muslim*, which is in fact a more accurate representation of the Arabic pronunciation. Both *Moslem* and *Muslim* add an *-s* to form the plural.

most, mostly Both *most* and *mostly* are adverbs and *mostly* is sometimes wrongly used in place of *most*:

It was the cyclist who was most (not *mostly*) to blame for the accident.

Mostly means 'for the most part' and is correctly used as follows:

By evening the work was mostly completed.

Most is also used in colloquial speech as a substitute for *very*, but is best avoided in writing:

He gave a most interesting account of his travels.

motivate, motivation These words first came into prominence in the domain of psychology and psychiatry, where they have a useful function to perform. However their increasing popularity has been at the expense of more suitable words such as *move* or *impulse*.

mow The past tense of this verb is *mowed* and the past participle *mown* or *mowed*. When the past participle is used as an adjective *mown* is the preferred form: *mown grass*.

MS, MSS *MS* is the contracted form for *manuscript* and *MSS* for *manuscripts*. However, since *MS* is always pronounced 'manuscript', it should be preceded by *a* and not *an*.

much, very As a general rule *much* is used with participles and *very* with adjectives: *much admired*, *much emphasized*, but *very bad*, *very pleasant*, etc. Some participles which have lost their verbal force are treated as adjectives and take *very*:

very pleased, very tired, very interested.

much more, much less These phrases are frequently a source of confusion. The general rule is that *much more* is used in an affirmative sentence:

It is hard enough to understand him, much more sympathize with him.

Much less frequently occurs in sentences which in fact require *much more* and many people would be tempted to use it in the above example. *Much less*, however, must be used only with negative sentences:

We did not even hear them, much less see them.

mucus, mucous Remember that *mucus* is the noun and *mucous* the adjective, *mucus* being defined as 'a secretion of the *mucous* membranes'.

mulatto A *mulatto* (plural *mulattos* or *mulattoes*) is the offspring of parents one of whom is white and the other a Negro. [See also *creole*, *quadroon*]

Muslim see Moslem

must This auxiliary verb implies necessity, obligation, or compulsion. Originally a past tense, it is now used only in the present:

Soldiers must obey orders.

Weaker obligations are expressed by the auxiliaries *ought to* and *should*. [See also *ought*, *shall*]

mute e The spelling of words or suffixes formed from words ending in mute *e* (silent or unpronounced *e*) has always been a source of confusion and uncertainty. The rules, to which there are unfortunately many exceptions, are as follows.

A mute *e* at the end of a word is retained before a suffix beginning with a consonant:

tamely, homeless, blameworthy, judgement (also spelt judgment), acknowledgement (also spelt acknowledgment).

but note the exceptions *truly*, *duly*.

A mute *e* at the end of a word is dropped before a suffix beginning with a vowel: *loving*, *proving whitish*. However, *e* is retained to prevent *c* or *g* becoming hard before a following *a* or *o*:

changeable, changeover, peaceable, traceable.

There are, in addition, a number of words such as *rateable* and *ratable*, *mileage* and *milage* in which alternate spellings exist. [See also *spelling*]

mutual see **common, reciprocal**

myth see **legend**

N

-n-, -nn- In a single-syllabled word followed by a suffix a final *n* is doubled if the vowel before it is a short one, as in *sun*, *sunny*, but not if the vowel is long, such as in *yawn*, *yawning*. With words of more than one syllable the same rules apply when the stress is on the second syllable, as in *beginning*, *refrained*, *remaining* or *buffoonery*, but the *n* does not double even after a short vowel when the stress is on the first syllable, as in *deafened*, *threatening* or *kittenish*.

naive This is now the accepted anglicized spelling of the French word *naïve* (masculine *naïf*). The nearest English meaning to it is ingenuous, unsophisticated or showing natural simplicity. It is a useful word, since there is no exact equivalent in English.

napkin, serviette *Serviette* is a term frowned on by many people as a genteel euphemism for *napkin* which, though an honest word, has a wider application with some less pleasant associations.

nationalize, naturalize To *nationalize* is to bring under the control or ownership of a nation, and is a term applied chiefly to land or industries. To *naturalize* means to confer the rights and privileges of citizenship on a foreign national. It is also applied to the introduction and successful adaptation of animals and plants to a region so that they thrive as if in their original natural surroundings.

native(s) Applied as a generic term to foreign nationals, especially those of Africa and Asia, the word is offensive, implying a patronage reminiscent of the days of colonialism. It is acceptable, however, if used in its specific sense, which could not be interpreted as disparaging:

He returned to his native land (he returned to the country where he was born),

and:

He was a native of France/Britain/Ireland/India,

or:

Only a native (of this town) would know his way through the back streets.

nature This is one of those words adopted by lovers of verbosity to deck out their adjectives:

It was a journey of an exploratory nature

would be more simply expressed as:

It was an exploratory journey,

and:

The dress she wore was of a diaphanous and flimsy nature

simply means:

She wore a diaphanous, flimsy dress.

But in the example:

The nature of his illness was never disclosed

the word is being used in its proper context.

naught, nought *Naught* is the archaic form, occasionally used in a poetical context, and *nought* is used in a strictly numerical sense:

Naught availed her, though she begged for mercy

and:

It's like a game of noughts and crosses.

near, nearly The adverbial use of *near*, for *nearly*, meaning 'almost', 'all but', is rarely used, except in dialect:

He was near exhausted

is more likely to be rendered as:

He was nearly exhausted

or:

He was near exhaustion.

nearby, near by *Nearby* is an adjective:

He called at the nearby farm for milk

and *near by* an adverb:

He called at the farm near by for milk.

But in modern usage *nearby* may also be accepted in an adverbial sense in place of *near by*.

Near East This is no longer a specific term, but a loose geographical definition incorporating the Balkan States, Egypt and the countries of South West Asia (Turkey, Lebanon, Syria, Israel, Jordan, Saudi Arabia, etc.).

need Confusion sometimes arises with this word, which occurs both as a verb and as a noun. The verb appears in:

He needs a new coat,

and:

A new coat is needed for winter.

In the construction:

He needs to have a new coat

the verb takes the infinitive in the usual way, but the negative:

He does not need to buy new clothes

can be expressed:

He need buy no new clothes.

Here the verb becomes an auxiliary like *must* and does not require the *to*. This is also true of a question:

Need he buy new clothes?

In the sentence:

He needs must purchase a coat

needs is an adverb meaning 'of necessity'. It is an archaic term used only occasionally in this context.

As a noun, *need* appears as:

He has need of a new coat

or:

He is in need of a new coat.

need, want *Need* is used in an objective sense; *want* is subjective. To become educated, a child may *need* to go to school. At the same time, the child may not *want* to go to school.
Colloquially *want* is sometimes substituted for *need* in the sense of 'ought to':

He wants to be careful he does not lose his wallet.

negatives Before condemning the double negative out of hand, it should be remembered that in some countries a repetition of negatives throughout a sentence serves to strengthen the negation, and at one time our own language followed a similar course. However, in modern usage two negatives are regarded as cancelling each other out and resulting in a positive:

I don't know nothing about it

means that I *do* know something about it. Even in educated speech it is very easy to slip unwittingly into a contradiction:

She said she had found nothing to make her doubt that it wasn't true.

The negative *that it wasn't true* should be a positive *was true* for the sentence to make its point.
If the first part of a sentence is negative, care must be taken that the rest of the sentence is consistent with the writer's intention:

No men will be recruited during the winter months but will be signed on in early spring.

The second part of the sentence has no subject of its own and is referring back to *no men*, which was clearly not intended. A fresh subject is needed – perhaps 'new recruits'.

Nobody wanted to go home by bus and agreed to take a taxi instead.

Nobody agreed? Again, a new subject is needed: *everyone* agreed.
The placing of the negative is important. In:

It is not believed to be a matter of choosing between fact and speculation but of making up our minds on the basis of probabilities

the main verb *it is believed* applies to the whole sentence and the negative to part of the sentence only. Here, by governing the main clause it reverses the meaning of the second part of the sentence:

It is not believed to be a matter of . . . making up our minds on the basis of probabilities.

The sentence should read:

It is believed to be not a matter of choosing between fact and speculation but of making up our minds on the basis of probabilities.

neither . . . nor If both the subjects joined by this correlative conjunction are singular, they will take a singular verb:

Neither the boy nor his dog was harmed.

If one of the subjects is singular and one plural, the verb may agree with the nearer subject:

Neither the captain nor his men were prepared for the attack

or:

Neither the men nor their captain was prepared for the attack.

However, it is more usual and sounds more natural to place the plural noun next to the verb and to use a plural verb, as in the first example.

More than two subjects may be included:

The answer was neither animal nor vegetable nor mineral,

but in:

Neither children, nor cats nor dogs nor any other kind of pet is welcome here.

It should read cats *or* dogs, since the meaning implies one category in which these terms are alternatives to each other and are not therefore correlated separately to the other subjects in the sentence.

Netherlands, The This is the proper name for the kingdom of Holland, the adjective for which is Dutch.

never Literally, this is 'not ever', and is used to emphasize a negative sentence:

I should never have allowed him to go.

This is stronger than:

I should not have allowed him to go.

However, it must be remembered that as a negative it should not be used with another one:

Nobody, however hard he tries, can never believe what I've been through

is therefore incorrect. For *never* substitute *ever*. The same rule applies in:

I promise I shan't never do it again

which would be better expressed as:

I promise I shall never do it again.

never so, ever so Once accepted in normal speech, *never so* was replaced by *ever so* in a construction such as:

She refused to listen to his protestations, spoke he never so gently.

This construction, too, has fallen out of use and today *ever so* occurs chiefly as a colloquial expression, frowned on as a vulgarism, and used in the sense of 'very':

I am ever so sorry.

nice One of the original meanings of this word was minute, fine or subtle, as of a distinction, or requiring delicacy or precision. Its commonest use today is as a blanket term meaning amiably pleasant, agreeable, delightful, or refined. It has been so overused and its meaning so broadened that it is almost valueless – ironic that a word once implying precision should now represent the opposite, and provide us with a vague, bland expression of pleasure. As a term of approval it is therefore best avoided.

nom de plume These French words, of which the literal translation is 'pen name', are the term for a writer who wishes to remain anonymous and uses a false name. The true French term for the same thing is *nom de guerre* (literally, 'war name').

nomenclature This is not just another more impressive word for 'name', but a word meaning a set or system of names of terms, such as is used in scientific or other fields requiring classificatory terminology. For example:

A club has just been started under the nomenclature of the Rosebery Committee Youth Association

is incorrect. A proper context is:

Linnaeus established the binomial system of scientific nomenclature.

non- A negative form which is often too easily used in place of a genuine word. There are many examples where it has a legitimate use because there is no single word as an alternative:

Because of the non-appearance of the star, the show was cancelled.

But in:

His non-positive approach was a handicap,

'negative' would be a preferable substitute.

none This pronoun may take a singular or a plural verb, according to which sense is most logical. So in a sentence such as:

He made us all stand up in turn; none of us was spared

none means 'not one' and therefore indicates a singular verb. But in:

Of the events which followed none are worth recording

none here means 'not any', referring to the events, and should therefore be followed by a plural verb. But applied to a collective term such as an amount or quantity, *none* in the sense of 'not any' would take a singular verb:

None of the money was spent.

non-restrictive see **restrictive**

nonsense The idiomatic use of this word:

This is nonsense

has long been accepted. What has been less readily assimilated is the use of the word with the indefinite article:

He made a nonsense of the test and had to take it again.

But events have overtaken the purists and this development of the idiom is now in such common use that its incursion into the language is unlikely to be repelled.

non-sequitur Literally, 'it does not follow'. This term means a statement or argument which does not relate to the premise which has gone before it:

She is a beautiful girl, so she is going to be a film star.

The second statement is not necessarily a consequence of the first.

nor Following neither, *nor* should always be used, just as *or* should always follow either. But in a negative sentence where the verb governs the whole sentence *nor* can have the effect of a double negative:

The purpose of education is not to stuff the heads of children with facts, nor with the doctrines nor prejudices of their teachers.

In this sentence *or* should be substituted.

However, if the verb with its negative applies to only one part of a sentence the second part must be reinforced by the negative *nor*:

He had little sense of achievement at the end of the day's work, nor did he have much in the way of material reward.

Where the verb is positive and the negative is attached to only one part of the sentence *nor* is attached to the other negative alternatives:

The use of a car is justified not just on the grounds of seniority, nor of distance nor time saving, but simply on account of expediency.

northerly see **easterly**

nostalgia, homesickness *Nostalgia* is defined as a longing and desire for home, family and friends. It has also acquired the additional meaning beyond homesickness of a yearning for times that have passed and this is the sense in which it is increasingly used. The meaning of *homesickness* is confined to the longing and desire for home, family and friends.

not There is nothing wrong with the idiomatic construction:

All women are not fools

but it is simpler to say:

Not all women are fools,

and easier to grasp the meaning at first glance.

The deliberate use of two negatives in a construction to convey a positive message is a peculiarly British quirk, having the effect of a gross understatement:

He exerted a not inconsiderable amount of energy in screwing up his courage to pop the question,

and:

She was not wholly unprepared for it.

Too much of this kind of irony can, however, easily become tedious. Used in an exclamation:

Not you again!

the force of the negative is in its positive meaning, equivalent to saying, 'So it's you again!'

Other idiomatic constructions where the sentence may be started with *not* are:

Not that I was one of them, but I understood how they felt,

and:

He called for volunteers and was greeted with silence. Not a man replied.

notable, noted *Notable* is worthy of notice, distinguished or prominent. *Noted* is celebrated or famous. In general, *notable* is applied to events or things and *noted* to people.

not only . . . but also A common error with this type of correlative conjunction is that it is often misplaced:

She must realize that not only are we interested in her present career but also in her future prospects

should be rephrased to read:

She must realize that we are interested not only in her present career but also in her future prospects.

The second sentence is better balanced. Each of the correlating conjunctions *not only . . . but also* is followed by a matching phrase, and the verb (*are interested*) is common to both. The important point to bear in mind is that the verb should come before the two correlating phrases since it governs both.

If one subject is singular and the other plural, the verb may agree with the subject nearest to it, though to avoid awkwardness it might be preferable to rephrase the sentence:

Not only the pupils but also their teacher has the right to express an opinion.

The more usual and natural-sounding way of expressing this would be to transpose the singular and plural nouns and use a plural verb:

Not only their teacher but also the pupils have the right to express an opinion.

notorious, famous *Notorious* means widely and publicly known for unfavourable reasons:

With his notorious weakness for drink, he soon spent all his money.

Famous is celebrated, renowned or well known for favourable reasons, though it may be used ironically:

One of the most famous of all generals was the Duke of Wellington.

It can also be used colloquially to mean excellent or first rate:

We had a famous night out on Saturday.

noun The modern tendency to use nouns as adjectives is deplored by some writers, especially in cases where there is a perfectly good adjective already in existence:

His home circumstances were unsatisfactory.

Domestic would be a better adjective than *home*. But since, as in that example, the alternative –

The circumstances at his home were unsatisfactory

– is often lengthier, there is quite a strong argument in support of the noun adjective, provided it does not result in ambiguity. This is especially liable to occur in newspaper headlines:

Police Chief Focus of Attack

Is this referring to the chief of police? Or are the police the chief focus? The ambiguity in such a headline has done its work, however, if it makes us look twice. The danger is that this kind of headline journalese tends to be used excessively in everyday speech. *The world food situation*, *the railway workers' strike*, *the Government Services Department report* – the proliferation of noun adjectives appear in longer and longer phrases until they require unravelling to make sense. A judicious use of the word 'of' would simplify them all.

number A common mistake is to use a plural verb when the subject is singular but the rest of the sentence is plural:

The attraction of the birds are chiefly in their songs.

It is *the attraction* that is the true subject of this sentence and the verb should therefore be singular. When two single subjects are offered as alternatives, the verb must remain singular, because they are independent of each other:

He must decide whether his wife or his sweetheart takes precedence in his affections.

But if one subject is singular and the other plural, the sentence can either be rephrased to avoid awkwardness, or the verb can follow the nearest subject:

He must decide whether his wife or his children come first.

Nouns of multitude are those words such as 'group' or 'party' which represent a collection of people as a single unit, and can be treated as either singular or plural. Where the group acts as one person, a singular verb may be preferable, but if it is thought of as a collection of individuals the plural form is better:

The committee decided it would meet again on the following day,

but:

The union were ready to call a full-scale strike.

The word *number* itself takes a plural verb if it suggests several units:

A number of children were playing in the snow,

but a singular verb if it refers to an amount or a total:

The number of people going abroad for holidays is higher than ever before.

numbers In general reading matter, numbers and fractions should be expressed in words, not in figures, unless particularly long or complicated. Twenty thousand may be written out, but it is preferable to present 20,345 in figures. Time may be expressed either way. Dates should be written in figures. Except in dates, where the name of the month is included, words and figures should never be mixed, and a sentence should never begin with a figure. This should always be spelt out.

O

O, Oh The interjection *O* is used only in poetry. *Oh* occurs in all other cases, usually followed by a comma, except in phrases such as 'Oh dear!', or 'Oh no!':

Oh, look at that lovely moon!

object, objective The words both mean an end towards which efforts are directed, or something aimed at, but *object* has several wider meanings as well, other than abstract ones, and can also denote purpose:

The object of the game is to see who can get the highest number of goals.

Originally a military term, *objective* is best reserved for a goal to be aimed at, an aim to be achieved:

His first objective is to win the support of the people, his next to win the support of the Government.

obliqueness, obliquity Both words mean the state of being oblique, but *obliquity* is more often used in a figurative sense meaning moral delinquency or mental perversity.

oblivious The meaning of this word is forgetful, without remembrance, not unaware or unconscious, with which it is often equated:

He was oblivious of the anger expressed on the faces of those behind him.

This is incorrect. *Unconscious* would be a more appropriate word here.

Oblivious to the rain that cascaded down, he watched, fascinated, as the bird fed her young.

This example is nearer the true meaning, but strictly speaking the correct preposition is *of*, not *to*.

obnoxious, noxious The original meaning of *obnoxious* is exposed or liable to harm or evil, but the more widely used sense today is objectionable, offensive or odious.
Noxious is harmful to health or, in a figurative sense, morally harmful, pernicious.

observance, observation *Observance* is the action of conforming to, obeying or following, or a celebration by proper procedure, ceremony or rite:

The observance of a cease-fire is vital to the peace negotiations.

Observation is the act of noticing, perceiving or watching; that which is learnt by observing. It can also mean a remark or comment:

Your observation about the weather could have a bearing on my own observations made in the bird sanctuary last spring.

In this example the word has been used in two of its senses.

obsolete, obsolescent Obsolete means no longer in use, discarded, out of date:

The hansom cab is an obsolete vehicle.

Obsolescent is tending to become out of date, passing out of use:

The piston-engined plane is obsolescent.

Obsolete is a stage beyond *obsolescent*.

obstacle, impediment *Obstacle* is something that stands in the way of progress:

Her mother's opposition to the marriage was an obstacle still to be overcome.

An *impediment* implies a physical defect, such as a speech disorder, an obstruction or hindrance:

Lame though he was, his impediment did not prevent him from undertaking a strenuous job.

occupant, occupier An *occupant* is one who is occupying a place, seat or compartment. An *occupier* is one who occupies living or office premises. The first suggests a temporary occupation, the second, one of a more permanent nature.

occur see **happen**

oculist, optician An *oculist* is a doctor who specializes in examination and treatment of the eye; an ophthalmologist. An *optician* is one who makes and sells glasses according to the prescriptions of an oculist. However, although he is not medically qualified an *optician* may also be competent to prescribe glasses for correcting defects of vision.

odious, odorous *Odious* is hateful or detestable. *Odorous* is having or diffusing an odour, especially a fragrant one.

-o(e)s Most of the commonest words ending in *-o*, such as *tomato*, *potato*, *hero*, *cargo*, take an *-e* in forming the plural: *potatoes*, *heroes*, *tomatoes*. So do words of a single syllable, such as *does* in 'does and don'ts', *noes* in 'yeses and noes' and *goes*. Words which occur less frequently in the plural, shortened words like *photo*, words in which the *-o* is preceded by a vowel, foreign words, especially of Italian origin, and many long words ending in *-o* do not take an additional *-e-* but invariably finish in *-os* in the plural. Some examples are:

concertos, photos, memos, folios, manifestos.

of This preposition is sometimes carelessly used when, in a complex sentence, a clause is introduced by one preposition and requires linking to another. A secondary use of *of* has perhaps just occurred and it is mistakenly repeated in place of the correct word:

She will be of most value to us for her knowledge of French and *of* her ability to speak fluently and clearly in public.

For should be substituted here for *of*.

It is also sometimes misplaced:

His chief ambition was the acquisition of a good job and of finding a comfortable home.

This should be amended to *the finding of* a comfortable home.

Never say *off of*. This is a vulgarism which is quite unacceptable:

He took it off of me

should be:

He took it from me.

official, officious The adjective *official* means pertaining to an office of trust or authority, authorized or possessing authority. *Officious* is pressing one's services upon others obtrusively:

I don't mind being told what to do by an official steward, but I refuse to be bossed by an officious underling!

O.K. This is a colloquialism that is universally accepted either in its initial form or spelt out as *okay*, but it should not be used in formal speech or writing. In a commercial context it is acceptable as an adjective, verb and noun.

olden This adjective is used only in the limited context of *olden days*.

Old English, Anglo-Saxon Both terms refer to the English language of the period before A.D. 1100.

older see **elder**

Olympian, Olympic *Olympian* is pertaining to Mount Olympus, home of the gods of ancient Greece. *Olympic* refers primarily to the Olympic games, though it can also mean the same as *Olympian*.

-on Some words ending in *-on* which are derived from Greek take *-a* in the plural, for example *criterion* and *criteria*, *ganglion* and *ganglia*, *phenomenon* and *phenomena*. With others, though an *-a* suffix would not be wrong, the English *-s* ending is usually employed, as in *skeletons*. Other words such as *tendon*, *nylon* or *siphon* take a different form in Greek and therefore should always be given the *-s* plural in English.

one Words compounded of *one* should be written:

anyone, everyone, someone, oneself, no one.

Some accidents can happen with the use of this pronoun:

One of the trains which runs to Waterloo has been cancelled.

This is wrong. The pronoun *which* is referring to the trains, so the verb of the subordinate clause should be in the plural:

One of the trains which run to Waterloo has been cancelled.

Another incorrect stentence is:

One of the longest, if not the longest, song was eliminated.

If the sentence is reduced to its bare essentials it will be seen to read: *One . . . was eliminated*. One what? *Of the longest . . . song*. This must clearly be amended to *songs*.

One may also be used as a pronoun either numerically:

There were one or two things I had to do,

or impersonally, standing in for a person or people in general:

One must work in order to live,

or as a 'false' personal pronoun, replacing the first person *I*:

One likes to feel one has been able to make a tiny contribution to this marvellous cause.

This last practice is condemned as an affectation and should be avoided.

If *one* has been used in a sentence it must not be changed halfway through to another pronoun:

It was bad enough to have one's shortcomings exposed, but to have to admit ignorance on my own pet subject was humiliating.

Either *one's* should be replaced by *my*, or *my* should give way to *one's* again.

One's is the only pronoun to take the apostrophe in the possessive case.

one another This is the correct form to use when referring to more than two people, for whom *each other* (*q.v.*) would be appropriate:

The two of them eyed each other suspiciously,

but:

All the members of the team helped one another to perfect their tactics.

However, in common usage *each other* is often used colloquially in this context.

In the possessive case it must be remembered that *one another* remains in the singular:

They helped to perfect one another's tactics.

ongoing This is a colloquial term which seems to have originated in the United States. It has become a vogue word meaning 'continuing', which is freely used in commercial circles in Britain. Provided it is not destroyed by overuse, it could become as useful a part of the English language as its opposite number *oncoming*:

The ongoing success of the company's export effort is reflected in the figures.

only This word is perhaps misplaced more frequently than any other. Its position in a sentence governs the entire meaning, as these examples will demonstrate:

Only she was wearing a bikini on the beach (nobody else was).
She was only wearing a bikini on the beach (ambiguous – could be 'Just imagine! That's all she was doing', or she was wearing nothing else, or it was just on the beach that she was wearing a bikini).
She was wearing only a bikini on the beach (and nothing else).
She was wearing a bikini only on the beach (and nowhere else).
She was wearing a bikini on the beach only (and nowhere else; possibly it was the only place where she was wearing anything at all).

It is not always best, however, to be too pedantic. What looks right and seems the position most acceptable in common usage for the sense intended may well be the most suitable, provided the meaning is absolutely clear and unambiguous.

onomatopoeia The formation of a name or word by imitating the sound associated with it: *buzz*, *cuckoo*, *clop*, for example, or of a phrase suggesting the sound:

'. . . murmuring of innumerable bees'.

on to, onto There has been disagreement for a long time between those who prefer to write this as two words and those who believe it should be one, and it remains a matter of choice. When it occurs as a separate adverb suggesting movement and as a preposition it must be regarded as two words, and written separately:

After visiting Coventry, he went on to Birmingham.

Onto should not be used unnecessarily if either *on* or *to* will do alone:

He put his gloves on the table

is quite sufficient. To say:

He put his gloves onto the table

implies that he moved them from somewhere else, and is a more deliberate action. But:

He drove on the motorway

has quite a different meaning from:

He drove onto the motorway,

and to make the distinction when necessary is perfectly valid.

onward, onwards *Onward* is both an adjective and an adverb and is more commonly used than *onwards*, which is an adverb only.

operator, operative An *operator* is a worker skilled in operating a machine. An operative, also a worker, is skilled in some branch of work, especially productive or industrial. *Operative* is a more loosely applied term and it is also a jargon word which, used as an adjective, has come to mean most effective or important:

In any society cooperation and mutual respect are vital to its success, and the operative word is respect.

Such usage is best avoided.

optimistic, pessimistic *Optimistic* was originally used to describe someone who believed that good ultimately predominates over evil, and *pessimistic* someone who thought that everything in the world naturally tends to evil. Both words have extended their meanings considerably. They are now vogue words, *optimistic* having come to mean disposed to take a favourable view of things and *pessimistic*, inclined to take the gloomiest possible view:

I am very optimistic about the Company's prospects for the coming year,

and:

The Chairman takes a pessimistic view about the country's prospects of curbing inflation.

optimum This is another vogue word suffering from overuse, especially in its figurative sense, and consequently in danger of losing its precise meaning – the best or most favourable conditions for the growth or reproduction of an organism. As an adjective it has come to be loosely used to mean 'best':

That model is the optimum in luxury at such a price.

But in the example:

A large, modern factory and up-to-date machinery offer the optimum conditions for successful expansion

there is a good case for it: in a figurative sense, the word is not far from its original meaning.

or In a sentence such as:

I am not old nor stupid

or could equally well be substituted for *nor*. The sentence can be read in two ways – either *I am not old, nor am I stupid*, or *old or stupid* could simply be regarded as interchangeable alternatives, in which case *or* is correct.

Sometimes *or* is incorrectly substituted for *and*:

No advantage or no profit will result from this transaction.

This implies that either there will be no advantage or there will be no profit, but not that there will be neither. *And* should be substituted for *or*, or alternatively it should be rewritten as *no advantage or profit*.

-or Many nouns, particularly those ending in -ate, which are derived from a Latin verb, end in *-or* instead of the English *-er*:

placate, placator; dictate, dictator; liberate, liberator

Others also take the *-or* ending:

collector, protector, director,

and some have alternative endings, *-er* when applied to people and *-or* for inanimate objects:

adapter or adaptor; conveyer or conveyor.

oral see **aural**

ordinance, ordnance An *ordinance* is a decree or command, an authoritative rule or law. *Ordnance* is cannon or artillery, or military weapons of all kinds.

orient, orientate The *Orient* is the name given to the East, applied to countries east of the Mediterranean, from the archaic word *orient* meaning east. It also means the lustre of a pearl. The verb *to orientate* is to place so as to face the east, or to place something in any definite position in relation to compass points or surroundings. It is also sometimes used figuratively. The verb *to orient* means the same thing, but is little used in Britain. In the United States, however, it is preferred.

Oriental, Eastern *Oriental* refers to those lands east of the Mediterranean. *Eastern* can apply to the eastern part of any country or continent. When used as proper names both words should be written with a capital letter, but as technical or geographical terms these adjectives are written with small initial letters:

The eastern part of Britain is flatter than the west.

ornate, ornamental *Ornate* is elaborately adorned, sumptuously splendid. *Ornamental* means used for ornament or decorative.

oscillate, osculate *To oscillate* is to swing to and fro like a pendulum. Figuratively it means to fluctuate between opinions and purposes. *To osculate* is to kiss, to bring into close contact.

other The phrase *on the other hand* is sometimes used where *on the contrary* is required. *On the other hand* introduces a supplementary statement to a first statement, whereas *on the contrary* proposes a contradiction:

The yield was hardly a lavish one; on the other hand, it was lower than usual.

This sentence clearly demands *on the contrary*. But:

He could see that she was feeling the cold. On the other hand, she made no complaint.

Here the phrase is correct. There is nothing contradictory about the second sentence, which is complementary to the first.

In a sentence such as:

He could do no other but accept the part he was offered,

but should be replaced by *than*.

otherwise A fault which is widely perpetrated is to use *otherwise* where *other* or *others* would be preferable:

Those who support libraries, teachers or otherwise, must bear a share of the costs,

and:

Not all the union's supporters, Labour or otherwise, agree with the decisions made.

In the first sentence a straight substitution of *others* for *otherwise* should be made. The second example might better be expressed as:

Not all the union's Labour or other supporters agree with the decisions made.

When meaning *or else*, the word *otherwise* is sufficient alone:

You must have a ticket or otherwise you won't get in.

Or is superfluous here. The sentence should read:

You must have a ticket, otherwise you won't get in.

ought Never say *you didn't ought to.* It is a vulgarism. *Ought* is the past tense of an old verb to *owe*, and it cannot be used with an auxiliary verb. The negative is simply *ought not to.* The verb must be followed by an infinitive, and is therefore incorrect expressed as:

He ought but doesn't want to pay,

which should be rephrased to read:

He ought to pay but doesn't want to.

Ought is stronger than *should*, expressing more of a general moral judgement, whereas *should* is simply a pious hope.

-our, -or Words with an *-our* ending such as *humour*, *valour*, and *vapour* lose the *u* if their adjectives end in *-ous*:

humorous, valorous, and vaporous,

but the *u* is retained for adjectives ending in *-able*, such as *honourable* or *favourable*.

In American usage such words are spelt without a *u*: *honor*, *color*, *favor*.

outdoor, outdoors The adjective is *outdoor*:

I like an outdoor swimming pool,

and the adverb is *outdoors*, as in *Let's eat outdoors*, but many consider the three-word phrase, *out of doors*, preferable to this.

outstanding This word can easily lead to ambiguity with its two meanings, 'prominent, conspicuous' or 'remaining unsettled, unpaid':

The figures are rather high but the quarterly report is outstanding.

Is it late? Or is it sensational? *Still outstanding* would clarify one of the meanings.

outward, outwards *Outward* is both an adjective and adverb, pertaining to what is seen or apparent, or to the outside of the body, or proceeding towards the outside:

Don't judge him by his outward appearance.

It is used in a wide range of senses, especially figuratively. *Outwards*, the adverb, is used chiefly in its literal sense of towards the outside, out:

He moved outwards from the curb, just as I was about to pass.

overall What has always been a versatile word, with its use as a noun meaning a garment, an adverb meaning all over, and an adjective describing the extent of a measurement, has now become a popular vogue word which is often used indiscriminately and meaninglessly:

She was elected with an overall majority of 47,

and:

The overall character of the area is rundown and derelict,

and:

After touring the factory, he made a short report to the Director giving his overall impressions.

In each of these examples the only contribution the word has made to the sentence is to fill up space.

overflow The past tense and past participle of this verb is *overflowed* not *overflown* or *overflew*. These are the past participle and past tense of *overfly*.

overlay, overlie *Overlay* is the past tense of *overlie* which, though transitive, corresponds to the verb *to lie* (*q.v.*). The past participle therefore is *overlain* and the present participle is *overlying*:

Heavy clouds have overlain the mountains all day.

There is also a transitive verb *to overlay*, meaning to lay something over something else. This corresponds to the verb *to lay* (*q.v.*), and the past tense and past participle is *overlaid*, the present participle *overlaying*:

She is overlaying the edges with a narrow embroidered ribbon.

overlook, oversee To *overlook* is to fail to notice or perceive, or to disregard. It also means to view from a higher position. To *oversee* is to supervise or manage, to observe without being seen.

oversea(s) There used to be a singular form *oversea* in use as an adjective, but this has been superseded by the plural form *overseas*, which is also an adverb:

The overseas branch is doing remarkably well.

overtone, undertone Both these words, taken from a musical analogy, are used metaphorically: *overtone* to suggest that a word or phrase means more than is apparent, and *undertone* to express a feeling that beyond the words, there is still a wealth of meaning left unsaid.

owing to, due to Too often *owing to* is used clumsily in place of *because*, *since* or *as*. On the other hand, as a preposition it is a better phrase than *due to*, which is creeping in on its preserves:

Owing to a signal failure, trains will be running 20 minutes late.

P

-p-, -pp- Single-syllable words ending in *p* double it before suffixes beginning with a vowel if the *p* is preceded by a single vowel:

mapped, slapping, foppish, sloppy.

If it is preceded by two vowels, a vowel and an *m* or a vowel and an *r* the *p* is not doubled:

peeping, sharply, heaped, looped, stamping.

In words of more than one syllable the same rule applies as for single-syllable words if the last syllable is stressed:

unmapped, enwrapping *but* unstamped.

There are however some words of more than one syllable which do not obey the rule. *Handicap*, *kidnap*, *worship* and some others are not stressed on the last syllable but nevertheless double the *p*:

handicapped, kidnapping, worshipper.

palaeo-, paleo- This is a Greek prefix meaning 'old' or 'ancient'. The form *palaeo* is preferred in British English, although *paleo* is the more common spelling in American English.

panacea This does not mean a remedy for a particular disease or an infallible cure, but a remedy for all diseases.

pandemic see **endemic**

pandit, pundit In India a *pandit* is a 'learned man' or 'scholar'. The spelling *pundit*, which is an alternative form, is now used to describe anyone who claims to be an expert or a specialist in a particular subject.

panic This verb has the present participle *panicking* and the past tense and past participle *panicked. Picnic* forms its present participle and past tense in the same way.

para- There are two prefixes with the form *para*, one of Greek and one of Latin origin. The Greek prefix, meaning 'beside', 'beyond', or 'aside', is used in words like *paradox*, *paraphrase* and *parallel*. The Latin prefix, meaning 'guard against', occurs in *parachute*, *parapet*, and *parasol*.

parable A short allegorical story designed to convey a truth or moral lesson. [See also *allegory*]

paradox This is a seemingly self-contradictory or absurd statement that yet expresses a truth.

paragraph This is a distinct section of written matter dealing with a particular point or topic. There are no rules for deciding the lengths of a paragraph, but it is important that it should link together related sentences, dealing in a unified manner with a single theme. If the paragraph becomes too long, it is sensible to split it up. On the other hand, paragraphs can be made quite short if each one deals with a separate topic.

parallel This verb does not double the *l* when suffixes are added: *paralleling*, *paralleled*, making it an exception among verbs ending in *-l*. [See also *-l-*, *-ll-*, *spelling*]

parameter This is another word whose popularity has led to a distortion and oversimplification of its very specialized meaning in mathematics. It is frequently used as a synonym for *boundary*, *limit* or *framework*, any of which is preferable.

parentheses see **brackets**

parody A *parody* is a humorous or satirical imitation of a literary work. Its purpose is frequently to ridicule the writer of the original by making fun of his work, but the imitation of another's style or mannerisms is often used to launch an attack upon an entirely different target.

parricide, patricide The similarity in spelling is sometimes a source of confusion. *Parricide* is the more general word and means the murder of a parent or anyone to whom reverence is due. *Patricide* is the act of killing one's father.

partially, partly There is some overlapping between these two adverbs, but they are not really interchangeable. *Partially* means 'to a certain or limited extent':

His opera was only partially completed at the time of his death.

Partly means 'as concerns one part' or 'not wholly':

The letter was written partly in ink and partly in pencil.

Whereas *partly* could be substituted for *partially* in the first example, *partially* would be quite wrong in the second.

participles The English verb has two participles, the present which ends in *-ing*, and the past which may end in *-n* or *-en* in strong verbs and *-ed*, *-d* and *-t* in weak verbs. The participles are used to form compound tenses of verbs, the present participle forming the present continuous, *I am talking*, and the past participle the perfect tense, *I have talked*. Both present and past participles can be used as adjectives as in *a winding road*, *a stolen car*. They are also employed to form an adjectival phrase which qualifies a noun or pronoun in the main clause:

Watching the children, he forgot about his troubles.
Exhausted by his long vigil, the soldier fell asleep.

For the common error of the misrelated or unattached particle see *unattached participle*.

particular This useful adjective is sometimes used as a superfluous addition to a demonstrative adjective like *this* or *that* in such phrases as:

We have nothing to add at this particular juncture.

part of speech This is the term given to the function that a word performs in a sentence. There are eight parts of speech: noun, pronoun, verb, adjective, adverb, preposition, conjunction and interjection, and each has an entry in this book.

passed, past The verb *pass* has *passed* as its past participle:

The time had passed very quickly.

The form *past* is used whenever the past participle is employed as an adjective:

During the past three months.

passive A verb is *active* if the subject performs an action, but *passive* if the subject receives an action or has an action performed upon it. In *the dog bites a boy* the verb is active but in *the boy is bitten by a dog* it is passive. The passive tends to be used in impersonal constructions, often to an excessive degree and in an apparent attempt to avoid personal responsibility: *it is regretted* and *it is thought*, where *I regret* or *we think* would be preferable. Another construction to be avoided is the double passive which always appears clumsy:

The plans which were proposed to be discussed.

past participle see **participles**

pathos This is the quality in art, literature and music which arouses feelings of pity or sympathetic sadness.

peaceable, peaceful Both adjectives are similar in meaning and to some extent interchangeable. *Peaceable* is 'disposed to peace or inclined to avoid strife' and is usually applied to people, their actions or feelings:

Peaceable intentions, peaceable folk.

Peaceful, which means 'characterized by peace, tranquil', is rarely applied to people and refers to situations, scenes, periods and activities:

A peaceful reign, a peaceful life.

pendant, pendent A *pendant* is a noun meaning 'a hanging ornament, as a necklace'. *Pendent* is an adjective meaning 'hanging' or 'suspended'. Confusion arises because *pendant* has the alternative spelling *pendent*, and *pendent* can be spelt *pendant*.

peninsula, peninsular *Peninsula* is the noun and *peninsular* the adjective, as in *The Peninsular War*.

people When used to mean the body of persons constituting a tribe or nation, *people* used generally to be followed by a singular verb. However, although it has its own plural, *peoples*, it now takes a plural verb:

The people of England are not easily intimidated.

In all its other senses *people* is followed by a plural verb.

per This Latin preposition has its uses in such phrases as *per annum*, *per cent*, where it is followed by another word in Latin. It should not be employed as a substitute for *a* or *an* in expressions like *two pounds per hour* or *thirty miles per hour*, although its use with English words is acceptable in *per day*, *per head*, *per person*, *per week*. *Per* should not be used instead of *by* in sentences like:

They sent the parcels per rail.

per capita This does not, strictly speaking, mean 'per head' but refers to a method of distributing property among a number of people or a payment made according to the number of people, an agreed amount being allowed for each. However, its meaning 'per head' or 'each person' is now firmly entrenched in the language in such phrases as *per capita income* and *consumption of alcohol per capita*.

percentage Do not use *percentage* to mean 'some' or 'a number of' as in:

This method has proved reliable in a percentage of cases.

Percentage should be used only to indicate the relationship of one number to another and is really meaningless unless preceded by an adjective such as 'low' or 'high'. [See also *proportion*]

perceptible, perceptive *Perceptible* means 'capable of being perceived', as in:

A perceptible difference of colour.

Perceptive means 'having the power of perceiving, quick to perceive':

He proved to be a perceptive writer.

perfect The adjective *perfect* is an absolute expression and cannot usually be preceded by *more* and *most*, since one thing cannot, strictly speaking, be *more perfect* than another. However, it has gained acceptance in the sense of 'coming close to perfection' in such phrases as:

You could not find a more perfect friend,

although care should be taken over its use.

perfect infinitive This is sometimes wrongly used after a perfect tense in such expressions as:

They would have liked to have watched the film.

Only one verb needs to be in the perfect tense and the sentence should be recast in one of two ways, depending on whether the action is viewed from the present or past:

They would like to have watched the film (present).

They would have liked to watch the film (past).

However, the use of the perfect infinitive after verbs like *seem* or *appear* can be justified:

They seemed to have found what they wanted.

In this instance *to have found what they wanted* refers to something which happened before the time indicated by *seemed*. The perfect infinitive is wrongly used in the following example:

I meant to have seen him yesterday.

Here the *to have seen* does not refer to a time prior to *meant* and the sentence must be:

I meant to see him yesterday.

periphrasis This means a roundabout way of speaking or writing and is to be avoided:

He made her the object of his most tender affections

means no more than:

He fell in love with her,

and is better expressed thus.

permanence, permanency Some distinction of meaning still exists between these two words. Both have the sense of 'the condition of being permanent', but *permanency*, the less common word, also refers to something which is permanent, such as a position or a job.

permissible, permissive *Permissible* means 'allowable or not prohibited':

It is permissible to leave your belongings in the cloakroom.

Permissive means 'granting permission to do something' without actual compulsion. In a broader sense it means 'sexually or morally tolerant':

We live in a permissive society.

permit, allow These verbs are often interchangeable but *permit* is a more positive word, suggesting formal assent or authorization:

The police will not permit you to park here.

Allow usually implies that there is no attempt to hinder or prohibit in any way:

They allow you to do what you like here.

permit to/of There is sometimes confusion about the use of the prepositions *to* and *of* after *permit*. Normally *permit* is followed by *to*. It can be followed by *of* only when it means 'to make possible' or 'to leave room for':

The problem permits of no other solution.

per proc., per pro., p.p. These are all abbreviations of the Latin phrase *per procurationem*, which means 'by the agency of'. They are used when one person signs a letter or form in the absence of the person who wrote it. The abbreviation, now usually *p.p.*, generally precedes the signature of the agent thus:

p.p. Jane Brown, John Smithson.

person In grammar distinction is made between the speaker (*first person*: I), the one addressed (*second person*: you) and anyone or anything else (*third person*: he, she, it). In the plural *we* is the first person, *you* the second person and *they* the third person. In English the verb changes only in the third person singular of the present tense: *he* or *she sings*, but *we sing*. [See also *pronoun*, *verb*]

personage, personality Both words are applied to people who are in some way different from the rest of us. A *personage* is someone of distinction or importance, as a high official or a member of the royal family. *Personality*, which is now the more common word, means a celebrity, particularly one who has achieved fame in the world of entertainment.

persona grata This Latin term means 'an acceptable person', particularly a diplomat who is acceptable to the government to which he is accredited:

He is persona grata with the new revolutionary regime.

personification This is a kind of metaphor in which the qualities or character of a person are attributed to inanimate objects or abstract notions:

Fortune smiles upon the brave.

perspicacious, perspicuous *Perspicacious* means 'having keen mental perception, shrewd or discerning' and is usually applied to people:

His perspicacious conduct of affairs was appreciated by all.

Perspicuous means 'clear to the understanding or clearly expressed' and usually refers to something written or spoken:

A perspicuous description of the situation.

The noun from *perspicacious* is *perspicacity* and that from *perspicuous* is *perspicuity*.

perturb, disturb Both verbs convey the idea of creating disorder or confusion and to some extent overlap. *Perturb* is now exclusively reserved for mental agitation or disquiet:

He was greatly perturbed by the news of his friend's illness.

Disturb usually refers to physical disorder, but it can also be used to express mental anguish.

phonograph, gramophone A *phonograph* is the U.S. term for a *gramophone*, which has now been more or less completely displaced by *record player*.

phrasal verb This is the term applied to the formation of new verbs by adding adverbial particles to a simple verb. This is a process which has enriched and continues to enrich the English language to a remarkable degree. Using verbs like *get*, *go*, *put* in combination with the adverbial particles (adverbs or prepositions) *in*, *out*, *up*, *down*, *out* and *over*, many new verbs can be formed.

phrase This means a sequence of two or more words in a sentence arranged in a grammatical construction and acting as a unit in the sentence. A *phrase* cannot stand alone since it does not have a verb, but must be seen in relation to the sentence as a whole.

pick, choose *Pick* is a more informal word than *choose* and suggests a rather more casual selection:

Pick any two cards.

Choose usually implies a deliberate decision made after weighing a number of possibilities:

We must choose our course of action very carefully.

picket, piquet A *picket* is 'a stake for driving into the ground', 'a group of people stationed by a trade union before a place of work' or 'a detached body of soldiers'. The spelling *piquet* should be reserved exclusively for the card game.

picnic see **panic**

pidgin, pigeon *Pidgin* is the usual form of this word in such phrases as *pidgin English*, although *pigeon* is also used.

piteous, pitiable, pitiful All three adjectives are applied to that which excites pity and provokes feelings of sympathy or contempt.

Pitiful means 'exciting pity' or 'contemptible':

A pitiful crippled child, a pitiful show of incompetence.

Pitiable means 'lamentable' or 'deplorable':

She was in a pitiable condition.

Piteous, now a less common word, means 'exciting or deserving pity' or 'appealing for pity':

A piteous state of misery.

plaid, tartan These two words are quite often confused. A *plaid* is a rectangular piece of cloth worn about the shoulders. A *tartan* is the name given to the distinctively patterned cloth out of which plaids and kilts are made.

pleonasm This is the use of more words than are necessary to express an idea. It is usually to be avoided but can be justified when used for the sake of emphasis. *Pleonasm* occurs in phrases like:

Continue to remain, the reason is because, an attempt to try and stop, the cause of the obstruction is due to.

plural forms As a general rule nouns in English add *-s* to the singular in order to form the plural. Those which already end in *-s* or *-ss* in the singular and those ending in *x*, *-z*, *-sh* or *-ch* make the plural by adding *-es*:

masses, bosses, foxes, bushes, wishes, coaches.

Some nouns, which have *-s* in the singular, do not change in the plural:

corps, mumps.

Others are used only in the plural:

forceps, alms, dregs.

Nouns ending in *-y* preceded by a consonant form their plurals by changing *-y* to *i* and adding *es*:

duty, duties; lady, ladies.

Nouns ending in *-y* preceded by a vowel form their plurals by adding *-s*:

donkey, donkeys; play, plays.

Nouns ending in *-o* may form their plurals in either *-os* or *-oes*:

cargo, cargoes; banjo, banjoes; potato, potatoes; photo, photos; folio, folios.

Generally, the more common words end in *-oes*, but see the entry *-o(e)s*. Nouns ending in *-f* or *-fe* usually form their plural by changing the *f* to *v* and adding *-es*:

leaf, leaves; thief, thieves; life, lives.

However, there are many such nouns which simply add an *-s*:

proof, proofs; cliff, cliffs; relief, reliefs.

Compound words normally form their plurals by adding *-s* to the most important part of the compound:

commander-in-chief, commanders-in-chief; brother-in-law, brothers-in-law; go-between, go-betweens; court-martial, courts-martial.

When the compound is considered as one word and normally written without a hyphen the *-s* is added at the end:

mouthful, mouthfuls; stepson, stepsons; sergeant-major, sergeant-majors.

The plural of proper nouns ending in *-s* is *-es*:

the Joneses, the Sallises, the Davises.

And names ending in *-y* do not change to *-ies* in the plural:

the four Henrys, the Barrys, the two Marys.

For plurals of foreign nouns, *i.e.*, those ending in *-a*, *-um*, *-ex* and *-is*, see *Latin and French plurals*.

poetess There are only a few words in which the ending *-ess* as a feminine designation is not considered derogatory, e.g. *actress* and *baroness*. The word *poet* should be used for either sex, or else *woman poet* if it is necessary to make a distinction.

poetic, poetical It is now very difficult to differentiate these two words and they are usually employed interchangeably. *Poetical* is perhaps a more neutral word and may simply mean 'of or pertaining to poetry':

Wordsworth's poetical works.

Poetic suggests the charm or qualities characteristic of poetry:

Poetic feeling, poetic licence, poetic justice.

point of view This is another phrase which has suffered severely from excess of popularity, and is often used as a rather clumsy roundabout way of saying something:

From the point of view of literary merit this book is worth reading.

This sentence would be better recast as:

This book is worth reading for its literary merit.

Do not use *point of view* where *view* or *views* alone would be sufficient:

They asked us for our point of view on the subject.

This would be better as:

They asked us for our views on the subject.

politics This may take either a singular or plural verb. When it is used to mean the 'science or art of political government' it generally takes the singular:

Politics is an attractive career for ambitious young men.

When *politics* is thought of as political beliefs, principles or opinions it takes a plural:

His politics are nothing to do with me.

port see **harbour**

portion, part Both words refer to something that is less than the whole. *Part* is the more general word:

Part of the building is to be let.

A *portion* is a part which has been allotted to a person:

Each received a portion of the cake.

possessive case The *possessive case* (also called the *genitive case*) is used to show ownership, origin, connection, authorship, association and duration:

John's book, the prime minister's speech, man's task, Shakespeare's works, a week's delay.

For use of the apostrophe *s* to express the possessive see *apostrophe*.

post- This Latin prefix, meaning 'behind', originally occurred only in words from Latin, but is now used freely to form words in English. It is usually written without a hyphen, except where it would produce an unsightly appearance:

postscript, postdate *but* post-Elizabethan, post-impressionism.

potent, potential These two words are occasionally used in error, the one for the other. *Potent* means 'powerful' or 'possessing great power or authority':

A potent drug, a potent ruler.

Potential means 'possible as opposed to actual', 'capable of becoming' or 'latent':

A potential prime minister, a potential source of trouble.

practicable, practical These adjectives are very close in some of their senses and an obvious source of confusion. *Practicable* means 'able to be done', 'capable of being put into practice or carried out in action':

This is a practicable way of carrying large quantities of goods.

Practical, when applied to people, means 'sensible or businesslike':

A practical man.

When applied to things it means 'efficient and workable' (as opposed to theoretical):

He put forward practical suggestions for ending the dispute.

practically It is not perhaps too late to regret the fact that *practically* is in danger of losing its other meanings and of becoming a mere synonym of *nearly* or *almost*. It is reasonable to say:

The work is practically completed,

since this means 'in practice completed'. But to say:

The team practically lost the match

is ambiguous since it can mean they did in fact lose it, although what is probably meant is that they *nearly* lost it.

practice, practise In English usage the noun is spelt with a *c* and the verb with an *s*. In American usage *practice* is used for both noun and verb.

pre- This prefix meaning 'before' or 'prior to' is normally written without a hyphen, except before another *e*:

prewar *but* pre-empt, pre-election.

precede, proceed *Precede* means 'to go before in place, order, rank or time':

There was some dispute over who should precede the archbishop in the ceremony.

Proceed means 'to go or move forwards, especially after stopping':

After the interruption at the entrance the party was allowed to proceed.

precipitate, precipitous These two adjectives are sometimes confused although their meanings are quite distinct. *Precipitate* means 'moving with great haste', 'sudden' or 'abrupt':

The soldiers made a precipitate retreat across the bridge.

Precipitous means 'like a precipice', 'extremely steep':

They followed a precipitous path down the hillside.

predicate In grammar the *predicate* is that part of a sentence or clause which expresses the action or state of the subject. It consists of the verb together with all the words it governs and those which modify it. In the sentences:

The children are here,
The girl cried bitterly,

the predicate is *are here* and *cried bitterly*. [See also *subject*]

predicate, predict These two verbs are occasionally confused. *Predicate*, a much rarer word, means 'to proclaim, affirm or assert'. *Predict* means 'to foretell or prophesy'.

preface, prefix When used as verbs *preface* and *prefix* are sometimes mistaken for each other. *Preface* is followed by *with* or *by*:

He prefaced his speech with a short reference to the financial situation.

His speech was prefaced by a short reference to the financial situation.

Prefix is followed by *to*:

He prefixed a title to his name.

Unlike *preface*, *prefix* cannot take as an object the thing to which something is added:

He prefixed his remarks with a few words of thanks.

This is not correct, and *prefaced* must be substituted for *prefixed*.

prefer This verb sometimes causes trouble because of doubt over which prepositions should follow it. It is usually followed by *to*:

I prefer beer to cider. She preferred flying to travelling by train.

The problem arises when *prefer* is followed by an infinitive. We cannot say:

They prefer to write to to read.

In this case *rather than* must be substituted:

They prefer to write rather than to read.

preferable This adjective is followed by *to* in comparisons:

I think my plan is preferable to yours.

Remember than *preferable* is already comparative and cannot be preceded by *more* or *most*.

prefix A prefix consists of one or more syllables attached to the beginning of a word which qualify or alter its meaning in some way. Common prefixes include *anti-*, *co-*, *ex-*, *in-*, *pre-* and *un-* and examples of their use are listed below:

aircraft, anti-aircraft; edition, coedition; president, ex-president; expensive, inexpensive; war, prewar; attractive, unattractive.

[See also *hyphens*]

preposition A preposition shows the relationship between a noun or pronoun and some other word in a sentence, clause or phrase, usually of time or place but also of means, manner and purpose:

Two minutes before noon, the dog jumped over the gate, through understanding, with great force, for future use.

In these examples *before*, *over*, *through*, *with* and *for* are all prepositions. Pronouns used as the object of prepositions are in the accusative or objective case:

After us, before him, by whom, with her, about them.

Prepositions generally come before their object but often follow and may even be placed at the end of a sentence (despite the protests of some authorities):

What is he talking about? It's the woman we are looking for.

prescribe, proscribe These two verbs are sometimes confused. *Prescribe* means 'to designate or order for use as a remedy' or 'to advise the use of':

She followed the course of treatment prescribed by the doctor.

Proscribe means 'to condemn as dangerous, to prohibit, banish or outlaw':

The terrorists were proscribed by the government.

present participle see **participles**

preserve see **reserve**

pretence, pretension Although there is some overlapping, the meanings of these two nouns are generally quite distinct. *Pretence* means 'make-believe' or 'a false show of something':

He made a pretence of friendship in order to deceive them.

Pretension means 'laying claim to something':

Her pretensions to superior merit were without foundation.

prevent The two correct constructions with *prevent* are:

We will prevent him from coming *or* we will prevent his coming.

We will prevent him coming is colloquial and best avoided in writing.

preventive, preventative There is no distinction in meaning between these two words. *Preventive* is, however, the preferred form, *preventative* being only rarely found.

prima facie This Latin phrase means 'at first appearance' or 'on a first impression' and is sometimes mistaken for *a priori* (*q.v.*).

principal, principle These two words are a rich source of confusion. Whether used as an adjective or a noun *principal* means 'chief':

The principal feature of the house, the principal of an educational institute.

Principle is a noun meaning 'a rule of conduct or action' or 'a fundamental doctrine':

The principles of government, a man of principle.

proceed see **precede**

programme, program *Programme* is the usual English form, *program* the American. The spelling *program* is however used in Britain in computer technology.

prohibit This verb can take a noun as its direct object:

They voted to prohibit the export of cattle.

But it can also be followed by *from* and a present participie:

They were prohibited from entering the building.

The use of *prohibit* and an infinitive is now archaic and an expression like *we prohibited them to come* is not correct.

pronoun A *pronoun* is a word which is used in place of a noun. There are several classes of pronoun including *personal* (I, you, him, her), *demonstrative* (this, that, these, those), *indefinite* (anybody, somebody, nobody, no one, each, both), and *relative* and *interrogative* (who, which, whose, whom, what, that). Care must be taken to ensure consistency in the use of pronouns, *i.e.* number and person must remain the same. Avoid sentences like:

We were frightened, for everywhere one saw evidence of violence.

We instead of *one* should be used in the second half of the sentence.

prophecy, prophesy These words are frequently mistaken for each other. *Prophecy* is the noun and *prophesy* the verb.

proportion This is another word whose meaning has been greatly enlarged, but not to the benefit of the English language. *Proportion* should be used to express the relationship of one size, quantity, number, etc. to another:

A man with a weekly salary of £100 who spends £60 on food may be rightly said to spend a large proportion of his income on food.

However, *proportion* is frequently used to mean a part or portion in relation to the whole without any idea of comparison:

A proportion of the work force failed to appear.

When it is preceded by *large* or *small*, this use of *proportion* is acceptable. It should not, however, be employed simply as a substitute for *a few* or *some* as in:

A proportion of the children were absent through sickness.

proportional, proportionate Both adjectives mean 'in due proportion'. The distinction between them is that *proportional* usually precedes its noun, *i.e.* is used attributively, and that *proportionate* usually follows its noun, *i.e.* is used predicatively:

A proportional share, proportional representation.
Each was given an amount which was considered proportionate to his needs.

proposition This is another word that has suffered excessive popularity. It is often confused with *proposal* in business matters and should only be used in preference to this word when terms are clearly stated and their advantages emphasized:

His proposition involved a 10% mark-up on all goods.

Proposition is also employed where words like *task*, *plan*, *job*, or *project*, would be far more suitable, and constant care should be exercised to see that it does not suffer from excessive abuse.

proscribe see **prescribe**

protagonist see **antagonist**

provided (that), providing *Provided (that)* is usually better than *providing*. It should be used only when there is a prior condition to be fulfilled:

She said she would go to church provided (that) I came with her.

Otherwise *if* is generally preferable.

punctuation see **brackets, colon, comma, dash, full stop, quotation marks, semicolon**

pundit see **pandit**

purport This is both a verb and a noun. As a verb it means 'to profess or claim' and is restricted in use. It cannot be used in the passive and it does not take a personal subject unless it is followed by the verb *to be*:

She purports to be an actress

is acceptable, but:

She purports to have acted in many plays

is not.

purposely, purposefully *Purposely* means 'intentionally' 'expressly':

He purposely tried to provoke her to anger.

Purposefully means 'resolutely', 'in a determined manner':

His mind made up, he walked purposefully into the room.

Q

quadroon A *quadroon* is the offspring of a white and a mulatto and is therefore one-fourth Negro. [See also *mulatto*]

qualitative, quantitative These words are quite frequently misspelt as *qualitive* and *quantitive*.

quantity This means 'a particular, indefinite or considerable amount of anything':

A small quantity of liquid.

It is better not to use it when referring to individuals or items, in which case *number* is to be preferred:

A large number (not *quantity*) of boxes.

question as to This rather ugly phrase has achieved a certain popularity, but good English requires that it should be avoided wherever possible. The *as to* can be omitted as redundant in such phrases as:

The question as to whether he would be elected president.

Alternatively, expressions like:

The question as to who would pay

can be changed *to the question of payment*.

question, beg the This means to assume without justification the very point raised in a question or to argue from an assumption which itself needs to be proved. Thus, in a discussion someone might say that prisons are necessary in order to avoid an increase in the crime rate, although it has not been proved that the provision of prisons does in fact keep down the rate of crime. *To beg the question* is also used colloquially to mean to evade the point at issue or to avoid giving a straight answer to a question.

question mark This is used at the end of a direct sentence:

Why didn't you come back last night?

It is not used at the end of an indirect or reported question:

He asked me why I didn't come back last night.

In instances where the question is in fact a request, although it has the form of a question, the tendency is to omit the question mark:

Will you please leave your hats and coats here.

quicker This is the comparative form of the adjective *quick* but it is frequently used as adverb instead of *more quickly*:

You can get there quicker by car.

In this instance *quicker* is really an equivalent to *sooner* rather than *faster*, and refers to the length of time taken.

quiet, quietness The main distinction between these two nouns is as follows. *Quiet* means 'freedom from disturbance' or 'a peaceful condition of affairs':

An atmosphere of quiet prevailed.

Quietness refers to a characteristic quality shown by a person or thing:

The quietness of the car's engine was surprising.

quite This is a word which tends to be used to excess. Unfortunately, its various senses are in some ways contradictory, since it can mean 'completely' or 'entirely' and also 'to a considerable extent':

The work is quite finished

but:

The house was quite attractive.

quotation marks The chief use of quotation marks or inverted commas is to set off spoken words from the rest of the text. They are used to enclose a direct quotation or direct speech:

'I must finish this report.'

Modern practice prefers single quotes (' ') to double ones (" "), but there are no absolute rules. When one set of quotes occurs within another set, as, for example, a quotation within a speech, use single quotes for the outer set and double quotes for the inner set:

> She asked, 'Have you any idea what the expression "begging the question" really means?'

Quotation marks should be placed before and after the paragraph, sentence, phrase, or word quoted. If a quotation consists of more than one paragraph, a single opening quotation mark should be placed at the beginning of each new paragraph, but the closing quotation mark should be placed only at the end of the final paragraph.

The use of other punctuation marks with quotation marks needs some careful study. A comma should be placed at the end of quoted matter before the quotation mark, since a punctuation mark usually refers to the group of words which precedes it:

> 'I must finish this report,' he said.

If a verb of saying is inserted in the middle of a sentence of direct speech, the insertion is preceded and followed by a comma:

> 'Before I go,' he declared, 'you must give me an answer.'

However, if the verb of saying is inserted in a continuous quotation which has no natural break, the first comma should fall outside the quotation marks:

> 'I will not', he declared, 'tolerate this.'

When the quoted matter forms a complete sentence which ends at the same point as the main sentence logic would require two full stops, one inside and one outside the quotation mark. In these instances it is usually better to place the full point inside the quotation mark:

> He said abruptly, 'I want that report to be ready by ten o'clock tomorrow morning.'

All punctuation used with quotation marks must be placed as far as possible according to sense. If a quotation ends with a question mark this must be placed before the closing quotation mark. If the question mark belongs to the whole sentence and not just to the quoted passage it should be placed after the closing quotation mark:

He asked, 'What are you doing here?'
What do you mean by 'I don't like it'?

Titles of articles within periodicals, chapters in books, single short poems, essays, etc. are usually placed within quotation marks:

He read Keats' poem 'Ode to a Nightingale'.

Quotation marks may be placed round letters, words, or phrases to which special attention is to be drawn. These are not separated off by a comma unless the sense demands it:

'A bunch of misfits' was his description of his colleagues.

Quotation marks should be placed around English translations of foreign words and phrases:

Qu'ils mangent de la brioche ('let them eat cake') is a saying attributed to Queen Marie Antoinette.

R

-r-, -rr- Single-syllable words ending in *r* double it before suffixes beginning with a vowel if the *r* is preceded by a single vowel:

tarring, furred, blurring, barred.

If it is preceded by two vowels the *r* is not doubled:

cheering, feared, soaring.

In words of more than one syllable the same rule applies as for single-syllable words if the last syllable is stressed:

deferring, preferred.

Otherwise they do not double the *r*:

conquering, entered.

Exceptions to the rule are words like *confer*, *prefer* and *refer* which, although stressed on the final syllable, shift the stress to a preceding syllable when suffixes other than verb endings are added:

conferring *but* conference, preferring *but* preferable, preference.

However, confer gives *conferrable*, which is, unfortunately, an exception to the exceptions noted above.

racket, racquet The spelling *racket* is now the generally accepted one both in the sense of 'disturbance' or 'noise' and in the sense of 'a bat for striking a ball.'

railroad, railway *Railroad* is the usual word in the United States and *railway* in Britain. *Railway*, however, is still used to some extent in the United States.

raise, rise Care is needed in the use of these words. *Raise* is a transitive verb and must therefore take a direct object:

He raised the stone above his head.

Rise is intransitive, that is, the verb is complete in itself without an object:

Prices are rising.

The noun *rise* is used in British English to mean an increase in salary, although the American version *raise* is edging its way into our vocabulary. *Raise* is also used in the United States to mean 'bring up' or 'rear'.

rapt, wrapped Identical pronunciation has led to some confusion in meaning. *Rapt* means 'deeply engrossed' or 'enraptured' as in *rapt in thought*. *Wrapped* means 'enclosed or enveloped in something', but it can be used figuratively as *wrapped up in* in the sense of 'engrossed or absorbed by'.

rare, scarce Both adjectives are used to describe what occurs only very occasionally or is found only in small amounts. *Rare* is applied to things which are seldom found, have scarcity value and may possess superior qualities:

A rare twelfth-century manuscript.

Scarce is applied to things which are in short supply, usually only temporarily:

Apples are scarce this year.

rase, raze *Rase* is the older form of this word, but it has now been generally supplanted by *raze*.

-re, -er There are many words ending in *-re* in British English which have *-er* in American usage:

centre, center; theatre, theater; sombre, somber.

However, British English has adopted such spellings as *diameter* and *filter* and shows a certain lack of consistency. [See also *American usage and spelling*]

re- This prefix has the meanings 'repetition' and 'backward motion' or 'withdrawal'. It is not usually hyphenated except when followed by an *e* as in *re-emerge*, *re-entry*, etc. However, it is also used with a hyphen to distinguish words with different meanings such as *recount* and *re-count* ('count again'), *recover* and *re-cover* ('cover again'), *reform* and *re-form* ('form again').

reaction This is another word whose increase in popularity has led to many unwarranted extensions of meaning. Its basic sense is, apart from its technical definitions, an action in response to some event, and it is properly used as follows:

The prime minister's hostile speech met with a strong reaction from his opponents.

However, it is constantly employed as a substitute for such words as *view*, *opinion*, *effect*, *response*, and sentences like:

What is your reaction?

would be better expressed as:

What is your view/opinion?

or simply:

What do you think?

readable, legible Both words may be used to mean 'capable of being read' or 'clear enough to be read', but this sense is usually confined to *legible*. *Readable* normally means 'interesting enough to be read'.

realistic Like the noun *reaction* this adjective has been over-exposed. It is now tending to displace such words as *sensible*, *reasonable*, *practical* and even *big* or *large*:

Quote me a realistic figure.

reason see **cause**

recall see **remember**

reciprocal, mutual These two words are to a certain extent synonymous: they both imply the idea of an exchange or balance between two or more people or groups of people. *Mutual* indicates an exchange of feeling or obligation:

Mutual esteem, mutual agreement.

Reciprocal can be used in the same way:

Reciprocal affection.

But it also indicates a relationship in which one service is given in return for another:

In view of the support they had given him they confidently expected reciprocal favours.

Whereas *mutual* involves the relationship of both parties *reciprocal* can be used to show the action of only one party with regard to the other. [See also *mutual*]

recollect see **remember**

recourse, resort, resource There is some overlapping of meaning between all three words. Both *recourse* and *resort* can be used for action undertaken for a certain purpose but the constructions are different:

To have recourse to desperate measures

is acceptable, and so is:

To resort to desperate measures,

but not:

To have resort to desperate measures.

The basic meaning of *resource* is 'a source of supply, support or aid'. It is occasionally wrongly substituted for *recourse* in *to have recourse to*, but it is also muddled with *resort* in the expression *in the last resort*. This frequently appears as *in the last resource* but the correct phrase with *resource* is *as a last resource*. Note that *recourse* and *resource* can be used only as nouns, but that *resort* is also a verb.

recrudescence This is another word which has suffered from excess of popularity. It is frequently used for any renewal of activity, although it is more properly applied to the outbreak or return of something disagreeable:

A recrudescence of violence.

redundant The basic meaning of *redundant* is 'excessive' or 'superfluous', but it has undergone various extensions of meaning for which it is wholly unsuited. It has been used as a synonym for *unnecessary*, *inappropriate*, *unsuitable* or *discontinued*, even by writers who ought to know better.

reference, testimonial *Reference* has had its meaning extended to include not only the person to whom one applies for testimony as to character or abilities, but also the written testimonial itself. The word *testimonial* is generally applied to a more formal document, but it does not differ essentially from *reference* in this respect.

reflection, reflexion It is very difficult to make a distinction between these two words. *Reflection* is now the much commoner spelling. *Reflexion* has the same senses as *reflection*, but it is also used in anatomy to mean 'the bending or folding back of a thing upon itself'.

reflective, reflexive *Reflective* is used as the adjective from *reflection*. *Reflexive* is now applied exclusively to grammar.

reflexive verbs and pronouns In grammar a *reflexive verb* is one which has an identical subject and object, as the verb *cut* in *he cut himself*. A *reflexive pronoun* is one that serves as the object of a *reflexive verb*, indicating identity of subject and object, as *himself* in *he cut himself*.

refute, deny These verbs are sometimes used as though they were synonyms, but there is an important difference between them. To *deny* something is to assert that it is not true:

He denied their allegations of corruption.

To *refute* something is to supply evidence that it is not true:

He refuted their allegations with documentary proof.

regard The prepositional phrases *with regard to*, *in regard to* and *as* regards are frequently used where a simpler construction with *in* or *about* would have been preferable. Note also the distinction between the two phrases *have regard to* ('to take into account or consideration') and *have regard for* ('to show respect or concern for'). Unlike verbs such as *consider* and *count*, *regard* cannot take two direct objects:

I consider it an insult

but:

I regard it as an insult.

regretful, regrettable *Regretful* means 'full of regret', 'sorrowful':

She was regretful for her lost youth.

Regrettable means 'causing regret':

Her hasty action was regrettable.

rehabilitate This means 'to restore to a healthy condition or a condition of respectability'. It should not be used simply as a synonym for *restore* or *repair* when referring to a building which has been damaged.

relation, relationship *Relation* and *relationship* both refer to the connection between people or things, but whereas *relation* has a number of different senses, most of them abstract, *relationship* is restricted to one or two meanings. Both can mean connection by blood or marriage but *relationship* has the additional sense of 'a particular connection' or 'a degree of similarity':

His relationship to the ruling family.
The relationship between art and sculpture.

relation, relative In the sense of 'one who is connected to another by marriage' *relation* and *relative* are virtually interchangeable. *Relation* is the more common word and tends to be used to refer to those with whom we are closely connected, but very often personal choice is the deciding factor in the selection of these words.

remember, recall, recollect All three verbs have the meaning of recalling to consciousness what exists in the memory. There are distinctions between them, which are worth noting, although they are often ignored in practice. *Remember*, the most common word, implies that a thing is present in the memory and can be brought to mind with only a slight effort:

I remember the days of my youth.

Recall implies a voluntary effort, possibly assisted by an association of ideas:

He recalled the words of the poem.

Recollect implies a conscious effort to remember something in particular:

I can't recollect the precise details of the car crash.

repairable, reparable Both adjectives mean 'capable of being repaired', but *repairable* is normally used only of material things:

Shoes which are still repairable.

Reparable is generally used of abstract things to be remedied or put right, such as a loss, a mistake or harm. The negative form, *irreparable* is far more common as in *an irreparable loss*. The negative of *repairable* is *unrepairable*.

repellant, repulsive Both words mean 'causing distaste or aversion' to an extent that drives one away, but *repulsive* implies a much stronger feeling and suggests violent reaction against what causes the repulsion.

repent, regret These two verbs are sometimes confused. *Repent* means 'to feel self-reproach or contrition for past action':

He repented his crimes.

Regret can mean the same as *repent*:

He regretted his misdeeds.

It does however, suggest, a far lesser degree of guilt than *repent* and is a much more general word.

repertoire, repertory Both words have the meaning of a list of dramas or musical pieces that a theatrical company or a musician can perform. *Repertoire* is the more usual word for this and *repertory* has the additional meanings of 'a type of theatrical company' and 'a stock or store of things of any kind':

His repertory of dirty jokes.

repetitious, repetitive Both adjectives mean 'characterized by repetition'. The main difference is that *repetitious* refers to undue or tedious repetition, whereas *repetitive* is a more neutral word.

replace This very useful word has frequently had to yield to *substitute*, which has often proved a less than satisfactory alternative. Care must be taken with the prepositions that follow *replace*:

We have replaced the old desks with new ones.
The old desks have been replaced by new ones.
The old desks have been replaced by the company with new ones.

[See also *substitute*]

require This verb is transitive, i.e. it takes a direct object, but it is often wrongly used as though it were an intransitive verb:

You require to have a letter from the manager

instead of the correct:

You require a letter from the manager.

requirement, requisite Both *requirement* and *requisite* refer to something that is necessary. A *requirement* is some quality which is needed in order to comply with certain conditions:

Requirements for admission to a university.

A *requisite* is something required by the nature of things or the circumstances of a particular case and is generally more specific:

The two requisites for this job are energy and initiative.

Requisite is also used for a concrete object:

Toilet requisites.

reserve, preserve Two of the various senses of these nouns are sometimes confused. A *reserve* is a tract of public land set aside for a special purpose, as a *a nature reserve*. A *preserve* is a place set apart for the protection and propagation of game or fish for sport.

resign This verb may be used with a direct object or alternatively followed by *from* when it means to give up an office or position:

He resigned the directorship.
He resigned from the company.

Note also:

To be resigned to one's fate.

resolution, motion Both words are used to refer to something to be debated and voted upon by a deliberative assembly. The difference is that a *resolution* may not be anything more than a formal determination or an expression of opinion:

The assembly passed a resolution deploring the recent outbreak of violence.

However, a *motion* leads to action:

The assembly passed a motion to adjourn.

resort, resource see **recourse**

respective, respectively These are words which are so often used incorrectly that it is probably better to avoid them altogether. The adverb *respectively* is properly employed when it shows the correct relationship between two groups of people or things. In:

Jane and Susan were given a book and a record respectively

it is made clear that Jane received a book and Susan a record. *Respectively* is often used superfluously, as in:

Peter, James and Charles respectively made successful appearances in the school concert.

The adjective *respective* is used correctly in:

The four teachers gave an account of how the new method was being used in their respective classes.

i.e., each in his own class. It is quite unnecessary, for example, in:

Each pupil gave his respective opinion,

since *respective* can add nothing to *each*.

restive, restless These adjectives are sometimes confused. *Restive* means 'impatient of control' or 'refractory', and *a restive horse* is one that offers resistance. *Restless* means 'unable to remain at rest', 'unquiet' or 'uneasy'. Thus, a *restive* horse may also be a *restless* one, but not necessarily.

restrictive and non-restrictive clauses A *restrictive clause* is one which limits or defines or makes specific:

Girls who laugh all the time are not very popular.

The relative clause, *who laugh all the time*, is essential to complete the meaning of the sentence. A *non-restrictive clause* is one which is not essential to the meaning but merely supplies additional information:

Jane, who laughs all the time, is not very popular.

The essential information, *Jane is not very popular*, has already been conveyed. *Non-restrictive clauses* are always set off by commas.

retrograde, retrogression, *Retrograde* is now the usual adjective accompanying the noun *retrogression*. The adjective *retrogressive* is not very commonly employed.

revenge see **avenge**

reverend, reverent It is important not to confuse these words. *Reverend* means 'worthy to be revered' or 'entitled to reverence'. *Reverent* means 'feeling or showing reverence', 'deeply respectful'.

reversal, reversion *Reversion* is occasionally used by mistake instead of *reversal*. *Reversal* is the noun which corresponds to the verb *reverse*. *Reversion* is linked with the verb *revert* and is mainly used in legal or scientific terminology.

reward see **award**

rhetorical question This is a question designed to produce a dramatic effect and not to elicit an answer. It is a favourite device of public speakers:

Who says we are not capable of defending ourselves?

rhyme, rime *Rhyme* is the established spelling, with *rime* as an alternative but now rarely used form.

right, rightly *Right* as an adverb has a number of other meanings, but both words are used in the sense of 'correctly, accurately or properly', although *rightly* tends to occur more frequently. *Right* can be used only after the verb but in some expressions both words are possible:

If I remember right *or* rightly.

Right should be used in preference to *rightly* when the meaning is 'so as to produce a correct or satisfactory result':

He guessed right. She was unable to do it right. Hold the pencil right.

Rightly must be used when the adverb is placed before the verb or when it modifies a whole sentence:

He rightly refused to answer.
She rightly guessed that he would not come.
They had not been rightly informed.

rise see **arise; raise**

rotary, rotatory Both words are used to mean 'turning round as on an axis', but *rotary* is the more common, especially when referring to machines.

round see **around**

rouse see **arouse**

rural, rustic Both adjectives refer to the country as opposed to the town. *Rural* is the usual term and may have a favourable sense:

Rural economy, the pleasures of rural life.

Rustic may be used with either a favourable or a pejorative meaning. It may suggest homeliness or lack of sophistication (*rustic simplicity*), or else something boorish, crude or uncouth (*rustic manners*). *Rustic* is also used to mean 'made of roughly dressed wood':

A rustic seat.

Russia, Russian *Russia*, strictly speaking, means either the Russian Empire overthrown in 1917 or else the largest of the constituent republics of the U.S.S.R., the corresponding adjective for each being *Russian*. However, both words are used loosely to refer to both the pre- and the post- revolutionary state. *Russian* as a noun can be applied to any inhabitant of the U.S.S.R., past or present, but it also has the narrower sense of a member of the Russian Soviet Republic. In speaking of the present-day country it is better to say either the *U.S.S.R.* or the *Soviet Union* rather than *Russia*.

S

-s-, -ss- There are so few single-syllable words ending in *-s* that the rules about doubling or not doubling the final consonant before a suffix beginning with a vowel can scarcely be applied. *Gas* has the plural *gases*, but the verb has *gassed*, *gassing*. In words of more than one syllable if the last syllable is not stressed the final *-s* is not usually doubled:

biased, canvases, bonuses, atlases.

However it should be noted that *focused* and *focusing* have the alternative forms *focussed* and *focussing*.

sabotage The first definition given in dictionaries is 'malicious damage to work, tools, machinery, etc.'. The word has now become so popular that both as a noun and a verb it is used to describe any kind of action which undermines or wrecks an agreement or scheme.

saccharin, saccharine The spelling *saccharin* is usually reserved for the noun and *saccharine* for the adjective meaning 'sweet', although the noun can also be spelt with an *'e'*.

sake This occurs in phrases like:

For heaven's sake, for mercy's sake.

When the noun preceding *sake* already ends in an *s* sound, the apostrophe *s* is not added:

For goodness sake.

salubrious, salutary *Salubrious* means 'favourable to health', especially of air or climate:

A salubrious resort.

Salutary also means 'conducive to health', but is more often used to imply moral benefit:

A salutary lesson in manners.

same The use of *same* or *the same* as a pronoun, which is still found in commercial English, is to be avoided. In a sentence like:

We have inspected the samples and are returning same

them should be substituted for *same*.

The use of *as* or *that* after *same* presents some difficulty. When the expression is intended to point out a resemblance *as* should be used:

She has the same hair style as her daughter.

However, *that* can be used when identification rather than resemblance is intended:

He was carrying the same book that he had with him last week.

same, similar Both words indicate a resemblance between things. *Same* means identical in every respect:

She wears the same clothes every day.

Similar means resembling in certain respects or in a general way, or having certain qualities in common:

Your views on the subject are similar to mine.

sanatory, sanitary These words may be occasionally confused because of the similarity in their spelling. *Sanatory*, which is a fairly uncommon word, means 'favourable to health', 'curative'. *Sanitary* means 'pertaining to health, especially with reference to cleanliness and precautions against disease'.

sanatorium, sanitarium *Sanatorium* is the usual English spelling. In American usage both *sanatorium* and *sanitarium* are found, although the latter is more common.

sanction This is a popular word whose various senses are in some ways contradictory. As a noun it means 'authoritative support given to an action' and, as a verb, 'to authorize or approve':

Their actions have been sanctioned by long usage.

In law a *sanction* is 'a provision enacting a penalty for disobedience':

They threatened to impose economic sanctions.

sarcasm This is a form of irony which takes the form of harsh or bitter derision and is intended to hurt the feelings of others. It is often expressed as the apparent opposite of what is intended:

A fine friend you turned out to be!

sardonic This means 'bitterly ironical' or 'sneering'. It can also mean 'sarcastic', but expresses a much milder form of sarcasm and may be directed against oneself as much as against anyone else:

The prisoner heard the jury's verdict with a sardonic smile.

satire This is the use of irony, sarcasm or ridicule in exposing, denouncing or deriding the shortcomings of society and of individuals. It often takes the form of a literary composition.

satiric, satirical Both adjectives mean exactly the same, but *satirical* is tending to oust *satiric* almost completely:

A satirical poet. Satirical remarks.

satisfy This verb has two quite distinct meanings: 'to fulfil desires, needs, etc.' and 'to give assurance to or convince'. The second meaning of *satisfy* is tending to displace *convince* and may lead to unfortunate ambiguity:

They were satisfied that no one could have escaped alive from the burning building.

save This is a preposition meaning 'except' or 'but', which is occasionally employed as an alternative to these words. It is, however, no longer in common use and adds an air of artificiality to any sentence in which it appears.

saw The usual past participle of *saw* is *sawn* but *sawed* is occasionally found.

scarce, scarcely *Scarce* as an adverb is now obsolete and *scarcely* should be used. *Scarcely*, like *hardly*, is followed by *when* and not *than*:

We had scarcely started when the front tyre went flat.

[See also *rare*]

sceptic, septic Similarity in spelling can lead to confusion between these two words, although their meanings are entirely different. *Sceptic* is a noun and means 'one who maintains a doubting or distrustful attitude towards people, ideas, etc.'. *Septic* is an adjective meaning 'affected by a microbe or bacteria'.

Scots, Scottish, Scotch *Scottish* is the usual adjective for 'belonging or pertaining to Scotland', but *Scots* can also be used in this sense and the two words apply to both people and things:

Scottish blood, Scots soldiers.

Scotch should be used only with reference to food, drink, animals, flowers and objects generally:

Scotch tweed, Scotch terrier, Scotch whisky.

scream, screech, shriek All three verbs refer to crying out in a loud, piercing way. *Scream* is often associated with pain or fear:

He screamed with anguish as he caught his finger in the door.

Screech refers to a harsh, disagreeable sound and may be used of birds or old women:

The screeching of crows in the night sky.

Shriek is usually associated with a shorter, sharper sound than *scream* and is frequently used of fear or pain of a more acute kind than is implied by *scream*:

She shrieked with terror at the sight.

scull, skull The similarity of these words may lead to confusion in spelling. A *scull* is an oar worked from side to side over the stern of boat as a means of propulsion. The *skull* is the bony framework of the head enclosing the brain.

seasonable, seasonal *Seasonable* means 'suitable to the season of the year':

We had some fine seasonable weather in August.

Seasonal means 'pertaining to or dependent on the seasons or some particular season':

To obtain seasonal work in the building trade.

seem Care must be taken in negative sentences to ensure that the negation applies to the main verb and not to *seem* when this is used as an auxiliary verb. This misplacement is frequent in colloquial speech but should not appear in the written language:

She can't seem to understand.

This is better expressed as:

She seems unable to understand.

seldom This is an adverb and should not be used as a predicative adjective, as in:

His trips abroad were seldom.

It can, however, be employed as a predicative adverb as follows:

It is seldom that we get the chance of a trip to London.

Seldom can also qualify a phrase:

When he stayed more than five minutes, which was seldom, we were all delighted.

self This should not be used as a substitute for *I* or *me* in such phrases as: *my friend and self* or *self and wife*. Likewise, *myself* should not appear instead of *I* or *me*. *My wife and myself* is better as *My wife and I*.

-self, -selves These endings are added to the personal pronouns to form either reflexive or intensive (emphatic) pronouns. The reflexive pronoun is used as an object which refers to the same person as the subject:

He cut himself.

The intensive pronoun is used to add emphasis:

They themselves persisted in denying everything.

semantics This is a branch of linguistics which is concerned with the study of the meaning of words and other linguistic forms.

semi(-) Most modern dictionaries tend not to hyphenate *semi* to the word with which it is compounded except to avoid an awkward combination of vowel sounds as in *semi-intoxicated.*

semicolon The semicolon indicates a longer pause or a more definite separation than the comma. It should be employed sparingly. It is used to separate main clauses in a sentence when these are not linked by a conjunction:

The man looked pleased when she arrived; the woman seemed indifferent.

It is used to separate main clauses linked by certain so-called conjunctive adverbs such as *indeed*, *nevertheless*, *moreover*, *hence*, *yet*, and *however*:

The plan has not worked; nevertheless, it was worth trying.

It is used to separate items in a series where the items themselves are already subdivided into a smaller series and thus helps to avoid ambiguity:

This book contains information about distribution and habitat; form, dimensions and colouring; life-cycle; and economic significance.

sensibility, sensitiveness, sensitivity All mean responsiveness or susceptibility. *Sensibility* denotes rather the capacity to respond to aesthetic stimuli:

The sensibility of a sculptor.

Sensitiveness is the quality of being sensitive or of responding to stimulation from outside:

Sensitiveness to light.

Sensitivity is used especially of capacity to respond in a physiological sense:

The sensitivity of a nerve.

sensible, sensitive The most common meaning of *sensible* is 'having or showing good sense or sound judgement'. It can, however, have the meaning of 'keenly aware', when it is usually followed by *of*:

Sensible of his errors.

In this instance it is close to one of the meanings of *sensitive*, 'readily affected by':

Sensitive to criticism.

sensual, sensuous Both words refer to what is experienced through the senses. *Sensual* is concerned with gratification derived from physical sensations, particularly sexual ones, and is usually pejorative:

A sensual delight in food. A man of crude sensual passions.

Sensuous is applied, with a favourable connotation, to what is perceived by or affects the senses:

The sensuous pleasure of good music.

sentence A sentence is a group of words that express a complete meaning. There are various types of sentences, expressing a statement, asking a question, issuing a command or making an exclamation, as in the following examples.

A sentence expressing a statement:

The Second World War ended in 1945.

A sentence asking a question:

What are we having for dinner?

A sentence expressing a command:

Get that window repaired at once.

A sentence expressing an exclamation:

Help! Fire! What a shame!

Sentences can also be divided up according to their structure. A simple sentence contains one subject and one predicate:

People are odd.

A compound sentence contains two or more independent clauses:

The door opened and a man stepped out.

A complex statement contains one or more dependent clauses in addition to the main clause:

When the concert finished (dependent clause) the audience clapped wildly.

sentinel, sentry Both words mean 'someone who stands guard' but *sentinel* is the more general word. *Sentry* is almost exclusively used in a military context.

sequence of tenses This means that the tense of verbs in subordinate clauses must be adjusted to suit the tense of the verb in the main clause. This does not usually present any great difficulty in English but it should be remembered that a main clause in a past tense can have a subordinate clause in the present tense if this expresses something which is true (or believed to be true) at all times:

They were taught that God is love.

sergeant, serjeant The form *sergeant* is used for the rank in the army and in the police force. *Serjeant* was a title formerly given to a member of a superior order of barristers. The spelling is preserved in *serjeant-at-arms*, an official of the Houses of Parliament.

service This is a comparatively recent verb meaning 'to make fit for service' and is useful in an age when motor vehicles are in regular need of attention. However, care should be taken to ensure that it does not usurp any of the various meanings of *serve*.

sestet, sextet These two words have the same origin. *Sestet* is now usually confined to poetry and means the last six lines of a sonnet. A *sextet* is a group of six, especially singers or players, or a musical composition for six voices or instruments.

sew, sow To *sew* meaning 'to attach with a needle or thread' has the past tense *sewed* and the past participle *sewn* or, rarely, *sewed.* To *sow* meaning 'to plant seeds' has the past tense *sowed* and the past participle *sown* or, rarely, *sowed.*

sewage, sewerage These words are sometimes confused. *Sewage* is the waste matter which passes through sewers. *Sewerage* is the removal of waste by means of sewers or a system of sewers, but it can be used to mean simply *sewage.*

shade, shadow Both words are used to describe an area of comparative darkness in relation to its surroundings. *Shade* indicates the diminished heat and brightness of a spot from which the sun's rays are cut off:

The tree provided sufficient shade.

Shade has no particular form or shape but *shadow* is often used to describe an object which intercepts the light:

He saw the shadow of a woman on the pavement.

Shakespeare; Shakespearian These are now the generally accepted spellings, the alternative forms being *Shakspeare, Shakespearean* and *Shaksperian.*

shall, will, should, would The correct use of these auxiliary verbs has always been a subject of controversy, but most authorities are agreed upon the following points. When a simple future is being expressed the forms are as follows:

I shall come	We shall come
You will come	You will come
He, she, it will come	They will come

I shall come to tea on Sunday. Mother will stay at home.

However, when the verb is used to express determination, obligation or permission the forms are changed:

I will come	We will come
You shall come	You shall come
He, she, it shall come	They shall come

I will come on Sunday no matter what she says.
You shall stay at home whether you like it or not.

The use of *should* and *would* is more complicated. When they express simple futurity from the point of past time (i.e. *he said he would come*) the pattern is the same as for *shall* and *will*.

I should come	We should come
You would come	You would come
He, she, it would come	They would come

However, *would* is frequently substituted for *should*, since *should* is not now generally used to represent past time.

Should is used with all three persons, singular and plural, to imply condition, obligation, doubt or supposition:

If I should be late. You should get up earlier than you do. He should arrive on time. If they should get here before me.

Would is used with all three persons, singular and plural, to represent determination, habitual action, or condition:

He said he would come despite their protests. She would go to bed regularly at nine o'clock. If they had the choice, they would come.

shambles The original meaning of *shambles* was a slaughter-house. It was extended to describe a scene of carnage or bloodshed. Such is its popularity that it is now used of any kind of chaos or disorder, much to the regret of some authorities.

shanty, chanty A *shanty* is a sailor's song. The original spelling was *chanty*, but *shanty* has now almost entirely displaced it.

sharp, sharply *Sharp* is still employed as an adverb when reference is made to abruptness or suddenness, punctuality and vigilance. It is also used in music:

He pulled the horse up sharp. Turn sharp right. Be here at six o'clock sharp. Look sharp! She was singing sharp.

Sharply is the adverb of the adjective *sharp* on all other occasions.

shear This verb has the past tense *sheared* and the past participle *sheared* or *shorn*. When the past participle is used as an adjective *shorn* is the usual form:

A shorn lamb.

shew, show The spelling *shew* was formerly quite common, but *show* is now the generally acceptable form. *Shew* is, however, still used in legal documents.

should see **shall**

shrink This verb has the past tense *shrank* or *shrunk* and the past participle *shrunk* or *shrunken*. When the past participle is used as an adjective the form *shrunken* is preferred:

A shrunken hand.

sic This is a Latin word meaning 'so', which is inserted after a word or phrase to show that it has been copied exactly from an original. It usually means that the writer knows he is quoting from something which is inaccurate and does not accept responsibility for it:

Brown wrote 'the author Graham Green (*sic*) is much overrated'.

The (*sic*) means that the writer is aware that *Green* should be spelt *Greene* but is quoting exactly.

sick see **ill**

significant This is a word which has achieved much popularity in recent years and unfortunately has undergone an unwarranted extension of meaning. It should not be used as a variant of *important* or *considerable* in such phrases as *a significant improvement* or *a significant change*.

simile This is a figure of speech which expresses a direct resemblance, in one or more particulars, of one thing to another:

He had a face like that of a frightened sheep.

simplistic, simplified Both adjectives mean 'made simpler' or 'made less complicated'. *Simplistic* is a new word which has currently become fashionable and tends to mean 'greatly simplified' or 'excessively simplified':

He is always proposing simplistic solutions to complex problems.

simulate see **dissimulate**

since When used as a conjunction *since* is normally followed by a verb in the past tense:

We have not heard from him since he joined the army. It is two hours since he left.

It is followed by a verb in the perfect tense when it refers to an action that is still continuing:

Since he has been here we have had no peace.

When *since* is used as an adverb it is usually preceded by a verb in the perfect tense and followed by an expression of time:

They have been here since six o'clock.

[See also *ago*]

sink This verb has the past tense *sank* (or rarely) *sunk*, and the past participle *sunk* or *sunken*. When the past participle is used as an adjective *sunken* is the usual form:

Sunken eyes.

slang It is not easy to offer a precise definition of slang but basically it is a language which differs from standard speech both in its choice of vocabulary and in its turns of phrase. Slang invents new words and gives established ones new meanings. It can be both imaginative and colourful, but if used excessively it becomes stale. It is considered by many to be inferior to standard speech, although numerous slang words do eventually win acceptance and respectability.

sled, sledge, sleigh All three words are used to describe a vehicle mounted on runners which moves over snow or ice. *Sled* is usually applied to a small *sledge*. *Sleigh* is often used for a horse-drawn vehicle. *Sledge* is the word most commonly employed for a vehicle which carries loads.

slovenly This is an adjective and for obvious reasons cannot take the ending *-ly* to form the adverb. Expressions such as 'in a slovenly manner' or 'in a slovenly way' must be used instead:

She dressed in a slovenly manner.

slow, slowly The adjective *slow* is used as an adverb in *go slow* and *run slow*. In the comparative and superlative forms *slower* and *slowest* are generally used as adverbs instead of *more slowly* and *most slowly*.

sly The normal comparative and superlative forms of this adjective are *slyer* and *slyest*, although *slier* and *sliest* are possible. The adverbial forms are *slyly* or (more rarely) *slily*.

small see **little**

smell This verb has either *smelt* or *smelled* in the past tense and in the past participle. When it means 'to give out an odour' it is followed by an adjective, not an adverb:

The flowers smell sweet.

so When *so* is used to introduce a clause expressing purpose or result it cannot stand alone but must be followed by *that* or *as to*:

He joined the club so that he could see her more often.

She stopped the car so that she could see more clearly *or* so as to be able to see more clearly.

The expression *to do so* is used to avoid repeating a verb:

Since she wanted to read I told her to do so.

It cannot, however, be employed as a substitute for a verb in the passive and the following is incorrect:

This door is not to be left open: anyone doing so will be severely reprimanded.

sociable, social Both adjectives are concerned with the relationship of people in society. *Sociable* means 'fond of the company of others' or 'friendly in company':

He was a good mixer and sociable at parties.

Social is a more neutral word, relating to society in general or to particular societies:

Man is a social animal. We have joined a social club.

soliloquy see **monologue**

soluble, solvable *Soluble* is used of both substances and problems and means 'capable of being dissolved' or 'capable of being solved'. *Solvable* means 'capable of being solved' and is applied only to problems.

some time, sometime Written as either two words or one word *some time* means 'an indefinite time' or 'some time or other':

The two men met in New York some time last year.

Written as one word *sometime* is used as an adjective meaning 'former':

Sometime senior lecturer in history.

sort This is a singular noun but it is frequently encountered with demonstrative adjectives in the plural in phrases like *these sort of*, *those sort of*. It is acceptable in conversation but it is advisable to avoid it in written English.

southerly see **easterly**

Soviet see **Russia**

sow see **sew**

speciality, specialty In British English *speciality* is the usual word, *specialty* being confined to the legal sense of a 'special agreement'. In American usage *specialty* is far more common and has some of the meanings of *speciality* in British English, notably 'a particular line of work'.

specially see **especially**

specie, species *Specie* means 'coined money' and cannot be used in the plural. *Species* meaning 'a group of individuals sharing common characteristics' is both singular and plural.

spelling The correct spelling of English words presents many formidable problems, some of which this *Guide to English Usage* can help to solve. There are a number of entries dealing with spelling including in particular *American usage and spelling*, *Latin and French plurals* and *plural forms*. However, it is useful to be able to summarize under one heading some of the main points which the reader will find treated under individual entries elsewhere in this book.

Words ending in a single consonant preceded by a single vowel double the consonant before suffixes beginning with a vowel, provided they are single-syllable words or have the stress on the past syllable:

bedding, drummer, regrettable, stopped, upsetting.

Single-syllable words ending in a consonant preceded by two vowels or another consonant, or words of more than one syllable which are not stressed on the last syllable do not double the final consonant:

roamed, limiting, heaped, peeping, seated.

For exceptions to the above rule see *-l-*, *-ll-* and *-p-*, *-pp-*.

Words ending in *y* and preceded by a consonant change *y* to *i* when a suffix is added:

easy, easily; party, parties; rely, reliable; mercy, merciful.

However, if the *y* is followed by *i* it is retained:

bury, burying; carry, carried; try, trying; occupy, occupied.

If *y* is preceded by a vowel it is usually retained:

employ, employable; play, plays; monkey, monkeys.

There are, however, some well-known exceptions to this rule:

pay, paid; say, said; gay, gaily.

In some cases final *y* is retained before suffixes although it is preceded by a consonant:

shy, shyness; sly, slyly; enjoy, enjoyment.

With words like *dry* and *fly* either *y* or *i* is permissible:

flier *or* flyer, drily *or* dryly.

Final *-ie* becomes *y* before *-ing*:

tie, tying (*but* tied); die, dying.

Final silent *-e* is usually dropped before a suffix beginning with a vowel:

shine, shining; believe, believable; name, naming.

However, when final silent *-e* is preceded by soft *c* or *g* it is usually retained in order to preserve the sound:

peace, peaceable; change, changeable; manage, manageable.

Final silent *-e* is also usually retained before a suffix beginning with a consonant:

elope, elopement; grave, gravely; achieve, achievement.

Final silent *-e* is retained in some words before *-ing* to prevent confusion over pronunciation and meaning:

dye, dyeing; singe, singeing.

Verbs ending in *c* add *k* before suffixes beginning with *e*, *i* or *y* so that the hard *c* is preserved:

picnic, picnicked, picnicking; mimic, mimicked, mimicking.

spin The generally accepted form of the past tense and past participle is *spun*. *Span* is still occasionally found, although some authorities consider it archaic.

spirituous, spiritual These words are sometimes confused. *Spirituous* means 'containing alcohol, alcoholic'. *Spiritual* means 'pertaining to the spirit or soul, as opposed to the body'.

split infinitive This is a construction in which an adverb is placed between *to* and the verb it goes with. Formerly grammarians condemned it out of hand, but strict observance of the rule frequently leads to awkward or ambiguous phrases, and a more flexible attitude is now adopted. In the two following sentences the position of *completely* alters the meaning and the infinitive must be split if the sense requires it:

He failed completely to finish the course = complete failure.
He failed to completely finish the course = partial failure.

The split infinitive is perfectly acceptable in such phrases as *to readily understand*, *to fully intend*, but it is still best avoided except in cases similar to those outlined above.

sprain, strain Both words (either as nouns or verbs) have the sense of injury done to muscles. *Sprain* suggests a sudden wrenching of the muscles or tendons, especially those of the wrist and ankle. *Strain* suggests a deformation caused by action over a long period (*to strain one's eyes*) or by the exertion of a muscle beyond its capacity:

The effort strained his heart.

sprint, spurt Both words are used to describe a spell of physical activity. A *sprint* is the name given to a race run at full speed. A *spurt* is a sudden increase in effort as might be needed in running or some other athletic sport.

staff, stave *Staff* is rarely used now in its old sense of 'stick'. However, its original plural *staves* has, by a process of back-formation, produced a new singular, *stave*. This has more or less replaced *staff* in the musical sense and is also used to mean a narrow, shaped piece of wood forming the side of a barrel. *Staffs* is now the normal plural of *staff*.

stanch, staunch When used as verbs both words mean 'to stop the flow of', but *stanch* is the more common form. *Staunch* is the usual spelling of the adjective meaning 'loyal, firm or steadfast'.

start see **begin**

stationary, stationery These words are frequently confused because of their spelling. *Stationary* is an adjective meaning 'standing still'. *Stationery* is a noun meaning writing materials, including, pens, pencils and envelopes.

stay see **stop**

stimulant, stimulus Both nouns are used to refer to something which incites mental or physical activity. However, the meaning of *stimulant* is usually limited to the effects of medicine or alcohol, and implies only a temporary increase in activity:

She was given stimulants to counteract her depression.

Stimulus is a more general word and is often used in a figurative sense:

The thought of the approaching strike was a stimulus to action.

stoic, stoical As an adjective *stoic* is generally attributive, i.e. it is placed before the noun. Moreover, it tends to have the original meaning of 'pertaining to Zeno's school of philosophy'. *Stoical* is used both attributively and predicatively, i.e. after the verb, and usually has the wider sense of 'impassive' or 'showing an austere fortitude':

He remained stoical although suffering much pain.

stop see **full stop**

stop, stay Apart from its basic sense of 'to cease moving' *stop* is quite frequently used in the sense of *stay*, i.e. 'to remain in a place'. Some authorities object to this use of *stop*, and it is probably better restricted to the idea of a short period which breaks a journey:

We stopped in New York overnight,

but:

They stayed in the country for nearly a year.

storey, story British English usage distinguishes between these two words, but the form *storey* meaning 'a floor of a building' has only recently been firmly established. In the United States *story* is the usual spelling for both 'a floor of a building' and 'a narrative'.

strategy, tactics *Strategy* is 'the planning and directing of large-scale military operations'. *Tactics* is 'the art of manoeuvring forces before or during a battle'.

stratum The usual plural is *strata*, but *stratums* is also found. [See *Latin and French plurals*]

string, strung, stringed The usual form of the past participle is *strung*, *stringed* being only rarely found. It is, however, used adjectivally as in *stringed instrument*.

subconscious see **unconscious**

subject In grammar the *subject*, together with the *predicate*, is an essential part of a sentence. The *subject* is the word or group of words which refer to the person who performs the action expressed in the predicate. The subject also determines the number and person of the verb. In the sentences:

John has a book.
We saw the train.
Who is that boy?

John, *we* and *who* are the subjects.

subject see **topic**

subjunctive The subjunctive mood of the verb is used to express a wish, condition, a mood of doubt, or a command. It is identical with the indicative of verbs except in the third person singular of the present tense, which drops the final *s*. Only the verb 'to be' has subjunctive forms in both present indicative and simple past tenses. The subjunctive is not much employed in present-day English except in conditional clauses and in subordinate clauses after verbs of asking, ordering and suggesting. In conditional clauses the subjunctive is used only when the condition is an unreal one, i.e. will not be fulfilled:

If he were to come (*but he won't*), he would tell us everything.

An example of the use of the subjunctive with verbs of asking and ordering is as follows:

He moved that the debate be adjourned until the next session.

It occurs in main clauses in certain set expressions:

Come what may. Peace be with you.

In fact the subjunctive in English is dying out and is frequently replaced by auxiliary verbs like *should*, *may* and *might*.

subnormal see **abnormal**

substitute, replace Care must be taken in the use of these words. *Substitute* means 'to put something in place of another' and *replace* means 'to take the place of'. The difference between them is illustrated in the following sentence:

When an encyclopedia is removed from a shelf and a dictionary put in its place, the dictionary is substituted for the encyclopedia and the encyclopedia is replaced by the dictionary.

succinct see **concise**

succubus see **incubus**

such When the pronoun *such* is followed by *as* it means 'of the kind specified':

There were monstrous animals such as I had never seen before.

When it is followed by *that* it implies a result or a consequence:

The density of the fog was such that we could scarcely see.

sufficient see **enough**

suffix A *suffix* consists of one or more syllables placed after a word to form a new word. It does not change the meaning in the way that a prefix does, but it does alter the grammatical function of the original word: a noun becomes an adjective, an adjective a noun or an adverb, etc. The endings of verbs are also suffixes. Examples of common suffixes are listed below:

bad, badly; go, going; desire, desirable; happy, happiness.

[See also *hyphens*]

suit, suite Both words are in fact the same, *suite* being a variant spelling of *suit*. Confusion arises over which spelling goes with which meaning. *Suit* is used for a set of clothes, a lawsuit, a set of cards, the courting of a woman and a petition to a person of high rank. *Suite* is used for a company of attendants, a connected series of rooms, a set of furniture, and a series of movements in music.

summon, summons The usual verb is *summon*. *Summons* is used only in the special legal sense of 'to serve with a summons'.

superior This unusual comparative form is followed by *to* and not *than*. When used in ordinary comparisons it must not be preceded by *more*:

The quality of his work is superior to that of his friends.

It cannot be preceded by *most* to form a superlative, but is used colloquially with *most* in the sense of 'displaying a feeling of being better than others', when it is no longer considered to be a true comparative:

He proved to be a most superior kind of individual.

superlative see **adjectives, comparison of**

supplement see **complement**

suppose, supposing Both words have very similar meanings. *Suppose* is generally used in the sense of 'to assume something for the sake of argument, without reference to its truth or falsity':

Suppose the factory workers go on strike, what shall we do?

Supposing is used in more realistic situations, in which something will or will not happen:

Supposing he gets here on time, we can start the meeting.

surprise When *surprise* means 'taken unawares' it is followed by the preposition *by*:

He was surprised by a burglar.

When it means 'astonished' it is followed by *at*:

We were surprised at his peculiar conduct.

susceptible When *susceptible* means 'liable to' or 'readily impressed' or 'impressionable' it is followed by *to*:

He was very susceptible to lavish praise.

When it means 'capable of' or 'admitting' it is usually followed by *of*:

His statement is susceptible of only one interpretation.

sustain This is often used as a synonym for 'receive' or 'suffer':

He sustained severe injuries when he fell down the steps.

However, in this sense *sustain* is rather formal and is better reserved for its original meaning of 'to bear (a burden)', or 'endure without giving way'.

swap, swop Both words can be used to mean 'exchange or barter', but *swop* is the more usual spelling.

swell This has the past tense *swelled*, and the past participle *swollen* or *swelled*. When the meaning is 'increase in numbers or quantity', *swelled* is the preferred form:

Their numbers were swelled by the arrival of large numbers of schoolchildren.

Swollen is used when the increase is considered to be a harmful or dangerous one:

The crowds of starving people were swollen by large numbers of sick and wounded.

sympathy This is usually followed by *for* when it means compassion or commiseration for someone:

He felt sympathy for the suffering woman.

It is generally followed by *with* when it expresses identity of view or understanding:

We are in sympathy with these people in their present difficulties.

syndrome In medicine this means a group of symptoms which, taken together, suggest a particular disease. It does not in itself mean a disease.

synonym A *synonym* is a word having approximately the same meaning and use as another, such as *royal* or *regal*. However, words which are called synonyms can rarely be substituted for one another in all their senses. We may talk about *royal power* or *regal power*, but we cannot use *a regal warrant* as an alternative to *a royal warrant*.

syntax see **grammar**

T

-t-, -tt- Single-syllable words ending in *t* double it before suffixes beginning with a vowel if the *t* is preceded by a single short vowel:

ratty, cutting, fatter, potted.

If, however, it is preceded by two vowels together or an *r* it is not doubled:

neater, sorting, seated, rooting.

Words of more than one syllable behave in the same way as single-syllable words if their last syllable is stressed and preceded by a single vowel:

besetting, befitted, abetter, regrettable.

They do not double the *t* otherwise:

unseated, maggoty, cosseting, hermitage.

-t and -ed verb endings There are a number of verbs whose past tense and past participle can end in either *-t* or *-ed*, such as *burnt* or *burned*. Other verbs of this kind are *dream*, *kneel*, *leap*, *learn*, *smell*, *spill*. English usage prefers the *-t* to the *-ed* ending, but American usage tends to favour *-ed*: *dreamed* rather than *dreamt*.

tableau This word of French origin normally takes *x* in the plural (*tableaux*), but most dictionaries give *tableaus* as an alternative.

talent, genius Both words are used to describe natural ability or aptitude of a high order. However, whereas *talent* is a capacity for achievement or success *genius* implies an exceptional natural ability for creative imagination or original thought.

tall, high Both words are to some extent interchangeable. *High* generally refers to distance from the ground or floor level:

A high mountain, a high window, high heels.

Tall is used of anything which is higher than usual of its kind or high in proportion to its breadth:

A tall girl, a tall building, a tall spire.

target This falls into the category of popular metaphors and is much overworked on that account. It is sensible to try to remember the literal meaning and that, to be successful, one must hit a *target* or, if unsuccessful, miss it. It is just possible to fall short of it but not to reach it, achieve it, obtain it, or do anything else with it. There are a number of other equally suitable words which can be substituted for *target*, including *aim*, *goal* and *objective*.

tartan see **plaid**

tasteful, tasty *Tasteful* means 'showing good taste'. *Tasty* originally had this meaning too, but is now almost wholly confined to what is pleasing to the taste. It is, however, considered a vulgarism by some authorities, and tends to be replaced by words like *appetizing* or *savoury*.

tautology This means saying the same thing twice over, especially the needless repetition of an idea in a sentence without adding anything to what is already there:

Their behaviour on all occasions was not always what we would have expected.

In the above sentence *on all occasions* is superfluous and adds nothing to the meaning.

temporal, temporary *Temporal* means 'pertaining to time' or 'concerned with the matters of this world':

He was dealing with temporal rather than spiritual matters.

Temporary means 'lasting for a time only':

He found temporary accommodation with friends.

tend, attend Both verbs can be used in the sense of 'to look after' or 'take charge of', but *attend* is always followed by *to*, whereas *tend* takes a direct object:

He attended to the needs of the children. The nurse was tending the sick.

tenses of verbs The tense of a verb indicates the time when an action takes place, either past, present or future.

The simple *present* tense shows that an action takes place now:

She cuts the cake.

The simple *past* tense shows that the action took place sometime in the past:

He drank the water.

The simple *future* tense shows that the action will take place in time to come:

You will receive a present.

The *perfect* tenses show that an action is complete at the present time, was completed at some time in the past or will be completed at some time in the future:

He has read the book. She had stayed at home. We shall have finished this evening.

[See also *verb*]

terminate This slightly pompous word frequently makes an appearance in official correspondence. In almost all cases it is better to use simpler words like *end*, *finish*, *conclude*, or *bring to an end*.

terminus, terminal In speaking of railways *terminus* is the normal word and its plural may be either *termini* or *terminuses*. For air travel use *terminal*.

than As a conjunction this is normally used only after a comparative adjective or adverb:

She is prettier than her sister. He can run faster than most of us.

Care must be taken with the case of pronouns after *than*. The same idea can be expressed in three different ways:

She is older than I am. She is older than I. She is older than me.

In the first two sentences *than* is a conjunction, but the use of *than I* in the second sentence is now considered rather pedantic. In the third sentence *than* can be considered as a preposition followed by a pronoun in the accusative case, *me*, and this usage is now acceptable in English. However, caution must be observed so as to avoid ambiguity in such sentences as:

You criticize her more than me.

If *than* is treated as a conjunction it means:

You criticize her more than you criticize me.

If *than* is treated as a preposition it means:

You criticize her more than I criticize her.

The last sentence could be better and unambiguously expressed as:

You criticize her more than I do.

Another common error is to follow *than* with an unnecessary *what*, which should be omitted in the following example:

It was cheaper than what we expected.

that, which Both are used as relative pronouns. Generally it is better not to use *which* where *that* would be sufficient and not to use either if the sentence can do without them:

There are the flowers (that/which) I bought.

In a restrictive clause, i.e. a clause that is essential to complete the meaning of the main clause, either *that* or *which* may be used:

Organic chemistry is a subject which/that has only limited appeal.

In a non-restrictive clause, i.e. one that is not essential to complete the meaning of the main clause, *which* (or *who*) must be used:

He asked me to stay to lunch, which had already been prepared.
The soldier, who had stayed in the hall, was too ill to walk any further.

That is sometimes introduced unnecessarily after a comparison. It should be omitted from the following example:

The sooner that he gets here, the better for all of us.

the The main function of the definite article *the* is to specify a particular thing which is distinct from others of the same kind, as opposed to *a* or *an*:

The apples are on the table. The girl is wearing an apron.

It is used in a generalizing sense to denote a particular member of a species as representative of the whole:

The fox is a quadruped.

The is used with adverbial force in such comparative expressions as:

The harder they try the more difficult they find it.

their Although the habit is frowned on by some authorities, this is often used in colloquial speech and also in writing as an equivalent of *his* and *hers*, since there is no singular possessive adjective covering both these words together:

I spoke to both Peter and Ann and each defended their point of view.

It is also used when the sex is not specified:

Everyone was told to bring a sample of their work.

theirs It should be noted that *theirs* is spelt without an apostrophe.

theism see **deism**

think When *think* is followed by *to* it can be used to mean 'remember' or 'occur to'. The usage is colloquial and not accepted by all, but seems to have established itself in conversation at least:

Did you think to lock the door?

though, although These words are more or less interchangeable, with some slight differences. *Although* is both a more emphatic and more imposing word than *though*. It tends to be used at the beginning of sentences, whereas the position of *though* is more flexible. It may be placed last in a sentence, which *although* cannot be.

thrash, thresh *Thrash* is in fact a variant of *thresh*, although the two words are now differentiated in sense. *Thrash* means 'to beat, especially as a means of punishment' or 'to defeat thoroughly'. It is also used figuratively meaning to 'discuss (a problem) exhaustively'. *Thresh* is used exclusively in the sense of separating grain or seeds from wheat and other crops.

through Used in the sense of 'up to and including' *through* is an Americanism:

From Sunday through Thursday.

It is, however, encroaching to some extent on British English.

thus This adverb is frequently used rather loosely before a participle, and care must be taken to ensure that the participle is correctly related to what precedes it:

His flat was destroyed by fire, thus making him homeless.

In the above sentence *making* refers back to his flat, but *his flat* did not make him *homeless* and so the sentence must be recast thus:

His flat was destroyed by fire and he was thus made homeless.

tight, tightly *Tight* can be used as adverb as well as an adjective and differs from *tightly* in that it emphasizes the result of an action:

He slammed the door tight. She screwed the bottle top on tight.

Tightly, on the other hand, generally refers to the manner in which something is carried out:

She grasped me tightly round the waist.

It can, however, be argued that in the expression *hold tight*, *tight* refers to manner just as much as it does to result.

till, until There is virtually no difference between these two words. Both have the meaning 'up to the time of', 'before' (with a negative). *Until* is more commonly used at the beginning of a sentence.

tire see **tyre**

titbit, tidbit *Titbit* is now the usual spelling in British English, although *tidbit* is the older form and the normal one in American usage.

titillate, titivate These verbs are often confused. *Titillate* means to stimulate or excite in an agreeable manner:

To titillate someone's fancy with the thought of good food.

Titivate means to make oneself spruce or to dress smartly:

The women were titivating themselves in preparation for the dance.

toilet, toilette The usual spelling is *toilet* for all meanings of the word, including lavatory, the act of dressing and the articles used in dressing. Most dictionaries, however, give *toilette* as an alternative form.

ton, tun A *ton* is a unit of weight equivalent to 2240 lbs as a *long ton* and to 2000 lbs as a *short ton*. A *tun* is a large cask for holding liquids, especially wine or beer.

too This is used before a past participle which has lost its verbal force and is purely an adjective:

He was too bewildered to notice.

When the past participle retains its verbal force *too much* is often substituted:

They were too much occupied with their own affairs to notice anyone else's problems.

It is often difficult to make a clear distinction between the two, and many writers would not bother to insert *much* in the second example.

topic, subject Both are used to mean a theme to be discussed or written about. *Topic* is, however, generally restricted to a particular part of a more wide-ranging subject:

Many aspects of the subject of race relations will provide topics for discussion.

total This undoubtedly useful word has in recent years suffered from a wave of popularity, which apparently began in the United States. It is now frequently used in place of words which are more suitable, such as *entire* or *complete*. *Total war* or *total eclipse* may be quite acceptable but *total control* is better expressed as *complete control*.

toward, towards As a preposition *towards* is the most common form in British English, but Americans seem to prefer the shorter word.

trace, vestige Both words are used to indicate signs of the existence of something. *Trace* is applied to a mark or slight evidence of something either past or present:

There were traces of blood on the staircarpet.

Vestige is more restricted in meaning and refers to a very slight remnant of something which no longer exists:

They found vestiges of an ancient civilization.

traffic This verb has the present participle *trafficking* and the past tense and past participle *trafficked*.

transcendent, transcendental These adjectives are frequently confused, because some of their senses overlap. *Transcendent* is used to mean going beyond ordinary limits, superior or pre-eminent:

A statesman of transcendent virtues.

Transcendental means going outside ordinary experience, idealistic or visionary:

He spoke about the benefits of transcendental meditation.

tranship, transship Dictionaries appear to be divided about the merits of these two spellings, with a slight bias in favour of *tranship*. *Trans-ship* is also found.

transient, transitory Both words are used in the sense of not lasting, temporary or fleeting. The distinction lies in the fact that *transient* has a special meaning in philosophy and *transitory* in law:

A transitory action.

transitive verb see **intransitive and transitive verbs**

transparent, translucent Both refer to matter through which light can pass. *Transparent* is the general word and means allowing things to be seen clearly through it:

In the transparent water of the swimming pool he could see a wristwatch lying at the bottom.

Translucent means letting light pass through in a diffuse manner so that objects beyond are not distinct:

He saw two vague shapes through the translucent glass.

transpire Many authorities deplore the use of this word in the sense of 'occur' or 'happen' and advocate that it should be confined to its original meaning of 'to become known gradually'. However, the popular sense is now so well established that nothing seems likely to shift it.

transport, transportation In American English the various meanings of the noun *transport* in British English are found mainly in *transportation*. In British English *transportation* usually, although not always, denotes the banishment of convicts to a penal colony.

trauma, traumatic Both the noun *trauma* and its adjective *traumatic* have achieved a popularity far beyond their original domain, that of medicine. *Trauma* means a bodily injury and, by extension, the condition which this produces. In psychiatry it denotes a deeply disturbing emotional experience which has a lasting effect. In everyday use *trauma*, and particularly *traumatic*, are used to describe any upsetting event.

travel This doubles the *l* in the present participle and past tenses (*travelling*, *travelled*), thus disobeying the rules about final consonants in unstressed syllables. However, American usage has *traveling* and *traveled*.

treble, triple Both words can be used as adjectives, verbs or nouns and in a sense are interchangeable. In practice, however, *treble* is the more usual form for the noun and verb and *triple* for the adjective. Moreover, *triple* as an adjective has the additional meaning of 'consisting of three parts' or 'threefold'.

trend, tendency Both words refer to an inclination towards a particular direction. *Trend* suggests something both firm and continuous, although the direction may be rather vague:

There is evidence of a trend in inflation rates.

Tendency is often used of a natural disposition or inclination:

He has a tendency to fall asleep at all hours.

triumphal, triumphant *Triumphal* means pertaining to or celebrating a triumph and is more restricted in meaning:

The emperor ordered a triumphal procession.

Triumphant means victorious or rejoicing in success:

They emerged triumphant after their ordeal in the boardroom.

try and The use of *try and* as an alternative to *try to* is now well established in conversation and is considered by many to be more a forceful variant:

Try and get here as fast as possible.

Try and cannot, however, be used in negative sentences or in the past tense and *try to* is always to be preferred in writing.

tsar This is now the preferred spelling, since it corresponds most closely to the Russian pronunciation. The alternatives *czar* and *tzar* are, however, frequently found.

turf The usual plural form is *turfs*. *Turves* is considered by some authorities to be archaic, but is still used in the sense of peat which has been cut for burning.

tyre, tire For a band of rubber fitted round the rim of a wheel *tyre* is the usual spelling in British English, although the form *tire* prevails in the United States.

U

ult., inst., prox. *Ult.* (last month), *inst.* (this month) and *prox.* (next month) are all examples of commercialese (see *jargon*). It is much better actually to name the month in question, which conveys the meaning intended more rapidly and more accurately. Fortunately the use of all three abbreviations seems to be dying out.

ultimatum This has *ultimatums* as the preferred form of the plural, with *ultimata* as an alternative.

-um, -ums, -a see **Latin and French plurals**

umpire, referee Both words are used of someone to whom a dispute is referred for decision. In sport they describe a person selected as a judge in certain games, who has the power to enforce rules and settle disputes. There is no real difference in function, the term *umpire* being used in cricket, tennis and hockey, and *referee* in football and boxing.

un- see **in-**

unanimous The word *unanimous* can be applied to a vote on a motion only when all those present are in agreement. If there are some abstentions, and provided nobody votes against, the motion is said to be carried *nem. con.* ('with no one dissenting').

unattached participle This is a participle that is related grammatically to a word which it was not intended to qualify or that has no word to which it can logically relate. It is a common error to leave participles unattached:

> Disturbed at the recent turn of events, it seems clear to us that prompt action is required.

This sentence should be recast along the following lines:

Disturbed at the recent turn of events, we see clearly that prompt action is required.

It is an equally common error to attach participles to the wrong noun:

Crossing the road, a lorry knocked him down.

This means grammatically that it was the lorry which was crossing the road. The sentence should be rephrased thus:

Crossing the road, he was knocked down by a lorry.

There are some participles which may be used without being related to a particular noun or pronoun, such as *considering*, *owing to* and *concerning*:

Considering the strain he had undergone, his appearance was normal.

unaware, unawares It is important to remember that *unaware* is the adjective and *unawares* the adverb:

She was unaware that she had already missed the train.
Arriving unexpectedly after lunch, they caught me unawares.

unconscious, subconscious Both words are used in psychology, as nouns and adjectives, to denote those mental processes of which the individual is unaware but which influence his conscious behaviour and conduct. *Unconscious* as an adjective also means 'oblivious of one's surroundings' or 'temporarily deprived of consciousness'.

under see **below**

underlay, underlie *Underlay* is a transitive verb meaning 'to provide (something) with support with something laid underneath it'. *Underlie,* which is a more common verb, is intransitive and means 'to lie under' or 'to be situated underneath'.

under the circumstances see **circumstances**

undiscriminating, indiscriminate Both adjectives mean 'making no distinction', but *undiscriminating* is normally used only of people:

He was undiscriminating in his choice of clothes.

Indiscriminate, which has the additional meaning of 'confused', or 'promiscuous', generally refers to behaviour, method or purpose:

The indiscriminate use of valuable material.

undue, unduly Both the adjective *undue*, which means 'unwarranted' or 'excessive', and its adverb *unduly* are often used when they add nothing to the meaning of the sentence in which they appear:

To exert undue influence

is quite acceptable but in:

There is no cause for undue haste

the *undue* is superfluous.

uneatable, inedible The main distinction between these two is that *uneatable* means unpalatable and is generally applied to something which could in normal circumstances be eaten:

The cold stew was uneatable.

Inedible, on the other hand, usually refers to something which could not be eaten under any circumstances:

There are many inedible plants.

unexceptionable, unexceptional see **exceptionable, exceptional**

uninterested see **disinterested**

unique This means 'of which there is only one' and if something is *unique* it is the only one of its kind in existence. This means that it cannot be qualified, as most adjectives can, by *very*, *more*, *less* or *most*. It is, however, permissible to use it with *almost* or *nearly*.

United Kingdom This term embraces Great Britain (England, Scotland and Wales) and Northern Ireland. The abbreviation *U.K.* can be used as an adjective, but should not be used as a noun except to save space. The *U.K. Government* is, strictly speaking, more accurate than the *British Government*, but *British* in this context is quite acceptable.

United States, U.S. The abbreviation *U.S.* should be used only as an adjective (*the U.S. Government*). It should not be used as a noun except to save space. *American* is generally preferable as an adjective to *U.S.* (*an American writer*, *an American farming community*), although it is a vaguer word than *U.S.* and can be applied to the whole of the Western Hemisphere. [See also *America*]

unlawful see **illegal**

unlike see **like**

unorganized, disorganized Both words mean 'lacking order', but *unorganized* is used of something which has never been properly organized or formed into a systematic whole. *Disorganized*, on the other hand, refers to an order or system which has been disrupted or overturned.

unreadable see **illegible**

unstructured This is a popular word, beloved of sociologists, and means 'informal' or 'unorganized'. It should be used with great caution, if at all.

until see **till**

upward, upwards *Upward* is both an adjective and an adverb, and *upwards* is an adverb only. *Upwards* is the more usual form of the adverb.

urban, urbane *Urban* means 'belonging to or situated in cities or towns'. *Urbane* means 'having the refinement and manners supposedly characteristic of city-dwellers'.

-us see **Latin and French plurals**

usage, use *Usage* is often employed where *use* would be the correct word, as in the following example:

There has been excessive usage of fuel during the recent cold spell.

Usage means 'the way in which something is used' or 'the habitual or customary way of doing something':

This car has received some rough usage. English usage changes over the years.

use In sentences in which *use* is preceded by *no*, *of* is usually but not always dropped:

This book is (of) no use to me.

In sentences of the following type it is always omitted:

It's no use asking for the impossible.

Of is, however, generally retained when *use* is preceded by *any* or *some*, and is always retained when *use* is not preceded by an adjective at all:

Will this be (of) any use to you? It must be of use to somebody.

use to, used to When *used to* refers to habitual or customary action it is followed by the infinitive:

He used to go to London every day.

Questions are usually formed with *do*:

Did you use to come only on Fridays?

It is possible to say *Used you to come . . .* ? but this is now very rare.

In negative sentences *used not to* is the correct form:

She used not to mind about the appearance of the house.

In negative questions *didn't use to* is the accepted phrase:

Didn't you use to work in Glasgow?

When *used to* is used as an adjective meaning 'accustomed to' it is followed by a present participle, a noun or a pronoun:

We became used to arriving late every day. I am used to a better standard of service.

utilize This is not really a longer variation of *use*, since it means 'to put to profitable use' and it should be avoided except when the sense requires it, as in the following:

We must utilize the energy available for both heating and lighting.

V

vacation This is the period of the year when the law courts and universities are closed. In America it is the normal word for holiday and is increasingly used with that meaning in Britain.

valet As a verb this has as its past tense *valeted* and present participle *valeting*. It thus obeys the rule that an unstressed final consonant is not doubled when followed by a suffix.

valour, valorous The adjective drops the *u*. The American spellings are *valor* and *valorous*.

valuable, valued *Valuable* is used of something which is known to have great value because of its usefulness or rarity. *Valued* means 'highly regarded or esteemed', but what it refers to may not be intrinsically *valuable*.

value Value must always be preceded by *of* when used with the verb *to be*:

Of what value has it been? This book is of no value whatsoever.

vantage see **advantage**

vapour Some words formed from *vapour* drop the *u*: *vaporous*, *vaporization*, but *vapouring*, *vapourish*. The American spelling is *vapor* and the *-or* form is found in all words derived from it.

variance The expression *at variance* is always followed by *with* and never by *from*.

venal, venial These adjectives are sometimes confused although their senses are quite different. *Venal* means 'open to bribery or corruption' and *venial* 'pardonable' or 'trivial', with reference to faults or shortcomings.

venture see **adventure**

venturesome see **adventurous**

verb The verb is a part of speech which expresses an action, a state or a condition. In form verbs are either strong or weak. Strong verbs show differences in tense by an internal vowel change:

sing, sang, sung; ride, rode, ridden.

Weak verbs use suffixes to show differences in tense, keeping the same vowel as in the present tense of the verb:

talk, talked; believe, believed; fill, filled.

Verbs can be either transitive or intransitive. A transitive verb requires an object to make its meaning complete:

The man finds the book.

An intransitive verb is complete in itself without an object:

She is coming. He slept. We shall go.

Some verbs do not fall into the categories of transitive or intransitive. The verb *to be* joins subject to predicate:

He is a good man.

Others like *become, grow* and *seem* link the subject with an adjective describing it:

She seems uneasy. They have grown old.

Auxiliary verbs are used with other verbs to express action or condition. They include *can*, *do*, *have*, *may*, *must* and *shall*:

I can come. Did she go? You must try. We shall see.

The persons of the verb are the speaker (first person), the one addressed (second person) and anyone or anything else (third person). The persons, singular and plural, are shown as follows:

I come	we come
you come	you come
he, she, it comes	they come

The tenses of the verb show the time when an action takes place – in the present, past or future:

I went, she has come, we shall try.

Verbs may be either active or passive. When the verb is active the subject performs the action expressed by the verb:

He read a book.

When the verb is passive the subject undergoes the action expressed by the verb:

The book was read.

The verb has three moods – indicative, imperative and subjunctive. The indicative mood expresses a statement of fact:

We shall have lamb for dinner.

The imperative mood is used to express a command or request:

Finish this work at once.

The subjunctive mood expresses doubt, command, condition or desire:

He asks that we come at once.
If he came, he wouldn't find us here.

Reflexive verbs have the same subject and object:

He shaved himself. The girl hurt herself.

verbal The basic meaning of verbal is 'pertaining to or consisting of words', but it is increasingly used to mean 'expressed in spoken words'. However, *oral* has the same sense, and it is probably better to use *oral* rather than *verbal* when referring to the spoken language in order to avoid any possibility of ambiguity as in *an oral examination*. Unfortunately, *verbal* continues to encroach upon the territory previously occupied by *oral*.

verbiage, verbosity Both mean an abundance of unnecessary words. *Verbiage* may be used of writing or speech, but *verbosity* generally refers to speech only.

verify, corroborate These words are often confused but have quite distinct meanings. *Verify* means to 'ascertain the truth of something':

It is essential to verify the prisoner's story.

Corroborate means 'to confirm' or 'to supply further evidence of the truth of something':

The police were able to corroborate the evidence provided by the witness.

vernacular This was originally used to mean the mother tongue as opposed to any foreign language. It is now generally applied to the language spoken by the people of a particular region or district – the native language – sometimes contrasted with the literary or learned language.

verso, recto *Verso* is the left-hand page of a book or manuscript and *recto* the right-hand page.

very see **much**

vestige see **trace**

via This means 'by way of' and is applied to a route:

We went to Spain via Paris.

It must not, however, be used to refer to a means of transport and in the following sentence is not acceptable:

We sent the consignment via rail to London.

viable This denotes the capacity of a foetus, having reached a certain stage of development, to exist outside the womb. It has suffered the fate of many popular words and has undergone an extension of meaning. It is now used as a synonym for *effective*, *practicable*, *durable*, *workable* and others, all of which would be far more suitable in most contexts.

vicious circle This is a situation in which the solution of one problem creates another or in which one difficulty inevitably produces another and so on.

vide This is a Latin word meaning 'see' and is used especially when making a reference from one part of a text to another.

view There are two important idiomatic expressions with *view* and care should be taken not to get them confused. *In view of* means 'considering' or 'taking into account':

In view of the gravity of our position, I suggest we ask for help.

With a view to means 'with the aim of':

I am going to Paris with a view to studying art.

vigour, vigorous The *u* is dropped in the adjective *vigorous*. In American usage the noun, too, is spelt without a *u*: *vigor*.

villain, villein A *villain* is a wicked person and a *villein* a serf under the feudal system. Some confusion may be caused by the fact that *villein* may also be spelt *villain*.

visit, visitation *Visitation* is a much more formal word than *visit* and its uses are strictly limited. It can mean a visit for the purpose of making an official inspection. It is also used for an affliction or punishment, especially one sent by God.

viz. This is short for *videlicet* which means 'that is to say' or 'namely', and is used to introduce examples or lists, or to specify what has previously been described more vaguely:

I have seen only three women on my visit to London, *viz.* Mary, Anne and Elizabeth.

Let us now discuss the person on whom our peaceful existence so much depends, *viz.* the ordinary policeman.

vocation see **avocation**

vogue words *Vogue words* are words which become fashionable at a particular period. Very often they are words with a specialized sense which have acquired a sudden popularity and an extension of meaning far beyond what they originally possessed. Such words, a number of which are mentioned in this *Guide to English Usage*, tend to be used far too frequently and to be lacking in clarity and precision. No one can predict what their future will be. Some disappear and others settle down to a respectable status, once their immediate fame has faded away. The only advice that can be given is that they should be used with great circumspection and that other words having a similar meaning should not be neglected.

W

wage, wages Both *wage* and *wages* are used in the sense of 'what is paid in return for work or services rendered'. *Wages* is no longer considered a singular noun and must be followed by a plural verb.

wagon, waggon The spelling *wagon* is now the more common one in both British and American usage.

wait see **await**

waive, wave These two words are quite distinct in origin but are sometimes muddled. *Waive* means 'to relinquish or forgo':

He waived his rights to the inheritance.

It is sometimes wrongly followed by *aside* in mistake for *wave aside*, which can mean 'to dismiss with a gesture'.

wake see **awake**

want, need The chief distinction between these verbs is that *want* means 'desire' and *need* implies a necessity.

We need food and water. He wants a new car.

In usage the distinction is often lost by the excessive use of *want*.

-ward, -wards In British English, as a general rule, *-ward* is used as a suffix for adjectives and *-wards* for adverbs:

He was a backward child. The children ran backwards.

In American English the suffix *-ward* is frequently used for adverbs.

waste, wastage There is a distinction between these two words, although in practice it is frequently blurred. *Wastage* means 'loss by use, wear, leakage or decay':

There was a considerable wastage of oil caused by an inefficient machine.

Waste means 'useless consumption or expenditure':

It is a waste of money to buy such an expensive gadget.

way, weigh Confusion between these words is caused by the fact that a ship is said to be *under way*, i.e. 'moving along' when it has *weighed anchor*, i.e. 'lifted its anchor'. Some dictionaries in fact accept *under weigh* as an alternative to *under way*.

we Apart from its usual meaning as the plural of *I*, *we* is used by a speaker or writer to refer to people in general, by a sovereign when alluding to himself or herself in formal speech, and by a newspaper editor in what is known as 'collective anonymity'.

wed, marry *Marry* is the usual word. *Wed*, which has as past tense and past participle either *wedded* or *wed*, is used in literature or journalism:

Bishop weds sex-kitten.

Wedded can also mean devoted to:

He was wedded to the idea of free trade.

well The phrase *as well as* forms a conjunction and not a preposition and, strictly speaking, in a sentence such as:

He is coming as well as me.

I should be substituted for *me*. However, *I* sounds artificial in such a context and it can be argued that the second *as* is in fact a preposition and is thus followed by a pronoun in the object case, *me*.

When *as well as* is followed by a verb great care must be taken. If the verb preceding *as well as* is a finite one it must be followed by a gerund:

She played tennis as well as taking part in other sports.

If it is an infinitive the *as well as* must be followed by an infinitive:

He must work hard as well as lead an active social life.

well- When *well-* is used with participle to form a compound adjective it is usually hyphenated:

a well-known story, a well-aimed blow.

However, when the adjective follows the verb *to be* the hyphen is usually omitted:

The story was well known. The blow was well aimed.

Welsh, Welch *Welsh* is the normal form of the adjective, *Welch* being used only as the name of certain regiments, such as *The Royal Welch Fusiliers.*

Welsh rabbit, Welsh rarebit The former is the original spelling of the name, but the fairly recent variant, *Welsh rarebit,* has made such inroads into the language that it is too late to do anything except to acknowledge the existence of both forms.

westerly see **easterly**

wet The past tense and past participle of this verb are either *wet* or *wetted. Wetted* tends to be used when the idea of a deliberate action is involved, but otherwise *wet* is the more common form:

He wetted his finger in the blood.

wharf The normal plural is *wharves* but *wharfs* is also found. [See also *plural forms*]

what When *what* is used as a relative pronoun there may be some difficulty in deciding whether it should be followed by a singular or a plural verb. If it means *that which* it takes a singular verb:

Don't ask for more work. What we have is enough to last all day.

If it means *those which* it takes a plural verb:

They had lots of tomatoes and what they couldn't eat were given to the neighbours.

As a relative pronoun *what* must never be substituted for *who, that* or *which. The book what I read* and *The man what I saw* are both substandard English.

whatever see **-ever, ever**

whether see **if**

which, what Both *which* and *what* may be used as interrogative adjectives, but there are differences between them. *Which* means a choice from a certain number either mentioned or implied:

Which hat did you buy? (of the half a dozen on display).

What implies a selection from an indefinite number:

What car are you going to buy? (It could be any one of a large variety of makes and models).

When *which* is used as an interrogative pronoun, choice from a select number is also implied:

Which of them belongs to you?

When *which* is used as a relative pronoun it can refer only to things or animals:

The cat which was sitting on the mat. The book which lay on the table.

As a relative pronoun *which* is normally linked with a specific antecedent, but it can refer back to a whole clause:

He announced that he was going to resign, which pleased everybody.

while It is probably wisest to use this conjunction only in the sense of 'throughout' or 'during the time that':

He laid the table while his wife prepared the lunch.

It is not wrong to use it to mean 'although':

While I do not agree with you, I am willing to accept your decision.

However, it can lead to ambiguity:

While he is lacking in experience he is doing the job well.

The use of *while* to mean 'on the other hand', 'but', or even 'and' should also be avoided:

At the impromptu concert the student played the organ while his friend recited a poem.

who, whom When *who* and *whom* are used as interrogative pronouns they can cause many difficulties. *Who* is the subject case and *whom* the object case:

Who was speaking just now? Whom did you see at the station?

Normally *whom* and not *who* should follow a preposition but when the preposition comes at the end of a sentence it is customary to use *who*:

Who is that letter addressed to?

Another problem arises when *who* and *whom* are employed as relative pronouns. *Whom* is often wrongly used because it is thought to be the object of a verb:

The boy whom we said would win came in last.

In fact *whom* is not the object of *said* but the subject of *would win* and should therefore be replaced by *who*.

Who and *whom* are generally used only with reference to people:

The boy who broke his leg.
The couple whom we met at the concert.

They can, however, be applied to animals:

The cat who was sitting on the window ledge.

whoever see **-ever, ever**

whose The old rule that *whose* should not be used of inanimate objects may now be safely ignored. It is the possessive case of both *who* and *which*:

The girl whose parents were killed in a car crash.
The house whose doors are painted green.

The latter is now considered preferable to:

The house the doors of which are painted green.

wide see **broad**

will see **shall**

-wise, -ways These suffixes are used with adverbs and both denote attitude or direction although *-wise* is the more common form. Some adverbs take only *-wise*, such as *clockwise* and others only *-ways*, such as *sideways*. Some can take both as *lengthwise* and *lengthways*. *-Wise* is in addition now used to mean 'with respect to' or 'concerning', being attached indiscriminately to all sorts of words: *jobwise*, *moneywise*, *weatherwise*. This new departure is generally deplored and not to be imitated, especially in writing.

wit, humour *Wit* is the ability to perceive and express in a prompt and skilful manner connections between ideas or unexpected analogies and relationships in such a way as to give pleasure and amusement:

His conversation was noted for its wit.

Humour is more the capacity of understanding and appreciating what is inherently amusing, comical, or absurd in a situation, in a person's character or in the foibles of human nature generally:

He was the first to see the humour of his ridiculous position.

without *Without* in the sense of 'outside' is now archaic. It is sometimes wrongly used with the meaning of *unless*:

She won't do it without you tell her first.

wont This is the past participle of a now obsolete verb. It is used as a predicative adjective meaning 'accustomed':

He was wont to spend his mornings in bed.

When the adjective precedes the noun the form is *wonted*:

She was at her wonted place by the fireside.

Wont is also used as a noun meaning 'custom' or 'habit'.

wool This has the adjective *woollen* and *woolly* in British English and *woolen* and *wooly* in American English. [See also *American usage and spelling*]

would see **shall**

wrapped see **rapt**

wrath, wroth, wrathful As a noun *wrath* means 'a fierce anger'. As an adjective it is the alternative and archaic form of *wroth* which means 'angry' and can only be used predicatively. *Wroth* is rarely found and *wrathful*, which is used as an attributive adjective with the same meaning, is not now very common:

A wrathful man.

wrong This can occasionally be used as an adverb alongside *wrongly* with the meaning of 'incorrectly' or 'in a wrong manner':

He got his answer wrong. She guessed wrong.

wrought This is an obsolete past tense and past participle of *work* and is used only with reference to some metals such as iron or silver:

wrought iron.

X

-x Some words taken from French form their plurals by adding *-x*. [See *Latin and French plurals*]

-x-, -ct- There are a number of nouns ending in *-ion* and adjectives in *-ive* which may be preceded by either *x* or *ct*. On the whole the *-ct-* spelling is preferred: *connection*, *connexion*; *deflection*, *deflexion*, although in one case (*reflection*, *reflexion*, *reflective*, *reflexive*) the different spellings have different meanings.

Y

-y and i The rule is that final *y* changes to *i* before a suffix if the *y* is preceded by a consonant:

duty, dutiful; happy, happiness; pretty, prettily.

Exceptions are certain single-syllable words including the following:

shy, shyness; dry, dryness; sly, slyness.

Before a suffix beginning with *i*, *y* does not change:

marry, marrying; bury, burying.

If the *y* is preceded by a vowel it is retained:

toy, toys; play, played; volley, volleying.

Exceptions are certain common single-syllable words:

day, daily; pay, paid; lay, laid.

Yankee The term was originally used to describe an inhabitant of New England and later an inhabitant of any of the northern states of the United States. During the American Civil War Federal soldiers were called Yankees. Only in Britain is it used indiscriminately to apply to any citizen of the United States.

ye This is an archaic spelling of the definite article *the*. The initial letter *y* is due to a misreading of a medieval letter which was subsequently replaced by *th*.

yet This is sometimes used with the archaic or dialectal sense of 'still' and care must be taken to avoid ambiguity. *Are they here yet?* may mean *Are they still here?* or, in standard English, *Have they arrived yet?*

Yiddish This is a language, basically German in content, with a vocabulary containing some Hebrew and Slavonic words, which was spoken by Jews in eastern Europe and by Jewish emigrants to other countries.

young, youthful Both adjectives refer to the early stage of life or development. *Young* is the general word for everything which is growing and is still immature:

A young girl, a young puppy, a young shoot.

Youthful, which is mainly applied to human beings, emphasizes the favourable aspects of youth, such as vigour and freshness:

Youthful high spirits, a youthful outlook on life.

yours Remember that this personal pronoun is always spelt without an apostrophe.

youth This noun has three distinct senses. It means the condition or period of being young:

In his youth he travelled widely.

It is also used to refer to young people generally:

The youth of the country is up in arms.

Finally, it can mean a young man and in this case takes an *s* in the plural:

Five youths ran across the road.

Z

-z-, -zz- All words ending in *z* have a double letter, with the exception of *quiz*. This follows the rules for single-syllable words with only one vowel and doubles the *z* when followed by a suffix:

quizzed, quizzing, quizzer.

zigzag This doubles the *g* in the present and past participles: *zigzagged*, *zigzagging*. The stress falls on the first syllable and it is thus an exception to the rule that words of more than one syllable do not double the final consonant before a suffix, unless the stress falls on the final syllable.